The Story of Psychology: A Timeline

by Charles L. Brewer, Furman University

B.C.E.

387 — Plato, who believed in innate ideas, suggests that the brain is the seat of mental processes.

335 — Aristotle, who denied the existence of innate ideas, suggests that the heart is the seat of mental processes.

C.E.

1604 — Johannes Kepler describes inverted image on the retina.

1605 — Francis Bacon publishes *The Proficiency and Advancement of Learning*.

1636 — Harvard College is founded.

1637 — René Descartes, the French philosopher and mathematician who proposed mind-body interaction and the doctrine of innate ideas, publishes *A Discourse on Method*.

1690 — John Locke, the British philosopher who rejected Descartes' notion of innate ideas and insisted that the mind at birth is a "blank slate" (*tabula rasa*), publishes *An Essay Concerning Human Understanding*, which stresses empiricism over speculation.

1774 — Franz Mesmer, an Austrian physician, performs his first supposed cure using "animal magnetism" (later called Mesmerism and hypnosis). In **1777** he was expelled from the practice of medicine in Vienna.

1793 — Philippe Pinel releases the first mental patients from their chains at the Bicêtre Asylum in France and advocates more humane treatment of mental patients.

1802 — Thomas Young publishes *A Theory of Color Vision* in England. (His theory was later called the trichromatic theory.)

1808 — Franz Joseph Gall, a German physician, describes phrenology, the belief that the shape of a person's skull reveals mental faculties and character traits.

1834 — Ernst Heinrich Weber publishes *The Sense of Touch*, in which he discusses the just noticeable difference *(jnd)* and what we now call Weber's Law.

1848 — Phineas Gage suffers massive brain damage when a large iron rod accidentally pierces his brain, leaving his intellect and memory intact but altering his personality.

1859 — Charles Darwin publishes *On the Origin of Species by Means of Natural Selection*, synthesizing much previous work on the theory of evolution, including that of Herbert Spencer, who coined the phrase "survival of the fittest."

1861 — Paul Broca, a French physician, discovers an area in the left frontal lobe of the brain (now called Broca's area) that is critical for the production of spoken language.

1901 — Ten founders establish the British Psychological Society.

1905 — Mary Whiton Calkins becomes the first woman president of the APA.

Ivan Petrovich Pavlov begins publishing studies of conditioning in animals.

Alfred Binet and Théodore Simon produce the first intelligence test for assessing the abilities and academic progress of Parisian schoolchildren.

1913 — John B. Watson outlines the tenets of behaviorism in a *Psychological Review* article, "Psychology as the Behaviorist Views It."

1914 — During World War I, Robert Yerkes and his staff develop a group intelligence test for evaluating U.S. military personnel, which increases the U.S. public's acceptance of psychological testing.

1920 — Leta Stetter Hollingworth publishes *The Psychology of Subnormal Children, an early classic. In 1921 she is cited in American Men of Science* for her research on the psychology of women.

Francis Cecil Sumner receives a Ph.D. degree in psychology from Clark University, becoming the first African-American to earn a psychology doctorate.

John B. Watson and Rosalie Rayner report conditioning a fear reaction in a child called "Little Albert."

1921 — Hermann Rorschach, a Swiss psychiatrist, introduces the Rorschach inkblot test.

1923 — Developmental psychologist Jean Piaget publishes *The Language and Thought of the Child*.

1924 — Mary Cover Jones reports reconditioning a fear reaction in a child (Peter), a forerunner of systematic desensitization developed by Joseph Wolpe.

1927 — In *Introduction to the Technique of Child Anal*[…] discusses psychoanalysis in the treatment of c[…]

1929 — Wolfgang Köhler publishes *Gestalt Psycholog*[…] behaviorism and outlines essential elements o[…] position and approach.

1931 — Margaret Floy Washburn becomes the first fem[…] (and the second female scientist in any discipli[…] the U.S. National Academy of Sciences.

1932 — In *The Wisdom of the Body*, Walter B. Cannon c[…] *homeostasis*, discusses the fight-or-flight resp[…] fies hormonal changes associated with stress.

D1074605

Turn the page to continue

1869 Francis Galton, Charles Darwin's cousin, publishes *Hereditary Genius*, in which he claims that intelligence is inherited. In **1876** he coins the expression "nature and nurture" to correspond with "heredity and environment."

1874 Carl Wernicke, a German neurologist and psychiatrist, shows that damage to a specific area in the left temporal lobe (now called Wernicke's area) disrupts ability to comprehend or produce spoken or written language.

1878 G. Stanley Hall receives from Harvard University's Department of Philosophy the first U.S. Ph.D. degree based on psychological research.

1879 Wilhelm Wundt establishes at the University of Leipzig, Germany, the first psychology laboratory, which becomes a Mecca for psychology students from all over the world.

1883 G. Stanley Hall, student of Wilhelm Wundt, establishes the first formal U.S. psychology laboratory at Johns Hopkins University.

1885 Hermann Ebbinghaus publishes *On Memory*, summarizing his extensive research on learning and memory, including the "forgetting curve."

1886 Joseph Jastrow receives from Johns Hopkins University the first Ph.D. degree in psychology awarded by a Department of Psychology in the United States.

1889 Alfred Binet and Henri Beaunis establish the first psychology laboratory in France at the Sorbonne, and the first International Congress of Psychology meets in Paris.

1890 William James, Harvard University philosopher and psychologist, publishes *The Principles of Psychology*, describing psychology as "the science of mental life."

1891 James Mark Baldwin establishes the first psychology laboratory in the British Commonwealth at the University of Toronto.

1892 G. Stanley Hall spearheads the founding of the American Psychological Association (APA) and becomes its first president.

1893 Mary Whiton Calkins (pictured) and Christine Ladd-Franklin are the first women elected to membership in the APA.

1894 Margaret Floy Washburn is the first woman to receive a Ph.D. degree in psychology (Cornell University).

Harvard University denies Mary Whiton Calkins admission to doctoral candidacy because of her gender, despite Hugo Münsterberg's claim that she was the best student he had ever had there.

1896 John Dewey publishes "The Reflex Arc Concept in Psychology," helping to formalize the school of psychology called functionalism.

1898 In "Animal Intelligence," Edward L. Thorndike, Columbia University, describes his learning experiments with cats in "puzzle boxes." In **1905**, he proposes the "law of effect."

1900 Sigmund Freud publishes *The Interpretation of Dreams*, his major theoretical work on psychoanalysis.

1933 Inez Beverly Prosser becomes the first African-American woman to receive a doctoral degree in psychology from a U.S. institution (Ph.D., University of Cincinnati).

1935 Christiana Morgan and Henry Murray introduce the Thematic Apperception Test to elicit fantasies from people undergoing psychoanalysis.

1936 Egas Moniz, Portuguese physician, publishes work on the first frontal lobotomies performed on humans.

1938 B. F. Skinner publishes *The Behavior of Organisms*, which describes operant conditioning of animals.

In *Primary Mental Abilities*, Louis L. Thurstone proposes seven such abilities.

Ugo Cerletti and Lucino Bini use electroshock treatment with a human patient.

1939 David Wechsler publishes the Wechsler-Bellevue intelligence test, forerunner of the Wechsler Intelligence Scale for Children (WISC) and the Wechsler Adult Intelligence Scale (WAIS).

Mamie Phipps Clark (pictured) receives a master's degree from Howard University. In collaboration with Kenneth B. Clark, she later extends her thesis, "The Development of Consciousness of Self in Negro Preschool Children," providing joint research cited in the U.S. Supreme Court's **1954** decision to end racial segregation in public schools.

Edward Alexander Bott helps found the Canadian Psychological Association. He becomes its first president in **1940**.

World War II provides many opportunities for psychologists to enhance the popularity and influence of psychology, especially in applied areas.

1943 Psychologist Starke Hathaway and physician J. Charnley McKinley publish the Minnesota Multiphasic Personality Inventory (MMPI).

1945 Karen Horney, who criticized Freud's theory of female sexual development, publishes *Our Inner Conflicts*.

1946 Benjamin Spock's first edition of *The Commonsense Book of Baby and Child Care* appears; the book will influence child rearing in North America for several decades.

1948 Alfred Kinsey and his colleagues publish *Sexual Behavior in the Human Male*, and they publish *Sexual Behavior in the Human Female* in **1953**.

B. F. Skinner's novel, *Walden Two*, describes a Utopian community based on positive reinforcement, which becomes a clarion call for applying psychological principles in everyday living, especially communal living.

Ernest R. Hilgard publishes *Theories of Learning*, which was required reading for several generations of psychology students in North America.

1949 Raymond B. Cattell publishes the Sixteen Personality Factor Questionnaire (16PF).

Continued on inside back cover

PSYCHOLOGY

TENTH EDITION IN MODULES

PSYCHOLOGY

TENTH EDITION IN MODULES

David G. Myers

Hope College
Holland, Michigan

WORTH PUBLISHERS

Senior Vice President, Editorial and Production: Catherine Woods
Publisher: Kevin Feyen
Executive Marketing Manager: Katherine Nurre
Marketing Assistant: Stephanie Ellis
Development Editors: Christine Brune, Nancy Fleming, Trish Morgan, Betty Probert
Director of Print and Digital Development: Tracey Kuehn
Media Editor: Peter Twickler
Supplements Editor: Betty Probert
Photo Editor: Bianca Moscatelli
Photo Researcher: Donna Ranieri
Art Director: Babs Reingold
Cover Designers: Lyndall Culbertson and Babs Reingold
Interior Designer: Charles Yuen
Layout Designer: Lee Ann McKevitt
Cover Artist: John Webster
Associate Managing Editor: Lisa Kinne
Project Editor: Jeanine Furino
Illustration Coordinators: Bill Page, Janice Donnola
Illustrations: TSI Graphics, Keith Kasnot, Todd Buck
Production Manager: Sarah Segal
Composition: TSI Graphics
Printing and Binding: RR Donnelley

Library of Congress Control Number: 2012930520

ISBN-13: 978-1-4641-0261-5
ISBN-10: 1-4641-0261-9

© 2013, 2010, 2007, 2004 by Worth Publishers

All rights reserved.

Printed in the United States of America

All royalties from the sale of this book are assigned to the David and Carol Myers Foundation, which exists to receive and distribute funds to other charitable organizations.

Worth Publishers
41 Madison Avenue
New York, NY 10010
www.worthpublishers.com

Photo Credits: Cover: *Woman's face:* © Tanner Productions/Corbis; *Trees:* Photodisc; *Drops of water/ripples:* Photodisc; *Human eye:* Digital Vision; *Cat:* Eric Isselée/Shutterstock; Bride/groom: bluehand/Shutterstock; *Sleeping baby:* Courtesy Kevin Feyen; *Smiling girl:* Tim Gainey/Alamy; *Man with glasses:* Tristan Savatier/Getty Images; *Rose:* Frank Chmura/Alamy; *Robins:* Lightscapes Photography Inc./Corbis; *Brain:* From *Mapping the Mind,* Rita Carter (c) 1989 University of California Press; *Elephant:* Johan Swanepoel/Alamy.
pp. x, xl, 14–15, 26–27. 42–43: *Open laptop:* Roman Sigaev/Shutterstock; *Single rose:* Galushko Sergey/Shutterstock; *Close-up of rose:* Frank Chmura/Alamy; *Sigmund Freud:* © Bettmann/Corbis; *Vintage desk:* Hemera Technologies/Getty Images; *Graduation cap:* Ewa Walicka/Shutterstock; *Student on laptop:* Lauren Burke/Getty Images; *Profile of man:* Blend Images/Getty Images; *Child and woman playing "peek a boo":* Laura Dwight; *Green tree:* Yuriy Kulyk/Shutterstock; *Plumeria tree:* Tungphoto/Shutterstock; *Trees in forest:* irin-k/Shutterstock; *Horse head/mouth:* Skye Hohmann/Alamy; *Woman:* Photodisc/Getty Images. **pp. x, 44–45, 59, 68, 81:** *Pills spilled out of container:* Stephen VanHorn/Shutterstock; *Brain with white burst inside:* LiquidLibrary/Jupiterimages; *White mouse:* American Images Inc/Getty Images; *Woman with hair in ponytail:* Paul Burley/Corbis; *Water:* Photodisc. **pp. xi, 82–83, 91, 109, 114, 129:** *Butterflies:* © Svetlana Larina/istockphoto; *Paper cup with coffee:* Vasca/Shutterstock; *Woman meditating:* INSADCO Photography/Alamy; *Sleeping toddler:* swissmacky/Shutterstock; *Kitten:* © Anna63|Dreamstime.com; *Sleeping adult male:* The Agency Collection/Punchstock; *Teenage boy:* Photodisc/Getty Images; *Blue sky with clouds:* Photodisc. **pp. xi, 130–131, 147, 167:** *Topiary bunny:* Icon Digital Featurepix/Alamy; *Earth:* heromen30/Shutterstock; *Mother helping daughter with homework:* Indeed/Getty Images; *Teens texting:* Allan Shoemake/Getty Images; *Dad interacting happily with child:* MGP/Getty Images; *Formal garden:* Alison Cornford-Matheson/Shutterstock; *Twin boys:* © Cold River Production/age fotostock; *Topiary plant:* Digital Vision/Getty Images; **pp. xi, 168–169, 176, 196, 207, 221:** *Checkerboard:* William Warner/Shutterstock; *Wedding rings:* DM7/Shutterstock; *Bucket in sand:* René Mansi/istockphoto; *Beach ball:* WendellandCarolyn/istockphoto; *Checkers:* © Floortje/istockphoto; *Parent using spoon to feed baby:* Asia Images/Getty Images; *Teenagers of different heights:* Rob Lewine/Getty Images; *Wedding couple doll:* bluehand/Shutterstock; *Baby boy crawling:* Juice Images/JupiterImages; *Girl pretend playing:* Image Source/Getty Images; *Pregnant woman on cell phone:* moodboard/JupiterImages; *Baby looking straight ahead:* Asia Images/Getty Images; **pp. xii, 222–223, 233, 256, 273:** *Herbs:* MARGRIT HIRSCH/Shutterstock; *Herbs in bucket:* Ivonne Wierink/Shutterstock; *Human eye:* Andrey Armyagov/Shutterstock; *Citrus:* Lauren Burke/Jupiterimages; *Child holding mother's face:* © Jose Luis Pelaez, Inc./Blend Images/Corbis; *Young man and cello:* sbarabu/Shutterstock; *Teen dancing with headphones (hand):* Photodisc/Jupiterimages; *Woman with eyes closed:* DK Stock/Getty Images; *Sheep:* Eric Isselée/Shutterstock. **pp. xii, 274–275, 285, 297, 309:** *Cat:* Eric Isselée/Shutterstock; *Dog on a tire:* Marina Jay/Shutterstock; *Pigeon:* Vitaly Titov & Maria Sidelnikova/Shutterstock; *Kids playing video games:* Stanislav Solntsev/Getty Images; *Lab rat in a maze:* Will & Deni McIntyre/Photo Researchers, Inc.; *Student working on computer:* Christopher Halloran/Shutterstock; *Young woman:* Digital Vision/Getty Images; *Neptune:* NASA/JPL; *Astronaut:* NASA; *Earth and Mars:* NASA/JPL; *Saturn:* NASA/JPL; *Venus:* NASA/JPL; *Jupiter:* NASA/JPL. **pp. xiii, 310–311, 322, 329, 333, 349:** *Cross section of tree trunk:* Jim Barber/Shutterstock; *Fossil shell in limestone:* Tim Burrett/Shutterstock; *Fossil fern imprint in a rock:* © Gabbro/Alamy; *Rock:* Corbis; *Mousetrap:* © Darren Matthews/Alamy; *Hot air balloon:* © D. Hurst/Alamy; *Chocolate chip cookie:* Peter Johansky/Index Stock/Corbis; *Young man with eyes closed, smiling:* Tim Kitchen/Digital Vision/Getty Images; *Cookie:* Jean Sandler/FeaturePics; *Clark's Nutcracker:* (c) Tim Zurowski/All Canada Photos/Corbis. **pp. xiii, 350–351, 364, 380, 391, 415:** *Stacked stones:* PIKSEL/istockphoto; *Toddler walking:* Jaimie Duplass/Shutterstock; *Woman playing basketball:* Blend Images/Jupiterimages; *Businesswoman explaining graph:* Jupiterimages; *Parrot:* Life on white/Alamy; *Elephant:* Johan Swanepoel/Alamy; *Violin and bow:* Bluemoon Stock/Jupiterimages; *Spider web with dew:* Gazelle Studios; *Chimp bests humans:* Tetsuro Matsuzawa/Primate Research Institute, Kyoto University; *Young woman sitting, portrait:* Photodisc/Getty Images; *Football:* Steve Collender/Shutterstock; *Chess pieces:* bitt24/shutterstock. **pp. xiv, 416–417, 434, 456, 471:** *Bird's eggs:* Duncan Usher/Foto Natura/Getty Images; *Laptop:* cloki/Shutterstock; *Bird's nest with five blue eggs:* Vishnevskiy Vasily/Shutterstock; *Twigs:* ivanastar/istockphoto; *Couple embracing each other:* Yuri Arcurs /Shutterstock; *Two teenage boys:* Photodisc/Jupiterimages; *Woman on treadmill:* PhotoObjects.net/Jupiterimages; *Luggage with chair attached:* www.rideoncarryon.com; *Young couple outdoors:* Petrenko Andriy/Shutterstock; *Teenager girl with braces:* CREATISTA/Shutterstock. **pp. xiv, 472–473, 483, 491, 503, 516, 528, 529:** *Young man:* © Ocean/Corbis; *Two women laughing:* Mark Andersen/Getty Images; *Person meditating in chair:* Dean Mitchell/Shutterstock; *Person jumping for joy:* RubberBall Selects/Alamy; *Women jumping and kicking:* Lev Olkha/Shutterstock; *Nun kneeling in the prayer position:* © PhotosIndia.com LLC/Alamy; *Baseball player:* © Sean Locke/istockphoto; *Cactus:* luchschen/Shutterstock; *Water:* Photodisc; *Tissues:* D. Hurst/Alamy; *Angry man:* Photo Spin, Inc./Alamy; *Man kissing dog:* Photos.com/Getty Images. **pp. xv, 530–531, 542, 546, 569:** *Hindu gods masks:* Bartosz Hadyniak/istockphoto; *Masks:* Perry Correll/shutterstock; *African mask:* brytta/istockphoto; *Colorful mask:* Hemera Technologies/Jupiterimages; *Expressive mask:* Hemera Technologies/Jupiterimages; *Happy dog:* Erik Lam /Shutterstock; *Centaur:* liquidlibrary/Jupiterimages; *Cheerful woman (mask):* Yuri Arcurs/Shutterstock; *Barry Manilow:* Trinity Mirror/Mirrorpix/Alamy; *Teen in blank t-shirt:* Timothy Large/Shutterstock. **pp. xv, 570–571, 578, 592, 607, 623:** *Penguins:* Benjamin Goode/istockphoto; *Stanley Milgram:* Courtesy of CUNY Graduate School and University Center; *Person with tattoo:* David Katzenstein/Photolibrary; *Football:* Todd Taulman/Shutterstock; *Baseball bat and baseball:* Jules Frazier/Jupiterimages; *Flamingoes flying:* Digitalvision; *Young woman smiling:* photosindia/Getty Images. **pp. xvi, 624–625, 636, 644, 656, 664, 673:** *Sea cliff:* Econ711|Dreamstime.com; *Woman looking depressed:* © cultura/Corbis; *Snake:* Hemera Technologies/Jupiterimages; *Mexican redknee tarantula:* Martin Harvey/Jupiterimages; *Broken glass* Thinkart|Dreamstime.com; *Depressed man:* Image Source/Getty Images; *Depressed man (gray shirt):* Brad Wenner/Getty Images. **pp. xvi, 674–675, 691, 703, 713:** *Crocus flowers:* Myotis/Shutterstock; *People in rainforest:* © Randy Faris/Corbis; *Chair:* Hemera Technologies/Jupiterimages; *Therapy session:* David Buffington/Getty Images; *Woman smiling:* Blend Images/Getty Images; *Woman in tank top:* Rubberball/Nicole Hill/Jupiterimages; *Prozac pill:* (c) John Greim/Agerotostock; *Woman consoling another:* Feng Li/Getty Images.

For James B. Maas

pioneering contributor to the teaching of psychology, master teacher, and supportive friend

ABOUT THE AUTHOR

DAVID MYERS received his psychology Ph.D. from the University of Iowa. He has spent his career at Hope College in Michigan, where he has taught dozens of introductory psychology sections. Hope College students have invited him to be their commencement speaker and voted him "outstanding professor."

His research and writings have been recognized by the Gordon Allport Intergroup Relations Prize, by a 2010 Honored Scientist award from the Federation of Associations in Behavioral & Brain Sciences, by a 2010 Award for Service on Behalf of Personality and Social Psychology, and by three honorary doctorates.

Myers' scientific articles have, with support from National Science Foundation grants, appeared in three dozen scientific periodicals, including *Science, American Scientist, Psychological Science*, and the *American Psychologist.* In addition to his scholarly writing and his textbooks for introductory and social psychology, he also digests psychological science for the general public. His writings have appeared in four dozen magazines, from *Today's Education* to *Scientific American.* He also has authored five general audience books, including *The Pursuit of Happiness* and *Intuition: Its Powers and Perils.*

David Myers has chaired his city's Human Relations Commission, helped found a thriving assistance center for families in poverty, and spoken to hundreds of college and community groups. Drawing on his experience, he also has written articles and a book (*A Quiet World*) about hearing loss, and he is advocating a transformation in American assistive listening technology (see www.hearingloop.org). He received the 2011 American Academy of Audiology Presidential Award for his work.

He bikes to work year-round and plays regular pickup basketball. David and Carol Myers have raised two sons and a daughter.

BRIEF CONTENTS

CONTENTS

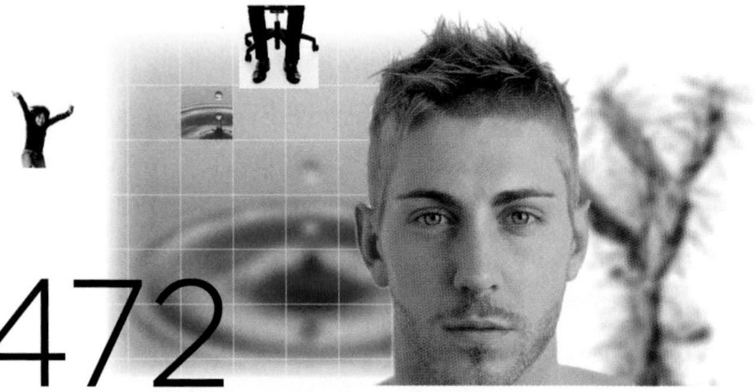

624 PSYCHOLOGICAL DISORDERS

674 THERAPY

PREFACE

Throughout its 10 editions, my unwavering vision for *Psychology* has been *to merge rigorous science with a broad human perspective that engages both mind and heart.* I aim to offer a state-of-the-art introduction to psychological science that speaks to students' needs and interests. I aspire to help students understand and appreciate the wonders of their everyday lives. And I seek to convey the inquisitive spirit with which psychologists *do* psychology.

I am genuinely enthusiastic about psychology and its applicability to our lives. Psychological science has the potential to expand our minds and enlarge our hearts. By studying and applying its tools, ideas, and insights, we can supplement our intuition with critical thinking, restrain our judgmentalism with compassion, and replace our illusions with understanding. By the time students complete this guided tour of psychology, they will also, I hope, have a deeper understanding of our moods and memories, about the reach of our unconscious, about how we flourish and struggle, about how we perceive our physical and social worlds, and about how our biology and culture in turn shape us. (See Tables 1 and 2, next page.)

Believing with Thoreau that "anything living is easily and naturally expressed in popular language," I seek to communicate psychology's scholarship with crisp narrative and vivid storytelling. "A writer's job," says my friend Mary Pipher, "is to tell stories that connect readers to all the people on Earth, to show these people as the complicated human beings they really are, with histories, families, emotions, and legitimate needs." Writing as a solo author, I hope to tell psychology's story in a way that is warmly personal as well as rigorously scientific. I love to reflect on connections between psychology and other realms, such as literature, philosophy, history, sports, religion, politics, and popular culture. And I love to provoke thought, to play with words, and to laugh. For his pioneering 1891 *Principles of Psychology*, William James sought "humor and pathos." And so do I.

I am grateful for the privilege of assisting with the teaching of this mind-expanding discipline to so many students, in so many countries, through so many different languages. To be entrusted with discerning and communicating psychology's insights is both an exciting honor and a great responsibility.

Creating this book is a team sport. Like so many human achievements, it is the product of a collective intelligence. Woodrow Wilson spoke for me: "I not only use all the brains I have, but all I can borrow." The thousands of instructors and millions of students across the globe who have taught or studied with this book (or both) have contributed immensely to its development. Much of this contribution has occurred spontaneously, through correspondence and conversations. For this edition, we also formally involved over 1250 researchers and teaching psychologists, along with many students, in our efforts to gather accurate and up-to-date information about the field of psychology and the content, study aids, and supplements needs of instructors and students in the introductory course. We look forward to continuing feedback as we strive, over future editions, to create an ever better book and teaching package.

TABLE 1 EVOLUTIONARY PSYCHOLOGY AND BEHAVIOR GENETICS

In addition to the coverage found in Modules 11-12, the **evolutionary perspective** is covered on the following pages:

In addition to the coverage found in Modules 11-12, **behavior genetics** is covered on the following pages:

TABLE 2 NEUROSCIENCE

In addition to the coverage found in Modules 4-6, **neuroscience** can be found on the following pages:

Why a Modular Book?

This 54-module text has been a longtime wish come true for me. It breaks out of the box by restructuring the material into a buffet of (a) short, digestible chapters (called modules) that (b) can be selected and assigned in any order.

Have we not all heard the familiar student complaint: "The chapters are too long!" A text's typical 30- to 50-page chapters cannot be read in a single sitting before the eyes grow weary and the mind wanders. So, why not parse the material into readable units? Ask your students whether they would prefer a 700-page book to be organized as fourteen 50-page chapters or as fifty 14-page chapters. You may be surprised at their overwhelming support for shorter chapters. Indeed, students digest material better when they process it in smaller chunks—as "spaced" rather than massed practice.

I have equally often heard from instructors bemoaning the fact that they "just can't get to everything" in the book. Sometimes instructors want to cover certain sections in a traditional, long chapter but not others. For example, in the typical Consciousness chapter, someone may want to cover Sleep and Hypnosis but not Drugs. In *Psychology, Tenth Edition in Modules*, instructors could easily choose to cover Module 8, Sleep and Dreams, and Module 9, Hypnosis, but not Module 10, Drugs and Consciousness.

How Is This Different From *Psychology, Tenth Edition*?

The primary differences between this book and my *Psychology*, tenth edition, text are organization and module independence.

Organization

This book really IS *Psychology*, tenth edition—just in a different format. So, this modular version contains all the updated research and innovative new coverage from *Psychology*, tenth edition. A very few sections have been moved around to accommodate the modular structure. For example, Rates of Psychological Disorders is a separate section at the end of the Psychological Disorders chapter in *Psychology*, tenth edition, but it is covered in the first of the Psychological Disorders modules in this modular version.

The Modules Are Independent

Each module in this book is self-standing rather than dependent upon the others for understanding. Cross-references to other parts of the book have been replaced with brief explanations. In some cases, illustrations or key terms are repeated to avoid possible confusion. No assumptions are made about what students have read prior to each module. This independence gives instructors ultimate flexibility in deciding which modules to use, and in what order. Connections among psychology's subfields and findings are still made—they are just made in a way that does not assume knowledge of other parts of the book.

What's NEW Since *Psychology, Ninth Edition in Modules*?

This tenth edition is the most carefully reworked and extensively updated of all the revisions to date. This new edition features improvements to the organization and presentation, especially to our system of supporting student learning and remembering.

NEW Study System Follows Best Practices From Learning and Memory Research

The new learning system harnesses the *testing effect,* which documents the benefits of actively retrieving information through self-testing. Thus, each module now offers new *Retrieval Practice* questions interspersed throughout. Creating these *desirable difficulties* for students along the way optimizes the testing effect, as does *immediate feedback* (via inverted answers beneath each question).

In addition, each main section of text begins with numbered questions that establish *learning objectives* and direct student reading. The Module Review section repeats these questions as a further self-testing opportunity (with answers in the Complete Module Reviews appendix). The Module Review section also offers a page-referenced list of key terms and concepts.

Over 1400 New Research Citations

My scrutiny of dozens of scientific periodicals and science news sources, enhanced by commissioned reviews and countless e-mails from instructors and students, enables my integrating our field's most important, thought-provoking, and student-relevant new discoveries. Part of the pleasure that sustains this work is learning something new every day! (For a complete list of significant changes to the content, see www.worthpub.com/myers.)

Reorganized Modules

In addition to the new pedagogy and updated coverage, I've introduced the following organizational changes:

- Module 1 concludes with a new section, "Improve Your Retention—And Your Grades!" This guide will help students replace ineffective and inefficient old habits with new habits that increase retention and success.
- Module 16, Adulthood, has been shortened by moving the Aging and Intelligence coverage to Module 30, Assessing Intelligence.
- The six Sensation and Perception modules have been condensed into three modules offering better integrated, more efficient coverage of the concepts (rather than offering all of sensation followed by all of perception). Coverage of the deaf experience is now in Module 28, Language and Thought.
- There is now a separate "Biology, Cognition, and Learning" module (Module 22) that more fully explores the biological and cognitive constraints on classical, operant, and observational learning.
- The Memory modules follow a new format, and more clearly explain how different brain networks process and retain memories. I worked closely with Janie Wilson (Professor of Psychology at Georgia Southern University and Vice President for Programming of the Society for the Teaching of Psychology) in the revision of this group of modules.
- Retitled Module 40, Psychodynamic Theories, offers improved coverage of modern-day psychodynamic approaches, which are now more clearly distinguished from their historical Freudian roots.
- The Social Psychology modules now follow the Personality modules.
- The Dissociative and Personality Disorders module (now Module 51) now also includes coverage of eating disorders, previously in the Hunger module.

Clinical Modules Were Carefully Reviewed and Significantly Improved

With helpful guidance from clinical psychologist colleagues, I have strengthened the clinical perspective, which has improved the Personality, Psychological Disorders, and Therapy modules, among others. For example, I cover problem-focused and emotion-focused coping strategies and the relationship of psychotherapy to cancer survival in Module 38, Stress and Health. Module 30, Assessing Intelligence, describes how psychologists use intelligence tests in clinical settings. Material from today's positive psychology is also woven throughout (see **TABLE 3**).

In addition, historical psychoanalysis and modern-day psychodynamic theories are now more clearly distinguished in Module 40, Psychodynamic Theories; Module 52, The Psychological Therapies; and Module 53, Evaluating Psychotherapies.

TABLE 3 EXAMPLES OF POSITIVE PSYCHOLOGY

Coverage of **positive psychology** topics can be found in the following modules:

Topic	Module
Altruism/Compassion	15, 29, 41, 46, 53
Coping	39
Courage	44, 46
Creativity	29, 42, 43
Emotional intelligence	29, 46
Empathy	14, 22, 37, 46, 52, 53
Flow	34
Gratitude	39, 46
Happiness/Life Satisfaction	16, 33, 34, 37, 39
Humility	43
Humor	39, 44
Justice	44, 46
Leadership	34, 42, 44
Love	12, 16, 33, 39, 42, 46, 47, 53
Morality	14, 15
Optimism	39, 42
Personal control	39
Resilience	14, 39, 46, 53
Self-discipline	14, 15, 32, 33, 34, 42
Self-efficacy	39, 42
Self-esteem	32, 33, 34, 39, 42
Spirituality	39, 44
Toughness (grit)	31, 34
Wisdom	1, 7, 15, 16, 27, 42, 43, 44, 46

New Time Management Section for Students

To help students maximize their reading, studying, and exam preparation efforts, a new student preface offers time management guidance.

Beautiful New Design and Contemporary New Photo Program

This new, more open and colorful design, chock-full of new photos and illustrations, provides a modern visual context for the book's up-to-date coverage.

Streamlined Coverage

The writing and presentation in every module has been tightened, with fewer overlapping examples and consolidated coverage of some topics (for example, including all of the deaf experience coverage in one module rather than spreading it across two). The net result, despite 1400 new citations, is some 20 fewer pages than in the ninth edition.

Dedicated Versions of Next-Generation Media

This tenth edition is accompanied by the dramatically enhanced **PsychPortal**, which adds new features (**LearningCurve** formative assessment activities and **Launch Pad** carefully crafted prebuilt assignments), while incorporating the full range of Worth's psychology media products (Video Tool Kit, PsychInvestigator, PsychSim). (For details, see p. 000.)

What Continues?

Eight Guiding Principles

Despite all the exciting changes, this new edition retains its predecessors' voice, as well as much of the content and organization. It also retains the goals—the guiding principles—that have animated the previous nine editions:

Facilitating the Learning Experience

1. **To teach critical thinking** By presenting research as intellectual detective work, I illustrate an inquiring, analytical mind-set. Whether students are studying development, cognition, or social behavior, they will become involved in, and see the rewards of, critical reasoning. Moreover, they will discover how an empirical approach can help them evaluate competing ideas and claims for highly publicized phenomena ranging from ESP and alternative therapies, to astrology and repressed and recovered memories.

2. **To integrate principles and applications** Throughout—by means of anecdotes, case histories, and the posing of hypothetical situations—I relate the findings of basic research to their applications and implications. Where psychology can illuminate pressing human issues—be they racism and sexism, health and happiness, or violence and war—I have not hesitated to shine its light.

3. **To reinforce learning at every step** Everyday examples and rhetorical questions encourage students to process the material actively. Concepts are presented and then frequently applied to reinforce learning. To help students learn and *retain* important concepts and terminology, the text offers numbered Learning Objective Questions at the beginning of each main section, Retrieval Practice self-tests throughout each module, a marginal glossary, and end-of-module key terms.

Demonstrating the Science of Psychology

4. **To exemplify the process of inquiry** I strive to show students not just the outcome of research, but how the research process works. Throughout, the book tries to excite the reader's curiosity. It invites readers to imagine themselves as participants in classic experiments. Several modules introduce research stories as mysteries that progressively unravel as one clue after another falls into place.

5. **To be as up-to-date as possible** Few things dampen students' interest as quickly as the sense that they are reading stale news. While retaining psychology's classic studies and concepts, I also present the discipline's most important recent developments. More than 1000 references in this edition are dated 2009–2011. Likewise, the new photos and everyday examples are drawn from today's world.

6. **To put facts in the service of concepts** My intention is not to fill students' intellectual file drawers with facts, but to reveal psychology's major concepts—to teach students how to think, and to offer psychological ideas worth thinking about. In each module, I place emphasis on those concepts I hope students will carry with them long after they complete the course. Always, I try to follow Albert Einstein's purported dictum that "everything should be made as simple as possible, but not simpler." Retrieval Practice questions throughout each module help students learn and retain the key concepts.

Promoting Big Ideas and Broadened Horizons

7. **To enhance comprehension by providing continuity** Because the book has a single author, many significant topics—such as cognitive neuroscience, dual processing, cultural and gender diversity, behavior genetics, human rationality and irrationality, empathy for and understanding of troubled lives—weave throughout the whole book, and students hear a consistent voice.

"The uniformity of a work," observed Edward Gibbon, "denotes the hand of a single artist."

8. **To convey respect for human unity and diversity** Throughout the book, readers will see evidence of our human kinship—our shared biological heritage, our common mechanisms of seeing and learning, hungering and feeling, loving and hating. They will also better understand the dimensions of our diversity—our *individual* diversity in development and aptitudes, temperament and personality, and disorder and health; and our *cultural* diversity in attitudes and expressive styles, child rearing and care for the elderly, and life priorities.

Continually Improving Cultural and Gender Diversity Coverage

This edition presents an even more thoroughly cross-cultural perspective on psychology (**TABLE 4** on the next page)—reflected in research findings, and text and photo examples. Coverage of the psychology of women and men is thoroughly integrated (see **TABLE 5** on the next page). In addition, I am working to offer a world-based psychology for our worldwide student readership. Thus, I continually search the world for research findings and text and photo examples, conscious that readers may be in Melbourne, Sheffield, Vancouver, or Nairobi. North American and European examples come easily, given that I reside in the United States, maintain contact with friends and colleagues in Canada, subscribe to several European periodicals, and live periodically in the U.K. This edition, for example, offers 135 British examples and 65 mentions of Australia and New Zealand. We are all citizens of a shrinking world, thanks to increased migration and the growing global economy. Thus, American students, too, benefit from information and examples that internationalize their world-consciousness. And if psychology seeks to explain *human* behavior (not just American or Canadian or Australian behavior), the broader the scope of studies presented, the more accurate is our picture of this world's people. My aim is to expose all students to the world beyond their own culture, and I continue to welcome input and suggestions from all readers.

Discussion of the relevance of cultural and gender diversity begins on the first page of the first module and continues throughout the text. Modules 11–12 provide focused coverage, encouraging students to appreciate cultural and gender differences and commonalities, and to consider the interplay of nature and nurture.

Strong Critical Thinking Coverage

I aim to introduce students to critical thinking throughout the book. Revised Learning Objective Questions at the beginning of each main section, and Retrieval Practice questions throughout each module, encourage critical reading to glean an understanding of important concepts. This tenth edition also includes the following opportunities for students to learn or practice their critical thinking skills.

- ***Module 2, Thinking Critically With Psychological Science, and Module 3, Research Strategies: How Psychologists Ask and Answer Questions,*** introduce students to psychology's research methods, emphasizing the fallacies of our everyday intuition and common sense and, thus, the need for psychological science. Critical thinking is introduced as a key term (p. 20). The Statistical Reasoning discussion encourages students to "focus on thinking smarter by applying simple statistical principles to everyday reasoning" (pp. 38–42).

TABLE 4 CULTURE AND MULTICULTURAL EXPERIENCE

Coverage of **culture and multicultural experience** can be found on the following pages:

TABLE 5 THE PSYCHOLOGY OF MEN AND WOMEN

Coverage of the **psychology of men and women** can be found on the following pages:

- ***"Thinking Critically About . . ." boxes*** are found throughout the book, modeling for students a critical approach to some key issues in psychology. For example, see the updated box "Thinking Critically About: The Fear Factor—Why We Fear the Wrong Things" (page 358).
- ***Detective-style stories*** throughout the narrative get students thinking critically about psychology's key research questions. For example, in Module 50, I present the causes of schizophrenia piece by piece, showing students how researchers put the puzzle together.
- ***"Apply this"*** and ***"Think about it"*** style discussions keep students active in their study of each module. In Module 44, for example, students take the perspective of participants in a Solomon Asch conformity experiment, and later in one of Stanley Milgram's obedience experiments. I've also asked students to join the fun by taking part in activities they can try along the way. For example, in Module 17, they try out a quick sensory adaptation activity. In Module 36, they try matching expressions to faces and test the effects of different facial expressions on themselves.
- ***Critical examinations of pop psychology*** spark interest and provide important lessons in thinking critically about everyday topics. For example, Module 18 includes a close examination of ESP, and Module 26 addresses the controversial topic of repression of painful memories.

See **TABLE 6** for a complete list of this text's coverage of critical thinking topics and Thinking Critically About boxes.

TABLE 6 CRITICAL THINKING AND RESEARCH EMPHASIS

Critical thinking coverage, and in-depth stories of psychology's **scientific research** process, can be found on the following pages:

Thinking Critically About . . . boxes:

Addiction, p. 114
The Evolutionary Perspective on Human Sexuality, p. 146
Can Subliminal Messages Control Our Behavior?, p. 227
ESP—Perception Without Sensation?, pp. 253-255
Does Viewing Media Violence Trigger Violent Behavior?, p. 308
The Fear Factor—Why We Fear the Wrong Things, pp. 358–359
Lie Detection, pp. 481–482
Complementary and Alternative Medicine, p. 526
How to Be a "Successful" Astrologer or Palm Reader, pp. 550–551
ADHD—Normal High Energy or Genuine Disorder?, p. 627
Insanity and Responsibility, p. 633
"Regressing" from Unusual to Usual, p. 693

Critical Examinations of Pop Psychology:

The need for psychological science, p. 15
Perceiving order in random events, pp. 17–18
Do we use only 10 percent of our brains?, pp. 73–74
Can hypnosis enhance recall? Coerce action? Be therapeutic? Alleviate pain?, pp. 110–112
Has the concept of "addiction" been stretched too far?, p. 116
Near-death experiences, p. 124
Critiquing the evolutionary perspective, p. 146
How much credit or blame do parents deserve?, pp. 149–150
Sensory restriction, pp. 250–251
Is there extrasensory perception?, pp. 253–254
Do other species exhibit language?, pp. 373–375
Complementary and alternative medicine, p. 526
How valid is the Rorschach test?, p. 538
Is repression a myth?, p. 40
Is Freud credible?, pp. 539–541
Is psychotherapy effective?, pp. 692–695
Evaluating alternative therapies, pp. 692–695
Do video games teach or release violence?, pp. 604–606

Thinking Critically With Psychological Science:

The limits of intuition and common sense, pp. 16–21
The scientific attitude, pp. 19–20
"Critical thinking" introduced as a key term, p. 20
The scientific method, pp. 26–27
Correlation and causation, pp. 31–34
Exploring cause and effect, pp. 34–35
Random assignment, p. 35
Independent and dependent variables, pp. 36–37
Statistical reasoning, pp. 38–42
Describing data, pp. 38–40
Making inferences, pp. 41–42

Scientific Detective Stories:

Is breast milk better than formula?, pp. 34–36
Our divided brains, pp. 76–78
Why do we sleep?, pp. 98–99
Why do we dream?, pp. 106–109
Is hypnosis an extension of normal consciousness or an altered state?, pp. 112–114
Twin and adoption studies, pp. 133–137
How a child's mind develops, pp. 179–186
Aging and intelligence, pp. 398–400
Parallel processing, pp. 239–240
How do we see in color?, pp. 241–242
How do we store memories in our brains?, pp. 323–324
How are memories constructed?, pp. 316–321
Do other species exhibit language?, pp. 373–375
Why do we feel hunger?, pp. 322–324
What determines sexual orientation?, pp. 442–448
The pursuit of happiness: Who is happy, and why?, pp. 495–502
Why—and in whom—does stress contribute to heart disease?, pp. 512–515
How and why is social support linked with health?, pp. 519–521
Self-esteem versus self-serving bias, pp. 565–568
What causes mood disorders?, pp. 647–655
Do prenatal viral infections increase risk of schizophrenia?, pp. 660-661
Is psychotherapy effective?, pp. 692–696
Why do people fail to help in emergencies?, pp. 615–616

APA Principles for Quality Undergraduate Education in Psychology

In February 2011, the American Psychological Association (APA) Council of Representatives approved the new *Principles for Quality Undergraduate Education in Psychology*, which had been assembled by the participants at the APA National Conference on Undergraduate Education in Psychology, organized by Diane F. Halpern (Claremont McKenna College, and past-president of APA). These principles were designed to help students develop appropriate workplace skills, solid academic preparation for continued studies, and the "knowledge, skills, and abilities that will enhance their personal lives." (See www.apa.org/education/undergrad/principles.aspx.)

Psychology departments in many schools hope to use these principles and their associated recommendations to help them establish their own benchmarks. Some instructors are eager to know whether a given text for the introductory course helps students get a good start at achieving these goals. *Psychology, Tenth Edition in Modules* will work nicely to help you begin to address these goals in your department. See www.worthpublishers.com/myers for a detailed guide to how *Psychology, Tenth Edition in Modules* corresponds to the 2011 APA Principles.

Next-Generation Multimedia

Psychology, Tenth Edition in Modules boasts impressive multimedia options. For more information about any of these choices, visit Worth Publishers' online catalog at www.worthpublishers.com.

PsychPortal With LearningCurve Quizzing

The tenth edition's dramatically enhanced **PsychPortal** (see **FIGURE 1**), adds new features (**LearningCurve** formative assessment activities and **Launch Pad** carefully crafted prebuilt assignments), while incorporating the full range of Worth's psychology media options (Video Tool Kit, PsychInvestigator, PsychSim).

FIGURE 1
PsychPortal opening page

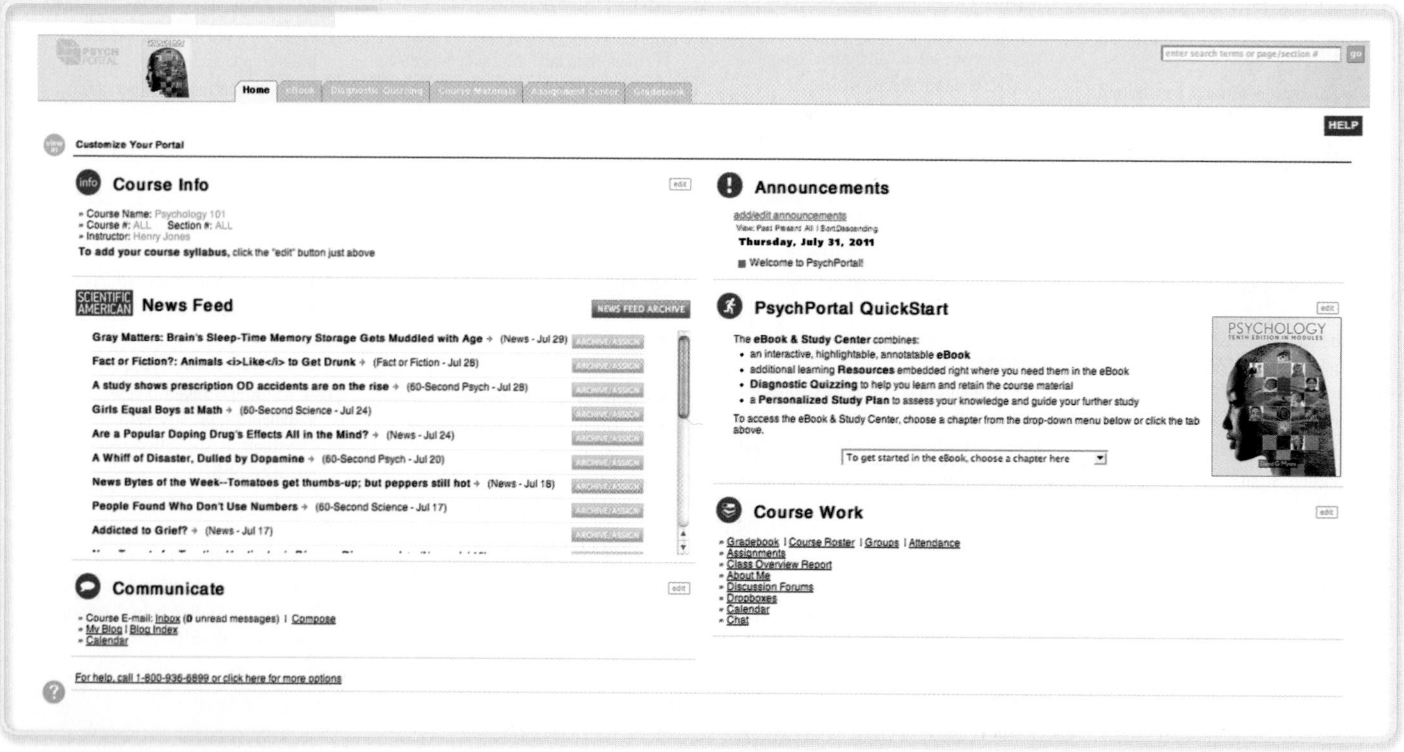

Based on the latest findings from learning and memory research, LearningCurve combines adaptive question selection, personalized study plans, immediate and valuable feedback, and state-of-the-art question analysis reports. LearningCurve's game-like nature keeps students engaged while helping them learn and *remember* key concepts.

Launch Pad offers a set of prebuilt assignments, carefully crafted by a group of instructional designers and instructors who have an abundance of teaching experience as well as deep familiarity with Worth Publishers' content. Each Launch Pad unit contains videos, activities, and formative assessment pieces to build student understanding for each topic, culminating with a randomized summative quiz to hold students accountable for the unit. Assign units in just a few clicks, and find scores in your gradebook upon submission. Launch Pad appeals not only to instructors who have been interested in adding an online component to their course but haven't been able to invest the time, but also to experienced online instructors curious to see how other colleagues might scaffold a series of online activities. Customize units as you wish, adding and dropping content to fit your course.

Student Resources

- eBook in various available formats
- Video Tool Kit for Introductory Psychology
- PsychInvestigator
- PsychSim 5.0
- PsychInquiry
- Psych2Go (audio downloads for study and review)
- Book Companion Site

Faculty Support

- **New! Faculty Lounge** (see **FIGURE 2**) is an online place to find and share favorite teaching ideas and materials, including videos, animations, images, PowerPoint® slides and lectures, news stories, articles, web links, and lecture activities. Includes publisher- as well as peer-provided resources—all faculty-reviewed for accuracy and quality.
- Instructor's Media Guide for Introductory Psychology
- Enhanced Course Management Solutions (including course cartridges)

Video and Presentation

- **New! Worth Introductory Psychology Videos,** produced in conjunction with ***Scientific American*** and ***Nature,*** is a breakthrough collection of NEW modular, tutorial videos on core psychology topics. This set includes animations, interviews with top scientists, and carefully selected archival footage and is available on flash drive and DVD, or as part of the new Worth Video Anthology for Introductory Psychology.
- **New! The Worth Video Anthology for Introductory Psychology** is a complete collection, all in one place, of our video clips from the **Video Tool Kit,** the **Digital Media Archive,** and the third edition of the ***Scientific American Frontiers Teaching Modules,*** as well as from the new ***Worth Introductory Psychology Videos*** co-produced with ***Scientific American*** and ***Nature.*** Available on DVD or flash drive, the set is accompanied by its own Faculty Guide.
- **New! Interactive Presentation Slides for Introductory Psychology** is an extraordinary series of PowerPoint® lectures. This is a dynamic, yet easy-to-use new way to engage

FIGURE 2
Sample from our Faculty Lounge site

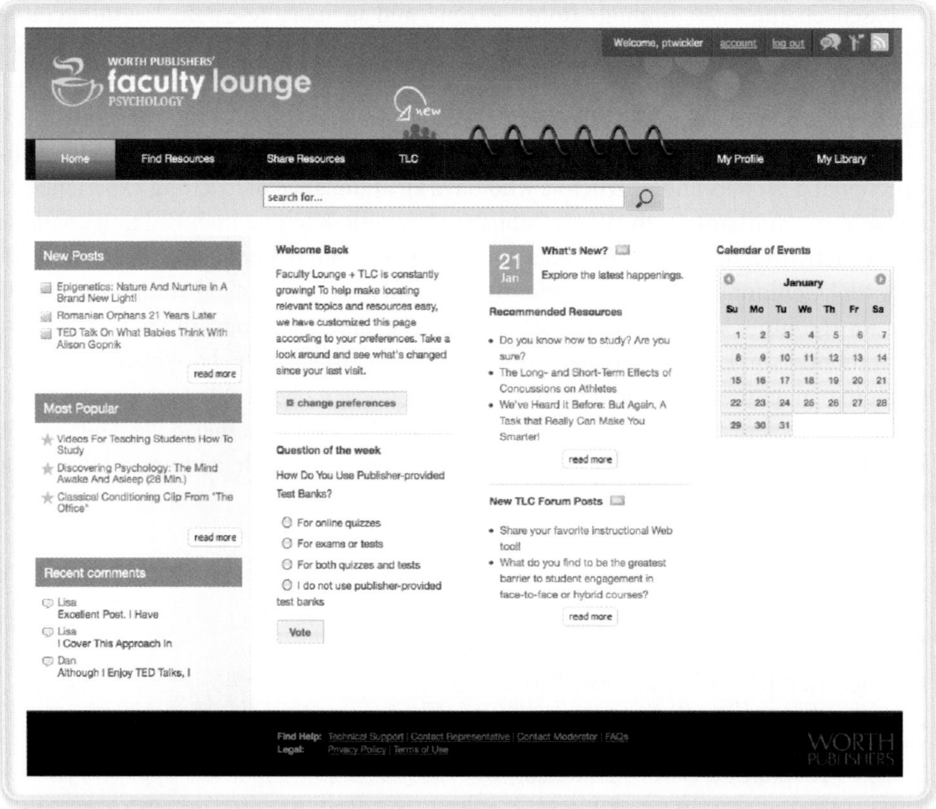

students during classroom presentations of core psychology topics. Provides opportunities for discussion and interaction. Includes an unprecedented number of embedded video clips and animations (including activities from our **ActivePsych** series).

Assessment

- **New! LearningCurve**
- Printed Test Bank
- Diploma Computerized Test Bank
- Online Quizzing
- i•clicker Radio Frequency Classroom Response System

Print

- Instructor's Resources
- Lecture Guides
- Study Guide
- *Pursuing Human Strengths: A Positive Psychology Guide*
- *Critical Thinking Companion*, Second Edition
- *Psychology and the Real World: Essays Illustrating Fundamental Contributions to Society.* This 2011 project of the FABBS Foundation brought together a virtual "Who's Who" of contemporary psychological scientists to describe—in clear, captivating ways—the research they have passionately pursued and what it means to the "real world." Each contribution is an original essay written for this project.

From Scientific American

- Improving the Mind & Brain: A *Scientific American* Special Issue
- *Scientific American* Reader to Accompany Myers

In Appreciation

If it is true that "whoever walks with the wise becomes wise" then I am wiser for all the wisdom and advice received from my colleagues. Aided by thousands of consultants and reviewers over the last two decades, this has become a better, more accurate book than one author alone (this author, at least) could write. As my editors and I keep reminding ourselves, all of us together are smarter than any one of us.

My indebtedness continues to each of the teacher-scholars whose influence I acknowledged in the nine previous editions, to the innumerable researchers who have been so willing to share their time and talent to help me accurately report their research, and to the 500 instructors who took the time to respond to our early information-gathering survey (with my apologies to those who were not able to participate when we met our cap of 500 within two hours of deploying the survey), and 400 more who took a later, smaller survey. I also appreciated having careful reviews of the entire tenth edition, as well as detailed consultation on the Memory coverage from Janie Wilson (Georgia Southern University, and Vice President for Programming of the Society of the Teaching of Psychology).

My gratitude extends to the colleagues who contributed criticism, corrections, and creative ideas related to the content, pedagogy, and format of this new edition and its teaching package. For their expertise and encouragement, and the gifts of their time to the teaching of psychology, I thank the reviewers and consultants listed below.

Lisa Abrams,
Hunter College

William Acker,
Chino Hills High School (CA)

Geri Acquard,
Walter Johnson High School (MD), and Howard Community College

Karen Albertini,
Penn State University

Jonathan Appel,
Tiffin University

Willow Aureala,
Hawaii Community College/University of Hawaii Center, W. H.

Hallie Baker,
Muskingum University

Meeta Banerjee,
Michigan State University

Joy Berrenberg,
University of Colorado, Denver

Joan Bihun,
University of Colorado, Denver

Megan Bradley,
Frostburg State University

Stephen Brasel,
Moody Bible Institute

Sherry Broadwell,
Georgia State University

Jane Brown,
Athens Technical College

Tamara Brown,
University of Kentucky

Mark Carter,
Baker University

Jenel Cavazos,
University of Oklahoma

Brian Charboneau,
Wekiva High School (FL)

Stephen Chew,
Samford University

Katherine Clemans,
University of Florida

James Collins,
Middle Georgia College

Ingrid Cominsky,
Onondaga Community College

Corey Cook,
University of Florida

Grant Corser,
Southern Utah University

Janet Dean,
Asbury University

Deanna DeGidio,
North Virginia Community College

Beth Dietz-Uhler,
Miami University

Stephanie Ding,
Del Mar College

William Dragon,
Cornell College

Kathryn Dumper,
Bainbridge College

David Dunaetz,
Azusa Pacific University

Julie Earles,
Florida Atlantic University

Kristin Flora,
Franklin College

James Foley,
The College of Wooster

Nicole Ford,
Walter Johnson High School (MD)

Lisa Fozio-Thielk,
Waubonsee Community College

Sue Frantz,
Highline Community College

Phyllis Freeman,
State University of New York, New Paltz

Julia Fullick,
Rollins College

Christopher Gade,
Dominican University of California

Becky Ganes,
Modesto Junior College

Gary Gillund,
The College of Wooster

William Goggin,
University of Southern Mississippi

Andrea Goldstein,
Keiser University

Chris Goode,
Georgia State University

Peter Graf,
University of British Columbia

Jeffrey Green,
Virginia Commonwealth University

Jerry J. Green,
Tarrant County College

Stephen Hampe,
Utica College

Marissa Harrison,
Penn State, Harrisburg

William Hart,
University of Alabama

Michael Hendery,
Southern New Hampshire University

Patricia Hinton,
Hiwassee College

Debra Hollister,
Valencia Community College

Richard Houston-Norton,
West Texas A & M University

Alishia Huntoon,
Oregon Institute of Technology

Matthew Isaak,
University of Louisiana, Lafayette

Diana Joy,
Community College of Denver

Bethany Jurs,
University of Wisconsin, Stout

Richard Keen,
Converse College

Barbara Kennedy,
Brevard Community College

April Kindrick,
South Puget Sound Community College

Kristina Klassen,
North Idaho College

Mark Kline,
Elon University

Larry Kollman,
North Iowa Area Community College

Lee Kooler,
Yosemite Community College

Kristine Kovak-Lesh,
Ripon University

Elizabeth Lanthier,
Northern Virginia Community College
Cathy Lawrenz,
Johnson County Community College
Fred Leavitt,
California State University, East Bay
Jennifer Levitas,
Strayer University
Gary Lewandowski,
Monmouth University
Peter Lifton,
Northeastern University
Mark Loftis,
Tennessee Technological University
Cecile Marczinski,
Northern Kentucky University
Monica Marsee,
University of New Orleans
Mary-Elizabeth Maynard,
Leominster High School (MA)
Judy McCown,
University of Detroit Mercy
Todd McKerchar,
Jacksonville State University
Michelle Merwin,
The University of Tennessee at Martin
Amy Miron,
Community College of Baltimore County
Charles Miron,
Community College of Baltimore County
Paulina Multhaupt,
Macomb Community College
Joel Nadler,
Southern Illinois University, Edwardsville
Carmelo Nina,
William Paterson University
Wendy North-Ollendorf,
Northwestern Connecticut Community College
Margaret Norwood,
Community College of Aurora
Lindsay Novak,
College of Saint Mary
Michie Odle,
State University of New York, Cortland
Caroline Olko,
Nassau Community College
Jennifer Peluso,
Florida Atlantic University
Marion Perlmutter,
University of Michigan
Maura PiLotti,
New Mexico Highlands University
Shane Pitts,
Birmingham-Southern College
Chantel Prat,
University of Washington
William Price,
North Country Community College
Chris K. Randall,
Kennesaw State University
Jenny Rinehart,
University of New Mexico
Vicki Ritts,
St. Louis Community College, Meramec
Alan Roberts,
Indiana University
Karena Rush,
Millersville University
Lisa Sanders,
Austin High School (TX)
Catherine Sanderson,
Amherst College
Kristina Schaefer,
Moorpark College
Cory Scherer,
Penn State, Schuylkill
Erin Schoeberl,
Mount Saint Mary College
Paul Schulman,
State University of New York Institute of Technology
Michael Schumacher,
Columbus State Community College
Jane Sheldon,
University of Michigan, Dearborn
Mark Sibiky,
Marietta College
Lisa Sinclair,
University of Winnipeg
Starlette Sinclair,
Georgia Institute of Technology
Stephanie Smith,
Indiana University Northwest

Michael Spiegler,
Providence College
George Spilich,
Washington College
Lynn Sprout,
Jefferson Community College
Kim Stark-Wroblewski,
University of Central Missouri
Krishna Stilianos,
Oakland Community College
Jaine Strauss,
Macalester College
Robert Strausser,
Baptist College for Health Sciences
James Sullivan,
Florida State University
Richard Tafalla,
University of Wisconsin, Stout
Michael Vallante,
Quinsigamond Community College
Amanda Vanderbur,
Zionsville Community High School (IN)
Jason Vasquez,
Illinois State University
Craig Vickio,
Bowling Green State University
Rachel Walker,
Charleston Southern University
Lou Ann Wallace,
University of Tennessee, Martin Parsons Center
Erica Weisgram,
University of Wisconsin, Stevens Point
Elizabeth Weiss,
The Ohio State University of Newark
Ryan Wessle,
Northwest Missouri State
Robert Westbrook,
Washington State Community College
Penny Williams,
Jackson Community College
William C. Williams,
Spokane Falls Community College
Jennifer Yanowitz,
Utica College
Tammy Zacchili,
Saint Leo University

At Worth Publishers a host of people played key roles in creating this tenth edition.

Although the information gathering is never ending, the formal planning began as the author-publisher team gathered for a two-day retreat in June 2010. This happy and creative gathering included John Brink, Thomas Ludwig, Richard Straub, and me from the author team, along with my assistants Kathryn Brownson and Sara Neevel. We were joined by Worth Publishers executives Tom Scotty, Elizabeth Widdicombe, Catherine Woods, Craig Bleyer, and Mark Resmer; editors Christine Brune, Kevin Feyen, Nancy Fleming, Tracey Kuehn, Betty Probert, and Trish Morgan; artistic director Babs Reingold; sales and marketing colleagues Tom Kling, Carlise Stembridge, John Britch, Lindsay Johnson, Cindi Weiss, Kari Ewalt, Mike Howard, and Matt Ours; and special guests Amy Himsel (El Camino Community College), Jennifer Peluso (Florida Atlantic University), Charlotte vanOyen Witvliet (Hope College), and Jennifer Zwolinski (University of San Diego). The input and brainstorming during this meeting of minds gave birth, among other things, to the study aids in this edition, the carefully revised clinical coverage, the decision to reduce the overall length, and the refreshing new design.

Christine Brune, chief editor for the last eight editions, is a wonder worker. She offers just the right mix of encouragement, gentle admonition, attention to detail, and passion for excellence. An author could not ask for more.

Development editor Nancy Fleming is one of those rare editors who is gifted both at "thinking big"—and with a kindred spirit to my own—while also applying her sensitive, graceful, line-by-line touches.

Editor Trish Morgan has amazed me once again with her meticulous eye, impressive knowledge, and deft editing.

Executive Editor Kevin Feyen is a valued team leader, thanks to his dedication, creativity, and sensitivity. Publisher Catherine Woods helped construct and execute the plan for this text and its supplements. Catherine was also a trusted sounding board as we faced a seemingly unending series of discrete decisions along the way. Peter Twickler coordinated production of the huge supplements package for this edition. Betty Probert efficiently edited and produced the print supplements and, in the process, helped fine-tune the whole book. Betty also took on the role of a Development Editor for the text for this edition, which allowed us to achieve our tight deadlines. Adam Frese and Nadina Persaud provided invaluable support in commissioning and organizing the multitude of reviews, sending information to professors, and handling numerous other daily tasks related to the book's development and production. Lee Ann McKevitt did a splendid job of laying out each page. Bianca Moscatelli and Donna Ranieri worked together to locate the myriad photos.

Tracey Kuehn, Director of Print and Digital Development, displayed tireless tenacity, commitment, and impressive organization in leading Worth's gifted artistic production team and coordinating editorial input throughout the production process. Production Manager Sarah Segal masterfully kept the book to its tight schedule, and Babs Reingold skillfully directed creation of the beautiful new design and art program. Production Manager Stacey Alexander, along with supplements production editors Jenny Chiu and Julio Espin, did their usual excellent work of producing the many supplements.

To achieve our goal of supporting the teaching of psychology, this teaching package not only must be authored, reviewed, edited, and produced, but also made available to teachers of psychology. For their exceptional success in doing that, our author team is grateful to Worth Publishers' professional sales and marketing team. We are especially grateful to Executive Marketing Manager Kate Nurre, Marketing Manager Lindsay Johnson, and National Psychology and Economics Consultant Tom Kling both for their tireless efforts to inform our teaching colleagues of our efforts to assist their teaching, and for the joy of working with them.

At Hope College, the supporting team members for this edition included Kathryn Brownson, who researched countless bits of information and proofed hundreds of pages. Kathryn has become a knowledgeable and sensitive adviser on many matters, and Sara Neevel has become our high-tech manuscript developer, par excellence.

Again, I gratefully acknowledge the influence and editing assistance of my writing coach, poet Jack Ridl, whose influence resides in the voice you will be hearing in the pages that follow. He, more than anyone, cultivated my delight in dancing with the language, and taught me to approach writing as a craft that shades into art.

After hearing countless dozens of people say that this book's supplements have taken their teaching to a new level, I reflect on how fortunate I am to be a part of a team in which everyone has produced on-time work marked by the highest professional standards. For their remarkable talents, their long-term dedication, and their friendship, I thank John Brink, Thomas Ludwig, and Richard Straub, and I welcome Jennifer Peluso (Florida Atlantic University) to our teaching package team. I am grateful for Jenny's excellent work—building on the many years of creative effort contributed by the late Martin Bolt.

Finally, my gratitude extends to the many students and instructors who have written to offer suggestions, or just an encouraging word. It is for them, and those about to begin their study of psychology, that I have done my best to introduce the field I love.

The day this book went to press was the day I started gathering information and ideas for the eleventh edition. Your input will again influence how this book continues to evolve. So, please, do share your thoughts.

Hope College
Holland, Michigan 49422-9000
davidmyers.org

TIME MANAGEMENT

Or, How to Be a Great Student and Still Have a Life!

—Richard O. Straub University of Michigan, Dearborn

© Nick Parkas

Motivated students: This course at Bunker Hill Community College meets at the increasingly popular time of midnight to 2:00 A.M., allowing shift workers, busy parents, and others to make it to class.

We all face challenges in our schedules. Some of you may be taking midnight courses, others squeezing in an online course in between jobs or after putting children to bed at night. Some of you may be veterans using military benefits to jump-start a new life.

How can you balance all of your life's demands and be successful? Time management. Manage the time you have so that you can find the time you need.

In this section, I will outline a simple, four-step process for improving the way you make use of your time.

1. Keep a time diary to understand how you are using your time. You may be surprised at how much time you're wasting.
2. Design a new schedule for using your time more effectively.
3. Make the most of your study time so that your new schedule will work for you.
4. If necessary, refine your new schedule, based on what you've learned.

How Are You Using Your Time Now?

Although everyone gets 24 hours in the day and seven days in the week, we fill those hours and days with different obligations and interests. If you are like most people, you probably use your time wisely in some ways, and not so wisely in others. Answering the questions in **TABLE 1** can help you find trouble spots—and hopefully more time for the things that matter most to you.

The next thing you need to know is how you *actually* spend your time. To find out, record your activities in a *time-use diary* for one week. Be realistic. Take notes on how much time you spend attending class, studying, working, commuting, meeting personal and family needs, fixing and eating meals, socializing (don't forget texting, Facebooking, and gaming), exercising, and anything else that occupies your time, including life's small practical tasks, which can take up plenty of your 24/7. As you record your activities, take notes on how you are feeling at various times of the day. When does your energy slump, and when do you feel most energetic?

Design a Better Schedule

Take a good look at your time-use diary. Where do you think you may be wasting time? Do you spend a lot of time commuting, for example? If so, could you use that time more productively? If you take public transportation, commuting is a great time to read and test yourself for review. If you drive, consider audio review files. (For audio review files for this text, see www.worthpublishers.com/Psych2Go.)

Did you remember to include time for meals, personal care, work schedules, family commitments, and other fixed activities?

How much time do you sleep? In the battle to meet all of life's daily commitments and interests, we tend to treat sleep as optional. Do your best to manage your life so that you can get enough sleep to feel rested. You will feel better and be healthier, and you will also do better academically and in relationships with your family and friends. (You will read more about this in Module 8.)

Are you dedicating enough time for focused study? Take a last look at your notes to see if any other patterns pop out. Now it's time to create a new and more efficient schedule.

Plan the Term

Before you draw up your new schedule, think ahead. Buy a portable calendar that covers the entire school term, with a writing space for each day. Using the course outlines provided by your instructors, enter the dates of all exams, term-paper deadlines, and other important assignments. Also be sure to enter your own long-range personal plans (work and family commitments, etc.). Carry this calendar with you each day. Keep it up to date, refer to it often, and change it as needed. Through this process, you will develop a regular schedule that will help you achieve success.

TABLE 1

Study Habits Survey

Answer the following questions, writing *Yes* or *No* for each line.

1. Do you usually set up a schedule to budget your time for studying, work, recreation, and other activities? ________
2. Do you often put off studying until time pressures force you to cram? ________
3. Do other students seem to study less than you do, but get better grades? ________
4. Do you usually spend hours at a time studying one subject, rather than dividing that time among several subjects? ________
5. Do you often have trouble remembering what you have just read in a textbook? ________
6. Before reading a module in a textbook, do you skim through it and read the section headings? ________
7. Do you try to predict test questions from your class notes and reading? ________
8. Do you usually try to summarize in your own words what you have just finished reading? ________
9. Do you find it difficult to concentrate for very long when you study? ________
10. Do you often feel that you studied the wrong material for a test? ________

Thousands of students have participated in similar surveys. Students who are fully realizing their academic potential usually respond as follows: (1) yes, (2) no, (3) no, (4) no, (5) no, (6) yes, (7) yes, (8) yes, (9) no, (10) no.

Do your responses fit that pattern? If not, you could benefit from improving your time management and study habits.

Plan Your Week

To pass those exams, meet those deadlines, and keep up with your life outside of class, you will need to convert your long-term goals into a daily schedule. Be realistic—you will be living with this routine for the entire school term. Here are some more things to add to that portable calendar.

1. Enter your class times, work hours, and any other fixed obligations. Be thorough. Allow plenty of time for such things as commuting, meals, and laundry.
2. Set up a study schedule for each course. Remember what you learned about yourself in the study habits survey (Table 1) and your time-use diary. Close-Up: More Tips for Effective Scheduling (next page) offers detailed guidance drawn from psychology's research.
3. After you have budgeted time for studying, fill in slots for other obligations, exercise, fun, and relaxation.

CLOSE-UP

More Tips for Effective Scheduling

There are a few other things you will want to keep in mind when you set up your schedule.

Spaced study is more effective than massed study. If you need 3 hours to study one subject, for example, it's best to divide that into shorter periods spaced over several days.

Alternate subjects, but avoid interference. Alternating the subjects you study in any given session will keep you fresh and will, surprisingly, increase your ability to remember what you're learning in each different area. Studying similar topics back-to-back, however, such as two different foreign languages, could lead to interference in your learning. (You will read more about this in Modules 23–26.)

Determine the amount of study time you need to do well in each course. The time you need depends upon the difficulty of your courses and the effectiveness of your study methods. Ideally, you would spend at least 1 to 2 hours studying for each hour spent in class. Increase your study time slowly by setting weekly goals that will gradually bring you up to the desired level.

Create a schedule that makes sense. Tailor your schedule to meet the demands of each course. For the course that emphasizes lecture notes, plan a daily review of your notes soon after each class. If you are evaluated for class participation (for example, in a language course), allow time for a review just before the class meets. Schedule study time for your most difficult (or least motivating) courses during hours when you are the most alert and distractions are fewest.

Schedule open study time. Life can be unpredictable. Emergencies and new obligations can throw off your schedule. Or you may simply need some extra time for a project or for review in one of your courses. Try to allow for some flexibility in your schedule each week.

Following these guidelines will help you find a schedule that works for you!

Make Every Minute of Your Study Time Count

How do you study from a textbook? Many students simply read and reread in a passive manner. As a result, they remember the wrong things—the catchy stories but not the main points that show up later in test questions. To make things worse, many students take poor notes during class. Here are some tips that will help you get the most from your class and your text.

Take Useful Class Notes

Good notes will boost your understanding and retention. Are yours thorough? Do they form a sensible outline of each lecture? If not, you may need to make some changes.

Keep Each Course's Notes Separate and Organized

If you have all your notes for a course in one location, you can flip back and forth easily to find answers to questions. Two options are (1) separate notebooks for each course, or (2) clearly marked sections in a shared ring binder. If pages are removable, you can reorganize as needed, adding new information and weeding out past mistakes. In either case, pages with lots of space are a good choice. You need room for notes, with a wide margin remaining to hold comments when you review and revise your notes after class.

Use an Outline Format

Use roman numerals for major points, letters for supporting arguments, and so on. (See **FIGURE 1** for a sample.) In some courses, taking notes will be easy, but some instructors may be less organized, and you will have to work harder to form your outline.

Clean Up Your Notes After Class

Try to reorganize your notes soon after class. Expand or clarify your comments and clean up any hard-to-read scribbles while the material is fresh in your mind. Write important questions in the margin next to notes that answer them. (For example: "What are the sleep stages?") This will help you when you review your notes before a test.

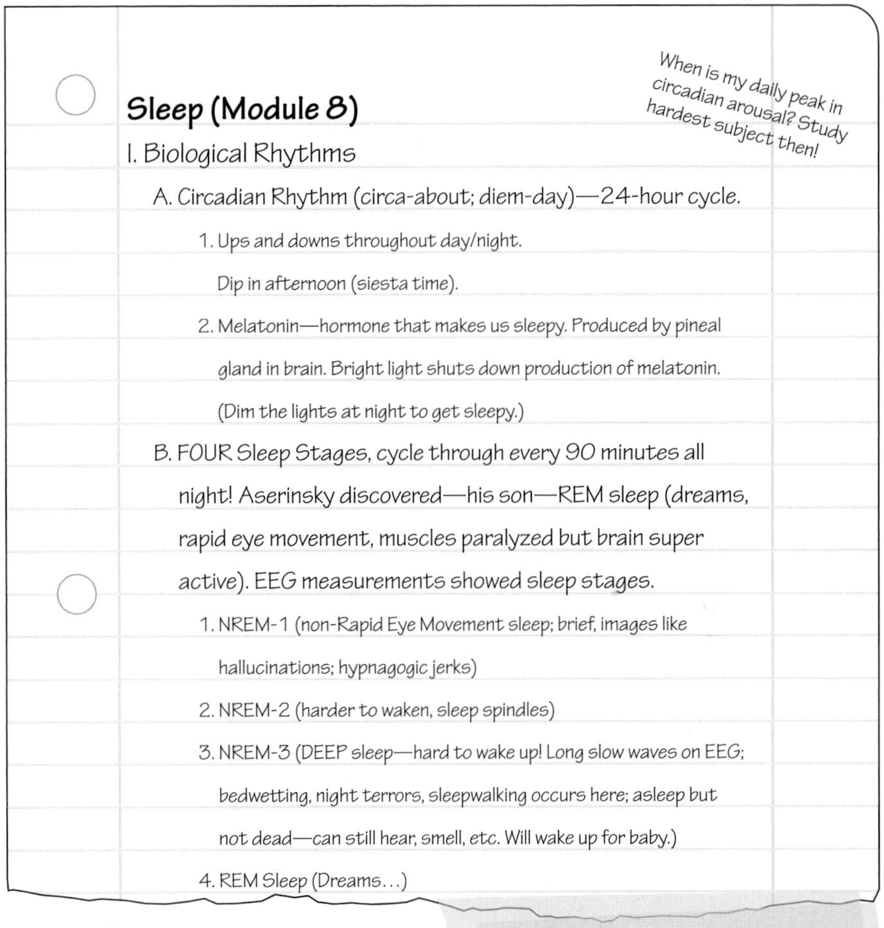

Sleep (Module 8)

When is my daily peak in circadian arousal? Study hardest subject then!

I. Biological Rhythms

A. Circadian Rhythm (circa-about; diem-day)—24-hour cycle.

1. Ups and downs throughout day/night. Dip in afternoon (siesta time).

2. Melatonin—hormone that makes us sleepy. Produced by pineal gland in brain. Bright light shuts down production of melatonin. (Dim the lights at night to get sleepy.)

B. FOUR Sleep Stages, cycle through every 90 minutes all night! Aserinsky discovered—his son—REM sleep (dreams, rapid eye movement, muscles paralyzed but brain super active). EEG measurements showed sleep stages.

1. NREM-1 (non-Rapid Eye Movement sleep; brief, images like hallucinations; hypnagogic jerks)

2. NREM-2 (harder to waken, sleep spindles)

3. NREM-3 (DEEP sleep—hard to wake up! Long slow waves on EEG; bedwetting, night terrors, sleepwalking occurs here; asleep but not dead—can still hear, smell, etc. Will wake up for baby.)

4. REM Sleep (Dreams…)

FIGURE 1
Sample class notes in outline form Here is a sample from a student's notes taken in outline form from a lecture on sleep.

Create a Study Space That Helps You Learn

It's easier to study effectively if your work area is well designed.

Organize Your Space

Work at a desk or table, not in your bed or a comfy chair that will tempt you to nap.

Minimize Distractions

Turn the TV off, turn off your phone, and close Facebook and other distracting windows on your computer. If you must listen to music to mask outside noise, play soft instrumentals, not vocal selections that will draw your mind to the lyrics.

Ask Others to Honor Your Quiet Time

Tell roommates, family, and friends about your new schedule. Try to find a study place where you are least likely to be disturbed.

Set Specific, Realistic Daily Goals

The simple note "7–8 P.M.: Study psychology" is too broad to be useful. Instead, break your studying into manageable tasks. For example, you will want to subdivide large reading assignments. If you aren't used to studying for long periods, start with relatively short periods of concentrated study, with breaks in between. This text has been broken into "modules" of readable length for you. In most cases, you should be able to read one whole module before taking a break. Limit your breaks to 5 or 10 minutes to stretch or move around a bit.

Your attention span is a good indicator of whether you are pacing yourself successfully. At this early stage, it's important to remember that you're in training. If your attention begins to wander, get up immediately and take a short break. It is better to study effectively for 15 minutes and then take a break than to fritter away 45 minutes out of your study hour. As your endurance develops, you can increase the length of study periods.

Use SQ3R to Help You Master This Text

David Myers organized this text by using a system called SQ3R (Survey, Question, Read, Retrieve, Review). Using SQ3R can help you to understand what you read, and to retain that information longer.

Applying SQ3R may feel at first as though it's taking more time and effort to "read" a module, but with practice, these steps will become automatic.

Survey

Before you read a module, survey its key parts. Scan the module outlines. Note that main sections have numbered learning objective questions to help you focus. Pay attention to headings, which indicate important subtopics, and to words set in bold type.

Surveying gives you the big picture of a module's content and organization. Understanding the module's logical sections will help you break your work into manageable pieces in your study sessions.

Question

As you survey, don't limit yourself to the numbered learning objective questions that appear throughout the modules. Jotting down additional questions of your own will cause you to look at the material in a new way. (You might, for example, scan this section's headings and ask "What does 'SQ3R' mean?") Information becomes easier to remember when you make it personally meaningful. Trying to answer your questions while reading will keep you in an active learning mode.

You will read more about SQ3R in Module 1.

Read

As you read, keep your questions in mind and actively search for the answers. If you come to material that seems to answer an important question that you haven't jotted down, stop and write down that new question.

Be sure to read everything. Don't skip photo or art captions, graphs, boxes, tables, or quotes. An idea that seems vague when you read about it may become clear when you see it in a graph or table. Keep in mind that instructors sometimes base their test questions on figures and tables.

Retrieve

When you have found the answer to one of your questions, close your eyes and mentally recite the question and its answer. Then write the answer next to the question in your own words. Trying to explain something in your own words will help you figure out where there are gaps in your understanding. These kinds of opportunities to practice *retrieving* develop the skills you will need when you are taking exams. If you study without ever putting your book and notes aside, you may develop false confidence about what you know. With the material available, you may be able to recognize the correct answer to your questions. But will you be able to recall it later, when you take an exam without having your mental props in sight?

Test your understanding as often as you can. Testing yourself is part of successful learning, because the act of testing forces your brain to work at remembering, thus establishing the memory more permanently (so you can find it later for the exam!). Use the self-testing opportunities throughout each module, including the periodic Retrieval Practice items. Also take advantage of the self-testing that is available on the free book companion website (www.worthpublishers.com/myers).

Review

After working your way through the module, read over your questions and your written answers. Take an extra few minutes to create a brief written summary covering all of your questions and answers. At the end of the module, you should take advantage of two important opportunities for self-testing and review—a list of the module's Learning

Objective Questions for you to try answering before checking Appendix B, Complete Module Reviews, and a list of the module's key terms for you to try to define before checking the referenced page.

Don't Forget About Rewards!

If you have trouble studying regularly, giving yourself a reward may help. What kind of reward works best? That depends on what you enjoy. You might start by making a list of 5 or 10 things that put a smile on your face. Spending time with a loved one, taking a walk or going for a bike ride, relaxing with a magazine or novel, or watching a favorite show can provide immediate rewards for achieving short-term study goals.

To motivate yourself when you're having trouble sticking to your schedule, allow yourself an immediate reward for completing a specific task. If running makes you smile, change your shoes, grab a friend, and head out the door! You deserve a reward for a job well done.

Do You Need to Revise Your New Schedule?

What if you've lived with your schedule for a few weeks, but you aren't making progress toward your academic and personal goals? What if your studying hasn't paid off in better grades? Don't despair and abandon your program, but do take a little time to figure out what's gone wrong.

Are You Doing Well in Some Courses But Not in Others?

Perhaps you need to shift your priorities a bit. You may need to allow more time for Chemistry, for example, and less time for some other course.

Have You Received a Poor Grade on a Test?

Did your grade fail to reflect the effort you spent preparing for the test? This can happen to even the hardest-working student, often on a first test with a new instructor. This common experience can be upsetting. "What do I have to do to get an A?" "The test was unfair!" "I studied the wrong material!"

Try to figure out what went wrong. Analyze the questions you missed, dividing them into two categories: class-based questions and text-based questions. How many questions did you miss in each category? If you find far more errors in one category than in the other, you'll have some clues to help you revise your schedule. Depending on the pattern you've found, you can add extra study time to review of class notes, or to studying the text.

Are You Trying to Study Regularly for the First Time and Feeling Overwhelmed?

Perhaps you've set your initial goals too high. Remember, the point of time management is to identify a regular schedule that will help you achieve success. Like any skill, time management takes practice. Accept your limitations and revise your schedule to work slowly up to where you know you need to be—perhaps adding 15 minutes of study time per day.

* * *

I hope that these suggestions help make you more successful academically, and that they enhance the quality of your life in general. Having the necessary skills makes any job a lot easier and more pleasant. Let me repeat my warning not to attempt to make too drastic a change in your lifestyle immediately. Good habits require time and self-discipline to develop. Once established, they can last a lifetime.

REVIEW

Time Management: Or, How to Be a Great Student and Still Have a Life!

1. How Are You Using Your Time Now?

- Identify your areas of weakness.
- Keep a time-use diary.
- Record the time you actually spend on activities.
- Record your energy levels to find your most productive times.

2. Design a Better Schedule

- Decide on your goals for the term and for each week.
- Enter class times, work times, social times (for family and friends), and time needed for other obligations and for practical activities.
- Tailor study times to avoid interference and to meet each course's needs.

3. Make Every Minute of Your Study Time Count

- Take careful class notes (in outline form) that will help you recall and rehearse material covered in lectures.
- Try to eliminate distractions to your study time, and ask friends and family to help you focus on your work.
- Set specific, realistic daily goals to help you focus on each day's tasks.
- Use the SQ3R system (survey, question, read, retrieve, review) to master material covered in your text.
- When you achieve your daily goals, reward yourself with something that you value.

4. Do You Need to Revise Your New Schedule?

- Allocate extra study time for courses that are more difficult, and a little less time for courses that are easy for you.
- Study your test results to help determine a more effective balance in your schedule.
- Make sure your schedule is not too ambitious. Gradually establish a schedule that will be effective for the long term.

PSYCHOLOGY

TENTH EDITION IN MODULES

Introduction to the History and Science of Psychology

Harvard astronomer Owen Gingerich (2006) reports that there are more than 100 billion galaxies. One of these, our own relative speck of a galaxy, has some 200 billion stars, many of which, like our Sun-star, are circled by planets. On the scale of outer space, we are less than a single grain of sand on all the oceans' beaches, and our lifetime but a relative nanosecond.

Yet there is nothing more awe inspiring and absorbing than our own inner space. Our brain, adds Gingerich, "is by far the most complex physical object known to us in the entire cosmos" (p. 29). Our consciousness—our mind somehow arising from matter—remains a profound mystery. Our thinking, emotions, and actions (and their interplay with others' thinking, emotions, and actions) fascinate us. Outer space staggers us with its enormity. But inner space enthralls us. Enter psychological science.

For people whose exposure to psychology comes from popular media, psychologists seem to analyze personality, offer counseling, and dispense child-rearing advice. Do they? *Yes*, and much more. Consider some of psychology's questions that you may wonder about:

- Have you ever found yourself reacting to something as one of your biological parents would—perhaps in a way you vowed you never would—and then wondered how much of your personality you inherited? *To what extent do genes predispose our person-to-person differences in personality? To what extent do home and community environments shape us?*

MODULES

1 The Story of Psychology

2 Thinking Critically With Psychological Science

3 Research Strategies: How Psychologists Ask and Answer Questions

- Have you ever worried about how to act among people of a different culture, race, gender, or sexual orientation? *In what ways are we alike as members of the human family? How do we differ?*
- Have you ever awakened from a nightmare and, with a wave of relief, wondered why you had such a crazy dream? *How often, and why, do we dream?*
- Have you ever played peekaboo with a 6-month-old and wondered why the baby finds the game so delightful? *What do babies actually perceive and think?*
- Have you ever wondered what fosters school and work success? *Are some people just born smarter? And why do some people get richer, think more creatively, or relate more sensitively?*
- Have you ever become depressed or anxious and wondered whether you'll ever feel "normal"? *What triggers our bad moods? What's the line between a normal mood swing and a* psychological disorder *for which someone should seek help?*
- Have you ever wondered how the Internet, video games, and electronic social networks affect people? *How do today's electronic media influence how we think and how we relate?*

Psychology is a science that seeks to answer such questions about us all—how and why we think, feel, and act as we do. In Module 1, we trace psychology's roots and survey its scope. In Module 2, we consider how psychological science can help you to think critically and to understand the dangers of relying on intuition and common sense. In Module 3, we survey psychology's methods—how psychologists ask and answer questions.

MODULE 1

The Story of Psychology

- What is Psychology?
- Contemporary Psychology

To assist your active learning of psychology, Learning Objectives, framed as questions, appear at the beginning of major sections. You can test your understanding by trying to answer the question before, and then again after, you read the section.

What Is Psychology?

Psychology's Roots

1-1 What are some important milestones in psychology's early development?

Once upon a time, on a planet in this neighborhood of the universe, there came to be people. Soon thereafter, these creatures became intensely interested in themselves and in one another: *"Who are we? What produces our thoughts? Our feelings? Our actions? And how are we to understand and manage those around us?"*

Psychological Science Is Born

To be human is to be curious about ourselves and the world around us. Before 300 B.C.E., the Greek naturalist and philosopher Aristotle theorized about learning and memory, motivation and emotion, perception and personality. Today we chuckle at some of his guesses, like his suggestion that a meal makes us sleepy by causing gas and heat to collect around the source of our personality, the heart. But credit Aristotle with asking the right questions.

Philosophers' thinking about thinking continued until the birth of psychology as we know it, on a December day in 1879, in a small, third-floor room at Germany's University of Leipzig. There, two young men were helping an austere, middle-aged professor, Wilhelm Wundt, create an experimental apparatus. Their machine measured the time lag between people's hearing a ball hit a platform and their pressing a telegraph key

Tim Gainey/Alamy

A smile is a smile the world around Throughout this book, you will see examples not only of our cultural and gender diversity but also of the similarities that define our shared human nature. People in different cultures vary in when and how often they smile, but a naturally happy smile *means* the same thing anywhere in the world.

JEWEL SAMAD/AFP/Getty Images/Newscom

A lesson in cultural differences During Barack Obama's 2011 state dinner with China's President Hu Jintao, both emphasized their commonalities, yet were acutely aware of their differences.

Wilhelm Wundt Wundt established the first psychology laboratory at the University of Leipzig, Germany.
© Bettmann/Corbis

Edward Bradford Titchener Titchener used introspection to search for the mind's structural elements.
Archives of the History of American Psychology, The University of Akron

(Hunt, 1993). Curiously, people responded in about one-tenth of a second when asked to press the key as soon as the sound occurred—and in about two-tenths of a second when asked to press the key as soon as they were consciously aware of perceiving the sound. (To be aware of one's awareness takes a little longer.) Wundt was seeking to measure "atoms of the mind"—the fastest and simplest mental processes. So began the first psychological laboratory, staffed by Wundt and by psychology's first graduate students.

Information sources are cited in parentheses, with name and date. Every citation can be found in the end-of-book References, with complete documentation that follows American Psychological Association style.

Before long, this new science of psychology became organized into different branches, or schools of thought, each promoted by pioneering thinkers. Two early schools were *structuralism* and *functionalism*. As physicists and chemists discerned the structure of matter, so Wundt's student Edward Bradford Titchener aimed to discover the mind's structure. To do so, he engaged people in self-reflective *introspection* (looking inward), training them to report elements of their experience as they looked at a rose, listened to a metronome, smelled a scent, or tasted a substance. What were their immediate sensations, their images, their feelings? And how did these relate to one another? Alas, introspection proved somewhat unreliable. It required smart, verbal people, and its results varied from person to person and experience to experience. As introspection waned, so did structuralism.

Hoping to assemble the mind's structure from simple elements was rather like trying to understand a car by examining its disconnected parts. Philosopher-psychologist William James thought it would be more fruitful to consider the evolved functions of our thoughts and feelings. Smelling is what the nose does; thinking is what the brain does. But *why* do the nose and brain do these things? Under the influence of evolutionary theorist Charles Darwin, James assumed that thinking, like smelling, developed because it was *adaptive*—it contributed to our ancestors' survival. Consciousness serves a function. It enables us to consider our past, adjust to our present, and plan our future. As a *functionalist*, James encouraged explorations of down-to-earth emotions, memories, willpower, habits, and moment-to-moment streams of consciousness.

William James and Mary Whiton Calkins Legendary teacher James mentored Calkins, who became a pioneering memory researcher and the first woman to be president of the American Psychological Association.
(left) Mary Evans Picture Library/Alamy; (right) Wellesley College Archives

Hemera Technologies / Getty Images

Margaret Floy Washburn The first woman to receive a psychology Ph.D., Washburn synthesized animal behavior research in *The Animal Mind.*

Center for the History of Psychology Archives of the History of American Psychology, The University of Akron

James' legacy stems partly from his Harvard mentoring and his writing. In 1890, over the objections of Harvard's president, he admitted Mary Whiton Calkins into his graduate seminar (Scarborough & Furumoto, 1987). (In those years women lacked even the right to vote.) When Calkins joined, the other students (all men) dropped out. So James tutored her alone. Later, she finished all of Harvard's Ph.D. requirements, outscoring all the male students on the qualifying exams. Alas, Harvard denied her the degree she had earned, offering her instead a degree from Radcliffe College, its undergraduate "sister" school for women. Calkins resisted the unequal treatment and refused the degree. She nevertheless went on to become a distinguished memory researcher and the American Psychological Association's (APA's) first female president in 1905.

The honor of being the first female psychology Ph.D. later fell to Margaret Floy Washburn, who also wrote an influential book, *The Animal Mind*, and became the second female APA president in 1921. But Washburn's gender barred doors for her, too. Although her thesis was the first foreign study Wundt published in the psychology journal he established, she could not join the all-male organization of experimental psychologists founded by Titchener, her own graduate adviser (Johnson, 1997). (What a different world from the recent past—1996 to 2012—when women were 8 of the 16 elected presidents of the science-oriented Association for Psychological Science. In the United States, Canada, and Europe, most psychology doctorates are now earned by women.)

Ewa Walicka/Shutterstock

James' writings moved the publisher Henry Holt to offer a contract for a textbook of the new science of psychology. James agreed and began work in 1878, with an apology for requesting two years to finish his writing. The text proved an unexpected chore and actually took him 12 years. (Why am I not surprised?) More than a century later, people still read the resulting *Principles of Psychology* and marvel at the brilliance and elegance with which James introduced psychology to the educated public.

Study Tip: Memory research reveals a *testing effect:* We retain information much better if we actively retrieve it by self-testing and rehearsing. (More on this in the Close-Up at the end of this module.) To bolster your learning and memory, take advantage of the *Retrieval Practice* opportunities you'll find throughout this text.

RETRIEVAL PRACTICE

- What event defined the start of scientific psychology?

ANSWER: Scientific psychology began in Germany in 1879 when Wilhelm Wundt opened the first psychology laboratory.

- Why did introspection fail as a method for understanding how the mind works?

ANSWER: People's self-reports varied, depending on the experience and the person's intelligence and verbal ability.

- __________ used introspection to define the mind's makeup; __________ focused on how mental processes enable us to adapt, survive, and flourish.

ANSWERS: Structuralism; functionalism

Psychological Science Develops

1-2 How did psychology continue to develop from the 1920s through today?

behaviorism the view that psychology (1) should be an objective science that (2) studies behavior without reference to mental processes. Most research psychologists today agree with (1) but not with (2).

humanistic psychology historically significant perspective that emphasized the growth potential of healthy people.

In the field's early days, many psychologists shared with the English essayist C. S. Lewis the view that "there is one thing, and only one in the whole universe which we know more about than we could learn from external observation." That one thing, Lewis said, is ourselves. "We have, so to speak, inside information" (1960, pp. 18–19). Wundt and Titchener focused on inner sensations, images, and feelings. James engaged in

John B. Watson and Rosalie Rayner Working with Rayner, Watson championed psychology as the science of behavior and demonstrated conditioned responses on a baby who became famous as "Little Albert."

(left) ©Underwood & Underwood/Corbis
(right) Center for the History of Psychology Archives of the History of American Psychology, The University of Akron

introspective examination of the stream of consciousness and of emotion. For these and other early pioneers, *psychology* was defined as "the science of mental life."

And so it continued until the 1920s, when the first of two provocative American psychologists appeared on the scene. John B. Watson, and later B. F. Skinner, dismissed introspection and redefined *psychology* as "the scientific study of observable behavior." After all, they said, science is rooted in observation. You cannot observe a sensation, a feeling, or a thought, but you *can* observe and record people's *behavior* as they respond to different situations. Many agreed, and the **behaviorists** were one of two major forces in psychology well into the 1960s.

Throughout the text, important concepts are **boldfaced.** As you study, you can find these terms with their definitions in a nearby margin and in the Glossary at the end of the book.

The other major force was *Freudian psychology,* which emphasized the ways our unconscious thought processes and our emotional responses to childhood experiences affect our behavior. (In other modules, we look more closely at Sigmund Freud's teachings, including his theory of personality, and his views on unconscious sexual conflicts and the mind's defenses against its own wishes and impulses.)

As the behaviorists had done in the early 1900s, two other groups rejected the definition of *psychology* that was current in the 1960s. The first, the **humanistic psychologists,** led by Carl Rogers and Abraham Maslow, found both Freudian psychology and behaviorism too limiting. Rather than focusing on the meaning of early childhood memories or the learning of conditioned responses, the humanistic psychologists drew attention to ways that current environmental influences can nurture or limit our growth potential, and to the importance of having our needs for love and acceptance satisfied.

B. F. Skinner A leading behaviorist, Skinner rejected introspection and studied how consequences shape behavior.

Bachrach/Getty Images

Sigmund Freud The controversial ideas of this famed personality theorist and therapist have influenced humanity's self-understanding.

© Bettmann/Corbis

The rebellion of a second group of psychologists during the 1960s is now known as the *cognitive revolution*, and it led the field back to its early interest in mental processes, such as the importance of how our mind processes and retains information. Cognitive psychology scientifically explores the ways we perceive, process, and remember information. **Cognitive neuroscience**, an interdisciplinary study, has enriched our understanding of the brain activity underlying mental activity. The cognitive approach has given us new ways to understand ourselves and to treat disorders such as depression.

To encompass psychology's concern with observable behavior *and* with inner thoughts and feelings, today we define **psychology** as the *science of behavior and mental processes.*

Let's unpack this definition. *Behavior* is anything an organism *does*—any action we can observe and record. Yelling, smiling, blinking, sweating, talking, and questionnaire-marking are all observable behaviors. *Mental processes* are the internal, subjective experiences we infer from behavior—sensations, perceptions, dreams, thoughts, beliefs, and feelings.

The key word in psychology's definition is *science*. Psychology, as I will emphasize throughout this book, is less a set of findings than a way of asking and answering questions. My aim, then, is not merely to report results but also to show you how psychologists play their game. You will see how researchers evaluate conflicting opinions and ideas. And you will learn how all of us, whether scientists or simply curious people, can think smarter when describing and explaining the events of our lives.

RETRIEVAL PRACTICE

- From the 1920s through the 1960s, the two major forces in psychology were __________ and __________ psychology.

ANSWERS: behaviorism; Freudian

- How did the cognitive revolution affect the field of psychology?

ANSWER: It recaptured the field's early interest in mental processes and made them legitimate topics for scientific study.

Contemporary Psychology

The young science of psychology developed from the more established fields of philosophy and biology. Wundt was both a philosopher and a physiologist. James was an American philosopher. Freud was an Austrian physician. Ivan Pavlov, who pioneered the study of learning, was a Russian physiologist. Jean Piaget, the last century's most influential observer of children, was a Swiss biologist. These "Magellans of the mind," as Morton Hunt (1993) has called them, illustrate psychology's origins in many disciplines and many countries.

Like those early pioneers, today's psychologists are citizens of many lands. The International Union of Psychological Science has 71 member nations, from Albania to Zimbabwe. In China, the first university psychology department began in 1978; in 2008 there were nearly 200 (Han, 2008; Tversky, 2008). Moreover, thanks to international publications, joint meetings, and the Internet, collaboration and communication now cross borders. Psychology is *growing* and it is *globalizing*. The story of psychology—the subject of this book—continues to develop in many places, at many levels, with interests ranging from the study of nerve cell activity to the study of international conflicts.

Psychology's Biggest Question

1-3 What is psychology's historic big issue?

Are our human traits present at birth, or do they develop through experience? This has been psychology's biggest and most persistent issue. But the debate over the **nature–nurture issue** is ancient. The Greek philosopher Plato (428–348 B.C.E.) assumed that we inherit character and intelligence and that certain ideas are inborn. Aristotle (384–322 B.C.E.) countered that there is nothing in the mind that does not first come in from the external world through the senses.

In the 1600s, European philosophers rekindled the debate. John Locke argued that the mind is a blank slate on which experience writes. René Descartes disagreed, believing

cognitive neuroscience the interdisciplinary study of the brain activity linked with cognition (including perception, thinking, memory, and language).

psychology the science of behavior and mental processes.

nature–nurture issue the longstanding controversy over the relative contributions that genes and experience make to the development of psychological traits and behaviors. Today's science sees traits and behaviors arising from the interaction of nature and nurture.

natural selection the principle that, among the range of inherited trait variations, those contributing to reproduction and survival will most likely be passed on to succeeding generations.

that some ideas are innate. Descartes' views gained support from a curious naturalist two centuries later. In 1831, an indifferent student but ardent collector of beetles, mollusks, and shells set sail on a historic round-the-world journey. The 22-year-old voyager, Charles Darwin, pondered the incredible species variation he encountered, including tortoises on one island that differed from those on nearby islands. Darwin's 1859 *On the Origin of Species* explained this diversity by proposing the evolutionary process of **natural selection:** From among chance variations, nature selects traits that best enable an organism to survive and reproduce in a particular environment. Darwin's principle of natural selection—what philosopher Daniel Dennett (1996) has called "the single best idea anyone has ever had,"—is still with us 150+ years later as biology's organizing principle. Evolution also has become an important principle for twenty-first-century psychology. This would surely have pleased Darwin, for he believed his theory explained not only animal structures (such as a polar bear's white coat) but also animal behaviors (such as the emotional expressions associated with human lust and rage).

Charles Darwin Darwin argued that natural selection shapes behaviors as well as bodies.

Vintage Images /Alamy

The nature–nurture issue recurs throughout this text as today's psychologists explore the relative contributions of biology and experience, asking, for example, how we humans are alike (because of our common biology and evolutionary history) and diverse (because of our differing environments). Are gender differences biologically predisposed or socially constructed? Is children's grammar mostly innate or formed by experience? How are intelligence and personality differences influenced by heredity and by environment? Are sexual behaviors more "pushed" by inner biology or "pulled" by external incentives? Should we treat psychological disorders—depression, for example—as disorders of the brain, disorders of thought, or both?

A nature-made nature–nurture experiment Because identical twins have the same genes, they are ideal participants in studies designed to shed light on hereditary and environmental influences on intelligence, personality, and other traits. Studies of identical and fraternal twins provide a rich array of findings that underscore the importance of both nature and nurture.

(left) WoodyStock /Alamy; (right) © Hola Images/agefotostock

Such debates continue. Yet over and over again we will see that in contemporary science the nature–nurture tension dissolves: *Nurture works on what nature endows.* Our species is biologically endowed with an enormous capacity to learn and adapt. Moreover, every psychological event (every thought, every emotion) is simultaneously a biological event. Thus, depression can be both a brain disorder and a thought disorder.

levels of analysis the differing complementary views, from biological to psychological to social-cultural, for analyzing any given phenomenon.

biopsychosocial approach an integrated approach that incorporates biological, psychological, and social-cultural levels of analysis.

RETRIEVAL PRACTICE

- What is natural selection?

ANSWER: This is the process by which nature selects from chance variations the traits that best enable an organism to survive and reproduce in a particular environment.

- What is contemporary psychology's position on the nature–nurture debate?

ANSWER: Psychological events often stem from the interaction of nature and nurture, rather than from either of them acting alone.

Psychology's Three Main Levels of Analysis

1-4 What are psychology's levels of analysis and related perspectives?

Each of us is a complex system that is part of a larger social system. But each of us is also composed of smaller systems, such as our nervous system and body organs, which are composed of still smaller systems—cells, molecules, and atoms.

These tiered systems suggest different **levels of analysis,** which offer complementary outlooks. It's like explaining why grizzly bears hibernate. Is it because hibernation helped their ancestors to survive and reproduce? Because their inner physiology drives them to do so? Because cold environments hinder food gathering during winter? Such perspectives are complementary because "everything is related to everything else" (Brewer, 1996). Together, different levels of analysis form an integrated **biopsychosocial approach,** which considers the influences of biological, psychological, and social-cultural factors (**FIGURE 1.1**).

Each level provides a valuable vantage point for looking at a behavior or mental process, yet each by itself is incomplete. Like different academic disciplines, psychology's varied perspectives ask different questions and have their own limits. One perspective may stress the biological, psychological, or social-cultural level more than another, but the different perspectives described in **TABLE 1.1** complement one another. Consider, for example, how they shed light on anger.

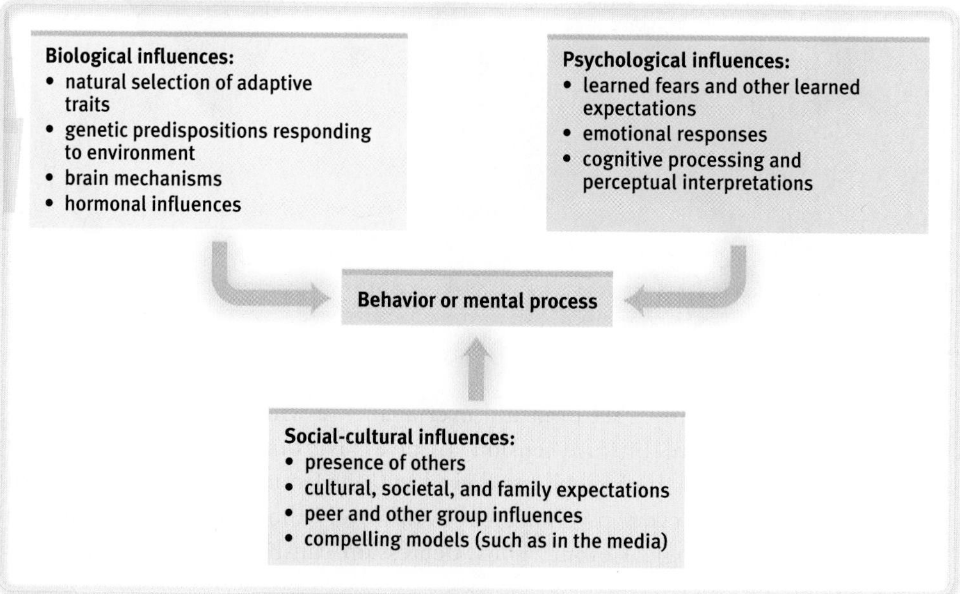

FIGURE 1.1
Biopsychosocial approach This integrated viewpoint incorporates various levels of analysis and offers a more complete picture of any given behavior or mental process.

TABLE 1.1

Psychology's Current Perspectives

Perspective	Focus	Sample Questions	Examples of Subfields Using This Perspective
Neuroscience	How the body and brain enable emotions, memories, and sensory experiences	How do pain messages travel from the hand to the brain? How is blood chemistry linked with moods and motives?	Biological; cognitive; clinical
Evolutionary	How the natural selection of traits has promoted the survival of genes	How does evolution influence behavior tendencies?	Biological; developmental; social
Behavior genetics	How our genes and our environment influence our individual differences	To what extent are psychological traits such as intelligence, personality, sexual orientation, and vulnerability to depression products of our genes? Of our environment?	Personality; developmental
Psychodynamic	How behavior springs from unconscious drives and conflicts	How can someone's personality traits and disorders be explained by unfulfilled wishes and childhood traumas?	Clinical; counseling; personality
Behavioral	How we learn observable responses	How do we learn to fear particular objects or situations? What is the most effective way to alter our behavior, say, to lose weight or stop smoking?	Clinical; counseling; industrial-organizational
Cognitive	How we encode, process, store, and retrieve information	How do we use information in remembering? Reasoning? Solving problems?	Cognitive; clinical; counseling; industrial-organizational
Social-cultural	How behavior and thinking vary across situations and cultures	How are we alike as members of one human family? How do we differ as products of our environment?	Developmental; social; clinical; counseling

- Someone working from a *neuroscience perspective* might study brain circuits that cause us to be "red in the face" and "hot under the collar."
- Someone working from the *evolutionary perspective* might analyze how anger facilitated the survival of our ancestors' genes.
- Someone working from the *behavior genetics perspective* might study how heredity and experience influence our individual differences in temperament.
- Someone working from the *psychodynamic perspective* might view an outburst as an outlet for unconscious hostility.
- Someone working from the *behavioral perspective* might attempt to determine which external stimuli trigger angry responses or aggressive acts.
- Someone working from the *cognitive perspective* might study how our interpretation of a situation affects our anger and how our anger affects our thinking.
- Someone working from the *social-cultural perspective* might explore how expressions of anger vary across cultural contexts.

The point to remember: Like two-dimensional views of a three-dimensional object, each of psychology's perspectives is helpful. But each by itself fails to reveal the whole picture.

JUERGEN SCHWARZ/AFP/Getty Images

RETRIEVAL PRACTICE

- What advantage do we gain by using the biopsychosocial approach in studying psychological events?

ANSWER: By incorporating different levels of analysis, the biopsychosocial approach can provide a more complete view than any one perspective could offer.

© The New Yorker Collection, 1986, J. B. Handelsman from cartoonbank.com. All Rights Reserved.

"I'm a social scientist, Michael. That means I can't explain electricity or anything like that, but if you ever want to know about people I'm your man."

Psychology's Subfields

1-5 What are psychology's main subfields?

Picturing a chemist at work, you probably envision a white-coated scientist surrounded by glassware and high-tech equipment. Picture a psychologist at work and you would be right to envision

- a white-coated scientist probing a rat's brain.
- an intelligence researcher measuring how quickly an infant shows boredom by looking away from a familiar picture.
- an executive evaluating a new "healthy lifestyles" training program for employees.
- someone at a computer analyzing data on whether adopted teens' temperaments more closely resemble those of their adoptive parents or their biological parents.
- a therapist listening carefully to a client's depressed thoughts.
- a traveler visiting another culture and collecting data on variations in human values and behaviors.
- a teacher or writer sharing the joy of psychology with others.

The cluster of subfields we call psychology is a meeting ground for different disciplines. "Psychology is a hub scientific discipline," said Association for Psychological Science president John Cacioppo (2007). Thus, it's a perfect home for those with wide-ranging interests. In its diverse activities, from biological experimentation to cultural comparisons, the tribe of psychology is united by a common quest: *describing and explaining behavior and the mind underlying it.*

Some psychologists conduct **basic research** that builds psychology's knowledge base. In the pages that follow we will meet a wide variety of such researchers, including *biological psychologists* exploring the links between brain and mind; *developmental psychologists* studying our changing abilities from womb to tomb; *cognitive psychologists* experimenting with how we perceive, think, and solve problems; *personality psychologists* investigating our persistent traits; and *social psychologists* exploring how we view and affect one another.

These and other psychologists also may conduct **applied research,** tackling practical problems. *Industrial-organizational psychologists,* for example, use psychology's concepts and methods in the workplace to help organizations and companies select and train employees, boost morale and productivity, design products, and implement systems.

Psychology in court Forensic psychologists apply psychology's principles and methods in the criminal justice system. They may assess witness credibility, or testify in court on a defendant's state of mind and future risk.

Image Source/ Punchstock

Ted Fitzgerald, Pool/ AP Photo

Although most psychology textbooks focus on psychological science, psychology is also a helping profession devoted to such practical issues as how to have a happy marriage, how to overcome anxiety or depression, and how to raise thriving children. As a science, psychology at its best bases such interventions on *evidence of effectiveness.* **Counseling psychologists** help people to cope with challenges and crises (including academic, vocational, and marital issues) and to improve their personal and social functioning. **Clinical psychologists** assess and treat mental, emotional, and behavior disorders. Both counseling and clinical psychologists administer and interpret tests, provide counseling and therapy, and sometimes conduct basic and applied research. By contrast, **psychiatrists,** who also may provide psychotherapy, are medical doctors licensed to prescribe drugs and otherwise treat physical causes of psychological disorders.

To balance historic psychology's focus on human problems, Martin Seligman and others (2002, 2005, 2011) have called for more research on human strengths and human flourishing. Their **positive psychology** scientifically explores "positive emotions, positive character traits, and enabling institutions." What, they ask, can psychology contribute to a "good life" that engages one's skills, and a "meaningful life" that points beyond oneself?

Rather than seeking to change people to fit their environment, **community psychologists** work to create social and physical environments that are healthy for all (Bradshaw et al., 2009; Trickett, 2009). For example, if school bullying is a problem, some psychologists will seek to change the bullies. Knowing that many students struggle with the transition from elementary to middle school, they might train individual kids how to cope. Community psychologists instead seek ways to adapt the school experience to early adolescent needs. To prevent bullying, they might study how the school and neighborhood foster bullying.

With perspectives ranging from the biological to the social, and with settings from the laboratory to the clinic, psychology relates to many fields. Psychologists teach in medical schools, law schools, and theological seminaries, and they work in hospitals, factories, and corporate offices. They engage in interdisciplinary studies, such as psychohistory (the psychological analysis of historical characters), psycholinguistics (the study of language and thinking), and psychoceramics (the study of crackpots).[1]

basic research pure science that aims to increase the scientific knowledge base.

applied research scientific study that aims to solve practical problems.

counseling psychology a branch of psychology that assists people with problems in living (often related to school, work, or marriage) and in achieving greater well-being.

clinical psychology a branch of psychology that studies, assesses, and treats people with psychological disorders.

psychiatry a branch of medicine dealing with psychological disorders; practiced by physicians who sometimes provide medical (for example, drug) treatments as well as psychological therapy.

positive psychology the scientific study of human functioning, with the goals of discovering and promoting strengths and virtues that help individuals and communities to thrive.

community psychology a branch of psychology that studies how people interact with their social environments and how social institutions affect individuals and groups.

[1] Confession: I wrote the last part of this sentence on April Fools' Day.

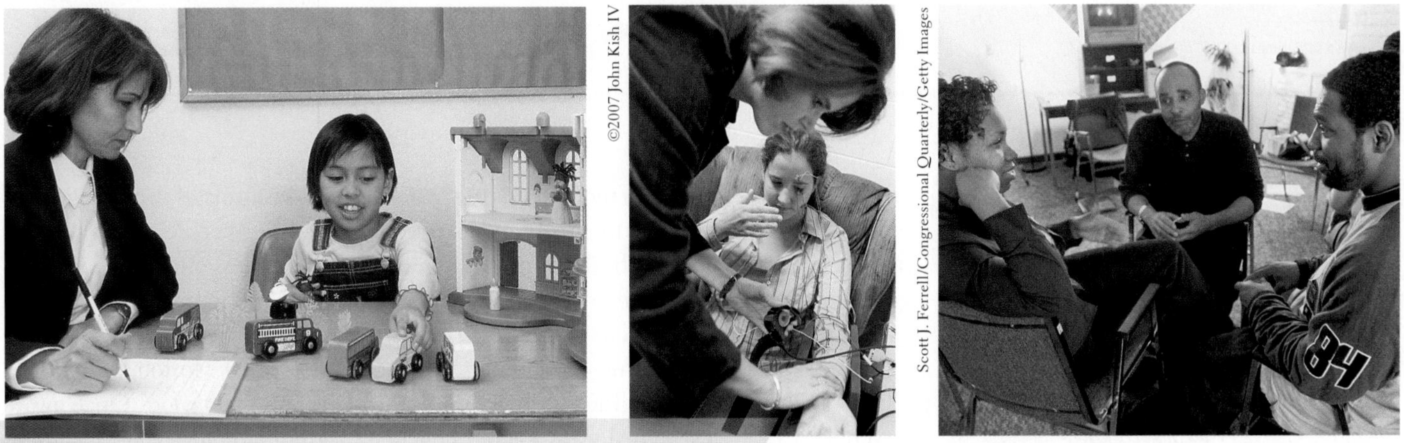

Michael Newman/Photo Edit

©2007 John Kish IV

Scott J. Ferrell/Congressional Quarterly/Getty Images

Psychology: A science and a profession Psychologists experiment with, observe, test, and treat behavior. Here we see psychologists testing a child, measuring emotion-related physiology, and doing face-to-face therapy.

CLOSE-UP

Improve Your Retention—and Your Grades!

1-6 How can psychological principles help you learn and remember?

Do you, like most students, assume that the way to cement your new learning is to reread? What helps even more—and what this book therefore encourages—is repeated self-testing and rehearsal of previously studied material. Memory researchers Henry Roediger and Jeffrey Karpicke (2006) call this phenomenon the **testing effect.** (It is also sometimes called the *retrieval practice effect* or *test-enhanced learning.*) They note that "testing is a powerful means of improving learning, not just assessing it." In one of their studies, students recalled the meaning of 40 previously learned Swahili words much better if tested repeatedly than if they spent the same time restudying the words (Karpicke & Roediger, 2008).

To master information you must *actively process it.* Your mind is not like your stomach, something to be filled passively; it is more like a muscle that grows stronger with exercise. Countless experiments reveal that people learn and remember best when they put material in their own words, rehearse it, and then retrieve and review it again.

The **SQ3R** study method incorporates these principles (McDaniel et al., 2009; Robinson, 1970). SQ3R is an acronym for its five steps: *S*urvey, *Q*uestion, *R*ead, *R*etrieve[2], *R*eview.

To study a module, first *survey,* taking a bird's-eye view. Scan the headings, and notice how the module is organized.

Before you read each main section, try to answer its numbered Learning Objective *Question* (for this box: "How can psychological principles help you learn and remember?"). Roediger and Bridgid Finn (2009) have found that, "trying and failing to retrieve the answer is actually helpful to learning." Those who test their understanding *before* reading, and discover what they don't yet know, will learn and remember better.

Then *read,* actively searching for the answer to the question. At each sitting, read only as much of the module (usually a single main section) as you can absorb without tiring. Read actively and critically. Ask questions. Take notes. Make the ideas your own: How does what you've read relate to your own life? Does it support or challenge your assumptions? How convincing is the evidence?

Having read a section, *retrieve* its main ideas. *Test yourself.* This will not only help you figure out what you know; the testing itself will help you learn and retain the information more effectively. Even better, test yourself repeatedly. To facilitate this, I am offering periodic *Retrieval Practice* opportunities throughout each module (see, for example, the questions in this module). After answering these questions for yourself, you can check the answers provided, and reread as needed.

Finally, *review:* Read over any notes you have taken, again with an eye on the module's organization, and quickly review the whole module. Write or say what a concept is before rereading to check your understanding.

Survey, question, read, retrieve, review. I have organized this book's modules to facilitate your use of the SQ3R study system. Each module

OJO Images Ltd/Alamy

[2] Also sometimes called "*Recite*."

Want to learn more? See Appendix A, Subfields of Psychology, at the end of this book, and go to the regularly updated ***Careers in Psychology*** at www.yourpsychportal.com/myers10einmodules to learn about the many interesting options available to those with bachelor's, master's, and doctoral degrees in psychology.

Psychology also influences modern culture. Knowledge transforms us. Learning about the solar system and the germ theory of disease alters the way people think and act. Learning about psychology's findings also changes people: They less often judge psychological disorders as moral failings, treatable by punishment and ostracism. They less often regard and treat women as men's mental inferiors. They less often view and rear children as ignorant, willful beasts in need of taming. "In each case," noted Morton Hunt (1990, p. 206), "knowledge has modified attitudes, and, through them, behavior." Once aware of psychology's well-researched ideas—about how body and mind connect, how a child's mind grows, how we construct our perceptions, how we remember (and misremember) our experiences, how people across the world differ (and are alike)—your mind may never again be quite the same.

But bear in mind psychology's limits. Don't expect it to answer the ultimate questions, such as those posed by Russian novelist Leo Tolstoy (1904): "Why should I live? Why begins with an outline that aids your *survey*. Headings and Learning Objective *Questions* suggest issues and concepts you should consider as you *read*. The material is organized into sections of readable length. The Retrieval Practice questions will challenge you to *retrieve* what you have learned, and thus better remember it. The end-of-module *Review* provides more opportunities for active processing and self-testing, focusing on the module's key terms and Learning Objective Questions. (Complete Module Reviews can be found in Appendix B, at the end of this book.) Survey, question, read . . .

Four additional study tips may further boost your learning:

Distribute your study time. One of psychology's oldest findings is that *spaced practice* promotes better retention than *massed practice*. You'll remember material better if you space your time over several study periods—perhaps one hour a day, six days a week—rather than cram it into one long study blitz. For example, rather than trying to read an entire module in a single sitting, read just one main section and then turn to something else. *Interleaving* your study of psychology with your study of other subjects boosts long-term retention and protects against overconfidence (Kornell & Bjork, 2008; Taylor & Rohrer, 2010).

Spacing your study sessions requires a disciplined approach to managing your time. (Richard O. Straub explains time management in a helpful preface at the beginning of this text.)

Learn to think critically. Whether you are reading or in class, note people's assumptions and values. What perspective or bias underlies an argument? Evaluate evidence. Is it anecdotal? Or is it based on informative experiments? Assess conclusions. Are there alternative explanations?

Process class information actively. Listen for the main ideas and sub-ideas of a lecture. *Write them down.* Ask questions during and after class. In class, as in your private study, process the information actively and you will understand and retain it better. As psychologist William James urged a century ago, *"No reception without reaction, no impression without . . . expression."* Make the information your own. Take notes in your own words. Relate what you read to what you already know. Tell someone else about it. (As any teacher will confirm, to teach is to remember.)

Overlearn. Psychology tells us that overlearning improves retention. We are prone to overestimating how much we know. You may understand a module as you read it, but that feeling of familiarity can be deceptively comforting. Using the Retrieval Practice opportunities, devote extra study time to testing your knowledge.

Memory experts Elizabeth Bjork and Robert Bjork (2011, p. 63) offer the bottom line for how to improve your retention and your grades:

> Spend less time on the input side and more time on the output side, such as summarizing what you have read from memory or getting together with friends and asking each other questions. Any activities that involve testing yourself—that is, activities that require you to retrieve or generate information, rather than just representing information to yourself—will make your learning both more durable and flexible.

RETRIEVAL PRACTICE

- The ________ ________ describes the enhanced memory that results from repeated retrieval (as in self-testing) rather than from simple rereading of new information.

ANSWER: testing effect

- What does the acronym SQ3R stand for?

ANSWER: Survey, Question, Read, Retrieve, and Review

testing effect enhanced memory after retrieving, rather than simply reading, information. Also sometimes referred to as a *retrieval practice effect* or *test-enhanced learning*.

SQ3R a study method incorporating five steps: *S*urvey, *Q*uestion, *R*ead, *R*etrieve, *R*eview.

should I do anything? Is there in life any purpose which the inevitable death that awaits me does not undo and destroy?"

Although many of life's significant questions are beyond psychology, some very important ones are illuminated by even a first psychology course. Through painstaking research, psychologists have gained insights into brain and mind, dreams and memories, depression and joy. Even the unanswered questions can renew our sense of mystery about "things too wonderful" for us yet to understand. And your study of psychology can help teach you how to ask and answer important questions—how to think critically as you evaluate competing ideas and claims.

Psychology deepens our appreciation for how we humans perceive, think, feel, and act. By so doing it can indeed enrich our lives and enlarge our vision. Through this book I hope to help guide you toward that end. As educator Charles Eliot said a century ago: "Books are the quietest and most constant of friends, and the most patient of teachers."

"Once expanded to the dimensions of a larger idea, [the mind] never returns to its original size."

Oliver Wendell Holmes, 1809–1894

RETRIEVAL PRACTICE

- Match the specialty on the left with the description on the right.

1. Clinical psychology
2. Psychiatry
3. Community psychology

a. Works to create social and physical environments that are healthy for all.
b. Studies, assesses, and treats people with psychological disorders but usually does not provide medical therapy.
c. Branch of medicine dealing with psychological disorders.

ANSWERS: 1. b, 2. c, 3. a

MODULE REVIEW

The Story of Psychology

Learning Objectives

RETRIEVAL PRACTICE Take a moment to answer each of these Learning Objective Questions (repeated here from within the module). Then turn to Appendix B, Complete Module Reviews, to check your answers. Research suggests that trying to answer these questions on your own will improve your long-term retention (McDaniel et al., 2009).

1-1: What are some important milestones in psychology's early development?

1-2: How did psychology continue to develop from the 1920s through today?

1-3: What is psychology's historic big issue?

1-4: What are psychology's levels of analysis and related perspectives?

1-5: What are psychology's main subfields?

1-6: How can psychological principles help you learn and remember?

Terms and Concepts to Remember

RETRIEVAL PRACTICE Test yourself on these terms by trying to write down the definition before flipping back to the referenced page to check your answer.

behaviorism, p. 5
humanistic psychology, p. 5
cognitive neuroscience, p. 6
psychology, p. 6
nature–nurture issue, p. 6
natural selection, p. 7
levels of analysis, p. 8
biopsychosocial approach, p. 8
basic research, p. 10
applied research, p. 10
counseling psychology, p. 11
clinical psychology, p. 11
psychiatry, p. 11
positive psychology, p. 11
community psychology, p. 11
testing effect, p. 12
SQ3R, p. 12

RETRIEVAL PRACTICE Gain an advantage, and benefit from immediate feedback, with the interactive self-testing resources at www.worthpublishers.com/myers.

MODULE 2

Thinking Critically With Psychological Science

- The Need for Psychological Science
- Frequently Asked Questions About Psychology

Hoping to satisfy their curiosity about people and to remedy their own woes, millions turn to "psychology." They listen to talk-radio counseling. They read articles on psychic powers. They attend stop-smoking hypnosis seminars. They immerse themselves in self-help websites and books on the meaning of dreams, the path to ecstatic love, and the roots of personal happiness.

Others, intrigued by claims of psychological truth, wonder: Do mothers and infants bond in the first hours after birth? How—and how much—does parenting shape children's personalities and abilities? Are first-born children more driven to achieve? Does psychotherapy heal?

In working with such questions, how can we separate uninformed opinions from examined conclusions? *How can we best use psychology to understand why people think, feel, and act as they do?*

The Need for Psychological Science

2-1 How do hindsight bias, overconfidence, and the tendency to perceive order in random events illustrate why science-based answers are more valid than those based on intuition and common sense?

Some people suppose that psychology merely documents and dresses in jargon what people already know: "So what else is new—you get paid for using fancy methods to prove what my grandmother knew?" Others place their faith in human intuition: "Buried deep within each and every one of us, there is an instinctive, heart-felt awareness that provides—if we allow it to—the most reliable guide," offered Prince Charles (2000). Former President George W. Bush described the feeling to journalist Bob Woodward (2002) in explaining his decision to launch the Iraq war: "I'm a gut player. I rely on my instincts."

Prince Charles and former President Bush have much company, judging from the long list of pop psychology books on "intuitive managing," "intuitive trading," and "intuitive healing." Today's psychological science does document a vast intuitive mind. As we will see, our thinking, memory, and attitudes operate on two levels—conscious and unconscious—with the larger part operating automatically, off-screen. Like jumbo jets, we fly mostly on autopilot.

So, are we smart to listen to the whispers of our inner wisdom, to simply trust "the force within"? Or should we more often be subjecting our intuitive hunches to skeptical scrutiny?

This much seems certain: We often underestimate intuition's perils. My geographical intuition tells me that Reno is east of Los Angeles, that Rome is south of New York, that Atlanta is east of Detroit. But I am wrong, wrong, and wrong.

Experiments have found people greatly overestimating their lie detection accuracy, their eyewitness recollections, their interviewee assessments, their risk predictions, and their stock-picking talents. "The first principle," said Richard Feynman (1997), "is that you must not fool yourself—and you are the easiest person to fool."

Indeed, observed novelist Madeleine L'Engle, "The naked intellect is an extraordinarily inaccurate instrument" (1973). Three phenomena—*hindsight bias, judgmental overconfidence*, and our *tendency to perceive patterns in random events*—illustrate why we cannot rely solely on intuition and common sense.

Asia Images Group Pte Ltd / Alamy

The limits of intuition Personnel interviewers tend to be overconfident of their gut feelings about job applicants. Their confidence stems partly from their recalling cases where their favorable impression proved right, and partly from their ignorance about rejected applicants who succeeded elsewhere.

"Those who trust in their own wits are fools."

Proverbs 28:26

hindsight bias the tendency to believe, after learning an outcome, that one would have foreseen it. (Also known as the *I-knew-it-all-along phenomenon.*)

"Life is lived forwards, but understood backwards."
Philosopher Søren Kierkegaard, 1813–1855

"Anything seems commonplace, once explained."
Dr. Watson to Sherlock Holmes

Did We Know It All Along? Hindsight Bias

Consider how easy it is to draw the bull's eye *after* the arrow strikes. After the stock market drops, people say it was "due for a correction." After the football game, we credit the coach if a "gutsy play" wins the game, and fault the coach for the "stupid play" if it doesn't. After a war or an election, its outcome usually seems obvious. Although history may therefore seem like a series of inevitable events, the actual future is seldom foreseen. No one's diary recorded, "Today the Hundred Years War began."

This **hindsight bias** (also known as the *I-knew-it-all-along phenomenon*) is easy to demonstrate: Give half the members of a group some purported psychological finding, and give the other half an opposite result. Tell the first group, "Psychologists have found that separation weakens romantic attraction. As the saying goes, 'Out of sight, out of mind.'" Ask them to imagine why this might be true. Most people can, and nearly all will then view this true finding as unsurprising.

Tell the second group the opposite, "Psychologists have found that separation strengthens romantic attraction. As the saying goes, 'Absence makes the heart grow fonder.'" People given this untrue result can also easily imagine it, and most will also see it as unsurprising. When two opposite findings both seem like common sense, there is a problem.

Such errors in our recollections and explanations show why we need psychological research. Just asking people how and why they felt or acted as they did can sometimes be misleading—not because common sense is usually wrong, but because common sense more easily describes what *has* happened than what *will* happen. As physicist Niels Bohr reportedly said, "Prediction is very difficult, especially about the future."

Some 100 studies have observed hindsight bias in various countries and among both children and adults (Blank et al., 2007). Nevertheless, Grandma's intuition is often right. As Yogi Berra once said, "You can observe a lot by watching." (We have Berra to thank for other gems, such as "Nobody ever comes here—it's too crowded," and "If the people don't want to come out to the ballpark, nobody's gonna stop 'em.") Because we're all behavior watchers, it would be surprising if many of psychology's findings had *not* been foreseen. Many people believe that love breeds happiness, and they are right, according to researchers who have found that we have a "deep need to belong." Indeed, note Daniel Gilbert, Brett Pelham, and Douglas Krull (2003), "good ideas in psychology usually have an oddly familiar quality, and the moment we encounter them we feel certain that we once came close to thinking the same thing ourselves and simply failed to write it down." Good ideas are like good inventions; once created, they seem obvious. (Why did it take so long for someone to invent suitcases on wheels and Post-it Notes?)

But sometimes Grandma's intuition, informed by countless casual observations, has it wrong. Psychological research has overturned popular ideas—that familiarity breeds contempt, that dreams predict the future, and that most of us use only 10 percent of our brain. It has also surprised us with discoveries about how the brain's chemical messengers control our moods and memories, about other animals' abilities, and about the effects of stress on our capacity to fight disease.

Hindsight bias When drilling its Deepwater Horizon oil well in 2010, BP employees took some shortcuts and ignored some warning signs, without intending to put their company and the environment at serious risk of devastation. *After* the resulting Gulf oil spill, with the benefit of 20/20 hindsight, the foolishness of those judgments became obvious.

REUTERS/U.S. Coast Guard/Handout

Overconfidence

We humans tend to think we know more than we do. Asked how sure we are of our answers to factual questions *(Is Boston north or south of Paris?)*, we tend to be more confident than correct.[1] Or consider these three anagrams, which Richard Goranson (1978) asked people to unscramble:

WREAT → WATER

ETRYN → ENTRY

GRABE → BARGE

About how many seconds do you think it would have taken you to unscramble each of these? Did hindsight influence you? Knowing the answers tends to make us overconfident—surely the solution would take only 10 seconds or so, when in reality the average problem solver spends 3 minutes, as you also might, given a similar anagram without the solution: OCHSA.[2]

Are we any better at predicting social behavior? University of Pennsylvania psychologist Philip Tetlock (1998, 2005) collected more than 27,000 expert predictions of world events, such as the future of South Africa or whether Quebec would separate from Canada. His repeated finding: These predictions, which experts made with 80 percent confidence on average, were right less than 40 percent of the time. Nevertheless, even those who erred maintained their confidence by noting they were "almost right." "The Québécois separatists *almost* won the secessionist referendum."

Overconfidence in history:

"We don't like their sound. Groups of guitars are on their way out."

Decca Records, in turning down a recording contract with the Beatles in 1962

"Computers in the future may weigh no more than 1.5 tons."

Popular Mechanics, 1949

"They couldn't hit an elephant at this distance."

General John Sedgwick just before being killed during a U.S. Civil War battle, 1864

RETRIEVAL PRACTICE

- Why, after friends start dating, do we often feel that we *knew* they were meant to be together?

ANSWER: We often suffer from hindsight bias—after we've learned a situation's outcome, that outcome seems familiar and therefore obvious.

Perceiving Order in Random Events

In our natural eagerness to make sense of our world—what poet Wallace Stevens called our "rage for order"—we are prone to perceive patterns. People see a face on the Moon, hear Satanic messages in music, perceive the Virgin Mary's image on a grilled cheese sandwich. Even in random data we often find order, because—here's a curious fact of life—*random sequences often don't look random* (Falk et al., 2009; Nickerson, 2002, 2005). In actual random sequences, patterns and streaks (such as repeating digits) occur more often than people expect (Oskarsson et al., 2009). To demonstrate this phenomenon for myself, I flipped a coin 51 times, with these results:

1. H	11. T	21. T	31. T	41. H	51. T
2. T	12. H	22. T	32. T	42. H	
3. T	13. H	23. H	33. T	43. H	
4. T	14. T	24. T	34. T	44. H	
5. H	15. T	25. T	35. T	45. T	
6. H	16. H	26. T	36. H	46. H	
7. H	17. T	27. H	37. T	47. H	
8. T	18. T	28. T	38. T	48. T	
9. T	19. H	29. H	39. H	49. T	
10. T	20. H	30. T	40. T	50. T	

Maciej Oleksy /Shutterstock

[1] Boston is south of Paris.

[2] The anagram solution: CHAOS.

© 1990 by Sidney Harris/*American Scientist* magazine.

Bizarre-looking, perhaps. But actually no more unlikely than any other number sequence.

Looking over the sequence, patterns jump out: Tosses 10 to 22 provided an almost perfect pattern of pairs of tails followed by pairs of heads. On tosses 30 to 38 I had a "cold hand," with only one head in nine tosses. But my fortunes immediately reversed with a "hot hand"—seven heads out of the next nine tosses. Similar streaks happen, about as often as one would expect in random sequences, in basketball shooting, baseball hitting, and mutual fund stock pickers' selections (Gilovich et al., 1985; Malkiel, 2007; Myers, 2002). These sequences often don't look random and so are overinterpreted. ("When you're hot, you're hot!")

What explains these streaky patterns? Was I exercising some sort of paranormal control over my coin? Did I snap out of my tails funk and get in a heads groove? No such explanations are needed, for these are the sorts of streaks found in any random data. Comparing each toss to the next, 23 of the 50 comparisons yielded a changed result—just the sort of near 50-50 result we expect from coin tossing. Despite seeming patterns, the outcome of one toss gives no clue to the outcome of the next.

However, some happenings seem so extraordinary that we struggle to conceive an ordinary, chance-related explanation (as applies to our coin tosses). In such cases, statisticians often are less mystified. When Evelyn Marie Adams won the New Jersey lottery *twice*, newspapers reported the odds of her feat as 1 in 17 trillion. Bizarre? Actually, 1 in 17 trillion are indeed the odds that a given person who buys a single ticket for two New Jersey lotteries will win both times. And given the millions of people who buy U.S. state lottery tickets, statisticians Stephen Samuels and George McCabe (1989) reported, it was "practically a sure thing" that someday, somewhere, someone would hit a state jackpot twice. Indeed, said fellow statisticians Persi Diaconis and Frederick Mosteller (1989), "with a large enough sample, any outrageous thing is likely to happen." An event that happens to but 1 in 1 billion people every day occurs about 7 times a day, 2500 times a year.

"The really unusual day would be one where nothing unusual happens."
Statistician Persi Diaconis (2002)

The point to remember: Hindsight bias, overconfidence, and our tendency to perceive patterns in random events often lead us to overestimate our intuition. But scientific inquiry can help us sift reality from illusion.

Roland Weihrauch/dpa/ picture-alliance/Newscom

Given enough random events, some weird-seeming streaks will occur During the 2010 World Cup, a German octopus—Paul, "the oracle of Oberhausen"—was offered two boxes, each with mussels and with a national flag on one side. Paul selected the right box eight out of eight times in predicting the outcome of Germany's seven matches and Spain's triumph in the final.

The Scientific Attitude: Curious, Skeptical, and Humble

2-2 How do the scientific attitude's three main components relate to critical thinking?

Underlying all science is, first, a hard-headed *curiosity*, a passion to explore and understand without misleading or being misled. Some questions *(Is there life after death?)* are beyond science. Answering them in any way requires a leap of faith. With many other ideas *(Can some people demonstrate ESP?)*, the proof is in the pudding. Let the facts speak for themselves.

Magician James Randi has used this *empirical approach* when testing those claiming to see auras around people's bodies:

Randi: Do you see an aura around my head?
Aura-seer: Yes, indeed.
Randi: Can you still see the aura if I put this magazine in front of my face?
Aura-seer: Of course.
Randi: Then if I were to step behind a wall barely taller than I am, you could determine my location from the aura visible above my head, right?

Randi told me that no aura seer has agreed to take this simple test.

No matter how sensible-seeming or wild an idea, the smart thinker asks: *Does it work?* When put to the test, can its predictions be confirmed? Subjected to such scrutiny, crazy-sounding ideas sometimes find support. During the 1700s, scientists scoffed at the notion that meteorites had extraterrestrial origins. When two Yale scientists challenged the conventional opinion, Thomas Jefferson jeered, "Gentlemen, I would rather believe that those two Yankee professors would lie than to believe that stones fell from Heaven." Sometimes scientific inquiry turns jeers into cheers.

More often, science becomes society's garbage disposal, sending crazy-sounding ideas to the waste heap, atop previous claims of perpetual motion machines, miracle cancer cures, and out-of-body travels into centuries past. To sift reality from fantasy, sense from nonsense, therefore requires a scientific attitude: being skeptical but not cynical, open but not gullible.

"To believe with certainty," says a Polish proverb, "we must begin by doubting." As scientists, psychologists approach the world of behavior with a *curious skepticism*, persistently asking two questions: *What do you mean? How do you know?*

When ideas compete, skeptical testing can reveal which ones best match the facts. Do parental behaviors determine children's sexual orientation? Can astrologers predict your future based on the position of the planets at your birth? Is electroconvulsive therapy (delivering an electric shock to the brain) an effective treatment for severe depression? As we will see, putting such claims to the test has led psychological scientists to answer *No* to the first two questions and *Yes* to the third.

The Amazing Randi The magician James Randi exemplifies skepticism. He has tested and debunked a variety of psychic phenomena.
AP Photo/Alan Diaz

"I'm a skeptic not because I do not want to believe but because I want to *know*. I believe that the truth is out there. But how can we tell the difference between what we would like to be true and what is actually true? The answer is science."

Michael Shermer, "I Want to Believe," *Scientific American*, 2009

Reprinted by permission of Universal Press Syndicate. © 1997 Wiley.

Putting a scientific attitude into practice requires not only curiosity and skepticism but also *humility*—an awareness of our own vulnerability to error and an openness to surprises and new perspectives. In the last analysis, what matters is not my opinion or yours, but the truths nature reveals in response to our questioning. If people or other animals don't behave as our ideas predict, then so much the worse for our ideas. This humble attitude was expressed in one of psychology's early mottos: "The rat is always right."

"My deeply held belief is that if a god anything like the traditional sort exists, our curiosity and intelligence are provided by such a god. We would be unappreciative of those gifts . . . if we suppressed our passion to explore the universe and ourselves."
Carl Sagan, *Broca's Brain*, 1979

Historians of science tell us that these three attitudes—curiosity, skepticism, and humility—helped make modern science possible. Some deeply religious people today may view science, including psychological science, as a threat. Yet, many of the leaders of the scientific revolution, including Copernicus and Newton, were deeply religious people acting on the idea that "in order to love and honor God, it is necessary to fully appreciate the wonders of his handiwork" (Stark, 2003a,b).

Of course, scientists, like anyone else, can have big egos and may cling to their preconceptions. Nevertheless, the ideal of curious, skeptical, humble scrutiny of competing ideas unifies psychologists as a community as they check and recheck one another's findings and conclusions.

Critical Thinking

The scientific attitude prepares us to think smarter. Smart thinking, called **critical thinking,** examines assumptions, discerns hidden values, evaluates evidence, and assesses conclusions. Whether reading a news report or listening to a conversation, critical thinkers ask questions. Like scientists, they wonder, How do they know that? What is this person's agenda? Is the conclusion based on anecdote and gut feelings, or on evidence? Does the evidence justify a cause-effect conclusion? What alternative explanations are possible?

Critical thinking, informed by science, helps clear the colored lenses of our biases. Consider: Does climate change threaten our future, and, if so, is it human-caused? In 2009, climate-action advocates interpreted an Australian heat wave and dust storms as evidence of climate change. In 2010, climate-change skeptics perceived North American bitter cold and East Coast blizzards as discounting global warming. Rather than having their understanding of climate change swayed by today's weather, or by their own political views, critical thinkers say, "Show me the evidence." Over time, is the Earth actually warming? Are the polar ice caps melting? Are vegetation patterns changing? And is human activity spewing gases that would lead us to expect such changes? When contemplating such issues, critical thinkers will consider the credibility of sources. They will look at the evidence *("Do the facts support them, or are they just makin' stuff up?")*. They will recognize multiple perspectives. And they will expose themselves to news sources that challenge their preconceived ideas.

"The real purpose of the scientific method is to make sure Nature hasn't misled you into thinking you know something you don't actually know."
Robert M. Pirsig, *Zen and the Art of Motorcycle Maintenance*, 1974

Has psychology's critical inquiry been open to surprising findings? The answer is plainly *Yes*. Some examples: massive losses of brain tissue early in life may have minimal long-term effects. Within days, newborns can recognize their mother's odor and voice. After brain damage, a person may be able to learn new skills yet be unaware of such learning. Diverse groups—men and women, old and young, rich and middle class, those with disabilities and without—report roughly comparable levels of personal happiness.

And has critical inquiry convincingly debunked popular presumptions? The answer is again *Yes*. The evidence indicates that sleepwalkers are *not* acting out their dreams. Our past experiences are *not* all recorded verbatim in our brains; with brain stimulation or hypnosis, one *cannot* simply "hit the replay button" and relive long-buried or repressed memories. Most people do *not* suffer from unrealistically low self-esteem, and high self-esteem is not all good. Opposites do *not* generally attract. In each of these instances and more, what has been learned is not what is widely believed.

critical thinking thinking that does not blindly accept arguments and conclusions. Rather, it examines assumptions, discerns hidden values, evaluates evidence, and assesses conclusions.

RETRIEVAL PRACTICE

- How does the scientific attitude contribute to critical thinking?

ANSWER: The scientific attitude combines (1) *curiosity* about the world around us, (2) *skepticism* toward various claims and ideas, and (3) *humility* about one's own understanding. Evaluating evidence, assessing conclusions, and examining our own assumptions are essential parts of critical thinking.

Frequently Asked Questions About Psychology

You are now prepared to think about psychological matters. Yet, even knowing this much, you may still be approaching psychology with a mixture of curiosity and apprehension. So before we plunge in, let's entertain some frequently asked questions.

2-3 Can laboratory experiments illuminate everyday life?

When you see or hear about psychological research, do you ever wonder whether people's behavior in the lab will predict their behavior in real life? For example, does detecting the blink of a faint red light in a dark room have anything useful to say about flying a plane at night? After viewing a violent, sexually explicit film, does an aroused man's increased willingness to push buttons that he thinks will electrically shock a woman really say anything about whether violent pornography makes a man more likely to abuse a woman?

Before you answer, consider: The experimenter *intends* the laboratory environment to be a simplified reality—one that simulates and controls important features of everyday life. Just as a wind tunnel lets airplane designers re-create airflow forces under controlled conditions, a laboratory experiment lets psychologists re-create psychological forces under controlled conditions.

An experiment's purpose is not to re-create the exact behaviors of everyday life but to test *theoretical principles* (Mook, 1983). In aggression studies, deciding whether to push a button that delivers a shock may not be the same as slapping someone in the face, but the principle is the same. *It is the resulting principles—not the specific findings—that help explain everyday behaviors.*

When psychologists apply laboratory research on aggression to actual violence, they are applying theoretical principles of aggressive behavior, principles they have refined through many experiments. Similarly, it is the principles of the visual system, developed from experiments in artificial settings (such as looking at red lights in the dark), that researchers apply to more complex behaviors such as night flying. And many investigations show that principles derived in the laboratory do typically generalize to the everyday world (Anderson et al., 1999).

The point to remember: Psychological science focuses less on particular behaviors than on seeking general principles that help explain many behaviors.

2-4 Does behavior depend on one's culture and gender?

What can psychological studies done in one time and place—often with people from what Joseph Henrich, Steven Heine, and Ara Norenzayan (2010) call the WEIRD cultures (Western, Educated, Industrialized, Rich, and Democratic cultures that contribute most study participants but are only 12 percent of humanity)—really tell us about people in general? As we will see time and again, **culture**—shared ideas and behaviors that one generation passes on to the next—matters. Our culture shapes our behavior. It influences our standards of promptness and frankness, our attitudes toward premarital sex and varying body shapes, our tendency to be casual or formal, our willingness to make eye contact, our conversational distance, and much, much more. Being aware of such differences, we can

culture the enduring behaviors, ideas, attitudes, values, and traditions shared by a group of people and transmitted from one generation to the next.

A cultured greeting Because culture shapes people's understanding of social behavior, actions that seem ordinary to us may seem quite odd to visitors from far away. Yet underlying these differences are powerful similarities. Supporters of newly elected leaders everywhere typically greet them with pleased deference, though not necessarily with bows and folded hands, as in India. Here influential and popular politician Sonia Gandhi greets some of her constituents shortly after her election.

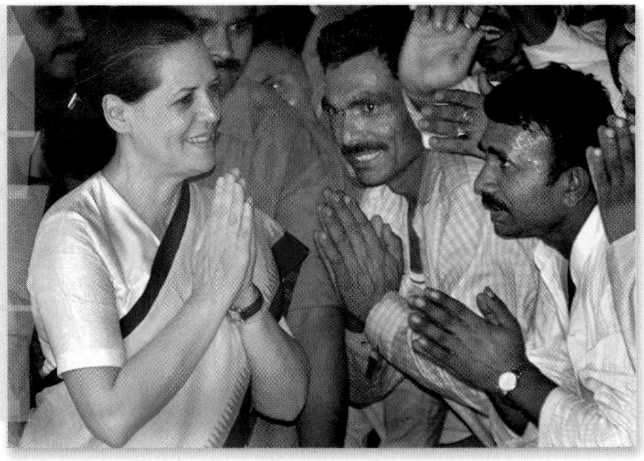

Ami Vitale/Getty Images

restrain our assumptions that others will think and act as we do. Given the growing mixing and clashing of cultures, our need for such awareness is urgent.

It is also true, however, that our shared biological heritage unites us as a universal human family. The same underlying processes guide people everywhere.

- People diagnosed with dyslexia, a reading disorder, exhibit the same brain malfunction whether they are Italian, French, or British (Paulesu et al., 2001).
- Variation in languages may impede communication across cultures. Yet all languages share deep principles of grammar, and people from opposite hemispheres can communicate with a smile or a frown.
- People in different cultures vary in feelings of loneliness. But across cultures, loneliness is magnified by shyness, low self-esteem, and being unmarried (Jones et al., 1985; Rokach et al., 2002).

We are each in certain respects like all others, like some others, and like no other. Studying people of all races and cultures helps us discern our similarities and our differences, our human kinship and our diversity.

You will see throughout this book that *gender* matters, too. Researchers report gender differences in what we dream, in how we express and detect emotions, and in our risk for alcohol dependence, depression, and eating disorders. Gender differences fascinate us, and studying them is potentially beneficial. For example, many researchers believe that women carry on conversations more readily to build relationships, while men talk more to give information and advice (Tannen, 2001). Knowing this difference can help us prevent conflicts and misunderstandings in everyday relationships.

But again, psychologically as well as biologically, women and men are overwhelmingly similar. Whether female or male, we learn to walk at about the same age. We experience the same sensations of light and sound. We feel the same pangs of hunger, desire, and fear. We exhibit similar overall intelligence and well-being.

"All people are the same; only their habits differ."

Confucius, 551–479 B.C.E

The point to remember: Even when specific attitudes and behaviors vary by gender or across cultures, as they often do, the underlying processes are much the same.

2-5 Why do psychologists study animals, and what ethical guidelines safeguard human and animal research participants?

Many psychologists study animals because they find them fascinating. They want to understand how different species learn, think, and behave. Psychologists also study animals to learn about people. We humans are not *like* animals; we *are* animals, sharing a common biology. Animal experiments have therefore led to treatments for human diseases—insulin for diabetes, vaccines to prevent polio and rabies, transplants to replace defective organs.

Humans are complex. But the same processes by which we learn are present in rats, monkeys, and even sea slugs. The simplicity of the sea slug's nervous system is precisely what makes it so revealing of the neural mechanisms of learning. Sharing such similarities, should we not respect our animal relatives? "We cannot defend our scientific work with animals on the basis of the similarities between them and ourselves and then defend it morally on the basis of differences," noted Roger Ulrich (1991). The animal protection movement protests the use of animals in psychological, biological, and medical research.

"Rats are very similar to humans except that they are not stupid enough to purchase lottery tickets."

Dave Barry, July 2, 2002

Out of this heated debate, two issues emerge. The basic one is whether it is right to place the well-being of humans above that of animals. In experiments on stress and cancer, is it right that mice get tumors in the hope that people might not? Should some monkeys be exposed to an HIV-like virus in the search for an AIDS vaccine? Is our use and consumption of other animals as natural as the behavior of carnivorous hawks, cats, and whales? The answers to such questions vary by culture. In Gallup surveys in Canada and the United States, about 60 percent of adults deem medical testing on animals "morally acceptable." In Britain, only 37 percent do (Mason, 2003).

"Please do not forget those of us who suffer from incurable diseases or disabilities who hope for a cure through research that requires the use of animals."

Psychologist Dennis Feeney (1987)

If we give human life first priority, what safeguards should protect the well-being of animals in research? One survey of animal researchers gave an answer. Some 98 percent supported government regulations protecting primates, dogs, and cats, and 74 percent supported regulations providing for the humane care of rats and mice (Plous & Herzog, 2000). Many professional associations and funding agencies already have such guidelines. British Psychological Society guidelines call for housing animals under reasonably natural living conditions, with companions for social animals (Lea, 2000). American Psychological Association guidelines state that researchers must ensure the "comfort, health, and humane treatment" of animals and minimize "infection, illness, and pain" (APA, 2002). The European Parliament now mandates standards for animal care and housing (Vogel, 2010).

"The greatness of a nation can be judged by the way its animals are treated."

Mahatma Gandhi, 1869–1948

Animals have themselves benefited from animal research. One Ohio team of research psychologists measured stress hormone levels in samples of millions of dogs brought each year to animal shelters. They devised handling and stroking methods to reduce stress and ease the dogs' transition to adoptive homes (Tuber et al., 1999). Other studies have helped improve care and management in animals' natural habitats. By revealing our behavioral kinship with animals and the remarkable intelligence of chimpanzees, gorillas, and other animals, experiments have also led to increased empathy and protection for them. At its best, a psychology concerned for humans and sensitive to animals serves the welfare of both.

Animal research benefiting animals Thanks partly to research on the benefits of novelty, control, and stimulation, these gorillas are enjoying an improved quality of life in New York's Bronx Zoo.

Ami Vitale/Getty Images

What about human participants? Does the image of white-coated scientists delivering electric shocks trouble you? If so, you'll be relieved to know that most psychological studies are free of such stress. With people, blinking lights, flashing words, and pleasant social interactions are more common. Moreover, psychology's experiments are mild compared with the stress and humiliation often inflicted by reality TV shows. In one episode of *The Bachelor*, a man dumped his new fiancée—on camera, at the producers' request—for the woman who earlier had finished second (Collins, 2009).

Occasionally, though, researchers do temporarily stress or deceive people, but only when they believe it is essential to a justifiable end, such as understanding and controlling violent behavior or studying mood swings. Some experiments won't work if participants know everything beforehand. (Wanting to be helpful, the participants might try to confirm the researcher's predictions.)

informed consent an ethical principle that research participants be told enough to enable them to choose whether they wish to participate.

debriefing the postexperimental explanation of a study, including its purpose and any deceptions, to its participants.

"It is doubtless impossible to approach any human problem with a mind free from bias."
Simone de Beauvoir, *The Second Sex,* 1953

The American Psychological Association's ethics code urges researchers to (1) obtain potential participants' **informed consent,** (2) protect them from harm and discomfort, (3) keep information about individual participants confidential, and (4) fully **debrief** people (explain the research afterward). Moreover, university ethics committees screen research proposals and safeguard participants' well-being.

2-6 Is psychology free of value judgments?

Psychology is definitely not value free. Values affect what we study, how we study it, and how we interpret results. Researchers' values influence their choice of topics. Should we study worker productivity or worker morale? Sex discrimination or gender differences? Conformity or independence? Values can also color "the facts." As we noted earlier, our preconceptions can bias our observations and interpretations; sometimes we see what we want or expect to see (**FIGURE 2.1**).

Mike Kemp/Getty Images

Even the words we use to describe something can reflect our values. Are the sex acts we do not practice "perversions" or "sexual variations"? In psychology and in everyday speech, labels describe and labels evaluate: One person's *rigidity* is another's *consistency.* One person's *faith* is another's *fanaticism.* One country's *enhanced interrogation techniques,* such as cold-water immersion, become *torture* when practiced by its enemies. Our labeling someone as *firm* or *stubborn, careful* or *picky, discreet* or *secretive* reveals our own attitudes.

Popular applications of psychology also contain hidden values. If you defer to "professional" guidance about how to live—how to raise children, how to achieve self-fulfillment, what to do with sexual feelings, how to get ahead at work—you are accepting value-laden advice. A science of behavior and mental processes can help us reach our goals. But it cannot decide what those goals should be.

If some people see psychology as merely common sense, others have a different concern—that it is becoming dangerously powerful. Is it an accident that astronomy is the oldest science and psychology the youngest? To some, exploring the external universe seems far safer than exploring our own inner universe. Might psychology, they ask, be used to manipulate people?

Knowledge, like all power, can be used for good or evil. Nuclear power has been used to light up cities—and to demolish them. Persuasive power has been used to educate people—and to deceive them. Although psychology does indeed have the power to deceive, its purpose is to enlighten. Every day, psychologists are exploring ways to enhance learning, creativity, and compassion. Psychology speaks to many of our world's great problems—war, overpopulation, prejudice, family crises, crime—all of which involve attitudes and behaviors. Psychology also speaks to our deepest longings—for nourishment, for love, for happiness. Psychology cannot address all of life's great questions, but it speaks to some mighty important ones.

FIGURE 2.1
What do you see? Our expectations influence what we perceive. Did you see a duck or a rabbit? Show some friends this image with the rabbit photo above covered up and see if they are more likely to perceive a duck lying on its back instead. (From Shepard, 1990).

© Roger Shepard

Office of Public Affairs at Columbia University

Psychology speaks In making its historic 1954 school desegregation decision, the U.S. Supreme Court cited the expert testimony and research of psychologists Kenneth Clark and Mamie Phipps Clark (1947). The Clarks reported that, when given a choice between Black and White dolls, most African-American children chose the White doll, which seemingly indicated internalized anti-Black prejudice.

RETRIEVAL PRACTICE

- How are human and animal research participants protected?

ANSWER: Animal protection legislation, laboratory regulation and inspection, and local ethics committees serve to protect human and animal welfare. University ethics committees screen research proposals. Ethical principles developed by the American Psychological Association and other organizations urge researchers using human participants to obtain *informed consent*, to protect them from harm and discomfort, to treat their personal information confidentially, and to fully *debrief* all participants.

MODULE REVIEW

Thinking Critically With Psychological Science

Learning Objectives

RETRIEVAL PRACTICE Take a moment to answer each of these Learning Objective Questions (repeated here from within the module). Then turn to Appendix B, Complete Module Reviews, to check your answers. Research suggests that trying to answer these questions on your own will improve your long-term retention (McDaniel et al., 2009).

2-1: How do hindsight bias, overconfidence, and the tendency to perceive order in random events illustrate why science-based answers are more valid than those based on intuition and common sense?

2-2: How do the scientific attitude's three main components relate to critical thinking?

2-3: Can laboratory experiments illuminate everyday life?

2-4: Does behavior depend on one's culture and gender?

2-5: Why do psychologists study animals, and what ethical guidelines safeguard human and animal research participants?

2-6: Is psychology free of value judgments?

Terms and Concepts to Remember

RETRIEVAL PRACTICE Test yourself on these terms by trying to write down the definition before flipping back to the referenced page to check your answer.

hindsight bias, p. 16
critical thinking, p. 20
culture, p. 21
informed consent, p. 24
debriefing, p. 24

RETRIEVAL PRACTICE Gain an advantage, and benefit from immediate feedback, with the interactive self-testing resources at www.worthpublishers.com/myers.

MODULE 3

- How *Do* Psychologists Ask and Answer Questions?
- Statistical Reasoning in Everyday Life

Research Strategies: How Psychologists Ask and Answer Questions

How *Do* Psychologists Ask and Answer Questions?

Psychologists arm their scientific attitude with the *scientific method*—a self-correcting process for evaluating ideas with observation and analysis. In its attempt to describe and explain human nature, psychological science welcomes hunches and plausible-sounding theories. And it puts them to the test. If a theory works—if the data support its predictions—so much the better for that theory. If the predictions fail, the theory will be revised or rejected.

The Scientific Method

3-1 How do theories advance psychological science?

In everyday conversation, we often use *theory* to mean "mere hunch." In science, a **theory** *explains* with principles that *organize* observations and *predict* behaviors or events. By organizing isolated facts, a theory simplifies. By linking facts with deeper principles, a theory offers a useful summary. As we connect the observed dots, a coherent picture emerges.

A good theory about the effects of sleep deprivation on memory, for example, helps us organize countless sleep-related observations into a short list of principles. Imagine that we observe over and over that people with poor sleep habits cannot answer questions in class, and they do poorly at test time. We might therefore theorize that sleep improves memory. So far so good: Our sleep-retention principle neatly summarizes a list of facts about the effects of sleep loss.

Yet no matter how reasonable a theory may sound—and it does seem reasonable to suggest that sleep loss could affect memory—we must put it to the test. A good theory produces testable predictions, called **hypotheses.** By enabling us to test and to reject or revise our theory, such predictions direct research. They specify what results would support the theory and what results would disconfirm it. To test our theory about the effects of sleep on memory, we might assess people's retention of course materials after a good night's sleep, or a shortened night's sleep (**FIGURE 3.1**).

Our theories can bias our observations. Having theorized that better memory springs from more sleep, we may see what we expect: We may perceive sleepy people's comments as less insightful. The urge to see what we expect is ever-present, both inside and outside the laboratory. According to the bipartisan U.S. Senate Select Committee on Intelligence (2004), preconceived expectations that Iraq had weapons of mass destruction led intelligence analysts to wrongly interpret ambiguous observations as confirming that theory (much as people's views of climate change may influence their interpretation of local weather events). This theory-driven conclusion then led to the preemptive U.S. invasion of Iraq.

As a check on their biases, psychologists report their research with precise **operational definitions** of procedures and concepts. *Hunger*, for example, might be defined as "hours without eating," *generosity* as "money contributed." Using these carefully worded statements, others can **replicate** (repeat) the original observations with different participants,

theory an explanation using an integrated set of principles that organizes observations and predicts behaviors or events.

hypothesis a testable prediction, often implied by a theory.

operational definition a statement of the procedures (operations) used to define research variables. For example, *human intelligence* may be operationally defined as "what an intelligence test measures."

replication repeating the essence of a research study, usually with different participants in different situations, to see whether the basic finding extends to other participants and circumstances.

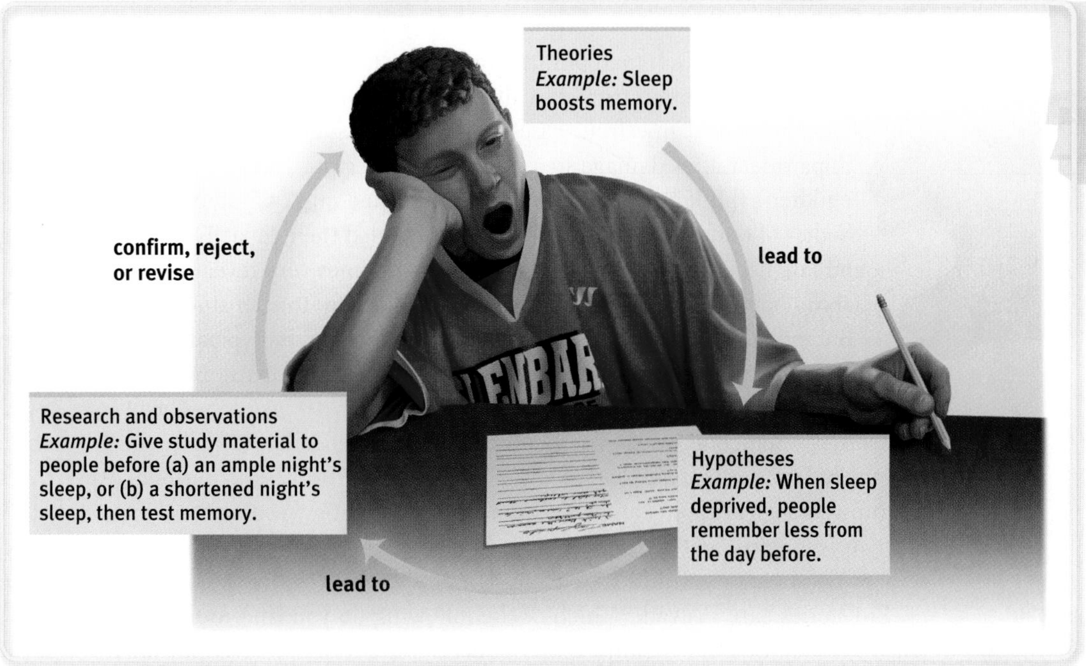

FIGURE 3.1
The scientific method A self-correcting process for asking questions and observing nature's answers.

materials, and circumstances. If they get similar results, confidence in the finding's reliability grows. The first study of hindsight bias (the tendency to believe, after learning an outcome, that one would have foreseen it) aroused psychologists' curiosity. Now, after many successful replications with differing people and questions, we feel sure of the phenomenon's power.

In the end, our theory will be useful if it (1) *organizes* a range of self-reports and observations, and (2) implies *predictions* that anyone can use to check the theory or to derive practical applications. (If people sleep more, will their retention improve?) Eventually, our research may lead to a revised theory that better organizes and predicts what we know. Or, our research may be replicated and supported by similar findings. (This has been the case for sleep and memory studies.)

As we will see next, we can test our hypotheses and refine our theories using *descriptive* methods (which describe behaviors, often through case studies, surveys, or naturalistic observations), *correlational* methods (which associate different factors), and *experimental* methods (which manipulate factors to discover their effects). To think critically about popular psychology claims, we need to understand these methods and know what conclusions they allow.

RETRIEVAL PRACTICE

- What does a good theory do?

ANSWER:
1. It *organizes* observed facts.
2. It implies hypotheses that offer testable *predictions* and, sometimes, practical applications.

- Why is replication important?

ANSWER: Psychologists watch eagerly for new findings, but they also proceed with caution—by awaiting other investigators' repeating the experiment to see if the finding will be confirmed (the result replicated).

Description

3-2 How do psychologists use case studies, naturalistic observation, and surveys to observe and describe behavior, and why is random sampling important?

The starting point of any science is description. In everyday life, we all observe and describe people, often drawing conclusions about why they act as they do. Professional psychologists do much the same, though more objectively and systematically, through

- *case studies* (analyses of special individuals).
- *naturalistic observation* (watching and recording the natural behavior of many individuals).
- *surveys* and interviews (by asking people questions).

The Case Study

Among the oldest research methods, the **case study** examines one individual in depth in the hope of revealing things true of us all. Some examples: Much of our early knowledge about the brain came from case studies of individuals who suffered a particular impairment after damage to a certain brain region. Jean Piaget taught us about children's thinking after carefully observing and questioning only a few children. Studies of only a few chimpanzees have revealed their capacity for understanding and language. Intensive case studies are sometimes very revealing. They show us what *can* happen, and they often suggest directions for further study.

But individual cases may mislead us if the individual is atypical. Unrepresentative information can lead to mistaken judgments and false conclusions. Indeed, anytime a researcher mentions a finding (*"Smokers die younger: 95 percent of men over 85 are nonsmokers"*) someone is sure to offer a contradictory anecdote (*"Well, I have an uncle who smoked two packs a day and lived to 89"*). Dramatic stories and personal experiences (even psychological case examples) command our attention and are easily remembered. Journalists understand that, and so begin an article about bank foreclosures with the sad story of one family put out of their house, not with foreclosure statistics. Stories move us. But stories can mislead. Which of the following do you find more memorable? (1) "In one study of 1300 dream reports concerning a kidnapped child, only 5 percent correctly envisioned the child as dead" (Murray & Wheeler, 1937). (2) "I know a man who dreamed his sister was in a car accident, and two days later she died in a head-on collision!" Numbers can be numbing, but the plural of *anecdote* is not *evidence*. As psychologist Gordon Allport (1954, p. 9) said, "Given a thimbleful of [dramatic] facts we rush to make generalizations as large as a tub."

The point to remember: Individual cases can suggest fruitful ideas. What's true of all of us can be glimpsed in any one of us. But to discern the general truths that cover individual cases, we must answer questions with other research methods.

Freud and Little Hans
Sigmund Freud's case study of 5-year-old Hans' extreme fear of horses led Freud to his theory of childhood sexuality. He conjectured that Hans felt an unconscious desire for his mother, feared castration by his rival father, and then transferred this fear into his phobia about being bitten by a horse. Today's psychological science discounts Freud's theory of childhood sexuality but acknowledges that much of the human mind operates outside our conscious awareness.
Skye Hohmann/Alamy

"'Well my dear,' said Miss Marple, 'human nature is very much the same everywhere, and of course, one has opportunities of observing it at closer quarters in a village.'"
Agatha Christie, *The Tuesday Club Murders*, 1933

RETRIEVAL PRACTICE

- Case studies do not allow us to learn about general principles that apply to all of us. Why not?

ANSWER: Case studies involve only one individual, so we can't know for sure whether the principles observed would apply to a larger population.

Naturalistic Observation

A second descriptive method records behavior in natural environments. These **naturalistic observations** range from watching chimpanzee societies in the jungle, to unobtrusively videotaping (and later systematically analyzing) parent-child interactions in different cultures, to recording racial differences in students' self-seating patterns in a school lunchroom.

Like the case study, naturalistic observation does not *explain* behavior. It *describes* it. Nevertheless, descriptions can be revealing. We once thought, for example, that only humans use tools. Then naturalistic observation revealed that chimpanzees sometimes insert a stick in a termite mound and withdraw it, eating the stick's load of termites. Such unobtrusive naturalistic observations paved the way for later studies of animal thinking, language, and emotion, which further expanded our understanding of our fellow animals. "Observations, made in the natural habitat, helped to show that the societies and behavior of animals are far more complex than previously supposed," chimpanzee observer Jane Goodall noted (1998). Thanks to researchers' observations, we know that chimpanzees and baboons use deception. Psychologists Andrew Whiten and Richard Byrne (1988) repeatedly saw one young baboon pretending to have been attacked by

case study an observation technique in which one person is studied in depth in the hope of revealing universal principles.

naturalistic observation observing and recording behavior in naturally occurring situations without trying to manipulate and control the situation.

Photo by Jack Kearse, Emory University for Yerkes National Primate Research Center

A natural observer Chimpanzee researcher Frans de Waal (2005) reported, "I am a born observer. . . . When picking a seat in a restaurant I want to face as many tables as possible. I enjoy following the social dynamics—love, tension, boredom, antipathy—around me based on body language, which I consider more informative than the spoken word. Since keeping track of others is something I do automatically, becoming a fly on the wall of an ape colony came naturally to me."

another as a tactic to get its mother to drive the other baboon away from its food. The more developed a primate species' brain, the more likely it is that the animals will display deceptive behaviors (Byrne & Corp, 2004).

Naturalistic observations also illuminate human behavior. Here are four findings you might enjoy.

- A *funny finding.* We humans laugh 30 times more often in social situations than in solitary situations. (Have you noticed how seldom you laugh when alone?) As we laugh, 17 muscles contort our mouth and squeeze our eyes, and we emit a series of 75-millisecond vowel-like sounds, spaced about one-fifth of a second apart (Provine, 2001).
- *Sounding out students.* What, really, are introductory psychology students saying and doing during their everyday lives? To find out, Matthias Mehl and James Pennebaker (2003) equipped 52 such students from the University of Texas with belt-worn Electronically Activated Recorders (EARs). For up to four days, the EAR captured 30 seconds of the students' waking hours every 12.5 minutes, thus enabling the researchers to eavesdrop on more than 10,000 half-minute life slices by the end of the study. On what percentage of the slices do you suppose they found the students talking with someone? What percentage captured the students at a computer? The answers: 28 and 9 percent. (What percentage of *your* waking hours are spent in these activities?)
- *What's on your mind?* To find out what was on the minds of their University of Nevada, Las Vegas, students, Christopher Heavey and Russell Hurlburt (2008) gave them beepers. On a half-dozen occasions, a beep interrupted students' daily activities, signaling them to pull out a notebook and record their inner experience at that moment. When the researchers later coded the reports in categories, they found five common forms of inner experience (**TABLE 3.1** on the next page).
- *Culture, climate, and the pace of life.* Naturalistic observation also enabled Robert Levine and Ara Norenzayan (1999) to compare the pace of life in 31 countries. (Their operational definition of *pace of life* included walking speed, the speed with which postal clerks completed a simple request, and the accuracy of public clocks.) Their conclusion: Life is fastest paced in Japan and Western Europe, and slower paced in economically less-developed countries. People in colder climates also tend to live at a faster pace (and are more prone to die from heart disease).

Naturalistic observation offers interesting snapshots of everyday life, but it does so without controlling for all the factors that may influence behavior. It's one thing to observe the pace of life in various places, but another to understand what makes some people walk faster than others.

RETRIEVAL PRACTICE

An EAR for naturalistic observation Psychologists Matthias Mehl and James Pennebaker have used Electronically Activated Recorders (EARs) to sample naturally occurring slices of daily life.

- What are the advantages and disadvantages of naturalistic observation, such as Mehl and Pennebaker used in this study?

ANSWER: The study by Mehl and Pennebaker carefully observed and recorded naturally occurring behaviors—outside the artificiality of the lab. Because this was not an experiment, the study did not reveal the factors that influence everyday speech.

Courtesy of Matthias Mehl

Creative Crop/Jupiterimages

TABLE 3.1

A Penny for Your Thoughts: The Inner Experience of University Students*

Inner Experience	Example	Frequency
Inner speech	Susan was saying to herself, "I've got to get to class."	26%
Inner seeing	Paul was imagining the face of a best friend, including her neck and head.	34%
Unsymbolized thinking	Alphonse was wondering whether the workers would drop the bricks.	22%
Feeling	Courtney was experiencing anger and its physical symptoms.	26%
Sensory awareness	Fiona was feeling the cold breeze on her cheek and her hair moving.	22%

* More than one experience could occur at once.

survey a technique for ascertaining the self-reported attitudes or behaviors of a particular group, usually by questioning a representative, random sample of the group.

population all the cases in a group being studied, from which samples may be drawn. (*Note:* Except for national studies, this does *not* refer to a country's whole population.)

random sample a sample that fairly represents a population because each member has an equal chance of inclusion.

The Survey

A **survey** looks at many cases in less depth. A survey asks people to report their behavior or opinions. Questions about everything from sexual practices to political opinions are put to the public. In recent surveys,

- half of all Americans reported experiencing more happiness and enjoyment than worry and stress on the previous day (Gallup, 2010).
- online Canadians reported using new forms of electronic communication and thus receiving 35 percent fewer e-mails in 2010 than 2008 (Ipsos, 2010a).
- 1 in 5 people across 22 countries reported believing that alien beings have come to Earth and now walk among us disguised as humans (Ipsos, 2010b).
- 68 percent of all humans—some 4.6 billion people—say that religion is important in their daily lives (Diener et al., 2011).

But asking questions is tricky, and the answers often depend on the ways questions are worded and respondents are chosen.

Wording Effects Even subtle changes in the order or wording of questions can have major effects. People are much more approving of "aid to the needy" than of "welfare," of "affirmative action" than of "preferential treatment," of "not allowing" televised cigarette ads and pornography than of "censoring" them, and of "revenue enhancers" than of "taxes." In 2009, three in four Americans in one national survey approved of giving people "a choice" of public, government-run, or private health insurance. Yet in another survey, most Americans were not in favor of "creating a public health care plan administered by the federal government that would compete directly with private health insurance companies" (Stein, 2009). Because wording is such a delicate matter, critical thinkers will reflect on how the phrasing of a question might affect people's expressed opinions.

This Modern World by Tom Tomorrow © 1991.

Random Sampling In everyday thinking, we tend to generalize from samples we observe, especially vivid cases. Given (a) a statistical summary of a professor's student evaluations and (b) the vivid comments of a biased sample—two irate students—an administrator's impression of the professor may be influenced as much by the two unhappy students as by the many favorable evaluations in the statistical summary. The temptation to ignore the *sampling bias* and to generalize from a few vivid but unrepresentative cases is nearly irresistible.

The point to remember: The best basis for generalizing is from a *representative sample.*

But it's not always possible to survey everyone in a group. So how do you obtain a representative sample—say, of the students at your college or university? How could you choose a group that would represent the total student **population,** the whole group you want to study and describe? Typically, you would seek a **random sample,** in which every person in the entire group has an equal chance of participating. You might number the names in the general student listing and then use a random number generator to pick your survey participants. (Sending each student a questionnaire wouldn't work because the conscientious people who returned it would not be a random sample.) Large representative samples are better than small ones, but a small representative sample of 100 is better than an unrepresentative sample of 500.

Political pollsters sample voters in national election surveys just this way. Using only 1500 randomly sampled people, drawn from all areas of a country, they can provide a remarkably accurate snapshot of the nation's opinions. Without random sampling, large samples—including call-in phone samples and TV or website polls—often merely give misleading results.

The point to remember: Before accepting survey findings, think critically: Consider the sample. You cannot compensate for an unrepresentative sample by simply adding more people.

With very large samples, estimates become quite reliable. *E* is estimated to represent 12.7 percent of the letters in written English. *E,* in fact, is 12.3 percent of the 925,141 letters in Melville's *Moby Dick,* 12.4 percent of the 586,747 letters in Dickens' *A Tale of Two Cities,* and 12.1 percent of the 3,901,021 letters in 12 of Mark Twain's works (*Chance News,* 1997).

RETRIEVAL PRACTICE

- What is *sampling bias,* and how do researchers avoid it?

ANSWER: *Random sampling* helps researchers avoid sampling bias, which occurs when a survey group is not representative of the population being studied.

Correlation

3-3 What are positive and negative correlations, and why do they enable prediction but not cause-effect explanation?

Describing behavior is a first step toward predicting it. Naturalistic observations and surveys often show us that one trait or behavior is related to another. In such cases, we say the two **correlate.** A statistical measure (the **correlation coefficient**) helps us figure how closely two things vary together, and thus how well either one *predicts* the other. Knowing how much aptitude test scores *correlate* with school success tells us how well the scores *predict* school success.

Throughout this book we will often ask how strongly two things are related: For example, how closely related are the personality scores of identical twins? How well do intelligence test scores predict vocational achievement? How closely is stress related to disease? In such cases, **scatterplots** can be very revealing.

Each dot in a scatterplot represents the values of two variables. The three scatterplots in FIGURE 3.2 illustrate the range of possible correlations from a perfect positive to a perfect negative. (Perfect correlations rarely occur in the "real world.") A correlation is positive if two sets of scores, such as height and weight, tend to rise or fall together.

correlation a measure of the extent to which two factors vary together, and thus of how well either factor predicts the other.

correlation coefficient a statistical index of the relationship between two things (from −1 to +1).

scatterplot a graphed cluster of dots, each of which represents the values of two variables. The slope of the points suggests the direction of the relationship between the two variables. The amount of scatter suggests the strength of the correlation (little scatter indicates high correlation).

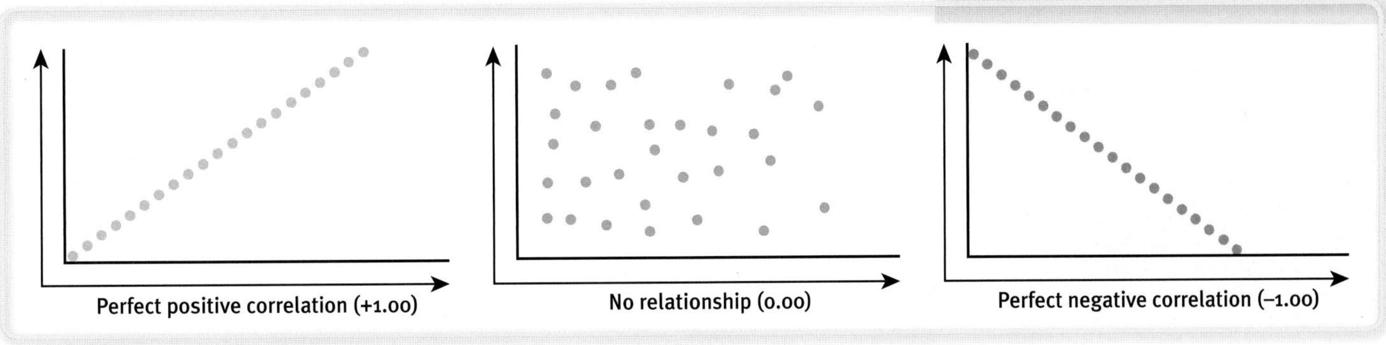

FIGURE 3.2 **Scatterplots, showing patterns of correlation** Correlations can range from +1.00 (scores on one measure increase in direct proportion to scores on another) to −1.00 (scores on one measure decrease precisely as scores rise on the other).

TABLE 3.2

Height and Temperamental Reactivity of 20 Men

Person	Height in Inches	Temperament
1	80	75
2	63	66
3	61	60
4	79	90
5	74	60
6	69	42
7	62	42
8	75	60
9	77	81
10	60	39
11	64	48
12	76	69
13	71	72
14	66	57
15	73	63
16	70	75
17	63	30
18	71	57
19	68	84
20	70	39

Saying that a correlation is "negative" says nothing about its strength or weakness. A correlation is negative if two sets of scores relate inversely, one set going up as the other goes down. The study of Nevada university students' inner speech discussed earlier in this module also included a correlational component. Students' reports of inner speech correlated negatively (–.36) with their scores on another measure: psychological distress. Those who reported more inner speech tended to report slightly *less* psychological distress.

Statistics can help us see what the naked eye sometimes misses. To demonstrate this for yourself, try an imaginary project. Wondering if tall men are more or less easygoing, you collect two sets of scores: men's heights and men's temperaments. You measure the heights of 20 men, and you have someone else independently assess their temperaments (from zero for extremely calm to 100 for highly reactive).

With all the relevant data right in front of you (**TABLE 3.2**), can you tell whether the correlation between height and reactive temperament is positive, negative, or close to zero?

Comparing the columns in Table 3.2, most people detect very little relationship between height and temperament. In fact, the correlation in this imaginary example is positive, +0.63, as we can see if we display the data as a scatterplot. In **FIGURE 3.3,** moving from left to right, the upward, oval-shaped slope of the cluster of points shows that our two imaginary sets of scores (height and temperament) tend to rise together.

If we fail to see a relationship when data are presented as systematically as in Table 3.2, how much less likely are we to notice them in everyday life? To see what is right in front of us, we sometimes need statistical illumination. We can easily see evidence of gender discrimination when given statistically summarized information about job level, seniority, performance, gender,

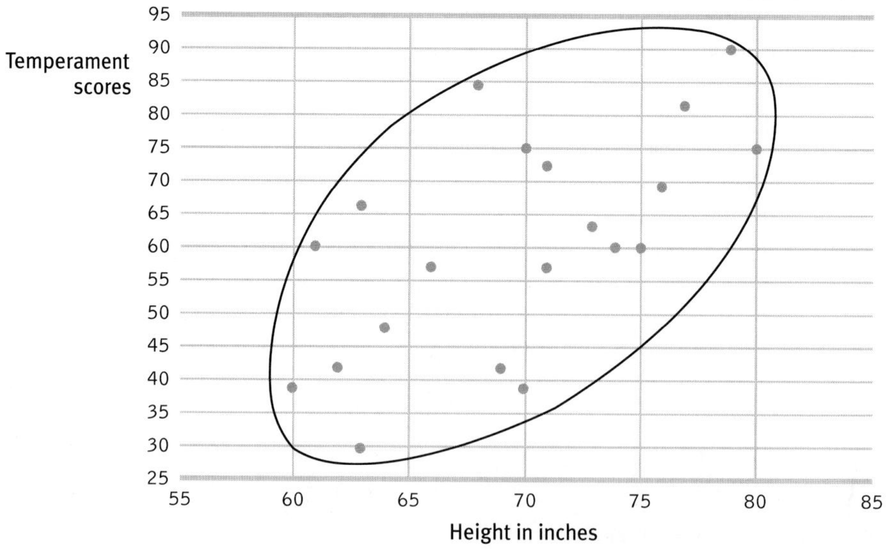

FIGURE 3.3
Scatterplot for height and reactive temperament This display of data from 20 imagined people (each represented by a data point) reveals an upward slope, indicating a positive correlation. The considerable scatter of the data indicates the correlation is much lower than +1.0.

and salary. But we often see no discrimination when the same information dribbles in, case by case (Twiss et al., 1989).

The point to remember: A correlation coefficient helps us see the world more clearly by revealing the extent to which two things relate.

RETRIEVAL PRACTICE

- Indicate whether each association is a positive correlation or a negative correlation.

1. The more children and youth use various media, the less happy they are with their lives (Kaiser, 2010). ________
2. The more sexual content teens see on TV, the more likely they are to have sex (Collins et al., 2004). ________
3. The longer children are breast-fed, the greater their later academic achievement (Horwood & Ferguson, 1998). ________
4. The more income rose among a sample of poor families, the fewer psychiatric symptoms their children experienced (Costello et al., 2003). ________

ANSWERS: 1. negative, 2. positive, 3. positive, 4. negative

Correlation and Causation

Correlations help us predict. The *New York Times* reports that U.S. counties with high gun ownership rates tend to have high murder rates (Luo, 2011). Gun ownership predicts homicide. What might explain this guns-homicide correlation?

I can almost hear someone thinking, "Well, of course, guns kill people, often in moments of passion." If so, that could be an example of A (guns) causes B (murder). But I can hear other readers saying, "Not so fast. Maybe people in dangerous places buy more guns for self-protection—maybe B causes A." Or maybe some third factor C causes both A and B.

© Nancy Brown/Getty Images

Another example: Self-esteem correlates negatively with (and therefore predicts) depression. (The lower people's self-esteem, the more they are at risk for depression.) So, does low self-esteem *cause* depression? If, based on the correlational evidence, you assume that it does, you have much company. A nearly irresistible thinking error is assuming that an association, sometimes presented as a correlation coefficient, proves causation. But no matter how strong the relationship, it does not.

As options 2 and 3 in **FIGURE 3.4** on the next page show, we'd get the same negative correlation between self-esteem and depression if depression caused people to be down on themselves, or if some third factor—such as heredity or brain chemistry—caused both low self-esteem and depression.

This point is so important—so basic to thinking smarter with psychology—that it merits one more example. A survey of over 12,000 adolescents found that the more teens feel loved by their parents, the less likely they are to behave in unhealthy ways—having early sex, smoking, abusing alcohol and drugs, exhibiting violence (Resnick et al., 1997). "Adults have a powerful effect on their children's behavior right through the high school years," gushed an Associated Press (AP) story reporting the finding. But this correlation comes with no built-in cause-effect arrow. The AP could as well have reported, "Well-behaved teens feel their parents' love and approval; out-of-bounds teens more often think their parents are disapproving jerks."

RETRIEVAL PRACTICE

Correlation and causation

- Length of marriage positively correlates with hair loss in men. Does this mean that marriage *causes* men to lose their hair (or that balding men make better husbands)?

ANSWER: In this case, as in many others, a third factor obviously explains the correlation: Golden anniversaries and baldness both accompany aging.

FIGURE 3.4
Three possible cause-effect relationships People low in self-esteem are more likely to report depression than are those high in self-esteem. One possible explanation of this negative correlation is that a bad self-image causes depressed feelings. But, as the diagram indicates, other cause-effect relationships are possible.

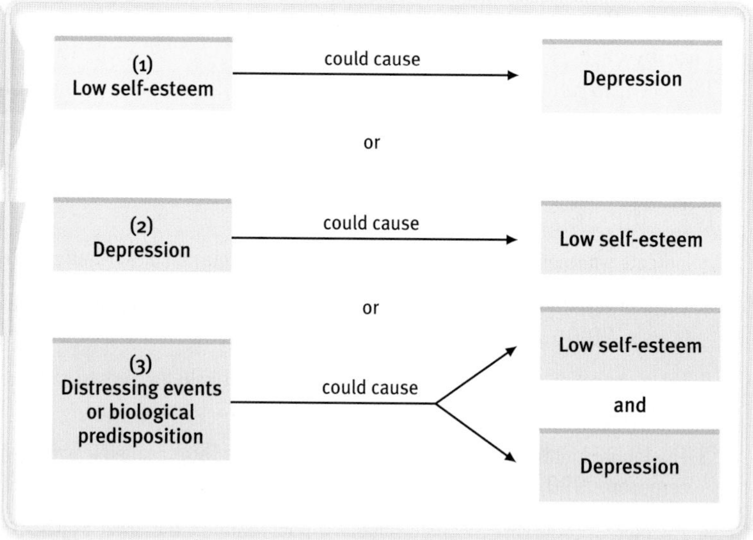

A *New York Times* writer reported a massive survey showing that "adolescents whose parents smoked were 50 percent more likely than children of nonsmokers to report having had sex." He concluded (would you agree?) that the survey indicated a causal effect—that "to reduce the chances that their children will become sexually active at an early age" parents might "quit smoking" (O'Neil, 2002).

The point to remember (turn the volume up here): *Association does not prove causation.*[1] Correlation indicates the *possibility* of a cause-effect relationship *but does not prove such.* Remember this principle and you will be wiser as you read and hear news of scientific studies.

Experimentation

3-4 What are the characteristics of experimentation that make it possible to isolate cause and effect?

Happy are they, remarked the Roman poet Virgil, "who have been able to perceive the causes of things." How might psychologists perceive causes in correlational studies, such as the correlation between breast feeding and intelligence?

Researchers have found that the intelligence scores of children who were breast-fed as infants are somewhat higher than the scores of children who were bottle-fed with cow's milk (Angelsen et al., 2001; Mortensen et al., 2002; Quinn et al., 2001). In Britain, breast-fed babies have also been more likely than their bottle-fed counterparts to eventually move into a higher social class (Martin et al., 2007). The "breast is best" intelligence effect shrinks when researchers compare breast-fed and bottle-fed children from the same families (Der et al., 2006).

What do such findings mean? Do smarter mothers (who in modern countries more often breast feed) have smarter children? Or, as some researchers believe, do the nutrients of mother's milk contribute to brain development? To find answers to such questions—to isolate cause and effect—researchers can **experiment.** Experiments enable researchers to isolate the effects of one or more

Lane Oatey /Getty Images

[1] Because many associations are stated as correlations, the famously worded principle is "Correlation does not prove causation." That's true, but it's also true of associations verified by other nonexperimental statistics (Hatfield et al., 2006).

factors by (1) *manipulating the factor(s) of interest* and (2) *holding constant ("controlling") other factors*. To do so, they often create an **experimental group**, in which people receive the treatment, and a contrasting **control group** that does not receive the treatment. To minimize any preexisting differences between the two groups, researchers **randomly assign** people to the two conditions. Random assignment effectively equalizes the two groups. If one-third of the volunteers for an experiment can wiggle their ears, then about one-third of the people in each group will be ear wigglers. So, too, with ages, attitudes, and other characteristics, which will be similar in the experimental and control groups. Thus, if the groups differ at the experiment's end, we can surmise that the treatment had an effect.

To experiment with breast feeding, one research team randomly assigned some 17,000 Belarus newborns and their mothers either to a breast-feeding promotion group or to a normal pediatric care program (Kramer et al., 2008). At three months of age, 43 percent of the infants in the experimental group were being exclusively breast-fed, as were 6 percent in the control group. At age 6, when nearly 14,000 of the children were restudied, those who had been in the breast-feeding promotion group had intelligence test scores averaging six points higher than their control condition counterparts.

No single experiment is conclusive, of course. But randomly assigning participants to one feeding group or the other effectively eliminated all factors except nutrition. This supported the conclusion that breast is indeed best for developing intelligence: If a behavior (such as test performance) changes when we vary an experimental factor (such as infant nutrition), then we infer the factor is having an effect.

The point to remember: Unlike correlational studies, which uncover naturally occurring relationships, an experiment manipulates a factor to determine its effect.

Consider, then, how we might assess therapeutic interventions. Our tendency to seek new remedies when we are ill or emotionally down can produce misleading testimonies. If three days into a cold we start taking vitamin C tablets and find our cold symptoms lessening, we may credit the pills rather than the cold naturally subsiding. In the 1700s, bloodletting *seemed* effective. People sometimes improved after the treatment; when they didn't, the practitioner inferred the disease was too advanced to be reversed. So, whether or not a remedy is truly effective, enthusiastic users will probably endorse it. To determine its effect, we must control for other factors.

And that is precisely how investigators evaluate new drug treatments and new methods of psychological therapy. They randomly assign participants in these studies to research groups. One group receives a treatment (such as a medication). The other group receives a pseudotreatment—an inert *placebo* (perhaps a pill with no drug in it). The participants are often *blind* (uninformed) about what treatment, if any, they are receiving. If the study is using a **double-blind procedure**, neither the participants nor the research assistants who administer the drug and collect the data will know which group is receiving the treatment.

In such studies, researchers can check a treatment's actual effects apart from the participants' and the staff's belief in its healing powers. Just *thinking* you are getting a treatment can boost your spirits, relax your body, and relieve your symptoms. This **placebo effect** is well documented in reducing pain, depression, and anxiety (Kirsch, 2010). And the more expensive the placebo, the more "real" it seems to us—a fake pill that costs $2.50 works better than one costing 10 cents (Waber et al., 2008). To know how effective a therapy really is, researchers must control for a possible placebo effect.

experiment a research method in which an investigator manipulates one or more factors (independent variables) to observe the effect on some behavior or mental process (the dependent variable). By *random assignment* of participants, the experimenter aims to control other relevant factors.

experimental group in an experiment, the group that is exposed to the treatment, that is, to one version of the *independent variable*.

control group in an experiment, the group that is *not* exposed to the treatment; contrasts with the experimental group and serves as a comparison for evaluating the effect of the treatment.

random assignment assigning participants to experimental and control groups by chance, thus minimizing preexisting differences between those assigned to the different groups.

double-blind procedure an experimental procedure in which both the research participants and the research staff are ignorant (blind) about whether the research participants have received the treatment or a placebo. Commonly used in drug-evaluation studies.

placebo [pluh-SEE-bo; Latin for "I shall please"] **effect** experimental results caused by expectations alone; any effect on behavior caused by the administration of an inert substance or condition, which the recipient assumes is an active agent.

RETRIEVAL PRACTICE

- What measure do researchers use to prevent the *placebo effect* from confusing their results?

ANSWER: Use of a *control group*, which is given a placebo and not the real treatment, allows results to be compared to the group that *is* given the real treatment, thus demonstrating whether the real treatment produces better results than *belief* in that treatment.

Independent and Dependent Variables

Here is an even more potent example: The drug Viagra was approved for use after 21 clinical trials. One trial was an experiment in which researchers randomly assigned 329 men with erectile dysfunction to either an experimental group (Viagra takers) or a control group (placebo takers). It was a double-blind procedure—neither the men nor the person giving them the pills knew what they were receiving. The result: At peak doses, 69 percent of Viagra-assisted attempts at intercourse were successful, compared with 22 percent for men receiving the placebo (Goldstein et al., 1998). Viagra worked.

This simple experiment manipulated just one factor: the drug dosage (none versus peak dose). We call this experimental factor the **independent variable** because we can vary it *independently* of other factors, such as the men's age, weight, and personality. These other factors, which can potentially influence the results of the experiment, are called **confounding variables.** Random assignment controls for possible confounding variables.

Experiments examine the effect of one or more independent variables on some measurable behavior, called the **dependent variable** because it can vary *depending* on what takes place during the experiment. Both variables are given precise *operational definitions,* which specify the procedures that manipulate the independent variable (the precise drug dosage and timing in this study) or measure the dependent variable (the questions that assessed the men's responses). These definitions provide a level of precision that enables others to repeat the study. (See **FIGURE 3.5** for the breast milk experiment's design.)

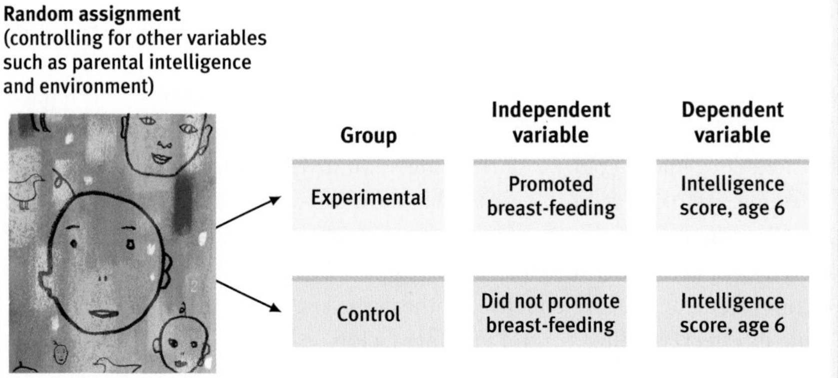

FIGURE 3.5
Experimentation To discern causation, psychologists may randomly assign some participants to an experimental group, others to a control group. Measuring the dependent variable (intelligence score in later childhood) will determine the effect of the independent variable (type of milk).

Let's pause to check your understanding using a simple psychology experiment: To test the effect of perceived ethnicity on the availability of a rental house, Adrian Carpusor and William Loges (2006) sent identically worded e-mail inquiries to 1115 Los Angeles–area landlords. The researchers varied the ethnic connotation of the sender's name and tracked the percentage of positive replies (invitations to view the apartment in person). "Patrick McDougall," "Said Al-Rahman," and "Tyrell Jackson" received, respectively, 89 percent, 66 percent, and 56 percent invitations. (Retrieval Practice: In this experiment, what was the independent variable? The dependent variable?[2])

Experiments can also help us evaluate social programs. Do early childhood education programs boost impoverished children's chances for success? What are the effects of different anti-smoking campaigns? Do school sex-education programs reduce teen pregnancies? To answer such questions, we can experiment: If an intervention is welcomed

independent variable the experimental factor that is manipulated; the variable whose effect is being studied.

confounding variable a factor other than the independent variable that might produce an effect in an experiment.

dependent variable the outcome factor; the variable that may change in response to manipulations of the independent variable.

[2]The independent variable, which the researchers manipulated, was the ethnicity-related names. The dependent variable, which they measured, was the positive response rate.

TABLE 3.3

Comparing Research Methods

Research Method	Basic Purpose	How Conducted	What Is Manipulated	Weaknesses
Descriptive	To observe and record behavior	Do case studies, naturalistic observations, or surveys	Nothing	No control of variables; single cases may be misleading
Correlational	To detect naturally occurring relationships; to assess how well one variable predicts another	Collect data on two or more variables; no manipulation	Nothing	Does not specify cause and effect
Experimental	To explore cause and effect	Manipulate one or more factors; use random assignment	The independent variable(s)	Sometimes not feasible; results may not generalize to other contexts; not ethical to manipulate certain variables

but resources are scarce, we could use a lottery to randomly assign some people (or regions) to experience the new program and others to a control condition. If later the two groups differ, the intervention's effect will be supported (Passell, 1993).

Let's recap. A *variable* is anything that can vary (infant nutrition, intelligence, TV exposure—anything within the bounds of what is feasible and ethical). Experiments aim to *manipulate* an *independent* variable, *measure* a *dependent* variable, and allow random assignment to *control* all other variables. An experiment has at least two different conditions: an *experimental condition* and a *comparison* or *control condition. Random assignment* works to equate the groups before any treatment effects occur. In this way, an experiment tests the effect of at least one independent variable (what we manipulate) on at least one dependent variable (the outcome we measure). **TABLE 3.3** compares the features of psychology's research methods.

RETRIEVAL PRACTICE

- By using *random assignment,* researchers are able to control for ____________ ____________, which are other factors besides the independent variable(s) that may influence research results.

ANSWER: confounding variables

- Match the term on the left with the description on the right.

1. double-blind procedure
2. random sampling
3. random assignment

a. helps researchers generalize from a small set of survey responses to a larger population

b. helps minimize preexisting differences between experimental and control groups

c. controls for the placebo effect; neither researchers nor participants know who receives the real treatment

ANSWERS: 1. c, 2. a, 3. b

- Why, when testing a new drug to control blood pressure, would we learn more about its effectiveness from giving it to half of the participants in a group of 1000 than to all 1000 participants?

ANSWER: To determine the drug's effectiveness, we must compare its effect on those randomly assigned to receive it (the experimental group) with the other half of the participants (control group), who receive a placebo. If we gave the drug to all 1000 participants, we would have no way of knowing if the drug is serving as a placebo or if it is actually medically effective.

© The New Yorker Collection, 2007, P. C. Vey from cartoonbank.com. All Rights Reserved.

"If I don't think it's going to work, will it still work?"

Statistical Reasoning in Everyday Life

Asked about the *ideal* wealth distribution in America, Democrats and Republicans were surprisingly similar. In the Democrats' ideal world, the richest 20 percent would possess 30 percent of the wealth. Republicans preferred a similar 35 percent (Norton & Ariely, 2011).

In descriptive, correlational, and experimental research, statistics are tools that help us see and interpret what the unaided eye might miss. Sometimes the unaided eye misses badly. Researchers Michael Norton and Dan Ariely (2011) invited 5522 Americans to estimate the percent of wealth possessed by the richest 20 percent in their country. Their average person's guess—58 percent—"dramatically underestimated" the actual wealth inequality. (The wealthiest 20 percent possess 84 percent of the wealth.)

Accurate statistical understanding benefits everyone. To be an educated person today is to be able to apply simple statistical principles to everyday reasoning. One needn't memorize complicated formulas to think more clearly and critically about data.

Off-the-top-of-the-head estimates often misread reality and then mislead the public. Someone throws out a big, round number. Others echo it, and before long the big, round number becomes public misinformation. A few examples:

- *Ten percent of people are lesbians or gay men.* Or is it 2 to 3 percent, as suggested by various national surveys?
- *We ordinarily use but 10 percent of our brain.* Or is it closer to 100 percent?
- *The human brain has 100 billion nerve cells.* Or is it more like 40 billion, as suggested by extrapolation from sample counts?

The point to remember: Doubt big, round, undocumented numbers.

Statistical illiteracy also feeds needless health scares (Gigerenzer et al., 2008, 2009, 2010). In the 1990s, the British press reported a study showing that women taking a particular contraceptive pill had a 100 percent increased risk of blood clots that could produce strokes. This caused thousands of women to stop taking the pill, leading to a wave of unwanted pregnancies and an estimated 13,000 additional abortions (which also are associated with increased blood clot risk). And what did the study find? A 100 percent increased risk, indeed—but only from 1 in 7000 to 2 in 7000. Such false alarms underscore the need to teach statistical reasoning and to present statistical information more transparently.

©Patrick Hardin

"Figures can be misleading—so I've written a song which I think expresses the real story of the firm's performance this quarter."

Describing Data

3-5 How can we describe data with measures of central tendency and variation?

Once researchers have gathered their data, they must organize them in some meaningful way. One way to do this is to convert the data into a simple *bar graph*, as in **FIGURE 3.6,** which displays a distribution of different brands of trucks still on the road after a decade. When reading statistical graphs such as this, take care. It's easy to design a graph to make a difference look big (Figure 3.6a) or small (Figure 3.6b). The secret lies in how you label the vertical scale (the *y-axis*).

The point to remember: Think smart. When viewing figures in magazines and on television, read the scale labels and note their range.

Measures of Central Tendency

The next step is to summarize the data using some *measure of central tendency,* a single score that represents a whole set of scores. The simplest measure is the **mode,** the most frequently occurring score or scores. The most commonly reported is the **mean,** or arithmetic average—the total sum of all the scores divided by the number of scores. On a divided highway, the median is the middle. So, too, with data: The **median** is the midpoint—the 50th percentile. If you arrange all the scores in order from the highest to the lowest, half will be above the median and half will be below it.

mode the most frequently occurring score(s) in a distribution.

mean the arithmetic average of a distribution, obtained by adding the scores and then dividing by the number of scores.

median the middle score in a distribution; half the scores are above it and half are below it.

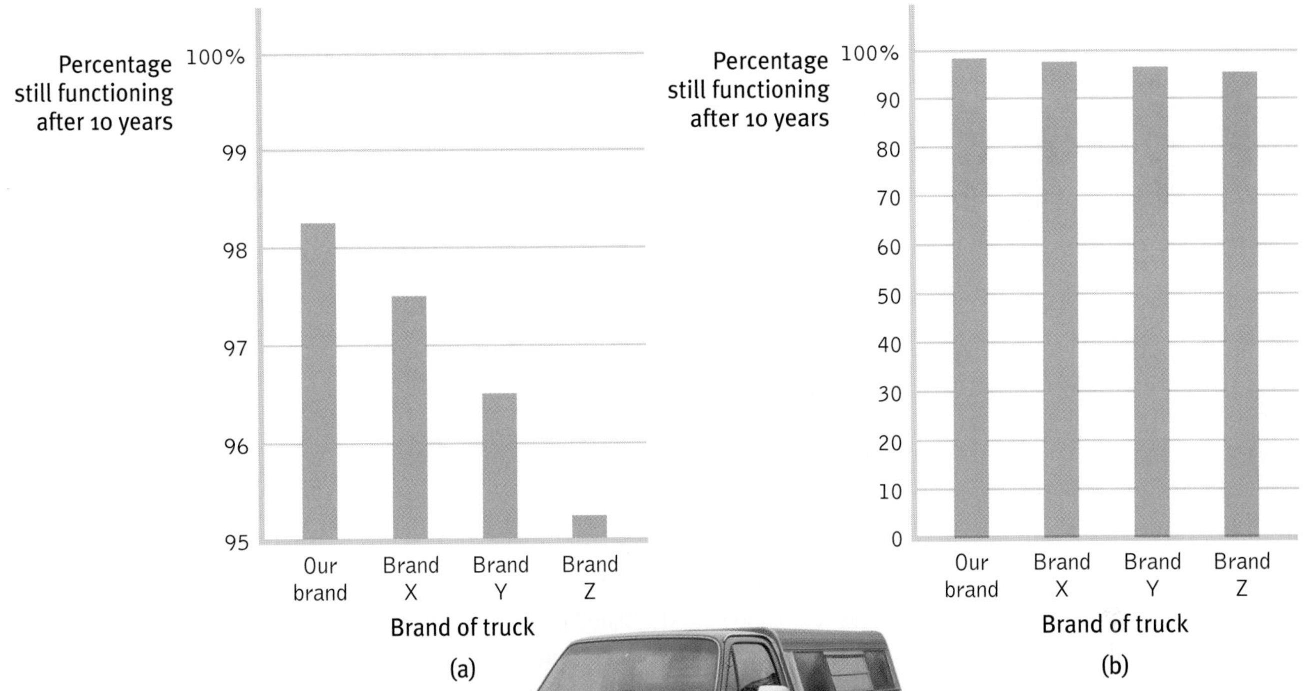

© Rick Sargeant/istockphoto

RETRIEVAL PRACTICE

FIGURE 3.6
Read the scale labels

- An American truck manufacturer offered graph (a)—with actual brand names included—to suggest the much greater durability of its trucks. What does graph (b) make clear about the varying durability, and how is this accomplished?

ANSWER: Note how the y-axis of each graph is labeled. The range for the y-axis labels in graph (a) is only from 95 to 100. The range for graph (b) is from 0 to 100. All the trucks rank as 95% and up, so almost all of them are "still functioning," which graph (b) makes clear.

Measures of central tendency neatly summarize data. But consider what happens to the mean when a distribution is lopsided, or *skewed*, by a few way-out scores. With income data, for example, the mode, median, and mean often tell very different stories (**FIGURE 3.7** on the next page). This happens because the mean is biased by a few extreme scores. When Microsoft co-founder Bill Gates sits down in an intimate café, its average (mean) customer instantly becomes a billionaire. But the customer's median wealth remains unchanged. Understanding this, you can see how a British newspaper could accurately run the headline "Income for 62% Is Below Average" (Waterhouse, 1993). Because the bottom *half* of British income earners receive only a *quarter* of the national income cake, most British people, like most people everywhere, make less than the mean. Mean and median tell different true stories.

The point to remember: Always note which measure of central tendency is reported. If it is a mean, consider whether a few atypical scores could be distorting it.

The average person has one ovary and one testicle.

Measures of Variation

Knowing the value of an appropriate measure of central tendency can tell us a great deal. But the single number omits other information. It helps to know something about the amount of *variation* in the data—how similar or diverse the scores are. Averages derived from scores with low variability are more reliable than averages based on scores with high variability. Consider a basketball player who scored between 13 and 17 points in each of her first 10 games in a season. Knowing this, we would be more confident that she would score near 15 points in her next game than if her scores had varied from 5 to 25 points.

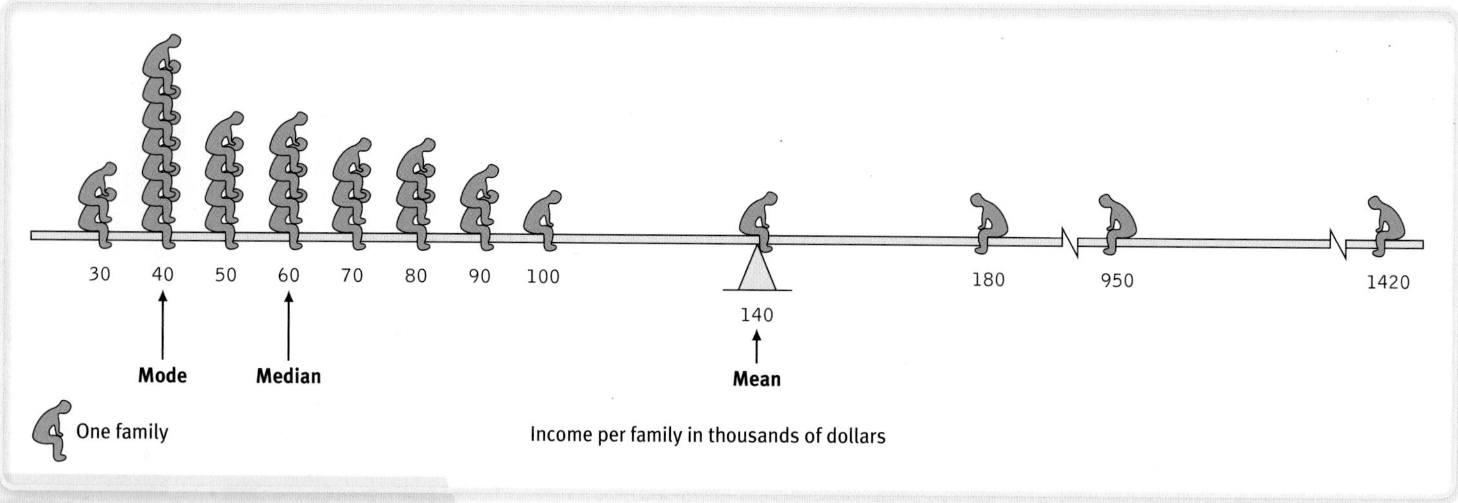

FIGURE 3.7

A skewed distribution This graphic representation of the distribution of a village's incomes illustrates the three measures of central tendency—mode, median, and mean. Note how just a few high incomes make the mean—the fulcrum point that balances the incomes above and below—deceptively high.

The **range** of scores—the gap between the lowest and highest scores—provides only a crude estimate of variation. A couple of extreme scores in an otherwise uniform group, such as the $950,000 and $1,420,000 incomes in Figure 3.7, will create a deceptively large range.

The more useful standard for measuring how much scores deviate from one another is the **standard deviation.** It better gauges whether scores are packed together or dispersed, because it uses information from each score. The computation (see Appendix B) assembles information about how much individual scores differ from the mean. If your college or university attracts students of a certain ability level, their intelligence scores will have a relatively small standard deviation compared with the more diverse community population outside your school.

You can grasp the meaning of the standard deviation if you consider how scores tend to be distributed in nature. Large numbers of data—heights, weights, intelligence scores, grades (though not incomes)—often form a symmetrical, *bell-shaped* distribution. Most cases fall near the mean, and fewer cases fall near either extreme. This bell-shaped distribution is so typical that we call the curve it forms the **normal curve.**

As **FIGURE 3.8** shows, a useful property of the normal curve is that roughly 68 percent of the cases fall within one standard deviation on either side of the mean. About 95 percent of cases fall within two standard deviations. Thus, about 68 percent of people taking an intelligence test will score within ±15 points of 100. About 95 percent will score within ±30 points.

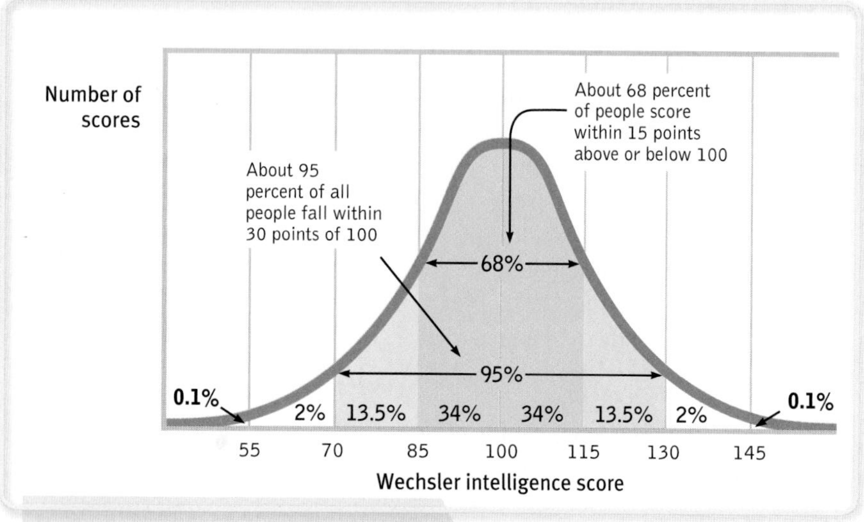

FIGURE 3.8

The normal curve Scores on aptitude tests tend to form a normal, or bell-shaped, curve. For example, the Wechsler Adult Intelligence Scale calls the average score 100.

RETRIEVAL PRACTICE

- The average of a distribution of scores is the ________. The score that shows up most often is the ________. The score right in the middle of a distribution (half the scores above it; half below) is the ________. We determine how much scores vary around the average in a way that includes information about the ________ of scores (difference between highest and lowest) by using the ________ ________ formula.

ANSWERS: mean; mode; median; range; standard deviation

Significant Differences

3-6 How do we know whether an observed difference can be generalized to other populations?

Data are "noisy." The average score in one group (breast-fed babies) could conceivably differ from the average score in another group (bottle-fed babies) not because of any real difference but merely because of chance fluctuations in the people sampled. How confidently, then, can we infer that an observed difference is not just a fluke—a chance result of your sampling? For guidance, we can ask how reliable and significant the differences are.

© The New Yorker Collection, 1988, Mirachi from cartoonbank.com. All Rights Reserved.

"The poor are getting poorer, but with the rich getting richer it all averages out in the long run."

When Is an Observed Difference Reliable?

In deciding when it is safe to generalize from a sample, we should keep three principles in mind.

1. **Representative samples are better than biased samples.** The best basis for generalizing is not from the exceptional and memorable cases one finds at the extremes but from a representative sample of cases. Research never randomly samples the whole human population. Thus, it pays to keep in mind what population a study has sampled.
2. **Less-variable observations are more reliable than those that are more variable.** As we noted in the example of the basketball player whose game-to-game points were consistent, an average is more reliable when it comes from scores with low variability.
3. **More cases are better than fewer.** An eager prospective student visits two university campuses, each for a day. At the first, the student randomly attends two classes and discovers both instructors to be witty and engaging. At the next campus, the two sampled instructors seem dull and uninspiring. Returning home, the student (discounting the small sample size of only two teachers at each institution) tells friends about the "great teachers" at the first school, and the "bores" at the second. Again, we know it but we ignore it: *Averages based on many cases are more reliable* (less variable) than averages based on only a few cases.

The point to remember: Smart thinkers are not overly impressed by a few anecdotes. Generalizations based on a few unrepresentative cases are unreliable.

When Is a Difference Significant?

Perhaps you've compared men's and women's scores on a laboratory test of aggression, and found a gender difference. But individuals differ. How likely is it that the difference you found was just a fluke? Statistical testing can estimate the probability of the result occurring by chance.

Here is the underlying logic: When averages from two samples are each reliable measures of their respective populations (as when each is based on many observations that have small variability), then their *difference* is likely to be reliable as well. (Example: The less the variability in women's and in men's aggression scores, the more confidence we would have that any observed gender difference is reliable.) And when the difference between the sample averages is *large*, we have even more confidence that the difference between them reflects a real difference in their populations.

PEANUTS reprinted by permission of UFS, Inc.

range the difference between the highest and lowest scores in a distribution.

standard deviation a computed measure of how much scores vary around the mean score.

normal curve *(normal distribution)* a symmetrical, bell-shaped curve that describes the distribution of many types of data; most scores fall near the mean (about 68 percent fall within one standard deviation of it) and fewer and fewer near the extremes.

statistical significance a statistical statement of how likely it is that an obtained result occurred by chance.

In short, when sample averages are reliable, and when the difference between them is relatively large, we say the difference has **statistical significance.** This means that the observed difference is probably not due to chance variation between the samples.

In judging statistical significance, psychologists are conservative. They are like juries who must presume innocence until guilt is proven. For most psychologists, proof beyond a reasonable doubt means not making much of a finding unless the odds of its occurring by chance, if no real effect exists, are less than 5 percent.

When reading about research, you should remember that, given large enough or homogeneous enough samples, a difference between them may be "statistically significant" yet have little practical significance. For example, comparisons of intelligence test scores among hundreds of thousands of first-born and later-born individuals indicate a highly significant tendency for first-born individuals to have higher average scores than their later-born siblings (Kristensen & Bjerkedal, 2007; Zajonc & Markus, 1975). But because the scores differ by only one to three points, the difference has little practical importance.

The point to remember: Statistical significance indicates the *likelihood* that a result will happen by chance. But this does not say anything about the *importance* of the result.

RETRIEVAL PRACTICE

- Can you solve this puzzle?

The registrar's office at the University of Michigan has found that usually about 100 students in Arts and Sciences have perfect marks at the end of their first term at the University. However, only about 10 to 15 students graduate with perfect marks. What do you think is the most likely explanation for the fact that there are more perfect marks after one term than at graduation (Jepson et al., 1983)?

ANSWER: Averages based on fewer courses are more variable, which guarantees a greater number of extremely low and high marks at the end of the first term.

MODULE REVIEW

Research Strategies: How Psychologists Ask and Answer Questions

Learning Objectives

RETRIEVAL PRACTICE Take a moment to answer each of these Learning Objective Questions (repeated here from within the module). Then turn to Appendix B, Complete Module Reviews, to check your answers. Research suggests that trying to answer these questions on your own will improve your long-term retention (McDaniel et al., 2009).

3-1: How do theories advance psychological science?

3-2: How do psychologists use case studies, naturalistic observation, and surveys to observe and describe behavior, and why is random sampling important?

3-3: What are positive and negative correlations, and why do they enable prediction but not cause-effect explanation?

3-4: What are the characteristics of experimentation that make it possible to isolate cause and effect?

3-5: How can we describe data with measures of central tendency and variation?

3-6: How do we know whether an observed difference can be generalized to other populations?

Terms and Concepts to Remember

RETRIEVAL PRACTICE Test yourself on these terms by trying to write down the definition before flipping back to the referenced page to check your answer.

theory, p. 26
hypothesis, p. 26
operational definition, p. 26
replication, p. 26
case study, p. 28
naturalistic observation, p. 28
survey, p. 30
population, p. 31
random sample, p. 31
correlation, p. 31
correlation coefficient, p. 31
scatterplot, p. 31
experiment, p. 34
experimental group, p. 35
control group, p. 35
random assignment, p. 35
double-blind procedure, p. 35
placebo effect, p. 35
independent variable, p. 36
confounding variable, p. 36
dependent variable, p. 36
mode, p. 38
mean, p. 38
median, p. 38
range, p. 40
standard deviation, p. 40
normal curve, p. 40
statistical significance, p. 42

RETRIEVAL PRACTICE Gain an advantage, and benefit from immediate feedback, with the interactive self-testing resources at www.worthpublishers.com/myers.

The Biology of Mind

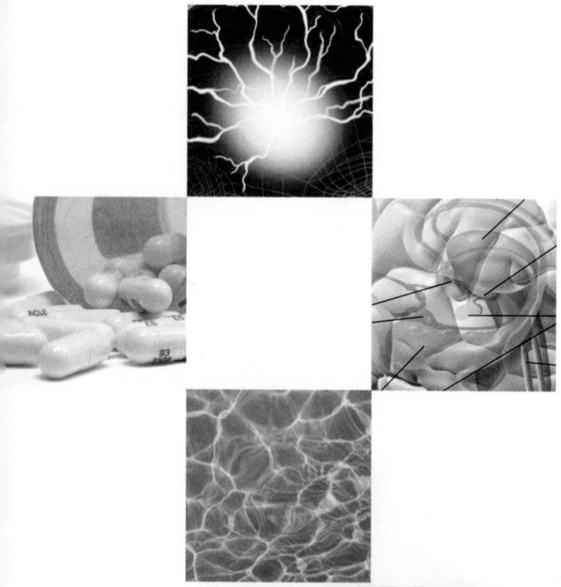

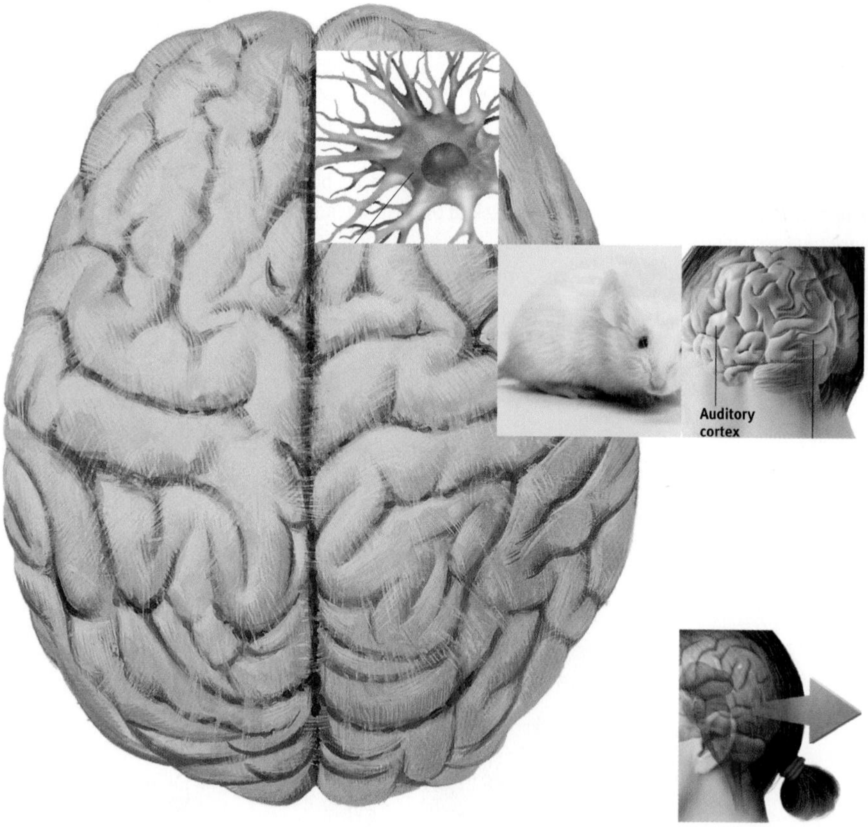

In 2000, a Virginia teacher began collecting sex magazines, visiting child pornography websites, and then making subtle advances on his young stepdaughter. When his wife called the police, he was arrested and later convicted of child molestation. Though put into a sexual addiction rehabilitation program, he still felt overwhelmed by his sexual urges. The day before being sentenced to prison, he went to his local emergency room complaining of a headache and thoughts of suicide. He was also distraught over his uncontrollable impulses, which led him to proposition nurses.

A brain scan located the problem—in his mind's biology. Behind his right temple there was an egg-sized brain tumor.

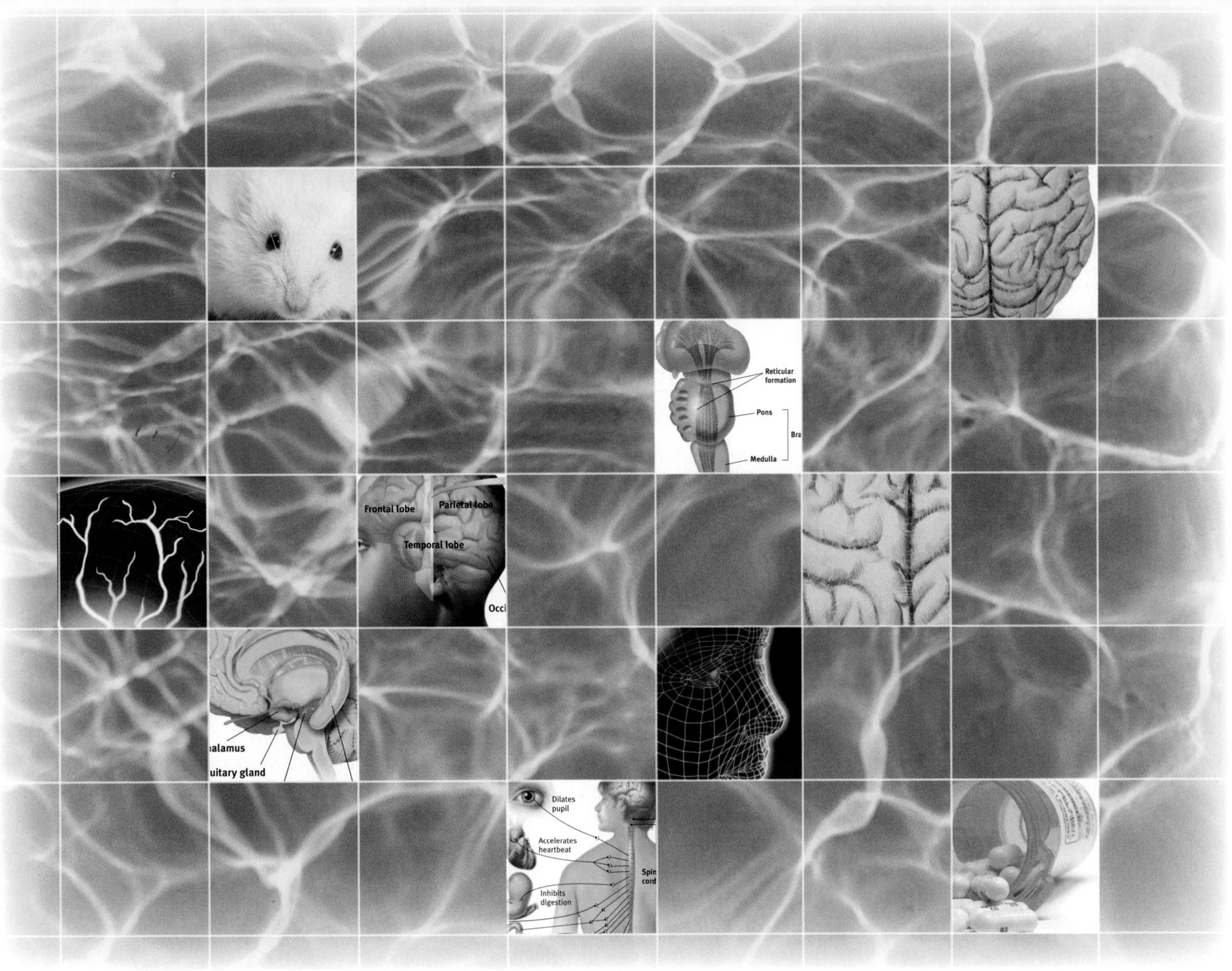

MODULES

4 Neural and Hormonal Systems

5 Tools of Discovery and Older Brain Structures

6 The Cerebral Cortex and Our Divided Brain

After surgeons removed the tumor, his lewd impulses faded and he returned home to his wife and stepdaughter. Alas, a year later the tumor partially grew back, and with it the sexual urges. A second tumor removal again lessened the urges (Burns & Swerdlow, 2003).

This case illustrates what you likely believe: that you reside in your head. If surgeons transplanted all your organs below your neck, and even your skin and limbs, you would *(Yes?)* still be you. An acquaintance of mine received a new heart from a woman who, in a rare operation, required a matched heart-lung transplant. When the two chanced to meet in their hospital ward, she introduced herself: "I think you have my heart." But only her heart. Her self, she assumed, still resided inside her skull. We rightly presume that our brain enables our mind. Indeed, no principle is more central to today's psychology, or to this book, than this: *Everything psychological is simultaneously biological.*

Throughout this text you will find examples of this interplay. In the next three modules, we start small and build from the bottom up—from nerve cells up to the brain. (Other modules in the text explore environmental influences, where we work from the top down as we consider how our thinking and emotions influence our brain and our health.)

MODULE 4

Neural and Hormonal Systems

- Biology, Behavior, and Mind
- Neural Communication
- The Nervous System
- The Endocrine System

Sidney Harris/Science Cartoons Plus

"Then it's agreed—you can't have a mind without a brain, but you can have a brain without a mind."

Biology, Behavior, and Mind

4-1 Why are psychologists concerned with human biology?

Your every idea, every mood, every urge is a biological happening. You love, laugh, and cry with your body. Without your body—your genes, your brain, your appearance—you would, indeed, be nobody. Although we find it convenient to talk separately of biological and psychological influences on behavior, we need to remember: To think, feel, or act without a body would be like running without legs.

Our understanding of how the brain gives birth to the mind has come a long way. The ancient Greek philosopher Plato correctly located the mind in the spherical head—his idea of the perfect form. His student, Aristotle, believed the mind was in the heart, which pumps warmth and vitality to the body. The heart remains our symbol for love, but science has long since overtaken philosophy on this issue. It's your brain, not your heart, that falls in love.

In the early 1800s, German physician Franz Gall proposed that *phrenology,* studying bumps on the skull, could reveal a person's mental abilities and character traits (**FIGURE 4.1**). At one point, Britain had 29 phrenological societies, and phrenologists traveled North America giving skull readings (Hunt, 1993). Using a false name, humorist Mark Twain put one famous phrenologist to the test. "He found a cavity [and] startled me by saying that that cavity represented the total absence of the sense of humor!" Three months later, Twain sat for a second reading, this time identifying himself. Now "the cavity was gone, and in its place was . . . the loftiest bump of humor he had ever encountered in his life-long

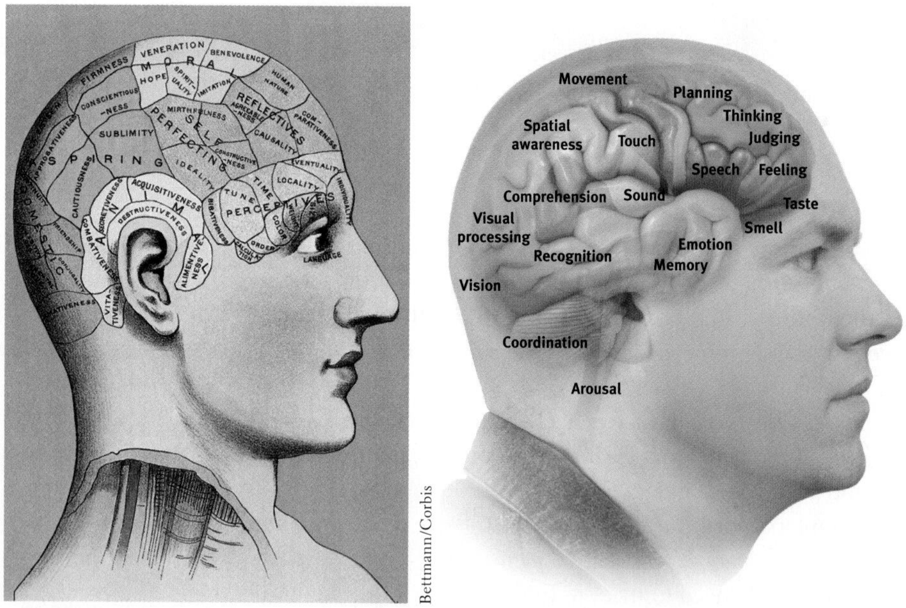

Bettmann/Corbis

FIGURE 4.1
A wrongheaded theory Despite initial acceptance of Franz Gall's speculations (left), bumps on the skull tell us nothing about the brain's underlying functions. Nevertheless, some of his assumptions have held true. Though they are not the functions Gall proposed, different parts of the brain do control different aspects of behavior, as suggested here at right (adapted from *The Human Brain Book*).

experience!" (Lopez, 2002). Although its initial popularity faded, phrenology succeeded in focusing attention on the *localization of function*—the idea that various brain regions have particular functions.

You and I are living in a time Gall could only dream about. By studying the links between biological activity and psychological events, those working from the **biological perspective** are announcing discoveries about the interplay of our biology and our behavior and mind at an exhilarating pace. Within little more than the past century, researchers seeking to understand the biology of the mind have discovered that

- the body is composed of cells.
- among these are nerve cells that conduct electricity and "talk" to one another by sending chemical messages across a tiny gap that separates them.
- specific brain systems serve specific functions (though not the functions Gall supposed).
- we integrate information processed in these different brain systems to construct our experience of sights and sounds, meanings and memories, pain and passion.
- our adaptive brain is wired by our experience.

We have also realized that we are each a system composed of subsystems that are in turn composed of even smaller subsystems. Tiny cells organize to form body organs. These organs form larger systems for digestion, circulation, and information processing. And those systems are part of an even larger system—the individual, who in turn is a part of a family, culture, and community. Thus, we are *biopsychosocial* systems. To understand our behavior, we need to study how these biological, psychological, and social systems work and interact.

"If I were a college student today, I don't think I could resist going into neuroscience."

Novelist Tom Wolfe, 2004

RETRIEVAL PRACTICE

- What do phrenology and psychology's biological perspective have in common?

ANSWER: They share a focus on the links between biology and behavior. Phrenology faded because it had no scientific basis—skull bumps don't reveal mental traits and abilities.

Neural Communication

For scientists, it is a happy fact of nature that the information systems of humans and other animals operate similarly—so similarly that you could not distinguish between small samples of brain tissue from a human and a monkey. This similarity allows researchers to study relatively simple animals, such as squids and sea slugs, to discover how our neural systems operate. It allows them to study other mammals' brains to understand the organization of our own. Cars differ, but all have engines, accelerators, steering wheels, and brakes. A Martian could study any one of them and grasp the operating principles. Likewise, animals differ, yet their nervous systems operate similarly. Though the human brain is more complex than a rat's, both follow the same principles.

Neurons

4-2 What are neurons, and how do they transmit information?

Our body's neural information system is complexity built from simplicity. Its building blocks are **neurons,** or nerve cells. To fathom our thoughts and actions, memories and moods, we must first understand how neurons work and communicate.

Neurons differ, but all are variations on the same theme (**FIGURE 4.2** on the next page). Each consists of a *cell body* and its branching fibers. The bushy **dendrite** fibers receive information and conduct it toward the cell body. From there, the cell's lengthy **axon** fiber passes the message through its terminal branches to other neurons or to muscles or glands. Dendrites listen. Axons speak.

Unlike the short dendrites, axons may be very long, projecting several feet through the body. A neuron carrying orders to a leg muscle, for example, has a cell body and axon roughly

biological perspective concerned with the links between biology and behavior. Includes psychologists working in neuroscience, behavior genetics, and evolutionary psychology. These researchers may call themselves *behavioral neuroscientists, neuropsychologists, behavior geneticists, physiological psychologists,* or *biopsychologists.*

neuron a nerve cell; the basic building block of the nervous system.

dendrites a neuron's bushy, branching extensions that receive messages and conduct impulses toward the cell body.

axon the neuron extension that passes messages through its branches to other neurons or to muscles or glands.

FIGURE 4.2
A motor neuron

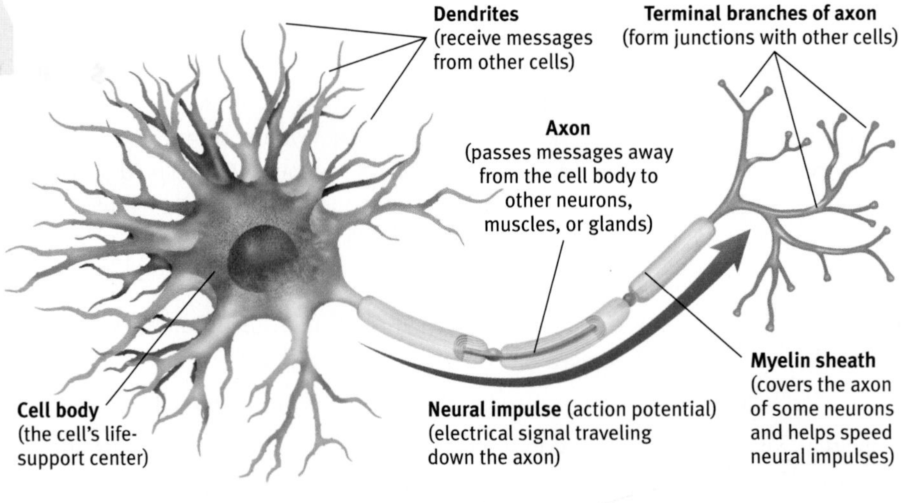

on the scale of a basketball attached to a rope 4 miles long. Much as home electrical wire is insulated, some axons are encased in a **myelin sheath**, a layer of fatty tissue that insulates them and speeds their impulses. As myelin is laid down up to about age 25, neural efficiency, judgment, and self-control grow (Fields, 2008). If the myelin sheath degenerates, *multiple sclerosis* results: Communication to muscles slows, with eventual loss of muscle control.

Neurons transmit messages when stimulated by signals from our senses or when triggered by chemical signals from neighboring neurons. In response, a neuron fires an impulse, called the **action potential**—a brief electrical charge that travels down its axon.

"I sing the body electric."
Walt Whitman, "Children of Adam" (1855)

Depending on the type of fiber, a neural impulse travels at speeds ranging from a sluggish 2 miles per hour to a breakneck 180 miles per hour. But even this top speed is 3 million times slower than that of electricity through a wire. We measure brain activity in milliseconds (thousandths of a second) and computer activity in nanoseconds (billionths of a second). Thus, unlike the nearly instantaneous reactions of a high-speed computer, your reaction to a sudden event, such as a child darting in front of your car, may take a quarter-second or more. Your brain is vastly more complex than a computer, but slower at executing simple responses. And if you are an elephant—whose round-trip message travel time from a yank on the tail to the brain and back to the tail is 100 times longer than for a tiny shrew—reflexes are slower yet (More et al., 2010).

Like batteries, neurons generate electricity from chemical events. In the neuron's chemistry-to-electricity process, ions (electrically charged atoms) are exchanged. The fluid outside an axon's membrane has mostly positively charged ions; a resting axon's fluid interior has mostly negatively charged ions. This positive-outside/negative-inside state is called the *resting potential*. Like a tightly guarded facility, the axon's surface is very selective about what it allows through its gates. We say the axon's surface is *selectively permeable*.

When a neuron fires, however, the security parameters change: The first section of the axon opens its gates, rather like sewer covers flipping open, and positively charged sodium ions flood through the cell membrane (**FIGURE 4.3**). This *depolarizes* that axon section, causing another axon channel to open, and then another, like a line of falling dominos, each tripping the next.

During a resting pause (the *refractory period*, rather like a web page pausing to refresh), the neuron pumps the positively charged sodium ions back outside. Then it can fire again. (In myelinated neurons, as in Figure 4.2, the action potential speeds up by hopping from the end of one myelin "sausage" to the next.) The mind boggles when imagining this electrochemical process repeating up to 100 or even 1000 times a second. But this is just the first of many astonishments.

"What one neuron tells another neuron is simply how much it is excited."
Francis Crick, *The Astonishing Hypothesis*, 1994

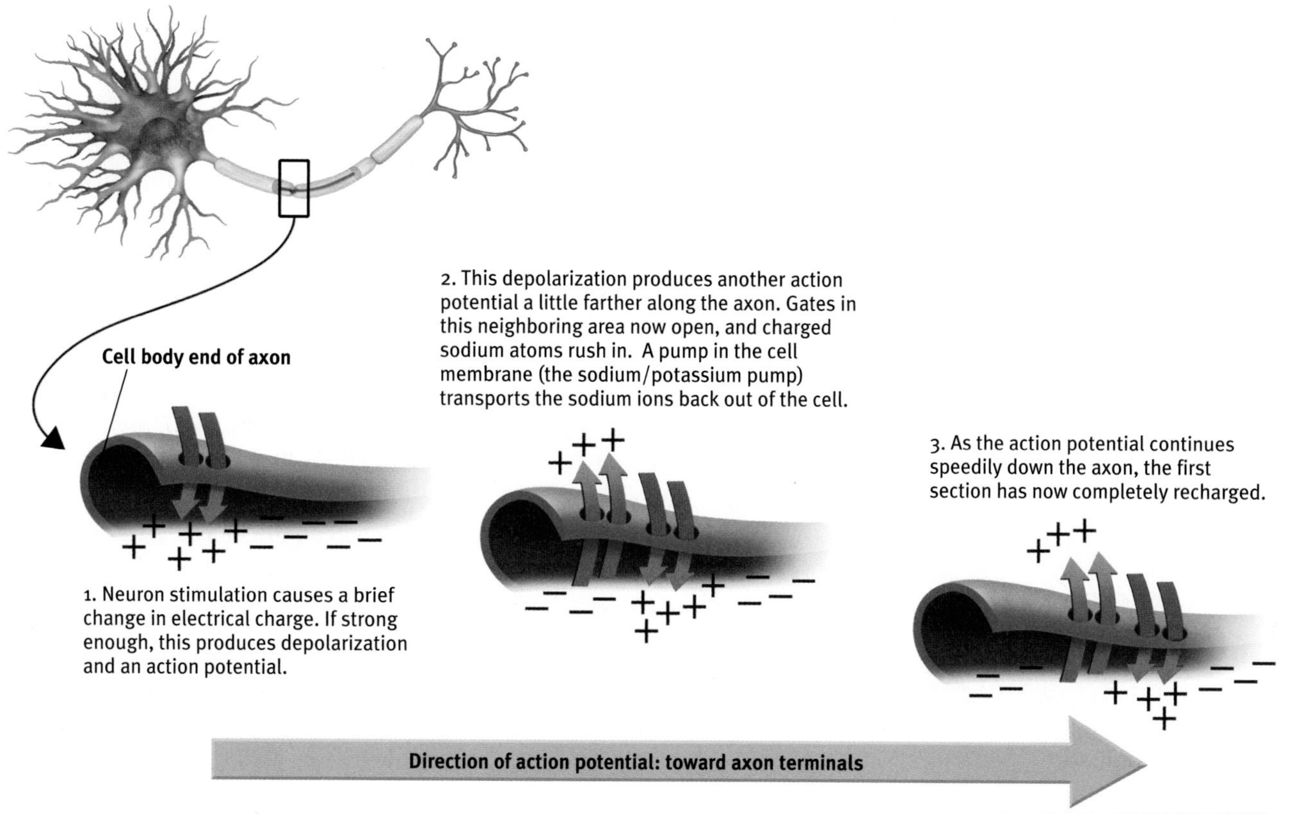

FIGURE 4.3
Action potential

Each neuron is itself a miniature decision-making device performing complex calculations as it receives signals from hundreds, even thousands, of other neurons. Most signals are *excitatory*, somewhat like pushing a neuron's accelerator. Some are *inhibitory*, more like pushing its brake. If excitatory signals minus inhibitory signals exceed a minimum intensity, or **threshold**, the combined signals trigger an action potential. (Think of it this way: If the excitatory party animals outvote the inhibitory party poopers, the party's on.) The action potential then travels down the axon, which branches into junctions with hundreds or thousands of other neurons or with the body's muscles and glands.

Increasing the level of stimulation above the threshold will not increase the neural impulse's intensity. The neuron's reaction is an *all-or-none response*: Like guns, neurons either fire or they don't. How, then, do we detect the intensity of a stimulus? How do we distinguish a gentle touch from a big hug? A strong stimulus can trigger *more* neurons to fire, and to fire more often. But it does not affect the action potential's strength or speed. Squeezing a trigger harder won't make a bullet go faster.

RETRIEVAL PRACTICE

- When a neuron fires an action potential, the information travels through the axon, the dendrites, and the axon's terminal branches, but not in that order. Place these three structures in the correct order.

ANSWER: dendrites, axon, axon's terminal branches

- How does our nervous system allow us to experience the difference between a slap and a tap on the back?

ANSWER: Stronger stimuli (the slap) cause more neurons to fire and to fire more frequently than happens with weaker stimuli (the tap).

myelin [MY-uh-lin] **sheath** a fatty tissue layer segmentally encasing the axons of some neurons; enables vastly greater transmission speed as neural impulses hop from one node to the next.

action potential a neural impulse; a brief electrical charge that travels down an axon.

threshold the level of stimulation required to trigger a neural impulse.

How Neurons Communicate

4-3 How do nerve cells communicate with other nerve cells?

Neurons interweave so intricately that even with a microscope you would have trouble seeing where one neuron ends and another begins. Scientists once believed that the axon of one cell fused with the dendrites of another in an uninterrupted fabric. Then British physiologist Sir Charles Sherrington (1857–1952) noticed that neural impulses were taking an unexpectedly long time to travel a neural pathway. Inferring that there must be a brief interruption in the transmission, Sherrington called the meeting point between neurons a **synapse.**

We now know that the axon terminal of one neuron is in fact separated from the receiving neuron by a *synaptic gap* (or *synaptic cleft*) less than a millionth of an inch wide. Spanish anatomist Santiago Ramón y Cajal (1852–1934) marveled at these near-unions of neurons, calling them "protoplasmic kisses." "Like elegant ladies air-kissing so as not to muss their makeup, dendrites and axons don't quite touch," notes poet Diane Ackerman (2004). How do the neurons execute this protoplasmic kiss, sending information across the tiny synaptic gap? The answer is one of the important scientific discoveries of our age.

"All information processing in the brain involves neurons 'talking to' each other at synapses."
Neuroscientist Solomon H. Snyder (1984)

When an action potential reaches the knob-like terminals at an axon's end, it triggers the release of chemical messengers, called **neurotransmitters** (**FIGURE 4.4**). Within

FIGURE 4.4
How neurons communicate

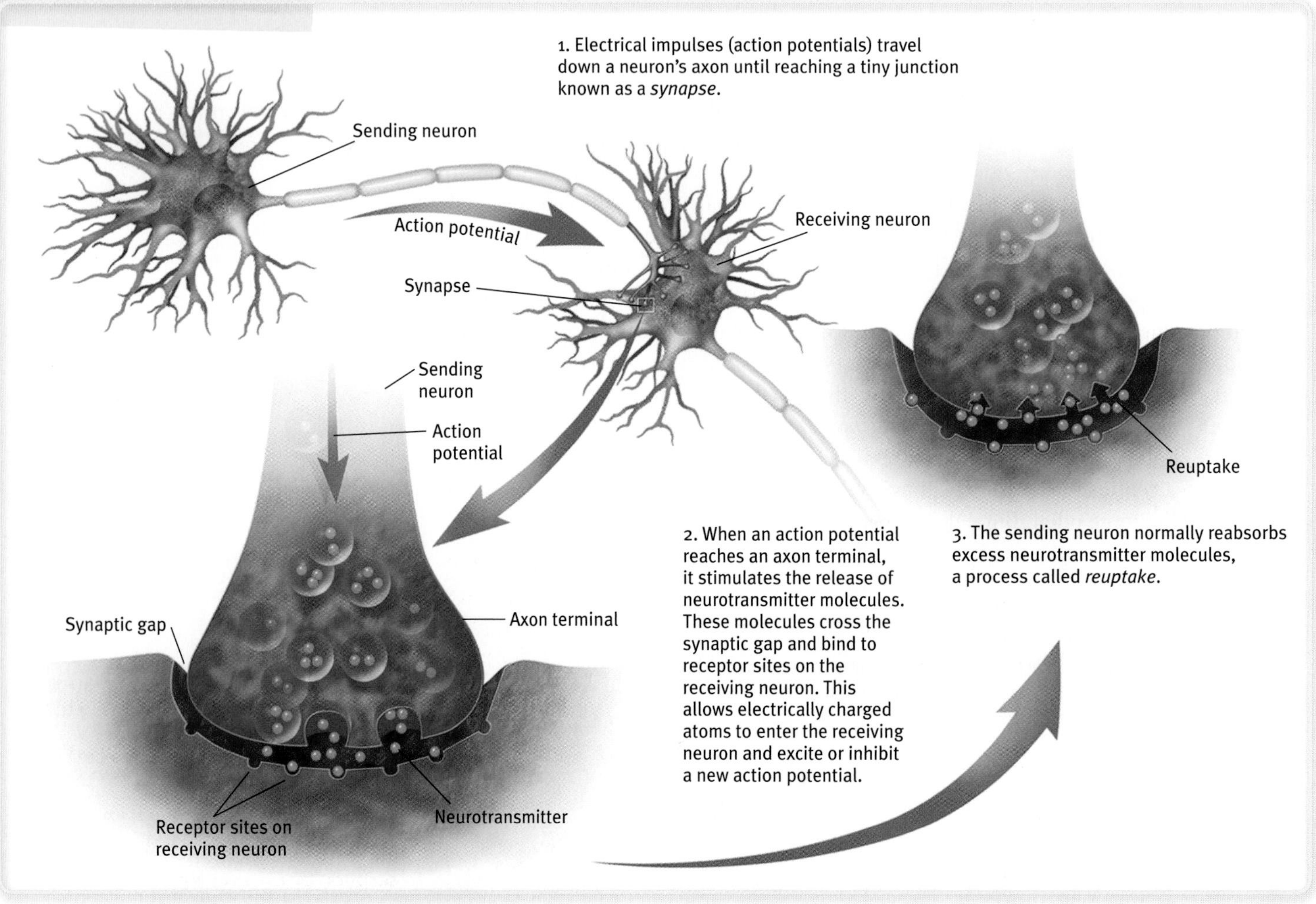

1/10,000th of a second, the neurotransmitter molecules cross the synaptic gap and bind to receptor sites on the receiving neuron—as precisely as a key fits a lock. For an instant, the neurotransmitter unlocks tiny channels at the receiving site, and electrically charged atoms flow in, exciting or inhibiting the receiving neuron's readiness to fire. Then, in a process called **reuptake,** the sending neuron reabsorbs the excess neurotransmitters.

RETRIEVAL PRACTICE

- What happens in the *synaptic gap?* What is *reuptake?*

ANSWERS: Neurons send neurotransmitters (chemical messengers) to one another across this tiny space between one neuron's terminal branch and the next neuron's dendrite. In reuptake, a sending neuron reabsorbs the extra neurotransmitters.

How Neurotransmitters Influence Us

4-4 How do neurotransmitters influence behavior, and how do drugs and other chemicals affect neurotransmission?

In their quest to understand neural communication, researchers have discovered dozens of different neurotransmitters and almost as many new questions: Are certain neurotransmitters found only in specific places? How do they affect our moods, memories, and mental abilities? Can we boost or diminish these effects through drugs or diet?

"When it comes to the brain, if you want to see the action, follow the neurotransmitters."

Neuroscientist Floyd Bloom (1993)

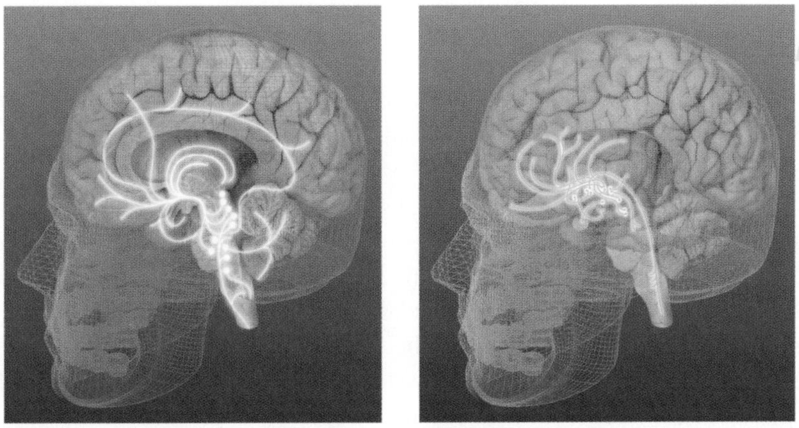

Serotonin pathways — Dopamine pathways

Both photos from *Mapping the Mind*, Rita Carter, © 1989 University of California Press

FIGURE 4.5

Neurotransmitter pathways Each of the brain's differing chemical messengers has designated pathways where it operates, as shown here for serotonin and dopamine (Carter, 1998).

Other modules explore neurotransmitter influences on hunger and thinking, depression and euphoria, addictions and therapy. For now, let's glimpse how neurotransmitters influence our motions and our emotions. A particular brain pathway may use only one or two neurotransmitters (**FIGURE 4.5**), and particular neurotransmitters may affect specific behaviors and emotions (**TABLE 4.1** on the next page). But neurotransmitter systems don't operate in isolation; they interact, and their effects vary with the receptors they stimulate. *Acetylcholine (ACh),* which is one of the best-understood neurotransmitters, plays a role in learning and memory. In addition, it is the messenger at every junction between motor neurons (which carry information from the brain and spinal cord to the body's tissues) and skeletal muscles. When ACh is released to our muscle cell receptors, the muscle contracts. If ACh transmission is blocked, as happens during some kinds of anesthesia, the muscles cannot contract and we are paralyzed.

Candace Pert and Solomon Snyder (1973) made an exciting discovery about neurotransmitters when they attached a radioactive tracer to morphine, showing where it was taken up in an animal's brain. The morphine, an opiate drug that elevates mood and eases pain,

synapse [SIN-aps] the junction between the axon tip of the sending neuron and the dendrite or cell body of the receiving neuron. The tiny gap at this junction is called the *synaptic gap* or *synaptic cleft.*

neurotransmitters chemical messengers that cross the synaptic gaps between neurons. When released by the sending neuron, neurotransmitters travel across the synapse and bind to receptor sites on the receiving neuron, thereby influencing whether that neuron will generate a neural impulse.

reuptake a neurotransmitter's reabsorption by the sending neuron.

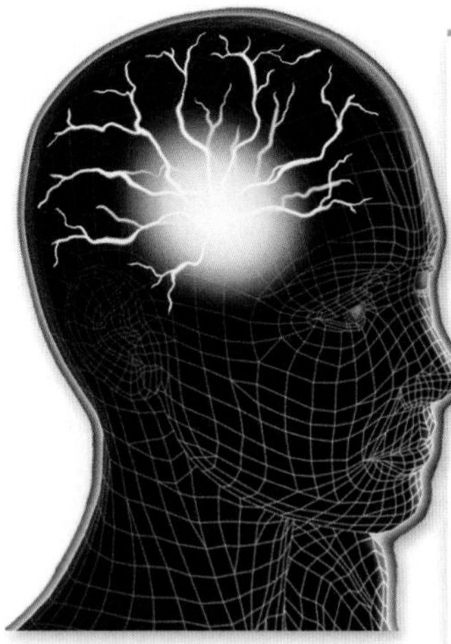
LiquidLibrary/Jupiterimages

TABLE 4.1

Some Neurotransmitters and Their Functions

Neurotransmitter	Function	Examples of Malfunctions
Acetylcholine (ACh)	Enables muscle action, learning, and memory.	With Alzheimer's disease, ACh-producing neurons deteriorate.
Dopamine	Influences movement, learning, attention, and emotion.	Oversupply linked to schizophrenia. Undersupply linked to tremors and decreased mobility in Parkinson's disease.
Serotonin	Affects mood, hunger, sleep, and arousal.	Undersupply linked to depression. Some antidepressant drugs raise serotonin levels.
Norepinephrine	Helps control alertness and arousal.	Undersupply can depress mood.
GABA (gamma-aminobutyric acid)	A major inhibitory neurotransmitter.	Undersupply linked to seizures, tremors, and insomnia.
Glutamate	A major excitatory neurotransmitter; involved in memory.	Oversupply can overstimulate brain, producing migraines or seizures (which is why some people avoid MSG, monosodium glutamate, in food).

Physician Lewis Thomas, on the endorphins: "There it is, a biologically universal act of mercy. I cannot explain it, except to say that I would have put it in had I been around at the very beginning, sitting as a member of a planning committee."

The Youngest Science, 1983

bound to receptors in areas linked with mood and pain sensations. But why would the brain have these "opiate receptors"? Why would it have a chemical lock, unless it also had a natural key to open it?

Researchers soon confirmed that the brain does indeed produce its own naturally occurring opiates. Our body releases several types of neurotransmitter molecules similar to morphine in response to pain and vigorous exercise. These **endorphins** (short for *endo*genous [produced within] m*orphine*) help explain good feelings such as the "runner's high," the painkilling effects of acupuncture, and the indifference to pain in some severely injured people. But once again, new knowledge led to new questions.

RETRIEVAL PRACTICE

- Serotonin, dopamine, and endorphins are all chemical messengers called ___________.

ANSWER: neurotransmitters

How Drugs and Other Chemicals Alter Neurotransmission

If indeed the endorphins lessen pain and boost mood, why not flood the brain with artificial opiates, thereby intensifying the brain's own "feel-good" chemistry? One problem is that when flooded with opiate drugs such as heroin and morphine, the brain may stop producing its own natural opiates. When the drug is withdrawn, the brain may then be deprived of any form of opiate, causing intense discomfort. For suppressing the body's own neurotransmitter production, nature charges a price.

Drugs and other chemicals affect brain chemistry at synapses, often by either exciting or inhibiting neurons' firing. *Agonist* molecules may be similar enough to a neurotransmitter to bind to its receptor and mimic its effects. Some opiate drugs are agonists and produce a temporary "high" by amplifying normal sensations of arousal or pleasure.

Antagonists also bind to receptors but their effect is instead to block a neurotransmitter's functioning.

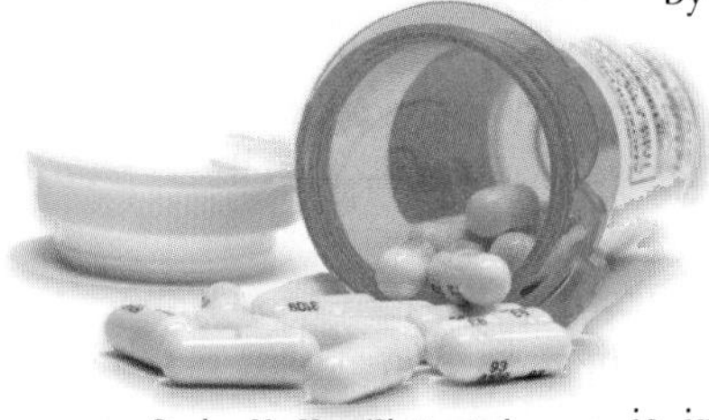
Stephen VanHorn/Shutterstock

endorphins [en-DOR-fins] "morphine within"—natural, opiate-like neurotransmitters linked to pain control and to pleasure.

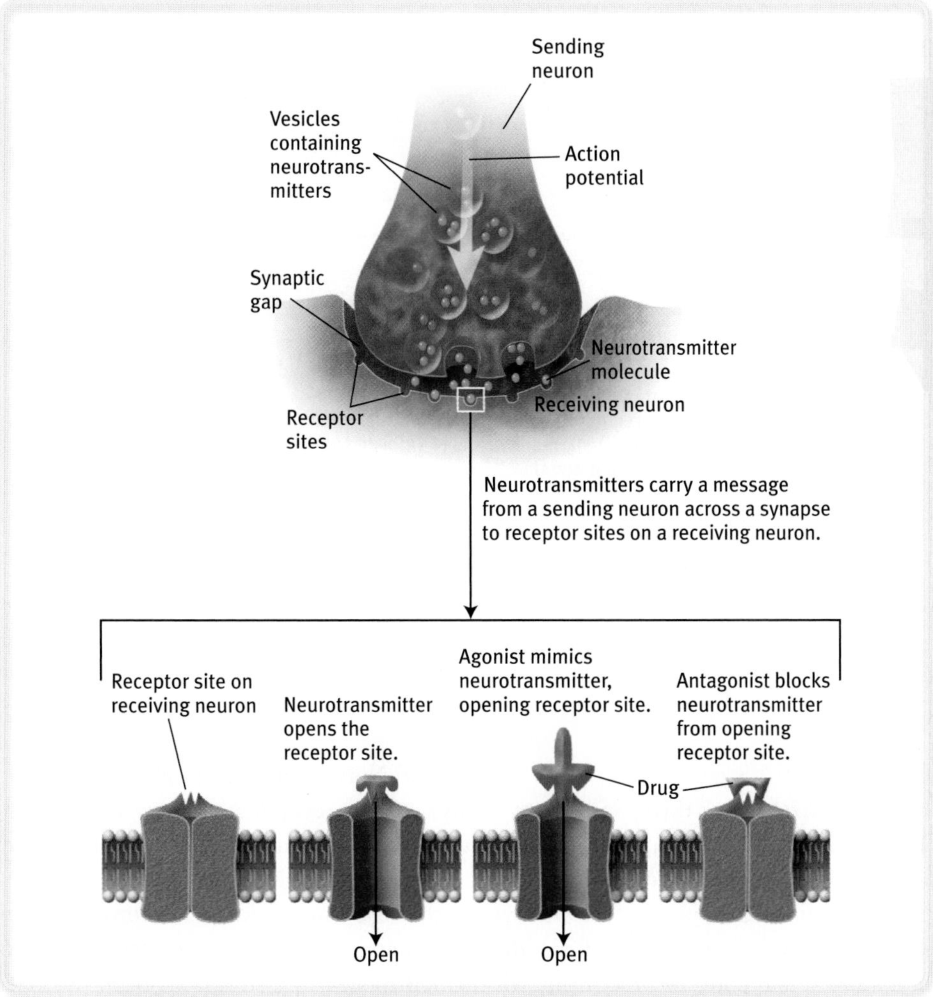

RETRIEVAL PRACTICE

FIGURE 4.6

Agonists and antagonists Curare poisoning paralyzes its victims by blocking ACh receptors involved in muscle movements. Morphine mimics endorphin actions. Which is an agonist, and which is an antagonist? (Art adapted from Higgins & George, 2008.)

ANSWER: Morphine is an agonist; curare is an antagonist.

Botulin, a poison that can form in improperly canned food, causes paralysis by blocking ACh release. (Small injections of botulin—Botox—smooth wrinkles by paralyzing the underlying facial muscles.) These antagonists are enough like the natural neurotransmitter to occupy its receptor site and block its effect, as in **FIGURE 4.6**, but are not similar enough to stimulate the receptor (rather like foreign coins that fit into, but won't operate, a candy machine). Curare, a poison some South American Indians have applied to hunting-dart tips, occupies and blocks ACh receptor sites on muscles, producing paralysis in animals struck by the darts.

The Nervous System

4-5 What are the functions of the nervous system's main divisions, and what are the three main types of neurons?

To live is to take in information from the world and the body's tissues, to make decisions, and to send back information and orders to the body's tissues. All this happens thanks to our body's **nervous system** (**FIGURE 4.7** on the next page). The brain and spinal cord form the **central nervous system (CNS)**, the body's decision maker. The **peripheral nervous system (PNS)** is responsible for gathering information and for

nervous system the body's speedy, electrochemical communication network, consisting of all the nerve cells of the peripheral and central nervous systems.

central nervous system (CNS) the brain and spinal cord.

peripheral nervous system (PNS) the sensory and motor neurons that connect the central nervous system (CNS) to the rest of the body.

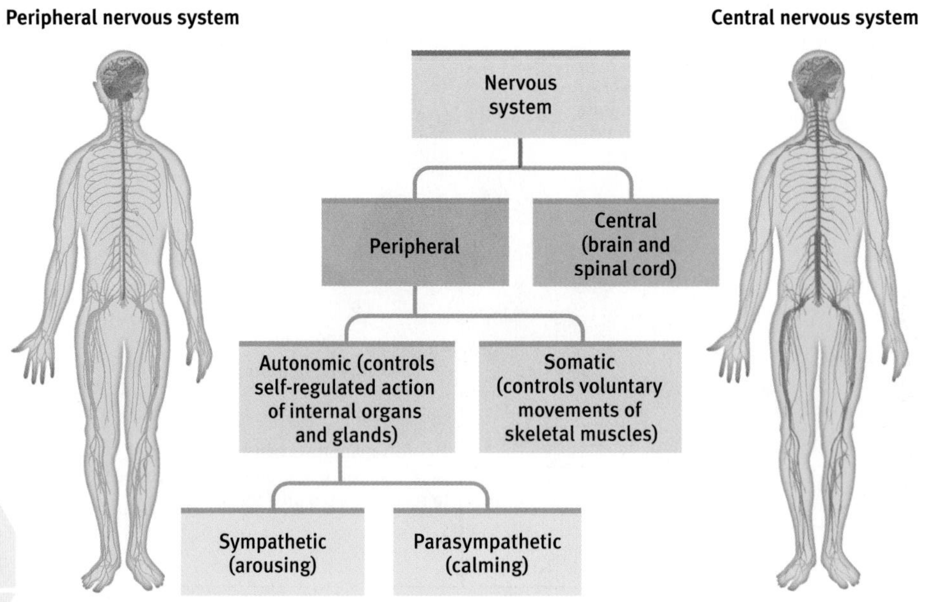

FIGURE 4.7
The functional divisions of the human nervous system

transmitting CNS decisions to other body parts. **Nerves,** electrical cables formed of bundles of axons, link the CNS with the body's sensory receptors, muscles, and glands. The optic nerve, for example, bundles a million axons into a single cable carrying the messages each eye sends to the brain (Mason & Kandel, 1991).

Information travels in the nervous system through three types of neurons. **Sensory neurons** carry messages from the body's tissues and sensory receptors inward to the brain and spinal cord for processing. **Motor neurons** carry instructions from the central nervous system out to the body's muscles. Between the sensory input and motor output, information is processed in the brain's internal communication system via its **interneurons.** Our complexity resides mostly in our interneuron systems. Our nervous system has a few million sensory neurons, a few million motor neurons, and billions and billions of interneurons.

nerves bundled axons that form neural "cables" connecting the central nervous system with muscles, glands, and sense organs.

sensory neurons neurons that carry incoming information from the sensory receptors to the brain and spinal cord.

motor neurons neurons that carry outgoing information from the brain and spinal cord to the muscles and glands.

interneurons neurons within the brain and spinal cord that communicate internally and intervene between the sensory inputs and motor outputs.

somatic nervous system the division of the peripheral nervous system that controls the body's skeletal muscles. Also called the *skeletal nervous system.*

autonomic [aw-tuh-NAHM-ik] **nervous system (ANS)** the part of the peripheral nervous system that controls the glands and the muscles of the internal organs (such as the heart). Its sympathetic division arouses; its parasympathetic division calms.

sympathetic nervous system the division of the autonomic nervous system that arouses the body, mobilizing its energy in stressful situations.

The Peripheral Nervous System

Our peripheral nervous system has two components—somatic and autonomic. Our **somatic nervous system** enables voluntary control of our skeletal muscles. As you reach the bottom of the next page, your somatic nervous system will report to your brain the current state of your skeletal muscles and carry instructions back, triggering your hand to turn the page.

Our **autonomic nervous system** (**ANS**) controls our glands and the muscles of our internal organs, influencing such functions as glandular activity, heartbeat, and digestion. Like an automatic pilot, this system may be consciously overridden, but usually operates on its own (autonomously).

The autonomic nervous system serves two important, basic functions (**FIGURE 4.8**). The **sympathetic nervous system** arouses and expends energy. If something alarms or challenges you (such as a longed-for job interview), your sympathetic nervous system will accelerate your heartbeat, raise your blood pressure, slow your

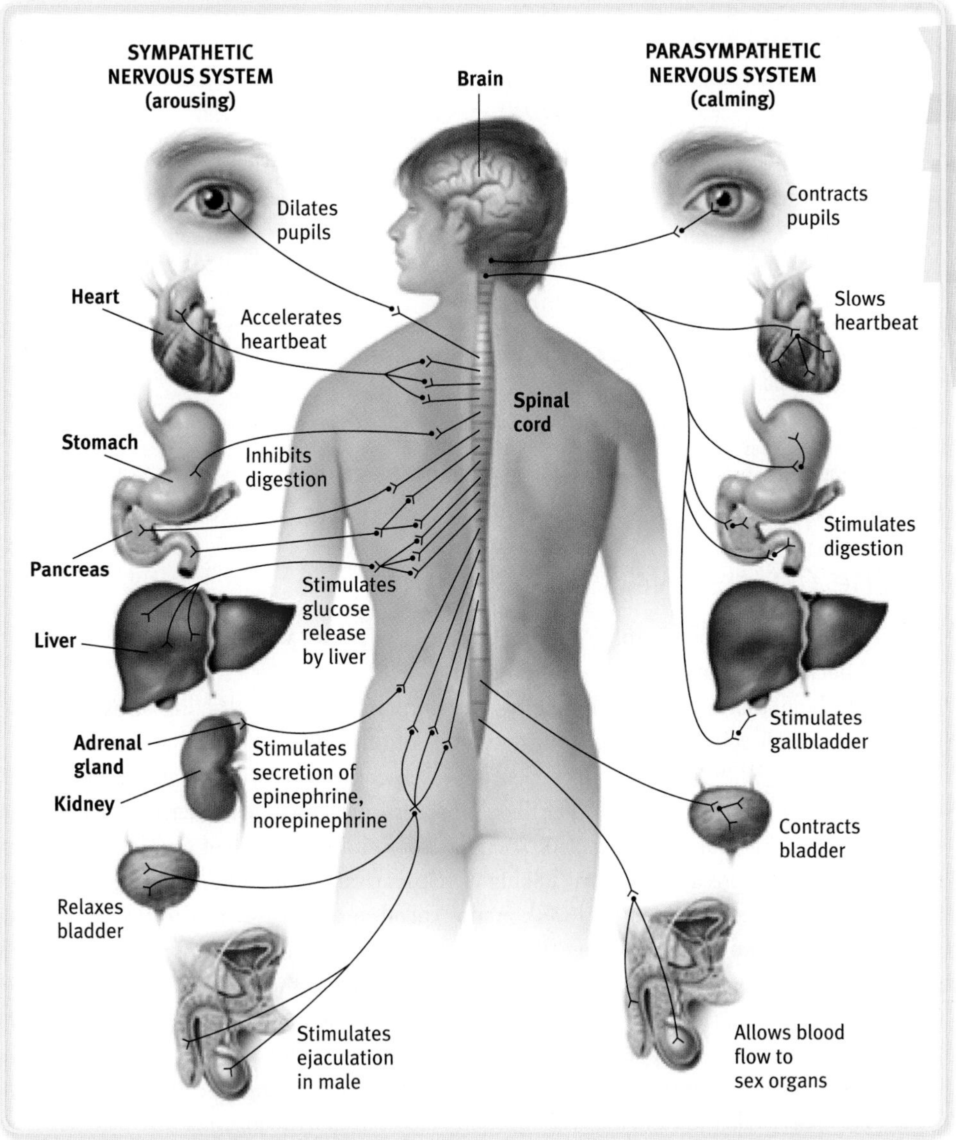

FIGURE 4.8
The dual functions of the autonomic nervous system The autonomic nervous system controls the more autonomous (or self-regulating) internal functions. Its sympathetic division arouses and expends energy. Its parasympathetic division calms and conserves energy, allowing routine maintenance activity. For example, sympathetic stimulation accelerates heartbeat, whereas parasympathetic stimulation slows it.

digestion, raise your blood sugar, and cool you with perspiration, making you alert and ready for action. When the stress subsides (the interview is over), your **parasympathetic nervous system** will produce the opposite effects, conserving energy as it calms you by decreasing your heartbeat, lowering your blood sugar, and so forth. In everyday situations, the sympathetic and parasympathetic nervous systems work together to keep you in a steady internal state.

I recently experienced my ANS in action. Before sending me into an MRI machine for a routine shoulder scan, the technician asked if I had issues with claustrophobia. "No, I'm fine," I assured her, with perhaps a hint of macho swagger. Moments later, as I found myself on my back, stuck deep inside a coffin-sized box and unable to move, my sympathetic nervous system had a different idea. As claustrophobia overtook me, my heart began pounding and I felt a desperate urge to escape. Just as I was about to cry out for release, I suddenly felt my calming parasympathetic nervous system kick in. My heart rate slowed and my body relaxed, though my arousal surged again before the 20-minute confinement ended. "You did well!" the technician said, unaware of my ANS roller-coaster ride.

parasympathetic nervous system the division of the autonomic nervous system that calms the body, conserving its energy.

RETRIEVAL PRACTICE

- Match the type of neuron to its description.

Type	Description
1. Motor neurons	a. carry incoming messages from sensory receptors to the CNS
2. Sensory neurons	b. communicate within the CNS and intervene between incoming and outgoing messages
3. Interneurons	c. carry outgoing messages from the CNS to muscles and glands

ANSWERS: 1. c, 2. a, 3. b

- What bodily changes does your autonomic nervous system (ANS) direct before and after you give an important speech?

ANSWER: Responding to this challenge, your ANS's *sympathetic* division will arouse you. It accelerates your heartbeat, raises your blood pressure and blood sugar, slows your digestion, and cools you with perspiration. After you give the speech, your ANS's *parasympathetic* division will reverse these effects.

The Central Nervous System

© Tom Swick

"The body is made up of millions and millions of crumbs."

From the simplicity of neurons "talking" to other neurons arises the complexity of the central nervous system's brain and spinal cord.

It is the brain that enables our humanity—our thinking, feeling, and acting. Tens of billions of neurons, each communicating with thousands of other neurons, yield an everchanging wiring diagram. With some 40 billion neurons, each connecting with roughly 10,000 other neurons, we end up with perhaps 400 trillion synapses—places where neurons meet and greet their neighbors (de Courten-Myers, 2005). A grain-of-sand-sized speck of your brain contains some 100,000 neurons and 1 billion "talking" synapses (Ramachandran & Blakeslee, 1998).

The brain's neurons cluster into work groups called *neural networks.* To understand why, Stephen Kosslyn and Olivier Koenig (1992, p. 12) have invited us to "think about why cities exist; why don't people distribute themselves more evenly across the countryside?" Like people networking with people, neurons network with nearby neurons with which they can have short, fast connections. As in **FIGURE 4.9,** each layer's cells connect with various cells in the neural network's next layer. Learning—to play the violin, speak a foreign language, solve a math problem—occurs as feedback strengthens connections. Neurons that fire together wire together.

The other part of the CNS, the *spinal cord,* is a two-way information highway connecting between the peripheral nervous system and the brain. Ascending neural fibers send up sensory information, and descending fibers send back motor-control information. The neural pathways governing our **reflexes,** our automatic responses to stimuli, illustrate the spinal cord's work. A

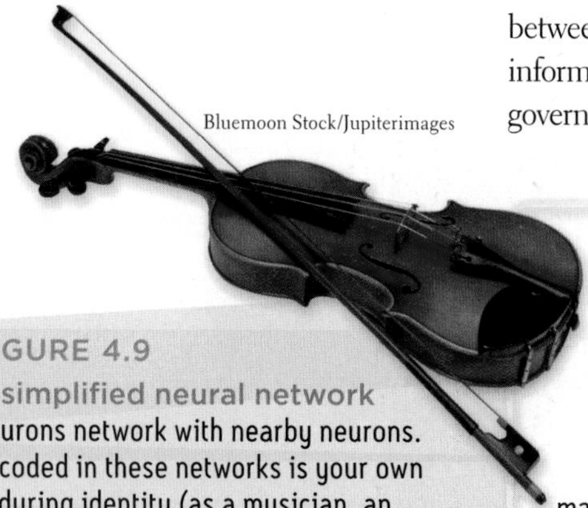

Bluemoon Stock/Jupiterimages

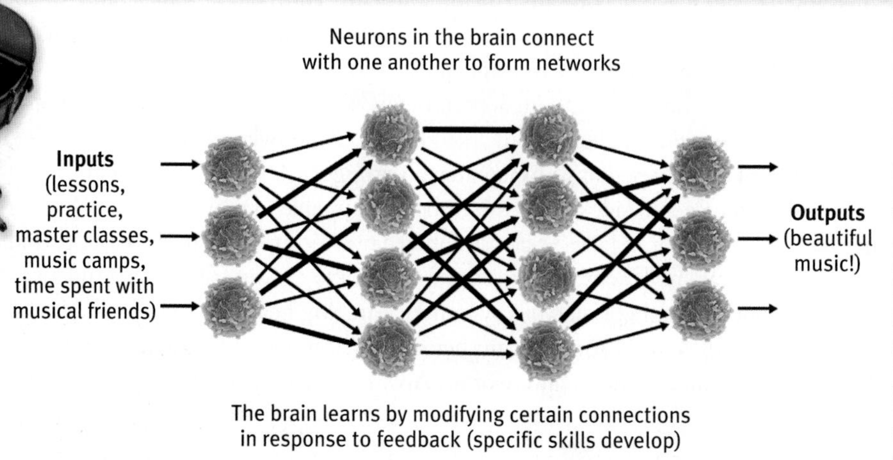

FIGURE 4.9
A simplified neural network
Neurons network with nearby neurons. Encoded in these networks is your own enduring identity (as a musician, an athlete, a devoted friend)—your sense of self that extends across the years. How neural networks organize themselves into complex circuits capable of learning, feeling, and thinking remains one of the great scientific mysteries. How does biology give birth to mind?

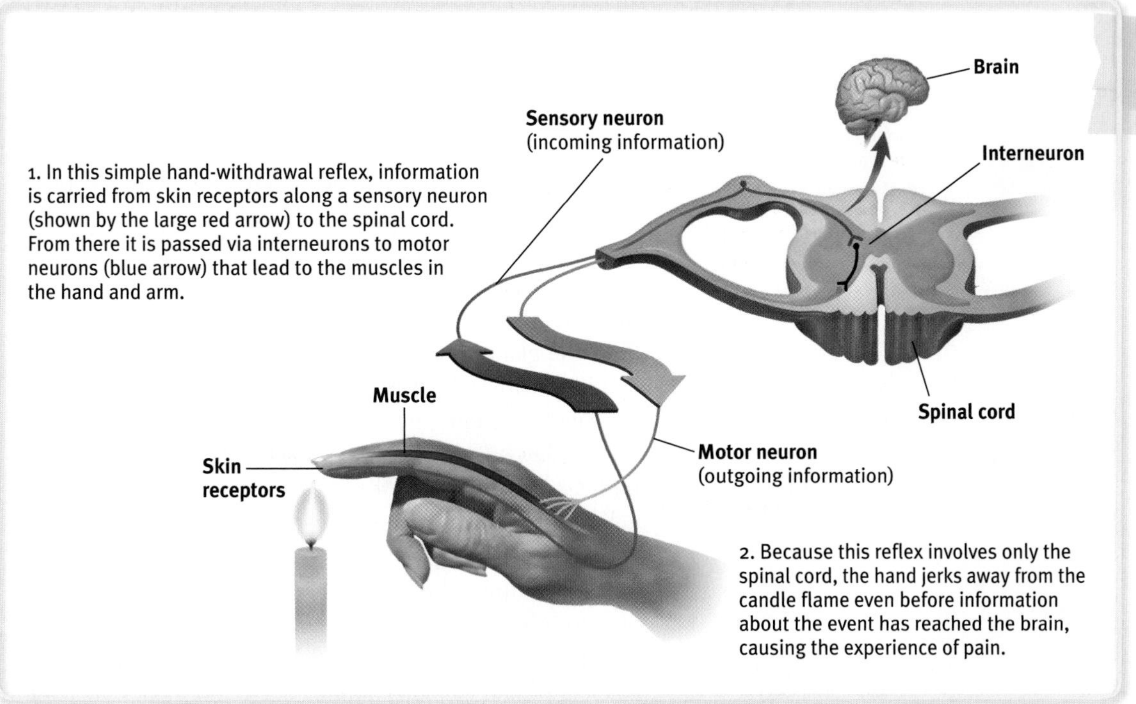

FIGURE 4.10
A simple reflex

simple spinal reflex pathway is composed of a single sensory neuron and a single motor neuron. These often communicate through an interneuron. The knee-jerk response, for example, involves one such simple pathway. A headless warm body could do it.

Another such pathway enables the pain reflex (**FIGURE 4.10**). When your finger touches a flame, neural activity (excited by the heat) travels via sensory neurons to interneurons in your spinal cord. These interneurons respond by activating motor neurons leading to the muscles in your arm. Because the simple pain-reflex pathway runs through the spinal cord and right back out, your hand jerks away from the candle's flame *before* your brain receives and responds to the information that causes you to feel pain. That's why it feels as if your hand jerks away not by your choice, but on its own.

Information travels to and from the brain by way of the spinal cord. Were the top of your spinal cord severed, you would not feel pain from your body below. Nor would you feel pleasure. With your brain literally out of touch with your body, you would lose all sensation and voluntary movement in body regions with sensory and motor connections to the spinal cord below its point of injury. You would exhibit the knee jerk without feeling the tap. When the brain center keeping the brakes on erections is severed, men paralyzed below the waist may be capable of an erection (a simple reflex) if their genitals are stimulated (Goldstein, 2000). Women similarly paralyzed may respond with vaginal lubrication. But, depending on where and how completely the spinal cord is severed, they may be genitally unresponsive to erotic images and have no genital feeling (Kennedy & Over, 1990; Sipski & Alexander, 1999). To produce bodily pain or pleasure, the sensory information must reach the brain.

"If the nervous system be cut off between the brain and other parts, the experiences of those other parts are nonexistent for the mind. The eye is blind, the ear deaf, the hand insensible and motionless."

William James, *Principles of Psychology,* 1890

The Endocrine System

4-6 How does the endocrine system transmit information and interact with the nervous system?

So far we have focused on the body's speedy electrochemical information system. Interconnected with your nervous system is a second communication system, the **endocrine system** (**FIGURE 4.11** on the next page). The endocrine system's glands secrete another form of chemical messengers, **hormones,** which travel through the bloodstream and affect other tissues, including the brain. When hormones act on the brain, they influence our interest in sex, food, and aggression.

reflex a simple, automatic response to a sensory stimulus, such as the knee-jerk response.

endocrine [EN-duh-krin] **system** the body's "slow" chemical communication system; a set of glands that secrete hormones into the bloodstream.

hormones chemical messengers that are manufactured by the endocrine glands, travel through the bloodstream, and affect other tissues.

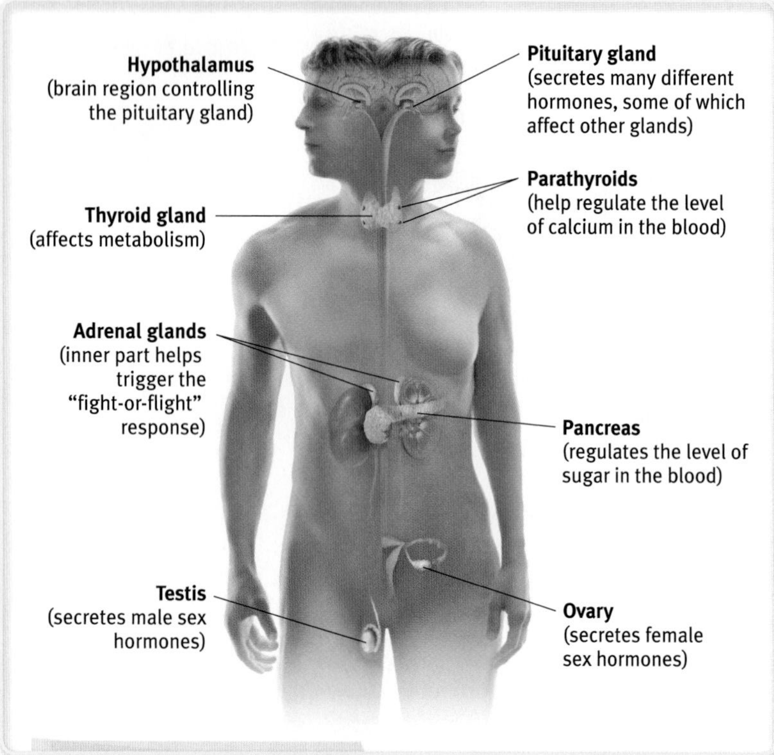

FIGURE 4.11
The endocrine system

Some hormones are chemically identical to neurotransmitters (the chemical messengers that diffuse across a synapse and excite or inhibit an adjacent neuron). The endocrine system and nervous system are therefore close relatives: Both produce molecules that act on receptors elsewhere. Like many relatives, they also differ. The speedy nervous system zips messages from eyes to brain to hand in a fraction of a second. Endocrine messages trudge along in the bloodstream, taking several seconds or more to travel from the gland to the target tissue. If the nervous system's communication delivers messages with the speed of a text message, the endocrine system is more like sending a letter.

But slow and steady sometimes wins the race. Endocrine messages tend to outlast the effects of neural messages. That helps explain why upset feelings may linger beyond our awareness of what upset us. When this happens, it takes time for us to "simmer down." In a moment of danger, for example, the ANS orders the **adrenal glands** on top of the kidneys to release *epinephrine* and *norepinephrine* (also called *adrenaline* and *noradrenaline*). These hormones increase heart rate, blood pressure, and blood sugar, providing us with a surge of energy. When the emergency passes, the hormones—and the feelings of excitement—linger a while.

The most influential endocrine gland is the **pituitary gland,** a pea-sized structure located in the core of the brain, where it is controlled by an adjacent brain area, the *hypothalamus.* The pituitary releases certain hormones. One is a growth hormone that stimulates physical development. Another, oxytocin, enables contractions associated with birthing, milk flow during nursing, and orgasm. Oxytocin also promotes pair bonding, group cohesion, and social trust (De Dreu et al., 2010). During a laboratory game, those given a nasal squirt of oxytocin rather than a placebo were more likely to trust strangers with their money (Kosfeld et al., 2005).

Pituitary secretions also influence the release of hormones by other endocrine glands. The pituitary, then, is a sort of master gland (whose own master is the hypothalamus). For example, under the brain's influence, the pituitary triggers your sex glands to release sex hormones. These in turn influence your brain and behavior. So, too, with stress. A stressful event triggers your hypothalamus to instruct your pituitary to release a hormone that causes your adrenal glands to flood your body with cortisol, a stress hormone that increases blood sugar.

This feedback system (brain ⟶ pituitary ⟶ other glands ⟶ hormones ⟶ body and brain) reveals the intimate connection of the nervous and endocrine systems. The nervous system directs endocrine secretions, which then affect the nervous system. Conducting and coordinating this whole electrochemical orchestra is that maestro we call the brain.

adrenal [ah-DREEN-el] **glands** a pair of endocrine glands that sit just above the kidneys and secrete hormones (epinephrine and norepinephrine) that help arouse the body in times of stress.

pituitary gland the endocrine system's most influential gland. Under the influence of the hypothalamus, the pituitary regulates growth and controls other endocrine glands.

RETRIEVAL PRACTICE

- Why is the pituitary gland called a "master gland"?

ANSWER: Responding to signals from the hypothalamus, the pituitary releases hormones that trigger other endocrine glands to secrete hormones that in turn influence brain and behavior.

- How are the nervous and endocrine systems alike, and how do they differ?

ANSWER: Both of these communication systems produce chemical molecules that act on the body's receptors to influence our behavior and emotions. The endocrine system, which secretes hormones into the bloodstream, delivers its messages much more slowly than the speedy nervous system, and the effects of the endocrine system's messages tend to linger much longer than those of the nervous system.

MODULE REVIEW

Neural and Hormonal Systems

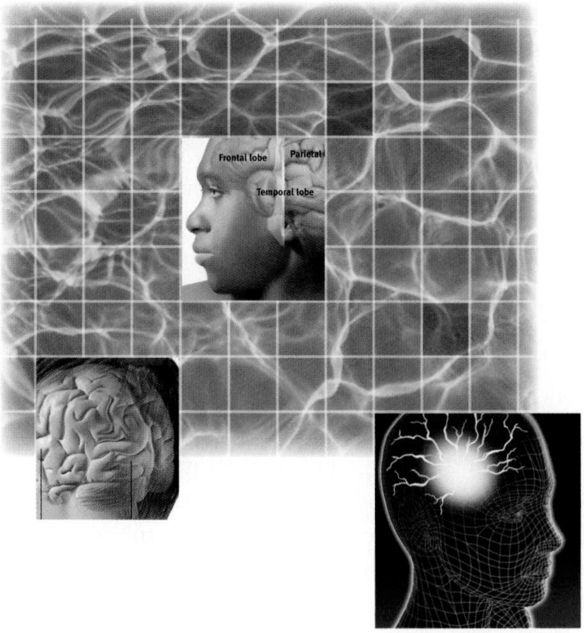

Learning Objectives

RETRIEVAL PRACTICE Take a moment to answer each of these Learning Objective Questions (repeated here from within the module). Then turn to Appendix B, Complete Module Reviews, to check your answers. Research suggests that trying to answer these questions on your own will improve your long-term retention (McDaniel et al., 2009).

4-1: Why are psychologists concerned with human biology?

4-2: What are neurons, and how do they transmit information?

4-3: How do nerve cells communicate with other nerve cells?

4-4: How do neurotransmitters influence behavior, and how do drugs and other chemicals affect neurotransmission?

4-5: What are the functions of the nervous system's main divisions, and what are the three main types of neurons?

4-6: How does the endocrine system transmit information and interact with the nervous system?

Terms and Concepts to Remember

RETRIEVAL PRACTICE Test yourself on these terms by trying to write down the definition before flipping back to the referenced page to check your answer.

biological perspective, p. 47
neuron, p. 47
dendrites, p. 47
axon, p. 47
myelin [MY-uh-lin] sheath, p. 48
action potential, p. 48
threshold, p. 49
synapse [SIN-aps], p. 50
neurotransmitters, p. 50
reuptake, p. 51
endorphins [en-DOR-fins], p. 52
nervous system, p. 53
central nervous system (CNS), p. 53
peripheral nervous system (PNS), p. 53
nerves, p. 54
sensory neurons, p. 54
motor neurons, p. 54
interneurons, p. 54
somatic nervous system, p. 54
autonomic [aw-tuh-NAHM-ik] nervous system (ANS), p. 54
sympathetic nervous system, p. 54
parasympathetic nervous system, p. 55
reflex, p. 56
endocrine [EN-duh-krin] system, p. 57
hormones, p. 57
adrenal [ah-DREEN-el] glands, p. 58
pituitary gland, p. 58

RETRIEVAL PRACTICE Gain an advantage, and benefit from immediate feedback, with the interactive self-testing resources at www.worthpublishers.com/myers.

MODULE 5

Tools of Discovery and Older Brain Structures

- The Tools of Discovery: Having Our Head Examined
- Older Brain Structures

© The New Yorker Collection, 1992, Gahan Wilson, from cartoonbank.com. All Rights Reserved.

"You're certainly a lot less fun since the operation."

"I am a brain, Watson. The rest of me is a mere appendix."

Sherlock Holmes, in Arthur Conan Doyle's "The Adventure of the Mazarin Stone"

In a jar on a display shelf in Cornell University's psychology department resides the well-preserved brain of Edward Bradford Titchener, a late-nineteenth-century experimental psychologist and proponent of the study of consciousness. Imagine yourself gazing at that wrinkled mass of grayish tissue, wondering if in any sense Titchener is still in there.[1]

You might answer that, without the living whir of electrochemical activity, there could be nothing of Titchener in his preserved brain. Consider, then, an experiment about which the inquisitive Titchener himself might have daydreamed. Imagine that just moments before his death, someone had removed Titchener's brain and kept it alive by feeding it enriched blood. Would Titchener still be in there? Further imagine that someone then transplanted the still-living brain into the body of a person whose own brain had been severely damaged. To whose home should the recovered patient return?

That we can imagine such questions illustrates how convinced we are that we live "somewhere north of the neck" (Fodor, 1999). And for good reason: The brain enables the mind—seeing, hearing, smelling, feeling, remembering, thinking, speaking, dreaming. Moreover, it is the brain that self-reflectively analyzes the brain. When we're thinking *about* our brain, we're thinking *with* our brain—by firing across millions of synapses and releasing billions of neurotransmitter molecules. The effect of hormones on experiences such as love reminds us that we would not be of the same mind if we were a bodiless brain. Brain + body = mind. Nevertheless, say neuroscientists, the *mind is what the brain does.* Brain, behavior, and cognition are an integrated whole. But precisely where and how are the mind's functions tied to the brain? Let's first see how scientists explore such questions.

The Tools of Discovery: Having Our Head Examined

5-1 How do neuroscientists study the brain's connections to behavior and mind?

A century ago, scientists had no tools high-powered yet gentle enough to explore the living human brain. Early *clinical observations* by physicians and others revealed some brain-mind connections. Damage to one side of the brain often caused numbness or paralysis on the body's opposite side, suggesting that the body's right side is wired to the brain's left side, and vice versa. Damage to the back of the brain disrupted vision, and to the left-front part of the brain produced speech difficulties. Gradually, these early explorers were mapping the brain.

Now, within a lifetime, a new generation of neural cartographers is probing and mapping the known universe's most amazing organ. Scientists can selectively **lesion** (destroy) tiny clusters of brain cells, leaving the surrounding tissue unharmed. In the laboratory, such studies have revealed, for example, that damage to one area of the hypothalamus in a rat's brain reduces eating, to the point of starvation, whereas damage in another area produces overeating.

lesion [LEE-zhuhn] tissue destruction. A brain lesion is a naturally or experimentally caused destruction of brain tissue.

[1] Carl Sagan's *Broca's Brain* (1979) inspired this question.

Today's neuroscientists can also electrically, chemically, or magnetically *stimulate* various parts of the brain and note the effect. Depending on the stimulated brain part, people may—to name a few examples—giggle, hear voices, turn their head, feel themselves falling, or have an out-of-body experience (Selimbeyoglu & Parvizi, 2010). Scientists can even snoop on the messages of individual neurons. With tips so small they can detect the electrical pulse in a single neuron, modern microelectrodes can, for example, now detect exactly where the information goes in a cat's brain when someone strokes its whisker. Researchers can also eavesdrop on the chatter of billions of neurons and can see color representations of the brain's energy-consuming activity.

© Philip Channing

Minding minds Neuroscientists Hanna Damasio and Antonio Damasio explore how the brain makes mind.

Right now, your mental activity is emitting telltale electrical, metabolic, and magnetic signals that would enable neuroscientists to observe your brain at work. Electrical activity in your brain's billions of neurons sweeps in regular waves across its surface. An **electroencephalogram (EEG)** is an amplified readout of such waves. Researchers record the brain waves through a shower-cap-like hat that is filled with electrodes covered with a conductive gel. Studying an EEG of the brain's activity is like studying a car engine by listening to its hum. With no direct access to the brain, researchers present a stimulus repeatedly and have a computer filter out brain activity unrelated to the stimulus. What remains is the electrical wave evoked by the stimulus (**FIGURE 5.1**).

"You must look into people, as well as at them," advised Lord Chesterfield in a 1746 letter to his son. Unlike EEGs, newer neuroimaging techniques give us that Superman-like ability to see inside the living brain. One such tool, the **PET (positron emission tomography) scan** (**FIGURE 5.2** on the next page), depicts brain activity by showing each brain area's consumption of its chemical fuel, the sugar glucose. Active neurons are glucose hogs, and after a person receives temporarily radioactive glucose, the PET scan can track the gamma rays released by this "food for thought" as the person performs a given task. Rather like weather radar showing rain activity, PET-scan "hot spots" show which brain areas are most active as the person does mathematical calculations, looks at images of faces, or daydreams.

In **MRI (magnetic resonance imaging)** brain scans, the person's head is put in a strong magnetic field, which aligns the spinning atoms of brain molecules. Then, a radio-wave pulse momentarily disorients the atoms. When the atoms return to their normal spin, they emit signals that provide a detailed picture of soft tissues, including the brain. MRI scans have revealed a larger-than-average neural area in the left hemisphere of musicians who display perfect pitch (Schlaug et al., 1995). They have also revealed

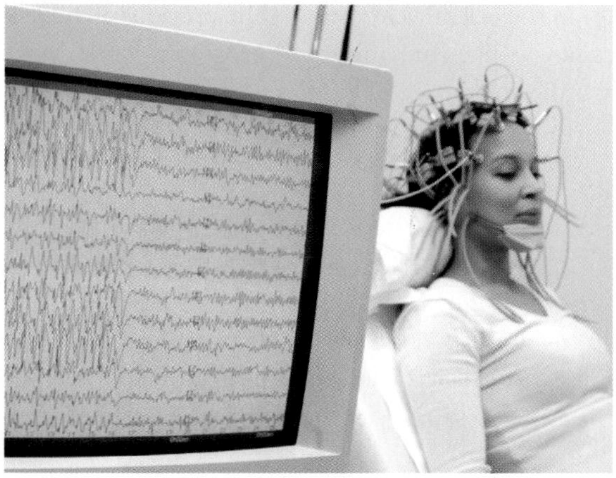

AJPhoto/Photo Researchers, Inc.

FIGURE 5.1
An electroencephalograph providing amplified tracings of waves of electrical activity in the brain

electroencephalogram (EEG) an amplified recording of the waves of electrical activity that sweep across the brain's surface. These waves are measured by electrodes placed on the scalp.

PET (positron emission tomography) scan a visual display of brain activity that detects where a radioactive form of glucose goes while the brain performs a given task.

MRI (magnetic resonance imaging) a technique that uses magnetic fields and radio waves to produce computer-generated images of soft tissue. MRI scans show brain anatomy.

FIGURE 5.2
The PET scan To obtain a PET scan, researchers inject volunteers with a low and harmless dose of a short-lived radioactive sugar. Detectors around the person's head pick up the release of gamma rays from the sugar, which has concentrated in active brain areas. A computer then processes and translates these signals into a map of the brain at work.

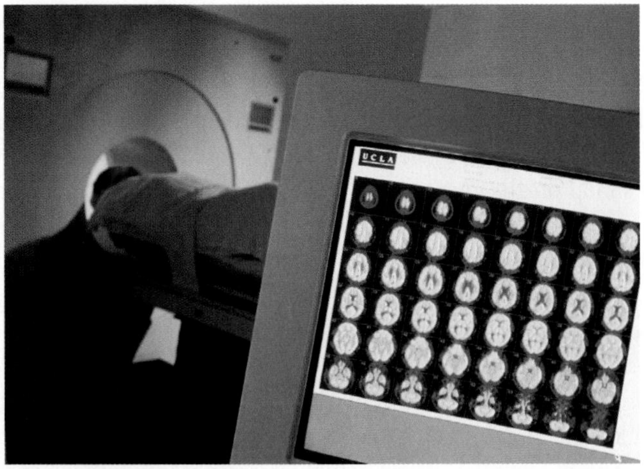

Mark Harmel/Getty Images

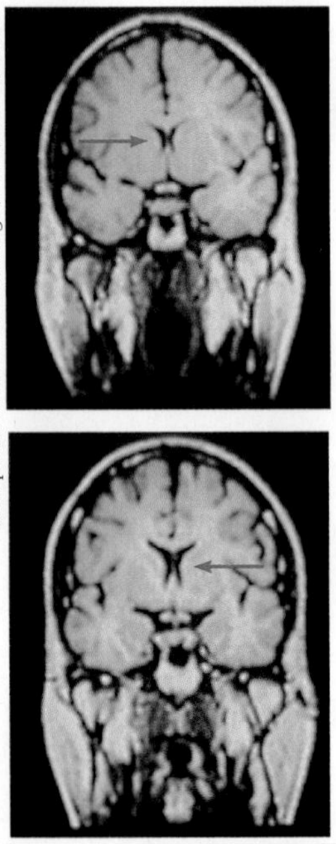

Both photos from Daniel Weinberger, M.D., CBDB, NIMH

FIGURE 5.3
MRI scan of a healthy individual (top) and a person with schizophrenia (bottom) Note the enlarged ventricle, the fluid-filled brain region at the tip of the arrow in the image on the bottom.

enlarged *ventricles*—fluid-filled brain areas (marked by the red arrows in **FIGURE 5.3**)—in some patients who have schizophrenia, a disabling psychological disorder.

A special application of MRI—**fMRI (functional MRI)**—can reveal the brain's functioning as well as its structure. Where the brain is especially active, blood goes. By comparing MRI scans taken less than a second apart, researchers can watch the brain "light up" (with increased oxygen-laden bloodflow) as a person performs different mental functions. As the person looks at a scene, for example, the fMRI machine detects blood rushing to the back of the brain, which processes visual information.

Such snapshots of the brain's changing activity are providing new insights—albeit sometimes overstated (Vul et al., 2009a,b)—into how the brain divides its labor. A mountain of recent fMRI studies suggests which brain areas are most active when people feel pain or rejection, listen to angry voices, think about scary things, feel happy, or become sexually excited. The technology enables a very crude sort of mind reading. After scanning 129 people's brains as they did eight different mental tasks (such as reading, gambling, or rhyming), neuroscientists were able, with 80 percent accuracy, to predict which of these mental activities people were doing (Poldrack et al., 2009). Other studies have explored brain activity associated with religious experience, though without settling the question of whether the brain is producing or perceiving God (Fingelkurts & Fingelkurts, 2009; Inzlicht et al., 2009; Kapogiannis et al., 2009).

* * *

Today's techniques for peering into the thinking, feeling brain are doing for psychology what the microscope did for biology and the telescope did for astronomy. From them we have learned more about the brain in the last 30 years than in the previous 30,000. To be learning about the neurosciences now is like studying world geography while Magellan was exploring the seas. This truly is the golden age of brain science.

RETRIEVAL PRACTICE

- Match the scanning technique with the correct description.

Technique	Description
1. fMRI scan	a. tracks radioactive glucose to reveal brain activity
2. PET scan	b. tracks successive images of brain tissue to show brain function
3. MRI scan	c. uses magnetic fields and radio waves to show brain anatomy

ANSWERS: 1. b, 2. a, 3. c

Older Brain Structures

5-2 What structures make up the brainstem, and what are the functions of the brainstem, thalamus, and cerebellum?

An animal's capacities come from its brain structures. In primitive animals, such as sharks, a not-so-complex brain primarily regulates basic survival functions: breathing, resting, and feeding. In lower mammals, such as rodents, a more complex brain enables emotion and greater memory. In advanced mammals, such as humans, a brain that processes more information enables increased foresight as well.

This increasing complexity arises from new brain systems built on top of the old, much as the Earth's landscape covers the old with the new. Digging down, one discovers the fossil remnants of the past—brainstem components performing for us much as they did for our distant ancestors.

fMRI (functional MRI) a technique for revealing bloodflow and, therefore, brain activity by comparing successive MRI scans. fMRI scans show brain function.

brainstem the oldest part and central core of the brain, beginning where the spinal cord swells as it enters the skull; the brainstem is responsible for automatic survival functions.

medulla [muh-DUL-uh] the base of the brainstem; controls heartbeat and breathing.

The Brainstem

The brain's oldest and innermost region is the **brainstem.** It begins where the spinal cord swells slightly after entering the skull. This slight swelling is the **medulla** (**FIGURE 5.4**). Here lie the controls for your heartbeat and breathing. As some brain-damaged patients in a vegetative state illustrate, we need no higher brain or conscious to orchestrate our heart's pumping and lungs' breathing. The brainstem handles those tasks.

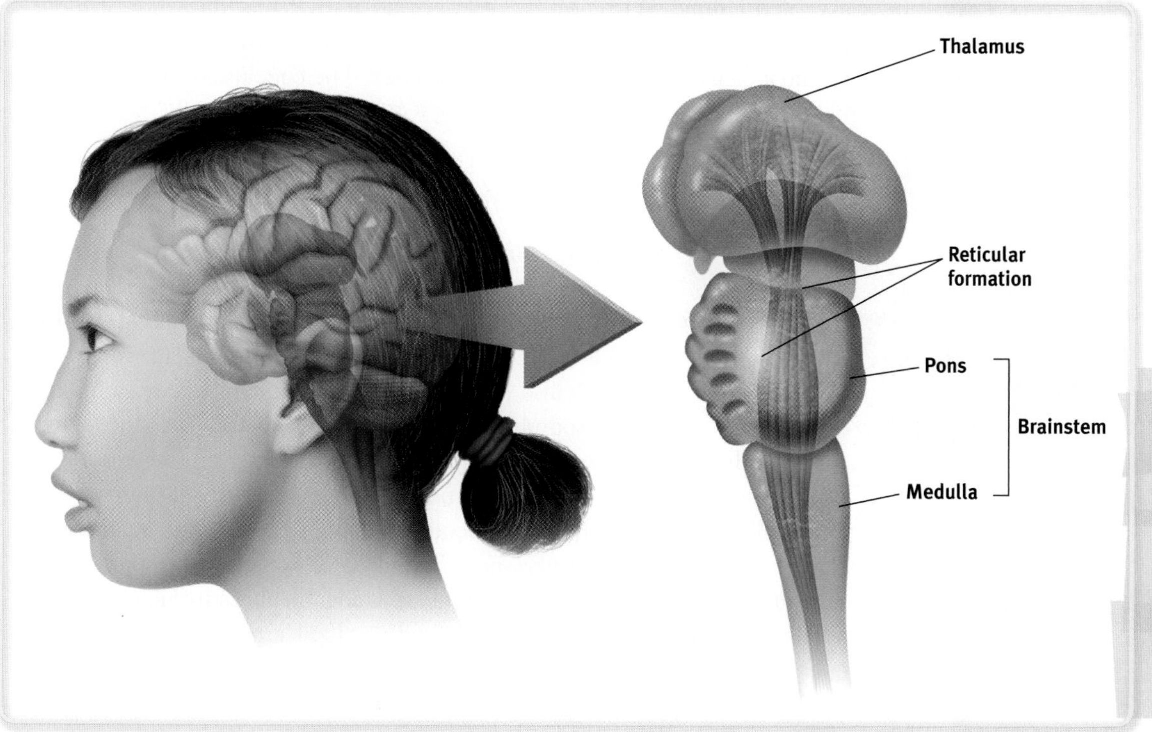

FIGURE 5.4
The brainstem and thalamus The brainstem, including the pons and medulla, is an extension of the spinal cord. The thalamus is attached to the top of the brainstem. The reticular formation passes through both structures.

Just above the medulla sits the *pons*, which helps coordinate movements. If a cat's brainstem is severed from the rest of the brain above it, the animal will still breathe and live—and even run, climb, and groom (Klemm, 1990). But cut off from the brain's higher regions, it won't purposefully run or climb to get food.

RETRIEVAL PRACTICE

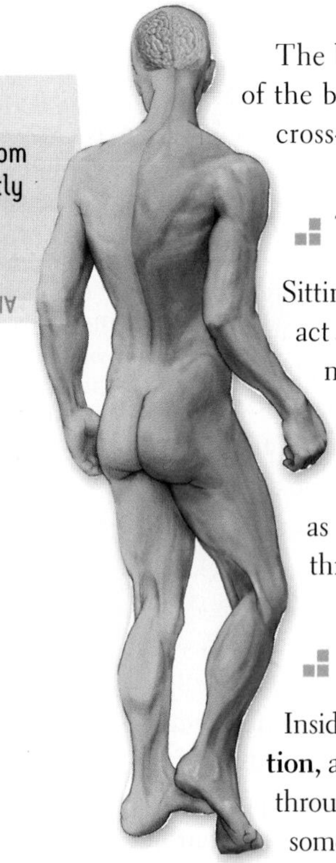

FIGURE 5.5
The body's wiring Nerves from the left side of the brain are mostly linked to the __________ side of the body, and vice versa.

ANSWER: right

The brainstem is a crossover point, where most nerves to and from each side of the brain connect with the body's opposite side (**FIGURE 5.5**). This peculiar cross-wiring is but one of the brain's many surprises.

The Thalamus

Sitting atop the brainstem is the **thalamus,** a pair of egg-shaped structures that act as the brain's sensory switchboard (Figure 5.4). The thalamus receives information from all the senses except smell and routes it to the higher brain regions that deal with seeing, hearing, tasting, and touching. The thalamus also receives some of the higher brain's replies, which it then directs to the medulla and to the cerebellum (see below). Think of the thalamus as being to sensory information what London is to England's trains: a hub through which traffic passes en route to various destinations.

The Reticular Formation

Inside the brainstem, between your ears, lies the **reticular** ("net-like") **formation,** a finger-shaped network of neurons that extends from the spinal cord right up through the thalamus. As the spinal cord's sensory input flows up to the thalamus, some of it travels through the reticular formation, which filters incoming stimuli and relays important information to other brain areas.

In 1949, Giuseppe Moruzzi and Horace Magoun discovered that electrically stimulating the reticular formation of a sleeping cat almost instantly produced an awake, alert animal. When Magoun *severed* a cat's reticular formation without damaging the nearby sensory pathways, the effect was equally dramatic: The cat lapsed into a coma from which it never awakened. The conclusion? The reticular formation enables arousal.

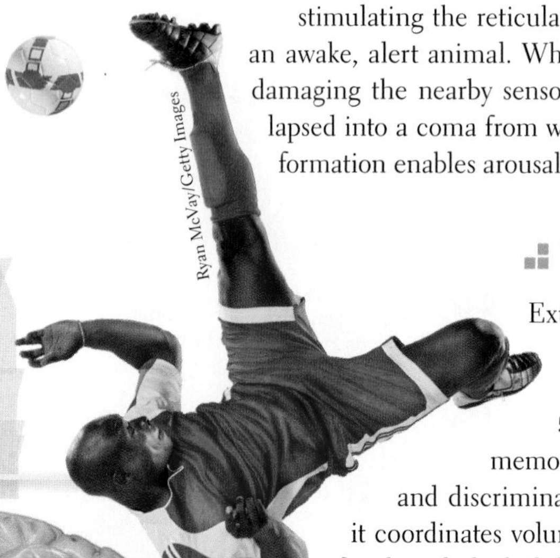

Ryan McVay/Getty Images

The Cerebellum

Extending from the rear of the brainstem is the baseball-sized **cerebellum,** meaning "little brain," which is what its two wrinkled halves resemble (**FIGURE 5.6**). The cerebellum enables nonverbal learning and memory. It also helps us judge time, modulate our emotions, and discriminate sounds and textures (Bower & Parsons, 2003). And it coordinates voluntary movement. When a soccer player executes a perfect bicycle kick (left), give his cerebellum some credit. If you injured your cerebellum, you would have difficulty walking, keeping your balance, or shaking hands. Your movements would be jerky and exaggerated. Gone would be any dreams of being a dancer or guitarist. Under alcohol's influence on the cerebellum, coordination suffers, as many a driver has learned after being pulled over and given a roadside test.

* * *

Note: These older brain functions all occur without any conscious effort. This illustrates another of our recurring themes: *Our brain processes most information outside of our awareness.* We are aware of the *results* of our brain's labor (say, our current visual experience) but not of *how* we construct the visual image. Likewise, whether we are asleep or awake, our brainstem manages its life-sustaining functions, freeing our newer brain regions to think, talk, dream, or savor a memory.

FIGURE 5.6
The brain's organ of agility Hanging at the back of the brain, the cerebellum coordinates our voluntary movements.

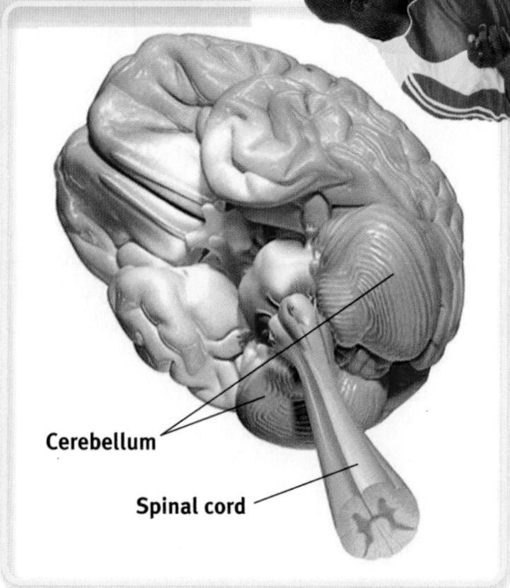

RETRIEVAL PRACTICE

- In what brain region would damage be most likely to (1) disrupt your ability to skip rope? (2) disrupt your ability to hear and taste? (3) perhaps leave you in a coma? (4) cut off the very breath and heartbeat of life?

ANSWERS: 1. cerebellum, 2. thalamus, 3. reticular formation, 4. medulla

thalamus [THAL-uh-muss] the brain's sensory switchboard, located on top of the brainstem; it directs messages to the sensory receiving areas in the cortex and transmits replies to the cerebellum and medulla.

reticular formation a nerve network that travels through the brainstem and plays an important role in controlling arousal.

cerebellum [sehr-uh-BELL-um] the "little brain" at the rear of the brainstem; functions include processing sensory input and coordinating movement output and balance.

The Limbic System

5-3 What are the limbic system's structures and functions?

Between the oldest and newest brain areas lies the **limbic system** (*limbus* means "border"). This system contains the *amygdala*, the *hypothalamus*, and the *hippocampus* (**FIGURE 5.7**). The hippocampus processes conscious memories. Animals or humans who lose their hippocampus to surgery or injury also lose their ability to form new memories of facts and events. Other modules explain how our two-track mind processes our memories. For now, let's look at the limbic system's links to emotions such as fear and anger, and to basic motives such as those for food and sex.

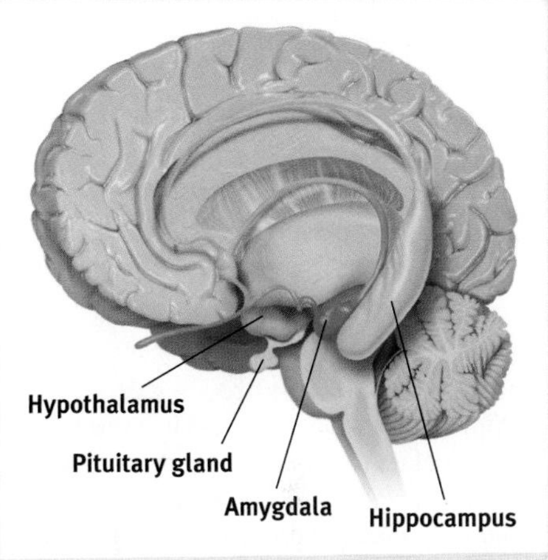

FIGURE 5.7
The limbic system This neural system sits between the brain's older parts and its cerebral hemispheres. The limbic system's hypothalamus controls the nearby pituitary gland.

The Amygdala

Research has linked the **amygdala,** two lima-bean-sized neural clusters, to aggression and fear. In 1939, psychologist Heinrich Klüver and neurosurgeon Paul Bucy surgically removed a rhesus monkey's amygdala, turning the normally ill-tempered animal into the most mellow of creatures. In studies with other wild animals, including the lynx, wolverine, and wild rat, researchers noted the same effect.

What then might happen if we electrically stimulated the amygdala of a normally placid domestic animal, such as a cat? Do so in one spot and the cat prepares to attack, hissing with its back arched, its pupils dilated, its hair on end. Move the electrode only slightly within the amygdala, cage the cat with a small mouse, and now it cowers in terror.

These and other experiments have confirmed the amygdala's role in rage and fear, including the perception of these emotions and the processing of emotional memories (Anderson & Phelps, 2000; Poremba & Gabriel, 2001). But we must be careful. The brain is not neatly organized into structures that correspond to our behavior categories. When we feel or act in aggressive or fearful ways, there is neural activity in many levels of our brain. Even within the limbic system, stimulating structures other than the amygdala can evoke aggression or fear. If you charge a car's dead battery, you can activate the engine. Yet the battery is merely one link in an integrated system.

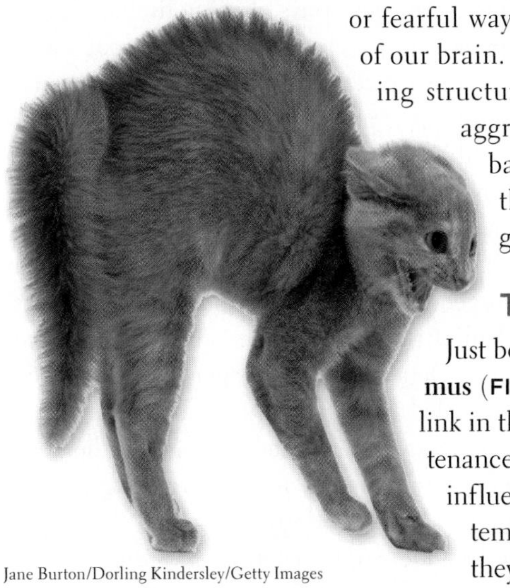

Jane Burton/Dorling Kindersley/Getty Images

The Hypothalamus

Just below (*hypo*) the thalamus is the **hypothalamus** (**FIGURE 5.8** on the next page), an important link in the command chain governing bodily maintenance. Some neural clusters in the hypothalamus influence hunger; others regulate thirst, body temperature, and sexual behavior. Together, they help maintain a steady internal state.

limbic system neural system (including the *hippocampus, amygdala,* and *hypothalamus*) located below the cerebral hemispheres; associated with emotions and drives.

amygdala [uh-MIG-duh-la] two lima-bean-sized neural clusters in the limbic system; linked to emotion.

hypothalamus [hi-po-THAL-uh-muss] a neural structure lying below (*hypo*) the thalamus; it directs several maintenance activities (eating, drinking, body temperature), helps govern the endocrine system via the pituitary gland, and is linked to emotion and reward.

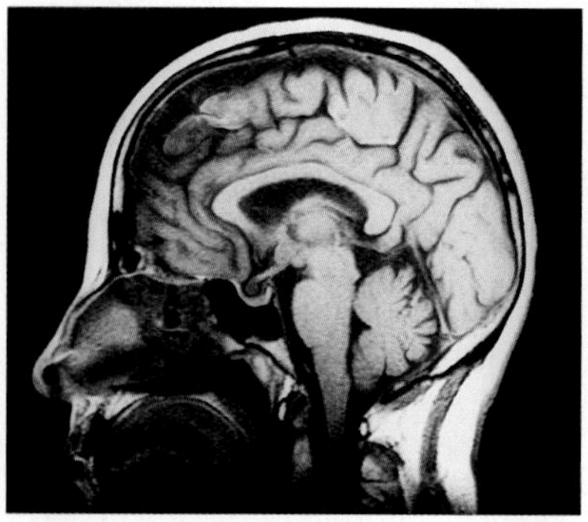

ISM/Phototake

FIGURE 5.8
The hypothalamus This small but important structure, colored yellow/orange in this MRI scan photograph, helps keep the body's internal environment in a steady state.

As the hypothalamus monitors the state of your body, it tunes into your blood chemistry and any incoming orders from other brain parts. For example, picking up signals from your brain's cerebral cortex that you are thinking about sex, your hypothalamus will secrete hormones. These hormones will in turn trigger the adjacent "master gland," your pituitary (see Figure 5.7), to influence your sex glands to release their hormones. These will intensify the thoughts of sex in your cerebral cortex. (Note the interplay between the nervous and endocrine systems: The brain influences the endocrine system, which in turn influences the brain.)

A remarkable discovery about the hypothalamus illustrates how progress in science often occurs—when curious, open-minded investigators make an unexpected observation. Two young McGill University neuropsychologists, James Olds and Peter Milner (1954), were trying to implant an electrode in a rat's reticular formation when they made a magnificent mistake: They placed the electrode incorrectly (Olds, 1975). Curiously, as if seeking more stimulation, the rat kept returning to the location where it had been stimulated by this misplaced electrode. On discovering that they had actually placed the device in a region of the hypothalamus, Olds and Milner realized they had stumbled upon a brain center that provides pleasurable rewards (Olds, 1975).

In a meticulous series of experiments, Olds (1958) went on to locate other "pleasure centers," as he called them. (What the rats actually experience only they know, and they aren't telling. Rather than attribute human feelings to rats, today's scientists refer to *reward centers*, not "pleasure centers.") When allowed to press pedals to trigger their own stimulation in these areas, rats would sometimes do so at a feverish pace—up to 7000 times per hour—until they dropped from exhaustion. Moreover, to get this stimulation, they would even cross an electrified floor that a starving rat would not cross to reach food (**FIGURE 5.9**).

FIGURE 5.9
Rat with an implanted electrode With an electrode implanted in a reward center of its hypothalamus, the rat readily crosses an electrified grid, accepting the painful shocks, to press a pedal that sends electrical impulses to that center.

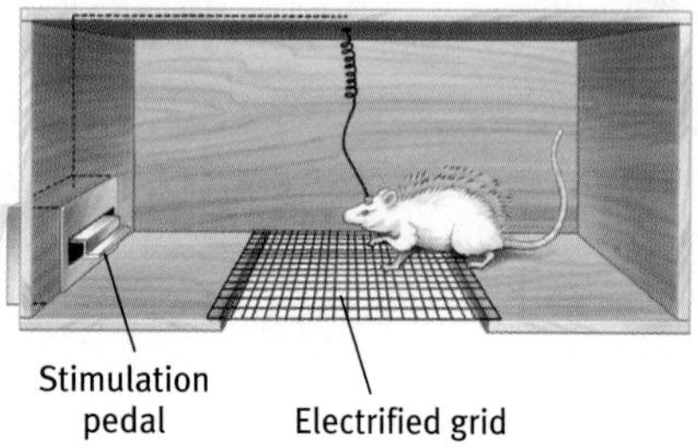

Other limbic system reward centers, such as the *nucleus accumbens* in front of the hypothalamus, were later discovered in many other species, including dolphins and monkeys. In fact, animal research has revealed both a general dopamine-related reward system and specific centers associated with the pleasures of eating, drinking, and sex. Animals, it seems, come equipped with built-in systems that reward activities essential to survival.

"If you were designing a robot vehicle to walk into the future and survive, . . . you'd wire it up so that behavior that ensured the survival of the self or the species—like sex and eating—would be naturally reinforcing."

Candace Pert (1986)

Contemporary researchers are experimenting with new ways of using limbic stimulation to control animals' actions in future applications, such as search-and-rescue operations. By rewarding rats for turning left or right, one research team trained previously caged rats to navigate natural environments (Talwar et al., 2002; **FIGURE 5.10**). By pressing buttons on a laptop, the researchers were then able to direct the rat—which carried a receiver, power source, and video camera on a backpack—to turn on cue, climb trees, scurry along branches, and turn around and come back down.

American Images Inc/Getty Images

Do humans have limbic centers for pleasure? Indeed we do. To calm violent patients, one neurosurgeon implanted electrodes in such areas. Stimulated patients reported mild pleasure; unlike Olds' rats, however, they were not driven to a frenzy (Deutsch, 1972; Hooper & Teresi, 1986).

Experiments have also revealed the effects of a dopamine-related reward system in people. One research team had people rate the desirability of different vacation destinations. Then, after receiving either a dopamine-increasing drug or a sugar pill, they imagined themselves vacationing at half the locations. A day later, when presented with pairs of vacation spots they had initially rated equally, only the dopamine takers preferred the places they had imagined under dopamine's influence (Sharot et al., 2009). The participants, it seems, associated the imagined experiences with dopamine-induced pleasant feelings.

Some researchers believe that addictive disorders, such as alcohol dependence, drug abuse, and binge eating, may stem from malfunctions in natural brain systems for pleasure and well-being. People genetically predisposed to this *reward deficiency syndrome* may crave whatever provides that missing pleasure or relieves negative feelings (Blum et al., 1996).

Sanjiv Talwar, SUNY Downstate

FIGURE 5.10 Ratbot on a pleasure cruise When stimulated by remote control, this rat could be guided to navigate across a field and even up a tree.

* * *

FIGURE 5.11 locates the brain areas we've discussed in this module.

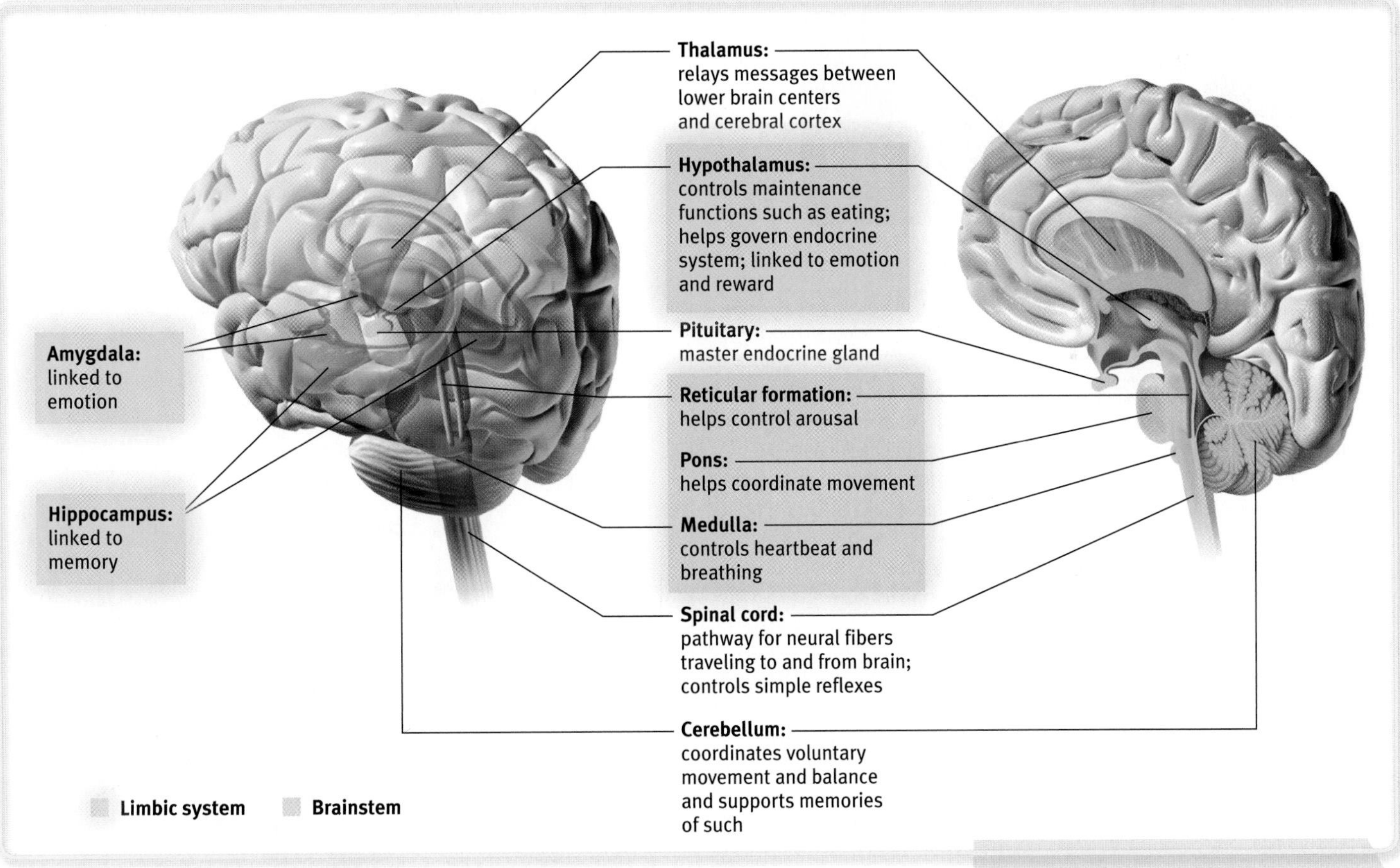

FIGURE 5.11 Review: Brain structures and their functions

RETRIEVAL PRACTICE

- What are the three key structures of the limbic system, and what functions do they serve?

ANSWER: (1) The *amygdala* is involved in aggression and fear responses. (2) The *hypothalamus* is involved in bodily maintenance, pleasurable rewards, and control of the hormonal systems. (3) The *hippocampus* processes memory.

MODULE REVIEW

Tools of Discovery and Older Brain Structures

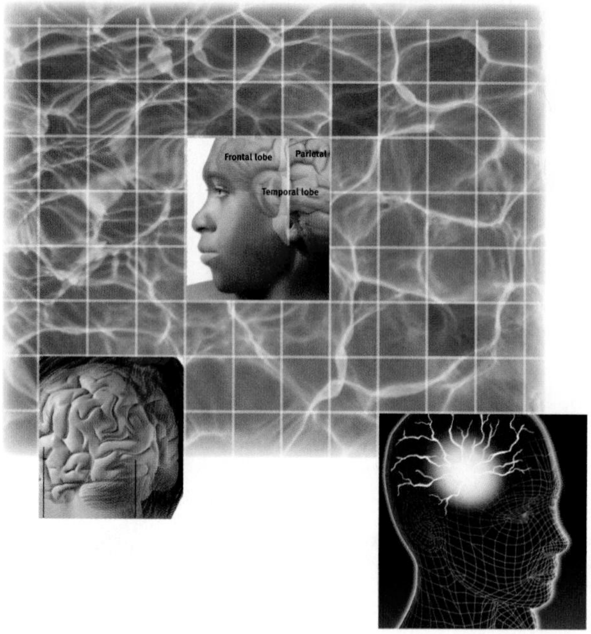

Learning Objectives

RETRIEVAL PRACTICE Take a moment to answer each of these Learning Objective Questions (repeated here from within the module). Then turn to Appendix B, Complete Module Reviews, to check your answers. Research suggests that trying to answer these questions on your own will improve your long-term retention (McDaniel et al., 2009).

5-1: How do neuroscientists study the brain's connections to behavior and mind?

5-2: What structures make up the brainstem, and what are the functions of the brainstem, thalamus, and cerebellum?

5-3: What are the limbic system's structures and functions?

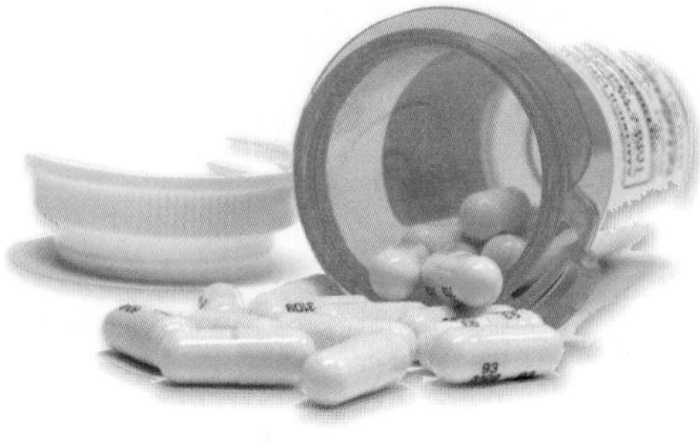

Terms and Concepts to Remember

RETRIEVAL PRACTICE Test yourself on these terms by trying to write down the definition before flipping back to the referenced page to check your answer.

lesion [LEE-zhuhn], p. 60
electroencephalogram (EEG), p. 61
PET (positron emission tomography) scan, p. 61
MRI (magnetic resonance imaging), p. 61
fMRI (functional MRI), p. 62
brainstem, p. 63
medulla [muh-DUL-uh], p. 63
thalamus [THAL-uh-muss], p. 64
reticular formation, p. 64
cerebellum [sehr-uh-BELL-um], p. 64
limbic system, p. 65
amygdala [uh-MIG-duh-la], p. 65
hypothalamus [hi-po-THAL-uh-muss], p. 65

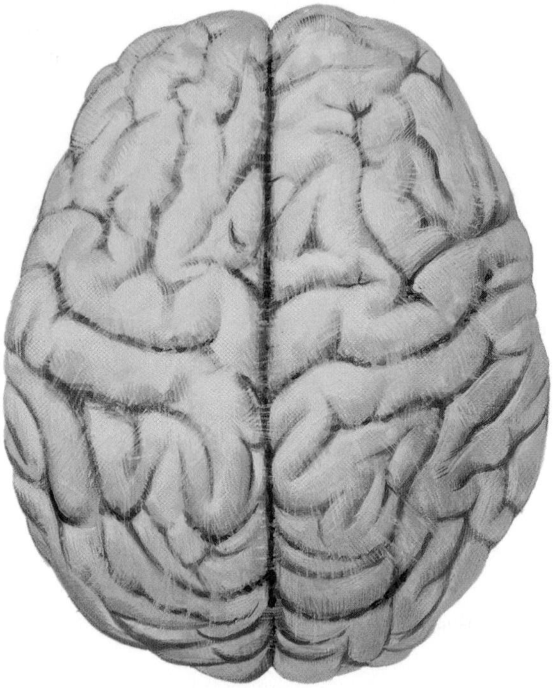

RETRIEVAL PRACTICE Gain an advantage, and benefit from immediate feedback, with the interactive self-testing resources at www.worthpublishers.com/myers.

MODULE 6

The Cerebral Cortex and Our Divided Brain

- The Cerebral Cortex
- Our Divided Brain
- Right-Left Differences in the Intact Brain

The Cerebral Cortex

6-1 What are the functions of the various cerebral cortex regions?

Older brain networks sustain basic life functions and enable memory, emotions, and basic drives. Newer neural networks within the *cerebrum*—the hemispheres that contribute 85 percent of the brain's weight—form specialized work teams that enable our perceiving, thinking, and speaking. Like other structures above the brainstem (including the thalamus, hippocampus, and amygdala), the cerebral hemispheres come as a pair. Covering those hemispheres, like bark on a tree, is the **cerebral cortex,** a thin surface layer of interconnected neural cells. It is your brain's thinking crown, your body's ultimate control and information-processing center.

As we move up the ladder of animal life, the cerebral cortex expands, tight genetic controls relax, and the organism's adaptability increases. Frogs and other small-cortex amphibians operate extensively on preprogrammed genetic instructions. The larger cortex of mammals offers increased capacities for learning and thinking, enabling them to be more adaptable. What makes us distinctively human mostly arises from the complex functions of our cerebral cortex.

The people who first dissected and labeled the brain used the language of scholars—Latin and Greek. Their words are actually attempts at graphic description: For example, *cortex* means "bark," *cerebellum* is "little brain," and *thalamus* is "inner chamber."

RETRIEVAL PRACTICE

- Which part of the human brain distinguishes us most from less complex animals?

ANSWER: The cerebral cortex

Structure of the Cortex

If you opened a human skull, exposing the brain, you would see a wrinkled organ, shaped somewhat like the meat of an oversized walnut. Without these wrinkles, a flattened cerebral cortex would require triple the area—roughly that of a large pizza. The brain's ballooning left and right hemispheres are filled mainly with axons connecting the cortex to the brain's other regions. The cerebral cortex—that thin surface layer—contains some 20 to 23 billion nerve cells and 300 trillion synaptic connections (de Courten-Myers, 2005). Being human takes a lot of nerve.

Supporting these billions of nerve cells are nine times as many spidery **glial cells** ("glue cells"). Neurons are like queen bees; on their own they cannot feed or sheathe themselves. Glial cells are worker bees. They provide nutrients and insulating myelin, guide neural connections, and mop up ions and neurotransmitters. Glia may also play a role in learning and thinking. By "chatting" with neurons they may participate in information transmission and memory (Fields, 2009; Miller, 2005).

In more complex animal brains, the proportion of glia to neurons increases. A postmortem analysis of Einstein's brain did not find more or larger-than-usual neurons, but it did reveal a much greater concentration of glial cells than found in an average Albert's head (Fields, 2004).

Each hemisphere's cortex is subdivided into four *lobes*, separated by prominent *fissures*, or folds (**FIGURE 6.1** on the next page). Starting at the front of your brain and moving over the top, there are the **frontal lobes** (behind your forehead), the **parietal lobes** (at the top and to the rear), and the **occipital lobes** (at the back of your head). Reversing direction and moving forward, just above your ears, you find the **temporal lobes.** Each of the four lobes carries out many functions, and many functions require the interplay of several lobes.

cerebral [seh-REE-bruhl] **cortex** the intricate fabric of interconnected neural cells covering the cerebral hemispheres; the body's ultimate control and information-processing center.

glial cells (glia) cells in the nervous system that support, nourish, and protect neurons; they may also play a role in learning and thinking.

frontal lobes portion of the cerebral cortex lying just behind the forehead; involved in speaking and muscle movements and in making plans and judgments.

parietal [puh-RYE-uh-tuhl] **lobes** portion of the cerebral cortex lying at the top of the head and toward the rear; receives sensory input for touch and body position.

occipital [ahk-SIP-uh-tuhl] **lobes** portion of the cerebral cortex lying at the back of the head; includes areas that receive information from the visual fields.

temporal lobes portion of the cerebral cortex lying roughly above the ears; includes the auditory areas, each receiving information primarily from the opposite ear.

FIGURE 6.1
The cortex and its basic subdivisions

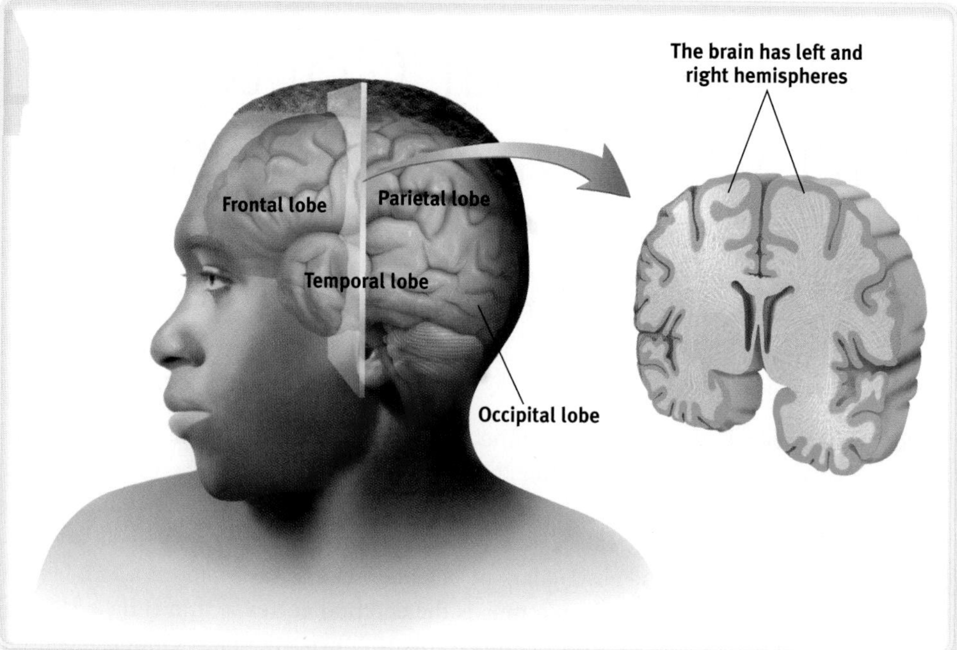

Functions of the Cortex

More than a century ago, surgeons found damaged cortical areas during autopsies of people who had been partially paralyzed or speechless. This rather crude evidence did not prove that specific parts of the cortex control complex functions like movement or speech. After all, if the entire cortex controlled speech and movement, damage to almost any area might produce the same effect. A TV with its power cord cut would go dead, but we would be fooling ourselves if we thought we had "localized" the picture in the cord.

Motor Functions

Scientists had better luck in localizing simpler brain functions. For example, in 1870, German physicians Gustav Fritsch and Eduard Hitzig made an important discovery: Mild electrical stimulation to parts of an animal's cortex made parts of its body move. The effects were selective: Stimulation caused movement only when applied to an arch-shaped region at the back of the frontal lobe, running roughly ear-to-ear across the top of the brain. Moreover, stimulating parts of this region in the left or right hemisphere caused movements of specific body parts on the *opposite* side of the body. Fritsch and Hitzig had discovered what is now called the **motor cortex.**

Mapping the Motor Cortex Lucky for brain surgeons and their patients, the brain has no sensory receptors. Knowing this, Otfrid Foerster and Wilder Penfield were able to map the motor cortex in hundreds of wide-awake patients by stimulating different cortical areas and observing the body's responses. They discovered that body areas requiring precise control, such as the fingers and mouth, occupy the greatest amount of cortical space (**FIGURE 6.2**).

In one of his many demonstrations of motor behavior mechanics, Spanish neuroscientist José Delgado stimulated a spot on a patient's left motor cortex, triggering the right hand to make a fist. Asked to keep the fingers open during the next stimulation, the patient, whose fingers closed despite his best efforts, remarked, "I guess, Doctor, that your electricity is stronger than my will" (Delgado, 1969, p. 114).

More recently, scientists were able to predict a monkey's arm motion a tenth of a second *before* it moved—by repeatedly measuring motor cortex activity preceding specific arm movements (Gibbs, 1996). Such findings have opened the door to research on brain-controlled computers.

RETRIEVAL PRACTICE

- Try moving your right hand in a circular motion, as if polishing a table. Then start your right foot doing the same motion, synchronized with your hand. Now reverse the right foot's motion, but not the hand's. Finally, try moving the *left* foot opposite to the right hand.

1. Why is reversing the right foot's motion so hard?
2. Why is it easier to move the left foot opposite to the right hand?

ANSWERS: 1. The right limbs' opposed activities interfere with each other because both are controlled by the same (left) side of your brain. 2. Opposite sides of your brain control your left and right limbs, so the reversed motion causes less interference.

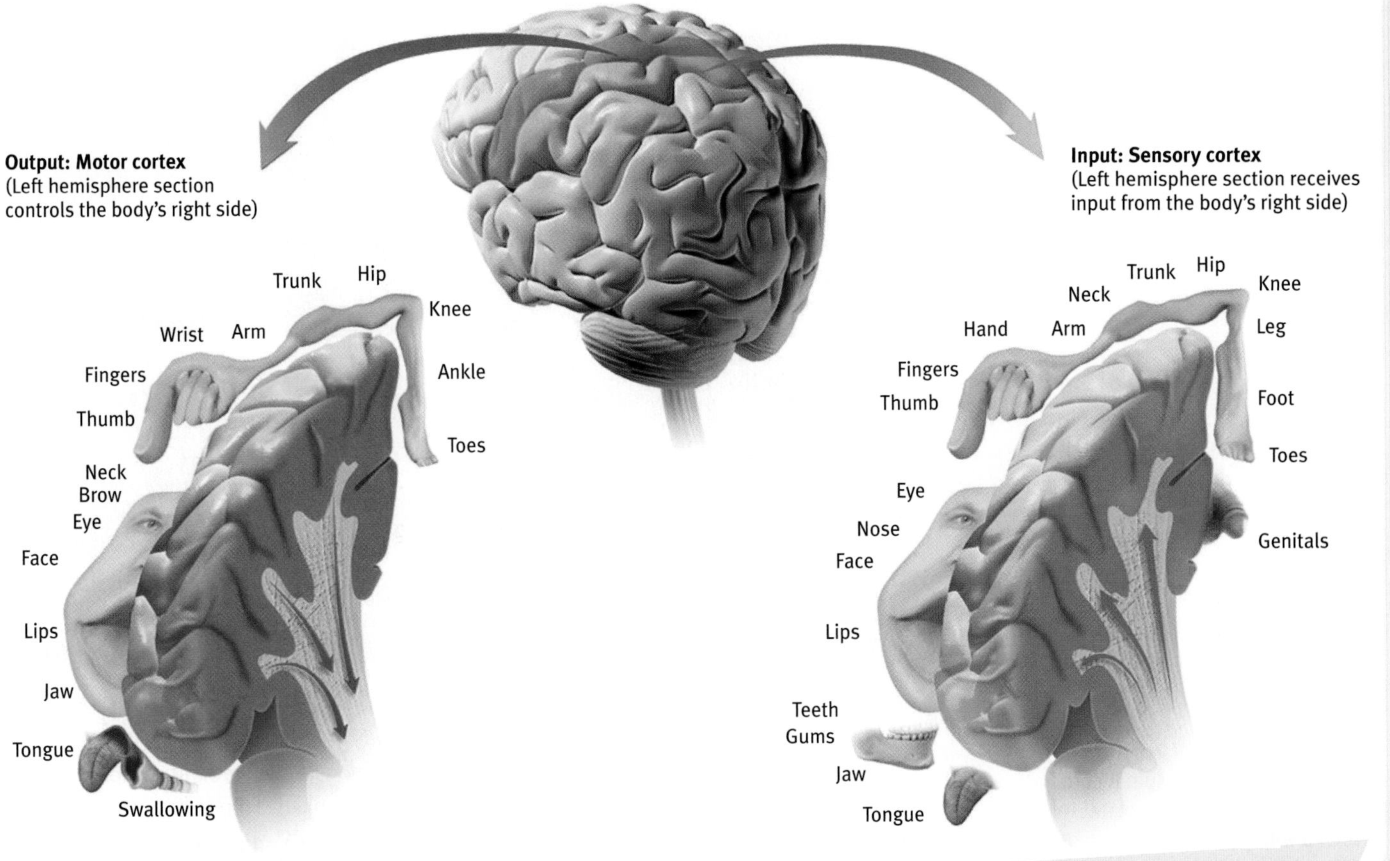

FIGURE 6.2

Left hemisphere tissue devoted to each body part in the motor cortex and the sensory cortex As you can see from this classic though inexact representation, the amount of cortex devoted to a body part is not proportional to that part's size. Rather, the brain devotes more tissue to sensitive areas and to areas requiring precise control. Thus, the fingers have a greater representation in the cortex than does the upper arm.

Brain-Computer Interfaces By eavesdropping on the brain, could we enable someone—perhaps a paralyzed person—to move a robotic limb? Could a *brain-computer interface* command a cursor to write an e-mail or search the Internet? To find out, Brown University brain researchers implanted 100 tiny recording electrodes in the motor cortexes of three monkeys (Nicolelis & Chapin, 2002; Serruya et al., 2002). As the monkeys used a joystick to move a cursor to follow a moving red target (to gain rewards), the researchers matched the brain signals with the arm movements. Then they programmed a computer to monitor the signals and operate the joystick. When a monkey merely thought about a move, the mind-reading computer moved the cursor with nearly the same proficiency as had the reward-seeking monkey. In a follow-up experiment (**FIGURE 6.3** on the next page), two monkeys were trained to control a robot arm that could grasp and deliver food (Velliste et al., 2008).

Research has also recorded messages not from the arm-controlling motor neurons, but from a brain area involved in planning and intention (Leuthardt et al., 2009; Musallam et al., 2004). In one study, a monkey seeking a juice reward awaited a cue telling it to reach toward a spot flashed on a screen in one of up to eight locations. A computer program captured the monkey's thinking by recording activity in its planning-intention brain area. By matching this neural activity to the monkey's subsequent pointing, the mind-reading researchers could program a cursor to move in response to the monkey's thoughts. Monkey think, computer do.

If this technique works, why not use it to capture the words a person can think but cannot say (for example, after a stroke)? Cal Tech neuroscientist Richard Andersen (2004, 2005) has speculated that researchers could implant electrodes in speech areas, then "ask a patient to think of different words and observe how the cells fire in different ways. So you build up your database, and then when the patient thinks of the word, you compare the signals with your database, and you can predict the words they're thinking. Then you take this output and connect it to a speech synthesizer. This would be identical to what we're doing for motor control."

motor cortex an area at the rear of the frontal lobes that controls voluntary movements.

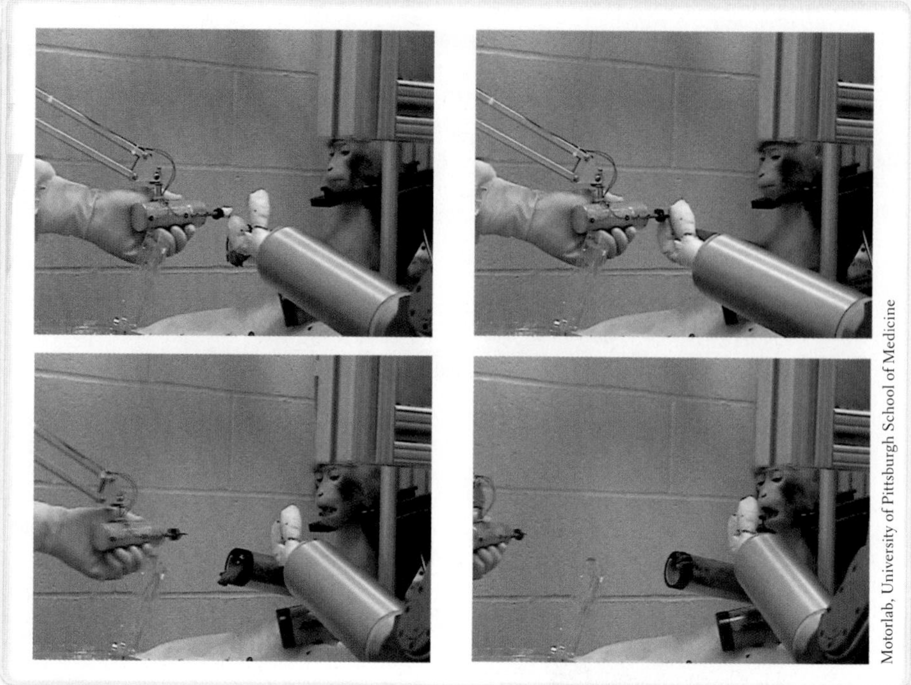

FIGURE 6.3
Mind over matter Guided by a tiny, 100-electrode brain implant, monkeys have learned to control a mechanical hand that can grab snacks and put them in their mouth (Velliste et al., 2008). Although not yet permanently effective, such implants raise hopes that people with paralyzed limbs may someday be able to use their own brain signals to control computers and robotic limbs.

Clinical trials of such *cognitive neural prosthetics* are now under way with people who have suffered paralysis or amputation (Andersen et al., 2010; Nurmikko et al., 2010). The first patient, a paralyzed 25-year-old man, was able to mentally control a TV, draw shapes on a computer screen, and play video games—all thanks to an aspirin-sized chip with 100 microelectrodes recording activity in his motor cortex (Hochberg et al., 2006). If everything psychological is also biological—if, for example, every thought is also a neural event—then microelectrodes perhaps could detect thoughts well enough to enable people to control events suggested by **FIGURE 6.4**.

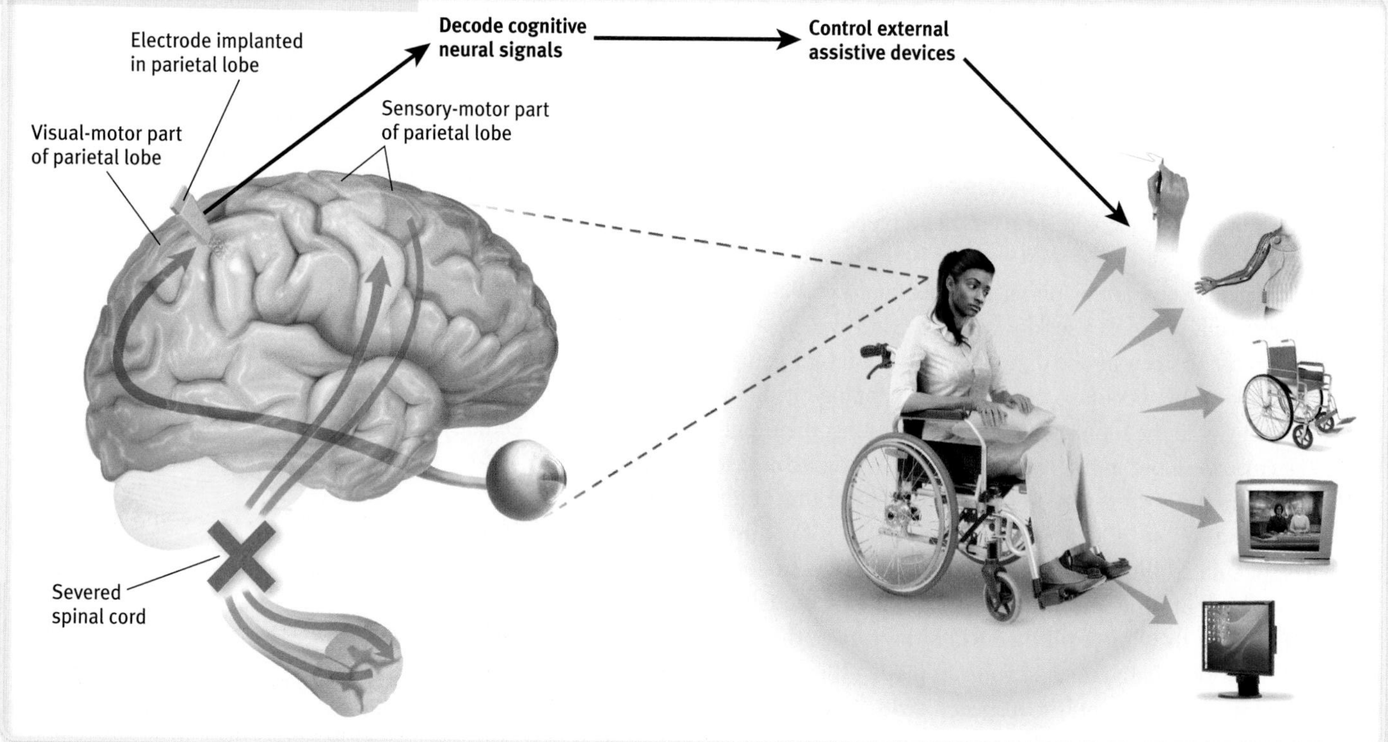

FIGURE 6.4
Brain-computer interaction A patient with a severed spinal cord has electrodes planted in a parietal lobe region involved with planning to reach one's arm. The resulting signal can enable the patient to move a robotic limb, stimulate muscles that activate a paralyzed limb, navigate a wheelchair, control a TV, and use the Internet. (Graphic adapted from Andersen et al., 2010.)

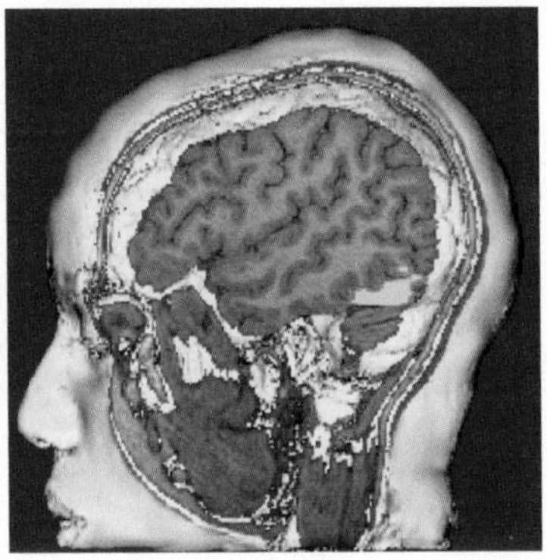

Courtesy of V. P. Clark, K. Keill, J. Ma. Maisog, S. Courtney, L. G. Ungerleider, and J. V. Haxby, National Institute of Mental Health

FIGURE 6.5
The brain in action This fMRI (functional MRI) scan shows the visual cortex in the occipital lobes activated (color represents increased bloodflow) as a research participant looks at a photo. When the person stops looking, the region instantly calms down.

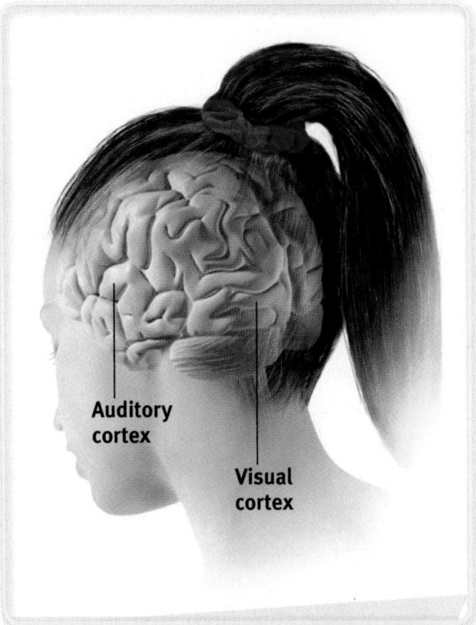

FIGURE 6.6
The visual cortex and auditory cortex The visual cortex of the occipital lobes at the rear of your brain receives input from your eyes. The auditory cortex, in your temporal lobes—above your ears—receives information from your ears.

Sensory Functions

If the motor cortex sends messages out to the body, where does the cortex receive the incoming messages? Penfield also identified the cortical area that specializes in receiving information from the skin senses and from the movement of body parts. This area at the front of the parietal lobes, parallel to and just behind the motor cortex, we now call the **sensory cortex** (Figure 6.2). Stimulate a point on the top of this band of tissue and a person may report being touched on the shoulder; stimulate some point on the side and the person may feel something on the face.

The more sensitive the body region, the larger the sensory cortex area devoted to it (Figure 6.2). Your supersensitive lips project to a larger brain area than do your toes, which is one reason we kiss with our lips rather than touch toes. Rats have a large area of the brain devoted to their whisker sensations, and owls to their hearing sensations.

Scientists have identified additional areas where the cortex receives input from senses other than touch. At this moment, you are receiving visual information in the visual cortex in your occipital lobes, at the very back of your brain (**FIGURES 6.5** and **6.6**). A bad enough bash there would make you blind. Stimulated there, you might see flashes of light or dashes of color. (In a sense, we *do* have eyes in the back of our head!) From your occipital lobes, visual information goes to other areas that specialize in tasks such as identifying words, detecting emotions, and recognizing faces.

Any sound you now hear is processed by your auditory cortex in your temporal lobes (just above your ears; see Figure 6.6). Most of this auditory information travels a circuitous route from one ear to the auditory receiving area above your opposite ear. If stimulated there, you might hear a sound. MRI scans of people with schizophrenia reveal active auditory areas in the temporal lobes during auditory hallucinations (Lennox et al., 1999). Even the phantom ringing sound experienced by people with hearing loss is—if heard in one ear—associated with activity in the temporal lobe on the brain's opposite side (Muhlnickel, 1998).

RETRIEVAL PRACTICE

- Our brain's __________ cortex registers and processes bodily input. The __________ cortex controls our voluntary movements.

ANSWERS: sensory, motor

Association Areas

So far, we have pointed out small cortical areas that either receive sensory input or direct muscular output. Together, these occupy about one-fourth of the human brain's thin, wrinkled cover. What, then, goes on in the vast regions of the cortex? In these **association areas** (the peach-colored areas in **FIGURE 6.7** on the next page), neurons are busy with higher mental functions—many of the tasks that make us human.

Electrically probing an association area won't trigger any observable response. So, unlike the sensory and motor areas, association area functions cannot be neatly mapped. Their silence has led to what Donald McBurney (1996, p. 44) has called "one of the hardiest weeds in the garden of psychology": the claim that we ordinarily use only 10 percent of our brains. (If

sensory cortex area at the front of the parietal lobes that registers and processes body touch and movement sensations.

association areas areas of the cerebral cortex that are not involved in primary motor or sensory functions; rather, they are involved in higher mental functions such as learning, remembering, thinking, and speaking.

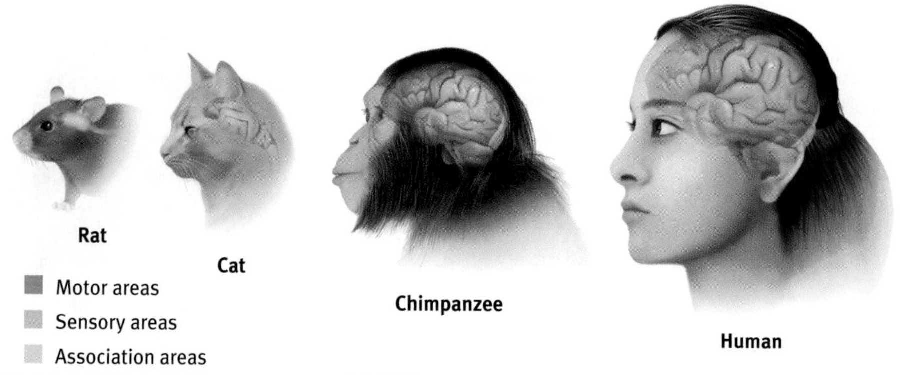

FIGURE 6.7
Areas of the cortex in four mammals More intelligent animals have increased "uncommitted" or association areas of the cortex. These vast areas of the brain are responsible for integrating and acting on information received and processed by sensory areas.

true, wouldn't this imply a 90 percent chance that a bullet to your brain would land in an unused area?) Surgically lesioned animals and brain-damaged humans bear witness that association areas are not dormant. Rather, these areas interpret, integrate, and act on sensory information and link it with stored memories—a very important part of thinking.

Association areas are found in all four lobes. In the frontal lobes, they enable judgment, planning, and processing of new memories. People with damaged frontal lobes may have intact memories, high scores on intelligence tests, and great cake-baking skills. Yet they would not be able to plan ahead to *begin* baking a cake for a birthday party (Huey et al., 2006).

Frontal lobe damage also can alter personality and remove a person's inhibitions. Consider the classic case of railroad worker Phineas Gage. One afternoon in 1848, Gage, then 25 years old, was packing gunpowder into a rock with a tamping iron. A spark ignited the gunpowder, shooting the rod up through his left cheek and out the top of his skull, leaving his frontal lobes massively damaged (**FIGURE 6.8**). To everyone's amazement, he was immediately able to sit up and speak, and after the wound healed he returned to work. But the affable, soft-spoken man was now irritable, profane, and dishonest. This person, said his friends, was "no longer Gage." Although his mental abilities and memories were intact, his personality was not. (Although Gage lost his job, he did, over time, adapt to his injury and find work as a stagecoach driver [Macmillan & Lena, 2010].)

More recent studies of people with damaged frontal lobes have revealed similar impairments. Not only may they become less inhibited (without the frontal lobe brakes on their impulses), but their moral judgments seem unrestrained by normal emotions. Would you advocate pushing someone in front of a runaway boxcar to save five others? Most people do not, but those with damage to a brain area behind the eyes often do (Koenigs et al., 2007). With their frontal lobes ruptured, people's moral compass seems to disconnect from their behavior.

Association areas also perform other mental functions. In the parietal lobes, parts of which were large and unusually shaped in Einstein's normal-weight brain, they enable mathematical and spatial reasoning (Witelson et al., 1999). In patients undergoing brain surgery, stimulation of one parietal lobe area produced a feeling of wanting to move an upper limb, the lips, or the tongue (but without any actual movement). With increased stimulation, patients falsely believed they actually had moved. Curiously, when surgeons stimulated a different association area near the motor cortex in the frontal lobes, the patients did move but had no awareness of doing so (Desmurget et al., 2009). These head-scratching findings suggest that our perception of moving flows not from the movement itself, but rather from our intention and the results we expected.

Yet another association area, on the underside of the right temporal lobe, enables us to recognize faces. If a stroke or head injury destroyed this area of your brain, you would still be able to describe facial features and to recognize someone's gender and approximate age, yet be strangely unable to identify the person as, say, Lady Gaga, or even your grandmother.

FIGURE 6.8
Phineas Gage reconsidered (a) Gage's skull was kept as a medical record. Using measurements and modern neuroimaging techniques, researchers have reconstructed the probable path of the rod through Gage's brain (Damasio et al., 1994). (b) This recently discovered photo shows Gage after his accident. The image has been reversed to show the features correctly. (Early photos, such as this one, are actually mirror images.)

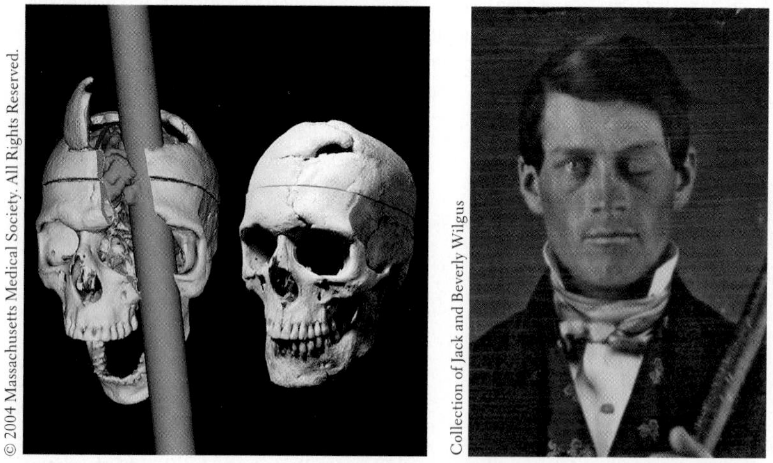

© 2004 Massachusetts Medical Society. All Rights Reserved.
Collection of Jack and Beverly Wilgus

(a) (b)

Nevertheless, we should be wary of using pictures of brain "hot spots" to create a new phrenology that locates complex functions in precise brain areas (Uttal, 2001). Complex mental functions don't reside in any one place. There is no one spot in a rat's small association cortex that, when damaged, will obliterate its ability to learn or remember a maze. Memory, language, and attention result from the synchronized activity among distinct brain areas (Knight, 2007). Ditto for religious experience. Reports of more than 40 distinct brain regions becoming active in different religious states, such as praying and meditating, indicate that there is no simple "God spot" (Fingelkurts & Fingelkurts, 2009). The big lesson: *Our mental experiences arise from coordinated brain activity.*

RETRIEVAL PRACTICE

- Why are association areas important?

ANSWER: Association areas are involved in higher mental functions—interpreting, integrating, and acting on information processed in sensory areas.

The Brain's Plasticity

6-2 To what extent can a damaged brain reorganize itself, and what is neurogenesis?

Our brains are sculpted not only by our genes but also by our experiences. MRI scans show that well-practiced pianists have a larger-than-usual auditory cortex area that encodes piano sounds (Bavelier et al., 2000; Pantev et al., 1998). In other modules, we focus more on how experience molds the brain. For now, let's turn to another aspect of the brain's **plasticity:** its ability to modify itself after damage.

Some of the effects of brain damage described earlier can be traced to two hard facts: (1) Severed neurons, unlike cut skin, usually do not regenerate. (If your spinal cord were severed, you would probably be permanently paralyzed.) And (2) some brain functions seem preassigned to specific areas. One newborn who suffered damage to temporal lobe facial recognition areas later remained unable to recognize faces (Farah et al., 2000). But there is good news: Some neural tissue can *reorganize* in response to damage. Under the surface of our awareness, the brain is constantly changing, building new pathways as it adjusts to little mishaps and new experiences.

Plasticity may also occur after serious damage, especially in young children (Kolb, 1989; see also **FIGURE 6.9**). *Constraint-induced therapy* aims to rewire brains and improve the dexterity of a brain-damaged child or even an adult stroke victim (Taub, 2004). By restraining a fully functioning limb, therapists force patients to use the "bad" hand or leg, gradually reprogramming the brain. One stroke victim, a surgeon in his fifties, was put to work cleaning tables, with his good arm and hand restrained. Slowly, the bad arm recovered its skills. As damaged-brain functions migrated to other brain regions, he gradually learned to write again and even to play tennis (Doidge, 2007).

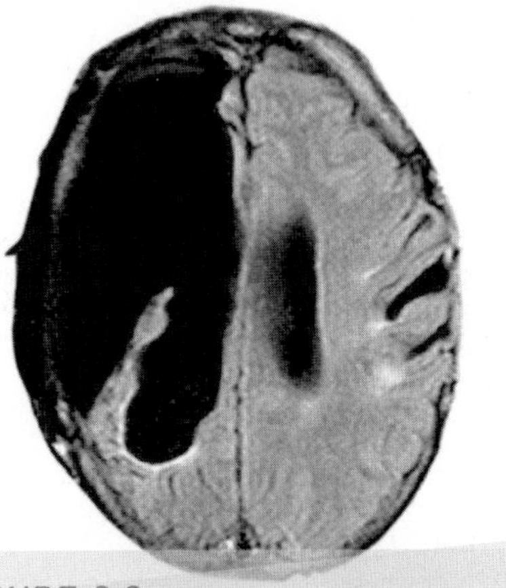

Joe McNally/Joe McNally Photography

FIGURE 6.9
Brain plasticity This 6-year-old had surgery to end her life-threatening seizures. Although most of an entire hemisphere was removed (see MRI of hemispherectomy above), her remaining hemisphere compensated by putting other areas to work. One Johns Hopkins medical team reflected on the child hemispherectomies they had performed. Although use of the opposite hand is compromised, they reported being "awed" by how well these children had retained their memory, personality, and humor (Vining et al., 1997). The younger the child, the greater the chance that the remaining hemisphere can take over the functions of the one that was surgically removed (Choi, 2008).

The brain's plasticity is good news for those blind or deaf. Blindness or deafness makes unused brain areas available for other uses (Amedi et al., 2005). If a blind person uses one finger to read Braille, the brain area dedicated to that finger expands as the sense of touch invades the visual cortex that normally helps people see (Barinaga, 1992a; Sadato et al., 1996). If magnetic stimulation temporarily "knocks out" the visual cortex, a lifelong-blind person will make more errors on a *language* task (Amedi et al., 2004).

plasticity the brain's ability to change, especially during childhood, by reorganizing after damage or by building new pathways based on experience.

Plasticity also helps explain why some studies find that deaf people have enhanced peripheral vision (Bosworth & Dobkins, 1999). In those people whose native language is sign, the temporal lobe area normally dedicated to hearing waits in vain for stimulation. Finally, it looks for other signals to process, such as those from the visual system.

Similar reassignment may occur when disease or damage frees up other brain areas normally dedicated to specific functions. If a slow-growing left hemisphere tumor disrupts language (which resides mostly in the left hemisphere), the right hemisphere may compensate (Thiel et al., 2006). If a finger is amputated, the sensory cortex that received its input will begin to receive input from the adjacent fingers, which then become more sensitive (Fox, 1984). So what do you suppose was the sexual intercourse experience of one patient whose lower leg had been amputated? (Note, too, in Figure 6.2, that the toes region is adjacent to the genitals.) "I actually experience my orgasm in my foot. And there it's much bigger than it used to be because it's no longer just confined to my genitals" (Ramachandran & Blakeslee, 1998, p. 36).

Although the brain often attempts self-repair by reorganizing existing tissue, it sometimes attempts to mend itself by producing new brain cells. This process, known as **neurogenesis**, has been found in adult mice, birds, monkeys, and humans (Jessberger et al., 2008). These baby neurons originate deep in the brain and may then migrate elsewhere and form connections with neighboring neurons (Aimone et al., 2010; Gould, 2007).

Master stem cells that can develop into any type of brain cell have also been discovered in the human embryo. If mass-produced in a lab and injected into a damaged brain, might neural stem cells turn themselves into replacements for lost brain cells? Might we someday be able to rebuild damaged brains, much as we reseed damaged lawns? Might new drugs spur the production of new nerve cells? Stay tuned. Today's biotech companies are hard at work on such possibilities. In the meantime, we can all benefit from other natural promoters of neurogenesis, such as exercise, sleep, and nonstressful but stimulating environments (Iso et al., 2007; Pereira et al., 2007; Stranahan et al., 2006).

Our Divided Brain

6-3 What do split brains reveal about the functions of our two brain hemispheres?

We have seen that our brain's look-alike left and right hemispheres serve differing functions. This *lateralization* is apparent after brain damage. Research collected over more than a century has shown that accidents, strokes, and tumors in the left hemisphere can impair reading, writing, speaking, arithmetic reasoning, and understanding. Similar lesions in the right hemisphere seldom have such dramatic effects.

Does this mean that the right hemisphere is just along for the ride—a silent, "subordinate" or "minor" hemisphere? Many believed this was the case until 1960, when researchers found that the "minor" right hemisphere was not so limited after all. The story of this discovery is a fascinating chapter in psychology's history.

Splitting the Brain

In 1961, two Los Angeles neurosurgeons, Philip Vogel and Joseph Bogen, speculated that major epileptic seizures were caused by an amplification of abnormal brain activity bouncing back and forth between the two cerebral hemispheres. If so, they wondered, could they put an end to this biological tennis game by severing the **corpus callosum** (see **FIGURE 6.10**)? This wide band of axon fibers connects the two hemispheres and carries messages between them. Vogel and Bogen knew that psychologists Roger Sperry, Ronald Myers, and Michael Gazzaniga had divided the brains of cats and monkeys in this manner, with no serious ill effects.

neurogenesis the formation of new neurons.

corpus callosum [KOR-pus kah-LOW-sum] the large band of neural fibers connecting the two brain hemispheres and carrying messages between them.

split brain a condition resulting from surgery that isolates the brain's two hemispheres by cutting the fibers (mainly those of the corpus callosum) connecting them.

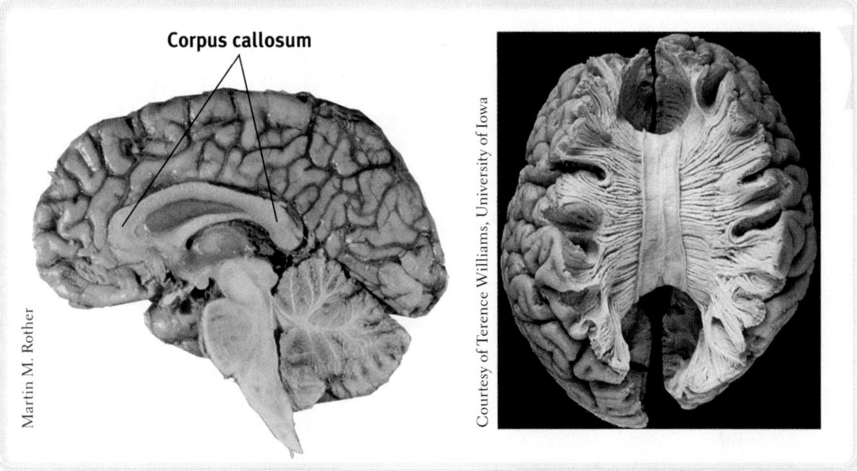

FIGURE 6.10
The corpus callosum This large band of neural fibers connects the two brain hemispheres. To photograph the half brain shown at left, a surgeon separated the hemispheres by cutting through the corpus callosum and lower brain regions. In the view on the right, brain tissue has been cut back to expose the corpus callosum and bundles of fibers coming out from it.

So the surgeons operated. The result? The seizures all but disappeared. The patients with these **split brains** were surprisingly normal, their personality and intellect hardly affected. Waking from surgery, one even joked that he had a "splitting headache" (Gazzaniga, 1967). By sharing their experiences, these patients have greatly expanded our understanding of interactions between the intact brain's two hemispheres.

To appreciate these findings, we need to focus for a minute on the peculiar nature of our visual wiring. As FIGURE 6.11 illustrates, information from the left half of your field of vision goes to your right hemisphere, and information from the right half of your visual field goes to your left hemisphere, which usually controls speech. (Note, however, that each eye receives sensory information from both the right and left visual fields.) Data received by either hemisphere are quickly transmitted to the other across the corpus callosum. In a person with a severed corpus callosum, this information sharing does not take place.

Knowing these facts, Sperry and Gazzaniga could send information to a patient's left or right hemisphere. As the person stared at a spot, they flashed a stimulus to its right or left. They could do this with you, too, but in your intact brain, the hemisphere receiving the information would instantly pass the news to the other side. Because the split-brain surgery had cut the communication lines between the hemispheres, the researchers could, with these patients, quiz each hemisphere separately.

In an early experiment, Gazzaniga (1967) asked these people to stare at a dot as he flashed HE·ART on a screen (FIGURE 6.12 on the next page). Thus, HE appeared in their left visual field (which transmits to the right hemisphere) and ART in the right field (which transmits to the left hemisphere). When he then asked them to *say* what they had seen, the patients reported that they had seen ART. But when asked to *point* to the word they had seen, they were startled when their left hand (controlled by the right hemisphere) pointed to HE. Given an opportunity to express itself, each hemisphere reported what it had seen. The right hemisphere (controlling the left hand) intuitively knew what it could not verbally report.

When a picture of a spoon was flashed to their right hemisphere, the patients could not *say* what they had viewed. But when asked to *identify* what they had viewed by feeling an assortment of hidden objects with their left hand, they readily selected the spoon. If the experimenter said, "Correct!" the patient might reply, "What? Correct? How could I possibly pick out the correct object when I don't know what I saw?" It is, of course, the left hemisphere doing the talking here, bewildered by what the nonverbal right hemisphere knows.

A few people who have had split-brain surgery have been for a time bothered by the unruly independence of their left hand, which might unbutton a shirt while the right hand buttoned it, or put grocery store items back on the shelf after the right hand put

FIGURE 6.11
The information highway from eye to brain

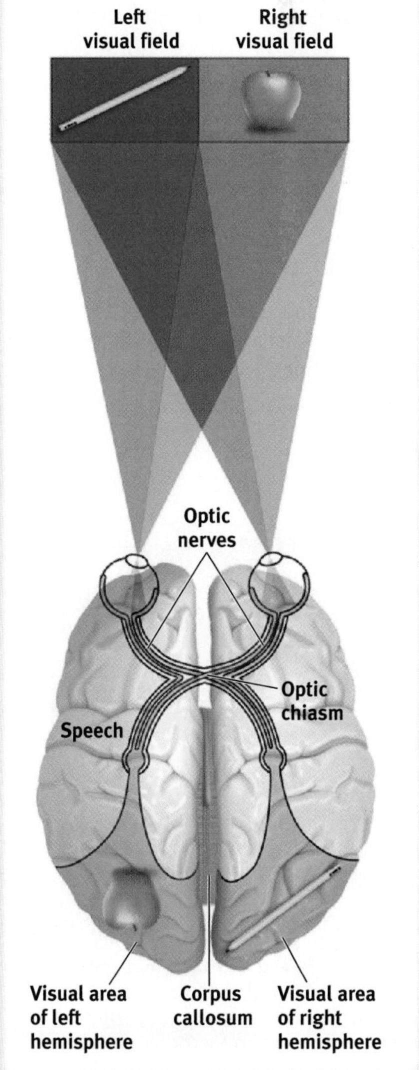

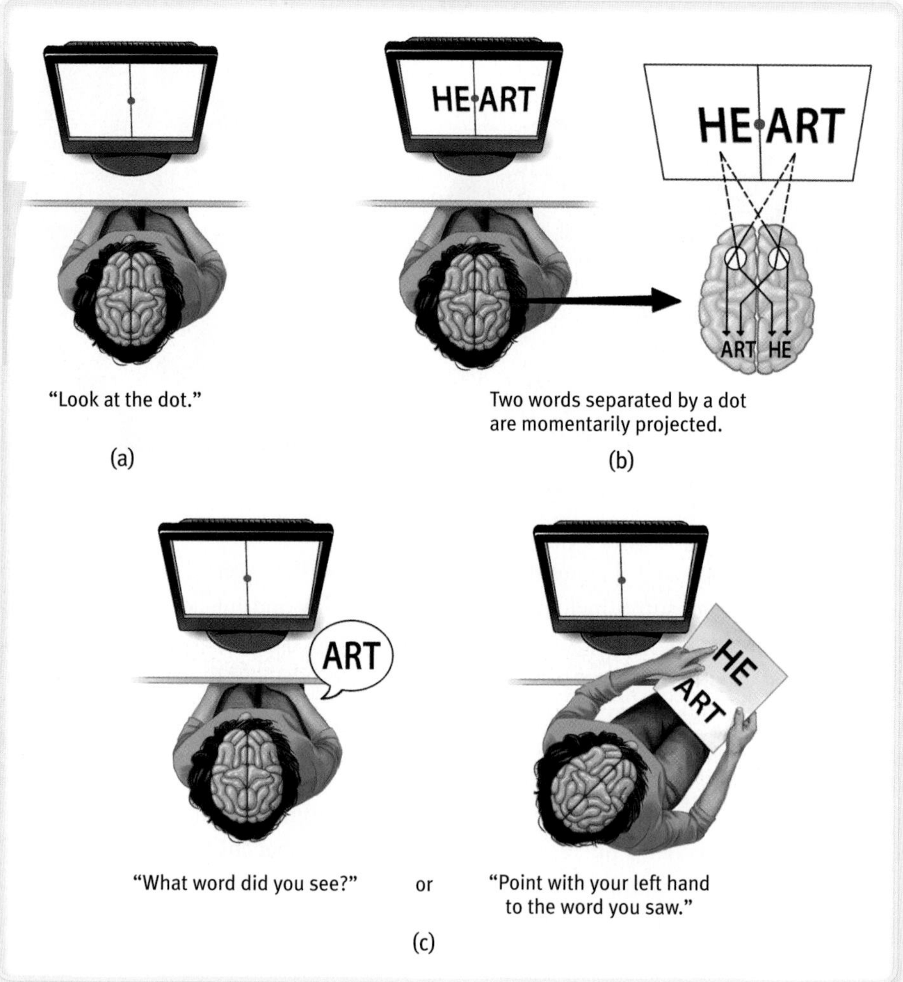

FIGURE 6.12
Testing the divided brain When an experimenter flashes the word HEART across the visual field, a woman with a split brain reports seeing the portion of the word transmitted to her left hemisphere. However, if asked to indicate with her left hand what she saw, she points to the portion of the word transmitted to her right hemisphere. (From Gazzaniga, 1983.)

"Do not let your left hand know what your right hand is doing."
Matthew 6:3

FIGURE 6.13
Try this! Joe, who has had split-brain surgery, can simultaneously draw two different shapes.

BBC

them in the cart. It was as if each hemisphere was thinking "I've half a mind to wear my green (blue) shirt today." Indeed, said Sperry (1964), split-brain surgery leaves people "with two separate minds." With a split brain, both hemispheres can comprehend and follow an instruction to copy—*simultaneously*—different figures with the left and right hands (Franz et al., 2000; see also **FIGURE 6.13**). (Reading these reports, I fantasize a patient enjoying a solitary game of "rock, paper, scissors"—left versus right hand.)

When the "two minds" are at odds, the left hemisphere does mental gymnastics to rationalize reactions it does not understand. If a patient follows an order sent to the right hemisphere ("Walk"), a strange thing happens. Unaware of the order, the left hemisphere doesn't know why the patient begins walking. Yet, when asked why, the patient doesn't say "I don't know." Instead, the interpretive left hemisphere improvises—"I'm going into the house to get a Coke." Gazzaniga (1988), who considers these patients "the most fascinating people on earth," concluded that the conscious left hemisphere is an "interpreter" or press agent that instantly constructs theories to explain our behavior.

RETRIEVAL PRACTICE

- (1) If we flash a red light to the right hemisphere of a person with a split brain, and flash a green light to the left hemisphere, will each observe its own color? (2) Will the person be aware that the colors differ? (3) What will the person verbally report seeing?

ANSWERS: 1. yes, 2. no, 3. green

an occasional night shift. You'll feel groggiest in the middle of the night but may gain new energy when your normal wake-up time arrives.

Age and experience can alter our circadian rhythm. Most 20-year-olds are evening-energized "owls," with performance improving across the day (May & Hasher, 1998). Most older adults are morning-loving "larks," with performance declining as the day wears on. By mid-evening, when the night has hardly begun for many young adults, retirement homes are typically quiet. At about age 20 (slightly earlier for women), we begin to shift from being owls to being larks (Roenneberg et al., 2004). Women become more morning oriented as they have children and also as they transition to menopause (Leonhard & Randler, 2009; Randler & Bausback, 2010). Morning types tend to do better in school, to take more initiative, and to be less vulnerable to depression (Randler, 2008, 2009; Randler & Frech, 2009).

Peter Chadwick/Photo Researchers, Inc.

Dolphins, porpoises, and whales sleep with one side of their brain at a time (Miller et al., 2008).

Sleep Stages

8-2 What is the biological rhythm of our sleeping and dreaming stages?

Sooner or later, sleep overtakes us and consciousness fades as different parts of our brain's cortex stop communicating (Massimini et al., 2005). But rather than emitting a constant dial tone, the sleeping brain has its own biological rhythm.

About every 90 minutes, we cycle through four distinct sleep stages. This simple fact apparently was unknown until 8-year-old Armond Aserinsky went to bed one night in 1952. His father, Eugene, a University of Chicago graduate student, needed to test an electroencephalograph he had repaired that day (Aserinsky, 1988; Seligman & Yellen, 1987). Placing electrodes near Armond's eyes to record the rolling eye movements then believed to occur during sleep, Aserinsky watched the machine go wild, tracing deep zigzags on the graph paper. Could the machine still be broken? As the night proceeded and the activity recurred, Aserinsky realized that the periods of fast, jerky eye movements were accompanied by energetic brain activity. Awakened during one such episode, Armond reported having a dream. Aserinsky had discovered what we now know as **REM sleep** (*r*apid *e*ye *m*ovement sleep).

Similar procedures used with thousands of volunteers showed the cycles were a normal part of sleep (Kleitman, 1960). To appreciate these studies, imagine yourself as a participant. As the hour grows late, you feel sleepy and yawn in response to reduced brain metabolism. (Yawning, which can be socially contagious, stretches your neck muscles and increases your heart rate, which increases your alertness [Moorcroft, 2003].) When you are ready for bed, a researcher comes in and tapes electrodes to your scalp (to detect your brain waves), on your chin (to detect muscle tension), and just outside the corners of your eyes (to detect eye movements) (**FIGURE 8.1** on the next page). Other devices will record your heart rate, respiration rate, and genital arousal.

When you are in bed with your eyes closed, the researcher in the next room sees on the EEG the relatively slow **alpha waves** of your awake but relaxed state (**FIGURE 8.2** on the next page). As you adapt to all this equipment, you grow tired and, in an unremembered moment, slip into **sleep** (**FIGURE 8.3** on the next page). The transition is marked by the slowed breathing and the irregular brain waves of non-REM stage 1 sleep. Using the new American Academy of Sleep Medicine classification of sleep stages, this is called NREM-1 (Silber et al., 2008).

REM sleep rapid eye movement sleep; a recurring sleep stage during which vivid dreams commonly occur. Also known as *paradoxical sleep,* because the muscles are relaxed (except for minor twitches) but other body systems are active.

alpha waves the relatively slow brain waves of a relaxed, awake state.

sleep periodic, natural, easily reversible loss of consciousness—as distinct from unconsciousness resulting from a coma, general anesthesia, or hibernation. (Adapted from Dement, 1999.)

FIGURE 8.1
Measuring sleep activity Sleep researchers measure brain-wave activity, eye movements, and muscle tension by electrodes that pick up weak electrical signals from the brain, eye, and facial muscles. (From Dement, 1978.)

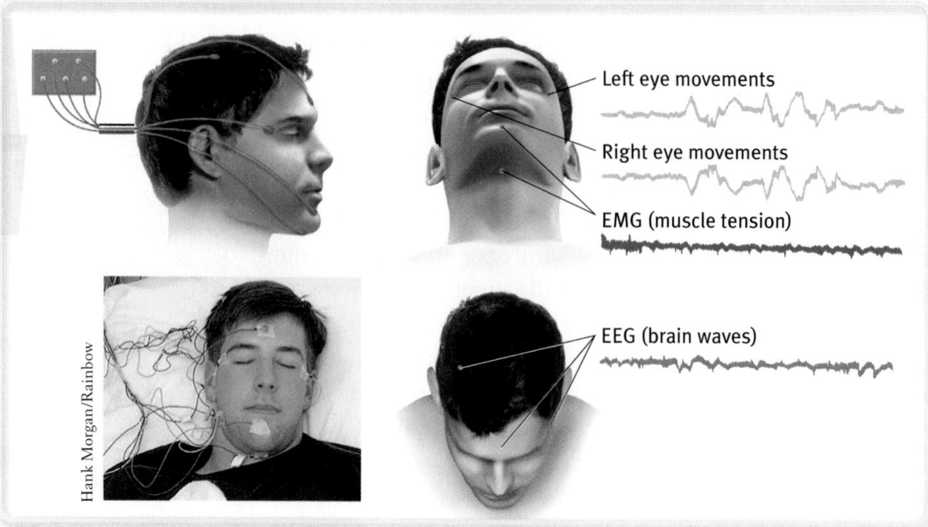

FIGURE 8.2
Brain waves and sleep stages The beta waves of an alert, waking state and the regular alpha waves of an awake, relaxed state differ from the slower, larger delta waves of deep NREM-3 sleep. Although the rapid REM sleep waves resemble the near-waking NREM-1 sleep waves, the body is more aroused during REM sleep than during NREM sleep. (Rebecca Spencer, University of Massachusetts, assisted with this figure.)

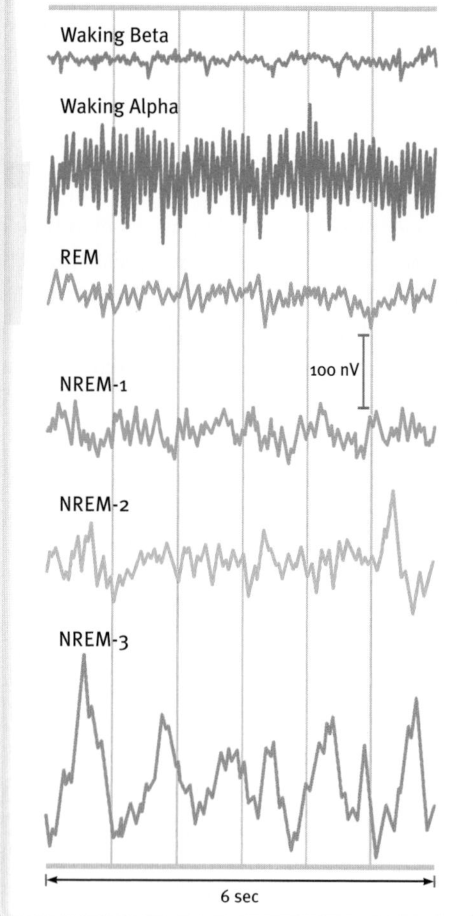

FIGURE 8.3
The moment of sleep We seem unaware of the moment we fall into sleep, but someone watching our brain waves could tell. (From Dement, 1999.)

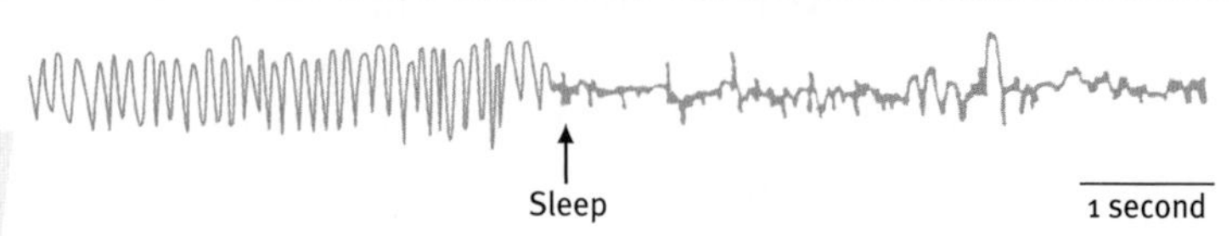

In one of his 15,000 research participants, William Dement (1999) observed the moment the brain's perceptual window to the outside world slammed shut. Dement asked this sleep-deprived young man, lying on his back with eyelids taped open, to press a button every time a strobe light flashed in his eyes (about every 6 seconds). After a few minutes the young man missed one. Asked why, he said, "Because there was no flash." But there was a flash. He missed it because (as his brain activity revealed) he had fallen asleep for 2 seconds, missing not only the flash 6 inches from his nose but also the awareness of the abrupt moment of entry into sleep.

During this brief NREM-1 sleep you may experience fantastic images resembling **hallucinations**—sensory experiences that occur without a sensory stimulus. You may have a sensation of falling (at which moment your body may suddenly jerk) or of floating weightlessly. These *hypnagogic* sensations may later be incorporated into your memories. People who claim to have been abducted by aliens—often shortly after getting into bed—commonly recall being floated off of or pinned down on their beds (Clancy, 2005).

To catch your own hypnagogic experiences, you might use your alarm's snooze function.

You then relax more deeply and begin about 20 minutes of NREM-2 sleep, with its periodic *sleep spindles*—bursts of rapid, rhythmic brain-wave activity (see Figure 8.2). Although you could still be awakened without too much difficulty, you are now clearly asleep.

Then you transition to the deep sleep of NREM-3. During this slow-wave sleep, which lasts for about 30 minutes, your brain emits large, slow **delta waves** and you are hard to awaken. (It is at the end of the deep, slow-wave NREM-3 sleep that children may wet the bed.)

REM Sleep

About an hour after you first fall asleep, a strange thing happens. Rather than continuing in deep slumber, you ascend from your initial sleep dive. Returning through NREM-2 (where you spend about half your night), you enter the most intriguing sleep phase—REM sleep (**FIGURE 8.4** on the next page). For about 10 minutes, your brain waves become rapid and saw-toothed, more like those of the nearly awake NREM-1 sleep. But unlike NREM-1, during REM sleep your heart rate rises, your breathing becomes rapid and irregular, and every half-minute or so your eyes dart around in momentary bursts of activity behind closed lids. These eye movements announce the beginning of a dream—often emotional, usually story-like, and richly hallucinatory. Because anyone watching a sleeper's eyes can notice these REM bursts, it is amazing that science was ignorant of REM sleep until 1952.

© 1994 by Sidney Harris.

"Boy are my eyes tired! I had REM sleep all night long."

Except during very scary dreams, your genitals become aroused during REM sleep. You have an erection or increased vaginal lubrication and clitoral engorgement, regardless of whether the dream's content is sexual (Karacan et al., 1966). Men's common "morning erection" stems from the night's last REM period, often just before waking. In young men, sleep-related erections outlast REM periods, lasting 30 to 45 minutes on average (Karacan et al., 1983; Schiavi & Schreiner-Engel, 1988). A typical 25-year-old man therefore has an erection during nearly half his night's sleep, a 65-year-old man for one-quarter. Many men troubled by *erectile dysfunction* (impotence) have sleep-related erections, suggesting the problem is not between their legs.

Horses, which spend 92 percent of each day standing and can sleep standing, must lie down for REM sleep (Morrison, 2003).

Your brain's motor cortex is active during REM sleep, but your brainstem blocks its messages. This leaves your muscles relaxed, so much so that, except for an occasional finger, toe, or facial twitch, you are essentially paralyzed. Moreover, you cannot easily be awakened. (This immobility may occasionally linger as you awaken from REM sleep, producing a disturbing experience of *sleep paralysis* [Santomauro & French, 2009].) REM sleep is thus sometimes called *paradoxical* sleep: The body is internally aroused, with waking-like brain activity, yet asleep and externally calm.

hallucinations false sensory experiences, such as seeing something in the absence of an external visual stimulus.

delta waves the large, slow brain waves associated with deep sleep.

FIGURE 8.4
The stages in a typical night's sleep People pass through a multi-stage sleep cycle several times each night, with the periods of deep sleep diminishing and REM sleep periods increasing in duration. As people age, sleep becomes more fragile, with awakenings common among older adults (Kamel et al., 2006; Neubauer, 1999).

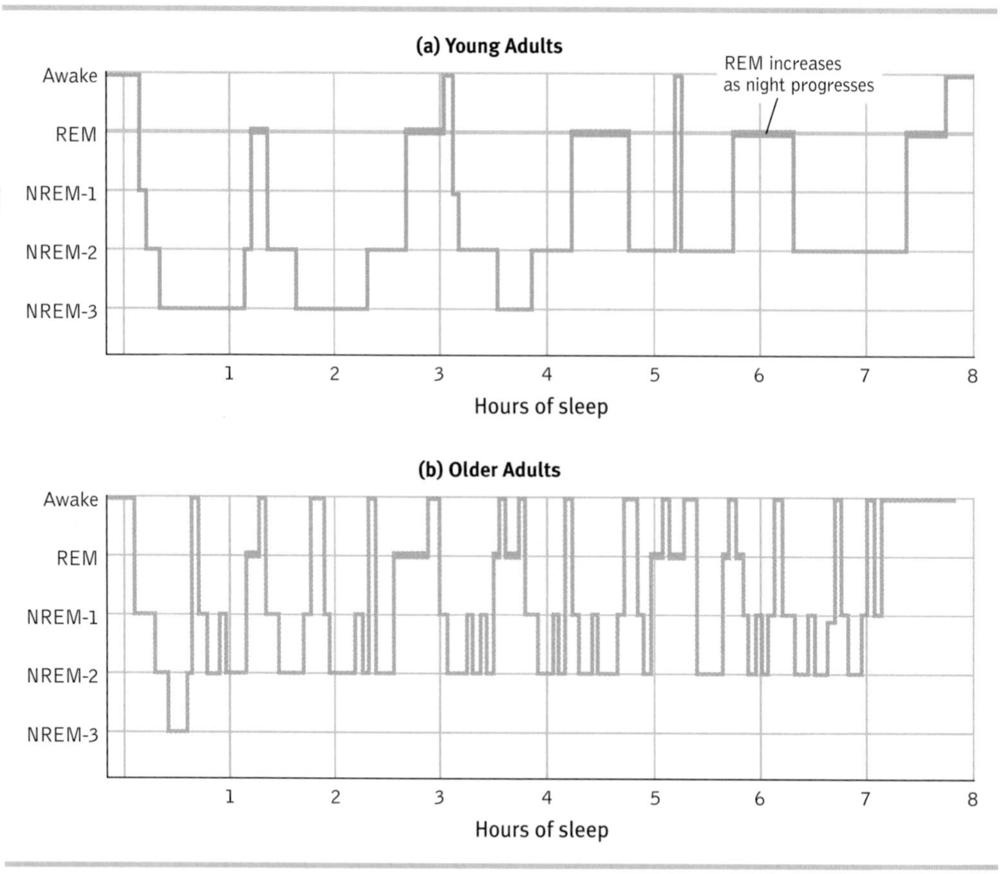

The sleep cycle repeats itself about every 90 minutes for younger adults (somewhat more frequently for older adults). As the night wears on, deep NREM-3 sleep grows shorter and disappears. The REM and NREM-2 sleep periods get longer (see Figure 8.4). By morning, we have spent 20 to 25 percent of an average night's sleep—some 100 minutes—in REM sleep. Thirty-seven percent of people report rarely or never having dreams "that you can remember the next morning" (Moore, 2004). Yet even they will, more than 80 percent of the time, recall a dream after being awakened during REM sleep. We spend about 600 hours a year experiencing some 1500 dreams, or more than 100,000 dreams over a typical lifetime—dreams swallowed by the night but not acted out, thanks to REM's protective paralysis.

People rarely snore during dreams. When REM starts, snoring stops.

RETRIEVAL PRACTICE

Safety in numbers? Why would communal sleeping provide added protection for those whose safety depends upon vigilance, such as these soldiers?

ANSWER: With each soldier cycling through the sleep stages independently, it is very likely that at any given time at least one of them will be awake or easily wakened in the event of a threat.

Uriel Sinai/Getty Images

RETRIEVAL PRACTICE

- Can you match the cognitive experience with the sleep stage?

1. NREM-1 — a. story-like dream
2. NREM-3 — b. fleeting images
3. REM — c. minimal awareness

ANSWERS: 1. b, 2. c, 3. a

- What are the four sleep stages, and in what order do we normally travel through those stages?

ANSWERS: REM, NREM-1, NREM-2, NREM-3; Normally we move through NREM-1, then NREM-2, then NREM-3, then back up through NREM-2 before we experience REM sleep.

What Affects Our Sleep Patterns?

8-3 How do biology and environment interact in our sleep patterns?

The idea that "everyone needs 8 hours of sleep" is untrue. Newborns sleep nearly two-thirds of their day, most adults no more than one-third. Still, there is more to our sleep differences than age. Some of us thrive with fewer than 6 hours per night; others regularly rack up 9 hours or more. Such sleep patterns are genetically influenced (Hor & Tafti, 2009). In studies of fraternal and identical twins, only the identical twins had strikingly similar sleep patterns and durations (Webb & Campbell, 1983). Today's researchers are discovering the genes that regulate sleep in humans and animals (Donlea et al., 2009; He et al., 2009).

Sleep patterns are also culturally influenced. In the United States and Canada, adults average 7 to 8 hours per night (Hurst, 2008; National Sleep Foundation, 2010; Robinson & Martin, 2009). (The weeknight sleep of many students and workers falls short of this average [NSF, 2008].) North Americans are nevertheless sleeping less than their counterparts a century ago. Thanks to modern light bulbs, shift work, and social diversions, those who would have gone to bed at 9:00 P.M. are now up until 11:00 P.M. or later. With sleep, as with waking behavior, biology and environment interact.

Bright morning light tweaks the circadian clock by activating light-sensitive retinal proteins. These proteins control the circadian clock by triggering signals to the brain's *suprachiasmatic nucleus* (SCN)—a pair of grain-of-rice-sized, 10,000-cell clusters in the hypothalamus (Wirz-Justice, 2009). The SCN does its job in part by causing the brain's pineal gland to decrease its production of the sleep-inducing hormone *melatonin* in the morning and to increase it in the evening (**FIGURE 8.5**).

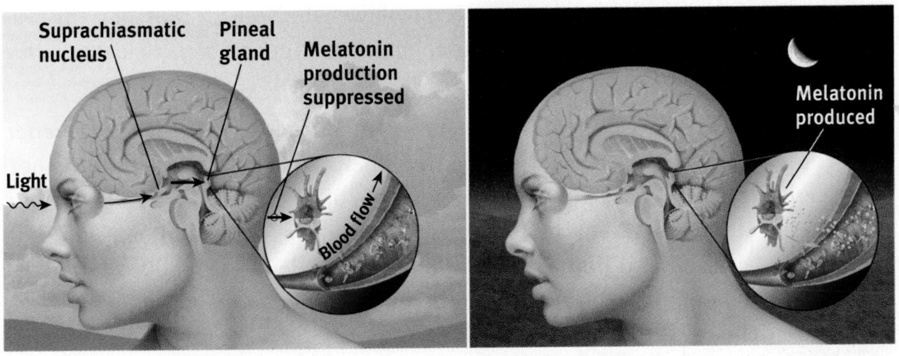

FIGURE 8.5
The biological clock Light striking the retina signals the suprachiasmatic nucleus (SCN) to suppress the pineal gland's production of the sleep hormone melatonin. At night, the SCN quiets down, allowing the pineal gland to release melatonin into the bloodstream.

If our natural circadian rhythm were attuned to a 23-hour cycle, would we instead need to discipline ourselves to stay up later at night and sleep in longer in the morning?

A circadian disadvantage: One study of a decade's 24,121 Major League Baseball games found that teams who had crossed three time zones before playing a multiday series had nearly a 60 percent chance of losing their first game (Winter et al., 2009).

Being bathed in light disrupts our 24-hour biological clock (Czeisler et al., 1999; Dement, 1999). Curiously—given that our ancestors' body clocks were attuned to the rising and setting Sun of the 24-hour day—many of today's young adults adopt something closer to a 25-hour day, by staying up too late to get 8 hours of sleep. For this, we can thank (or blame) Thomas Edison, inventor of the light bulb. This helps explain why, until our later years, we must discipline ourselves to go to bed and force ourselves to get up. Most animals, too, when placed under unnatural constant illumination will exceed a 24-hour day. Artificial light delays sleep.

Sleep often eludes those who stay up late and sleep in on weekends, and then go to bed earlier on Sunday evening in preparation for the new workweek (Oren & Terman, 1998). They are like New Yorkers whose biology is on California time. For North Americans who fly to Europe and need to be up when their circadian rhythm cries "*SLEEP*" bright light (spending the next day outdoors) helps reset the biological clock (Czeisler et al., 1986, 1989; Eastman et al., 1995).

RETRIEVAL PRACTICE

- The __________ nucleus helps monitor the brain's release of melatonin, which affects our __________ rhythm.

ANSWERS: suprachiasmatic, circadian

Sleep Theories

8-4 What are sleep's functions?

Our sleep patterns differ from person to person and from culture to culture. But why do we have this need for sleep?

Psychologists believe sleep may have evolved for five reasons.

1. ***Sleep protects.*** When darkness shut down the day's hunting, food gathering, and travel, our distant ancestors were better off asleep in a cave, out of harm's way. Those who didn't try to navigate around rocks and cliffs at night were more likely to leave descendants. This fits a broader principle: A species' sleep pattern tends to suit its ecological niche (Siegel, 2009). Animals with the greatest need to graze and the least ability to hide tend to sleep less. (For a sampling of animal sleep times, see **FIGURE 8.6.**)
2. ***Sleep helps us recuperate.*** It helps restore and repair brain tissue. Bats and other animals with high waking metabolism burn a lot of calories, producing a lot of *free radicals*, molecules that are toxic to neurons. Sleeping a lot gives resting neurons time to repair themselves, while pruning or weakening unused connections (Gilestro et al., 2009; Siegel, 2003; Vyazovskiy et al., 2008). Think of it this way: When consciousness leaves your house, brain construction workers come in for a makeover.
3. ***Sleep helps restore and rebuild our fading memories of the day's experiences.*** Sleep consolidates our memories—it strengthens and stabilizes neural memory traces (Racsmány et al., 2010; Rasch & Born, 2008). People trained to perform tasks therefore recall them better after a night's sleep, or even after a short nap, than after several hours awake (Stickgold & Ellenbogen, 2008). Among older adults, more sleep leads to better memory of recently learned material (Drummond, 2010). After sleeping well, seniors remember more. And in both

"Sleep faster, we need the pillows."
Yiddish proverb

"Corduroy pillows make headlines."
Anonymous

"Remember to sleep, because you need sleep to remember."
James B. Maas, 2010

humans and rats, neural activity during slow-wave sleep re-enacts and promotes recall of prior novel experiences (Peigneux et al., 2004; Ribeiro et al., 2004). Sleep, it seems, strengthens memories in a way that being awake does not.

4. ***Sleep feeds creative thinking.*** On occasion, dreams have inspired noteworthy literary, artistic, and scientific achievements, such as the dream that clued chemist August Kekulé to the structure of benzene (Ross, 2006). More commonplace is the boost that a complete night's sleep gives to our thinking and learning. After working on a task, then sleeping on it, people solve problems more insightfully than do those who stay awake (Wagner et al., 2004). They also are better at spotting connections among novel pieces of information (Ellenbogen et al., 2007). To think smart and see connections, it often pays to sleep on it.
5. ***Sleep supports growth.*** During deep sleep, the pituitary gland releases a growth hormone. This hormone is necessary for muscle development. A regular full night's sleep can also "*dramatically* improve your athletic ability," report James Maas and Rebecca Robbins (see Close-Up: Sleep and Athletic Performance on the next page). As we age, we release less of this hormone and spend less time in deep sleep (Pekkanen, 1982).

Given all the benefits of sleep, it's no wonder that sleep loss hits us so hard.

FIGURE 8.6
Animal sleep time Would you rather be a brown bat and sleep 20 hours a day or a giraffe and sleep 2 hours (data from NIH, 2010)?
Kruglov_Orda/Shutterstock; Courtesy of Andrew D. Myers; © Anna63/Dreamstime.com; Steffen Foerster Photography/Shutterstock; The Agency Collection/Punchstock; Eric Isselée/Shutterstock; pandapaw/Shutterstock

RETRIEVAL PRACTICE

- What five theories explain our need for sleep?

ANSWERS: (1) Sleep has survival value. (2) Sleep helps us restore and repair brain tissue. (3) During sleep we consolidate memory traces. (4) Sleep fuels creativity. (5) Sleep plays a role in the growth process.

Sleep Deprivation and Sleep Disorders

8-5 How does sleep loss affect us, and what are the major sleep disorders?

When our body yearns for sleep but does not get it, we begin to feel terrible. Trying to stay awake, we will eventually lose. In the tiredness battle, sleep always wins.

Effects of Sleep Loss

Today, more than ever, our sleep patterns leave us not only sleepy but drained of energy and feelings of well-being. After a succession of 5-hour nights, we accumulate a sleep debt that need not be entirely repaid but cannot be satisfied by one long sleep. "The brain keeps an accurate count of sleep debt for at least two weeks," reported sleep researcher William Dement (1999, p. 64).

Obviously, then, we need sleep. Sleep commands roughly one-third of our lives—some 25 years, on average. But why?

Allowed to sleep unhindered, most adults will sleep at least 9 hours a night (Coren, 1996). With that much sleep, we awake refreshed, sustain better moods, and perform

In 1989, Michael Doucette was named America's Safest Driving Teen. In 1990, while driving home from college, he fell asleep at the wheel and collided with an oncoming car, killing both himself and the other driver. Michael's driving instructor later acknowledged never having mentioned sleep deprivation and drowsy driving (Dement, 1999).

CLOSE-UP

Sleep and Athletic Performance

Exercise improves sleep. What's not as widely known, report James Maas and Rebecca Robbins (2010), is that sleep improves athletic performance. Well-rested athletes have faster reaction times, more energy, and greater endurance, and teams that build 8 to 10 hours of daily sleep into their training show improved performance. Top violinists also report sleeping 8.5 hours a day on average, and rate practice and sleep as the two most important improvement-fostering activities (Ericsson et al., 1993).

Slow-wave sleep, which occurs mostly in the first half of a night's sleep, produces the human growth hormone necessary for muscle development. REM sleep and NREM-2 sleep, which occur mostly in the final hours of a long night's sleep, help strengthen the neural connections that build enduring memories, including the "muscle memories" learned while practicing tennis or shooting baskets.

The optimal exercise time is late afternoon or early evening, Maas and Robbins advise, when the body's natural cooling is most efficient. Early morning workouts are ill-advised, because they increase the risk of injury and rob athletes of valuable sleep. Heavy workouts within three hours of bedtime should also be avoided because the arousal disrupts falling asleep. Precision muscle training, such as shooting free throws, may, however, benefit when followed by sleep.

Maas has been a sleep consultant for college and professional athletes and teams. On Maas's advice, the Orlando Magic cut early morning practices. He also advised one young woman, Sarah Hughes, who felt stymied in her efforts to excel in figure-skating competition. "Cut the early morning practice," he instructed, as part of the recommended sleep regimen. Soon thereafter, Hughes' performance scores increased, ultimately culminating in her 2002 Olympic gold medal.

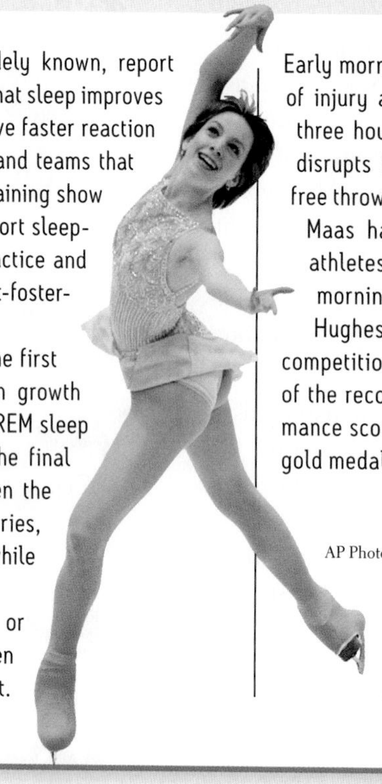

AP Photo/Lionel Cironneau

Ample sleep supports skill learning and high performance This was the experience of Olympic gold medalist Sarah Hughes.

Reuters/China Daily (China)

Sleepless and suffering These fatigued, sleep-deprived earthquake rescue workers in China may experience a depressed immune system, impaired concentration, and greater vulnerability to accidents.

more efficient and accurate work. The U.S. Navy and the National Institutes of Health have demonstrated the benefits of unrestricted sleep in experiments in which volunteers spent 14 hours daily in bed for at least a week. For the first few days, the volunteers averaged 12 hours of sleep a day or more, apparently paying off a sleep debt that averaged 25 to 30 hours. That accomplished, they then settled back to 7.5 to 9 hours nightly and felt energized and happier (Dement, 1999). In one Gallup survey (Mason, 2005), 63 percent of adults who reported getting the sleep they needed also reported being "very satisfied" with their personal life (as did only 36 percent of those needing more sleep). And when 909 working women reported on their daily moods, the researchers were struck by what mattered little (such as money, so long as the person was not battling poverty), and what mattered a lot: less time pressure at work and a good night's sleep (Kahneman et al., 2004). Perhaps it's not surprising, then, that when asked if they had felt well rested on the previous day, 3 in 10 Americans said they had not (Pelham, 2010).

College and university students are especially sleep deprived; 69 percent in one national survey reported "feeling tired" or "having little energy" on several or more days in the last two weeks (AP, 2009). In another survey, 28 percent of high school students acknowledged falling asleep in class at least once a week (Sleep Foundation, 2006). When the going gets boring, the students start snoring. (To test whether you are one of the many sleep-deprived students, see **TABLE 8.1.**)

Sleep loss is a predictor of depression. Researchers who studied 15,500 young people, 12 to 18 years old, found that those who slept 5 or fewer hours a night had a 71 percent higher risk of depression than their peers who slept 8 hours or more (Gangwisch et al., 2010). This link does not appear to reflect sleep difficulties caused by depression. When children and youth are followed through time, sleep loss predicts depression rather than vice versa (Gregory et al., 2009). Moreover, REM sleep's processing of emotional experiences helps protect against depression (Walker & van der Helm, 2009). After a good night's sleep, we often do feel better the next day. And that may help to explain why parentally enforced bedtimes predict less depression, and why pushing back school start time leads to improved adolescent sleep, alertness, and mood (Gregory et al., 2009; Owens et al., 2010).

Even when awake, students often function below their peak. And they know it: Four in five teens and three in five 18- to 29-year-olds wish they could get more sleep on weekdays (Mason, 2003, 2005). Yet that teen who staggers glumly out of bed in response to an unwelcome alarm, yawns through morning classes, and feels half-depressed much of the day may be energized at 11 P.M. and mindless of the next day's looming sleepiness (Carskadon, 2002). "Sleep deprivation has consequences—difficulty studying, diminished productivity, tendency to make mistakes, irritability, fatigue," noted Dement (1999, p. 231). A large sleep debt "makes you stupid."

In a 2001 Gallup poll, 61 percent of men, but only 47 percent of women, said they got enough sleep.

TABLE 8.1

Cornell University psychologist James Maas has reported that most students suffer the consequences of sleeping less than they should. To see if you are in that group, answer the following true-false questions:

True	False	
____	____	1. I need to set an alarm in order to wake up at the appropriate time.
____	____	2. It's a struggle for me to get out of bed in the morning.
____	____	3. Weekday mornings I hit snooze several times to get more sleep.
____	____	4. I feel tired, irritable, and stressed out during the week.
____	____	5. I have trouble concentrating and remembering.
____	____	6. I feel slow with critical thinking, problem solving, and being creative.
____	____	7. I often fall asleep watching TV.
____	____	8. I often fall asleep in boring meetings or lectures or in warm rooms.
____	____	9. I often fall asleep after heavy meals or after a low dose of alcohol.
____	____	10. I often fall asleep while relaxing after dinner.
____	____	11. I often fall asleep within five minutes of getting into bed.
____	____	12. I often feel drowsy while driving.
____	____	13. I often sleep extra hours on weekend mornings.
____	____	14. I often need a nap to get through the day.
____	____	15. I have dark circles around my eyes.

If you answered "true" to three or more items, you probably are not getting enough sleep. To determine your sleep needs, Maas recommends that you "go to bed 15 minutes earlier than usual every night for the next week—and continue this practice by adding 15 more minutes each week—until you wake without an alarm and feel alert all day." (Quiz reprinted with permission from James B. Maas, *Power sleep: The revolutionary program that prepares your mind and body for peak performance* [New York: HarperCollins, 1999].)

insomnia recurring problems in falling or staying asleep.

narcolepsy a sleep disorder characterized by uncontrollable sleep attacks. The sufferer may lapse directly into REM sleep, often at inopportune times.

It can also make you fatter. Sleep deprivation increases *ghrelin*, a hunger-arousing hormone, and decreases its hunger-suppressing partner, *leptin*. It also increases cortisol, a stress hormone that stimulates the body to make fat. Sure enough, children and adults who sleep less than normal are fatter than those who sleep more (Chen et al., 2008; Knutson et al., 2007; Schoenborn & Adams, 2008). And experimental sleep deprivation of adults increases appetite and eating (Nixon et al., 2008; Patel et al., 2006; Spiegel et al., 2004; Van Cauter et al., 2007). This may help explain the common weight gain among sleep-deprived students (although a review of 11 studies reveals that the mythical "freshman 15" is, on average, closer to a "first-year 4" [Hull et al., 2007]).

In addition to making us more vulnerable to obesity, sleep deprivation can suppress immune cells that fight off viral infections and cancer (Motivala & Irwin, 2007). One experiment exposed volunteers to a cold virus. Those who had been averaging less then 7 hours sleep a night were 3 times more likely to develop a cold than were those sleeping 8 or more hours a night (Cohen et al., 2009). Sleep's protective effect may help explain why people who sleep 7 to 8 hours a night tend to outlive those who are chronically sleep deprived, and why older adults who have no difficulty falling or staying asleep tend to live longer than their sleep-deprived agemates (Dement, 1999; Dew et al., 2003). When infections do set in, we typically sleep more, boosting our immune cells.

Sleep deprivation slows reactions and increases errors on visual attention tasks similar to those involved in screening airport baggage, performing surgery, and reading X-rays (Lim & Dinges, 2010). The result can be devastating for driving, piloting, and equipment operating. Driver fatigue has contributed to an estimated 20 percent of American traffic accidents (Brody, 2002) and to some 30 percent of Australian highway deaths (Maas, 1999). Consider, too, the timing of the 1989 *Exxon Valdez* oil spill; Union Carbide's 1984 Bhopal, India, disaster; and the 1979 Three Mile Island and 1986 Chernobyl nuclear accidents: All occurred after midnight, when operators in charge were likely to be drowsiest and unresponsive to signals requiring an alert response. So it was in 2011 when sleeping air controllers at several U.S. airports could not be roused by pilots seeking clearance to land after midnight. When sleepy frontal lobes confront an unexpected situation, misfortune often results.

Stanley Coren capitalized on what is, for many North Americans, a semi-annual sleep-manipulation experiment—the "spring forward" to "daylight savings" time and "fall backward" to "standard" time. Searching millions of records, Coren found that in both Canada and the United States, accidents increased immediately after the time change that shortens sleep (**FIGURE 8.7**).

FIGURE 8.7

Canadian traffic accidents On the Monday after the spring time change, when people lose one hour of sleep, accidents increase, as compared with the Monday before. In the fall, traffic accidents normally increase because of greater snow, ice, and darkness, but they diminish after the time change. (Adapted from Coren, 1996.)

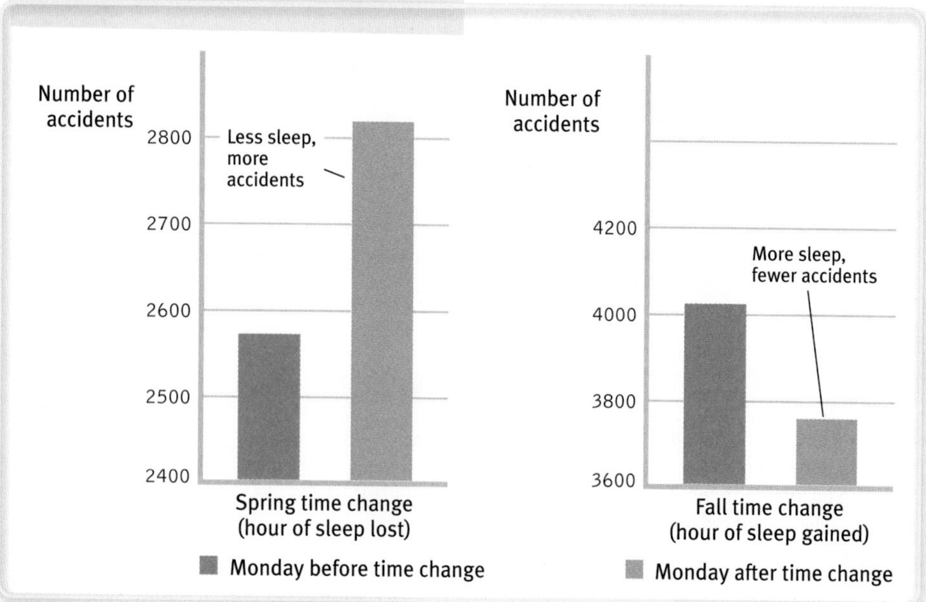

FIGURE 8.8 summarizes the effects of sleep deprivation. But there is good news! Psychologists have discovered a treatment that strengthens memory, increases concentration, boosts mood, moderates hunger and obesity, fortifies the disease-fighting immune system, and lessens the risk of fatal accidents. Even better news: The treatment feels good, it can be self-administered, the supplies are limitless, and it's available free! If you are a typical university-age student, often going to bed near 2:00 A.M. and dragged out of bed six hours later by the dreaded alarm, the treatment is simple: Each night just go to bed a bit earlier.

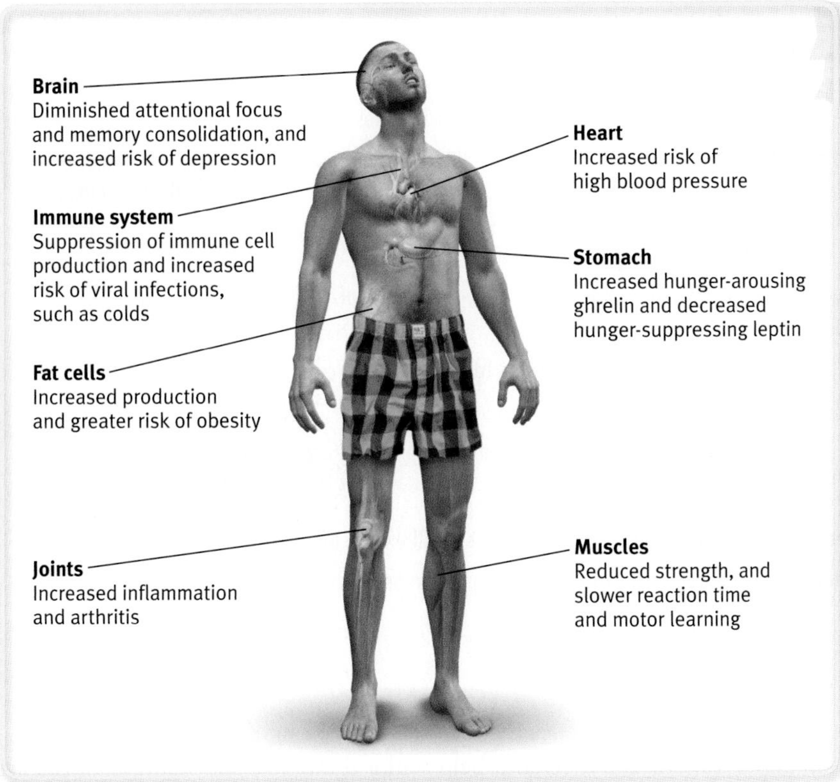

FIGURE 8.8
How sleep deprivation affects us

Major Sleep Disorders

No matter what their normal need for sleep, 1 in 10 adults, and 1 in 4 older adults, complain of **insomnia**—not an occasional inability to sleep when anxious or excited, but persistent problems in falling or staying asleep (Irwin et al., 2006).

From middle age on, awakening occasionally during the night becomes the norm, not something to fret over or treat with medication (Vitiello, 2009). Ironically, insomnia is worsened by fretting about one's insomnia. In laboratory studies, insomnia complainers do sleep less than others, but they typically overestimate—by about double—how long it takes them to fall asleep. They also underestimate by nearly half how long they actually have slept. Even if we have been awake only an hour or two, we may *think* we have had very little sleep because it's the waking part we remember.

The most common quick fixes for true insomnia—sleeping pills and alcohol—can aggravate the problem, reducing REM sleep and leaving the person with next-day blahs. Such aids can also lead to *tolerance*—a state in which increasing doses are needed to produce an effect. An ideal sleep aid would mimic the natural chemicals that are abundant during sleep, without side effects. Until scientists can supply this magic pill, sleep experts have offered some tips for getting better quality sleep (TABLE 8.2 on the next page).

Falling asleep is not the problem for people with **narcolepsy** (from *narco*, "numbness," and *lepsy*, "seizure"), who have sudden attacks of overwhelming sleepiness, usually lasting less than 5 minutes. Narcolepsy attacks can occur at the most inopportune times, perhaps just after taking a terrific swing at a softball or when laughing loudly, shouting angrily, or having sex (Dement, 1978, 1999). In severe cases, the person collapses directly into a brief period of REM sleep, with loss of muscular tension. People with narcolepsy—1 in 2000 of us, estimated the Stanford University Center for Narcolepsy (2002)—must therefore live with extra caution. As a traffic menace, "snoozing is second only to boozing," says the American Sleep Disorders Association, and those with narcolepsy are especially at risk (Aldrich, 1989).

"The lion and the lamb shall lie down together, but the lamb will not be very sleepy."

Woody Allen, in the movie *Love and Death*, 1975

"Sleep is like love or happiness. If you pursue it too ardently it will elude you."

Wilse Webb, *Sleep: The Gentle Tyrant*, 1992

Imagine observing a person with narcolepsy in medieval times. Might such symptoms (especially the instant dreams from dropping into REM sleep) have seemed like demon possession?

TABLE 8.2

Some Natural Sleep Aids

- Exercise regularly but not in the late evening. (Late afternoon is best.)
- Avoid caffeine after early afternoon, and avoid food and drink near bedtime. The exception would be a glass of milk, which provides raw materials for the manufacture of serotonin, a neurotransmitter that facilitates sleep.
- Relax before bedtime, using dimmer light.
- Sleep on a regular schedule (rise at the same time even after a restless night) and avoid naps.
- Hide the clock face so you aren't tempted to check it repeatedly.
- Reassure yourself that temporary sleep loss causes no great harm.
- Realize that for any stressed organism, being vigilant is natural and adaptive. A personal conflict during the day often means a fitful sleep that night (Åkerstedt et al., 2007; Brissette & Cohen, 2002). And a traumatic stressful event can take a lingering toll on sleep (Babson & Feldner, 2010). Managing your stress levels will enable more restful sleeping.
- If all else fails, settle for less sleep, either going to bed later or getting up earlier.

AP Photo/Paul Sakuma, File

Economic recession and stress can rob sleep A National Sleep Foundation (2009) survey found 27 percent of people reporting sleeplessness related to the economy, their personal finances, and employment, as seems evident in this man looking for work.

The Granger Collection, New York

Did Brahms need his own lullabies? Cranky, overweight, and nap-prone, Johannes Brahms exhibited common symptoms of sleep apnea (Margolis, 2000).

Researchers have discovered genes that cause narcolepsy in dogs and humans (Miyagawa et al., 2008; Taheri, 2004). Genes help sculpt the brain, and neuroscientists are searching the brain for narcolepsy-linked abnormalities. One team discovered a relative absence of a hypothalamic neural center that produces *orexin* (also called hypocretin), a neurotransmitter linked to alertness (Taheri et al., 2002; Thannickal et al., 2000). (That discovery has led to the clinical testing of a new sleeping pill that works by blocking orexin's arousing activity.) Narcolepsy, it is now clear, is a brain disease; it is not just "in your mind." And this gives hope that narcolepsy might be effectively relieved by a drug that mimics the missing orexin and can sneak through the blood-brain barrier (Fujiki et al., 2003; Siegel, 2000). In the meantime, physicians are prescribing other drugs to relieve narcolepsy's sleepiness in humans.

Although 1 in 20 of us have **sleep apnea**, it was unknown before modern sleep research. *Apnea* means "with no breath," and people with this condition intermittently stop breathing during sleep. After an airless minute or so, decreased blood oxygen arouses them and they wake up enough to snort in air for a few seconds, in a process that repeats hundreds of times each night, depriving them of slow-wave sleep. Apnea sufferers don't recall these episodes the next day. So, despite feeling fatigued and depressed—and hearing their mate's complaints about their loud "snoring"—many are unaware of their disorder (Peppard et al., 2006).

Sleep apnea is associated with obesity, and as the number of obese Americans has increased, so has this disorder, particularly among overweight men, including some football players (Keller, 2007). Other warning signs are loud snoring, daytime sleepiness and irritability, and (possibly) high blood pressure, which increases the risk of a stroke or heart attack (Dement, 1999). If one doesn't mind looking a little goofy in the dark (imagine a snorkeler at a slumber party), the treatment—a masklike device with an air pump that keeps the sleeper's airway open—can effectively relieve apnea symptoms.

Unlike sleep apnea, **night terrors** target mostly children, who may sit up or walk around, talk incoherently, experience doubled heart and breathing rates, and appear terrified (Hartmann, 1981). They seldom wake up fully during an episode and recall little or nothing the next morning—at most, a fleeting, frightening image. Night terrors are not nightmares (which, like other dreams, typically occur during early morning REM sleep); night terrors usually occur during the first few hours of NREM-3.

Sleepwalking—another NREM-3 sleep disorder—and *sleeptalking* are usually childhood disorders, and like narcolepsy, they run in families. (Sleeptalking—usually garbled or nonsensical—can occur during any sleep stage [Mahowald & Ettinger, 1990].) Occasional childhood sleepwalking occurs for about one-third of those with a sleepwalking fraternal twin and half of those with a sleepwalking identical twin. The same is true for sleeptalking (Hublin et al., 1997, 1998). Sleepwalking is usually harmless. After returning to bed on their own or with the help of a family member, few sleepwalkers recall their trip the next morning. About 20 percent of 3- to 12-year-olds have at least one episode of sleepwalking, usually lasting 2 to 10 minutes; some 5 percent have repeated episodes (Giles et al., 1994). Young children, who have the deepest and lengthiest NREM-3 sleep, are the most likely to experience both night terrors and sleepwalking. As we grow older and deep NREM-3 sleep diminishes, so do night terrors and sleepwalking. After being sleep deprived, we sleep more deeply, which increases any tendency to sleepwalk (Zadra et al., 2008).

sleep apnea a sleep disorder characterized by temporary cessations of breathing during sleep and repeated momentary awakenings.

night terrors a sleep disorder characterized by high arousal and an appearance of being terrified; unlike nightmares, night terrors occur during NREM-3 sleep, within two or three hours of falling asleep, and are seldom remembered.

dream a sequence of images, emotions, and thoughts passing through a sleeping person's mind. Dreams are notable for their hallucinatory imagery, discontinuities, and incongruities, and for the dreamer's delusional acceptance of the content and later difficulties remembering it.

Dreams

Now playing at an inner theater near you: the premiere showing of a sleeping person's vivid dream. This never-before-seen mental movie features captivating characters wrapped in a plot so original and unlikely, yet so intricate and so seemingly real, that the viewer later marvels at its creation.

Waking from a troubling dream, wrenched by its emotions, who among us has not wondered about this weird state of consciousness? How can our brain so creatively, colorfully, and completely construct this alternative, conscious world? In the shadowland between our dreaming and waking consciousness, we may even wonder for a moment which is real.

Discovering the link between REM-sleep and dreaming opened a new era in dream research. Instead of relying on someone's hazy recall hours or days after having a dream, researchers could catch dreams as they happened. They could awaken people during or within 3 minutes after a REM sleep period and hear a vivid account.

Photofest/Warner Bros. Pictures

A dreamy take on dreamland The 2010 movie *Inception* creatively plays off our interest in finding meaning in our dreams, and in understanding the layers of our consciousness.

What We Dream

8-6 What do we dream?

Daydreams tend to involve the familiar details of our life—perhaps picturing ourselves explaining to an instructor why a paper will be late, or replaying in our minds personal encounters we relish or regret. REM **dreams**—"hallucinations of the sleeping mind"(Loftus & Ketcham, 1994, p. 67)—are vivid, emotional, and bizarre—so vivid we may confuse them with reality. Awakening from a nightmare, a 4-year-old may be sure there is a bear in the house.

"I do not believe that I am now dreaming, but I cannot prove that I am not."

Philosopher Bertrand Russell (1872–1970)

We spend six years of our life in dreams, many of which are anything but sweet. For both women and men, 8 in 10 dreams are marked by at least one negative event or emotion (Domhoff, 2007). Common themes are repeatedly failing in an attempt to do something; of being attacked, pursued, or rejected; or of experiencing misfortune (Hall et al., 1982). Dreams with sexual imagery occur less often than you might think. In one study, only 1 in 10 dreams among young men and 1 in 30 among young women had sexual content (Domhoff, 1996). More commonly, the story line of our dreams incorporates traces of previous days' nonsexual experiences and preoccupations (De Koninck, 2000):

Would you suppose that people dream if blind from birth? Studies in France, Hungary, Egypt, and the United States all found blind people dreaming of using their nonvisual senses—hearing, touching, smelling, tasting (Buquet, 1988; Taha, 1972; Vekassy, 1977).

MAXINE

© 2001 Mariam Henley

"For what one has dwelt on by day, these things are seen in visions of the night."
Menander of Athens (342–292 B.C.E.), *Fragments*

- After suffering a trauma, people commonly report nightmares, which help extinguish daytime fears (Levin & Nielsen, 2007, 2009). One sample of Americans recording their dreams during September 2001 reported an increase in threatening dreams following the 9/11 attack (Propper et al., 2007).
- After playing the computer game *Tetris* for 7 hours and then being awakened repeatedly during their first hour of sleep, 3 in 4 people reported experiencing images of the game's falling blocks (Stickgold et al., 2000).
- Compared to city-dwellers, people in hunter-gatherer societies more often dream of animals (Mestel, 1997). Compared with nonmusicians, musicians report twice as many dreams of music (Uga et al., 2006).

A popular sleep myth: If you dream you are falling and hit the ground (or if you dream of dying), you die. (Unfortunately, those who could confirm these ideas are not around to do so. Some people, however, have had such dreams and are alive to report them.)

Our two-track mind is also monitoring our environment while we sleep. Sensory stimuli—a particular odor or a phone's ringing—may be instantly and ingeniously woven into the dream story. In a classic experiment, researchers lightly sprayed cold water on dreamers' faces (Dement & Wolpert, 1958). Compared with sleepers who did not get the cold-water treatment, these people were more likely to dream about a waterfall, a leaky roof, or even about being sprayed by someone.

So, could we learn a foreign language by hearing it played while we sleep? If only it were so easy. While sleeping, we can learn to associate a sound with a mild electric shock (and to react to the sound accordingly). But we do not remember recorded information played while we are soundly asleep (Eich, 1990; Wyatt & Bootzin, 1994). In fact, anything that happens during the 5 minutes just before we fall asleep is typically lost from memory (Roth et al., 1988). This explains why sleep apnea patients, who repeatedly awaken with a gasp and then immediately fall back to sleep, do not recall the episodes. It also explains why dreams that momentarily awaken us are mostly forgotten by morning. To remember a dream, get up and stay awake for a few minutes.

"Follow your dreams, except for that one where you're naked at work."
Attributed to Henny Youngman

Why We Dream

8-7 What are the functions of dreams?

Dream theorists have proposed several explanations of why we dream, including these:

To satisfy our own wishes. In 1900, in his landmark book *The Interpretation of Dreams*, Sigmund Freud offered what he thought was "the most valuable of all the discoveries it has been my good fortune to make." He proposed that dreams provide a psychic safety valve that discharges otherwise unacceptable feelings. He viewed a dream's **manifest content** (the apparent and remembered story line) as a censored, symbolic version of its **latent content**, the unconscious drives and wishes that would be threatening if expressed directly. Although most dreams have no overt sexual imagery, Freud nevertheless believed that most adult dreams could be "traced back by analysis to erotic wishes." Thus, a gun might be a disguised representation of a penis.

Freud considered dreams the key to understanding our inner conflicts. However, his critics say it is time to wake up from Freud's dream theory, which is a scientific nightmare. Based on the accumulated science, "there is no reason to believe any of Freud's specific claims about dreams and their purposes," observed dream researcher William Domhoff (2003). Some contend that even if dreams are symbolic, they could be interpreted any way one wished. Others maintain that dreams hide nothing. A dream about a gun is a dream about a gun. Legend has it that even Freud, who loved to smoke cigars, acknowledged that "sometimes, a cigar is just a cigar." Freud's wish-fulfillment theory of dreams has in large part given way to other theories.

manifest content according to Freud, the remembered story line of a dream (as distinct from its latent, or hidden, content).

latent content according to Freud, the underlying meaning of a dream (as distinct from its manifest content).

"When people interpret [a dream] as if it were meaningful and then sell those interpretations, it's quackery."
Sleep researcher J. Allan Hobson (1995)

To file away memories. The *information-processing* perspective proposes that dreams may help sift, sort, and fix the day's experiences in our memory. Some studies support this view. When tested the next day after learning a task, those deprived of both slow-wave and REM sleep did not do as well as those who slept undisturbed on their new learning (Stickgold et al., 2000, 2001). People who hear unusual phrases or learn to find hidden visual images before bedtime remember less the next morning if awakened every time they begin REM sleep than they do if awakened during other sleep stages (Empson & Clarke, 1970; Karni & Sagi, 1994).

Brain scans confirm the link between REM sleep and memory. The brain regions that buzz as rats learn to navigate a maze, or as people learn to perform a visual-discrimination task, buzz again during later REM sleep (Louie & Wilson, 2001; Maquet, 2001). So precise are these activity patterns that scientists can tell where in the maze the rat would be if awake. Others, unpersuaded by these studies, note that memory consolidation may also occur during non-REM sleep (Siegel, 2001; Vertes & Siegel, 2005). This much seems true: A night of solid sleep (and dreaming) has an important place in our lives. To sleep, perchance to remember.

This is important news for students, many of whom, observed researcher Robert Stickgold (2000), suffer from a kind of sleep bulimia—binge-sleeping on the weekend. "If you don't get good sleep and enough sleep after you learn new stuff, you won't integrate it effectively into your memories," he warned. That helps explain why secondary students with high grades have averaged 25 minutes more sleep a night than their lower-achieving classmates (Wolfson & Carskadon, 1998).

To develop and preserve neural pathways. Perhaps dreams, or the brain activity associated with REM sleep, serve a *physiological* function, providing the sleeping brain with periodic stimulation. This theory makes developmental sense. We know that stimulating experiences preserve and expand the brain's neural pathways. Infants, whose neural networks are fast developing, spend much of their abundant sleep time in REM sleep (**FIGURE 8.9** on the next page).

Rapid eye movements also stir the liquid behind the cornea; this delivers fresh oxygen to corneal cells, preventing their suffocation.

To make sense of neural static. Other theories propose that dreams erupt from neural activation spreading upward from the brainstem (Antrobus, 1991; Hobson, 2003, 2004, 2009). According to one version, dreams are the brain's attempt to make sense of random neural activity. Much as a neurosurgeon can produce hallucinations by stimulating different parts of a patient's cortex, so can stimulation originating within the brain. These internal stimuli activate brain areas that process visual images, but not the visual cortex area, which receives raw input from the eyes. As Freud might have expected, PET scans of sleeping people also reveal increased activity in the emotion-related limbic system (in the amygdala) during REM sleep. In contrast, frontal lobe regions responsible for inhibition and logical thinking seem to idle, which may explain why our dreams are less inhibited than we are when awake (Maquet et al., 1996). Add the limbic system's emotional tone to the brain's visual bursts and—Voila!—we dream. Damage either the limbic system or the visual centers active during dreaming, and dreaming itself may be impaired (Domhoff, 2003).

Question: Does eating spicy foods cause one to dream more?
Answer: Any food that causes you to awaken more increases your chance of recalling a dream (Moorcroft, 2003).

swissmacky/Shutterstock

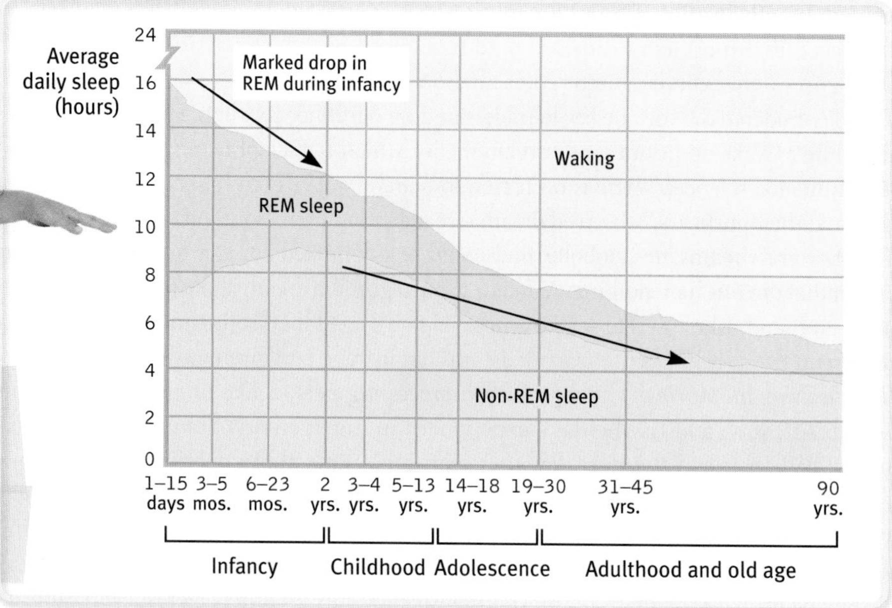

FIGURE 8.9

Sleep across the life span As we age, our sleep patterns change. During our first few months, we spend progressively less time in REM sleep. During our first 20 years, we spend progressively less time asleep. (Adapted from Snyder & Scott, 1972.)

To reflect cognitive development. Some dream researchers dispute both the Freudian and neural activation theories, preferring instead to see dreams as part of brain maturation and cognitive development (Domhoff, 2010, 2011; Foulkes, 1999). For example, prior to age 9, children's dreams seem more like a slide show and less like an active story in which the dreamer is an actor. Dreams overlap with waking cognition and feature coherent speech. They simulate reality by drawing on our concepts and knowledge. They engage brain networks that also are active during daydreaming. Unlike the idea that dreams arise from bottom-up brain activation, the cognitive perspective emphasizes our mind's top-down control of our dream content (Nir & Tononi, 2010).

REM rebound the tendency for REM sleep to increase following REM sleep deprivation (created by repeated awakenings during REM sleep).

TABLE 8.3 compares major dream theories. Although sleep researchers debate dreams' function—and some are skeptical that dreams serve any function—there is one thing they agree on: We need REM sleep. Deprived of it by repeatedly being awakened, people return more and more quickly to the REM stage after falling back to sleep. When finally allowed to sleep undisturbed, they literally sleep like babies—with increased REM sleep,

TABLE 8.3

Dream Theories

Theory	Explanation	Critical Considerations
Freud's wish-fulfillment	Dreams provide a "psychic safety valve"—expressing otherwise unacceptable feelings; contain manifest (remembered) content and a deeper layer of latent content—a hidden meaning.	Lacks any scientific support; dreams may be interpreted in many different ways.
Information-processing	Dreams help us sort out the day's events and consolidate our memories.	But why do we sometimes dream about things we have not experienced?
Physiological function	Regular brain stimulation from REM sleep may help develop and preserve neural pathways.	This does not explain why we experience meaningful dreams.
Neural activation	REM sleep triggers neural activity that evokes random visual memories, which our sleeping brain weaves into stories.	The individual's brain is weaving the stories, which still tells us something about the dreamer.
Cognitive development	Dream content reflects dreamers' cognitive development—their knowledge and understanding.	Does not address the neuroscience of dreams.

a phenomenon called **REM rebound.** Withdrawing REM-suppressing sleeping medications also increases REM sleep, but with accompanying nightmares.

Most other mammals also experience REM rebound, suggesting that the causes and functions of REM sleep are deeply biological. That REM sleep occurs in mammals—and not in animals such as fish, whose behavior is less influenced by learning—also fits the information-processing theory of dreams.

So does this mean that because dreams serve physiological functions and extend normal cognition, they are psychologically meaningless? Not necessarily. Every psychologically meaningful experience involves an active brain. We are once again reminded of a basic principle: *Biological and psychological explanations of behavior are partners, not competitors.*

RETRIEVAL PRACTICE

- What five theories explain why we dream?

ANSWERS: (1) Freud's wish-fulfillment (dreams as a psychic safety valve), (2) information-processing (dreams sort the day's events and form memories), (3) physiological function (dreams pave neural pathways), (4) neural activation (dreams trigger random neural activity that the mind weaves into stories), (5) cognitive development (dreams reflect the dreamer's developmental stage)

MODULE REVIEW

Sleep and Dreams

Learning Objectives

RETRIEVAL PRACTICE Take a moment to answer each of these Learning Objective Questions (repeated here from within the module). Then turn to Appendix B, Complete Module Reviews, to check your answers. Research suggests that trying to answer these questions on your own will improve your long-term retention (McDaniel et al., 2009).

8-1: How do our biological rhythms influence our daily functioning?

8-2: What is the biological rhythm of our sleeping and dreaming stages?

8-3: How do biology and environment interact in our sleep patterns?

8-4: What are sleep's functions?

8-5: How does sleep loss affect us, and what are the major sleep disorders?

8-6: What do we dream?

8-7: What are the functions of dreams?

Terms and Concepts to Remember

RETRIEVAL PRACTICE Test yourself on these terms by trying to write down the definition before flipping back to the referenced page to check your answer.

circadian [ser-KAY-dee-an] rhythm, p. 92
REM sleep, p. 93
alpha waves, p. 93
sleep, p. 93
hallucinations, p. 95
delta waves, p. 95
insomnia, p. 103
narcolepsy, p. 103
sleep apnea, p.104
night terrors, p. 104
dream, p. 105
manifest content, p. 106
latent content, p. 106
REM rebound, p. 109

RETRIEVAL PRACTICE Gain an advantage, and benefit from immediate feedback, with the interactive self-testing resources at www.worthpublishers.com/myers.

- Frequently Asked Questions About Hypnosis
- Explaining the Hypnotized State

MODULE 9

Hypnosis

9-1 What is hypnosis, and what powers does a hypnotist have over a hypnotized subject?

Imagine you are about to be hypnotized. The hypnotist invites you to sit back, fix your gaze on a spot high on the wall, and relax. In a quiet voice the hypnotist suggests, "Your eyes are growing tired. . . . Your eyelids are becoming heavy . . . . now heavier and heavier. . . . They are beginning to close. . . . You are becoming more deeply relaxed. . . . Your breathing is now deep and regular. . . . Your muscles are becoming more and more relaxed. Your whole body is beginning to feel like lead."

After a few minutes of this *hypnotic induction*, you may experience **hypnosis.** When the hypnotist suggests, "Your eyelids are shutting so tight that you cannot open them even if you try," it may indeed seem beyond your control to open your eyelids. Told to forget the number 6, you may be puzzled when you count 11 fingers on your hands. Invited to smell a sensuous perfume that is actually ammonia, you may linger delightedly over its pungent odor. Told that you cannot see a certain object, such as a chair, you may indeed report that it is not there, although you manage to avoid the chair when walking around (illustrating the *dual-processing* talents of that mind of yours).

But is hypnosis really an *altered* state of consciousness? Let's start with some frequently asked questions.

Frequently Asked Questions About Hypnosis

Hypnotists have no magical mind-control power. Their power resides in the subjects' openness to suggestion, their ability to focus on certain images or behaviors (Bowers, 1984). But how open to suggestions are we?

- ***Can anyone experience hypnosis?*** To some extent, we are all open to suggestion. When people stand upright with their eyes closed and are told that they are swaying back and forth, most will indeed sway a little. In fact, *postural sway* is one of the items assessed on the Stanford Hypnotic Susceptibility Scale. People who respond to such suggestions without hypnosis are the same people who respond with hypnosis (Kirsch & Braffman, 2001).

  Highly hypnotizable people—say, the 20 percent who can carry out a suggestion not to smell or react to a bottle of ammonia held under their nose—typically become deeply absorbed in imaginative activities (Barnier & McConkey, 2004; Silva & Kirsch, 1992). Many researchers refer to this as hypnotic ability—the ability to focus attention totally on a task, to become imaginatively absorbed in it, to entertain fanciful possibilities.

- ***Can hypnosis enhance recall of forgotten events?*** Most people wrongly believe that our experiences are all "in there," recorded in our brain and available for recall if only we can break through our own defenses (Loftus, 1980). But 60 years of memory research disputes such beliefs. We do not encode everything that occurs around us. We permanently store only some of our experiences, and we may be unable to retrieve some memories we have stored.

  "Hypnotically refreshed" memories combine fact with fiction. Since 1980, thousands of people have reported being abducted by UFOs, but most such reports have come from people who are predisposed to believe in aliens, are highly hypnotizable, and have undergone hypnosis (Newman & Baumeister, 1996; Nickell, 1996). Without

"Hypnosis is not a psychological truth serum and to regard it as such has been a source of considerable mischief."

Researcher Kenneth Bowers (1987)

either person being aware of what is going on, a hypnotist's hints—"Did you hear loud noises?"—can plant ideas that become the subject's pseudomemory.

So should testimony obtained under hypnosis be admissible in court? American, Australian, and British courts have agreed it should not. They generally ban testimony from witnesses who have been hypnotized (Druckman & Bjork, 1994; Gibson, 1995; McConkey, 1995).

- ***Can hypnosis force people to act against their will?*** Researchers have induced hypnotized people to perform an apparently dangerous act: plunging one hand briefly into fuming "acid," then throwing the "acid" in a researcher's face (Orne & Evans, 1965). Interviewed a day later, these people emphatically denied their acts and said they would never follow such orders.

  Had hypnosis given the hypnotist a special power to control others against their will? To find out, researchers Martin Orne and Frederich Evans unleashed that enemy of so many illusory beliefs—the control group. Orne asked other individuals to *pretend* they were hypnotized. Laboratory assistants, unaware that those in the experiment's control group had not been hypnotized, treated both groups the same. The result? All the *un*hypnotized participants (perhaps believing that the laboratory context assured safety) performed the same acts as those who were hypnotized.

- ***Can hypnosis help people heal or relieve their pain?*** *Hypnotherapists* try to help patients harness their own healing powers (Baker, 1987). **Posthypnotic suggestions** have helped alleviate headaches, asthma, and stress-related skin disorders.

  In one statistical digest of 18 studies, the average client whose therapy was supplemented with hypnosis showed greater improvement than 70 percent of other therapy patients (Kirsch et al., 1995, 1996). Hypnosis seemed especially helpful for the treatment of obesity. However, drug, alcohol, and smoking addictions have not responded well to hypnosis (Nash, 2001). In controlled studies, hypnosis speeds the disappearance of warts, but so do the same positive suggestions given without hypnosis (Spanos, 1991, 1996).

  Hypnosis *can* relieve pain (Druckman & Bjork, 1994; Jensen, 2008). When unhypnotized people put their arm in an ice bath, they feel intense pain within 25 seconds. When hypnotized people do the same after being given suggestions to feel no pain, they indeed report feeling little pain. As some dentists know, light hypnosis can reduce fear, thus reducing hypersensitivity to pain.

hypnosis a social interaction in which one person (the hypnotist) suggests to another (the subject) that certain perceptions, feelings, thoughts, or behaviors will spontaneously occur.

posthypnotic suggestion a suggestion, made during a hypnosis session, to be carried out after the subject is no longer hypnotized; used by some clinicians to help control undesired symptoms and behaviors.

"It wasn't what I expected. But facts are facts, and if one is proved to be wrong, one must just be humble about it and start again."

Agatha Christie's Miss Marple

o44/ZUMA Press/Newscom

Stage hypnotist

Hypnosis inhibits pain-related brain activity. In surgical experiments, hypnotized patients have required less medication, recovered sooner, and left the hospital earlier than unhypnotized control patients (Askay & Patterson, 2007; Hammond, 2008; Spiegel, 2007). Nearly 10 percent of us can become so deeply hypnotized that even major surgery can be performed without anesthesia. Half of us can gain at least some pain relief from hypnosis. The surgical use of hypnosis has flourished in Europe, where one Belgian medical team has performed more than 5000 surgeries with a combination of hypnosis, local anesthesia, and a mild sedative (Song, 2006).

RETRIEVAL PRACTICE

- When is the use of hypnosis potentially harmful, and when can hypnosis be used to help?

ANSWER: Hypnosis can be harmful if used to "hypnotically refresh" memories, which may plant false memories. But posthypnotic suggestions have helped alleviate some ailments, and hypnosis can also help control pain.

Explaining the Hypnotized State

9-2 Is hypnosis an extension of normal consciousness or an altered state?

We have seen that hypnosis involves heightened suggestibility. We have also seen that hypnotic procedures do not endow a person with special powers but can sometimes help people overcome stress-related ailments and cope with pain. So, just what *is* hypnosis? Psychologists have proposed two explanations.

Hypnosis as a Social Phenomenon

Our attentional spotlight and interpretations powerfully influence our ordinary perceptions. Might hypnotic phenomena reflect such workings of normal consciousness, as well as the power of social influence (Lynn et al., 1990; Spanos & Coe, 1992)? Advocates of the *social influence theory of hypnosis* believe they do.

Does this mean that subjects consciously fake hypnosis? *No*—like actors caught up in their roles, they begin to feel and behave in ways appropriate for "good hypnotic subjects." The more they like and trust the hypnotist, the more they allow that person to direct their attention and fantasies (Gfeller et al., 1987). "The hypnotist's ideas become the subject's thoughts," explained Theodore Barber (2000), "and the subject's thoughts produce the hypnotic experiences and behaviors." Told to scratch their ear later when they hear the word *psychology*, subjects will likely do so—but only if they think the experiment is still under way. If an experimenter eliminates their motivation for acting hypnotized—by stating that hypnosis reveals their "gullibility"—subjects become unresponsive. Such findings support the idea that hypnotic phenomena are an extension of normal social and cognitive processes.

These views illustrate a principle Stanley Milgram (1974) demonstrated: *An authoritative person in a legitimate context can induce people—hypnotized or not—to perform some unlikely acts.* Or as hypnosis researcher Nicholas Spanos (1982) put it, "The overt behaviors of hypnotic subjects are well within normal limits."

Hypnosis as Divided Consciousness

Other hypnosis researchers believe hypnosis is more than inducing someone to play the role of "good subject." How, they ask, can we explain why hypnotized subjects sometimes carry out suggested behaviors on cue, even when they believe no one is watching

(Perugini et al., 1998)? And why does distinctive brain activity accompany hypnosis (Oakley & Halligan, 2009)? In one experiment, deeply hypnotized people were asked to imagine a color, and areas of their brain lit up as if they were really seeing the color. To the hypnotized person's brain, mere imagination had become a compelling hallucination (Kosslyn et al., 2000). In another experiment, researchers invited hypnotizable and nonhypnotizable people to say the color of letters. This is an easy task, but it slows if, say, green letters form the conflicting word RED (Raz et al., 2005). When easily hypnotized people were given a suggestion to focus on the color and to perceive the letters as irrelevant gibberish, they were much less slowed by the word-color conflict. (Brain areas that decode words and detect conflict remained inactive.)

These results would not have surprised famed researcher Ernest Hilgard (1986, 1992), who believed hypnosis involves not only social influence but also a special dual-processing state of **dissociation**—a split between different levels of consciousness. Hilgard viewed hypnotic dissociation as a vivid form of everyday mind splits—similar to doodling while listening to a lecture or typing the end of a sentence while starting a conversation. Hilgard felt that when, for example, hypnotized people lower their arm into an ice bath, as in **FIGURE 9.1**, the hypnosis dissociates the sensation of the pain stimulus (of which the subjects are still aware) from the emotional suffering that defines their experience of pain. The ice water therefore feels cold—very cold—but not painful.

"The total possible consciousness may be split into parts which co-exist but mutually ignore each other."

William James, *Principles of Psychology,* 1890

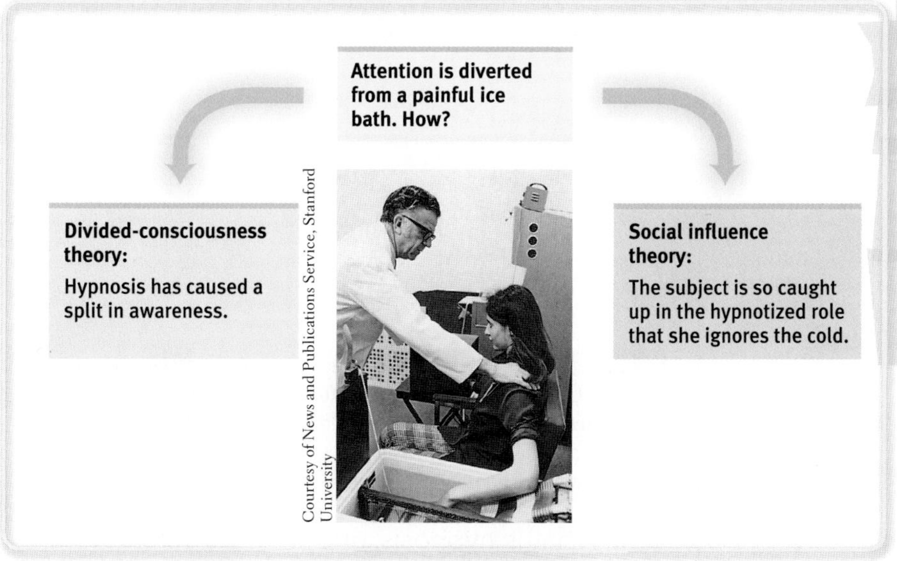

FIGURE 9.1
Dissociation or role playing? This hypnotized woman tested by Ernest Hilgard exhibited no pain when her arm was placed in an ice bath. But asked to press a key if some part of her felt the pain, she did so. To Hilgard, this was evidence of dissociation, or divided consciousness. Proponents of social influence theory, however, maintain that people responding this way are caught up in playing the role of "good subject."

Another form of dual processing—*selective attention*—may also play a role in hypnotic pain relief. PET scans show that hypnosis reduces brain activity in a region that processes painful stimuli, but not in the sensory cortex, which receives the raw sensory input (Rainville et al., 1997). Hypnosis does not block sensory input, but it may block our attention to those stimuli. This helps explain why an injured athlete, caught up in the competition, may feel little or no pain until the game ends.

Although the divided-consciousness theory of hypnosis is controversial, this much seems clear: There is, without doubt, much more to thinking and acting than we are conscious of. Our information processing, which starts with selective attention, is divided into simultaneous conscious and nonconscious realms. In hypnosis as in life, *much of our behavior occurs on autopilot.* We have two-track minds, as a biopsychosocial approach helps demonstrate (**FIGURE 9.2** on the next page).

dissociation a split in consciousness, which allows some thoughts and behaviors to occur simultaneously with others.

FIGURE 9.2
Levels of analysis for hypnosis
Using a biopsychosocial approach, researchers explore hypnosis from complementary perspectives.

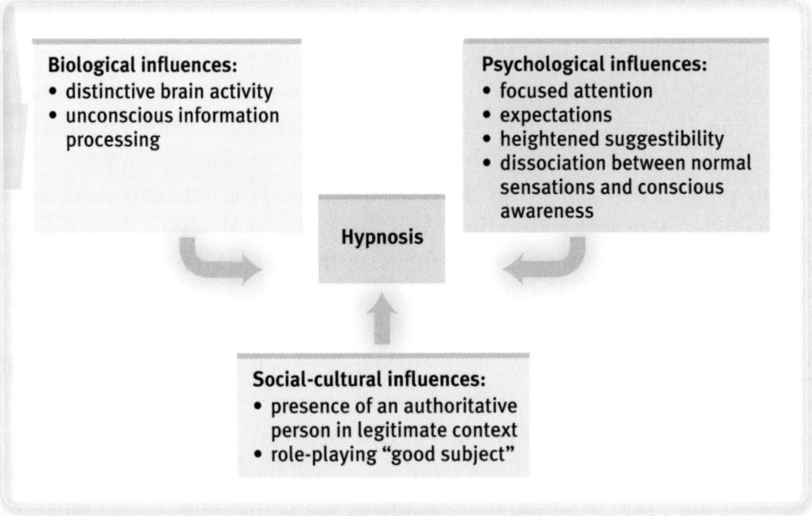

RETRIEVAL PRACTICE

- Hilgard believed that hypnosis involves a state of divided consciousness called ___________. His beliefs have been challenged by researchers who suggest ___________ influence is involved.

ANSWERS: dissociation; social

MODULE REVIEW

Hypnosis

Learning Objectives

RETRIEVAL PRACTICE Take a moment to answer each of these Learning Objective Questions (repeated here from within the module). Then turn to Appendix B, Complete Module Reviews, to check your answers. Research suggests that trying to answer these questions on your own will improve your long-term retention (McDaniel et al., 2009).

9-1: What is hypnosis, and what powers does a hypnotist have over a hypnotized subject?

9-2: Is hypnosis an extension of normal consciousness or an altered state?

Terms and Concepts to Remember

RETRIEVAL PRACTICE Test yourself on these terms by trying to write down the definition before flipping back to the referenced page to check your answer.

hypnosis, p. 110
posthypnotic suggestion, p. 111
dissociation, p. 113

MODULE 10

Drugs and Consciousness

- Tolerance, Dependence, and Addiction
- Types of Psychoactive Drugs
- Influences on Drug Use

Let's imagine a day in the life of a legal-drug user. It begins with a wake-up latte. By midday, several cigarettes have calmed frazzled nerves before an appointment at the plastic surgeon's office for wrinkle-smoothing Botox injections. A diet pill before dinner helps stem the appetite, and its stimulating effects can later be partially offset with a glass of wine and two Tylenol PMs. And if performance needs enhancing, there are beta blockers for onstage performers, Viagra for middle-aged men, hormone-delivering "libido patches" for middle-aged women, and Adderall for students hoping to focus their concentration. Before drifting off into REM-depressed sleep, our hypothetical drug user is dismayed by news reports of pill-sharing, pill-popping college students.

Most of us manage to use some nonprescription drugs in moderation and without disrupting our lives. But some of us develop self-harming *substance-related disorders.* The substances these people are using are **psychoactive drugs,** chemicals that change perceptions and moods. A drug's overall effect depends not only on its *biological* effects but also on the *psychology* of the user's expectations, which vary with social contexts and cultures (Ward, 1994). If one culture assumes that a particular drug produces euphoria (or aggression or sexual arousal) and another does not, each culture may find its expectations fulfilled. In the pages that follow, we'll take a closer look at these interacting forces in the use and potential abuse of particular psychoactive drugs. But first, let's see how our bodies react to the ongoing use of psychoactive drugs.

psychoactive drug a chemical substance that alters perceptions and moods.

tolerance the diminishing effect with regular use of the same dose of a drug, requiring the user to take larger and larger doses before experiencing the drug's effect.

addiction compulsive drug craving and use, despite adverse consequences.

withdrawal the discomfort and distress that follow discontinuing the use of an addictive drug.

physical dependence a physiological need for a drug, marked by unpleasant withdrawal symptoms when the drug is discontinued.

psychological dependence a psychological need to use a drug, such as to relieve negative emotions.

Tolerance, Dependence, and Addiction

10-1 What are tolerance, dependence, and addiction, and what are some common misconceptions about addiction?

Why might a person who rarely drinks alcohol get buzzed on one can of beer while a long-term drinker shows few effects until the second six-pack? The answer is **tolerance.** With continued use of alcohol and some other drugs (marijuana is an exception), the user's brain chemistry adapts to offset the drug effect (a process called *neuroadaptation*). To experience the same effect, the user requires larger and larger doses (**FIGURE 10.1**). In alcohol tolerance, for example, the person's brain, heart, and liver suffer damage from the chronic, excessive amounts of alcohol being "tolerated." These ever-increasing doses can become a serious threat to health and may lead to **addiction:** The person craves and uses the substance despite its adverse consequences. (See Thinking Critically About: Addiction on the next page.) Worldwide, reports the World Health Organization (2008), 90 million people suffer from such problems related to alcohol and other drugs.

Regular users often try to fight their addiction. But abruptly stopping the drug may lead to the undesirable side effects of **withdrawal.** As the body responds to the drug's absence, the user may feel physical pain and intense cravings, indicating **physical dependence.** People can also develop **psychological dependence,** particularly for stress-relieving drugs, such as alcohol. Although not always physically addictive, such drugs may nevertheless become

RETRIEVAL PRACTICE

FIGURE 10.1

Drug tolerance What is the process that leads to drug tolerance?

ANSWER: With repeated exposure to a psychoactive drug, the drug's effect lessens. Thus, it takes bigger doses to get the desired effect.

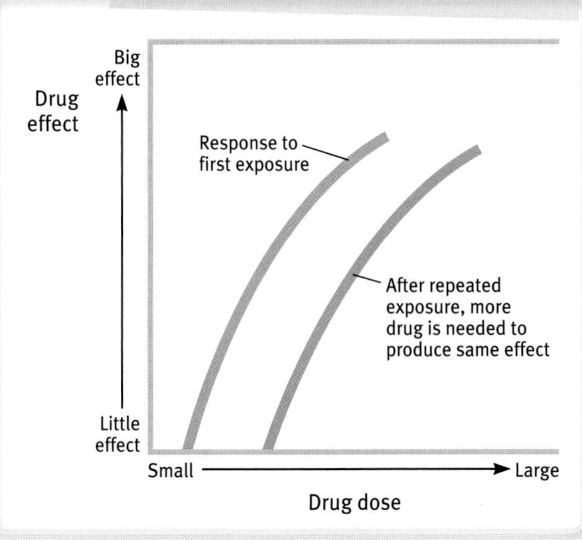

THINKING CRITICALLY ABOUT

Addiction

In recent pop psychology, the supposedly irresistible seduction of addiction has been extended to cover many behaviors formerly considered bad habits or even sins. Has the concept been stretched too far? Are addictions as irresistible as commonly believed? Let's consider three big questions.

1. **Do addictive drugs quickly corrupt?** For example, does morphine taken to control pain often lead to heroin abuse? Generally not. People given morphine to control pain rarely develop the cravings of the addict who uses morphine as a mood-altering drug (Melzack, 1990). Some—perhaps 10 percent—do indeed have a hard time using a psychoactive drug in moderation or stopping altogether. But controlled, occasional users far outnumber those who become addicted to drugs such as alcohol and marijuana (Gazzaniga, 1988; Siegel, 1990). "Even for a very addictive drug like cocaine, only 15 to 16 percent of people become addicted within 10 years of first use," observed Terry Robinson and Kent Berridge (2003).
2. **Does overcoming an addiction require therapy?** Addictions can be powerful, and some addicts do benefit from therapy or group support. Alcoholics Anonymous has supported many people in overcoming their alcohol dependence. But the recovery rates of treated and untreated groups differ less than one might suppose. Moreover, viewing addiction as an uncontrollable disease can undermine people's self-confidence and their belief that they can change. And that, critics say, would be unfortunate, for many people do voluntarily stop using addictive drugs, without any treatment. Most of America's 41 million ex-smokers kicked the habit on their own, usually after prior failed efforts or treatments.
3. **Can we extend the concept of addiction to cover not just drug dependencies, but a whole spectrum of repetitive, pleasure-seeking behaviors?** We can, and we have, but should we? The addiction-as-disease-needing-treatment idea has been suggested for a host of driven, excessive behaviors—eating, shopping, gambling, work, and sex. Used not as a metaphor ("I'm a science fiction addict") but as reality, "addiction" can become an all-purpose excuse. Moreover, labeling a behavior doesn't explain it. Attributing serial adultery, as in the case of Tiger Woods, to a "sex addiction" does not explain the sexual impulsiveness, say critics (Radford, 2010).

David Horsey/Seattlepi.com

A social networking addiction?

Sometimes, though, behaviors such as gambling, video gaming, or online surfing do become compulsive and dysfunctional, much like abusive drug taking (Gentile, 2009; Griffiths, 2001; Hoeft et al., 2008). Some Internet users, for example, do display an apparent inability to resist logging on, and staying on, even when this excessive use impairs their work and relationships (Ko et al., 2005). Are we justified in stretching the addiction concept to cover such social behaviors? Stay tuned. Debates over the addiction-as-disease model continue.

an important part of the user's life, often as a way of relieving negative emotions. For someone who is either physically or psychologically dependent, obtaining and using the drug can become the day's focus (**TABLE 10.1**).

The odds of getting hooked after trying various drugs:

Tobacco	32%
Heroin	23%
Alcohol	15%
Marijuana	9%

Source: National Academy of Science, Institute of Medicine (Brody, 2003).

TABLE 10.1

What Is Substance Dependence?

According to the American Psychiatric Association's *Diagnostic and Statistical Manual of Mental Disorders,* the presence of three or more of the following indicates *dependence* on a substance.

- Tolerance (with repeated use, desired effect requires larger doses)
- Withdrawal (discomfort and distress when discontinued)
- Taking the substance longer or in greater amounts than intended
- Failure to regulate use
- Much time devoted to obtaining the substance
- Normal activities abandoned or reduced
- Continued use despite knowledge that using the substance worsens problems

Types of Psychoactive Drugs

The three major categories of psychoactive drugs are *depressants*, *stimulants*, and *hallucinogens*. All do their work at the brain's synapses, stimulating, inhibiting, or mimicking the activity of the brain's own chemical messengers, the neurotransmitters.

depressants drugs (such as alcohol, barbiturates, and opiates) that reduce neural activity and slow body functions.

Depressants

10-2 What are depressants, and what are their effects?

Depressants are drugs such as alcohol, barbiturates (tranquilizers), and opiates that calm neural activity and slow body functions.

Alcohol

True or false? In small amounts, alcohol is a stimulant.

False. Low doses of alcohol may, indeed, enliven a drinker, but they do so by acting as a *disinhibitor*—they slow brain activity that controls judgment and inhibitions. Alcohol is an equal-opportunity drug: It increases (disinhibits) helpful tendencies—as when tipsy restaurant patrons leave extravagant tips (Lynn, 1988). And it increases harmful tendencies, as when sexually aroused men become more disposed to sexual aggression. One University of Illinois campus survey showed that before sexual assaults, 80 percent of the male assailants and 70 percent of the female victims had been drinking (Camper, 1990). Another survey of 89,874 American collegians found alcohol or drugs involved in 79 percent of unwanted sexual intercourse experiences (Presley et al., 1997).

When drinking, both men and women are more disposed to casual sex (Davis et al., 2006; Ebel-Lam et al., 2009; Grello et al., 2006). Alcohol + sex = the perfect storm. More than 600 studies have explored the link between drinking and risky sex, with the overwhelming majority finding the two correlated (Cooper, 2006). *The urges you would feel if sober are the ones you will more likely act upon when intoxicated.*

"That is not one of the seven habits of highly effective people."

© The New Yorker Collection 1998 Leo Cullum from cartoonbank.com. All Rights Reserved.

Slowed Neural Processing Low doses of alcohol relax the drinker by slowing sympathetic nervous system activity. In larger doses, alcohol can become a staggering problem: Reactions slow, speech slurs, skilled performance deteriorates. Paired with sleep deprivation, alcohol is a potent sedative. Add these physical effects to lowered inhibitions, and the result can be deadly. Worldwide, several hundred thousand lives are lost each year in alcohol-related accidents and violent crime. When sober, most drinkers believe that driving under the influence of alcohol is wrong, and they insist they would not do so. Yet, as blood-alcohol levels rise and moral judgments falter, people's qualms about drinking and driving lessen. Virtually all will drive home from a bar, even if given a breathalyzer test and told they are intoxicated (Denton & Krebs, 1990; MacDonald et al., 1995). If heavy drinking follows a period of moderate drinking (which depresses the vomiting response), people may poison themselves with an overdose that their bodies would normally throw up.

Dangerous disinhibition Alcohol consumption leads to feelings of invincibility, which become especially dangerous behind the wheel of a car, such as this one totaled by a teenage drunk driver. This Colorado University Alcohol Awareness Week exhibit prompted many students to post their own anti-drinking pledges (white flags).

Ray Ng/Time & Life Pictures/Getty Images

Memory Disruption Alcohol disrupts memory formation. Thus, heavy drinkers may not recall people they met the night before or what they said or did while intoxicated. These blackouts result partly from the way alcohol suppresses REM sleep, which helps fix the day's experiences into permanent memories.

Heavy drinking can also have long-term effects on the brain and cognition. In rats, at a developmental period corresponding to human adolescence, binge drinking contributes to nerve cell

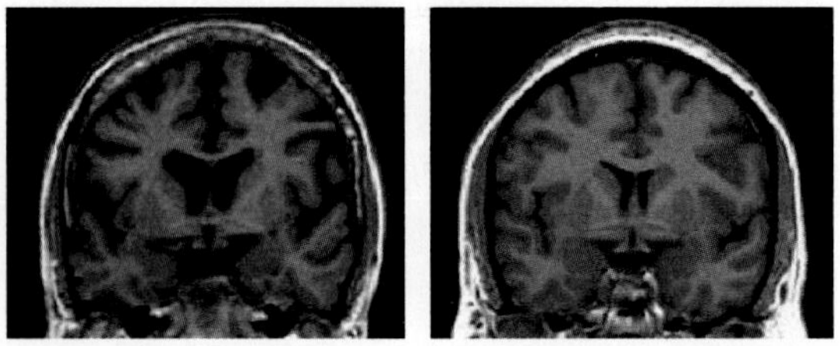

Daniel Hommer, NIAAA, NIH, HHS

Scan of woman with alcohol dependence

Scan of woman without alcohol dependence

FIGURE 10.2
Alcohol dependence shrinks the brain MRI scans show brain shrinkage in women with alcohol dependence (left) compared with women in a control group (right).

death and reduces the birth of new nerve cells. It also impairs the growth of synaptic connections (Crews et al., 2006, 2007).

In those with **alcohol dependence**, prolonged and excessive drinking can shrink the brain (**FIGURE 10.2**). Women, who have less of a stomach enzyme that digests alcohol, are especially vulnerable (Wuethrich, 2001). Girls and young women can become addicted to alcohol more quickly than boys and young men do, and they are at risk for lung, brain, and liver damage at lower consumption levels (CASA, 2003).

Reduced Self-Awareness and Self-Control Alcohol also reduces self-awareness (Hull et al., 1986). In one experiment, those who consumed alcohol (rather than a placebo beverage) were doubly likely to be caught mind-wandering during a reading task, yet were *less* likely to notice that they zoned out (Sayette et al., 2009). Alcohol also produces a sort of "myopia": It focuses attention on an arousing situation, such as a provocation, and distracts attention from normal inhibitions and future consequences (Giancola et al., 2010; Steele & Josephs, 1990).

Reduced self-awareness may help explain why people who want to suppress their awareness of failures or shortcomings are more likely to drink than are those who feel good about themselves. Losing a business deal, a game, or a romantic partner sometimes elicits a drinking binge.

Expectancy Effects As with other psychoactive drugs, users' expectations influence their behavior. When people *believe* that alcohol affects social behavior in certain ways, and *believe*, rightly or wrongly, that they have been drinking alcohol, they will behave accordingly (Moss & Albery, 2009). In a now-classic experiment, researchers gave Rutgers University men (who had volunteered for a study on "alcohol and sexual stimulation") either an alcoholic or a nonalcoholic drink (Abrams & Wilson, 1983). (Both had strong tastes that masked any alcohol.) In each group, half the participants thought they were drinking alcohol and half thought they were not. After watching an erotic movie clip, the men who *thought* they had consumed alcohol were more likely to report having strong sexual fantasies and feeling guilt free. Being able to *attribute* their sexual responses to alcohol released their inhibitions—whether or not they had actually consumed any alcohol. Alcohol's effect lies partly in that powerful sex organ, the mind.

Barbiturates

Like alcohol, the **barbiturate** drugs, or *tranquilizers*, depress nervous system activity. Barbiturates such as Nembutal, Seconal, and Amytal are sometimes prescribed to induce sleep or reduce anxiety. In larger doses, they can impair memory and judgment. If combined with alcohol—as sometimes happens when people take a sleeping pill after an evening of heavy drinking—the total depressive effect on body functions can be lethal.

Opiates

The **opiates**—opium and its derivatives, morphine and heroin—also depress neural functioning. Pupils constrict, breathing slows, and lethargy sets in as blissful pleasure replaces pain and anxiety. For this short-term pleasure, opiate users may pay a long-term price: a gnawing craving for another fix, a need for progressively larger doses (as tolerance develops), and the extreme discomfort of withdrawal. When repeatedly flooded with an artificial opiate, the brain eventually stops producing *endorphins*, its own opiates. If the artificial opiate is then withdrawn, the brain lacks the normal level of these painkilling neurotransmitters. Those who cannot or choose not to tolerate this state may pay an ultimate price—death by overdose. *Methadone*, a synthetic opiate prescribed as a substitute for heroin or for relief of common pain, can also produce tolerance and dependence.

alcohol dependence (popularly known as alcoholism). Alcohol use marked by tolerance, withdrawal if suspended, and a drive to continue use.

barbiturates drugs that depress central nervous system activity, reducing anxiety but impairing memory and judgment.

opiates opium and its derivatives, such as morphine and heroin; they depress neural activity, temporarily lessening pain and anxiety.

stimulants drugs (such as caffeine, nicotine, and the more powerful amphetamines, cocaine, Ecstasy, and methamphetamine) that excite neural activity and speed up body functions.

amphetamines drugs that stimulate neural activity, causing speeded-up body functions and associated energy and mood changes.

nicotine a stimulating and highly addictive psychoactive drug in tobacco.

RETRIEVAL PRACTICE

- Alcohol, barbiturates, and opiates are all in a class of drugs called __________.

ANSWER: depressants

Stimulants

10-3 What are stimulants, and what are their effects?

Vasca/Shutterstock

A **stimulant** excites neural activity and speeds up body functions. Pupils dilate, heart and breathing rates increase, and blood sugar levels rise, causing a drop in appetite. Energy and self-confidence also rise.

Stimulants include caffeine, nicotine, the **amphetamines**, cocaine, *methamphetamine* ("speed"), and Ecstasy. People use stimulants to feel alert, lose weight, or boost mood or athletic performance. Unfortunately, stimulants can be addictive. You may know this if you are one of the many people who use caffeine daily in your coffee, tea, soda, or energy drinks. If cut off from your usual dose, you may crash into fatigue, headaches, irritability, and depression (Silverman et al., 1992). A mild dose of caffeine typically lasts three or four hours, which—if taken in the evening—may be long enough to impair sleep.

Nicotine

One of the most addictive stimulants is **nicotine**, found in cigarettes and other tobacco products. Imagine that cigarettes were harmless—except, once in every 25,000 packs, an occasional innocent-looking one is filled with dynamite instead of tobacco. Not such a bad risk of having your head blown off. But with 250 million packs a day consumed worldwide, we could expect more than 10,000 gruesome daily deaths (more than three times the 9/11 fatalities each and every day)—surely enough to have cigarettes banned everywhere.[1]

The lost lives from these dynamite-loaded cigarettes approximate those from today's actual cigarettes. A teen-to-the-grave smoker has a 50 percent chance of dying from the habit, and each year, tobacco kills nearly 5.4 million of its 1.3 billion customers worldwide. (Imagine the outrage if terrorists took down an equivalent of 25 loaded jumbo jets today, let alone tomorrow and every day thereafter.) By 2030, annual deaths are expected to increase to 8 million. That means that *1 billion* twenty-first-century people may be killed by tobacco (WHO, 2008). Eliminating smoking would increase life expectancy more than any other preventive measure. Why, then, do so many people smoke?

Smoking usually begins during early adolescence. (If you are in college or university, and if by now the cigarette manufacturers haven't made you their devoted customer, they almost surely never will.) Adolescents, self-conscious and often thinking the world is watching their every move, are vulnerable to smoking's allure. They may first light up to imitate glamorous celebrities, or to project a mature image, or to get the social reward of being accepted by other smokers (Cin et al., 2007; Tickle et al., 2006). Mindful of these tendencies, cigarette companies have effectively modeled smoking with themes that appeal to youths: sophistication, independence, adventure-seeking, social approval. Typically, teens who start smoking also have friends who smoke, who suggest its pleasures, and who offer them cigarettes (Rose et al., 1999). Among teens whose parents and best friends are nonsmokers, the smoking rate is close to zero (Moss et al., 1992; also see **FIGURE 10.3** on the next page).

"There is an overwhelming medical and scientific consensus that cigarette smoking causes lung cancer, heart disease, emphysema, and other serious diseases in smokers. Smokers are far more likely to develop serious diseases, like lung cancer, than nonsmokers."

Philip Morris Companies Inc., 1999

Smoke a cigarette and nature will charge you 12 minutes—ironically, just about the length of time you spend smoking it (*Discover,* 1996).

---

[1] This analogy, adapted here with world-based numbers, was suggested by mathematician Sam Saunders, as reported by K. C. Cole (1998).

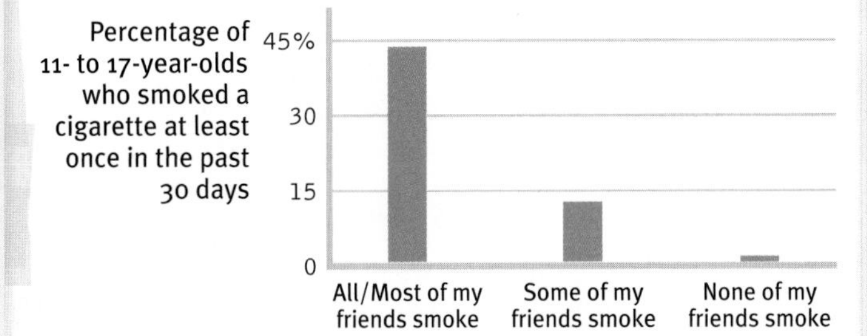

FIGURE 10.3
Peer influence Kids don't smoke if their friends don't (Philip Morris, 2003). A correlation-causation question: Does the close link between teen smoking and friends' smoking reflect peer influence? Teens seeking similar friends? Or both?

James Devaney/WireImage

Nic-A-Teen Virtually nobody starts smoking past the vulnerable teen years. Eager to hook customers whose addiction will give them business for years to come, cigarette companies target teens. Portrayals of smoking by popular actors, such as Robert Pattinson in *Remember Me,* entice teens to imitate.

Those addicted to nicotine find it very hard to quit because tobacco products are as powerfully and quickly addictive as heroin and cocaine. Attempts to quit even within the first weeks of smoking often fail (DiFranza, 2008). As with other addictions, smokers become *dependent,* and they develop *tolerance.* Quitting causes nicotine-withdrawal symptoms, including craving, insomnia, anxiety, irritability, and distractibility. When nicotine-deprived, smokers trying to focus on a task experience a tripled rate of mind wandering (Sayette et al., 2010). When not craving a cigarette, smokers underestimate the power of their future cravings when deprived (Sayette et al., 2008).

All it takes to relieve this aversive state is a cigarette—a portable nicotine dispenser. Within 7 seconds, a rush of nicotine signals the central nervous system to release a flood of neurotransmitters (**FIGURE 10.4**). Epinephrine and norepinephrine diminish

Humorist Dave Barry (1995) recalling why he smoked his first cigarette the summer he turned 15: "Arguments against smoking: 'It's a repulsive addiction that slowly but surely turns you into a gasping, gray-skinned, tumor-ridden invalid, hacking up brownish gobs of toxic waste from your one remaining lung.' Arguments for smoking: 'Other teenagers are doing it.' Case closed! Let's light up!"

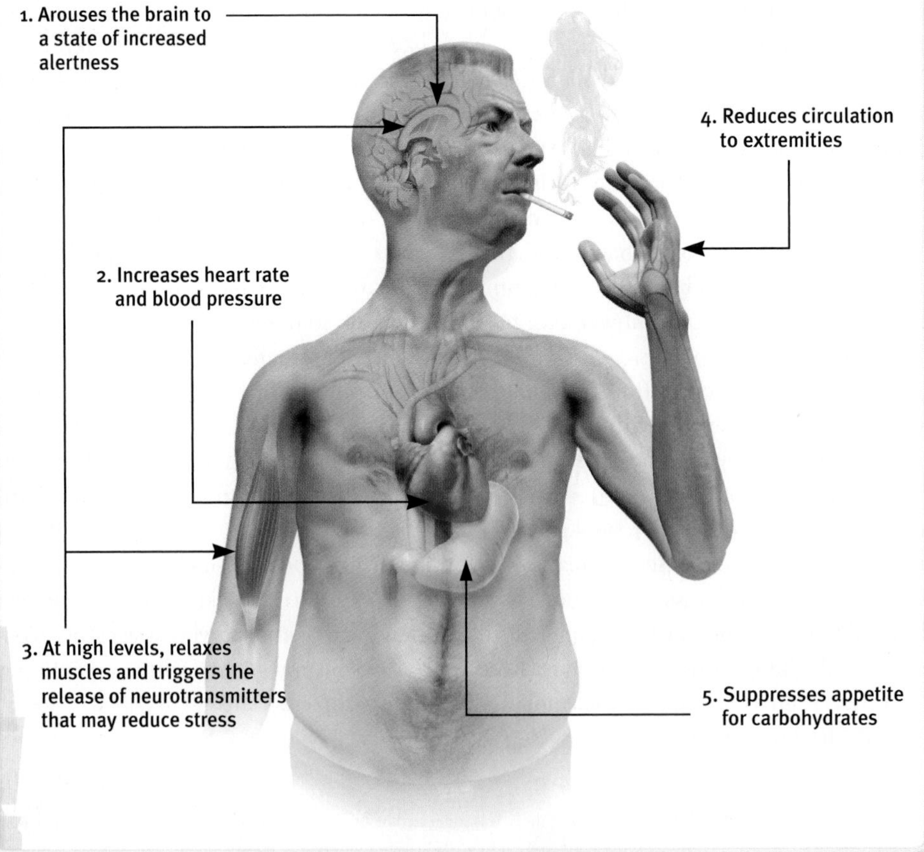

FIGURE 10.4
Where there's smoke . . . : The physiological effects of nicotine Nicotine reaches the brain within 7 seconds, twice as fast as intravenous heroin. Within minutes, the amount in the blood soars.

appetite and boost alertness and mental efficiency. Dopamine and opioids calm anxiety and reduce sensitivity to pain (Nowak, 1994; Scott et al., 2004).

These rewards keep people smoking, even among the 8 in 10 smokers who wish they could stop (Jones, 2007). Each year, fewer than 1 in 7 smokers who want to quit will be able to resist. Even those who know they are committing slow-motion suicide may be unable to stop (Saad, 2002).

Asked "If you had to do it all over again, would you start smoking?" more than 85 percent of adult smokers answer *No* (Slovic et al., 2002).

Nevertheless, repeated attempts seem to pay off. Half of all Americans who have ever smoked have quit, sometimes aided by a nicotine replacement drug and with encouragement from a telephone counselor or a support group. Success is equally likely whether smokers quit abruptly or gradually (Fiore et al., 2008; Lichtenstein et al., 2010; Lindson et al., 2010). For those who endure, the acute craving and withdrawal symptoms gradually dissipate over the ensuing six months (Ward et al., 1997). After a year's abstinence, only 10 percent will relapse in the next year (Hughes, 2010). These nonsmokers may live not only healthier but also happier lives. Smoking correlates with higher rates of depression, chronic disabilities, and divorce (Doherty & Doherty, 1998; Vita et al., 1998). Healthy living seems to add both years to life and life to years.

"To cease smoking is the easiest thing I ever did; I ought to know because I've done it a thousand times."
Mark Twain (1835–1910)

RETRIEVAL PRACTICE

- Why do tobacco companies try so hard to get customers hooked as teens?

ANSWER: Adults are well aware that nicotine is powerfully addictive, expensive, and deadly. Teens may also be aware of these facts but choose to smoke anyway as an act of rebellion or in an attempt to be cool. Especially for those who start paving the neural pathways young, once hooked, it is very hard to quit using nicotine, and tobacco companies as a result may have a customer for a very long time.

Cocaine

Cocaine use offers a fast track from euphoria to crash. The recipe for Coca-Cola originally included an extract of the coca plant, creating a cocaine tonic for tired elderly people. Between 1896 and 1905, Coke was indeed "the real thing." But no longer. Cocaine is now snorted, injected, or smoked. It enters the bloodstream quickly, producing a rush of euphoria that depletes the brain's supply of the neurotransmitters dopamine, serotonin, and norepinephrine (**FIGURE 10.5** on the next page). Within the hour, a crash of agitated depression follows as the drug's effect wears off. Many regular cocaine users chasing this high become addicted. In the lab, cocaine-addicted monkeys have pressed levers more than 12,000 times to gain one cocaine injection (Siegel, 1990).

"Cocaine makes you a new man. And the first thing that new man wants is more cocaine."
Comedian George Carlin (1937–2008)

In situations that trigger aggression, ingesting cocaine may heighten reactions. Caged rats fight when given foot shocks, and they fight even more when given cocaine *and* foot shocks. Likewise, humans ingesting high doses of cocaine in laboratory experiments impose higher shock levels on a presumed opponent than do those receiving a placebo (Licata et al., 1993). Cocaine use may also lead to emotional disturbances, suspiciousness, convulsions, cardiac arrest, or respiratory failure.

In national surveys, 3 percent of U.S. high school seniors and 6 percent of British 18- to 24-year-olds reported having tried cocaine during the past year (ACMD, 2009; Johnston et al., 2011). Nearly half had smoked *crack*. This faster-working crystallized form of cocaine produces a briefer but more intense high followed by a more intense crash. The craving for more wanes after several hours, only to return several days later (Gawin, 1991).

Cocaine's psychological effects depend in part on the dosage and form consumed. But as with all psychoactive drugs, the situation and the user's expectations and personality play a role. Given a placebo, cocaine users who *thought* they were taking cocaine often had a cocaine-like experience (Van Dyke & Byck, 1982).

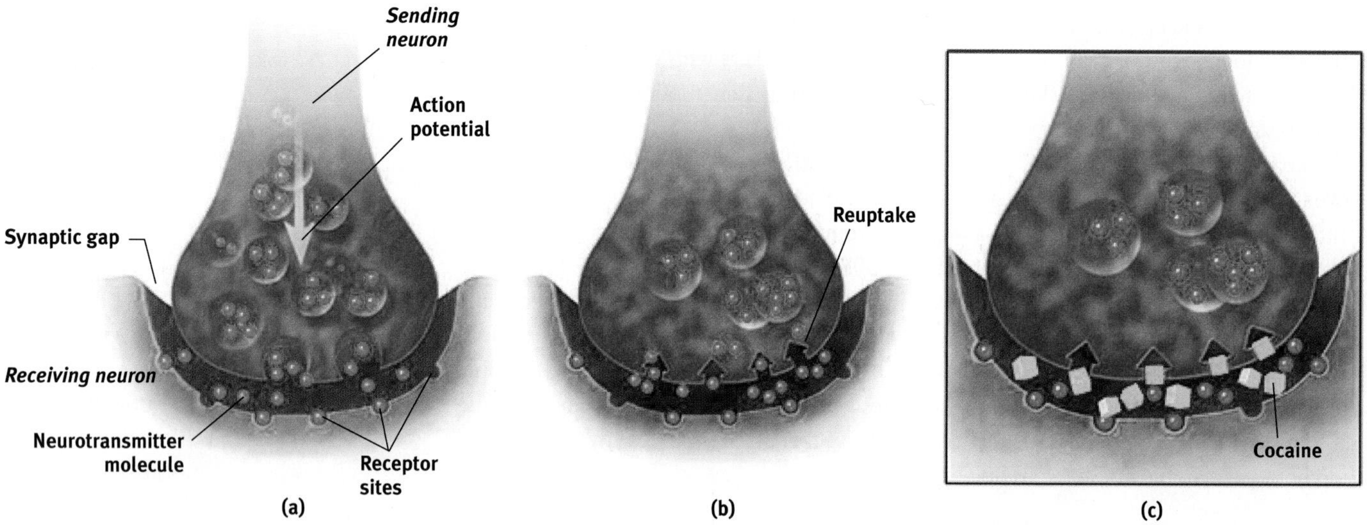

Neurotransmitters carry a message from a sending neuron across a synapse to receptor sites on a receiving neuron.

The sending neuron normally reabsorbs excess neurotransmitter molecules, a process called reuptake.

By binding to the sites that normally reabsorb neurotransmitter molecules, cocaine blocks reuptake of dopamine, norepinephrine, and serotonin (Ray & Ksir, 1990). The extra neurotransmitter molecules therefore remain in the synapse, intensifying their normal mood-altering effects and producing a euphoric rush. When the cocaine level drops, the absence of these neurotransmitters produces a crash.

FIGURE 10.5
Cocaine euphoria and crash

Methamphetamine

Methamphetamine is chemically related to its parent drug, *amphetamine* (NIDA, 2002, 2005) but has even greater effects. Methamphetamine triggers the release of the neurotransmitter dopamine, which stimulates brain cells that enhance energy and mood. The result can include eight hours or so of heightened energy and euphoria. Its aftereffects may include irritability, insomnia, hypertension, seizures, social isolation, depression, and occasional violent outbursts (Homer et al., 2008). Over time, methamphetamine may reduce baseline dopamine levels, leaving the user with depressed functioning.

Dramatic drug-induced decline This woman's methamphetamine addiction led to obvious physical changes. Her decline is evident in these two photos, taken at age 36 (left) and, after four years of addiction, at age 40 (right).

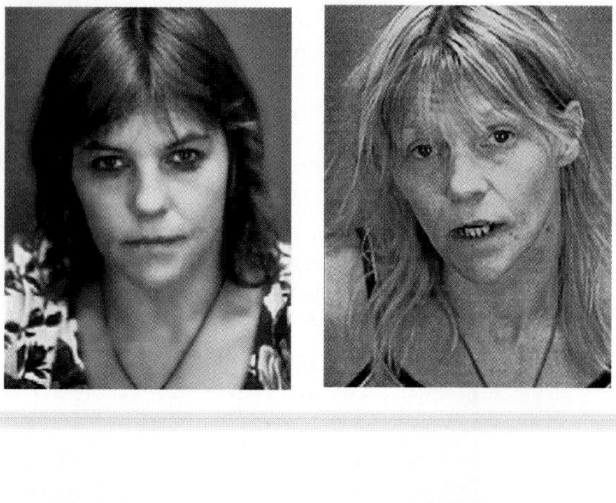
National Pictures/Topham/The Image Works

Ecstasy

Ecstasy, a street name for **MDMA** (methylenedioxymethamphetamine), is both a stimulant and a mild hallucinogen. As an amphetamine derivative, it triggers dopamine release. But its major effect is releasing stored serotonin and blocking its reuptake, thus prolonging serotonin's feel-good flood (Braun, 2001). Users feel the effect about a half-hour after taking an Ecstasy pill. For three or four hours, they experience high energy, emotional elevation, and (given a social context) connectedness with those around them ("I love everyone").

During the 1990s, Ecstasy's popularity soared as a "club drug" taken at nightclubs and all-night raves (Landry, 2002). The drug's popularity crosses national borders, with an estimated 60 million tablets consumed annually in Britain (ACMD, 2009). There are, however, reasons not to be ecstatic about Ecstasy. One is its dehydrating effect, which—when combined with prolonged dancing—can lead to severe overheating, increased blood pressure, and death. Another is that long-term, repeated leaching of brain serotonin can damage serotonin-producing neurons, leading to decreased output and increased risk of permanently depressed

AP Photo/Dale Sparks

The hug drug MDMA, known as Ecstasy, produces a euphoric high and feelings of intimacy. But repeated use destroys serotonin-producing neurons and may permanently deflate mood and impair memory.

mood (Croft et al., 2001; McCann et al., 2001; Roiser et al., 2005). Ecstasy also suppresses the disease-fighting immune system, impairs memory, slows thought, and disrupts sleep by interfering with serotonin's control of the circadian clock (Laws & Kokkalis, 2007; Pacifici et al., 2001; Schilt et al., 2007). Ecstasy delights for the night but dispirits the morrow.

Hallucinogens

10-4 What are hallucinogens, and what are their effects?

Hallucinogens distort perceptions and evoke sensory images in the absence of sensory input (which is why these drugs are also called *psychedelics*, meaning "mind-manifesting"). Some, such as LSD and MDMA (Ecstasy), are synthetic. Others, including the mild hallucinogen marijuana, are natural substances.

LSD

Albert Hofmann, a chemist, created—and on one Friday afternoon in April 1943 accidentally ingested—**LSD** (lysergic acid diethylamide). The result—"an uninterrupted stream of fantastic pictures, extraordinary shapes with intense, kaleidoscopic play of colors"—reminded him of a childhood mystical experience that had left him longing for another glimpse of "a miraculous, powerful, unfathomable reality" (Siegel, 1984; Smith, 2006).

The emotions of an LSD trip vary from euphoria to detachment to panic. The user's current mood and expectations color the emotional experience, but the perceptual distortions and hallucinations have some commonalities. Whether provoked to hallucinate by drugs, loss of oxygen, or extreme sensory deprivation, the brain hallucinates in basically the same way (Siegel, 1982). The experience typically begins with simple geometric forms, such as a lattice, cobweb, or spiral. The next phase consists of more meaningful images; some may be superimposed on a tunnel or funnel, others may be replays of past emotional experiences. As the hallucination peaks, people frequently feel separated from their body and experience dreamlike scenes so real that they may become panic-stricken or harm themselves.

methamphetamine a powerfully addictive drug that stimulates the central nervous system, with speeded-up body functions and associated energy and mood changes; over time, appears to reduce baseline dopamine levels.

Ecstasy (MDMA) a synthetic stimulant and mild hallucinogen. Produces euphoria and social intimacy, but with short-term health risks and longer-term harm to serotonin-producing neurons and to mood and cognition.

hallucinogens psychedelic ("mind-manifesting") drugs, such as LSD, that distort perceptions and evoke sensory images in the absence of sensory input.

LSD *(lysergic acid diethylamide)* a powerful hallucinogenic drug; also known as acid.

FIGURE 10.6
Near-death vision or hallucination? Psychologist Ronald Siegel (1977) reported that people under the influence of hallucinogenic drugs often see "a bright light in the center of the field of vision. . . . The location of this point of light create[s] a tunnel-like perspective." This is very similar to others' near-death experiences.

These sensations are strikingly similar to the **near-death experience,** an altered state of consciousness reported by about 15 percent of those who are revived from cardiac arrest (Agrillo, 2011; Greyson, 2010). Many experience visions of tunnels (**FIGURE 10.6**), bright lights or beings of light, a replay of old memories, and out-of-body sensations (Siegel, 1980). Given that oxygen deprivation and other insults to the brain are known to produce hallucinations, it is difficult to resist wondering whether a brain under stress manufactures the near-death experience. Following temporal lobe seizures, patients have reported similarly profound mystical experiences. So have solitary sailors and polar explorers while enduring monotony, isolation, and cold (Suedfeld & Mocellin, 1987).

Marijuana

For 5000 years, hemp has been cultivated for its fiber. The leaves and flowers of this plant, which are sold as marijuana, contain **THC** (delta-9-tetrahydrocannabinol). Marijuana is a difficult drug to classify. Whether smoked (getting to the brain in about 7 seconds) or eaten (causing its peak concentration to be reached at a slower, unpredictable rate), THC produces a mix of effects. Marijuana is a mild hallucinogen, amplifying sensitivity to colors, sounds, tastes, and smells. But like alcohol, marijuana relaxes, disinhibits, and may produce a euphoric high. Both drugs impair the motor coordination, perceptual skills, and reaction time necessary for safely operating an automobile or other machine. "THC causes animals to misjudge events," reported Ronald Siegel (1990, p. 163). "Pigeons wait too long to respond to buzzers or lights that tell them food is available for brief periods; and rats turn the wrong way in mazes."

Marijuana and alcohol also differ. The body eliminates alcohol within hours. THC and its by-products linger in the body for a week or more, which means that regular users may achieve a high with smaller amounts of the drug than would be needed by occasional users. This is contrary to the usual path of tolerance, in which repeat users need to take larger doses to feel the same effect.

A user's experience can vary with the situation. If the person feels anxious or depressed, using marijuana may intensify these feelings. The more often the person uses marijuana, especially during adolescence, the greater the risk of anxiety or depression (Bambico et al., 2010; Hall, 2006; Murray et al., 2007). Daily use bodes a worse outcome than infrequent use.

Marijuana also disrupts memory formation and interferes with immediate recall of information learned only a few minutes before. Such cognitive effects outlast the period of smoking (Messinis et al., 2006). Heavy adult use for over 20 years is associated with a shrinkage of brain areas that process memories and emotions (Yücel et al., 2008). Prenatal exposure through maternal marijuana use impairs brain development (Berghuis et al., 2007; Huizink & Mulder, 2006).

Some states and countries have passed laws allowing marijuana to be used for medical purposes to relieve the pain and nausea associated with diseases such as AIDS and cancer (Munsey, 2010; Watson et al., 2000). In such cases, the Institute of Medicine recommends delivering the THC with medical inhalers. Marijuana smoke, like cigarette smoke, is toxic and can cause cancer, lung damage, and pregnancy complications.

How does marijuana alter thinking, movements, and moods and relieve pain? Scientists shed light on this question with the discovery of concentrations of THC-sensitive receptors in the brain's frontal lobes, limbic system, and motor cortex (Iversen, 2000). As the 1970s discovery of receptors for morphine put researchers on the trail of morphine-like neurotransmitters (the endorphins), so this more recent discovery of *cannabinoid receptors* has led to a successful hunt for naturally occurring THC-like molecules that bind with cannabinoid receptors. These molecules may naturally control pain. If so, this would help explain why marijuana is effective for pain relief.

* * *

near-death experience an altered state of consciousness reported after a close brush with death (such as through cardiac arrest); often similar to drug-induced hallucinations.

THC the major active ingredient in marijuana; triggers a variety of effects, including mild hallucinations.

TABLE 10.2

A Guide to Selected Psychoactive Drugs

Drug	Type	Pleasurable Effects	Adverse Effects
Alcohol	Depressant	Initial high followed by relaxation and disinhibition	Depression, memory loss, organ damage, impaired reactions
Heroin	Depressant	Rush of euphoria, relief from pain	Depressed physiology, agonizing withdrawal
Caffeine	Stimulant	Increased alertness and wakefulness	Anxiety, restlessness, and insomnia in high doses; uncomfortable withdrawal
Methamphet-amine	Stimulant	Euphoria, alertness, energy	Irritability, insomnia, hypertension, seizures
Cocaine	Stimulant	Rush of euphoria, confidence, energy	Cardiovascular stress, suspiciousness, depressive crash
Nicotine	Stimulant	Arousal and relaxation, sense of well-being	Heart disease, cancer
Ecstasy (MDMA)	Stimulant; mild hallucinogen	Emotional elevation, disinhibition	Dehydration, overheating, depressed mood, impaired cognitive and immune functioning
Marijuana	Mild hallucinogen	Enhanced sensation, relief of pain, distortion of time, relaxation	Impaired learning and memory, increased risk of psychological disorders, lung damage from smoke

Despite their differences, the psychoactive drugs summarized in **TABLE 10.2** share a common feature: They trigger negative aftereffects that offset their immediate positive effects and grow stronger with repetition. And that helps explain both tolerance and withdrawal. As the opposing, negative aftereffects grow stronger, it takes larger and larger doses to produce the desired high *(tolerance)*, causing the aftereffects to worsen in the drug's absence *(withdrawal)*. This in turn creates a need to switch off the withdrawal symptoms by taking yet more of the drug (which may lead to *addiction*).

RETRIEVAL PRACTICE

"How strange would appear to be this thing that men call pleasure! And how curiously it is related to what is thought to be its opposite, pain! . . . Wherever the one is found, the other follows up behind."

Plato, *Phaedo,* fourth century B.C.E.

- How does this pleasure-pain description apply to the repeated use of psychoactive drugs?

ANSWER: Psychoactive drugs create pleasure by altering brain chemistry. With repeated use of the drug, the brain develops tolerance and needs more of the drug to achieve the desired effect. As the body becomes dependent, discontinuing use of the substance produces painful withdrawal symptoms, because addiction has changed the brain's neurochemistry.

Influences on Drug Use

10-5 Why do some people become regular users of consciousness-altering drugs?

Drug use by North American youth increased during the 1970s. Then, with increased drug education and a more realistic and deglamorized media depiction of taking drugs, drug use declined sharply. After the early 1990s, the cultural antidrug voice softened, and drugs for a time were again glamorized in some music and films. Consider these marijuana-related trends:

- In the University of Michigan's annual survey of 15,000 U.S. high school seniors, the proportion who believe there is "great risk" in regular marijuana use rose from 35 percent in 1978 to 79 percent in 1991, then retreated to 47 percent in 2010 (Johnston et al., 2011).
- After peaking in 1978, marijuana use by U.S. high school seniors declined through 1992, then rose, but has recently been tapering off (see **FIGURE 10.7**). Among Canadian 15- to 24-year-olds, 23 percent report using marijuana monthly, weekly, or daily (Health Canada, 2009).

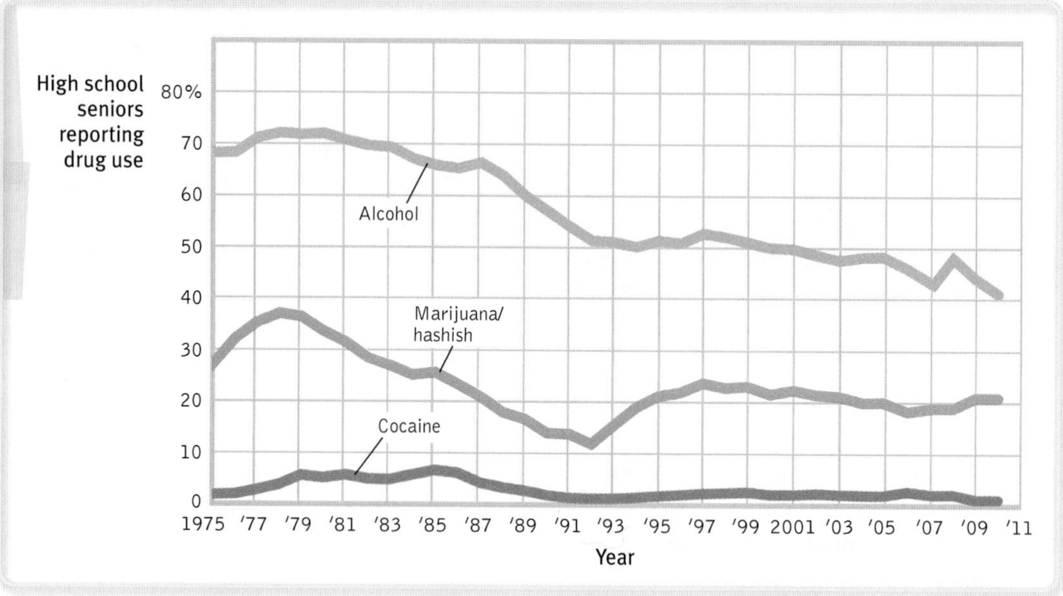

FIGURE 10.7
Trends in drug use The percentage of U.S. high school seniors who report having used alcohol, marijuana, or cocaine during the past 30 days declined from the late 1970s to 1992, when it partially rebounded for a few years. (From Johnston et al., 2011.)

For some adolescents, occasional drug use represents thrill seeking. Why, though, do others become regular drug users? In search of answers, researchers have engaged biological, psychological, and social-cultural levels of analysis.

Biological Influences

Some people may be biologically vulnerable to particular drugs. For example, evidence accumulates that heredity influences some aspects of alcohol abuse problems, especially those appearing by early adulthood (Crabbe, 2002):

- Adopted individuals are more susceptible to alcohol dependence if one or both biological parents have a history of it.
- Having an identical rather than fraternal twin with alcohol dependence puts one at increased risk for alcohol problems (Kendler et al., 2002). In marijuana use also, identical twins more closely resemble each other than do fraternal twins.
- Boys who at age 6 are excitable, impulsive, and fearless (genetically influenced traits) are more likely as teens to smoke, drink, and use other drugs (Masse & Tremblay, 1997).
- Researchers have bred rats and mice that prefer alcoholic drinks to water. One such strain has reduced levels of the brain chemical NPY. Mice engineered to *overproduce* NPY are very sensitive to alcohol's sedating effect and drink little (Thiele et al., 1998).
- Researchers have identified genes that are more common among people and animals predisposed to alcohol dependence, and they are seeking genes that contribute to tobacco addiction (NIH, 2006; Nurnberger & Bierut, 2007). These culprit genes seemingly produce deficiencies in the brain's natural dopamine reward system: While

Warning signs of alcohol dependence

- Drinking binges
- Regretting things done or said when drunk
- Feeling low or guilty after drinking
- Failing to honor a resolve to drink less
- Drinking to alleviate depression or anxiety
- Avoiding family or friends when drinking

triggering temporary dopamine-produced pleasure, the addictive drugs disrupt normal dopamine balance. Studies of how drugs reprogram the brain's reward systems raise hopes for anti-addiction drugs that might block or blunt the effects of alcohol and other drugs (Miller, 2008; Wilson & Kuhn, 2005).

Culture and alcohol

Percentage drinking weekly or more:

United States	30%
Canada	40%
Britain	58%

(Gallup Poll, from Moore, 2006)

Psychological and Social-Cultural Influences

Biological, psychological, and social-cultural influences interact to produce behavior, including drug use (**FIGURE 10.8**). One psychological factor that has appeared in studies of youth and young adults is the feeling that life is meaningless and directionless (Newcomb & Harlow, 1986). This feeling is common among school dropouts who subsist without job skills, without privilege, and with little hope.

Sometimes the psychological influence is obvious. Many heavy users of alcohol, marijuana, and cocaine have experienced significant stress or failure and are depressed. Girls with a history of depression, eating disorders, or sexual or physical abuse are at risk for substance addiction. So are youth undergoing school or neighborhood transitions (CASA, 2003; Logan et al., 2002). Collegians who have not yet achieved a clear identity are also at greater risk (Bishop et al., 2005). By temporarily dulling the pain of self-awareness, alcohol and other drugs may offer a way to avoid coping with depression, anger, anxiety, or insomnia. The relief may be temporary, but behavior is often controlled more by its immediate consequences than by its later ones.

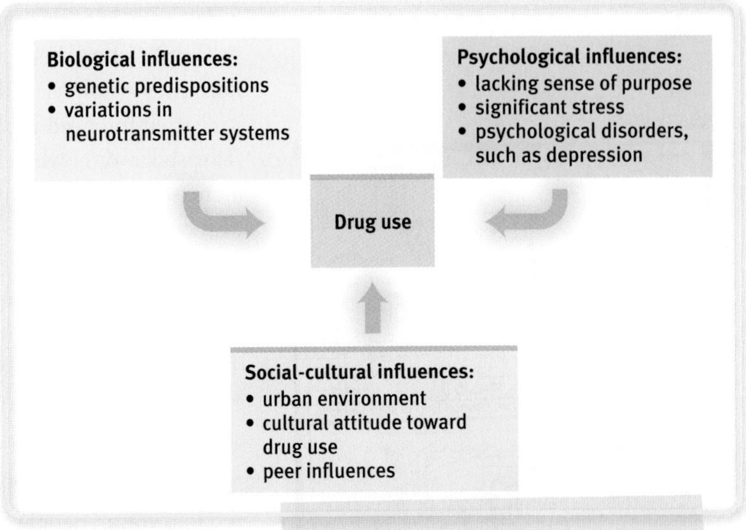

FIGURE 10.8
Levels of analysis for drug use
The biopsychosocial approach enables researchers to investigate drug use from complementary perspectives.

Especially for teenagers, drug use can have social roots. Teens are also exposed to smoking in movies. Those with high exposure are three times as likely as other teens to try smoking and become smokers. And that correlation is not a result of personality, parenting style, or family economics, which researchers controlled for (Heatherton & Sargent, 2009). Most teen drinking is done for social reasons, not as a way to cope with problems (Kuntsche et al., 2005). When young unmarried adults leave home, alcohol and other drug use increases; when they marry and have children, it decreases (Bachman et al., 1997).

Rates of drug use also vary across cultural and ethnic groups. One survey of 100,000 teens in 35 European countries found that marijuana use in the prior 30 days ranged from zero to 1 percent in Romania and Sweden to 20 to 22 percent in Britain, Switzerland, and France (ESPAD, 2003). Independent U.S. government studies of drug use in households nationwide and among high schoolers in all regions reveal that African-American teens have sharply lower rates of drinking, smoking, and cocaine use (Johnston et al., 2007). Alcohol and other drug addiction rates have also been low among those actively religious, and extremely low among Orthodox Jews, Mormons, the Amish, and Mennonites (Trimble, 1994; Yeung et al., 2009). Relatively drug-free small towns and rural areas tend to constrain any genetic predisposition to drug use (Legrand et al., 2005). So does active parental monitoring (Lac & Crano, 2009). For those whose genetic predispositions nudge them toward substance use, cities offer more opportunities and less supervision.

Whether in cities or rural areas, peers influence attitudes about drugs. They also throw the parties and provide (or don't provide) the drugs. If an adolescent's friends use drugs, the odds are that he or she will, too. If the friends do not, the opportunity may not even arise. Teens who come from happy families, who do not begin drinking before age 15, and who do well in school tend not to use drugs, largely because they rarely associate with those who do (Bachman et al., 2007; Hingson et al., 2006; Odgers et al., 2008).

TABLE 10.3

Facts About "Higher" Education

College and university students drink more alcohol than their nonstudent peers and exhibit 2.5 times the general population's rate of substance abuse.
Fraternity and sorority members report nearly twice the binge drinking rate of nonmembers.
Since 1993, campus smoking rates have declined, alcohol use has been steady, and abuse of prescription opioids, stimulants, tranquilizers, and sedatives has increased, as has marijuana use.

Source: NCASA, 2007.

Peer influence is more than what friends do or say. Adolescents' expectations—what they *believe* friends are doing and favoring—influence their behavior (Vitória et al., 2009). One study surveyed sixth graders in 22 U.S. states. How many believed their friends had smoked marijuana? About 14 percent. How many of those friends acknowledged doing so? Only 4 percent (Wren, 1999). University students are not immune to such misperceptions: Drinking dominates social occasions partly because students overestimate their fellow students' enthusiasm for alcohol and underestimate their views of its risks (Prentice & Miller, 1993; Self, 1994) (**TABLE 10.3**). When students' overestimates of peer drinking are corrected, alcohol use often subsides (Moreira et al., 2009).

People whose beginning use of drugs was influenced by their peers are more likely to stop using when friends stop or the social network changes (Kandel & Raveis, 1989). One study that followed 12,000 adults over 32 years found that smokers tend to quit in clusters (Christakis & Fowler, 2008). Within a social network, the odds of a person's quitting increased when a spouse, friend, or co-worker stopped smoking. Similarly, most soldiers who became drug addicted while in Vietnam ceased their drug use after returning home (Robins et al., 1974).

SNAPSHOTS

© Jason Love

As always with correlations, the traffic between friends' drug use and our own may be two-way: Our friends influence us. Social networks matter. But we also select as friends those who share our likes and dislikes.

What do the findings on drug use suggest for drug prevention and treatment programs? Three channels of influence seem possible:

- Educate young people about the long-term costs of a drug's temporary pleasures.
- Help young people find other ways to boost their self-esteem and purpose in life.
- Attempt to modify peer associations or to "inoculate" youths against peer pressures by training them in refusal skills.

People rarely abuse drugs if they understand the physical and psychological costs, feel good about themselves and the direction their lives are taking, and are in a peer group that disapproves of using drugs. These educational, psychological, and social-cultural factors may help explain why 26 percent of U.S. high school dropouts, but only 6 percent of those with a postgraduate education, report smoking (CDC, 2011).

RETRIEVAL PRACTICE

- Studies have found that people who begin drinking in the early teens are much more likely to become alcohol dependent than those who begin at age 21 or after. What possible explanations might there be for this correlation between early use and later abuse?

ANSWER: Possible explanations include (a) a biological predisposition to both early use and later abuse; (b) brain changes and taste preferences triggered by early use; and (c) enduring habits, attitudes, activities, or peer relationships that foster alcohol abuse.

MODULE REVIEW

Drugs and Consciousness

Learning Objectives

RETRIEVAL PRACTICE Take a moment to answer each of these Learning Objective Questions (repeated here from within the module). Then turn to Appendix B, Complete Module Reviews, to check your answers. Research suggests that trying to answer these questions on your own will improve your long-term retention (McDaniel et al., 2009).

10-1: What are tolerance, dependence, and addiction, and what are some common misconceptions about addiction?

10-2: What are depressants, and what are their effects?

10-3: What are stimulants, and what are their effects?

10-4: What are hallucinogens, and what are their effects?

10-5: Why do some people become regular users of consciousness-altering drugs?

Terms and Concepts to Remember

RETRIEVAL PRACTICE Test yourself on these terms by trying to write down the definition before flipping back to the referenced page to check your answer.

psychoactive drug, p. 115
tolerance, p. 115
addiction, p. 115
withdrawal, p. 115
physical dependence, p. 115
psychological dependence, p. 115
depressants, p. 117
alcohol dependence, p. 118
barbiturates, p. 118
opiates, p. 118
stimulants, p. 119
amphetamines, p. 119
nicotine, p. 119
methamphetamine, p. 122
Ecstasy (MDMA), p. 122
hallucinogens, p. 123
LSD, p. 123
near-death experience, p. 124
THC, p. 124

RETRIEVAL PRACTICE Gain an advantage, and benefit from immediate feedback, with the interactive self-testing resources at www.worthpublishers.com/myers.

Nature, Nurture, and Human Diversity

What makes you you? In important ways, we are each unique. We look different. We sound different. We have varying personalities, interests, and cultural and family backgrounds.

We are also the leaves of one tree. Our human family shares not only a common biological heritage—cut us and we bleed—but also common behavioral tendencies. Our shared brain architecture predisposes us to sense the world, develop language, and feel hunger through identical mechanisms. Whether we live in the Arctic or the tropics, we prefer sweet tastes to sour. We divide the color spectrum into similar colors. And we feel drawn to behaviors that produce and protect offspring.

Our kinship appears in our social behaviors as well. Whether named Wong, Nkomo, Smith, or Gonzales, we start fearing strangers at about eight months, and as adults we prefer the company of those with attitudes and attributes similar to our own. Coming from different parts of the globe, we know how to read one another's smiles and frowns. As members of one

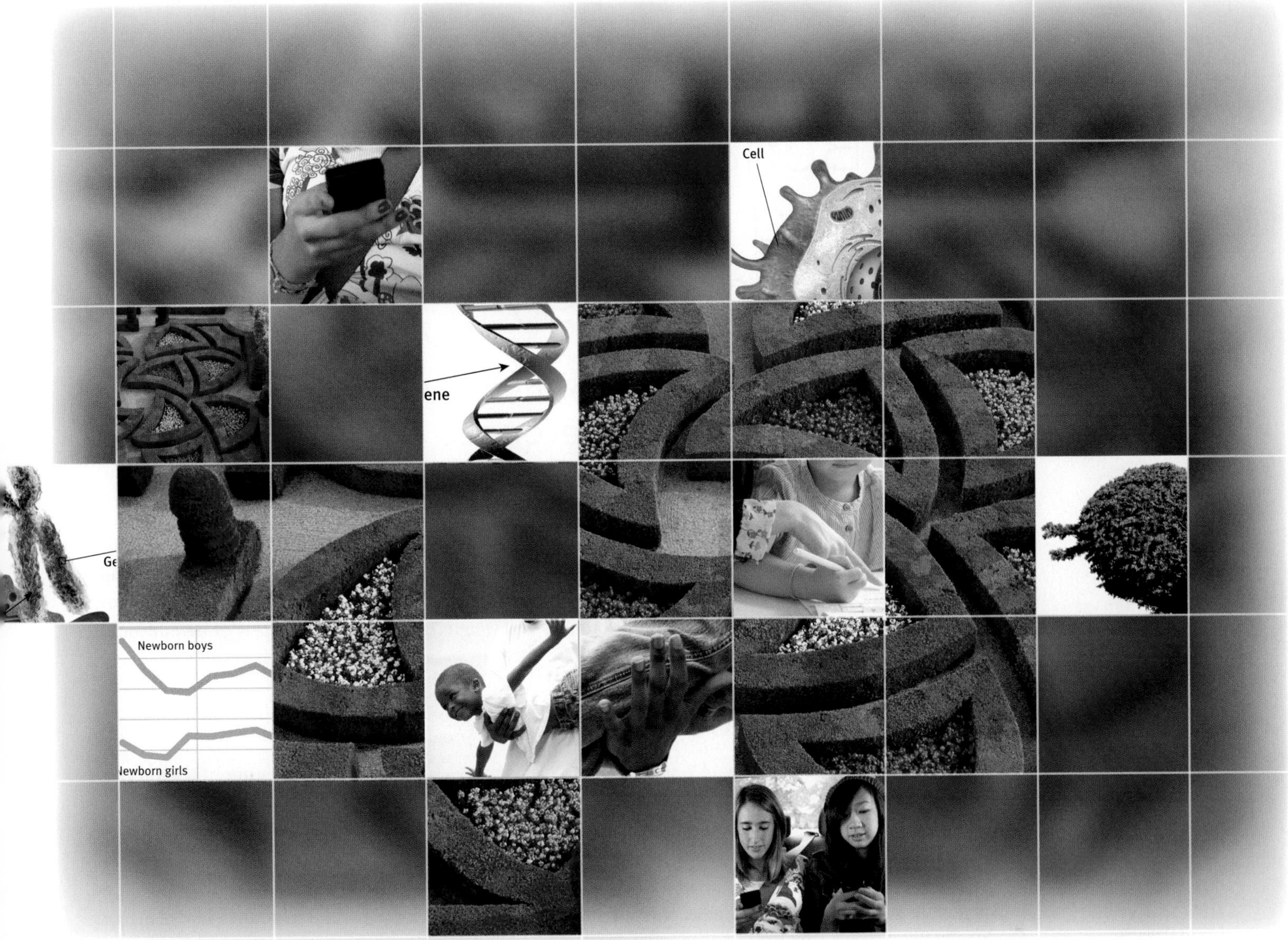

MODULES

11
Behavior Genetics and Evolutionary Psychology

12
Culture, Gender, and Other Environmental Influences

species, we affiliate, conform, return favors, punish offenses, organize hierarchies of status, and grieve a child's death. A visitor from outer space could drop in anywhere and find humans dancing and feasting, singing and worshiping, playing sports and games, laughing and crying, living in families and forming groups. Taken together, such universal behaviors define our human nature.

What causes our striking diversity, and also our shared human nature? How much are human differences shaped by our differing genes? And how much by our *environment*—by every external influence, from maternal nutrition while in the womb to social support while nearing the tomb? To what extent are we formed by our upbringing? By our culture? By our current circumstances? By people's reactions to our genetic dispositions? Modules 11 and 12 tell us something of the complex story of how our genes (nature) and environments (nurture) define us.

- Behavior Genetics: Predicting Individual Differences
- Evolutionary Psychology: Understanding Human Nature

Behavior Genetics and Evolutionary Psychology

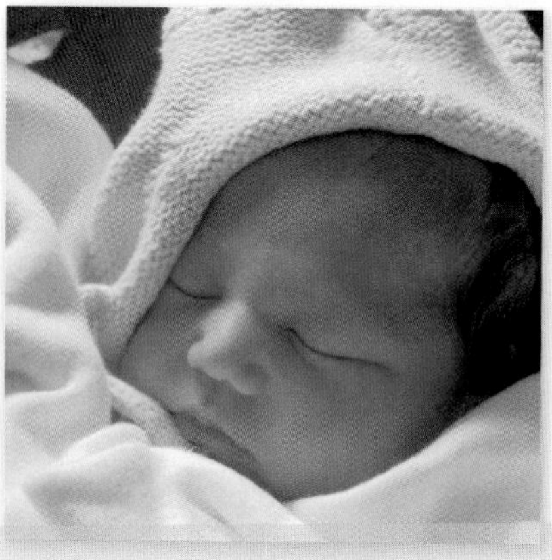

Courtesy of Kevin Feyen

The nurture of nature Parents everywhere wonder: Will my baby grow up to be peaceful or aggressive? Homely or attractive? Successful or struggling at every step? What comes built in, and what is nurtured—and how? Research reveals that nature and nurture together shape our development—every step of the way.

© The New Yorker Collection, 1999, Danny Shanahan from cartoonbank.com. All Rights Reserved.

"Thanks for almost everything, Dad."

"Your DNA and mine are 99.9 percent the same. . . . At the DNA level, we are clearly all part of one big worldwide family."
Francis Collins, Human Genome Project director, 2007

"We share half our genes with the banana."
Evolutionary biologist Robert May, president of Britain's Royal Society, 2001

Behavior Genetics: Predicting Individual Differences

11-1 What are genes, and how do behavior geneticists explain our individual differences?

If Jaden Agassi, son of tennis stars Andre Agassi and Stefanie Graf, grows up to be a tennis star, should we attribute his superior talent to his Grand Slam genes? To his growing up in a tennis-rich environment? To high expectations? Such questions intrigue **behavior geneticists,** who study our differences and weigh the effects and interplay of heredity and **environment.**

Genes: Our Codes for Life

Behind the story of our body and of our brain—surely the most awesome thing on our little planet—is the heredity that interacts with our experience to create both our universal human nature and our individual and social diversity. Barely more than a century ago, few would have guessed that every cell nucleus in your body contains the genetic master code for your entire body. It's as if every room in Dubai's Burj Khalifa (the world's tallest building) had a book containing the architect's plans for the entire structure. The plans for your own book of life run to 46 chapters—23 donated by your mother's egg and 23 by your father's sperm. Each of these 46 chapters, called a **chromosome,** is composed of a coiled chain of the molecule **DNA** *(deoxyribonucleic acid).* **Genes,** small segments of the giant DNA molecules, form the words of those chapters (**FIGURE 11.1**). All told, you have 20,000 to 25,000 gene words. Genes can be either active *(expressed)* or inactive. Environmental events "turn on" genes, rather like hot water enabling a tea bag to express its flavor. When turned on, genes provide the code for creating *protein molecules,* our body's building blocks.

Genetically speaking, every other human is nearly your identical twin. Human **genome** researchers have discovered the common sequence within human DNA. It is this shared genetic profile that makes us humans, rather than chimpanzees or tulips.

Actually, we aren't all that different from our chimpanzee cousins; with them we share about 96 percent of our DNA sequence (Mikkelsen et al., 2005). At "functionally important" DNA sites, reported one molecular genetics team, the human-chimpanzee DNA similarity is 99.4 percent (Wildman et al., 2003). Yet that wee difference matters. Despite some remarkable abilities, chimpanzees grunt. Shakespeare intricately wove 17,677 words to form his literary masterpieces.

Small differences matter among chimpanzees, too. Two species, common chimpanzees and bonobos, differ by much less than 1 percent of their genomes, yet they display markedly differing behaviors. Chimpanzees are aggressive and male dominated. Bonobos are peaceable and female led.

Geneticists and psychologists are interested in the occasional variations found at particular gene sites in human DNA. Slight person-to-person variations from the common pattern give clues to our uniqueness—why one person has a disease that another does not, why one person is short and another tall, why one is outgoing and another shy.

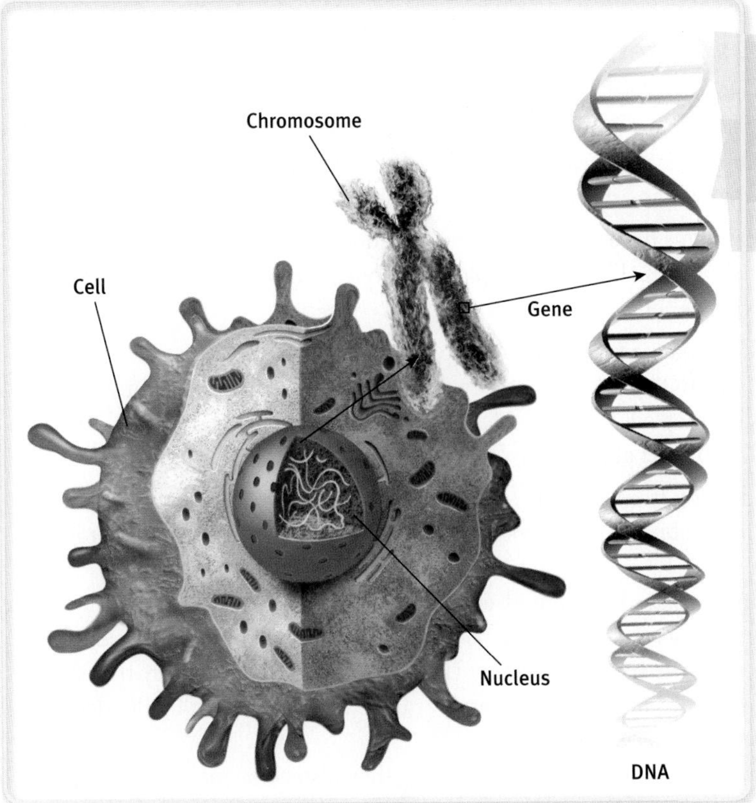

FIGURE 11.1
The human building blocks
The nucleus of every human cell contains chromosomes, each of which is made up of two strands of DNA connected in a double helix.

RETRIEVAL PRACTICE

- Put the following cell structures in order from smallest to largest: nucleus, gene, chromosome.

ANSWER: gene, chromosome, nucleus

- When the mother's egg and the father's sperm unite, each contributes 23 __________.

ANSWER: chromosomes

Most of our traits are influenced by many genes. How tall you are, for example, reflects the size of your face, vertebrae, leg bones, and so forth—each of which may be influenced by different genes interacting with your environment. Complex traits such as intelligence, happiness, and aggressiveness are similarly influenced by groups of genes. Thus our genetic predispositions—our genetically influenced traits—help explain both our shared human nature and our human diversity.

Twin and Adoption Studies

To scientifically tease apart the influences of environment and heredity, behavior geneticists would need to design two types of experiments. The first would ... environment while varying heredity. The second ... the home environment. Such experimen... happily for our purposes, nature has done ...

Courtesy of Güher and Süher Pekinel

behavior genetics the study of the relative power and limits of genetic and environmental influences on behavior.

environment every nongenetic influence, from prenatal nutrition to the people and things around us.

chromosomes threadlike structures made of DNA molecules that contain the genes.

DNA *(deoxyribonucleic acid)* a complex molecule containing the genetic information that makes up the chromosomes.

genes the biochemical units of heredity that make up the chromosomes; segments of DNA capable of synthesizing protein.

genome the complete instructions for making an organism, consisting of all the genetic material in that organism's chromosomes.

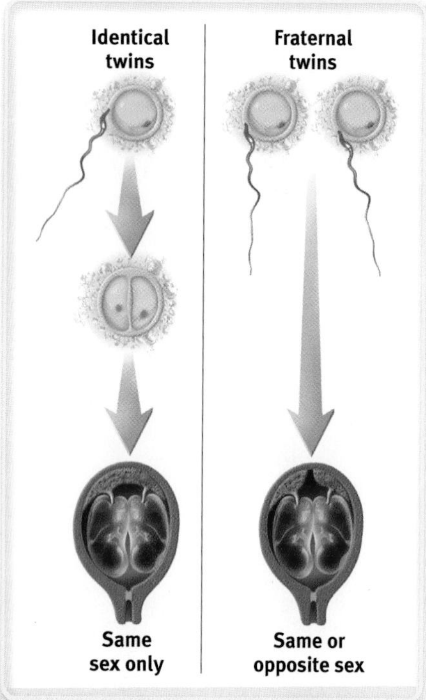

FIGURE 11.2
Same fertilized egg, same genes; different eggs, different genes Identical twins develop from a single fertilized egg, fraternal twins from two.

Identical Versus Fraternal Twins

Identical twins develop from a single *(monozygotic)* fertilized egg that splits in two. Thus they are *genetically* identical—nature's own human clones (**FIGURE 11.2**). Indeed, they are clones who share not only the same genes but the same conception and uterus, and usually the same birth date and cultural history. Two slight qualifications:

- Although identical twins have the same genes, they don't always have the same *number of copies* of those genes. That helps explain why one twin may be more at risk for certain illnesses (Bruder et al., 2008).
- Most identical twins share a placenta during prenatal development, but one of every three sets has two separate placentas. One twin's placenta may provide slightly better nourishment, which may contribute to identical twin differences (Davis et al., 1995; Phelps et al., 1997; Sokol et al., 1995).

Fraternal twins develop from separate *(dizygotic)* fertilized eggs. As womb-mates, they share a fetal environment, but they are genetically no more similar than ordinary brothers and sisters.

Shared genes can translate into shared experiences. A person whose identical twin has Alzheimer's disease, for example, has a 60 percent risk of getting the disease; if the affected twin is fraternal, the risk is 30 percent (Plomin et al., 1997). To study the effects of genes and environments, hundreds of researchers have studied some 800,000 identical and fraternal twin pairs (Johnson et al., 2009).

Are identical twins, being genetic clones of one another, also behaviorally more similar than fraternal twins? Studies of thousands of twin pairs in Sweden, Finland, and Australia find that on both extraversion (outgoingness) and neuroticism (emotional instability), identical twins are much more similar than fraternal twins. If genes influence traits such as emotional instability, might they also influence the social effects of such traits? To find out, Matt McGue and David Lykken (1992) studied divorce rates among 1500 same-sex, middle-aged twin pairs. Their result: If you have a fraternal twin who has divorced, the odds of your divorcing are 1.6 times greater than if you have a not-divorced twin. If you have an identical twin who has divorced, the odds of your divorcing are 5.5 times greater. From such data, McGue and Lykken estimate that people's differing divorce risks are about 50 percent attributable to genetic factors.

Dennis MacDonald/Photo Edit

©Lee Snider/The Image Works

Index Stock Imagery/Newscom

More twins Curiously, twinning rates vary by race. The rate among Caucasians is roughly twice that of Asians and half that of Africans. In Africa and Asia, most twins are identical. In Western countries, most twins are fraternal, and fraternal twins are increasing with the use of fertility drugs (Hall, 2003; Steinhauer, 1999).

Identical twins, more than fraternal twins, also report being treated alike. So, do their experiences rather than their genes account for their similarity? *No.* Studies have shown that identical twins whose parents treated them alike were not psychologically more alike than identical twins who were treated less similarly (Loehlin & Nichols, 1976). In explaining individual differences, genes matter.

Separated Twins

Imagine the following science fiction experiment: A mad scientist decides to separate identical twins at birth, then rear them in differing environments. Better yet, consider a *true* story:

On a chilly February morning in 1979, some time after divorcing his first wife, Linda, Jim Lewis awoke in his modest home next to his second wife, Betty. Determined that this marriage would work, Jim made a habit of leaving love notes to Betty around the house. As he lay in bed he thought about others he had loved, including his son, James Alan, and his faithful dog, Toy.

Jim was looking forward to spending part of the day in his basement woodworking shop, where he had put in many happy hours building furniture, picture frames, and other items, including a white bench now circling a tree in his front yard. Jim also liked to spend free time driving his Chevy, watching stock-car racing, and drinking Miller Lite beer.

Jim was basically healthy, except for occasional half-day migraine headaches and blood pressure that was a little high, perhaps related to his chain-smoking habit. He had become overweight a while back but had shed some of the pounds. Having undergone a vasectomy, he was done having children.

What was extraordinary about Jim Lewis, however, was that at that same moment (I am not making this up) there existed another man—also named Jim—for whom all these things (right down to the dog's name) were also true.[1] This other Jim—Jim Springer—just happened, 38 years earlier, to have been his fetal partner. Thirty-seven days after their birth, these genetically identical twins were separated, adopted by blue-collar families, and reared with no contact or knowledge of each other's whereabouts until the day Jim Lewis received a call from his genetic clone (who, having been told he had a twin, set out to find him).

One month later, the brothers became the first twin pair tested by University of Minnesota psychologist Thomas Bouchard and his colleagues, beginning a study of separated twins that extends to the present (Holden, 1980a,b; Wright, 1998). Their voice intonations and inflections were so similar that, hearing a playback of an earlier interview, Jim Springer guessed "That's me." Wrong—it was his brother. Given tests measuring their personality, intelligence, heart rate, and brain waves, the Jim twins—despite 38 years of separation—were virtually as alike as the same person tested twice. Both married women named Dorothy Jane Scheckelburger. Okay, the last item is a joke. But as Judith Rich Harris (2006) notes, it is hardly weirder than some other reported similarities.

Sweden has the world's largest national twin registry—140,000 living and dead twin pairs—which forms part of a massive registry of over 600,000 twins currently being sampled in the world's largest twin study (Wheelwright, 2004; www.genomeutwin.org).

"In some domains it looks as though our identical twins reared apart are . . . just as similar as identical twins reared together. Now that's an amazing finding and I can assure you none of us would have expected that degree of similarity."

Thomas Bouchard (1981)

Bouchard's famous twin research was, appropriately enough, conducted in Minneapolis, the "Twin City" (with St. Paul), and home to the Minnesota Twins baseball team.

[1] Actually, this description of the two Jims errs in one respect: Jim Lewis named his son James Alan. Jim Springer named his James Allan.

©2006 Bob Sacha

Identical twins are people two Identical twins Jim Lewis and Jim Springer were separated shortly after birth and raised in different homes without awareness of each other. Research has shown remarkable similarities in the life choices of separated identical twins, lending support to the idea that genes influence personality.

identical twins twins who develop from a single (monozygotic) fertilized egg that splits in two, creating two genetically identical organisms.

fraternal twins twins who develop from separate (dizygotic) fertilized eggs. They are genetically no closer than brothers and sisters, but they share a fetal environment.

Aided by publicity in magazine and newspaper stories, Bouchard (2009) and his colleagues located and studied 74 pairs of identical twins reared apart. They continued to find similarities not only of tastes and physical attributes but also of personality (characteristic patterns of thinking, feeling, and acting), abilities, attitudes, interests, and even fears.

In Sweden, Nancy Pedersen and her co-workers (1988) identified 99 separated identical twin pairs and more than 200 separated fraternal twin pairs. Compared with equivalent samples of identical twins reared together, the separated identical twins had somewhat less identical personalities. Still, separated twins were more alike if genetically identical than if fraternal. And separation shortly after birth (rather than, say, at age 8) did not amplify their personality differences.

Coincidences are not unique to twins. Patricia Kern of Colorado was born March 13, 1941, and named Patricia Ann Campbell. Patricia DiBiasi of Oregon also was born March 13, 1941, and named Patricia Ann Campbell. Both had fathers named Robert, worked as bookkeepers, and at the time of this comparison had children ages 21 and 19. Both studied cosmetology, enjoyed oil painting as a hobby, and married military men, within 11 days of each other. They are not genetically related. (From an AP report, May 2, 1983.)

Stories of startling twin similarities do not impress Bouchard's critics, who remind us that "the plural of *anecdote* is not *data*." They contend that if any two strangers were to spend hours comparing their behaviors and life histories, they would probably discover many coincidental similarities. If researchers created a control group of biologically unrelated pairs of the same age, sex, and ethnicity, who had not grown up together but who were as similar to one another in economic and cultural background as are many of the separated twin pairs, wouldn't these pairs also exhibit striking similarities (Joseph, 2001)? Bouchard replies that separated fraternal twins do not exhibit similarities comparable to those of separated identical twins.

Even the more impressive data from personality assessments are clouded by the reunion of many of the separated twins some years before they were tested. Moreover, identical twins share an appearance, and the responses it evokes. Adoption agencies also tend to place separated twins in similar homes. Despite these criticisms, the striking twin-study results helped shift scientific thinking toward a greater appreciation of genetic influences.

Biological Versus Adoptive Relatives

For behavior geneticists, nature's second real-life experiment—adoption—creates two groups: *genetic relatives* (biological parents and siblings) and *environmental relatives* (adoptive parents and siblings). For any given trait, we can therefore ask whether adopted children are more like their biological parents, who contributed their genes, or their adoptive parents, who contribute a home environment. While sharing that home environment, do adopted siblings also come to share traits?

"We carry to our graves the essence of the zygote that was first us."
Mary Pipher, *Seeking Peace: Chronicles of the Worst Buddhist in the World,* 2009

The stunning finding from studies of hundreds of adoptive families is that people who grow up together, whether biologically related or not, do not much resemble one another in personality (McGue & Bouchard, 1998; Plomin, 2011; Rowe, 1990). In traits such as extraversion and agreeableness, adoptees are more similar to their biological parents than to their caregiving adoptive parents.

Nature or nurture or both? When talent runs in families, as with Wynton Marsalis, Branford Marsalis, and Delfeayo Marsalis, how do heredity and environment together do their work?

AP Photo/Charles Sykes

The finding is important enough to bear repeating: *The environment shared by a family's children has virtually no discernible impact on their personalities.* Two adopted children reared in the same home are no more likely to share personality traits with each other than with the child down the block. Heredity shapes other primates' personalities, too. Macaque monkeys raised by foster mothers exhibit social behaviors that resemble their biological, rather than foster, mothers (Maestripieri, 2003). Add all this to the similarity of identical twins, whether they grow up together or apart, and the effect of a shared rearing environment seems shockingly modest.

What we have here is perhaps "the most important puzzle in the history of psychology," contended Steven Pinker (2002): *Why are children in the same family so different?* Why does shared family environment have so little effect on children's personalities? Is it because each sibling experiences unique peer influences and life events? Because sibling relationships ricochet off each other, amplifying their differences? Because siblings—despite sharing half their genes—have very different combinations of genes and may evoke very different kinds of parenting? Such questions fuel behavior geneticists' curiosity.

"Mom may be holding a full house while Dad has a straight flush, yet when Junior gets a random half of each of their cards his poker hand may be a loser."

David Lykken (2001)

The minimal shared-environment effect does not mean that adoptive parenting is a fruitless venture. The genetic leash may limit the family environment's influence on personality, but parents do influence their children's attitudes, values, manners, faith, and politics (Reifman & Cleveland, 2007). A pair of adopted children or identical twins *will*, especially during adolescence, have more similar religious beliefs if reared together (Koenig et al., 2005). Parenting matters!

The greater uniformity of adoptive homes—mostly healthy, nurturing homes—helps explain the lack of striking differences when comparing child outcomes of different adoptive homes (Stoolmiller, 1999).

Moreover, in adoptive homes, child neglect and abuse and even parental divorce are rare. (Adoptive parents are carefully screened; natural parents are not.) So it is not surprising that, despite a somewhat greater risk of psychological disorder, most adopted children thrive, especially when adopted as infants (Loehlin et al., 2007; van IJzendoorn & Juffer, 2006; Wierzbicki, 1993). Seven in eight report feeling strongly attached to one or both adoptive parents. As children of self-giving parents, they grow up to be more self-giving and altruistic than average (Sharma et al., 1998). Many score higher than their biological parents on intelligence tests, and most grow into happier and more stable adults. In one Swedish study, infant adoptees grew up with fewer problems than were experienced by children whose biological mothers had initially registered them for adoption but then decided to raise the children themselves (Bohman & Sigvardsson, 1990). Regardless of personality differences between parents and their adoptees, most children benefit from adoption.

RETRIEVAL PRACTICE

- How do researchers use twin and adoption studies to learn about psychological principles?

ANSWER: Researchers compare the traits and behaviors of identical twins (same genes) and fraternal twins (sharing half their genes—similar to any sibling). They also compare adopted children with their adoptive and biological parents. Some studies compare twins raised together or separately. These studies help us determine how much variation among individuals is due to genetic makeup and how much to environmental factors.

Temperament and Heredity

As most parents will tell you after having their second child, babies differ even before gulping their first breath. Heredity predisposes one quickly apparent aspect of personality—**temperament,** or emotional excitability (Rothbart, 2007). From their first weeks of life, some infants are reactive, intense, and fidgety. Others are easygoing, quiet, and placid. *Difficult* babies are more irritable, intense, and unpredictable. *Easy* babies are cheerful, relaxed, and predictable in feeding and sleeping. *Slow-to-warm-up* infants tend to resist or withdraw from new people and situations (Chess & Thomas, 1987; Thomas & Chess, 1977). And temperament differences typically persist. Consider:

- The most emotionally reactive newborns tend also to be the most reactive 9-month-olds (Wilson & Matheny, 1986; Worobey & Blajda, 1989).
- Exceptionally inhibited and fearful 2-year-olds often are still relatively shy as 8-year-olds; about half will become introverted adolescents (Kagan et al., 1992, 1994).

temperament a person's characteristic emotional reactivity and intensity.

© The New Yorker Collection, 1999, Barbara Smaller from cartoonbank.com. All Rights Reserved.

"Oh, he's cute, all right, but he's got the temperament of a car alarm."

© The New Yorker Collection, 1999, Nick Downes from cartoonbank.com. All Rights Reserved.

"I thought that sperm-bank donors remained anonymous."

molecular genetics the subfield of biology that studies the molecular structure and function of genes.

- The most emotionally intense preschoolers tend to be relatively intense young adults (Larsen & Diener, 1987). In one study of more than 900 New Zealanders, emotionally reactive and impulsive 3-year-olds developed into somewhat more impulsive, aggressive, and conflict-prone 21-year-olds (Caspi, 2000).

The genetic effect appears in physiological differences. Anxious, inhibited infants have high and variable heart rates and a reactive nervous system. When facing new or strange situations, they become more physiologically aroused (Kagan & Snidman, 2004). One form of a gene that regulates the neurotransmitter serotonin predisposes a fearful temperament and, in combination with unsupportive caregiving, an inhibited child (Fox et al., 2007). Such evidence adds to the emerging conclusion that our biologically rooted temperament helps form our enduring personality (McCrae et al., 2000, 2007; Rothbart et al., 2000).

The New Frontier: Molecular Genetics

11-2 What is the promise of molecular genetics research?

Behavior geneticists have progressed beyond asking, "Do genes influence behavior?" The new frontier of behavior-genetics research draws on "bottom-up" **molecular genetics** as it seeks to identify *specific genes* influencing behavior.

As we have already seen, most human traits are influenced by teams of genes. For example, twin and adoption studies tell us that heredity influences body weight, but there is no single "obesity gene." More likely, some genes influence how quickly the stomach tells the brain, "I'm full." Others might dictate how much fuel the muscles need, how many calories are burned off by fidgeting, and how efficiently the body converts extra calories into fat (Vogel, 1999). Given that genes typically are not solo players, a goal of *molecular behavior genetics* is to find some of the many genes that together orchestrate traits such as body weight, sexual orientation, and extraversion (Holden, 2008; Tsankova et al., 2007).

Genetic tests can now reveal at-risk populations for many dozens of diseases. The search continues in labs worldwide, where molecular geneticists are teaming with psychologists to pinpoint genes that put people at risk for such genetically influenced disorders as learning disabilities, depression, schizophrenia, and alcohol dependence. Worldwide research efforts are under way, for example, to sleuth the genes that make people vulnerable to the emotional swings of bipolar disorder, formerly known as manic-depressive disorder. To tease out the implicated genes, molecular behavior geneticists find families that have had the disorder across several generations. They draw blood or take cheek swabs from both affected and unaffected family members. Then they examine their DNA, looking for differences. "The most powerful potential for DNA," note Robert Plomin and John Crabbe (2000), "is to predict risk so that steps can be taken to prevent problems before they happen."

Aided by inexpensive DNA-scanning techniques, medical personnel are becoming able to give would-be parents a readout on how their fetus's genes differ from the normal pattern and what this might mean. With this benefit come risks. Might labeling a fetus "at risk for a learning disorder" lead to discrimination? Prenatal screening poses ethical dilemmas. In China and India, where boys are highly valued, testing for an offspring's sex has enabled selective abortions resulting in millions—yes, millions—of "missing women."

Assuming it were possible, should prospective parents take their eggs and sperm to a genetics lab for screening before combining them to produce an embryo? Should we enable parents to screen their fertilized eggs for health—and for brains or beauty? Progress is a double-edged sword, raising both hopeful possibilities and difficult problems. By selecting out certain traits, we may deprive ourselves of future Handels and van Goghs, Churchills and Lincolns, Tolstoys and Dickinsons—troubled people all.

Heritability

11-3 What is heritability, and how does it relate to individuals and groups?

heritability the proportion of variation among individuals that we can attribute to genes. The heritability of a trait may vary, depending on the range of populations and environments studied.

Using twin and adoption studies, behavior geneticists can mathematically estimate the **heritability** of a trait—the extent to which variation among individuals can be attributed to their differing genes. If the heritability of intelligence is, say, 50 percent, this does *not* mean that *your* intelligence is 50 percent genetic. (The heritability of height is 90 percent, but this does not mean that a 60-inch-tall woman can credit her genes for 54 inches and her environment for the other 6 inches.) Rather, it means that genetic influence explains 50 percent of the observed *variation among people*. This point is so often misunderstood that I repeat: We can never say what percentage of an *individual's* personality or intelligence is inherited. It makes no sense to say that your personality is due *x* percent to your heredity and *y* percent to your environment. Heritability refers instead to the extent to which *differences among people* are attributable to genes.

Even this conclusion must be qualified, because heritability can vary from study to study. Consider humorist Mark Twain's (1835–1910) fantasy of raising boys in barrels to age 12, feeding them through a hole. If we were to follow his suggestion, the boys would all emerge with lower-than-normal intelligence scores at age 12. Yet, given their equal environments, their test score differences could be explained only by their heredity. In this case, heritability—differences due to genes—would be near 100 percent.

As environments become more similar, heredity as a source of differences necessarily becomes more important. If all schools were of uniform quality, all families equally loving, and all neighborhoods equally healthy, then heritability would *increase* (because differences due to environment would *decrease*). At the other extreme, if all people had similar heredities but were raised in drastically different environments (some in barrels, some in luxury homes), heritability would be much lower.

© The New Yorker Collection, 2003, Michael Shaw from cartoonbank.com. All Rights Reserved.

"The title of my science project is 'My Little Brother: Nature or Nurture.'"

Can we extend this thinking to differences between groups? If genetic influences help explain individual diversity in traits such as aggressiveness, for example, can the same be said of group differences between men and women, or between people of different races? Not necessarily. Individual differences in height and weight, for example, are highly heritable; yet nutritional rather than genetic influences explain why, as a group, today's adults are taller and heavier than those of a century ago. The two groups differ, but not because human genes have changed in a mere century's eyeblink of time. Although height is 90 percent heritable, South Koreans, with their better diets, average six inches taller than North Koreans, who come from the same genetic stock (Johnson et al., 2009).

As with height and weight, so with personality and intelligence scores: Heritable individual differences need not imply heritable group differences. If some individuals are genetically disposed to be more aggressive than others, that needn't explain why some groups are more aggressive than others. Putting people in a new social context can change their aggressiveness. Today's peaceful Scandinavians carry many genes inherited from their Viking warrior ancestors.

RETRIEVAL PRACTICE

- Those studying the heritability of a trait try to determine how much of our individual variation in that trait is due to our ___________.

ANSWER: genes

Gene-Environment Interaction

11-4 How do heredity and environment work together?

Among our similarities, the most important—the behavioral hallmark of our species—is our enormous adaptive capacity. Some human traits, such as having two eyes, develop the same in virtually every environment. But other traits are expressed only in particular environments. Go barefoot for a summer and you will develop toughened, callused feet—a biological adaptation to friction. Meanwhile, your shod neighbor will remain a

"Men's natures are alike; it is their habits that carry them far apart."

Confucius, *Analects*, 500 B.C.E.

Dim154/Shutterstock

"Heredity deals the cards; environment plays the hand."
Psychologist Charles L. Brewer (1990)

tenderfoot. The difference between the two of you is, of course, an effect of environment. But it is also the product of a biological mechanism—adaptation. Our shared biology enables our developed diversity (Buss, 1991).

An analogy may help: Genes and environment—nature and nurture—work together like two hands clapping. Genes are *self-regulating.* Rather than acting as blueprints that lead to the same result no matter the context, genes react. An African butterfly that is green in summer turns brown in fall, thanks to a temperature-controlled genetic switch. The genes that produce brown in one situation produce green in another. So, too, people with identical genes but differing experiences will have similar but not identical minds. One twin may fall in love with someone quite different from the co-twin's love.

Asking whether our personality is more a product of our genes or our environment is like asking whether the area of a field is more the result of its length or its width. We could, however, ask whether the differing areas of various fields are more the result of *differences* in their length or their width, and also whether person-to-person personality differences are influenced more by nature or nurture.

To say that genes and experience are *both* important is true. But more precisely, they **interact.** Imagine two babies, one genetically predisposed to be attractive, sociable, and easygoing, the other less so. Assume further that the first baby attracts more affectionate and stimulating care and so develops into a warmer and more outgoing person. As the two children grow older, the more naturally outgoing child more often seeks activities and friends that encourage further social confidence.

What has caused their resulting personality differences? Neither heredity nor experience dances alone. Environments trigger gene activity. And our genetically influenced traits *evoke* significant responses in others. Thus, a child's impulsivity and aggression may evoke an angry response from a teacher who reacts warmly to the child's model classmates. Parents, too, may treat their own children differently; one child elicits punishment, another does not. In such cases, the child's nature and the parents' nurture interact. Neither operates apart from the other. Gene and scene dance together.

Evocative interactions may help explain why identical twins reared in different families recall their parents' warmth as remarkably similar—almost as similar as if they had had the same parents (Plomin et al., 1988, 1991, 1994). Fraternal twins have more differing recollections of their early family life—even if reared in the same family! "Children experience us as different parents, depending on their own qualities," noted Sandra Scarr (1990). Moreover, a selection effect may be at work. As we grow older, we select environments well suited to our natures.

Recall that genes can be either active (expressed, as the hot water activates the tea bag) or inactive. A new field, **epigenetics** (meaning "in addition to" or "above and beyond" genetics), is studying the molecular mechanisms by which environments trigger genetic expression. Although genes have the potential to influence development, environmental triggers can switch them on or off, much as your computer's software directs your printer. One such *epigenetic mark* is an organic methyl molecule attached to part of a DNA strand (FIGURE 11.3). It instructs the cell to ignore any gene present in that DNA stretch, thereby preventing the DNA from producing the proteins coded by that gene.

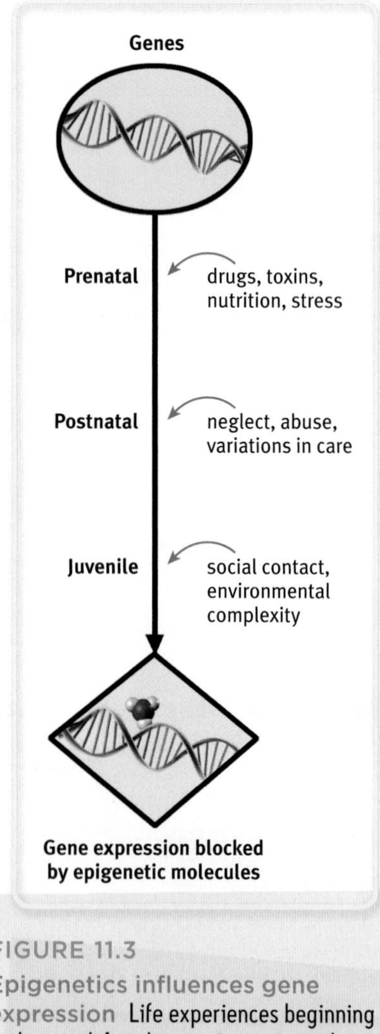

FIGURE 11.3
Epigenetics influences gene expression Life experiences beginning in the womb lay down epigenetic marks—organic methyl molecules—that can block the expression of any gene in the associated DNA segment (from Champagne, 2010).

Environmental factors such as diet, drugs, and stress can affect the epigenetic molecules that regulate gene expression. In one experiment, infant rats deprived of their mothers' normal licking had more molecules that blocked access to the "on" switch for developing the brain's stress hormone receptors. When stressed, the animals had more free-floating stress hormones and were more stressed out (Champagne et al., 2003; Champagne & Mashoodh, 2009). Child abuse may similarly affect its victims. Humans who have committed suicide exhibit the same epigenetic effect if they had suffered a history of child abuse (McGowan et al., 2009). Researchers now wonder if epigenetics might help solve some scientific mysteries, such as why only one member of an identical twin pair may develop a genetically influenced mental disorder, and how experience leaves its fingerprints in our brains.

miniature toy, but they could not use the model to locate an actual stuffed dog behind a couch in a real room. Three-year-olds—only 6 months older—usually went right to the actual stuffed animal in the real room, showing they *could* think of the model as a symbol for the room. Piaget probably would have been surprised.

theory of mind people's ideas about their own and others' mental states—about their feelings, perceptions, and thoughts, and the behaviors these might predict.

concrete operational stage in Piaget's theory, the stage of cognitive development (from about 6 or 7 to 11 years of age) during which children gain the mental operations that enable them to think logically about concrete events.

Theory of Mind

When Little Red Riding Hood realized her "grandmother" was really a wolf, she swiftly revised her ideas about the creature's intentions and raced away. Preschoolers, although still egocentric, develop this ability to infer others' mental states when they begin forming a **theory of mind** (a term first coined by psychologists David Premack and Guy Woodruff [1978], to describe chimpanzees' seeming ability to read intentions).

Infants as young as 7 months show some knowledge of others' beliefs (Kovács et al., 2010). With time, the ability to take another's perspective develops. They come to understand what made a playmate angry, when a sibling will share, and what might make a parent buy a toy. And they begin to tease, empathize, and persuade. Between about 3½ and 4½, children worldwide come to realize that others may hold false beliefs (Callaghan et al., 2005; Sabbagh et al., 2006). Jennifer Jenkins and Janet Astington (1996) showed Toronto children a Band-Aids box and asked them what was inside. Expecting Band-Aids, the children were surprised to discover that the box actually contained pencils. Asked what a child who had never seen the box would think was inside, 3-year-olds typically answered "pencils." By age 4 to 5, the children's theory of mind had leapt forward, and they anticipated their friends' false belief that the box would hold Band-Aids.

In a follow-up experiment, children viewed a doll named Sally leaving her ball in a red cupboard (**FIGURE 14.10**). Another doll, Anne, then moves the ball to a blue cupboard. Researchers then pose a question: When Sally returns, where will she look for the ball? Children with *autism* (see Close-Up: Autism and "Mind Blindness" on the next page) have difficulty understanding that Sally's state of mind differs from their own—that Sally, not knowing the ball has been moved, will return to the red cupboard. They also have difficulty reflecting on their own mental states. They are, for example, less likely to use the personal pronouns *I* and *me.* Deaf children with hearing parents and minimal communication opportunities have had similar difficulty inferring others' states of mind (Peterson & Siegal, 1999).

FIGURE 14.10
Testing children's theory of mind This simple problem illustrates how researchers explore children's presumptions about others' mental states. (Inspired by Baron-Cohen et al., 1985.)

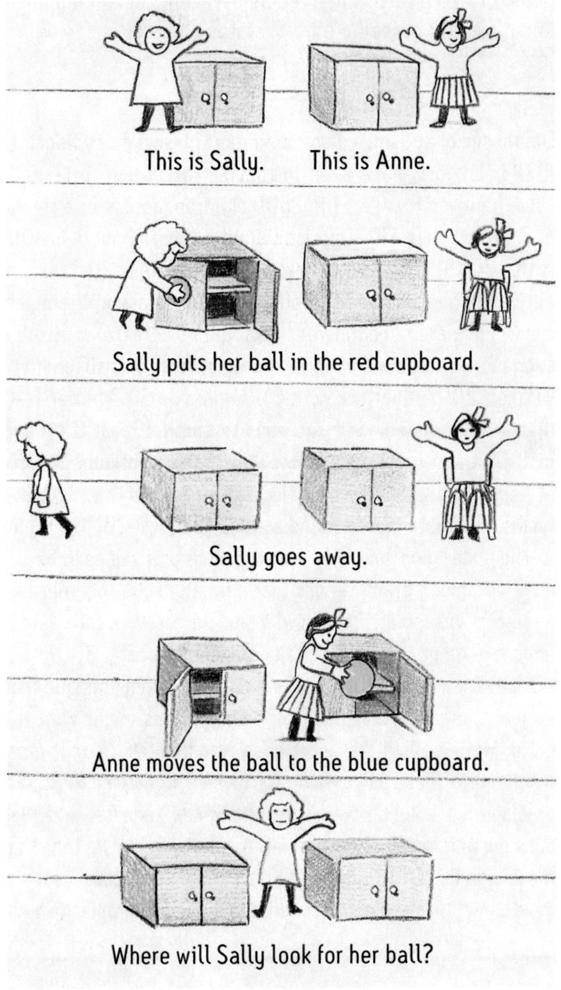

Concrete Operational Stage

By age 6 or 7, said Piaget, children enter the **concrete operational stage.** Given concrete (physical) materials, they begin to grasp conservation. Understanding that change in form does not mean change in quantity, they can mentally pour milk back and forth between glasses of different shapes. They also enjoy jokes that use this new understanding:

> Mr. Jones went into a restaurant and ordered a whole pizza for his dinner. When the waiter asked if he wanted it cut into 6 or 8 pieces, Mr. Jones said, "Oh, you'd better make it 6, I could never eat 8 pieces!" (McGhee, 1976)

Piaget believed that during the concrete operational stage, children become able to comprehend mathematical transformations and conservation. When my daughter, Laura, was 6, I was astonished at her inability to reverse simple arithmetic. Asked, "What is 8 plus 4?" she required 5 seconds to compute "12," and another 5 seconds to then compute 12 minus 4. By age 8, she could answer a reversed question instantly.

CLOSE-UP

Autism and "Mind-Blindness"

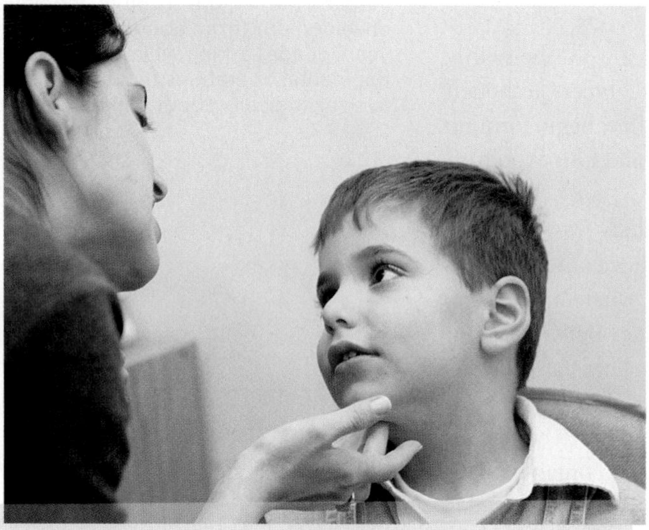

Ozier Muhammad/The New York Times/Redux

Autism This speech-language pathologist is helping a boy with autism learn to form sounds and words. Autism, which afflicts four boys for every girl, is marked by deficient social communication and difficulty grasping others' states of mind.

Diagnoses of **autism,** a disorder marked by social deficiencies and repetitive behaviors, have been increasing, according to recent estimates. Once believed to affect 1 in 2500 children, autism or a related disorder now affects 1 in 110 American children and about 1 in 100 in Britain (CDC, 2009; Lilienfeld & Arkowitz, 2007; NAS, 2011). The increase in autism diagnoses has been offset by a decrease in the number of children considered "cognitively disabled" or "learning disabled," which suggests a relabeling of children's disorders (Gernsbacher et al., 2005; Grinker, 2007; Shattuck, 2006). A massive $6.7 billion National Children's Study now under way aims to enroll 100,000 pregnant women in 105 countries and to follow their babies until they turn 21—partly in hopes of explaining the rising rates of autism, as well as premature births, childhood obesity, and asthma (Belluck, 2010; Murphy, 2008).

The underlying source of autism's symptoms seems to be poor communication among brain regions that normally work together to let us take another's viewpoint. People with autism are therefore said to have an *impaired theory of mind* (Rajendran & Mitchell, 2007; Senju et al., 2009). They have difficulty inferring others' thoughts and feelings. They do not appreciate that playmates and parents might view things differently. Mind reading that most of us find intuitive *(Is that face conveying a smirk or a sneer?)* is difficult for those with autism. Most children learn that another child's pouting mouth signals sadness, and that twinkling eyes mean happiness or mischief. A child with autism fails to understand these signals (Frith & Frith, 2001). In hopes of a cure, desperate parents have sometimes subjected children to dubious therapies (Shute, 2010).

Autism spectrum disorder is a term used to encompass a range of variations, one of which is *Asperger syndrome,* a high-functioning form of autism. Asperger syndrome is marked by normal intelligence, often accompanied by exceptional skill or talent in a specific area, but deficient social and communication skills and a tendency to become distracted by irrelevant stimuli (Remington et al., 2009).

Autism afflicts four boys for every girl. Children for whom amniotic fluid analyses indicated high prenatal testosterone develop more masculine and autistic traits (Auyeung et al., 2009). Psychologist Simon Baron-Cohen (2008, 2009) argues that autism represents an "extreme male brain." Girls are naturally predisposed to be "empathizers," he contends. They are better at reading facial expressions and gestures though less so if given testosterone (van Honk et al., 2011). Reading faces is a challenging task for those with autism. And, although the sexes overlap, boys are, he believes, better "systemizers"—understanding things according to rules or laws, as in mathematical and mechanical systems.

"If two 'systemizers' have a child, this will increase the risk of the child having autism," Baron-Cohen theorizes. And because of *assortative mating*—people's tendency to seek spouses who share their interests—two systemizers will indeed often mate. "I do not discount environmental factors," he notes. "I'm just saying, don't forget about biology."

Twin and sibling studies provide some evidence for biology's influence. If one identical twin is diagnosed with autism, the chances are

Miller Mobley/Redux

Autism case number 1 In 1943, Donald Gray Triplett, an "odd" child with unusual gifts and social deficits, was the first person to receive the diagnosis of a previously unreported condition, which psychiatrist Leo Kanner termed *autism*. In 2010, at age 77, Triplett was still living in his native home and Mississippi town, where he often played golf (Donvan & Zucker, 2010).

50 to 70 percent that the co-twin will be as well (Lichtenstein et al., 2010; Sebat et al., 2007). A younger sibling of a child with autism also is at a heightened risk (Sutcliffe, 2008). Random genetic mutations in sperm-producing cells may also play a role. As men age, these mutations become more frequent, which may help explain why an over-40 man has a much higher risk of fathering a child with autism than does a man under 30 (Reichenberg et al., 2007). Researchers are now sleuthing autism spectrum disorder's telltale signs in the brain's synaptic and gray matter (Crawley, 2007; Ecker et al., 2010; Garber, 2007).

Biology's role in autism also appears in brain-function studies. People without autism often yawn after seeing others yawn. And as they view and imitate another's smiling or frowning, they feel something of what the other is feeling. Not so among those with autism spectrum disorder, who are less imitative and show much less activity in brain areas involved in mirroring others' actions (Dapretto et al., 2006; Perra et al., 2008; Senju et al., 2007). When people with autism watch another person's hand movements, for example, their brain displays less than normal mirroring activity (Oberman & Ramachandran, 2007; Théoret et al., 2005). Scientists are continuing to explore and vigorously debate the idea that the brains of people with autism have "broken mirrors" (Gallese et al., 2011).

Seeking to "systemize empathy," Baron-Cohen and his Cambridge University colleagues (2007; Golan et al., 2010) collaborated with Britain's National Autistic Society and a film production company. Knowing that television shows with vehicles have been popular among kids with autism, they created animations that grafted emotion-conveying faces onto toy tram, train, and tractor characters in a pretend boy's bedroom (**FIGURE 14.11**). After the boy leaves for school, the characters come to life and have experiences that lead them to display various emotions (which I predict you would enjoy viewing at www.thetransporters.com). The children were surprisingly able to generalize what they had learned to a new, real context. By the intervention's end, their previously deficient ability to recognize emotions on real faces now equaled that of children without autism.

autism a disorder that appears in childhood and is marked by deficient communication, social interaction, and understanding of others' states of mind.

RETRIEVAL PRACTICE

- What does *theory of mind* have to do with autism?

ANSWER: Theory of mind focuses on our ability to understand our own and others' mental states. Those with autism struggle with this ability.

FIGURE 14.11

Transported into a world of emotion (a) A research team at Cambridge University's Autism Research Centre introduced children with autism to emotions experienced and displayed by toy vehicles. (b) After four weeks of viewing animations, the children displayed a markedly increased ability to recognize emotions not only in the toy faces but also in humans.

© Crown copyright MMVI, www.thetransporters.com, courtesy Changing Media Development

(a) Emotion-conveying faces are grafted onto toy trains.

"The neighbor's dog has bitten people before. He is barking at Louise."

Point to the face that shows how Louise is feeling.

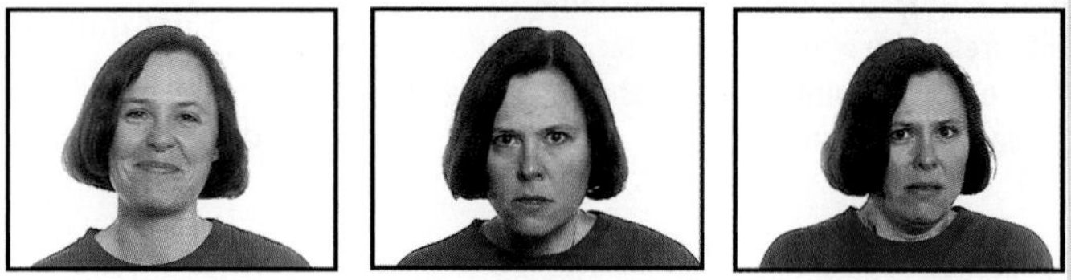

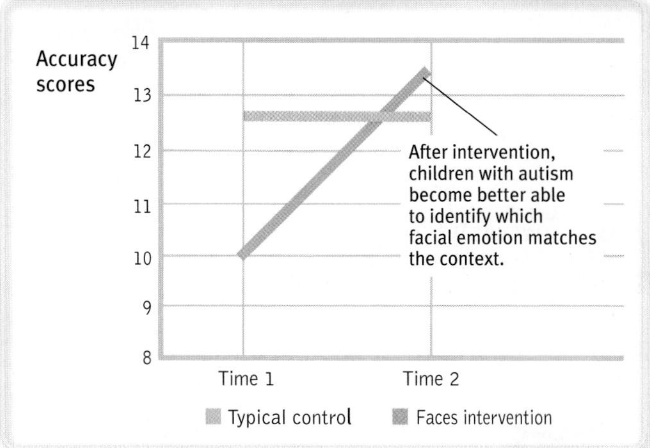

(b) Children match the correct face with the story and photo. (The graph above shows data for two trials.)

formal operational stage in Piaget's theory, the stage of cognitive development (normally beginning about age 12) during which people begin to think logically about abstract concepts.

stranger anxiety the fear of strangers that infants commonly display, beginning by about 8 months of age.

attachment an emotional tie with another person; shown in young children by their seeking closeness to the caregiver and showing distress on separation.

Formal Operational Stage

By age 12, our reasoning expands from the purely concrete (involving actual experience) to encompass abstract thinking (involving imagined realities and symbols). As children approach adolescence, said Piaget, many become capable of thinking more like scientists. They can ponder hypothetical propositions and deduce consequences: *If* this, *then* that. Systematic reasoning, what Piaget called **formal operational** thinking, is now within their grasp.

Although full-blown logic and reasoning await adolescence, the rudiments of formal operational thinking begin earlier than Piaget realized. Consider this simple problem:

> If John is in school, then Mary is in school. John is in school. What can you say about Mary?

Formal operational thinkers have no trouble answering correctly. But neither do most 7-year-olds (Suppes, 1982).

James V. Wertsch/Washington University

Lev Vygotsky (1896–1934) Vygotsky, a Russian developmental psychologist, pictured here with his daughter, studied how a child's mind feeds on the language of social interaction.

An Alternative Viewpoint: Lev Vygotsky's Scaffolding

As Piaget was forming his theory of cognitive development, Russian psychologist Lev Vygotsky (1896–1934) was also studying how children think and learn. He noted that by age 7, they increasingly think in words and use words to solve problems. They do this, he said, by internalizing their culture's language and relying on inner speech (Fernyhough, 2008). Parents who say *"No, no!"* when pulling a child's hand away from a cake are giving the child a self-control tool. When the child later needs to resist temptation, he may likewise say *"No, no!"* Second graders who muttered to themselves while doing math problems grasped third-grade math better the following year (Berk, 1994). Whether out loud or inaudibly, talking to themselves helps children control their behavior and emotions and master new skills.

Where Piaget emphasized how the child's mind grows through interaction with the physical environment, Vygotsky emphasized how the child's mind grows through interaction with the *social* environment. If Piaget's child was a young scientist, Vygotsky's was a young apprentice. By mentoring children and giving them new words, parents and others provide a temporary *scaffold* from which children can step to higher levels of thinking (Renninger & Granott, 2005). Language, an important ingredient of social mentoring, provides the building blocks for thinking, noted Vygotsky (who was born the same year as Piaget, but died prematurely of tuberculosis).

RETRIEVAL PRACTICE

- Object permanence, pretend play, conservation, and abstract logic are developmental milestones for which of Piaget's stages, respectively?

ANSWER: Object permanence for the sensorimotor stage, pretend play for the preoperational stage, conservation for the concrete operational stage, and abstract logic for the formal operational stage.

- Match the developmental phenomena (1-8) to the correct cognitive developmental stage (a-d).

a. Sensorimotor b. Preoperational c. Concrete operational d. Formal operational

1. Thinking about abstract concepts, such as "freedom."
2. Intense fear of unknown people.
3. Enjoying imaginary play (such as dress-up).
4. Ability to reason with maturity about moral values.
5. Understanding that physical properties stay the same even when objects change form.
6. Ability to reverse math operations.
7. Understanding that something is not gone for good when it disappears from sight as when Mom "disappears" behind the shower curtain.
8. Difficulty taking another's point of view (as when blocking someone's view of the TV).

ANSWERS: 1. d, 2. a, 3. b, 4. d, 5. c, 6. c, 7. a, 8. b

Family Circus ® Bil Keane

©Bil Keane, Inc. Reprinted with special permission of King Features Syndicate.

"Don't you remember, Grandma? You were in it with me."

Reflecting on Piaget's Theory

What remains of Piaget's ideas about the child's mind? Plenty—enough to merit his being singled out by *Time* magazine as one of the twentieth century's 20 most influential scientists and thinkers and rated in a survey of British psychologists as the last century's greatest psychologist (*Psychologist*, 2003). Piaget identified significant cognitive milestones and stimulated worldwide interest in how the mind develops. His emphasis was less on the ages at which children typically reach specific milestones than on their sequence. Studies around the globe, from aboriginal Australia to Algeria to North America, have confirmed that human cognition unfolds basically in the sequence Piaget described (Lourenco & Machado, 1996; Segall et al., 1990).

"Assessing the impact of Piaget on developmental psychology is like assessing the impact of Shakespeare on English literature."
Developmental psychologist Harry Beilin (1992)

However, today's researchers see development as more continuous than did Piaget. By detecting the beginnings of each type of thinking at earlier ages, they have revealed conceptual abilities Piaget missed. Moreover, they see formal logic as a smaller part of cognition than he did. Piaget would not be surprised that today, as part of our own cognitive development, we are adapting his ideas to accommodate new findings.

Implications for Parents and Teachers

Future parents and teachers remember: Young children are incapable of adult logic. Preschoolers who block one's view of the TV simply have not learned to take another's viewpoint. What seems simple and obvious to us—getting off a teeter-totter will cause a friend on the other end to crash—may be incomprehensible to a 3-year-old. Also remember that children are not passive receptacles waiting to be filled with knowledge. Better to build on what they already know, engaging them in concrete demonstrations and stimulating them to think for themselves. And, finally, accept children's cognitive immaturity as adaptive. It is nature's strategy for keeping children close to protective adults and providing time for learning and socialization (Bjorklund & Green, 1992).

"Childhood has its own way of seeing, thinking, and feeling, and there is nothing more foolish than the attempt to put ours in its place."
Philosopher Jean-Jacques Rousseau, 1798

Social Development

14-3 How do parent-infant attachment bonds form?

From birth, babies in all cultures are social creatures, developing an intense bond with their caregivers. Infants come to prefer familiar faces and voices, then to coo and gurgle when given a parent's attention. At about 8 months, soon after object permanence emerges and children become mobile, a curious thing happens: They develop **stranger anxiety.** They may greet strangers by crying and reaching for familiar caregivers. "No! Don't leave me!" their distress seems to say. Children this age have schemas for familiar faces; when they cannot assimilate the new face into these remembered schemas, they become distressed (Kagan, 1984). Once again, we see an important principle: *The brain, mind, and social-emotional behavior develop together.*

Stranger anxiety A newly emerging ability to evaluate people as unfamiliar and possibly threatening helps protect babies 8 months and older.

© Christina Kennedy/PhotoEdit

Origins of Attachment

One-year-olds typically cling tightly to a parent when they are frightened or expect separation. Reunited after being apart, they shower the parent with smiles and hugs. No social behavior is more striking than the intense and mutual infant-parent bond. This **attachment** bond is a powerful survival impulse that keeps infants close to their caregivers. Infants become attached to those—typically their parents—who are comfortable and familiar. For many years, psychologists reasoned that infants became attached to those who satisfied their need for nourishment. It made sense. But an accidental finding overturned this explanation.

FIGURE 14.12
The Harlows' mothers
Psychologists Harry Harlow and Margaret Harlow raised monkeys with two artificial mothers—one a bare wire cylinder with a wooden head and an attached feeding bottle, the other a cylinder with no bottle but covered with foam rubber and wrapped with terry cloth. The Harlows' discovery surprised many psychologists: The infants much preferred contact with the comfortable cloth mother, even while feeding from the nourishing mother.

Body Contact

During the 1950s, University of Wisconsin psychologists Harry Harlow and Margaret Harlow bred monkeys for their learning studies. To equalize experiences and to isolate any disease, they separated the infant monkeys from their mothers shortly after birth and raised them in sanitary individual cages, which included a cheesecloth baby blanket (Harlow et al., 1971). Then came a surprise: When their blankets were taken to be laundered, the monkeys became distressed.

The Harlows recognized that this intense attachment to the blanket contradicted the idea that attachment derives from an association with nourishment. But how could they show this more convincingly? To pit the drawing power of a food source against the contact comfort of the blanket, they created two artificial mothers. One was a bare wire cylinder with a wooden head and an attached feeding bottle, the other a cylinder wrapped with terry cloth.

When raised with both, the monkeys overwhelmingly preferred the comfy cloth mother (**FIGURE 14.12**). Like other infants clinging to their live mothers, the monkey babies would cling to their cloth mothers when anxious. When exploring their environment, they used her as a *secure base*, as if attached to her by an invisible elastic band that stretched only so far before pulling them back. Researchers soon learned that other qualities—rocking, warmth, and feeding—made the cloth mother even more appealing.

For some people a perceived relationship with God functions as do other attachments, by providing a secure base for exploration and a safe haven when threatened (Granqvist et al., 2010; Kirkpatrick, 1999).

Human infants, too, become attached to parents who are soft and warm and who rock, feed, and pat. Much parent-infant emotional communication occurs via touch (Hertenstein et al., 2006), which can be either soothing (snuggles) or arousing (tickles). Human attachment also consists of one person providing another with a secure base from which to explore and a safe haven when distressed. As we mature, our secure base and safe haven shift—from parents to peers and partners (Cassidy & Shaver, 1999). But at all ages we are social creatures. We gain strength when someone offers, by words and actions, a safe haven: "I will be here. I am interested in you. Come what may, I will support you" (Crowell & Waters, 1994).

Familiarity

Contact is one key to attachment. Another is familiarity. In many animals, attachments based on familiarity form during a **critical period**—an optimal period when certain events must take place to facilitate proper development (Bornstein, 1989). For goslings, ducklings, or chicks, that period falls in the hours shortly after hatching, when the first moving object they see is normally their mother. From then on, the young fowl follow her, and her alone.

critical period an optimal period early in the life of an organism when exposure to certain stimuli or experiences produces normal development.

imprinting the process by which certain animals form attachments during a critical period very early in life.

Konrad Lorenz (1937) explored this rigid attachment process, called **imprinting.** He wondered: What would ducklings do if he was the first moving creature they observed? What they did was follow him around: Everywhere that Konrad went, the ducks were sure to go. Although baby birds imprint best to their own species, they also will imprint to a variety of moving objects—an animal of another species, a box

Mark Peterson/Redux

Imprinting Whooping cranes normally learn to migrate by following their parents. These cranes, reared from eggs, have imprinted on a crane-costumed ultralight pilot, who can then guide them to winter nesting grounds (Mooallem, 2009).

on wheels, a bouncing ball (Colombo, 1982; Johnson, 1992). Once formed, this attachment is difficult to reverse.

Children—unlike ducklings—do not imprint. However, they do become attached to what they've known. *Mere exposure* to people and things fosters fondness. Children like to reread the same books, rewatch the same movies, reenact family traditions. They prefer to eat familiar foods, live in the same familiar neighborhood, attend school with the same old friends. Familiarity is a safety signal. Familiarity breeds content.

RETRIEVAL PRACTICE

- What distinguishes imprinting from attachment?

ANSWER: Attachment is the normal process by which we form emotional ties with important others. Imprinting occurs in animals that have a critical period very early in their development during which they must form their attachments, and they do so in an inflexible manner.

Attachment Differences

14-4 How have psychologists studied attachment differences, and what have they learned?

What accounts for children's attachment differences? To answer this question, Mary Ainsworth (1979) designed the *strange situation* experiment. She observed mother-infant pairs at home during their first six months. Later she observed the 1-year-old infants in a strange situation (usually a laboratory playroom). Such research has shown that about 60 percent of infants display *secure attachment.* In their mother's presence they play comfortably, happily exploring their new environment. When she leaves, they become distressed; when she returns, they seek contact with her.

Other infants avoid attachment or show *insecure attachment,* marked either by anxiety or avoidance of trusting relationships. They are less likely to explore their surroundings; they may even cling to their mother. When she leaves, they either cry loudly and remain upset or seem indifferent to her departure and return (Ainsworth, 1973, 1989; Kagan, 1995; van IJzendoorn & Kroonenberg, 1988).

Ainsworth and others found that sensitive, responsive mothers—those who noticed what their babies were doing and responded appropriately—had infants who exhibited secure attachment (De Wolff & van IJzendoorn, 1997). Insensitive, unresponsive mothers—mothers who attended to their babies when they felt like doing so but ignored them at other times—often had infants who were insecurely attached. The Harlows' monkey studies, with unresponsive artificial mothers, produced even more striking effects. When put in strange situations without their artificial mothers, the deprived infants were terrified (**FIGURE 14.13**).

But is attachment style the *result* of parenting? Or is attachment style the result of genetically influenced *temperament*—a person's characteristic emotional reactivity and intensity? Shortly after birth, some babies are noticeably *difficult*—irritable, intense, and unpredictable. Others are *easy*—cheerful, relaxed, and feeding and sleeping on predict-

FIGURE 14.13

Social deprivation and fear In the Harlows' experiments, monkeys raised with artificial mothers were terror-stricken when placed in strange situations without those mothers. (Today's climate of greater respect for animal welfare prevents such primate studies.)

Harlow Primate Laboratory, University of Wisconsin

d85/ZUMA Press/Newscom

Full-time dad Financial analyst Walter Cranford, shown here with his baby twins, is one of a growing number of stay-at-home dads. Cranford says the experience has made him appreciate how difficult the work can be: "Sometimes at work you can just unplug, but with this you've got to be going all the time."

able schedules (Chess & Thomas, 1987). By neglecting such inborn differences, the parenting studies, noted Judith Harris (1998), are like "comparing foxhounds reared in kennels with poodles reared in apartments." So to separate nature and nurture, we would need to vary parenting while controlling temperament. (Pause and think: If you were the researcher, how might you have done this?)

Dutch researcher Dymphna van den Boom's solution was to randomly assign 100 temperamentally difficult 6- to 9-month-olds to either an experimental group, in which mothers received personal training in sensitive responding, or to a control group, in which they did not. At 12 months of age, 68 percent of the infants in the experimental group were rated securely attached, as were only 28 percent of the control group infants. Other studies support the idea that intervention programs can increase parental sensitivity and, to a lesser extent, infant attachment security (Bakermans-Kranenburg et al., 2003; Van Zeijl et al., 2006).

As these examples indicate, researchers have more often studied mother care than father care. Infants who lack a caring mother are said to suffer "maternal deprivation"; those lacking a father's care merely experience "father absence." This reflects a wider attitude in which "fathering a child" has meant impregnating, and "mothering" has meant nurturing. But fathers are more than just mobile sperm banks. Across nearly 100 studies worldwide, a father's love and acceptance have been comparable to a mother's love in predicting their offspring's health and well-being (Rohner & Veneziano, 2001). In one mammoth British study following 7259 children from birth to adulthood, those whose fathers were most involved in parenting (through outings, reading to them, and taking an interest in their education) tended to achieve more in school, even after controlling for other factors such as parental education and family wealth (Flouri & Buchanan, 2004).

Children's anxiety over separation from parents peaks at around 13 months, then gradually declines (**FIGURE 14.14**). This happens whether they live with one parent or two, are cared for at home or in a day-care center, live in North America, Guatemala, or the Kalahari Desert. Does this mean our need for and love of others also fades away? Hardly. Our capacity for love grows, and our pleasure in touching and holding those we love never ceases. The power of early attachment does nonetheless gradually relax, allowing us to move out into a wider range of situations, communicate with strangers more freely, and stay emotionally attached to loved ones despite distance.

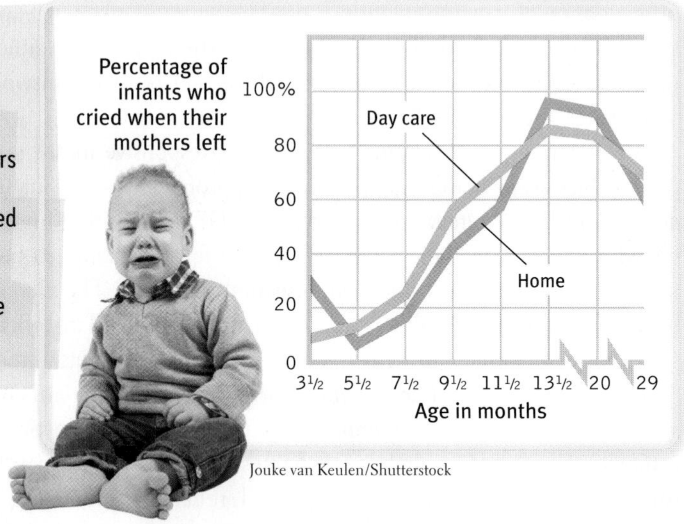

Jouke van Keulen/Shutterstock

FIGURE 14.14
Infants' distress over separation from parents
In an experiment, groups of infants were left by their mothers in an unfamiliar room. In both groups, the percentage who cried when the mother left peaked at about 13 months. Whether the infant had experienced day care made little difference. (From Kagan, 1976.)

Attachment Styles and Later Relationships

Developmental theorist Erik Erikson (1902–1994), working with his wife, Joan Erikson, believed that securely attached children approach life with a sense of **basic trust**—a sense that the world is predictable and reliable. He attributed basic trust not to environment or inborn temperament, but to early parenting. He theorized that infants blessed with sensitive, loving caregivers form a lifelong attitude of trust rather than fear.

"Out of the conflict between trust and mistrust, the infant develops hope, which is the earliest form of what gradually becomes faith in adults."
Erik Erikson (1983)

Although debate continues, many researchers now believe that our early attachments form the foundation for our adult relationships and our comfort with affection and intimacy (Birnbaum et al., 2006; Fraley, 2002). Our adult styles of romantic love tend to exhibit either secure, trusting attachment; insecure, anxious attachment; or the avoidance of attachment (Feeney & Noller, 1990; Rholes & Simpson, 2004; Shaver & Mikulincer, 2007). These adult attachment styles in turn affect relationships with one's own children, as avoidant people find parenting more stressful and unsatisfying (Rholes et al., 2006).

basic trust according to Erik Erikson, a sense that the world is predictable and trustworthy; said to be formed during infancy by appropriate experiences with responsive caregivers.

Attachment style is also associated with motivation (Elliot & Reis, 2003). Securely attached people exhibit less fear of failure and a greater drive to achieve. But say this for those (nearly half of all humans) who exhibit insecure attachments: Anxious or avoidant tendencies have helped our groups detect or escape dangers (Ein-Dor et al., 2010).

Deprivation of Attachment

14-5 Does childhood neglect, abuse, or family disruption affect children's attachments?

If secure attachment nurtures social competence, what happens when circumstances prevent a child from forming attachments? In all of psychology, there is no sadder research literature. Babies locked away at home under conditions of abuse or extreme neglect are often withdrawn, frightened, even speechless. The same is true of those reared in institutions without the stimulation and attention of a regular caregiver, as was tragically illustrated during the 1970s and 1980s in Romania. Having decided that economic growth for his impoverished country required more human capital, Nicolae Ceauşescu, Romania's Communist dictator, outlawed contraception, forbade abortion, and taxed families with fewer than five children. The birthrate indeed skyrocketed. But unable to afford the children they had been coerced into having, many families abandoned them to government-run orphanages with untrained and overworked staff. Child-to-caregiver ratios often were 15 to 1 (and you thought parenting triplets was a strain), so the children were deprived of healthy attachments with at least one adult. When tested after Ceauşescu was assassinated in 1989, these children had lower intelligence scores and double the 20 percent rate of anxiety symptoms found in children assigned to quality foster care settings (Nelson et al., 2009). Dozens of other studies across 19 countries have confirmed that orphaned children tend to fare better on later intelligence tests if raised in family homes. This is especially so for those placed at an early age (van IJzendoorn et al., 2008).

"What is learned in the cradle, lasts to the grave."
French proverb

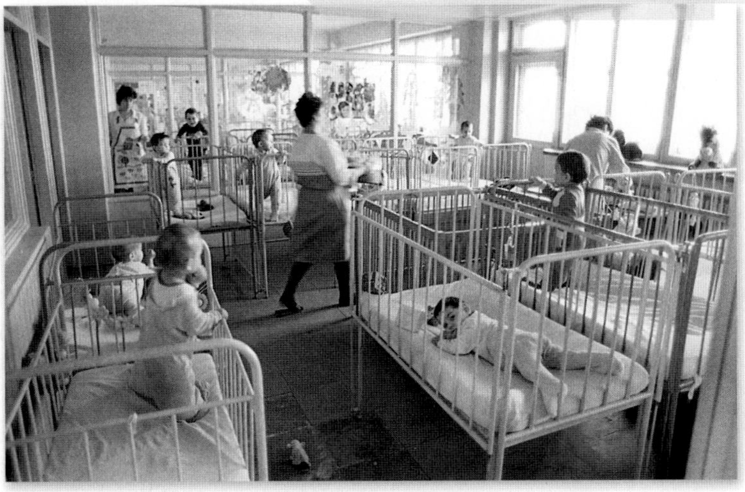

The deprivation of attachment In this Romanian orphanage, the 250 children between ages one and five outnumbered caregivers 10 to 1.

Mike Carroll mike@carrollmj.com

Most children growing up under adversity (as did the surviving children of the Holocaust) are *resilient*; they become normal adults (Helmreich, 1992; Masten, 2001). So do most victims of childhood sexual abuse, noted Harvard researcher Susan Clancy (2010), while emphasizing that using children for sex is revolting and never the victim's fault.

But others, especially those who experience no sharp break from their abusive past, don't bounce back so readily. The Harlows' monkeys raised in total isolation, without even an artificial mother, bore lifelong scars. As adults, when placed with other monkeys their age, they either cowered in fright or lashed out in aggression. When they reached sexual maturity, most were incapable of mating. If artificially impregnated, females often were neglectful, abusive, even murderous toward their first-born. Another primate experiment confirmed the abuse-breeds-abuse phenomenon. In one study, 9 of 16 females who had been abused by their mothers became abusive parents, as did *no* female raised by a nonabusive mother (Maestripieri, 2005).

In humans, too, the unloved may become the unloving. Most abusive parents—and many condemned murderers—have reported being neglected or battered as children (Kempe & Kempe, 1978; Lewis et al., 1988). Some 30 percent of people who have been abused later abuse their children—a rate lower than that found in the primate study, but four times the U.S. national rate of child abuse (Dumont et al., 2007; Kaufman & Zigler, 1987).

Although most abused children do *not* later become violent criminals or abusive parents, extreme early trauma may nevertheless leave footprints on the brain. Abused children exhibit hypersensitivity to angry faces (Pollak, 2008). As adults, they exhibit stronger startle responses (Jovanovic et al., 2009). If repeatedly threatened and attacked while young, normally placid golden hamsters grow up to be cowards when caged with same-sized hamsters, or bullies when caged with weaker ones (Ferris, 1996). Such animals show changes in the brain chemical serotonin, which calms aggressive impulses. A similarly sluggish serotonin response has been found in abused children who become aggressive teens and adults. "Stress can set off a ripple of hormonal changes that permanently wire a child's brain to cope with a malevolent world," concluded abuse researcher Martin Teicher (2002).

Such findings help explain why young children who have survived severe or prolonged physical abuse, childhood sexual abuse, or wartime atrocities are at increased risk for health problems, psychological disorders, substance abuse, and criminality (Freyd et al., 2005; Kendall-Tackett et al., 1993, 2004; Wegman & Stetler, 2009). Abuse victims are at considerable risk for depression *if* they carry a gene variation that spurs stress-hormone production (Bradley et al., 2008). As we will see again and again, behavior and emotion arise from a particular environment interacting with particular genes.

We adults also suffer when our attachment bonds are severed. Whether through death or separation, a break produces a predictable sequence. Agitated preoccupation with the lost partner is followed by deep sadness and, eventually, the beginnings of emotional detachment and a return to normal living (Hazan & Shaver, 1994). Newly separated couples who have long ago ceased feeling affection are sometimes surprised at their desire to be near the former partner. Deep and longstanding attachments seldom break quickly. Detaching is a process, not an event.

Day Care

14-6 How does day care affect children?

In the mid-twentieth century, when Mom-at-home was the social norm, researchers asked, "Is day care bad for children? Does it disrupt children's attachments to their parents?" For the high-quality day-care programs usually studied, the answer was *No.* In *Mother Care/Other Care,* developmental psychologist Sandra Scarr (1986) explained that children are "biologically sturdy individuals . . . who can thrive in a wide variety of life situations." Scarr spoke for many developmental psychologists, whose research has uncovered no major impact of maternal employment on children's development, attachments, and achievements (Friedman & Boyle, 2008; Goldberg et al., 2008; Lucas-Thompson et al., 2010).

Research then shifted to the effects of differing quality of day care on different types and ages of children (Vandell et al., 2010). Scarr (1997) explained: Around the world, "high-quality child care consists of warm, supportive interactions with adults in a safe, healthy, and stimulating environment. . . . Poor care is boring and unresponsive to children's needs."

self-concept all our thoughts and feelings about ourselves, in answer to the question, "Who am I?"

Even well-run orphanages can produce healthy, thriving children. In Africa and Asia, where many children are losing parents to AIDS and other diseases, orphanages typically are unlike those in Ceauşescu's Romania, and the children living in quality orphanages fare about as well as those living in communities (Whetten et al., 2009).

Children's ability to thrive under varied types of responsive caregiving should not surprise us, given cultural variations in attachment patterns. Westernized attachment features one or two caregivers and their offspring. In other cultures, such as the Efe of Zaire, multiple caregivers are the norm (Field, 1996; Whaley et al., 2002). Even before the mother holds her newborn, the baby is passed among several women. In the weeks to come, the infant will be constantly held (and fed) by other women. The result is strong multiple attachments. As an African proverb says, "It takes a village to raise a child."

AP Photo/Imperial Valley Press, Cuauhtemoc Beltran

An example of high-quality day care Research has shown that young children thrive socially and intellectually in safe, stimulating environments with a ratio of one caregiver for every three or four children.

One ongoing study in 10 American cities has followed 1100 children since the age of 1 month. The researchers found that at ages 4½ to 6, children who had spent the most time in day care had slightly advanced thinking and language skills. They also had an increased rate of aggressiveness and defiance (NICHD, 2002, 2003, 2006). To developmental psychologist Eleanor Maccoby (2003), the positive correlation between increased rate of problem behaviors and time spent in child care suggested "some risk for some children spending extended time in some day-care settings as they're now organized." But the child's temperament, the parents' sensitivity, and the family's economic and educational level influenced aggression more than time spent in day care.

There is little disagreement that the children who merely exist for 9 hours a day in understaffed centers deserve better. What all children need is a consistent, warm relationship with people whom they can learn to trust. The importance of such relationships extends beyond the preschool years, as Finnish psychologist Lea Pulkkinen (2006) observed in her career-long study of 285 individuals tracked from age 8 to 42. Her finding—that adult monitoring of children predicts favorable outcomes—led her to undertake, with support from Finland's parliament, a nationwide program of adult-supervised activities for all first and second graders (Pulkkinen, 2004; Rose, 2004).

Self-Concept

14-7 How do children's self-concepts develop?

Infancy's major social achievement is attachment. *Childhood's* major social achievement is a positive sense of self. By the end of childhood, at about age 12, most children have developed a **self-concept**—an understanding and assessment of who they are. Parents often wonder when and how this sense of self develops. "Is my baby girl aware of herself—does she know she is a person distinct from everyone else?"

Kate Nurre/Worth Publishers

Self-awareness Mirror images fascinate infants from the age of about 6 months. Only at about 18 months, however, does the child recognize that the image in the mirror is "me."

Self-aware animals After prolonged exposure to mirrors, several species—chimpanzees, orangutans, gorillas, dolphins, elephants, and magpies—have similarly demonstrated self-recognition of their mirror image (Gallup, 1970; Reis & Marino, 2001; Prior et al., 2008). In an experiment by Joshua Plotnik and colleagues (2006), Happy, an Asian elephant, when facing a mirror, repeatedly used her trunk to touch an "X" painted above her eye (but not a similar mark above the other eye that was visible only under black light). As one report said, "She's Happy and she knows it!"

AP Photo/National Academy of Sciences, Courtesy of Joshua Plotnik, Frans de Waal, and Diana Reiss

Of course we cannot ask the baby directly, but we can again capitalize on what she can do—letting her *behavior* provide clues to the beginnings of her self-awareness. In 1877, biologist Charles Darwin offered one idea: Self-awareness begins when we recognize ourselves in a mirror. To see whether a child recognizes that the girl in the mirror is indeed herself, researchers sneakily dabbed color on the nose. At about 6 months, children reach out to touch their mirror image as if it were another child (Courage & Howe, 2002; Damon & Hart, 1982, 1988, 1992). By 15 to 18 months, they begin to touch their own noses when they see the colored spot in the mirror (Butterworth, 1992; Gallup & Suarez, 1986). Apparently, 18-month-olds have a schema of how their face should look, and they wonder, "What is that spot doing on *my* face?"

By school age, children's self-concept has blossomed into more detailed descriptions that include their gender, group memberships, psychological traits, and similarities and differences compared with other children (Newman & Ruble, 1988; Stipek, 1992). They come to see themselves as good and skillful in some ways but not others. They form a concept of which traits, ideally, they would like to have. By age 8 or 10, their self-image is quite stable.

Children's views of themselves affect their actions. Children who form a positive self-concept are more confident, independent, optimistic, assertive, and sociable (Maccoby, 1980). So how can parents encourage a positive yet realistic self-concept?

Parenting Styles

14-8 What are three parenting styles, and how do children's traits relate to them?

Some parents spank, some reason. Some are strict, some are lax. Some show little affection, some liberally hug and kiss. Do such differences in parenting styles affect children?

The most heavily researched aspect of parenting has been how, and to what extent, parents seek to control their children. Investigators have identified three parenting styles:

1. ***Authoritarian*** parents impose rules and expect obedience: "Don't interrupt." "Keep your room clean." "Don't stay out late or you'll be grounded." "Why? Because I said so."
2. ***Permissive*** parents submit to their children's desires. They make few demands and use little punishment.
3. ***Authoritative*** parents are both demanding and responsive. They exert control by setting rules and enforcing them, but they also explain the reasons for rules. And, especially with older children, they encourage open discussion when making the rules and allow exceptions.

Too hard, too soft, and just right, these styles have been called. Research indicates that children with the highest self-esteem, self-reliance, and social competence usually have warm, concerned, *authoritative* parents (Baumrind, 1996; Buri et al., 1988; Coopersmith, 1967). Those with authoritarian parents tend to have less social skill and self-esteem, and those with permissive parents tend to be more aggressive and immature. The participants in most studies have been middle-class White families, and some critics suggest that effective parenting may vary by culture. Yet studies with families of other races and in more than 200 cultures worldwide have confirmed the social and academic correlates of loving and authoritative parenting (Rohner & Veneziano, 2001; Sorkhabi, 2005; Steinberg & Morris, 2001). For example, two studies of thousands of Germans found that those whose parents had maintained a curfew exhibited better adjustment and greater achievements in young adulthood than did those with permissive parents (Haase et al., 2008). And the effects are stronger when children are embedded in *authoritative communities* with connected adults who model a good life (Commission on Children at Risk, 2003).

A word of caution: The association between certain parenting styles (being firm but open) and certain childhood outcomes (social competence) is correlational. *Correlation is not causation.* Here are two possible alternative explanations for this parenting-competence link.

- Children's traits may influence parenting. Parental warmth and control vary somewhat from child to child, even in the same family (Holden & Miller, 1999). Perhaps socially mature, agreeable, easygoing children *evoke* greater trust and warmth from their parents. Twin studies have supported this possibility (Kendler, 1996).
- Some underlying third factor may be at work. Perhaps, for example, competent parents and their competent children share genes that predispose social competence. Twin studies have also supported this possibility (South et al., 2008).

Parents who struggle with conflicting advice should remember that *all advice reflects the advice-giver's values.* For those who prize unquestioning obedience from a child, an authoritarian style may have the desired effect. For those who value children's sociability and self-reliance, authoritative firm-but-open parenting is advisable.

The investment in raising a child buys many years not only of joy and love but of worry and irritation. Yet for most people who become parents, a child is one's biological and social legacy—one's personal investment in the human future. To paraphrase psychiatrist Carl Jung, we reach backward into our parents and forward into our children, and through their children into a future we will never see, but about which we must therefore care.

"You are the bows from which your children as living arrows are sent forth."

Kahlil Gibran, *The Prophet,* 1923

RETRIEVAL PRACTICE

- The three parenting styles have been called "too hard, too soft, and just right." Which one is "too hard," which one "too soft," and which one "just right," and why?

ANSWER: The authoritarian style would be too hard, the permissive style too soft, and the authoritative style just right. Parents using the authoritative style tend to have children with high self-esteem, self-reliance, and social competence.

MODULE REVIEW

Infancy and Childhood

Learning Objectives

RETRIEVAL PRACTICE Take a moment to answer each of these Learning Objective Questions (repeated here from within the module). Then turn to Appendix B, Complete Module Reviews, to check your answers. Research suggests that trying to answer these questions on your own will improve your long-term retention (McDaniel et al., 2009).

14-1: During infancy and childhood, how do the brain and motor skills develop?

14-2: From the perspectives of Piaget, Vygotsky, and today's researchers, how does a child's mind develop?

14-3: How do parent-infant attachment bonds form?

14-4: How have psychologists studied attachment differences, and what have they learned?

14-5: Does childhood neglect, abuse, or family disruption affect children's attachments?

14-6: How does day care affect children?

14-7: How do children's self-concepts develop?

14-8: What are three parenting styles, and how do children's traits relate to them?

Terms and Concepts to Remember

RETRIEVAL PRACTICE Test yourself on these terms by trying to write down the definition before flipping back to the referenced page to check your answer.

maturation, p.177
cognition, p. 179
schema, p. 179
assimilation, p. 179
accommodation, p. 179
sensorimotor stage, p. 180
object permanence, p. 180
egocentrism, p. 182
preoperational stage, p. 182
conservation, p. 182
theory of mind, p. 183
concrete operational stage, p. 183
autism, p. 184
formal operational stage, p. 186
stranger anxiety, p. 187
attachment, p. 187
critical period, p. 188
imprinting, p. 188
basic trust, p. 191
self-concept, p. 193

RETRIEVAL PRACTICE Gain an advantage, and benefit from immediate feedback, with the interactive self-testing resources at www.worthpublishers.com/myers.

MODULE 15

Adolescence

- Physical Development
- Cognitive Development
- Social Development
- Emerging Adulthood

15-1 How is adolescence defined, and what physical changes mark this period?

Many psychologists once believed that childhood sets our traits. Today's developmental psychologists see development as lifelong. At a five-year high school reunion, former best friends may be surprised at their divergence; a decade later, they may have trouble sustaining a conversation.

As the *life-span perspective* emerged, psychologists began to look at how maturation and experience shape us not only in infancy and childhood, but also in adolescence and beyond. **Adolescence**—the years spent morphing from child to adult—starts with the physical beginnings of sexual maturity and ends with the social achievement of independent adult status (which means that in some cultures, where teens are self-supporting, adolescence hardly exists).

In industrialized countries, what are the teen years like? In Leo Tolstoy's *Anna Karenina*, the teen years were "that blissful time when childhood is just coming to an end, and out of that vast circle, happy and gay, a path takes shape." But another teenager, Anne Frank, writing in her diary while hiding from the Nazis, described tumultuous teen emotions:

> My treatment varies so much. One day Anne is so sensible and is allowed to know everything; and the next day I hear that Anne is just a silly little goat who doesn't know anything at all and imagines that she's learned a wonderful lot from books. . . . Oh, so many things bubble up inside me as I lie in bed, having to put up with people I'm fed up with, who always misinterpret my intentions.

G. Stanley Hall (1904), one of the first psychologists to describe adolescence, believed that this tension between biological maturity and social dependence creates a period of "storm and stress." Indeed, after age 30, many who grow up in independence-fostering Western cultures look back on their teenage years as a time they would not want to relive, a time when their peers' social approval was imperative, their sense of direction in life was in flux, and their feeling of alienation from their parents was deepest (Arnett, 1999; Macfarlane, 1964).

But for many, adolescence is a time of vitality without the cares of adulthood, a time of rewarding friendships, of heightened idealism and a growing sense of life's exciting possibilities.

© Andy Singer/Funny Times

How will you look back on your life 10 years from now? Are you making choices that someday you will recollect with satisfaction?

Physical Development

Adolescence begins with **puberty,** the time when we mature sexually. Puberty follows a surge of hormones, which may intensify moods and which trigger a two-year period of rapid physical development, usually beginning at about age 11 in girls and at about age 13 in boys. About the time of puberty, boys' growth propels them to greater height than their female counterparts (**FIGURE 15.1** on the next page). During this growth spurt, the **primary sex characteristics**—the reproductive organs and external genitalia—develop dramatically. So do **secondary sex characteristics,** the nonreproductive traits such as breasts and hips in girls, facial hair and deepened voice in boys, pubic and underarm hair in both sexes (**FIGURE 15.2** on the next page). A year or two before puberty, however, boys and girls often feel the first stirrings of attraction toward those of the other (or their own) sex (McClintock & Herdt, 1996).

adolescence the transition period from childhood to adulthood, extending from puberty to independence.

puberty the period of sexual maturation, during which a person becomes capable of reproducing.

primary sex characteristics the body structures (ovaries, testes, and external genitalia) that make sexual reproduction possible.

secondary sex characteristics nonreproductive sexual characteristics, such as female breasts and hips, male voice quality, and body hair.

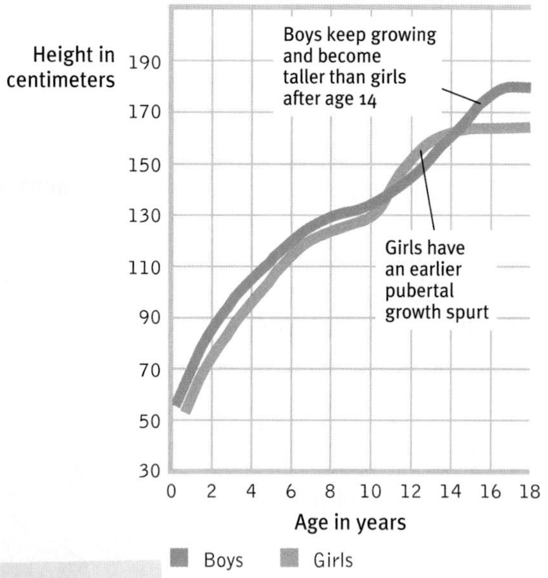

Rob Lewine/Getty Images

FIGURE 15.1
Height differences Throughout childhood, boys and girls are similar in height. At puberty, girls surge ahead briefly, but then boys overtake them at about age 14. (Data from Tanner, 1978.) Recent studies suggest that sexual development and growth spurts are beginning somewhat earlier than was the case a half-century ago (Herman-Giddens et al., 2001).

In girls, puberty starts with breast development, which now sometimes begins before age 10 (Biro et al., 2010). But puberty's landmarks are the first ejaculation in boys *(spermarche)*, usually by about age 14, and the first menstrual period in girls, (**menarche**—meh-NAR-key), usually within a year of age 12½ (Anderson et al., 2003). Menarche appears to occur a few months earlier, on average, for girls who have experienced stresses related to father absence, sexual abuse, or insecure attachments (Belsky et al., 2010; Vigil et al., 2005; Zabin et al., 2005). Nearly all adult women recall their first menstrual period and remember experiencing a mixture of feelings—pride, excitement, embarrassment, and apprehension (Greif & Ulman, 1982; Woods et al., 1983). Girls who have been prepared for menarche usually experience it as a positive life transition. Most men similarly recall their first ejaculation, which usually occurs as a nocturnal emission (Fuller & Downs, 1990).

Just as in the earlier life stages, the *sequence* of physical changes in puberty (for example, breast buds and visible pubic hair before menarche) is far more predictable

FIGURE 15.2
Body changes at puberty At about age 11 in girls and age 13 in boys, a surge of hormones triggers a variety of physical changes.

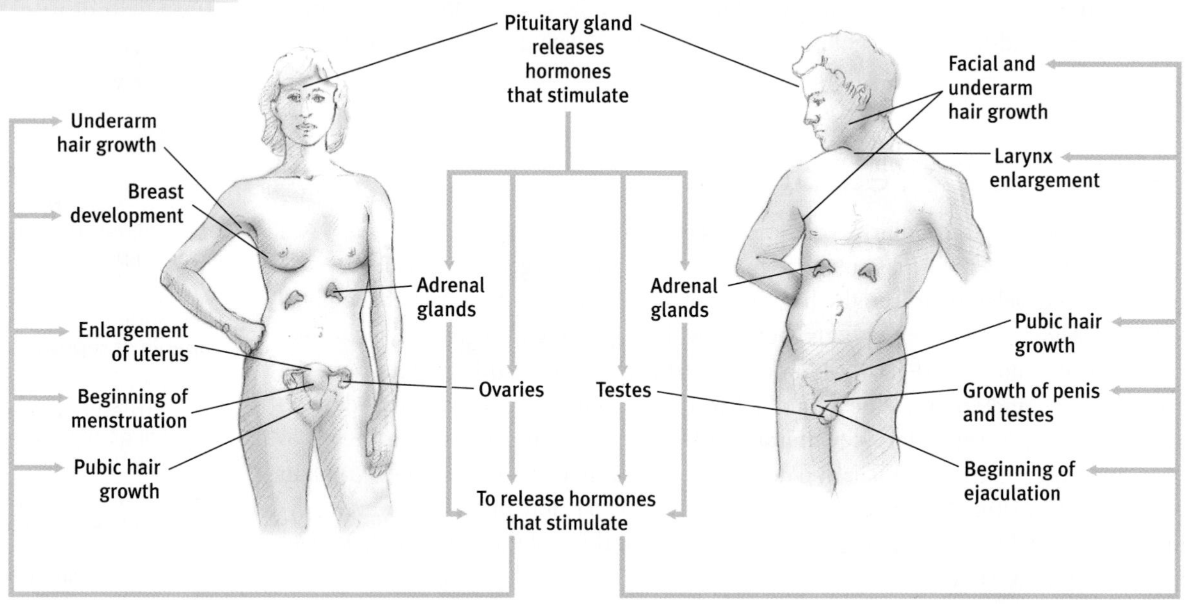

than their *timing*. Some girls start their growth spurt at 9, some boys as late as age 16. Though such variations have little effect on height at maturity, they may have psychological consequences. For boys, early maturation has mixed effects. Boys who are stronger and more athletic during their early teen years tend to be more popular, self-assured, and independent, though also more at risk for alcohol use, delinquency, and premature sexual activity (Conley & Rudolph, 2009; Copeland et al., 2010; Lynne et al., 2007). For girls, early maturation can be a challenge (Mendle et al., 2007). If a young girl's body and hormone-fed feelings are out of sync with her emotional maturity and her friends' physical development and experiences, she may begin associating with older adolescents or may suffer teasing or sexual harassment (Ge & Natsuaki, 2009).

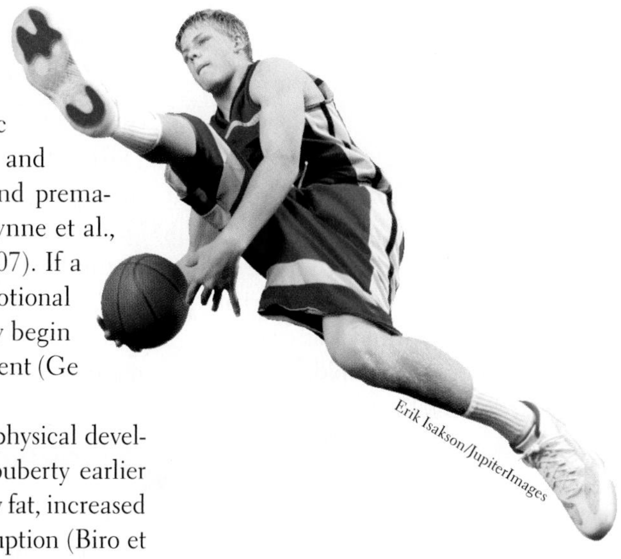

Erik Isakson/JupiterImages

It is not only when we mature that counts, but how people react to our physical development. Girls in various countries are developing breasts and reaching puberty earlier today than in the past, a phenomenon variously attributed to increased body fat, increased hormone-mimicking chemicals, and increased stress related to family disruption (Biro et al., 2010). Researchers wonder: If early puberty is disadvantageous for girls, are today's girls paying a price? Remember: *Nature and nurture interact*. There is some evidence that, as adults, girls who matured early may exhibit more apprehensive responses to male faces and voices (Belles et al., 2010).

An adolescent's brain is also a work in progress. Until puberty, brain cells increase their connections, like trees growing more roots and branches. Then, during adolescence, comes a selective *pruning* of unused neurons and connections (Blakemore, 2008). What we don't use, we lose. It's rather like traffic engineers reducing congestion by eliminating certain streets and constructing new beltways that move traffic more efficiently.

As teens mature, their frontal lobes also continue to develop. The growth of *myelin*, the fatty tissue that forms around axons and speeds neurotransmission, enables better communication with other brain regions (Kuhn, 2006; Silveri et al., 2006). These developments bring improved judgment, impulse control, and long-term planning.

© The New Yorker Collection, 2006, Barbara Smaller from cartoonbank.com. All Rights Reserved.

"Young man, go to your room and stay there until your cerebral cortex matures."

Frontal lobe maturation nevertheless lags behind the emotional limbic system. Puberty's hormonal surge and limbic system development help explain teens' occasional impulsiveness, risky behaviors, and emotional storms—slamming doors and turning up the music (Casey et al., 2008). No wonder younger teens (whose unfinished frontal lobes aren't yet fully equipped for making long-term plans and curbing impulses) so often succumb to the tobacco corporations, which most adult smokers could tell them they will later regret. Teens actually don't underestimate the risks of smoking—or fast driving or unprotected sex. They just, when reasoning from their gut, weigh the benefits more heavily (Reyna & Farley, 2006; Steinberg, 2007, 2010). They seek thrills and rewards, but they can't yet locate the brake pedal controlling their impulses.

So, when Junior drives recklessly and academically self-destructs, should his parents reassure themselves that "he can't help it; his frontal cortex isn't yet fully grown"? They can at least take hope: The brain with which Junior begins his teens differs from the brain with which he will end his teens. Unless he slows his brain development with heavy drinking—leaving him prone to impulsivity and addiction—his frontal lobes will continue maturing until about age 25 (Beckman, 2004; Crews et al., 2007).

"If a gun is put in the control of the prefrontal cortex of a hurt and vengeful 15-year-old, and it is pointed at a human target, it will very likely go off."

National Institutes of Health brain scientist Daniel R. Weinberger, "A Brain Too Young for Good Judgment," 2001

In 2004, the American Psychological Association joined seven other medical and mental health associations in filing U.S. Supreme Court briefs, arguing against the death penalty for 16- and 17-year-olds. The briefs documented the teen brain's immaturity "in areas that bear upon adolescent decision making." Teens are "less guilty by reason of adolescence," suggested psychologist Laurence Steinberg and law professor Elizabeth Scott (2003; Steinberg et al., 2009). In 2005, by a 5-to-4 margin, the Court concurred, declaring juvenile death penalties unconstitutional.

menarche [meh-NAR-key] the first menstrual period.

Cognitive Development

15-2 How did Piaget, Kohlberg, and later researchers describe adolescent cognitive and moral development?

During the early teen years, reasoning is often self-focused. Adolescents may think their private experiences are unique, something parents just could not understand: "But, Mom, *you* don't really know how it feels to be in love" (Elkind, 1978). Capable of thinking about their own thinking, and about other people's thinking, they also begin imagining what others are thinking about *them.* (They might worry less if they understood their peers' similar self-absorption.) Gradually, though, most begin to reason more abstractly.

"When the pilot told us to brace and grab our ankles, the first thing that went through my mind was that we must all look pretty stupid."

Jeremiah Rawlings, age 12, after a 1989 DC-10 crash in Sioux City, Iowa

Developing Reasoning Power

When adolescents achieve the intellectual summit Jean Piaget called *formal operations,* they apply their new abstract reasoning tools to the world around them. They may think about what is ideally possible and compare that with the imperfect reality of their society, their parents, and even themselves. They may debate human nature, good and evil, truth and justice. Their sense of what's fair changes from simple equality to equity—to what's proportional to merit (Almås et al., 2010). Having left behind the concrete images of early childhood, they may now seek a deeper conception of God and existence (Elkind, 1970; Worthington, 1989). Reasoning hypothetically and deducing consequences also enables adolescents to detect inconsistencies and spot hypocrisy in others' reasoning. This can lead to heated debates with parents and silent vows never to lose sight of their own ideals (Peterson et al., 1986).

© The New Yorker Collection, 1992, Koren from cartoonbank.com. All Rights Reserved.

"Ben is in his first year of high school, and he's questioning all the right things."

Developing Morality

Two crucial tasks of childhood and adolescence are discerning right from wrong and developing character—the psychological muscles for controlling impulses. To be a moral person is to *think* morally and *act* accordingly. Jean Piaget and Lawrence Kohlberg proposed that moral reasoning guides moral actions. A newer view builds on psychology's game-changing new recognition that much of our functioning occurs not on the "high road" of deliberate, conscious thinking but on the "low road" of unconscious, automatic thinking.

Moral Reasoning

Piaget (1932) believed that children's moral judgments build on their cognitive development. Agreeing with Piaget, Lawrence Kohlberg (1981, 1984) sought to describe the development of *moral reasoning,* the thinking that occurs as we consider right and wrong.

Demonstrating their reasoning ability Although on opposite sides of the immigration policy debate, these teens are all demonstrating their ability to think logically about abstract topics. According to Piaget, they are in the final cognitive stage, formal operations.

Richard B. Levine/Newsome

Jeff Malet/Newscom

Kohlberg posed moral dilemmas (for example, whether a person should steal medicine to save a loved one's life) and asked children, adolescents, and adults whether the action was right or wrong. He then analyzed their answers for evidence of stages of moral thinking. His findings led him to propose three basic levels of moral thinking: preconventional, conventional, and postconventional (**TABLE 15.1**). Kohlberg claimed these levels form a moral ladder. As with all stage theories, the sequence is unvarying. We begin on the bottom rung and ascend to varying heights. Kohlberg's critics have noted that his postconventional stage is culturally limited, appearing mostly among people who prize individualism (Eckensberger, 1994; Miller & Bersoff, 1995).

Reuters/Eduardo Munoz

Moral reasoning Survivors of the 2010 Haiti earthquake were faced with a moral dilemma: Should they steal household necessities? Their reasoning likely reflected different levels of moral thinking, even if they behaved similarly.

Moral Intuition

Psychologist Jonathan Haidt (2002, 2006, 2010) believes that much of our morality is rooted in *moral intuitions*—"quick gut feelings, or affectively laden intuitions." According to this intuitionist view, the mind makes moral judgments as it makes aesthetic judgments—quickly and automatically. We *feel* disgust when seeing people engaged in degrading or subhuman acts. Even a disgusting taste in the mouth heightens people's disgust over various moral digressions (Eskine et al., 2011). We *feel* elevation—a tingly, warm, glowing feeling in the chest—when seeing people display exceptional generosity, compassion, or courage. These feelings in turn trigger moral reasoning, says Haidt.

One woman recalled driving through her snowy neighborhood with three young men as they passed "an elderly woman with a shovel in her driveway. I did not think much of it, when one of the guys in the back asked the driver to let him off there. . . . When I saw him jump out of the back seat and approach the lady, my mouth dropped in shock as I realized that he was offering to shovel her walk for her." Witnessing this unexpected goodness triggered elevation: "I felt like jumping out of the car and hugging this guy. I felt like singing and running, or skipping and laughing. I felt like saying nice things about people" (Haidt, 2000).

"Could human morality really be run by the moral emotions," Haidt wonders, "while moral reasoning struts about pretending to be in control?" Consider the desire to punish. Laboratory games reveal that the desire to punish wrongdoings is mostly driven not by reason (such as an objective calculation that punishment deters crime) but rather by emotional reactions, such as moral outrage (Darley, 2009). After the emotional fact, moral reasoning—our mind's press secretary—aims to convince us and others of the logic of what we have intuitively felt.

This intuitionist perspective on morality finds support in a study of moral paradoxes. Imagine seeing a runaway trolley headed for five people. All will certainly be killed unless you throw a switch that diverts the trolley onto another track, where it will kill one person. Should you throw the switch? Most say *Yes*. Kill one, save five.

TABLE 15.1

Kohlberg's Levels of Moral Thinking

Level (approximate age)	Focus	Example
Preconventional morality (before age 9)	Self-interest; obey rules to avoid punishment or gain concrete rewards.	"If you save your dying wife, you'll be a hero."
Conventional morality (early adolescence)	Uphold laws and rules to gain social approval or maintain social order.	"If you steal the drug for her, everyone will think you're a criminal."
Postconventional morality (adolescence and beyond)	Actions reflect belief in basic rights and self-defined ethical principles.	"People have a right to live."

Now imagine the same dilemma, except that your opportunity to save the five requires you to push a large stranger onto the tracks, where he will die as his body stops the trolley. Kill one, save five? The logic is the same, but most say *No*. Seeking to understand why, a Princeton research team led by Joshua Greene (2001) used brain imaging to spy on people's neural responses as they contemplated such dilemmas. Only when given the body-pushing type of moral dilemma did their brain's emotion areas light up. Despite the identical logic, the personal dilemma engaged emotions that altered moral judgment.

While the new moral psychology illustrates the many ways moral intuitions trump moral reasoning, others reaffirm the importance of moral reasoning. The religious and moral reasoning of the Amish, for example, shapes their practices of forgiveness, communal life, and modesty (Narvaez, 2010). Joshua Greene (2010) likens our moral cognition to a camera. Usually, we rely on the automatic point-and-shoot. But sometimes we use reason to manually override the camera's automatic impulse.

Moral Action

"It is a delightful harmony when doing and saying go together."
Michel Eyquem de Montaigne (1533–1592)

Our moral thinking and feeling surely affect our moral talk. But sometimes talk is cheap and emotions are fleeting. Morality involves *doing* the right thing, and what we do also depends on social influences. As political theorist Hannah Arendt (1963) observed, many Nazi concentration camp guards during World War II were ordinary "moral" people who were corrupted by a powerfully evil situation.

Today's character education programs tend to focus on the whole moral package—thinking, feeling, and *doing* the right thing. As children's *thinking* matures, their *behavior* also becomes less selfish and more caring (Krebs & Van Hesteren, 1994; Miller et al., 1996). Today's programs also teach children *empathy* for others' feelings, and the self-discipline needed to restrain one's own impulses—to delay small gratifications now to enable bigger rewards later. Those who do learn to *delay gratification* become more socially responsible, academically successful, and productive (Funder & Block, 1989; Mischel et al., 1988, 1989). In service-learning programs, teens tutor, clean up their neighborhoods, and assist the elderly. The result? The teens' sense of competence and desire to serve increase, and their school absenteeism and drop-out rates diminish (Andersen, 1998; Piliavin, 2003). Moral action feeds moral attitudes.

© The New Yorker Collection, 1987, Victor from cartoonbank.com. All Rights Reserved.

"This might not be ethical. Is that a problem for anybody?"

RETRIEVAL PRACTICE

- According to Kohlberg, __________ morality focuses on upholding laws and social rules, __________ morality focuses on self-interest, and __________ morality focuses on self-defined ethical principles.

ANSWERS: conventional; preconventional; postconventional

Social Development

15-3 What are the social tasks and challenges of adolescence?

"Somewhere between the ages of 10 and 13 (depending on how hormone-enhanced their beef was), children entered adolescence, a.k.a. 'the de-cutening.'"
Jon Stewart et al., *Earth (The Book)*, 2010

Theorist Erik Erikson (1963) contended that each stage of life has its own *psychosocial* task, a crisis that needs resolution. Young children wrestle with issues of *trust*, then *autonomy* (independence), then *initiative*. School-age children strive for *competence*, feeling able and productive. The adolescent's task is to synthesize past, present, and future possibilities into a clearer sense of self (**TABLE 15.2**). Adolescents wonder, "Who am I as an individual? What do I want to do with my life? What values should I live by? What do I believe in?" Erikson called this quest the adolescent's *search for identity*.

TABLE 15.2

Erikson's Stages of Psychosocial Development

Stage (approximate age)	Issue	Description of Task
Infancy (to 1 year)	Trust vs. mistrust	If needs are dependably met, infants develop a sense of basic trust.
Toddlerhood (1 to 3 years)	Autonomy vs. shame and doubt	Toddlers learn to exercise their will and do things for themselves, or they doubt their abilities.
Preschool (3 to 6 years)	Initiative vs. guilt	Preschoolers learn to initiate tasks and carry out plans, or they feel guilty about their efforts to be independent.
Elementary school (6 years to puberty)	Competence vs. inferiority	Children learn the pleasure of applying themselves to tasks, or they feel inferior.
Adolescence (teen years into 20s)	Identity vs. role confusion	Teenagers work at refining a sense of self by testing roles and then integrating them to form a single identity, or they become confused about who they are.
Young adulthood (20s to early 40s)	Intimacy vs. isolation	Young adults struggle to form close relationships and to gain the capacity for intimate love, or they feel socially isolated.
Middle adulthood (40s to 60s)	Generativity vs. stagnation	In middle age, people discover a sense of contributing to the world, usually through family and work, or they may feel a lack of purpose.
Late adulthood (late 60s and up)	Integrity vs. despair	Reflecting on his or her life, an older adult may feel a sense of satisfaction or failure.

© Ron Chapple/Corbis

Competence vs. inferiority

© Oliver Rossi/Corbis

Intimacy vs. isolation

As sometimes happens in psychology, Erikson's interests were bred by his own life experience. As the son of a Jewish mother and a Danish Gentile father, Erikson was "doubly an outsider," reported Morton Hunt (1993, p. 391). He was "scorned as a Jew in school but mocked as a Gentile in the synagogue because of his blond hair and blue eyes." Such episodes fueled his interest in the adolescent struggle for identity.

Forming an Identity

To refine their sense of identity, adolescents in individualistic cultures usually try out different "selves" in different situations. They may act out one self at home, another with friends, and still another at school or on Facebook. If two situations overlap—as when a teenager brings friends home—the discomfort can be considerable. The teen asks, "Which self should I be? Which is the real me?" The resolution is a self-definition that unifies the various selves into a consistent and comfortable sense of who one is—an **identity.**

identity our sense of self; according to Erikson, the adolescent's task is to solidify a sense of self by testing and integrating various roles.

social identity the "we" aspect of our self-concept; the part of our answer to "Who am I?" that comes from our group memberships.

For both adolescents and adults, group identities are often formed by how we differ from those around us. When living in Britain, I become conscious of my Americanness. When spending time with my daughter in Africa, I become conscious of my minority (White) race. When surrounded by women, I am mindful of my gender identity. For international students, for those of a minority ethnic group, for people with a disability, for those on a team, a **social identity** often forms around their distinctiveness.

But not always. Erikson noticed that some adolescents forge their identity early, simply by adopting their parents' values and expectations. (Traditional, less individualistic cultures teach adolescents who they are, rather than encouraging them to decide on their own.) Other adolescents may adopt the identity of a particular peer group—jocks, preps, geeks, goths.

"Self-consciousness, the recognition of a creature by itself as a 'self,' [cannot] exist except in contrast with an 'other,' a something which is not the self."

C. S. Lewis, *The Problem of Pain,* 1940

Tristan Savatier/Getty Images

Wiklund, Juliana/Getty Images

Who shall I be today? By varying the way they look, adolescents try out different "selves." Although we eventually form a consistent and stable sense of identity, the self we present may change with the situation.

Most young people do develop a sense of contentment with their lives. When American teens were asked whether a series of statements described them, 81 percent said *Yes* to "I would choose my life the way it is right now." The other 19 percent agreed that "I wish I were somebody else" (Lyons, 2004). Reflecting on their existence, 75 percent of American collegians say they "discuss religion/spirituality" with friends, "pray," and agree that "we are all spiritual beings" and "search for meaning/purpose in life" (Astin et al., 2004; Bryant & Astin, 2008). This would not surprise Stanford psychologist William Damon and his colleagues (2003), who have contended that a key task of adolescence is to achieve a purpose—a desire to accomplish something personally meaningful that makes a difference to the world beyond oneself.

The late teen years, when many people in industrialized countries begin attending college or working full time, provide new opportunities for trying out possible roles. Many college seniors have achieved a clearer identity and a more positive self-concept than they had as first-year students (Waterman, 1988). Collegians who have achieved a clear sense of identity are less prone to alcohol abuse (Bishop et al., 2005).

Several nationwide studies indicate that young Americans' self-esteem falls during the early to mid-teen years, and, for girls, depression scores often increase. But then self-image rebounds during the late teens and twenties (Robins et al., 2002; Twenge & Campbell, 2001; Twenge & Nolen-Hoeksema, 2002). Late adolescence is also a time when agreeableness and emotional stability scores increase (Klimstra et al., 2009).

Erikson contended that the adolescent identity stage is followed in young adulthood by a developing capacity for **intimacy,** the ability to form emotionally close relationships. Romantic relationships, which tend to be emotionally intense, are reported by some two in three North American 17-year-olds, but fewer among those in collectivist countries such as China (Collins et al., 2009; Li et al., 2010). Those who enjoy high-quality (intimate, supportive) relationships with family and friends tend also to enjoy similarly high-quality romantic relationships in adolescence, which set the stage for healthy adult relationships. Such relationships are, for most of us, a source of great pleasure. When Mihaly Csikszentmihalyi [chick-SENT-me-hi] and Jeremy Hunter (2003) used a beeper to sample the daily experiences of American teens, they found them unhappiest when alone and happiest when with friends. As Aristotle long ago recognized, we humans are "the social animal."

Parent and Peer Relationships

15-4 How do parents and peers influence adolescents?

As adolescents in Western cultures seek to form their own identities, they begin to pull away from their parents (Shanahan et al., 2007). The preschooler who can't be close enough to her mother, who loves to touch and cling to her, becomes the 14-year-old who wouldn't be caught dead holding hands with Mom. The transition occurs gradually (**FIGURE 15.3**). By adolescence, arguments occur more often, usually over mundane things—household chores, bedtime, homework (Tesser et al., 1989). Parent-child conflict during the transition to adolescence tends to be greater with first-born than with second-born children, and greater with mothers than with fathers (Burk et al., 2009; Shanahan et al., 2007).

© David Sipress

"She says she's someone from your past who gave birth to you, and raised you, and sacrificed everything so you could have whatever you wanted."

For a minority of parents and their adolescents, differences lead to real splits and great stress (Steinberg & Morris, 2001). But most disagreements are at the level of harmless bickering. And most adolescents—6000 of them in 10 countries, from Australia to Bangladesh

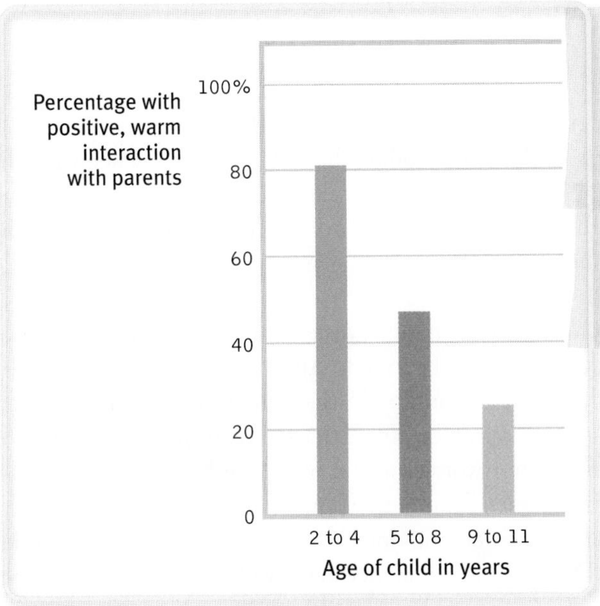

FIGURE 15.3
The changing parent-child relationship Interviews from a large, national study of Canadian families reveal that the typically close, warm relationships between parents and preschoolers loosen as children become older. (Data from Statistics Canada, 1999.)

intimacy in Erikson's theory, the ability to form close, loving relationships; a primary developmental task in late adolescence and early adulthood.

"I love u guys."

Emily Keyes' final text message to her parents before dying in a Colorado school shooting, 2006

to Turkey—said they like their parents (Offer et al., 1988). "We usually get along but . . . ," adolescents often reported (Galambos, 1992; Steinberg, 1987).

Positive parent-teen relations and positive peer relations often go hand in hand. High school girls who have the most affectionate relationships with their mothers tend also to enjoy the most intimate friendships with girlfriends (Gold & Yanof, 1985). And teens who feel close to their parents tend to be healthy and happy and to do well in school (Resnick et al., 1997). Of course, we can state this correlation the other way: Misbehaving teens are more likely to have tense relationships with parents and other adults.

Adolescence is typically a time of diminishing parental influence and growing peer influence. Asked in a survey if they had "ever had a serious talk" with their child about illegal drugs, 85 percent of American parents answered *Yes*. But if the parents had indeed given this earnest advice, many teens had apparently tuned it out: Only 45 percent could recall such a talk (Morin & Brossard, 1997).

Heredity does much of the heavy lifting in forming individual temperament and personality differences, and peer influences do much of the rest. Most teens are herd animals. They talk, dress, and act more like their peers than their parents. What their friends are, they often become, and what "everybody's doing," they often do. In teen calls to hotline counseling services, peer relationships have been the most discussed topic (Boehm et al., 1999). In 2008, according to a Nielsen study, the average American 13- to 17-year-old sent or received more than 1700 text messages a month (Steinhauer & Holson, 2008). Many adolescents become absorbed by social networking, sometimes with a compulsive use that produces "Facebook fatigue." Online communication stimulates intimate self-disclosure—both for better (support groups) and for worse (online predators and extremist groups) (Subrahmanyam & Greenfield, 2008; Valkenburg & Peter, 2009).

For those who feel excluded, the pain is acute. "The social atmosphere in most high schools is poisonously clique-driven and exclusionary," observed social psychologist Elliot Aronson (2001). Most excluded "students suffer in silence. . . . A small number act out in violent ways against their classmates." Those who withdraw are vulnerable to loneliness, low self-esteem, and depression (Steinberg & Morris, 2001). Peer approval matters.

Teens see their parents as having more influence in other areas—for example, in shaping their religious faith and in thinking about college and career choices (*Emerging Trends*, 1997). A Gallup Youth Survey reveals that most share their parent's political views (Lyons, 2005).

The New Yorker Collection, 2010, Barbara Smaller, from cartoonbank.com. All Rights Reserved.

"It's you who don't understand me—I've been fifteen, but you have never been forty-eight."

© 2002, Margaret Shulock. Reprinted with special permission of King Features Syndicate.

Nine times out of ten, it's all about peer pressure.

emerging adulthood for some people in modern cultures, a period from the late teens to mid-twenties, bridging the gap between adolescent dependence and full independence and responsible adulthood.

Emerging Adulthood

15-5 What is emerging adulthood?

In the Western world, adolescence now roughly corresponds to the teen years. At earlier times, and in other parts of the world today, this slice of life has been much smaller (Baumeister & Tice, 1986). Shortly after sexual maturity, young people would assume adult responsibilities and status. The event might be celebrated with an elaborate initiation—a public *rite of passage*. The new adult would then work, marry, and have children.

When schooling became compulsory in many Western countries, independence was put on hold until after graduation. From Europe to Australia, adolescents are now taking more time to establish themselves as adults. In the United States, for example, the average age at first marriage has increased more than 4 years since 1960 (to 28 for men, 26 for women). In 1960, 3 in 4 women and 2 in 3 men had, by age 30, finished school, left home, become financially independent, married, and had a child. Today, fewer than half of 30-year-old women and one-third of men have achieved these five milestones (Henig, 2010). Delayed independence has overlapped with an earlier onset of puberty. Earlier sexual maturity may be related both to girls' increased body fat (which can support pregnancy and nursing) and to weakened parent-child bonds, including absent fathers (Ellis, 2004).

© The New Yorker Collection, 2007, William Haefeli from cartoonbank.com. All Rights Reserved.

"When I was your age, I was an adult."

Together, later independence and earlier sexual maturity have widened the once-brief interlude between biological maturity and social independence (**FIGURE 15.4**). In prosperous communities, the time from 18 to the mid-twenties is an increasingly not-yet-settled phase of life, which some now call **emerging adulthood** (Arnett, 2006, 2007; Reitzle, 2006). No longer adolescents, these emerging adults, having not yet assumed full adult responsibilities and independence, feel "in between." After high school, those who enter the job market or go to college may be managing their own time and priorities more than ever before. Yet they may be doing so from their parents' home—unable to afford their own place and perhaps still emotionally dependent as well. Recognizing today's more gradually emerging adulthood, the U.S. government now allows dependent children up to age 26 to remain on their parents' health insurance (Cohen, 2010).

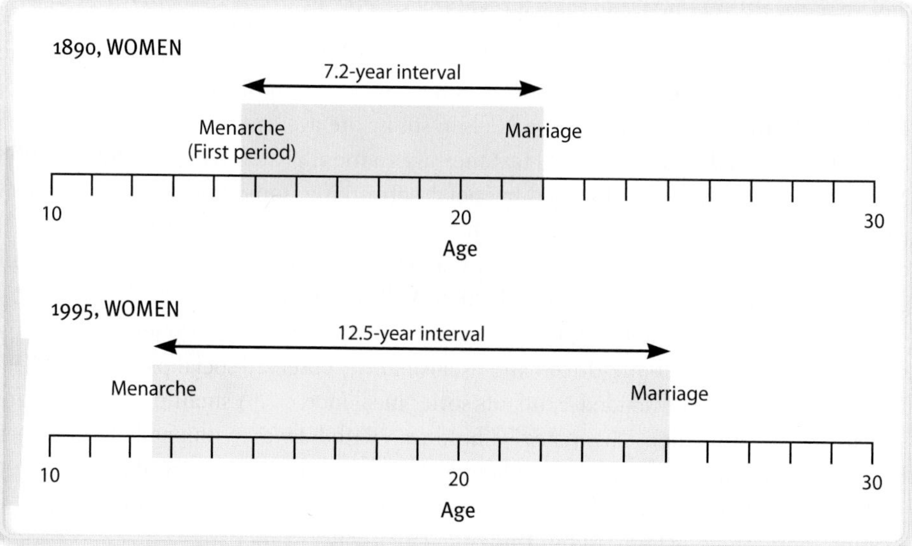

FIGURE 15.4

The transition to adulthood is being stretched from both ends In the 1890s, the average interval between a woman's first menstrual period and marriage, which typically marked a transition to adulthood, was about 7 years; in industrialized countries today it is about 12 years (Guttmacher, 1994, 2000). Although many adults are unmarried, later marriage combines with prolonged education and earlier menarche to help stretch out the transition to adulthood.

RETRIEVAL PRACTICE

- Match the psychosocial development stage below (1–8) with the issue that Erikson believed we wrestle with at that stage (a–h).

1. Infancy
2. Toddlerhood
3. Preschool
4. Elementary school
5. Adolescence
6. Young adulthood
7. Middle adulthood
8. Late adulthood

a. Generativity vs. stagnation
b. Integrity vs. despair
c. Initiative vs. guilt
d. Intimacy vs. isolation
e. Identity vs. role confusion
f. Competence vs. inferiority
g. Trust vs. mistrust
h. Autonomy vs. shame and doubt

ANSWERS: 1. g, 2. h, 3. c, 4. f, 5. e, 6. d, 7. a, 8. b

MODULE REVIEW

Adolescence

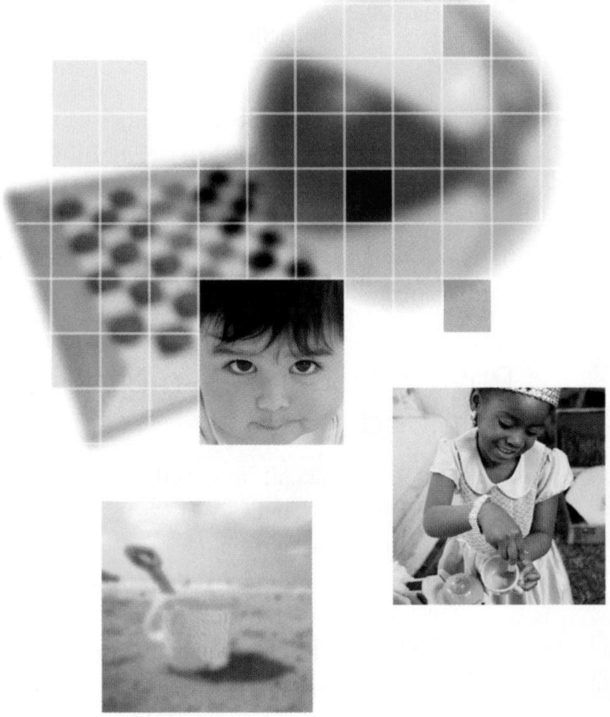

Learning Objectives

RETRIEVAL PRACTICE Take a moment to answer each of these Learning Objective Questions (repeated here from within the module). Then turn to Appendix B, Complete Module Reviews, to check your answers. Research suggests that trying to answer these questions on your own will improve your long-term retention (McDaniel et al., 2009).

15-1: How is adolescence defined, and what physical changes mark this period?

15-2: How did Piaget, Kohlberg, and later researchers describe adolescent cognitive and moral development?

15-3: What are the social tasks and challenges of adolescence?

15-4: How do parents and peers influence adolescents?

15-5: What is emerging adulthood?

Terms and Concepts to Remember

RETRIEVAL PRACTICE Test yourself on these terms by trying to write down the definition before flipping back to the referenced page to check your answer.

adolescence, p. 197
puberty, p. 197
primary sex characteristics, p. 197
secondary sex characteristics, p. 197
menarche [meh-NAR-key], p. 198
identity, p. 203
social identity, p. 203
intimacy, p. 204
emerging adulthood, p 206

RETRIEVAL PRACTICE Gain an advantage, and benefit from immediate feedback, with the interactive self-testing resources at www.worthpublishers.com/myers.

MODULE 16

- Physical Development
- Cognitive Development
- Social Development

Adulthood

Barbara Smaller/Funny Times

"I just don't know what to do with myself in that long stretch after college but before social security."

How old does a person have to be before you think of him or her as old? The average 18- to 29-year-old says 67. The average person 60 and over says 76 (Yankelovich, 1995).

"I am still learning."

Michelangelo, 1560, at age 85

At one time, psychologists viewed the center-of-life years between adolescence and old age as one long plateau. No longer. Those who follow the unfolding of people's adult lives now believe our development continues across the life span.

It is more difficult to generalize about adulthood stages than about life's early years. If you know that James is a 1-year-old and Jamal is a 10-year-old, you could say a great deal about each child. Not so with adults who differ by a similar number of years. The boss may be 30 or 60; the marathon runner may be 20 or 50; the 19-year-old may be a parent who supports a child or a child who receives an allowance. Yet our life courses are in some ways similar. Physically, cognitively, and especially socially, we differ at age 50 from our 25-year-old selves. In the discussion that follows, we recognize these differences and use three terms: *early adulthood* (roughly twenties and thirties), *middle adulthood* (to age 65), and *late adulthood* (the years after 65). Within each of these stages, people will vary widely in physical, psychological, and social development.

Physical Development

16-1 What physical changes occur during middle and late adulthood?

Like the declining daylight after the summer solstice, our physical abilities—muscular strength, reaction time, sensory keenness, and cardiac output—all begin an almost imperceptible decline in our mid-twenties. Athletes are often the first to notice. World-class sprinters and swimmers peak by their early twenties. Women—who mature earlier than men—also peak earlier. But most of us—especially those of us whose daily lives do not require top physical performance—hardly perceive the early signs of decline.

Rick Doyle/Corbis

Adult abilities vary widely Ninety-three-year-olds: Don't try this. In 2002, George Blair became the world's oldest barefoot water-skier, 18 days after his eighty-seventh birthday, and did it again in 2008 at age 93.

Physical Changes in Middle Adulthood

Post-40 athletes know all too well that physical decline gradually accelerates. As a 68-year-old who plays basketball, I now find myself occasionally not racing for that loose ball. But even diminished vigor is sufficient for normal activities. Moreover, during early and middle adulthood, physical vigor has less to do with age than with a person's health and exercise habits. Many of today's physically fit 50-year-olds run four miles with ease, while sedentary 25-year-olds find themselves huffing and puffing up two flights of stairs.

Aging also brings a gradual decline in fertility, especially for women. For a 35- to 39-year-old woman, the chances of getting pregnant after a single act of intercourse are only half those of a woman 19 to 26 (Dunson et al., 2002). Men experience a gradual decline in sperm count, testosterone level, and speed of erection and ejaculation. Women experience **menopause,** as menstrual cycles end, usually within a few years of age 50. Expectations and attitudes influence the emotional impact of this event. Is it a sign of lost femininity and growing old? Or is it liberation from menstrual periods and fears of pregnancy? As is often the case, expectations influence perceptions. Some men may similarly experience distress related to a perception of declining virility and physical capacities, but most age without such problems.

Data from Africa support an evolutionary theory of menopause: Infants with a living maternal grandmother—typically a caring and invested family member without young children of her own—have had a greater chance of survival (Shanley et al., 2007).

© The New Yorker Collection, 1999, Tom Cheney from cartoonbank.com. All Rights Reserved.

"Happy fortieth. I'll take the muscle tone in your upper arms, the girlish timbre of your voice, your amazing tolerance for caffeine, and your ability to digest french fries. The rest of you can stay."

With age, sexual activity lessens. Nearly 9 in 10 Americans in their late twenties reported having had vaginal intercourse in the past year, compared with 22 percent of women and 43 percent of men who were over 70 (Herbenick et al., 2010; Reece et al., 2010). Nevertheless, most men and women remain capable of satisfying sexual activity, and most express satisfaction with their sex life. This was true of 70 percent of Canadians surveyed (ages 40 to 64) and 75 percent of Finns (ages 65 to 74) (Kontula & Haavio-Mannila, 2009; Wright, 2006). In one survey, 75 percent of respondents reported being sexually active into their 80s (Schick et al., 2010). And in an American Association of Retired Persons sexuality survey, it was not until age 75 or older that most women and nearly half of men reported little sexual desire (DeLamater & Sill, 2005). Given good health and a willing partner, the flames of desire, though simmered down, live on. As Alex Comfort (1992, p. 240) jested, "The things that stop you having sex with age are exactly the same as those that stop you riding a bicycle (bad health, thinking it looks silly, no bicycle)."

Physical Changes in Later Life

Is old age "more to be feared than death" (Juvenal, *Satires*)? Or is life "most delightful when it is on the downward slope" (Seneca, *Epistulae ad Lucilium*)? What is it like to grow old?

Life Expectancy

From 1950 to 2010, life expectancy at birth increased worldwide from 49 years to 69 years—and to 80 and beyond in some developed countries (PRB, 2010; Sivard, 1996). What a gift—two decades more of life! In China, the United States, Britain, Canada, and Australia (to name some countries where students read this book), life expectancy has risen to 75, 78, 79, 81 and 82, respectively (CIA, 2010). This increasing life expectancy (humanity's greatest achievement, say some) combines with decreasing birthrates to make older adults a bigger and bigger population segment, which provides an increasing demand for hearing aids, retirement villages, and nursing homes. Today, 1 in 10 people worldwide are 60 or older. The United Nations (2001, 2010) projects that number will double to 2 in 10 by 2050 (and to nearly 4 in 10 in Europe).

Throughout the life span, males are more prone to dying. Although 126 male embryos begin life for every 100 females, the sex ratio is down to 105 males for every 100 females at birth (Strickland, 1992). During the first year, male infants' death rates exceed females' by one-fourth. Worldwide, women outlive men by 4 years (PRB, 2010). (Rather than marrying a man older than themselves, 20-year-old women who want a husband who shares their life expectancy should wait for the 16-year-old boys to mature.) By age 100, women outnumber men 5 to 1.

But few of us live to 100. Disease strikes. The body ages. Its cells stop reproducing. It becomes frail and vulnerable to tiny insults—hot weather, a fall, a mild infection—that at age 20 would have been trivial. Tips of chromosomes, called *telomeres,* wear down, much as the tip of a shoelace frays. This wear is accentuated by smoking, obesity, or stress. As telomeres shorten, aging cells may die without being replaced with perfect genetic replicas (Epel, 2009).

menopause the time of natural cessation of menstruation; also refers to the biological changes a woman experiences as her ability to reproduce declines.

World record for longevity? French woman Jeanne Calment, the oldest human in history with authenticated age, died in 1998 at age 122. At age 100, she was still riding a bike. At age 114, she became the oldest film actor ever, by portraying herself in *Vincent and Me.* She is shown at left at age 20 in 1895.

public domain/wikimedia commons

© Eric Fougère/Kipa/Corbis

Aging researchers

Betsy Streeter

"For some reason, possibly to save ink, the restaurants had started printing their menus in letters the height of bacteria."

Dave Barry, *Dave Barry Turns Fifty*, 1998

Low stress and good health habits also enable longevity, as does the human spirit. Chronic anger and depression increase our risk of premature death. Researchers have even observed an intriguing *death-deferral* phenomenon (Shimizu & Pelham, 2008). In one recent 15-year-period, 2000 to 3000 more Americans died on the two days after Christmas than on Christmas and the two days before (**FIGURE 16.1**). The death rate also increases when people reach their birthdays, and when they survive until after other milestones, like the first day of the new millennium.

Sensory Abilities

Although physical decline begins in early adulthood, we are not usually acutely aware of it until later life, when the stairs get steeper, the print gets smaller, and other people seem to mumble more. Visual sharpness diminishes, and distance perception and adaptation to light-level changes are less acute. Muscle strength, reaction time, and stamina also diminish, as do the sense of smell and hearing. In Wales, teens' loitering around a convenience store has been discouraged by a device that emits an aversive high-pitched sound that almost no one over 30 can hear (Lyall, 2005). Some students have also used that pitch to their advantage with cell-phone ringtones that their instructors cannot hear (Vitello, 2006).

With age, the eye's pupil shrinks and its lens becomes less transparent, reducing the amount of light reaching the retina. A 65-year-old retina receives only about one-third as much light as its 20-year-old counterpart (Kline & Schieber, 1985). Thus, to see as well as

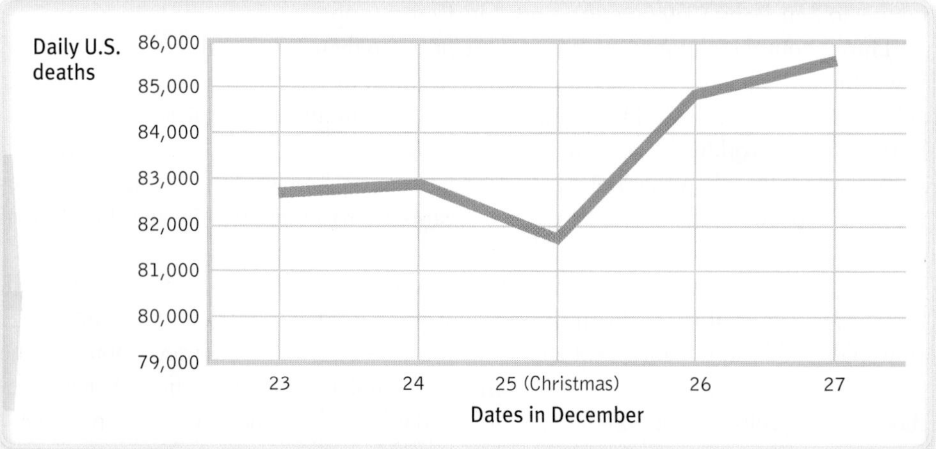

FIGURE 16.1
Postponing a date with the Grim Reaper? The total number of daily U.S. deaths from 1987 to 2002 increased on the days following Christmas. To researchers Mitsuru Shimizu and Brett Pelham (2008), this adds to the growing evidence of a death-deferral phenomenon.

a 20-year-old when reading or driving, a 65-year-old needs three times as much light—a reason for buying cars with untinted windshields. This also explains why older people sometimes ask younger people, "Don't you need better light for reading?"

Most stairway falls taken by older people occur on the top step, precisely where the person typically descends from a window-lit hallway into the darker stairwell (Fozard & Popkin, 1978). Our knowledge of aging could be used to design environments that would reduce such accidents (National Research Council, 1990).

Health

For those growing older, there is both bad and good news about health. The bad news: The body's disease-fighting immune system weakens, making older people more susceptible to life-threatening ailments such as cancer and pneumonia. The good news: Thanks partly to a lifetime's accumulation of antibodies, people over 65 suffer fewer short-term ailments, such as common flu and cold viruses. They are, for example, half as likely as 20-year-olds and one-fifth as likely as preschoolers to suffer upper respiratory flu each year (National Center for Health Statistics, 1990).

Aging levies a tax on the brain by slowing our neural processing. Up to the teen years, we process information with greater and greater speed (Fry & Hale, 1996; Kail, 1991). But compared with teens and young adults, older people take a bit more time to react, to solve perceptual puzzles, even to remember names (Bashore et al., 1997; Verhaeghen & Salthouse, 1997). The lag is greatest on complex tasks (Cerella, 1985; Poon, 1987). At video games, most 70-year-olds are no match for a 20-year-old. And, as **FIGURE 16.2** indicates, fatal accident rates per mile driven increase sharply after age 75. By age 85, they exceed the 16-year-old level. Nevertheless, because older people drive less, they account for fewer than 10 percent of crashes (Coughlin et al., 2004).

Brain regions important to memory begin to atrophy during aging (Schacter, 1996). In young adulthood, a small, gradual net loss of brain cells begins, contributing by age 80 to a brain-weight reduction of 5 percent or so. Late-maturing frontal lobes help account for teen impulsivity. Late in life, atrophy of the inhibition-controlling frontal lobes seemingly explains older people's occasional blunt questions ("Have you put on weight?") and frank comments (von Hippel, 2007).

Some good news: Exercise slows aging. Active older adults tend to be mentally quick older adults. Physical exercise not only enhances muscles, bones, and energy and helps to prevent obesity and heart disease, it also stimulates brain cell development and neural connections, thanks perhaps to increased oxygen and nutrient flow (Erickson et al., 2010; Pereira et al., 2007). That may help explain why sedentary older adults randomly assigned to aerobic exercise programs exhibit enhanced memory, sharpened judgment, and reduced risk of dementia (Colcombe et al., 2004; Liang et al., 2010; Nazimek, 2009).

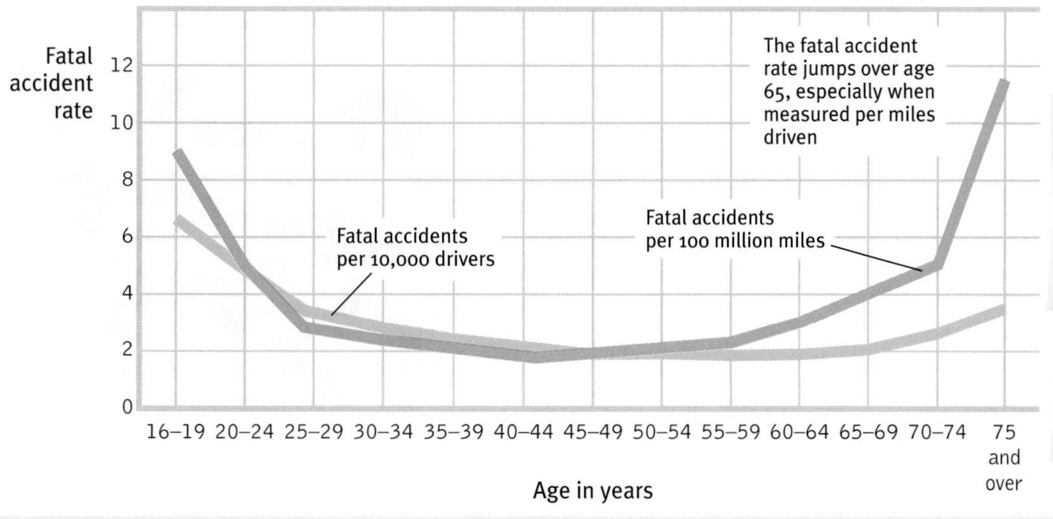

FIGURE 16.2
Age and driver fatalities Slowing reactions contribute to increased accident risks among those 75 and older, and their greater fragility increases their risk of death when accidents happen (NHTSA, 2000). Would you favor driver exams based on performance, not age, to screen out those whose slow reactions or sensory impairments indicate accident risk?

Exercise promotes neurogenesis (the birth of new nerve cells) in the hippocampus, a brain region important for memory, and helps maintain the telomeres protecting the ends of chromosomes (Cherkas et al., 2008; Erickson, 2009; Pereira et al., 2007). We are more likely to rust from disuse than to wear out from overuse.

Dementia and Alzheimer's Disease

Most people who live into their nineties do so with clear minds, but some, unfortunately, suffer a substantial loss of brain cells in a process that is *not* normal aging. A series of small strokes, a brain tumor, or alcohol dependence can progressively damage the brain, causing that mental erosion we call *dementia.* Heavy mid-life smoking more than doubles later dementia risk (Rusanen et al., 2011). The feared brain ailment *Alzheimer's disease* strikes 3 percent of the world's population by age 75. Up to age 95, the incidence of mental disintegration doubles roughly every 5 years (**FIGURE 16.3**).

"We're keeping people alive so they can live long enough to get Alzheimer's disease."

Steve McConnell, Alzheimer's Association Vice President, 2007

Alzheimer's destroys even the brightest of minds. First memory deteriorates, then reasoning. (Occasionally forgetting where you laid the car keys is no cause for alarm; forgetting how to get home may suggest Alzheimer's.) Robert Sayre (1979) recalled his father shouting at his afflicted mother to "think harder," while his mother, confused, embarrassed, on the verge of tears, randomly searched the house for lost objects. As the disease runs its course, after 5 to 20 years, the person becomes emotionally flat, then disoriented and disinhibited, then incontinent, and finally mentally vacant—a sort of living death, a mere body stripped of its humanity.

Underlying the symptoms of Alzheimer's are a loss of brain cells and a deterioration of neurons that produce the neurotransmitter acetylcholine, vital to memory and thinking. An autopsy reveals two telltale abnormalities in these acetylcholine-producing neurons: shriveled protein filaments in the cell body, and flecks of a free-floating protein fragment that accumulate as plaque at neuron tips. Long before its symptoms occur, new technologies can now test for the Alzheimer's susceptibility gene or check spinal fluid for the culprit protein fragments (De Meyer et al., 2010; Luciano et al., 2009). Such discoveries have stimulated a race to invent and test drugs that may forestall the disease, such as by blocking an enzyme that snips off the protein fragments (Kolata, 2010; Stix, 2010). The recent discovery of five associated genes may help (Hollingworth et al., 2011).

A diminishing sense of smell is associated with the pathology that foretells Alzheimer's (Wilson et al., 2007). In people at risk for Alzheimer's, brain scans (**FIGURE 16.4**) also

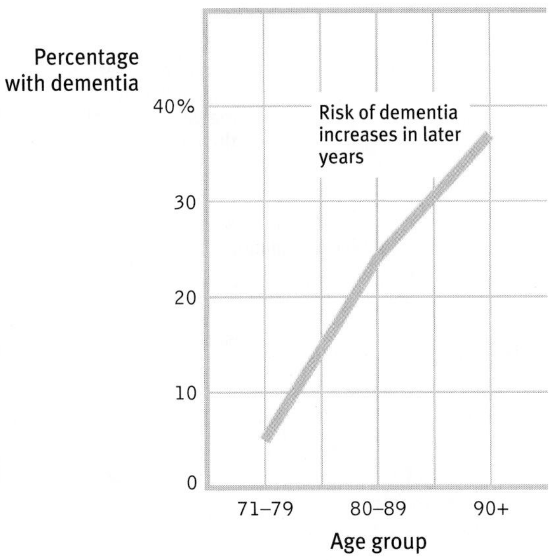

Alan Oddie/PhotoEdit

FIGURE 16.3
Incidence of dementia (mental disintegration) by age The risk of dementia due to Alzheimer's disease or a series of strokes increases with age (Brookmeyer et al., 2011). Still, most people who live into their nineties do so with clear minds.

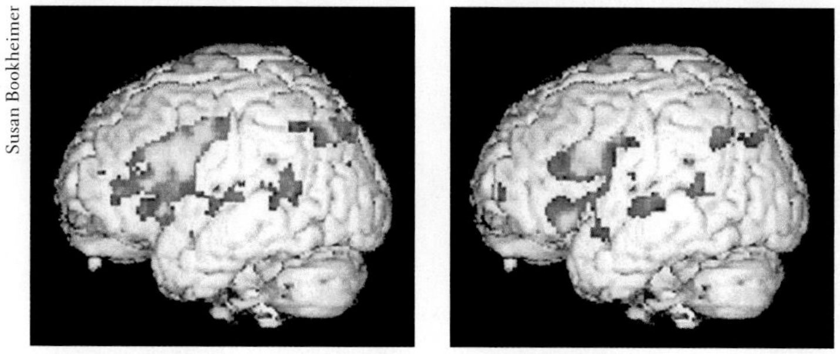

FIGURE 16.4
Predicting Alzheimer's disease During a memory test, MRI scans of the brains of people at risk for Alzheimer's (left) revealed more intense activity (yellow, followed by orange and red) when compared with normal brains (right). As brain scans and genetic tests make it possible to identify those likely to suffer Alzheimer's, would you want to be tested? At what age?

reveal—before symptoms appear—the telltale degeneration of critical brain cells and diminished activity in Alzheimer's-related brain areas (Apostolova et al., 2006; Johnson et al., 2006; Wu & Small, 2006). When people are memorizing words, scans also show diffuse brain activity, as if more exertion was required to achieve the same performance (Bookheimer et al., 2000).

Alzheimer's is somewhat less common among those who exercise their minds as well as their bodies. As with muscles, so with the brain: Those who use it, less often lose it. When given memory tests, those in their sixties do better if they live in countries where people work into their sixties; in countries where people retire earlier, memory declines earlier (Rohwedder & Willis, 2010).

Cognitive Development

16-2 How does memory change with age?

Among the most intriguing developmental psychology questions is whether adult cognitive abilities, such as memory, intelligence, and creativity, parallel the gradually accelerating decline of physical abilities.

As we age, we remember some things well. Looking back in later life, people asked to recall the one or two most important events over the last half-century tend to name events from their teens or twenties (Conway et al., 2005; Rubin et al., 1998). Whatever people experience around this time of life—the events of 9/11, the civil rights movement, World War II—becomes pivotal (Pillemer, 1998; Schuman & Scott, 1989). Our teens and twenties are a time of so many memorable "firsts"—first date, first job, first day at college or university, first meeting in-laws.

FIGURE 16.5
Tests of recall Recalling new names introduced once, twice, or three times is easier for younger adults than for older ones. (Data from Crook & West, 1990.)

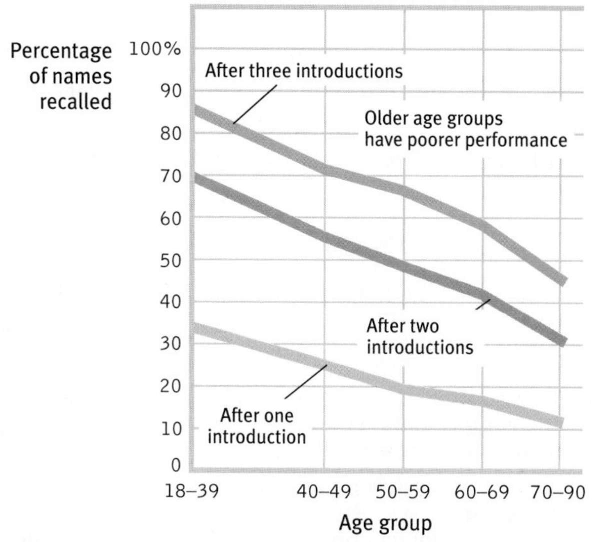

Early adulthood is indeed a peak time for some types of learning and remembering. In one test of recall, people (1205 of them) watched videotapes as 14 strangers said their names, using a common format: "Hi, I'm Larry" (Crook & West, 1990). Then those strangers reappeared and gave additional details. For example, saying "I'm from Philadelphia" provided visual *and* voice cues for remembering the person's name. As **FIGURE 16.5** shows, after a second and third replay of the introductions, everyone remembered more names, but younger adults consistently surpassed older adults.

Perhaps it is not surprising, then, that nearly two-thirds of people over age 40 say their memory is worse than it was 10 years ago (KRC, 2001). In fact, how well older people remember depends on the task. In another experiment (Schonfield & Robertson, 1966), when asked to *recognize* 24 words they had earlier tried to memorize, people showed only a minimal decline in memory. When asked to *recall* that information without clues, the decline was greater (**FIGURE 16.6** on the next page).

FIGURE 16.6
Recall and recognition in adulthood In this experiment, the ability to *recall* new information declined during early and middle adulthood, but the ability to *recognize* new information did not. (From Schonfield & Robertson, 1966.)

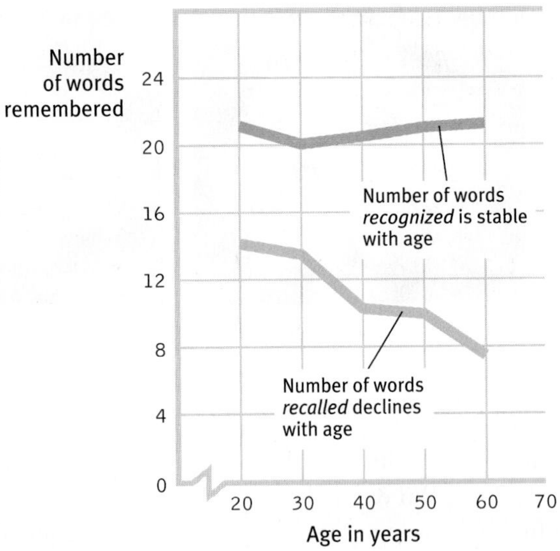

Teens and young adults surpass both young children and 70-year-olds at *prospective memory* ("Remember to . . .") (Zimmerman & Meier, 2006). But older people's prospective memory remains strong when events help trigger a memory (as when walking by a convenience store triggers "Pick up milk!"). Time-based tasks ("Client meeting at 3:00 P.M.") and especially habitual tasks ("Take medications at 9:00 A.M., 2:00 P.M., and 6:00 P.M.") can be challenging (Einstein et al., 1990, 1995, 1998). To minimize such problems, older adults rely more on time management and reminder cues, such as notes to themselves (Henry et al., 2004). This might have helped John Basinger, who, at age 76, was to be interviewed by a local paper regarding a psychology journal article on his late-life memorization of all 12 volumes of John Milton's epic poem *Paradise Lost* (Seamon et al., 2010; Weir, 2010). He forgot a scheduled meeting with the reporter. When calling to apologize, he noted the irony of forgetting his interview about memory.

In our capacity to learn and remember, as in other areas of development, we differ. Younger adults vary in their abilities to learn and remember, but 70-year-olds vary much more. "Differences between the most and least able 70-year-olds become much greater than between the most and least able 50-year-olds," reports Oxford researcher Patrick Rabbitt (2006). Some 70-year-olds perform below nearly all 20-year-olds; other 70-year-olds match or outdo the average 20-year-old.

No matter how quick or slow we are, remembering seems also to depend on the type of information we are trying to retrieve. If the information is meaningless—nonsense syllables or unimportant events—then the older we are, the more errors we are likely to make. If the information is *meaningful*, as was *Paradise Lost* for John Basinger, older people's rich web of existing knowledge will help them to hold it. But they may take longer than younger adults to *produce* the words and things they know: Quick-thinking game show winners are usually young or middle-aged adults (Burke & Shafto, 2004). Older people's capacity to learn and remember *skills* declines less than their verbal recall (Graf, 1990; Labouvie-Vief & Schell, 1982; Perlmutter, 1983).

If you are within five years of 20, what experiences from your last year will you likely never forget? (This is the time of your life you may best remember when you are 50.)

Other modules explore another dimension of cognitive development: intelligence. **Cross-sectional studies** (comparing people of different ages) and **longitudinal studies** (restudying people over time) have identified mental abilities that do and do not change as people age. Age is less a predictor of memory and intelligence than is proximity to death. Tell me whether someone is 8 months or 8 years from death and, regardless of age, you've given me a clue to that person's mental ability. Especially in the last three or four years of life, cognitive decline typically accelerates (Wilson et al., 2007). Researchers call this near-death drop *terminal decline* (Backman & MacDonald, 2006).

cross-sectional study a study in which people of different ages are compared with one another.

longitudinal study research in which the same people are restudied and retested over a long period.

Social Development

16-3 What themes and influences mark our social journey from early adulthood to death?

social clock the culturally preferred timing of social events such as marriage, parenthood, and retirement.

Many differences between younger and older adults are created by significant life events. A new job means new relationships, new expectations, and new demands. Marriage brings the joy of intimacy and the stress of merging two lives. The three years surrounding the birth of a child bring increased life satisfaction for most parents (Dyrdal & Lucas, 2011). The death of a loved one creates an irreplaceable loss. Do these adult life events shape a sequence of life changes?

Adulthood's Ages and Stages

As people enter their forties, they undergo a transition to middle adulthood, a time when they realize that life will soon be mostly behind instead of ahead of them. Some psychologists have argued that for many the *midlife transition* is a crisis, a time of great struggle, regret, or even feeling struck down by life. The popular image of the midlife crisis is an early-forties man who forsakes his family for a younger girlfriend and a hot sports car. But the fact—reported by large samples of people—is that unhappiness, job dissatisfaction, marital dissatisfaction, divorce, anxiety, and suicide do *not* surge during the early forties (Hunter & Sundel, 1989; Mroczek & Kolarz, 1998). Divorce, for example, is most common among those in their twenties, suicide among those in their seventies and eighties. One study of emotional instability in nearly 10,000 men and women found "not the slightest evidence" that distress peaks anywhere in the midlife age range.

"Midway in the journey of our life I found myself in a dark wood, for the straight way was lost."

Dante, *The Divine Comedy*, 1314

For the 1 in 4 adults who does report experiencing a life crisis, the trigger is not age, but a major event, such as illness, divorce, or job loss (Lachman, 2004). Some middle-aged adults describe themselves as a "sandwich generation," simultaneously supporting their aging parents and their emerging adult children or grandchildren (Riley & Bowen, 2005).

Life events trigger transitions to new life stages at varying ages. The **social clock**—the definition of "the right time" to leave home, get a job, marry, have children, and retire—varies from era to era and culture to culture. The once-rigid sequence for many Western women—of student to worker to wife to at-home mom to worker again—has loosened. Contemporary women occupy these roles in any order or all at once. The social clock still ticks, but people feel freer about being out of sync with it.

Even *chance events*, such as romantic attraction, can have lasting significance, by deflecting us down one road rather than another (Bandura, 1982). Albert Bandura (2005) recalls the ironic true story of a book editor who came to one of Bandura's lectures on the "Psychology of Chance Encounters and Life Paths"—and ended up marrying the woman who happened to sit next to him. The sequence that led to my authoring this book (which was not my idea) began with my being seated near, and getting to know, a distinguished colleague at an international conference. Chance events can change our lives.

"The important events of a person's life are the products of chains of highly improbable occurrences."

Joseph Traub, "Traub's Law," 2003

©The New Yorker Collection, 2006, John Donohue from cartoonbank.com. All Rights Reserved.

Adulthood's Commitments

Two basic aspects of our lives dominate adulthood. Erik Erikson called them *intimacy* (forming close relationships) and *generativity* (being productive and supporting future generations). Researchers have chosen various terms—*affiliation* and *achievement*, *attachment* and *productivity*, *connectedness* and *competence*. Sigmund Freud (1935) put it most simply: The healthy adult, he said, is one who can *love* and *work*.

Lisa B./Corbis

Love Intimacy, attachment, commitment—love by whatever name—is central to healthy and happy adulthood.

Love

We typically flirt, fall in love, and commit—one person at a time. "Pairbonding is a trademark of the human animal," observed anthropologist Helen Fisher (1993). From an evolutionary perspective, relatively monogamous pairing makes sense: Parents who cooperated to nurture their children to maturity were more likely to have their genes passed along to posterity than were parents who didn't.

Adult bonds of love are most satisfying and enduring when marked by a similarity of interests and values, a sharing of emotional and material support, and intimate self-disclosure. Couples who seal their love with commitment—via (in one Vermont study) marriage for heterosexual couples and civil unions for homosexual couples—more often endure (Balsam et al., 2008). Marriage bonds are especially likely to last when couples marry after age 20 and are well educated. Compared with their counterparts of 40 years ago, people in Western countries *are* better educated and marrying later. Yet, ironically, they are nearly twice as likely to divorce. (Both Canada and the United States now have about one divorce for every two marriages [Bureau of the Census, 2007], and in Europe, divorce is only slightly less common.) The divorce rate partly reflects women's lessened economic dependence and men and women's rising expectations. We now hope not only for an enduring bond, but also for a mate who is a wage earner, caregiver, intimate friend, and warm and responsive lover.

Might test-driving life together in a "trial marriage" minimize divorce risk? In one Gallup survey of American twenty-somethings, 62 percent thought it would (Whitehead & Popenoe, 2001). In reality, in Europe, Canada, and the United States, those who cohabit before marriage have had *higher* rates of divorce and marital dysfunction than those who did not cohabit (Jose et al., 2010). The risk appears greatest for those cohabiting prior to engagement (Goodwin et al., 2010; Rhoades et al., 2009).

American children born to cohabiting parents are about five times more likely to experience their parents' separation than are children born to married parents (Osborne et al., 2007). Two factors contribute. First, cohabiters tend to be initially less committed to the ideal of enduring marriage. Second, they become even less marriage-supporting while cohabiting.

What do you think? Does marriage correlate with happiness because marital support and intimacy breed happiness, because happy people more often marry and stay married, or both?

Nonetheless, the institution of marriage endures. Worldwide, reports the United Nations, 9 in 10 heterosexual adults marry. And marriage is a predictor of happiness, sexual satisfaction, income, and physical and mental health (Scott et al., 2010). National Opinion Research Center surveys of more than 48,000 Americans since 1972 reveal that 40 percent of married adults, though only 23 percent of unmarried adults, have reported being "very happy." Lesbian couples, too, report greater well-being than those who are alone (Peplau & Fingerhut, 2007; Wayment & Peplau, 1995). Moreover, neighborhoods with high marriage rates typically have low rates of social pathologies such as crime, delinquency, and emotional disorders among children (Myers & Scanzoni, 2005).

bluehand/Shutterstock

Marriages that last are not always devoid of conflict. Some couples fight but also shower each other with affection. Other couples never raise their voices yet also seldom praise each other or nuzzle. Both styles can last. After observing the interactions of 2000 couples, John Gottman (1994) reported one indicator of marital success: at least a five-to-one ratio of positive to negative interactions. Stable marriages provide five times more instances of smiling, touching, complimenting, and laughing than of sarcasm, criticism, and insults. So, if you want to predict which newlyweds will stay together, don't pay attention to how passionately they are in love. The couples

DM7/Shutterstock

who make it are more often those who refrain from putting down their partners. To prevent a cancerous negativity, successful couples learn to fight fair (to state feelings without insulting) and to steer conflict away from chaos with comments like "I know it's not your fault" or "I'll just be quiet for a moment and listen."

Often, love bears children. For most people, this most enduring of life changes is a happy event. "I feel an overwhelming love for my children unlike anything I feel for anyone else," said 93 percent of American mothers in a national survey (Erickson & Aird, 2005). Many fathers feel the same. A few weeks after the birth of my first child I was suddenly struck by a realization: "So *this* is how my parents felt about me!"

When children begin to absorb time, money, and emotional energy, satisfaction with the marriage itself may decline (Doss et al., 2009). This is especially likely among employed women who, more than they expected, carry the traditional burden of doing the chores at home. Putting effort into creating an equitable relationship can thus pay double dividends: a more satisfying marriage, which breeds better parent-child relations (Erel & Burman, 1995).

Although love bears children, children eventually leave home. This departure is a significant and sometimes difficult event. For most people, however, an empty nest is a happy place (Adelmann et al., 1989; Gorchoff et al., 2008). Many parents experience a "postlaunch honeymoon," especially if they maintain close relationships with their children (White & Edwards, 1990). As Daniel Gilbert (2006) has said, "The only known symptom of 'empty nest syndrome' is increased smiling."

"Our love for children is so unlike any other human emotion. I fell in love with my babies so quickly and profoundly, almost completely independently of their particular qualities. And yet 20 years later I was (more or less) happy to see them go—I had to be happy to see them go. We are totally devoted to them when they are little and yet the most we can expect in return when they grow up is that they regard us with bemused and tolerant affection."

Developmental psychologist Alison Gopnik, "The Supreme Infant," 2010

If you have left home, did your parents suffer the "empty nest syndrome"—a feeling of distress focusing on a loss of purpose and relationship? Did they mourn the lost joy of listening for you in the wee hours of Saturday morning? Or did they seem to discover a new freedom, relaxation, and (if married) renewed satisfaction with their own relationship?

Work

For many adults, the answer to "Who are you?" depends a great deal on the answer to "What do you do?" For women and men, choosing a career path is difficult, especially during bad economic times. Even in the best of times, few students in their first two years of college or university can predict their later careers.

In the end, happiness is about having work that fits your interests and provides you with a sense of competence and accomplishment. It is having a close, supportive companion who cheers your accomplishments (Gable et al., 2006). And for some, it includes having children who love you and whom you love and feel proud of.

RETRIEVAL PRACTICE

- Freud defined the healthy adult as one who is able to __________ and to __________.

ANSWERS: love; work

Hill Street Studios/Getty Images

© Jose Luis Pelaez Inc/Blend Images/Corbis

Job satisfaction and life satisfaction Work can provide us with a sense of identity and competence and opportunities for accomplishment. Perhaps this is why challenging and interesting occupations enhance people's happiness.

"Hope I die before I get old."

Pete Townshend, of the Who (written at age 20)

© Andonghun/agefotostock

Well-Being Across the Life Span

16-4 Do self-confidence and life satisfaction vary with life stages?

To live is to grow older. This moment marks the oldest you have ever been and the youngest you will henceforth be. That means we all can look back with satisfaction or regret, and forward with hope or dread. When asked what they would have done differently if they could relive their lives, people's most common answer is "Taken my education more seriously and worked harder at it" (Kinnier & Metha, 1989; Roese & Summerville, 2005). Other regrets—"I should have told my father I loved him," "I regret that I never went to Europe"—also focus less on mistakes made than on the things one *failed* to do (Gilovich & Medvec, 1995).

From the teens to midlife, people typically experience a strengthening sense of identity, confidence, and self-esteem (Huang, 2010; Robins & Trzesniewski, 2005). In later life, challenges arise: Income shrinks, work is often taken away, the body deteriorates, recall fades, energy wanes, family members and friends die or move away, and the great enemy, death, looms ever closer. And for those in the terminal decline phase, life satisfaction does decline as death approaches (Gerstorf et al., 2008).

Small wonder that most presume that happiness declines in later life (Lacey et al., 2006). But worldwide, as Gallup researchers discovered, most find that the over-65 years are not notably unhappy (**FIGURE 16.7**). If anything, positive feelings, supported by enhanced emotional control, grow after midlife and negative feelings subside (Stone et al., 2010; Urry & Gross, 2010). Older adults increasingly use words that convey positive emotions (Pennebaker & Stone, 2003), and they attend less and less to negative information. Compared with younger adults, for example, they are slower to perceive negative faces and more attentive to positive news (Carstensen & Mikels, 2005; Scheibe & Carstensen, 2010). Older adults also have fewer problems in their social relationships (Fingerman & Charles, 2010), and they experience less intense anger, stress, and worry (Stone et al., 2010).

"When you were born, you cried and the world rejoiced. Live your life in a manner so that when you die the world cries and you rejoice."

Native American proverb

The aging brain may help nurture these positive feelings. Brain scans of older adults show that the amygdala, a neural processing center for emotions, responds less actively to negative events (but not to positive events), and it interacts less with the hippocampus, a brain memory processing center (Mather et al., 2004; St. Jacques et al., 2010; Williams et al., 2006). Brainwave reactions to negative images also diminish with age (Kisley et al., 2007).

"At 20 we worry about what others think of us. At 40 we don't care what others think of us. At 60 we discover they haven't been thinking about us at all."

Anonymous

Moreover, at all ages, the bad feelings we associate with negative events fade faster than do the good feelings we associate with positive events (Walker et al., 2003). This contributes to most older people's sense that life, on balance, has been mostly good.

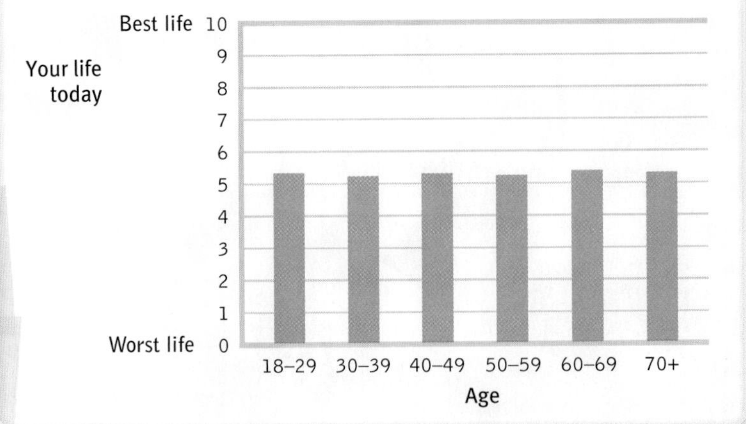

FIGURE 16.7

Age and life satisfaction The Gallup Organization asked 142,682 people worldwide to rate their lives on a ladder, from 0 ("the worst possible life") to 10 ("the best possible life"). Age gave no clue to life satisfaction (Crabtree, 2010).

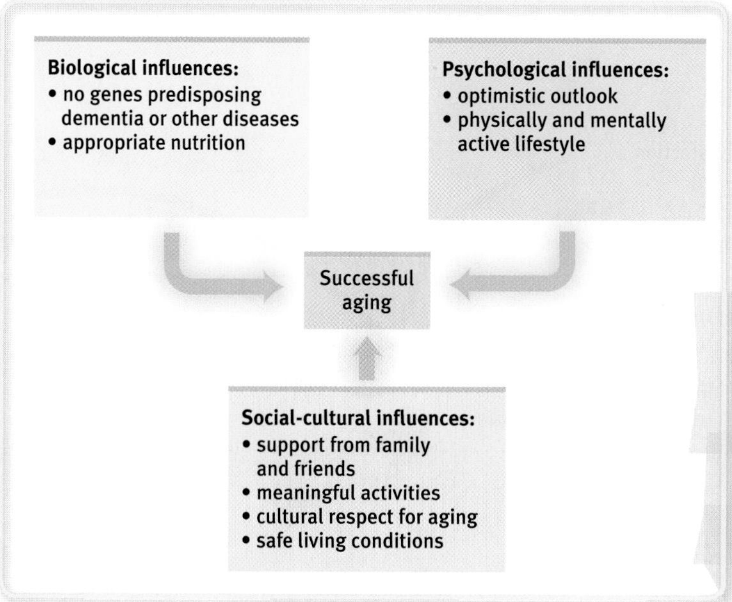

FIGURE 16.8
Biopsychosocial influences on successful aging Numerous biological, psychological, and social-cultural factors affect the way we age. With the right genes, we have a good chance of aging successfully if we maintain a positive outlook and stay mentally and physically active, as well as connected to family and friends in the community.

Given that growing older is an outcome of living (an outcome most prefer to early dying), the positivity of later life is comforting. More and more people flourish into later life, thanks to biological, psychological, and social-cultural influences (**FIGURE 16.8**).

The resilience of well-being across the life span obscures some interesting age-related emotional differences. Psychologists Mihaly Csikszentmihalyi [chick-SENT-me-hi] and Reed Larson (1984) mapped people's emotional terrain by periodically signaling them with electronic beepers to report their current activities and feelings. They found that teenagers typically come down from elation or up from gloom in less than an hour, but adult moods are less extreme and more enduring. As the years go by, feelings mellow (Costa et al., 1987; Diener et al., 1986). Highs become less high, lows less low. Compliments provoke less elation and criticisms less despair, as both become merely additional feedback atop a mountain of accumulated praise and blame. As we age, life therefore becomes less of an emotional roller coaster.

"The best thing about being 100 is *no peer pressure*."

Lewis W. Kuester, 2005, on turning 100

"At 70, I would say the advantage is that you take life more calmly. You know that 'this, too, shall pass'!"

Eleanor Roosevelt, 1954

RETRIEVAL PRACTICE

- What are some of the most significant challenges and rewards of growing old?

ANSWERS: Challenges: decline of muscular strength, reaction times, stamina, sensory keenness, cardiac output, and immune system functioning. Rewards: positive feelings tend to grow, negative emotions are less intense, and risk of depression often decreases.

Death and Dying

16-5 A loved one's death triggers what range of reactions?

Warning: If you begin reading the next paragraph, you will die.

But of course, if you hadn't read this, you would still die in due time. Death is our inevitable end. Most of us will also suffer and cope with the deaths of relatives and friends. Usually, the most difficult separation is from a spouse—a loss suffered by five times more women than men. When, as usually happens, death comes at an expected late-life time, the grieving may be relatively short-lived. (**FIGURE 16.9** on the next page shows the typical emotional path before and after a spouse's death.)

Grief is especially severe when a loved one's death comes suddenly and before its expected time on the social clock. The sudden illness or accident claiming a 45-year-old

"Love—why, I'll tell you what love is: It's you at 75 and her at 71, each of you listening for the other's step in the next room, each afraid that a sudden silence, a sudden cry, could mean a lifetime's talk is over."

Brian Moore, *The Luck of Ginger Coffey*, 1960

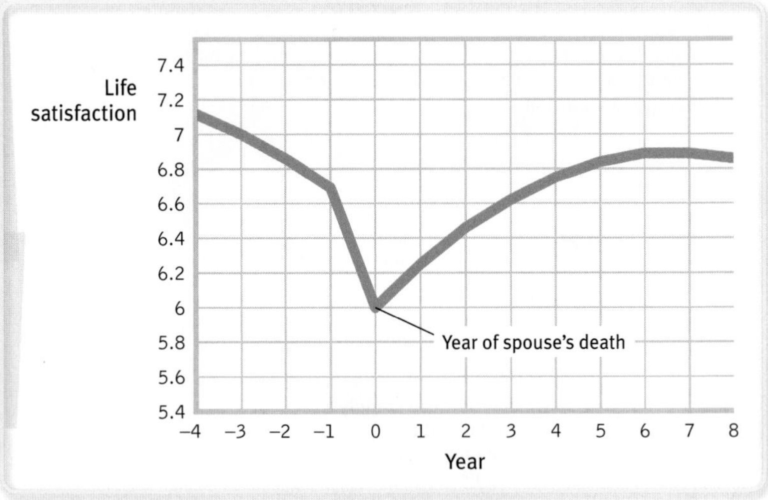

FIGURE 16.9
Life satisfaction before, during the year of, and after a spouse's death Richard Lucas and his collaborators (2003) examined longitudinal annual surveys of more than 30,000 Germans. The researchers identified 513 married people who had experienced a spouse's death and had not remarried. In this group, life satisfaction began to dip during the prewidowhood year, dropped significantly during the year of the spouse's death, and then eventually rebounded to nearly the earlier level. (*Source:* Richard Lucas.)

life partner or a child may trigger a year or more of memory-laden mourning that eventually subsides to a mild depression (Lehman et al., 1987).

For some, however, the loss is unbearable. One Danish long-term study of more than 1 million people found that about 17,000 of them had suffered the death of a child under 18. In the five years following that death, 3 percent of them had a first psychiatric hospitalization. This rate was 67 percent higher than the rate recorded for parents who had not lost a child (Li et al., 2005).

"Consider, friend, as you pass by, as you are now, so once was I. As I am now, you too shall be. Prepare, therefore, to follow me."
Scottish tombstone epitaph

Even so, reactions to a loved one's death range more widely than most suppose. Some cultures encourage public weeping and wailing; others hide grief. Within any culture, individuals differ. Given similar losses, some people grieve hard and long, others less so (Ott et al., 2007). Contrary to popular misconceptions, however,

- terminally ill and bereaved people do not go through identical predictable stages, such as denial before anger (Friedman & James, 2008; Nolen-Hoeksema & Larson, 1999). A Yale study following 233 bereaved individuals through time did, however, find that yearning for the loved one reached a high point four months after the loss, with anger peaking, on average, about a month later (Maciejewski et al., 2007).
- those who express the strongest grief immediately do not purge their grief more quickly (Bonanno & Kaltman, 1999; Wortman & Silver, 1989).
- bereavement therapy and self-help groups offer support, but there is similar healing power in the passing of time, the support of friends, and the act of giving support and help to others (Baddeley & Singer, 2009; Brown et al., 2008; Neimeyer & Currier, 2009). Grieving spouses who talk often with others or receive grief counseling adjust about as well as those who grieve more privately (Bonanno, 2001, 2004; Genevro, 2003; Stroebe et al., 2001, 2002, 2005).

We can be grateful for the waning of death-denying attitudes. Facing death with dignity and openness helps people complete the life cycle with a sense of life's meaningfulness and unity—the sense that their existence has been good and that life and death are parts of an ongoing cycle. Although death may be unwelcome, life itself can be affirmed even at death. This is especially so for people who review their lives not with despair but with what Erik Erikson called a sense of *integrity*—a feeling that one's life has been meaningful and worthwhile.

The New Yorker Collection, 2008, William Hamilton, from cartoonbank.com. All Rights Reserved.

"I'm nothing, and yet I'm all I can think about."

MODULE REVIEW

Adulthood

Learning Objectives

RETRIEVAL PRACTICE Take a moment to answer each of these Learning Objective Questions (repeated here from within the module). Then turn to Appendix B, Complete Module Reviews, to check your answers. Research suggests that trying to answer these questions on your own will improve your long-term retention (McDaniel et al., 2009).

16-1: What physical changes occur during middle and late adulthood?

16-2: How does memory change with age?

16-3: What themes and influences mark our social journey from early adulthood to death?

16-4: Do self-confidence and life satisfaction vary with life stages?

16-5: A loved one's death triggers what range of reactions?

Terms and Concepts to Remember

RETRIEVAL PRACTICE Test yourself on these terms by trying to write down the definition before flipping back to the referenced page to check your answer.

menopause, p. 209
cross-sectional study, p. 214
longitudinal study, p. 214
social clock, p. 215

RETRIEVAL PRACTICE Gain an advantage, and benefit from immediate feedback, with the interactive self-testing resources at www.worthpublishers.com/myers.

Sensation and Perception

I have perfect vision," explains my colleague, Heather Sellers, an acclaimed writer and teacher. Her vision may be fine, but there is a problem with her perception. She cannot recognize faces.

In her memoir, *You Don't Look Like Anyone I Know,* Sellers (2010) tells of awkward moments resulting from her lifelong *prosopagnosia*—face blindness.

> In college, on a date at the Spaghetti Station, I returned from the bathroom and plunked myself down in the wrong booth, facing the wrong man. I remained unaware he was not my date even as my date (a stranger to me) accosted Wrong Booth Guy, and then stormed out of the Station. I can't distinguish actors in movies and on television. I do not recognize myself in photos or videos. I can't recognize my step-sons in the soccer pick-up line; I failed to determine which husband was mine at a party, in the mall, at the market.

Her inability to recognize faces means that people sometimes perceive her as snobby or aloof. "Why did you walk past me?" a neighbor might later ask. Similar to those of us with hearing loss who fake hearing during trite social conversation, Sellers sometimes fakes recognition. She often smiles at people she passes, in case she knows them. Or she pretends to know the person with whom she is talking. (To avoid the stress associated with such perception failures, people with serious hearing loss or with prosopagnosia often shy away from busy social situations.) But there is an upside:

MODULES

17 Basic Principles of Sensation and Perception

18 Vision and Perceptual Organization and Interpretation

19 The Nonvisual Senses

When encountering someone who previously irritated her, she typically won't feel ill will, because she doesn't recognize the person.

Unlike Sellers, most of us have a functioning area on the underside of our brain's right hemisphere that helps us recognize a familiar human face as soon as we detect it—in only one-seventh of a second (Jacques & Rossion, 2006). This ability illustrates a broader principle. *Nature's sensory gifts enable each animal to obtain essential information.* Some examples:

- Frogs, which feed on flying insects, have cells in their eyes that fire only in response to small, dark, moving objects. A frog could starve to death knee-deep in motionless flies. But let one zoom by and the frog's "bug detector" cells snap awake.
- Male silkworm moths' odor receptors can detect one-billionth of an ounce of sex attractant per second released by a female one mile away. That is why there continue to be silkworms.
- Human ears are most sensitive to sound frequencies that include human voices, especially a baby's cry.

In these modules, we'll look more closely at what psychologists have learned about how we sense and perceive the world around us. Module 17 begins by considering some basic principles. We will then explore vision and perceptual organization and interpretation (Module 18), and look at the nonvisual senses (Module 19).

MODULE 17

- Transduction
- Thresholds
- Sensory Adaptation
- Perceptual Set
- Context Effects
- Emotion and Motivation

Basic Principles of Sensation and Perception

17-1 What are *sensation* and *perception?* What do we mean by *bottom-up processing* and *top-down processing?*

Heather Sellers' curious mix of "perfect vision" and face blindness illustrates the distinction between *sensation* and *perception.* When she looks at a friend, her **sensation** is normal: Her senses detect the same information yours would, and they transmit that information to her brain. And her **perception**—the processes by which her brain organizes and interprets sensory input—is *almost* normal. Thus, she may recognize people from their hair, gait, voice, or particular physique, just not their face. Her experience is much like the struggle you or I would have trying to recognize a specific penguin in a group of waddling penguins.

In our everyday experiences, sensation and perception blend into one continuous process. In this module, we slow down that process to study its parts, but in real life, our sensory and perceptual processes work together to help us decipher the world around us.

- Our **bottom-up processing** starts at the sensory receptors and works up to higher levels of processing.
- Our **top-down processing** constructs perceptions from the sensory input by drawing on our experience and expectations.

© Sandro Del-Prete/www.sandrodelprete.com

FIGURE 17.1
What's going on here? Our sensory and perceptual processes work together to help us sort out the complex images, including the hidden couple in Sandro Del-Prete's drawing, *The Flowering of Love.*

As our brain absorbs the information in **FIGURE 17.1**, bottom-up processing enables our sensory systems to detect the lines, angles, and colors that form the flower and leaves. Using top-down processing we interpret what our senses detect.

But *how* do we do it? How do we create meaning from the blizzard of sensory stimuli bombarding our bodies 24 hours a day? Meanwhile, in a silent, cushioned, inner world, our brain floats in utter darkness. By itself, it sees nothing. It hears nothing. It feels nothing. *So, how does the world out there get in?* To phrase the question scientifically: How do we construct our representations of the external world? How do a campfire's flicker, crackle, and smoky scent activate neural connections? And how, from this living neurochemistry, do we create our conscious experience of the fire's motion and temperature, its aroma and beauty? In search of answers to such questions, let's look at some processes that cut across all our sensory systems.

sensation the process by which our sensory receptors and nervous system receive and represent stimulus energies from our environment.

perception the process of organizing and interpreting sensory information, enabling us to recognize meaningful objects and events.

bottom-up processing analysis that begins with the sensory receptors and works up to the brain's integration of sensory information.

top-down processing information processing guided by higher-level mental processes, as when we construct perceptions drawing on our experience and expectations.

transduction conversion of one form of energy into another. In sensation, the transforming of stimulus energies, such as sights, sounds, and smells, into neural impulses our brain can interpret.

Transduction

17-2 What three steps are basic to all our sensory systems?

Every second of every day, our sensory systems perform an amazing feat: They convert one form of energy into another. Vision processes light energy. Hearing processes sound waves. All our senses

- *receive* sensory stimulation, often using specialized receptor cells.
- *transform* that stimulation into neural impulses.
- *deliver* the neural information to our brain.

The process of converting one form of energy into another that our brain can use is called **transduction.** How do we see? Hear? Feel pain? Taste? Smell? Keep our balance?

In each case, there are three steps to consider—receiving, transforming, and delivering the information to the brain. Let's see what **psychophysics** has discovered about the physical energy we can detect and its effects on our psychological experiences.

RETRIEVAL PRACTICE

- What is the rough distinction between sensation and perception?

ANSWER: *Sensation* is the bottom-up process by which the physical sensory system receives and represents stimuli. *Perception* is the top-down mental process of organizing and interpreting sensory input.

Thresholds

17-3 What are the absolute and difference thresholds, and do stimuli below the absolute threshold have any influence on us?

At this moment, you and I are being struck by X-rays and radio waves, ultraviolet and infrared light, and sound waves of very high and very low frequencies. To all of these we are blind and deaf. Other animals with differing needs detect a world that lies beyond our experience. Migrating birds stay on course aided by an internal magnetic compass. Bats and dolphins locate prey using sonar, bouncing echoing sound off objects. Bees navigate on cloudy days by detecting invisible (to us) polarized light.

The shades on our own senses are open just a crack, allowing us a restricted awareness of this vast sea of energy. But for our needs, this is enough.

Absolute Thresholds

To some kinds of stimuli we are exquisitely sensitive. Standing atop a mountain on an utterly dark, clear night, most of us could see a candle flame atop another mountain 30 miles away. We could feel the wing of a bee falling on our cheek. We could smell a single drop of perfume in a three-room apartment (Galanter, 1962).

German scientist and philosopher Gustav Fechner (1801–1887) studied our awareness of these faint stimuli and called them our **absolute thresholds**—the minimum stimulation necessary to detect a particular light, sound, pressure, taste, or odor 50 percent of the time. To test your absolute threshold for sounds, a hearing specialist would expose each of your ears to varying sound levels. For each tone, the test would define where half the time you could detect the sound and half the time you could not. That 50-50 point would define your absolute threshold.

Detecting a weak stimulus, or signal, depends not only on the signal's strength (such as a hearing-test tone) but also on our psychological state—our experience, expectations, motivation, and alertness. **Signal detection theory** predicts when we will detect weak signals (measured as our ratio of "hits" to "false alarms"). Signal detection theorists seek to understand why people respond differently to the same stimuli, and why the same person's reactions vary as circumstances change. Exhausted parents will notice the faintest whimper from a newborn's cradle while failing to notice louder, unimportant sounds. Lonely, anxious people at speed-dating events also respond with a low threshold, and thus tend to be unselective in reaching out to potential dates (McClure et al., 2010).

Stimuli you cannot detect 50 percent of the time are **subliminal**—below your absolute threshold (**FIGURE 17.2** on the next page). Under certain conditions, you can be affected by stimuli so weak that you don't consciously notice them. An unnoticed image or word can reach your visual cortex and briefly **prime** your response to a later question. In a

psychophysics the study of relationships between the physical characteristics of stimuli, such as their intensity, and our psychological experience of them.

absolute threshold the minimum stimulation needed to detect a particular stimulus 50 percent of the time.

signal detection theory a theory predicting how and when we detect the presence of a faint stimulus (*signal*) amid background stimulation (*noise*). Assumes there is no single absolute threshold and that detection depends partly on a person's experience, expectations, motivation, and alertness.

subliminal below one's absolute threshold for conscious awareness.

priming the activation, often unconsciously, of certain associations, thus predisposing one's perception, memory, or response.

Try out this old riddle on a couple of friends. "You're driving a bus with 12 passengers. At your first stop, 6 passengers get off. At the second stop, 3 get off. At the third stop, 2 more get off but 3 new people get on. What color are the bus driver's eyes?" Do your friends detect the signal—who is the bus driver?—amid the accompanying noise?

RETRIEVAL PRACTICE

Signal detection

What three factors will make it more likely that you correctly detect a text message?

ANSWER: (1) You are expecting a text message. (2) It is important that you see the text message and respond. (3) You are alert.

© Inspirestock/Corbis

FIGURE 17.2
Absolute threshold Can I detect this sound? An *absolute threshold* is the intensity at which a person can detect a stimulus half the time. Hearing tests locate these thresholds for various frequency levels.

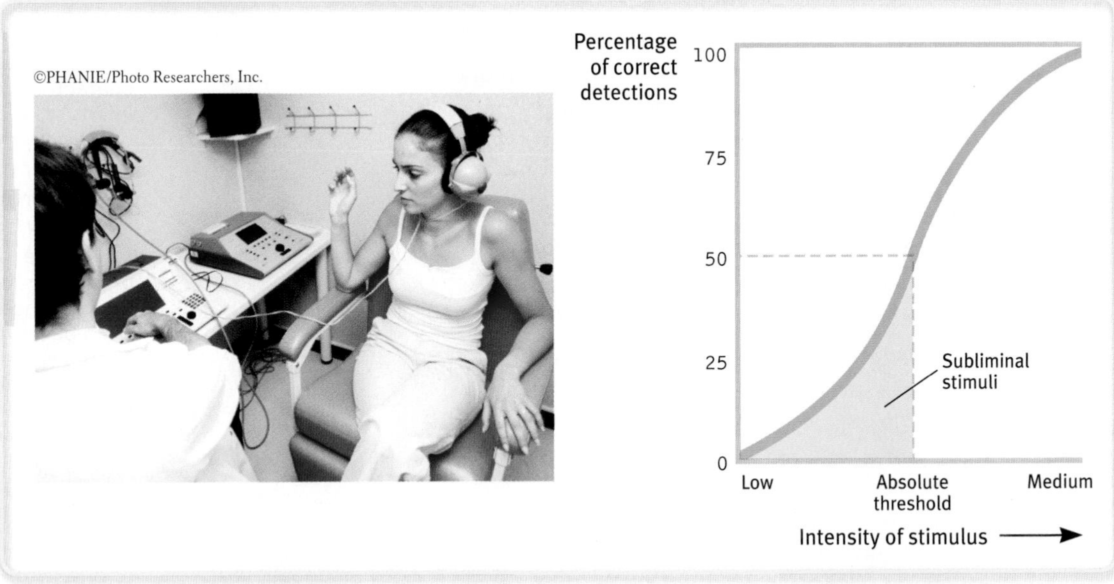

"The heart has its reasons which reason does not know."
Pascal, *Pensées,* 1670

FIGURE 17.3
The hidden mind After an image of a nude man or woman was flashed to one side or another, then masked before being perceived, people's attention was unconsciously drawn to images in a way that reflected their sexual orientation (Jiang et al., 2006).

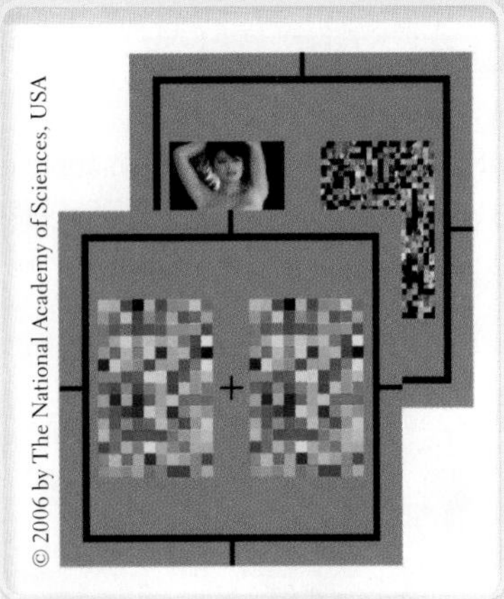

typical experiment, the image or word is quickly flashed, then replaced by a *masking stimulus* that interrupts the brain's processing before conscious perception (Van den Bussche et al., 2009). Consider one such experiment, which also illustrates the deep reality of sexual orientation. Researchers asked people to gaze at the center of a screen, and then flashed a photo of a nude person to one side and a scrambled version of the photo to the other side (Jiang et al., 2006). Because the images were immediately masked by a colored checkerboard, the volunteers saw nothing but flashes of color and were unable to guess where the nude had appeared. Then the researchers flashed a geometric figure to one side or the other, followed by the masking stimulus, and asked the volunteers to give the figure's angle (**FIGURE 17.3**). Straight men were more accurate when the geometric figure appeared where a nude *woman* had been a moment earlier. Gay men and straight women guessed more accurately when the geometric figure replaced a nude *man*. As other experiments confirm, we can evaluate a stimulus even when we are not aware of it—and even when we are unaware of our evaluation (Ferguson & Zayas, 2009).

How do we feel or respond to what we do not know and cannot describe? An imperceptibly brief stimulus often triggers a weak response that *can* be detected by brain scanning (Blankenburg et al., 2003; Haynes & Rees, 2005, 2006). It's only when the stimulus triggers synchronized activity in several brain areas does it reach consciousness (Dehaene, 2009). Once again we see the dual-track mind at work: *Much of our information processing occurs automatically, out of sight, off the radar screen of our conscious mind.*

So can we be controlled by subliminal messages? For more on that question, see Thinking Critically About: Can Subliminal Messages Control Our Behavior?

Difference Thresholds

To function effectively, we need absolute thresholds low enough to allow us to detect important sights, sounds, textures, tastes, and smells. We also need to detect small differences among stimuli. A musician must detect minute discrepancies when tuning an instrument. Parents must detect the sound of their own child's voice amid other children's voices. Even after living two years in Scotland, sheep *baa's* all sound alike to my ears. But not to those of ewes, which I have observed streaking, after shearing, directly to the *baa* of their lamb amid the chorus of other distressed lambs.

difference threshold the minimum difference between two stimuli required for detection 50 percent of the time. We experience the difference threshold as a *just noticeable difference* (or *jnd*).

Weber's law the principle that, to be perceived as different, two stimuli must differ by a given percentage (rather than a given amount).

THINKING CRITICALLY ABOUT

Can Subliminal Messages Control Our Behavior?

Hoping to penetrate our unconscious, entrepreneurs offer audio and video programs to help us lose weight, stop smoking, or improve our memories. Soothing ocean sounds may mask messages we cannot consciously hear: "I am thin"; "Smoke tastes bad"; or "I do well on tests—I have total recall of information." Such claims make two assumptions: (1) We can unconsciously sense subliminal (literally, "below threshold") stimuli. (2) Without our awareness, these stimuli have extraordinary suggestive powers. Can we? Do they?

Babs Reingold

Subliminal persuasion? Although subliminally presented stimuli *can* subtly influence people, experiments discount attempts at subliminal advertising and self-improvement. (The playful message here is not actually subliminal—because you can easily perceive it.)

As we have seen, subliminal *sensation* is a fact. Remember that an "absolute" threshold is merely the point at which we can detect a stimulus *half the time.* At or slightly below this threshold, we will still detect the stimulus some of the time.

But does this mean that claims of subliminal *persuasion* are also facts? The near-consensus among researchers is *No.* The laboratory research reveals a *subtle, fleeting* effect. Priming thirsty people with the subliminal word *thirst* might therefore, for a moment, make a thirst-quenching beverage ad more persuasive (Strahan et al., 2002). Likewise, priming thirsty people with Lipton Ice Tea may increase their choosing the primed brand (Karremans et al., 2006; Veltkamp et al., 2011; Verwijmeren et al., 2011a,b). But the subliminal-message hucksters claim something different: a *powerful, enduring* effect on behavior.

To test whether subliminal recordings have this enduring effect, Anthony Greenwald and his colleagues (1991, 1992) randomly assigned university students to listen daily for five weeks to commercial subliminal messages claiming to improve either self-esteem or memory. But the researchers played a practical joke and switched half the labels. Some students who thought they were receiving affirmations of self-esteem were actually hearing the memory-enhancement message. Others got the self-esteem message but thought their memory was being recharged.

Were the recordings effective? Students' test scores for self-esteem and memory, taken before and after the five weeks, revealed no effects. Yet the students *perceived* themselves receiving the benefits they *expected.* Those who *thought* they had heard a memory recording *believed* their memories had improved. Those who thought they had heard a self-esteem recording believed their self-esteem had grown. (Reading this research, one hears echoes of the testimonies that ooze from mail-order catalogs. Some customers, having bought what is not supposed to be heard [and having indeed not heard it!] offer testimonials like, "I really know that your tapes were invaluable in reprogramming my mind.")

Over a decade, Greenwald conducted 16 double-blind experiments evaluating subliminal self-help recordings. His results were uniform: Not one of the recordings helped more than a placebo (Greenwald, 1992). And placebos work only because we *believe* they will work.

The **difference threshold** (or the *just noticeable difference [jnd]*) is the minimum difference a person can detect between any two stimuli half the time. That difference threshold increases with the size of the stimulus. Thus, if you add 1 ounce to a 10-ounce weight, you will detect the difference; add 1 ounce to a 100-ounce weight and you probably will not.

In the nineteenth century, Ernst Weber noted something so simple and so widely applicable that we still refer to it as **Weber's law.** This law states that for an average person to perceive a difference, two stimuli must differ by a constant *proportion* (not a constant *amount*). The exact proportion varies, depending on the stimulus. Two lights, for example, must differ in intensity by 8 percent. Two objects must differ in weight by 2 percent. And two tones must differ in frequency by only 0.3 percent (Teghtsoonian, 1971).

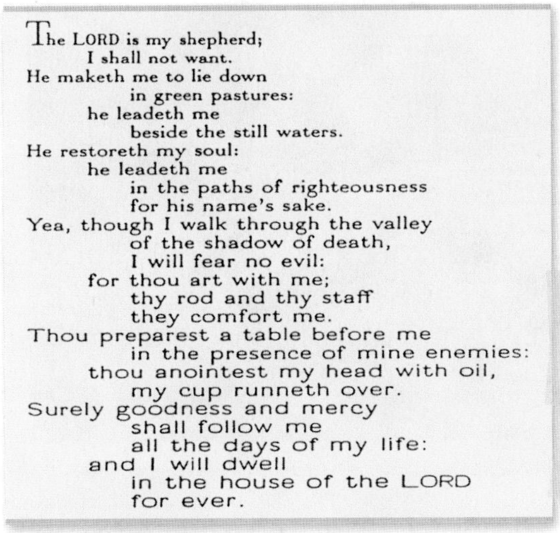
The LORD is my shepherd;
I shall not want.
He maketh me to lie down
in green pastures:
he leadeth me
beside the still waters.
He restoreth my soul:
he leadeth me
in the paths of righteousness
for his name's sake.
Yea, though I walk through the valley
of the shadow of death,
I will fear no evil:
for thou art with me;
thy rod and thy staff
they comfort me.
Thou preparest a table before me
in the presence of mine enemies:
thou anointest my head with oil,
my cup runneth over.
Surely goodness and mercy
shall follow me
all the days of my life:
and I will dwell
in the house of the LORD
for ever.

The difference threshold In this computer-generated copy of the Twenty-third Psalm, each line of the typeface increases slightly. How many lines are required for you to experience a just noticeable difference?

sensory adaptation diminished sensitivity as a consequence of constant stimulation.

perceptual set a mental predisposition to perceive one thing and not another.

RETRIEVAL PRACTICE

- Using sound as your example, illustrate the distinctions among these concepts: absolute threshold, subliminal stimulation, and difference threshold.

ANSWER: *Absolute threshold* is the minimum stimulation needed to detect a particular sound (such as an approaching bike on the sidewalk behind us) 50 percent of the time. *Subliminal stimulation* happens when, without our awareness, our sensory system processes that sound (when it is below our absolute threshold). A *difference threshold* is the minimum difference for us to distinguish between two sounds.

Sensory Adaptation

17-4 What is the function of sensory adaptation?

"We need above all to know about changes; no one wants or needs to be reminded 16 hours a day that his shoes are on."

Neuroscientist David Hubel (1979)

Entering your neighbors' living room, you smell a musty odor. You wonder how they can stand it, but within minutes you no longer notice it. **Sensory adaptation** has come to your rescue. When we are constantly exposed to a stimulus that does not change, we become less aware of it because our nerve cells fire less frequently. (To experience sensory adaptation, move your watch up your wrist an inch: You will feel it—but only for a few moments.)

Why, then, if we stare at an object without flinching, does it *not* vanish from sight? Because, unnoticed by us, our eyes are always moving. This continual flitting from one spot to another ensures that stimulation on the eyes' receptors continually changes (**FIGURE 17.4**).

What if we actually could stop our eyes from moving? Would sights seem to vanish, as odors do? To find out, psychologists have devised ingenious instruments that maintain a constant image on the eye's inner surface. Imagine that we have fitted a volunteer, Mary, with one of these instruments—a miniature projector mounted on a contact lens (**FIGURE 17.5a**). When Mary's eye moves, the image from the projector moves as well. So everywhere that Mary looks, the scene is sure to go.

If we project images through this instrument, what will Mary see? At first, she will see the complete image. But within a few seconds, as her sensory system begins to fatigue, things get weird. Bit by bit, the image vanishes, only to reappear and then disappear—often in fragments (Figure 17.5b).

Although sensory adaptation reduces our sensitivity, it offers an important benefit: freedom to focus on *informative* changes in our environment without being distracted by background chatter. Stinky or heavily perfumed people don't notice their odor because, like you and me, they adapt to what's constant and detect only change. Our sensory receptors are alert to novelty; bore them with repetition and they free our attention for more important things. We will see this principle again and again: *We perceive the world not exactly as it is, but as it is useful for us to perceive it.*

Our sensitivity to changing stimulation helps explain television's attention-grabbing power. Cuts, edits, zooms, pans, sudden noises—all demand attention. The phenomenon is irresistible

FIGURE 17.4
The jumpy eye Our gaze jumps from one spot to another every third of a second or so, as eye-tracking equipment illustrated in this photograph of Edinburgh's Princes Street Gardens (Henderson, 2007). The circles represent fixations, and the numbers indicate the time of fixation in milliseconds (300 milliseconds = three-tenths of a second).

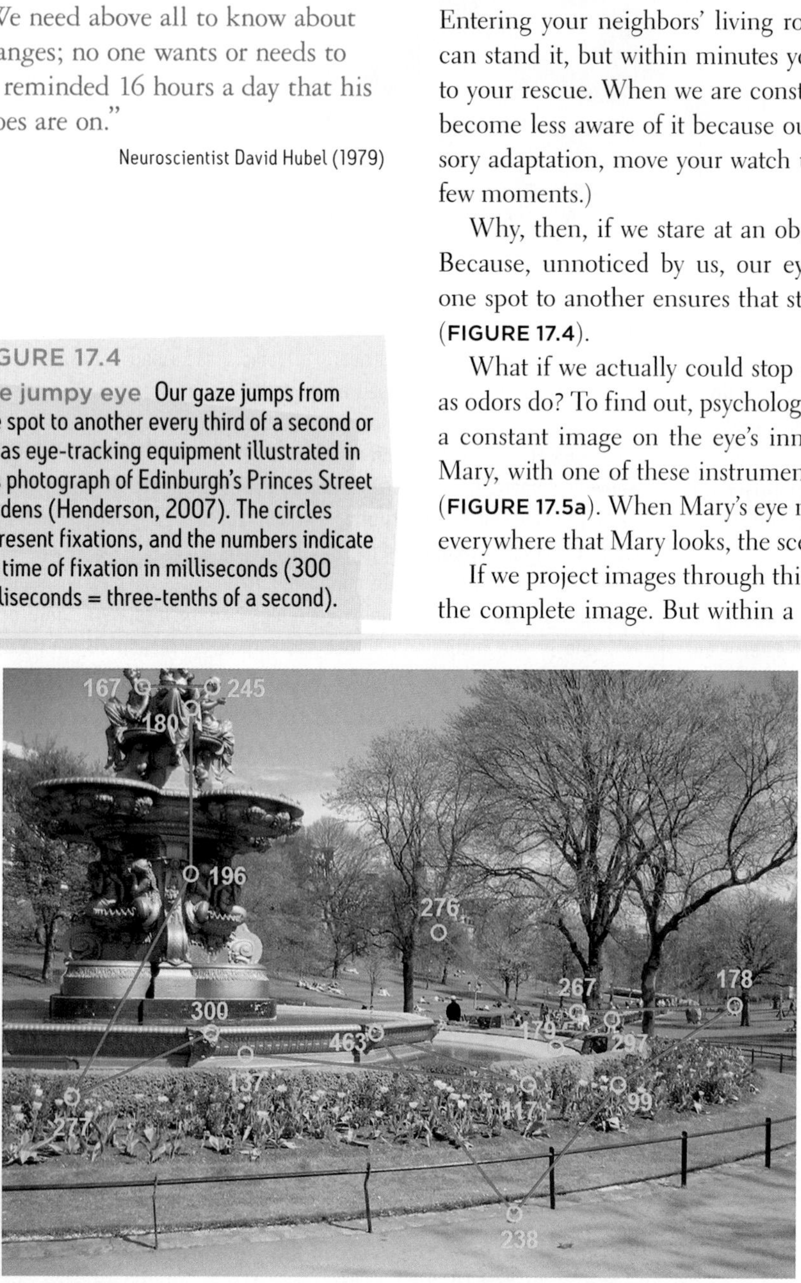

John M. Henderson

Two physical characteristics of light help determine our sensory experience of them. Light's **wavelength**—the distance from one wave peak to the next (FIGURE 18.2a)—determines its **hue** (the color we experience, such as the tulip's red petals or green leaves). **Intensity,** the amount of energy in light waves (determined by a wave's *amplitude,* or height), influences brightness (Figure 18.2b). To understand *how* we transform physical energy into color and meaning, we first need to understand vision's window, the eye.

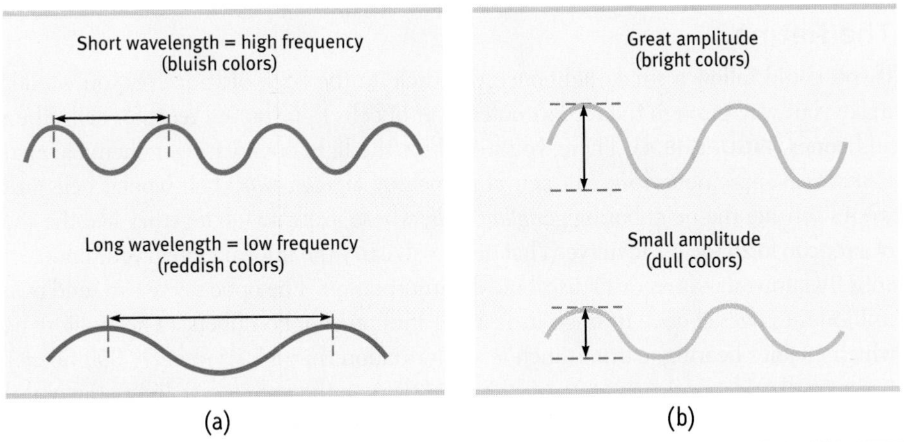

FIGURE 18.2
The physical properties of waves (a) Waves vary in wavelength (the distance between successive peaks). Frequency, the number of complete wavelengths that can pass a point in a given time, depends on the wavelength. The shorter the wavelength, the higher the frequency. (b) Waves also vary in amplitude (the height from peak to trough). Wave amplitude determines the intensity of colors.

The Eye

Light enters the eye through the *cornea,* which protects the eye and bends light to provide focus (FIGURE 18.3). The light then passes through the **pupil,** a small adjustable opening. Surrounding the pupil and controlling its size is the **iris,** a colored muscle that dilates or constricts in response to light intensity and even to inner emotions. (When we're feeling amorous, our telltale dilated pupils and dark eyes subtly signal our interest.) Each iris is so distinctive that an iris-scanning machine can confirm your identity.

Behind the pupil is a **lens** that focuses incoming light rays into an image on the **retina,** a multilayered tissue on the eyeball's sensitive inner surface. The lens focuses the rays by changing its curvature in a process called **accommodation.**

For centuries, scientists knew that when an image of a candle passes through a small opening, it casts an inverted mirror image on a dark wall behind. If the retina receives this sort of upside-down image, as in Figure 18.3, how can we see the world right side up? The ever-curious Leonardo da Vinci had an idea: Perhaps the eye's watery fluids bend the light rays, reinverting the image to the upright position as

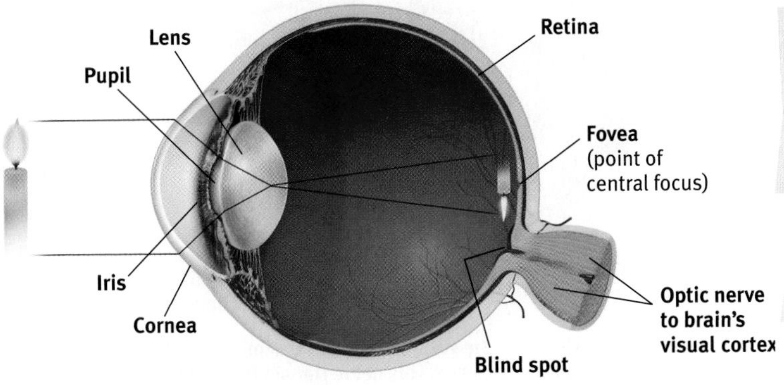

FIGURE 18.3
The eye Light rays reflected from a candle pass through the cornea, pupil, and lens. The curvature and thickness of the lens change to bring nearby or distant objects into focus on the retina. Rays from the top of the candle strike the bottom of the retina, and those from the left side of the candle strike the right side of the retina. The candle's image on the retina thus appears upside-down and reversed.

rods retinal receptors that detect black, white, and gray; necessary for peripheral and twilight vision, when cones don't respond.

cones retinal receptor cells that are concentrated near the center of the retina and that function in daylight or in well-lit conditions. The cones detect fine detail and give rise to color sensations.

optic nerve the nerve that carries neural impulses from the eye to the brain.

blind spot the point at which the optic nerve leaves the eye, creating a "blind" spot because no receptor cells are located there.

fovea the central focal point in the retina, around which the eye's cones cluster.

it reaches the retina. But then in 1604, the astronomer and optics expert Johannes Kepler showed that the retina does receive upside-down images of the world (Crombie, 1964). And how could we understand such a world? "I leave it," said the befuddled Kepler, "to natural philosophers."

Eventually, the answer became clear: The retina doesn't "see" a whole image. Rather, its millions of receptor cells convert particles of light energy into neural impulses and forward those to the brain. *There,* the impulses are reassembled into a perceived, upright--seeming image.

The Retina

If you could follow a single light-energy particle to the back of your eye, you would first make your way through the retina's outer layer of cells to its buried receptor cells, the **rods** and **cones** (**FIGURE 18.4**). There, you would see the light energy trigger chemical changes that would spark neural signals, activating nearby *bipolar cells.* The bipolar cells in turn would activate the neighboring *ganglion cells,* whose axons twine together like the strands of a rope to form the **optic nerve.** That nerve will carry the information to your brain, where your thalamus stands ready to distribute the information. The optic nerve can send nearly 1 million messages at once through its nearly 1 million ganglion fibers. (The auditory nerve, which enables hearing, carries much less information through its mere 30,000 fibers.) We pay a small price for this eye-to-brain highway. Where the optic nerve leaves the eye, there are no receptor cells—creating a **blind spot** (**FIGURE 18.5**). Close one eye and you won't see a black hole, however. Without seeking your approval, your brain fills in the hole.

Experiments are under way to restore vision for those with blindness, using a bionic retina (a 2-millimeter-diameter microchip with photoreceptors that stimulate damaged retinal cells), and with a video camera and computer that stimulate the visual cortex. In test trials, both devices have enabled blind people to gain partial sight (Boahen, 2005; Steenhuysen, 2002).

Rods and cones differ in where they're found and in what they do (**TABLE 18.1**). *Cones* cluster in and around the **fovea,** the retina's area of central focus (see Figure 18.3). Many have their own hotline to the brain: Each one transmits to a single bipolar cell that helps relay the cone's individual message to the visual cortex, which devotes a large area to input from the fovea. These direct connections preserve the cones' precise information, making them better able to detect fine detail.

Rods have no such hotline; they share bipolar cells with other rods, sending combined messages. To experience this rod-cone difference in sensitivity to details, pick a word in

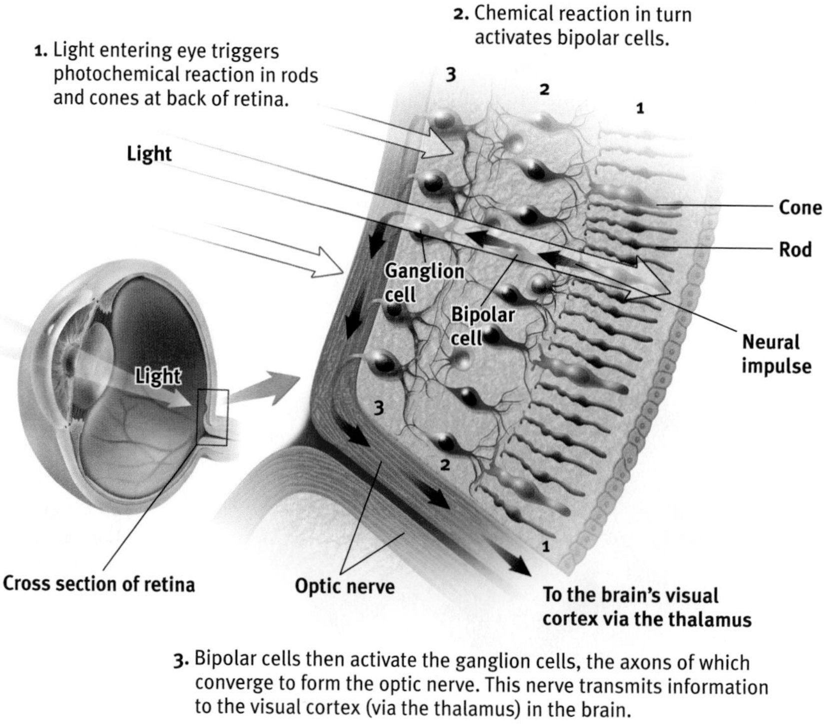

FIGURE 18.4
The retina's reaction to light

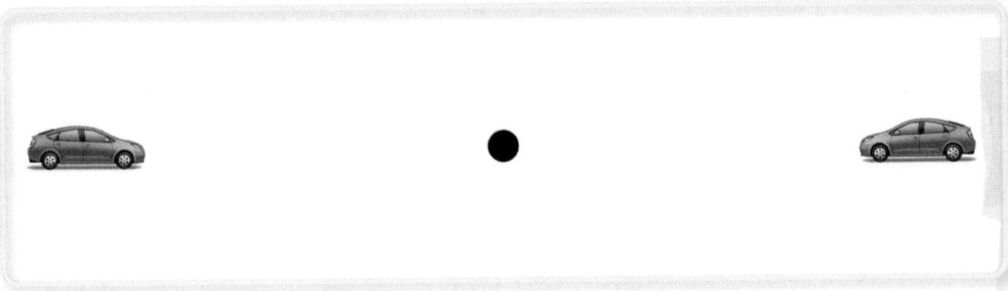

RETRIEVAL PRACTICE

FIGURE 18.5

The blind spot There are no receptor cells where the optic nerve leaves the eye (see Figure 18.4). This creates a blind spot in your vision. To demonstrate, first close your left eye, look at the spot, and move the page to a distance from your face at which one of the cars disappears (which one do you predict it will be?). Repeat with the other eye closed—and note that now the other car disappears. Can you explain why?

ANSWER: The blind spot does not normally impair your vision, because your eyes are moving and because one eye catches what the other misses. Your blind spot is on the nose side of each retina, which means that objects to your right may fall onto the right eye's blind spot. Objects to your left may fall on the left eye's blind spot.

this sentence and stare directly at it, focusing its image on the cones in your fovea. Notice that words a few inches off to the side appear blurred? Their image strikes the outer regions of your retina, where rods predominate. Thus, when driving or biking, you can detect a car in your peripheral vision well before perceiving its details.

Cones also enable you to perceive color. In dim light they become ineffectual, so you see no colors. Rods, which enable black-and-white vision, remain sensitive in dim light. Several rods will funnel their faint energy output onto a single bipolar cell. Thus, cones and rods each provide a special sensitivity—cones to detail and color, and rods to faint light.

TABLE 18.1

Receptors in the Human Eye: Rod-Shaped Rods and Cone-Shaped Cones

	Cones	Rods
Number	6 million	120 million
Location in retina	Center	Periphery
Sensitivity in dim light	Low	High
Color sensitivity	High	Low
Detail sensitivity	High	Low

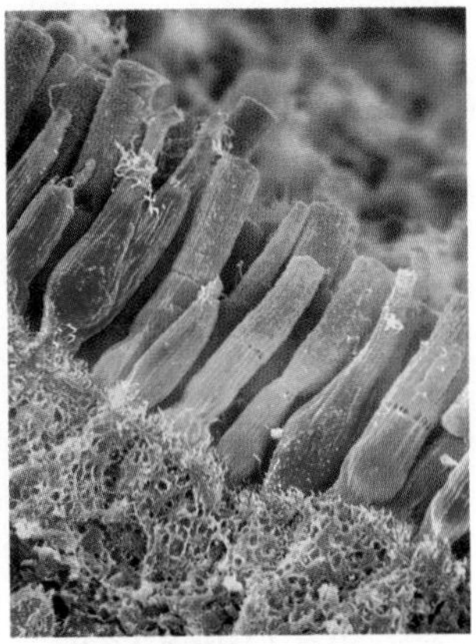

Omikron/Photo Researchers, Inc.

When you enter a darkened theater or turn off the light at night, your eyes adapt. Your pupils dilate to allow more light to reach your retina, but it typically takes 20 minutes or more before your eyes fully adapt. You can demonstrate dark adaptation by closing or covering one eye for up to 20 minutes. Then make the light in the room not quite bright enough to read this book with your open eye. Now open the dark-adapted eye and read (easily). This period of dark adaptation matches the average natural twilight transition between the Sun's setting and darkness. How wonderfully made we are.

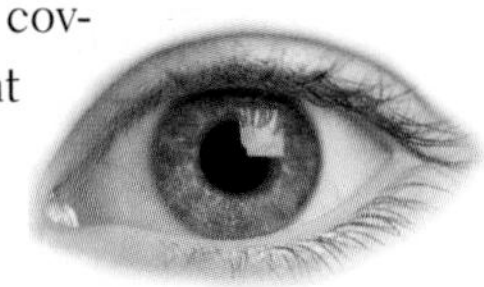

Andrey Armyagov/Shutterstock

RETRIEVAL PRACTICE

- Some nocturnal animals, such as toads, mice, rats, and bats, have impressive night vision thanks to having many more ___________ (rods/cones) than ___________ (rods/cones) in their retinas. These creatures probably have very poor ___________ (color/black and white) vision.

ANSWERS: rods; cones; color

- Cats are also able to open their ___________ much wider than we can, which allows more light into their eyes so they can see better at night.

ANSWER: pupils

Visual Information Processing

18-2 How do the eye and the brain process visual information?

Visual information percolates through progressively more abstract levels on its path through the thalamus and on to the visual cortex. At the entry level, information processing begins in the retina's neural layers, which are actually brain tissue that migrated to the eye during early fetal development. These layers don't just pass along electrical impulses; they also help to encode and analyze sensory information. The third neural layer in a frog's eye, for example, contains "bug detector" cells that fire only in response to moving fly-like stimuli.

After processing by your retina's nearly 130 million receptor rods and cones, information travels to your bipolar cells, then to your million or so ganglion cells, and through their axons making up the optic nerve to your brain. Any given retinal area relays its information to a corresponding location in the visual cortex, in the occipital lobe at the back of your brain (**FIGURE 18.6**).

FIGURE 18.6

Pathway from the eyes to the visual cortex Ganglion axons forming the optic nerve run to the thalamus, where they synapse with neurons that run to the visual cortex.

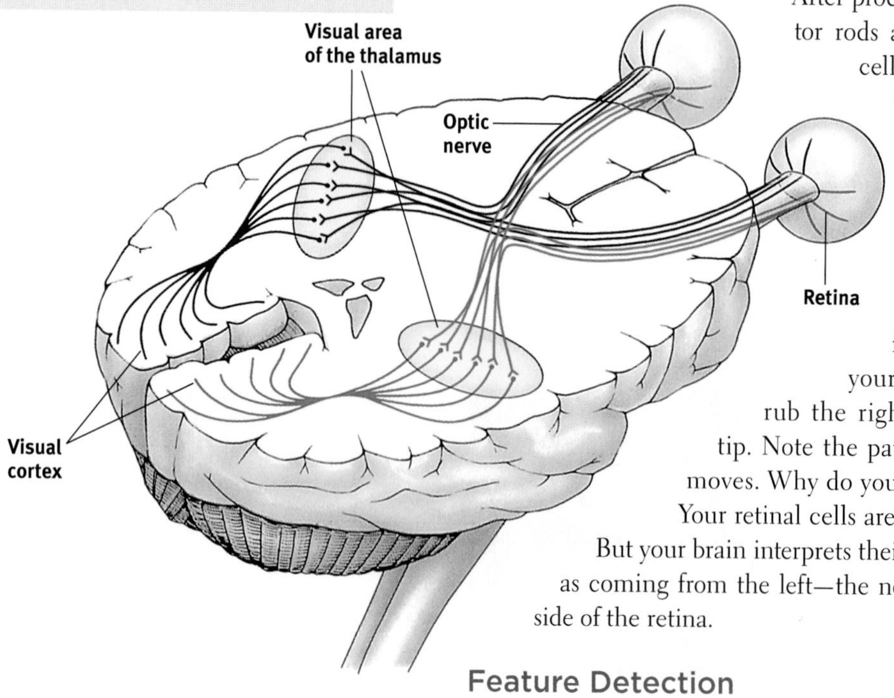

The same sensitivity that enables retinal cells to fire messages can lead them to misfire, as you can demonstrate for yourself. Turn your eyes to the left, close them, and then gently rub the right side of your right eyelid with your fingertip. Note the patch of light to the left, moving as your finger moves. Why do you see light? Why at the left?

Your retinal cells are so responsive that even pressure triggers them. But your brain interprets their firing as light. Moreover, it interprets the light as coming from the left—the normal direction of light that activates the right side of the retina.

Feature Detection

David Hubel and Torsten Wiesel (1979) received a Nobel Prize for their work on **feature detectors.** These specialized neurons in the occipital lobe's visual cortex receive information from individual ganglion cells in the retina. Feature detector cells derive their name from their ability to respond to a scene's specific features—to particular edges, lines, angles, and movements. These cells pass this information to other cortical areas, where teams of cells *(supercell clusters)* respond to more complex patterns. One temporal lobe area by your right ear (**FIGURE 18.7**) enables you to perceive faces and, thanks to a specialized neural network, to recognize them from varied viewpoints (Connor, 2010). If this region were

feature detectors nerve cells in the brain that respond to specific features of the stimulus, such as shape, angle, or movement.

parallel processing the processing of many aspects of a problem simultaneously; the brain's natural mode of information processing for many functions, including vision. Contrasts with the step-by-step (serial) processing of most computers and of conscious problem solving.

FIGURE 18.7

Face recognition processing In social animals such as humans, a dedicated brain system (shown here in a right-facing brain) assigns considerable neural bandwidth to the crucial task of face recognition.

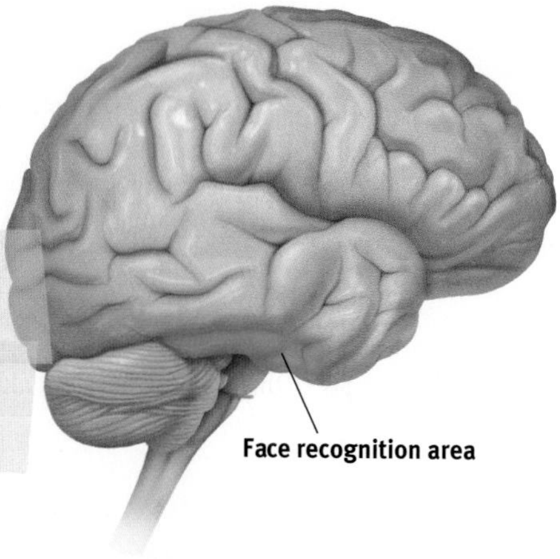

damaged, you might recognize other forms and objects, but not familiar faces. When researchers temporarily disrupt the brain's face-processing areas with magnetic pulses, people are unable to recognize faces.

They will, however, be able to recognize houses, because the brain's face-perception occurs separately from its object-perception (McKone et al., 2007; Pitcher et al., 2007). Thus, functional MRI (fMRI) scans show different brain areas lighting up when people view varied objects (Downing et al., 2001). Brain activity is so specific (**FIGURE 18.8**) that, with the help of brain scans, "we can tell if a person is looking at a shoe, a chair, or a face, based on the pattern of their brain activity," noted one researcher (Haxby, 2001).

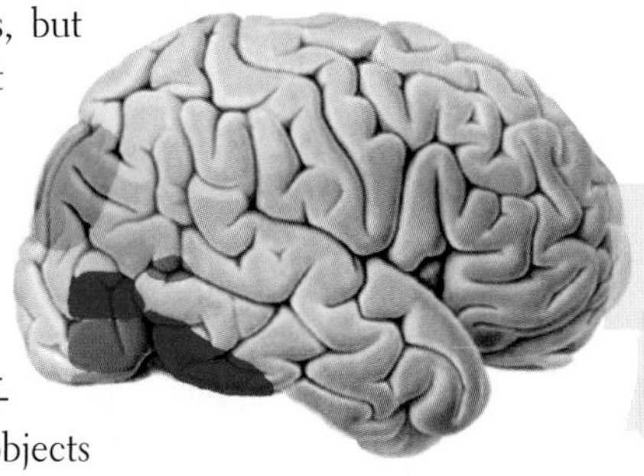

Faces | Chairs | Houses | Houses and chairs

FIGURE 18.8
The telltale brain Looking at faces, houses, and chairs activates different brain areas in this right-facing brain.

Research shows that for biologically important objects and events, monkey brains (and surely ours as well) have a "vast visual encyclopedia" distributed as specialized cells (Perrett et al., 1988, 1992, 1994). These cells respond to one type of stimulus, such as a specific gaze, head angle, posture, or body movement. Other supercell clusters integrate this information and fire only when the cues collectively indicate the direction of someone's attention and approach. This instant analysis, which aided our ancestors' survival, also helps a soccer goalkeeper anticipate the direction of an impending kick, and a driver anticipate a pedestrian's next movement.

Reuters/Claro Cortes IV (China)

Well-developed supercells In this 2007 World Cup match, Brazil's Marta instantly processed visual information about the positions and movements of Australia's defenders and goalkeeper (Melissa Barbieri) and somehow managed to get the ball around them all and into the net.

Parallel Processing

Our brain achieves these and other remarkable feats by means of **parallel processing:** doing many things at once. To analyze a visual scene, the brain divides it into subdimensions—color, motion, form, depth—and works on each aspect simultaneously (Livingstone & Hubel, 1988). We then construct our perceptions by integrating the separate but parallel work of these different visual teams (**FIGURE 18.9**).

FIGURE 18.9
Parallel processing Studies of patients with brain damage suggest that the brain delegates the work of processing color, motion, form, and depth to different areas. After taking a scene apart, the brain integrates these subdimensions into the perceived image. How does the brain do this? The answer to this question is the Holy Grail of vision research.

To recognize a face, your brain integrates information projected by your retinas to several visual cortex areas, compares it to stored information, and enables you to recognize the face: *Grandmother!* Scientists are debating whether this stored information is contained in a single cell or distributed over a network. Some supercells—"grandmother cells"—do appear to respond very selectively to 1 or 2 faces in 100 (Bowers, 2009). The whole facial recognition process requires tremendous brain power—30 percent of the cortex (10 times the brain area devoted to hearing).

Destroy or disable a neural workstation for a visual subtask, and something peculiar results, as happened to "Mrs. M." (Hoffman, 1998). Since a stroke damaged areas near the rear of both sides of her brain, she has been unable to perceive movement. People in a room seem "suddenly here or there but I have not seen them moving." Pouring tea into a cup is a challenge because the fluid appears frozen—she cannot perceive it rising in the cup.

After stroke or surgery damage to the brain's visual cortex, others have experienced *blindsight*. Shown a series of sticks, they report seeing nothing. Yet when asked to guess whether the sticks are vertical or horizontal, their visual intuition typically offers the correct response. When told, "You got them all right," they are astounded. There is, it seems, a second "mind"—a parallel processing system—operating unseen. These separate visual systems for perception and action illustrate dual processing—the two-track mind.

* * *

Think about the wonders of visual processing. As you look at that tiger in the zoo, information enters your eyes, is transduced, and is sent to your brain as millions of neural impulses. As your brain buzzes with activity, various areas focus on different aspects of the tiger's image. Finally, in some as yet mysterious way, these separate teams pool their work to produce a meaningful image, which you compare with previously stored images and recognize: a crouching tiger (**FIGURE 18.10**).

Think, too, about what is happening as you read this page. The printed squiggles are transmitted by reflected light rays onto your retina, which triggers a process that sends formless nerve impulses to several areas of your brain, which integrates the information and decodes meaning, thus completing the transfer of information across time and space from my mind to your mind. That all of this happens instantly, effortlessly, and continuously is indeed awesome. As Roger Sperry (1985) observed, the "insights of science give added, not lessened, reasons for awe, respect, and reverence."

"I am . . . wonderfully made."
King David, Psalm 139:14

FIGURE 18.10
A simplified summary of visual information processing

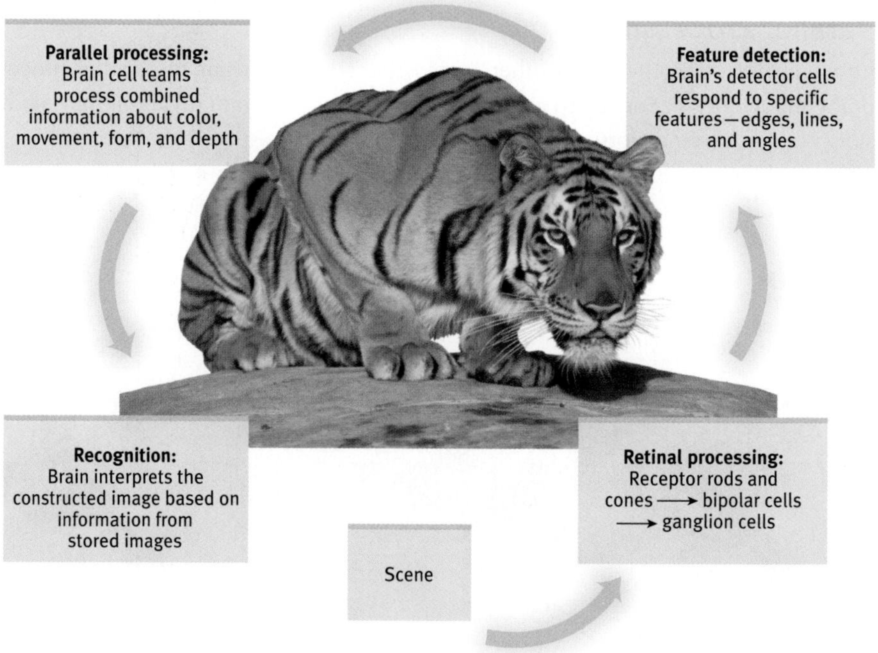

RETRIEVAL PRACTICE

- What is the rapid sequence of events that occurs when you see and recognize a friend?

ANSWER: Light waves reflect off the person and travel into your eye, where the receptor cells in your retina convert the light waves' energy into neural impulses sent to your brain. Your brain processes the subdimensions of this visual input—including color, depth, movement, and form—separately but simultaneously. It interprets this information based on previously stored information and your expectations into a conscious perception of your friend.

Young-Helmholtz trichromatic (three-color) theory the theory that the retina contains three different color receptors—one most sensitive to red, one to green, one to blue—which, when stimulated in combination, can produce the perception of any color.

Color Vision

18-3 What theories help us understand color vision?

We talk as though objects possess color: "A tomato is red." Perhaps you have pondered the old question, "If a tree falls in the forest and no one hears it, does it make a sound?" We can ask the same of color: If no one sees the tomato, is it red?

The answer is No. First, the tomato is everything *but* red, because it *rejects* (reflects) the long wavelengths of red. Second, the tomato's color is our mental construction. As Isaac Newton (1704) noted, "The [light] rays are not colored." Color, like all aspects of vision, resides not in the object but in the theater of our brains, as evidenced by our dreaming in color.

One of vision's most basic and intriguing mysteries is how we see the world in color. How, from the light energy striking the retina, does the brain manufacture our experience of color—and of such a multitude of colors? Our difference threshold for colors is so low that we can discriminate more than 1 million different color variations (Neitz et al., 2001). At least most of us can. For about 1 person in 50, vision is color deficient—and that person is usually male, because the defect is genetically sex linked.

"Only mind has sight and hearing; all things else are deaf and blind."
Epicharmus, *Fragments,* 550 B.C.E.

Why is some people's vision deficient? To answer that question, we need to understand how normal color vision works. Modern detective work on this mystery began in the nineteenth century, when Hermann von Helmholtz built on the insights of an English physicist, Thomas Young. Knowing that any color can be created by combining the light waves of three primary colors—red, green, and blue—Young and von Helmholtz inferred that the eye must have three corresponding types of color receptors. Years later, researchers measured the response of various cones to different color stimuli and confirmed the **Young-Helmholtz trichromatic (three-color) theory,** which implies that the receptors do their color magic in teams of three. Indeed, the retina has three types of color receptors, each especially sensitive to one of three colors. And those colors are, in fact, red, green, and blue. When we stimulate combinations of these cones, we see other colors. For example, there are no receptors especially sensitive to yellow. We see yellow when mixing red and green light, which stimulates both red-sensitive and green-sensitive cones.

Most people with color-deficient vision are not actually "colorblind." They simply lack functioning red- or green-sensitive cones, or sometimes both. Their vision—perhaps unknown to them, because their lifelong vision *seems* normal—is monochromatic (one-color) or dichromatic (two-color) instead of trichromatic, making it impossible to distinguish the red and green in **FIGURE 18.11** (Boynton, 1979). Dogs, too, lack receptors for the wavelengths of red, giving them only limited, dichromatic color vision (Neitz et al., 1989).

But how is it that people blind to red and green can often still see yellow? And why does yellow appear to be a pure color and not a mixture of red and green, the way purple is of red and blue? As Ewald Hering soon noted, trichromatic theory leaves some parts of the color vision mystery unsolved.

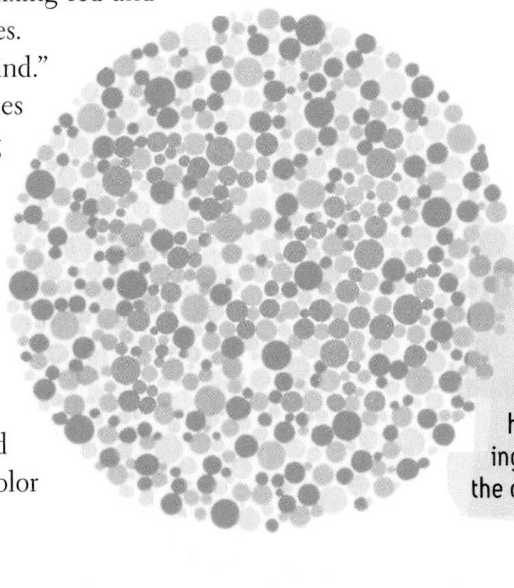

FIGURE 18.11 Color-deficient vision People who suffer red-green deficiency have trouble perceiving the number within the design.

FIGURE 18.12
Afterimage effect Stare at the center of the flag for a minute and then shift your eyes to the dot in the white space beside it. What do you see? (After tiring your neural response to black, green, and yellow, you should see their opponent colors.) Stare at a white wall and note how the size of the flag grows with the projection distance!

Hering, a physiologist, found a clue in *afterimages*. Stare at a green square for a while and then look at a white sheet of paper, and you will see red, green's *opponent color*. Stare at a yellow square and its opponent color, blue, will appear on the white paper. (To experience this, try the flag demonstration in **FIGURE 18.12**.) Hering surmised that there must be two additional color processes, one responsible for red-versus-green perception, and one for blue-versus-yellow.

Indeed, a century later, researchers also confirmed Hering's **opponent-process theory.** Three sets of opponent retinal processes—*red-green*, *yellow-blue*, and *white-black*—enable color vision. In the retina and in the thalamus (where impulses from the retina are relayed en route to the visual cortex), some neurons are turned "on" by red but turned "off" by green. Others are turned on by green but off by red (DeValois & DeValois, 1975). Like red and green marbles sent down a narrow tube, "red" and "green" messages cannot both travel at once. So we do not experience a reddish green. (Red and green are thus opponents.) But red and blue travel in separate channels, so we *can* see a reddish-blue magenta.

So how do we explain afterimages, such as in the flag demonstration? By staring at green, we tire our green response. When we then stare at white (which contains all colors, including red), only the red part of the green-red pairing will fire normally.

The present solution to the mystery of color vision is therefore roughly this: Color processing occurs in two stages. The retina's red, green, and blue cones respond in varying degrees to different color stimuli, as the Young-Helmholtz trichromatic theory suggested. Their signals are then processed by the nervous system's opponent-process cells, as Hering's theory proposed.

RETRIEVAL PRACTICE

- What are two key theories of color vision? Are they contradictory or complementary? Explain.

ANSWER: The *Young-Helmholtz trichromatic theory* shows that the retina contains color receptors for red, green, and blue. The *opponent-process theory* shows that we have opponent-process cells in the retina for red-green, yellow-blue, and white-black. These theories are complementary and outline the two stages of color vision: (1) The retina's receptors for red, green, and blue respond to different color stimuli. (2) The receptors' signals are then processed by the opponent-process cells on their way to the visual cortex in the brain.

Visual Organization

18-4 How did the Gestalt psychologists understand perceptual organization, and how do figure-ground and grouping principles contribute to our perceptions?

It's one thing to understand how we see shapes and colors. But how do we organize and interpret those sights (or sounds or tastes or smells) so that they become meaningful perceptions—a rose in bloom, a familiar face, a sunset?

Early in the twentieth century, a group of German psychologists noticed that when given a cluster of sensations, people tend to organize them into a **gestalt,** a German word meaning a "form" or a "whole." For example, look at **FIGURE 18.13**. Note that the individual elements of this figure, called a *Necker cube*, are really nothing but eight blue circles, each containing three converging white lines. When we view these elements all together, however, we see a cube that sometimes reverses direction. This phenomenon nicely illustrates a favorite saying of Gestalt psychologists: In perception, the whole may exceed the sum of its parts. If we combine sodium (a corrosive metal) with chlorine (a poisonous gas), something very different emerges—table salt. Likewise, a unique perceived form emerges from a stimulus' components (Rock & Palmer, 1990).

Over the years, the Gestalt psychologists demonstrated many principles we use to organize our sensations into perceptions. Underlying all of them is a fundamental truth: *Our brain does more than register information about the world.* Perception is not just opening a shutter and letting a picture print itself on the brain. We filter incoming information and construct perceptions. Mind matters.

FIGURE 18.13

A Necker cube What do you see: circles with white lines, or a cube? If you stare at the cube, you may notice that it reverses location, moving the tiny X in the center from the front edge to the back. At times, the cube may seem to float in front of the page, with circles behind it. At other times, the circles may become holes in the page through which the cube appears, as though it were floating behind the page. There is far more to perception than meets the eye. (From Bradley et al., 1976.)

Form Perception

Imagine designing a video-computer system that, like your eye-brain system, can recognize faces at a glance. What abilities would it need?

Figure and Ground

To start with, the video-computer system would need to separate faces from their backgrounds. Likewise, in our eye-brain system, our first perceptual task is to perceive any object (the *figure*) as distinct from its surroundings (the *ground*). Among the voices you hear at a party, the one you attend to becomes the figure; all others are part of the ground. As you read, the words are the figure; the white paper is the ground. Sometimes the same stimulus can trigger more than one perception. In FIGURE 18.14, the **figure-ground** relationship continually reverses—but always we organize the stimulus into a figure seen against a ground.

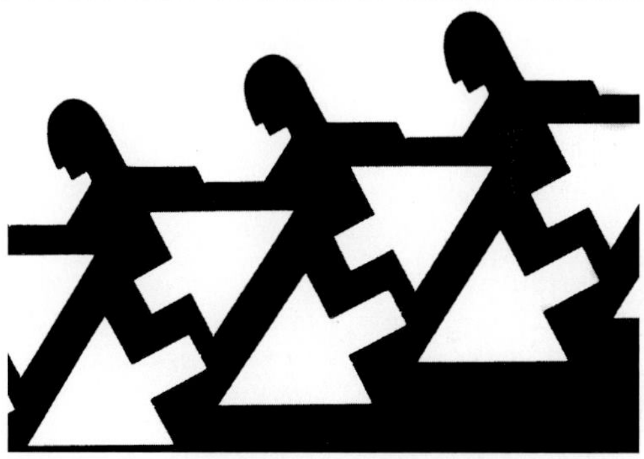

Time Saving Suggestion, © 2003 Roger N. Shepard.

FIGURE 18.14

Reversible figure and ground

Grouping

Having discriminated figure from ground, we (and our video-computer system) must also organize the figure into a *meaningful* form. Some basic features of a scene—such as color, movement, and light-dark contrast—we process instantly and automatically (Treisman, 1987). Our minds bring order and form to stimuli by following certain rules for **grouping**. These rules, identified by the Gestalt psychologists and applied even by infants, illustrate how the perceived whole differs from the sum of its parts (Quinn et al., 2002; Rock & Palmer, 1990). Three examples:

Proximity We group nearby figures together. We see not six separate lines, but three sets of two lines.

Continuity We perceive smooth, continuous patterns rather than discontinuous ones. This pattern could be a series of alternating semicircles, but we perceive it as two continuous lines—one wavy, one straight.

Closure We fill in gaps to create a complete, whole object. Thus we assume that the circles on the left are complete but partially blocked by the (illusory) triangle. Add nothing more than little line segments to close off the circles and your brain stops constructing a triangle.

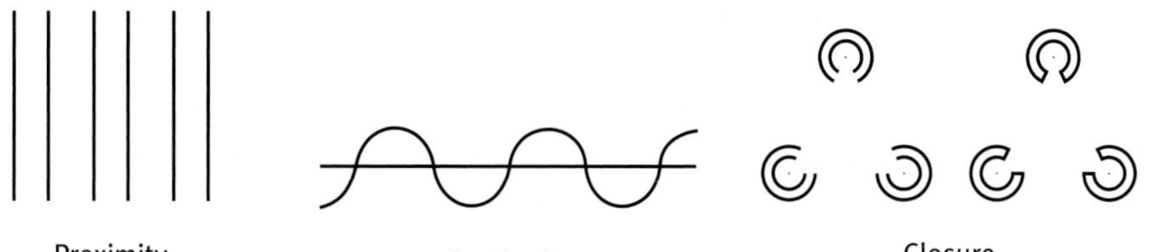

opponent-process theory the theory that opposing retinal processes (red-green, yellow-blue, white-black) enable color vision. For example, some cells are stimulated by green and inhibited by red; others are stimulated by red and inhibited by green.

gestalt an organized whole. Gestalt psychologists emphasized our tendency to integrate pieces of information into meaningful wholes.

figure-ground the organization of the visual field into objects (the *figures*) that stand out from their surroundings (the *ground*).

grouping the perceptual tendency to organize stimuli into coherent groups.

Photo by Walter Wick. Reprinted from *GAMES* Magazine. © 1983 PCS Games Limited Partnership.

FIGURE 18.15
Grouping principles What's the secret to this impossible doghouse? You probably perceive this doghouse as a gestalt—a whole (though impossible) structure. Actually, your brain imposes this sense of wholeness on the picture. As Figure 18.19 shows, Gestalt grouping principles such as closure and continuity are at work here.

Such principles usually help us construct reality. Sometimes, however, they lead us astray, as when we look at the doghouse in **FIGURE 18.15.**

RETRIEVAL PRACTICE

- In terms of perception, a band's lead singer would be considered __________ (figure/ground), and the other musicians would be considered __________ (figure/ground).

ANSWERS: figure; ground

- What do we mean when we say that, in perception, "the whole is greater than the sum of its parts"?

ANSWER: Gestalt psychologists used this saying to describe our perceptual tendency to organize clusters of sensations into meaningful forms or coherent groups.

Depth Perception

18-5 How do we use binocular and monocular cues to perceive the world in three dimensions and perceive motion?

From the two-dimensional images falling on our retinas, we somehow organize three-dimensional perceptions. **Depth perception** enables us to estimate an object's distance from us. At a glance, we can estimate the distance of an oncoming car or the height of a house. Depth perception is partly innate, as Eleanor Gibson and Richard Walk (1960) discovered using a model of a cliff with a drop-off area (which was covered by sturdy glass). Gibson's inspiration for these **visual cliff** experiments occurred while she was picnicking on the rim of the Grand Canyon. She wondered: Would a toddler peering over the rim perceive the dangerous drop-off and draw back?

Back in their Cornell University laboratory, Gibson and Walk placed 6- to 14-month-old infants on the edge of a safe canyon and had the infants' mothers coax them to crawl out onto the glass (**FIGURE 18.16**). Most infants refused to do so, indicating that they could perceive depth.

Had they *learned* to perceive depth? Learning seems to be part of the answer because crawling, no matter when it begins, seems to increase infants' wariness of heights (Campos et al., 1992). Yet, the researchers observed, mobile newborn animals come prepared to perceive depth. Even those with virtually no visual experience—including young kittens, a day-old

depth perception the ability to see objects in three dimensions although the images that strike the retina are two-dimensional; allows us to judge distance.

visual cliff a laboratory device for testing depth perception in infants and young animals.

FIGURE 18.16
Visual cliff Eleanor Gibson and Richard Walk devised this miniature cliff with a glass-covered drop-off to determine whether crawling infants and newborn animals can perceive depth. Even when coaxed, infants are reluctant to venture onto the glass over the cliff.

goat, and newly hatched chicks—will not venture across the visual cliff. Thus, it seems that biological maturation predisposes us to be wary of heights and experience amplifies that fear.

How do we do it? *How* do we transform two differing two-dimensional retinal images into a single three-dimensional perception? Our brain constructs these perceptions using information supplied by one or both eyes.

Binocular Cues

Try this: With both eyes open, hold two pens or pencils in front of you and touch their tips together. Now do so with one eye closed. With one eye, the task becomes noticeably more difficult, demonstrating the importance of **binocular cues** in judging the distance of nearby objects. Two eyes are better than one.

Because your eyes are about 2½ inches apart, your retinas receive slightly different images of the world. By comparing these two images, your brain can judge how close an object is to you. The greater the **retinal disparity,** or difference between the two images, the closer the object. Try it. Hold your two index fingers, with the tips about half an inch apart, directly in front of your nose, and your retinas will receive quite different views. If you close one eye and then the other, you can see the difference. (You may also create a finger sausage, as in FIGURE 18.17.) At a greater distance—say, when you hold your fingers at arm's length—the disparity is smaller.

We could easily build this feature into our video-computer system. Moviemakers can simulate or exaggerate retinal disparity by filming a scene with two cameras placed a few

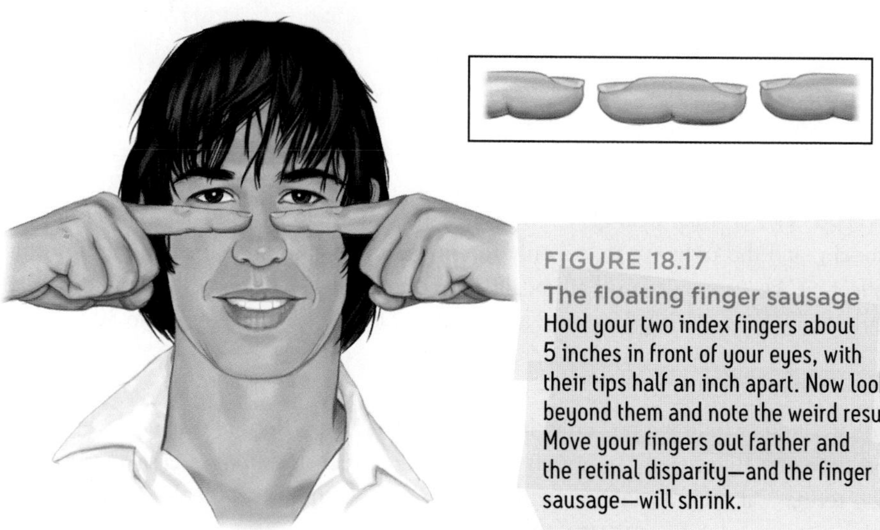

FIGURE 18.17
The floating finger sausage Hold your two index fingers about 5 inches in front of your eyes, with their tips half an inch apart. Now look beyond them and note the weird result. Move your fingers out farther and the retinal disparity—and the finger sausage—will shrink.

binocular cues depth cues, such as retinal disparity, that depend on the use of two eyes.

retinal disparity a binocular cue for perceiving depth: By comparing images from the retinas in the two eyes, the brain computes distance—the greater the disparity (difference) between the two images, the closer the object.

FIGURE 18.18
Monocular depth cues

Image courtesy Shaun P. Vecera, Ph.D., adapted from stimuli that appeared in Vecera et al., 2002

Relative height We perceive objects higher in our field of vision as farther away. Because we assume the lower part of a figure-ground illustration is closer, we perceive it as figure (Vecera et al., 2002). Invert this illustration and the black will become ground, like a night sky.

Relative motion As we move, objects that are actually stable may appear to move. If while riding on a bus you fix your gaze on some point—say, a house—the objects beyond the fixation point will appear to move with you. Objects in front of the point will appear to move backward. The farther an object is from the fixation point, the faster it will seem to move.

Relative size If we assume two objects are similar in size, *most* people perceive the one that casts the smaller retinal image as farther away.

Rene Magritte, *The Blank Signature*, oil on canvas, National Gallery of Art, Washington. Collection of Mr. and Mrs. Paul Mellon. Photo by Richard Carafelli.

Interposition If one object partially blocks our view of another, we perceive it as closer. The depth cues provided by interposition make this an impossible scene.

Linear perspective Parallel lines appear to meet in the distance. The sharper the angle of convergence, the greater the perceived distance.

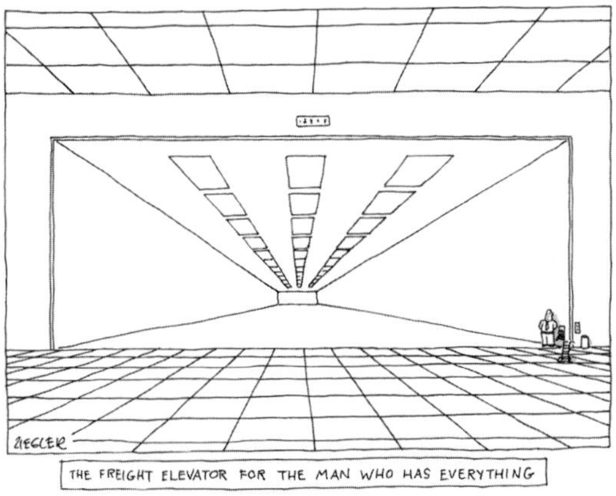

©The New Yorker Collection, 2002, Jack Ziegler from cartoonbank.com. All Rights Reserved.

Light and shadow Shading produces a sense of depth consistent with our assumption that light comes from above. If you invert this illustration, the hollow will become a hill.

From "Perceiving Shape From Shading" by Vilayanur S. Ramachandran. Copyright © 1988 by Scientific American, Inc. All Rights Reserved.

Carnivorous animals, including humans, have eyes that enable forward focus on a prey and offer binocular vision-enhanced depth perception. Grazing herbivores, such as horses and sheep, typically have eyes on the sides of their skull. Although lacking binocular depth perception, they have sweeping peripheral vision.

inches apart. Viewers then wear glasses that allow the left eye to see only the image from the left camera, and the right eye to see only the image from the right camera. The resulting 3-D effect, as *Avatar* movie fans will recall, mimics or exaggerates normal retinal disparity. Similarly, twin cameras in airplanes can take photos of terrain for integration into 3-D maps.

Monocular Cues

How do we judge whether a person is 10 or 100 meters away? Retinal disparity won't help us here, because there won't be much difference between the images cast on our right and left retinas. At such distances, we depend on **monocular cues** (depth cues available to each eye separately). See **FIGURE 18.18** for some examples.

RETRIEVAL PRACTICE

- How do we normally perceive depth?

ANSWER: We are normally able to perceive depth thanks to the binocular cues that are based on our retinal disparity, and monocular cues including relative height, relative size, interposition, linear perspective, light and shadow, and relative motion.

Motion Perception

Imagine that you could perceive the world as having color, form, and depth but that you could not see motion. Not only would you be unable to bike or drive, you would have trouble writing, eating, and walking.

Normally your brain computes motion based partly on its assumption that shrinking objects are retreating (not getting smaller) and enlarging objects are approaching. But you are imperfect at motion perception. Large objects, such as trains, appear to move more slowly than smaller objects, such as cars moving at the same speed. (Perhaps at an airport you've noticed that jumbo jets seem to land more slowly than little jets.)

To catch a fly ball, softball or cricket players (unlike drivers) want to achieve a collision—with the ball that's flying their way. To accomplish that, they follow an unconscious rule—one they can't explain but know intuitively: Run to keep the ball at a constantly increasing angle of gaze (McBeath et al., 1995). A dog catching a Frisbee does the same (Shaffer et al., 2004).

The brain also perceives continuous movement in a rapid series of slightly varying images (a phenomenon called *stroboscopic movement*). As film animation artists know well, you can create this illusion by flashing 24 still pictures a second. The motion we then see in popular action adventures is not in the film, which merely presents a superfast slide show. We construct that motion in our heads, just as we construct movement in blinking marquees and holiday lights. When two adjacent stationary lights blink on and off in quick succession, we perceive a single light moving back and forth between them. Lighted signs exploit this **phi phenomenon** with a succession of lights that creates the impression of, say, a moving arrow.

Perceptual Constancy

18-6 How do perceptual constancies help us organize our sensations into meaningful perceptions?

So far, we have noted that our video-computer system must perceive objects as we do—as having a distinct form, location, and perhaps motion. Its next task is to recognize objects without being deceived by changes in their color, brightness, shape, or size—a top-down process called **perceptual constancy.** Regardless of the viewing angle, distance, and illumination, we can identify people and things in less time than it takes to draw a breath, a feat that challenges even advanced computers and has intrigued researchers for decades. This would be a monumental challenge for a video-computer system.

Color and Brightness Constancies

Color does not reside in an object. Our experience of color depends on the object's *context.* If you view an isolated tomato through a paper tube, its color would seem to change as the light—and thus the wavelengths reflected from its surface—changed. But if you viewed that tomato as one item in a bowl of fresh vegetables, its color would remain roughly constant as the lighting shifts. This perception of consistent color is known as **color constancy.**

Though we take color constancy for granted, this ability is truly remarkable. A blue poker chip under indoor lighting reflects wavelengths that match those reflected by a sunlit gold chip (Jameson, 1985). Yet bring a bluebird indoors and it won't look like a goldfinch.

monocular cues depth cues, such as interposition and linear perspective, available to either eye alone.

phi phenomenon an illusion of movement created when two or more adjacent lights blink on and off in quick succession.

perceptual constancy perceiving objects as unchanging (having consistent shapes, size, brightness, and color) even as illumination and retinal images change.

color constancy perceiving familiar objects as having consistent color, even if changing illumination alters the wavelengths reflected by the object.

"Sometimes I wonder: Why is that Frisbee getting bigger? And then it hits me."

Anonymous

"From there to here, from here to there, funny things are everywhere."

Dr. Seuss, *One Fish, Two Fish, Red Fish, Blue Fish,* 1960

FIGURE 18.19

The solution Another view of the impossible doghouse in Figure 18.15 reveals the secrets of this illusion. From the photo angle in Figure 18.15, the grouping principle of closure leads us to perceive the boards as continuous.

Photo by Walter Wick. Reprinted from GAMES Magazine. © 1983 PCS Games Limited Partnership.

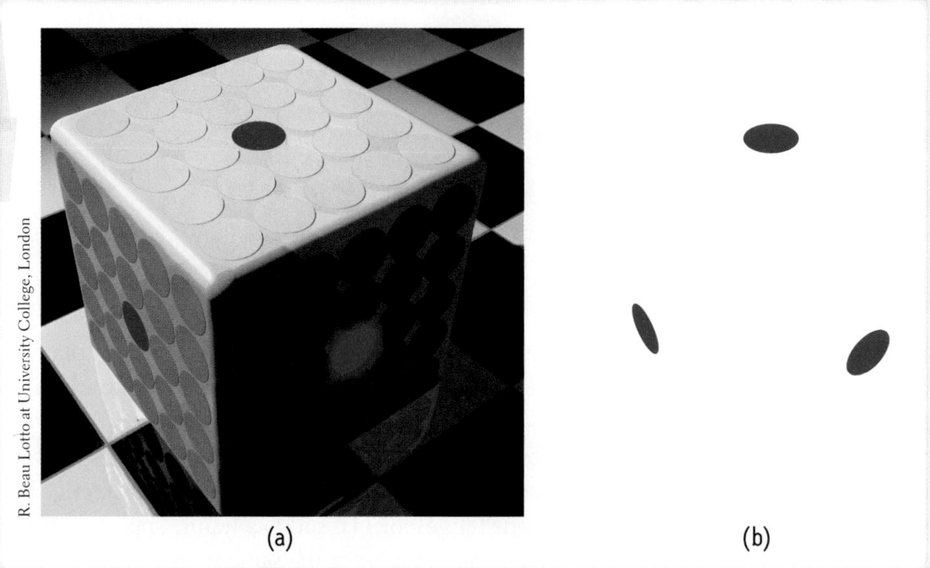

FIGURE 18.20
Color depends on context Believe it or not, these three blue disks are identical in color (a). Remove the surrounding context and see what results (b).

FIGURE 18.21
Relative luminance Squares A and B are identical in color, believe it or not. (If you don't believe me, photocopy the illustration, cut out the squares, and compare.) But we perceive B as lighter, thanks to its surrounding context.

The color is not in the bird's feathers. You and I see color thanks to our brain's computations of the light reflected by an object *relative to the objects surrounding it*. (But only if we grew up with normal light, it seems. Monkeys raised under a restricted range of wavelengths later have great difficulty recognizing the same color when illumination varies [Sugita, 2004].) **FIGURE 18.20** dramatically illustrates the ability of a blue object to appear very different in three different contexts. Yet we have no trouble seeing these disks as blue.

Similarly, *brightness constancy* (also called *lightness constancy*) depends on context. We perceive an object as having a constant brightness even while its illumination varies. This perception of constancy depends on *relative luminance*—the amount of light an object reflects *relative to its surroundings* (**FIGURE 18.21**). White paper reflects 90 percent of the light falling on it; black paper, only 10 percent. Although a black paper viewed in sunlight may reflect 100 times more light than does a white paper viewed indoors, it will still look black (McBurney & Collings, 1984). But if you view sunlit black paper through a narrow tube so nothing else is visible, it may look gray, because in bright sunshine it reflects a fair amount of light. View it without the tube and it is again black, because it reflects much less light than the objects around it.

This principle—that we perceive objects not in isolation but in their environmental context—matters to artists, interior decorators, and clothing designers. Our perception of the color and brightness of a wall or of a streak of paint on a canvas is determined not just by the paint in the can but by the surrounding colors. The take-home lesson: *Comparisons govern our perceptions.*

FIGURE 18.22
Perceiving shape Do the tops of these tables have different dimensions? They appear to. But—believe it or not—they are identical. (Measure and see.) With both tables, we adjust our perceptions relative to our viewing angle.

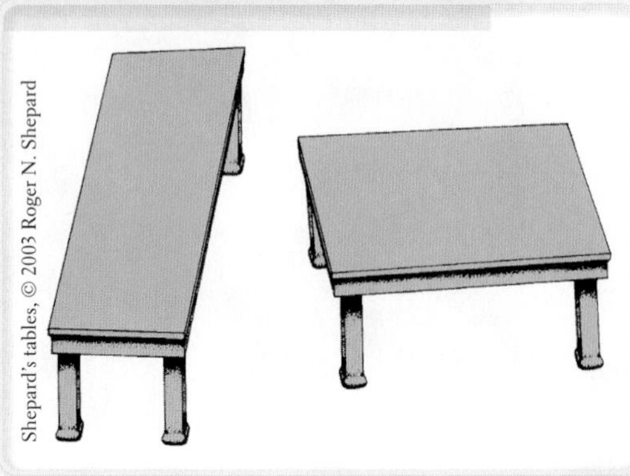

Shape and Size Constancies

Sometimes an object whose actual shape cannot change *seems* to change shape with the angle of our view (**FIGURE 18.22**). More often, thanks to *shape constancy*, we perceive the form of familiar objects, such as the door in **FIGURE 18.23**, as constant even while our retinas receive changing images of them. Our brain manages this feat thanks to visual cortex neurons that rapidly learn to associate different views of an object (Li & DiCarlo, 2008).

Thanks to *size constancy*, we perceive objects as having a constant size, even while our distance from them varies. We assume a car is large enough to carry people, even when we see its tiny image from two blocks away. This assumption also illustrates the close connection between perceived *distance* and perceived *size*. Perceiving an object's distance gives us cues to its size. Likewise, knowing its general size—that the object is a car—provides us with cues to its distance.

Even in size-distance judgments, however, we consider an object's context. This interplay between perceived size and perceived distance helps explain several well-known illusions, including the *Moon illusion:* The Moon looks up to 50 percent larger when near the horizon than when high in the sky. Can you imagine why? For at least 22 centuries, scholars have debated this question (Hershenson, 1989). One reason is that cues to objects' distances make the horizon Moon appear farther away. If it's farther away, our brain assumes, it must be larger than the Moon high in the night sky (Kaufman & Kaufman, 2000). Take away the distance cue, by looking at the horizon Moon through a paper tube, and it will immediately shrink.

FIGURE 18.23
Shape constancy A door casts an increasingly trapezoidal image on our retinas as it opens, yet we still perceive it as rectangular.

Size-distance relationships also explain why in **FIGURE 18.24** the two same-age girls seem so different in size. As the diagram reveals, the girls are actually about the same size, but the room is distorted. Viewed with one eye through a peephole, the room's trapezoidal walls produce the same images you would see in a normal rectangular room viewed with both eyes. Presented with the camera's one-eyed view, your brain makes the reasonable assumption that the room *is* normal and each girl is therefore the same distance from you. Given the different sizes of the girls' images on your retinas, your brain ends up calculating that the girls must be very different in size.

Perceptual illusions reinforce a fundamental lesson: Perception is not merely a projection of the world onto our brain. Rather, our sensations are disassembled into information bits that our brain then reassembles into its own functional model of the external world. During this reassembly process, our assumptions—such as the usual relationship between distance and size—can lead us astray. *Our brain constructs our perceptions.*

* * *

Form perception, depth perception, motion perception, and perceptual constancies illuminate how we organize our visual experiences. Perceptual organization applies to our other senses, too. It explains why we perceive a clock's steady tick not as a *tick-tick-tick-tick* but as grouped sounds, say, *TICK-tick, TICK-tick.* Listening to an unfamiliar language, we have trouble hearing where one word stops and the next one begins. Listening to our own language, we automatically hear distinct words. This, too, reflects perceptual organization. But it is more, for we even organize a string of letters—THEDOGATEMEAT—into words that make an intelligible phrase, more likely "The dog ate meat" than "The do gate me at" (McBurney & Collings, 1984). This process involves not only the organization we've been discussing, but also interpretation—discerning meaning in what we perceive.

FIGURE 18.24
The illusion of the shrinking and growing girls This distorted room, designed by Adelbert Ames, appears to have a normal rectangular shape when viewed through a peephole with one eye. The girl in the right corner appears disproportionately large because we judge her size based on the false assumption that she is the same distance away as the girl in the far corner.

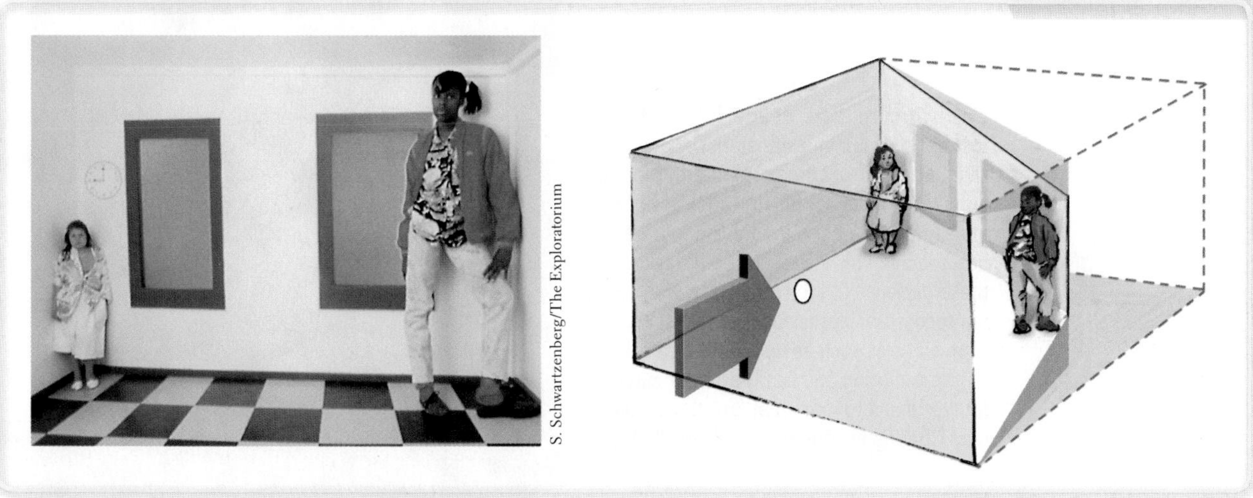

S. Schwartzenberg/The Exploratorium

"Let us then suppose the mind to be, as we say, white paper void of all characters, without any ideas: How comes it to be furnished? . . . To this I answer, in one word, from EXPERIENCE."

John Locke, *An Essay Concerning Human Understanding,* 1690

Visual Interpretation

Philosophers have debated whether our perceptual abilities should be credited to our nature or our nurture. To what extent do we *learn* to perceive? German philosopher Immanuel Kant (1724–1804) maintained that knowledge comes from our *inborn* ways of organizing sensory experiences. Indeed, we come equipped to process sensory information. But British philosopher John Locke (1632–1704) argued that through our experiences we also *learn* to perceive the world. Indeed, we learn to link an object's distance with its size. So, just how important is experience? How radically does it shape our perceptual interpretations?

Experience and Visual Perception

18-7 What does research on restored vision, sensory restriction, and perceptual adaptation reveal about the effects of experience on perception?

Restored Vision and Sensory Restriction

Writing to John Locke, William Molyneux wondered whether "a man *born* blind, and now adult, taught by his *touch* to distinguish between a cube and a sphere" could, if made to see, visually distinguish the two. Locke's answer was *No,* because the man would never have *learned* to see the difference.

Molyneux's hypothetical case has since been put to the test with a few dozen adults who, though blind from birth, have gained sight (Gregory, 1978; von Senden, 1932). Most had been born with cataracts—clouded lenses that allowed them to see only diffused light, rather as someone might see a foggy image through a Ping-Pong ball sliced in half. After cataract surgery, the patients could distinguish figure from ground and could sense colors—suggesting that these aspects of perception are innate. But much as Locke supposed, they often could not visually recognize objects that were familiar by touch.

Learning to see At age 3, Mike May lost his vision in an explosion. Decades later, after a new cornea restored vision to his right eye, he got his first look at his wife and children. Alas, although signals were now reaching his visual cortex, it lacked the experience to interpret them. May could not recognize expressions, or faces, apart from features such as hair. Yet he can see an object in motion and has learned to navigate his world and to marvel at such things as dust floating in sunlight (Abrams, 2002).

AP Photo/Marcio Jose Sanchez

Seeking to gain more control than is provided by clinical cases, researchers have outfitted infant kittens and monkeys with goggles through which they could see only diffuse, unpatterned light (Wiesel, 1982). After infancy, when the goggles were removed, these animals exhibited perceptual limitations much like those of humans born with cataracts. They could distinguish color and brightness, but not the form of a circle from that of a square. Their eyes had not degenerated; their retinas still relayed signals to their visual cortex. But lacking stimulation, the cortical cells had not developed normal connections. Thus, the animals remained functionally blind to shape. Experience guides, sustains, and maintains the brain's neural organization as it forms the pathways that affect our perceptions.

In both humans and animals, similar sensory restrictions later in life do no permanent harm. When researchers cover the eye of an adult animal for several months, its vision will be unaffected after the eye patch is removed. When surgeons remove cataracts that develop during late adulthood, most people are thrilled at the return to normal vision.

The effect of sensory restriction on infant cats, monkeys, and humans suggests there is a *critical period* for normal sensory and perceptual development. Nurture sculpts what nature has endowed. In less dramatic ways, it continues to do so throughout our lives. Despite concerns about their social costs, action video games sharpen spatial skills such as visual attention, eye-hand coordination and speed, and tracking multiple objects (Spence & Feng, 2010).

Experiments on the perceptual limitations and advantages produced by early sensory deprivation provide a partial answer to the enduring question about experience: Does the effect of early experience last a lifetime? For some aspects of perception, the answer is clearly *Yes:* "Use it *soon* or lose it." We retain the imprint of some early sensory experiences far into the future.

perceptual adaptation in vision, the ability to adjust to an artificially displaced or even inverted visual field.

Perceptual Adaptation

Given a new pair of glasses, we may feel slightly disoriented, even dizzy. Within a day or two, we adjust. Our **perceptual adaptation** to changed visual input makes the world seem normal again. But imagine a far more dramatic new pair of glasses—one that shifts the apparent location of objects 40 degrees to the left. When you first put them on and toss a ball to a friend, it sails off to the left. Walking forward to shake hands with the person, you veer to the left.

Could you adapt to this distorted world? Chicks cannot. When fitted with such lenses, they continue to peck where food grains *seem* to be (Hess, 1956; Rossi, 1968). But we humans adapt to distorting lenses quickly. Within a few minutes your throws would again be accurate, your stride on target. Remove the lenses and you would experience an aftereffect: At first your throws would err in the *opposite* direction, sailing off to the right; but again, within minutes you would readapt.

Indeed, given an even more radical pair of glasses—one that literally turns the world upside down—you could still adapt. Psychologist George Stratton (1896) experienced this when he invented, and for eight days wore, optical headgear that flipped left to right *and* up to down, making him the first person to experience a right-side-up retinal image while standing upright. The ground was up, the sky was down.

At first, when Stratton wanted to walk, he found himself searching for his feet, which were now "up." Eating was nearly impossible. He became nauseated and depressed. But he persisted, and by the eighth day he could comfortably reach for an object in the right direction and walk without bumping into things. When Stratton finally removed the headgear, he readapted quickly.

In later experiments, people wearing the optical gear have even been able to ride a motorcycle, ski the Alps, and fly an airplane (Dolezal, 1982; Kohler, 1962). The world around them still seemed above their heads or on the wrong side. But by actively moving about in these topsy-turvy worlds, they adapted to the context and learned to coordinate their movements.

Courtesy of Hubert Dolezal

Perceptual adaptation "Oops, missed," thought researcher Hubert Dolezal as he viewed the world through inverting goggles. Yet, believe it or not, kittens, monkeys, and humans can adapt to an inverted world.

Sensory information travels to these areas of the brain's cerebral cortex:

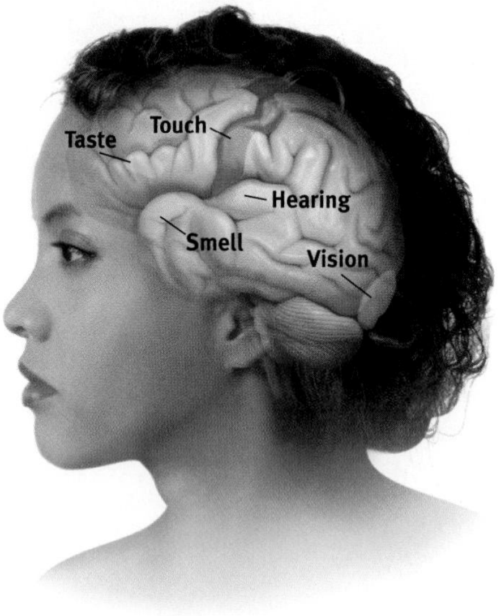

TABLE 18.2

Summarizing the Senses

Sensory System	Source	Receptors
Vision	Light waves striking the eye	Rods and cones in the retina
Hearing	Sound waves striking the outer ear	Cochlear hair cells in the inner ear
Touch	Pressure, warmth, cold on the skin	Skin receptors detect pressure, warmth, cold, and pain
Taste	Chemical molecules in the mouth	Basic tongue receptors for sweet, sour, salty, bitter, and umami
Smell	Chemical molecules breathed in through the nose	Millions of receptors at top of nasal cavity
Body position—kinesthesis	Any change in position of a body part, interacting with vision	Kinesthetic sensors all over the body
Body movement—vestibular sense	Movement of fluids in the inner ear caused by head/body movement	Hairlike receptors in the semi-circular canals and vestibular sacs

* * *

Vision has been our primary focus in this module, but for a summary of it and our other sensory systems, see **TABLE 18.2**. The river of perception is fed by sensation, cognition, and emotion. And that is why we need multiple levels of analysis (**FIGURE 18.25**).

If perception is the product of these three sources, what can we say about extrasensory perception, which claims that perception can occur apart from sensory input? For more on that question, see, Thinking Critically About ESP—Perception Without Sensation?

* * *

To feel awe, mystery, and a deep reverence for life, we need look no further than our own perceptual system and its capacity for organizing formless nerve impulses into colorful sights, vivid sounds, and evocative smells. As Shakespeare's Hamlet recognized, "There are more things in Heaven and Earth, Horatio, than are dreamt of in your philosophy." Within our ordinary sensory and perceptual experiences lies much that is truly extraordinary—surely much more than has so far been dreamt of in our psychology.

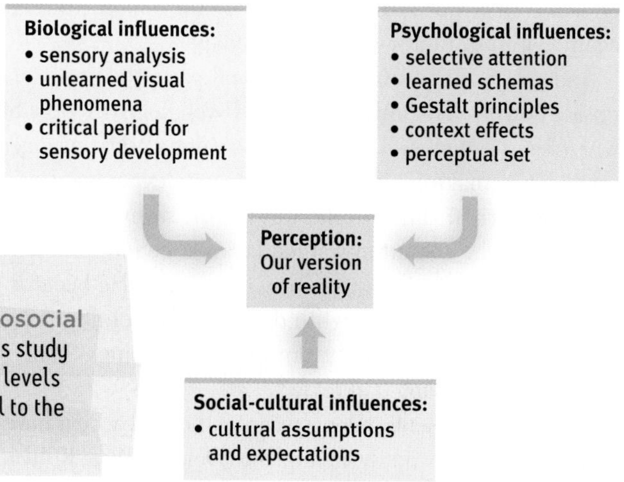

FIGURE 18.25
Perception is a biopsychosocial phenomenon Psychologists study how we perceive with different levels of analysis, from the biological to the social-cultural.

THINKING CRITICALLY ABOUT

ESP—Perception Without Sensation?

18-8 What are the claims of ESP, and what have most research psychologists concluded after putting these claims to the test?

Without sensory input, are we capable of **extrasensory perception (ESP)**? Are there indeed people—any people—who can read minds, see through walls, or foretell the future? Nearly half of Americans believe there are (AP, 2007; Moore, 2005).

The most testable and, for this module, most relevant parapsychological concepts are

- *telepathy:* mind-to-mind communication.
- *clairvoyance:* perceiving remote events, such as a house on fire in another state.
- *precognition:* perceiving future events, such as an unexpected death in the next month.

Closely linked is *psychokinesis,* or "mind over matter," such as levitating a table or influencing the roll of a die. (The claim is illustrated by the wry request, "Will all those who believe in psychokinesis please raise my hand?")

If ESP is real, we would need to overturn the scientific understanding that we are creatures whose minds are tied to our physical brains and whose perceptual experiences of the world are built of sensations. Sometimes new evidence does overturn our scientific preconceptions. Science, as we will see throughout this book, offers us various surprises—about the extent of the unconscious mind, about the effects of emotions on health, about what heals and what doesn't, and much more.

© Dan Piraro, Bizarro.

Most research psychologists and scientists—including 96 percent of the scientists in the U.S. National Academy of Sciences—are skeptical that paranormal phenomena exist (McConnell, 1991). But reputable universities in many locations, including Great Britain, the Netherlands, and Australia, have added faculty chairs or research units in **parapsychology** (Turpin, 2005). These researchers perform scientific experiments searching for possible ESP and other paranormal phenomena. Before seeing how parapsychologists do research on ESP, let's consider some popular beliefs.

Premonitions or Pretensions?

Can psychics see into the future? Although one might wish for a psychic stock forecaster, the tallied forecasts of "leading psychics" reveal meager accuracy. During the 1990s, the tabloid psychics were all wrong in predicting surprising events. (Madonna did not become a gospel singer, the Statue of Liberty did not lose both its arms in a terrorist blast, Queen Elizabeth did not abdicate her throne to enter a convent.) And the new-century psychics have missed the big-news events. Where were the psychics on 9/10 when we needed them? Why, despite a $50 million reward offered, could none of them help locate Osama bin Laden after 9/11, or step forward to predict the impending stock crashes in 2008? In 30 years, unusual predictions have almost never come true, and psychics have virtually never anticipated any of the year's headline events (Emory, 2004, 2006). In 2010, when a mine collapse trapped 33 miners, the Chilean government reportedly consulted four psychics. Their verdict? "They're all dead" (Kraul, 2010). But 69 days later, all 33 were rescued.

Moreover, the hundreds of psychic visions offered to police departments have been no more accurate than guesses made by others (Nickell, 1994, 2005; Radford, 2010; Reiser, 1982). But their sheer volume does increase the odds of an occasional correct guess, which psychics can then report to the media. Police departments are wise to all this. When researchers asked the police departments of America's 50 largest cities whether they ever had used psychics, 65 percent said *No* (Sweat & Durm, 1993). Of those that had, not one had found them helpful. Vague predictions can also later be interpreted ("retrofitted")

extrasensory perception (ESP) the controversial claim that perception can occur apart from sensory input; includes telepathy, clairvoyance, and precognition.

parapsychology the study of paranormal phenomena, including ESP and psychokinesis.

(Continued on next page)

to match events that provide a perceptual set for "understanding" them. Nostradamus, a sixteenth-century French psychic, explained in an unguarded moment that his ambiguous prophecies "could not possibly be understood till they were interpreted after the event and by it."

Are the spontaneous "visions" of everyday people any more accurate? Do dreams, for example, foretell the future, as people from both Eastern and Western cultures tend to believe—making some people more reluctant to fly after dreaming of a plane crash (Morewedge & Norton, 2009)? Or do they only seem to do so when we recall or reconstruct them in light of what has already happened? Two Harvard psychologists tested the prophetic power of dreams after superhero aviator Charles Lindbergh's baby son was kidnapped and murdered in 1932, but before the body was discovered (Murray & Wheeler, 1937). When invited to report their dreams about the child, 1300 visionaries submitted dream reports. How many accurately envisioned the child dead? Five percent. And how many also correctly anticipated the body's location—buried among trees? Only 4 of the 1300. Although this number was surely no better than chance, to those 4 dreamers the accuracy of their apparent precognitions must have seemed uncanny.

Given the billions of events in the world each day, and given enough days, some stunning coincidences are sure to occur. By one careful estimate, chance alone would predict that more than a thousand times a day someone on Earth will think of another person and then within the next five minutes will learn of that person's death (Charpak & Broch, 2004). Thus, when explaining an astonishing event, we should "give chance a chance" (Lilienfeld, 2009). With enough time and people, the improbable becomes inevitable.

Putting ESP to Experimental Test

When faced with claims of mind reading or out-of-body travel or communication with the dead, how can we separate bizarre ideas from those that sound bizarre but are true? At the heart of science is a simple answer: *Test them to see if they work.* If they do, so much the better for the ideas. If they don't, so much the better for our skepticism.

This scientific attitude has led both believers and skeptics to agree that what parapsychology needs is a reproducible phenomenon and a theory to explain it. Parapsychologist Rhea White (1998) spoke for many in saying that "the image of parapsychology that comes to my mind, based on nearly 44 years in the field, is that of a small airplane [that] has been perpetually taxiing down the runway of the Empirical Science Airport since 1882 . . . its movement punctuated occasionally by lifting a few feet off the ground only to bump back down on the tarmac once again. It has never taken off for any sustained flight."

How might we test ESP claims in a controlled, reproducible experiment? An experiment differs from a staged demonstration. In the laboratory, the experimenter controls what the "psychic" sees and hears. On stage, the psychic controls what the audience sees and hears.

The search for a valid and reliable test of ESP has resulted in thousands of experiments. After digesting data from 30 such studies, parapsychologist Lance Storm and his colleagues (2010a,b) concluded that, given participants with experience or belief in ESP, there is "consistent and reliable" parapsychological evidence. Psychologist Ray Hyman (2010), who has been scrutinizing parapsychological research since 1957, replies that if this is the best evidence, it fails to impress: "Parapsychology will achieve scientific acceptability only when it provides a positive theory with . . . independently replicable evidence. This is something it has yet to achieve after more than a century."

Daryl Bem (2011), a respected social psychologist, has been a skeptic of stage psychics; he once quipped that "a psychic is an actor

---

"To be sure of hitting the target, shoot first and call whatever you hit the target."

Writer-artist Ashleigh Brilliant, 1933–

"A person who talks a lot is sometimes right."

Spanish proverb

"At the heart of science is an essential tension between two seemingly contradictory attitudes—an openness to new ideas, no matter how bizarre or counterintuitive they may be, and the most ruthless skeptical scrutiny of all ideas, old and new."

Carl Sagan (1987)

Magician Harry Houdini after fooling Sir Arthur Conan Doyle with a pseudo-psychic trick: "Now I beg of you, Sir Arthur, do not jump to the conclusion that certain things you see are necessarily 'supernatural,' or with the work of 'spirits,' just because you cannot explain them."

Quoted by William Kalush and Larry Sloman, *The Secret Life of Houdini*, 2007

Courtesy of Claire Cole

Testing psychic powers in the British population Hertfordshire University psychologist Richard Wiseman created a "mind machine" to see if people can influence or predict a coin toss. Using a touch-sensitive screen, visitors to festivals around the country were given four attempts to call heads or tails. Using a random-number generator, a computer then decided the outcome. When the experiment concluded in January 2000, nearly 28,000 people had predicted 110,972 tosses—with 49.8 percent correct.

playing the role of a psychic" (1984). Yet he has reignited hopes for replicable evidence with nine experiments that seemed to show people anticipating future events. In one, when an erotic scene was about to appear on a screen in one of two randomly selected positions, Cornell University participants guessed right 53.1 percent of the time (beating 50 percent by a small but statistically significant margin). In another, people viewed a set of words, took a recall test of those words, and then rehearsed a randomly selected subset of those words. People better remembered the rehearsed words—even when the rehearsal took place *after* the recall test. The upcoming rehearsal—a future event—apparently affected their ability to recall words.

Bem wonders if his "anomalous" findings reflect an evolutionary advantage to those who can precognitively anticipate future dangers. Critics scoff. "If any of his claims were true," wrote cognitive scientist Douglas Hofstadter (2011), "then all of the bases underlying contemporary science would be toppled, and we would have to rethink everything about the nature of the universe." Moreover, if future events retroactively affect present feelings, then why can't people intuitively predict casino outcomes or stock market futures?

Despite Bem's paper having survived critical reviews by a top-tier journal, other critics found the methods "badly flawed" (Alcock, 2011) or the statistical analyses "biased" (Wagenmakers et al., 2011). "A result—especially one of this importance—must recur several times in tests by independent and skeptical researchers to gain scientific credibility," observed astronomer David Helfand (2011). "I have little doubt that Professor Bem's experiments will fail this test."

Anticipating such skepticism, Bem has made his computer materials available to anyone who wishes to replicate his studies, and replications are now under way. One research team has already conducted five replications of Bem's recall experiments at various universities and found no precognition (Galak et al., 2011). Regardless of the outcomes, science will have done its work. It will have been open to a finding that challenges its own worldview, and then, through follow-up research, it will have assessed its validity. And that is how science sifts crazy-sounding ideas, leaving most on the historical waste heap while occasionally surprising us.

One skeptic, magician James Randi, has had a longstanding offer of $1 million to be given "to anyone who proves a genuine psychic power under proper observing conditions" (Randi, 1999; Thompson, 2010). French, Australian, and Indian groups have made similar offers of up to 200,000 euros (CFI, 2003). Large as these sums are, the scientific seal of approval would be worth far more. To refute those who say there is no ESP, one need only produce a single person who can demonstrate a single, reproducible ESP event. (To refute those who say pigs can't talk would take but one talking pig.) So far, no such person has emerged.

RETRIEVAL PRACTICE

- What is the field of study that researches claims of extrasensory perception (ESP)?

ANSWER: parapsychology

MODULE REVIEW

Vision and Perceptual Organization and Interpretation

Learning Objectives

RETRIEVAL PRACTICE Take a moment to answer each of these Learning Objective Questions (repeated here from within the module). Then turn to Appendix B, Complete Module Reviews, to check your answers. Research suggests that trying to answer these questions on your own will improve your long-term retention (McDaniel et al., 2009).

18-1: What is the energy that we see as visible light, and how does the eye transform light energy into neural messages?

18-2: How do the eye and the brain process visual information?

18-3: What theories help us understand color vision?

18-4: How did the Gestalt psychologists understand perceptual organization, and how do figure-ground and grouping principles contribute to our perceptions?

18-5: How do we use binocular and monocular cues to perceive the world in three dimensions and perceive motion?

18-6: How do perceptual constancies help us organize our sensations into meaningful perceptions?

18-7: What does research on restored vision, sensory restriction, and perceptual adaptation reveal about the effects of experience on perception?

18-8: What are the claims of ESP, and what have most research psychologists concluded after putting these claims to the test?

Terms and Concepts to Remember

RETRIEVAL PRACTICE Test yourself on these terms by trying to write down the definition before flipping back to the referenced page to check your answer.

wavelength, p. 235
hue, p. 235
intensity, p. 235
pupil, p. 235
iris, p. 235
lens, p. 235
retina, p. 235
accommodation, p. 235
rods, p. 236
cones, p. 236
optic nerve, p. 236
blind spot, p. 236
fovea, p. 236
feature detectors, p. 238
parallel processing, p. 239
Young-Helmholtz trichromatic (three-color) theory, p. 241
opponent-process theory, p. 242
gestalt, p. 242
figure-ground, p. 243
grouping, p. 243
depth perception, p. 244
visual cliff, p. 244
binocular cues, p. 245
retinal disparity, p. 245
monocular cues, p. 246
phi phenomenon, p. 247
perceptual constancy, p. 247
color constancy, p. 247
perceptual adaptation, p. 251
extrasensory perception (ESP), p. 253
parapsychology, p. 253

RETRIEVAL PRACTICE Gain an advantage, and benefit from immediate feedback, with the interactive self-testing resources at www.worthpublishers.com/myers.

Touch sensations involve more than tactile stimulation, however. A self-administered tickle produces less somatosensory cortex activation than does the same tickle from something or someone else (Blakemore et al., 1998). (The brain is wise enough to be most sensitive to unexpected stimulation.)

FIGURE 19.5
Warm + cold = hot When ice-cold water passes through one coil and comfortably warm water through another, we perceive the combined sensation as burning hot.

Pain

19-5 How can we best understand and control pain?

Be thankful for occasional pain. Pain is your body's way of telling you something has gone wrong. Drawing your attention to a burn, a break, or a sprain, pain orders you to change your behavior—"Stay off that turned ankle!" The rare people born without the ability to feel pain may experience severe injury or even die before early adulthood. Without the discomfort that makes us occasionally shift position, their joints fail from excess strain, and without the warnings of pain, the effects of unchecked infections and injuries accumulate (Neese, 1991).

More numerous are those who live with chronic pain, which is rather like an alarm that won't shut off. The suffering of such people, and of those with persistent or recurring backaches, arthritis, headaches, and cancer-related pain, prompts two questions: What is pain? How might we control it?

Understanding Pain

Our pain experiences vary widely. Women are more pain sensitive than men are (Wickelgren, 2009). Individual pain sensitivity varies, too, depending on genes, physiology, experience, attention, and surrounding culture (Gatchel et al., 2007; Reimann et al., 2010). Thus, feeling pain reflects *bottom-up* sensations and *top-down* processes.

Biological Influences There is no one type of stimulus that triggers pain (as sound waves trigger hearing). Instead, there are different *nociceptors*—sensory receptors that detect hurtful temperatures, pressure, or chemicals (**FIGURE 19.6** on the next page).

A pain-free, problematic life Ashlyn Blocker (right), shown here with her mother and sister, has a rare genetic disorder. She feels neither pain nor extreme hot and cold. She must frequently be checked for accidentally self-inflicted injuries that she herself cannot feel. "Some people would say [that feeling no pain is] a good thing," says her mother. "But no, it's not. Pain's there for a reason. It lets your body know something's wrong and it needs to be fixed. I'd give anything for her to feel pain" (quoted by Bynum, 2004).

AP Photo/Stephen Morton

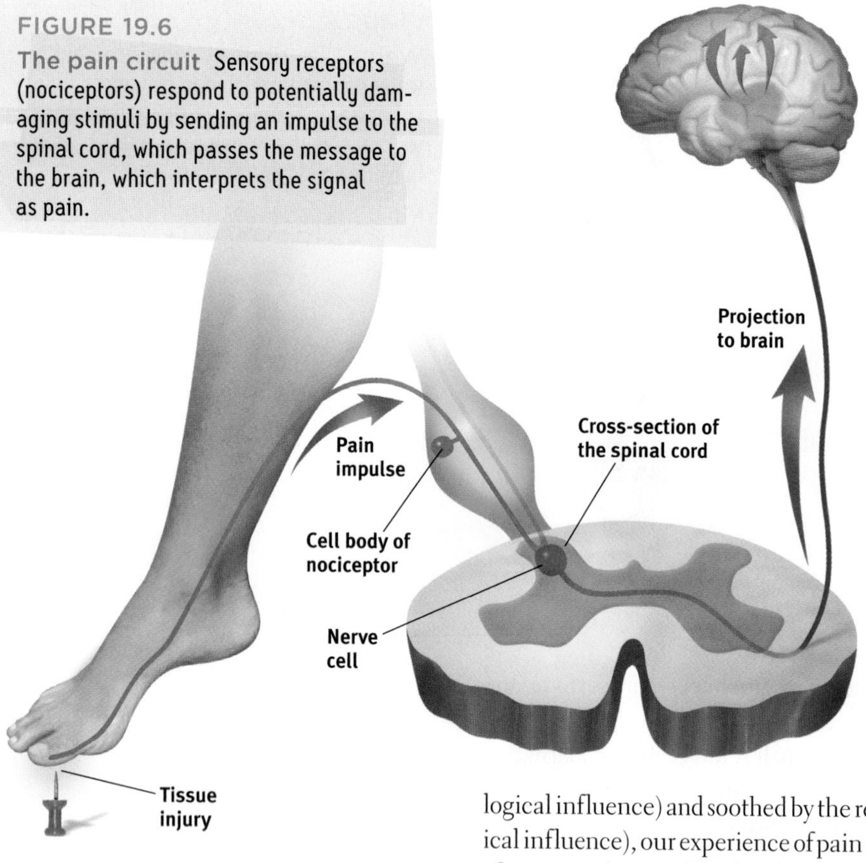

FIGURE 19.6
The pain circuit Sensory receptors (nociceptors) respond to potentially damaging stimuli by sending an impulse to the spinal cord, which passes the message to the brain, which interprets the signal as pain.

Although no theory of pain explains all available findings, psychologist Ronald Melzack and biologist Patrick Wall's (1965, 1983) classic **gate-control theory** provides a useful model. The spinal cord contains small nerve fibers that conduct most pain signals, and larger fibers that conduct most other sensory signals. Melzack and Wall theorized that the spinal cord contains a neurological "gate." When tissue is injured, the small fibers activate and open the gate, and you feel pain. Large-fiber activity closes the gate, blocking pain signals and preventing them from reaching the brain. Thus, one way to treat chronic pain is to stimulate (by massage, electric stimulation, or acupuncture) "gate-closing" activity in the large neural fibers (Wall, 2000).

But pain is not merely a physical phenomenon of injured nerves sending impulses to a definable brain area—like pulling on a rope to ring a bell. Melzack and Wall noted that brain-to-spinal-cord messages can also close the gate, helping to explain some striking influences on pain. When we are distracted from pain (a psychological influence) and soothed by the release of our naturally painkilling *endorphins* (a biological influence), our experience of pain diminishes. Sports injuries may go unnoticed until the after-game shower. People who carry a gene that boosts the availability of endorphins are less bothered by pain, and their brain is less responsive to pain (Zubieta et al., 2003). Others carry a mutated gene that disrupts pain circuit neurotransmission and experience little pain (Cox et al., 2006). Such discoveries may point the way toward new pain medications that mimic these genetic effects.

The brain can also create pain, as it does in people's experiences of *phantom limb sensations*, when it misinterprets the spontaneous central nervous system activity that occurs in the absence of normal sensory input. As the dreamer may see with eyes closed, so some 7 in 10 amputees may feel pain or movement in nonexistent limbs (Melzack, 1992, 2005). (An amputee may also try to step off a bed onto a phantom limb or to lift a cup with a phantom hand.) Even those born without a limb sometimes perceive sensations from the absent arm or leg. The brain, Melzack (1998) surmises, comes prepared to anticipate "that it will be getting information from a body that has limbs."

Playing with pain In a 2010 Super Bowl playoff game, Vikings quarterback Brett Favre seriously injured his ankle and hamstring. He was taken out of the game briefly but came back and played through the pain, which reclaimed his attention after the game's end.

AP Photo/Paul Abell

A similar phenomenon occurs with other senses. People with hearing loss often experience the sound of silence: phantom sounds—a ringing-in-the-ears sensation known as *tinnitus*. Those who lose vision to glaucoma, cataracts, diabetes, or macular degeneration may experience phantom sights—nonthreatening hallucinations (Ramachandran & Blakeslee, 1998). Some with nerve damage have had taste phantoms, such as ice water seeming sickeningly sweet (Goode, 1999). Others have experienced phantom smells, such as nonexistent rotten food. The point to remember: *We feel, see, hear, taste, and smell with our brain*, which can sense even without functioning senses.

Psychological Influences The psychological effects of distraction are clear in the stories of athletes who, focused on winning, play through the pain. We also seem to edit our *memories* of pain, which often differ from the pain we actually experienced. In experiments, and after medical procedures, people overlook a pain's duration. Their memory snapshots instead record two factors: their pain's *peak* moment (which can lead them to recall variable pain, with peaks, as worse [Stone et al., 2005]), and how much pain they felt at the *end*.

In one experiment, researchers asked people to immerse one hand in painfully cold water for 60 seconds, and then the other hand in the same painfully cold water for 60 seconds followed by a slightly less painful 30 seconds more (Kahneman et al., 1993). Which experience would you expect to recall as most painful? Curiously, when asked which trial they would prefer to repeat, most preferred the longer trial, with more net pain—but less pain at the end. Physicians have used this principle with patients undergoing colon exams—lengthening the discomfort by a minute, but lessening its intensity (Kahneman, 1999). Although the extended milder discomfort added to their net pain experience, patients experiencing this taper-down treatment later recalled the exam as less painful than did those whose pain ended abruptly. (If, at the end of a painful root canal, the oral surgeon asks if you'd like to go home or to have a few more minutes of milder discomfort, there's a case to be made for prolonging your hurt.)

"When belly with bad pains doth swell, It matters naught what else goes well."

Sadi, *The Gulistan*, 1258

"Pain is increased by attending to it."

Charles Darwin, *Expression of Emotions in Man and Animals*, 1872

Social-Cultural Influences Our perception of pain also varies with our social situation and our cultural traditions. We tend to perceive more pain when others also seem to be experiencing pain (Symbaluk et al., 1997). This may help explain other apparent social aspects of pain, as when pockets of Australian keyboard operators during the mid-1980s suffered outbreaks of severe pain during typing or other repetitive work—without any discernible physical abnormalities (Gawande, 1998). Sometimes the pain in sprain is mainly in the brain—literally. When feeling empathy for another's pain, a person's own brain activity may partly mirror that of the other's brain in pain (Singer et al, 2004).

Thus, our perception of pain is a biopsychosocial phenomenon (**FIGURE 19.7**). Viewing pain this way can help us better understand how to cope with pain and treat it.

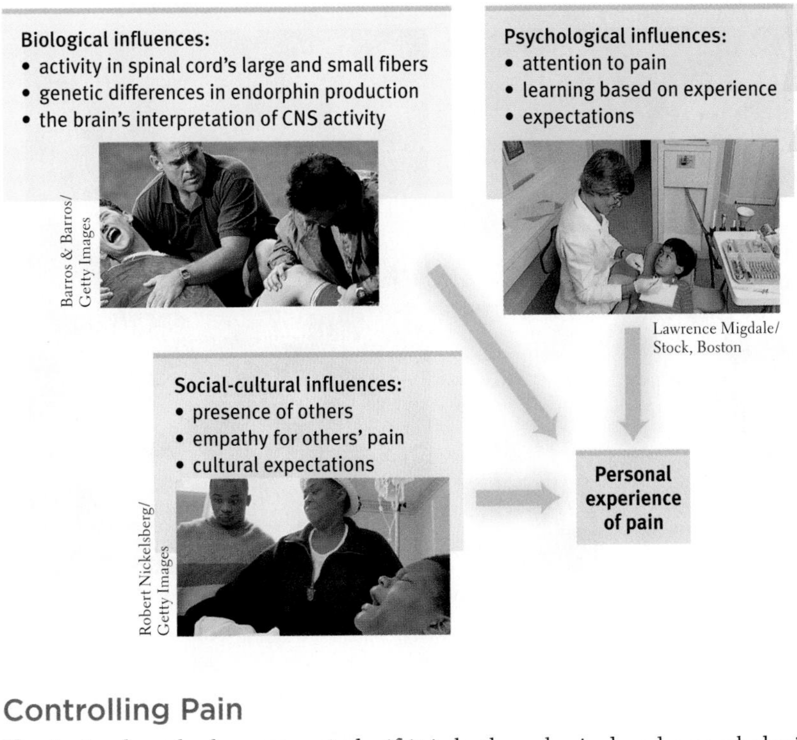

FIGURE 19.7 Biopsychosocial approach to pain Our experience of pain is much more than neural messages sent to the brain.

Controlling Pain

If pain is where body meets mind—if it is both a physical and a psychological phenomenon—then it should be treatable both physically and psychologically. Depending on the type of symptoms, pain control clinics select one or more therapies from a list that includes drugs, surgery, acupuncture, electrical stimulation, massage, exercise, hypnosis, relaxation training, and thought distraction.

gate-control theory the theory that the spinal cord contains a neurological "gate" that blocks pain signals or allows them to pass on to the brain. The "gate" is opened by the activity of pain signals traveling up small nerve fibers and is closed by activity in larger fibers or by information coming from the brain.

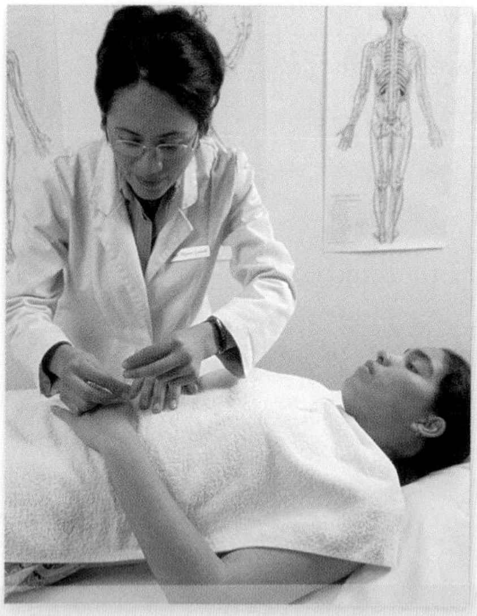
Gary Conner/PhototakeUSA.com

Acupuncture: A jab well done This acupuncturist is attempting to help this woman gain relief from back pain by using needles on points of the patient's hand.

Even an inert placebo can help, by dampening the central nervous system's attention and responses to painful experiences—mimicking analgesic drugs (Eippert et al., 2009; Wager, 2005). After being injected in the jaw with a stinging saltwater solution, men in one experiment received a placebo said to relieve pain, and they immediately felt better. Being given fake pain-killing chemicals caused the brain to dispense real ones, as indicated by activity in an area that releases natural pain-killing opiates (Scott et al., 2007; Zubieta et al., 2005). "Believing becomes reality," noted one commentator (Thernstrom, 2006), as "the mind unites with the body."

Another experiment pitted two placebos—fake pills and pretend acupuncture—against each other (Kaptchuk et al., 2006). People with persistent arm pain (270 of them) received either sham acupuncture (with trick needles that retracted without puncturing the skin) or blue cornstarch pills that looked like pills often prescribed for strain injury. A fourth of those receiving the nonexistent needle pricks and 31 percent of those receiving the pills complained of side effects, such as painful skin or dry mouth and fatigue. After two months, both groups were reporting less pain, with the fake acupuncture group reporting the greater pain drop.

Distracting people with pleasant images *("Think of a warm, comfortable environment")* or drawing their attention away from the painful stimulation *("Count backward by 3's")* is an especially effective way to activate pain-inhibiting circuits and to increase pain tolerance (Edwards et al., 2009). A well-trained nurse may distract needle-shy patients by chatting with them and asking them to look away when inserting the needle. For burn victims receiving excruciating wound care, an even more effective distraction comes from immersion in a computer-generated 3-D world, like the snow scene in **FIGURE 19.8**. Functional MRI (fMRI) scans reveal that playing in the virtual reality reduces the brain's pain-related activity (Hoffman, 2004). Because pain is in the brain, diverting the brain's attention may bring relief.

Image by Todd Richards and Aric Bills, U.W., ©Hunter Hoffman, www.vrpain.com

FIGURE 19.8
Virtual-reality pain control For burn victims undergoing painful skin repair, an escape into virtual reality can powerfully distract attention, thus reducing pain and the brain's response to painful stimulation. The fMRI scans on the right illustrate a lowered pain response when the patient is distracted.

Taste

19-6 How do we experience taste and smell, and how do they interact?

Like touch, our sense of taste involves several basic sensations. Taste's sensations were once thought to be sweet, sour, salty, and bitter, with all others stemming from mixtures of these four (McBurney & Gent, 1979). Then, as investigators searched for specialized nerve fibers for the four taste sensations, they encountered a receptor for what we now know is a fifth—the savory meaty taste of *umami*, best experienced as the flavor enhancer monosodium glutamate.

Tastes exist for more than our pleasure (see **TABLE 19.1**). Pleasureful tastes attracted our ancestors to energy- or protein-rich foods that enabled their survival. Aversive tastes deterred them from new foods that might be toxic. We see the inheritance of this biological wisdom in today's 2- to 6-year-olds, who are typically fussy eaters, especially when offered new meats or bitter-tasting vegetables, such as spinach and brussels sprouts (Cooke et al., 2003). Meat and plant toxins were both potentially dangerous sources of food poisoning for our ancestors, especially for children. Given repeated small tastes of disliked new foods, children will, however, typically begin to accept them (Wardle et al., 2003).

Taste is a chemical sense. Inside each little bump on the top and sides of your tongue are 200 or more taste buds, each containing a pore that catches food chemicals. Into each taste bud pore, 50 to 100 taste receptor cells project antenna-like hairs that sense food molecules. Some receptors respond mostly to sweet-tasting molecules, others to salty-, sour-, umami-, or bitter-tasting ones. It doesn't take much to trigger a response that alerts your brain's temporal lobe. If a stream of water is pumped across your tongue, the addition of a concentrated salty or sweet taste for but one-tenth of a second will get your attention (Kelling & Halpern, 1983). When a friend asks for "just a taste" of your soft drink, you can squeeze off the straw after a mere instant.

Taste receptors reproduce themselves every week or two, so if you burn your tongue with hot food it hardly matters. However, as you grow older, the number of taste buds decreases, as does taste sensitivity (Cowart, 1981). (No wonder adults enjoy strong-tasting foods that children resist.) Smoking and alcohol use accelerate these declines. Those who lose their sense of taste report that food tastes like "straw" and is hard to swallow (Cowart, 2005).

Essential as taste buds are, there's more to taste than meets the tongue. Expectations can influence taste. When told a sausage roll was "vegetarian," people in one experiment found it decidedly inferior to its identical partner labeled "meat" (Allen et al., 2008). In another experiment, being told that a wine cost $90 rather than its real $10 price made it taste better and triggered more activity in a brain area that responds to pleasant experiences (Plassmann et al., 2008).

TABLE 19.1

The Survival Functions of Basic Tastes

Taste	Indicates
Sweet	Energy source
Salty	Sodium essential to physiological processes
Sour	Potentially toxic acid
Bitter	Potential poisons
Umami	Proteins to grow and repair tissue

(Adapted from Cowart, 2005.)

Lauren Burke/Jupiterimages

Sensory Interaction

Taste also illustrates another curious phenomenon. Hold your nose, close your eyes, and have someone feed you various foods. A slice of apple may be indistinguishable from a chunk of raw potato. A piece of steak may taste like cardboard. Without their smells, a cup of cold coffee may be hard to distinguish from a glass of red wine. To savor a taste, we normally breathe the aroma through our nose—which is why eating is not much fun when you have a bad cold. Smell can also change our perception of taste: A drink's strawberry odor enhances our perception of its sweetness. This is **sensory interaction** at work—the principle that one sense may influence another. Smell plus texture plus taste equals flavor.

Sensory interaction similarly influences what we hear. If I (as a person with hearing loss) watch a video with simultaneous captioning, I have no trouble hearing the words I am seeing (and may therefore think I don't need the captioning). If I then turn off the captioning, I suddenly realize I need it (**FIGURE 19.9** on the next page). But what do you suppose happens if we *see* a speaker saying one syllable while we *hear* another? Surprise: We may perceive a third syllable that blends both inputs. Seeing the mouth movements for *ga* while hearing *ba* we may perceive *da*—a phenomenon known as the *McGurk effect*, after its discoverers, psychologist Harry McGurk and his assistant John MacDonald (1976).

sensory interaction the principle that one sense may influence another, as when the smell of food influences its taste.

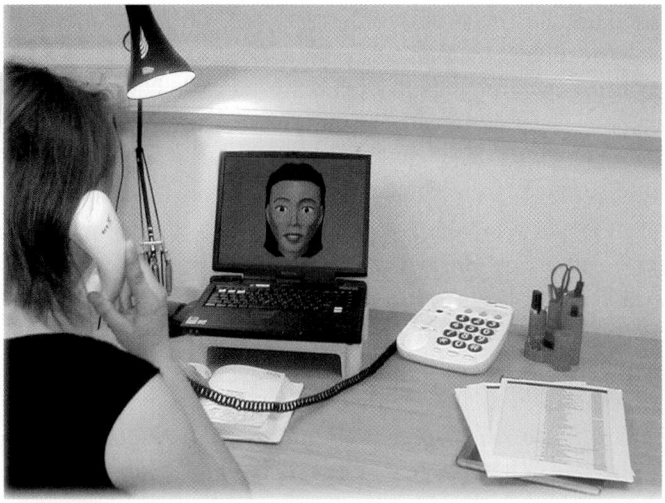

FIGURE 19.9
Sensory interaction When a hard-of-hearing listener sees an animated face forming the words being spoken at the other end of a phone line, the words become easier to understand (Knight, 2004). The eyes guide the ears.

Our senses—tasting, smelling, hearing, seeing, touching—are not totally separate information channels. In interpreting the world, our brain blends their inputs. It even blends our tactile and social judgments:

- After holding a warm drink rather than a cold one, people are more likely to rate someone more warmly, feel closer to them, and behave more generously (IJzerman & Semin, 2009; Williams & Bargh, 2008). Physical warmth promotes social warmth.
- After being given the cold shoulder by others in an experiment, people judge the room as colder than do those treated warmly (Zhong & Leonardelli, 2008). Social exclusion literally feels cold.
- Holding a heavy rather than light clipboard makes job candidates seem more important. Holding rough objects makes social interactions seem more difficult (Ackerman et al., 2010).
- When leaning to the left—by sitting in a left- rather than right-leaning chair, squeezing a hand-grip with the left hand, or using a mouse with their left hand—people lean more left in their expressed political attitudes (Oppenheimer & Trail, 2010).

These examples of **embodied cognition** illustrate how brain circuits that process our bodily sensations connect with brain circuits responsible for cognition.

Vision and touch also illustrate sensory interaction. A weak flicker of light that we have trouble perceiving becomes more visible when accompanied by a short burst of sound (Kayser, 2007). In detecting events, the brain can combine simultaneous visual and touch signals, thanks to neurons projecting from the somatosensory cortex back to the visual cortex (Macaluso et al., 2000).

Touch also interacts with taste. Depending on its texture, a potato chip "tastes" fresh or stale (Smith, 2011). Touch even interacts with hearing. One experiment blew a puff of air (such as our mouths produce when saying *pa* and *ta*) on the neck or hands as people heard either these sounds or the more airless sounds *ba* or *da*. To my surprise (and yours?), the people more often misheard *ba* or *da* as *pa* or *ta* when played with the faint puff (Gick & Derrick, 2009). Thanks to sensory interaction, they were hearing with their skin.

So, the senses interact: As we attempt to decipher our world, our brain blends inputs from our seeing, hearing, touching, tasting, and smelling channels. In a few select individuals, the senses become joined in a phenomenon called *synaesthesia*, where one sort of sensation (such as hearing sound) produces another (such as seeing color). Thus, hearing music or seeing a specific number may activate color-sensitive cortex regions and

embodied cognition in psychological science, the influence of bodily sensations, gestures, and other states on cognitive preferences and judgments.

trigger a sensation of color (Brang et al., 2008; Hubbard et al., 2005). Seeing the number 3 may evoke a taste sensation (Ward, 2003). For many people, an odor, perhaps of mint or chocolate, can evoke a sensation of taste (Stevenson & Tomiczek, 2007).

Impress your friends with your new word for the day: People unable to see are said to experience blindness. People unable to hear experience deafness. People unable to smell experience *anosmia.*

Smell

Inhale, exhale. Inhale, exhale. Breaths come in pairs—except at two crucial moments: birth and death. Between those two moments, you will daily inhale and exhale nearly 20,000 breaths of life-sustaining air, bathing your nostrils in a stream of scent-laden molecules. The resulting experiences of smell *(olfaction)* are strikingly intimate: You inhale something of whatever or whoever it is you smell.

Like taste, smell is a chemical sense. We smell something when molecules of a substance carried in the air reach a tiny cluster of 5 million or more receptor cells at the top of each nasal cavity (**FIGURE 19.10**). These olfactory receptor cells, waving like sea anemones on a reef, respond selectively—to the aroma of a cake baking, to a wisp of smoke, to a friend's fragrance. Instantly, they alert the brain through their axon fibers.

Tish1/Shutterstock

Even nursing infants and their mothers have a literal chemistry to their relationship. They quickly learn to recognize each other's scents (McCarthy, 1986). Aided by smell, a mother fur seal returning to a beach crowded with pups will find her own. Our own sense of smell is less impressive than the acuteness of our seeing and hearing. Looking out across a garden, we see its forms and colors in exquisite detail and hear a variety of birds singing, yet we smell little of it without sticking our nose into the blossoms.

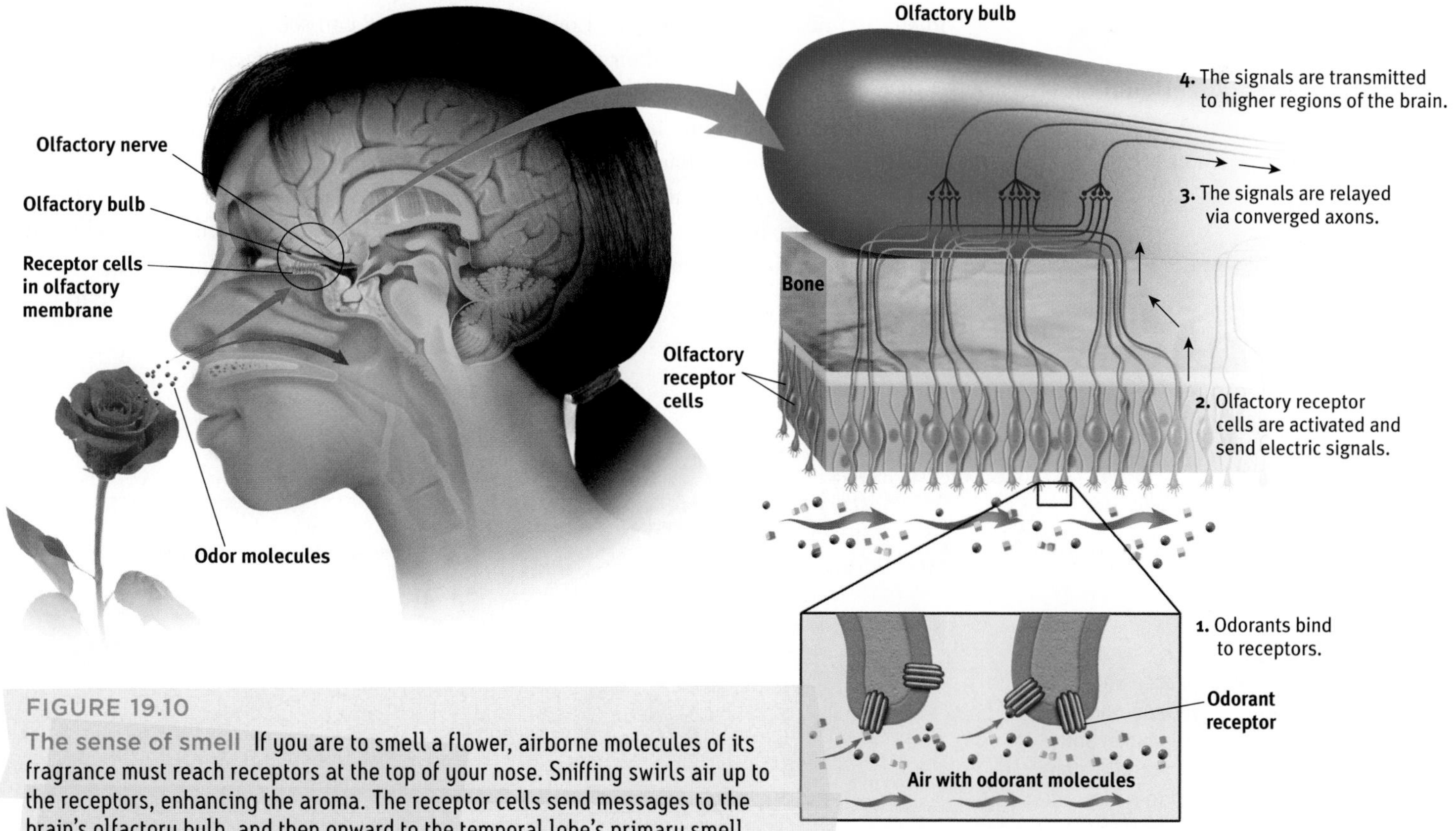

FIGURE 19.10
The sense of smell If you are to smell a flower, airborne molecules of its fragrance must reach receptors at the top of your nose. Sniffing swirls air up to the receptors, enhancing the aroma. The receptor cells send messages to the brain's olfactory bulb, and then onward to the temporal lobe's primary smell cortex and to the parts of the limbic system involved in memory and emotion.

kinesthesis [kin-ehs-THEE-sehs] the system for sensing the position and movement of individual body parts.

Odor molecules come in many shapes and sizes—so many, in fact, that it takes many different receptors to detect them. A large family of genes designs the 350 or so receptor proteins that recognize particular odor molecules (Miller, 2004). Linda Buck and Richard Axel (1991) discovered (in work for which they received a 2004 Nobel Prize) that these receptor proteins are embedded on the surface of nasal cavity neurons. As a key slips into a lock, so odor molecules slip into these receptors. Yet we don't seem to have a distinct receptor for each detectable odor. This suggests that some odors trigger a combination of receptors, in patterns that are interpreted by the olfactory cortex. As the English alphabet's 26 letters can combine to form many words, so odor molecules bind to different receptor arrays, producing the 10,000 odors we can detect (Malnic et al., 1999). It is the combinations of olfactory receptors, which activate different neuron patterns, that allow us to distinguish between the aromas of fresh-brewed and hours-old coffee (Zou et al., 2005).

Women have a better sense of smell than men do (Wickelgren, 2009; Wysocki & Gilbert, 1989). Smokers and people with Alzheimer's disease, Parkinson's disease, or alcohol dependence typically experience a diminished sense of smell (Doty, 2001). Although gender and physical condition influence our ability to identify scents, this ability typically peaks in early adulthood and gradually declines thereafter (**FIGURE 19.11**). Despite our skill at discriminating scents, we aren't very good at describing them. Words more readily portray the sound of coffee brewing than its aroma. Compared with how we experience and remember sights and sounds, smells are primitive and certainly harder to describe and recall (Richardson & Zucco, 1989; Zucco, 2003).

"There could be a stack of truck tires burning in the living room, and I wouldn't necessarily smell it. Whereas my wife can detect a lone spoiled grape two houses away."

Dave Barry, 2005

As any dog or cat with a good nose could tell us, we each have our own identifiable chemical signature. (One noteworthy exception: A dog will follow the tracks of one identical twin as though they had been made by the other [Thomas, 1974].) Animals that have many times more olfactory receptors than we do also use their sense of smell to communicate and to navigate. Long before the shark can see its prey, or the moth its mate, olfactory cues direct their way, as they also do for migrating salmon returning to their home stream. If exposed in a hatchery to one of two odorant chemicals, they will, when returning two years later, seek whichever stream near their release site is spiked with the familiar smell (Barinaga, 1999).

Humans have 10 to 20 million olfactory receptors. A bloodhound has some 200 million (Herz, 2001).

For humans, too, the attractiveness of smells depends on learned associations (Herz, 2001). Babies are not born with a built-in preference for the smell of their mother's breast; as they nurse, their preference builds. As good experiences become associated with a particular scent, people come to like that scent, which helps explain why people in the

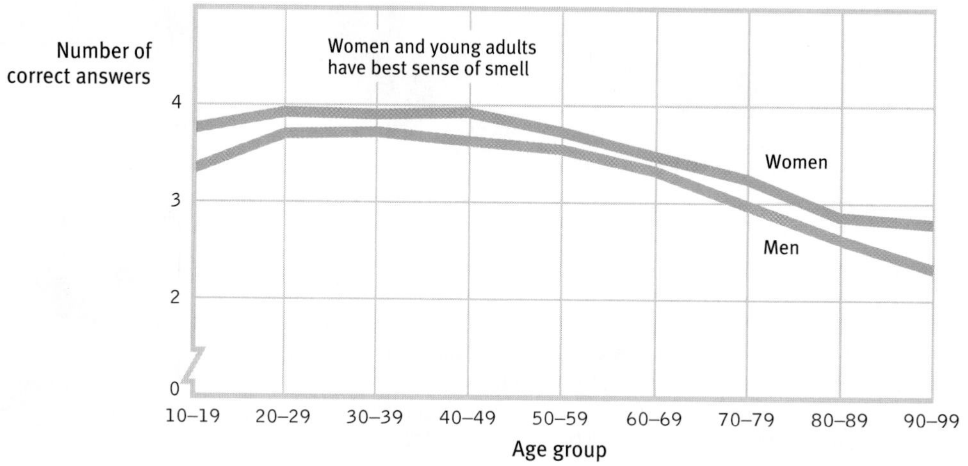

FIGURE 19.11
Age, sex, and sense of smell Among the 1.2 million people who responded to a *National Geographic* scratch-and-sniff survey, women and younger adults most successfully identified six sample odors. (From Wysocki & Gilbert, 1989.)

United States tend to like the smell of wintergreen (which they associate with candy and gum) more than do those in Great Britain (where it often is associated with medicine). In another example of odors evoking unpleasant emotions, researchers frustrated Brown University students with a rigged computer game in a scented room (Herz et al., 2004). Later, if exposed to the same odor while working on a verbal task, the students' frustration was rekindled and they gave up sooner than others exposed to a different odor or no odor.

Though it's difficult to recall odors by name, we have a remarkable capacity to recognize long-forgotten odors and their associated memories (Engen, 1987; Schab, 1991). The smell of the sea, the scent of a perfume, or an aroma of a favorite relative's kitchen can bring to mind a happy time. It's a phenomenon that was understood by the British travel agent chain Lunn Poly. To evoke memories of lounging on sunny, warm beaches, the company once piped the aroma of coconut suntan oil into its shops (Fracassini, 2000).

Our brain's circuitry helps explain an odor's power to evoke feelings and memories (**FIGURE 19.12**). A hotline runs between the brain area receiving information from the nose and the brain's ancient limbic centers associated with memory and emotion. Thus, when put in a foul-smelling room, people expressed harsher judgments of immoral acts (such as lying or keeping a found wallet) and more negative attitudes toward gay men (Inbar et al., 2011; Schnall et al., 2008).

Smell is indeed primitive. Eons before the elaborate analytical areas of our cerebral cortex had fully evolved, our mammalian ancestors sniffed for food—and for predators. New York's governor candidate Carl Paladino understood how primitive, disgusting smells can affect judgments. He mailed a flyer that smelled of rotting garbage with a message attacking his opponent—whom he then defeated 62 to 38 percent in the Republican primary (Liberman & Pizarro, 2010).

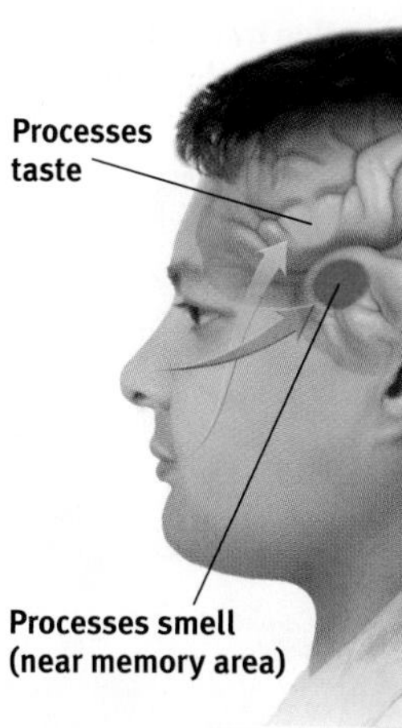

FIGURE 19.12
Taste, smell, and memory Information from the taste buds (yellow arrow) travels to an area between the frontal and temporal lobes of the brain. It registers in an area not far from where the brain receives information from our sense of smell, which interacts with taste. The brain's circuitry for smell (red circle) also connects with areas involved in memory storage, which helps explain why a smell can trigger a memory.

RETRIEVAL PRACTICE

- How does our system for sensing smell differ from our sensory systems for touch and taste?

ANSWER: We have four basic touch senses and five taste sensations. But we have no basic smell receptors. Instead, different combinations of odor receptors send messages to the brain, enabling us to recognize some 10,000 different smells.

Body Position and Movement

19-7 How do we sense our body's position and movement?

Important sensors in your joints, tendons, bones, and ears, as well as your skin sensors enable your **kinesthesis**—your sense of the position and movement of your body parts. By closing your eyes or plugging your ears you can momentarily imagine being without sight or sound. But what would it be like to live without touch or kinesthesis—without, therefore, being able to sense the positions of your limbs when you wake during the night? Ian Waterman of Hampshire, England, knows. In 1972, at age 19, Waterman contracted a rare viral infection that destroyed the nerves enabling his sense of light touch and of body position and movement. People with this condition report feeling disembodied, as though their body is dead, not real, not theirs (Sacks, 1985). With prolonged practice, Waterman has learned to walk and eat—by visually focusing on his limbs and directing them accordingly. But if the lights go out, he crumples to the floor (Azar, 1998). Even for the rest of us, vision interacts with kinesthesis. Stand with your right heel in front of your left toes. Easy. Now close your eyes and you will probably wobble.

Bodies in space These high school competitive cheer team members can thank their inner ears for the information that enables their brains to monitor their bodies' position so expertly.

© Robert Kanavel

Sensory information travels to these areas of the brain's cerebral cortex:

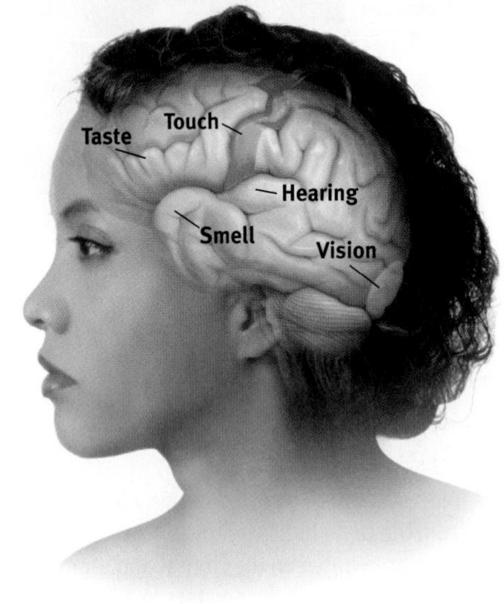

TABLE 19.2

Summarizing the Senses

Sensory System	Source	Receptors
Vision	Light waves striking the eye	Rods and cones in the retina
Hearing	Sound waves striking the outer ear	Cochlear hair cells in the inner ear
Touch	Pressure, warmth, cold on the skin	Skin receptors detect pressure, warmth, cold, and pain
Taste	Chemical molecules in the mouth	Basic tongue receptors for sweet, sour, salty, bitter, and umami
Smell	Chemical molecules breathed in through the nose	Millions of receptors at top of nasal cavity
Body position—kinesthesis	Any change in position of a body part, interacting with vision	Kinesthetic sensors all over the body
Body movement—vestibular sense	Movement of fluids in the inner ear caused by head/body movement	Hairlike receptors in the semicircular canals and vestibular sacs

A companion **vestibular sense** monitors your head's (and thus your body's) position and movement. The biological gyroscopes for this sense of equilibrium are in your inner ear. The *semicircular canals*, which look like a three-dimensional pretzel (Figure 19.2a), and the *vestibular sacs*, which connect the canals with the cochlea, contain fluid that moves when your head rotates or tilts. This movement stimulates hairlike receptors, which send messages to the cerebellum at the back of the brain, thus enabling you to sense your body position and to maintain your balance.

If you twirl around and then come to an abrupt halt, neither the fluid in your semicircular canals nor your kinesthetic receptors will immediately return to their neutral state. The dizzy aftereffect fools your brain with the sensation that you're still spinning. This illustrates a principle that underlies perceptual illusions: Mechanisms that normally give us an accurate experience of the world can, under special conditions, fool us. Understanding how we get fooled provides clues to how our perceptual system works.

* * *

For a summary of our sensory systems, see **TABLE 19.2**.

RETRIEVAL PRACTICE

- Where are vestibular sense receptors located?

ANSWER: the inner ear

vestibular sense the sense of body movement and position, including the sense of balance.

MODULE REVIEW

The Nonvisual Senses

Learning Objectives

RETRIEVAL PRACTICE Take a moment to answer each of these Learning Objective Questions (repeated here from within the module). Then turn to Appendix B, Complete Module Reviews, to check your answers. Research suggests that trying to answer these questions on your own will improve your long-term retention (McDaniel et al., 2009).

19-1: What are the characteristics of air pressure waves that we hear as sound, and how does the ear transform sound energy into neural messages?

19-2: What theories help us understand pitch perception?

19-3: How do we locate sounds?

19-4: How do we sense touch?

19-5: How can we best understand and control pain?

19-6: How do we experience taste and smell, and how do they interact?

19-7: How do we sense our body's position and movement?

Terms and Concepts to Remember

RETRIEVAL PRACTICE Test yourself on these terms by trying to write down the definition before flipping back to the referenced page to check your answer.

audition, p. 257
frequency, p. 257
pitch, p. 257
middle ear, p. 258
cochlea [KOHK-lee-uh], p. 258
inner ear, p. 258
sensorineural hearing loss, p. 258
conduction hearing loss, p. 258
cochlear implant, p. 260
place theory, p. 261
frequency theory, p. 261
gate-control theory, p. 264
sensory interaction, p. 267
embodied cognition, p. 268
kinesthesis [kin-ehs-THEE-sehs], p. 271
vestibular sense, p. 272

RETRIEVAL PRACTICE Gain an advantage, and benefit from immediate feedback, with the interactive self-testing resources at www.worthpublishers.com/myers.

Learning

When a chinook salmon first emerges from its egg in a stream's gravel bed, its genes provide most of the behavioral instructions it needs for life. It knows instinctively how and where to swim, what to eat, and most spectacularly, where to go and when and how to return to its birthplace. Guided by the scent of its home stream, it pursues an upstream odyssey to its ancestral spawning ground and seeks out the best gravel and water flow for breeding. It then mates and, its life mission accomplished, dies.

Unlike salmon, we are not born with a genetic plan for life. Much of what we do we learn from experience. Although we

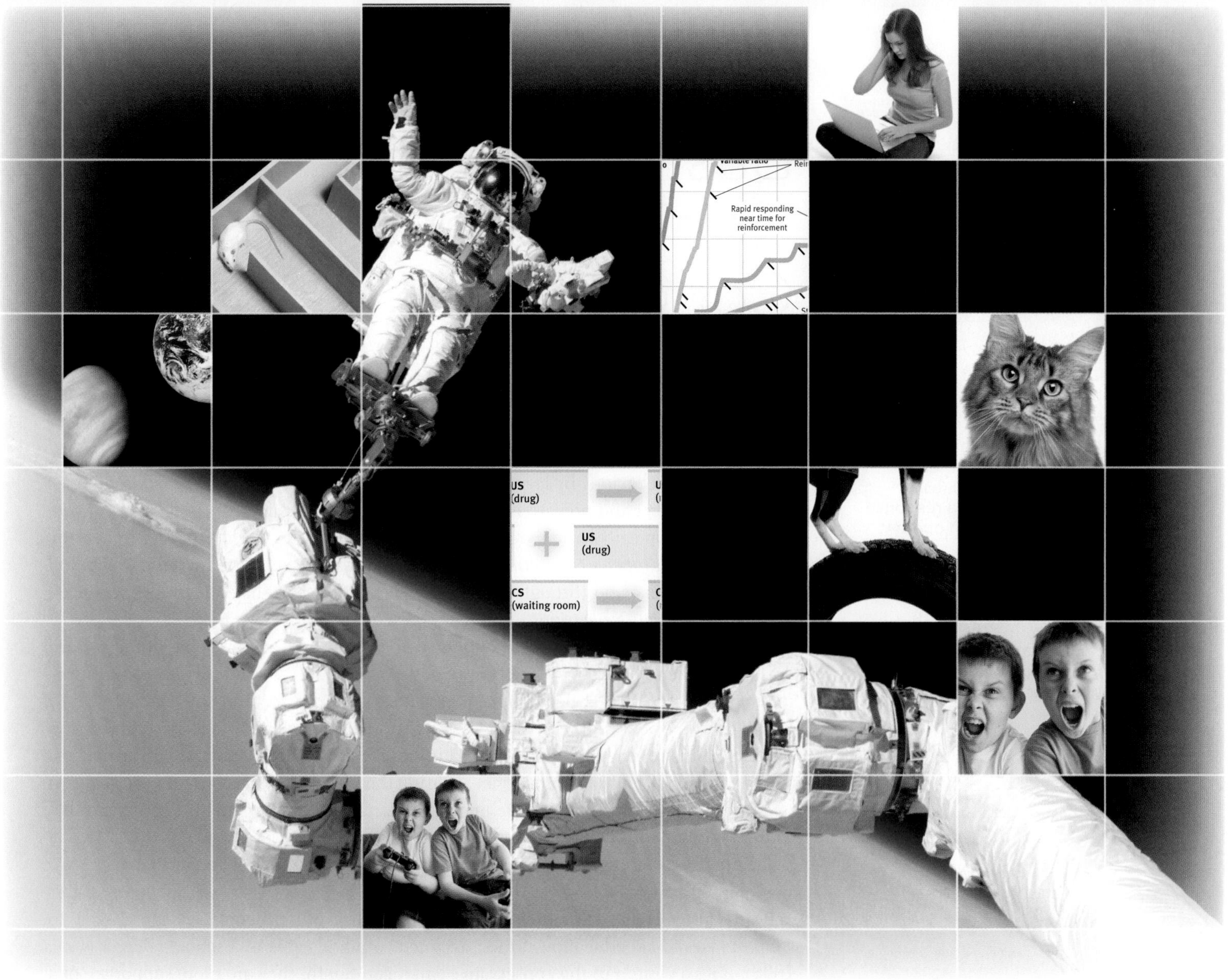

MODULES

struggle to find the life direction a salmon is born with, our learning gives us more flexibility. We can learn how to build grass huts or snow shelters, submarines or space stations, and thereby adjust to almost any environment. Indeed, nature's most important gift to us may be our *adaptability*—our capacity to learn new behaviors that help us cope with changing circumstances.

Learning breeds hope. What is learnable we can potentially teach—a fact that encourages parents, educators, coaches, and animal trainers. What has been learned we can potentially change by new learning—an assumption that underlies counseling, psychotherapy, and rehabilitation programs. No matter how unhappy, unsuccessful, or unloving we are, that need not be the end of our story.

No topic is closer to the heart of psychology than *learning*. Psychologists study infants' learning, and the learning of visual perceptions, of a drug's expected effect, and of gender roles. They also consider how learning shapes our thought and language, our motivations and emotions, our personalities and attitudes. In other modules we see how the brain stores and retrieves learning, but Modules 21 through 23 examine classical conditioning, operant conditioning, the effects of biology and cognition on learning, and learning by observation.

MODULE 20

- How Do We Learn?
- Classical Conditioning

Basic Learning Concepts and Classical Conditioning

learning the process of acquiring new and relatively enduring information or behaviors.

associative learning learning that certain events occur together. The events may be two stimuli (as in classical conditioning) or a response and its consequence (as in operant conditioning).

stimulus any event or situation that evokes a response.

cognitive learning the acquisition of mental information, whether by observing events, by watching others, or through language.

How Do We Learn?

20-1 What is learning, and what are some basic forms of learning?

Psychologists define **learning** as the process of acquiring new and relatively enduring information or behaviors. By learning, we humans are able to adapt to our environments. We learn to expect and prepare for significant events such as food or pain *(classical conditioning)*. We typically learn to repeat acts that bring rewards and to avoid acts that bring unwanted results *(operant conditioning)*. We learn new behaviors by observing events and by watching others, and through language we learn things we have neither experienced nor observed *(cognitive learning)*. But *how* do we learn?

More than 200 years ago, philosophers such as John Locke and David Hume echoed Aristotle's conclusion from 2000 years earlier: We learn by *association*. Our minds naturally connect events that occur in sequence. Suppose you see and smell freshly baked bread, eat some, and find it satisfying. The next time you see and smell fresh bread, you will expect that eating it will again be satisfying. So, too, with sounds. If you associate a sound with a frightening consequence, hearing the sound alone may trigger your fear. As one 4-year-old exclaimed after watching a TV character get mugged, "If I had heard that music, I wouldn't have gone around the corner!" (Wells, 1981).

Learned associations often operate subtly. Give people a red pen (associated with error marking) rather than a black pen and, when correcting essays, they will spot more errors and give lower grades (Rutchick et al., 2010). When voting, people are more likely to support taxes to aid education if their assigned voting place is in a school (Berger et al., 2008). If it's a church in the conservative American South, they are more supportive of a same-sex marriage ban (Rutchick, 2010).

Learned associations also feed our habitual behaviors (Wood & Neal, 2007). As we repeat behaviors in a given context—sleeping in a certain posture in bed, walking certain routes on campus, eating popcorn in a movie theater—the behaviors become associated with the contexts. Our next experience of the context then evokes our habitual response. How long does it take to form such habits? To find out, one British research team asked 96 university students to choose some healthy behavior (such as running before dinner or eating fruit with lunch), to do it daily for 84 days, and to record whether the behavior felt automatic (something they did without thinking and would find it hard not to do). On average, behaviors became habitual after about 66 days (Lally et al., 2010). (Is there something you'd like to make a routine part of your life? Just do it every day for two months, or a bit longer for exercise, and you likely will find yourself with a new habit.)

Most of us would be unable to name the order of the songs on our favorite CD or playlist. Yet, hearing the end of one piece cues (by association) an anticipation of the next. Likewise, when singing your national anthem, you associate the end of each line with the beginning of the next. (Pick a line out of the middle and notice how much harder it is to recall the *previous* line.)

Other animals also learn by association. Disturbed by a squirt of water, the sea slug *Aplysia* protectively withdraws its gill. If the squirts continue, as happens naturally in choppy water, the withdrawal response diminishes. But if the sea slug repeatedly receives an electric shock just after being squirted, its response to the squirt instead grows stronger. The animal has associated the squirt with the impending shock.

Complex animals can learn to associate their own behavior with its outcomes. An aquarium seal will repeat behaviors, such as slapping and barking, that prompt people to toss it a herring.

By linking two events that occur close together, both animals are exhibiting **associative learning.** The sea slug associates the squirt with an impending shock; the seal associates

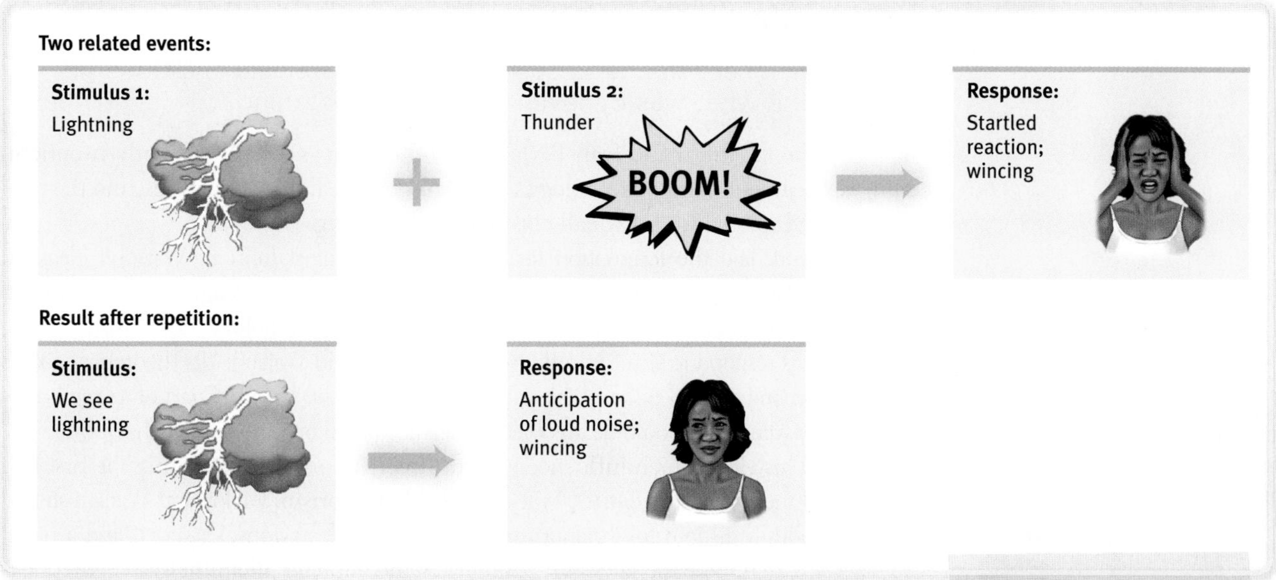

FIGURE 20.1
Classical conditioning

slapping and barking with a herring treat. Each animal has learned something important to its survival: predicting the immediate future.

This process of learning associations is *conditioning*, and it takes two main forms:

- In *classical conditioning*, we learn to associate two stimuli and thus to anticipate events. (A **stimulus** is any event or situation that evokes a response.) We learn that a flash of lightning signals an impending crack of thunder; when lightning flashes nearby, we start to brace ourselves (**FIGURE 20.1**).
- In *operant conditioning*, we learn to associate a response (our behavior) and its consequence. Thus we (and other animals) learn to repeat acts followed by good results (**FIGURE 20.2**) and avoid acts followed by bad results.

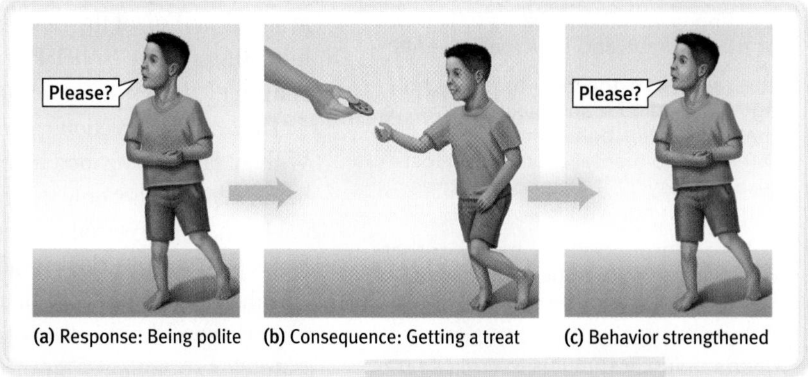

FIGURE 20.2
Operant conditioning

To simplify, we will explore these two types of associative learning separately. Often, though, they occur together, as on one Japanese cattle ranch, where the clever rancher outfitted his herd with electronic pagers, which he calls from his cell phone. After a week of training, the animals learn to associate two stimuli—the beep on their pager and the arrival of food (classical conditioning). But they also learn to associate their hustling to the food trough with the pleasure of eating (operant conditioning).

Conditioning is not the only form of learning. Through **cognitive learning** we acquire mental information that guides our behavior. *Observational learning*, one form of cognitive learning, lets us learn from others' experiences. Chimpanzees, for example, sometimes learn behaviors merely by watching others perform them. If one animal sees another solve a puzzle and gain a food reward, the observer may perform the trick more quickly. So, too, in humans: We look and we learn.

Let's look more closely now at classical conditioning.

RETRIEVAL PRACTICE

- Why are habits, such as having something sweet with that cup of coffee, so hard to break?

ANSWER: Habits form when we repeat behaviors in a given context and, as a result, learn associations—often without our awareness. For example, we may have eaten a sweet pastry with a cup of coffee often enough to associate the flavor of the coffee with the treat, so that the cup of coffee alone just doesn't seem right anymore!

Classical Conditioning

20-2 What are the basic components of classical conditioning, and what was behaviorism's view of learning?

For many people, the name Ivan Pavlov (1849–1936) rings a bell. His early twentieth-century experiments—now psychology's most famous research—are classics, and the phenomenon he explored we justly call **classical conditioning.**

Pavlov's work laid the foundation for many of psychologist John B. Watson's ideas. In searching for laws underlying learning, Watson (1913) urged his colleagues to discard reference to inner thoughts, feelings, and motives. The science of psychology should instead study how organisms respond to stimuli in their environments, said Watson: "Its theoretical goal is the prediction and control of behavior. Introspection forms no essential part of its methods." Simply said, psychology should be an objective science based on observable behavior.

Ivan Pavlov "Experimental investigation . . . should lay a solid foundation for a future true science of psychology" (1927).

Sovfoto

This view, which influenced North American psychology during the first half of the twentieth century, Watson called **behaviorism.** Pavlov and Watson shared both a disdain for "mentalistic" concepts (such as consciousness) and a belief that the basic laws of learning were the same for all animals—whether dogs or humans. Few researchers today propose that psychology should ignore mental processes, but most now agree that classical conditioning is a basic form of learning by which all organisms adapt to their environment.

Pavlov's Experiments

Pavlov was driven by a lifelong passion for research. After setting aside his initial plan to follow his father into the Russian Orthodox priesthood, Pavlov received a medical degree at age 33 and spent the next two decades studying the digestive system. This work earned him Russia's first Nobel Prize in 1904. But his novel experiments on learning, which consumed the last three decades of his life, earned this feisty scientist his place in history.

Pavlov's new direction came when his creative mind seized on an incidental observation. Without fail, putting food in a dog's mouth caused the animal to salivate. Moreover, the dog began salivating not only to the taste of the food, but also to the mere sight of the food, or the food dish, or the person delivering the food, or even the sound of that person's approaching footsteps. At first, Pavlov considered these "psychic secretions" an annoyance—until he realized that these **respondent behaviors** pointed to a simple but important form of learning.

Pavlov and his assistants tried to imagine what the dog was thinking and feeling as it drooled in anticipation of the food. This only led them into fruitless debates. So, to explore the phenomenon more objectively, they experimented. To eliminate other possible influences, they isolated the dog in a small room, secured it in a harness, and attached a device to divert its saliva to a measuring instrument. From the next room, they presented food—first by sliding in a food bowl, later by blowing meat powder into the dog's mouth at a precise moment. They then paired various **neutral stimuli (NS)**—events the dog could see or hear but didn't associate with food—with food in the dog's mouth. If a sight or sound regularly signaled the arrival of food, would the dog learn the link? If so, would it begin salivating in anticipation of the food?

The answers proved to be *Yes* and *Yes*. Just before placing food in the dog's mouth to produce salivation, Pavlov sounded a tone. After several pairings of tone and food, the dog, now anticipating the meat powder, began salivating to the tone alone. In later experiments, a buzzer[1], a light, a touch on the leg, even the sight of a circle set off the drooling.

classical conditioning a type of learning in which one learns to link two or more stimuli and anticipate events.

behaviorism the view that psychology (1) should be an objective science that (2) studies behavior without reference to mental processes. Most research psychologists today agree with (1) but not with (2).

respondent behavior behavior that occurs as an automatic response to some stimulus.

neutral stimulus (NS) in classical conditioning, a stimulus that elicits no response before conditioning.

unconditioned response (UR) in classical conditioning, an unlearned, naturally occurring response (such as salivation) to an unconditioned stimulus (US) (such as food in the mouth).

unconditioned stimulus (US) in classical conditioning, a stimulus that unconditionally—naturally and automatically—triggers a response (UR).

conditioned response (CR) in classical conditioning, a learned response to a previously neutral (but now conditioned) stimulus (CS).

conditioned stimulus (CS) in classical conditioning, an originally irrelevant stimulus that, after association with an unconditioned stimulus (US), comes to trigger a conditioned response (CR).

[1] The "buzzer" (English translation) was perhaps Pavlov's supposed bell—a small electric bell (Tully, 2003).

(This procedure works with people, too. When hungry young Londoners viewed abstract figures before smelling peanut butter or vanilla, their brain soon responded in anticipation to the abstract images alone [Gottfried et al., 2003].)

A dog doesn't learn to salivate in response to food in its mouth. Food in the mouth automatically, *unconditionally*, triggers a dog's salivary reflex (**FIGURE 20.3**). Thus, Pavlov called the drooling an **unconditioned response (UR)**. And he called the food an **unconditioned stimulus (US)**.

FIGURE 20.3
Pavlov's classic experiment Pavlov presented a neutral stimulus (a tone) just before an unconditioned stimulus (food in mouth). The neutral stimulus then became a conditioned stimulus, producing a conditioned response.

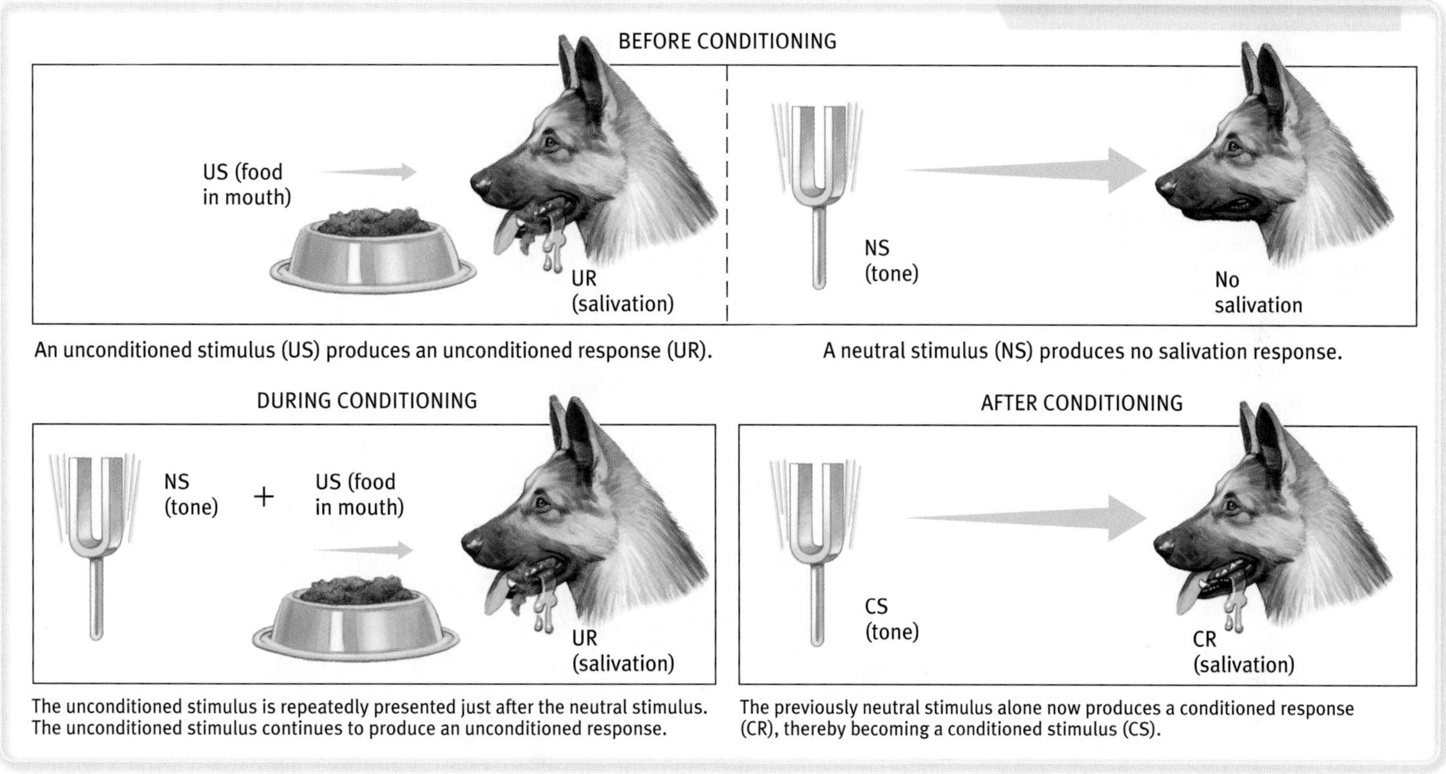

Salivation in response to the tone, however, is learned. Because it is *conditional* upon the dog's associating the tone and the food, we call this response the **conditioned response (CR).** The stimulus that used to be neutral (in this case, a previously meaningless tone that now triggers the salivation) is the **conditioned stimulus (CS).** Distinguishing these two kinds of stimuli and responses is easy: Conditioned = learned; *un*conditioned = *un*learned.

If Pavlov's demonstration of associative learning was so simple, what did he do for the next three decades? What discoveries did his research factory publish in his 532

PEANUTS

PEANUTS reprinted by permission of United Feature Syndicate, Inc.

papers on salivary conditioning (Windholz, 1997)? He and his associates explored five major conditioning processes: *acquisition, extinction, spontaneous recovery, generalization,* and *discrimination.*

> **RETRIEVAL PRACTICE**
>
> - An experimenter sounds a tone just before delivering an air puff to your blinking eye. After several repetitions, you blink to the tone alone. What is the NS? The US? The UR? The CS? The CR?
>
> ANSWERS: NS = tone before procedure; US = air puff; UR = blink to air puff; CS = tone after procedure; CR = blink to tone

Acquisition

20-3 In classical conditioning, what are the processes of acquisition, extinction, spontaneous recovery, generalization, and discrimination?

To understand the **acquisition,** or initial learning, of the stimulus-response relationship, Pavlov and his associates had to confront the question of timing: How much time should elapse between presenting the NS (the tone, the light, the touch) and the US (the food)? In most cases, not much—half a second usually works well.

What do you suppose would happen if the food (US) appeared before the tone (NS) rather than after? Would conditioning occur? Not likely. With but a few exceptions, conditioning doesn't happen when the NS follows the US. *Remember, classical conditioning is biologically adaptive because it helps humans and other animals prepare for good or bad events.* To Pavlov's dogs, the originally neutral tone became a (CS) after signaling an important biological event—the arrival of food (US). To deer in the forest, the snapping of a twig (CS) may signal a predator's approach (US). If the good or bad event has already occurred, the tone or the sound won't help the animal prepare.

More recent research on male Japanese quail shows how a CS can signal another important biological event (Domjan, 1992, 1994, 2005). Just before presenting a sexually approachable female quail, the researchers turned on a red light. Over time, as the red light continued to herald the female's arrival, the light caused the male quail to become excited. They developed a preference for their cage's red-light district, and when a female appeared, they mated with her more quickly and released more semen and sperm (Matthews et al., 2007). All in all, the quail's capacity for classical conditioning gives it a reproductive edge.

Eric Isselée/Shutterstock

In humans, too, objects, smells, and sights associated with sexual pleasure—even a geometric figure in one experiment—can become conditioned stimuli for sexual arousal (Byrne, 1982). Onion breath does not usually produce sexual arousal. But when repeatedly paired with a passionate kiss, it can become a CS and do just that (**FIGURE 20.4**). The larger lesson: *Conditioning helps an animal survive and reproduce—by responding to cues that help it gain food, avoid dangers, locate mates, and produce offspring* (Hollis, 1997).

Through **higher-order conditioning,** a new NS can become a new CS. All that's required is for it to become associated with a previously conditioned stimulus. If a tone regularly signals food and produces salivation, then a light that becomes associated with the tone may also begin to trigger salivation. Although this higher-order conditioning (also called *second-order conditioning*) tends to be weaker than first-order conditioning, it influences our everyday lives. Imagine that something makes us very

acquisition in classical conditioning, the initial stage, when one links a neutral stimulus and an unconditioned stimulus so that the neutral stimulus begins triggering the conditioned response. In operant conditioning, the strengthening of a reinforced response.

higher-order conditioning a procedure in which the conditioned stimulus in one conditioning experience is paired with a new neutral stimulus, creating a second (often weaker) conditioned stimulus. For example, an animal that has learned that a tone predicts food might then learn that a light predicts the tone and begin responding to the light alone. (Also called *second-order conditioning.*)

extinction the diminishing of a conditioned response; occurs in classical conditioning when an unconditioned stimulus (US) does not follow a conditioned stimulus (CS); occurs in operant conditioning when a response is no longer reinforced.

spontaneous recovery the reappearance, after a pause, of an extinguished conditioned response.

Remember:
NS = Neutral Stimulus
US = Unconditioned Stimulus
UR = Unconditioned Response
CS = Conditioned Stimulus
CR = Conditioned Response

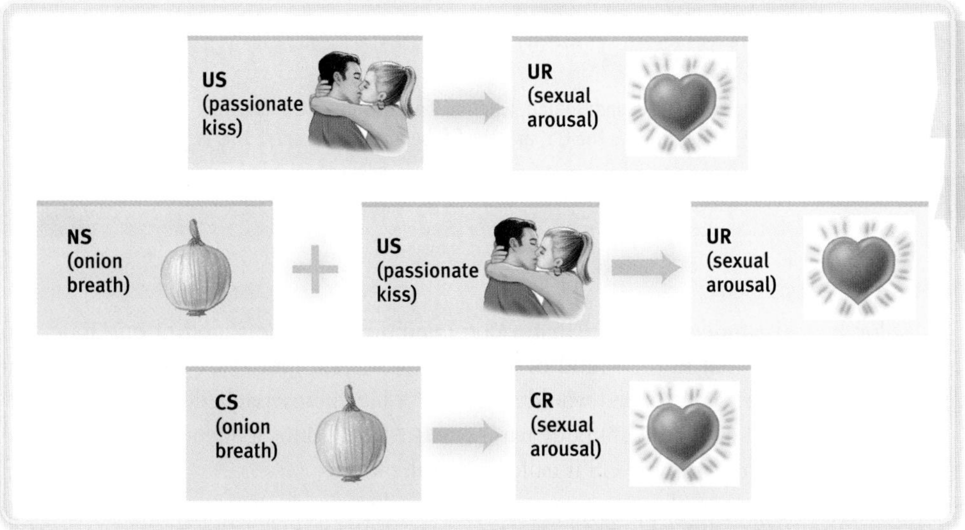

FIGURE 20.4
An unexpected CS Psychologist Michael Tirrell (1990) recalled: "My first girlfriend loved onions, so I came to associate onion breath with kissing. Before long, onion breath sent tingles up and down my spine. Oh what a feeling!"

afraid (perhaps a guard dog associated with a previous dog bite). If something else, such as the sound of a barking dog, brings to mind that guard dog, the bark alone may make us feel a little afraid.

RETRIEVAL PRACTICE

- If the aroma of cake baking sets your mouth to watering, what is the US? The CS? The CR?

ANSWERS: The cake (and its taste) are the US. The associated aroma is the CS. Salivation to the aroma is the CR.

Extinction and Spontaneous Recovery

What would happen, Pavlov wondered, if after conditioning, the CS occurred repeatedly without the US? If the tone sounded again and again, but no food appeared, would the tone still trigger salivation? The answer was mixed. The dogs salivated less and less, a reaction known as **extinction**, the diminished responding that occurs when the CS (tone) no longer signals an impending US (food). But a different picture emerged when Pavlov allowed several hours to elapse before sounding the tone again. After the delay, the dogs would again begin salivating to the tone (**FIGURE 20.5**). This **spontaneous recovery**—the reappearance of a (weakened) CR after a pause—suggested to Pavlov that extinction was suppressing the CR rather than eliminating it.

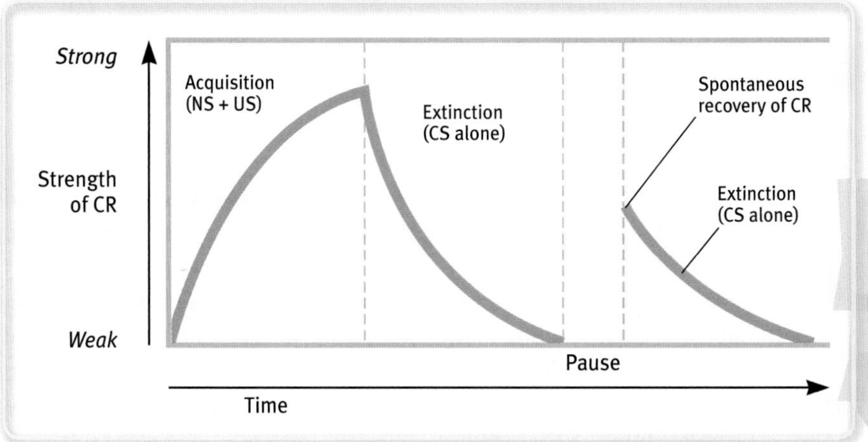

FIGURE 20.5
Idealized curve of acquisition, extinction, and spontaneous recovery The rising curve shows that the CR rapidly grows stronger as the NS becomes a CS as it is repeatedly paired with the US *(acquisition)*, then weakens as the CS is presented alone *(extinction)*. After a pause, the CR reappears *(spontaneous recovery)*.

RETRIEVAL PRACTICE

- The first step of classical conditioning, when an NS becomes a CS, is called __________. When a US no longer follows the CS, and the CR becomes weakened, this is __________.

ANSWERS: acquisition; extinction

Generalization

Pavlov and his students noticed that a dog conditioned to the sound of one tone also responded somewhat to the sound of a new and different tone. Likewise, a dog conditioned to salivate when rubbed would also drool a bit when scratched (Windholz, 1989) or when touched on a different body part (**FIGURE 20.6**). This tendency to respond likewise to stimuli similar to the CS is called **generalization.**

Generalization can be adaptive, as when toddlers taught to fear moving cars also become afraid of moving trucks and motorcycles. And generalized fears can linger. One Argentine writer who underwent torture still recoils with fear when he sees black shoes—his first glimpse of his torturers as they approached his cell. Generalized anxiety reactions have been demonstrated in laboratory studies comparing abused with nonabused children (**FIGURE 20.7**). When an angry face appears on a computer screen, abused children's brain-wave responses are dramatically stronger and longer lasting (Pollak et al., 1998).

FIGURE 20.6
Generalization Pavlov demonstrated generalization by attaching miniature vibrators to various parts of a dog's body. After conditioning salivation to stimulation of the thigh, he stimulated other areas. The closer a stimulated spot was to the dog's thigh, the stronger the conditioned response. (From Pavlov, 1927.)

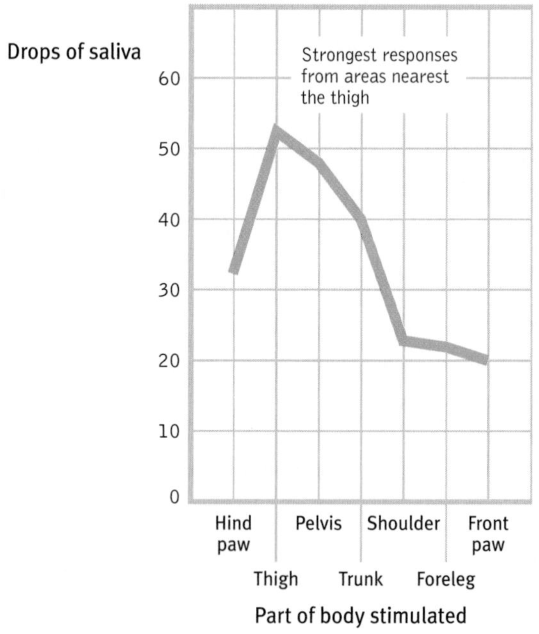

FIGURE 20.7
Child abuse leaves tracks in the brain Abused children's sensitized brains react more strongly to angry faces (Pollak et al., 1998). This generalized anxiety response may help explain their greater risk of psychological disorder.

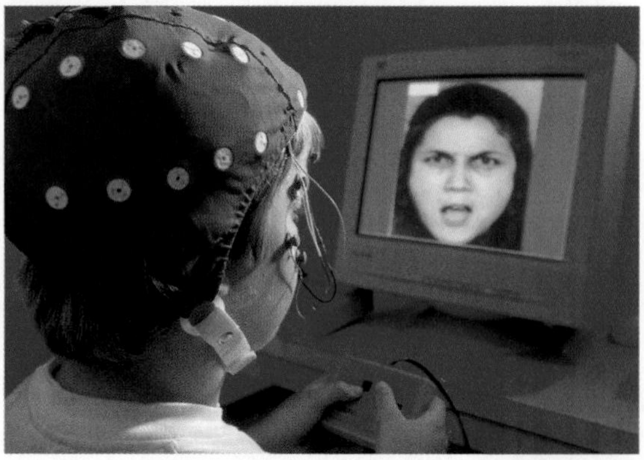
© UW–Madison News & Public Affairs. Photo by Jeff Miller

Stimuli similar to naturally disgusting objects will, by association, also evoke some disgust, as otherwise desirable fudge does when shaped to resemble dog feces (Rozin et al., 1986). Researchers have also found that we like unfamiliar people more if they look somewhat like someone we've learned to like rather than dislike (Verosky & Todorov, 2010). (They find this by subtly morphing the facial features of someone we've learned to like or dislike onto a novel face.) In each of these human examples, people's emotional reactions to one stimulus have generalized to similar stimuli.

MODULE REVIEW

Basic Learning Concepts and Classical Conditioning

Learning Objectives

RETRIEVAL PRACTICE Take a moment to answer each of these Learning Objective Questions (repeated here from within the module). Then turn to Appendix B, Complete Module Reviews, to check your answers. Research suggests that trying to answer these questions on your own will improve your long-term retention (McDaniel et al., 2009).

20-1: What is learning, and what are some basic forms of learning?

20-2: What are the basic components of classical conditioning, and what was behaviorism's view of learning?

20-3: In classical conditioning, what are the processes of acquisition, extinction, spontaneous recovery, generalization, and discrimination?

20-4: Why does Pavlov's work remain so important, and what have been some applications of his work to human health and well-being?

Terms and Concepts to Remember

RETRIEVAL PRACTICE Test yourself on these terms by trying to write down the definition before flipping back to the referenced page to check your answer.

learning, p. 276
associative learning, p. 276
stimulus, p. 277
cognitive learning, p. 277
classical conditioning, p. 278
behaviorism, p. 278
respondent behavior, p. 278
neutral stimulus (NS), p. 278
unconditioned response (UR), p. 279
unconditioned stimulus (US), p. 279
conditioned response (CR), p. 279
conditioned stimulus (CS), p. 279
acquisition, p. 280
higher-order conditioning, p. 280
extinction, p. 281
spontaneous recovery, p. 281
generalization, p. 282
discrimination, p. 283

RETRIEVAL PRACTICE Gain an advantage, and benefit from immediate feedback, with the interactive self-testing resources at www.worthpublishers.com/myers.

MODULE 21

Operant Conditioning

- Skinner's Experiments
- Skinner's Legacy
- Contrasting Classical and Operant Conditioning

21-1 What is operant conditioning, and how is operant behavior reinforced and shaped?

It's one thing to classically condition a dog to salivate at the sound of a tone, or a child to fear moving cars. To teach an elephant to **learn** how to walk on its hind legs or a child how to say *please*, we turn to operant conditioning.

Classical conditioning and operant conditioning are both forms of **associative learning,** yet their difference is straightforward:

- *Classical conditioning* forms associations between **stimuli** (a *conditioned stimulus*, or CS, and the *unconditioned stimulus*, or US, it signals). It also involves *respondent behavior*—actions that are automatic responses to a stimulus (such as salivating in response to meat powder and later in response to a tone).
- In **operant conditioning,** organisms associate their own actions with consequences. Actions followed by reinforcers increase; those followed by punishers often decrease. Behavior that *operates* on the environment to *produce* rewarding or punishing stimuli is called *operant behavior.*

learning the process of acquiring new and relatively enduring information or behaviors.

associative learning learning that certain events occur together. The events may be two stimuli (as in classical conditioning) or a response and its consequence (as in operant conditioning).

stimulus any event or situation that evokes a response.

operant conditioning a type of learning in which behavior is strengthened if followed by a reinforcer or diminished if followed by a punisher.

law of effect Thorndike's principle that behaviors followed by favorable consequences become more likely, and that behaviors followed by unfavorable consequences become less likely.

RETRIEVAL PRACTICE

- With __________ conditioning, we learn associations between events we do not control. With __________ conditioning, we learn associations between our behavior and resulting events.

ANSWERS: classical; operant

Skinner's Experiments

B. F. Skinner (1904–1990) was a college English major and an aspiring writer who, seeking a new direction, entered psychology graduate school. He went on to become modern behaviorism's most influential and controversial figure. Skinner's work elaborated on what psychologist Edward L. Thorndike (1874–1949) called the **law of effect:** Rewarded behavior is likely to recur (**FIGURE 21.1**). Using Thorndike's law of effect as a starting point, Skinner developed a behavioral technology that revealed principles of *behavior control.* These principles also enabled him to teach pigeons such unpigeon-like behaviors as walking in a

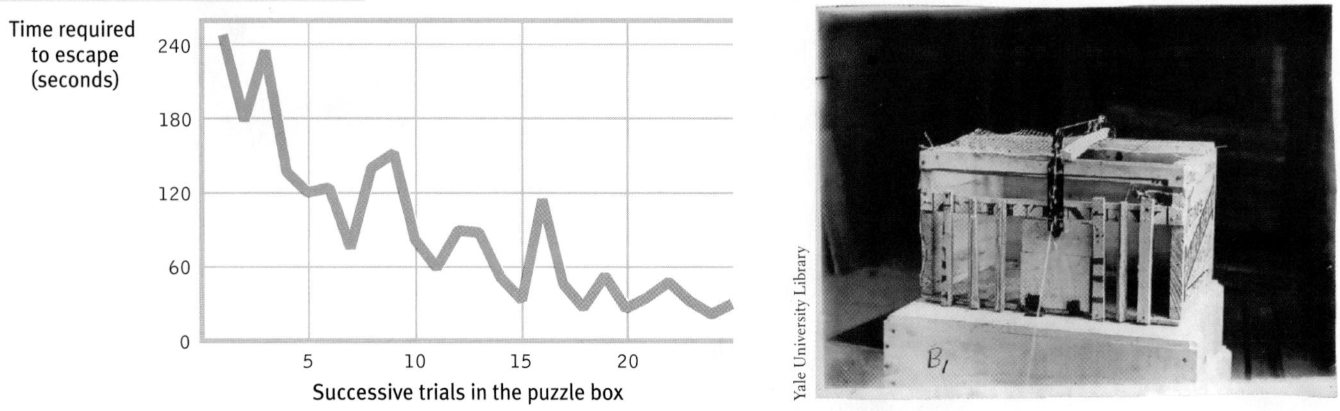

Yale University Library

FIGURE 21.1
Cat in a puzzle box Thorndike used a fish reward to entice cats to find their way out of a puzzle box (right) through a series of maneuvers. The cats' performance tended to improve with successive trials (left), illustrating Thorndike's *law of effect.* (Adapted from Thorndike, 1898.)

Eric Isselée/Shutterstock

figure 8, playing Ping-Pong, and keeping a missile on course by pecking at a screen target.

For his pioneering studies, Skinner designed an **operant chamber,** popularly known as a *Skinner box* (**FIGURE 21.2**). The box has a bar (a lever) that an animal presses—or a key (a disc) the animal pecks—to release a reward of food or water. It also has a device that records these responses. This design creates a stage on which rats and others animals act out Skinner's concept of **reinforcement:** any event that strengthens (increases the frequency of) a preceding response. What is reinforcing depends on the animal and the conditions. For people, it may be praise, attention, or a paycheck. For hungry and thirsty rats, food and water work well. Skinner's experiments have done far more than teach us how to pull habits out of a rat. They have explored the precise conditions that foster efficient and enduring learning.

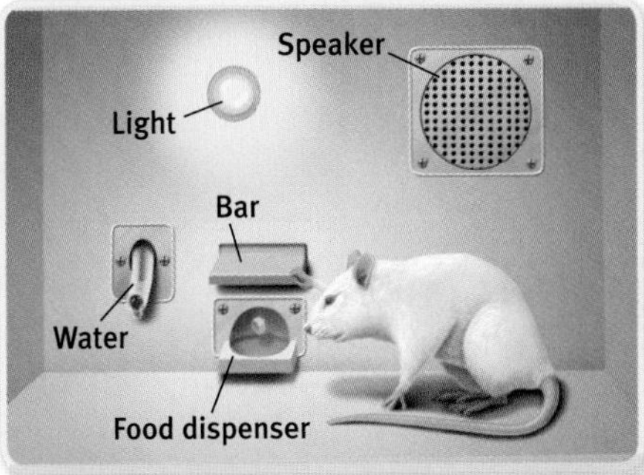

FIGURE 21.2
A Skinner box Inside the box, the rat presses a bar for a food reward. Outside, a measuring device (not shown here) records the animal's accumulated responses.

Shaping Behavior

Imagine that you wanted to condition a hungry rat to press a bar. Like Skinner, you could tease out this action with **shaping,** gradually guiding the rat's actions toward the desired behavior. First, you would watch how the animal naturally behaves, so that you could build on its existing behaviors. You might give the rat a bit of food each time it approaches the bar. Once the rat is approaching regularly, you would give the food only when it moves close to the bar, then closer still. Finally, you would require it to touch the bar to get food. With this method of *successive approximations*, you reward responses that are ever-closer to the final desired behavior, and you ignore all other responses. By making rewards contingent on desired behaviors, researchers and animal trainers gradually shape complex behaviors.

Shaping can also help us understand what nonverbal organisms perceive. Can a dog distinguish red and green? Can a baby hear the difference between lower- and higher-pitched tones? If we can shape them to respond to one stimulus and not to another, then we know they can perceive the difference. Such experiments have even shown that some animals can form concepts. When experimenters reinforced pigeons for pecking after seeing a human face, but not after seeing other images, the pigeon's behavior showed that it could recognize human faces (Herrnstein & Loveland, 1964). In this experiment, the human face was a *discriminative stimulus.* Like a green traffic light, discriminative stimuli signal that a response will be reinforced. After being trained to discriminate among classes of events or objects—flowers, people, cars, chairs—pigeons can usually identify the category in which a new pictured object belongs (Bhatt et al., 1988; Wasserman, 1993). They have even been trained to discriminate between the music of Bach and Stravinsky (Porter & Neuringer, 1984).

Reuters/Corbis

Reinforcers vary with circumstances What is reinforcing (a heat lamp) to one animal (a cold meerkat) may not be to another (an overheated child). What is reinforcing in one situation (a cold snap at the Taronga Zoo in Sydney) may not be in another (a sweltering summer day).

Khamis Ramadhan

Shaping rats to save lives A Gambian giant pouched rat, having been shaped to sniff out land mines, receives a bite of banana after successfully locating a mine during training in Mozambique.

operant chamber in operant conditioning research, a chamber (also known as a *Skinner box*) containing a bar or key that an animal can manipulate to obtain a food or water reinforcer; attached devices record the animal's rate of bar pressing or key pecking.

reinforcement in operant conditioning, any event that *strengthens* the behavior it follows.

shaping an operant conditioning procedure in which reinforcers guide behavior toward closer and closer approximations of the desired behavior.

In everyday life, we continually reinforce and shape others' behavior, said Skinner, though we may not mean to do so. Billy's whining, for example, annoys his parents, but look how they typically respond:

Billy: Could you tie my shoes?
Father: (Continues reading paper.)
Billy: Dad, I need my shoes tied.
Father: Uh, yeah, just a minute.
Billy: DAAAAD! TIE MY SHOES!
Father: How many times have I told you not to whine? Now, which shoe do we do first?

Billy's whining is reinforced, because he gets something desirable—his dad's attention. Dad's response is reinforced because it gets rid of something aversive—Billy's whining.

Or consider a teacher who pastes gold stars on a wall chart beside the names of children scoring 100 percent on spelling tests. As everyone can then see, some children consistently do perfect work. The others, who take the same test and may have worked harder than the academic all-stars, get no rewards. The teacher would be better advised to apply the principles of operant conditioning—to reinforce all spellers for gradual improvements (successive approximations toward perfect spelling of words they find challenging).

Types of Reinforcers

21-2 How do positive and negative reinforcement differ, and what are the basic types of reinforcers?

Up to now, we've mainly been discussing **positive reinforcement,** which strengthens a response by *presenting* a typically pleasurable stimulus after a response. But, as we saw in the whining Billy story, there are *two* basic kinds of reinforcement (**TABLE 21.1**).

TABLE 21.1

Ways to Increase Behavior

Operant Conditioning Term	Description	Examples
Positive reinforcement	Add a desirable stimulus	Pet a dog that comes when you call it; pay the person who paints your house.
Negative reinforcement	Remove an aversive stimulus	Take painkillers to end pain; fasten seat belt to end loud beeping.

Negative reinforcement *strengthens* a response by *reducing or removing* something negative. Billy's whining was *positively* reinforced, because Billy got something desirable—his father's attention. His dad's response to the whining (tying Billy's shoes) was negatively reinforced, because it ended an aversive event—Billy's whining. Similarly, taking aspirin may relieve your headache, and hitting snooze will silence your annoying alarm. These welcome results provide negative reinforcement and increase the odds that you will repeat these behaviors. For drug addicts, the negative reinforcement of ending withdrawal pangs can be a compelling reason to resume using (Baker et al., 2004). Note that *negative reinforcement is not punishment.* (Some friendly advice: Repeat the last five words in your mind.) Rather,

positive reinforcement increasing behaviors by presenting positive reinforcers. A positive reinforcer is any stimulus that, when *presented* after a response, strengthens the response.

negative reinforcement increasing behaviors by stopping or reducing negative stimuli. A negative reinforcer is any stimulus that, when *removed* after a response, strengthens the response. (*Note:* negative reinforcement is not punishment.)

primary reinforcer an innately reinforcing stimulus, such as one that satisfies a biological need.

conditioned reinforcer a stimulus that gains its reinforcing power through its association with a primary reinforcer; also known as a *secondary reinforcer.*

negative reinforcement *removes* a punishing (aversive) event.

Sometimes negative and positive reinforcement coincide. Imagine a worried student who, after goofing off and getting a bad exam grade, studies harder for the next exam. This increased effort may be *negatively* reinforced by reduced anxiety, and *positively* reinforced by a better grade. Whether it works by reducing something aversive, or by giving something desirable, *reinforcement is any consequence that strengthens behavior.*

Dave Coverly/Dist. by Creators Syndicate, Inc.

RETRIEVAL PRACTICE

- How is operant conditioning at work in this cartoon?

ANSWER: If the child follows her older friend's instructions, she will negatively reinforce her caregivers by ceasing her cries when they grant her wishes. The parents will positively reinforce her whines with a treat.

Primary and Conditioned Reinforcers

Getting food when hungry or having a painful headache go away is innately satisfying. These **primary reinforcers** are unlearned. **Conditioned reinforcers,** also called *secondary reinforcers*, get their power through learned association with primary reinforcers. If a rat in a Skinner box learns that a light reliably signals a food delivery, the rat will work to turn on the light. The light has become a conditioned reinforcer. Our lives are filled with conditioned reinforcers—money, good grades, a pleasant tone of voice—each of which has been linked with more basic rewards. If money is a conditioned reinforcer—if people's desire for money is derived from their desire for food—then hunger should also make people more money-hungry, reasoned one European research team (Briers et al., 2006). Indeed, in their experiments, people were less likely to donate to charity when food deprived, and less likely to share money with fellow participants when in a room with hunger-arousing aromas.

Immediate and Delayed Reinforcers

Let's return to the imaginary shaping experiment in which you were conditioning a rat to press a bar. Before performing this "wanted" behavior, the hungry rat will engage in a sequence of "unwanted" behaviors—scratching, sniffing, and moving around. If you present food immediately after any one of these behaviors, the rat will likely repeat that rewarded behavior. But what if the rat presses the bar while you are distracted, and you delay giving the reinforcer? If the delay lasts longer than about 30 seconds, the rat will not learn to press the bar. You will have reinforced other incidental behaviors—more sniffing and moving—that intervened after the bar press.

Unlike rats, humans do respond to delayed reinforcers: the paycheck at the end of the week, the good grade at the end of the semester, the trophy at the end of the season. Indeed, to function effectively we must learn to delay gratification. In laboratory testing, some 4-year-olds show this ability. In choosing a candy, they prefer having a big reward tomorrow to munching on a small one right now. Learning to control our impulses in order to achieve more valued rewards is a big step toward maturity (Logue, 1998a,b). No wonder children who make such choices have tended to become socially competent and high-achieving adults (Mischel et al., 1989).

"Oh, not bad. The light comes on, I press the bar, they write me a check. How about you?"

© The New Yorker Collection, 1993, Tom Cheney from cartoonbank.com. All Rights Reserved.

To our detriment, small but immediate consequences (the enjoyment of watching late-night TV, for example) are sometimes more alluring than big but delayed consequences (feeling alert tomorrow). For many teens, the immediate gratification of risky,

reinforcement schedule a pattern that defines how often a desired response will be reinforced.

continuous reinforcement reinforcing the desired response every time it occurs.

partial (intermittent) reinforcement reinforcing a response only part of the time; results in slower acquisition of a response but much greater resistance to extinction than does continuous reinforcement.

fixed-ratio schedule in operant conditioning, a reinforcement schedule that reinforces a response only after a specified number of responses.

variable-ratio schedule in operant conditioning, a reinforcement schedule that reinforces a response after an unpredictable number of responses.

fixed-interval schedule in operant conditioning, a reinforcement schedule that reinforces a response only after a specified time has elapsed.

variable-interval schedule in operant conditioning, a reinforcement schedule that reinforces a response at unpredictable time intervals.

unprotected sex in passionate moments prevails over the delayed gratifications of safe sex or saved sex. And for many people, the immediate rewards of today's gas-guzzling vehicles, air travel, and air conditioning prevail over the bigger future consequences of global climate change, rising seas, and extreme weather.

Reinforcement Schedules

21-3 How do different reinforcement schedules affect behavior?

In most of our examples, the desired response has been reinforced every time it occurs. But **reinforcement schedules** vary. With **continuous reinforcement,** learning occurs rapidly, which makes this the best choice for mastering a behavior. But *extinction* also occurs rapidly. When reinforcement stops—when we stop delivering food after the rat presses the bar—the behavior soon stops. If a normally dependable candy machine fails to deliver a chocolate bar twice in a row, we stop putting money into it (although a week later we may exhibit spontaneous recovery by trying again).

Real life rarely provides continuous reinforcement. Salespeople do not make a sale with every pitch. But they persist because their efforts are occasionally rewarded. This persistence is typical with **partial (intermittent) reinforcement** schedules, in which responses are sometimes reinforced, sometimes not. Learning is slower to appear, but *resistance to extinction* is greater than with continuous reinforcement. Imagine a pigeon that has learned to peck a key to obtain food. If you gradually phase out the food delivery until it occurs only rarely, in no predictable pattern, the pigeon may peck 150,000 times without a reward (Skinner, 1953). Slot machines reward gamblers in much the same way—occasionally and unpredictably. And like pigeons, slot players keep trying, time and time again. With intermittent reinforcement, hope springs eternal.

Lesson for parents: Partial reinforcement also works with children. *Occasionally* giving in to children's tantrums for the sake of peace and quiet intermittently reinforces the tantrums. This is the very best procedure for making a behavior persist.

Skinner (1961) and his collaborators compared four schedules of partial reinforcement. Some are rigidly fixed, some unpredictably variable.

Fixed-ratio schedules reinforce behavior after a set number of responses. Coffee shops may reward us with a free drink after every 10 purchased. In the laboratory, rats may be reinforced on a fixed ratio of, say, one food pellet for every 30 responses. Once conditioned, animals will pause only briefly after a reinforcer before returning to a high rate of responding (**FIGURE 21.3**).

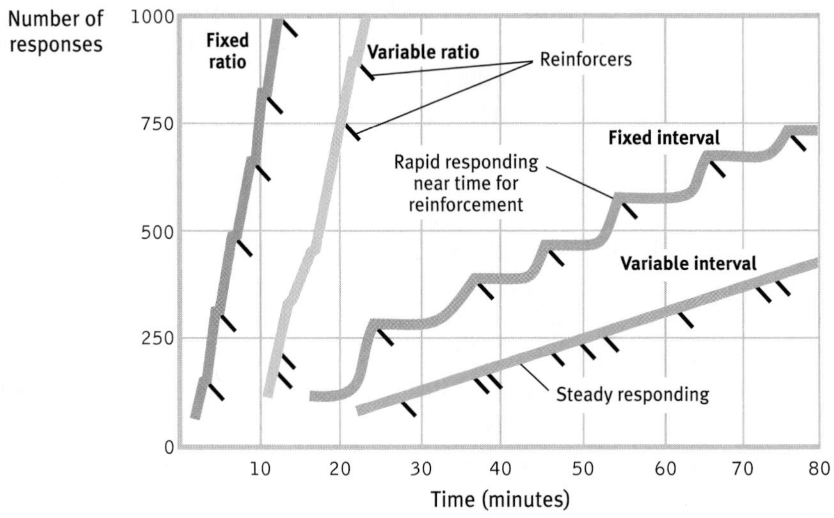

FIGURE 21.3
Intermittent reinforcement schedules Skinner's laboratory pigeons produced these response patterns to each of four reinforcement schedules. (Reinforcers are indicated by diagonal marks.) For people, as for pigeons, reinforcement linked to number of responses (a *ratio schedule*) produces a higher response rate than reinforcement linked to amount of time elapsed (an *interval schedule*). But the predictability of the reward also matters. An unpredictable *(variable)* schedule produces more consistent responding than does a predictable *(fixed)* schedule.

Adapted from "Teaching machines" by B. F. Skinner. Copyright © 1961, Scientific American, Inc. All Rights Reserved.

Variable-ratio schedules provide reinforcers after a seemingly unpredictable number of responses. This is what slot-machine players and fly-casting anglers experience—unpredictable reinforcement—and what makes gambling and fly fishing so hard to extinguish even when both are getting nothing for something. Because reinforcers increase as the number of responses increases, variable-ratio schedules produce high rates of responding.

"The charm of fishing is that it is the pursuit of what is elusive but attainable, a perpetual series of occasions for hope."

Scottish author John Buchan (1875–1940)

Fixed-interval schedules reinforce the first response after a fixed time period. Animals on this type of schedule tend to respond more frequently as the anticipated time for reward draws near. People check more frequently for the mail as the delivery time approaches. A hungry child jiggles the Jell-O more often to see if it has set. Pigeons peck keys more rapidly as the time for reinforcement draws nearer. This produces a choppy stop-start pattern rather than a steady rate of response (see Figure 21.3).

Variable-interval schedules reinforce the first response after *varying* time intervals. Like the message that finally rewards persistence in rechecking for e-mail or a Facebook response, variable-interval schedules tend to produce slow, steady responding. This makes sense, because there is no knowing when the waiting will be over (**TABLE 21.2**).

Vitaly Titov & Maria Sidelnikova/Shutterstock

TABLE 21.2

Schedules of Reinforcement

	Fixed	Variable
Ratio	*Every so many:* reinforcement after every *nth* behavior, such as buy 10 coffees, get 1 free, or pay per product unit produced	*After an unpredictable number:* reinforcement after a random number of behaviors, as when playing slot machines or fly casting
Interval	*Every so often:* reinforcement for behavior after a fixed time, such as Tuesday discount prices	*Unpredictably often:* reinforcement for behavior after a random amount of time, as in checking for a Facebook response

In general, response rates are higher when reinforcement is linked to the number of responses (a ratio schedule) rather than to time (an interval schedule). But responding is more consistent when reinforcement is unpredictable (a variable schedule) than when it is predictable (a fixed schedule). Animal behaviors differ, yet Skinner (1956) contended that the reinforcement principles of operant conditioning are universal. It matters little, he said, what response, what reinforcer, or what species you use. The effect of a given reinforcement schedule is pretty much the same: "Pigeon, rat, monkey, which is which? It doesn't matter. . . . Behavior shows astonishingly similar properties."

RETRIEVAL PRACTICE

- Telemarketers are reinforced by which schedule? People checking the oven to see if the cookies are done are on which schedule? Airline frequent-flyer programs that offer a free flight after every 25,000 miles of travel are using which reinforcement schedule?

ANSWERS: Telemarketers are reinforced on a variable-ratio schedule (after a varying number of calls). Cookie checkers are reinforced on a fixed-interval schedule. Frequent-flyer programs use a fixed-ratio schedule.

punishment an event that tends to *decrease* the behavior that it follows.

Punishment

21-4 How does punishment differ from negative reinforcement, and how does punishment affect behavior?

Reinforcement increases a behavior; **punishment** does the opposite. A *punisher* is any consequence that *decreases* the frequency of a preceding behavior (**TABLE 21.3**). Swift and sure punishers can powerfully restrain unwanted behavior. The rat that is shocked after touching a forbidden object and the child who is burned by touching a hot stove will learn not to repeat those behaviors. Some punishments, though unintentional, are nevertheless quite effective: A dog that has learned to come running at the sound of an electric can opener will stop coming if its owner runs the machine to attract the dog and banish it to the basement.

Criminal behavior, much of it impulsive, is also influenced more by swift and sure punishers than by the threat of severe sentences (Darley & Alter, 2011). Thus, when Arizona introduced an exceptionally harsh sentence for first-time drunk drivers, the drunk-driving rate changed very little. But when Kansas City police started patrolling a high crime area to increase the sureness and swiftness of punishment, that city's crime rate dropped dramatically.

How should we interpret the punishment studies in relation to parenting practices? Many psychologists and supporters of nonviolent parenting note four major drawbacks of physical punishment (Gershoff, 2002; Marshall, 2002).

1. ***Punished behavior is suppressed, not forgotten. This temporary state may (negatively) reinforce parents' punishing behavior.*** The child swears, the parent swats, the parent hears no more swearing and feels the punishment successfully stopped the behavior. No wonder spanking is a hit with so many U.S. parents of 3- and 4-year-olds—more than 9 in 10 of whom acknowledged spanking their children (Kazdin & Benjet, 2003).
2. ***Punishment teaches discrimination among situations.*** In operant conditioning, *discrimination* occurs when an organism learns that certain responses, but not others, will be reinforced. Did the punishment effectively end the child's swearing? Or did the child simply learn that it's not okay to swear around the house, though okay elsewhere?
3. ***Punishment can teach fear.*** In operant conditioning, *generalization* occurs when an organism's response to similar stimuli is also reinforced. A punished child may associate fear not only with the undesirable behavior but also with the person who delivered the punishment or the place it occurred. Thus, children may learn to fear a punishing teacher and try to avoid school, or may become more anxious (Gershoff et al., 2010). For such reasons, most European countries and most U.S. states now ban hitting children in schools and child-care institutions (www.stophitting.com). Eleven countries, including those in Scandinavia, further outlaw hitting by parents, providing children the same legal protection given to spouses (EPOCH, 2000).
4. ***Physical punishment may increase aggression by modeling aggression as a way to cope with problems.*** Studies find that spanked children are at increased risk for aggression (and depression and low self-esteem). We know, for example, that many aggressive delinquents and abusive parents come from abusive families (Straus & Gelles, 1980; Straus et al., 1997).

TABLE 21.3

Ways to Decrease Behavior

Type of Punisher	Description	Possible Examples
Positive punishment	Administer an aversive stimulus	Spray water on a barking dog; give a traffic ticket for speeding
Negative punishment	Withdraw a rewarding stimulus	Take away a teen's driving privileges; revoke a library card for nonpayment of fines

Some researchers note a problem. Well, yes, they say, physically punished children may be more aggressive, for the same reason that people who have undergone psychotherapy are more likely to suffer depression—because they had preexisting problems that triggered the treatments (Larzelere, 2000, 2004). Which is the chicken and which is the egg? Correlations don't hand us an answer.

If one adjusts for preexisting antisocial behavior, then an occasional single swat or two to misbehaving 2- to 6-year-olds looks more effective (Baumrind et al., 2002; Larzelere & Kuhn, 2005). That is especially so if two other conditions are met:

1. The swat is used only as a backup when milder disciplinary tactics, such as a time-out (removing them from reinforcing surroundings) fail.
2. The swat is combined with a generous dose of reasoning and reinforcing.

Other researchers remain unconvinced. After controlling for prior misbehavior, they report that more frequent spankings of young children predict future aggressiveness (Grogan-Kaylor, 2004; Taylor et al., 2010).

Parents of delinquent youths are often unaware of how to achieve desirable behaviors without screaming or hitting their children (Patterson et al., 1982). Training programs can help transform dire threats ("You clean up your room this minute or no dinner!") into positive incentives ("You're welcome at the dinner table after you get your room cleaned up"). Stop and think about it. Aren't many threats of punishment just as forceful, and perhaps more effective, when rephrased positively? Thus, "If you don't get your homework done, there'll be no car" would better be phrased as . . . .

In classrooms, too, teachers can give feedback on papers by saying, "No, but try this . . ." and "Yes, that's it!" Such responses reduce unwanted behavior while reinforcing more desirable alternatives. Remember: *Punishment tells you what not to do; reinforcement tells you what to do.*

What punishment often teaches, said Skinner, is how to avoid it. Most psychologists now favor an emphasis on reinforcement: Notice people doing something right and affirm them for it.

RETRIEVAL PRACTICE

- Fill in the four blanks below with one of the following terms: positive reinforcement (PR), negative reinforcement (NR), positive punishment (PP), and negative punishment (NP). I have provided the first answer (PR) for you.

Type of Stimulus	Give It	Take It Away
Desired (for example, a teen's use of the car):	1. PR	2.____
Undesired/aversive (for example, an insult):	3.____	4.____

ANSWERS: 1. PR (positive reinforcement); 2. NP (negative punishment); 3. PP (positive punishment); 4. NR (negative reinforcement)

Skinner's Legacy

21-5 Why did Skinner's ideas provoke controversy, and how might his operant conditioning principles be applied at school, in sports, at work, and at home?

B. F. Skinner stirred a hornet's nest with his outspoken beliefs. He repeatedly insisted that external influences (not internal thoughts and feelings) shape behavior. And he urged people to use operant principles to influence others' behavior at school, work, and home. Knowing that behavior is shaped by its results, he said we should use rewards to evoke more desirable behavior.

Skinner's critics objected, saying that he dehumanized people by neglecting their personal freedom and by seeking to control their actions. Skinner's reply: External consequences already haphazardly control people's behavior. Why not administer those consequences toward human betterment? Wouldn't reinforcers be more humane than the punishments used in homes, schools, and prisons? And if it is humbling to think that our history has shaped us, doesn't this very idea also give us hope that we can shape our future?

Bachrach/Getty Images

B. F. Skinner "I am sometimes asked, 'Do you think of yourself as you think of the organisms you study?' The answer is yes. So far as I know, my behavior at any given moment has been nothing more than the product of my genetic endowment, my personal history, and the current setting" (1983).

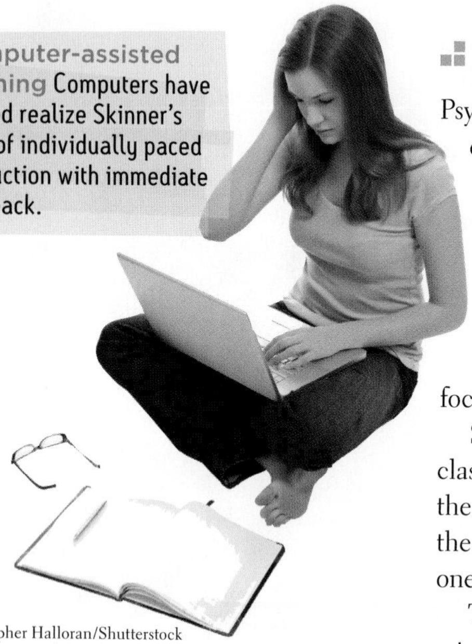

Computer-assisted learning Computers have helped realize Skinner's goal of individually paced instruction with immediate feedback.

Christopher Halloran/Shutterstock

Applications of Operant Conditioning

Psychologists are applying operant conditioning principles to help people with a variety of challenges, from moderating high blood pressure to gaining social skills. Reinforcement technologies are also at work in schools, sports, workplaces, and homes (Flora, 2004).

At School

A generation ago, Skinner envisioned a day when teaching machines and textbooks would shape learning in small steps, immediately reinforcing correct responses. He believed such machines and texts would revolutionize education and free teachers to focus on each student's special needs.

Stand in Skinner's shoes for a moment and imagine two math teachers, each with a class of students ranging from whiz kids to slow learners. Teacher A gives the whole class the same lesson, knowing that the bright kids will breeze through the math concepts, and the slower ones will be frustrated and fail. With so many different children, how could one teacher guide them individually?

Teacher B, faced with a similar class, paces the material according to each student's rate of learning and provides prompt feedback, with positive reinforcement, to both the slow and the fast learners. Thinking as Skinner did, how might you achieve the individualized instruction of Teacher B?

Computers were Skinner's final hope. "Good instruction demands two things," he said. "Students must be told immediately whether what they do is right or wrong and, when right, they must be directed to the step to be taken next." Thus, the computer could be Teacher B—pacing math drills to the student's rate of learning, quizzing the student to find gaps in understanding, giving immediate feedback, and keeping flawless records. To the end of his life, Skinner (1986, 1988, 1989) believed his ideal was achievable. The predicted education revolution has not occurred, partly because the early teaching machines often trained rote learning, not deep processing. Today's interactive student software, web-based learning, and online testing bring us closer to achieving Skinner's ideal.

In Sports

The key to shaping behavior in athletic performance, as elsewhere, is first reinforcing small successes and then gradually increasing the challenge. Golf students can learn putting by starting with very short putts, and then, as they build mastery, eventually stepping back farther and farther. Novice batters can begin with half swings at an oversized ball pitched from 10 feet away, giving them the immediate pleasure of smacking the ball. As the hitters' confidence builds with their success and they achieve mastery at each level, the pitcher gradually moves back—to 15, then 22, 30, and 40.5 feet—and eventually introduces a standard baseball. Compared with children taught by conventional methods, those trained by this behavioral method have shown faster skill improvement (Simek & O'Brien, 1981, 1988).

© The New Yorker Collection, 1989, Ziegler from cartoonbank.com. All Rights Reserved.

At Work

Knowing that reinforcers influence productivity, many organizations have invited employees to share the risks and rewards of company ownership. Others focus on reinforcing a job well done. Rewards are most likely to increase productivity if the desired performance has been well defined and is achievable. The message for managers? *Reward specific, achievable behaviors, not vaguely defined "merit."*

Operant conditioning also reminds us that reinforcement should be *immediate.* IBM legend Thomas Watson understood. When he observed an achievement, he wrote the employee a check on the spot (Peters & Waterman, 1982). But rewards need not be material, or lavish. An effective manager may simply walk the floor and sincerely affirm people for good work, or write notes of appreciation for a completed project. As Skinner said, "How much richer would the whole world be if the reinforcers in daily life were more effectively contingent on productive work?"

At Home

As we have seen, parents can learn from operant conditioning practices. Parent-training researchers remind us that by saying, "Get ready for bed" but caving in to protests or defiance, parents reinforce such whining and arguing (Wierson & Forehand, 1994). Exasperated, they may then yell or gesture menacingly. When the child, now frightened, obeys, that reinforces the parents' angry behavior. Over time, a destructive parent-child relationship develops.

To disrupt this cycle, parents should remember that basic rule of shaping: *Notice people doing something right and affirm them for it.* Give children attention and other reinforcers when they are behaving *well.* Target a specific behavior, reward it, and watch it increase. When children misbehave or are defiant, don't yell at them or hit them. Simply explain the misbehavior and give them a time-out.

Finally, we can use operant conditioning in our own lives (see Close-Up: Training Our Partners). To reinforce your own desired behaviors (perhaps to exercise more often) and extinguish the undesired ones (to stop smoking, for example) psychologists suggest taking these steps:

1. ***State your goal in measurable terms, and announce it.*** You might, for example, aim to boost your study time by an hour a day and share that goal with some close friends.
2. ***Monitor how often you engage in your desired behavior.*** You might log your current study time, noting under what conditions you do and don't study. (When I began writing textbooks, I logged how I spent my time each day and was amazed to discover how much time I was wasting.)

"I wrote another five hundred words. Can I have another cookie?"

© The New Yorker Collection, 2001, Mick Stevens from cartoonbank.com. All Rights Reserved.

CLOSE-UP

Training Our Partners

By Amy Sutherland

For a book I was writing about a school for exotic animal trainers, I started commuting from Maine to California, where I spent my days watching students do the seemingly impossible: teaching hyenas to pirouette on command, cougars to offer their paws for a nail clipping, and baboons to skateboard.

I listened, rapt, as professional trainers explained how they taught dolphins to flip and elephants to paint. Eventually it hit me that the same techniques might work on that stubborn but lovable species, the American husband.

The central lesson I learned from exotic animal trainers is that I should reward behavior I like and ignore behavior I don't. After all, you don't get a sea lion to balance a ball on the end of its nose by nagging. The same goes for the American husband.

Back in Maine, I began thanking Scott if he threw one dirty shirt into the hamper. If he threw in two, I'd kiss him. Meanwhile, I would step over any soiled clothes on the floor without one sharp word, though I did sometimes kick them under the bed. But as he basked in my appreciation, the piles became smaller.

I was using what trainers call "approximations," rewarding the small steps toward learning a whole new behavior. . . . Once I started thinking this way, I couldn't stop. At the school in California, I'd be scribbling notes on how to walk an emu or have a wolf accept you as a pack member, but I'd be thinking, "I can't wait to try this on Scott. . . ."

After two years of exotic animal training, my marriage is far smoother, my husband much easier to love. I used to take his faults personally; his dirty clothes on the floor were an affront, a symbol of how he didn't care enough about me. But thinking of my husband as an exotic species gave me the distance I needed to consider our differences more objectively.

Excerpted with permission from Sutherland, A., (2006, June 25). What Shamu taught me about a happy marriage, *New York Times.*

respondent behavior behavior that occurs as an automatic response to some stimulus.

operant behavior behavior that operates on the environment, producing consequences.

3. ***Reinforce the desired behavior.*** To increase your study time, give yourself a reward (a snack or some activity you enjoy) only after you finish your extra hour of study. Agree with your friends that you will join them for weekend activities only if you have met your realistic weekly studying goal.
4. ***Reduce the rewards gradually.*** As your new behaviors become more habitual, give yourself a mental pat on the back instead of a cookie.

Contrasting Classical and Operant Conditioning

21-6 How does operant conditioning differ from classical conditioning?

Both classical and operant conditioning are forms of associative learning. Both involve *acquisition, extinction, spontaneous recovery, generalization,* and *discrimination*. But these two forms of learning also differ. Through classical (Pavlovian) conditioning, we associate different stimuli we do not control, and we respond automatically (**respondent behaviors**) (TABLE 21.4). Through operant conditioning, we associate our own behaviors that act on our environment to produce rewarding or punishing stimuli (**operant behaviors**) with their consequences.

"O! This learning, what a thing it is."
William Shakespeare, *The Taming of the Shrew,* 1597

TABLE 21.4

Comparison of Classical and Operant Conditioning

	Classical Conditioning	Operant Conditioning
Basic idea	Organism associates events	Organism associates behavior and resulting events
Response	Involuntary, automatic	Voluntary, operates on environment
Acquisition	Associating events; NS is paired with US and becomes CS	Associating response with a consequence (reinforcer or punisher)
Extinction	CR decreases when CS is repeatedly presented alone	Responding decreases when reinforcement stops
Spontaneous recovery	The reappearance, after a rest period, of an extinguished CR	The reappearance, after a rest period, of an extinguished response
Generalization	The tendency to respond to stimuli similar to the CS	Organism's response to similar stimuli is also reinforced
Discrimination	The learned ability to distinguish between a CS and other stimuli that do not signal a US	Organism learns that certain responses, but not others, will be reinforced

RETRIEVAL PRACTICE

- Salivating in response to a tone paired with food is a(n) __________ behavior; pressing a bar to obtain food is a(n) __________ behavior.

ANSWERS: respondent; operant

MODULE REVIEW

Operant Conditioning

Learning Objectives

RETRIEVAL PRACTICE Take a moment to answer each of these Learning Objective Questions (repeated here from within the module). Then turn to Appendix B, Complete Module Reviews, to check your answers. Research suggests that trying to answer these questions on your own will improve your long-term retention (McDaniel et al., 2009).

21-1: What is operant conditioning, and how is operant behavior reinforced and shaped?

21-2: How do positive and negative reinforcement differ, and what are the basic types of reinforcers?

21-3: How do different reinforcement schedules affect behavior?

21-4: How does punishment differ from negative reinforcement, and how does punishment affect behavior?

21-5: Why did Skinner's ideas provoke controversy, and how might his operant conditioning principles be applied at school, in sports, at work, and at home?

21-6: How does operant conditioning differ from classical conditioning?

Terms and Concepts to Remember

RETRIEVAL PRACTICE Test yourself on these terms by trying to write down the definition before flipping back to the referenced page to check your answer.

learning, p. 286
associative learning, p. 286
stimulus, p. 286
operant conditioning, p. 286
law of effect, p. 286
operant chamber, p. 287
reinforcement, p. 287
shaping, p. 287
positive reinforcement, p. 288
negative reinforcement, p. 288
primary reinforcer, p. 289
conditioned reinforcer, p. 289
reinforcement schedule, p. 290
continuous reinforcement, p. 290
partial (intermittent) reinforcement, p. 290
fixed-ratio schedule, p. 290
variable-ratio schedule, p. 291
fixed-interval schedule, p. 291
variable-interval schedule, p. 291
punishment, p. 292
respondent behavior, p.296
operant behavior, p. 296

RETRIEVAL PRACTICE Gain an advantage, and benefit from immediate feedback, with the interactive self-testing resources at www.worthpublishers.com/myers.

MODULE 22

- Biology, Cognition, and Learning
- Learning by Observation

Effects of Biology and Cognition, and Learning by Observation

learning the process of acquiring new and relatively enduring information or behaviors.

Biology, Cognition, and Learning

From drooling dogs, running rats, and pecking pigeons we have learned much about the basic processes of **learning** through *classical* and *operant conditioning*. But conditioning principles don't tell us the whole story. Today's learning theorists recognize that learning is the product of the interaction of biological, psychological, and social-cultural influences (**FIGURE 22.1**).

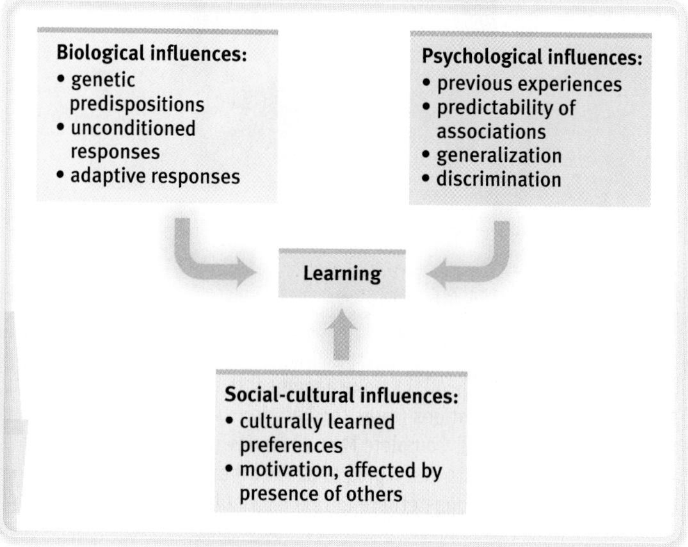

FIGURE 22.1
Biopsychosocial influences on learning Our learning results not only from environmental experiences, but also from cognitive and biological influences.

Biological Constraints on Conditioning

22-1 How do biological constraints affect classical and operant conditioning?

Ever since Charles Darwin, scientists have assumed that all animals share a common evolutionary history and thus share commonalities in their makeup and functioning. Ivan Pavlov and John B. Watson, for example, believed the basic laws of learning were essentially similar in all animals. So it should make little difference whether one studied pigeons or people. Moreover, it seemed that any natural response could be conditioned to any *neutral stimulus*.

Limits on Classical Conditioning

In 1956, learning researcher Gregory Kimble proclaimed, "Just about any activity of which the organism is capable can be conditioned and . . . these responses can be conditioned to any stimulus that the organism can perceive" (p. 195). Twenty-five years later, he humbly acknowledged that "half a thousand" scientific reports had proven him wrong (Kimble, 1981). More than the early behaviorists realized, an animal's capacity for conditioning is constrained by its biology. Each species' predispositions prepare it to learn the associations that enhance its survival. Environments are not the whole story.

John Garcia was among those who challenged the prevailing idea that all associations can be learned equally well. While researching the effects of radiation on laboratory animals, Garcia and Robert Koelling (1966) noticed that rats began to avoid drinking water from the plastic bottles in radiation chambers. Could classical conditioning be the culprit? Might the rats have linked the plastic-tasting water (a *conditioned stimulus*, or CS) to the sickness (*unconditioned response*, or UR) triggered by the radiation (*unconditioned stimulus*, or US)?

To test their hunch, Garcia and Koelling exposed the rats to a particular taste, sight, or sound (CS) and later also to radiation or drugs (US) that led to nausea and vomiting (UR). Two startling findings emerged: First, even if sickened as late as several hours after tasting a particular novel flavor, the rats thereafter avoided that flavor. This appeared to violate the Pavlovian notion that for conditioning to occur, the US must immediately follow the CS.

Courtesy of John Garcia

John Garcia As the laboring son of California farmworkers, Garcia attended school only in the off-season during his early childhood years. After entering junior college in his late twenties, and earning his Ph.D. in his late forties, he received the American Psychological Association's Distinguished Scientific Contribution Award "for his highly original, pioneering research in conditioning and learning." He was also elected to the National Academy of Sciences.

Second, the sickened rats developed aversions to tastes but not to sights or sounds. This contradicted the behaviorists' idea that any perceivable stimulus could serve as a CS. But it made adaptive sense. For rats, the easiest way to identify tainted food is to taste it; if sickened after sampling a new food, they thereafter avoid it. This response, called *taste aversion*, makes it difficult to eradicate a population of "bait-shy" rats by poisoning.

Humans, too, seem biologically prepared to learn some associations rather than others. If you become violently ill four hours after eating contaminated mussels, you will probably develop an aversion to the taste of mussels but usually not to the sight of the associated restaurant, its plates, the people you were with, or the music you heard there. (In contrast, birds, which hunt by sight, appear biologically primed to develop aversions to the *sight* of tainted food [Nicolaus et al., 1983].)

Antonio S./Shutterstock

Taste aversion If you became violently ill after eating mussels, you probably would have a hard time eating them again. Their smell and taste would have become a CS for nausea. This learning occurs readily because our biology prepares us to learn taste aversions to toxic foods.

Garcia's early findings on taste aversion were met with an onslaught of criticism. As the German philosopher Arthur Schopenhauer (1788–1860) once said, important ideas are first ridiculed, then attacked, and finally taken for granted. Leading journals refused to publish Garcia's work: The findings are impossible, said some critics. But, as often happens in science, Garcia and Koelling's taste-aversion research is now basic textbook material.

It is also a good example of experiments that begin with the discomfort of some laboratory animals and end by enhancing the welfare of many others. In one conditioned taste-aversion study, coyotes and wolves were tempted into eating sheep carcasses laced with a sickening poison. Thereafter, they developed an aversion to sheep meat; two wolves later penned with a live sheep seemed actually to fear it (Gustavson et al., 1974, 1976). These studies not only saved the sheep from their predators, but also saved the sheep-shunning coyotes and wolves from angry ranchers and farmers who had wanted to destroy them. Similar applications have prevented baboons from raiding African gardens, raccoons from attacking chickens, ravens and crows from feeding on crane eggs, and Mexican wolves from preying on sheep. In all these cases, research helped preserve both the prey and their predators, who occupy an important ecological niche (Dingfelder, 2010; Garcia & Gustavson, 1997).

Such research supports Darwin's principle that natural selection favors traits that aid survival. Our ancestors who readily learned taste aversions were unlikely to eat the same toxic food again and were more likely to survive and leave descendants. Nausea, like anxiety, pain, and other bad feelings, serves a good purpose. Like a low-oil warning on a car dashboard, each alerts the body to a threat (Neese, 1991).

blickwinkel/Alamy

Animal taste aversion As an alternative to killing wolves and coyotes that preyed on sheep, some ranchers have sickened the animals with lamb laced with a drug.

In an example illustrating how a CS can signal an important biological event, Japanese quail were conditioned to get excited by a red light that signaled a receptive female's arrival. Michael Domjan and his colleagues (2004) report that such conditioning is even speedier, stronger, and more durable when the CS is *ecologically relevant*—something similar to stimuli associated with sexual activity in the natural environment, such as the stuffed head of a female quail. In the real world, observes Domjan (2005), conditioned stimuli have a natural association with the unconditioned stimuli they predict.

"All animals are on a voyage through time, navigating toward futures that promote their survival and away from futures that threaten it. Pleasure and pain are the stars by which they steer."

Psychologists Daniel T. Gilbert and Timothy D. Wilson, "Prospection: Experiencing the Future," 2007

The tendency to learn behaviors favored by natural selection may help explain why we humans seem to be naturally disposed to learn associations between the color red and sexuality. Female primates display red when nearing ovulation. In human females, enhanced bloodflow produces the red blush of flirtation and sexual excitation. Does the frequent pairing of red and sex—with Valentine's hearts, red-light districts, and red lipstick—naturally enhance men's attraction to women? Experiments (**FIGURE 22.2**) suggest that, without men's awareness, it does (Elliot & Niesta, 2008). In follow-up studies, men who viewed a supposed female conversation partner in a red rather than green shirt chose to sit closer to where they expected her to sit and to ask her more intimate questions (Kayser et al., 2010). And it's not just men: Women tend to perceive men as more attractive when seen on a red background or in red clothing (Elliot et al., 2010).

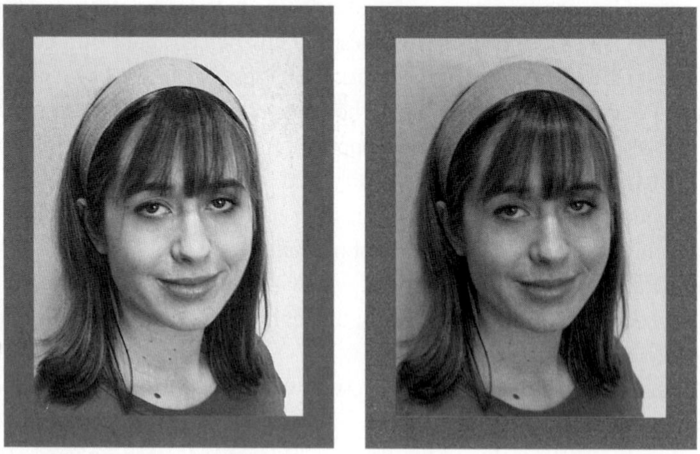

Courtesy of Kathryn Brownson, Hope College

FIGURE 22.2
Romantic red In a series of experiments that controlled for other factors (such as the brightness of the image), men found women more attractive and sexually desirable when framed in red (Elliot & Niesta, 2008).

"Once bitten, twice shy."

G. F. Northall, *Folk-Phrases*, 1894

A genetic predisposition to associate a CS with a US that follows predictably and immediately is adaptive: Causes often immediately precede effects. Often, but not always, as we saw in the taste-aversion findings. At such times, our predispositions can trick us. When chemotherapy triggers nausea and vomiting more than an hour following treatment, cancer patients may over time develop classically conditioned nausea (and sometimes anxiety) to the sights, sounds, and smells associated with the clinic (**FIGURE 22.3**) (Hall, 1997). Merely returning to the clinic's waiting room or seeing the nurses can provoke these conditioned feelings (Burish & Carey, 1986; Davey, 1992). Under normal circumstances, such revulsion to sickening stimuli would be adaptive.

FIGURE 22.3
Nausea conditioning in cancer patients

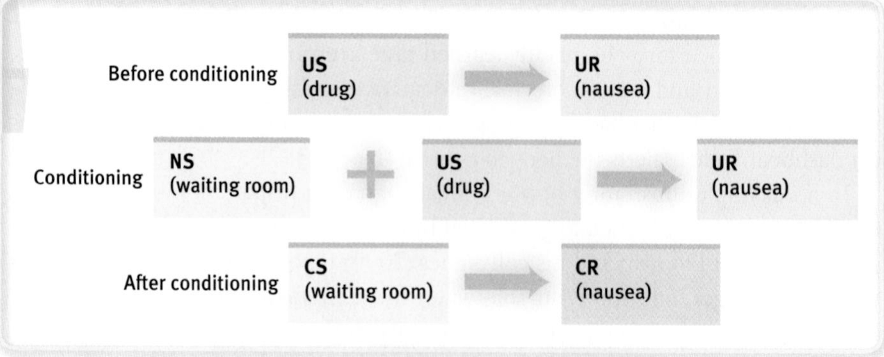

Limits on Operant Conditioning

As with classical conditioning, nature sets limits on each species' capacity for operant conditioning. Mark Twain (1835–1910) said it well: "Never try to teach a pig to sing. It wastes your time and annoys the pig."

We most easily learn and retain behaviors that reflect our biological predispositions. Thus, using food as a reinforcer, you could easily condition a hamster to dig or to rear up, because these are among the animal's natural food-searching behaviors. But you won't be so successful if you use food as a reinforcer to shape face washing and other hamster behaviors that aren't normally associated with food or hunger (Shettleworth, 1973). Similarly, you could easily teach pigeons to flap their wings to avoid being shocked, and to peck to obtain food: Fleeing with their wings and eating with their beaks are natural pigeon behaviors. However, pigeons would have a hard time learning to peck to avoid a shock, or to flap their wings to obtain food (Foree & LoLordo, 1973). The principle: *Biological constraints predispose organisms to learn associations that are naturally adaptive.*

Natural athletes Animals can most easily learn and retain behaviors that draw on their biological predispositions, such as dogs' inborn tendency to rely on all four feet for mobility and balance.

In the early 1940s, University of Minnesota graduate students Marian Breland and Keller Breland witnessed the power of operant conditioning (1961; Bailey & Gillaspy, 2005). Their mentor was B. F. Skinner. Impressed with his results, they began training dogs, cats, chickens, parakeets, turkeys, pigs, ducks, and hamsters. The rest is history. The company they formed spent the next half-century training more than 15,000 animals from 140 species for movies, traveling shows, amusement parks, corporations, and the government. And along the way, the Brelands themselves mentored others, including Sea World's first director of training.

In their early training days, the Brelands presumed that operant principles would work on almost any response an animal could make. But they too learned about biological constraints. In one act, pigs trained to pick up large wooden "dollars" and deposit them in a piggy bank began to drift back to their natural ways. They dropped the coin, pushed it with their snouts as pigs are prone to do, picked it up again, and then repeated the sequence—delaying their food reinforcer. This *instinctive drift* occurred as the animals reverted to their biologically predisposed patterns.

For more information on animal behavior, see books by (I am not making this up) Robin Fox and Lionel Tiger.

Cognition's Influence on Conditioning

22-2 How do cognitive processes affect classical and operant conditioning?

Cognitive Processes and Classical Conditioning

In their dismissal of "mentalistic" concepts such as consciousness, Pavlov and Watson underestimated the importance not only of biological constraints on an organism's learning capacity, but also the effects of cognitive processes (thoughts, perceptions, expectations). Through **cognitive learning** we acquire mental information that guides our behavior. The early behaviorists believed that rats' and dogs' learned behaviors could be reduced to mindless mechanisms, so there was no need to consider cognition. But Robert Rescorla and Allan Wagner (1972) showed that an animal can learn the *predictability* of an event. If a shock always is preceded by a tone, and then may also be preceded by a light that accompanies the tone, a rat will react with fear to the tone but not to the light. Although the light is always followed by the shock, it adds no new information; the tone is a better predictor. The more predictable the association, the stronger the conditioned response. It's as if the animal learns an *expectancy*, an awareness of how likely it is that the US will occur.

"All brains are, in essence, anticipation machines."

Daniel C. Dennett, *Consciousness Explained*, 1991

cognitive learning the acquisition of mental information, whether by observing events, by watching others, or through language.

Associations can influence attitudes (Hofmann et al., 2010). When British children viewed novel cartoon characters alongside either ice cream (*Yum!*) or brussels sprouts (*Yuk!*), they came to like best the ice-cream-associated characters (Field, 2006). Other researchers have

cognitive map a mental representation of the layout of one's environment. For example, after exploring a maze, rats act as if they have learned a cognitive map of it.

latent learning learning that occurs but is not apparent until there is an incentive to demonstrate it.

intrinsic motivation a desire to perform a behavior effectively for its own sake.

extrinsic motivation a desire to perform a behavior to receive promised rewards or avoid threatened punishment.

observational learning learning by observing others.

modeling the process of observing and imitating a specific behavior.

classically conditioned adults' attitudes, using little-known Pokémon characters (Olson & Fazio, 2001). The participants, playing the role of a security guard monitoring a video screen, viewed a stream of words, images, and Pokémon characters. Their task, they were told, was to respond to one target Pokémon character by pressing a button. Unnoticed by the participants, when two other Pokémon characters appeared on the screen, one was consistently associated with various positive words and images (such as *awesome* or a hot fudge sundae); the other appeared with negative words and images (such as *awful* or a cockroach). Without any conscious memory for the pairings, the participants formed more gut-level liking for the characters associated with the positive stimuli.

Follow-up studies indicate that conditioned likes and dislikes are even stronger when people notice and are aware of the associations they have learned (Shanks, 2010). Cognition matters.

Such experiments help explain why classical conditioning treatments that ignore cognition often have limited success. For example, people receiving therapy for alcohol dependence may be given alcohol spiked with a nauseating drug. Will they then associate alcohol with sickness? If classical conditioning were merely a matter of "stamping in" stimulus associations, we might hope so, and to some extent this does occur. However, one's awareness that the nausea is induced by the drug, not the alcohol, often weakens the association between drinking alcohol and feeling sick. So, even in classical conditioning, it is (especially with humans) not simply the CS-US association but also the thought that counts.

Cognitive Processes and Operant Conditioning

B. F. Skinner granted the biological underpinnings of behavior and the existence of private thought processes. Nevertheless, many psychologists criticized him for discounting the importance of these influences.

A mere eight days before dying of leukemia in 1990, Skinner stood before the American Psychological Association convention. In this final address, he again resisted the growing belief that cognitive processes (thoughts, perceptions, expectations) have a necessary place in the science of psychology and even in our understanding of conditioning. He viewed "cognitive science" as a throwback to early twentieth-century introspectionism. For Skinner, thoughts and emotions were behaviors that follow the same laws as other behaviors.

Nevertheless, the evidence of cognitive processes cannot be ignored. For example, animals on a *fixed-interval reinforcement schedule* respond more and more frequently as the time approaches when a response will produce a reinforcer. Although a strict behaviorist would object to talk of "expectations," the animals behave as if they expected that repeating the response would soon produce the reward.

Evidence of cognitive processes has also come from studying rats in mazes. Rats exploring a maze, given no obvious rewards, seem to develop a **cognitive map**, a mental representation of the maze. When an experimenter then places food in the maze's goal box, these rats run the maze as quickly and efficiently as other rats that were previously reinforced with food for this result. Like people sightseeing in a new town, the exploring rats seemingly experienced **latent learning** during their earlier tours. That learning became apparent only when there was some incentive to demonstrate it. Children, too, may learn from watching a parent but demonstrate the learning only much later, as needed. The point to remember: *There is more to learning than associating a response with a consequence; there is also cognition.* Psychologists have presented some striking evidence of animals' cognitive abilities in solving problems and in using aspects of language.

© The New Yorker Collection, 2000, Pat Byrnes, from cartoonbank.com. All Rights Reserved.

"Bathroom? Sure, it's just down the hall to the left, jog right, left, another left, straight past two more lefts, then right, and it's at the end of the third corridor on your right."

The cognitive perspective has also shown us the limits of rewards: Promising people a reward for a task they already enjoy can backfire. Excessive rewards can destroy **intrinsic motivation**—the desire to perform a behavior effectively and for its own sake. In experiments, children have been promised a payoff for playing with an interesting puzzle or toy. Later, they played with the toy *less* than other unpaid children did (Deci et al., 1999;

Tang & Hall, 1995). Likewise, rewarding children with toys or candy for reading diminishes the time they spend reading (Marinak & Gambrell, 2008). It is as if they think, "If I have to be bribed into doing this, it must not be worth doing for its own sake."

To sense the difference between intrinsic motivation and **extrinsic motivation** (behaving in certain ways to gain external rewards or avoid threatened punishment), think about your experience in this course. Are you feeling pressured to finish this reading before a deadline? Worried about your grade? Eager for the credits that will count toward graduation? If *Yes*, then you are extrinsically motivated (as, to some extent, almost all students must be). Are you also finding the material interesting? Does learning it make you feel more competent? If there were no grade at stake, might you be curious enough to want to learn the material for its own sake? If *Yes*, intrinsic motivation also fuels your efforts.

Youth sports coaches who aim to promote enduring interest in an activity, not just to pressure players into winning, should focus on the intrinsic joy of playing and of reaching one's potential (Deci & Ryan, 1985, 2009). Giving people choices also enhances their intrinsic motivation (Patall et al., 2008). Nevertheless, rewards used to signal a job well done (rather than to bribe or control someone) can be effective (Boggiano et al., 1985). "Most improved player" awards, for example, can boost feelings of competence and increase enjoyment of a sport. Rightly administered, rewards can raise performance and spark creativity (Eisenberger & Aselage, 2009; Henderlong & Lepper, 2002). And extrinsic rewards (such as the admissions scholarships and jobs that often follow good grades) are here to stay. **TABLE 22.1** compares the biological and cognitive influences on classical and operant conditioning.

Will and Deni McIntyre/Photo Researchers

Latent learning Animals, like people, can learn from experience, with or without reinforcement. After exploring a maze for 10 days, rats received a food reward at the end of the maze. They quickly demonstrated their prior learning of the maze—by immediately completing it as quickly as (and even faster than) rats that had been reinforced for running the maze. (From Tolman & Honzik, 1930.)

TABLE 22.1

Biological and Cognitive Influences on Conditioning

	Classical Conditioning	Operant Conditioning
Cognitive processes	Organisms develop expectation that CS signals the arrival of US.	Organisms develop expectation that a response will be reinforced or punished; they also exhibit latent learning, without reinforcement.
Biological predispositions	Natural predispositions constrain what stimuli and responses can easily be associated.	Organisms best learn behaviors similar to their natural behaviors; unnatural behaviors instinctively drift back toward natural ones.

Learning by Observation

22-3 What is observational learning, and how do some scientists believe it is enabled by mirror neurons?

Cognition is certainly a factor in **observational learning,** in which higher animals, especially humans, learn without direct experience, by watching and imitating others. A child who sees his sister burn her fingers on a hot stove learns not to touch it. We learn our native languages and various other specific behaviors by observing and imitating others, a process called **modeling.**

Picture this scene from an experiment by Albert Bandura, the pioneering researcher of observational learning (Bandura et al., 1961). A preschool child works on a drawing. An adult in another part of the room is building with Tinkertoys. As the child watches, the adult gets up and for nearly 10 minutes pounds, kicks, and throws around the room a large inflated Bobo doll, yelling, "Sock him in the nose. . . . Hit him down. . . . Kick him."

The child is then taken to another room filled with appealing toys. Soon the experimenter returns and tells the child she has decided to save these good toys "for the other children." She takes the now-frustrated child to a third room containing a few toys, including a Bobo doll. Left alone, what does the child do?

Compared with children not exposed to the adult model, those who viewed the model's actions were more likely to lash out at the doll. Observing the aggressive outburst apparently

Albert Bandura "The Bobo doll follows me wherever I go. The photographs are published in every introductory psychology text and virtually every undergraduate takes introductory psychology. I recently checked into a Washington hotel. The clerk at the desk asked, 'Aren't you the psychologist who did the Bobo doll experiment?' I answered, 'I am afraid that will be my legacy.' He replied, 'That deserves an upgrade. I will put you in a suite in the quiet part of the hotel'" (2005).

Courtesy of Albert Bandura, Stanford University

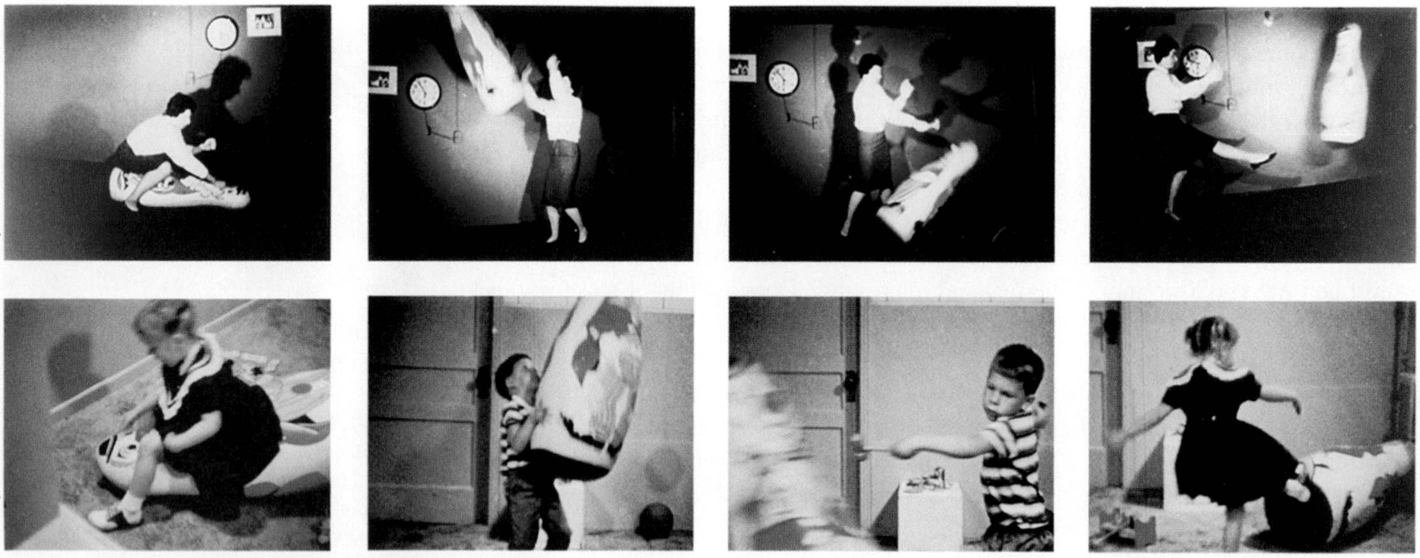

Courtesy of Albert Bandura, Stanford University

FIGURE 22.4
The famous Bobo doll experiment Notice how the children's actions directly imitate the adult's.

lowered their inhibitions. But *something more* was also at work, for the children imitated the very acts they had observed and used the very words they had heard (**FIGURE 22.4**).

That "something more," Bandura suggests, was this: By watching a model, we experience *vicarious reinforcement* or *vicarious punishment*, and we learn to anticipate a behavior's consequences in situations like those we are observing. We are especially likely to learn from people we perceive as similar to ourselves, as successful, or as admirable. fMRI scans show that when people observe someone winning a reward (and especially when it's someone likable and similar to themselves) their own brain reward systems activate, much as if they themselves had won the reward (Mobbs et al., 2009). When we identify with someone, we experience their outcomes vicariously. Lord Chesterfield (1694–1773) had the idea: "We are, in truth, more than half what we are by imitation."

Mirror neurons at work?

David Sipress

"Your back is killing me!"

Mirrors and Imitation in the Brain

On a 1991 hot summer day in Parma, Italy, a lab monkey awaited its researchers' return from lunch. The researchers had implanted wires next to its motor cortex, in a frontal lobe brain region that enabled the monkey to plan and enact movements. The monitoring device would alert the researchers to activity in that region of the monkey's brain. When the monkey moved a peanut into its mouth, for example, the device would buzz. That day, as one of the researchers reentered the lab, ice cream cone in hand, the monkey stared at him. As the researcher raised the cone to lick it, the monkey's monitor buzzed—as if the motionless monkey had itself moved (Blakeslee, 2006; Iacoboni, 2008, 2009).

The same buzzing had been heard earlier, when the monkey watched humans or other monkeys move peanuts to their mouths. The flabbergasted researchers, led by Giacomo Rizzolatti (2002, 2006), had, they believed, stumbled onto a previously unknown type of neuron. These presumed **mirror neurons** may provide a neural basis for everyday imitation and observational learning. When a monkey grasps, holds, or tears something, these neurons fire. And they likewise fire when the monkey observes another doing so. When one monkey sees, its neurons mirror what another monkey does.

mirror neurons frontal lobe neurons that some scientists believe fire when performing certain actions or when observing another doing so. The brain's mirroring of another's action may enable imitation and empathy.

Imitation is widespread in other species. In one experiment, a monkey watching another selecting certain pictures to gain treats learned to imitate the order of choices (**FIGURE 22.5**). In other research, rhesus macaque monkeys rarely made up quickly after a fight—unless they grew up with forgiving older macaques. Then, more often than not, their fights, too, were quickly followed by reconciliation (de Waal & Johanowicz, 1993). Rats, pigeons, crows, and

©Herb Terrace

FIGURE 22.5
Cognitive imitation Monkey A (far left) watched Monkey B touch four pictures on a display screen in a certain order to gain a banana. Monkey A learned to imitate that order, even when shown the same pictures in a different configuration (Subiaul et al., 2004).

gorillas all observe others and learn (Byrne et al., 2011; Dugatkin, 2002). Chimpanzees observe and imitate all sorts of novel foraging and tool use behaviors, which are then transmitted from generation to generation within their local culture (Hopper et al., 2008; Whiten et al., 2007).

In humans, imitation is pervasive. Our catchphrases, hem lengths, ceremonies, foods, traditions, vices, and fads all spread by one person copying another. Imitation shapes even very young humans' behavior (Bates & Byrne, 2010). Shortly after birth, a baby may imitate an adult who sticks out his tongue. By 8 to 16 months, infants imitate various novel gestures (Jones, 2007). By age 12 months (**FIGURE 22.6**), they look where an adult is looking (Meltzoff et al., 2009). And by age 14 months, children imitate acts modeled on TV (Meltzoff, 1988; Meltzoff & Moore, 1989, 1997). Even as 2½-year-olds, when many of their mental abilities are near those of adult chimpanzees, young humans surpass chimps at social tasks such as imitating another's solution to a problem (Herrmann et al., 2007). Children see, children do.

So strong is the human predisposition to learn from watching adults that 2- to 5-year-old children *overimitate*. Whether living in urban Australia or rural Africa, they copy even irrelevant adult actions. Before reaching for a toy in a plastic jar, they will first stroke the jar with a feather if that's what they have observed (Lyons et al., 2007). Or, imitating an adult, they will wave a stick over a box and then use the stick to push on a knob that opens the box—when all they needed to do to open the box was to push on the knob (Nielsen & Tomaselli, 2010).

"Children need models more than they need critics."

Joseph Joubert, *Pensées,* 1842

Humans, like monkeys, have brains that support empathy and imitation. Researchers cannot insert experimental electrodes in human brains, but they can use fMRI scans to see brain activity associated with performing and with observing actions. So, is the human capacity to simulate another's action and to share in another's experience due to specialized mirror neurons? Or is it due to distributed brain networks? That issue is currently being debated (Gallese et al. 2011; Iacoboni, 2008, 2009; Mukamel et al., 2010). Regardless, children's brains enable their empathy and their ability to infer another's mental state, an ability known as *theory of mind.*

FIGURE 22.6
Imitation This 12-month-old infant sees an adult look left, and immediately follows her gaze. (From Meltzoff et al., 2009.)

Meltzoff, A. N., Kuhl, P. K., Movellan, J., & Sejnowski, T. J. (2009). Foundations for a new science of learning. *Science, 325,* 284–288.

FIGURE 22.7
Experienced and imagined pain in the brain Brain activity related to actual pain (top) is mirrored in the brain of an observing loved one (bottom). Empathy in the brain shows up in emotional brain areas, but not in the somatosensory cortex, which receives the physical pain input.

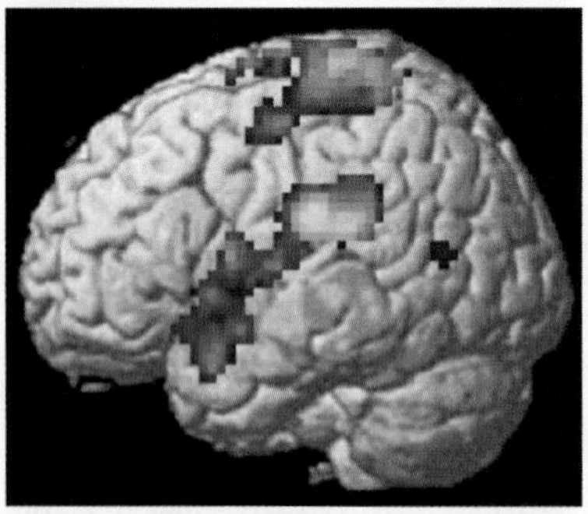
Pain

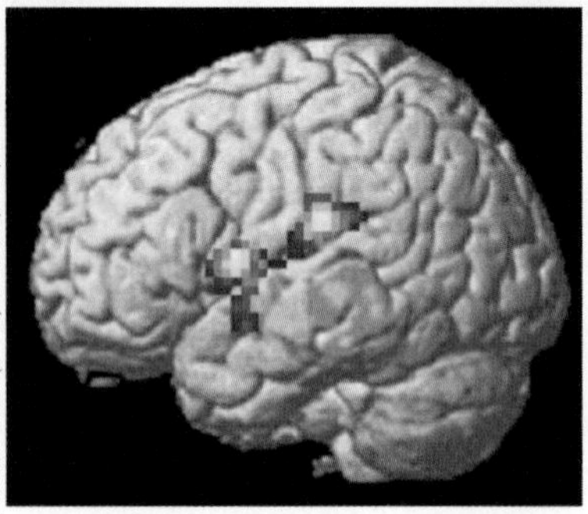
Empathy

Reprinted with permission from The American Association for the Advancement of Science. Subiaul et al. (2004). *Science, 305,* 407–410. AAAS.

The brain's response to observing others makes emotions contagious. Through its neurological echo, our brain simulates and vicariously experiences what we observe. So real are these mental instant replays that we may misremember an action we have observed as an action we have performed (Lindner et al., 2010). But through these reenactments, we grasp others' states of mind. Observing others' postures, faces, voices, and writing styles, we unconsciously synchronize our own to theirs—which helps us feel what they are feeling (Bernieri et al., 1994; Ireland & Pennebaker, 2010). We find ourselves yawning when they yawn, laughing when they laugh.

When observing movie characters smoking, smokers' brains spontaneously simulate smoking, which helps explain their cravings (Wagner et al., 2011). Seeing a loved one's pain, our faces mirror the other's emotion. But as **FIGURE 22.7** shows, so do our brains. In this fMRI scan, the pain imagined by an empathic romantic partner has triggered some of the same brain activity experienced by the loved one actually having the pain (Singer et al., 2004). Even fiction reading may trigger such activity, as we mentally simulate (and vicariously experience) the experiences described (Mar & Oatley, 2008; Speer et al., 2009). The bottom line: *Brain activity underlies our intensely social nature.*

Applications of Observational Learning

So the big news from Bandura's studies and the mirror-neuron research is that we look, we mentally imitate, and we learn. Models—in our family or neighborhood, or on TV—may have effects—good or bad.

Prosocial Effects

22-4 What is the impact of prosocial modeling and of antisocial modeling?

The good news is that **prosocial** (positive, helpful) models can have prosocial effects. Many business organizations effectively use *behavior modeling* to help new employees learn communications, sales, and customer service skills (Taylor et al., 2005). Trainees gain these skills faster when they are able to observe the skills being modeled effectively by experienced workers (or actors simulating them).

prosocial behavior positive, constructive, helpful behavior. The opposite of antisocial behavior.

People who exemplify nonviolent, helpful behavior can also prompt similar behavior in others. India's Mahatma Gandhi and America's Martin Luther King, Jr., both drew on the power of modeling, making nonviolent action a powerful force for social change in both countries. Parents are also powerful models. European Christians who risked their lives to rescue Jews from the Nazis usually had a close relationship with at least one parent who modeled a strong moral or humanitarian concern; this was also true for U.S. civil rights activists in the 1960s (London, 1970; Oliner & Oliner, 1988). The observational learning of morality begins early. Socially responsive toddlers who readily imitate their parents tend to become preschoolers with a strong internalized conscience (Forman et al., 2004).

A model caregiver This girl is learning orphan-nursing skills, as well as compassion, by observing her mentor in this Humane Society program. As the sixteenth-century proverb states, "Example is better than precept."

Zumapress/Newscom

Models are most effective when their actions and words are consistent. Sometimes, however, models say one thing and do another. To encourage children to read, read to them and surround them with books and people who read. To increase the odds that your children will practice your religion, worship and attend religious activities with them. Many parents seem to operate according to the principle "Do as I *say,* not as I do." Experiments suggest that children learn to do both (Rice & Grusec, 1975; Rushton, 1975). Exposed to a hypocrite, they tend to imitate the hypocrisy—by doing what the model did and saying what the model said.

Antisocial Effects

The bad news is that observational learning may have *antisocial effects.* This helps us understand why abusive parents might have aggressive children, and why many men who beat their wives had wife-battering fathers (Stith et al., 2000). Critics note that being aggressive could be passed along by parents' genes. But with monkeys we know it can be environmental. In study after study, young monkeys separated from their mothers and subjected to high levels of aggression grew up to be aggressive themselves (Chamove, 1980). The lessons we learn as children are not easily replaced as adults, and they are sometimes visited on future generations.

TV is a powerful source of observational learning. While watching TV, children may "learn" that bullying is an effective way to control others, that free and easy sex brings pleasure without later misery or disease, or that men should be tough and women gentle. And they have ample time to learn such lessons. During their first 18 years, most children in developed countries spend more time watching TV than they spend in school. In the United States, where 9 in 10 teens watch TV daily, someone who lives to age 75 will have spent 9 years staring at the tube (Gallup, 2002; Kubey & Csikszentmihalyi, 2002). The average teen watches TV more than 4 hours a day, the average adult 3 hours (Robinson & Martin, 2009; Strasburger et al., 2010). With CNN reaching 212 countries, and MTV's networks broadcasting in 33 languages, television has created a global pop culture.

TV viewers are learning about life from a rather peculiar storyteller, one that reflects the culture's mythology but not its reality. During the late twentieth century, the average child viewed some 8000 TV murders and 100,000 other acts of violence before finishing elementary school (Huston et al., 1992). Between 1998 and 2006, prime-time violence reportedly increased another 75 percent (PTC, 2007). If we include cable programming and watching movies at home, the violence numbers escalate. An analysis of more than 3000 network and cable programs aired in the 1996–1997 season revealed that nearly 6 in 10 featured violence, that 74 percent of the violence went unpunished, that 58 percent did not show the victims' pain, that nearly half the incidents involved "justified" violence, and that nearly half involved an attractive perpetrator. These conditions define the recipe for the *violence-viewing effect* described in many studies (Donnerstein, 1998, 2011). To read more about this effect, see Thinking Critically About: Does Viewing Media Violence Trigger Violent Behavior?

David Strickler/The Image Works

Children see, children do? Children who often experience physical punishment tend to display more aggression.

"The problem with television is that the people must sit and keep their eyes glued to a screen: The average American family hasn't time for it. Therefore the showmen are convinced that . . . television will never be a serious competitor of [radio] broadcasting."

New York Times, 1939

RETRIEVAL PRACTICE

- Jason's parents and older friends all smoke, but they advise him not to. Juan's parents and friends don't smoke, but they say nothing to deter him from doing so. Will Jason or Juan be more likely to start smoking?

ANSWER: Jason may be more likely to smoke, because observational learning studies suggest that children tend to do as others do and say what they say.

* * *

Bandura's work—like that of Ivan Pavlov, John Watson, B. F. Skinner, and thousands of others who advanced our knowledge of learning principles—illustrates the impact that can result from single-minded devotion to a few well-defined problems and ideas. All of these researchers defined the issues and impressed on us the importance of learning. As their legacy demonstrates, intellectual history is often made by people who risk going to extremes in pushing ideas to their limits (Simonton, 2000).

TV's greatest effect may stem from what it displaces. Children and adults who spend 4 hours a day watching TV spend 4 fewer hours in active pursuits—talking, studying, playing, reading, or socializing with friends. What would you have done with your extra time if you had never watched TV, and how might you therefore be different?

RETRIEVAL PRACTICE

- Match the examples (1-5) to the appropriate underlying learning principle (a-e):

a. Classical conditioning
b. Operant conditioning
c. Latent learning
d. Observational learning
e. Biological predispositions

1. Knowing the way from your bed to the bathroom in the dark
2. Your little brothers getting in a fight after watching a violent action movie
3. Salivating when you smell brownies in the oven
4. Disliking the taste of chili after being violently sick a few hours after eating chili
5. Your dog racing to greet you on your arrival home

ANSWERS: 1. c, 2. d, 3. a, 4. e, 5. b

THINKING CRITICALLY ABOUT

Does Viewing Media Violence Trigger Violent Behavior?

Was the judge who in 1993 tried two British 10-year-olds for their murder of a 2-year-old right to suspect that the pair had been influenced by "violent video films"? Were the American media right to think that the teen assassins who killed 13 of their Columbine High School classmates had been influenced by repeated exposure to *Natural Born Killers* and splatter games such as *Doom?* To understand whether violence viewing leads to violent behavior, researchers have done some 600 correlational and experimental studies (Anderson & Gentile, 2008; Comstock, 2008; Murray, 2008).

Correlational studies do support this link:

- In the United States and Canada, homicide rates doubled between 1957 and 1974, just when TV was introduced and spreading. Moreover, census regions with later dates for TV service also had homicide rates that jumped later.
- White South Africans were first introduced to TV in 1975. A similar near-doubling of the homicide rate began after 1975 (Centerwall, 1989).
- Elementary schoolchildren with heavy exposure to media violence (via TV, videos, and video games) also tend to get into more fights (**FIGURE 22.8**). As teens, they also are at greater risk for violent behavior (Boxer et al., 2009).

But remember, correlation need not mean causation. So these studies do not prove that viewing violence causes aggression (Freedman, 1988; McGuire, 1986). Maybe aggressive children prefer violent programs. Maybe abused or neglected children are both more aggressive and more often left in front of the TV. Maybe violent programs simply reflect, rather than affect, violent trends.

To pin down causation, psychologists experimented. They randomly assigned some viewers to observe violence and others to watch entertaining nonviolence. Does viewing cruelty prepare people, when irritated, to react more cruelly? To some extent, it does. This is especially so when an attractive person commits seemingly justified, realistic violence that goes unpunished and causes no visible pain or harm (Donnerstein, 1998, 2011).

The violence-viewing effect seems to stem from at least two factors. One is *imitation* (Geen & Thomas, 1986). Children as young as 14 months will imitate acts they observe on TV (Meltzoff & Moore, 1989, 1997). As they watch, their brains simulate the behavior, and after this inner rehearsal they become more likely to act it out. Thus, in one experiment, violent play increased sevenfold immediately after children viewed *Power Rangers* episodes (Boyatzis et al., 1995). As happened in the Bobo doll experiment, children often precisely imitated the models' violent acts—in this case, flying karate kicks.

Prolonged exposure to violence also *desensitizes* viewers. They become more indifferent to it when later viewing a brawl, whether on TV or in real life (Fanti et al., 2009; Rule & Ferguson, 1986). Adult males who spent three evenings watching sexually violent movies became progressively less bothered by the rapes and slashings. Compared with those in a control group, the film watchers later expressed less sympathy for domestic violence victims, and they rated the victims' injuries as less severe (Mullin & Linz, 1995). Likewise, moviegoers were less likely to help an injured woman pick up her crutches if they had just watched a violent rather than a nonviolent movie (Bushman & Anderson, 2009).

Drawing on such findings, the American Academy of Pediatrics (2009) has advised pediatricians that "media violence can contribute to aggressive behavior, desensitization to violence, nightmares, and fear of being harmed." Indeed, an evil psychologist could hardly imagine a better way to make people indifferent to brutality than to expose them to a graded series of scenes, from fights to killings to the mutilations in slasher movies (Donnerstein et al., 1987). Watching cruelty fosters indifference.

> "Thirty seconds worth of glorification of a soap bar sells soap. Twenty-five minutes worth of glorification of violence sells violence."
>
> **U.S. Senator Paul Simon, Remarks to the Communitarian Network, 1993**

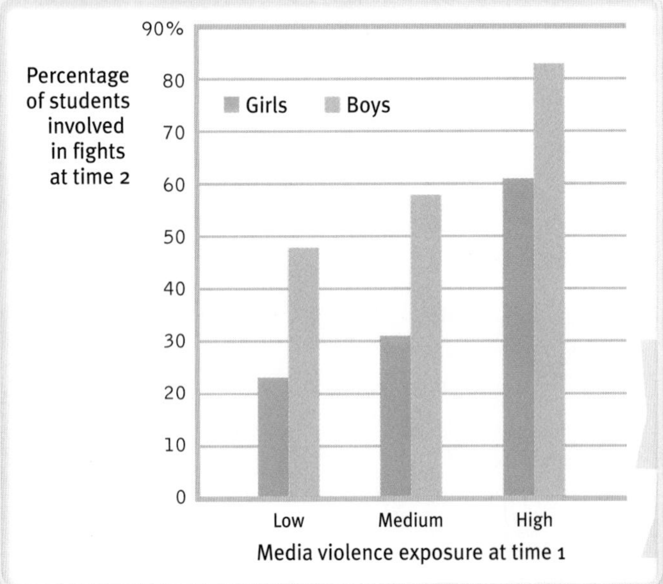

FIGURE 22.8
Heavy exposure to media violence predicts future aggressive behavior Researchers studied more than 400 third- to fifth-graders. After controlling for existing differences in hostility and aggression, the researchers reported increased aggression in those heavily exposed to violent TV, videos, and video games (Gentile et al., 2004).

MODULE REVIEW

Effects of Biology and Cognition, and Learning by Observation

Learning Objectives

RETRIEVAL PRACTICE Take a moment to answer each of these Learning Objective Questions (repeated here from within the module). Then turn to Appendix B, Complete Module Reviews, to check your answers. Research suggests that trying to answer these questions on your own will improve your long-term retention (McDaniel et al., 2009).

22-1: How do biological constraints affect classical and operant conditioning?

22-2: How do cognitive processes affect classical and operant conditioning?

22-3: What is observational learning, and how do some scientists believe it is enabled by mirror neurons?

22-4: What is the impact of prosocial modeling and of antisocial modeling?

Terms and Concepts to Remember

RETRIEVAL PRACTICE Test yourself on these terms by trying to write down the definition before flipping back to the referenced page to check your answer.

learning, p. 298
cognitive learning, p. 301
cognitive map, p. 302
latent learning, p. 302
intrinsic motivation, p. 302
extrinsic motivation, p. 303
observational learning, p. 303
modeling, p. 303
mirror neurons, p. 304
prosocial behavior, p. 306

RETRIEVAL PRACTICE Gain an advantage, and benefit from immediate feedback, with the interactive self-testing resources at www.worthpublishers.com/myers.

Memory

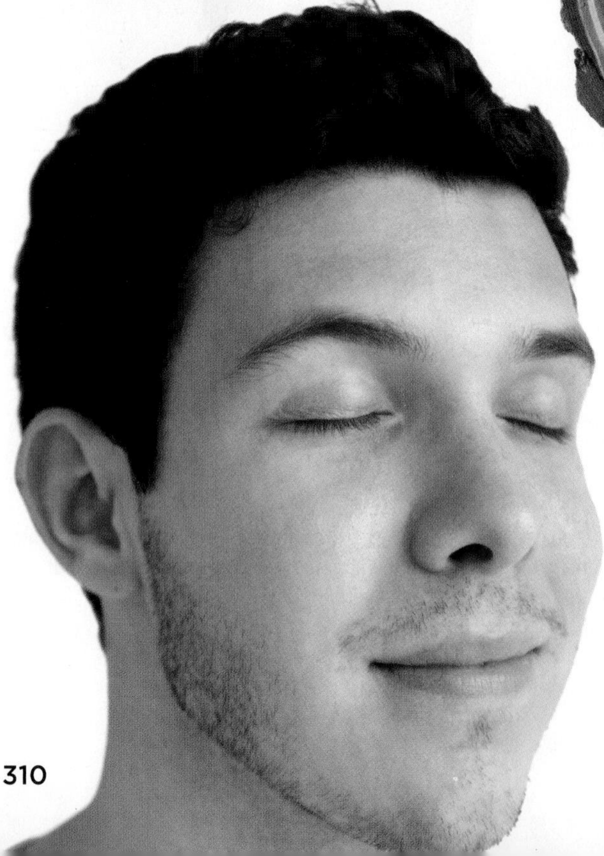

These 10th edition Memory modules are co-authored by Janie Wilson, Professor of Psychology at Georgia Southern University and Vice President for Programming of the Society for the Teaching of Psychology.

Be thankful for memory. We take it for granted, except when it malfunctions. But it is our memory that accounts for time and defines our life. It is our memory that enables us to recognize family, speak

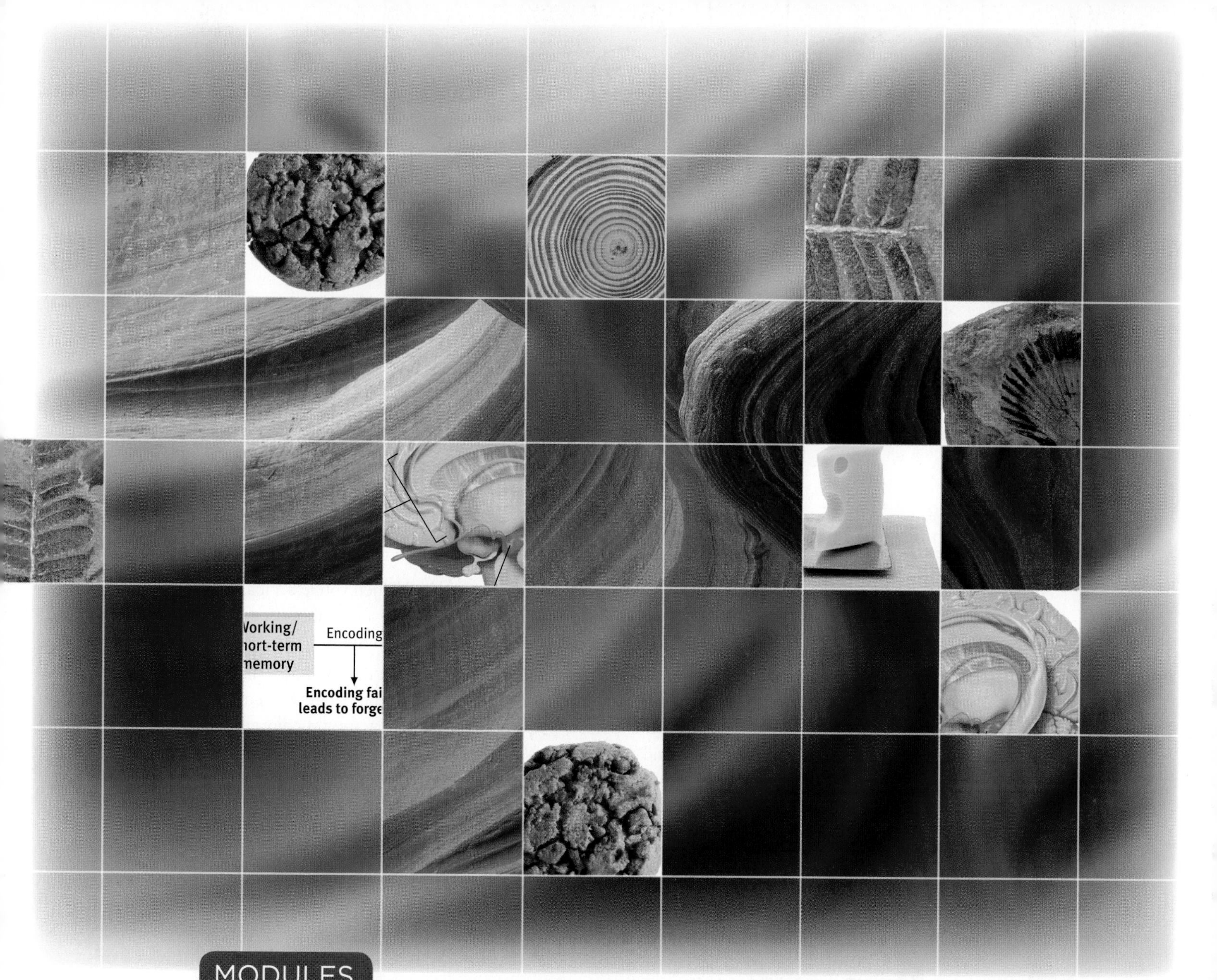

MODULES

23 Studying and Building Memories

24 Storage: Retaining Information in the Brain

25 Retrieval

26 Forgetting, Memory Construction, and Improving Memory

our language, find our way home, and locate food and water. It is our memory that enables us to enjoy an experience and then mentally replay and enjoy it again. Our shared memories help bind us together as Irish or Aussies, as Serbs or Albanians. And it is our memory that occasionally pits us against those whose offenses we cannot forget.

In large part, we are what we remember. Without memory—our storehouse of accumulated learning—there would be no savoring of past joys, no guilt or anger over painful recollections. We would instead live in an enduring present, each moment fresh. But each person would be a stranger, every language foreign, every task—dressing, cooking, biking—a new challenge. You would even be a stranger to yourself, lacking that continuous sense of self that extends from your distant past to your momentary present.

Modules 23 through 26 explore how we *do* manage to build, store, retrieve, and also forget memories, concluding with tips on how to improve memory.

MODULE 23

- Studying Memory
- Building Memories

Studying and Building Memories

Studying Memory

23-1 What is memory?

Memory is learning that has persisted over time, information that has been stored and can be retrieved. To a psychologist, evidence that learning persists takes three forms:

- **recall**—retrieving information that is not currently in your conscious awareness but that was learned at an earlier time. A fill-in-the-blank question tests your recall.
- **recognition**—identifying items previously learned. A multiple-choice question tests your recognition.
- **relearning**—learning something more quickly when you learn it a second or later time. When you study for a final exam or engage a language used in early childhood, you will relearn the material more easily than you did initially.

Research on memory's extremes has helped us understand how memory works. At age 92, my father suffered a small stroke that had but one peculiar effect. He was as mobile as before. His genial personality was intact. He knew us and enjoyed poring over family photo albums and reminiscing about his past. But he had lost most of his ability to lay down new memories of conversations and everyday episodes. He could not tell me what day of the week it was, or what he'd had for lunch. Told repeatedly of his brother-in-law's death, he was surprised and saddened each time he heard the news.

At the other extreme are people who would be gold medal winners in a memory Olympics. Russian journalist Shereshevskii, or S, had merely to listen while other reporters scribbled notes (Luria, 1968). You and I could parrot back a string of about 7—maybe even 9—digits. S could repeat up to 70, if they were read about 3 seconds apart in an otherwise silent room. Moreover, he could recall digits or words backwards as easily as forward. His accuracy was unerring, even when recalling a list as much as 15 years later. "Yes, yes," he might recall. "This was a series you gave me once when we were in your apartment. . . . You were sitting at the table and I in the rocking chair. . . . You were wearing a gray suit. . . ."

© The New Yorker Collection, 1987, W. Miller from cartoonbank.com. All Rights Reserved.

Amazing? Yes, but consider your own impressive memory. You remember countless voices, sounds, and songs; tastes, smells, and textures; faces, places, and happenings. Imagine viewing more than 2500 slides of faces and places for 10 seconds each. Later, you see 280 of these slides, paired with others you've never seen. Actual participants in this experiment recognized 90 percent of the slides they had viewed in the first round (Haber, 1970). In a follow-up experiment, people exposed to 2800 images for only 3 seconds each spotted the repeats with 82 percent accuracy (Konkle et al., 2010).

Or imagine yourself looking at a picture fragment, such as the one in **FIGURE 23.1**. Also imagine that you had seen the complete picture for a couple of seconds 17 years earlier. This, too, was a real experiment, and participants who had previously seen the complete drawings were more likely to identify the objects than were members of a control group (Mitchell, 2006). Moreover, the picture memory reappeared even for those who did not consciously recall participating in the long-ago experiment!

How do we accomplish such memory feats? How does our brain pluck information out of the world around us and tuck that information away for later use? How can we

memory the persistence of learning over time through the storage and retrieval of information.

recall a measure of memory in which the person must retrieve information learned earlier, as on a fill-in-the-blank test.

recognition a measure of memory in which the person need only identify items previously learned, as on a multiple-choice test.

relearning a measure of memory that assesses the amount of time saved when learning material again.

FIGURE 23.1
What is this? People who had, 17 years earlier, seen the complete image (in Figure 23.4 when you turn the page) were more likely to recognize this fragment, even if they had forgotten the earlier experience (Mitchell, 2006).

remember things we have not thought about for years, yet forget the name of someone we met a minute ago? How are memories stored in our brains? Why will you be likely, later in this module, to misrecall this sentence: *"The angry rioter threw the rock at the window"*? In this module, we'll consider some of these fascinating questions.

Measures of Retention

23-2 What are three measures of retention?

Recall, recognition, and relearning speed are three ways that psychologists measure retention of memories. Long after you cannot recall most of the people in your high school graduating class, you may still be able to recognize their yearbook pictures from a photographic lineup and pick their names from a list of names. In one experiment, people who had graduated 25 years earlier could not recall many of their old classmates, but they could recognize 90 percent of their pictures and names (Bahrick et al., 1975). If you are like most students, you, too, could probably recognize more names of Snow White's Seven Dwarfs than you could recall (Miserandino, 1991).

Our recognition memory is impressively quick and vast. "Is your friend wearing a new or old outfit?" "Old." "Is this five-second movie clip from a film you've ever seen?" "Yes." "Have you ever seen this person before—this minor variation on the same old human features (two eyes, one nose, and so on)?" "No." Before the mouth can form our answer to any of millions of such questions, the mind knows, and knows that it knows.

Our speed at *relearning* also reveals memory. German philosopher Hermann Ebbinghaus (1850–1909) showed this more than a century ago in his learning experiments, using nonsense syllables. He randomly selected a sample of syllables, practiced them, and tested himself. To get a feel for his experiments, rapidly read aloud, eight times over, the following list (from Baddeley, 1982), then look away and try to recall the items:

JIH, BAZ, FUB, YOX, SUJ, XIR, DAX, LEQ, VUM, PID, KEL, WAV, TUV, ZOF, GEK, HIW.

Both Photos Spanky's Yearbook Archive

Remembering things past Even if Oprah Winfrey and Brad Pitt had not become famous, their high school classmates would most likely still recognize their yearbook photos.

FIGURE 23.2
Ebbinghaus' retention curve
Ebbinghaus found that the more times he practiced a list of nonsense syllables on day 1, the fewer repetitions he required to relearn it on day 2. Speed of relearning is one measure of memory retention. (From Baddeley, 1982.)

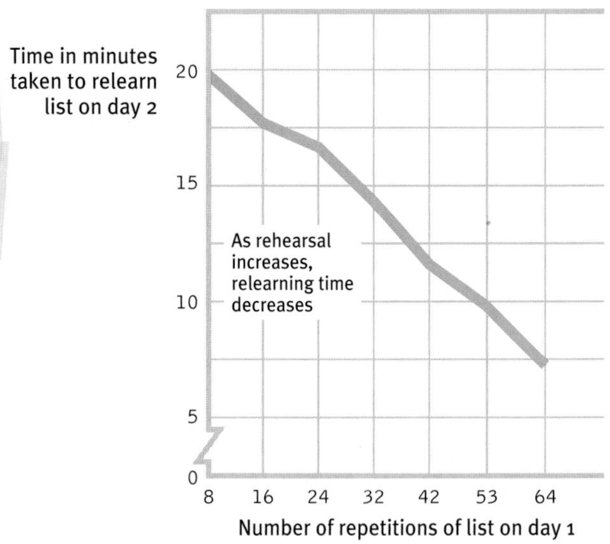

The day after learning such a list, Ebbinghaus could recall few of the syllables. But they weren't entirely forgotten. As **FIGURE 23.2** portrays, the more frequently he repeated the list aloud on day 1, the fewer repetitions he required to *relearn* the list on day 2. Additional rehearsal *(overlearning)* of verbal information increases retention, especially when practice is distributed over time.

The point to remember: Tests of recognition and of time spent relearning demonstrate that *we remember more than we can recall.*

RETRIEVAL PRACTICE

- If you want to be sure to remember what you're learning for an upcoming test, would it be better to use *recall* or *recognition* to check your memory? Why?

ANSWER: It would be better to test your memory with *recall* (such as with short-answer or fill-in-the-blank self-test questions) rather than *recognition* (such as with multiple-choice questions). Recalling information is harder than recognizing it, so if you can recall it that means your retention of the material is better than if you could only recognize it, and your chances of test success are therefore greater.

encoding the processing of information into the memory system—for example, by extracting meaning.

storage the retention of encoded information over time.

retrieval the process of getting information out of memory storage.

sensory memory the immediate, very brief recording of sensory information in the memory system.

short-term memory activated memory that holds a few items briefly, such as seven digits of a phone number while dialing, before the information is stored or forgotten.

long-term memory the relatively permanent and limitless storehouse of the memory system. Includes knowledge, skills, and experiences.

working memory a newer understanding of short-term memory that focuses on conscious, active processing of incoming auditory and visual-spatial information, and of information retrieved from long-term memory.

Memory Models

23-3 How do psychologists describe the human memory system?

Architects make miniature house models to help clients imagine their future homes. Similarly, psychologists create memory models to help us think about how our brain forms and retrieves memories. *Information-processing models* are analogies that compare human memory to a computer's operations. Thus, to remember any event, we must

- *get information into our brain,* a process called **encoding.**
- *retain that information,* a process called **storage.**
- later *get the information back out,* a process called **retrieval.**

Like all analogies, computer models have their limits. Our memories are less literal and more fragile than a computer's. Moreover, most computers process information sequentially, even while alternating between tasks. Our dual-track brain processes many things simultaneously (some of them unconsciously) by means of *parallel processing.* To focus on this complex, simultaneous processing, one information-processing model, *connectionism,*

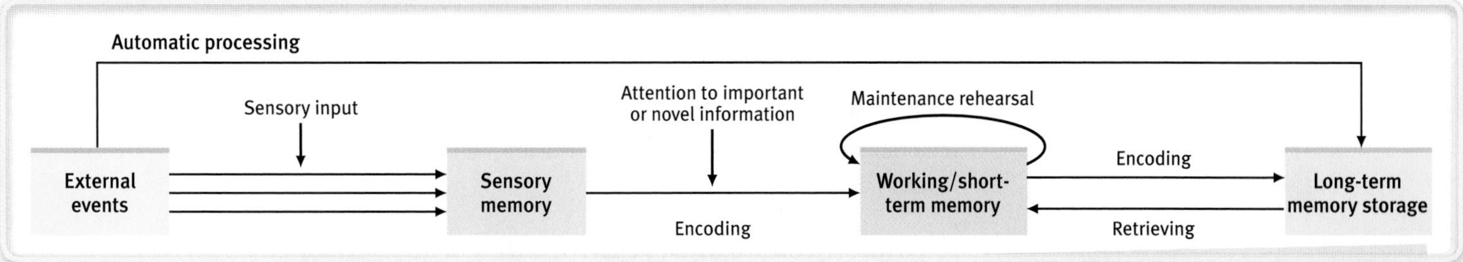

FIGURE 23.3
A modified three-stage processing model of memory Atkinson and Shiffrin's classic three-step model helps us to think about how memories are processed, but today's researchers recognize other ways long-term memories form. For example, some information slips into long-term memory via a "back door," without our consciously attending to it *(automatic processing)*. And so much active processing occurs in the short-term memory stage that many now prefer the term *working memory*.

views memories as products of interconnected neural networks. Specific memories arise from particular activation patterns within these networks. Every time you learn something new, your brain's neural connections change, forming and strengthening pathways that allow you to interact with and learn from your constantly changing environment.

To explain our memory-forming process, Richard Atkinson and Richard Shiffrin (1968) proposed a three-stage model:

1. We first record to-be-remembered information as a fleeting **sensory memory.**
2. From there, we process information into **short-term memory,** where we encode it through *rehearsal.*
3. Finally, information moves into **long-term memory** for later retrieval.

Other psychologists have updated this model (**FIGURE 23.3**) to include important newer concepts, including *working memory* and *automatic processing.*

Working Memory

Alan Baddeley and others (Baddeley, 2001, 2002; Engle, 2002) challenged Atkinson and Shiffrin's view of short-term memory as a small, brief storage space for recent thoughts and experiences. Research shows that this stage is not just a temporary shelf for holding incoming information. It's an active desktop where your brain processes information, making sense of new input and linking it with long-term memories. Whether we hear *eye-screem* as "ice cream" or "I scream" will depend on how the context and our experience guide us in interpreting and encoding the sounds. To focus on the active processing that takes place in this middle stage, psychologists use the term **working memory.** Right now, you are using your working memory to link the information you're reading with your previously stored information (Cowan, 2010; Kail & Hall, 2001).

The pages you are reading may enter working memory through vision. You might also repeat the information using auditory rehearsal. As you integrate these memory inputs with your existing long-term memory, your attention is focused. Baddeley (2002) suggested the *central executive* handles this focused processing (**FIGURE 23.5**).

FIGURE 23.4
Now you know People who had seen this complete image were, 17 years later, more likely to recognize the fragment in Figure 23.1.

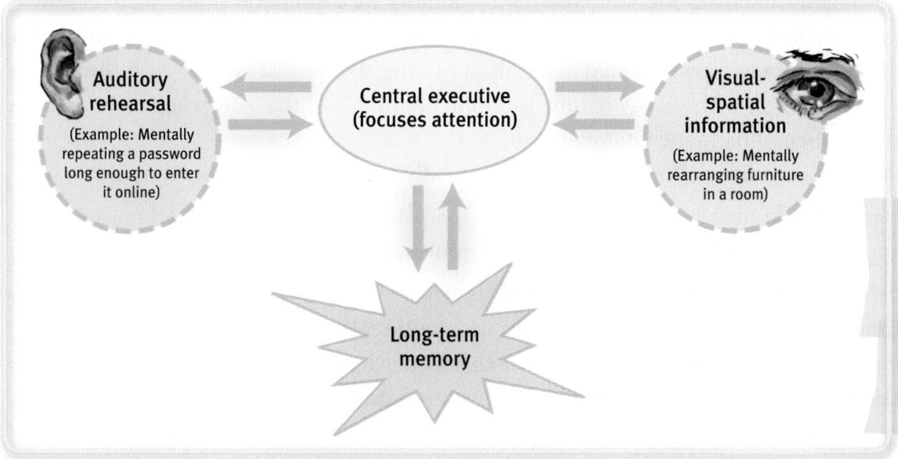

FIGURE 23.5
Working memory Alan Baddeley's (2002) model of working memory, simplified here, includes *visual* and *auditory rehearsal* of new information. A hypothetical *central executive* (manager) focuses attention and pulls information from long-term memory to help make sense of new information.

Without focused attention, information often fades. In one experiment, people read and typed new information they would later need, such as "An ostrich's eye is bigger than its brain." If they knew the information would be available online they invested less energy in remembering, and remembered the trivia less well (Sparrow et al., 2011). Sometimes Google replaces rehearsal.

Dual-Track Memory: Effortful Versus Automatic Processing

23-4 How are explicit and implicit memories distinguished?

Atkinson and Shiffrin's model focused on how we process our **explicit memories**—the facts and experiences that we can consciously know and declare (thus, also called *declarative memories*). But our mind operates on two tracks. It processes explicit memories through conscious, **effortful processing.** But behind the scenes, outside the Atkinson-Shiffrin stages, other information skips our conscious encoding and barges directly into storage. This **automatic processing,** which happens without our awareness, produces **implicit memories** (also called *nondeclarative memories*).

The two-track memory system reinforces an important principle of parallel processing: Mental feats such as vision, thinking, and memory may seem to be single abilities, but they are not. Rather, we split information into different components for separate and simultaneous processing.

RETRIEVAL PRACTICE

- What two new concepts update the classic Atkinson-Shiffrin three-stage information-processing model?

ANSWER: (1) We form some memories (*implicit memories*) through *automatic processing*, without our awareness. The Atkinson-Shiffrin model focused only on conscious, *explicit memories*. (2) The newer concept of a *working memory* emphasizes the active processing that we now know takes place in Atkinson-Shiffrin's short-term memory stage.

- What are two basic functions of *working memory?*

ANSWER: (1) Active processing of incoming visual and auditory information, and (2) focusing our spotlight of attention.

Building Memories

Encoding and Automatic Processing

23-5 What information do we automatically process?

Our implicit memories include *procedural* memory for automatic skills, such as how to ride a bike, and classically conditioned *associations* among stimuli. Visiting your dentist, you may, thanks to a conditioned association linking the dentist's office with the painful drill, find yourself with sweaty palms. You didn't plan to feel that way when you got to the dentist's office; it happened *automatically.*

Without conscious effort you also automatically process information about

- ***space.*** While studying, you often encode the place on a page where certain material appears; later, when you want to retrieve information about automatic processing, you may visualize the location of that information on this page.
- ***time.*** While going about your day, you unintentionally note the sequence of its events. Later, realizing you've left your coat somewhere, the event sequence your brain automatically encoded will enable you to retrace your steps.
- ***frequency.*** You effortlessly keep track of how many times things happen, as when you suddenly realize, *This is the third time I've run into her today.*

explicit memory memory of facts and experiences that one can consciously know and "declare." (Also called *declarative memory.*)

effortful processing encoding that requires attention and conscious effort.

automatic processing unconscious encoding of incidental information, such as space, time, and frequency, and of well-learned information, such as word meanings.

implicit memory retention independent of conscious recollection. (Also called *nondeclarative memory.*)

iconic memory a momentary sensory memory of visual stimuli; a photographic or picture-image memory lasting no more than a few tenths of a second.

echoic memory a momentary sensory memory of auditory stimuli; if attention is elsewhere, sounds and words can still be recalled within 3 or 4 seconds.

Our two-track mind engages in impressively efficient information processing. As one track automatically tucks away many routine details, the other track is free to focus on conscious, effortful processing.

Encoding and Effortful Processing

Automatic processing happens so effortlessly that it is difficult to shut off. When you see words in your native language, perhaps on the side of a delivery truck, you can't help but read them and register their meaning. *Learning* to read wasn't automatic. You may recall working hard to pick out letters and connect them to certain sounds. But with experience and practice, your reading became automatic. Imagine now learning to read reversed sentences like this:

.citamotua emoceb nac gnissecorp luftroffE

At first, this requires effort, but after enough practice, you would also perform this task much more automatically. We develop many skills in this way. We learn to drive, to text, to speak a new language with effort, but then these tasks become automatic.

Sensory Memory

23-6 How does sensory memory work?

Effortful processing begins with sensory memory (recall Figure 23.3), which feeds our active working memory. Our sensory memory records a momentary image of a scene or an echo of a sound. How much of this page could you sense and recall with less exposure than a lightning flash? In one experiment (Sperling, 1960), people viewed three rows of three letters each, for only one-twentieth of a second (**FIGURE 23.6**). After the nine letters disappeared, they could recall only about half of them.

Was it because they had insufficient time to glimpse them? *No.* The researcher, George Sperling, cleverly demonstrated that people actually *could* see and recall all the letters, but only momentarily. Rather than ask them to recall all nine letters at once, he sounded a high, medium, or low tone immediately *after* flashing the nine letters. This tone directed participants to report only the letters of the top, middle, or bottom row, respectively. Now they rarely missed a letter, showing that all nine letters were momentarily available for recall.

Sperling's experiment demonstrated **iconic memory,** a fleeting sensory memory of visual stimuli. For a few tenths of a second, our eyes register a photographic or picture-image memory of a scene, and we can recall any part of it in amazing detail. But if Sperling delayed the tone signal by more than half a second, the image faded and participants again recalled only about half the letters. Our visual screen clears quickly, as new images are superimposed over old ones.

We also have an impeccable, though fleeting, memory for auditory stimuli, called **echoic memory** (Cowan, 1988; Lu et al., 1992). Picture yourself in conversation, as your attention veers to the TV. If your mildly irked companion tests you by asking, "What did I just say?" you can recover the last few words from your mind's echo chamber. Auditory echoes tend to linger for 3 or 4 seconds.

FIGURE 23.6
Momentary photographic memory When George Sperling flashed a group of letters similar to this for one-twentieth of a second, people could recall only about half of the letters. But when signaled to recall a particular row immediately after the letters had disappeared, they could do so with near-perfect accuracy.

K	Z	R
Q	B	T
S	G	N

Capacity of Short-Term and Working Memory

23-7 What is the capacity of our short-term and working memory?

George Miller (1956) proposed that short-term memory can retain about seven information bits (give or take two). Other researchers have confirmed that we can, if nothing distracts us, recall about seven digits, or about six letters or five words (Baddeley et al., 1975). How quickly do our short-term memories disappear? To find out, Lloyd Peterson and Margaret Peterson (1959) asked people to remember three-consonant groups, such as *CHJ*. To prevent rehearsal, the researchers asked them, for example, to start at 100 and

The Magical Number Seven has become psychology's contribution to an intriguing list of magic sevens—the seven wonders of the world, the seven seas, the seven deadly sins, the seven primary colors, the seven musical scale notes, the seven days of the week—seven magical sevens.

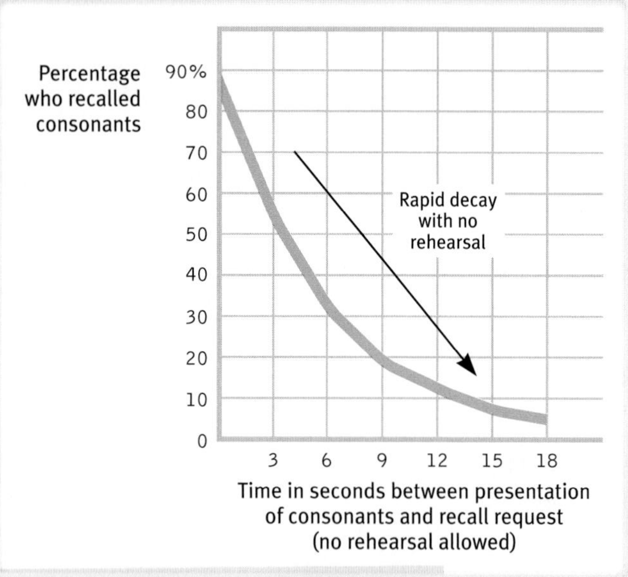

FIGURE 23.7
Short-term memory decay Unless rehearsed, verbal information may be quickly forgotten. (From Peterson & Peterson, 1959; see also Brown, 1958.)

count aloud backwards by threes. After 3 seconds, people recalled the letters only about half the time; after 12 seconds, they seldom recalled them at all (**FIGURE 23.7**). Without the active processing that we now understand to be a part of the "working memory" concept, short-term memories have a limited life.

Working-memory capacity varies, depending on age and other factors. Compared with children and older adults, young adults have more working-memory capacity, so they can use their mental workspace more efficiently. This means their ability to multitask is relatively greater. But whatever our age, we do better and more efficient work when focused, without distractions, on one task at a time. The bottom line: It's probably a bad idea to try to watch TV, text your friends, and write a psychology paper all at the same time (Willingham, 2010)!

Unlike short-term memory capacity, working-memory capacity appears to reflect intelligence level (Cowan, 2008; Shelton et al., 2010). Imagine seeing a letter of the alphabet, then a simple question, then another letter, followed by another question, and so on. In such experiments, those who could juggle the most mental balls—who could remember the most letters despite the interruptions—tended in everyday life to exhibit high intelligence and an ability to maintain their focus (Kane et al., 2007; Unsworth & Engle, 2007). When beeped to report in at various times, they were less likely than others to report that their mind was wandering.

Effortful Processing Strategies

23-8 What are some effortful processing strategies that can help us remember new information?

Research shows that several effortful processing strategies can boost our ability to form new memories. Later, when we try to retrieve a memory, these strategies can make the difference between success and failure.

Chunking Glance for a few seconds at row 1 of **FIGURE 23.8**, then look away and try to reproduce what you saw. Impossible, yes? But you can easily reproduce the second row, which is no less complex. Similarly, you will probably find row 4 much easier to remember than row 3, although both contain the same letters. And you could remember the sixth cluster more easily than the fifth, although both contain the same words. As these units demonstrate, **chunking** information—organizing items into familiar, manageable units—enables us to recall it more easily. Try remembering 43 individual numbers and letters. It would be impossible, unless chunked into, say, seven meaningful chunks, such as "Try remembering 43 individual numbers and letters." ☺

FIGURE 23.8
Effects of chunking on memory When we organize information into meaningful units, such as letters, words, and phrases, we recall it more easily. (From Hintzman, 1978.)

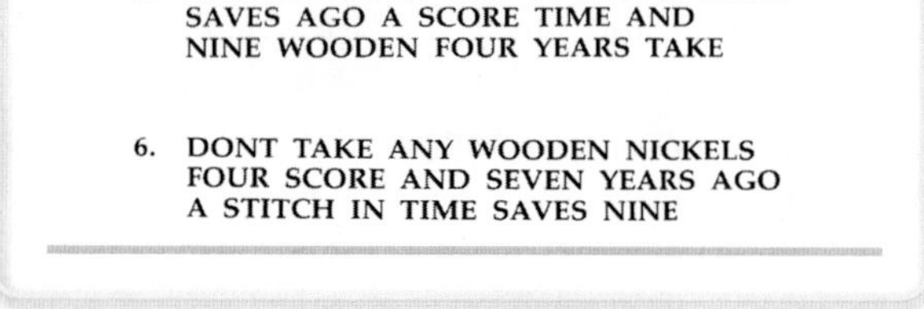

Chunking usually occurs so naturally that we take it for granted. If you are a native English speaker, you can reproduce perfectly the 150 or so line segments that make up the words in the three phrases of item 6 in Figure 23.8. It would astonish someone unfamiliar with the language. I am similarly awed at a Chinese reader's ability to glance at **FIGURE 23.9** and then reproduce all the strokes; or of a varsity basketball player's recall of the positions of the players after a 4-second glance at a basketball play (Allard & Burnett, 1985). We all remember information best when we can organize it into personally meaningful arrangements.

Mnemonics To help them encode lengthy passages and speeches, ancient Greek scholars and orators also developed **mnemonics** (nih-MON-iks). Many of these memory aids use vivid imagery, because we are particularly good at remembering mental pictures. We more easily remember concrete, visualizable words than we do abstract words. (When I quiz you later, which three of these words—*bicycle, void, cigarette, inherent, fire, process*—will you most likely recall?) If you still recall the rock-throwing rioter sentence, it is probably not only because of the meaning you encoded but also because the sentence painted a mental image.

The *peg-word system* harnesses our superior visual-imagery skill. This mnemonic requires you to memorize a jingle: *One is a bun; two is a shoe; three is a tree; four is a door; five is a hive; six is sticks; seven is heaven; eight is a gate; nine is swine; ten is a hen.* Without much effort, you will soon be able to count by peg words instead of numbers: *bun, shoe, tree* . . . and then to visually associate the peg words with to-be-remembered items. Now you are ready to challenge anyone to give you a grocery list to remember. Carrots? Stick them into the imaginary bun. Milk? Fill the shoe with it. Paper towels? Drape them over the tree branch. Think *bun, shoe, tree* and you see their associated images: carrots, milk, paper towels. With few errors, you will be able to recall the items in any order and to name any given item (Bugelski et al., 1968). Memory whizzes understand the power of such systems. A study of star performers in the World Memory Championships showed them not to have exceptional intelligence, but rather to be superior at using mnemonic strategies (Maguire et al., 2003).

春
夏
秋
冬

FIGURE 23.9
An example of chunking—for those who read Chinese After looking at these characters, can you reproduce them exactly? If so, you are literate in Chinese.

Chunking and mnemonic techniques combined can be great memory aids for unfamiliar material. Want to remember the colors of the rainbow in order of wavelength? Think of the mnemonic ROY G. BIV (*r*ed, *o*range, *y*ellow, *g*reen, *b*lue, *i*ndigo, *v*iolet). Need to recall the names of North America's five Great Lakes? Just remember HOMES (*H*uron, *O*ntario, *M*ichigan, *E*rie, *S*uperior). In each case, we chunk information into a more familiar form by creating a word (called an *acronym*) from the first letters of the to-be-remembered items.

Hierarchies When people develop expertise in an area, they process information not only in chunks but also in *hierarchies* composed of a few broad concepts divided and subdivided into narrower concepts and facts. This section, for example, aims to help you organize memory concepts (**FIGURE 23.10**).

Organizing knowledge in hierarchies helps us retrieve information efficiently, as Gordon Bower and his colleagues (1969) demonstrated by presenting words either randomly or grouped into categories. When the words were organized into categories, recall was two to three times better. Such results show the benefits of organizing what you study—of giving special attention to module outlines, headings, the numbered "Learning Objective" questions (such as 23-8, left), Retrieval Practice questions, and module reviews. Taking lecture and text notes in outline format—a type of hierarchical organization—may also prove helpful.

Distributed Practice We retain information (such as classmates' names) better when our encoding is distributed over time. More than 300 experiments over the last century have consistently revealed the benefits of this **spacing effect** (Cepeda et al., 2006). *Massed practice* (cramming) can produce speedy short-term learning and feelings of confidence. But to paraphrase pioneer memory researcher Hermann Ebbinghaus (1885), those who learn quickly also forget quickly. *Distributed practice* produces better

chunking organizing items into familiar, manageable units; often occurs automatically.

mnemonics [nih-MON-iks] memory aids, especially those techniques that use vivid imagery and organizational devices.

spacing effect the tendency for distributed study or practice to yield better long-term retention than is achieved through massed study or practice.

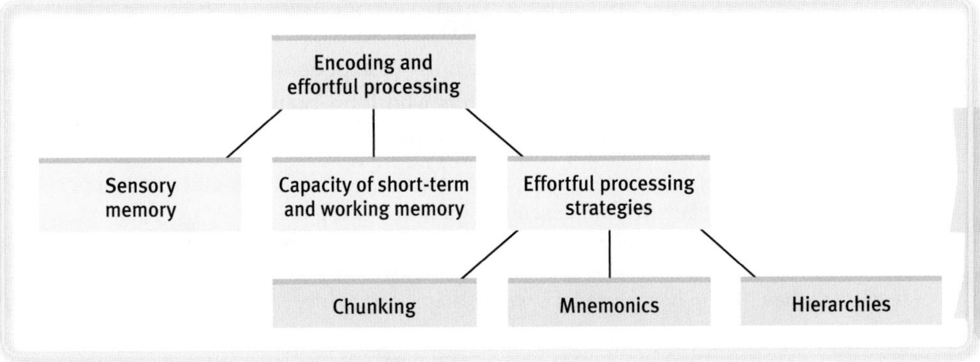

FIGURE 23.10
Organization benefits memory When we organize words or concepts into hierarchical groups, as illustrated here with concepts in this section, we remember them better than when we see them presented randomly.

long-term recall. After you've studied long enough to master the material, further study becomes inefficient (Rohrer & Pashler, 2007). Better to spend that extra reviewing time later—a day later if you need to remember something 10 days hence, or a month later if you need to remember something 6 months hence (Cepeda et al., 2008).

"The mind is slow in unlearning what it has been long in learning."
Roman philosopher Seneca (4 B.C.E.–65 C.E.)

Spreading your learning over several months, rather than over a shorter term, can help you retain information for a lifetime. In a 9-year experiment, Harry Bahrick and three of his family members (1993) practiced foreign language word translations for a given number of times, at intervals ranging from 14 to 56 days. Their consistent finding: The longer the space between practice sessions, the better their retention up to 5 years later.

One effective way to distribute practice is repeated self-testing, a phenomenon that researchers Henry Roediger and Jeffrey Karpicke (2006) call the **testing effect**. In this text, for example, the Retrieval Practice features offer such an opportunity. Better to practice retrieval (as any exam will demand) than merely to reread material (which may lull you into a false sense of mastery).

The point to remember: Spaced study and self-assessment beat cramming and rereading.

Levels of Processing

23-9 What are the levels of processing, and how do they affect encoding?

Memory researchers have discovered that we process verbal information at different levels, and that depth of processing affects our long-term retention. **Shallow processing** encodes on a very basic level, such as a word's letters or, at a more intermediate level, a word's sound. **Deep processing** encodes *semantically*, based on the meaning of the words. The deeper (more meaningful) the processing, the better our retention.

In one classic experiment, researchers Fergus Craik and Endel Tulving (1975) flashed words at people. Then they asked the viewers a question that would elicit different levels of processing. To experience the task yourself, rapidly answer the following sample questions:

Sample Questions to Elicit Processing	Word Flashed	Yes	No
1. Is the word in capital letters?	CHAIR	______	______
2. Does the word rhyme with train?	brain	______	______
3. Would the word fit in this sentence? The girl put the ______ on the table.	doll	______	______

Which type of processing would best prepare you to recognize the words at a later time? In Craik and Tulving's experiment, the deeper, semantic processing triggered by the third question yielded a much better memory than did the shallower processing elicited by the second question or the very shallow processing elicited by question 1 (which was especially ineffective) (**FIGURE 23.11**).

Making Material Personally Meaningful

If new information is not meaningful or related to our experience, we have trouble processing it. Put yourself in the place of the students who John Bransford and Marcia Johnson (1972) asked to remember the following recorded passage:

> The procedure is actually quite simple. First you arrange things into different groups. Of course, one pile may be sufficient depending on how much there is to do. . . . After the procedure is completed one arranges the materials into different groups again. Then they can be put into their appropriate places. Eventually they will be used once more and the whole cycle will then have to be repeated. However, that is part of life.

testing effect enhanced memory after retrieving, rather than simply reading, information. Also sometimes referred to as a *retrieval practice effect* or *test-enhanced learning*.

shallow processing encoding on a basic level based on the structure or appearance of words.

deep processing encoding semantically, based on the meaning of the words; tends to yield the best retention.

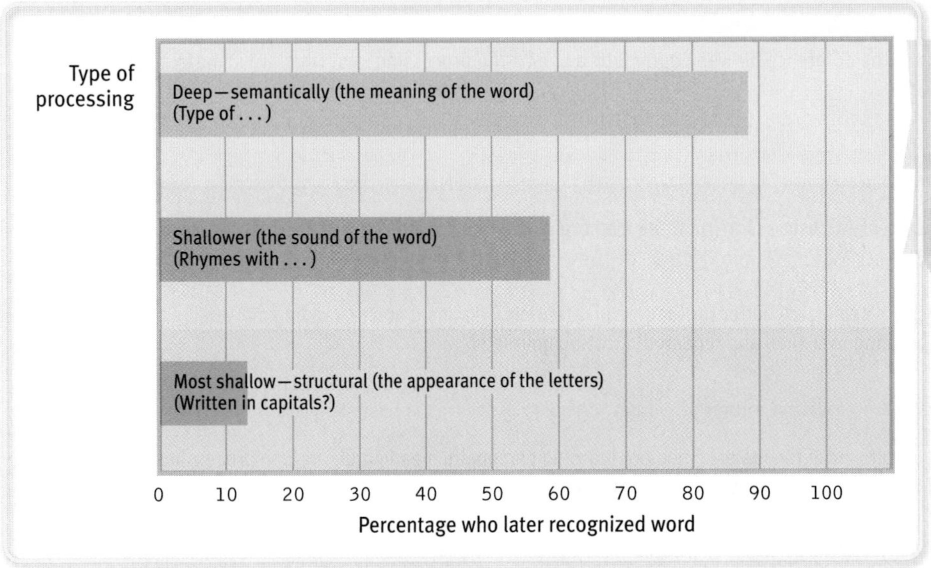

FIGURE 23.11
Levels of processing Processing a word deeply—by its meaning (semantically)—produces better recognition of it at a later time than does shallower processing by attending to its appearance or sound. (From Craik & Tulving, 1975.)

When the students heard the paragraph you have just read, without a meaningful context, they remembered little of it. When told the paragraph described washing clothes (something meaningful to them), they remembered much more of it—as you probably could now after rereading it.

Can you repeat the sentence about the rioter that I gave you at this module's beginning? ("The angry rioter threw . . .") Perhaps, like those in an experiment by William Brewer (1977), you recalled the sentence by the meaning you encoded when you read it (for example, "The angry rioter threw the rock *through* the window") and not as it was written ("The angry rioter threw the rock *at* the window"). Referring to such mental mismatches, Gordon Bower and Daniel Morrow (1990) have likened our minds to theater directors who, given a raw script, imagine the finished stage production. Asked later what we heard or read, we recall not the literal text but *what we encoded*. Thus, studying for an exam, you may remember your lecture notes rather than the lecture itself.

In the discussion of mnemonics, I gave you six words and told you I would quiz you about them later. How many of these words can you now recall? Of these, how many are high-imagery words? How many are low-imagery? (You can check your list against the six inverted words below.)

Bicycle, void, cigarette, inherent, fire, process

We can avoid some of these mismatches by rephrasing what we see and hear into meaningful terms. From his experiments on himself, Ebbinghaus estimated that, compared with learning nonsense material, learning meaningful material required one-tenth the effort. As memory researcher Wayne Wickelgren (1977, p. 346) noted, "The time you spend thinking about material you are reading and relating it to previously stored material is about the most useful thing you can do in learning any new subject matter."

Psychologist-actor team Helga Noice and Tony Noice (2006) have described how actors inject meaning into the daunting task of learning "all those lines." They do it by first coming to understand the flow of meaning: "One actor divided a half-page of dialogue into three [intentions]: 'to flatter,' 'to draw him out,' and 'to allay his fears.'" With this meaningful sequence in mind, the actor more easily remembers the lines.

We have especially good recall for information we can meaningfully relate to ourselves. Asked how well certain adjectives describe someone else, we often forget them; asked how well the adjectives describe us, we remember the words well. This tendency, called the *self-reference effect*, is especially strong in members of individualistic Western cultures (Symons & Johnson, 1997; Wagar & Cohen, 2003). Information deemed "relevant to me" is processed more deeply and remains more accessible. Knowing this, you can profit from taking time to find personal meaning in what you are studying.

The point to remember: The amount remembered depends both on the time spent learning and on your making it meaningful for deep processing.

RETRIEVAL PRACTICE

- What is the difference between *automatic* and *effortful* processing, and what are some examples of each?

ANSWER: *Automatic* processing occurs unconsciously (automatically) for such things as the sequence and frequency of a day's events, and reading and comprehending words in our own language. *Effortful* processing requires attention and awareness and happens, for example, when we work hard to learn new material in class, or new lines for a play.

- At which of Atkinson-Shiffrin's three memory stages would *iconic* and *echoic* memory occur?

ANSWER: sensory memory

- Which strategies are better for long-term retention: cramming and re-reading material, or spreading out learning over time and repeatedly testing yourself?

ANSWER: Although cramming may lead to short-term gains in knowledge, distributed practice and repeated self-testing will result in the greatest long-term retention.

- If you try to make the material you are learning personally meaningful, are you processing at a shallow or a deep level? Which level leads to greater retention?

ANSWER: Making material personally meaningful involves processing at a deep level, because you are processing *semantically*—based on the meaning of the words. Deep processing leads to greater retention.

MODULE REVIEW

Studying and Building Memories

Learning Objectives

RETRIEVAL PRACTICE Take a moment to answer each of these Learning Objective Questions (repeated here from within the module). Then turn to Appendix B, Complete Module Reviews, to check your answers. Research suggests that trying to answer these questions on your own will improve your long-term retention (McDaniel et al., 2009).

23-1: What is memory?

23-2: What are three measures of retention?

23-3: How do psychologists describe the human memory system?

23-4: How are explicit and implicit memories distinguished?

23-5: What information do we automatically process?

23-6: How does sensory memory work?

23-7: What is the capacity of our short-term and working memory?

23-8: What are some effortful processing strategies that can help us remember new information?

23-9: What are the levels of processing, and how do they affect encoding?

Terms and Concepts to Remember

RETRIEVAL PRACTICE Test yourself on these terms by trying to write down the definition before flipping back to the referenced page to check your answer.

memory, p. 312
recall, p. 312
recognition, p. 312
relearning, p. 312
encoding, p. 314
storage, p. 314
retrieval, p. 314
sensory memory, p. 315
short-term memory, p. 315
long-term memory, p. 315
working memory, p. 315
explicit memory, p. 316
effortful processing, p. 316
automatic processing, p. 316
implicit memory, p. 316
iconic memory, p. 317
echoic memory, p. 317
chunking, p. 318
mnemonics [nih-MON-iks], p. 318
spacing effect, p. 319
testing effect, p. 320
shallow processing, p. 320
deep processing, p. 320

Source Amnesia

Among the frailest parts of a memory is its source. We may recognize someone but have no idea where we have seen the person. We may dream an event and later be unsure whether it really happened. We may misrecall how we learned about something (Henkel et al., 2000). Psychologists are not immune to the process. Famed child psychologist Jean Piaget was startled as an adult to learn that a vivid, detailed memory from his childhood—a nursemaid's thwarting his kidnapping—was utterly false. He apparently constructed the memory from repeatedly hearing the story (which his nursemaid, after undergoing a religious conversion, later confessed had never happened). In attributing his "memory" to his own experiences, rather than to his nursemaid's stories, Piaget experienced **source amnesia** (also called *source misattribution*). Misattribution is at the heart of many false memories. Authors and songwriters sometimes suffer from it. They think an idea came from their own creative imagination, when in fact they are unintentionally plagiarizing something they earlier read or heard.

Debra Poole and Stephen Lindsay (1995, 2001, 2002) demonstrated source amnesia among preschoolers. They had the children interact with "Mr. Science," who engaged them in activities such as blowing up a balloon with baking soda and vinegar. Three months later, on three successive days, their parents read them a story describing some things the children had experienced with Mr. Science and some they had not. When a new interviewer asked what Mr. Science had done with them—"Did Mr. Science have a machine with ropes to pull?"—4 in 10 children spontaneously recalled him doing things that had happened only in the story.

Source amnesia also helps explain **déjà vu** (French for "already seen"). Two-thirds of us have experienced this fleeting, eerie sense that "I've been in this exact situation before." It happens most commonly to well-educated, imaginative young adults, especially when tired or stressed (Brown, 2003, 2004; McAneny, 1996). Some wonder, "How could I recognize a situation I'm experiencing for the first time?" Others may think of reincarnation ("I must have experienced this in a previous life") or precognition ("I viewed this scene in my mind before experiencing it").

Alan Brown and Elizabeth Marsh (2009) devised an intriguing way to induce déjà vu in the laboratory. They invited participants to view symbols on a computer screen and to report whether they had ever seen them before. What the viewers didn't know was that these symbols had earlier been subliminally flashed on the screen, too briefly for conscious awareness. The result? Half the participants reported experiencing déjà vu—a sense of familiarity without awareness of why. Brown and Marsh suggest that real-life experiences may include glancing very briefly at a visual scene, looking away without consciously processing it, then looking again—only to feel the uncanny sense of having seen it before.

The key to déjà vu seems to be familiarity with a stimulus without a clear idea of where we encountered it before (Cleary, 2008). Normally, we experience a feeling of *familiarity* (thanks to temporal lobe processing) before we consciously remember details (thanks to hippocampus and frontal lobe processing). When these functions (and brain regions) are out of sync, we may experience a feeling of familiarity without conscious recall. Our amazing brains try to make sense of such an improbable situation, and we get an eerie feeling that we're reliving some earlier part of our life. After all, the situation is familiar, even though we have no idea why. Our source amnesia forces us to do our best to make sense of an odd moment.

source amnesia attributing to the wrong source an event we have experienced, heard about, read about, or imagined. (Also called *source misattribution.*) Source amnesia, along with the misinformation effect, is at the heart of many false memories.

déjà vu that eerie sense that "I've experienced this before." Cues from the current situation may subconsciously trigger retrieval of an earlier experience.

"Do you ever get that strange feeling of vujà dé? Not déjà vu; vujà dé. It's the distinct sense that, somehow, something just happened that has never happened before. Nothing seems familiar. And then suddenly the feeling is gone. Vujà dé."

George Carlin (1937–2008), in *Funny Times*, December 2001

Discerning True and False Memories

Because memory is reconstruction as well as reproduction, we can't be sure whether a memory is real by how real it feels. Much as perceptual illusions may seem like real perceptions, unreal memories *feel* like real memories.

False memories created by suggested misinformation and misattributed sources not only can feel as real as true memories, they can be very persistent. Imagine that I were to read aloud a list of words such as *candy, sugar, honey,* and *taste.* Later, I ask you to recognize the presented words from a larger list. If you are at all like the people tested by Henry Roediger and Kathleen McDermott (1995), you would err three out of four times—by falsely remembering a nonpresented similar word, such as *sweet.* We more easily remember the gist than the words themselves.

Memory construction helps explain why 79 percent of 200 convicts exonerated by later DNA testing had been misjudged based on faulty eyewitness identification (Garrett, 2008). It explains why "hypnotically refreshed" memories of crimes so easily incorporate errors, some of which originate with the hypnotist's leading questions *("Did you hear loud noises?").* It explains why dating partners who fall in love *over*estimate their first impressions of one another *("It was love at first sight"),* while those who break up *under*estimate their earlier liking *("We never really clicked")* (McFarland & Ross, 1987). And it explains why people asked how they felt 10 years ago about marijuana or gender issues have recalled attitudes closer to their current views than to the views they had actually reported a decade earlier (Markus, 1986). Thanks to *hindsight bias,* how people feel today tends to be how they recall they have always felt (Mazzoni & Vannucci, 2007).

One research team interviewed 73 ninth-grade boys and then reinterviewed them 35 years later. When asked to recall how they had reported their attitudes, activities, and experiences, most men recalled statements that matched their actual prior responses at a rate no better than chance. Only 1 in 3 now remembered receiving physical punishment, though as ninth-graders 82 percent had said they had (Offer et al., 2000). As George Vaillant (1977, p. 197) noted after following adult lives through time, "It is all too common for caterpillars to become butterflies and then to maintain that in their youth they had been little butterflies. Maturation makes liars of us all."

Children's Eyewitness Recall

26-3 How reliable are young children's eyewitness descriptions, and why are reports of repressed and recovered memories so hotly debated?

If memories can be sincere, yet sincerely wrong, might children's recollections of sexual abuse be prone to error? "It would be truly awful to ever lose sight of the enormity of child abuse," observed Stephen Ceci (1993). Yet Ceci and Maggie Bruck's (1993, 1995) studies of children's memories have made them aware of how easily children's memories can be molded. For example, they asked 3-year-olds to show on anatomically correct dolls where a pediatrician had touched them. Of the children who had not received genital examinations, 55 percent pointed to either genital or anal areas.

In other experiments, the researchers studied the effect of suggestive interviewing techniques (Bruck & Ceci, 1999, 2004). In one study, children chose a card from a deck of possible happenings, and an adult then read the card to them. For example, "Think real hard, and tell me if this ever happened to you. Can you remember going to the hospital with a mousetrap on your finger?" In interviews, the same adult repeatedly asked children to think about several real and fictitious events. After 10 weeks of this, a new adult asked the same question. The stunning result: 58 percent of preschoolers produced false (often vivid) stories regarding one or more events they had never experienced (Ceci et al., 1994). Here's one of those stories:

> My brother Colin was trying to get Blowtorch [an action figure] from me, and I wouldn't let him take it from me, so he pushed me into the wood pile where the mousetrap was. And then my finger got caught in it. And then we went to the hospital, and my mommy, daddy, and Colin drove me there, to the hospital in our van, because it was far away. And the doctor put a bandage on this finger.

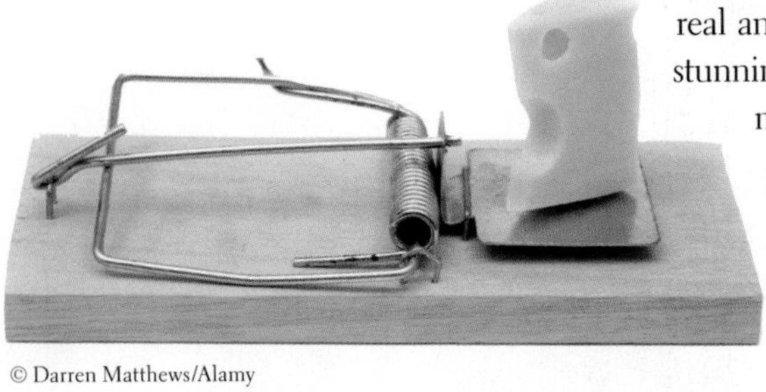

© Darren Matthews/Alamy

Given such detailed stories, professional psychologists who specialize in interviewing children could not reliably separate the real memories from the false ones. Nor could the children themselves. Colin's brother, reminded that his parents had told him several times that the mousetrap incident never happened—that he had imagined it—protested, "But it really did happen. I remember it!" In another experiment, preschoolers merely overheard an erroneous remark that a magician's missing rabbit had gotten loose in their classroom. Later, when the children were suggestively questioned, 78 percent of them recalled actually seeing the rabbit (Principe et al., 2006). "[The] research leads me to worry about the possibility of false allegations. It is not a tribute to one's scientific integrity to walk down the middle of the road if the data are more to one side," said Ceci (1993).

Does this mean that children can never be accurate eyewitnesses? *No.* If questioned about their experiences in neutral words they understand, children often accurately recall what happened and who did it (Goodman, 2006; Howe, 1997; Pipe, 1996). When interviewers use less suggestive, more effective techniques, even 4- to 5-year-old children produce more accurate recall (Holliday & Albon, 2004; Pipe et al., 2004). Children are especially accurate when they have not talked with involved adults prior to the interview and when their disclosure is made in a first interview with a neutral person who asks nonleading questions.

Like children (whose frontal lobes have not fully matured), older adults—especially those whose frontal lobe functioning has declined—are more susceptible than young adults to false memories. This makes older adults more vulnerable to scams, as when a repairperson overcharges by falsely claiming, "I told you it would cost x, and you agreed to pay" (Jacoby et al., 2005; Jacoby & Rhodes, 2006; Roediger & Geraci, 2007; Roediger & McDaniel, 2007).

Repressed or Constructed Memories of Abuse?

There are two tragedies related to adult recollections of child abuse. One happens when people don't believe abuse survivors who tell their secret. The other happens when innocent people are falsely accused. What, then, shall we say about clinicians who have guided people in "recovering" childhood abuse memories? Were these well-intentioned therapists triggering false memories that damaged innocent adults? Or were they uncovering the truth?

The research on source amnesia and the misinformation effect raises concerns about therapist-guided recovered memories. Some have reasoned with patients that "people who've been abused often have your symptoms, so you probably were abused. Let's see if, aided by hypnosis or drugs, or helped to dig back and visualize your trauma, you can recover it." Patients exposed to such techniques may then form an image of a threatening person. With further visualization, the image grows more vivid. The patient ends up stunned, angry, and ready to confront or sue the remembered abuser. The equally stunned and devastated parent or relative vigorously denies the accusation.

Critics are not questioning the professionalism of most therapists. Nor are they questioning the accusers' sincerity; even if false, their memories are heartfelt. Critics' charges are specifically directed against clinicians who use "memory work" techniques, such as "guided imagery," hypnosis, and dream analysis to recover memories. "Thousands of families were cruelly ripped apart," with "previously loving adult daughters" suddenly accusing fathers (Gardner, 2006). Irate clinicians have countered that those who argue that recovered memories of abuse never happen are adding to abused people's trauma and playing into the hands of child molesters.

In an effort to find a sensible common ground that might resolve psychology's "memory war," professional organizations (the American Medical, American Psychological, and American Psychiatric Associations; the Australian Psychological Society; the British Psychological Society; and the Canadian Psychiatric Association) have convened study panels and issued public statements. Those committed to protecting abused children and those committed to protecting wrongly accused adults have agreed on the following:

- ***Sexual abuse happens.*** And it happens more often than we once supposed. Although sexual abuse can leave its victims at risk for problems ranging from sexual dysfunction to depression (Freyd et al., 2007), there is no characteristic "survivor syndrome"—no group of symptoms that lets us spot victims of sexual abuse (Kendall-Tackett et al., 1993).

- ***Injustice happens.*** Some innocent people have been falsely convicted. And some guilty people have evaded responsibility by casting doubt on their truth-telling accusers.
- ***Forgetting happens.*** Many of those actually abused were either very young when abused or may not have understood the meaning of their experience—circumstances under which forgetting is common. Forgetting isolated past events, both negative and positive, is an ordinary part of everyday life.
- ***Recovered memories are commonplace.*** Cued by a remark or an experience, we all recover memories of long-forgotten events, both pleasant and unpleasant. What many psychologists debate is twofold: Does the unconscious mind sometimes *forcibly repress* painful experiences? If so, can these experiences be retrieved by certain therapist-aided techniques? (Memories that surface naturally are more likely to be verified [Geraerts et al., 2007].)
- ***Memories of things happening before age 3 are unreliable.*** We cannot reliably recall happenings from our first three years. This *infantile amnesia* happens because our brain pathways have not yet developed enough to form the kinds of memories we will form later in life. Most psychologists—including most clinical and counseling psychologists—therefore doubt "recovered" memories of abuse during infancy (Gore-Felton et al., 2000; Knapp & VandeCreek, 2000). The older a child was when suffering sexual abuse, and the more severe the abuse, the more likely it is to be remembered (Goodman et al., 2003).
- ***Memories "recovered" under hypnosis or the influence of drugs are especially unreliable.*** Under hypnosis, people will incorporate all kinds of suggestions into their memories, even memories of "past lives."
- ***Memories, whether real or false, can be emotionally upsetting.*** Both the accuser and the accused may suffer when what was born of mere suggestion becomes, like an actual trauma, a stinging memory that drives bodily stress (McNally, 2003, 2007). Some people knocked unconscious in unremembered accidents know this all too well. They have later developed stress disorders after being haunted by memories they constructed from photos, news reports, and friends' accounts (Bryant, 2001).

"When memories are 'recovered' after long periods of amnesia, particularly when extraordinary means were used to secure the recovery of memory, there is a high probability that the memories are false."

Royal College of Psychiatrists Working Group on Reported Recovered Memories of Child Sexual Abuse (Brandon et al., 1998)

© The New Yorker Collection, 1993, Lorenz from cartoonbank.com. All Rights Reserved.

The debate over repression and childhood sexual abuse, like many other scientific debates, has stimulated new research and new theories. Richard McNally and Elke Geraerts (2009) contend that victims of most childhood sexual abuse do not repress their abuse; rather, they simply stop devoting thought and emotion to it. McNally and Geraerts believe this letting go of the memory is most likely when

- the experience, when it occurred, was strange, uncomfortable, and confusing, rather than severely traumatic.
- the abuse happened once or only a few times.
- victims have not spent time thinking about the abuse, either because of their own resilience or because no reminders are available.

McNally and Geraerts agree that victims do sometimes accurately and spontaneously recall memories of childhood abuse. But these memories usually occur outside of therapy. Moreover, people who recall abuse spontaneously rarely form false memories when in a lab setting. Conversely, those who form memories of abuse during suggestive therapy tend to have vivid imaginations and score high on false-memory tests in the lab (Clancy et al., 2000; McNally, 2003).

So, does *repression* of threatening memories ever occur? Psychologists continue to have heated debates on this topic, which is the cornerstone of Freud's theory and a recurring theme in much popular psychology. But this much appears certain: The most common response to a traumatic experience (witnessing a loved one's murder, being terrorized by a hijacker or a rapist, losing everything in a natural disaster) is not banishment of the experience into the unconscious. Rather, such experiences are typically etched on the mind as vivid, persistent, haunting memories (Porter & Peace, 2007). As Robert Kraft (2002) said of the experience of those trapped in the Nazi death camps, "Horror sears memory, leaving . . . the consuming memories of atrocity."

RETRIEVAL PRACTICE

- What—given the commonality of source amnesia—might life be like if we remembered all our waking experiences and all our dreams?

ANSWER: Real experiences would be confused with those we dreamed. When meeting someone, we might therefore be unsure whether we were reacting to something they previously did or to something we dreamed they did.

Improving Memory

26-4 How can you use memory research findings to do better in this and other courses?

Biology's findings benefit medicine. Botany's findings benefit agriculture. So, too, can psychology's research on memory benefit education. Here for easy reference is a summary of concrete suggestions that could help you remember information when you need it. The SQ3R—Survey, Question, Read, Retrieve, Review—study technique used in this book incorporates several of these strategies.

Study repeatedly. To master material, use distributed (spaced) practice. To learn a concept, give yourself many separate study sessions. Take advantage of life's little intervals—riding a bus, walking across campus, waiting for class to start. New memories are weak; exercise them and they will strengthen. To memorize specific facts or figures, Thomas Landauer (2001) has advised, "rehearse the name or number you are trying to memorize, wait a few seconds, rehearse again, wait a little longer, rehearse again, then wait longer still and rehearse yet again. The waits should be as long as possible without losing the information." Reading complex material with minimal rehearsal yields little retention. Rehearsal and critical reflection help more. It pays to study actively.

Make the material meaningful. You can build a network of retrieval cues by taking text and class notes in your own words. Apply the concepts to your own life. Form images. Understand and organize information. Relate the material to what you already know or have experienced. As William James (1890) suggested, "Knit each new thing on to some acquisition already there." Restate concepts in your own words. Mindlessly repeating someone else's words won't supply many retrieval cues. On an exam, you may find yourself stuck when a question uses phrasing different from the words you memorized.

Thinking and memory Actively thinking as we read, by rehearsing and relating ideas, and by making the material personally meaningful, yields the best retention.

© Sigrid Olsson/PhotoAlto/Corbis

Activate retrieval cues. Mentally re-create the situation and the mood in which your original learning occurred. Jog your memory by allowing one thought to cue the next.

Use mnemonic devices. Associate items with peg-words. Make up a story that incorporates vivid images of the items. Chunk information into acronyms. Create rhythmic rhymes (*"i before e, except after c"*).

Minimize interference. Study before sleep. Do not schedule back-to-back study times for topics that are likely to interfere with each other, such as Spanish and French.

Sleep more. During sleep, the brain reorganizes and consolidates information for long-term memory. Sleep deprivation disrupts this process.

Test your own knowledge, both to rehearse it and to find out what you don't yet know. Don't be lulled into overconfidence by your ability to recognize information. Test your recall using the Retrieval Practice items found throughout each module, and the numbered Learning Objective Questions in the Review section at the end of each module. Outline sections on a blank page. Define the terms and concepts listed at each module's end before turning back to their definitions. Take practice tests; the websites and study guides that accompany many texts, including this one, are a good source for such tests.

RETRIEVAL PRACTICE

- What are the recommended memory strategies you just read about?

ANSWER: Study repeatedly to boost long-term recall. Schedule spaced (not crammed) study times. Spend more time rehearsing or actively thinking about the material. Make the material personally meaningful, with well-organized and vivid associations. Refresh your memory by returning to contexts and moods to activate retrieval cues. Use mnemonic devices. Minimize interference. Plan for a complete night's sleep. Test yourself repeatedly—retrieval practice is a proven retention strategy.

MODULE REVIEW

Forgetting, Memory Construction, and Improving Memory

Learning Objectives

RETRIEVAL PRACTICE Take a moment to answer each of these Learning Objective Questions (repeated here from within the module). Then turn to Appendix B, Complete Module Reviews, to check your answers. Research suggests that trying to answer these questions on your own will improve your long-term retention (McDaniel et al., 2009).

26-1: Why do we forget?

26-2: How do misinformation, imagination, and source amnesia influence our memory construction? How do we decide whether a memory is real or false?

26-3: How reliable are young children's eyewitness descriptions, and why are reports of repressed and recovered memories so hotly debated?

26-4: How can you use memory research findings to do better in this and other courses?

Terms and Concepts to Remember

RETRIEVAL PRACTICE Test yourself on these terms by trying to write down the definition before flipping back to the referenced page to check your answer.

anterograde amnesia, p. 335
retrograde amnesia, p. 335
proactive interference, p.338
retroactive interference, p. 338
repression, p. 339
misinformation effect, p. 341
source amnesia, p. 343
déjà vu, p. 343

RETRIEVAL PRACTICE Gain an advantage, and benefit from immediate feedback, with the interactive self-testing resources at www.worthpublishers.com/myers.

Thinking, Language, and Intelligence

Throughout history, we humans have both bemoaned our foolishness and celebrated our wisdom. The poet T. S. Eliot was struck by "the hollow men . . . Headpiece filled with straw." But Shakespeare's Hamlet extolled the human species as "noble in reason! . . . infinite in faculties! . . . in apprehension how like a god!" Throughout this text, we likewise marvel at both our abilities and our errors.

We study the human brain—three pounds of wet tissue the size of a small cabbage, yet containing circuitry more complex than the planet's telephone networks. We appreciate the amazing abilities of newborns. We marvel at our sensory system,

MODULES

- **27** Thinking
- **28** Language and Thought
- **29** Introduction to Intelligence
- **30** Assessing Intelligence
- **31** Genetic and Environmental Influences on Intelligence

translating visual stimuli into nerve impulses, distributing them for parallel processing, and reassembling them into colorful perceptions. We ponder our memory's enormous capacity, and the ease with which our two-track mind processes information, with and without our awareness. Little wonder that our species has had the collective genius to invent the camera, the car, and the computer; to unlock the atom and crack the genetic code; to travel out to space and into our brain's depths.

Yet we also see that our species is kin to the other animals, influenced by the same principles that produce learning in rats and pigeons. We note that we not-so-wise humans are easily deceived by perceptual illusions, pseudopsychic claims, and false memories.

In Modules 27 and 28, we encounter further instances of these two images of the human condition—the rational and the irrational. We will consider how we use and misuse the information we receive, perceive, store, and retrieve. We will look at our gift for language and consider how and why it develops. And we will reflect on how deserving we are of our species name, *Homo sapiens*—wise human.

In Modules 29 through 31, we focus on an ongoing debate about intelligence, in which psychologists and others pick sides on two major questions: (1) Does each of us have an inborn general mental capacity (intelligence), and (2) can we quantify this capacity as a meaningful number?

- Concepts
- Problem Solving: Strategies and Obstacles
- Forming Good and Bad Decisions and Judgments
- Do Other Species Share Our Cognitive Skills?

Thinking

Concepts

27-1 What is cognition, and what are the functions of concepts?

Psychologists who study **cognition** focus on the mental activities associated with thinking, knowing, remembering, and communicating information. One of these activities is forming **concepts**—mental groupings of similar objects, events, ideas, and people. The concept *chair* includes many items—a baby's high chair, a reclining chair, a dentist's chair—all of which are for sitting. Concepts simplify our thinking. Imagine life without them. We would need a different name for every person, event, object, and idea. We could not ask a child to "throw the ball" because there would be no concept of *throw* or *ball*. Instead of saying, "They were angry," we would have to describe expressions, intensities, and words. Concepts such as *ball* and *anger* give us much information with little cognitive effort.

We often form our concepts by developing **prototypes**—a mental image or best example of a category (Rosch, 1978). People more quickly agree that "a robin is a bird" than that "a penguin is a bird." For most of us, the robin is the birdier bird; it more closely resembles our bird prototype. And the more closely something matches our prototype of a concept—bird or car—the more readily we recognize it as an example of the concept.

© Oleksiy Maksymenko/agefotostock

Toying with our prototypes It takes a bit longer to conceptualize a Smart Car as an actual car, because it looks more like a toy than our mental prototype for "car."

Once we place an item in a category, our memory of it later shifts toward the category prototype, as it did for Belgian students who viewed ethnically blended faces. For example, when viewing a blended face in which 70 percent of the features were Caucasian and 30 percent were Asian, the students categorized the face as Caucasian (**FIGURE 27.1**). Later, as their memory shifted toward the Caucasian prototype, they were more likely to remember an 80 percent Caucasian face than the 70 percent Caucasian they had actually seen (Corneille et al., 2004). Likewise, if shown a 70 percent Asian face, they later remembered a more prototypically Asian face. So, too, with gender: People who viewed 70 percent male faces categorized them as male (no surprise there) and then later misremembered them as even more prototypically male (Huart et al., 2005).

Move away from our prototypes, and category boundaries may blur. Is a tomato a fruit? Is a 17-year-old female a girl or a woman? Is a whale a fish or a mammal? Because a whale fails to match our "mammal" prototype, we are slower to recognize it as a mammal. Similarly, when symptoms don't fit one of our disease prototypes, we are slow to perceive an illness (Bishop, 1991). People whose heart attack symptoms (shortness of breath, exhaustion, a dull weight in the chest) don't match their heart attack prototype (sharp chest

FIGURE 27.1
Categorizing faces influences recollection Shown a face that was 70 percent Caucasian, people tended to classify the person as Caucasian and to recollect the face as more Caucasian than it was. (From Corneille et al., 2004.)

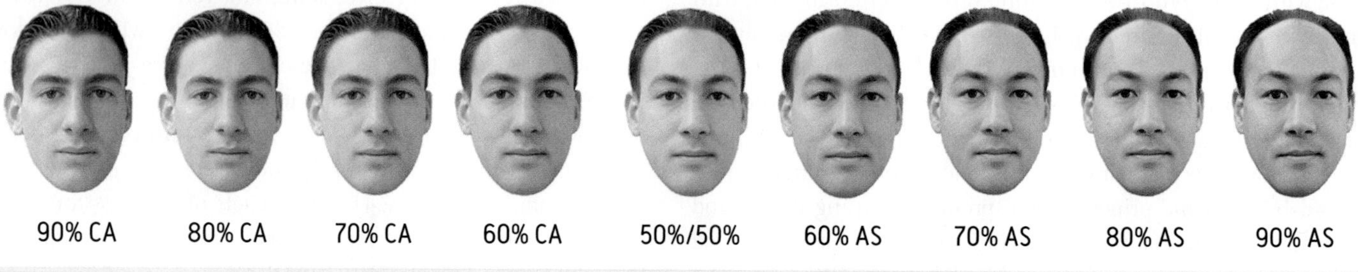

Courtesy of Olivier Corneille

Overconfidence

overconfidence the tendency to be more confident than correct—to overestimate the accuracy of our beliefs and judgments.

belief perseverance clinging to one's initial conceptions after the basis on which they were formed has been discredited.

Sometimes our judgments and decisions go awry simply because we are more confident than correct. Across various tasks, people overestimate their performance (Metcalfe, 1998). If 60 percent of people correctly answer a factual question, such as "Is absinthe a liqueur or a precious stone?," they will typically average 75 percent confidence (Fischhoff et al., 1977). (It's a licorice-flavored liqueur.) This tendency to overestimate the accuracy of our knowledge and judgments is **overconfidence**.

It was an overconfident BP that, before its exploded drilling platform spewed oil into the Gulf of Mexico, downplayed safety concerns, and then downplayed the spill's magnitude (Mohr et al., 2010; Urbina, 2010). It is overconfidence that drives stockbrokers and investment managers to market their ability to outperform stock market averages, despite overwhelming evidence to the contrary (Malkiel, 2004). A purchase of stock X, recommended by a broker who judges this to be the time to buy, is usually balanced by a sale made by someone who judges this to be the time to sell. Despite their confidence, buyer and seller cannot both be right.

Bianca Moscatelli/Worth Publishers

Predict your own behavior When will you finish reading this module?

History is full of leaders who were more confident than correct. And classrooms are full of overconfident students who expect to finish assignments and write papers ahead of schedule (Buehler et al., 1994). In fact, the projects generally take about twice the number of days predicted.

Anticipating how much we will accomplish, we also overestimate our future leisure time (Zauberman & Lynch, 2005). Believing we will have more time next month than we do today, we happily accept invitations and assignments, only to discover we're just as busy when the day rolls around. Failing to appreciate our potential for error and believing we will have more money next year, we take out loans or buy on credit. Despite our painful underestimates, we remain overly confident of our next prediction.

Overconfidence can have adaptive value. People who err on the side of overconfidence live more happily. They make tough decisions more easily, and they seem more credible than others (Baumeister, 1989; Taylor, 1989). Moreover, given prompt and clear feedback, as weather forecasters receive after each day's predictions, people can learn to be more realistic about the accuracy of their judgments (Fischhoff, 1982). The wisdom to know when we know a thing and when we do not is born of experience.

"When you know a thing, to hold that you know it; and when you do not know a thing, to allow that you do not know it; this is knowledge."
Confucius (551–479 B.C.E.), *Analects*

Belief Perseverance

Our overconfidence in our judgments is startling; equally startling is our tendency to cling to our beliefs in the face of contrary evidence. **Belief perseverance** often fuels social conflict, as it did in a classic study of people with opposing views of capital punishment (Lord et al., 1979). Each side studied two supposedly new research findings, one supporting and the other refuting the claim that the death penalty deters crime. Each side was more impressed by the study supporting its own beliefs, and each readily disputed the other study. Thus, showing the pro- and anti-capital-punishment groups the *same* mixed evidence actually *increased* their disagreement.

If you want to rein in the belief perseverance phenomenon, a simple remedy exists: *Consider the opposite*. When the same researchers repeated the capital-punishment study, they asked some participants to be "as *objective* and *unbiased* as possible" (Lord et al., 1984). The plea did nothing to reduce biased evaluations of evidence. They asked another group to consider "whether you would have made the same high or low evaluations had exactly the same study produced results on the *other* side of the issue." Having imagined and pondered *opposite* findings, these people became much less biased in their evaluations of the evidence.

THINKING CRITICALLY ABOUT

The Fear Factor—Why We Fear the Wrong Things

After 9/11, many people feared flying more than driving. In a 2006 Gallup survey, only 40 percent of Americans reported being "not afraid at all" to fly. Yet from 2005 to 2007 Americans were—mile for mile—170 times more likely to die in an automobile or pickup truck crash than on a scheduled flight (National Safety Council, 2010). In 2009 alone, 33,808 Americans were killed in motor vehicle accidents—that's 650 dead people *each week*. Meanwhile, in 2009 (as in 2007 and 2008) *zero* died from scheduled airline accidents.

In a late 2001 essay, I calculated that if—because of 9/11—we flew 20 percent less and instead drove half those unflown miles, about 800 more people would die in the year after 9/11 (Myers, 2001). German psychologist Gerd Gigerenzer (2004, 2006) later checked this estimate against actual accident data. (Why didn't I think of that?) U.S. traffic deaths did indeed increase significantly in the last three months of 2001 (**FIGURE 27.6**). By the end of 2002, Gigerenzer estimated, 1600 Americans had "lost their lives on the road by trying to avoid the risk of flying." Despite our greater fear of flying, flying's greatest danger is, for most people, the drive to the airport.

Why do we fear the wrong things? Why do we judge terrorism to be a greater risk than accidents? Psychologists have identified four influences that feed fear and cause us to ignore higher risks.

1. *We fear what our ancestral history has prepared us to fear.* Human emotions were road tested in the Stone Age. Our old brain prepares us to fear yesterday's risks: snakes, lizards, and spiders (which

AP/Wide World Photos

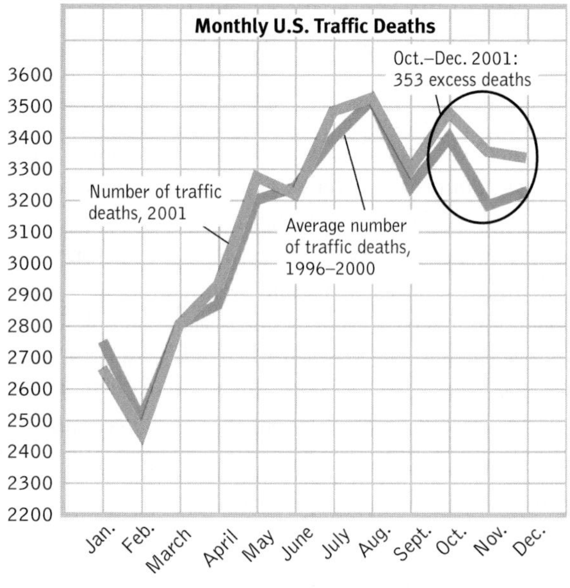

FIGURE 27.6
Scared onto deadly highways Images of 9/11 etched a sharper image in American minds than did the millions of fatality-free flights on U.S. airlines during 2002 and after. Dramatic events are readily available to memory, and they shape our perceptions of risk. In the three months after 9/11, those faulty perceptions led more Americans to travel, and some to die, by car. (Adapted from Gigerenzer, 2004.)

© The New Yorker Collection, 1973, Fradon from cartoonbank.com. All Rights Reserved.

"I'm happy to say that my final judgment of a case is almost always consistent with my prejudgment of the case."

The more we come to appreciate why our beliefs might be true, the more tightly we cling to them. Once we have explained to ourselves why we believe a child is "gifted" or has a "learning disability," or why candidate X or Y will be a better commander-in-chief, or why company Z is a stock worth owning, we tend to ignore evidence undermining our belief. Prejudice persists. Once beliefs form and get justified, it takes more compelling evidence to change them than it did to create them.

The Effects of Framing

Framing, the way we present an issue, sways our decisions and judgments. Imagine two surgeons explaining a surgery risk. One tells patients that 10 percent of people die during this surgery. The other tells patients that 90 percent will survive. The information is the same. The effect is not. In surveys, both patients and physicians said the risk seems greater when they hear that 10 percent will *die* (Marteau, 1989; McNeil et al., 1988; Rothman & Salovey, 1997). Similarly, 9 in 10 college students rated a condom as combined now kill a tiny fraction of the number killed by modern-day threats, such as cars and cigarettes). Yesterday's risks also prepare us to fear confinement and heights, and therefore flying.

2. *We fear what we cannot control.* Driving we control; flying we do not.
3. *We fear what is immediate.* The dangers of flying are mostly telescoped into the moments of takeoff and landing. The dangers of driving are diffused across many moments to come, each trivially dangerous.
4. *Thanks to the availability heuristic, we fear what is most readily available in memory.* Powerful, vivid images, like that of United Flight 175 slicing into the World Trade Center, feed our judgments of risk. Thousands of safe car trips have extinguished our anxieties about driving. Similarly, we remember (and fear) widespread disasters (hurricanes, tornadoes, earthquakes) that kill people dramatically, in bunches. But we fear too little the less dramatic threats that claim lives quietly, one by one, continuing into the distant future. Bill Gates has noted that each year a half-million children worldwide die from rotavirus. This is the equivalent of four 747s full of children every day, and we hear nothing of it (Glass, 2004).

The news, and our own memorable experiences, can make us disproportionately fearful of infinitesimal risks. As one risk analyst explained, "If it's in the news, don't worry about it. The very definition of *news* is 'something that hardly ever happens'" (Schneier, 2007). Despite people's fear of dying in a terrorist attack on an airplane, the last decade produced one terrorist attempt for every 10.4 million flights—less than one-twentieth the chance of any one of us being struck by lightning (Silver, 2009).

The point to remember: It is perfectly normal to fear purposeful violence from those who hate us. When terrorists strike again, we will all recoil in horror. But smart thinkers will check their fears against the facts and resist those who aim to create a culture of fear. By so doing, we take away the terrorists' most omnipresent weapon: exaggerated fear.

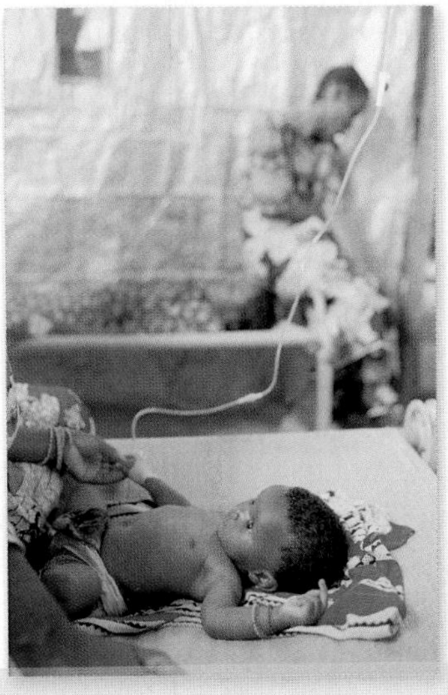

Ian Berry/Magnum Photos

Dramatic deaths in bunches breed concern and fear The memorable 2010 Haitian earthquake that killed some 250,000 people stirred an outpouring of justified concern. Meanwhile, according to the World Health Organization, a silent earthquake of poverty-related malaria was killing about that many people, mostly in Africa, every four months.

"Fearful people are more dependent, more easily manipulated and controlled, more susceptible to deceptively simple, strong, tough measures and hard-line postures."

Media researcher George Gerbner to U.S. Congressional Subcommittee on Communications, 1981

effective if told it had a supposed "95 percent success rate" in stopping the HIV virus. Only 4 in 10 judged it effective when told it had a "5 percent failure rate" (Linville et al., 1992). To scare people, frame risks as numbers, not percentages. People told that a chemical exposure is projected to kill 10 of every 10 million people (imagine 10 dead people!) feel more frightened than if told the fatality risk is an infinitesimal .000001 (Kraus et al., 1992).

Framing can be a powerful persuasion tool. Carefully posed options can nudge people toward decisions that could benefit them or society as a whole (Thaler & Sunstein, 2008).

- *Why choosing to be an organ donor depends on where you live.* In many European countries as well as the United States, people can decide whether they want to be organ donors when renewing their driver's license. In some countries, the default option is *Yes*, but people can opt out. Nearly 100 percent of the people in opt-out countries agree to be donors. In the United States, Britain, and Germany, the default option is *No*, but people can "opt in." There, only about 25 percent agree to be donors (Johnson & Goldstein, 2003).

framing the way an issue is posed; how an issue is framed can significantly affect decisions and judgments.

- *How to help employees decide to save for their retirement.* A 2006 U.S. pension law recognized the framing effect. Before that law, employees who wanted to contribute to a 401(k) retirement plan typically had to choose a lower take-home pay, which few people will do. Companies can now automatically enroll their employees in the plan but allow them to opt out (which would raise the employees' take-home pay). In both plans, the decision to contribute is the employee's. But under the new "opt-out" arrangement, enrollments in one analysis of 3.4 million workers soared from 59 to 86 percent (Rosenberg, 2010).
- *How to help save the planet.* Some psychologists are asking: With the climate warming, but concerns lessening among the British and Americans, are there better ways to frame these issues (Krosnick, 2010; Rosenthal, 2010)? For example, although a "carbon tax" may be the most effective way to curb greenhouse gases, many people oppose new taxes. But they are more supportive of funding energy development or carbon capture with a "carbon offset" fee (Hardisty et al., 2010).

The point to remember: Those who understand the power of framing can use it to influence our decisions.

The Perils and Powers of Intuition

27-4 How do smart thinkers use intuition?

We have seen how our irrational thinking can plague our efforts to see problems clearly, make wise decisions, form valid judgments, and reason logically. Moreover, these perils of intuition feed gut fears and prejudices. And they persist even when people are offered extra pay for thinking smart, even when they are asked to justify their answers, and even when they are expert physicians or clinicians (Shafir & LeBoeuf, 2002). So, are our heads indeed filled with straw?

Good news: Cognitive scientists are also revealing intuition's powers. Here is a summary of some of the high points:

- *Intuition is huge.* Today's cognitive science offers many examples of unconscious influences on our judgments (clear support for the principle of *dual processing*) (Custers & Aarts, 2010). Consider: Most people guess that the more complex the choice, the smarter it is to make decisions rationally rather than intuitively (Inbar et al., 2010). Actually, Dutch psychologists have shown that in making complex decisions, we benefit by letting our brain work on a problem without thinking about it (Strick et al., 2010). In one series of experiments, they showed three groups of people complex information (about apartments or roommates or art posters or soccer matches). They invited one group to state their preference immediately after reading information about each of four options. A second group, given several minutes to analyze the information, made slightly smarter decisions. But wisest of all, in study after study, was the third group, whose attention was distracted for a time, enabling their minds to process the complex information unconsciously. Critics of this research remind us that deliberate, conscious thought also is part of smart thinking (Gonzáles-Vallejo et al., 2008; Lassiter et al., 2009; Newell et al., 2008; Payne et al., 2008). Nevertheless, letting a problem "incubate" while we attend to other things can pay dividends (Sio & Ormerod, 2009). Facing a difficult decision involving lots of facts, we're wise to gather all the information we can, and then say, "Give me some time *not* to think about this." By taking time to sleep on it, we let our unconscious mental machinery work on, and await, the intuitive result of our unconscious processing.
- *Intuition is usually adaptive.* Our instant, intuitive reactions enable us to react quickly. Our fast and frugal heuristics, for example, enable us to intuitively assume that fuzzy looking objects are far away—which they usually are, except on foggy mornings. Our learned associations surface as gut feelings, the intuitions of our two-track mind.

If a stranger looks like someone who previously harmed or threatened us, we may—without consciously recalling the earlier experience—react warily. People's automatic, unconscious associations with a political position can even predict their future decisions *before* they consciously make up their minds (Galdi et al., 2008).

- *Intuition is recognition born of experience.* It is implicit knowledge—what we've learned but can't fully explain, such as how to ride a bike. We see this tacit expertise in chess masters playing "blitz chess," where every move is made after barely more than a glance. They can look at a board and intuitively know the right move (Burns, 2004). We see it in experienced nurses, firefighters, art critics, car mechanics, and hockey players. And in you, too, for anything in which you have developed a special skill. In each case, what feels like instant intuition is an acquired ability to size up a situation in an eyeblink. As Nobel laureate psychologist Herbert Simon (2001) observed, intuition is analysis "frozen into habit."

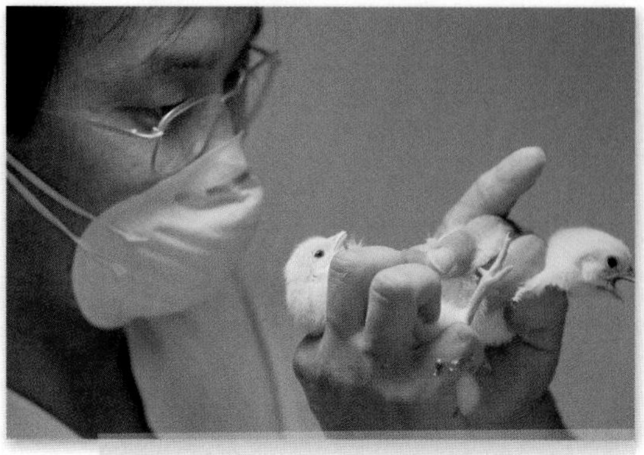

Jean-Philippe Ksiazek/AFP

Chick sexing When acquired expertise becomes an automatic habit, as it is for experienced chicken sexers, it feels like intuition. At a glance, they just know, yet cannot easily tell you how they know.

The bottom line: Intuition can be perilous, especially when we overfeel and underthink, as we do when judging risks. Today's psychological science reminds us to check our intuitions against reality, but also enhances our appreciation for intuition. Our two-track mind makes sweet harmony as smart, critical thinking listens to the creative whispers of our vast unseen mind, and then evaluates evidence, tests conclusions, and plans for the future.

RETRIEVAL PRACTICE

- Match the process or strategy listed below (1–9) with the descriptions.

1. Algorithm	4. Heuristics	7. Overconfidence
2. Intuition	5. Fixation	8. Framing
3. Insight	6. Confirmation bias	9. Belief perseverance

a. Inability to view problems from a new angle; focuses thinking but hinders creative problem solving.

b. Methodological rule or procedure that guarantees solution but requires time and effort.

c. Fast, automatic, unthinking feelings and thoughts based on our experience; huge and adaptive but can lead us to overfeel and underthink.

d. Simple thinking shortcuts that allow us to act quickly and efficiently, but put us at risk for errors.

e. Sudden Aha! reaction that provides instant realization of the solution.

f. Tendency to search for support for our own views and ignore contradictory evidence.

g. Ignoring evidence that proves our beliefs are wrong; closes our mind to new ideas.

h. Overestimating the accuracy of our beliefs and judgments; allows us to be happy and to make decisions easily, but puts us at risk for errors.

i. Wording a question or statement so that it evokes a desired response; can influence others' decisions and produce a misleading result.

ANSWERS: 1. b, 2. c, 3. e, 4. d, 5. a, 6. f, 7. h, 8. i, 9. g

Do Other Species Share Our Cognitive Skills?

27-5 What do we know about animal thinking?

Animals are smarter than we often realize. As the pioneering psychologist Margaret Floy Washburn explained in her 1908 book, *The Animal Mind,* animal consciousness and intelligence can be inferred from their behavior.

Life on white/Alamy

Using Concepts and Numbers

Even pigeons—mere birdbrains—can sort objects (pictures of cars, cats, chairs, flowers) into categories, or concepts. Shown a picture of a never-before-seen chair, the pigeon will reliably peck a key that represents "chairs" (Wasserman, 1995). The great apes also form concepts, such as "cat" and "dog." After monkeys learn these concepts, certain frontal lobe neurons in their brains fire in response to new "catlike" images, others to new "doglike" images (Freedman et al., 2001).

Until his death in 2007, Alex, an African Grey parrot, categorized and named objects (Pepperberg, 2006, 2009). Among his jaw-dropping numerical skills was the ability to comprehend numbers up to 6. He could speak the number of objects. He could add two small clusters of objects and announce the sum. He could indicate which of two numbers was greater. And he gave correct answers when shown various groups of objects. Asked, for example, "What color four?" (meaning "What's the color of the objects of which there are four?"), he could speak the answer.

Displaying Insight

Psychologist Wolfgang Köhler (1925) showed that we are not the only creatures to display insight. He placed a piece of fruit and a long stick outside the cage of a chimpanzee named Sultan, beyond his reach. Inside the cage, he placed a short stick, which Sultan grabbed, using it to try to reach the fruit. After several failed attempts, he dropped the stick and seemed to survey the situation. Then suddenly, as if thinking "Aha!" Sultan jumped up and seized the short stick again. This time, he used it to pull in the longer stick—which he then used to reach the fruit. What is more, apes will even exhibit foresight, by storing a tool they can use to retrieve food the next day (Mulcahy & Call, 2006).

Using Tools and Transmitting Culture

Like humans, many other species invent behaviors and transmit cultural patterns to their peers and offspring (Boesch-Achermann & Boesch, 1993). Forest-dwelling chimpanzees select different tools for different purposes—a heavy stick for making holes, a light, flexible stick for fishing for termites (Sanz et al., 2004). They break off the reed or stick, strip off any leaves, carry it to a termite mound, twist it just so, and carefully remove it. Termites for lunch! (This is very reinforcing for a chimpanzee.) One anthropologist, trying to mimic the animal's deft fishing moves, failed miserably.

Researchers have found at least 39 local customs related to chimpanzee tool use, grooming, and courtship (Whiten & Boesch, 2001). One group may slurp termites directly from a stick, another group may pluck them off individually. One group may break nuts with a stone hammer, another with a wooden hammer. These group differences, along with differing styles of communication and hunting, are not genetic; they are the chimpanzee version of cultural diversity. Several experiments have brought chimpanzee cultural transmission into the laboratory (Horner et al., 2006). If Chimpanzee A obtains food either by sliding or by lifting a door, Chimpanzee B will then typically do the same to get food. And so will Chimpanzee C after observing Chimpanzee B. Across a chain of six animals, chimpanzees see, and chimpanzees do.

Other animals have also shown surprising cognitive talents (**FIGURE 27.7**).

Chris Bird & Nathan Emery (a)
Michael Nichols/National Geographic Image (b)
Mathias Osvath (c)
Copyright Amanda K. Coakes (d)

FIGURE 27.7
Tool-using animals (a) New Caledonian crows studied by Christopher Bird and Nathan Emery (2009) quickly learned to raise the water level in a tube and nab a floating worm by dropping stones into the water. Other crows have used twigs to probe for insects, and bent strips of metal to reach food. (b) Capuchin monkeys have learned not only to use heavy rocks to crack open palm nuts, but also to test stone hammers and select a sturdier, less crumbly one (Visalberghi et al., 2009). (c) One male chimpanzee in Sweden's Furuvik Zoo was observed every morning collecting stones into a neat little pile, which later in the day he used as ammunition to pelt visitors (Osvath, 2009). (d) Dolphins form coalitions, cooperatively hunt, and learn tool use from one another (Bearzi & Stanford, 2010). This bottlenose dolphin in Shark Bay, Western Australia, belongs to a small group that uses marine sponges as protective nose guards when probing the sea floor for fish (Krützen et al., 2005).

Other Cognitive Skills

A baboon knows everyone's voice within its 80-member troop (Jolly, 2007). Sheep can recognize and remember individual faces (Morell, 2008). Chimpanzees and two species of monkeys can even read your intent. They would show more interest in a food container you have intentionally grasped rather than in one you flopped your hand on, as if by accident (Wood et al., 2007). Great apes and dolphins have demonstrated self-awareness (by recognizing themselves in a mirror). So have elephants, which in tests also display their abilities to learn, remember, discriminate smells, empathize, cooperate, teach, and spontaneously use tools (Byrne et al., 2009). As social creatures, chimpanzees have shown altruism, cooperation, and group aggression. Like humans, they will kill their neighbor to gain land, and they grieve over dead relatives (Anderson et al., 2010; Biro et al., 2010; Mitani et al., 2010).

Johan Swanepoel/Alamy

* * *

Returning to our debate about how deserving we humans are of our name *Homo sapiens*, let's pause to issue an interim report card. On decision making and risk assessment, our error-prone species might rate a C+. On problem solving, where humans are inventive yet vulnerable to fixation, we would probably receive a better mark, perhaps a B. On cognitive efficiency, our fallible but quick heuristics earn us an A. And when it comes to learning and adapting to our culture, the awestruck experts would surely award the human species an A+.

What time is it now? When I asked you (in the section on overconfidence) to estimate how quickly you would finish this module, did you underestimate or overestimate?

MODULE REVIEW

Thinking

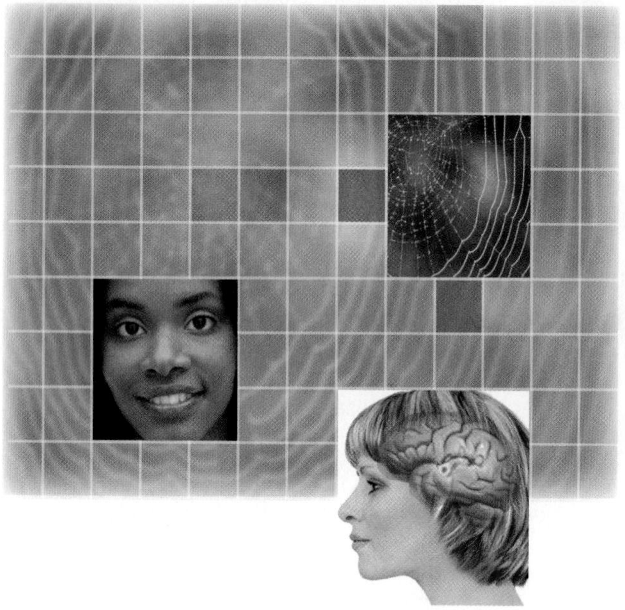

Learning Objectives

RETRIEVAL PRACTICE Take a moment to answer each of these Learning Objective Questions (repeated here from within the module). Then turn to Appendix B, Complete Module Reviews, to check your answers. Research suggests that trying to answer these questions on your own will improve your long-term retention (McDaniel et al., 2009).

27-1: What is cognition, and what are the functions of concepts?

27-2: What cognitive strategies assist our problem solving, and what obstacles hinder it?

27-3: What is intuition, and how can the availability heuristic, overconfidence, belief perseverance, and framing influence our decisions and judgments?

27-4: How do smart thinkers use intuition?

27-5: What do we know about animal thinking?

Terms and Concepts to Remember

RETRIEVAL PRACTICE Test yourself on these terms by trying to write down the definition before flipping back to the referenced page to check your answer.

cognition, p. 352
concept, p. 352
prototype, p. 352
algorithm, p. 353
heuristic, p. 353
insight, p. 353
confirmation bias, p. 354
mental set, p. 354
intuition, p. 355
availability heuristic, p. 355
overconfidence, p. 357
belief perseverance, p. 357
framing, p. 358

RETRIEVAL PRACTICE Gain an advantage, and benefit from immediate feedback, with the interactive self-testing resources at www.worthpublishers.com/myers.

MODULE 28

Language and Thought

- Language Structure
- Language Development
- The Brain and Language
- Do Other Species Have Language?
- Thinking and Language

Imagine an alien species that could pass thoughts from one head to another merely by pulsating air molecules in the space between them. Perhaps these weird creatures could inhabit a future Spielberg movie?

Actually, we are those creatures. When we speak, our brain and voice apparatus conjure up air pressure waves that we send banging against another's eardrum—enabling us to transfer thoughts from our brain into theirs. As cognitive scientist Steven Pinker (1998) has noted, we sometimes sit for hours "listening to other people make noise as they exhale, because those hisses and squeaks contain *information*." And thanks to all those funny sounds created in our heads from the air-pressure waves we send out, we get people's attention, we get them to do things, and we maintain relationships (Guerin, 2003). Depending on how you vibrate the air after opening your mouth, you may get slapped or kissed.

But **language** is more than vibrating air. As I create this paragraph, my fingers on a keyboard generate electronic binary numbers that are translated into squiggles of dried carbon pressed onto the page in front of you. When transmitted by reflected light rays into your retina, the printed squiggles trigger formless nerve impulses that project to several areas of your brain, which integrate the information, compare it to stored information, and decode meaning. Thanks to language, information is moving from my mind to yours. Monkeys mostly know what they see. Thanks to language (spoken, written, or signed) we comprehend much that we've never seen and that our distant ancestors never knew. Today, notes Daniel Gilbert (2006), "The average newspaper boy in Pittsburgh knows more about the universe than did Galileo, Aristotle, Leonardo, or any of those other guys who were so smart they only needed one name."

To Pinker (1990), language is "the jewel in the crown of cognition." If you were able to retain one cognitive ability, make it language, suggests researcher Lera Boroditsky (2009). Without sight or hearing, you could still have friends, family, and a job. But without language, could you have these things? "Language is so fundamental to our experience, so deeply a part of being human, that it's hard to imagine life without it."

language our spoken, written, or signed words and the ways we combine them to communicate meaning.

AP Photo/M. Spencer Green

Language transmits knowledge Whether spoken, written, or signed, language—the original wireless communication—enables mind-to-mind information transfer, and with it the transmission of civilization's accumulated knowledge across generations.

phoneme in a language, the smallest distinctive sound unit.

morpheme in a language, the smallest unit that carries meaning; may be a word or a part of a word (such as a prefix).

grammar in a language, a system of rules that enables us to communicate with and understand others. In a given language, *semantics* is the set of rules for deriving meaning from sounds, and *syntax* is the set of rules for combining words into grammatically sensible sentences.

Language Structure

28-1 What are the structural components of a language?

Consider how we might go about inventing a language. For a spoken language, we would need three building blocks:

- **Phonemes** are the smallest distinctive sound units in a language. To say *bat,* English speakers utter the phonemes *b, a,* and *t.* (Phonemes aren't the same as letters. *Chat* also has three phonemes—*ch, a,* and *t.*) Linguists surveying nearly 500 languages have identified 869 different phonemes in human speech, but no language uses all of them (Holt, 2002; Maddieson, 1984). English uses about 40; other languages use anywhere from half to more than twice that many. As a general rule, consonant phonemes carry more information than do vowel phonemes. *The treth ef thes stetement shed be evedent frem thes bref demenstretien.*
- **Morphemes** are the smallest units that carry meaning in a given language. In English, a few morphemes are also phonemes—the personal pronoun *I* and the article *a,* for instance. But most morphemes combine two or more phonemes. Some, like *bat,* are words. Others—like the prefix *pre-* in *preview* or the suffix *-ed* in *adapted*—are parts of words.
- **Grammar** is the system of rules that enables us to communicate with one another. Grammatical rules guide us in deriving meaning from sounds *(semantics)* and in ordering words into sentences *(syntax).*

Language becomes increasingly complex as we move from one level to the next. In English, for example, 40 or so phonemes can be combined to form more than 100,000 morphemes, which alone or in combination produce the 616,500 word forms in the *Oxford English Dictionary.* Using those words, we can then create an infinite number of sentences, most of which (like this one) are original. Like life constructed from the genetic code's simple alphabet, language is complexity built of simplicity. I know that you can know why I worry that you think this sentence is starting to get too complex, but that complexity—and our capacity to communicate and comprehend it—is what distinguishes human language capacity (Hauser et al., 2002; Premack, 2007).

From *The Wall Street Journal*—permission Cartoon Features Syndicate.

"Let me get this straight now. Is what you want to build a jean factory or a gene factory?"

RETRIEVAL PRACTICE

- How many morphemes are in the word cats? How many phonemes?

ANSWERS: Two morphemes—cat and s, and four phonemes—c, a, t, and s

Language Development

Make a quick guess: How many words did you learn during the years between your first birthday and your high school graduation? Although you use only 150 words for about half of what you say, you probably learned about 60,000 words in your native language during those years (Bloom, 2000; McMurray, 2007). That averages (after age 2) to nearly 3500 words each year, or nearly 10 each day! How you did it—how those 3500 words could so far outnumber the roughly 200 words your schoolteachers consciously taught you each year—is one of the great human wonders.

Could you even state all your language's rules of syntax (the correct way to string words together to form sentences)? Most of us cannot. Yet, before you were able to add

you, too, will notice your attention being drawn to your other senses. In one experiment, people who had spent 90 minutes sitting quietly blindfolded became more accurate in their location of sounds (Lewald, 2007). When kissing, lovers minimize distraction and increase sensitivity by closing their eyes.

People who lose one channel of sensation do seem to compensate with a slight enhancement of their other sensory abilities (Backman & Dixon, 1992; Levy & Langer, 1992). Blind musicians are more likely than sighted ones to develop perfect pitch (Hamilton, 2000). Blind people are also more accurate than sighted people at locating a sound source with one ear plugged (Gougoux et al., 2005; Lessard et al., 1998). And when reading Braille—requiring sensitive touch perception—they make use of the spare processing power of their visual cortex (Amedi et al., 2003).

In deaf cats, brain areas normally used for hearing donate themselves to the visual system (Lomber et al., 2010). So, too, in people who have been deaf from birth: They exhibit enhanced attention to their peripheral vision (Bavelier et al., 2006). Their auditory cortex, starved for sensory input, remains largely intact but becomes responsive to touch and to visual input (Emmorey et al., 2003; Finney et al., 2001; Penhune et al., 2003). (For more on living without hearing, see Close-Up: Living in a Silent World.)

CLOSE-UP

Living in a Silent World

The world's 500 million people who live with hearing loss are a diverse group (Phonak, 2007). Some are profoundly deaf; others (more men than women) have hearing loss (Agrawal et al., 2008). Some were deaf prelingually; others have known the hearing world. Some sign and identify with the language-based Deaf culture. Others, especially those who lost their hearing after speaking a language, are "oral" and converse with the hearing world by reading lips or reading written notes. Still others move between the two cultures.

The challenges of life without hearing may be greatest for children. Unable to communicate in customary ways, signing playmates may struggle to coordinate their play with speaking playmates. School achievement may also suffer, because academic subjects are rooted in *spoken* languages. Adolescents may feel socially excluded, with a resulting low self-confidence.

Children who grow up around other deaf people more often identify with Deaf culture and feel positive self-esteem. If raised in a signing household, whether by deaf or hearing parents, they also express higher self-esteem and feel more accepted (Bat-Chava, 1993, 1994).

Adults whose hearing becomes impaired later in life also face challenges. When older people with hearing loss must expend effort to hear words, they have less remaining cognitive capacity available to remember and comprehend them (Wingfield et al., 2005). In several studies, people with hearing loss, especially those not wearing hearing aids, have reported feeling sadder, being less socially engaged, and more often experiencing others' irritation (Chisolm et al., 2007; Fellinger et al., 2007; Kashubeck-West & Meyer, 2008; National Council on Aging, 1999). They also may experience a sort of shyness: "It's almost universal among the deaf to want to cause hearing people as little fuss as possible," observed Henry Kisor (1990, p. 244), a Chicago newspaper editor and columnist who lost his hearing at age 3. "We can be self-effacing and diffident to the point of invisibility. Sometimes this tendency can be crippling. I must fight it all the time." Helen Keller, both blind and deaf, noted that "Blindness cuts people off from things. Deafness cuts people off from people."

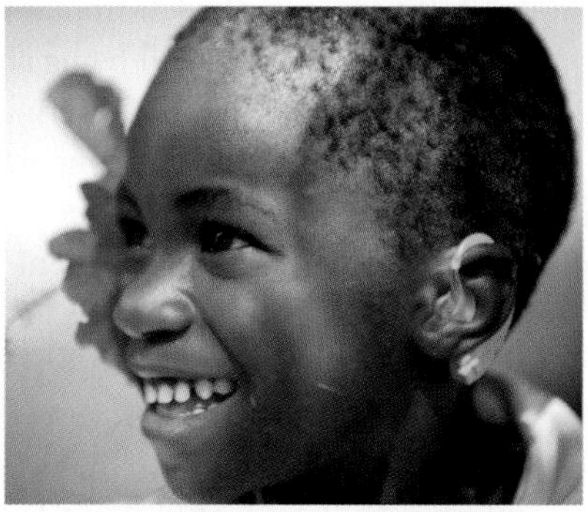
© Andy Richter/Aurora Photos/Corbis

Hearing improved

I understand. My mother, with whom we communicated by writing notes on an erasable "magic pad," spent her last dozen years in an utterly silent world, largely withdrawn from the stress and strain of trying to interact with people outside a small circle of family and old friends. With my own hearing declining on a trajectory toward hers, I find myself sitting front and center at plays and meetings, seeking quiet corners in restaurants, and asking my wife to make necessary calls to friends whose accents differ from ours. I do benefit from cool technology (see www.hearingloop.org) that, at the press of a button, can transform my hearing aids into in-the-ear loudspeakers for the broadcast of phone, TV, and public address system sound. Yet I still experience frustration when, with or without hearing aids, I can't hear the joke everyone else is guffawing over; when, after repeated tries, I just can't catch that exasperated person's question and can't fake my way around it; when family members give up and say, "Oh, never mind" after trying three times to tell me something unimportant.

As she aged, my mother came to feel that seeking social interaction was simply not worth the effort. I share newspaper columnist Kisor's belief that communication is worth the effort (p. 246): "So, . . . I will grit my teeth and plunge ahead." To reach out, to connect, to communicate with others, even across a chasm of silence, is to affirm our humanity as social creatures.

RETRIEVAL PRACTICE

- What was the premise of researcher Noam Chomsky's work in language development?

ANSWER: He believed that we are born with a built-in readiness to learn the grammar rules of language.

- Why is it so difficult to learn a new language in adulthood?

ANSWER: Our brain's *critical period* for language learning is in childhood, when we can absorb language structure almost effortlessly. As we move past that stage in our brain's development, our ability to learn a new language diminishes dramatically.

The Brain and Language

28-4 What brain areas are involved in language processing and speech?

We think of speaking and reading, or writing and reading, or singing and speaking as merely different examples of the same general ability—language. But consider this curious finding: **Aphasia,** an impairment of language, can result from damage to any of several cortical areas. Even more curious, some people with aphasia can speak fluently but cannot read (despite good vision), while others can comprehend what they read but cannot speak. Still others can write but not read, read but not write, read numbers but not letters, or sing but not speak. These cases suggest that language is complex, and that different brain areas must serve different language functions.

Indeed, in 1865, French physician Paul Broca reported that after damage to an area of the left frontal lobe (later called **Broca's area**) a person would struggle to *speak* words while still being able to sing familiar songs and comprehend speech.

In 1874, German investigator Carl Wernicke discovered that after damage to an area of the left temporal lobe (**Wernicke's area**) people could speak only meaningless words. Asked to describe a picture that showed two boys stealing cookies behind a woman's back, one patient responded: "Mother is away her working her work to get her better, but when she's looking the two boys looking the other part. She's working another time" (Geschwind, 1979). Damage to Wernicke's area also disrupts understanding.

Today's neuroscience has confirmed brain activity in Broca's and Wernicke's areas during language processing (**FIGURE 28.2**). But neuroscience is refining our understanding of how our brain processes language. We now know that Broca's area processes language through a series of neural computations (Sahin et al., 2009). Language functions are distributed across other brain areas as well. Functional MRI scans show that different neural networks are activated by nouns and verbs, or objects and actions; by different vowels; and by reading stories of visual versus motor experiences (Shapiro et al., 2006;

aphasia impairment of language, usually caused by left-hemisphere damage either to Broca's area (impairing speaking) or to Wernicke's area (impairing understanding).

Broca's area controls language expression—an area of the frontal lobe, usually in the left hemisphere, that directs the muscle movements involved in speech.

Wernicke's area controls language reception—a brain area involved in language comprehension and expression; usually in the left temporal lobe.

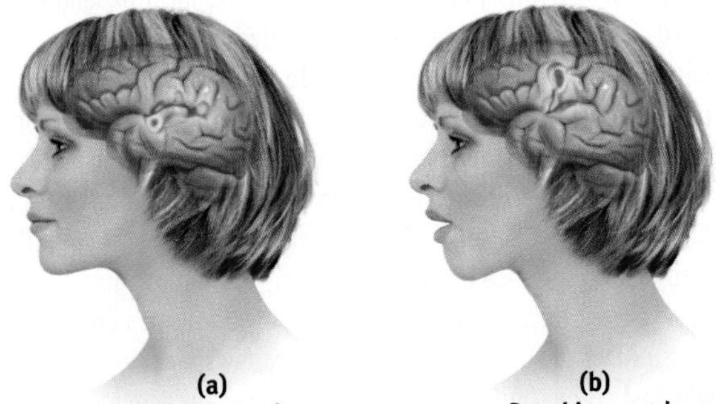

FIGURE 28.2 Brain activity when hearing and speaking words

(a) Hearing words (auditory cortex and Wernicke's area)

(b) Speaking words (Broca's area and the motor cortex)

Speer et al., 2009). Different neural networks also enable one's native language and a second language learned later in life (Perani & Abutalebi, 2005).

And here's another funny fMRI finding. Jokes that play on meaning *("Why don't sharks bite lawyers? . . . Professional courtesy")* are processed in a different brain area than jokes that play on words (*"What kind of lights did Noah use on the ark? . . . Flood lights"*) (Goel & Dolan, 2001).

The big point to remember is this: In processing language, as in other forms of information processing, *the brain operates by dividing its mental functions—speaking, perceiving, thinking, remembering—into subfunctions.* Your conscious experience of reading this page *seems* indivisible, but your brain is computing each word's form, sound, and meaning using different neural networks (Posner & Carr, 1992). We can also see this division of processing in vision, for which the brain engages specialized subtasks, such as discerning color, depth, movement, and form. And in vision as in language, a localized trauma that destroys one of these neural work teams may cause people to lose just one aspect of processing. In visual processing, a stroke may destroy the ability to perceive movement but not color. In language processing, a stroke may impair the ability to speak distinctly without harming the ability to read.

Think about it: What you experience as a continuous, indivisible stream of experience is actually but the visible tip of a subdivided information-processing iceberg.

"It is the way systems interact and have a dynamic interdependence that is—unless one has lost all sense of wonder—quite awe-inspiring."

Simon Conway Morris, "The Boyle Lecture," 2005

RETRIEVAL PRACTICE

- __________ __________ is the part of the brain that, if damaged, might impair your ability to *speak* words. If you damage __________ __________, you might impair your ability to understand language.

ANSWERS: Broca's area; Wernicke's area

Do Other Species Have Language?

28-5 Do other animals share our capacity for language?

Humans have long and proudly proclaimed that language sets us above all other animals. "When we study human language," asserted linguist Noam Chomsky (1972), "we are approaching what some might call the 'human essence,' the qualities of mind that are, so far as we know, unique [to humans]."

If in our use of language we humans are, as the psalmist long ago rhapsodized, "little lower than God," where, then, do other animals fit in the scheme of things? Are they "little lower than humans?" Let's see what research on animal language can tell us.

Without doubt, animals show impressive comprehension and communication. Consider vervet monkeys. They sound different alarm cries for different predators: a barking call for a leopard, a cough for an eagle, and a chuttering for a snake. Hearing the leopard alarm, other vervets climb the nearest tree. Hearing the eagle alarm, they rush into the bushes. Hearing the snake chutter, they stand up and scan the ground (Byrne, 1991). To indicate such things as a type of threat—an eagle, leopard, falling tree, or neighboring group—monkeys will combine six different calls into a 25-call sequence (Balter, 2010). But is this language, in the sense that humans use language? This question has launched thousands of studies, most of them with chimpanzees.

In the late 1960s, psychologists Allen Gardner and Beatrix Gardner (1969) aroused enormous scientific and public interest when they built on chimpanzees' natural tendencies for gestured communication and taught sign language to a chimpanzee named Washoe (c. 1965–2007). After four years, Washoe could use 132 signs; by her life's end, she was using 245 signs (Metzler et al., 2010; Sanz et al., 1998). After moving to a Central Washington University primate center, Washoe and other chimpanzees showed continued vocabulary growth (Metzler et al., 2010).

During the 1970s, as more and more reports came in, it seemed apes might indeed be "little lower than human" (**FIGURE 28.3** on the next page). One *New York Times* reporter, having learned sign language from his deaf parents, visited Washoe and exclaimed, "Suddenly I realized I was conversing with a member of another species in my native tongue." Other chimpanzees were stringing signs together to form sentences, as Washoe

Jim Cummins/Getty Images

FIGURE 28.3
Talking hands Chimpanzees' use of sign language builds upon their natural gestured words (such as a hand extended for "I want some"). Among wild chimpanzees, researchers have identified 66 distinct gestures (Hobaiter & Byrne, 2011). Human language appears to have evolved from such gestured communications (Corballis, 2002, 2003; Pollick & de Waal, 2007). Even today, gestures are naturally associated with spontaneous speech, especially speech that has spatial content. Both gesture and speech communicate, and when they convey the same rather than different information (as they do in baseball's sign language), we humans understand faster and more accurately (Hostetter, 2011; Kelly et al., 2010). Outfielder William Hoy, the first deaf player to join the major leagues (1892), invented hand signals for "Strike!" "Safe!" (shown here) and "Yerr Out!" (Pollard, 1992). Referees in all sports now use invented signs, and fans are fluent in sports sign language.

did, signing, "You me go out, please." Some word combinations seemed very creative—saying *water bird* for "swan" or *elephant baby* for a long-nosed Pinocchio doll, or *apple-which-is-orange* for "orange" (Patterson, 1978; Rumbaugh, 1977).

By the late 1970s, some psychologists were growing skeptical. Were the chimps language champs or were the researchers chumps? Consider, said the skeptics:

- Ape vocabularies and sentences are simple, rather like those of a 2-year-old child. And unlike speaking or signing children, who easily soak up dozens of new words a week (and 60,000 by adulthood), apes gain their limited vocabularies only with great difficulty (Wynne, 2004, 2008). Saying that apes can learn language because they can sign words is like saying humans can fly because they can jump.
- Chimpanzees can make signs or push buttons in sequence to get a reward. But pigeons, too, can peck a sequence of keys to get grain (Straub et al., 1979). The apes' signing might be nothing more than aping their trainers' signs and learning that certain arm movements produce rewards (Terrace, 1979).
- Studies of *perceptual set* show that when information is unclear, we tend to see what we want or expect to see. Interpreting chimpanzee signs as language may be little more than the trainers' wishful thinking (Terrace, 1979). When Washoe signed *water bird*, she may have been separately naming *water* and *bird*.
- "Give orange me give eat orange me eat orange . . ." is a far cry from the exquisite syntax of a 3-year-old (Anderson, 2004; Pinker, 1995). To the child, "You tickle" and "Tickle you" communicate different ideas. A chimpanzee, lacking human syntax, might use the same sequence of signs for both phrases.

Controversy can stimulate progress, and in this case, it triggered more evidence of chimpanzees' abilities to think and communicate. One surprising finding was that Washoe trained her adopted son Loulis to use the signs she had learned. It started like this. After her second infant died, Washoe became withdrawn when told, "Baby dead, baby gone, baby finished." Two weeks later, researcher caretaker Roger Fouts (1992, 1997) signed better news: "I have baby for you." Washoe reacted with instant excitement. Hair on end, she swaggered and panted while signing over and again, "Baby, my baby." It took several hours for the foster mom and infant to warm to each other, but then Washoe broke the ice by signing, "Come baby" and cuddling Loulis. In the months that followed, Loulis, without human assistance, picked up 68 signs, simply by observing Washoe and three other language-trained chimps signing together.

Copyright Baus/Krzeslowski

Comprehending canine Border collie Rico has a 200 (human) word vocabulary. If asked to retrieve a toy with a name he has never heard, Rico will pick out a new toy from a group of familiar items (Kaminski et al., 2004). Hearing that name for the second time four weeks later, Rico more often than not retrieves the same toy. Another border collie, Chaser, has set an animal record by learning 1022 object names (Pilley & Reid, 2011). Like a 3-year-old child, she can also categorize them by function and shape. She can "fetch a ball" or "fetch a doll."

Even more stunning was a report that Kanzi, a bonobo with a reported 384-word vocabulary, could understand syntax (rules of word order) in spoken English (Savage-Rumbaugh et al., 1993, 2009). Kanzi happened onto language while observing his adoptive mother during her language training. To someone who doesn't understand syntax, "Can you show me the light?" and "Can you bring me the [flash]light?" and "Can you turn the light on?" might all seem the same. Kanzi, who appears to have the grammatical abilities of a human 2-year-old, knows the difference. Given stuffed animals and asked—for the first time—to "make the dog bite the snake," he put the snake to the dog's mouth.

Paul Fusco/Magnum Photos

But is this language? Chimpanzees' ability to express themselves in American Sign Language (ASL) raises questions about the very nature of language. Here, the trainer is asking, "What is this?" The sign in response is "Baby." Does the response constitute language?

So, how should we interpret these studies? Are humans the only language-using species? If by *language* we mean verbal or signed expression of complex grammar, most psychologists would now agree that humans alone possess language. If we mean, more simply, an ability to communicate through a meaningful sequence of symbols, then apes are indeed capable of language.

One thing is certain: Studies of animal language and thinking have moved psychologists toward a greater appreciation of other species, not only for the traits we share with them but also for their own remarkable abilities. In the past, many psychologists doubted that other species could plan, form concepts, count, use tools, show compassion, or use language (Thorpe, 1974). Today, thanks to animal researchers, we know better. It's true that humans alone are capable of complex sentences. Moreover, 2½-year-old children display some cognitive abilities, such as following an actor's gaze to a target, that are unmatched even by chimpanzees (Herrmann et al., 2010). Nevertheless, other species do exhibit insight, show family loyalty, communicate with one another, care for one another, and transmit cultural patterns across generations. Accepting and working out what this means in terms of the moral rights of other animals is an unfinished task for our own thinking species.

RETRIEVAL PRACTICE

- If your dog barks at a stranger at the front door, does this qualify as language? What if the dog yips in a telltale way to let you know she needs to go out?

ANSWER: These are definitely communications. But if language consists of words and the grammatical rules we use to combine them to communicate meaning, few scientists would label a dog's barking and yipping as language.

Thinking and Language

28-6 What is the relationship between language and thinking, and what is the value of thinking in images?

Thinking and language intricately intertwine. Asking which comes first is one of psychology's chicken-and-egg questions. Do our ideas come first and we wait for words to name them? Or are our thoughts conceived in words and therefore unthinkable without them?

Language Influences Thinking

Linguist Benjamin Lee Whorf (1956) contended that language determines the way we think: "Language itself shapes a [person's] basic ideas." The Hopi, who have no past tense for their verbs, could not readily *think* about the past, said Whorf.

Whorf's **linguistic determinism** hypothesis is too extreme. We all think about things for which we have no words. (Can you think of a shade of blue you cannot name?) And

linguistic determinism Whorf's hypothesis that language determines the way we think.

we routinely have *unsymbolized* (wordless, imageless) thoughts, as when someone, while watching two men carry a load of bricks, wondered whether the men would drop them (Heavey & Hurlburt, 2008; Hurlburt & Akhter, 2008).

Nevertheless, to those who speak two dissimilar languages, such as English and Japanese, it seems obvious that a person may think differently in different languages (Brown, 1986). Unlike English, which has a rich vocabulary for self-focused emotions such as anger, Japanese has more words for interpersonal emotions such as sympathy (Markus & Kitayama, 1991). Many bilinguals report that they have different senses of self, depending on which language they are using (Matsumoto, 1994). In one series of studies with bilingual Israeli Arabs (who speak both Arabic and Hebrew), participants thought differently about their social world, with differing automatic associations with Arabs and Jews, depending on which language the testing session used (Danziger & Ward, 2010).

Before reading on, use a pen or pencil to sketch this idea: "The girl pushes the boy." Now see the inverted comment below.

How did you illustrate "the girl pushes the boy"? Anne Maass and Aurore Russo (2003) report that people whose language reads from left to right mostly position the pushing girl on the left. Those who read and write Arabic, a right-to-left language, mostly place her on the right. This spatial bias appears only in those old enough to have learned their culture's writing system (Dobel et al., 2007).

Bilingual individuals may even reveal different personality profiles when taking the same test in their two languages (Dinges & Hull, 1992). This happened when China-born, bilingual University of Waterloo students were asked to describe themselves in English or Chinese (Ross et al., 2002). The English-language self-descriptions fit typical Canadian profiles: Students expressed mostly positive self-statements and moods. Responding in Chinese, the same students gave typically Chinese self-descriptions: They reported more agreement with Chinese values and roughly equal positive and negative self-statements and moods. "Learn a new language and get a new soul," says a Czech proverb. Similar personality changes have been shown when bicultural, bilingual Americans and Mexicans shifted between the cultural frames associated with English and Spanish (Ramírez-Esparza et al., 2006).

So our words may not *determine* what we think, but they do *influence* our thinking (Boroditsky, 2011). We use our language in forming categories. In Brazil, the isolated Piraha tribespeople have words for the numbers 1 and 2, but numbers above that are simply "many." Thus, if shown 7 nuts in a row, they find it very difficult to lay out the same number from their own pile (Gordon, 2004).

Words also influence our thinking about colors. Whether we live in New Mexico, New South Wales, or New Guinea, we *see* colors much the same, but we use our native language to *classify* and *remember* colors (Davidoff, 2004; Roberson et al., 2004, 2005). If your language is English, you might view three colors and call two of them "yellow" and one of them "blue." Later you would likely see and recall the yellows as being more similar. But if you are a member of Papua New Guinea's Berinmo tribe, which has words

Culture and color Papua New Guinea Berinmo tribe children have words for different shades of "yellow," so they might more quickly spot and recall yellow variations. Here and everywhere, "the languages we speak profoundly shape the way we think, the way we see the world, the way we live our lives," notes psychologist Lera Boroditsky (2009).

Prisma Bildagentur AG/Alamy

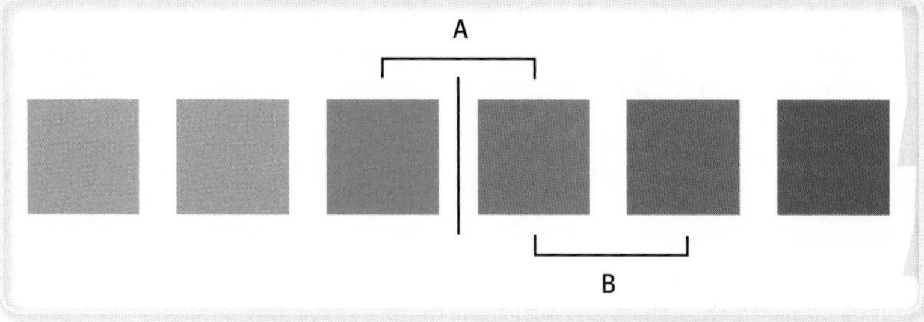

FIGURE 28.4
Language and perception When people view blocks of equally different colors, they perceive those with different names as more different. Thus, the "green" and "blue" in contrast A may appear to differ more than the two similarly different blues in contrast B (Özgen, 2004).

for two different shades of yellow, you would more speedily perceive and better recall the distinctions between the two yellows. And if your language is Russian, which has distinct names for different shades of blue, such as *goluboy* and *sinly*, you might remember the blue better. Words matter.

Perceived differences grow when we assign different names to colors. On the color spectrum, blue blends into green—until we draw a dividing line between the portions we call "blue" and "green." Although equally different on the color spectrum, two different items that share the same color name (as the two "blues" do in **FIGURE 28.4**, contrast B) are harder to distinguish than two items with different names ("blue" and "green," as in Figure 28.4, contrast A) (Özgen, 2004).

Perceived distances between cities also grow when two cities are in different countries or states rather than in the same (Burris & Branscombe, 2005; Mishra & Mishra, 2010).

Given words' subtle influence on thinking, we do well to choose our words carefully. Does it make any difference whether I write, "A child learns language as *he* interacts with *his* caregivers" or "Children learn language as *they* interact with *their* caregivers"? Many studies have found that it does. When hearing the generic *he* (as in "the artist and his work") people are more likely to picture a male (Henley, 1989; Ng, 1990). If *he* and *his* were truly gender free, we shouldn't skip a beat when hearing that "man, like other mammals, nurses his young."

To expand language is to expand the ability to think. In young children, thinking develops hand in hand with language (Gopnik & Meltzoff, 1986). Indeed, it is very difficult to think about or conceptualize certain abstract ideas (commitment, freedom, or rhyming) without language! And what is true for preschoolers is true for everyone: *It pays to increase your word power.* That's why most textbooks, including this one, introduce new words—to teach new ideas and new ways of thinking. And that's also why psychologist Steven Pinker (2007) titled his book on language *The Stuff of Thought.*

"All words are pegs to hang ideas on."
Henry Ward Beecher, *Proverbs from Plymouth Pulpit*, 1887

Increased word power helps explain what McGill University researcher Wallace Lambert (1992; Lambert et al., 1993) calls the *bilingual advantage.* Although their vocabulary in each language is somewhat smaller than that of people speaking a single language, bilingual people are skilled at inhibiting one language while using the other. And thanks to their well-practiced "executive control" over language, they also are better at inhibiting their attention to irrelevant information (Bialystock & Craik, 2010). This superior attentional control is evident from 7 months of age into adulthood (Emmorey et al., 2008; Kovacs & Mehler, 2009).

Lambert helped devise a Canadian program that immerses English-speaking children in French. (The number of non-Quebec children enrolled rose from 65,000 in 1981 to 300,000 in 2007 [Statistics Canada, 2010].) For most of their first three years in school, the English-speaking children are taught entirely in French, and thereafter gradually shift to classes mostly in English. Not surprisingly, the children attain a natural French fluency unrivaled by other methods of language teaching. Moreover, compared with similarly capable children in control groups, they do so without detriment to their English fluency, and with increased aptitude scores, creativity, and appreciation for French-Canadian culture (Genesee & Gándara, 1999; Lazaruk, 2007).

Many native English speakers, including most Americans, are monolingual. Most humans are bilingual or multilingual. Does monolingualism limit people's ability to comprehend the thinking of other cultures?

Whether we are in the linguistic minority or majority, language links us to one another. Language also connects us to the past and the future. "To destroy a people, destroy their language," observed poet Joy Harjo.

RETRIEVAL PRACTICE

- Benjamin Lee Whorf's controversial hypothesis, called _________ _________, suggested that we cannot think about things unless we have words for those concepts or ideas.

ANSWER: linguistic determinism

Thinking in Images

When you are alone, do you talk to yourself? Is "thinking" simply conversing with yourself? Without a doubt, words convey ideas. But aren't there times when ideas precede words? To turn on the cold water in your bathroom, in which direction do you turn the handle? To answer, you probably thought not in words but with *implicit* (nondeclarative, procedural) memory—a mental picture of how you do it.

"When we see a person walking down the street talking to himself, we generally assume that he is mentally ill. But we all talk to ourselves continuously—we just have the good sense of keeping our mouths shut. . . . It's as though we are having a conversation with an imaginary friend possessed of infinite patience. Who are we talking to?"
Sam Harris, "We Are Lost in Thought," 2011

Indeed, we often think in images. Artists think in images. So do composers, poets, mathematicians, athletes, and scientists. Albert Einstein reported that he achieved some of his greatest insights through visual images and later put them into words. Pianist Liu Chi Kung showed the value of thinking in images. One year after placing second in the 1958 Tschaikovsky piano competition, Liu was imprisoned during China's cultural revolution. Soon after his release, after seven years without touching a piano, he was back on tour, the critics judging his musicianship better than ever. How did he continue to develop without practice? "I did practice," said Liu, "every day. I rehearsed every piece I had ever played, note by note, in my mind" (Garfield, 1986).

For someone who has learned a skill, such as ballet dancing, even *watching* the activity will activate the brain's internal simulation of it, reported one British research team after collecting fMRIs as people watched videos (Calvo-Merino et al., 2004). So too, will imagining a physical experience, which activates some of the same neural networks that are active during the actual experience (Grèzes & Decety, 2001). Small wonder, then, that mental practice has become a standard part of training for Olympic athletes (Suinn, 1997).

One experiment on mental practice and basketball foul shooting tracked the University of Tennessee women's team over 35 games (Savoy & Beitel, 1996). During that time, the team's free-throw shooting increased from approximately 52 percent in games following standard physical practice to some 65 percent after mental practice. Players had repeatedly imagined making foul shots under various conditions, including being "trash-talked" by their opposition. In a dramatic conclusion, Tennessee won the national championship game in overtime, thanks in part to their foul shooting.

Mental rehearsal can also help you achieve an academic goal, as researchers demonstrated with two groups of introductory psychology students facing a midterm exam one week later (Taylor et al., 1998). (Scores of other students formed a control group, not engaging in any mental simulation.) The first group spent five minutes each day visualizing themselves scanning the posted grade list, seeing their A, beaming with joy, and feeling proud. This *outcome simulation* had little effect, adding only 2 points to their exam-scores average. Another group spent five minutes each day visualizing themselves effectively studying—reading the textbook, going over notes, eliminating distractions,

Blend Images/Jupiterimages

declining an offer to go out. This *process simulation* paid off: This second group began studying sooner, spent more time at it, and beat the others' average by 8 points. *The point to remember:* It's better to spend your fantasy time planning how to get somewhere than to dwell on the imagined destination.

* * *

What, then, should we say about the relationship between thinking and language? As we have seen, language influences our thinking. But if thinking did not also affect language, there would never be any new words. And new words and new combinations of old words express new ideas. The basketball term *slam dunk* was coined after the act itself had become fairly common. So, let us say that *thinking affects our language, which then affects our thought* (**FIGURE 28.5**).

FIGURE 28.5
The interplay of thought and language
The traffic runs both ways between thinking and language. Thinking affects our language, which affects our thought.

Psychological research on thinking and language mirrors the mixed views of our species by those in fields such as literature and religion. The human mind is simultaneously capable of striking intellectual failures and of striking intellectual power. Misjudgments are common and can have disastrous consequences. So we do well to appreciate our capacity for error. Yet our efficient heuristics—our snap judgment strategies—often serve us well. Moreover, our ingenuity at problem solving and our extraordinary power of language mark humankind as almost "infinite in faculties."

RETRIEVAL PRACTICE

- What is "mental practice," and how can it help you to prepare for an upcoming event?

ANSWER: Mental practice uses visual imagery to mentally rehearse future behaviors, activating some of the same brain areas used during the actual behaviors. Visualizing the details of the process is more effective than visualizing only your end goal.

MODULE REVIEW

Language and Thought

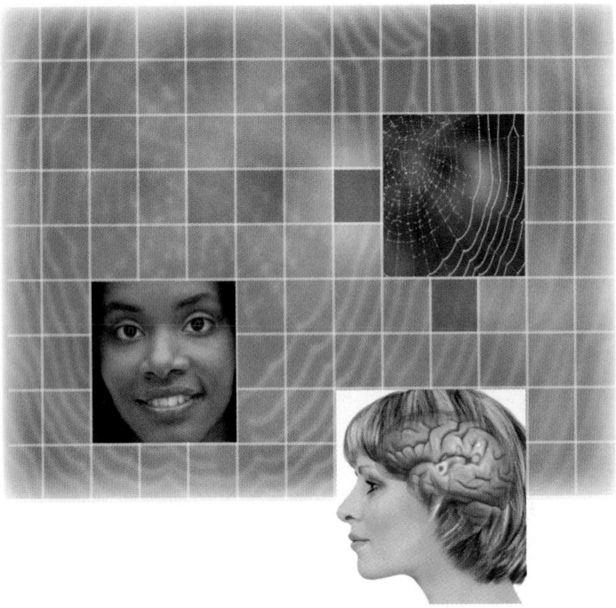

Learning Objectives

RETRIEVAL PRACTICE Take a moment to answer each of these Learning Objective Questions (repeated here from within the module). Then turn to Appendix B, Complete Module Reviews, to check your answers. Research suggests that trying to answer these questions on your own will improve your long-term retention (McDaniel et al., 2009).

28-1: What are the structural components of a language?

28-2: What are the milestones in language development?

28-3: How do we acquire language?

28-4: What brain areas are involved in language processing and speech?

28-5: Do other animals share our capacity for language?

28-6: What is the relationship between language and thinking, and what is the value of thinking in images?

Terms and Concepts to Remember

RETRIEVAL PRACTICE Test yourself on these terms by trying to write down the definition before flipping back to the referenced page to check your answer.

language, p. 365
phoneme, p. 366
morpheme, p. 366
grammar, p. 366
babbling stage, p. 367
one-word stage, p. 368
two-word stage, p. 368
telegraphic speech, p. 368
aphasia, p. 372
Broca's area, p. 372
Wernicke's area, p. 372
linguistic determinism, p. 375

RETRIEVAL PRACTICE Gain an advantage, and benefit from immediate feedback, with the interactive self-testing resources at www.worthpublishers.com/myers.

Intelligence and Creativity

29-4 What is creativity, and what fosters it?

Pierre de Fermat, a seventeenth-century mischievous genius, challenged mathematicians of his day to match his solutions to various number theory problems. His most famous challenge—*Fermat's last theorem*—baffled the greatest mathematical minds, even after a $2 million prize (in today's dollars) was offered in 1908 to whoever first created a proof.

Princeton mathematician Andrew Wiles had pondered the problem for more than 30 years and had come to the brink of a solution. One morning, out of the blue, the final "incredible revelation" struck him. "It was so indescribably beautiful; it was so simple and so elegant. I couldn't understand how I'd missed it. . . . It was the most important moment of my working life" (Singh, 1997, p. 25).

Wiles' incredible moment illustrates **creativity**—the ability to produce ideas that are both novel and valuable (Hennessey & Amabile, 2010). Studies suggest that a certain level of aptitude—a score above 120 on a standard intelligence test—supports creativity. Those who score exceptionally high in quantitative aptitude as 13-year-olds are more likely to obtain graduate science and math degrees and create published or patented work (Park et al., 2008; Robertson et al., 2010). Intelligence matters. Yet, there is more to creativity than what intelligence tests reveal. Indeed, the two kinds of thinking engage different brain areas. Intelligence tests, which demand a single correct answer, require *convergent thinking*. Injury to the left parietal lobe damages this ability. Creativity tests *(How many uses can you think of for a brick?)* require *divergent thinking*. Injury to certain areas of the frontal lobes can leave reading, writing, and arithmetic skills intact but destroy imagination (Kolb & Whishaw, 2006).

After picking up a Nobel Prize in Stockholm, physicist Richard Feynman stopped in Queens, New York, to look at his high school record. "My grades were not as good as I remembered," he reported, "and my IQ was [a good, though unexceptional] 124" (Faber, 1987).

Although there is no agreed-upon creativity measure—there is no Creativity Quotient (CQ) corresponding to an IQ score—Sternberg and his colleagues have identified five components of creativity (Sternberg, 1988, 2003; Sternberg & Lubart, 1991, 1992):

1. ***Expertise***—a well-developed base of knowledge—furnishes the ideas, images, and phrases we use as mental building blocks. "Chance favors only the prepared mind," observed Louis Pasteur. The more blocks we have, the more chances we have to combine them in novel ways. Wiles' well-developed base of knowledge put the needed theorems and methods at his disposal.

2. ***Imaginative thinking skills*** provide the ability to see things in novel ways, to recognize patterns, and to make connections. Having mastered a problem's basic elements, we redefine or explore it in a new way. Copernicus first developed expertise regarding the solar system and its planets, and then creatively defined the system as revolving around the Sun, not the Earth. Wiles' imaginative solution combined two partial solutions.

3. ***A venturesome personality*** seeks new experiences, tolerates ambiguity and risk, and perseveres in overcoming obstacles. Inventor Thomas Edison tried countless substances before finding the right one for his light bulb filament. Wiles said he labored in near-isolation from the mathematics community partly to stay focused and avoid distraction.

4. ***Intrinsic motivation*** is being driven more by interest, satisfaction, and challenge than by external pressures (Amabile & Hennessey, 1992). Creative people focus less on extrinsic motivators—meeting deadlines, impressing people, or making money—than on the pleasure and stimulation of the work itself. Asked how he solved such difficult scientific problems, Isaac Newton reportedly answered, "By thinking about them all the time." Wiles concurred: "I was so obsessed by this problem that . . . I was thinking about it all the time—[from] when I woke up in the morning to when I went to sleep at night" (Singh & Riber, 1997).

creativity the ability to produce novel and valuable ideas.

© 1991 Leigh Rubin. Creator's Syndicate Inc.

"For the love of God, is there a doctor in the house?"

© The New Yorker Collection, 2006, Christopher Weyant from cartoonbank.com. All Rights Reserved.

Everyone held up their crackers as David threw the cheese log into the ceiling fan.

Reprinted with permission of Paul Soderblom.

Imaginative thinking Cartoonists often display creativity as they see things in new ways or make unusual connections.

5. ***A creative environment*** sparks, supports, and refines creative ideas. After studying the careers of 2026 prominent scientists and inventors, Dean Keith Simonton (1992) noted that the most eminent were mentored, challenged, and supported by their colleagues. Many had the *emotional intelligence* needed to network effectively with peers. Even Wiles stood on the shoulders of others and wrestled his problem with the collaboration of a former student. Creativity-fostering environments support innovation, team-building, and communication (Hülsheger et al., 2009). They also support contemplation. After Jonas Salk solved a problem that led to the polio vaccine while in a monastery, he designed the Salk Institute to provide contemplative spaces where scientists could work without interruption (Sternberg, 2006).

The New Yorker Collection, 2010, Mick Stevens, from cartoonbank.com. All Rights Reserved.

A creative environment.

For those seeking to boost the creative process, research offers some ideas:

- ***Develop your expertise.*** Ask yourself what you care about and most enjoy. Follow your passion and become an expert at something.
- ***Allow time for incubation.*** Given sufficient knowledge available for novel connections, a period of inattention to a problem ("sleeping on it") allows for unconscious processing to form associations (Zhong et al., 2008). So think hard on a problem, then set it aside and come back to it later.
- ***Set aside time for the mind to roam freely.*** Take time away from attention-absorbing television, social networking, and video gaming. Jog, go for a long walk, or meditate.
- ***Experience other cultures and ways of thinking.*** Living abroad sets the creative juices flowing. Even after controlling for other variables, students who have spent time abroad are more adept at working out creative solutions to problems (Leung et al., 2008; Maddux et al., 2009, 2010). Multicultural experiences expose us to multiple perspectives and facilitate flexible thinking.

Emotional Intelligence

29-5 What are the four components of emotional intelligence?

Also distinct from academic intelligence is *social intelligence*—the know-how involved in successfully comprehending social situations. People with high social intelligence can read social situations the way a skilled football player reads the defense or a seafarer reads the weather. The concept was first proposed in 1920 by psychologist Edward Thorndike, who noted, "The best mechanic in a factory may fail as a foreman for lack of social intelligence" (Goleman, 2006, p. 83). Later psychologists have marveled that high-aptitude people are "not, by a wide margin, more effective . . . in achieving better marriages, in successfully raising their children, and in achieving better mental and physical well-being" (Epstein & Meier, 1989). Others have explored the difficulty that some smart people have processing and managing social information (Cantor & Kihlstrom, 1987; Weis & Süß, 2007). This idea is especially significant for an aspect of social intelligence that John Mayer, Peter Salovey, and David Caruso (2002, 2008) have called **emotional intelligence.** They have developed a test that assesses four emotional intelligence components:

emotional intelligence the ability to perceive, understand, manage, and use emotions.

- ***Perceiving*** emotions (to recognize them in faces, music, and stories)
- ***Understanding*** emotions (to predict them and how they change and blend)
- ***Managing*** emotions (to know how to express them in varied situations)
- ***Using*** emotions to enable adaptive or creative thinking

Mayer, Salovey, and Caruso caution against stretching "emotional intelligence" to include varied traits such as self-esteem and optimism. Rather, emotionally intelligent people are both socially and self-aware. And in both the United States and Germany, those scoring high on managing emotions enjoy higher-quality interactions with friends (Lopes et al., 2004). They avoid being hijacked by overwhelming depression, anxiety, or anger. Being sensitive to emotional cues, they know what to say to soothe a grieving friend, encourage a colleague, and manage a conflict.

Emotional intelligence is less a matter of conscious effort than of one's unconscious processing of emotional information (Fiori, 2009). Yet the outgrowths of this automatic processing become visible. Across dozens of studies in many countries, those scoring high in emotional intelligence exhibit somewhat better job performance (Joseph & Newman, 2010; Van Rooy & Viswesvaran, 2004; Zeidner et al., 2008). They also can delay gratification in pursuit of long-range rewards, rather than being overtaken by immediate impulses. They are emotionally in tune with others, and thus often succeed in career, marriage, and parenting situations where academically smarter (but emotionally less intelligent) people fail (Cherniss, 2001a,b; Ciarrochi et al., 2006).

Brain-damage reports have provided extreme examples of the results of diminished emotional intelligence in people with high general intelligence. Neuroscientist Antonio Damasio (1994) tells of Elliot, who had a brain tumor removed: "I never saw a tinge of emotion in my many hours of conversation with him, no sadness, no impatience, no frustration." Shown disturbing pictures of injured people, destroyed communities, and natural disasters, Elliot showed—and realized he felt—no emotion. He knew but he could not feel. Unable to intuitively adjust his behavior in response to others' feelings, Elliot lost his job. He went bankrupt. His marriage collapsed. He remarried and divorced again. At last report, he was dependent on a disability check and custodial care from a sibling.

Some scholars, however, are concerned that emotional intelligence stretches the concept of intelligence too far. Multiple-intelligence man Howard Gardner (1999) welcomes our stretching the concept into the realms of space, music, and information about ourselves and others. But let us also, he says, respect emotional sensitivity, creativity, and motivation as important but different. Stretch "intelligence" to include everything we prize and it will lose its meaning.

"I worry about [intelligence] definitions that collapse assessments of our cognitive powers with statements about the kind of human beings we favor."

Howard Gardner, "Rethinking the Concept of Intelligence," 2000

Is Intelligence Neurologically Measurable?

You know it: You are smarter than some people and not as smart as others. Question: What in that heart of smarts—your brain—creates this difference? Is it your brain's relative *size?* The amount of certain brain *tissue?* Your brain networks' *efficiency?*

Brain Size and Complexity

29-6 To what extent is intelligence related to brain anatomy?

After the brilliant English poet Lord Byron died in 1824, doctors discovered that his brain was a massive 5 pounds, not the normal 3 pounds. Three years later, Beethoven died and his brain was found to have exceptionally numerous and deep convolutions. Such observations set brain scientists off studying the brains of other geniuses at their wits' end (Burrell, 2005). Do people with big brains have big smarts?

Alas, some geniuses had small brains, and some dim-witted criminals had brains like Byron's. More recent studies that directly measure brain volume using MRI scans do reveal correlations of about +.33 between brain size (adjusted for body size) and intelligence score (Carey, 2007; McDaniel, 2005). Bigger is better.

One review of 37 brain-imaging studies revealed associations between intelligence and brain size and activity in specific areas, especially within the frontal and parietal lobes (Jung & Haier, 2007; Tang et al., 2010). Intelligence is having ample gray matter (mostly neural cell bodies) plus ample white matter (axons) that make for efficient communication between brain centers (Deary et al., 2009; Haier et al., 2009).

Sandra Witelson would not have been surprised. With the brains of 91 Canadians as a comparison base, Witelson and her colleagues (1999) seized an opportunity to study Einstein's brain. Although not notably heavier or larger in total size than the typical Canadian's brain, Einstein's brain was 15 percent larger in the parietal lobe's lower region—which just happens to be a center for processing mathematical and spatial information.

RETRIEVAL PRACTICE

- Correlations do not indicate cause-effect, but they do tell us whether two things are associated in some way. A correlation of -1.0, represents perfect __________ (agreement/disagreement) between two sets of scores—as one score goes up, the other score goes __________ (up/down). A correlation of __________ represents no association. The highest correlation, +1.0, represents perfect __________ (agreement/disagreement)—as the first score goes up, the other score goes __________ (up/down).

ANSWERS: disagreement; down; zero; agreement; up

Brain Function

29-7 To what extent is intelligence related to neural processing speed?

The correlations between brain anatomy and intelligence only begin to explain intelligence differences. Searching for other explanations, neuroscientists are studying the brain's functioning.

As people contemplate a variety of questions like those found on intelligence tests, a frontal lobe area just above the outer edge of the eyebrows becomes especially active—in the left brain for verbal questions, and on both sides for spatial questions (Duncan et al., 2000). Information from various brain areas seems to converge here, suggesting to researcher John Duncan (2000) that it may be a "global workspace for organizing and coordinating information" and that some people may be "blessed with a workspace that functions very, very well."

Functioning well means functioning efficiently. Brain scans reveal that smart people use less energy to solve problems (Haier, 2009). They are like skilled athletes, for whom agile moves can seem effortless. Agile minds come with agile brains.

Kiselev Andrey Valerevich/Shutterstock

So, are more intelligent people literally more quick-witted, much as today's speedier computer chips enable ever more powerful computing? On some tasks they seem to be. Verbal intelligence scores are predictable from the speed with which people retrieve information from memory (Hunt, 1983). Those who recognize quickly that *sink* and *wink* are different words, or that A and *a* share the same name, tend to score high in verbal ability. Extremely precocious 12- to 14-year-old college students are especially quick in responding to such tasks (Jensen, 1989). To try to define *quick-wittedness*, researchers are taking a close look at speed of perception and speed of neural processing.

Across many studies, the correlation between intelligence score and the speed of taking in perceptual information tends to be about +.3 to +.5 (Deary & Der, 2005; Sheppard & Vernon, 2008). A typical experiment flashes an incomplete stimulus, as in **FIGURE 29.3,** then

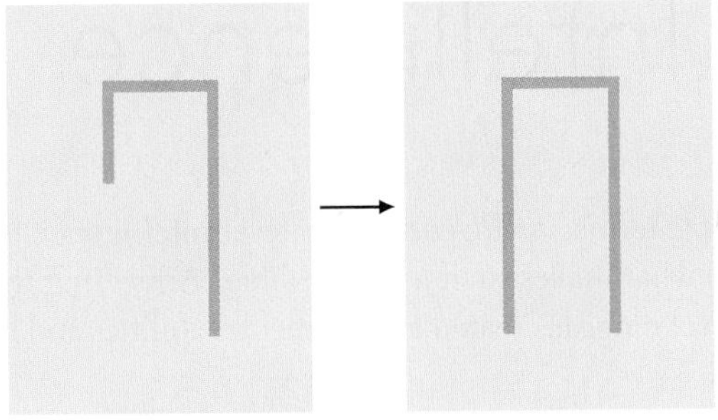

FIGURE 29.3
An inspection time task A stimulus is flashed before being overridden by a masking image. How long would you need to glimpse the stimulus at the left to answer the question? People who can perceive the stimulus very quickly tend to score somewhat higher on intelligence tests. (Adapted from Deary & Stough, 1996.)

a *masking image*—another image that overrides the lingering afterimage of the incomplete stimulus. The researcher then asks participants whether the long side appeared on the right or left. Those whose brains require the least inspection time to register a simple stimulus tend to score somewhat higher on intelligence tests (Caryl, 1994; Deary & Caryl, 1993; Reed & Jensen, 1992).

Perhaps people who process more quickly accumulate more information. Or perhaps, as one Australian-Dutch research team has found, processing speed and intelligence correlate not because one causes the other but because they share an underlying genetic influence (Luciano et al., 2005).

MODULE REVIEW

Introduction to Intelligence

Learning Objectives

RETRIEVAL PRACTICE Take a moment to answer each of these Learning Objective Questions (repeated here from within the module). Then turn to Appendix B, Complete Module Reviews, to check your answers. Research suggests that trying to answer these questions on your own will improve your long-term retention (McDaniel et al., 2009).

29-1: How is *intelligence* defined?

29-2: What are the arguments for and against considering intelligence as one general mental ability?

29-3: How do Gardner's and Sternberg's theories of multiple intelligences differ?

29-4: What is creativity, and what fosters it?

29-5: What are the four components of emotional intelligence?

29-6: To what extent is intelligence related to brain anatomy?

29-7: To what extent is intelligence related to neural processing speed?

Terms and Concepts to Remember

RETRIEVAL PRACTICE Test yourself on these terms by trying to write down the definition before flipping back to the referenced page to check your answer.

intelligence, p. 381
intelligence test, p. 381
general intelligence (*g*), p. 382
factor analysis, p. 382
savant syndrome, p. 383
creativity, p. 387
emotional intelligence, p. 389

MODULE 30

- The Origins of Intelligence Testing
- Modern Tests of Mental Abilities
- Principles of Test Construction
- The Dynamics of Intelligence

Assessing Intelligence

How do we assess intelligence? In simple terms, *intelligence* is whatever **intelligence tests** measure. So, what are these tests, and what makes such a test credible? Answering these questions begins with a look at why psychologists created tests of mental abilities and how they have used those tests.

The Origins of Intelligence Testing

30-1 When and why were intelligence tests created?

Some societies concern themselves with promoting the collective welfare of the family, community, and society. Other societies emphasize individual opportunity. Plato, a pioneer of the individualist tradition, wrote more than 2000 years ago in *The Republic* that "no two persons are born exactly alike; but each differs from the other in natural endowments, one being suited for one occupation and the other for another." As heirs to Plato's individualism, people in Western societies have pondered how and why individuals differ in mental ability.

Western attempts to assess such differences began in earnest over a century ago. The English scientist Francis Galton (1822–1911) had a fascination with measuring human traits. When his cousin Charles Darwin proposed that nature selects successful traits through the survival of the fittest, Galton wondered if it might be possible to measure "natural ability" and to encourage those of high ability to mate with one another. At the 1884 London Exposition, more than 10,000 visitors received his assessment of their "intellectual strengths" based on such things as reaction time, sensory acuity, muscular power, and body proportions. But alas, on these measures, well-regarded adults and students did not outscore others. Nor did the measures correlate with each other.

Although Galton's quest for a simple intelligence measure failed, he gave us some statistical techniques that we still use (as well as the phrase "nature and nurture"). And his persistent belief in the inheritance of genius—reflected in his book, *Hereditary Genius*—illustrates an important lesson from both the history of intelligence research and the history of science: Although science itself strives for objectivity, individual scientists are affected by their own assumptions and attitudes.

Alfred Binet: Predicting School Achievement

The modern intelligence-testing movement began at the turn of the twentieth century, when France passed a law requiring that all children attend school. Some children, including many newcomers to Paris, seemed incapable of benefiting from the regular school curriculum and in need of special classes. But how could the schools objectively identify children with special needs?

Alfred Binet "Some recent philosophers have given their moral approval to the deplorable verdict that an individual's intelligence is a fixed quantity, one which cannot be augmented. We must protest and act against this brutal pessimism" (Binet, 1909, p. 141).

National Library of Medicine

intelligence test a method for assessing an individual's mental aptitudes and comparing them with those of others, using numerical scores.

By age 4, however, children's performance on intelligence tests begins to predict their adolescent and adult scores. The consistency of scores over time increases with the age of the child. The remarkable stability of aptitude scores by late adolescence is seen in a U.S. Educational Testing Service study of 23,000 students who took the SAT and then later took the GRE (Angoff, 1988). On either test, verbal scores correlated only modestly with math scores—revealing that these two aptitudes are distinct. Yet scores on the SAT verbal test correlated +.86 with the scores on the GRE verbal tests taken four to five years later. An equally astonishing +.86 correlation occurred between the two math tests. Given the time lapse and differing educational experiences of these 23,000 students, the stability of their aptitude scores is remarkable.

Ironically, SAT and GRE scores correlate better with each other than either does with its intended criterion, school achievement. Thus, their reliability far exceeds their predictive validity. If either test was much affected by coaching, luck, or how one feels on the test day (as so many people believe), such reliability would be impossible.

Ian Deary and his colleagues (2004, 2009) recently set a record for long-term follow-up. Their amazing longitudinal studies have been enabled by their country, Scotland, doing something that no nation has done before or since. On June 1, 1932, essentially every child in the country who had been born in 1921—87,498 children around age 11—was given an intelligence test. The aim was to identify working-class children who would benefit from further education. Sixty-five years later to the day, Patricia Whalley, the wife of Deary's co-worker, Lawrence Whalley, discovered the test results on dusty storeroom shelves at the Scottish Council for Research in Education, not far from Deary's Edinburgh University office. "This will change our lives," Deary replied when Whalley told him the news.

And so it has, with dozens of studies of the stability and the predictive capacity of these early test results. For example, when the intelligence test administered to 11-year-old Scots in 1932 was readministered to 542 survivors as turn-of-the-millennium 80-year-olds, the correlation between the two sets of scores—after some 70 years of varied life experiences—was striking (**FIGURE 30.7**). A later study that followed Scots born in 1936 from ages 11 to 70 confirmed the remarkable stability of intelligence, independent of life circumstance (Johnson et al., 2010).

High-scoring 11-year-olds also were more likely to be living independently as 77-year-olds and were less likely to have suffered late-onset Alzheimer's disease (Starr et al., 2000; Whalley et al., 2000). Among girls scoring in the highest 25 percent, 70 percent were still alive at age 76—as were only 45 percent of those scoring in the lowest 25 percent (**FIGURE 30.8** on the next page). (World War II prematurely ended the lives of many of the male test-takers.) Follow-up studies with other large samples confirm the phenomenon: More intelligent children and adults live healthier and longer (Deary et al., 2008, 2010; Der et

"Whether you live to collect your old-age pension depends in part on your IQ at age 11."

Ian Deary, "Intelligence, Health, and Death," 2005

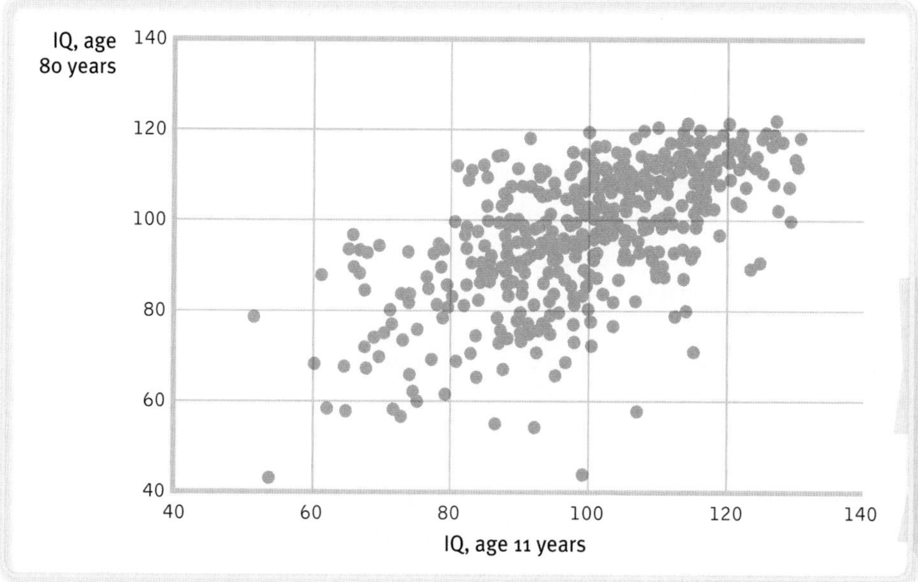

FIGURE 30.7
Intelligence endures When Ian Deary and his colleagues (2004) retested 80-year-old Scots, using an intelligence test they had taken as 11-year-olds, their scores across seven decades correlated +.66. (When 207 survivors were again retested at age 87, the correlation with their age 11 scores was +.51 [Gow et al., 2011].)

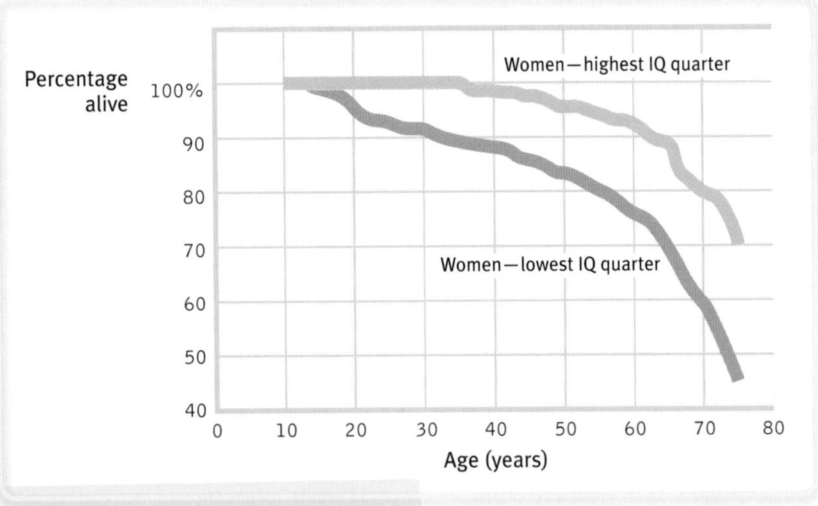

FIGURE 30.8

Living smart Women scoring in the highest 25 percent on the Scottish national intelligence test at age 11 tended to live longer than those who scored in the lowest 25 percent. (From Whalley & Deary, 2001.)

al., 2009; Weiss et al., 2009). One study that followed 93 nuns found that those exhibiting less verbal ability in essays written when entering convents in their teens were more at risk for Alzheimer's disease after age 75 (Snowdon et al., 1996).

Pause a moment: Have you any ideas why more intelligent people might live longer? Deary (2008) reports four possible explanations:

1. Intelligence facilitates more education, better jobs, and a healthier environment.
2. Intelligence encourages healthy living: less smoking, better diet, more exercise.
3. Prenatal events or early childhood illnesses might have influenced both intelligence and health.
4. A "well-wired body," as evidenced by fast reaction speeds, perhaps fosters both intelligence and longevity.

Extremes of Intelligence

30-6 What are the traits of those at the low and high intelligence extremes?

intellectual disability a condition of limited mental ability, indicated by an intelligence score of 70 or below and difficulty in adapting to the demands of life; varies from mild to profound. (Formerly referred to as *mental retardation.*)

Down syndrome a condition of mild to severe intellectual disability and associated physical disorders caused by an extra copy of chromosome 21.

One way to glimpse the validity and significance of any test is to compare people who score at the two extremes of the normal curve. The two groups should differ noticeably, and they do.

The Low Extreme

At one extreme of the normal curve are those with unusually low intelligence test scores. To be labeled as having an **intellectual disability** (formerly referred to as *mental retardation*), a person must have both a low test score and difficulty adapting to the normal demands of independent living. American Association on Intellectual and Developmental Disabilities (Schalock et al., 2010) guidelines specify performance that is approximately two standard deviations below average. For an intelligence test with 100 as average and a standard deviation of 15, that means (allowing for some variation in one's test score) an IQ of approximately 70 or below. The second criteria is a comparable limitation in adaptive behavior as expressed in

- ***conceptual skills,*** such as language, literacy, and concepts of money, time, and number,
- ***social skills,*** such as interpersonal skills, social responsibility, and the ability to follow basic rules and laws and avoid being victimized, and
- ***practical skills,*** such as daily personal care, occupational skill, and travel and health care.

Intellectual disability is a developmental condition that is apparent before age 18, sometimes with a known physical cause. **Down syndrome,** for example, is a disorder of varying severity caused by an extra chromosome 21 in the person's genetic makeup.

Consider one reason why people diagnosed with a mild intellectual disability—those just below the 70 score—might be better able to live independently today than many decades ago, when they were institutionalized. Recall that, thanks to the Flynn effect, the tests have been periodically restandardized. As that happened, individuals who scored near 70 on earlier tests suddenly lost about 6 IQ points. Two people with the same ability level could thus be classified differently, depending on when they were tested (Kanaya et al., 2003; Reynolds et al., 2010). As the boundary shifts, more people become eligible for special education and for Social Security payments

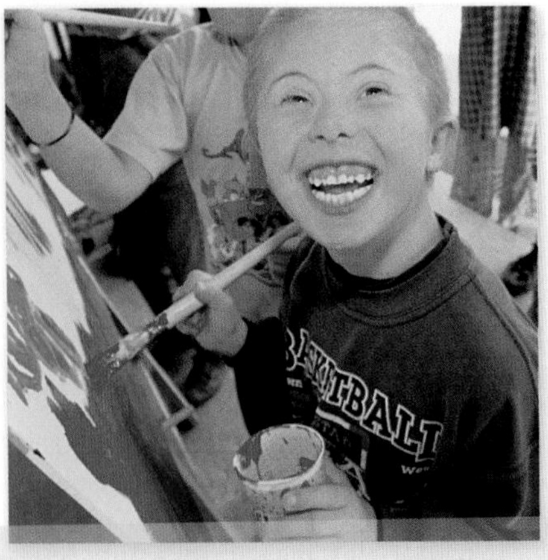

Reuters/Claudia Daut

Mainstreaming in Chile Most Chilean children with Down syndrome attend separate schools for children with special needs. However, this boy is a student at the Altamira School, where children with differing abilities share the classrooms.

Other studies find that around ovulation, women fantasize more about sex with desirable partners, wear more sexually attractive clothing, and have slightly higher voice pitch (Bryant & Haselton, 2009; Pillsworth & Haselton, 2006; Sheldon et al., 2006). After sniffing a T-shirt worn by a woman, men display higher testosterone levels if she was ovulating rather than nonovulating (Miller & Maner, 2010, 2011). In a study of 5300 strip-club lap dancers, their hourly tips almost doubled on the days near ovulation, compared with days during menstruation (Miller et al., 2007).

Women's sexuality differs from that of other mammalian females in being more responsive to testosterone level (van Anders & Dunn, 2009). If a woman's natural testosterone level drops, as happens with removal of the ovaries or adrenal glands, her sexual interest may wane. But testosterone-replacement therapy sometimes restores diminished sexual appetite. That is the finding of experiments with hundreds of surgically or naturally menopausal women, for whom a testosterone-replacement patch restored sexual activity, arousal, and desire more than did a placebo (Braunstein et al., 2005; Buster et al., 2005; Petersen & Hyde, 2011). For men with abnormally low testosterone levels, testosterone-replacement therapy often increases sexual desire and also energy and vitality (Yates, 2000).

In men, normal fluctuations in testosterone levels, from man to man and hour to hour, have little effect on sexual drive (Byrne, 1982). Indeed, fluctuations in male hormones are partly a *response* to sexual stimulation. In the presence of an attractive female, Australian skateboarders' testosterone surges, which contributes to riskier moves and more crash landings (Ronay & von Hippel, 2010). Thus, sexual arousal can be a cause as well as a consequence of increased testosterone levels. At the other end of the mating spectrum, studies in both North America and China find that married fathers tend to have lower testosterone levels than do bachelors and married men without children (Gray et al., 2006).

Although normal short-term hormonal changes have little effect on men's and women's desire, large hormonal shifts over the life span have a greater effect. A person's interest in dating and sexual stimulation usually increases with the pubertal surge in sex hormones. If the hormonal surge is precluded—as it was during the 1600s and 1700s for prepubertal boys who were castrated to preserve their soprano voices for Italian opera—the normal development of sex characteristics and sexual desire does not occur (Peschel & Peschel, 1987). When adult men are castrated, sex drive typically falls as testosterone levels decline sharply (Hucker & Bain, 1990). Male sex offenders taking Depo-Provera, a drug that reduces testosterone levels to that of a prepubertal boy, similarly lose much of their sexual urge (Bilefsky, 2009; Money et al., 1983). In later life, as sex hormone levels decline, the frequency of sexual fantasies and intercourse declines as well (Leitenberg & Henning, 1995).

To summarize: We might compare human sex hormones, especially testosterone, to the fuel in a car. Without fuel, a car will not run. But if the fuel level is minimally adequate, adding more fuel to the gas tank won't change how the car runs. The analogy is imperfect, because hormones and sexual motivation interact. However, it correctly suggests that biology is a necessary but not sufficient explanation of human sexual behavior. The hormonal fuel is essential, but so are the psychological stimuli that turn on the engine, keep it running, and shift it into high gear.

"Fill'er up with testosterone."

© The New Yorker Collection, 1993, Robert Mankoff from cartoonbank.com. All Rights Reserved.

The Psychology of Sex

Hunger and sex are different sorts of motivations. Hunger responds to a *need.* If we do not eat, we die. Sex is not in this sense a need. (We may feel like dying, but we do not.) Nevertheless, there are similarities between hunger and sexual motivation. Both depend on internal physiological factors. Both reflect the interplay of excitatory and inhibitory responses—the body's acceleration and braking systems (Bancroft et al., 2009). And both are influenced by external

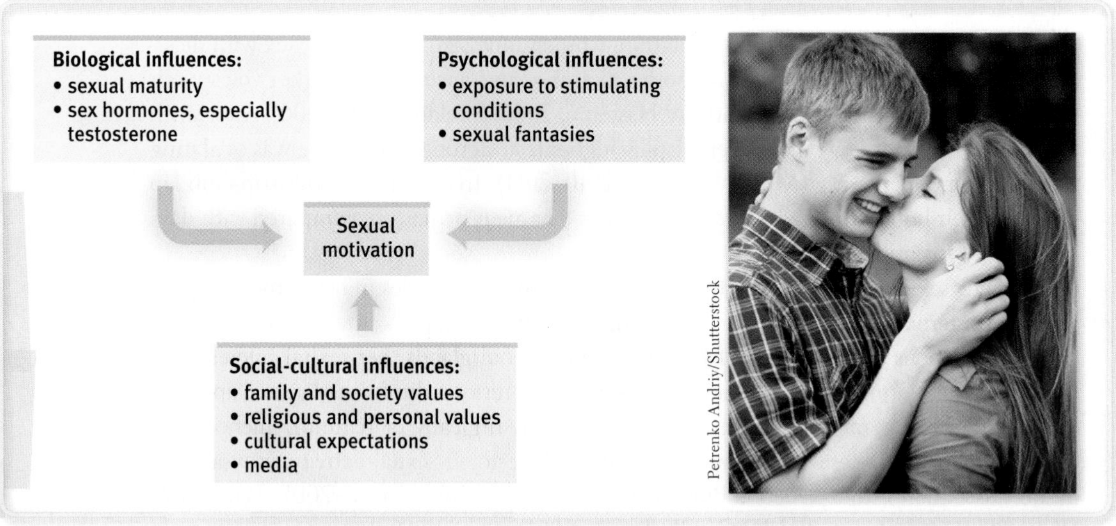

FIGURE 33.1
Levels of analysis for sexual motivation
Compared with our motivation for eating, our sexual motivation is less influenced by biological factors. Psychological and social-cultural factors play a bigger role.

and imagined stimuli, and by cultural expectations (**FIGURE 33.1**). Thus, despite the shared biology that underlies sexual motivation, the 281 expressed reasons for having sex (at last count) range widely—from "to get closer to God" to "to get my boyfriend to shut up" (Buss, 2008; Meston & Buss, 2007).

© Anthony Singer

"Ours is a society which stimulates interest in sex by constant titillation. . . . Cinema, television, and all the formidable array of our marketing technology project our very effective forms of titillation and our prejudices about man as a sexy animal into every corner of every hovel in the world."
Germaine Greer, 1984

External Stimuli

Many studies confirm that men become aroused when they see, hear, or read erotic material. Surprising to many (because sexually explicit materials are marketed mostly to men) is that most women—at least the less-inhibited women who volunteer to participate in such studies—report or exhibit nearly as much arousal to the same stimuli (Heiman, 1975; Stockton & Murnen, 1992). (Their brains do, however, respond differently, with fMRI scans revealing a more active amygdala in men viewing erotica [Hamann et al., 2004].) In 132 such experiments, men's feelings of sexual arousal have much more closely mirrored their (more obvious) genital response than have women's (Chivers et al., 2010).

People may find sexual arousal either pleasing or disturbing. (Those who wish to control their arousal often limit their exposure to such materials, just as those wishing to control hunger limit their exposure to tempting cues.) With repeated exposure, the emotional response to any erotic stimulus often lessens, or *habituates*. During the 1920s, when Western women's hemlines first reached the knee, an exposed leg was a mildly erotic stimulus.

Can sexually explicit material have adverse effects? Research indicates that it can. Depictions of women being sexually coerced—and liking it—tend to increase viewers' acceptance of the false idea that women enjoy rape, and they tend to increase male viewers' willingness to hurt women (Malamuth & Check, 1981; Zillmann, 1989). Viewing images of sexually attractive women and men may also lead people to devalue their own partners and relationships. After male collegians viewed TV or magazine depictions of sexually attractive women, they often found an average woman, or their own girlfriend or wife, less attractive (Kenrick & Gutierres, 1980; Kenrick et al., 1989; Weaver et al., 1984). Viewing X-rated sex films similarly tends to diminish people's satisfaction with their own sexual partner (Zillmann, 1989). Perhaps reading or watching erotica creates expectations that few men and women can fulfill.

Imagined Stimuli

The brain, it has been said, is our most significant sex organ. The stimuli inside our head—our imagination—can influence sexual arousal and desire. People who, because of a spinal-cord injury, have no genital sensation can still feel sexual desire (Willmuth, 1987). Consider, too, the erotic potential of dreams. Sleep researchers have discovered that genital arousal accompanies all types of dreams, even though most dreams have no sexual content.

But in nearly all men and some 40 percent of women, dreams sometimes contain sexual imagery that leads to orgasm (Wells, 1986). In men, nighttime orgasm and nocturnal emissions ("wet dreams") are more likely when orgasm has not occurred recently.

Wide-awake people become sexually aroused not only by memories of prior sexual activities but also by fantasies. Happy individuals in blossoming new relationships might fantasize about hoped-for future marriage and intimacy. In one survey of masturbation-related fantasies (Hunt, 1974), 19 percent of women and 10 percent of men reported imagining being "taken" by someone overwhelmed with desire for them. Fantasy is not reality, however. To paraphrase Susan Brownmiller (1975), there's a big difference between fantasizing that Christian Bale just won't take no for an answer and having a hostile person actually force himself on you.

About 95 percent of both men and women say they have sexual fantasies. Men (whether gay or straight) fantasize about sex more often, more physically, and less romantically. They also prefer less personal and faster-paced sexual content in books and videos (Leitenberg & Henning, 1995). Fantasizing about sex does *not* indicate a sexual problem or dissatisfaction. If anything, sexually active people have more sexual fantasies.

RETRIEVAL PRACTICE

- What factors affect our sexual expression?

ANSWER: Our genes and sex hormones (testosterone and the estrogens) influence our sexual behavior. Psychological stimuli and cultural attitudes and expectations also affect the ways we express our sexuality.

Adolescent Sexuality

33-3 What factors influence teen pregnancy and risk of sexually transmitted infections?

Adolescents' physical maturation fosters a sexual dimension to their emerging identity. Yet sexual expression varies dramatically with time and culture. Among American women born before 1900, a mere 3 percent had experienced premarital sex by age 18 (Smith, 1998). A century later, about half of U.S. ninth- to twelfth-graders reported having had sexual intercourse (CDC, 2010). Teen intercourse rates are roughly similar in Western Europe and in Latin America, but much lower in Arab and Asian countries and among North Americans of Asian descent (McLaughlin et al., 1997; Wellings et al., 2006). Given the wide variation across time and place, it's no surprise that twin research has found that environmental factors accounted for almost three-fourths of the individual variation in age of sexual initiation (Bricker et al., 2006). Family and cultural values matter.

Teen Pregnancy

Compared with European teens, American teens have a higher rate of teen pregnancy (Call et al., 2002; Sullivan/Anderson, 2009). What contributes to teen pregnancy?

Minimal communication about birth control Many teenagers are uncomfortable discussing contraception with their parents, partners, and peers. Teens who talk freely with parents and are in an exclusive relationship with a partner with whom they communicate openly are more likely to use contraceptives (Aspy et al., 2007; Milan & Kilmann, 1987). In a 2009 national survey, some 3 in 4 sexually active American 14- to 17-year-olds reported using condoms (Fortenberry et al., 2010).

"Condoms should be used on every conceivable occasion."

Anonymous

Guilt related to sexual activity In another survey, 72 percent of sexually active 12- to 17-year-old American girls said they regretted having had sex (Reuters, 2000). Sexual inhibitions or ambivalence can restrain sexual activity, but if passion overwhelms intentions they may also reduce attempts at birth control (Gerrard & Luus, 1995; MacDonald & Hynie, 2008).

Alcohol use Sexually active teens are typically alcohol-using teens (Zimmer-Gembeck & Helfand, 2008), and those who use alcohol prior to sex are less likely to use condoms (Kotchick et al., 2001). By depressing the brain centers that control judgment, inhibition, and self-awareness, alcohol disarms normal restraints, a phenomenon well known to sexually coercive males.

"All of us who make motion pictures are teachers, teachers with very loud voices."

Film producer George Lucas, Academy Award ceremonies, 1992

CLOSE-UP

The Sexualization of Girls

As you have surely noticed, TV, the Internet, music videos and lyrics, movies, magazines, sports media, and advertising often portray women and even girls as sexual objects. The frequent result, report both an American Psychological Association (APA, 2007) task force and the Scottish Parliament (2010), is harm to their self-image, and unhealthy sexual development.

Sexualization occurs when girls

- are led to value themselves in terms of their sexual appeal.
- compare themselves to narrowly defined beauty standards.
- see themselves as sexual beings for others' use.

In experiments, the task force reported, being made self-conscious about one's body, such as by wearing a swimsuit, disrupts thinking when doing math computations or logical reasoning. Sexualization also contributes to eating disorders and depression, and to unrealistic expectations regarding sexuality.

© T. Arroyo/JPegFoto/ PictureGroup via AP Images

Mindful of today's sexualizing media, the APA has some suggestions for countering these messages. Parents, teachers, and others can teach girls "to value themselves for who they are rather than how they look." They can teach boys "to value girls as friends, sisters, and girlfriends, rather than as sexual objects." And they can help girls and boys develop "media literacy skills" that enable them to recognize and resist the message that women are sexual objects and that a thin, sexy look is all that matters.

Keeping abreast of hypersexuality An analysis of the 60 top-selling video games found 489 characters, 86 percent of whom were males (like most of the game players). The female characters were much more likely than the male characters to be "hypersexualized"—partially nude or revealingly clothed, with large breasts and tiny waists (Downs & Smith, 2010).

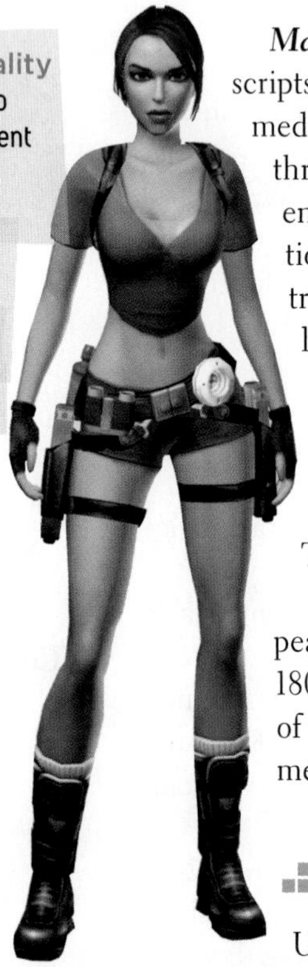
Eidos Scripps Howard Photo Service/Newscom

Mass media norms of unprotected promiscuity Media help write the "social scripts" that affect our perceptions and actions. So what sexual scripts do today's media write on our minds? An average hour of prime-time television on the three major U.S. networks has contained 15 sexual acts, words, and innuendos. The partners are usually unmarried, with no prior romantic relationship, and few communicate any concern for birth control or sexually transmitted infections (Brown et al., 2002; Kunkel, 2001; Sapolsky & Tabarlet, 1991). The more sexual content adolescents view (even when controlling for other predictors of early sexual activity), the more likely they are to perceive their peers as sexually active, to develop sexually permissive attitudes, and to experience early intercourse (Escobar-Chaves et al., 2005; Martino et al., 2005; Ward & Friedman, 2006). (See Close-Up: The Sexualization of Girls.)

In recent history, the pendulum of sexual values has swung from the European eroticism of the early 1800s to the conservative Victorian era of the late 1800s, from the libertine flapper era of the 1920s to the family values period of the 1950s. The pendulum may have begun a new swing toward commitment in the twenty-first century, with declining teen birth rates since 1991.

Sexually Transmitted Infections

Unprotected sex has led to increased rates of *sexually transmitted infections* (*STIs;* also called *STDs* for *sexually transmitted diseases*). Two-thirds of new infections occur in people under 25 (CASA, 2004). Teenage girls, because of their not yet fully mature biological development and lower levels of protective antibodies, are especially vulnerable (Dehne & Riedner, 2005; Guttmacher, 1994). A Centers for Disease Control study of sexually experienced 14- to 19-year-old U.S. females found 39.5 percent had STIs (Forhan et al., 2008).

To comprehend the mathematics of infection transmission, imagine that over the course of a year, Pat has sex with 9 people, each of whom over the same period has sex with 9 other people, who in turn have sex with 9 others. How many "phantom" sex partners (past partners of partners) will Pat have? Laura Brannon and Timothy Brock (1993) report that the actual number—511—is more than five times the estimate given by the average student. Or consider this: If someone uses a birth control method that is 98 percent effective in preventing pregnancy or infection, a 2 percent chance of failure in the first such use accumulates to a risk of nearly 50 percent after 30 such uses. Moreover, when people feel drawn to a partner, they become motivated to underestimate risks (Knäuper el al., 2005).

Given these odds, the rapid spread of STIs is not surprising. Condoms offer limited protection against certain skin-to-skin STIs, such as herpes (Medical Institute, 1994; NIH, 2001). Across the available studies, condoms have, however, been 80 percent effective in preventing transmission of HIV (human immunodeficiency virus—the virus that causes AIDS) from an infected partner (Weller & Davis-Beaty, 2002; WHO, 2003). The effects were clear when Thailand promoted 100 percent condom use by commercial sex workers. Over a four-year period, as condom use soared from 14 to 94 percent, the annual number of bacterial STIs plummeted from 410,406 to 27,362 (WHO, 2000). In the United States, reports the Centers for Disease Control and Prevention, women's condom use during first premarital sex increased from 34 percent before 1985 to 72 percent between 2005 and 2008 (Mosher & Jones, 2010).

STI facts of life have led to another response: a greater emphasis on teen abstinence within some comprehensive sex-education programs. A government-commissioned study of four urban, school-based abstinence programs found that 49 percent of students not participating had sex over the next four to six years. And how many participating in the abstinence programs did so? An identical 49 percent (Trenholm et al., 2007). A National Longitudinal Study of Adolescent Health followed abstinence pledgers and nonpledgers (matched samples of similarly conservative teens who had never had sex). Five years later, the pledgers—82 percent of whom denied having ever pledged—were just as likely to have had premarital sex (Rosenbaum, 2009). However, a more recent experiment offered African-American middle school students an abstinence education program rooted in social psychological theory and research. In the ensuing two years, only 34 percent of those who participated started having sex, compared with 49 percent of those randomly assigned to a health promotion control group (Jemmott et al., 2010).

The National Longitudinal Study of Adolescent Health among 12,000 teens has also found several predictors of sexual restraint:

High intelligence Teens with high rather than average intelligence test scores more often delay sex, partly because they appreciate possible negative consequences and are more focused on future achievement than on here-and-now pleasures (Halpern et al., 2000).

Religious engagement Actively religious teens and adults more often reserve sex for marital commitment (Lucero et al., 2008).

Father presence In studies following hundreds of New Zealand and U.S. girls from age 5 to 18, a father's absence was linked to sexual activity before age 16 and to teen pregnancy (Ellis et al., 2003). These associations held even after adjusting for other adverse influences, such as poverty. Close family attachments—families that eat together and where parents know their teens' activities and friends—also predict later sexual initiation (Coley et al., 2008).

Participation in service learning programs Several experiments have found lower pregnancy rates among teens volunteering as tutors or teachers' aides or participating in community projects than found among comparable teens randomly assigned to control conditions (Kirby, 2002; O'Donnell et al., 2002). Researchers are unsure why. Does service learning promote a sense of personal competence, control, and responsibility? Does it encourage more future-oriented thinking? Or does it simply reduce opportunities for unprotected sex?

RETRIEVAL PRACTICE

- Which THREE of the following five factors contribute to unplanned teen pregnancies?

  a. Alcohol use
  b. Higher intelligence level
  c. Ignorance
  d. Mass media models
  e. Increased communication about options

  ANSWERS: a., c., d

- The use of condoms during sex __________ (does/doesn't) reduce the risk of getting HIV and __________ (does/doesn't) fully protect against skin-to-skin STIs.

  ANSWERS: does; doesn't

Sexual Orientation

33-4 What has research taught us about sexual orientation?

To motivate is to energize and direct behavior. So far, we have considered the energizing of sexual motivation but not its direction. We express the direction of our sexual interest in our **sexual orientation**—our enduring sexual attraction toward members of our own sex *(homosexual orientation)* or the other sex *(heterosexual orientation)*. We experience this attraction in our interests, thoughts, and fantasies (who's that person in your imagination?). Cultures vary in their attitudes toward homosexuality. In Chile, 32 percent of people say homosexuality "is never justified," as do 98 percent of Kenyans and Nigerians (Pew, 2006). Yet whether a culture condemns or accepts homosexuality, heterosexuality prevails and homosexuality survives.

Gay men and lesbians often recall childhood play preferences like those of the other sex (Bailey & Zucker, 1995). But most homosexual people report not becoming aware of same-sex attraction until during or shortly after puberty, and not thinking of themselves as gay or lesbian (their socially influenced identity) until later in their teens or twenties (Garnets & Kimmel, 1990; Hammack, 2005). As adolescents, their friendship quality is similar to that of "straight" teenagers, and as adults, their partnerships are "remarkably similar" in love and satisfaction to those of heterosexual couples (Busseri et al., 2006; Peplau & Fingerhut, 2007).

Sexual Orientation Statistics

How many people are exclusively homosexual? About 10 percent, as the popular press has often assumed? Nearly 25 percent, as average Americans estimated in a 2011 Gallup survey (Morales, 2011)? Not according to more than a dozen national surveys that have explored sexual orientation in Europe and the United States, using methods protecting the respondents' anonymity. The most accurate figure seems to be about 3 percent of men and 1 or 2 percent of women (Chandra et al., 2011; Herbenick et al., 2010a). Estimates derived from the sexual activity of unmarried partners reported in the 2000 U.S. Census suggest that 2.5 percent of the population is gay or lesbian (Tarmann, 2002). Fewer than 1 percent of survey respondents—for example, only 12 people out of 7076 Dutch adults in one survey (Sandfort et al., 2001)—reported being actively bisexual. A larger number of adults—13 percent of women and 5 percent of men in a U.S. National Center for Health Statistics survey—report some same-sex sexual contact during their lives (Chandra et al., 2011). And more people report having had an occasional homosexual fantasy.

In one British survey, of the 18,876 people contacted, 1 percent were seemingly asexual, having "never felt sexually attracted to anyone at all" (Bogaert, 2004, 2006b).

What does it feel like to be homosexual in a heterosexual culture? If you are heterosexual, one way to understand is to imagine how you would feel if you were shunned or fired for openly admitting or displaying your feelings toward someone of the other sex; if you overheard people making crude jokes about heterosexual people; if most movies, TV shows, and advertisements portrayed (or implied) homosexuality; and if your family members were pleading with you to change your heterosexual lifestyle and to enter into a homosexual marriage.

sexual orientation an enduring sexual attraction toward members of either one's own sex (homosexual orientation) or the other sex (heterosexual orientation).

STAN HONDA/AFP/Getty Images

Driven to suicide In 2010, Rutgers University student Tyler Clementi jumped off this bridge after his sexual encounter with another man was posted online. Reports then surfaced of other gay teens who had reacted in a similarly tragic fashion after being taunted.

Sexual orientation is not an indicator of mental health. "Homosexuality, in and of itself, is not associated with mental disorders or emotional or social problems," declares the American Psychological Association (2007). Moreover, same-sex civil unions provide emotional, social, and health benefits similar to those of heterosexual unions (Herek, 2006; King & Bartlett, 2006; Kurdek, 2005). But some homosexual individuals, especially during adolescence and if feeling rejected by parents or harassed by peers, struggle with their sexual attractions and may contemplate suicide (Balsam et al., 2005; Kitts, 2005; Plöderl & Fartacek, 2005; Ryan et al., 2009). They may at first try to ignore or deny their desires, hoping they will go away. But they don't. Then they may try to change, through psychotherapy, willpower, or prayer. But the feelings typically persist, as do those of heterosexual people—who are similarly incapable of becoming homosexual (Haldeman, 1994, 2002; Myers & Scanzoni, 2005). Moreover, our sexual orientation is so basic to who we are that some research suggests it operates automatically—without our awareness (Jiang et al., 2006).

Most of today's psychologists therefore view sexual orientation as neither willfully chosen nor willfully changed. "Efforts to change sexual orientation are unlikely to be successful and involve some risk of harm," declared a 2009 American Psychological Association report. Sexual orientation in some ways is like handedness: Most people are one way, some the other. A very few are truly ambidextrous. Regardless, the way one is endures.

This conclusion is most strongly established for men. Compared with men's sexual orientation, women's tends to be less strongly felt and potentially more fluid and changing (Chivers, 2005; Diamond, 2008; Peplau & Garnets, 2000). Men's lesser sexual variability is apparent in many ways, notes Roy Baumeister (2000). Across time, across cultures, across situations, and across differing levels of education, religious observance, and peer influence, adult women's sexual drive and interests are more flexible and varying than are adult men's. Women, more than men, for example, prefer to alternate periods of high sexual activity with periods of almost none, and are somewhat more likely than men to feel and act on bisexual attractions (Mosher et al., 2005). Baumeister calls women's more varying sexuality a gender difference in *erotic plasticity*.

In men, a high sex drive is associated with increased attraction to women (if heterosexual) or men (if homosexual). In women, a high sex drive is associated with increased attraction to both men and women (Lippa, 2006, 2007a). When shown pictures of heterosexual couples, in either erotic or nonerotic contexts, heterosexual men look mostly at the woman while heterosexual women look more equally at both the man and the woman (Lykins et al., 2008). Likewise, heterosexual men gaze more at female than male swimsuit models, while heterosexual

AP Photo/Stephen J. Carerra

Personal values affect sexual orientation less than they affect other forms of sexual behavior Compared with people who rarely attend religious services, for example, those who attend regularly are one-third as likely to have lived together before marriage, and they report having had many fewer sex partners. But (if male) they are just as likely to be homosexual (Smith, 1998).

women gaze more equally at both (Lippa et al., 2010). And when shown sexually explicit film clips, men's genital and subjective sexual arousal is mostly to preferred sexual stimuli (for heterosexual viewers, depictions of women). Women respond more nonspecifically to depictions of sexual activity involving males or females (Chivers et al., 2007).

Origins of Sexual Orientation

If our sexual orientation is indeed something we do not choose and seemingly cannot change (most clearly so for males), then where do these preferences—heterosexual or homosexual—come from? See if you can anticipate the conclusions that have emerged from hundreds of research studies by responding *Yes* or *No* to the following questions:

Note that the scientific question is not "What causes homosexuality?" (or "What causes heterosexuality?") but "What causes differing sexual orientations?" In pursuit of answers, psychological science compares the backgrounds and physiology of people whose sexual orientations *differ.*

1. Is homosexuality linked with problems in a child's relationships with parents, such as with a domineering mother and an ineffectual father, or a possessive mother and a hostile father?
2. Does homosexuality involve a fear or hatred of people of the other gender, leading individuals to direct their sexual desires toward members of their own sex?
3. Is sexual orientation linked with levels of sex hormones currently in the blood?
4. As children, were most homosexuals molested, seduced, or otherwise sexually victimized by an adult homosexual?

The answer to all these questions appears to be *No* (Storms, 1983). In interviews with nearly 1000 homosexuals and 500 heterosexuals, Kinsey Institute investigators assessed nearly every imaginable psychological cause of homosexuality—parental relationships, childhood sexual experiences, peer relationships, dating experiences (Bell et al., 1981; Hammersmith, 1982). Their findings: Homosexuals are no more likely than heterosexuals to have been smothered by maternal love or neglected by their father. And consider this: If "distant fathers" were more likely to produce homosexual sons, then shouldn't boys growing up in father-absent homes more often be gay? (They are not.) And shouldn't the rising number of such homes have led to a noticeable increase in the gay population? (It has not.) Most children raised by gay or lesbian parents grow up straight and well-adjusted (Gartrell & Bos, 2010).

Homosexual people do, however, appear more often in certain populations. One study (Ludwig, 1995) of the biographies of 1004 eminent people found homosexual and bisexual people especially overrepresented among poets (24 percent), fiction writers (21 percent), and artists and musicians (15 percent). Gay more than straight men also express interest in occupations that attract many women, such as decorator, florist, and flight attendant (Lippa, 2002). (Given that some 96 percent of men are not gay, most men in such occupations may nevertheless be straight.)

Men who have older brothers are also somewhat more likely to be gay, report Ray Blanchard (1997, 2008a,b) and Anthony Bogaert (2003)—about one-third more likely for each additional older brother. If the odds of homosexuality are roughly 2 percent among first sons, they would rise to nearly 3 percent among second sons, 4 percent for third sons, and so on for each additional older brother (see **FIGURE 33.2**). The reason for this curious phenomenon—the *fraternal birth-order effect*—is unclear. Blanchard suspects a defensive maternal immune response to foreign substances produced by male fetuses. With each pregnancy with a male fetus, the maternal antibodies may become stronger and may prevent the fetus' brain from developing in a male-typical pattern. Consistent with this biological explanation, the fraternal birth-order effect occurs only in men with older brothers born to the same mother (whether reared together or not). Sexual orientation is unaffected by adoptive brothers (Bogaert, 2006b). The birth-order effect on sexual orientation is not found among women with older sisters, women who were womb-mates of twin brothers, and men who are not right-handed (Rose et al., 2002).

FIGURE 33.2
The fraternal birth-order effect
Researcher Ray Blanchard (2008a) offers these approximate curves depicting a man's likelihood of homosexuality as a function of his number of older brothers. This correlation has been found in several studies, but only among right-handed men.

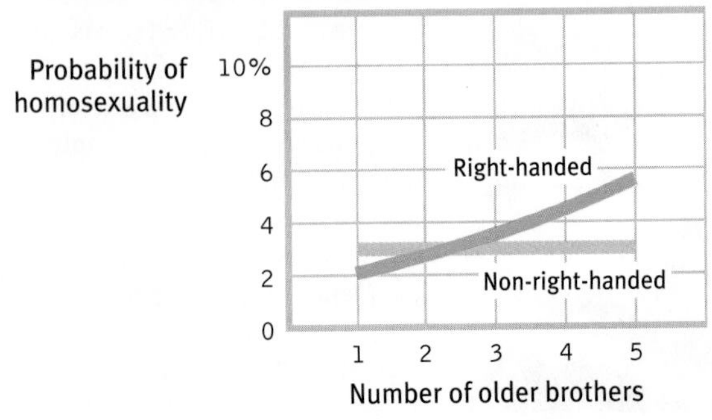

So, what else might influence sexual orientation? One theory has proposed that people develop same-sex erotic attachments if segregated by gender at the time their sex drive matures (Storms, 1981). Indeed, gay men tend to recall going through puberty somewhat earlier, when peers are more likely to be all males (Bogaert et al., 2002). But even in tribal cultures in which homosexual behavior is expected of all boys before marriage, heterosexuality prevails (Hammack, 2005; Money, 1987). (As this illustrates, homosexual *behavior* does not always indicate a homosexual *orientation*.)

The bottom line from a half-century's theory and research: If there are environmental factors that influence sexual orientation, we do not yet know what they are. This reality has motivated researchers to consider more carefully other possible biological influences on orientation by studying homosexuality in the animal world, as well as differing brain centers, genetics, and prenatal hormone exposure.

© The Boston Globe/John Tlumacki

Juliet and Juliet Boston's beloved swan couple, "Romeo and Juliet," were discovered actually to be, as are many other animal partners, a same-sex pair. Biologist Bruce Bagemihl (1999) has identified several hundred species in which at least occasional same-sex relations have been observed, including grizzlies, gorillas, monkeys, flamingos, owls, and albatrosses. Some degree of homosexuality seems to be a natural part of the animal world.

The Brain and Sexual Orientation

Researcher Simon LeVay (1991) studied sections of the hypothalamus taken from deceased heterosexual and homosexual people. As a gay scientist, LeVay wanted to do "something connected with my gay identity." To avoid biasing the results, he did a *blind study*, not knowing which donors were gay. For nine months he peered through his microscope at a cell cluster he thought might be important. Then, one morning, he broke the code: One cell cluster was reliably larger in heterosexual men than in women and homosexual men. "I was almost in a state of shock," LeVay said (1994). "I took a walk by myself on the cliffs over the ocean. I sat for half an hour just thinking what this might mean."

It should not surprise us that in other ways, too, brains differ with sexual orientation (Savic & Lindström, 2008; Swaab, 2008). Remember our maxim: *Everything psychological is simultaneously biological.* But when do such brain differences begin? At conception? In the womb? During childhood or adolescence? Does experience produce these differences? Or is it genes or prenatal hormones (or genes via prenatal hormones)?

LeVay does not view the hypothalamus as a sexual orientation center; rather, he sees it as an important part of the neural pathway engaged in sexual behavior. He acknowledges that sexual behavior patterns may influence the brain's anatomy. In fish, birds, rats, and humans, brain structures vary with experience—including sexual experience, reports sex researcher Marc Breedlove (1997). But LeVay believes it more likely that brain anatomy influences sexual orientation. His hunch seems confirmed by the discovery of a similar hypothalamic difference between the male sheep that do and don't display same-sex attraction (Larkin et al., 2002; Roselli et al., 2002, 2004). Moreover, report University of London psychologists Qazi Rahman and Glenn Wilson (2003), "the neuroanatomical correlates of male homosexuality differentiate very early postnatally, if not prenatally."

Responses to hormone-derived sexual scents also point to a brain difference (Savic et al., 2005). When straight women are given a whiff of a scent derived from men's sweat, their hypothalamus lights up in an area governing sexual arousal. Gay men's brains respond similarly to the men's scent. But straight men's brains show the arousal response only to a female hormone derivative. Other studies of brain responses to sex-related sweat odors and to pictures of male and female faces find similar gay-straight differences (Kranz & Ishai, 2006; Martins et al., 2005).

"Gay men simply don't have the brain cells to be attracted to women."

Simon LeVay, *The Sexual Brain,* 1993

Genes and Sexual Orientation

Are these sex-related brain differences genetically influenced? Evidence does indicate a genetic influence on sexual orientation. "First, homosexuality does appear to run in families," note Brian Mustanski and Michael Bailey (2003). "Second, twin studies have established that genes play a substantial role in explaining individual differences in sexual orientation." Identical twins are somewhat more likely than fraternal twins to share a homosexual orientation (Alanko et al., 2010; Långström et al., 2008, 2010). (Because sexual orientations differ in many identical twin pairs, especially female twins, we know that other factors besides genes are also at work.)

By genetic manipulations, experimenters have created female fruit flies that during courtship act like males (pursuing other females) and males that act like females (Demir & Dickson, 2005). "We have shown that a single gene in the fruit fly is sufficient to determine all aspects of the flies' sexual orientation and behavior," explained Barry Dickson (2005). With humans, it's likely that multiple genes, possibly in interaction with other influences, shape sexual orientation. One study financed by the U.S. National Institutes of Health is analyzing the genes of more than 1000 gay brothers in search of such genetic markers.

Researchers have speculated about possible reasons why "gay genes" might exist. Given that same-sex couples cannot naturally reproduce, why would such genes survive in the human gene pool? One possible answer is kin selection. Evolutionary psychologists remind us that many of our genes also reside in our biological relatives. Perhaps, then, gay people's genes live on through their supporting the survival and reproductive success of their nieces, nephews, and other relatives (who also carry many of the same genes). Gay men make generous uncles, suggests one study of Samoans (Vasey & VanderLaan, 2010).

"Studies indicate that male homosexuality is more likely to be transmitted from the mother's side of the family."

Robert Plomin, John DeFries, Gerald McClearn, and Michael Rutter, *Behavioral Genetics,* 1997

An alternative "fertile females" theory suggests that maternal genetics may be at work (Bocklandt et al., 2006). Recent Italian studies confirm what others have found—that homosexual men have more homosexual relatives on their mother's side than on their father's (Camperio-Ciani et al., 2004, 2009; Zietsch et al., 2008). And, compared with the maternal relatives of heterosexual men, the maternal relatives of homosexual men produce more offspring. Perhaps the genes that dispose women to be strongly attracted to men, and therefore to have more children, also dispose men (including some of their male relatives) to be attracted to men (LeVay, 2011).

Prenatal Hormones and Sexual Orientation

Elevated rates of homosexual orientation in identical *and* fraternal twins suggest that not just shared genes but also a shared prenatal environment may be a factor. In animals and some human cases, prenatal hormone conditions have altered a fetus' sexual orientation. German researcher Gunter Dorner (1976, 1988) pioneered research on the influence of prenatal hormones by manipulating a fetal rat's exposure to male hormones, thereby "inverting" its sexual orientation. In other studies, when pregnant sheep were injected with testosterone during a critical period of fetal development, their female offspring later showed homosexual behavior (Money, 1987).

A critical period for the human brain's neural-hormonal control system may exist between the middle of the second and fifth months after conception (Ellis & Ames, 1987; Gladue, 1990; Meyer-Bahlburg, 1995). Exposure to the hormone levels typically experienced by female fetuses during this time appears to predispose the person (whether female or male) to be attracted to males in later life. "Prenatal sex hormones control the sexual differentiation of brain centers involved in sexual behaviors," notes Simon LeVay (2011, p. 216). Thus, female fetuses most exposed to testosterone, and male fetuses least exposed to testosterone, appear most likely later to exhibit gender-atypical traits and to experience same-sex desires.

"Modern scientific research indicates that sexual orientation is . . . partly determined by genetics, but more specifically by hormonal activity in the womb."

Glenn Wilson and Qazi Rahman, *Born Gay: The Psychobiology of Sex Orientation,* 2005

On several traits, gays and lesbians appear to fall midway between straight females and males (**TABLE 33.1**; see also LeVay, 2011; Rahman & Koerting, 2008). For example, lesbians' cochlea and hearing systems develop in a way that is intermediate between those of heterosexual females and heterosexual males, which seems attributable to prenatal hormonal influence (McFadden, 2002). Gay men tend to be shorter and lighter, even at birth, than straight men, while women in same-sex marriages were mostly heavier than average at birth (Bogaert, 2010; Frisch & Zdravkovic, 2010). Fingerprint ridge counts may also differ: Although most

TABLE 33.1

Biological Correlates of Sexual Orientation

Gay-straight trait differences

Sexual orientation is part of a package of traits. Studies—some in need of replication—indicate that homosexuals and heterosexuals differ in the following biological and behavioral traits.

- spatial abilities
- fingerprint ridge counts
- auditory system development
- handedness
- occupational preferences
- relative finger lengths
- gender nonconformity
- age of onset of puberty in males
- male body size
- sleep length
- physical aggression
- walking style

On average (the evidence is strongest for males), results for gays and lesbians fall between those of straight men and straight women. Three biological influences—brain, genetic, and prenatal—may contribute to these differences.

Brain differences

- One hypothalamic cell cluster is smaller in women and gay men than in straight men.
- Anterior commissure is larger in gay men than in straight men.
- Gay men's hypothalamus reacts as do straight women's to the smell of sex-related hormones.

Genetic influences

- Shared sexual orientation is higher among identical twins than among fraternal twins.
- Sexual attraction in fruit flies can be genetically manipulated.
- Male homosexuality often appears to be transmitted from the mother's side of the family.

Prenatal influences

- Altered prenatal hormone exposure may lead to homosexuality in humans and other animals.
- Right-handed men with several older biological brothers are more likely to be gay, possibly due to a maternal immune-system reaction.

people have more fingerprint ridges on their right hand than on their left, some studies find a greater right-left difference in heterosexual males than in females and gay males (Hall & Kimura, 1994; Mustanski et al., 2002; Sanders et al., 2002). Given that fingerprint ridges are complete by the sixteenth fetal week, this difference may be due to prenatal hormones. Prenatal hormones also are a possible explanation for why data from 20 studies revealed that "homosexual participants had 39 percent greater odds of being non-right-handed," and why men with older biological brothers are also more likely to be left-handed (Blanchard, 2008; Lalumière et al., 2000). In addition to these and other natural markers of sexual orientation, faces and facial expressions can enable people's "gaydar" to identify gays and lesbians with better than chance accuracy (Freeman et al., 2010; Rule & Ambady, 2008; Rule et al., 2011). Such differences often appear early, in the gender nonconformity of many (but not all) "pre-gay" children. In one study, raters viewed video clips of children without being told their later sexual orientation. The average pre-gay child was rated as more gender nonconforming than the average pre-straight child, especially after age 10 (Rieger et al., 2008).

Another you-never-would-have-guessed-it gay-straight difference appears in studies showing that gay men's spatial abilities resemble those typical of straight women (Cohen, 2002; Gladue, 1994; McCormick & Witelson, 1991; Sanders & Wright, 1997). On mental rotation tasks such as the one illustrated in **FIGURE 33.3** on the next page, straight men tend to outscore women. (So do women who were womb-mates of a male co-twin [Vuoksimaa et al., 2010].) Studies by Qazi Rahman and colleagues (2003, 2008) find that, as on a number of other measures, the scores of gays and lesbians fall between those of heterosexual males and females.

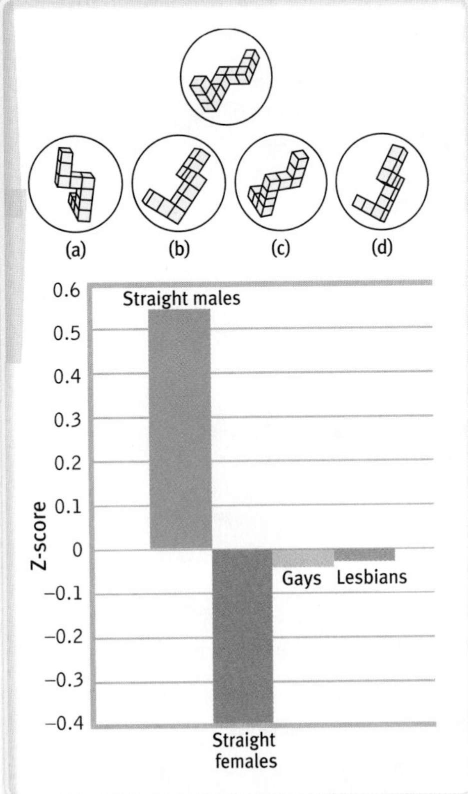

FIGURE 33.3
Spatial abilities and sexual orientation Which of the four figures can be rotated to match the target figure at the top? Straight males tend to find this an easier task than do straight females, with gays and lesbians intermediate. (From Rahman et al., 2003, with 60 people tested in each group.)

Answer: Figures a and d.

But straight women and gays both outperform straight men at remembering objects' spatial locations in tasks like those found in memory games (Hassan & Rahman, 2007).

The consistency of the brain, genetic, and prenatal findings has swung the pendulum toward a biological explanation of sexual orientation (Rahman & Wilson, 2003; Rahman & Koerting, 2008). This helps explain why sexual orientation is so difficult to change, and why a BBC Internet study of more than 200,000 people found the same gay-straight differences in personality and interests worldwide (Lippa, 2007a,b, 2008).

Still, some people wonder: Should the cause of sexual orientation matter? Perhaps it shouldn't, but people's assumptions matter. Those who believe that sexual orientation is biologically disposed also express more accepting attitudes toward homosexual people (Allen et al., 1996; Haslam & Levy, 2006; Kaiser, 2001; Whitley, 1990).

To gay and lesbian activists, the new biological research is a double-edged sword (Diamond, 1993; Roan, 2010). If sexual orientation, like skin color and sex, is genetically influenced, that offers a further rationale for civil rights protection. Moreover, it may alleviate parents' concerns about their children being unduly influenced by gay teachers and role models. At the same time, this research raises the troubling possibility that genetic markers of sexual orientation could someday be identified through fetal testing, that a fetus could be aborted simply for being predisposed to an unwanted orientation, or that hormonal treatment in the womb might engineer a desired orientation.

"There is no sound scientific evidence that sexual orientation can be changed."
UK Royal College of Psychiatrists, 2009

RETRIEVAL PRACTICE

- Which THREE of the following five factors have researchers found to have an effect on sexual orientation?

  a. A domineering mother
  b. Size of certain cell clusters in the hypothalamus
  c. Prenatal hormone exposure
  d. A distant or ineffectual father
  e. For men, having multiple older biological brothers

ANSWERS: b., c., e

Sex and Human Values

33-5 Is scientific research on sexual motivation value free?

Recognizing that values are both personal and cultural, most sex researchers and educators strive to keep their writings value free. But the very words we use to describe behavior can reflect our personal values. Whether we label certain sexual behaviors as "perversions" or as part of an "alternative sexual lifestyle" depends on our attitude toward the behaviors. Labels describe, but they also evaluate.

Sex education separated from the context of human values may also give some students the idea that sexual intercourse is simply a recreational activity. Diana Baumrind

(1982), a University of California child-rearing expert, observed that an implication that adults are neutral about adolescent sexual activity is unfortunate, because "promiscuous recreational sex poses certain psychological, social, health, and moral problems that must be faced realistically." One recent study asked 2035 married people when they started having sex (while controlling for education, religious engagement, and relationship length). Those whose relationship first developed to a deep commitment, such as marriage, reported greater relationship satisfaction and stability—and better sex (Busby et al., 2010).

Perhaps we can agree that the knowledge provided by sex research is preferable to ignorance, and yet also agree that researchers' values should be stated openly, enabling us to debate them and to reflect on our own values. We should remember that scientific research on sexual motivation does not aim to define the personal meaning of sex in our own lives. You could know every available fact about sex—that the initial spasms of male and female orgasm come at 0.8-second intervals, that the female nipples expand 10 millimeters at the peak of sexual arousal, that systolic blood pressure rises some 60 points and the respiration rate to 40 breaths per minute—but fail to understand the human significance of sexual intimacy.

Surely one significance of sexual intimacy is its expression of our profoundly social nature. Sex is a socially significant act. Men and women can achieve orgasm alone, yet most people find greater satisfaction—and experience a much greater surge in the prolactin hormone associated with sexual satisfaction and satiety—after intercourse and orgasm with their loved one (Brody & Tillmann, 2006). With the satisfaction of intimacy and relationship surpassing the satisfaction of self-stimulation, there is a yearning for closeness in sexual motivation. Sex at its human best is life-uniting and love-renewing.

A sharing of love For most adults, a sexual relationship fulfills not only a biological motive but also a social need for intimacy.

Yuri Arcurs/Shutterstock

The Need to Belong

33-6 What evidence points to our human need to belong?

Separated from friends or family—isolated in prison, alone at a new school, living in a foreign land—most people feel keenly their lost connections with important others. We are what Aristotle called *the social animal.* "Without friends," wrote Aristotle in his *Nichomachean Ethics,* "no one would choose to live, though he had all other goods." We have a need to affiliate with others, even to become strongly attached to certain others in enduring, close relationships. Human beings, contended the personality theorist Alfred Adler, have an "urge to community" (Ferguson, 1989, 2001, 2010). Roy Baumeister and Mark Leary (1995) have assembled evidence for this deep *need to belong.*

Photodisc

Aiding Survival

Social bonds boosted our ancestors' survival rate. By keeping children close to their caregivers, attachments served as a powerful survival impulse. As adults, those who formed attachments were more likely to reproduce and to co-nurture their offspring to maturity. To be "wretched" literally means, in its Middle English origin *(wrecche),* to be without kin nearby.

Survival also was enhanced by cooperation. In solo combat, our ancestors were not the toughest predators. But as hunters, they learned that six hands were better than two. As foragers, they gained protection from predators and enemies by traveling in groups. Those who felt a need to belong survived and reproduced most successfully, and their genes now predominate. We are innately social creatures. People in every society on Earth belong to groups and prefer and favor "us" over "them."

Do you have close friends—people with whom you freely disclose your ups and downs? Having someone who rejoices with us over good news helps us feel even better about the good news, as well as about the friendship (Reis et al., 2010). People who feel supported by close relationships also live with better health and at lower risk for psychological disorder and premature death than do those who lack social support. Married people, for example, are less at risk for depression, suicide, and early death than are unattached people.

"We must love one another or die."
W. H. Auden "September 1, 1939"

Wanting to Belong

The need to belong colors our thoughts and emotions. We spend a great deal of time thinking about actual and hoped-for relationships. When relationships form, we often feel joy. Falling in mutual love, people have been known to feel their cheeks ache from their irrepressible grins. Asked, "What is necessary for your happiness?" or "What is it that makes your life meaningful?" most people mention—before anything else—close, satisfying relationships with family, friends, or romantic partners (Berscheid, 1985). Happiness hits close to home.

Pause a moment to consider: What was your most satisfying moment in the past week? Kennon Sheldon and his colleagues (2001) asked that question of American and South Korean collegians, then asked them to rate how much this peak experience had satisfied various needs. In both countries, the satisfaction of self-esteem and relatedness-belonging needs were the top two contributors to the peak moment. Another study found that *very* happy university students are not distinguished by their money but by their "rich and satisfying close relationships" (Diener & Seligman, 2002). The need to belong runs deeper, it seems, than any need to be rich. When our need for relatedness is satisfied in balance with two other basic psychological needs—*autonomy* (a sense of personal control) and *competence*—the result is a deep sense of well-being (Deci & Ryan, 2002, 2009; Milyavskaya et al., 2009; Sheldon & Niemiec, 2006). To feel connected, free, and capable is to enjoy a good life.

South Africans have a word for the human bonds that define us all. *Ubuntu* [oo-BOON-too], explained Desmond Tutu (1999), expresses the fact that "my humanity is caught up, is inextricably bound up, in yours." A Zulu maxim captures the idea: *Umuntu ngumuntu ngabantu*—"a person is a person through other persons."

When we feel included, accepted, and loved by those important to us, our self-esteem rides high. Indeed, say Mark Leary and his colleagues (1998), self-esteem is a gauge of how valued and accepted we feel. Much of our social behavior therefore aims to increase our belonging—our social acceptance and inclusion. To avoid rejection, we generally conform to group standards and seek to make favorable impressions. To win friendship and esteem, we monitor our behavior, hoping to create the right impressions. Seeking love and belonging, we spend billions on clothes, cosmetics, and diet and fitness aids—all motivated by our quest for acceptance.

Like sexual motivation, which feeds both love and exploitation, the need to belong feeds both deep attachments and menacing threats. Out of our need to define a "we" come loving families, faithful friendships, and team spirit, but also teen gangs, ethnic rivalries, and fanatic nationalism.

Sustaining Relationships

For most of us, familiarity breeds liking, not contempt. Thrown together in groups at school, at summer camp, on a vacation cruise, we later resist breaking those social bonds—we promise to call, to write, to come back for reunions. Parting, we feel distress.

When the fear of being alone seems worse than the pain of emotional or physical abuse, attachments can keep people in abusive relationships. Even when bad relationships break, people suffer. After separations, feelings of loneliness and anger—and sometimes even a strange desire to be near the former partner—linger. In one 16-nation survey, and in U.S. surveys, separated and divorced people have been half as likely as married people to say they were "very happy" (Inglehart, 1990; NORC, 2010).

AP/Wide World Photos

The need to connect Six days a week, women from the Philippines work as "domestic helpers" in 154,000 Hong Kong households. On Sundays, they throng to the central business district to picnic, dance, sing, talk, and laugh. "Humanity could stage no greater display of happiness," reported one observer (*Economist,* 2001).

Our fear of being alone has some basis in reality. Children who move through a series of foster homes or through repeated family relocations, with repeated disruption of budding attachments, may come to have difficulty forming deep attachments (Oishi & Schimmack, 2011). And children reared in institutions without a sense of belonging to anyone, or locked away at home under extreme neglect, become pathetic creatures—withdrawn, frightened, speechless.

Much as life's best moments occur when close relationships begin—making a new friend, falling in love, having a baby—life's worst moments are when close relationships end (Jaremka et al., 2011). When something threatens or dissolves our social ties, anxiety, loneliness, jealousy, or guilt may overwhelm us. The bereaved often feel life is empty, pointless. Even the first weeks living on a college campus away from home can be distressing. For immigrants and refugees moving alone to new places, the stress and loneliness can be depressing. Social isolation also puts us at risk for mental decline and ill health (Cacioppo & Hawkley, 2009). But if feelings of acceptance and connection increase, so will self-esteem, positive feelings, and desires to help rather than hurt others (Blackhart et al., 2009; Buckley & Leary, 2001). After years of placing individual refugee and immigrant families in isolated communities, U.S. policies began to encourage *chain migration* (Pipher, 2002). The second refugee Sudanese family settling in a town generally has an easier adjustment than the first.

The Pain of Ostracism

Sometimes, though, our need to belong is denied. Perhaps you can recall feeling excluded or ignored or shunned. Perhaps you received the silent treatment. Perhaps others avoided you, or averted their eyes in your presence, or even mocked you behind your back. If you are like others, even just being a linguistic outsider among people speaking a different language may have left you feeling excluded (Dotan-Eliaz, 2009).

Social psychologist Kipling Williams (2007, 2009) and his colleagues have studied such experiences of *ostracism*—of social exclusion—in both natural and laboratory settings. Worldwide, humans control social behavior via the punishing effects of severe ostracism—of exile, imprisonment, and solitary confinement. For children, even a brief time-out in isolation can be punishing. Asked to describe personal episodes that made them feel especially good about themselves, people often think of some achievement. But asked what made them feel especially *bad* about themselves, they will—about four times in five—describe a relationship difficulty (Pillemer et al., 2007).

Being shunned—given the cold shoulder or the silent treatment, with others' eyes avoiding yours—threatens one's need to belong (Williams & Zadro, 2001). "It's the

The need to belong Because of the human desire for connection, solitary confinement is, with the exception of torture, the worst punishment.

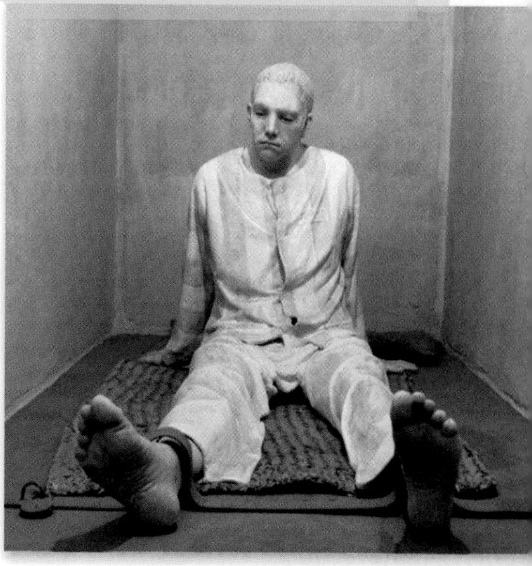

Robin Nelson/ZUMA Press/ Newscom

AFP/Getty Images

A violent response to social exclusion Although most socially excluded teens do not commit violence, ostracism is a risk factor. This teen, described by a classmate as someone his peers taunted as "freak, dork, nerd, stuff like that," went on a shooting spree at his suburban California high school, killing 2 and wounding 13 (Bowles & Kasindorf, 2001).

meanest thing you can do to someone, especially if you know they can't fight back. I never should have been born," said Lea, a lifelong victim of the silent treatment by her mother and grandmother. Like Lea, people often respond to social ostracism with depressed moods, initial efforts to restore their acceptance, and then withdrawal. After two years of silent treatment by his employer, Richard reported, "I came home every night and cried. I lost 25 pounds, had no self-esteem and felt that I wasn't worthy."

To experience ostracism is to experience real pain, as Williams and his colleagues were surprised to discover in their studies of *cyber-ostracism* (Gonsalkorale & Williams, 2006). (Perhaps you can recall the feeling of being ignored in a chat room or having e-mail go unanswered.) Such ostracism, they discovered, even by strangers or by a despised outgroup, such as the Australian branch of the KKK, takes a toll: It elicits increased activity in brain areas, such as the *anterior cingulate cortex*, that also activate in response to physical pain (Kross et al., 2011; Lieberman & Eisenberger, 2009). That helps explain a surprising finding: The pain-reliever acetaminophen (as in Tylenol and Anacin) lessens *social* as well as physical pain (DeWall et al., 2010). Psychologically, we seem to experience social pain with the same emotional unpleasantness that marks physical pain (MacDonald & Leary, 2005). Pain, whatever its source, focuses our attention and motivates corrective action.

Feelings of love (the opposite of ostracism) activate brain reward systems. In one experiment, deeply-in-love university students felt markedly less pain when looking at their beloved's picture (rather than viewing someone else's photo, or being distracted by a word task). The pleasure of love is a natural painkiller (Younger et al., 2010).

Rejected and unable to remedy the situation, people may seek new friends or gain stress relief by a strengthened religious faith (Aydin et al., 2010). Or they may turn nasty. In a series of experiments, Jean Twenge and her collaborators (2001, 2002, 2007; Baumeister et al., 2002; Maner et al., 2007) told some students (who had taken a personality test) that they were "the type likely to end up alone later in life," or that people they had met didn't want them in a group that was forming. They told other students that they would have "rewarding relationships throughout life," or that "everyone chose you as someone they'd like to work with." Those excluded became much more likely to engage in self-defeating behaviors and to underperform on aptitude tests. The rejection also interfered with their empathy for others and made them more likely to act in disparaging or aggressive ways against those who had excluded them (blasting them with noise, for example). "If intelligent, well-adjusted, successful . . . students can turn aggressive in response to a small laboratory experience of social exclusion," noted the research team, "it is disturbing to imagine the aggressive tendencies that might arise from . . . chronic exclusion from desired groups in actual social life." Indeed, reports Williams (2007), ostracism "weaves through case after case of school violence."

Note: The researchers later *debriefed* and reassured the participants.

RETRIEVAL PRACTICE

- How have students reacted in studies where they were made to feel rejected and unwanted? What helps explain these results?

ANSWER: These students' basic *need to belong* seems to have been disrupted. They engaged in more self-defeating behaviors, underperformed on aptitude tests, and displayed less empathy and more aggression.

Social Networking

33-7 How does social networking influence us?

As social creatures, we live for connection. Asked what he had learned from studying 238 Harvard University men from the 1930s to the end of their lives, researcher George Vaillant (2009) replied, "The only thing that really matters in life are your relationships to other people."

Mobile Networks and Social Media

Look around and see humans connecting: talking, but also texting, posting, chatting, social gaming, or e-mailing. The changes in how we connect are fast and vast.

- Cell phones have been history's most rapidly adopted technology. At the end of 2010, the world had 6.9 billion people and 5.3 billion mobile cell-phone subscriptions (ITU, 2010). Asia and Europe lead the way. In India, the 618 million people with mobile phone access are reportedly almost double the 366 million with access to a toilet (*Harper's*, 2010). But American youth are up with the world: 85 percent of 15- to 18-year-olds are cell-phone users (Kaiser, 2010).
- Texting and e-mailing are displacing phone talking, which now accounts for less than half of U.S. mobile network traffic (Wortham, 2010). Moreover, in Canada and elsewhere, texting, Facebook, and other messaging technology have led to declining e-mails (IPSOS, 2010a).
- Ninety percent of U.S. teens text, up from 50 percent in 2006. Half (mostly females) send 50 or more texts daily; one-third send 200 (Lenhart, 2010). For many, it's as though friends, for better or worse, are always present.
- How many of us are using social networking sites, such as Facebook? Among 2010's entering American collegians, 94 percent were (Pryor et al., 2010). If a "critical mass" of your friends are on a social network, its lure becomes hard to resist. If you don't check in, you may feel you're missing out. Such is our need to belong. The average number of Facebook friends is about 125—near the 150 people with whom evolutionary psychologist Robin Dunbar (1992, 2010) estimates we can have meaningful, supportive relationships (also a typical size of tribal villages).

Thomas Northcut/Jupiterimages

"There's no question in my mind about what stands at the heart of the communication revolution—the human desire to connect."

Skype President Josh Silverman, 2009

The Social Effects of Social Networking

By connecting like-minded people, the Internet serves as a social amplifier. It also functions as an online dating matchmaker. As electronic communication becomes part of the "new normal," researchers are exploring how these changes affect our relationships.

Are Social Networking Sites Making Us More, or Less, Socially Isolated? When online communication in chat rooms and during social games was mostly between strangers in the Internet's early years, adolescents and adults who spent more time online spent less time with friends, and their offline relationships suffered as a result (Kraut et al., 1998; Mesch, 2001; Nie, 2001). Even today, lonely people tend to spend greater-than-average time online (Bonetti et al., 2010; Stepanikova et al., 2010). Social networkers are also less likely to know their real-world neighbors and are "64 percent less likely than non-Internet users to rely on neighbors for help in caring for themselves or a family member" (Pew, 2009).

But some things are changing. The Internet is diversifying our social networks. (I am now connected to other hearing-technology advocates across the world.) And despite the decrease in neighborliness, social networking is mostly strengthening our connections with people we already know (DiSalvo, 2010; Valkenburg & Peter, 2010). If your Facebook page helps you connect with friends, stay in touch with extended family, or find support in facing challenges, then you are not alone (Rainie et al., 2011). And if you are like other students, two days of Facebook deprivation would be followed by a glut of Facebook use, much as you would eat voraciously after a two-day food fast (Sheldon et al., 2011).

ICP-UK/Alamy

© 2009 Isabella Bannerman. King Features Syndicate

Does Electronic Communication Stimulate Healthy Self-Disclosure? Confiding in others can be a healthy way of coping with day-to-day challenges. When communicating electronically rather than face to face, we often are less focused on others' reactions, less self-conscious, and thus less inhibited. We become more willing to share joys, worries, and vulnerabilities. Sometimes this is taken to an extreme, as when "sexting" teens send nude photos of themselves, youth are "cyber-bullied," or hate groups post messages promoting bigotry or crimes. More often, however, the increased self-disclosure serves to deepen friendships (Valkenburg & Peter, 2010). Although electronic networking pays dividends, nature has designed us for face-to-face communication, which appears to be the better predictor of life satisfaction (Killingsworth & Gilbert, 2010; Lee et al., 2011). Texting and e-mailing are rewarding, but eye-to-eye conversation with family and friends is even more so.

Do Social Networking Profiles and Posts Reflect People's Actual Personalities? We've all heard stories of Internet predators hiding behind false personalities, values, and motives. Generally, however, social networks reveal people's real personalities. In one study, participants completed a personality test twice. In one test, they described their "actual personality"; in the other, they described their "ideal self." Volunteers then used the participants' Facebook profiles to create an independent set of personality ratings. The ratings based on Facebook profiles were much closer to the participants' actual personalities than to their ideal personalities (Back et al., 2010). In another study, people who seemed most likable on their Facebook page also seemed most likable in face-to-face meetings (Weisbuch et al., 2009). So, your Facebook profile may indeed reflect the real you!

Does Social Networking Promote Narcissism? A secure and positive self-esteem can benefit our health and well-being, but self-esteem gone awry becomes *narcissism*. Narcissistic people are self-important, self-focused, and self-promoting. Some personality tests assess narcissism with items such as "I like to be the center of attention." Given our constant social comparison—our measuring ourselves against others—many Facebook users can't resist comparing numbers of friends. Those who score high on narcissism are especially active on social networking sites. They collect more superficial "friends." They offer more staged, glamorous photos. And, not surprisingly, they *seem* more narcissistic to strangers viewing their pages (Buffardi & Campbell, 2008).

Social networking sites are not just a gathering place for narcissists. They are also a feeding trough. In one study, college students were randomly assigned either to edit and explain their MySpace page for 15 minutes, or to use that time to study and explain a Google Maps routing (Freeman & Twenge, 2010). After completing their tasks, all were tested. Who then scored higher on a narcissism measure? Those who had spent the time focused on themselves.

Maintaining Balance and Focus

So social networks connect us. But they can also, as you've surely noticed, become a gigantic time- and attention-sucking diversion. In both Taiwan and the United States, excessive online socializing and gaming have been associated with lower grades (Chen &

Fu, 2008; Kaiser Foundation, 2010). In one U.S. survey, 47 percent of the heaviest users of the Internet and other media were receiving mostly C grades or lower, as were 23 percent of the lightest users (Kaiser Foundation, 2010). Except for sleep, the heaviest users may be almost constantly connected.

In today's world, each of us is challenged to find a healthy balance between our real-world tasks, our time with people, and our online sharing. If you're trying to maintain a healthy balance of online connecting with friends and meeting your real-world responsibilities, experts offer some practical suggestions.

- ***Monitor your time.*** Keep a log of how you use your time. Then ask yourself, "Does my time use reflect my priorities? Am I spending more time online than I intended? Is my time online interfering with school or work performance? Have family or friends commented on this?"
- ***Monitor your feelings.*** Again, ask yourself, "Am I emotionally distracted by excessive online preoccupations? When I get up from my computer, how do I feel?"
- ***"Hide" your more distracting online friends.*** And in your own postings, practice the golden rule. Before you post, ask yourself, "Is this something I'd care about reading if someone else posted it?"
- ***Try turning off your handheld devices or leaving them elsewhere.*** Selective attention—the flashlight of your mind—can be in only one place at a time. "One of the most stubborn, persistent phenomenon of the mind," notes cognitive psychologist Daniel Willingham (2010), "is that when you do two things at once, you don't do either one as well as when you do them one at a time." When you want to study or work productively, squelch the temptation to check for e-mails, messages, or posts. And disable sound alerts and pop-ups. These distractions can interrupt your work and hijack your attention just when you've managed to get focused.
- ***Try a Facebook fast (give it up for an hour, a day, or a week) or a time-controlled social media diet (check in only after homework is done, or only during a lunch break).*** Take notes on what you're losing and gaining on your new "diet."
- ***Replenish your focus with a nature walk.*** University of Michigan researchers report that a walk in the woods, unlike walking a busy street, replenishes people's capacity for focused attention (Berman et al., 2008). People learn better after a peaceful walk that restores their fatigued attention.

"The solution is not to bemoan technology but to develop strategies of self-control, as we do with every other temptation in life."

Psychologist Steven Pinker, "Mind Over Mass Media," 2010

DOONESBURY © 2011 G. B. Trudeau. Reprinted with permission of UNIVERSAL UCLICK. All Rights Reserved.

RETRIEVAL PRACTICE

- Social networking tends to __________ (strengthen/weaken) your relationships with people you already know, __________ (increase/decrease) your self-disclosure, and __________ (reveal/hide) your true personality.

ANSWERS: strengthen; increase; reveal

MODULE REVIEW

Sexual Motivation and the Need to Belong

Learning Objectives

RETRIEVAL PRACTICE Take a moment to answer each of these Learning Objective Questions (repeated here from within the module). Then turn to Appendix B, Complete Module Reviews, to check your answers. Research suggests that trying to answer these questions on your own will improve your long-term retention (McDaniel et al., 2009).

33-1: What physiological factors affect human sexual behavior, and what disorders disrupt the sexual response cycle?

33-2: How do hormones, and external and internal stimuli, influence human sexual motivation?

33-3: What factors influence teen pregnancy and risk of sexually transmitted infections?

33-4: What has research taught us about sexual orientation?

33-5: Is scientific research on sexual motivation value free?

33-6: What evidence points to our human need to belong?

33-7: How does social networking influence us?

Terms and Concepts to Remember

RETRIEVAL PRACTICE Test yourself on these terms by trying to write down the definition before flipping back to the referenced page to check your answer.

sexual response cycle, p. 435
refractory period, p. 436
sexual disorder, p. 436
estrogens, p. 436
testosterone, p. 436
sexual orientation, p. 442

RETRIEVAL PRACTICE Gain an advantage, and benefit from immediate feedback, with the interactive self-testing resources at www.worthpublishers.com/myers.

MODULE 34

Motivation at Work

- Personnel Psychology
- Organizational Psychology: Motivating Achievement
- The Human Factor

34-1 What is "flow," and what are the three subfields of industrial-organizational psychology?

For most of us, work is life's biggest single waking activity. To live is to work. Work helps satisfy several levels of need identified in Maslow's pyramid of needs. Work supports us. Work connects us. Work defines us. Meeting someone for the first time, and wondering "Who are you?" we may ask, "So, what do you do?"

Amy Wrzesniewski and her colleagues (1997, 2001) have identified person-to-person variations in people's attitudes toward their work. Across various occupations, some people view their work as a *job*, an unfulfilling but necessary way to make money. Others view their work as a *career*, an opportunity to advance from one position to a better position. The rest—those who view their work as a *calling*, a fulfilling and socially useful activity—report the highest satisfaction with their work and with their lives.

This finding would not surprise Mihaly Csikszentmihalyi (1990, 1999). He has observed that people's quality of life increases when they are purposefully engaged. Between the anxiety of being overwhelmed and stressed, and the apathy of being underwhelmed and bored, lies a zone in which people experience **flow.** Can you recall being in a zoned-out flow state while playing a video game or text messaging? If so, then perhaps you can sympathize with the two Northwest Airlines pilots who in 2009 were so focused on their laptops that they missed Earth-to-pilot messages from their control tower. The pilots flew 150 miles past their Minneapolis destination—and lost their jobs.

Csikszentmihalyi [chick-SENT-me-hi] formulated the flow concept after studying artists who spent hour after hour painting or sculpting with enormous concentration. Immersed in a project, they worked as if nothing else mattered, and then, when finished, they promptly forgot about it. The artists seemed driven less by the external rewards of producing art—money, praise, promotion—than by the intrinsic rewards of creating the work.

Csikszentmihalyi's later observations—of dancers, chess players, surgeons, writers, parents, mountain climbers, sailors, and farmers; of Australians, North Americans, Koreans, Japanese, and Italians; of people from their teens to their golden years—confirmed an overriding principle: It's exhilarating to flow with an activity that fully engages our skills. Flow experiences boost our sense of self-esteem, competence, and well-being. Idleness may sound like bliss, but purposeful work enriches our lives. Busy people are happier (Hsee et al., 2010; Robinson & Martin, 2008). One research team interrupted people on about a quarter-million occasions (using an iPhone application), and found people's minds wandering 47 percent of the time. They were, on average, happier when *not* mind-wandering (Killingsworth & Gilbert, 2010).

Sometimes, notes Gene Weingarten (2002), a humor writer knows "when to just get out of the way." Here are some sample job titles from the U.S. Department of Labor *Dictionary of Occupational Titles:* Animal impersonator, human projectile, banana ripening-room supervisor, impregnator, impregnator helper, dope sprayer, finger waver, rug scratcher, egg smeller, bottom buffer, cookie breaker, brain picker, hand pouncer, bosom presser, and mother repairer.

Have you ever noticed that when you are immersed in an activity, time flies? And that when you are watching the clock, it seems to move more slowly? French researchers have confirmed that the more we attend to an event's duration, the longer it seems to last (Couli et al., 2004).

Hill Street Studios/Matthew Palmer/Jupiterimages

Disrupted flow Internet-related distractions can disrupt flow. It takes time to refocus mental concentration after the distraction of an e-mail or text message.

flow a completely involved, focused state of consciousness, with diminished awareness of self and time, resulting from optimal engagement of one's skills.

CLOSE-UP

I/O Psychology at Work

As scientists, consultants, and management professionals, industrial-organizational psychologists are found working in varied areas:

Personnel Psychology

Selecting and placing employees

- Developing and validating assessment tools for selecting, placing, and promoting workers
- Analyzing job content
- Optimizing worker placement

Training and developing employees

- Identifying needs
- Designing training programs
- Evaluating training programs

Appraising performance

- Developing criteria
- Measuring individual performance
- Measuring organizational performance

Organizational Psychology

Developing organizations

- Analyzing organizational structures
- Maximizing worker satisfaction and productivity
- Facilitating organizational change

Enhancing quality of work life

- Expanding individual productivity
- Identifying elements of satisfaction
- Redesigning jobs

Human Factors (Engineering) Psychology

- Designing optimum work environments
- Optimizing person-machine interactions
- Developing systems technologies

Source: Adapted from the Society of Industrial and Organizational Psychology (www.siop.org).

The modern workforce The editorial team that supports the creation of this book and its teaching package works both in-house and remotely from far-flung places. Clockwise from top left are Nancy Fleming in Massachusetts, Kevin Feyen in New York, Betty Probert and Don Probert in Florida, Christine Brune in Alaska, Trish Morgan in Alberta, Tracey Kuehn in New York, and Kathryn Brownson in Michigan.

In many nations, work has been changing, from farming to manufacturing to *knowledge work*. More and more work is outsourced to temporary employees and consultants or done by telecommuters who communicate electronically from virtual workplaces in remote locations. As work changes, will our attitudes toward our work also change? Will our satisfaction with work increase or decrease? Will the *psychological contract*—the sense of mutual obligations between workers and employers—become more or less trusting and secure? These are among the questions that fascinate psychologists who study work-related behavior.

Industrial-organizational (I/O) psychology applies psychology's principles to the workplace (see Close-Up: I/O Psychology at Work). Here we consider three of I/O psychology's subfields:

- **Personnel psychology** applies psychology's methods and principles to selecting and evaluating workers. Personnel psychologists match people with jobs, by identifying and placing well-suited candidates.
- **Organizational psychology** considers how work environments and management styles influence worker motivation, satisfaction, and productivity. Organizational psychologists modify jobs and supervision in ways that boost morale and productivity.
- **Human factors psychology** explores how machines and environments can be optimally designed to fit human abilities. Human factors psychologists study people's natural perceptions and inclinations to create user-friendly machines and work settings.

RETRIEVAL PRACTICE

- What is the value of finding flow in our work?

ANSWER: We become more likely to view our work as fulfilling and socially useful.

Personnel Psychology

34-2 How do personnel psychologists help organizations with employee selection, work placement, and performance appraisal?

Psychologists can assist organizations at various stages of selecting and assessing employees. They may help identify needed job skills, decide upon selection methods, recruit and evaluate applicants, introduce and train new employees, and appraise their performance.

industrial-organizational (I/O) psychology the application of psychological concepts and methods to optimizing human behavior in workplaces.

personnel psychology a subfield of I/O psychology that focuses on employee recruitment, selection, placement, training, appraisal, and development.

organizational psychology a subfield of I/O psychology that examines organizational influences on worker satisfaction and productivity and facilitates organizational change.

human factors psychology a subfield of I/O psychology that explores how people and machines interact and how machines and physical environments can be made safe and easy to use.

Harnessing Strengths

As a new AT&T human resources executive, psychologist Mary Tenopyr (1997) was assigned to solve a problem: Customer-service representatives were failing at a high rate. After concluding that many of the hires were ill-matched to the demands of their new job, Tenopyr developed a new selection instrument:

1. She asked new applicants to respond to various questions (without as yet making any use of their responses).
2. She followed up later to assess which of the applicants excelled on the job.
3. She identified the individual items on the earlier test that best predicted who would succeed.

The happy result of her data-driven work was a new test that enabled AT&T to identify likely-to-succeed customer-service representatives. Personnel selection techniques such as this one aim to match people's strengths with work that enables them and their organization to flourish. Marry the strengths of people with the tasks of organizations and the result is often prosperity and profit.

Your strengths are any enduring qualities that can be productively applied. Are you naturally curious? Persuasive? Charming? Persistent? Competitive? Analytical? Empathic? Organized? Articulate? Neat? Mechanical? Any such trait, if matched with suitable work, can function as a strength (Buckingham, 2007). (See Close-Up: Discovering Your Strengths on the next page.)

Gallup researchers Marcus Buckingham and Donald Clifton (2001) have argued that the first step to a stronger organization is instituting a *strengths-based selection system.* Thus, as a manager, you would first identify a group of the most effective people in any role—the ones you would want to hire more of—and compare their strengths with those of a group of the least effective people in that role. In defining these groups, you would try to measure performance as objectively as possible. In one Gallup study of more than 5000 telecommunications customer-service representatives, those evaluated most favorably by their managers were strong in "harmony" and "responsibility," while those actually rated most effective by customers were strong in energy, assertiveness, and eagerness to learn.

An example: If you needed to hire new people in software development, and you had discovered that your best software developers are analytical, disciplined, and eager to learn, you would focus employment ads less on experience than on the identified strengths. Thus "Do you take a logical and systematic approach to problem solving [*analytical*]? Are you a perfectionist who strives for timely completion of your projects [*disciplined*]? Do you want

Artistic strengths At age 21, Henri Matisse was a sickly and often depressed lawyer's clerk. When his mother gave him a box of paints to cheer him up one day, he felt the darkness lift and his energy surge. He began to fill his days with painting and drawing and went on to art school and a life as one of the world's great painters. For Matisse, doing art felt like "a comfortable armchair." That is how exercising our strengths often feels.

© CNAC/MNAM/Dist. Réunion des Musées Nationaux/Art Resource, NY

CLOSE-UP

Discovering Your Strengths

You can use some of the techniques personnel psychologists have developed to identify your own strengths and pinpoint types of work that will likely prove satisfying and successful. Buckingham and Clifton (2001) have suggested asking yourself these questions:

- What activities give me pleasure? (Bringing order out of chaos? Playing host? Helping others? Challenging sloppy thinking?)
- What activities leave me wondering, "When can I do this again?" (Rather than, "When will this be over?")
- What sorts of challenges do I relish? (And which do I dread?)
- What sorts of tasks do I learn easily? (And which do I struggle with?)

Some people find themselves in flow—their skills engaged and time flying—when teaching or selling or writing or cleaning or consoling or creating or repairing. If an activity feels good, if it comes easily, if you look forward to it, then look deeper and see your strengths at work.

Satisfied and successful people devote far less time to correcting their deficiencies than to accentuating their strengths. Top performers are "rarely well rounded," Buckingham and Clifton found (p. 26). Instead, they have sharpened their existing skills. Given the persistence of our traits and temperaments, we should focus not on our deficiencies, but rather on identifying and employing our talents. There may be limits to the benefits of assertiveness training if you are extremely shy, of public speaking courses if you tend to be nervous and soft-spoken, or of drawing classes if you express your artistic side in stick figures.

But identifying your talents can help you recognize the activities you learn quickly and find absorbing. Knowing your strengths, you can develop them further.

to master Java, C++, and PHP *[eager to learn]*? If you can say *Yes* to these questions, then please call . . ."

Identifying people's strengths and matching strengths to work is a first step toward workplace effectiveness. To assess applicants' strengths and decide who is best-suited to the job, personnel managers use various tools (Sackett & Lievens, 2008), including ability tests, personality tests, and behavioral observations in "assessment centers" that stimulate job tasks. Here we focus on job interviews.

Do Interviews Predict Performance?

Interviewers tend to feel confident in their ability to predict long-term job performance from an unstructured, get-acquainted interview. What's therefore shocking is how error-prone those predictions are. Whether predicting job or graduate school success, interviewers' judgments are weak predictors. From their review of 85 years of personnel-selection research, I/O psychologists Frank Schmidt and John Hunter (1998; Schmidt, 2002) determined that for all but less-skilled jobs, general mental ability best predicts on-the-job performance. Subjective overall evaluations from informal interviews are more useful than handwriting analysis (which is worthless). But informal interviews are less informative than aptitude tests, work samples, job knowledge tests, and past job performance. If there's a contest between what our gut tells us about someone and what test scores, work samples, and past performance tell us, we should distrust our gut.

"Interviews are a terrible predictor of performance."

Laszlo Bock, Google's Vice President, People Operations, 2007

The Interviewer Illusion

Richard Nisbett (1987) has labeled interviewers' overrating their discernment as the *interviewer illusion*. "I have excellent interviewing skills, so I don't need reference checking as much as someone who doesn't have my ability to read people," is a comment sometimes heard by I/O consultants. Four factors explain this gap between interviewers' overconfidence and the resulting reality:

"Between the idea and reality . . . falls the shadow."

T. S. Eliot, *The Hollow Men*, 1925

- *Interviews disclose the interviewee's good intentions, which are less revealing than habitual behaviors* (Ouellette & Wood, 1998). Intentions matter. People can change. But the best predictor of the person we will be is the person we have been. Compared with work-avoiding university students, those who engage in their tasks are more likely, a decade and more later, to be engaged workers (Salmela-Aro et al., 2009). Educational attainments predict job performance partly because people who have shown up for school each day and done their tasks also tend to show up for work and do their tasks (Ng & Feldman, 2009). Wherever we go, we take ourselves along.

- *Interviewers more often follow the successful careers of those they have hired than the successful careers of those they have rejected and lost track of.* This missing feedback prevents interviewers from getting a reality check on their hiring ability.
- *Interviewers presume that people are what they seem to be in the interview situation.* When meeting others, we discount the enormous influence of varying situations and mistakenly presume that what we see is what we will get. But mountains of research on everything from chattiness to conscientiousness reveal that how we behave reflects not only our enduring traits but also the details of the particular situation (such as wanting to impress in a job interview).
- *Interviewers' preconceptions and moods color how they perceive interviewees' responses* (Cable & Gilovich, 1998; Macan & Dipboye, 1994). If interviewers instantly like a person who perhaps is similar to themselves, they may interpret the person's assertiveness as indicating "confidence" rather than "arrogance." If told certain applicants have been prescreened, interviewers are disposed to judge them more favorably.

Traditional *unstructured interviews* do provide a sense of someone's personality—their expressiveness, warmth, and verbal ability, for example. But unstructured interviews also give interviewees considerable power to control the impression they are making in the interview situation (Barrick et al., 2009). The interview may thus create a false impression of the person's behavior toward others in different situations. Hoping to improve prediction and selection, personnel psychologists have put people in simulated work situations, scoured sources for information on past performance, aggregated evaluations from multiple interviews, administered tests, and developed job-specific interviews.

Structured Interviews

Unlike casual conversation aimed at getting a feel for someone, **structured interviews** offer a disciplined method of collecting information. A personnel psychologist may analyze a job, script questions, and train interviewers. The interviewers then put the same questions, in the same order, to all applicants, and rate each applicant on established scales.

In an unstructured interview, someone might ask, "How organized are you?" "How well do you get along with people?" or "How do you handle stress?" Street-smart applicants know how to score high: "Although I sometimes drive myself too hard, I handle stress by prioritizing and delegating, and by making sure I leave time for sleep and exercise."

By contrast, structured interviews pinpoint strengths (attitudes, behaviors, knowledge, and skills) that distinguish high performers in a particular line of work. The process includes outlining job-specific situations and asking candidates to explain how they would handle them, and how they handled similar situations in their prior employment. "Tell me about a time when you were caught between conflicting demands, without time to accomplish both. How did you handle that?"

To reduce memory distortions and bias, the interviewer takes notes and makes ratings as the interview proceeds and avoids irrelevant and follow-up questions. The structured interview therefore feels less warm, but that can be explained to the applicant: "This conversation won't typify how we relate to each other in this organization."

A review of 150 findings revealed that structured interviews had double the predictive accuracy of unstructured seat-of-the-pants interviews (Schmidt & Hunter, 1998; Wiesner & Cronshaw, 1988). Structured interviews also reduce bias, such as against overweight applicants (Kutcher & Bragger, 2004). Thanks partly to its greater reliability and partly to its job-analysis focus, the predictive power of one structured interview is roughly equal to

structured interviews interview process that asks the same job-relevant questions of all applicants, each of whom is rated on established scales.

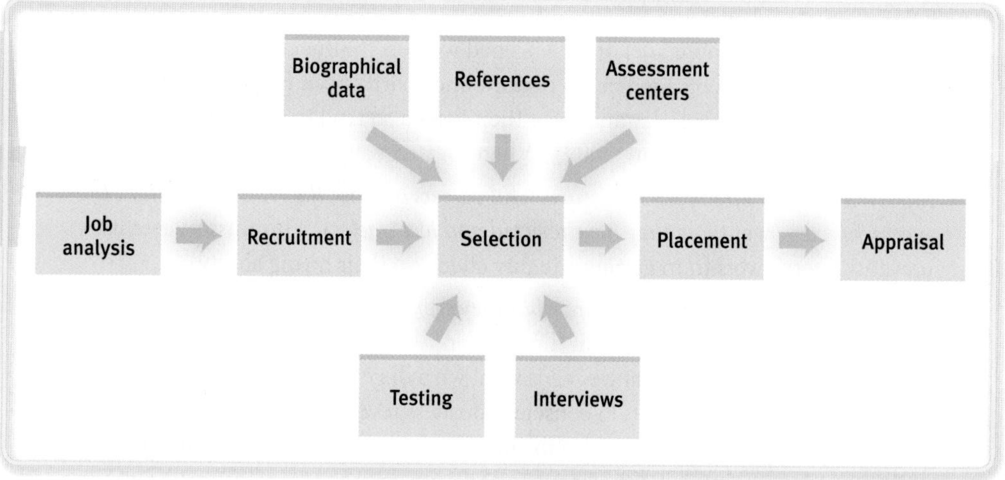

FIGURE 34.1
Personnel psychologists' tasks Personnel psychologists consult in human resources activities, from job definition to employee appraisal.

that of the average judgment from three or four unstructured interviews (Huffcutt et al., 2001; Schmidt & Zimmerman, 2004).

If, instead, we let our intuitions bias the hiring process, notes Malcolm Gladwell (2000, p. 86), then "all we will have done is replace the old-boy network, where you hired your nephew, with the new-boy network, where you hire whoever impressed you most when you shook his hand. Social progress, unless we're careful, can merely be the means by which we replace the obviously arbitrary with the not so obviously arbitrary."

To recap, personnel psychologists assist organizations in analyzing jobs, recruiting well-suited applicants, selecting and placing employees, and appraising their performance (**FIGURE 34.1**)—the topic we turn to next.

Appraising Performance

Performance appraisal serves organizational purposes: It helps decide who to retain, how to appropriately reward and pay people, and how to better harness employee strengths, sometimes with job shifts or promotions. Performance appraisal also serves individual purposes: Feedback affirms workers' strengths and helps motivate needed improvements.

Performance appraisal methods include

- *checklists* on which supervisors simply check specific behaviors that describe the worker ("always attends to customers' needs," "takes long breaks").
- *graphic rating scales* on which a supervisor checks, perhaps on a five-point scale, how often a worker is dependable, productive, and so forth.
- *behavior rating scales* on which a supervisor checks scaled behaviors that describe a worker's performance. If rating the extent to which a worker "follows procedures," the supervisor might mark the employee somewhere between "often takes shortcuts" and "always follows established procedures" (Levy, 2003).

FIGURE 34.2
360-degree feedback With multisource 360-degree feedback, our knowledge, skills, and behaviors are rated by ourselves and surrounding others. Professors, for example, may be rated by their department chairs, their students, and their colleagues. After receiving all these ratings, professors discuss the 360-degree feedback with their department chair.

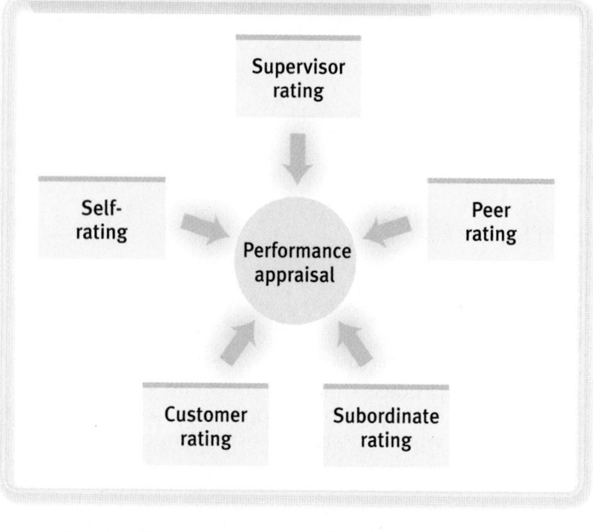

In some organizations, performance feedback comes not only from supervisors but also from all organizational levels. If you join an organization that practices *360-degree feedback* (**FIGURE 34.2**), you will rate yourself, your manager, and your other colleagues, and you will be rated by your manager, other colleagues, and customers (Green, 2002). The net result is often more open communication and more complete appraisal.

Performance appraisal, like other social judgments, is vulnerable to bias (Murphy & Cleveland, 1995). *Halo errors* occur when one's overall evaluation of an employee, or of a personal trait such as their friendliness, biases ratings of their specific work-related behaviors, such as their reliability. *Leniency* and *severity errors* reflect evaluators' tendencies to be either too easy or too harsh on everyone. *Recency errors* occur when raters focus only on easily

Setting Specific, Challenging Goals

In everyday life, our achievement goals sometimes involve approaching high levels of mastery or performance (such as mastering the material for this class and getting a high grade) and sometimes involve avoiding failure (Elliot & McGregor, 2001). In many situations, specific, challenging goals motivate achievement, especially when combined with progress reports (Johnson et al., 2006; Latham & Locke, 2007). Specific, measurable objectives, such as "finish gathering the history paper information by Friday," serve to direct attention, promote effort, motivate persistence, and stimulate creative strategies.

When people state goals together with *subgoals* and *implementation intentions*—action plans that specify when, where, and how they will march toward achieving those goals—they become more focused in their work, and on-time completion becomes more likely (Burgess et al., 2004; Fishbach et al., 2006; Koestner et al., 2002). Through a task's ups and downs, people best sustain their mood and motivation when they focus on immediate goals (such as daily study) rather than distant goals (such as a course grade). Better to have one's nose to the grindstone than one's eye on the ultimate prize (Houser-Marko & Sheldon, 2008). Thus, before beginning each new edition of this book, my editor, my associates, and I *manage by objectives*—we agree on target dates for the completion and editing of each chapter draft.) If we focus on achieving each of these short-term goals, the prize—an on-time book—takes care of itself. So, to motivate high productivity, effective leaders work with people to define explicit goals, subgoals, and implementation plans, and then provide feedback on progress.

task leadership goal-oriented leadership that sets standards, organizes work, and focuses attention on goals.

social leadership group-oriented leadership that builds teamwork, mediates conflict, and offers support.

Choosing an Appropriate Leadership Style

Leadership varies from a boss-focused directive style to a democratic style that empowers workers in setting goals and strategies. Which works best may depend on the situation and the leader. The best leadership style for leading a discussion may not be the best style for leading troops on a charge (Fiedler, 1981). Moreover, different leaders are suited to different styles. Some excel at **task leadership**—setting standards, organizing work, and focusing attention on goals. Being goal-oriented, task leaders are good at keeping a group centered on its mission. Typically, they have a directive style, which can work well if the leader is bright enough to give good orders (Fiedler, 1987).

"I'm the decider, and I decide what's best."

Former U.S. President George W. Bush, 2006

Other managers excel at **social leadership**—explaining decisions, mediating conflicts, and building high-achieving teams (Evans & Dion, 1991). Social leaders often have a democratic style: They delegate authority and welcome the participation of team members. Many experiments show that social leadership is good for morale. Subordinates usually feel more satisfied and motivated, and perform better, when they participate in decision making (Cawley et al., 1998; Pereira & Osburn, 2007). Moreover, groups solve problems with greater "collective intelligence" when group members are sensitive to one another and participate equally (Woolley et al., 2010).

Positive coaching Larry Brown has been an adviser to the youth sports organization The Positive Coaching Alliance. He was observed during practices offering his players 4 to 5 positive comments for every negative comment (Insana, 2005). In 2004, he coached his underdog Detroit Pistons to the National Basketball Association championship.

Kirthmon F. Dozier/KRT/Newscom

Because effective leadership styles vary with the situation and the person, the once-popular *great person theory of leadership*—that all great leaders share certain traits—now seems overstated (Vroom & Jago, 2007; Wielkiewicz & Stelzner, 2005). The same coach may seem great or inferior depending on the strength of the team and its competition. But a leader's personality does matter (Zaccaro, 2007). Effective leaders tend to be neither extremely assertive (impairing social relationships) or unassertive (limiting task leadership) (Ames, 2008). Effective leaders of laboratory groups, work teams, and large corporations also tend to exude *charisma* (House & Singh, 1987; Shamir et al., 1993). Their charisma blends a goal-based *vision*, clear *communication*, and optimism that *inspires* others to follow.

In one study of 50 Dutch companies, the firms with highest morale had chief executives who most inspired their colleagues "to transcend their own self-interests for the sake of the collective" (de Hoogh et al., 2004). *Transformational leadership* of this kind motivates

© The New Yorker Collection, 1988, Anthony Tabèr from cartoonbank.com. All Rights Reserved.

others to identify with and commit themselves to the group's mission. Transformational leaders, many of whom are natural extraverts, articulate high standards, inspire people to share their vision, and offer personal attention (Bono & Judge, 2004). The frequent result is more engaged, trusting, and effective workers (Turner et al., 2002). As leaders, women more than men tend to exhibit transformational leadership qualities. Alice Eagly (2007) believes this helps explain why companies with women in top management have recently tended to enjoy superior financial results, even after controlling for such variables as company size.

Peter Smith and Monir Tayeb (1989) compiled data from studies in India, Taiwan, and Iran indicating that effective managers—whether in coal mines, banks, or government offices—often exhibit a high degree of *both* task and social leadership. As achievement-minded people, effective managers certainly care about how well work is done, yet at the same time they are sensitive to their subordinates' needs. In one national survey of American workers, those in family-friendly organizations offering flexible-time hours reported feeling greater loyalty to their employers (Roehling et al., 2001). A work environment that satisfies one's need to belong also energizes employees. Employees who enjoy high-quality colleague relationships also engage their work with more vigor (Carmeli et al., 2009). Gallup researchers have asked more than 15 million employees worldwide if they have a "best friend at work." The 30 percent who do "are *seven times* as likely to be engaged in their jobs" as those who don't, report Tom Rath and James Harter (2010).

"Good leaders don't ask more than their constituents can give, but they often ask—and get—more than their constituents intended to give or thought it was possible to give."
John W. Gardner, *Excellence*, 1984

Many successful businesses have also increased employee participation in making decisions, a management style common in Sweden and Japan and increasingly elsewhere (Naylor, 1990; Sundstrom et al., 1990). Although managers often think better of work they have directly supervised, studies reveal a *voice effect*: If given a chance to voice their opinion during a decision-making process, people will respond more positively to the decision (van den Bos & Spruijt, 2002). They will also feel more empowered, and likely, therefore, more creative (Hennessey & Amabile, 2010; Huang et al., 2010). And, as we noted earlier, positive, engaged employees are a mark of thriving organizations.

The ultimate in employee participation is the employee-owned company. One such company in my town, the Fleetwood Group, is a 165-employee manufacturer of educational furniture and wireless electronic clickers. When its founder gave 45 percent of the company to his employees, who later bought out other family stockholders, Fleetwood became one of America's first companies with an employee stock ownership plan (ESOP). Today, every employee owns part of the company and as a group they own 100 percent. The more years employees work, the more they own, yet no one owns more than 5 percent. Like every corporate president, Doug Ruch works for his stockholders—who also just happen to be his employees.

As a company that endorses faith-inspired "servant leadership" and "respect and care for each team member-owner," Fleetwood is free to place people above profits. Thus, when orders lagged during the recent recession, the employee-owners decided that job security meant more to them than profits. So the company paid otherwise idle workers to do community service—answering phones at non-profit agencies, building Habitat for Humanity houses, and the like.

Fleetwood employees "act like they own the place," notes Ruch. Employee ownership attracts and retains talented people, "drives dedication," and gives Fleetwood "a sustainable competitive advantage," he contends. With stock growth averaging 17 percent a year, Fleetwood was named the 2006 National ESOP of the year.

We have considered *personnel psychology* (the I/O subfield that focuses on employee selection, placement, appraisal, and development). And we have considered *organizational psychology* (the I/O subfield that focuses on worker satisfaction and productivity, and on organizational change). Finally, we turn to *human factors psychology*, which explores the human-machine interface.

RETRIEVAL PRACTICE

- What characteristics are important for *transformational leaders?*

ANSWER: *Transformational leaders* are able to inspire others to share a vision and commit themselves to a group's mission. They tend to be naturally extraverted and set high standards.

The Human Factor

34-5 How do human factors psychologists work to create user-friendly machines and work settings?

Designs sometimes neglect the human factor. Psychologist Donald Norman, an MIT alumnus with a Ph.D., bemoaned the complexity of assembling his new HDTV, related components, and seven remotes into a usable home theater system: "I was VP of Advanced Technology at Apple. I can program dozens of computers in dozens of languages. I understand television, really, I do. . . . It doesn't matter: I am overwhelmed."

How much easier life might be if engineers would routinely work with human factors psychologists to test their designs and instructions on real people. Human factors psychologists help to design appliances, machines, and work settings that fit our natural perceptions and inclinations. Bank ATM machines are internally more complex than remote controls ever were, yet, thanks to human factors psychologists working with engineers, ATMs are easier to operate. Digital recorders have solved the TV recording problem with a simple select-and-click menu system ("record that one"). Apple has similarly engineered easy usability with the iPhone and iPad.

Norman (2001) hosts a website (www.jnd.org) that illustrates good designs that fit people (see **FIGURE 34.4**). Human factors psychologists also work at designing efficient environments. An ideal kitchen layout, researchers have found, stores needed items close to their usage point and near eye level. It locates work areas to enable doing tasks in order, such as with a refrigerator, stove, and sink in a triangle. It creates counters that enable hands to work at or slightly below elbow height (Boehm-Davis, 2005).

Understanding human factors can help prevent accidents. By studying the human factor in driving accidents, psychologists seek to devise ways to reduce the distractions, fatigue, and inattention that contribute to 1.3 million annual worldwide traffic fatalities (Lee, 2008). Two-thirds of commercial air accidents have been caused by human error (Nickerson, 1998). After beginning commercial flights in the 1960s, the Boeing 727 was involved in several landing accidents caused by pilot error. Psychologist Conrad Kraft (1978) noted a common setting for these accidents: All took place at night, and all involved landing short of the runway after crossing a dark stretch of water or unilluminated ground. Kraft reasoned that, beyond the runway, city lights would project a larger retinal image if on rising terrain. This would make the ground seem farther away than it was. By

FIGURE 34.4
Designing products that fit people Human factors psychologist Donald Norman offers these and other examples of effectively designed products.

Courtesy www.rideoncarryon.com

The Ride On Carry On foldable chair attachment, "designed by a flight attendant mom," enables a small suitcase to double as a stroller.

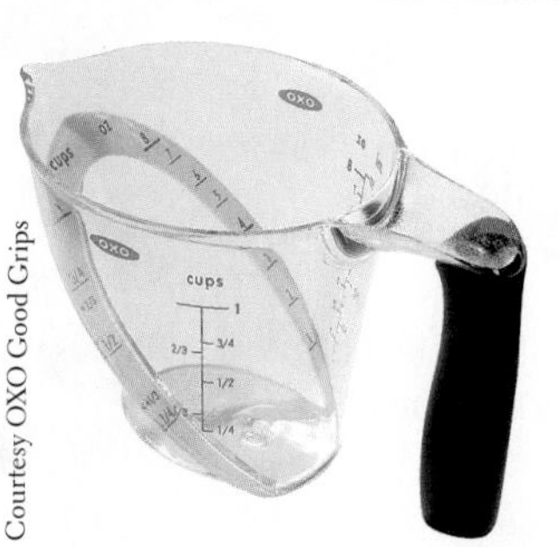
Courtesy OXO Good Grips

The Oxo measuring cup allows the user to see the quantity from above.

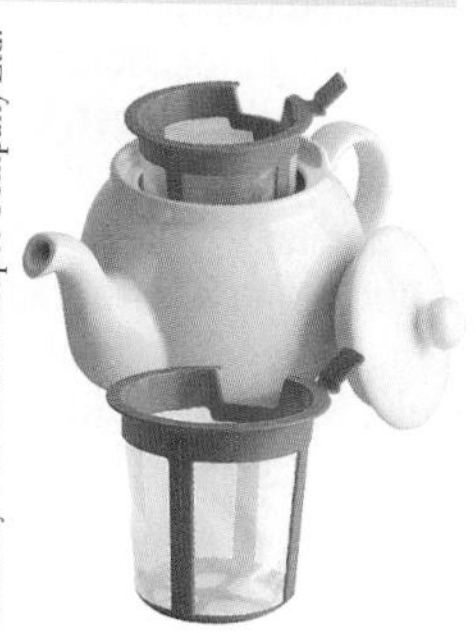
Courtesy The London Teapot Company Ltd.

The Chatsford Teapot comes with a built-in strainer.

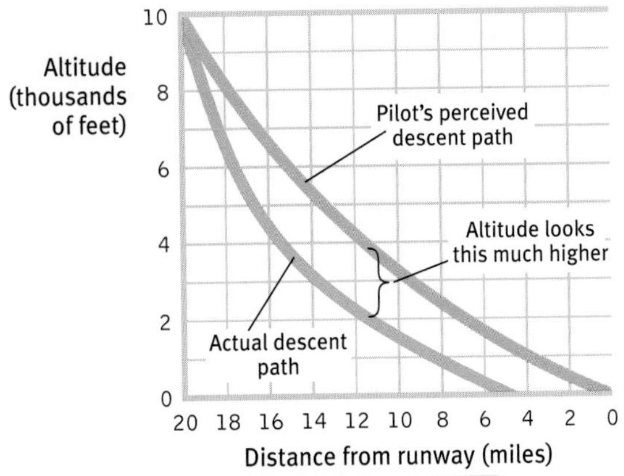

FIGURE 34.5
The human factor in accidents Lacking distance cues when approaching a runway from over a dark surface, pilots simulating a night landing tended to fly too low. (From Kraft, 1978.)

re-creating these conditions in flight simulations, Kraft discovered that pilots were deceived into thinking they were flying higher than their actual altitudes (**FIGURE 34.5**). Aided by Kraft's finding, the airlines began requiring the co-pilot to monitor the altimeter—calling out altitudes during the descent—and the accidents diminished.

Later Boeing psychologists worked on other human factors problems (Murray, 1998): How should airlines best train and manage mechanics to reduce the maintenance errors that underlie about 50 percent of flight delays and 15 percent of accidents? What illumination and typeface would make on-screen flight data easiest to read? How could warning messages be most effectively worded—as an action statement ("Pull Up") rather than a problem statement ("Ground Proximity")?

Consider, finally, the available *assistive listening* technologies in various theaters, auditoriums, and places of worship. One technology, commonly available in the United States, requires a headset attached to a pocket-sized receiver that detects infrared or FM signals from the room's sound system. The well-meaning people who design, purchase, and install these systems correctly understand that the technology puts sound directly into the user's ears. Alas, few people with hearing loss undergo the hassle and embarrassment of locating, requesting, wearing, and returning a conspicuous headset. Most such units therefore sit in closets. Britain, the Scandinavian countries, and Australia have instead installed *loop systems* (see www.hearingloop.org) that broadcast customized sound directly through a person's own hearing aid. When suitably equipped, a hearing aid can be transformed by a discrete touch of a switch into an in-the-ear loudspeaker. Offered convenient, inconspicuous, personalized sound, many more people elect to use assistive listening.

Designs that enable safe, easy, and effective interactions between people and technology often seem obvious after the fact. Why, then, aren't they more common? Technology developers sometimes mistakenly assume that others share their expertise—that what's clear to them will similarly be clear to others (Camerer et al., 1989; Nickerson, 1999). When people rap their knuckles on a table to convey a familiar tune (try this with a friend), they often expect their listener to recognize it. But for the listener, this is a near-impossible task (Newton, 1991). When you know a thing, it's hard to mentally simulate what it's like not to know, and that is called the *curse of knowledge*.

The human factor in safe landings Advanced cockpit design and rehearsed emergency procedures aided pilot Chesley "Sully" Sullenberger, a U.S. Air Force Academy graduate who studied psychology and human factors. In January 2009, Sullenberger's instantaneous decisions safely guided his disabled airplane onto New York City's Hudson River, where all 155 of the passengers and crew were safely evacuated.

AP Photo/Steven Day

The point to remember: Designers and engineers should consider human abilities and behaviors by designing things to fit people, user-testing their inventions before production and distribution, and being mindful of the curse of knowledge.

RETRIEVAL PRACTICE

- What are the three main divisions within industrial-organizational psychology?

ANSWER: personnel, organizational, human factors

* * *

Identifiable physiological mechanisms drive some motives, such as hunger (though learned tastes and cultural expectations matter, too). Other motives, such as achievement at work, are more obviously driven by psychological factors, such as an intrinsic quest for mastery and the external rewards of recognition. What unifies all motives is their common effect: the energizing and directing of behavior.

MODULE REVIEW

Motivation at Work

Learning Objectives

RETRIEVAL PRACTICE Take a moment to answer each of these Learning Objective Questions (repeated here from within the module). Then turn to Appendix B, Complete Module Reviews, to check your answers. Research suggests that trying to answer these questions on your own will improve your long-term retention (McDaniel et al., 2009).

34-1: What is "flow," and what are the three subfields of industrial-organizational psychology?

34-2: How do personnel psychologists help organizations with employee selection, work placement, and performance appraisal?

34-3: What is achievement motivation? What is the role of organizational psychologists?

34-4: What are some effective leadership techniques?

34-5: How do human factors psychologists work to create user-friendly machines and work settings?

Terms and Concepts to Remember

RETRIEVAL PRACTICE Test yourself on these terms by trying to write down the definition before flipping back to the referenced page to check your answer.

flow, p. 457
industrial-organizational (I/O) psychology, p. 458
personnel psychology, p. 458
organizational psychology, p. 458
human factors psychology, p. 458
structured interviews, p. 461
achievement motivation, p. 463
grit, p. 464
task leadership, p. 467
social leadership, p. 467

RETRIEVAL PRACTICE Gain an advantage, and benefit from immediate feedback, with the interactive self-testing resources at www.worthpublishers.com/myers.

Emotions, Stress, and Health

No one needs to tell you that feelings add color to your life, or that in times of stress they can disrupt your life, or save it. Fear, anger, sadness, joy, and love are psychological states that also entail physical reactions. Nervous about an important encounter, we feel stomach butterflies. Anxious over public speaking, we frequent the bathroom. Smoldering over a family conflict, we get a splitting headache.

You can surely recall a time when emotion overwhelmed you. I retain a flashbulb memory for the day I went to a huge store to drop off film and brought along Peter, my toddler first-born child. As I set Peter down on his feet and prepared to complete the paperwork, a passerby warned, "You'd better be careful or you'll lose that boy!" Not more than a few breaths later, after dropping the film in the slot, I turned and found no Peter beside me.

With mild anxiety, I peered around one end of the counter. No Peter in sight. With slightly more anxiety, I peered around the other end. No Peter there, either. Now, with my heart accelerating, I circled the neighboring counters. Still no Peter anywhere. As anxiety turned to panic, I began racing up and down the store aisles. He was nowhere to be found. Apprised of my alarm, the store manager used the public-address system to ask customers to assist in looking for a missing child. Soon after, I passed the customer who had warned me. "I told you that you were going to

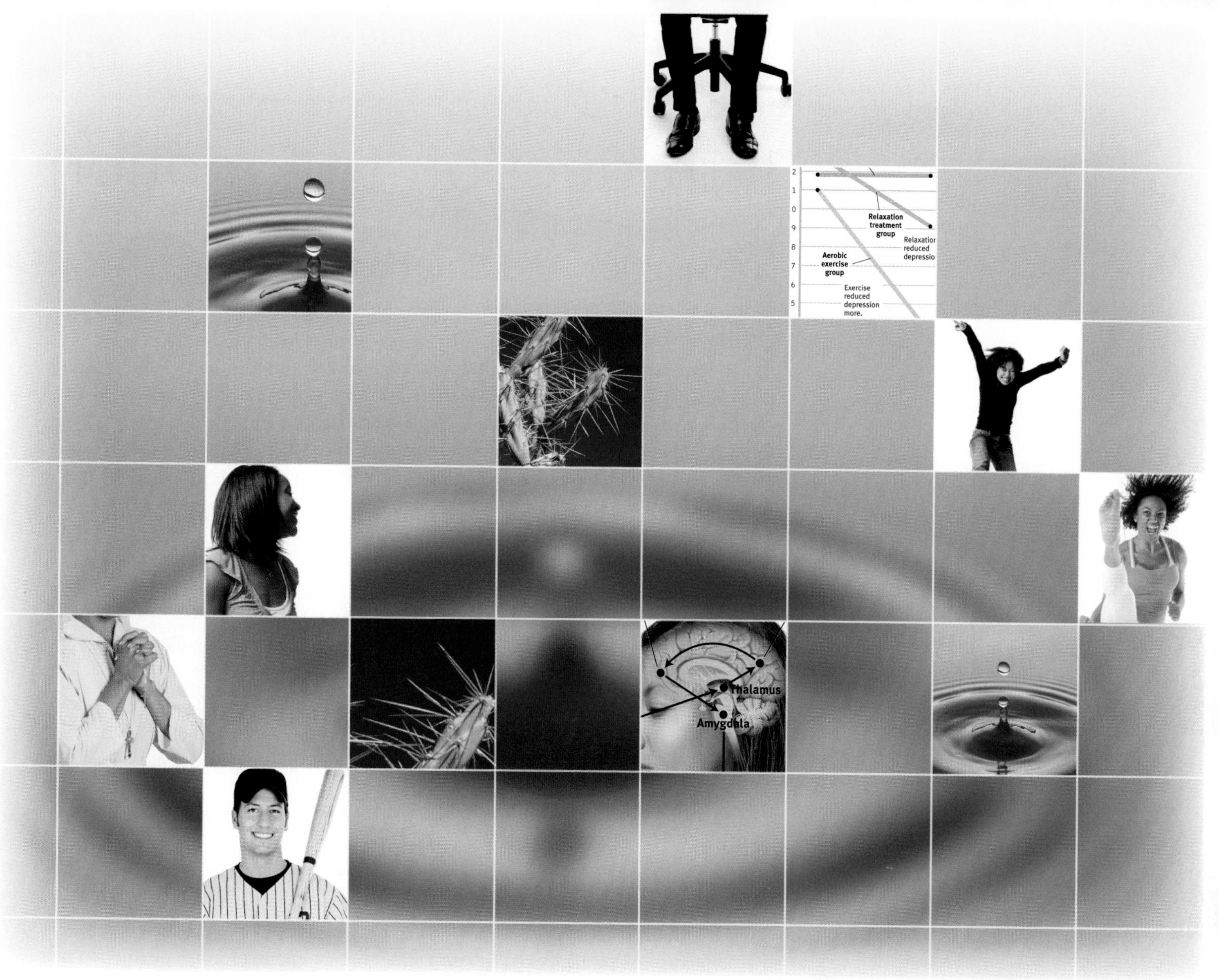

MODULES

35 Introduction to Emotion

36 Expressed Emotion

37 Experienced Emotion

38 Stress and Health

39 Promoting Health

lose him!" he now scorned. With visions of kidnapping (strangers routinely adored that beautiful child), I braced for the possibility that my negligence had caused me to lose what I loved above all else, and that I might have to return home and face my wife without our only child.

But then, as I passed the customer service counter yet again, there he was, having been found and returned by some obliging customer. In an instant, the arousal of terror spilled into ecstasy. Clutching my son, with tears suddenly flowing, I found myself unable to speak my thanks and stumbled out of the store awash in grateful joy.

So, how do psychologists think about and study emotions, stress, and health? In Module 35, we examine theories that explore the interplay of physiological activation, expressive behavior, and conscious experience. We then turn to the bodily responses involved in emotional expression. Module 36 explains how we express our emotions. In Module 37, we focus on experiencing our emotions with an in-depth look at anger and happiness. Module 38 looks at a key question health psychologists ask: How do our emotions and personality influence our risk of disease? And Module 39 explores the attitudes and behaviors that may help prevent illness and promote health and well-being.

MODULE 35

Introduction to Emotion

- Cognition and Emotion
- Embodied Emotion

Cognition and Emotion

35-1 How do arousal and expressive behaviors interact in emotion?

Courtesy of David G. Myers

As my panicked search for Peter illustrates, **emotions** are a mix of *bodily arousal* (heart pounding); *expressive behaviors* (quickened pace); and *conscious experience*, including thoughts (*"Is this a kidnapping?"*) and feelings (panic, fear, joy).

The puzzle for psychologists is figuring out how these three pieces fit together. To do that, we need answers to two big questions:

- A chicken-and-egg debate: Does your bodily arousal come *before* or *after* your emotional feelings? (Did I first notice my racing heart and faster step, and then feel terror about losing Peter? Or did my sense of fear come first, stirring my heart and legs to respond?)
- How do *thinking* (cognition) and *feeling* interact? Does cognition always come before emotion? (Did I think about a kidnapping threat before I reacted emotionally?)

Historical emotion theories, as well as current research, have sought to answer these questions.

Not only emotion, but most psychological phenomena (vision, sleep, memory, sex, and so forth) can be approached these three ways—physiologically, behaviorally, and cognitively.

Historical Emotion Theories

James-Lange Theory: Arousal Comes Before Emotion

Common sense tells most of us that we cry because we are sad, lash out because we are angry, tremble because we are afraid. First comes conscious awareness, then the feeling. But to pioneering psychologist William James, this commonsense view of emotion had things backwards. Rather, "We feel sorry because we cry, angry because we strike, afraid because we tremble" (1890, p. 1066). James' idea was also proposed by Danish physiologist Carl Lange, and so is called the **James-Lange theory.** James and Lange would guess that I noticed my racing heart and then, shaking with fright, felt the whoosh of emotion. My feeling of fear followed my body's response.

Joy expressed According to the James-Lange theory, we don't just smile because we share our teammates' joy. We also share the joy because we are smiling with them.

REUTERS/Matt Sullivan

Cannon-Bard Theory: Arousal and Emotion Occur Simultaneously

Physiologist Walter Cannon (1871–1945) disagreed with James and Lange. Does a racing heart signal fear or anger or love? The body's responses—heart rate, perspiration, and body temperature—are too similar, and they change too slowly, to *cause* the different emotions, said Cannon. He, and later another physiologist, Philip Bard, concluded that our bodily responses and experienced emotions occur separately but simultaneously. So, according to the **Cannon-Bard theory,** my heart began pounding *as* I experienced fear. The emotion-triggering stimulus traveled to my sympathetic nervous system, causing my body's arousal. *At the same time,* it traveled to my brain's cortex, causing my awareness of my emotion. My pounding heart did not cause my feeling of fear, nor did my feeling of fear cause my pounding heart.

The Cannon-Bard theory has been challenged by studies of people with severed spinal cords, including a survey of 25 soldiers who suffered such injuries in World War II (Hohmann, 1966). Those with *lower-spine injuries,* who had lost sensation only in their legs, reported little change in their emotions' intensity. Those with *high spinal cord injury,* who could feel nothing below the neck, did report changes. Some reactions were much less intense than before the injuries. Anger, one man confessed, "just doesn't have the heat to it that it used to. It's a mental kind of anger." Other emotions, those expressed mostly in body areas above the neck, were felt *more* intensely. These men reported increases in weeping, lumps in the throat, and getting choked up when saying good-bye, worshipping, or watching a touching movie. Our bodily responses seemingly feed our experienced emotions.

But most researchers now agree that our emotions also involve cognition (Averill, 1993; Barrett, 2006). Whether we fear the man behind us on the dark street depends entirely on whether we interpret his actions as threatening or friendly.

RETRIEVAL PRACTICE

- According to the Cannon-Bard theory, (a) our *physiological response* to a stimulus (for example, a pounding heart), and (b) the *emotion* we experience (for example, fear) occur __________ (simultaneously/sequentially). According to the James-Lange theory, (a) and (b) occur __________ (simultaneously/sequentially).

ANSWERS: simultaneously; sequentially (first the physiological response, and then the experienced emotion)

Cognition Can Define Emotion: Schachter and Singer

35-2 To experience emotions, must we consciously interpret and label them?

Stanley Schachter and Jerome Singer (1962) believed that an emotional experience requires a conscious interpretation of arousal: Our physical reactions and our thoughts (perceptions, memories, and interpretations) together create emotion. In their **two-factor theory,** emotions therefore have two ingredients: physical arousal and cognitive appraisal.

Consider how arousal spills over from one event to the next. Imagine arriving home after an invigorating run and finding a message that you got a longed-for job. With arousal lingering from the run, would you feel more elated than if you received this news after awakening from a nap?

To explore this *spillover effect*, Schachter and Singer injected college men with the hormone epinephrine, which triggers feelings of arousal. Picture yourself as a participant: After receiving the injection, you go to a waiting room, where you find yourself with another person (actually an accomplice of the experimenters) who is acting either euphoric or irritated. As you observe this person, you begin to feel your heart race, your body flush, and your breathing become more rapid. If you had been told to expect these effects from the injection, what would you feel? The actual volunteers felt little emotion—because they attributed their arousal to the drug. But if you had been told the injection would produce no effects, what would you feel? Perhaps you would react as another group of participants did. They "caught" the apparent emotion of the other person in the waiting room. They became happy if the accomplice was acting euphoric, and testy if the accomplice was acting irritated.

Reuters/Corbis

The spillover effect Arousal from a soccer match can fuel anger, which can descend into rioting or other violent confrontations.

emotion a response of the whole organism, involving (1) physiological arousal, (2) expressive behaviors, and (3) conscious experience.

James-Lange theory the theory that our experience of emotion is our awareness of our physiological responses to emotion-arousing stimuli.

Cannon-Bard theory the theory that an emotion-arousing stimulus simultaneously triggers (1) physiological responses and (2) the subjective experience of emotion.

two-factor theory the Schachter-Singer theory that to experience emotion one must (1) be physically aroused and (2) cognitively label the arousal.

This discovery—that a stirred-up state can be experienced as one emotion or another, depending on how we interpret and label it—has been replicated in dozens of experiments (Reisenzein, 1983; Sinclair et al., 1994; Zillmann, 1986). As researcher Daniel Gilbert (2006) has noted, "Feelings that one interprets as fear in the presence of a sheer drop may be interpreted as lust in the presence of a sheer blouse." *The point to remember:* Arousal fuels emotion; cognition channels it.

RETRIEVAL PRACTICE

- According to Schachter and Singer, two factors lead to our experience of an emotion: (1) physiological arousal and (2) __________ appraisal.

ANSWER: cognitive

Cognition May Not Precede Emotion: Zajonc, LeDoux, and Lazarus

But is the heart always subject to the mind? Must we *always* interpret our arousal before we can experience an emotion? Robert Zajonc (pronounced ZI-yence; 1980, 1984a) contended that we actually have many emotional reactions apart from, or even before, our interpretation of a situation. Perhaps you can recall liking something or someone immediately, without knowing why.

For example, when people repeatedly view stimuli flashed too briefly for them to interpret, they come to prefer those stimuli. Unaware of having previously seen them, they nevertheless rather like them. We have an acutely sensitive automatic radar for emotionally significant information, such that even a subliminally flashed stimulus can prime us to feel better or worse about a follow-up stimulus (Murphy et al., 1995; Zeelenberg et al., 2006). In experiments, thirsty people were given a fruit-flavored drink after viewing a subliminally flashed (thus unperceived) face. Those exposed to a happy face drank about 50 percent more than those exposed to a neutral face (Berridge & Winkielman, 2003). Those flashed an angry face drank substantially less.

Neuroscientists are charting the neural pathways of both "bottom-up" and "top-down" emotions (Ochsner et al., 2009). Our emotional responses can follow two different brain pathways. Some emotions (especially more complex feelings like hatred and love) travel a "high-road." A stimulus following this path would travel (by way of the thalamus) to the brain's cortex (**FIGURE 35.1a**). There, it would be analyzed and labeled before the command is sent out, via the amygdala (an emotion-control center), to respond.

But sometimes our emotions (especially simple likes, dislikes, and fears) take what Joseph LeDoux (2002) has called the "low road," a neural shortcut that bypasses the cortex. Following the low-road pathway, a fear-provoking stimulus would travel from the eye or ear (again via the thalamus) directly to the amygdala (Figure 35.1b). This shortcut, bypassing the cortex, enables our greased-lightning emotional response before our intellect intervenes. Like speedy reflexes that also operate apart from the brain's thinking cortex, the amygdala reactions are so fast that we may be unaware of what's transpired (Dimberg et al., 2000). In one fascinating experiment, researchers used fMRI scans to observe the amygdala's response to subliminally presented fearful eyes (**FIGURE 35.2**) (Whalen et al., 2004). Although they were flashed too quickly for people to consciously perceive them, the fearful eyes triggered increased amygdala activity. A control condition that presented happy eyes did not trigger this activity.

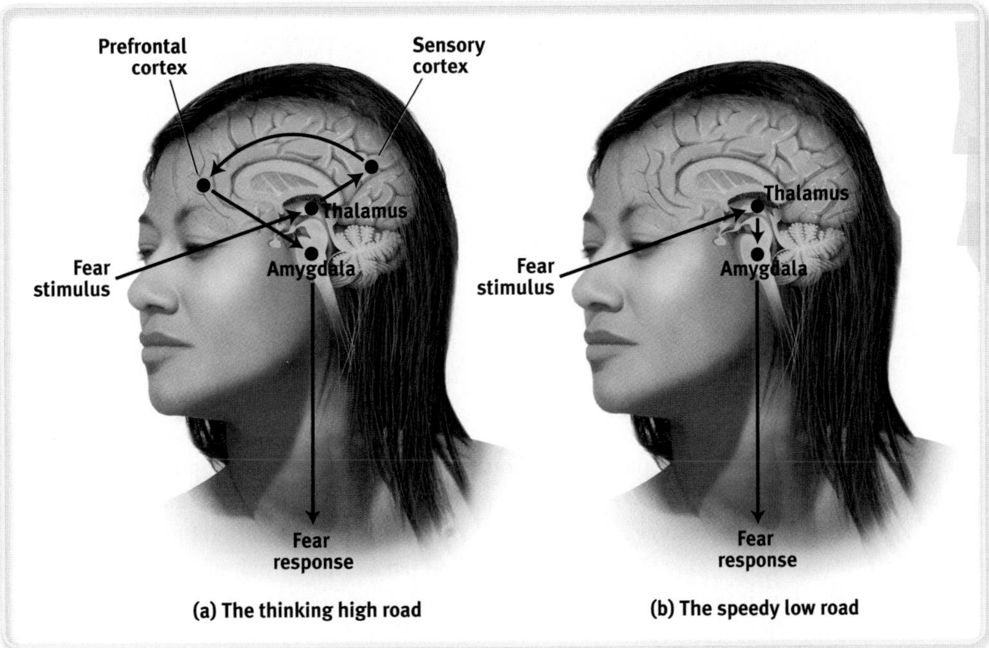

FIGURE 35.1
The brain's pathways for emotions In the two-track brain, sensory input may be routed (a) to the cortex (via the thalamus) for analysis and then transmission to the amygdala; or (b) directly to the amygdala (via the thalamus) for an instant emotional reaction.

The amygdala sends more neural projections up to the cortex than it receives back, which makes it easier for our feelings to hijack our thinking than for our thinking to rule our feelings (LeDoux & Armony, 1999). Thus, in the forest, we can jump at the sound of rustling bushes nearby and leave it to our cortex to decide later whether the sound was made by a snake or by the wind. Such experiences support Zajonc's belief that *some* of our emotional reactions involve no deliberate thinking.

Emotion researcher Richard Lazarus (1991, 1998) conceded that our brains process vast amounts of information without our conscious awareness, and that some emotional responses do not require *conscious* thinking. Much of our emotional life operates via the automatic, speedy low road. But, he asked, how would we *know* what we are reacting to if we did not in some way appraise the situation? The appraisal may be effortless and we may not be conscious of it, but it is still a mental function. To know whether a stimulus is good or bad, the brain must have some idea of what it is (Storbeck et al., 2006). Thus, said Lazarus, emotions arise when we *appraise* an event as harmless or dangerous, whether we truly *know* it is or not. We appraise the sound of the rustling bushes as the presence of a threat. Later, we realize that it was "just the wind."

Courtesy of Paul J. Whalen, Ph.D., Dartmouth College, www.whalenlab.info

FIGURE 35.2
The brain's sensitivity to threats Even when fearful eyes (left) were flashed too briefly for people to consciously perceive them, fMRI scans revealed that their hypervigilant amygdala was alerted (Whalen et al., 2004). The eyes on the right did not have this effect.

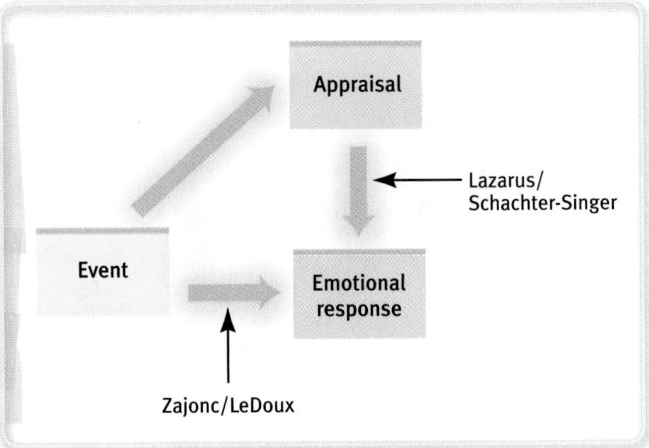

FIGURE 35.3
Two pathways for emotions Zajonc and LeDoux have emphasized that some emotional responses are immediate, before any conscious appraisal. Lazarus, Schachter, and Singer emphasized that our appraisal and labeling of events also determine our emotional responses. Neuroscientists are charting the neural pathways of both "bottom-up" and "top-down" emotions (Ochsner et al., 2009).

So, as Zajonc and LeDoux have demonstrated, some emotional responses—especially simple likes, dislikes, and fears—involve no conscious thinking (**FIGURE 35.3**). We may fear a big spider, even if we "know" it is harmless. Such responses are difficult to alter by changing our thinking. We may automatically like one person more than another. This instant appeal can even influence our political decisions if we vote (as many people do) for a candidate we *like* over the candidate expressing positions closer to our own (Westen, 2007).

But as Lazarus, Schachter, and Singer predicted, our memories, expectations, and interpretations also influence our feelings about politics. Moreover, highly emotional people are intense partly because of their interpretations. They may *personalize* events as being somehow directed at them, and they may *generalize* their experiences by blowing single incidents out of proportion (Larsen et al., 1987). Thus, learning to *think* more positively can help people *feel* better. Although the emotional low road functions automatically, the thinking high road allows us to retake some control over our emotional life. Together, automatic emotion and conscious thinking weave the fabric of our emotional lives. (**TABLE 35.1** summarizes these emotion theories.)

TABLE 35.1
Summary of Emotion Theories

Theory	Explanation of Emotions	Example
James-Lange	Our awareness of our specific bodily response to emotion-arousing stimuli	We observe our heart racing after a threat and then feel afraid.
Cannon-Bard	Bodily response + simultaneous subjective experience	Our heart races as we experience fear.
Schachter-Singer	Two factors: General arousal + a conscious cognitive label	Arousal could be labeled as fear or excitement, depending on context.
Zajonc; LeDoux	Instant, before cognitive appraisal	We automatically react to a sound in the forest before appraising it.
Lazarus	Appraisal ("Is it dangerous or not?")—sometimes without our awareness—defines emotion	The sound is "just the wind."

RETRIEVAL PRACTICE

- Emotion researchers have disagreed about whether emotional responses occur in the absence of cognitive processing. How would you characterize the approach of each of the following researchers: Zajonc, LeDoux, Lazarus, Schachter, and Singer?

ANSWERS: Zajonc and LeDoux suggested that we experience some emotions without any conscious, cognitive appraisal. Lazarus, Schachter, and Singer emphasized the importance of appraisal and cognitive labeling in our experience of emotion.

Embodied Emotion

Whether you are falling in love or grieving a death, you need little convincing that emotions involve the body. Feeling without a body is like breathing without lungs. Some physical responses are easy to notice. Other emotional responses we experience without awareness.

Emotions and the Autonomic Nervous System

35-3 What is the link between emotional arousal and the autonomic nervous system? How does arousal affect performance?

In a crisis, the *sympathetic division* of your *autonomic nervous system (ANS)* mobilizes your body for action, directing your adrenal glands to release the stress hormones epinephrine (adrenaline) and norepinephrine (noradrenaline) (**FIGURE 35.4**). To provide energy, your liver pours extra sugar into your bloodstream. To help burn the sugar, your respiration increases to supply needed oxygen. Your heart rate and blood pressure increase. Your digestion slows, diverting blood from your internal organs to your muscles. With blood sugar driven into the large muscles, running becomes easier. Your pupils dilate, letting in more light. To cool your stirred-up body, you perspire. If wounded, your blood would clot more quickly.

"Fear lends wings to his feet."
Virgil, *Aeneid,* 19 B.C.E.

FIGURE 35.4
Emotional arousal Like a crisis control center, the autonomic nervous system arouses the body in a crisis and calms it when danger passes.

Autonomic Nervous System Controls Physiological Arousal

Sympathetic division (arousing)		Parasympathetic division (calming)
Pupils dilate	EYES	Pupils contract
Decreases	SALIVATION	Increases
Perspires	SKIN	Dries
Increases	RESPIRATION	Decreases
Accelerates	HEART	Slows
Inhibits	DIGESTION	Activates
Secrete stress hormones	ADRENAL GLANDS	Decrease secretion of stress hormones
Reduced	IMMUNE SYSTEM FUNCTIONING	Enhanced

Arousal affects performance in different ways, depending on the task. When taking an exam, it pays to be moderately aroused—alert but not trembling with nervousness (**FIGURE 35.5** on the next page). But too little arousal (as when sleepy) can be disruptive, and prolonged high arousal can tax the body.

When the crisis passes, the *parasympathetic division* of your ANS gradually calms your body, as stress hormones slowly leave your bloodstream. After your next crisis, think of this: Without any conscious effort, your body's response to danger is wonderfully coordinated and adaptive—preparing you to *fight or flee.*

RETRIEVAL PRACTICE

FIGURE 35.5

Arousal and performance Performance peaks at lower levels of arousal for difficult tasks, and at higher levels for easy or well-learned tasks. (1) How might this phenomenon affect runners? (2) How might this phenomenon affect anxious test-takers facing a difficult exam? (3) How might the performance of anxious students be affected by relaxation training?

ANSWERS: (1) Runners tend to excel when aroused by competition. (2) High anxiety in test-takers may disrupt their performance. (3) Teaching anxious students how to relax before an exam can enable them to perform better (Hembree, 1988).

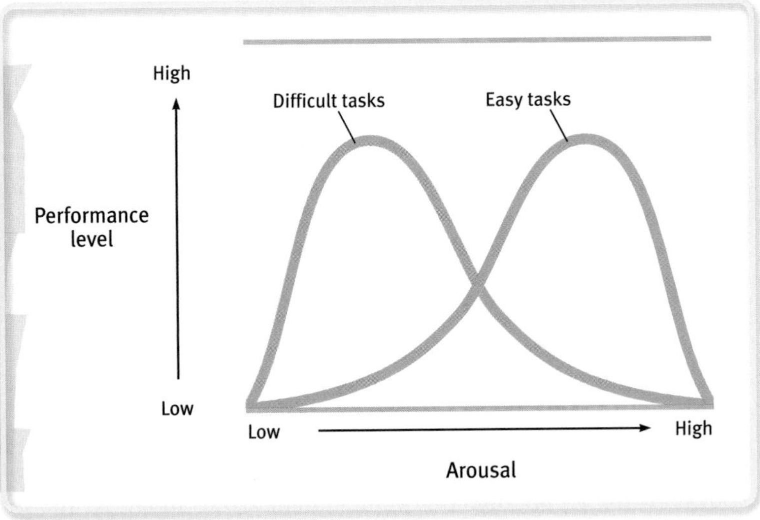

The Physiology of Emotions

35-4 Do different emotions activate different physiological and brain-pattern responses?

"No one ever told me that grief felt so much like fear. I am not afraid, but the sensation is like being afraid. The same fluttering in the stomach, the same restlessness, the yawning. I keep on swallowing."

C. S. Lewis, *A Grief Observed*, 1961

Imagine conducting an experiment measuring the physiological responses of emotion. In each of four rooms, you have someone watching a movie: In the first, the person is viewing a horror show; in the second, an anger-provoking film; in the third, a sexually arousing film; in the fourth, a boring film. From the control center you monitor each person's perspiration, breathing, and heart rate. Could you tell who is frightened? Who is angry? Who is sexually aroused? Who is bored?

With training, you could probably pick out the bored viewer. But discerning physiological differences among fear, anger, and sexual arousal would be much more difficult (Barrett, 2006). Different emotions do not have sharply distinct biological signatures.

Nor do they engage sharply distinct brain regions. Consider the broad emotional portfolio of the *insula*, a neural center deep inside the brain. The insula is activated when we experience various social emotions, such as lust, pride, and disgust. In brain scans, it "lights up" when people bite into some disgusting food, smell the same disgusting food, think about biting into a disgusting cockroach, or feel moral disgust over a sleazy business exploiting a saintly widow (Sapolsky, 2010).

Nevertheless, despite their similarities, sexual arousal, fear, anger, and disgust *feel* different to you and me, and they often *look* different to others. We may appear "paralyzed with fear" or "ready to explode." Research has pinpointed some real, though subtle, physiological distinctions among the emotions. For example, the finger temperatures and hormone secretions that accompany fear and rage do sometimes differ (Ax, 1953; Levenson, 1992). Fear and joy, although they prompt similar increased heart rate, stimulate different facial muscles. During fear, your brow muscles tense. During joy, muscles in your cheeks and under your eyes pull into a smile (Witvliet & Vrana, 1995).

Some emotions also differ in their brain circuits (Panksepp, 2007). Compared with observers watching angry faces, those watching (and subtly mimicking) fearful faces show more activity in their amygdala, an emotion control center (Whalen et al., 2001). Brain scans and EEG recordings show that emotions also activate different areas of the brain's cortex. When you experience negative emotions such as disgust, your right prefrontal cortex tends to be more active than the left. Depression-prone people, and those with generally negative personalities, also show more right-frontal activity (Harmon-Jones et al., 2002).

Emotional arousal Elated excitement and panicky fear involve similar physiological arousal. That allows us to flip rapidly between the two emotions.

FotoStor.co.uk/Alamy

Positive moods tend to trigger more left frontal lobe activity. People with positive personalities—exuberant infants and alert, enthusiastic, energized, and persistently goal-directed adults—also show more activity in the left frontal lobe than in the right (Davidson, 2000, 2003; Urry et al., 2004). Indeed, the more a person's baseline frontal lobe activity tilts left—or is made to tilt left by perceptual activity—the more upbeat the person typically is (Drake & Myers, 2006).

To sum up, we can't easily see differences in emotions from tracking heart rate, breathing, and perspiration. But facial expressions and brain activity can vary with the emotion. So, do we, like Pinocchio, give off telltale signs when we lie? For more on that question, see Thinking Critically About: Lie Detection.

In 1966, a young man named Charles Whitman killed his wife and mother and then climbed to the top of a tower at the University of Texas and shot 38 people. An autopsy later revealed a tumor pressing against his amygdala, which may have contributed to his violence.

RETRIEVAL PRACTICE

- How do the two divisions of the autonomic nervous system affect our emotional responses?

ANSWER: The *sympathetic division* of the ANS arouses us for more intense experiences of emotion, pumping out the stress hormones epinephrine and norepinephrine to prepare our body for fight or flight. The *parasympathetic division* of the ANS takes over when a crisis passes, restoring our body to a calm physiological and emotional state.

THINKING CRITICALLY ABOUT

Lie Detection

35-5 How effective are polygraphs in using body states to detect lies?

Can a *lie detector*—a **polygraph**—reveal lies? Polygraphs don't literally detect lies. Instead, they measure emotion-linked changes in breathing, cardiovascular activity, and perspiration. If you were taking this test, an examiner would monitor these responses as you answered questions. She might ask, "In the last 20 years, have you ever taken something that didn't belong to you?" This item is a control question, aimed at making everyone a little nervous. If you lie and say *"No!"* (as many people do) the polygraph will detect arousal. This response will establish a baseline, a useful comparison for your responses to *critical questions ("Did you ever steal anything from your previous employer?")*. If your responses to critical questions are weaker than to control questions, the examiner will infer you are telling the truth.

Critics point out two problems: First, our physiological arousal is much the same from one emotion to another. Anxiety, irritation, and guilt all prompt similar physiological reactivity. Second, many innocent people do respond with heightened tension to the accusations implied by the critical questions (**FIGURE 35.6**). Many rape victims, for example, "fail" these tests when reacting emotionally but truthfully (Lykken, 1991).

polygraph a machine, commonly used in attempts to detect lies, that measures several of the physiological responses (such as perspiration and cardiovascular and breathing changes) accompanying emotion.

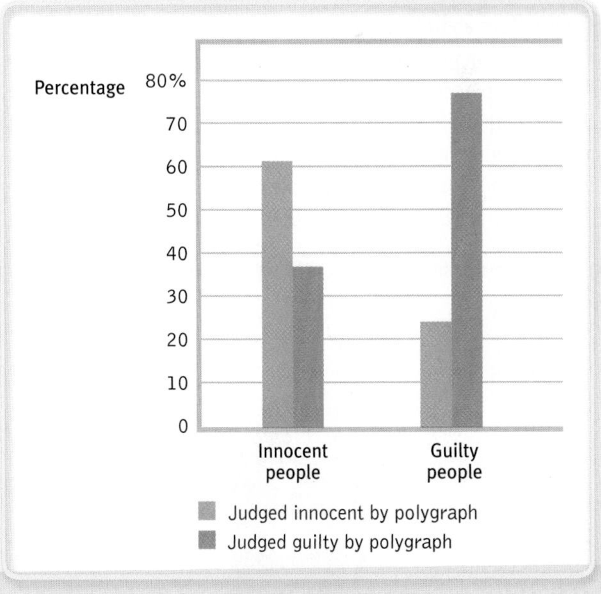

FIGURE 35.6
How often do lie detection tests lie? In one study, polygraph experts interpreted the polygraph data of 100 people who had been suspects in theft crimes (Kleinmuntz & Szucko, 1984). Half the suspects were guilty and had confessed; the other half had been proven innocent. Had the polygraph experts been the judges, more than one-third of the innocent would have been declared guilty, and one-fourth of the guilty would have been declared innocent.

Continued on the next page.

Lie Detection

A 2002 U.S. National Academy of Sciences report noted that "no spy has ever been caught [by] using the polygraph." It is not for lack of trying. The FBI, CIA, and Departments of Defense and Energy in the United States have tested tens of thousands of employees, and polygraph use in Europe has also increased (Meijer & Verschuere, 2010). Meanwhile Aldrich Ames, a Russian spy within the CIA, went undetected. Ames took many "polygraph tests and passed them all," noted Robert Park (1999). "Nobody thought to investigate the source of his sudden wealth—after all, he was passing the lie detector tests."

A more effective approach to lie detection uses a *guilty knowledge test,* which assesses a suspect's physiological responses to crime-scene details known only to the police and the guilty person (Ben-Shakhar & Elaad, 2003). If a camera and computer had been stolen, for example, only a guilty person should react strongly to the brand names of the stolen items. Given enough such specific probes, an innocent person will seldom be wrongly accused.

Research teams are now exploring new ways to nab liars. Psychologist Paul Ekman (2003) has done research (and has trained law enforcement officers) in detecting fleeting signals of deceit in facial expressions. Eyeblinks, for example, decrease during the cognitive demands of lying, and increase afterward (Leal & Vrij, 2008). Other researchers are developing software that analyzes facial microexpressions (Adelson, 2004; Newman et al., 2003) or compares the language of truth-tellers and of liars (who use fewer first-person pronouns and more negative-emotion words).

"Forensic neuroscience" researchers are going straight to the seat of deceit—the brain. EEG recordings have revealed brain waves that indicate familiarity with crime information. fMRI scans have shown liars' brains lighting up in places that honest people's brains do not (Langleben et al., 2006, 2008; Lui & Rosenfeld, 2009). Pinocchio's giveaway signal of lying may be not the length of his nose, but rather the telltale activity in places such as his left frontal lobe and anterior cingulate cortex, which become active when the brain inhibits truth-telling (**FIGURE 35.7**). A new U.S. $10 million Law and Neuroscience Project, led by psychologist Michael Gazzaniga, aims to assess appropriate uses of the new technology in identifying terrorists, convicting criminals, and protecting the innocent. In 2010, a U.S. federal court declared that fMRI lie detection is not yet ready for courtroom use (Miller, 2010). Many neuroscientists concur (Gazzaniga, 2011; Wagner, 2010). Others argue that jurors' and judges' seat-of-the-pants judgments "are worse than the science that is excluded" (Schauer, 2010).

James Salzano/0Salzano Photo

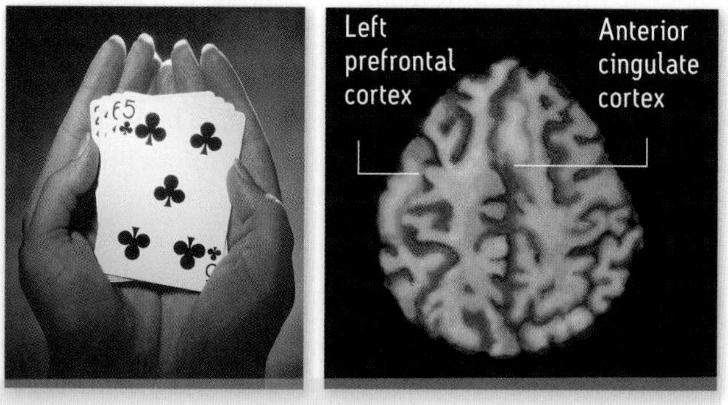

Lucy Reading/Lucy Illustrations

FIGURE 35.7
Liar, liar, brain's on fire An fMRI scan identified two brain areas that became especially active when a participant lied about holding a five of clubs.

MODULE REVIEW

Introduction to Emotion

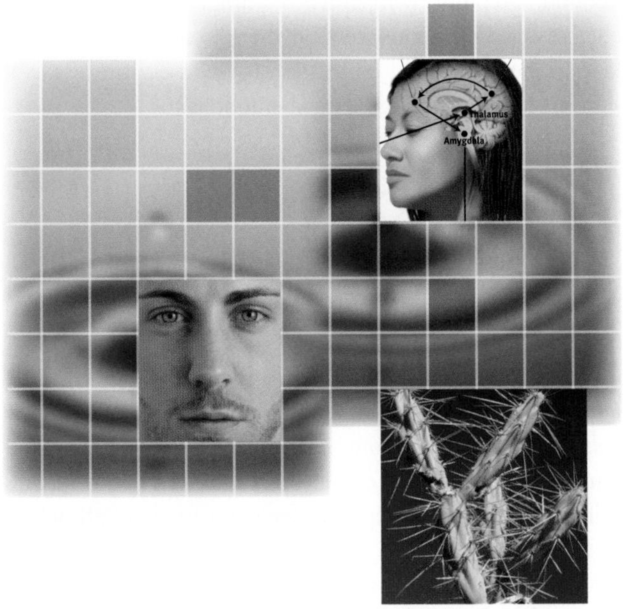

Learning Objectives

RETRIEVAL PRACTICE Take a moment to answer each of these Learning Objective Questions (repeated here from within the module). Then turn to Appendix B, Complete Module Reviews, to check your answers. Research suggests that trying to answer these questions on your own will improve your long-term retention (McDaniel et al., 2009).

35-1: How do arousal and expressive behaviors interact in emotion?

35-2: To experience emotions, must we consciously interpret and label them?

35-3: What is the link between emotional arousal and the autonomic nervous system? How does arousal affect performance?

35-4: Do different emotions activate different physiological and brain-pattern responses?

35-5: How effective are polygraphs in using body states to detect lies?

Terms and Concepts to Remember

RETRIEVAL PRACTICE Test yourself on these terms by trying to write down the definition before flipping back to the referenced page to check your answer.

emotion, p. 474
James-Lange theory, p. 474
Cannon-Bard theory, p. 474
two-factor theory, p. 475
polygraph, p. 481

RETRIEVAL PRACTICE Gain an advantage, and benefit from immediate feedback, with the interactive self-testing resources at www.worthpublishers.com/myers.

MODULE 36

Expressed Emotion

- Detecting Emotion in Others
- Gender, Emotion, and Nonverbal Behavior
- Culture and Emotional Expression
- The Effects of Facial Expressions

"Your face, my thane, is a book where men may read strange matters."

Lady Macbeth to her husband, in William Shakespeare's *Macbeth*

Expressive behavior implies emotion. Dolphins, with smiles seemingly plastered on their faces, appear happy. To decipher people's emotions we read their bodies, listen to their voice tones, and study their faces. Does nonverbal language vary with culture—or is it universal? And do our expressions influence our experienced emotions?

Detecting Emotion in Others

36-1 How do we communicate nonverbally?

To Westerners, a firm handshake conveys an outgoing, expressive personality (Chaplin et al., 2000). A gaze, an averted glance, or a stare communicate intimacy, submission, or dominance (Kleinke, 1986). When two people are passionately in love, they typically spend time—quite a bit of time—gazing into each other's eyes (Rubin, 1970). Would such gazes stir these feelings between strangers? To find out, researchers asked unacquainted male-female pairs to gaze intently for two minutes either at each other's hands or into each other's eyes. After separating, the eye gazers reported feeling a tingle of attraction and affection (Kellerman et al., 1989).

Most of us read nonverbal cues well. Shown 10 seconds of video from the end of a speed-dating interaction, people can often detect whether one person is attracted to another (Place et al., 2009). We are especially good at detecting nonverbal threats. In a series of subliminally flashed words, we more often sense the presence of negative ones, such as *snake* or *bomb* (Dijksterhuis & Aarts, 2003). In a crowd of faces, a single angry face "pops out" faster than a single happy one (Hansen & Hansen, 1988; Pinkham et al., 2010). And even when hearing another language, most of us readily detect anger (Scherer et al., 2001).

Experience can sensitize us to particular emotions, as shown by experiments using a series of faces (like those in **FIGURE 36.1**) that morph from anger to fear (or sadness). Viewing such faces, physically abused children are much quicker than other children to spot the signals of anger. Shown a face that is 60 percent fear and 40 percent anger, they are as likely to perceive anger as fear. Their perceptions become sensitively attuned to glimmers of danger that nonabused children miss.

Hard-to-control facial muscles reveal signs of emotions you may be trying to conceal. Lifting just the inner part of your eyebrows, which few people do consciously, reveals distress or worry. Eyebrows raised and pulled together signal fear. Activated muscles under the eyes and raised cheeks suggest a natural smile. A feigned smile, such as one we make for a photographer, often continues for more than 4 or 5 seconds. Most authentic expressions have faded by that time. Feigned smiles are also switched on and off more abruptly than is a genuine happy smile (Bugental, 1986).

Our brains are rather amazing detectors of subtle expressions. Just *how* amazing was clear when researchers filmed teachers talking to unseen schoolchildren (Babad et al., 1991). A mere 10-second clip of either the teacher's voice or face provided enough clues for both young and old viewers to determine whether the teacher liked and admired a child. In other experiments, even glimpsing a face for one-tenth of a second enabled people to judge others' attractiveness or trustworthiness or to rate politicians' competence and predict their voter support (Willis & Todorov, 2006). "First impressions . . . occur with astonishing speed," note Christopher Olivola and Alexander Todorov (2010).

A silent language of emotion Hindu classic dance uses the face and body to effectively convey 10 different emotions (Hejmadi et al., 2000).

Network Photographers/Alamy

Genes matter. In one study of 254 identical and fraternal twins, about 50 percent of the difference among people's happiness ratings was heritable—attributable to genes. (Lykken & Tellegen, 1996). Other twin studies report similar or slightly less heritability (Bartels & Boomsma, 2009; Lucas, 2008; Nes et al., 2010). Identical twins raised apart are often similarly happy.

But our personal history and our culture matter, too. On the personal level, as we have seen, our emotions tend to balance around a level defined by our experience. On the cultural level, groups vary in the traits they value. Self-esteem and achievement matter more to Westerners, who value individualism. Social acceptance and harmony matter more to those in communal cultures such as Japan that stress family and community (Diener et al., 2003; Uchida & Kitayama, 2009).

Depending on our genes, our outlook, and our recent experiences, our happiness seems to fluctuate around our "happiness set point," which disposes some people to be ever upbeat and others more negative. Even so, after following thousands of lives over two decades, researchers have determined that our satisfaction with life is not fixed (Lucas & Donnellan, 2007). Happiness rises and falls, and can be influenced by factors that are under our control. A striking example: In a long-term German study, married partners were as similarly satisfied with their lives as were identical twins (Schimmack & Lucas, 2007). Genes matter. But as this study hints, relationship quality matters, too. (For research-based hints on enhancing your own happiness, see Close-Up: Want to Be Happier?)

Studies of chimpanzees in zoos reveal that happiness in chimpanzees, as rated by 200 employees, is also genetically influenced (Weiss et al., 2000, 2002).

© The New Yorker Collection, 1996, J. B. Handelsman from cartoonbank.com. All Rights Reserved.

"I could cry when I think of the years I wasted accumulating money, only to learn that my cheerful disposition is genetic."

CLOSE-UP

Want to Be Happier?

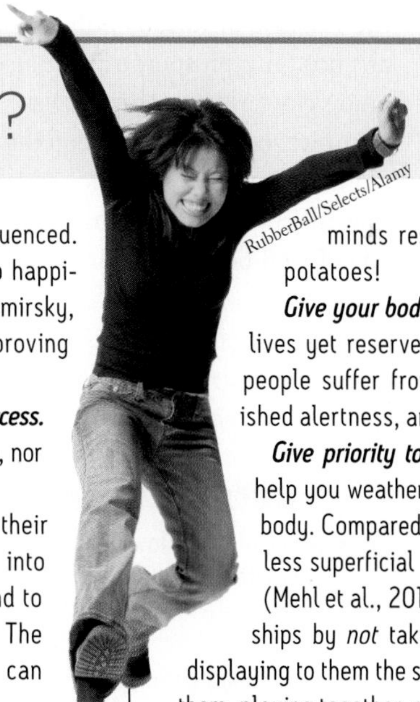

RubberBall/Selects/Alamy

Your happiness, like your cholesterol level, is genetically influenced. Yet as cholesterol is also influenced by diet and exercise, so happiness is partly under your control (Nes, 2010; Sin & Lyubomirsky, 2009). Here are some research-based suggestions for improving your mood and increasing your satisfaction with life.

Realize that enduring happiness may not come from financial success. We adapt to change by adjusting our expectations. Neither wealth, nor any other circumstance we long for, will guarantee happiness.

Take control of your time. Happy people feel in control of their lives. To master your use of time, set goals and break them into daily aims. This may be frustrating at first because we all tend to overestimate how much we will accomplish in any given day. The good news is that we generally *underestimate* how much we can accomplish in a year, given just a little progress every day.

Act happy. People who are manipulated into a smiling expression feel better. So put on a happy face. Talk as *if* you feel positive self-esteem, are optimistic, and are outgoing. We can often act our way into a happier state of mind.

Seek work and leisure that engage your skills. Happy people often are in a zone called *flow*—absorbed in tasks that challenge but don't overwhelm them. The most expensive forms of leisure (sitting on a yacht) often provide less flow experience than simpler forms, such as gardening, socializing, or craft work. Money also buys more happiness when spent on experiences that you can look forward to, enjoy, and remember than when spent on material stuff (Carter & Gilovich, 2010). As pundit Art Buchwald said, "The best things in life aren't things."

Join the "movement" movement. Aerobic exercise can relieve mild depression and anxiety as it promotes health and energy. Sound minds reside in sound bodies. Off your duffs, couch potatoes!

Give your body the sleep it wants. Happy people live active lives yet reserve time for renewing sleep and solitude. Many people suffer from sleep debt, with resulting fatigue, diminished alertness, and gloomy moods.

Give priority to close relationships. Intimate friendships can help you weather difficult times. Confiding is good for soul and body. Compared with unhappy people, happy people engage in less superficial small talk and more meaningful conversations (Mehl et al., 2010). So resolve to nurture your closest relationships by *not* taking your loved ones for granted. This means displaying to them the sort of kindness you display to others, affirming them, playing together, and sharing together.

Focus beyond self. Reach out to those in need. Happiness increases helpfulness (those who feel good do good). But doing good also makes one feel good.

Count your blessings and record your gratitude. Keeping a gratitude journal heightens well-being (Emmons, 2007; Seligman et al., 2005). Try pausing each day to savor good moments, and to record positive events and why they occurred. Express your gratitude to others.

Nurture your spiritual self. For many people, faith provides a support community, a reason to focus beyond self, and a sense of purpose and hope. That helps explain why people active in faith communities report greater-than-average happiness and often cope well with crisis.

Digested from David G. Myers, *The Pursuit of Happiness* (Harper).

FIGURE 37.8

Declining well-being in Egypt and Tunisia prior to popular revolts In Gallup surveys, the percentage of people who were "thriving" (rating their life satisfaction 7 or higher and projecting their next five years at 8 or higher on a 10-step scale) declined in advance of 2011 demonstrations that led to a change of government (Clifton & Morales, 2011).

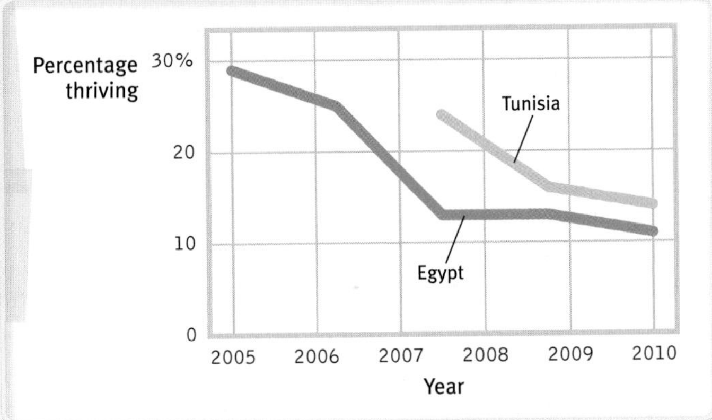

If we can enhance our happiness on an individual level, could we use happiness research to refocus our national priorities more on advancing psychological well-being? Many psychologists believe we could. Ed Diener (2006, 2009), supported by 52 colleagues, has proposed ways in which nations might measure national well-being. "Policymakers should be interested in subjective well-being not only because of its inherent value to citizens, but also because individuals' subjective well-being can have positive spillover benefits for the society as a whole." Happiness research offers new ways to assess the impacts of various public policies, argue Diener and his colleagues. Happy societies are not only prosperous, but also places where people trust one another, feel free, and enjoy close relationships (Oishi & Schimmack, 2010). Thus, when debating the minimum wage, economic inequality, tax rates, divorce laws, health care, and neighborhood planning, people's psychological well-being should be a prime consideration—a point now affirmed by the Canadian, French, German, and British governments, which have added well-being measures to their national agendas (Cohen, 2011; Gertner, 2010; Stiglitz, 2009). The predictive power of national well-being assessments was apparent in 2011, as the governments of Egypt and Tunisia succumbed to popular uprisings in the aftermath of declining life satisfaction (**FIGURE 37.8**).

RETRIEVAL PRACTICE

- Which of the following factors do NOT predict self-reported happiness? Which factors are better predictors?

  a. Age
  b. Personality traits
  c. Close relationships
  d. Gender
  e. "Flow" in work and leisure
  f. Religious faith

ANSWERS: Age and gender (a. and d.) do NOT effectively predict happiness levels. Better predictors are personality traits, close relationships, "flow" in work and leisure, and religious faith (b., c., e., and f.).

MODULE REVIEW

Experienced Emotion

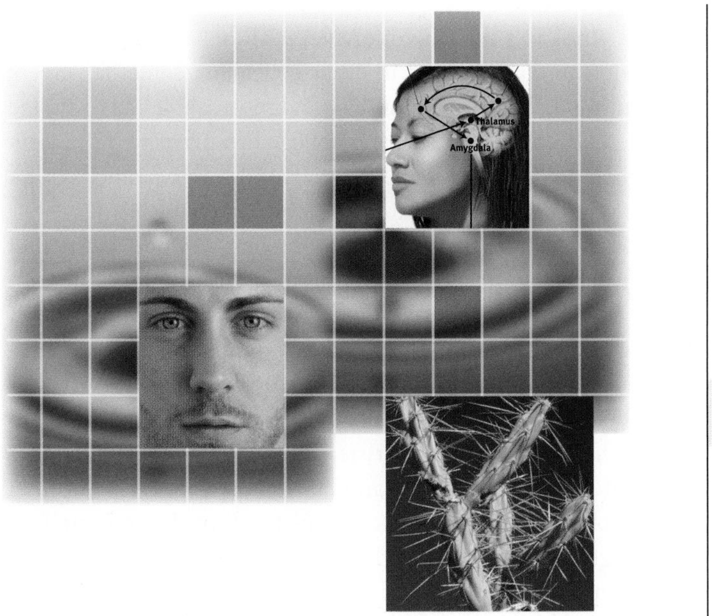

Learning Objectives

RETRIEVAL PRACTICE Take a moment to answer each of these Learning Objective Questions (repeated here from within the module). Then turn to Appendix B, Complete Module Reviews, to check your answers. Research suggests that trying to answer these questions on your own will improve your long-term retention (McDaniel et al., 2009).

37-1: What are some basic emotions, and what two dimensions help differentiate them?

37-2: What are the causes and consequences of anger?

37-3: What are the causes and consequences of happiness?

Terms and Concepts to Remember

RETRIEVAL PRACTICE Test yourself on these terms by trying to write down the definition before flipping back to the referenced page to check your answer.

catharsis, p. 493
feel-good, do-good phenomenon, p. 495
subjective well-being, p. 495
adaptation-level phenomenon, p. 499
relative deprivation, p. 499

RETRIEVAL PRACTICE **Gain an advantage, and benefit from immediate feedback, with the interactive self-testing resources at www.worthpublishers.com/myers.**

MODULE 38

- Stress: Some Basic Concepts
- Stress and Illness

Stress and Health

How often do you experience stress in your daily life? Never? Rarely? Sometimes? Or frequently? When pollsters put a similar question to other collegians, some 85 percent recalled experiencing stress during the last three months—and most said it had disrupted their school work at least once (AP, 2009). On entering college or university, 18 percent of men and 39 percent of women reported having been "frequently overwhelmed" by all they had to do during the past year (Pryor et al., 2010).

Stress often strikes without warning. Imagine being 21-year-old Ben Carpenter on the world's wildest and fastest wheelchair ride. As he crossed an intersection on a sunny summer afternoon in 2007, the light changed. A large truck, whose driver didn't see him, started moving into the intersection. As they bumped, Ben's wheelchair turned to face forward, and its handles got stuck in the truck's grille. Off they went, the driver unable to hear Ben's cries for help. As they sped down the highway about an hour from my home, passing motorists caught the bizarre sight of a truck pushing a wheelchair at 50 miles per hour and started calling 911. (The first caller: "You are not going to believe this. There is a semi truck pushing a guy in a wheelchair on Red Arrow highway!") Lucky for Ben, one passerby was an undercover police officer. Pulling a quick U-turn, he followed the truck to its destination a couple of miles from where the wild ride had started, and informed the disbelieving driver that he had a passenger hooked in his grille. "It was very scary," said Ben, who has muscular dystrophy.

AP Photo/Michigan State Police

Extreme stress Ben Carpenter experienced the wildest of rides after his wheelchair got stuck in a truck's grille.

Ben Carpenter clearly had a stressful experience. He reacted fairly calmly. How would you react? In this module, we answer basic questions about stress. What is it? How does it affect us? How do our emotions, personality, attitudes, and behaviors influence our risk of disease? To study how stress and healthy and unhealthy behaviors influence health and illness, psychologists and physicians created the interdisciplinary field of *behavioral medicine*, integrating behavioral and medical knowledge. **Health psychology** provides psychology's contribution to behavioral medicine. Let's consider some of psychology's findings on stress.

Stress: Some Basic Concepts

38-1 What events provoke stress responses, and how do we respond and adapt to stress?

Stress is a slippery concept. We sometimes use the word informally to describe threats or challenges ("Ben was under a lot of stress"), and at other times our responses ("Ben experienced acute stress"). To a psychologist, the dangerous truck ride was a *stressor*. Ben's physical and emotional responses were a *stress reaction*. And the process by which he related to the threat was *stress*. Thus, **stress** is the process of appraising and responding to a threatening or challenging event (**FIGURE 38.1**). Stress arises less from events themselves than from how we

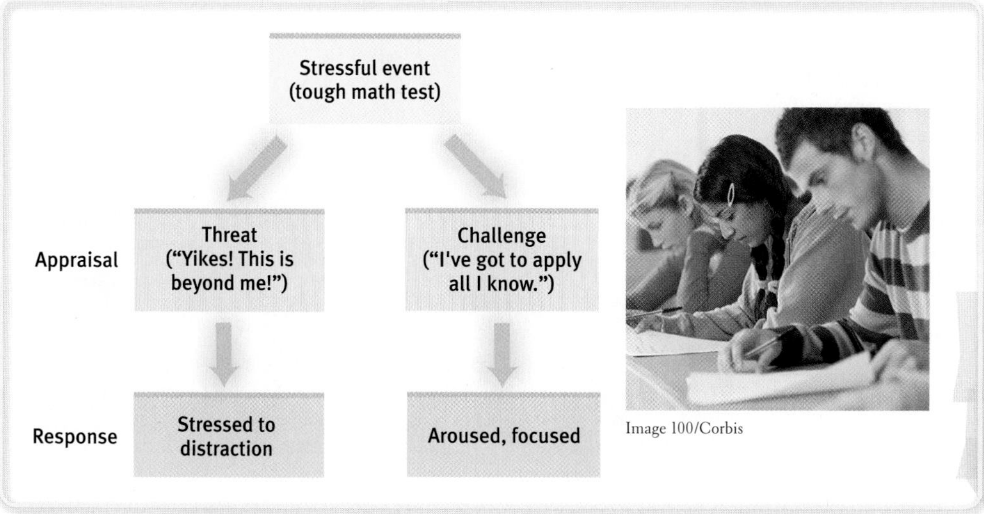

FIGURE 38.1
Stress appraisal The events of our lives flow through a psychological filter. How we appraise an event influences how much stress we experience and how effectively we respond.

appraise them (Lazarus, 1998). One person, alone in a house, ignores its creaking sounds and experiences no stress; someone else suspects an intruder and becomes alarmed. One person regards a new job as a welcome challenge; someone else appraises it as risking failure.

When short-lived, or when perceived as challenges, stressors can have positive effects. A momentary stress can mobilize the immune system for fending off infections and healing wounds (Segerstrom, 2007). Stress also arouses and motivates us to conquer problems. In the Gallup World Poll, those who are stressed but not depressed report being energized and satisfied with their lives—the opposite of the lethargy of those depressed but not stressed (Ng et al., 2009). Championship athletes, successful entertainers, and great teachers and leaders all thrive and excel when aroused by a challenge (Blascovich et al., 2004). Having conquered cancer or rebounded from a lost job, some people emerge with stronger self-esteem and a deepened spirituality and sense of purpose. Indeed, some stress early in life is conducive to later emotional resilience (Landauer & Whiting, 1979). Adversity can beget growth.

Extreme or prolonged stress can harm us. Children who suffer severe or prolonged abuse are later at risk of chronic disease (Repetti et al., 2002). Troops who had post-traumatic stress reactions to heavy combat in the Vietnam war later suffered greatly elevated rates of circulatory, digestive, respiratory, and infectious diseases (Boscarino, 1997). People who lose their jobs, especially later in their working life, are at increased risk of heart problems and death (Gallo et al., 2006; Sullivan & von Wachter, 2009).

So there is an interplay between our heads and our health. Before exploring that interplay, let's look more closely at stressors and stress reactions.

Stressors—Things That Push Our Buttons

Stressors fall into three main types: catastrophes, significant life changes, and daily hassles. All can be toxic.

Catastrophes

Catastrophes are unpredictable large-scale events, such as wars, earthquakes, and famines. Nearly everyone appraises catastrophes as threatening. We often give aid and comfort to one another after such events, but damage to emotional and physical health can be significant. In surveys taken in the three weeks after the 9/11 terrorist attacks, for example, two-thirds of Americans said they were having some trouble concentrating and sleeping (Wahlberg, 2001). In the New York area, people were especially likely to report such symptoms, and sleeping pill prescriptions rose by a reported 28 percent (HMHL, 2002; NSF, 2010). In the four months after Hurricane Katrina, New Orleans' suicide rate reportedly tripled (Saulny, 2006).

health psychology a subfield of psychology that provides psychology's contribution to behavioral medicine.

stress the process by which we perceive and respond to certain events, called *stressors,* that we appraise as threatening or challenging.

Daniel Morel/AFP/Getty/Newscom

Toxic stress On the day of its 1994 earthquake, Los Angeles experienced a fivefold increase in sudden-death heart attacks. Most occurred in the first two hours after the quake and near its center and were unrelated to physical exertion (Muller & Verrier, 1996). The 2010 Haiti earthquake and its aftermath, shown here, surely also triggered stress-related ills.

For those who respond to catastrophes by relocating to another country, the stress is twofold. The trauma of uprooting and family separation combine with the challenges of adjusting to the new culture's language, ethnicity, climate, and social norms (Pipher, 2002; Williams & Berry, 1991). In the first half-year, before their morale begins to rebound, newcomers often experience culture shock and deteriorating well-being (Marovizky & Samid, 2008). Such relocations may become increasingly common due to climate change in years to come.

Significant Life Changes

Life transitions are often keenly felt. Even happy events, such as getting married, can be stressful. Many changes—leaving home, becoming divorced, losing a job, having a loved one die—often happen during young adulthood. The stress of those years was clear in a survey in which 15,000 Canadian adults were asked whether "You are trying to take on too many things at once." Responses indicated highest stress levels among young adults. Young adult stress appeared again when 650,000 Americans were asked if they had experienced a lot of stress "yesterday" (**FIGURE 38.2**).

Some psychologists study the health effects of life changes by following people over time. Others compare the life changes recalled by those who have or have not suffered a specific health problem, such as a heart attack. These studies indicate that people recently widowed, fired, or divorced are more vulnerable to disease (Dohrenwend et al., 1982; Strully, 2009). In one Finnish study of 96,000 widowed people, their risk of death doubled in the week following their partner's death (Kaprio et al., 1987). Experiencing a cluster of crises—losing a job, home, and partner, for example—puts one even more at risk.

FIGURE 38.2

Age and stress A Gallup-Healthways survey of 650,000 Americans during 2008 and 2009 found daily stress highest among younger adults (Newport & Pelham, 2009).

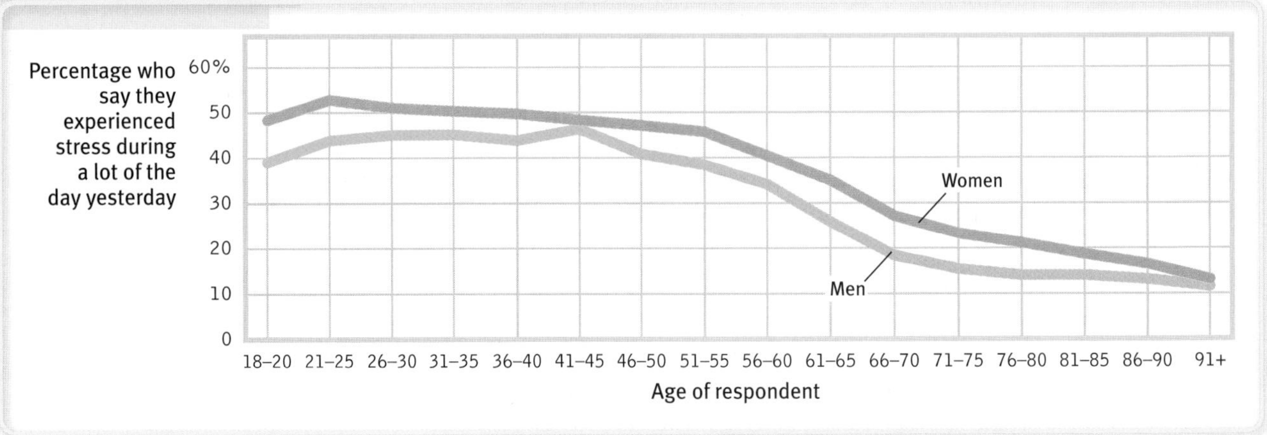

general adaptation syndrome (GAS) Selye's concept of the body's adaptive response to stress in three phases—alarm, resistance, exhaustion.

Daily Hassles

Events don't have to remake our lives to cause stress. Stress also comes from *daily hassles*—rush-hour traffic, aggravating housemates, long lines at the store, too many things to do, family frustrations, and friends who won't pick up their phone (Kohn & Macdonald, 1992; Repetti et al., 2009; Ruffin, 1993). Some people can simply shrug off such hassles. For others, however, the everyday annoyances add up and take a toll on health and well-being.

Many people face more significant daily hassles. As the Great Recession of 2008–2009 bottomed out, Americans' most oft-cited stressors related to money (76 percent), work (70 percent), and the economy (65 percent) (APA, 2010). Such stressors are well-known to residents of impoverished areas, where many people routinely face inadequate income, unemployment, solo parenting, and overcrowding.

Prolonged stress takes a toll on our cardiovascular system. Daily pressures may be compounded by anti-gay prejudice or racism, which—like other stressors—can have both psychological and physical consequences (Pascoe & Richman, 2009; Rostosky et al., 2009; Swim et al., 2009). Thinking that some of the people you encounter each day will dislike you, distrust you, or doubt your abilities makes daily life stressful. Such stress takes a toll on the health of many African-Americans, driving up blood pressure levels (Mays et al., 2007; Ong et al., 2009).

The Stress Response System

Medical interest in stress dates back to Hippocrates (460–377 B.C.E.). In the 1920s, Walter Cannon (1929) confirmed that the stress response is part of a unified mind-body system. He observed that extreme cold, lack of oxygen, and emotion-arousing events all trigger an outpouring of the stress hormones epinephrine and norepinephrine from the core of the adrenal glands. When alerted by any of a number of brain pathways, the sympathetic nervous system increases heart rate and respiration, diverts blood from digestion to the skeletal muscles, dulls feelings of pain, and releases sugar and fat from the body's stores. All this prepares the body for the wonderfully adaptive response that Cannon called *fight or flight*.

"You've got to know when to hold'em; know when to fold'em. Know when to walk away, and know when to run."

Kenny Rogers, "The Gambler," 1978

Since Cannon's time, physiologists have identified an additional stress response system. On orders from the cerebral cortex (via the hypothalamus and pituitary gland), the outer part of the adrenal glands secretes *glucocorticoid* stress hormones such as *cortisol*. The two systems work at different speeds, explains biologist Robert Sapolsky (2003): "In a fight-or-flight scenario, epinephrine is the one handing out guns; glucocorticoids are the ones drawing up blueprints for new aircraft carriers needed for the war effort." The epinephrine guns were firing at high speed during an experiment inadvertently conducted on a British Airways San Francisco to London flight. Three hours after takeoff, a mistakenly played message told passengers the plane was about to crash into the sea. Although the flight crew immediately recognized the error and tried to calm the terrified passengers, several required medical assistance (Associated Press, 1999).

Canadian scientist Hans Selye's (1936, 1976) 40 years of research on stress extended Cannon's findings. His studies of animals' reactions to various stressors, such as electric shock and surgery, helped make stress a major concept in both psychology and medicine. Selye proposed that the body's adaptive response to stress is so general that, like a single burglar alarm, it sounds, no matter what intrudes. He named this response the **general adaptation syndrome (GAS)**, and he saw it as a three-phase process (**FIGURE 38.3** on the next page). Let's say you suffer a physical or an emotional trauma. In Phase 1, you have an *alarm reaction*, as your sympathetic nervous system is suddenly activated. Your heart rate zooms. Blood is diverted to your skeletal muscles. You feel the faintness of shock.

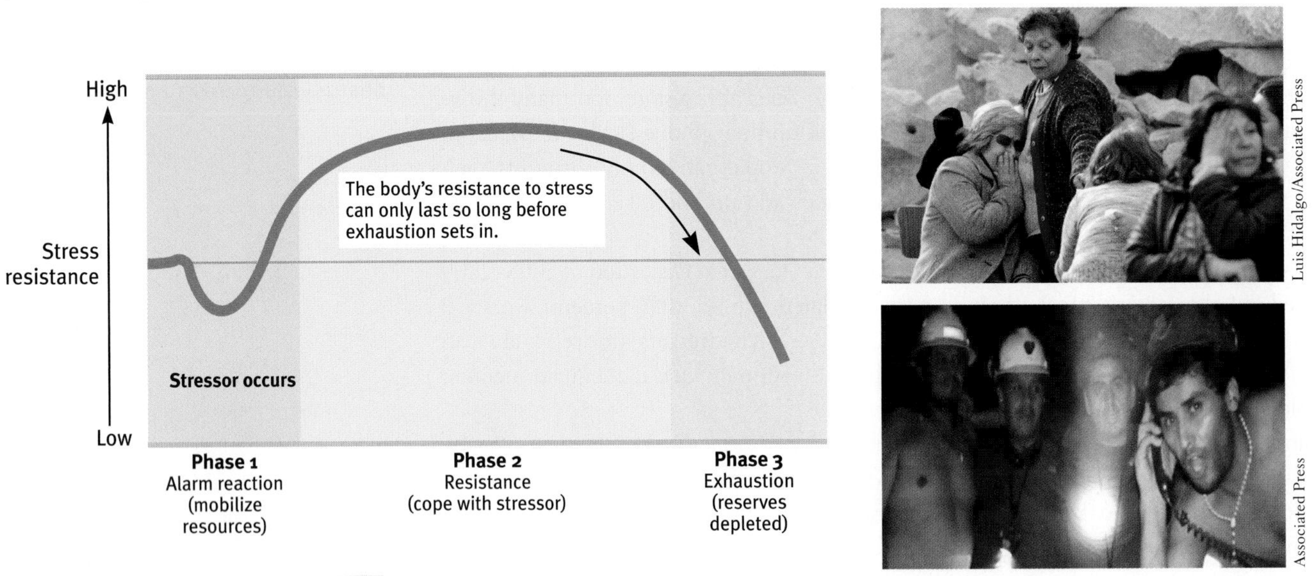

Luis Hidalgo/Associated Press

Associated Press

FIGURE 38.3
Selye's general adaptation syndrome When a gold and copper mine in Chile collapsed in 2010, family and friends rushed to the scene, fearing the worst. Many of those holding vigil outside the mine were nearly exhausted with the stress of waiting and worrying when, after 18 days, they received news that all 33 of the miners inside were alive and well.

With your resources mobilized, you are now ready to fight back. During Phase 2, *resistance*, your temperature, blood pressure, and respiration remain high. Your adrenal glands pump hormones into your bloodstream. You are fully engaged, summoning all your resources to meet the challenge.

As time passes, with no relief from stress, your body's reserves begin to run out. You have reached Phase 3, *exhaustion*. With exhaustion, you become more vulnerable to illness or even, in extreme cases, collapse and death.

Selye's basic point: Although the human body copes well with temporary stress, prolonged stress can damage it. The brain's production of new neurons slows and some neural circuits degenerate (Dias-Ferreira et al., 2009; Mirescu & Gould, 2006). One study found shortening of *telomeres*, pieces of DNA at the ends of chromosomes, in women who suffered enduring stress as caregivers for children with serious disorders (Epel et al., 2004). Telomere shortening is a normal part of the aging process; when telomeres get too short, the cell can no longer divide and it ultimately dies. The most stressed women had cells that looked a decade older than their chronological age, which may help explain why severe stress seems to age people. Even fearful, easily stressed rats have been found to die sooner (after about 600 days) than their more confident siblings, which average 700-day life spans (Cavigelli & McClintock, 2003).

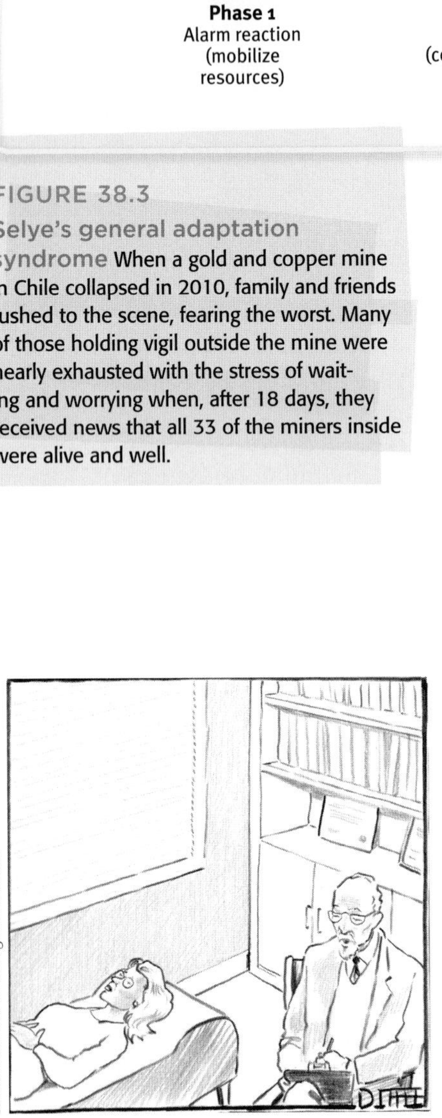

© The New Yorker Collection, 2007, Matthew Diffee from cartoonbank.com. All Rights Reserved.

"You may be suffering from what's known as full-nest syndrome."

Fortunately, there are other options for dealing with stress. One is a common response to a loved one's death: Withdraw. Pull back. Conserve energy. Faced with an extreme disaster, such as a ship sinking, some people become paralyzed by fear. Another stress response, found especially among women, is to seek and give support (Taylor et al., 2000, 2006). This **tend-and-befriend** response is demonstrated in the outpouring of help after natural disasters.

Facing stress, men more often than women tend to socially withdraw, turn to alcohol, or become aggressive. Women more often respond to stress by nurturing and banding together. This may in part be due to *oxytocin*, a stress-moderating hormone associated with pair bonding in animals and released by cuddling, massage, and breast feeding in humans (Campbell, 2010; Taylor, 2006). Gender differences in stress responses are reflected in brain scans: Women's brains become more active in areas important for face processing and empathy; men's become less active (Mather et al., 2010).

It often pays to spend our resources in fighting or fleeing an external threat. But we do so at a cost. When stress is momentary, the cost is small. When stress persists, we may pay a much higher price, with lowered resistance to infections and other threats to mental and physical well-being.

RETRIEVAL PRACTICE

- Stress response system: When alerted to a negative, uncontrollable event, our __________ nervous system arouses us. Heart rate and respiration __________ (increase/decrease). Blood is diverted from digestion to the skeletal __________. The body releases sugar and fat. All this prepares the body for the __________ - __________ - __________ response.

ANSWERS: sympathetic; increase; muscles; fight-or-flight

tend and befriend under stress, people (especially women) often provide support to others (tend) and bond with and seek support from others (befriend).

psychophysiological illness literally, "mind-body" illness; any stress-related physical illness, such as hypertension and some headaches.

psychoneuroimmunology the study of how psychological, neural, and endocrine processes together affect the immune system and resulting health.

lymphocytes the two types of white blood cells that are part of the body's immune system: *B lymphocytes* form in the *b*one marrow and release antibodies that fight bacterial infections; *T lymphocytes* form in the *t*hymus and other lymphatic tissue and attack cancer cells, viruses, and foreign substances.

Stress and Illness

38-2 How does stress make us more vulnerable to disease?

Not so long ago, the term *psychosomatic* described psychologically caused physical symptoms. In common usage, the term came to mean that the symptoms were unreal—"merely" psychosomatic. To avoid such connotations and to better describe the genuine physiological effects of psychological states, most experts today refer instead to stress-related **psychophysiological illnesses,** such as hypertension and some headaches. Stress also leaves us less able to fight off disease. A relatively new field—**psychoneuroimmunology**—has emerged to study these mind-body interactions (Kiecolt-Glaser, 2009). This awkward name makes sense when said slowly: Your thoughts and feelings *(psycho)* influence your brain *(neuro)*, which influences the endocrine hormones that affect your disease-fighting *immune* system. And this new field is the study of *(ology)* those interactions.

Hundreds of new experiments reveal the nervous and endocrine systems' influence on the immune system (Sternberg, 2009). You can think of the immune system as a complex surveillance system. When it functions properly, it keeps you healthy by isolating and destroying bacteria, viruses, and other invaders. Four types of cells are active in these search-and-destroy missions (**FIGURE 38.4**). Two are types of white blood cells, called **lymphocytes.**

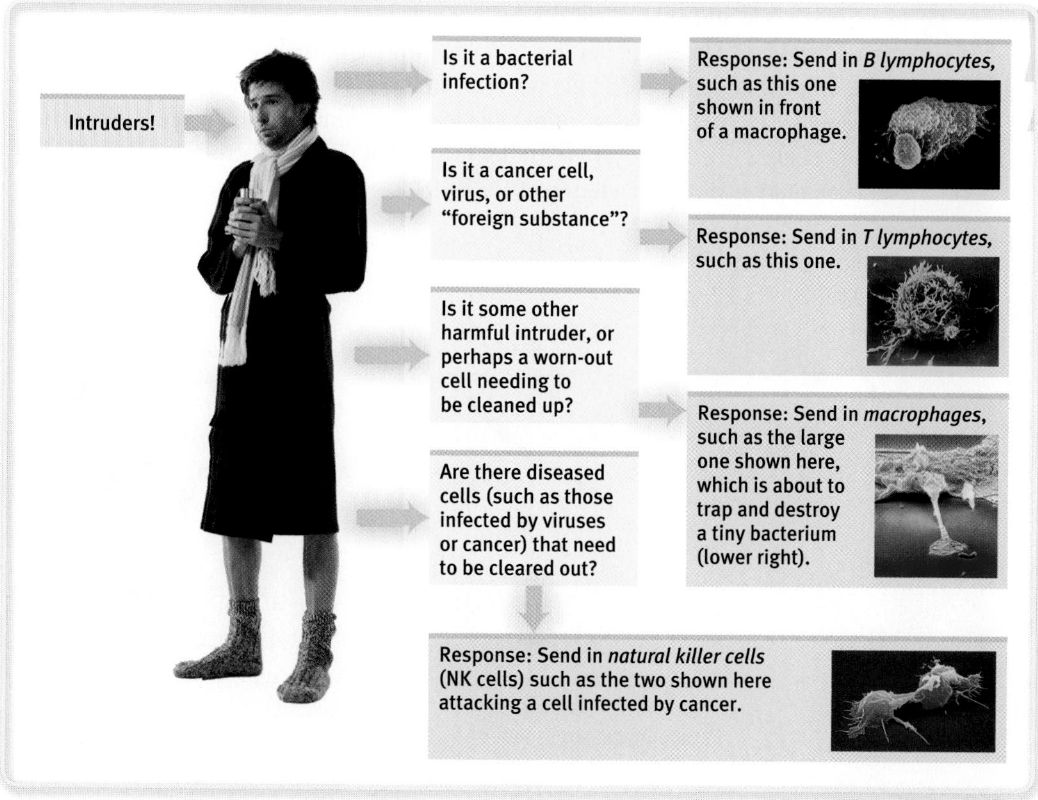

FIGURE 38.4 A simplified view of immune responses

Man with scarf: Fuse/Getty Images; *B lymphocyte*: CNRI/Photo Researchers; *T lymphocyte*: NIBSC/Photo Researchers; *macrophage*: Lennart Nilsson/Boehringer Ingelheim International GmbH; *NK cells*: Eye of Science/Photo Researchers

B lymphocytes form in the *b*one marrow and release antibodies that fight bacterial infections. *T lymphocytes* form in the *t*hymus and other lymphatic tissue and attack cancer cells, viruses, and foreign substances—even "good" ones, such as transplanted organs. The third agent is the *macrophage* ("big eater"), which identifies, pursues, and ingests harmful invaders and worn-out cells. And, finally, the *natural killer cells* (NK cells) pursue diseased cells (such as those infected by viruses or cancer). Your age, nutrition, genetics, body temperature, and stress all influence your immune system's activity.

When your immune system doesn't function properly, it can err in two directions. Responding too strongly, it may attack the body's own tissues, causing some forms of arthritis or an allergic reaction. Underreacting, it may allow a dormant herpes virus to erupt or cancer cells to multiply. Women are immunologically stronger than men, making them less susceptible to infections, but this very strength also makes them more susceptible to self-attacking diseases, such as lupus and multiple sclerosis (Morell, 1995; Pido-Lopez et al., 2001).

"In the eyes of God or biology or what have you, it is just very important to have women."

Immunologist Normal Talal (1995)

Your immune system is not a headless horseman. The brain regulates the secretion of stress hormones, which lessens the disease-fighting lymphocytes. Immune suppression appears when animals are stressed by physical restraints, unavoidable electric shocks, noise, crowding, cold water, social defeat, or separation from their mothers (Maier et al., 1994). One six-month study monitored immune responses in 43 monkeys over six months (Cohen et al., 1992). Twenty-one were stressed by being housed with new roommates—three or four new monkeys—each month. By the end of the experiment, the socially disrupted monkeys' immune systems were weaker than those of monkeys left in stable groups. Human immune systems react similarly. Two examples:

- *Surgical wounds heal more slowly in stressed people.* In one experiment, dental students received punch wounds (precise small holes punched in the skin). Compared with wounds placed during summer vacation, those placed three days before a major exam healed 40 percent more slowly (Kiecolt-Glaser et al., 1998). Marriage conflict also slows punch-wound healing (Kiecolt-Glaser et al., 2005).
- *Stressed people are more vulnerable to colds.* Researchers dropped a cold virus into the noses of stressed and relatively unstressed people (**FIGURE 38.5**). Among those living stress-filled lives, 47 percent developed colds. Among those living relatively free of stress, only 27 percent did. In follow-up research, the happiest and most relaxed people were likewise markedly less vulnerable to an experimentally delivered cold virus (Cohen et al., 2003, 2006). Other studies reveal that major life stress increases the risk of a respiratory infection (Pedersen et al., 2010).

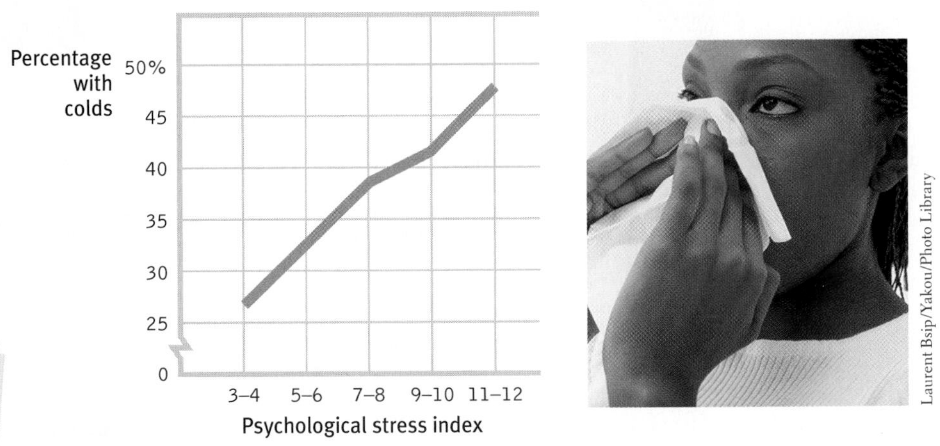

FIGURE 38.5
Stress and colds In an experiment by Sheldon Cohen and colleagues (1991), people with the highest life stress scores were also most vulnerable when exposed to an experimentally delivered cold virus.

D. Hurst/Alamy

The stress effect on immunity makes physiological sense. It takes energy to track down invaders, produce swelling, and maintain fevers. Thus, when diseased, your body reduces muscular energy output by inactivity and increased sleep. Stress does the opposite. It creates a competing energy need. During an aroused fight-or-flight reaction, your stress responses divert energy from your disease-fighting immune system and send it to your muscles and brain. This renders you more vulnerable to illness. *The bottom line:* Stress does not make us sick, but it does alter our immune functioning, which leaves us less able to resist infection.

Let's consider some ways that stress might affect AIDS, cancer, and heart disease.

RETRIEVAL PRACTICE

- The field of __________ studies mind-body interactions, including the effects of psychological, neural, and endocrine functioning on the immune system and overall health.

ANSWER: psychoneuroimmunology

- What general effect does stress have on our overall health?

ANSWER: Stress tends to reduce our immune system's ability to function properly, so that higher stress generally leads to greater incidence of physical illness.

Stress and AIDS

We know that stress suppresses immune functioning. What does this mean for people with AIDS *(acquired immune deficiency syndrome)*? As its name tells us, AIDS is an immune disorder, caused by the *human immunodeficiency virus (HIV)*. AIDS has become the world's fourth leading cause of death and Africa's number one killer.

Ironically, if a disease is spread by human contact (as AIDS is, through the exchange of bodily fluids, primarily semen and blood), and if it kills slowly (as AIDS does), it can be lethal to more people. Those who acquire HIV often spread it in the highly contagious first few weeks before they know they are infected. Worldwide, some 2.6 million people—slightly more than half of them women—became infected with HIV in 2009, often without their awareness (UNAIDS, 2010). Years after the initial infection, when AIDS appears, people have difficulty fighting off other diseases, such as pneumonia. More than 25 million people worldwide have died of AIDS (UNAIDS, 2010). (In the United States, where "only" a half-million of these fatalities have occurred, AIDS has killed more people than did combat in all the twentieth-century wars.)

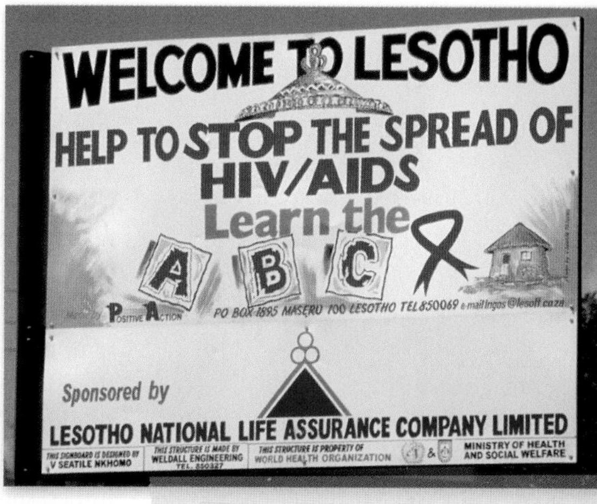

UNAIDS/G. Pirozzi

Africa is ground zero for AIDS In Lesotho, Uganda, and elsewhere, prevention efforts include the "ABC" Campaign—*A*bstinence, *B*e faithful, and use *C*ondoms.

Stress cannot give people AIDS. But could stress and negative emotions speed the transition from HIV infection to AIDS in someone already infected? Might stress predict a faster decline in those with AIDS? The answer to both questions seems to be *Yes* (Bower et al., 1998; Kiecolt-Glaser & Glaser, 1995; Leserman et al., 1999). HIV-infected men who experience stressful events, such as the loss of a partner, exhibit somewhat greater immune suppression and travel a faster course in this disease.

In North America and Western Europe, 74 percent of people with AIDS are men. In Sub-Saharan Africa, 60 percent of people with AIDS are women (UNAIDS, 2010).

Would efforts to reduce stress help control the disease? Again, the answer appears to be *Yes*. Educational initiatives, bereavement support groups, cognitive therapy, relaxation training, and exercise programs that reduce distress have all had positive consequences for HIV-positive people (Baum & Posluszny, 1999; McCain et al., 2008; Schneiderman, 1999). But the benefits are small, compared with available drug treatments.

Although AIDS is now more treatable than ever before, preventing HIV infection is a far better option. This is the focus of many educational programs, such as the ABC (*a*bstinence, *b*eing faithful, *c*ondom use) program that has been used with seeming success in Uganda (Altman, 2004; USAID, 2004).

Stress and Cancer

Stress does not create cancer cells. But in a healthy, functioning immune system, lymphocytes, macrophages, and NK cells search out and destroy cancer cells and cancer-damaged cells. If stress weakens the immune system, might this weaken a person's ability to

coronary heart disease the clogging of the vessels that nourish the heart muscle; the leading cause of death in many developed countries.

Type A Friedman and Rosenman's term for competitive, hard-driving, impatient, verbally aggressive, and anger-prone people.

Type B Friedman and Rosenman's term for easygoing, relaxed people.

fight off cancer? To explore a possible connection between stress and cancer, experimenters have implanted tumor cells in rodents or given them *carcinogens* (cancer-producing substances). They then exposed some rodents to uncontrollable stress, such as inescapable shocks, which weakened their immune systems. Those rodents were indeed more prone to developing cancer (Sklar & Anisman, 1981). Their tumors developed sooner and grew larger than in nonstressed rodents.

Does this stress-cancer link also hold with humans? The results are mixed. Some studies find that people are at increased risk for cancer within a year after experiencing depression, helplessness, or bereavement (Chida et al., 2008; Steptoe et al., 2010). In one large Swedish study, the risk of colon cancer was 5.5 times greater among people with a history of workplace stress than among those who reported no such problems. This difference was not attributable to group differences in age, smoking, drinking, or physical characteristics (Courtney et al., 1993). Other studies, however, have found no link between stress and human cancer (Coyne et al., 2010; Petticrew et al., 1999, 2002). Concentration camp survivors and former prisoners of war, for example, do not have elevated cancer rates.

"I didn't give myself cancer."

Mayor Barbara Boggs Sigmund, 1939–1990, Princeton, New Jersey

One danger in hyping reports on emotions and cancer is that some patients may then blame themselves for their illness: "If only I had been more expressive, relaxed, and hopeful." A corollary danger is a "wellness macho" among the healthy, who take credit for their "healthy character" and lay a guilt trip on the ill: "She has cancer? That's what you get for holding your feelings in and being so nice." Dying thus becomes the ultimate failure.

It's important enough to repeat: *Stress does not create cancer cells.* At worst, it may affect their growth by weakening the body's natural defenses against multiplying malignant cells (Antoni & Lutgendorf, 2007). Although a relaxed, hopeful state may enhance these defenses, we should be aware of the thin line that divides science from wishful thinking. The powerful biological processes at work in advanced cancer or AIDS are not likely to be completely derailed by avoiding stress or maintaining a relaxed but determined spirit (Anderson, 2002; Kessler et al., 1991). And that explains why research consistently indicates that psychotherapy does not extend cancer patients' survival (Coyne et al., 2007, 2009; Coyne & Tennen, 2010).

When organic causes of illness are unknown, it is tempting to invent psychological explanations. Before the germ that causes tuberculosis was discovered, personality explanations of TB were popular (Sontag, 1978).

Stress and Heart Disease

38-3 Why are some of us more prone than others to coronary heart disease?

Stress is much more closely linked to **coronary heart disease**, North America's leading cause of death. In this disease, the blood vessels that nourish the heart muscle gradually close. Hypertension and a family history of the disease increase the risk of coronary heart disease. So do many behavioral factors (smoking, obesity, a high-fat diet, physical inactivity), physiological factors (an elevated cholesterol level), and psychological factors (stress responses and personality traits).

In a now-classic study, Meyer Friedman, Ray Rosenman, and their colleagues tested the idea that stress increases vulnerability to heart disease by measuring the blood cholesterol level and clotting speed of 40 U.S. male tax accountants at different times of year (Friedman & Ulmer, 1984). From January through March, the test results were completely normal. Then, as the accountants began scrambling to finish their clients' tax returns before the April 15 filing deadline, their cholesterol and clotting measures rose to dangerous levels. In May and June, with the deadline past, the measures returned to normal. Stress predicted heart attack risk for these men. The researchers' hunch had paid off, launching a classic nine-year study of more than 3000 healthy men, aged 35 to 59.

Photo Spin, Inc./Alamy

At the start of the study, the researchers interviewed each man for 15 minutes, noting his work and eating habits, manner of talking, and other behavioral patterns. Those who seemed the most reactive, competitive, hard-driving, impatient, time-conscious, supermotivated, verbally aggressive, and easily angered they called **Type A.** The roughly equal number who were more easygoing they called **Type B.** Which group do you suppose turned out to be the most coronary-prone?

In both India and America, Type A bus drivers are literally hard-driving: They brake, pass, and honk their horns more often than their more easygoing Type B colleagues (Evans et al., 1987).

Nine years later, 257 men had suffered heart attacks, and 69 percent of them were Type A. Moreover, not one of the "pure" Type Bs—the most mellow and laid back of their group—had suffered a heart attack.

As often happens in science, this exciting discovery provoked enormous public interest. But after that initial honeymoon period, researchers wanted to know more. Was the finding reliable? If so, what is the toxic component of the Type A profile: Time-consciousness? Competitiveness? Anger?

More than 700 studies have now explored possible psychological correlates or predictors of cardiovascular health (Chida & Hamer, 2008; Chida & Steptoe, 2009). These reveal that Type A's toxic core is negative emotions—especially the anger associated with an aggressively reactive temperament. When we are harassed or challenged, our active sympathetic nervous system redistributes bloodflow to our muscles, pulling it away from our internal organs. One of those organs, the liver, which normally removes cholesterol and fat from the blood, can't do its job. Type A individuals are more often "combat ready." Thus, excess cholesterol and fat may continue to circulate in their blood and later get deposited around the heart. Further stress—sometimes conflicts brought on by their own abrasiveness—may trigger altered heart rhythms. In people with weakened hearts, this altered pattern can cause sudden death (Kamarck & Jennings, 1991). Hostility also correlates with other risk factors, such as smoking, drinking, and obesity (Bunde & Suls, 2006). In important ways, people's minds and hearts interact.

"The fire you kindle for your enemy often burns you more than him."
Chinese proverb

Bannerman © 7/94

Hundreds of other studies of young and middle-aged men and women have confirmed the finding that people who react with anger over little things are the most coronary-prone. Suppressing negative emotions only heightens the risk (Kupper & Denollet, 2007). One study followed 13,000 middle-aged people for 5 years. Among those with normal blood pressure, people who had scored high on anger were three times more likely to have had heart attacks, even after researchers controlled for smoking and weight (Williams et al., 2000). Another study followed 1055 male medical students over an average of 36 years. Those who had reported being hot tempered were five times more likely to have had a heart attack by age 55 (Chang et al., 2002). As others have noted, rage "seems to lash back and strike us in the heart muscle" (Spielberger & London, 1982).

Pessimism seems to be similarly toxic. Laura Kubzansky and her colleagues (2001) studied 1306 initially healthy men who a decade earlier had scored as optimists, pessimists, or neither. Even after other risk factors such as smoking had been ruled out, pessimists were more than twice as likely as optimists to develop heart disease (**FIGURE 38.6**).

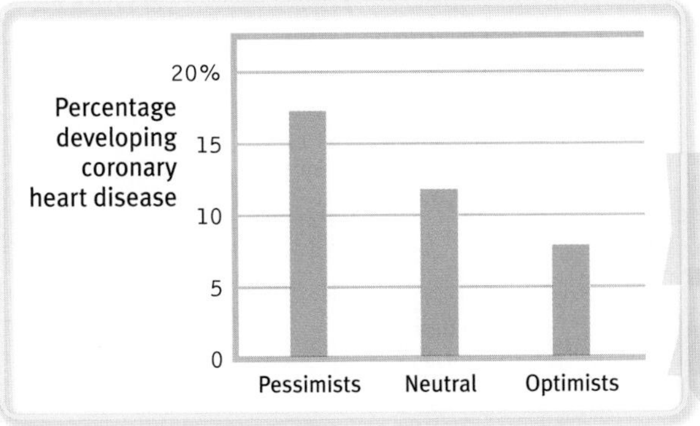

FIGURE 38.6
Pessimism and heart disease A Harvard School of Public Health team found pessimistic men at doubled risk of developing heart disease over a 10-year period. (From Kubzansky et al., 2001.)

"A cheerful heart is a good medicine, but a downcast spirit dries up the bones."

Proverbs 17:22

© Sean Locke/istockphoto

Depression, too, can be lethal. Happy people tend to be healthier and to outlive their unhappy peers (Diener & Chan, 2011; Siahpush et al., 2008). Even a big, happy smile predicts longevity, as Ernest Abel and Michael Kruger (2010) discovered when they examined the photographs of 150 Major League Baseball players who had appeared in the 1952 *Baseball Register* and had died by 2009. On average, the nonsmilers had died at 73, compared with an average 80 years for those with a broad, genuine smile.

The accumulated evidence from 57 studies suggests that "depression substantially increases the risk of death, especially death by unnatural causes and cardiovascular disease" (Wulsin et al., 1999). After following 63,469 women over a dozen years, researchers found more than a doubled rate of heart attack death among those who initially scored as depressed (Whang et al., 2009). In the years following a heart attack, people with high scores for depression are four times more likely than their low-scoring counterparts to develop further heart problems (Frasure-Smith & Lesperance, 2005). Depression is disheartening.

Depressed people tend to smoke more and exercise less (Whooley et al., 2008), but stress itself is also disheartening:

- When following 17,415 middle-aged American women, researchers found an 88 percent increased risk of heart attacks among those facing significant work stress (Slopen et al., 2010).
- In Denmark, a study of 12,116 female nurses found that those reporting "much too high" work pressures had a 40 percent increased risk of heart disease (Allesøe et al., 2010).
- In the United States, a 10-year study of middle-aged workers found that involuntary job loss more than doubled their risk of a heart attack (Gallo et al., 2006). A 14-year study of 1059 women found that those with five or more trauma-related stress symptoms had three times the normal risk of heart disease (Kubzansky et al., 2009).

Research suggests that heart disease and depression may both result when chronic stress triggers persistent inflammation (Matthews, 2005; Miller & Blackwell, 2006). After a heart attack, stress and anxiety increase the risk of death or of another attack (Roest et al., 2010). As we have seen, stress disrupts the body's disease-fighting immune system, enabling the body to focus its energies on fleeing or fighting the threat. Yet stress hormones enhance one immune response, the production of proteins that contribute to inflammation. Thus, people who experience social threats, including children reared in harsh families, are more prone to inflammation responses (Dickerson et al., 2009; Miller & Chen, 2010). Inflammation fights infections; if you cut yourself, inflammation recruits infection-fighting cells. But persistent inflammation can produce problems such as asthma or clogged arteries, and worsen depression (see **FIGURE 38.7**). Researchers are now uncovering the molecular mechanisms by which stress, in some people, activates genes that control inflammation (Cole et al., 2010).

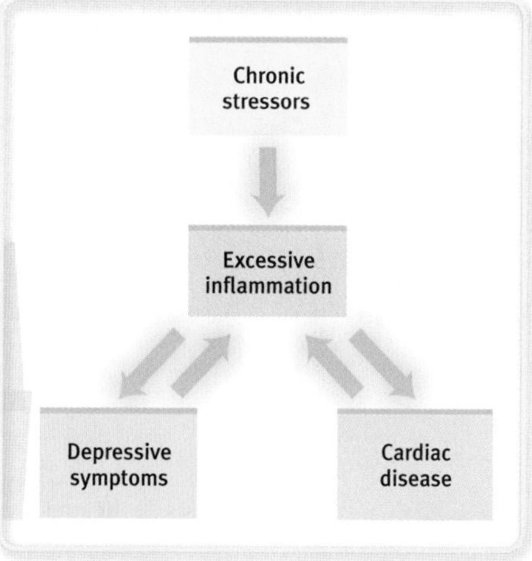

FIGURE 38.7
Stress→inflammation→heart disease and depression Gregory Miller and Ekin Blackwell (2006) report that chronic stress leads to persistent inflammation, which heightens the risk of both depression and clogged arteries.

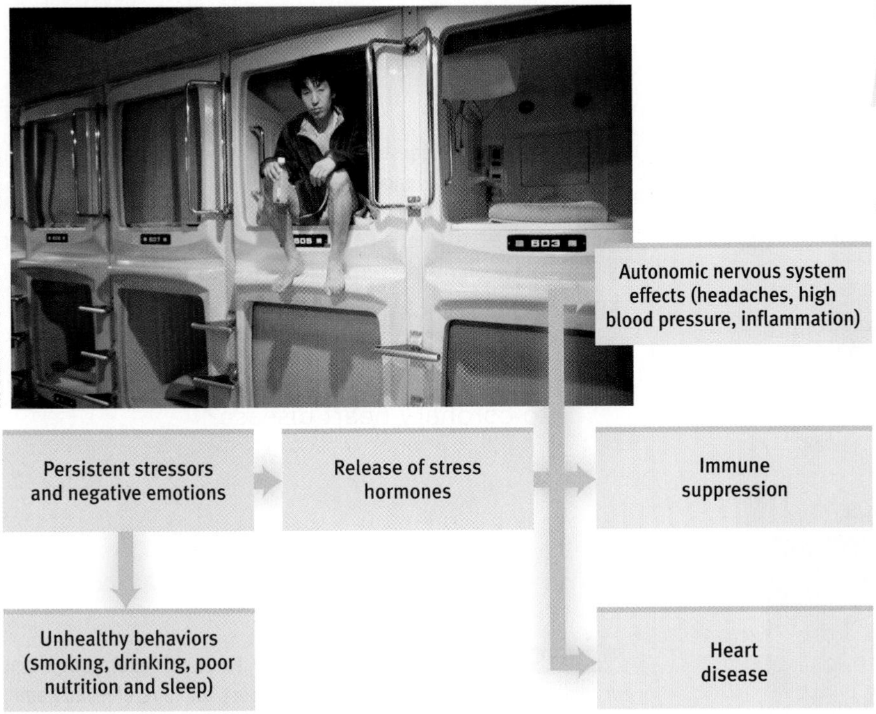

Ko Sasaki/The New York Times/Redux

FIGURE 38.8
Stress can have a variety of health-related consequences This is especially so when stress is experienced by angry, depressed, or anxious people. Job and income loss caused by the recent economic recession has created stress for many people, such as this jobless Japanese man living in a Tokyo "capsule hotel."

* * *

We can view the stress effect on our disease resistance as a price we pay for the benefits of stress (**FIGURE 38.8**). Stress invigorates our lives by arousing and motivating us. An unstressed life would hardly be challenging or productive.

Behavioral medicine research provides a reminder of one of contemporary psychology's overriding themes: *Mind and body interact; everything psychological is simultaneously physiological.* Psychological states are physiological events that influence other parts of our physiological system. Just pausing to *think* about biting into an orange section—the sweet, tangy juice from the pulpy fruit flooding across your tongue—can trigger salivation. As the Indian sage Santi Parva recognized more than 4000 years ago, "Mental disorders arise from physical causes, and likewise physical disorders arise from mental causes." There is an interplay between our heads and our health. We are biopsychosocial systems.

RETRIEVAL PRACTICE

- Which component of the Type A personality has been linked most closely to coronary heart disease?

ANSWER: Feeling angry and negative much of the time

MODULE REVIEW

Stress and Health

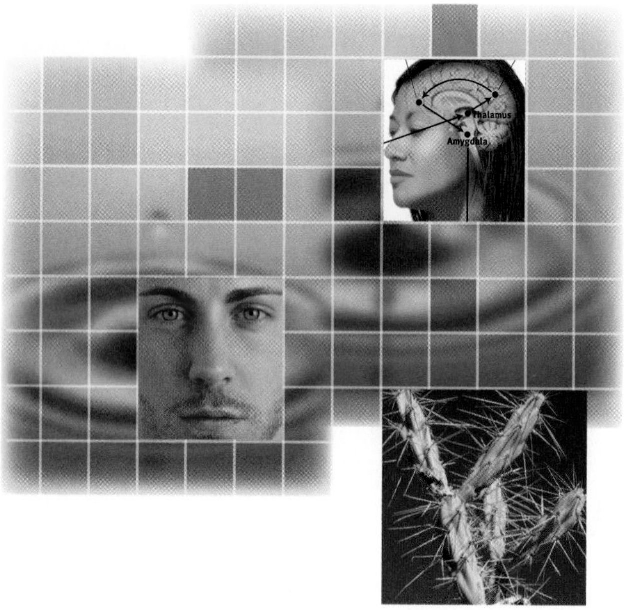

Learning Objectives

RETRIEVAL PRACTICE Take a moment to answer each of these Learning Objective Questions (repeated here from within the module). Then turn to Appendix B, Complete Module Reviews, to check your answers. Research suggests that trying to answer these questions on your own will improve your long-term retention (McDaniel et al., 2009).

38-1: What events provoke stress responses, and how do we respond and adapt to stress?

38-2: How does stress make us more vulnerable to disease?

38-3: Why are some of us more prone than others to coronary heart disease?

Terms and Concepts to Remember

RETRIEVAL PRACTICE Test yourself on these terms by trying to write down the definition before flipping back to the referenced page to check your answer.

health psychology, p. 504
stress, p. 504
general adaptation syndrome (GAS), p. 507
tend and befriend, p. 508
psychophysiological illness, p. 509
psychoneuroimmunology, p. 509
lymphocytes, p. 509
coronary heart disease, p. 512
Type A, p. 513
Type B, p. 513

RETRIEVAL PRACTICE Gain an advantage, and benefit from immediate feedback, with the interactive self-testing resources at www.worthpublishers.com/myers.

MODULE 39

Promoting Health

- Coping With Stress
- Reducing Stress

Promoting health begins with implementing strategies that prevent illness and enhance wellness. Traditionally, people have thought about their health only when something goes wrong—visiting a physician for diagnosis and treatment. That, say health psychologists, is like ignoring a car's maintenance and going to a mechanic only when the car breaks down. Health maintenance includes alleviating stress, preventing illness, and promoting well-being.

coping alleviating stress using emotional, cognitive, or behavioral methods.

problem-focused coping attempting to alleviate stress directly—by changing the stressor or the way we interact with that stressor.

emotion-focused coping attempting to alleviate stress by avoiding or ignoring a stressor and attending to emotional needs related to one's stress reaction.

Coping With Stress

39-1 In what ways do people cope with stress, and how does a perceived lack of control affect health?

Stressors are unavoidable. This fact, coupled with the fact that persistent stress correlates with heart disease, depression, and lowered immunity, gives us a clear message. We need to learn to **cope** with the stress in our lives, alleviating it with emotional, cognitive, or behavioral methods. We address some stressors directly, with **problem-focused coping.** For example, if our impatience leads to a family fight, we may go directly to that family member to work things out. We tend to use problem-focused strategies when we feel a sense of control over a situation and think we can change the circumstances, or at least change ourselves to deal with the circumstances more capably. We turn to **emotion-focused coping** when we cannot—or *believe* we cannot—change a situation. If, despite our best efforts, we cannot get along with that family member, we may search for relief from stress by confiding in friends and reaching out for support and comfort. When challenged, some of us tend to respond with cool problem-focused coping, others with emotion-focused coping (Connor-Smith & Flachsbart, 2007).

Emotion-focused strategies can move us toward better long-term health, as when we seek emotional distance from a damaging relationship or keep busy with hobbies to avoid thinking about an old addiction. Emotion-focused strategies can be maladaptive, however, as when students worried about not keeping up with the reading in class go out to party to get it off their mind. Sometimes a problem-focused strategy (catching up with the reading) more effectively reduces stress and promotes long-term health and satisfaction.

Several factors affect our ability to cope successfully. Among them are our feelings of personal control, our explanatory style, and our supportive connections.

Perceived Control

If two rats receive simultaneous shocks, but one can turn a wheel to stop the shocks (as illustrated in **FIGURE 39.1**), the helpless rat, but not the wheel turner, becomes more susceptible to ulcers and lowered immunity to disease (Laudenslager & Reite, 1984). In humans, too, uncontrollable threats trigger the strongest stress responses (Dickerson & Kemeny, 2004). For example, a bacterial infection often combines with uncontrollable stress to produce the most severe ulcers (Overmier & Murison, 1997). To cure the ulcer, kill the bug with antibiotics and control the stomach's acid secretions with reduced stress.

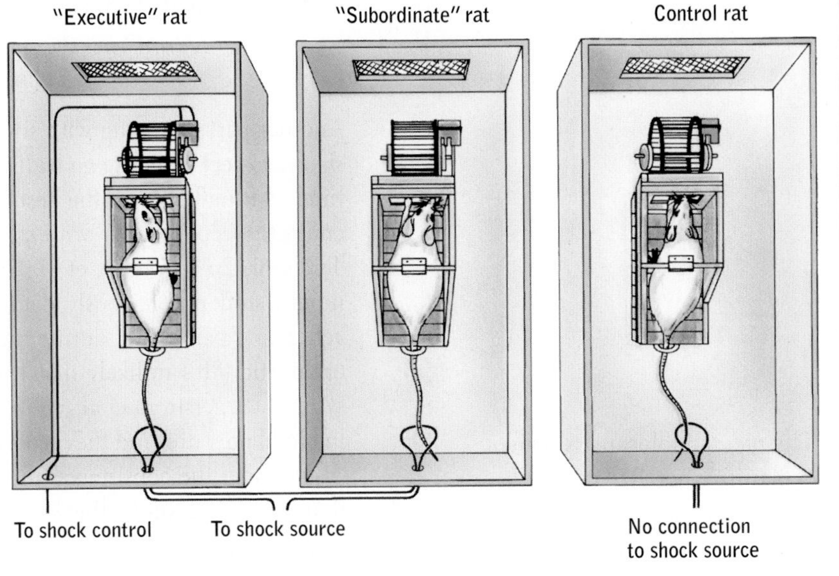

FIGURE 39.1
Health consequences of a loss of control The "executive" rat at the left can switch off the tail shock by turning the wheel. Because it has control over the shock, it is no more likely to develop ulcers than is the unshocked control rat on the right. The "subordinate" rat in the center receives the same shocks as the executive rat, but with no control over the shocks. It is, therefore, more likely to develop ulcers. (Adapted from Weiss, 1977.)

Perceiving a loss of control, we become more vulnerable to ill health. Elderly nursing home residents who have little perceived control over their activities tend to decline faster and die sooner than do those given more control (Rodin, 1986). Workers given control over their work environment—by being able to adjust office furnishings and control interruptions and distractions—also experience less stress (O'Neill, 1993). This helps explain why British civil service workers at the executive grades outlive those at clerical or laboring grades, and why Finnish workers with low job stress are less than half as likely to die of strokes or heart disease as are those with a demanding job and little control. The more control workers have, the longer they live (Bosma et al., 1997, 1998; Kivimaki et al., 2002; Marmot et al., 1997).

Control may also help explain a well-established link between economic status and longevity (Jokela et al., 2009). In one study of 843 grave markers in an old graveyard in Glasgow, Scotland, those with the costliest, highest pillars (indicating the most affluence) tended to have lived the longest (Carroll et al., 1994). Likewise, those living in Scottish regions with the least overcrowding and unemployment have the greatest longevity. There and elsewhere, high economic status predicts a lower risk of heart and respiratory diseases (Sapolsky, 2005). Wealthy predicts healthy among children, too (Chen, 2004). With higher economic status comes reduced risks of low birth weight, infant mortality, smoking, and violence. Even among other primates, those at the bottom of the social pecking order are more likely than their higher-status companions to become sick when exposed to a coldlike virus (Cohen et al., 1997). But for those high-status baboons and monkeys who frequently have to physically defend their dominant position, high status also entails stress (Sapolsky, 2005).

Why does perceived loss of control predict health problems? Animal studies show—and human studies confirm—that losing control provokes an outpouring of stress hormones. When rats cannot control shock or when primates or humans feel unable to control their environment, stress hormone levels rise, blood pressure increases, and immune responses drop (Rodin, 1986; Sapolsky, 2005). Captive animals therefore experience more stress and are more vulnerable to disease than are wild animals (Roberts, 1988). The crowding that occurs in high-density neighborhoods, prisons, and college and university dorms is another source of diminished feelings of control—and of elevated levels of stress hormones and blood pressure (Fleming et al., 1987; Ostfeld et al., 1987).

RETRIEVAL PRACTICE

- To cope with stress, we tend to use ___________- focused (emotion/problem) strategies when we feel in control of our world, and ___________-focused (emotion/problem) strategies when we believe we cannot change a situation.

ANSWERS: problem; emotion

Optimism and Health

39-2 What are the links among basic outlook on life, social support, stress, and health?

Another part of coping with stress is our outlook—what we expect from the world. *Pessimists* expect things to go badly. *Optimists* agree with statements such as, "In uncertain times, I usually expect the best." People with an optimistic outlook expect to have more control, to cope better with stressful events, and to enjoy better health (Aspinwall & Tedeschi, 2010; Carver et al., 2010; Rasmussen et al., 2009). During a semester's last month, students previously identified as optimistic reported less fatigue and fewer coughs, aches, and pains. And during the stressful first few weeks of law school, those who were optimistic ("It's unlikely that I will fail") enjoyed better moods and stronger immune systems (Segerstrom et al., 1998). Optimists also respond to stress with smaller increases in blood pressure, and they recover more quickly from heart bypass surgery.

The oldest Holocaust survivor explaining her 107 years: "In a word: optimism. I look at the good. When you are relaxed, your body is always relaxed."
Alice Herz-Sommer, 2010

Consider the consistency and startling magnitude of the optimism and positive emotions factor in several other studies:

- One research team followed 941 Dutch people, ages 65 to 85, for nearly a decade (Giltay et al., 2004, 2007). Among those in the lowest optimism quartile, 57 percent died, as did only 30 percent of the top optimism quartile.

- When Finnish researchers followed 2428 men for up to a decade, the number of deaths among those with a bleak, hopeless outlook was more than double that found among their optimistic counterparts (Everson et al., 1996). American researchers found the same when following 4256 Vietnam-era veterans (Phillips et al., 2009).
- A now-famous study followed up on 180 Catholic nuns who had written brief autobiographies at about 22 years of age and had thereafter lived similar lifestyles. Those who had expressed happiness, love, and other positive feelings in their autobiographies lived an average 7 years longer than their more dour counterparts (Danner et al., 2001). By age 80, some 54 percent of those expressing few positive emotions had died, as had only 24 percent of the most positive spirited.

PhotosIndia.com LLC/Alamy

Social Support

Social support—feeling liked and encouraged by intimate friends and family—promotes both happiness and health. In massive investigations, some following thousands of people for several years, close relationships have predicted health. People are less likely to die early if supported by close relationships (Uchino, 2009). When Brigham Young University researchers combined data from 148 studies totaling more than 300,000 people worldwide, they confirmed a striking effect of social support (Holt-Lunstad et al., 2010). During the studies, those with ample social connections had survival rates about 50 percent greater than those with meager connections. The impact of meager connections appeared roughly equal to the effect of smoking 15 cigarettes a day or being alcohol-dependent, and double the effect of not exercising or being obese. People aren't the only creatures to benefit from friends. Among baboons, strong social bonds with relatives and friends similarly predicts longevity (Silk et al., 2010).

People need people. Some fill this need by connecting with friends, family, co-workers, members of a faith community, or other support groups. Others connect in positive, happy, supportive marriages. People in low-conflict marriages live longer, healthier lives than the unmarried (De Vogli et al., 2007; Kaplan & Kronick, 2006; Sbarra, 2009). This correlation holds regardless of age, sex, race, and income (National Center for Health Statistics, 2004). One seven-decades-long study found that at age 50, healthy aging is better predicted by a good marriage than by a low cholesterol level (Vaillant, 2002). But the married versus never-married health gap has shrunk (Liu, 2009).

How can we explain the link between social support and health? Is it because middle-aged and older adults who live alone are more likely to smoke, be obese, and have high cholesterol—and therefore to have a doubled risk of heart attacks (Nielsen et al., 2006)? Or because healthy people are more supportive and marriage-prone? Possibly. But research indicates some other possibilities.

Social support calms us and reduces blood pressure and stress hormones. More than 50 studies support this finding (Graham et al., 2006; Uchino et al., 1996, 1999). To see if social support might calm people's response to threats, one research team subjected happily married women, while lying in an fMRI machine, to the threat of electric shock to an ankle (Coan et al., 2006). During the experiment, some women held their husband's hand. Others held the hand of an unknown person or no hand at all. While awaiting the occasional shocks, women holding their husband's hand showed less activity in threat-responsive areas. This soothing benefit was greatest for those reporting the highest-quality marriages. Supportive family and friends—human and nonhuman—help buffer threats. After stressful events, Medicare patients who have a dog or other companionable pet are less likely to visit their doctor (Siegel, 1990). (See Close-Up: Pets Are Friends, Too on the next page.)

Social support fosters stronger immune functioning. Volunteers in studies of resistance to cold viruses showed this effect (Cohen et al., 1997, 2004). In those studies, healthy volunteers inhaled nasal drops laden with a cold virus and were quarantined and observed

Laughter among friends is good medicine Laughter arouses us, massages muscles, and then leaves us feeling relaxed (Robinson, 1983). Humor (though not hostile sarcasm) may defuse stress, ease pain, and strengthen immune activity (Ayan, 2009; Berk et al., 2001; Kimata, 2001). People who laugh a lot also tend to have lower rates of heart disease (Clark et al., 2001).

Getty Images/Rubberball

CLOSE-UP

Pets Are Friends, Too

Have you ever wished for a friend who would love you just as you are? One who would never judge you? Who would be there for you, no matter your mood? For many tens of millions of people that friend exists, and it is a loyal dog or a friendly cat.

Many people describe their pet as a cherished family member who helps them feel calm, happy, and valued. Can pets also help people handle stress? If so, might pets have healing power? The evidence is, as yet, mixed and meager (Herzog, 2010). But Deborah Wells (2009) and Karen Allen (2003) have reported that pets have sometimes been found to increase the odds of survival after a heart attack, to relieve depression among AIDS patients, and to lower the level of blood pressure and blood lipids that contribute to cardiovascular risk. As nursing pioneer Florence Nightingale (1860) foresaw, "A small pet animal is often an excellent companion for the sick." In one study, women's blood pressure rose as they struggled with challenging math problems in the presence of a best friend or even a spouse, but much less so when accompanied by their dog (Allen, 2003).

So, would pets be good medicine for people who do not have pets? To find out, Allen experimented. The participants were a group of stockbrokers who lived alone, described their work as stressful, and had high blood pressure. She randomly selected half to adopt an animal shelter cat or dog. When later facing stress, all participants experienced higher blood pressure. But among the new pet owners, the increase was less than half as high as the increase in the no-pet group. The effect was greatest for pet owners with few social contacts or friends. Allen's conclusion: For lowering blood pressure, pets are no substitute for effective drugs and exercise. But for those who enjoy animals, and especially for those who live alone, they are a healthy pleasure.

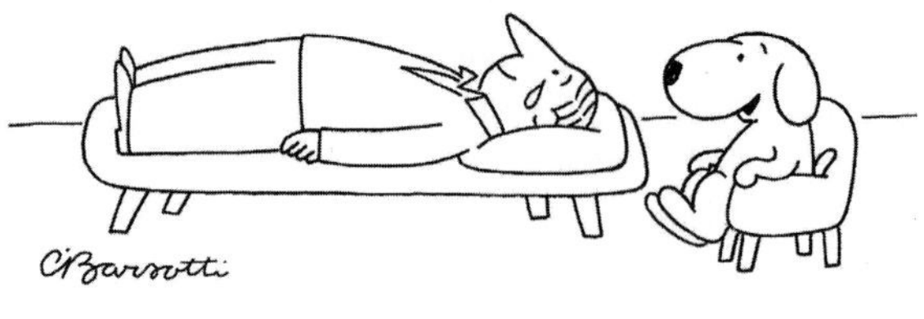

The New Yorker Collection, 2002, Charles Barsotti, from cartoonbank.com. All Rights Reserved.

"Well, I think you're wonderful"

for five days. (In these experiments, more than 600 volunteers received $800 each to endure this experience.) Age, race, sex, smoking, and other health habits being equal, those with the most social ties were least likely to catch a cold. If they did catch one, they produced less mucus. More sociability meant less susceptibility. The cold fact is that the effect of social ties is nothing to sneeze at!

Close relationships give us an opportunity for "open heart therapy," a chance to confide painful feelings (Frattaroli, 2006). Talking about a stressful event can temporarily arouse us, but in the long run it calms us, by calming limbic system activity (Lieberman et al., 2007; Mendolia & Kleck, 1993). In one study, 33 Holocaust survivors spent two hours recalling their experiences, many in intimate detail never before disclosed (Pennebaker et al., 1989). In the weeks following, most watched a tape of their recollections and showed it to family and friends. Those who were most self-disclosing had the most improved health 14 months later. Confiding is good for the body and the soul. In another study of surviving spouses of people who had committed suicide or died in car accidents, those who bore their grief alone had more health problems than those who could express it openly (Pennebaker & O'Heeron, 1984).

"Woe to one who is alone and falls and does not have another to help."
Ecclesiastes 4:10

Suppressing emotions can be detrimental to physical health. When health psychologist James Pennebaker (1985) surveyed more than 700 undergraduate women, about 1 in 12 of them reported a traumatic sexual experience in childhood. The sexually abused women—

© Baby Blues Partnership, Distributed by King Features Syndicate especially those who had kept their secret to themselves—reported more headaches and stomach ailments than did other women who had experienced nonsexual traumas, such as parental death or divorce. Another study, of 437 Australian ambulance drivers, confirmed the ill effects of suppressing one's emotions after witnessing traumas (Wastell, 2002).

Even writing about personal traumas in a diary can help (Burton & King, 2008; Hemenover, 2003; Lyubomirsky et al., 2006). In one experiment, volunteers who did so had fewer health problems during the ensuing four to six months (Pennebaker, 1990). As one participant explained, "Although I have not talked with anyone about what I wrote, I was finally able to deal with it, work through the pain instead of trying to block it out. Now it doesn't hurt to think about it."

If we are aiming to exercise more, drink less, quit smoking, or be a healthy weight, our social ties can tug us away from or toward our goal. Studies of networks of thousands of people followed over years suggest that clusters of friends may "infect" one another with either bad health practices or good behaviors (Christakis & Fowler, 2009). Obesity, for example, spreads within networks in ways that seem not merely to reflect people's seeking out similar others.

Photos.com/Getty Images

RETRIEVAL PRACTICE

- Some research finds that people with companionable pets are less likely than those without pets to visit their doctors after stressful events (Siegel, 1990). How can the health benefits from social support shed light on this finding?

ANSWER: Feeling social support—even from a pet—might calm people, and lead to lower levels of stress hormones and blood pressure.

Reducing Stress

Having a sense of control, developing more optimistic thinking, and building social support can help us *experience* less stress and thus improve our health. Moreover, these factors interrelate: People who are upbeat about themselves and their future tend also to enjoy health-promoting social ties (Stinson et al., 2008). But sometimes we cannot alleviate stress and simply need to *manage* our stress. Aerobic exercise, relaxation, meditation, and spiritual communities may help us gather inner strength and lessen stress effects.

"Is there anyone here who specializes in stress management?"

© The New Yorker Collection, 1993, Edward Koren from cartoonbank.com. All Rights Reserved.

Aerobic Exercise

39-3 How effective is aerobic exercise as a way to manage stress and improve well-being?

Aerobic exercise is sustained, oxygen-consuming, exercise—such as jogging, swimming or biking—that increases heart and lung fitness. It's hard to find bad things to say about exercise. By one estimate, moderate exercise adds not only to your quantity of life—two additional years, on average—but also to your quality of life, with more energy and better mood (Seligman, 1994).

Exercise helps fight heart disease by strengthening the heart, increasing bloodflow, keeping blood vessels open, and lowering both blood pressure and the blood pressure reaction to stress (Ford, 2002; Manson, 2002). Compared with inactive adults, people who exercise suffer half as many heart attacks (Powell et al., 1987; Visich & Fletcher, 2009). Exercise makes the muscles hungry for the fats that, if not used by the muscles, contribute to clogged arteries (Barinaga, 1997). In one 20-year study of adult Finnish twins, other things being equal, daily conditioning exercise reduced death risk by 43 percent (Kujala et al., 1998). Regular exercise in later life also predicts better cognitive functioning and reduced risk of dementia and Alzheimer's disease (Kramer & Erickson, 2007).

aerobic exercise sustained exercise that increases heart and lung fitness; may also alleviate depression and anxiety.

The genes passed down to us from our distant ancestors were those that enabled the physical activity essential to hunting, foraging, and farming. In muscle cells, those genes, when activated by exercise, respond by producing proteins. In the modern inactive person, these genes produce lower quantities of proteins and leave us susceptible to more than 20 chronic diseases, such as type-2 diabetes, cardiovascular disease, Alzheimer's disease, and cancer (Booth & Neufer, 2005). Inactivity is thus potentially toxic.

Does exercise also boost the spirit? Many studies reveal that aerobic exercise can reduce stress, depression, and anxiety. Americans, Canadians, and Britons who do aerobic exercise at least three times a week manage stress better, exhibit more self-confidence, feel more vigor, and feel less depressed and fatigued than their inactive peers (McMurray, 2004; Mead et al., 2010; Puetz et al., 2006). And in a 21-country survey of university students, physical exercise was a "strong" and consistent predictor of life satisfaction (Grant et al., 2009).

But we could state this observation another way: Stressed and depressed people exercise less. These findings are correlations, and cause and effect are unclear. To sort out cause and effect, researchers experiment. They randomly assign stressed, depressed, or anxious people either to an aerobic exercise group or to a control group. One classic experiment randomly assigned mildly depressed female college students to three groups. One-third participated in a program of aerobic exercise. Another third took part in a program of relaxation exercises. The remaining third (the control group) formed a no-treatment group (McCann & Holmes, 1984). As **FIGURE 39.2** shows, 10 weeks later, the women in the aerobic exercise program reported the greatest decrease in depression. Many had, quite literally, run away from their troubles. Dozens of other experiments confirm that exercise prevents or reduces depression and anxiety (Conn, 2010; Rethorst et al., 2009; Windle et al., 2010). Vigorous exercise provides a substantial and immediate mood boost (Watson, 2000). Even a 10-minute walk stimulates two hours of increased well-being by raising energy levels and lowering tension (Thayer, 1987, 1993).

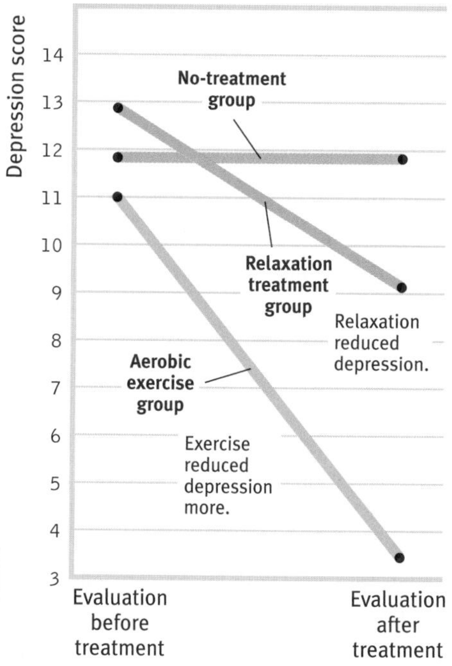

Lev Olkha/Shutterstock

FIGURE 39.2
Aerobic exercise and depression Mildly depressed college women who participated in an aerobic exercise program showed markedly reduced depression, compared with those who did relaxation exercises or received no treatment. (From McCann & Holmes, 1984.)

Some studies indicate that not only is exercise as effective as drugs, it better prevents symptom recurrence (Babyak et al., 2000; Salmon, 2001). In exploring *why* aerobic exercise alleviates negative emotions, researchers have found that exercise in some ways works like an antidepressant drug. Exercise increases arousal, thus counteracting depression's low arousal state. It often leads to muscle relaxation and sounder sleep. It also orders up mood-boosting chemicals from our body's internal pharmacy—neurotransmitters such as norepinephrine, serotonin, and the endorphins (Jacobs, 1994; Salmon, 2001). And it may foster *neurogenesis*. In mice, exercise causes the brain to produce a molecule that acts as a natural antidepressant, by stimulating the production of new, stress-resistant neurons (Hunsberger et al., 2007; Reynolds, 2009; van Praag, 2009). On a simpler level, the sense of accomplishment and improved physique and body image that often accompany a successful exercise routine may enhance one's self-image, leading to a better emotional state. Exercise (at least a half-hour on five or more days of the week) is like a drug that prevents and treats disease, increases energy, calms anxiety, and boosts mood—a drug we would all take, if available. Yet few people (only 1 in 4 in the United States) take advantage of it (Mendes, 2010).

Kathryn Brownson

The mood boost When one's energy or spirits are sagging, few things reboot the day better than exercising (as I can confirm from my daily noontime basketball). Aerobic exercise appears to counteract depression partly by increasing arousal (replacing depression's low-arousal state) and by doing naturally what antidepressants do—increasing the brain's serotonin activity.

Relaxation and Meditation

39-4 In what ways might relaxation and meditation influence stress and health?

Knowing the damaging effects of stress, could we learn to counteract our stress responses by altering our thinking and lifestyle? In the late 1960s, some respected psychologists, including Neal Miller, began experimenting with *biofeedback*, a system of recording, amplifying, and feeding back information about subtle physiological responses, many controlled by the autonomic nervous system. Biofeedback instruments mirror the results of a person's own efforts, enabling the person to learn which techniques do (or do not) control a particular physiological response. After a decade of study, however, the initial claims for biofeedback seemed overblown and oversold (Miller, 1985). In 1995, a National Institutes of Health panel declared that biofeedback works best on tension headaches.

Simple methods of relaxation, which require no expensive equipment, produce many of the results biofeedback once promised. Figure 39.2 pointed out that aerobic exercise reduces depression. But did you notice in that figure that depression also decreased among women in the relaxation treatment group? More than 60 studies have found that relaxation procedures can also help alleviate headaches, hypertension, anxiety, and insomnia (Nestoriuc et al., 2008; Stetter & Kupper, 2002). Such findings would not surprise Meyer Friedman and his colleagues. They tested relaxation in a program designed to help Type A heart attack survivors reduce their risk of future attacks, by randomly assigning hundreds of middle-aged men to one of two groups. The first group received standard advice from cardiologists about medications, diet, and exercise habits. The second group received similar advice, but they also were taught ways of modifying their lifestyles. They learned to slow down and relax by walking, talking, and eating more slowly. They learned to smile at others and laugh at themselves. They learned to admit their mistakes; to take time to enjoy life; and to renew their religious faith. The training paid off (**FIGURE 39.3** on the next page). During the next three years, the group that learned to modify their lifestyle had half as many repeat heart attacks as did the first group. This, wrote the exuberant Friedman, was an unprecedented, spectacular reduction in heart-attack recurrence. A smaller-scale British study similarly divided heart-attack–prone people into control and lifestyle modification groups (Eysenck & Grossarth-Maticek, 1991). During the next 13 years, that study also showed a 50 percent reduction in death rate among

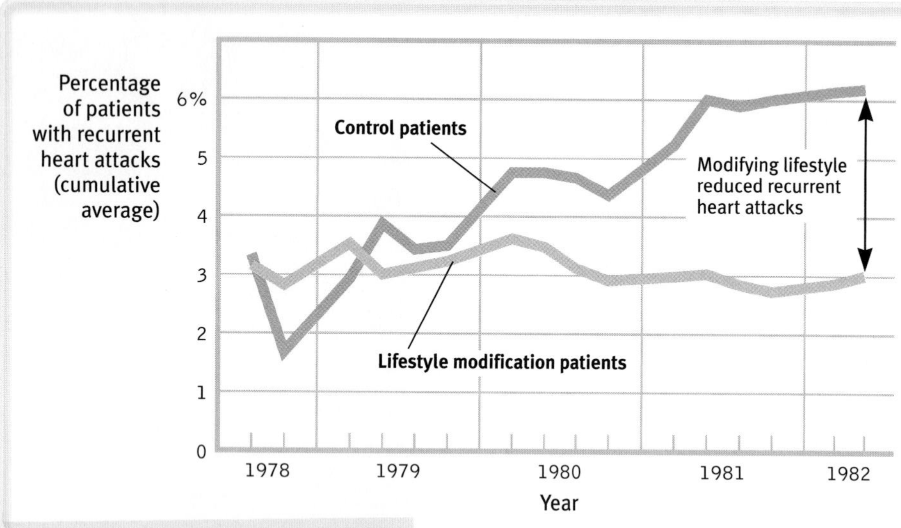

David Madison/Jupiterimages

➤ FIGURE 39.3

Recurrent heart attacks and lifestyle modification The San Francisco Recurrent Coronary Prevention Project offered counseling from a cardiologist to survivors of heart attacks. Those who were also guided in modifying their Type A lifestyle suffered fewer repeat heart attacks. (From Friedman & Ulmer, 1984.)

people trained to alter their thinking and lifestyle. After suffering a heart attack at age 55, Friedman started taking his own behavioral medicine—and lived to age 90 (Wargo, 2007).

Cardiologist Herbert Benson (1996) became intrigued with reports that experienced meditators could lower their blood pressure, heart rate, and oxygen consumption and raise their fingertip temperature. His research led him to what he now calls the *relaxation response*, a state of calm marked by relaxed muscles, slowed breathing and heart rate, and decreased blood pressure. According to Benson, relaxation practiced once or twice daily has lasting stress-reducing benefits.

To experience the relaxation response, the Benson-Henry Institute for Mind Body Medicine recommends these steps: Sit quietly in a comfortable position. Close your eyes. Relax your muscles, starting with your feet, then your calves, and upward through your thighs, shoulders, neck, and head. Breathe slowly. As you exhale each breath, repeat a focus word, phrase, or prayer—something drawn from your own belief system. When other thoughts intrude, don't worry. Just return to your repetition and continue for 10 to 20 minutes. When finished, sit quietly for another minute or two, then open your eyes and sit for a few more moments.

Meditation is a modern phenomenon with a long history: "Sit down alone and in silence. Lower your head, shut your eyes, breathe out gently, and imagine yourself looking into your own heart. . . . As you breathe out, say 'Lord Jesus Christ, have mercy on me.' . . . Try to put all other thoughts aside. Be calm, be patient, and repeat the process very frequently" (Gregory of Sinai, died 1346).

Tibetan Buddhists deep in meditation and Franciscan nuns deep in centering prayer report a diminished sense of self, space, and time. Brain scans reveal the neural footprints of such spiritual feelings during these mystical experiences: A part of the parietal lobe that tracks our location in space is less active than usual, and a frontal lobe area involved in focused attention is more active (Cahn & Polich, 2006; Newberg & D'Aquili, 2001). Another difference appears in the brain's left frontal lobe. In Buddhist monks who are experienced in meditation, this area displays elevated levels of activity usually associated with positive emotions.

Was this high rate of activity a *result* of meditation, or simply a correlation unrelated to cause and effect? To find out, the researchers experimented, comparing "before" and "after" brain scans of volunteers who were not experienced meditators (Davidson et al., 2003). First, they took baseline scans of volunteers' normal levels of brain activity. They then randomly assigned them either to a

Dean Mitchell/Shutterstock

control group or to an eight-week course in *mindfulness meditation*, which has been shown to lessen anxiety and depression (Hofmann et al., 2010). Compared with both the control group and their own baseline, the meditation participants showed noticeably more left-hemisphere activity after the training, and they also had improved immune functioning. Such effects may help explain the results of another study, which found that hypertension patients assigned to meditation training had (compared with other treatment groups) a 30 percent lower cardiovascular death rate over the ensuing 19 years (Schneider et al., 2005). This benefit may result from the lessened anxiety and improved mood that accompanies meditation (Hofmann et al., 2010). The U.S. National Institutes of Health include relaxation and meditation techniques as part of complementary and alternative medicine. For more on that topic, see Thinking Critically About Complementary and Alternative Medicine on the next page.

And then there are the mystics who seek to use the mind's power to enable novocaine-free cavity repair. Their aim: transcend dental medication.

Faith Communities and Health

39-5 What is the faith factor, and what are some possible explanations for this link?

A wealth of studies has revealed another curious correlation, called the *faith factor*. Religiously active people tend to live longer than those who are not religiously active. In the twenty-first century's first decade alone, some 1800 studies explored connections between spirituality and health and healing (Koenig et al., 2011). In one study, researchers compared the death rates for 3900 Israelis living either in one of two groups of communities. The first group contained 11 religiously orthodox collective settlements; the second group contained 11 matched, nonreligious collective settlements (Kark et al., 1996). The researchers found that, over a 16-year period, "belonging to a religious collective was associated with a strong protective effect" not explained by age or economic differences. In every age group, religious community members were about half as likely to have died as were their nonreligious counterparts. This difference is roughly comparable to the gender difference in mortality.

How should we interpret such findings? Skeptical researchers remind us that correlations can leave many factors uncontrolled (Sloan et al., 1999, 2000, 2002, 2005). Here is one obvious possibility: Women are more religiously active than men, and women outlive men. Does religious involvement merely reflect this gender-longevity link? One 8-year study by the National Institutes of Health, for example, followed 92,395 women, ages 50 to 79. Even after controlling for many factors, women attending religious services weekly (or more) experienced an approximately 20 percent reduced risk of death during the study period (Schnall et al., 2010). But the association between religious

THINKING CRITICALLY ABOUT

Complementary and Alternative Medicine

complementary and alternative medicine (CAM) as yet unproven health care treatments intended to supplement (complement) or serve as alternatives to conventional medicine, and which typically are not widely taught in medical schools, used in hospitals, or reimbursed by insurance companies. When research shows a therapy to be safe and effective, it usually then becomes part of accepted medical practice.

39-6 What is complementary and alternative medicine, and how is it best assessed through scientific research?

In China, herbal therapies have long flourished, as have acupuncture and acupressure therapies that claim to correct "imbalances of energy flow" (called Qi or Chi) at identifiable points close to the skin. In Germany, herbal remedies and homeopathy are popular. Such remedies are part of **complementary and alternative medicine (CAM),** which also includes relaxation, massage therapy, spiritual healing, chiropractic, and aromatherapy. Facing political pressure to explore CAM techniques, the U.S. National Institutes of Health (NIH) established the National Center for Complementary and Alternative Medicine, which the center defines as health care treatments not taught widely in medical schools, not usually reimbursed by insurance companies, and not used in hospitals (**TABLE 39.1**).

So what shall we make of CAM? Some aspects, such as lifestyle changes and stress management, have acknowledged validity. And certain techniques have proved useful for specific ailments, as acupuncture, massage therapy, and aromatherapy have for pain relief in cancer patients (Fellowes et al., 2004). Do the other aspects offer, as some believe, a new medical paradigm?

Critics point out that people consult physicians for diagnosable, curable diseases and turn to CAM techniques for either incurable illnesses or when well but feeling subpar. And given two influences—*spontaneous remission* and the *placebo effect*—CAM practices are bound to seem effective, whether they are or not. Thus, an otherwise healthy person with a cold may try an herbal remedy and then credit the natural disappearance of symptoms to CAM. During cyclical diseases, such as arthritis and allergies, CAM may seem especially effective as people seek therapy during the downturn and presume its effectiveness during the ensuing upturn.

The healing power of belief was clear in one German study of 302 migraine headache patients, which found that 51 percent of those receiving acupuncture treatment obtained relief, as did only 15 percent of those in a waiting list control group. But among a third group that received "sham acupuncture" (needles inserted at nonacupuncture points), 53 percent enjoyed relief. Such results indicate "a powerful placebo effect" (Linde et al., 2005).

As always, the way to discern what works and what does not is to experiment: Randomly assign patients to receive the therapy or a placebo control. Then ask the critical question: When neither the therapist nor the patient knows who is getting the real therapy, is the real therapy effective?

Much of today's mainstream medicine began as yesterday's alternative medicine. Natural botanical life has given us digitalis (from purple foxglove), morphine (from the opium poppy), and penicillin (from penicillium mold). In each case, the active ingredient was verified in controlled trials. We have medical and public health science to thank for the antibiotics, vaccines, surgical procedures, sanitation, and emergency medicine that helped lengthen our life expectancy by three decades during the last century.

"CAM changes continually," notes the National Center for Complementary and Alternative Medicine (2006), "as those therapies that are proven to be safe and effective become adopted into conventional health care." Indeed, said *New England Journal of Medicine* editors Marcia Angell and Jerome Kassirer (1998), "There cannot be two kinds of medicine—conventional and alternative. There is only medicine that has been adequately tested and medicine that has not, medicine that works and medicine that may or may not work. Once a treatment has been tested rigorously, it no longer matters whether it was considered alternative at the outset."

TABLE 39.1

Five Domains of Complementary and Alternative Medicine

Alternative medical system	Therapies used in place of conventional medicine, including homeopathy in Western cultures and traditional Chinese medicine and Ayurveda practices in non-Western cultures.
Mind-body interventions	Techniques designed to enhance the mind's capacity to affect bodily functions and symptoms, including meditation, prayer, mental healing, and therapies using creative outlets such as art, music, or dance.
Biologically based therapies	Therapies using natural substances such as herbs, foods, and vitamins.
Manipulative and body-based methods	Techniques such as chiropractic or osteopathic manipulation and massage therapy, which manipulate or move one or more body parts.
Energy therapies	Techniques using presumed energy fields. Biofield therapies, such as qi gong, Reiki, and therapeutic touch, are intended to affect energy fields that purportedly surround and penetrate the human body. Bioelectromagnetic-based therapies involve the unconventional use of electromagnetic fields, such as pulsed or magnetic fields.

Source: Adapted from the National Center for Complementary and Alternative Medicine, NIH http://nccam.nih.gov/health/whatiscam.

involvement and life expectancy is also found among men (Benjamins et al., 2010; McCullough et al., 2000, 2005, 2009). A 28-year study that followed 5286 Californians found that, after controlling for age, gender, ethnicity, and education, frequent religious attenders were 36 percent less likely to have died in any year (**FIGURE 39.4**). In another 8-year controlled study of more than 20,000 people (Hummer et al., 1999), this effect translated into a life expectancy at age 20 of 83 years for frequent attenders at religious services and 75 years for infrequent attenders.

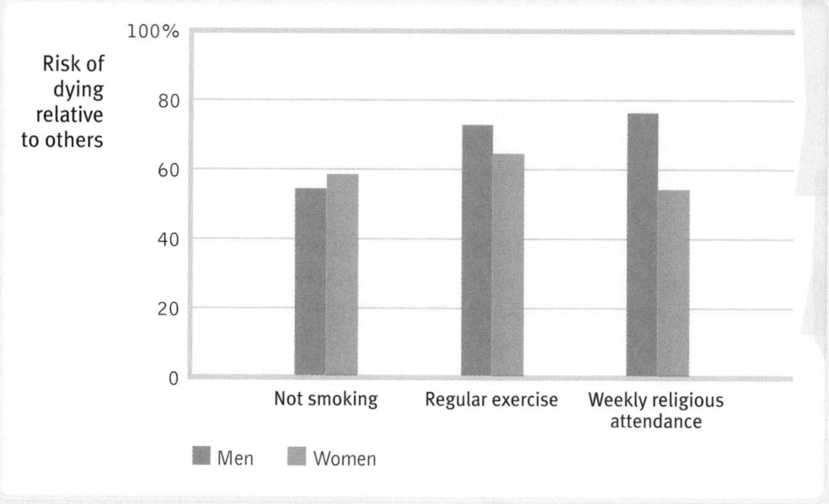

FIGURE 39.4
Predictors of longer life: Not smoking, frequent exercise, and regular religious attendance Epidemiologist William Strawbridge and his co-workers (1997, 1999; Oman et al., 2002) followed 5286 Alameda, California, adults over 28 years. After adjusting for age and education, the researchers found that not smoking, regular exercise, and religious attendance all predicted a lowered risk of death in any given year. Women attending weekly religious services, for example, were only 54 percent as likely to die in a typical study year as were nonattenders.

These correlational findings do not indicate that nonattenders can add 8 years to their lives if they start attending services and change nothing. But the findings do indicate that religious involvement is a *predictor* of health and longevity, just as nonsmoking and exercise are. Can you imagine what intervening variables might account for the correlation?

First, religion promotes *self-control* (McCullough & Willoughby, 2009). Religiously active people therefore tend to have healthier lifestyles; they smoke and drink much less (Koenig & Vaillant, 2009; Park, 2007; Strawbridge et al., 2001). One Gallup survey of 550,000 Americans found that 15 percent of the very religious were smokers, as were 28 percent of the nonreligious (Newport et al., 2010). But such lifestyle differences are not great enough to explain the dramatically reduced mortality in the religious settlements, say the Israeli researchers. In American studies, too, about 75 percent of the longevity difference remained when researchers controlled for unhealthy behaviors, such as inactivity and smoking (Musick et al., 1999).

Could *social support* explain the faith factor (Ai et al., 2007; George et al., 2002)? In Judaic, Christian, and Islamic religions, faith is a communal experience. To belong to one of these faith communities is to have access to a support network. Religiously active people are there for one another when misfortune strikes. Moreover, religion encourages marriage, another predictor of health and longevity. In the Israeli religious settlements, for example, divorce has been almost nonexistent. But even after controlling for social support, gender, unhealthy behaviors, and preexisting health problems, the mortality studies still find that religiously engaged people tend to live longer (Chida et al., 2009).

Researchers therefore speculate that a third set of intervening variables help protect religiously active people from stress and enhance their well-being. Those benefits may flow from a stable, coherent worldview, a sense of hope for the long-term future, feelings of ultimate acceptance, and the relaxed meditation of prayer or Sabbath observance

FIGURE 39.5
Possible explanations for the correlation between religious involvement and health/longevity

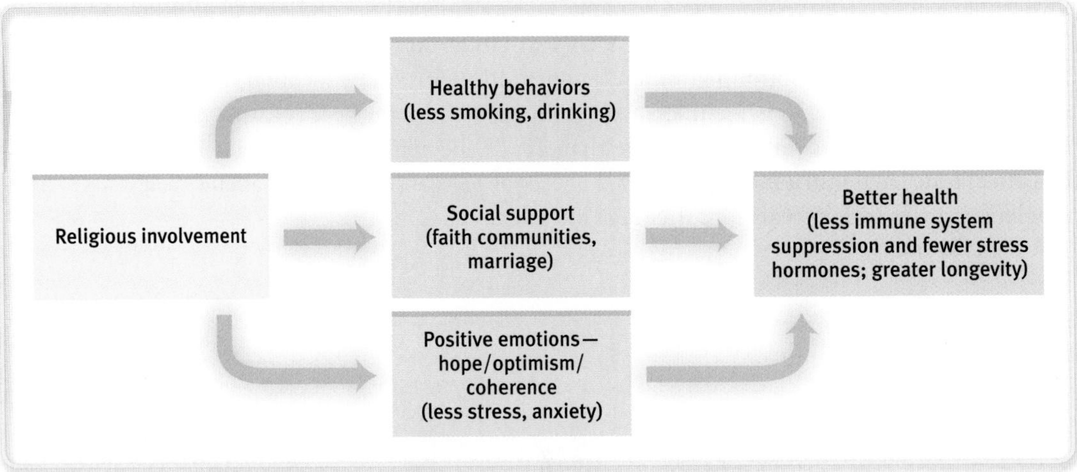

(**FIGURE 39.5**). These variables might also help to explain other recent findings among the religiously active, such as healthier immune functioning, fewer hospital admissions, and, for AIDS patients, fewer stress hormones and longer survival (Ironson et al., 2002; Koenig & Larson, 1998; Lutgendorf et al., 2004).

RETRIEVAL PRACTICE

- What are some of the tactics we can use to manage successfully the stress we cannot avoid?

ANSWERS: Aerobic exercise, relaxation procedures, meditation, and religious engagement

MODULE REVIEW

Promoting Health

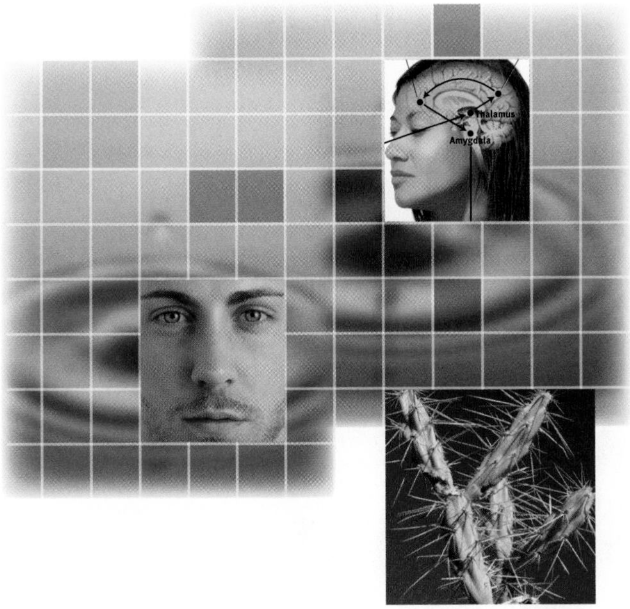

Learning Objectives

RETRIEVAL PRACTICE Take a moment to answer each of these Learning Objective Questions (repeated here from within the module). Then turn to Appendix B, Complete Module Reviews, to check your answers. Research suggests that trying to answer these questions on your own will improve your long-term retention (McDaniel et al., 2009).

39-1: In what ways do people cope with stress, and how does a perceived lack of control affect health?

39-2: What are the links among basic outlook on life, social support, stress, and health?

39-3: How effective is aerobic exercise as a way to manage stress and improve well-being?

39-4: In what ways might relaxation and meditation influence stress and health?

39-5: What is the faith factor, and what are some possible explanations for this link?

39-6: What is complementary and alternative medicine, and how is it best assessed through scientific research?

Terms and Concepts to Remember

RETRIEVAL PRACTICE Test yourself on these terms by trying to write down the definition before flipping back to the referenced page to check your answer.

RETRIEVAL PRACTICE Gain an advantage, and benefit from immediate feedback, with the interactive self-testing resources at www.worthpublishers.com/myers.

Personality

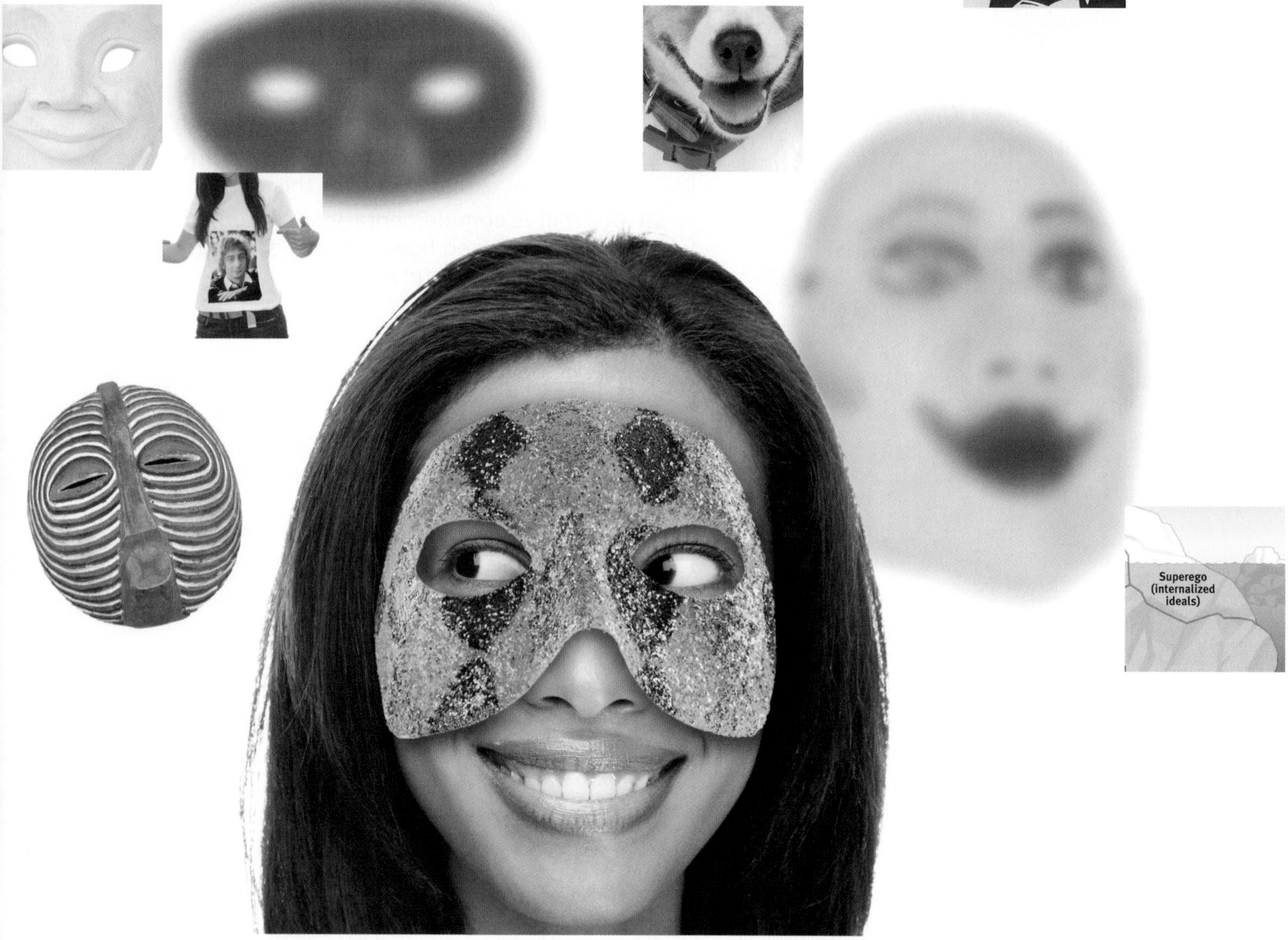

Lord of the Rings hobbit-hero Frodo Baggins knew that throughout his difficult journey there was one who would never fail him—his loyal and ever-cheerful companion, Sam Gamgee. Even before they left their beloved homes in the Shire, Frodo warned Sam that the journey would not be easy.

> "It is going to be very dangerous, Sam. It is already dangerous. Most likely neither of us will come back."
>
> "If you don't come back, sir, then I shan't, that's certain," said Sam. "[The Elves told me] 'Don't you leave him!' Leave him! I said. I never mean to. I am going with him, if he climbs to the Moon; and if any of those Black Riders try to stop him, they'll have Sam Gamgee to reckon with." (J.R.R. Tolkien, *The Fellowship of the Ring*, p. 96)

And so they did! Later in the story, when it becomes clear that Frodo's path will lead him into the dreaded land of Mordor, it is Sam who insists he will be at Frodo's side, come what may. It is Sam who lifts Frodo's spirits with songs and stories from their boyhood. And it is Sam whom Frodo leans upon when he can barely take another step. When Frodo is overcome by the evil of the ring he carries, it is Sam who saves him. In the end, it is Sam who helps Frodo successfully reach the end of his journey. Sam Gamgee—cheerful, optimistic, emotionally stable—never falters in his faithfulness or his belief that they will overcome the threatening darkness.

As he appears and reappears throughout the series, Tolkien's Sam Gamgee exhibits the distinctive and enduring behaviors that

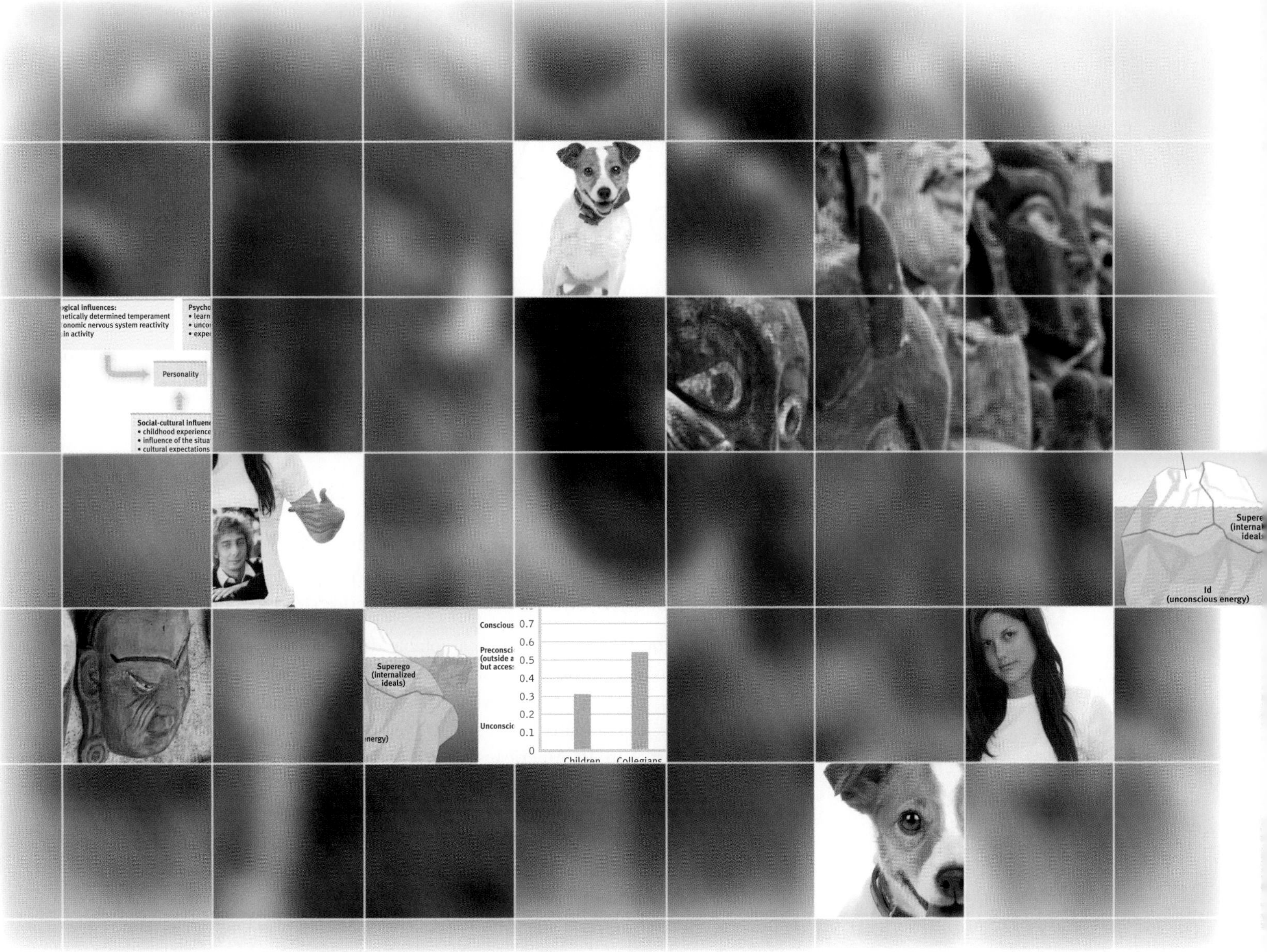

MODULES

40 Psychodynamic Theories

41 Humanistic Theories

42 Trait Theories, Social-Cognitive Theories, and the Self

define **personality**—a person's characteristic pattern of thinking, feeling, and acting. Other modules focus on our similar ways of developing, perceiving, learning, remembering, thinking, and feeling. Modules 40 through 42 focus on what makes us each unique.

Much of this book deals with personality. Psychologists study biological influences on personality; personality development across the life span; personality-related aspects of learning, motivation, emotion, and health; social influences on personality; and disorders of personality.

Two historically significant theories have become part of our cultural legacy. Sigmund Freud's *psychoanalytic* theory proposed that childhood sexuality and unconscious motivations influence personality (Module 40). The *humanistic* approach focused on our inner capacities for growth and self-fulfillment (Module 41). These sweeping perspectives on human nature laid the foundation for later personality theorists and are complemented by newer scientific research on specific aspects of personality (Module 42). Today's personality researchers study the basic dimensions of personality, the biological roots of these dimensions, and the interaction of persons and environments. They also study self-esteem, self-serving bias, and cultural influences on one's sense of self. And they study the unconscious mind—with findings that probably would have surprised Freud himself.

MODULE 40

Psychodynamic Theories

- Freud's Psychoanalytic Perspective: Exploring the Unconscious
- The Neo-Freudian and Psychodynamic Theorists
- Assessing Unconscious Processes
- Evaluating Freud's Psychoanalytic Perspective and Modern Views of the Unconscious

Psychodynamic theories of personality view human behavior as a dynamic interaction between the conscious and unconscious mind, including associated motives and conflicts. These theories are descended from Freud's psychoanalysis, which first focused clinical attention on our unconscious mind.

Freud's Psychoanalytic Perspective: Exploring the Unconscious

40-1 How did Sigmund Freud's treatment of psychological disorders lead to his view of the unconscious mind?

Sigmund Freud, 1856–1939
"I was the only worker in a new field."

© Bettmann/Corbis

"The female . . . acknowledges the fact of her castration, and with it, too, the superiority of the male and her own inferiority; but she rebels against this unwelcome state of affairs."
Sigmund Freud, *Female Sexuality*, 1931

Ask 100 people on the street to name a notable deceased psychologist, suggested Keith Stanovich (1996, p. 1), and "Freud would be the winner hands down." In the popular mind, he is to psychology's history what Elvis Presley is to rock music's history. Freud's influence lingers in psychiatry and clinical psychology, but also in literary and film interpretation. Almost 9 in 10 American college courses that reference psychoanalysis are outside of psychology departments (Cohen, 2007). His early twentieth-century concepts penetrate our twenty-first-century language. Without realizing their source, we may speak of *ego*, *repression*, *projection*, *complex* (as in "inferiority complex"), *sibling rivalry*, *Freudian slips*, and *fixation*. So, who was Freud, and what did he teach?

Like all of us, Sigmund Freud was a product of his times. His Victorian era was a time of tremendous discovery and scientific advancement, but it is also known today as a time of sexual repression and male dominance. Men's and women's roles were clearly defined, with male superiority assumed and only male sexuality generally acknowledged (discreetly).

Long before entering the University of Vienna in 1873, young Freud showed signs of independence and brilliance. He so loved reading plays, poetry, and philosophy that he once ran up a bookstore debt beyond his means. As a teen he often took his evening meal in his tiny bedroom in order to lose no time from his studies. After medical school he set up a private practice specializing in nervous disorders. Before long, however, he faced patients whose disorders made no neurological sense. For example, a patient might have lost all feeling in a hand—yet there is no sensory nerve that, if damaged, would numb the entire hand and nothing else. Freud's search for a cause for such disorders set his mind running in a direction destined to change human self-understanding.

Might some neurological disorders have psychological causes? Observing patients led Freud to his "discovery" of the unconscious. He speculated that lost feeling in one's hand might be caused by a fear of touching one's genitals; that unexplained blindness or deafness might be caused by not wanting to see or hear something that aroused intense anxiety. After some early unsuccessful trials with hypnosis, Freud turned to **free association,** in which he told the patient to relax and say whatever came to mind, no matter how embarrassing or trivial. He assumed that a line of mental dominoes had fallen from his patients' distant past to their troubled present. Free association, he believed, would allow him to retrace that line, following a chain of thought leading into the patient's unconscious, where painful unconscious memories, often from childhood, could be retrieved and released. Freud called his theory of personality and the associated treatment techniques **psychoanalysis.**

personality an individual's characteristic pattern of thinking, feeling, and acting.

psychodynamic theories view personality with a focus on the unconscious and the importance of childhood experiences.

free association in psychoanalysis, a method of exploring the unconscious in which the person relaxes and says whatever comes to mind, no matter how trivial or embarrassing.

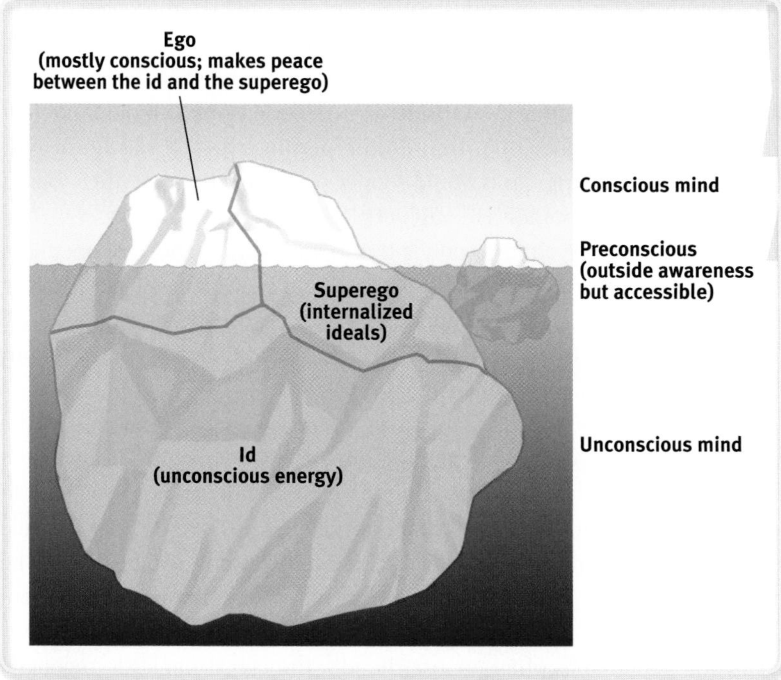

FIGURE 40.1
Freud's idea of the mind's structure
Psychologists have used an iceberg image to illustrate Freud's idea that the mind is mostly hidden beneath the conscious surface. Note that the id is totally unconscious, but ego and superego operate both consciously and unconsciously. Unlike the parts of a frozen iceberg, however, the id, ego, and superego interact.

Basic to Freud's theory was his belief that the mind is mostly hidden (**FIGURE 40.1**). Our conscious awareness is like the part of an iceberg that floats above the surface. Beneath our awareness is the larger **unconscious** mind with its thoughts, wishes, feelings, and memories. Some of these thoughts we store temporarily in a *preconscious* area, from which we can retrieve them into conscious awareness. Of greater interest to Freud was the mass of unacceptable passions and thoughts that he believed we *repress*, or forcibly block from our consciousness because they would be too unsettling to acknowledge. Freud believed that without our awareness, these troublesome feelings and ideas powerfully influence us, sometimes gaining expression in disguised forms—the work we choose, the beliefs we hold, our daily habits, our troubling symptoms.

For Freud the determinist, nothing was ever accidental. He believed he could glimpse the unconscious seeping not only into people's free associations, beliefs, habits, and symptoms but also into slips of the tongue and pen. He illustrated with a financially stressed patient who, not wanting any large pills, said, "Please do not give me any bills, because I cannot swallow them." Similarly, Freud viewed jokes as expressions of repressed sexual and aggressive tendencies, and dreams as the "royal road to the unconscious." The remembered content of dreams (their *manifest content*) he believed to be a censored expression of the dreamer's unconscious wishes (the dream's *latent content*). In his dream analyses, Freud searched for patients' inner conflicts.

"*Good morning, beheaded—uh, I mean beloved.*"

© The New Yorker Collection, 1983, Dana Fradon from cartoonbank.com. All Rights Reserved.

"I remember your name perfectly but I just can't think of your face."

Oxford professor W. A. Spooner, 1844–1930, famous for his linguistic flip-flops *(spoonerisms)*. Spooner rebuked one student for "fighting a liar in the quadrangle" and another who "hissed my mystery lecture," adding "You have tasted two worms."

Personality Structure

40-2 What was Freud's view of personality?

In Freud's view, human personality—including its emotions and strivings—arises from a conflict between impulse and restraint—between our aggressive, pleasure-seeking biological urges and our internalized social controls over these urges. Freud believed personality arises from our efforts to resolve this basic conflict—to express these impulses in ways that bring satisfaction without also bringing guilt or punishment. To understand the mind's dynamics during this conflict, Freud proposed three interacting systems: the *id*, *ego*, and *superego* (Figure 40.1).

psychoanalysis Freud's theory of personality that attributes thoughts and actions to unconscious motives and conflicts; the techniques used in treating psychological disorders by seeking to expose and interpret unconscious tensions.

unconscious according to Freud, a reservoir of mostly unacceptable thoughts, wishes, feelings, and memories. According to contemporary psychologists, information processing of which we are unaware.

id a reservoir of unconscious psychic energy that, according to Freud, strives to satisfy basic sexual and aggressive drives. The id operates on the *pleasure principle,* demanding immediate gratification.

ego the largely conscious, "executive" part of personality that, according to Freud, mediates among the demands of the id, superego, and reality. The ego operates on the *reality principle,* satisfying the id's desires in ways that will realistically bring pleasure rather than pain.

superego the part of personality that, according to Freud, represents internalized ideals and provides standards for judgment (the conscience) and for future aspirations.

The **id's** unconscious psychic energy constantly strives to satisfy basic drives to survive, reproduce, and aggress. The id operates on the *pleasure principle:* It seeks immediate gratification. To envision an id-dominated person, think of a newborn infant crying out for satisfaction, caring nothing for the outside world's conditions and demands. Or think of people with a present rather than future time perspective—those who heavily use tobacco, alcohol, and other drugs, and would sooner party now than sacrifice today's pleasure for future success and happiness (Keough et al., 1999).

As the **ego** develops, the young child responds to the real world. The ego, operating on the *reality principle,* seeks to gratify the id's impulses in realistic ways that will bring long-term pleasure. (Imagine what would happen if, lacking an ego, we expressed all our unrestrained sexual or aggressive impulses.) The ego contains our partly conscious perceptions, thoughts, judgments, and memories.

Around age 4 or 5, Freud theorized, a child's ego recognizes the demands of the newly emerging **superego,** the voice of our moral compass (conscience) that forces the ego to consider not only the real but the *ideal.* The superego focuses on how we *ought* to behave. It strives for perfection, judging actions and producing positive feelings of pride or negative feelings of guilt. Someone with an exceptionally strong superego may be virtuous yet guilt-ridden; another with a weak superego may be wantonly self-indulgent and remorseless.

Because the superego's demands often oppose the id's, the ego struggles to reconcile the two. It is the personality "executive," mediating among the impulsive demands of the id, the restraining demands of the superego, and the real-life demands of the external world. If chaste Jane feels sexually attracted to John, she may satisfy both id and superego by joining a volunteer organization that John attends regularly.

© The New Yorker Collection, 1987, Woodman from cartoonbank.com. All Rights Reserved.

"Fifty is plenty." "Hundred and fifty."

The ego struggles to reconcile the demands of superego and id, said Freud.

Personality Development

40-3 What developmental stages did Freud propose?

Analysis of his patients' histories convinced Freud that personality forms during life's first few years. He concluded that children pass through a series of **psychosexual stages,** during which the id's pleasure-seeking energies focus on distinct pleasure-sensitive areas of the body called *erogenous zones* (TABLE 40.1). Each stage offers its own challenges, which Freud saw as conflicting tendencies.

Freud believed that during the *phallic stage,* for example, boys seek genital stimulation, and they develop both unconscious sexual desires for their mother and jealousy and hatred for their father, whom they consider a rival. Given these feelings, he thought boys also experience guilt and a lurking fear of punishment, perhaps by castration, from their father. Freud called this collection of feelings the **Oedipus complex**

Science Cartoons Plus

"I heard that as soon as we become aware of our sexual impulses, whatever they are, we'll have to hide them."

TABLE 40.1

Freud's Psychosexual Stages

Stage	Focus
Oral (0–18 months)	Pleasure centers on the mouth—sucking, biting, chewing
Anal (18–36 months)	Pleasure focuses on bowel and bladder elimination; coping with demands for control
Phallic (3–6 years)	Pleasure zone is the genitals; coping with incestuous sexual feelings
Latency (6 to puberty)	A phase of dormant sexual feelings
Genital (puberty on)	Maturation of sexual interests

MODULE 41

Humanistic Theories

- Abraham Maslow's Self-Actualizing Person
- Carl Rogers' Person-Centered Perspective
- Assessing the Self
- Evaluating Humanistic Theories

41-1 How did humanistic psychologists view personality, and what was their goal in studying personality?

By the 1960s, some personality psychologists had become discontented with the sometimes bleak focus on drives and conflicts in psychodynamic theory and the mechanistic psychology of B. F. Skinner's behaviorism. In contrast to Freud's study of the base motives of "sick" people, these **humanistic theorists** focused on the ways "healthy" people strive for self-determination and self-realization. In contrast to behaviorism's scientific objectivity, they studied people through their own self-reported experiences and feelings.

Two pioneering theorists—Abraham Maslow (1908–1970) and Carl Rogers (1902–1987)—offered a "third-force" perspective that emphasized human potential.

humanistic theories view personality with a focus on the potential for healthy personal growth.

self-actualization according to Maslow, one of the ultimate psychological needs that arises after basic physical and psychological needs are met and self-esteem is achieved; the motivation to fulfill one's potential.

Abraham Maslow's Self-Actualizing Person

Maslow proposed that we are motivated by a *hierarchy of needs*. If our physiological needs are met, we become concerned with personal safety; if we achieve a sense of security, we then seek to love, to be loved, and to love ourselves; with our love needs satisfied, we seek self-esteem. Having achieved self-esteem, we ultimately seek **self-actualization** (the process of fulfilling our potential) and *self-transcendence* (meaning, purpose, and communion beyond the self).

Maslow (1970) developed his ideas by studying healthy, creative people rather than troubled clinical cases. He based his description of self-actualization on a study of those, such as Abraham Lincoln, who seemed notable for their rich and productive lives. Maslow reported that such people shared certain characteristics: They were self-aware and self-accepting, open and spontaneous, loving and caring, and not paralyzed by others' opinions. Secure in their sense of who they were, their interests were problem-centered rather than self-centered. They focused their energies on a particular task, one they often regarded as their mission in life. Most enjoyed a few deep relationships rather than many superficial ones. Many had been moved by spiritual or personal *peak experiences* that surpassed ordinary consciousness.

These, said Maslow, are mature adult qualities, ones found in those who have learned enough about life to be compassionate, to have outgrown their mixed feelings toward their parents, to have found their calling, to have "acquired enough courage to be unpopular, to be unashamed about being openly virtuous, etc." Maslow's work with college students led him to speculate that those likely to become self-actualizing adults were likeable, caring, "privately affectionate to those of their elders who deserve it," and "secretly uneasy about the cruelty, meanness, and mob spirit so often found in young people."

Abraham Maslow "Any theory of motivation that is worthy of attention must deal with the highest capacities of the healthy and strong person as well as with the defensive maneuvers of crippled spirits" (*Motivation and Personality,* 1970, p. 33).

© Bettmann/Corbis

Carl Rogers' Person-Centered Perspective

Fellow humanistic psychologist Carl Rogers agreed with much of Maslow's thinking. Rogers believed that people are basically good and are endowed with self-actualizing tendencies. Unless thwarted by an environment that inhibits growth, each of us is like an acorn, primed for growth and fulfillment. Rogers (1980) believed that a growth-promoting climate required three conditions.

The picture of empathy Being open and sharing confidences is easier when the listener shows real understanding. Within such relationships people can relax and fully express their true selves.

Dylan Martinez/Reuters

A father *not* offering unconditional positive regard:

© The New Yorker Collection, 2001, Pat Byrnes from cartoonbank.com. All Rights Reserved.

"Just remember, son, it doesn't matter whether you win or lose—unless you want Daddy's love."

- ***Genuineness:*** When people are *genuine*, they are open with their own feelings, drop their facades, and are transparent and self-disclosing.
- ***Acceptance:*** When people are *accepting*, they offer **unconditional positive regard,** an attitude of grace that values us even knowing our failings. It is a profound relief to drop our pretenses, confess our worst feelings, and discover that we are still accepted. In a good marriage, a close family, or an intimate friendship, we are free to be spontaneous without fearing the loss of others' esteem.
- ***Empathy:*** When people are *empathic*, they share and mirror others' feelings and reflect their meanings. "Rarely do we listen with real understanding, true empathy," said Rogers. "Yet listening, of this very special kind, is one of the most potent forces for change that I know."

Genuineness, acceptance, and empathy are, Rogers believed, the water, sun, and nutrients that enable people to grow like vigorous oak trees. For "as persons are accepted and prized, they tend to develop a more caring attitude toward themselves" (Rogers, 1980, p. 116). As persons are empathically heard, "it becomes possible for them to listen more accurately to the flow of inner experiencings."

Writer Calvin Trillin (2006) recalls an example of parental genuineness and acceptance at a camp for children with severe disorders, where his wife, Alice, worked. L., a "magical child," had genetic diseases that meant she had to be tube-fed and could walk only with difficulty. Alice recalled,

> One day, when we were playing duck-duck-goose, I was sitting behind her and she asked me to hold her mail for her while she took her turn to be chased around the circle. It took her a while to make the circuit, and I had time to see that on top of the pile [of mail] was a note from her mom. Then I did something truly awful. . . . I simply had to know what this child's parents could have done to make her so spectacular, to make her the most optimistic, most enthusiastic, most hopeful human being I had ever encountered. I snuck a quick look at the note, and my eyes fell on this sentence: "If God had given us all of the children in the world to choose from, L., we would only have chosen you." Before L. got back to her place in the circle, I showed the note to Bud, who was sitting next to me. "Quick. Read this," I whispered. "It's the secret of life."

Maslow and Rogers would have smiled knowingly. For them a central feature of personality is one's **self-concept**—all the thoughts and feelings we have in response to the question, "Who am I?" If our self-concept is positive, we tend to act and perceive the world positively. If it is negative—if in our own eyes we fall far short of our *ideal self*—said Rogers, we feel dissatisfied and unhappy. A worthwhile goal for therapists, parents, teachers, and friends is therefore, he said, to help others know, accept, and be true to themselves.

Assessing the Self

41-2 How did humanistic psychologists assess a person's sense of self?

Humanistic psychologists sometimes assessed personality by asking people to fill out questionnaires that would evaluate their self-concept. One questionnaire, inspired by Carl Rogers, asked people to describe themselves both as they would *ideally* like to be and as they *actually* are. When the ideal and the actual self are nearly alike, said Rogers, the self-concept is positive. Assessing his clients' personal growth during therapy, he looked for successively closer ratings of actual and ideal selves.

Some humanistic psychologists believed that any standardized assessment of personality, even a questionnaire, is depersonalizing. Rather than forcing the person to respond to narrow categories, these humanistic psychologists presumed that interviews and intimate conversation would provide a better understanding of each person's unique experiences.

unconditional positive regard according to Rogers, an attitude of total acceptance toward another person.

self-concept all our thoughts and feelings about ourselves, in answer to the question, "Who am I?"

Evaluating Humanistic Theories

41-3 How have humanistic theories influenced psychology? What criticisms have they faced?

One thing said of Freud can also be said of the humanistic psychologists: Their impact has been pervasive. Maslow's and Rogers' ideas have influenced counseling, education, child rearing, and management.

They have also influenced—sometimes in ways they did not intend—much of today's popular psychology. Is a positive self-concept the key to happiness and success? Do acceptance and empathy nurture positive feelings about oneself? Are people basically good and capable of self-improvement? Many people answer *Yes, Yes,* and *Yes.* Responding to a 1992 *Newsweek* Gallup poll, 9 in 10 people rated self-esteem as very important for "motivating a person to work hard and succeed." Given a choice, today's North American collegians say they'd rather get a self-esteem boost, such as a compliment or good grade on a paper, than enjoy a favorite food or sexual activity (Bushman et al., 2011). Humanistic psychology's message has been heard.

© The New Yorker Collection, 1979, Dana Fradon from cartoonbank.com. All Rights Reserved.

"We do pretty well when you stop to think that people are basically good."

The prominence of the humanistic perspective set off a backlash of criticism. First, said the critics, its concepts are vague and *subjective.* Consider Maslow's description of self-actualizing people as open, spontaneous, loving, self-accepting, and productive. Is this a scientific description? Isn't it merely a description of the theorist's own values and ideals? Maslow, noted M. Brewster Smith (1978), offered impressions of his own personal heroes. Imagine another theorist who began with a different set of heroes—perhaps Napoleon, John D. Rockefeller, Sr., and Margaret Thatcher. This theorist would likely describe self-actualizing people as "undeterred by others' needs and opinions," "motivated to achieve," and "comfortable with power."

Critics also objected to the idea that, as Rogers put it, "The only question which matters is, 'Am I living in a way which is deeply satisfying to me, and which truly expresses me?'" (quoted by Wallach & Wallach, 1985). The *individualism* encouraged by humanistic psychology—trusting and acting on one's feelings, being true to oneself, fulfilling oneself—can, the critics have said, lead to self-indulgence, selfishness, and an erosion of moral restraints (Campbell & Specht, 1985; Wallach & Wallach, 1983). Indeed, it is those who focus beyond themselves who are most likely to experience social support, to enjoy life, and to cope effectively with stress (Crandall, 1984).

Humanistic psychologists reply that a secure, nondefensive self-acceptance is actually the first step toward loving others. Indeed, people who feel intrinsically liked and accepted—for who they are, not just for their achievements—exhibit less defensive attitudes (Schimel et al., 2001).

A final accusation leveled against humanistic psychology is that it is *naive,* that it fails to appreciate the reality of our human capacity for evil. Faced with climate change, overpopulation, terrorism, and the spread of nuclear weapons, we may become apathetic from either of two rationalizations. One is a starry-eyed optimism that denies the threat ("People are basically good; everything will work out"). The other is a dark despair ("It's hopeless; why try?"). Action requires enough realism to fuel concern and enough optimism to provide hope. Humanistic psychology, say the critics, encourages the needed hope but not the equally necessary realism about evil.

RETRIEVAL PRACTICE

- How did *humanistic psychology* provide a fresh perspective?

ANSWER: This movement sought to turn psychology's attention away from drives and conflicts and toward our growth potential, with a focus on the way healthy people strive for self-determination and self-realization, which was in contrast to psychodynamic theory and strict behaviorism.

- What does it mean to be *empathic?* How about *self-actualized?* Which humanistic psychologists used these terms?

ANSWERS: To be *empathic* is to share and mirror another person's feelings. Carl Rogers believed that people nurture growth in others by being empathic. Abraham Maslow proposed that *self-actualization* is the motivation to fulfill one's potential, and one of the ultimate psychological needs (the other is self-transcendence).

MODULE REVIEW

Humanistic Theories

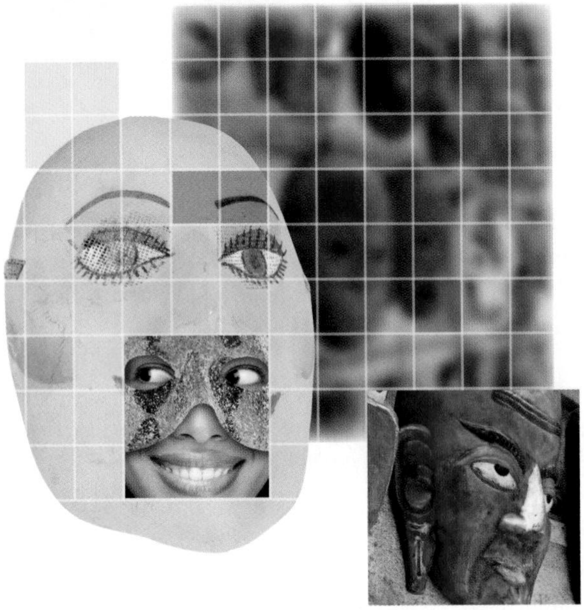

Learning Objectives

RETRIEVAL PRACTICE Take a moment to answer each of these Learning Objective Questions (repeated here from within the module). Then turn to Appendix B, Complete Module Reviews, to check your answers. Research suggests that trying to answer these questions on your own will improve your long-term retention (McDaniel et al., 2009).

41-1: How did humanistic psychologists view personality, and what was their goal in studying personality?

41-2: How did humanistic psychologists assess a person's sense of self?

41-3: How have humanistic theories influenced psychology? What criticisms have they faced?

Terms and Concepts to Remember

RETRIEVAL PRACTICE Test yourself on these terms by trying to write down the definition before flipping back to the referenced page to check your answer.

humanistic theories, p. 543
self-actualization, p. 543
unconditional positive regard, p. 544
self-concept, p. 544

RETRIEVAL PRACTICE Gain an advantage, and benefit from immediate feedback, with the interactive self-testing resources at www.worthpublishers.com/myers.

MODULE 42

Trait Theories, Social-Cognitive Theories, and the Self

- Trait Theories
- Social-Cognitive Theories
- Exploring the Self

Trait Theories

42-1 How do psychologists use traits to describe personality?

In J.R.R. Tolkien's *Lord of the Rings*, Frodo Baggins' faithful companion, Sam Gamgee, is unwaveringly loyal and optimistic. In psychology, trait researchers attempt to define personality in terms of such stable and enduring behavior patterns. This perspective can be traced in part to a remarkable meeting in 1919, when Gordon Allport, a curious 22-year-old psychology student, interviewed Sigmund Freud in Vienna. Allport soon discovered just how preoccupied the founder of psychoanalysis was with finding hidden motives, even in Allport's own behavior during the interview. That experience ultimately led Allport to do what Freud did not do—to describe personality in terms of fundamental **traits**—people's characteristic behaviors and conscious motives (such as the curiosity that actually motivated Allport to see Freud). Meeting Freud, said Allport, "taught me that [psychoanalysis], for all its merits, may plunge too deep, and that psychologists would do well to give full recognition to manifest motives before probing the unconscious." Allport came to define personality in terms of identifiable behavior patterns. He was concerned less with *explaining* individual traits than with *describing* them.

Like Allport, Isabel Briggs Myers (1987) and her mother, Katharine Briggs, wanted to describe important personality differences. They attempted to sort people according to Carl Jung's personality types, based on their responses to 126 questions. The *Myers-Briggs Type Indicator (MBTI)*, available in 21 languages, has been taken by more than 2 million people a year, mostly for career counseling, leadership training, and work-team development (CPP, 2008). It offers choices, such as "Do you usually value sentiment more than logic, or value logic more than sentiment?" Then it counts the test-taker's preferences, labels them as indicating, say, a "feeling type" or "thinking type," and feeds them back to the person in complimentary terms. Feeling types, for example, are told they are sensitive to values and are "sympathetic, appreciative, and tactful"; thinking types are told they "prefer an objective standard of truth" and are "good at analyzing." (Every type has its strengths, so everyone is affirmed.)

Most people agree with their announced type profile, which mirrors their declared preferences. They may also accept their label as a basis for being matched with work partners and tasks that supposedly suit their temperaments. A National Research Council report noted, however, that despite the test's popularity in business and career counseling, its initial use outran research on its value as a predictor of job performance, and "the popularity of this instrument in the absence of proven scientific worth is troublesome" (Druckman & Bjork, 1991, p. 101; see also Pittenger, 1993). Although research on the MBTI has been accumulating since those cautionary words were expressed, the test remains mostly a counseling and coaching tool, not a research instrument.

Exploring Traits

Classifying people as one or another distinct personality type fails to capture their full individuality. We are each a unique complex of multiple traits. So how else could we describe our personalities? We might describe an apple by placing it along several trait dimensions—

trait a characteristic pattern of behavior or a disposition to feel and act, as assessed by self-report inventories and peer reports.

Stephen Colbert: The extravert Trait labels such as *extraversion* can describe our temperament and typical behaviors.

Ida Mae Astute/ABC via Getty Images

relatively large or small, red or green, sweet or sour. By placing people on several trait dimensions simultaneously, psychologists can describe countless individual personality variations.

What trait dimensions describe personality? If you had an upcoming blind date, what personality traits might give you an accurate sense of the person? Allport and his associate H. S. Odbert (1936) counted all the words in an unabridged dictionary with which one could describe people. There were almost 18,000! How, then, could psychologists condense the list to a manageable number of basic traits?

Factor Analysis

One technique is *factor analysis*, a statistical procedure used to identify clusters *(factors)* of test items that tap basic components of a trait (such as, for intelligence, spatial ability, or verbal skill). Imagine that people who describe themselves as outgoing also tend to say that they like excitement and practical jokes and dislike quiet reading. Such a statistically correlated cluster of behaviors reflects a basic factor, or trait—in this case, *extraversion*.

British psychologists Hans Eysenck and Sybil Eysenck [EYE-zink] believed that we can reduce many of our normal individual variations to two or three dimensions, including *extraversion–introversion* and *emotional stability–instability* (**FIGURE 42.1**). People in 35 countries around the world, from China to Uganda to Russia, have taken the *Eysenck Personality Questionnaire*. When their answers were analyzed, the extraversion and emotionality factors inevitably emerged as basic personality dimensions (Eysenck, 1990, 1992). The Eysencks believed that these factors are genetically influenced, and research supports this belief.

Biology and Personality

Brain-activity scans of extraverts add to the growing list of traits and mental states that have been explored with brain-imaging procedures. (That list includes intelligence, impulsivity, addictive cravings, lying, sexual attraction, aggressiveness, empathy, spiritual experience, and even racial and political attitudes [Olson, 2005].) Such studies indicate that extraverts seek stimulation because their normal *brain arousal* is relatively low. For example, PET scans show that a frontal lobe area involved in behavior inhibition is less active in extraverts than in introverts (Johnson et al., 1999). Dopamine and dopamine-related neural activity tend to be higher in extraverts (Wacker et al., 2006).

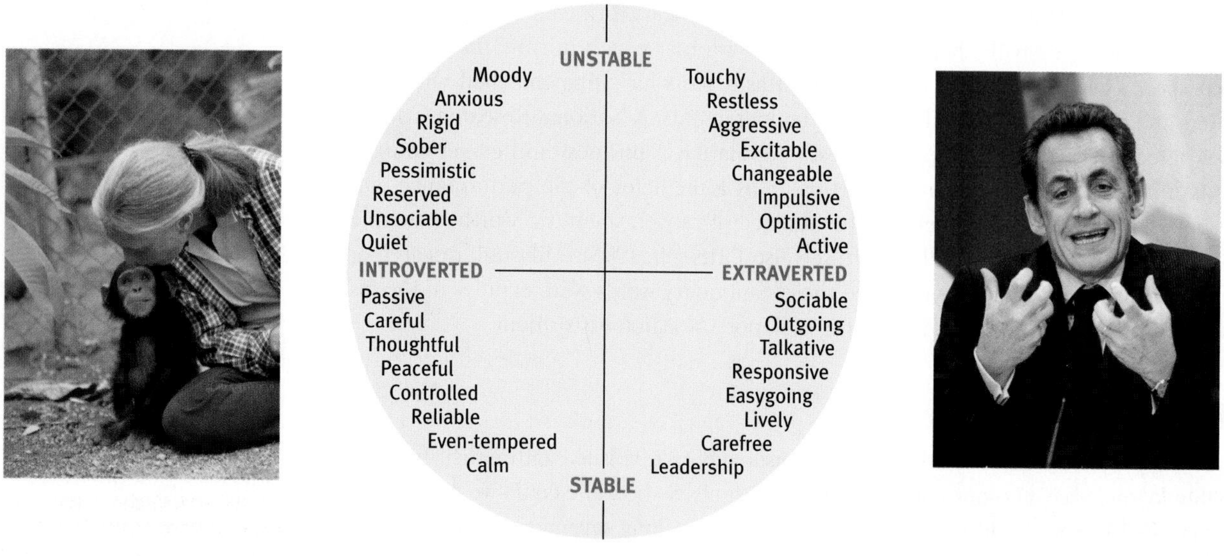

© Karl Ammann/Corbis

HOANG DINH NAM/AFP/Getty Images

FIGURE 42.1
Two personality dimensions
Map-makers can tell us a lot by using two axes (north-south and east-west). Two primary personality factors (extraversion–introversion and stability–instability) are similarly useful as axes for describing personality variation. Varying combinations define other, more specific traits. (From Eysenck & Eysenck, 1963.) Those who are naturally introverted, such as primatologist Jane Goodall, may be particularly gifted in field studies. Successful politicians, including French President Nicolas Sarkozy, are often natural extraverts.

Our biology influences our personality in other ways as well. Our *genes* have much to say about the temperament and behavioral style that help define our personality. Jerome Kagan, for example, has attributed differences in children's shyness and inhibition to their *autonomic nervous system reactivity.* Given a reactive autonomic nervous system, we respond to stress with greater anxiety and inhibition. The fearless, curious child may become the rock-climbing or fast-driving adult.

Samuel Gosling and his colleagues (2003; Jones & Gosling, 2005) report that personality differences among dogs (in energy, affection, reactivity, and curious intelligence) are as evident, and as consistently judged, as personality differences among humans. Monkeys, chimpanzees, orangutans, and even birds also have stable personalities (Weiss et al., 2006). Among the Great Tit (a European relative of the American chickadee), bold birds more quickly inspect new objects and explore trees (Groothuis & Carere, 2005; Verbeek et al., 1994). By selective breeding, researchers can produce bold or shy birds. Both have their place in natural history. In lean years, bold birds are more likely to find food; in abundant years, shy birds feed with less risk.

Erik Lam/Shutterstock

RETRIEVAL PRACTICE

- Which two primary dimensions did Hans and Sybil Eysenck propose for describing personality variation?

ANSWER: introversion–extraversion and emotional stability–instability

Assessing Traits

42-2 What are personality inventories, and what are their strengths and weaknesses as trait-assessment tools?

If stable and enduring traits guide our actions, can we devise valid and reliable tests of them? Several trait assessment techniques exist—some more valid than others (see Thinking Critically About: How to Be a "Successful" Astrologer or Palm Reader on the next page). Some provide quick assessments of a single trait, such as extraversion, anxiety, or self-esteem. **Personality inventories**—longer questionnaires covering a wide range of feelings and behaviors—assess several traits at once.

The classic personality inventory is the **Minnesota Multiphasic Personality Inventory (MMPI).** Although it assesses "abnormal" personality tendencies rather than normal personality traits, the MMPI illustrates a good way of developing a personality inventory. One of its creators, Starke Hathaway (1960), compared his effort to that of Alfred Binet. Binet developed the first intelligence test by selecting items that identified children who would probably have trouble progressing normally in French schools. Like Binet's items, the MMPI items were **empirically derived.** From a large pool of items, Hathaway and his colleagues selected those on which particular diagnostic groups differed. They then grouped the questions into 10 clinical scales, including scales that assess depressive tendencies, masculinity–femininity, and introversion–extraversion.

Hathaway and others initially gave hundreds of true-false statements ("No one seems to understand me"; "I get all the sympathy I should"; "I like poetry") to groups of psychologically disordered patients and to "normal" people. They retained any statement—no matter how silly it sounded—on which the patient group's answer differed from that of the normal group. "Nothing in the newspaper interests me except the comics" may seem senseless, but it just so happened that depressed people were more likely to answer *True.* (Nevertheless, people have had fun spoofing the MMPI with their own mock items: "Weeping brings tears to my eyes," "Frantic screams make me nervous," and "I stay in the bathtub until I look like a raisin" [Frankel et al., 1983].) Today's MMPI-2 also has scales assessing, for instance, work attitudes, family problems, and anger.

personality inventory a questionnaire (often with *true-false* or *agree-disagree* items) on which people respond to items designed to gauge a wide range of feelings and behaviors; used to assess selected personality traits.

Minnesota Multiphasic Personality Inventory (MMPI) the most widely researched and clinically used of all personality tests. Originally developed to identify emotional disorders (still considered its most appropriate use), this test is now used for many other screening purposes.

empirically derived test a test (such as the MMPI) developed by testing a pool of items and then selecting those that discriminate between groups.

THINKING CRITICALLY ABOUT

How to Be a "Successful" Astrologer or Palm Reader

"A petite fortune-teller who escapes from prison is a small medium at large."

Anonymous

Can we discern people's traits from the alignment of the stars and planets at the time of their birth? From their handwriting? From lines on their palms?

Astronomers scoff at the naiveté of astrology—the constellations have shifted in the millennia since astrologers formulated their predictions (Kelly, 1997, 1998). Humorists mock it: "No offense," writes Dave Barry, "but if you take the horoscope seriously your frontal lobes are the size of Raisinets." Psychologists instead ask questions: Does it work? Can astrologers surpass chance when given someone's birth date and asked to identify the person from a short lineup of different personality descriptions? Can people pick out their own horoscopes from a lineup of horoscopes? Do people's astrological signs correlate with predicted traits?

The consistent answers have been *No, No, No,* and *No* (British Psychological Society, 1993; Carlson, 1985; Kelly, 1997, Reichardt, 2010). For example, one researcher examined census data from 20 million married people in England and Wales and found that "astrological sign has no impact on the probability of marrying—and staying married to—someone of any other sign" (Voas, 2008).

Cihan Demirok, CIDEPIX/Shutterstock

liquidlibrary/Jupiterimages

© 2000 by Rob Pudim

Graphologists, who make predictions from handwriting samples, have similarly been found to do no better than chance when trying to discern people's occupations from examining several pages of their handwriting (Beyerstein & Beyerstein, 1992; Dean et al., 1992). Nevertheless, graphologists—and introductory psychology students—will often *perceive* correlations between personality and handwriting even where there are none (King & Koehler, 2000).

If all these perceived correlations evaporate under close scrutiny, how do astrologers, palm readers, and crystal-ball gazers persuade

In contrast to the subjectivity of most projective tests, personality inventories are scored objectively—so objectively that a computer can administer and score them. (The computer can also provide descriptions of people who previously responded similarly.) Objectivity does not, however, guarantee validity. For example, individuals taking the MMPI for employment purposes can give socially desirable answers to create a good impression. But in so doing they may also score high on a *lie scale* that assesses faking (as when people respond *false* to a universally true statement such as "I get angry sometimes"). The objectivity of the MMPI has contributed to its popularity and to its translation into more than 100 languages.

The Big Five Factors

42-3 Which traits seem to provide the most useful information about personality variation?

Today's trait researchers believe that simple trait factors, such as the Eysencks' introverted–extraverted and stability–instability dimensions, are important, but they do not tell the whole story. A slightly expanded set of factors—dubbed the *Big Five*—does a better job (Costa & McCrae, 2009). If a test specifies where you are on the five dimensions (conscientiousness, millions of people worldwide to buy their services? Ray Hyman (1981), palm reader turned research psychologist, has revealed some of their suckering methods.

The first technique, the "stock spiel," builds on the observation that each of us is in some ways like no one else and in other ways just like everyone. That some things are true of us all enables the "seer" to offer statements that seem impressively accurate: "I sense that you worry about things more than you let on, even to your best friends." A number of such generally true statements can be combined into a personality description. Imagine that you take a personality test and then receive the following character sketch:

> You have a strong need for other people to like and to admire you. You have a tendency to be critical of yourself. . . . You pride yourself on being an independent thinker and do not accept other opinions without satisfactory proof. You have found it unwise to be too frank in revealing yourself to others. At times you are extraverted, affable, sociable; at other times you are introverted, wary, and reserved. Some of your aspirations tend to be pretty unrealistic (Davies, 1997; Forer, 1949).

In experiments, college students have received stock assessments like this one, drawn from statements in a newsstand astrology book. When they think the bogus, generic feedback was prepared just for them and when it is favorable, they nearly always rate the description as either "good" or "excellent" (Davies, 1997). Even skeptics, given a flattering description attributed to an astrologer, begin to think that "maybe there's something to this astrology stuff after all" (Glick et al., 1989). An astrologer, it has been said, is someone "prepared to tell you what you think of yourself" (Jones, 2000). This acceptance of stock, positive descriptions is called the *Barnum effect,* named in honor of master showman P. T. Barnum's dictum, "We've got something for everyone."

A second technique used by seers is to "read" our clothing, physical features, gestures, and reactions. An expensive wedding ring and black dress might, for example, suggest a wealthy woman who was recently widowed.

"Perhaps you'd like a second opinion?"

The New Yorker Collection, 2010, Mick Stevens, from cartoonbank.com. All Rights Reserved.

You, too, could read such clues, says Hyman. If people seek you out for a reading, start with some safe sympathy: "I sense you're having some problems lately. You seem unsure what to do. I get the feeling another person is involved." Then tell them what they want to hear. Memorize some Barnum statements from astrology and fortune-telling manuals and use them liberally. Tell people it is their responsibility to cooperate by relating your message to their specific experiences. Later they will recall that you predicted those specific details. Phrase statements as questions, and when you detect a positive response assert the statement strongly. Finally, be a good listener, and later, in different words, reveal to people what they earlier revealed to you. If you dupe them, they will come.

Better yet, beware of those who, by exploiting people with these techniques, are fortune takers rather than fortune tellers.

agreeableness, neuroticism, openness, and extraversion; see **TABLE 42.1** on the next page), it has said much of what there is to say about your personality. Around the world—across 56 nations and 29 languages in one study (Schmitt et al., 2007)—people describe others in terms roughly consistent with this list. The Big Five may not be the last word. (Some researchers report it takes only two or three factors—such as conscientiousness, agreeableness, and extraversion—to describe the basic personality dimensions [Block, 2010; De Raad et al., 2010].) But for now, at least, five is the winning number in the personality lottery (Heine & Buchtel, 2009; McCrae, 2009). The Big Five—today's "common currency for personality psychology" (Funder, 2001)—has been the most active personality research topic since the early 1990s and is currently our best approximation of the basic trait dimensions.

Big Five research has explored various questions:

- ***How stable are these traits?*** In adulthood, the Big Five traits are quite stable, with some tendencies (emotional instability, extraversion, and openness) waning a bit during early and middle adulthood, and others (agreeableness and conscientiousness) rising (McCrae, 2011; Vaidya et al., 2002). Conscientiousness increases the most during people's twenties, as people mature and learn to manage their jobs and relationships.

Hemera Technologies/ Jupiterimages

TABLE 42.1

The "Big Five" Personality Factors

(*Memory tip:* Picturing a **CANOE** will help you recall these.)

Disorganized Careless Impulsive	**C**onscientiousness	Organized Careful Disciplined
Ruthless Suspicious Uncooperative	**A**greeableness	Soft-hearted Trusting Helpful
Calm Secure Self-satisfied	**N**euroticism (emotional stability vs. instability)	Anxious Insecure Self-pitying
Practical Prefers routine Conforming	**O**penness	Imaginative Prefers variety Independent
Retiring Sober Reserved	**E**xtraversion	Sociable Fun-loving Affectionate

Source: Adapted from McCrae & Costa (1986, 2008).

Agreeableness increases the most during people's thirties and continues to increase through their sixties (Srivastava et al., 2003).

- ***How heritable are they?*** Heritability (the extent to which individual differences are attributable to genes) varies with the diversity of people studied, but it generally runs 50 percent or a tad more for each dimension, and genetic influences are similar in different nations (Loehlin et al., 1998; Yamagata et al., 2006). Many genes, each having small effects, combine to influence our traits (McCrae et al., 2010). Researchers have also identified brain areas associated with the various Big Five traits, such as a frontal lobe area that is sensitive to reward and is larger in extraverts (DeYoung et al., 2010).
- ***Do the Big Five traits predict other behavioral attributes?*** *Yes.* If people report being outgoing, conscientious, and agreeable, "they probably are telling the truth," reports Big Five researcher Robert McCrae (2011). Here are some examples:
  - Shy introverts are more likely than extraverts to prefer communicating by e-mail rather than face-to-face (Hertel et al., 2008).
  - Highly conscientious people earn better high school and university grades (Poropat, 2009). They also are more likely to be morning types (sometimes called "larks"); evening types ("owls") are marginally more extraverted (Jackson & Gerard, 1996).
  - If one partner scores lower than the other on agreeableness, stability, and openness, marital and sexual satisfaction may suffer (Botwin et al., 1997; Donnellan et al., 2004).
  - Our traits infuse our language. In text messaging, extraversion predicts use of personal pronouns, agreeableness predicts positive emotion words, and neuroticism (emotional instability) predicts negative emotion words (Holtgraves, 2011).

By exploring such questions, Big Five research has sustained trait psychology and renewed appreciation for the importance of personality. Traits matter.

RETRIEVAL PRACTICE

- What are the *Big Five* personality factors, and what are the strengths of using these factors?

ANSWER: The Big Five personality factors are conscientiousness, agreeableness, neuroticism (emotional stability vs. instability), openness, and extraversion (CANOE). These factors may be objectively measured, with validity, and research suggests that these factors are relatively stable across the life span and apply to all cultures in which they have been studied.

Evaluating Trait Theories

42-4 Does research support the consistency of personality traits over time and across situations?

Are our personality traits stable and enduring? Or does our behavior depend on where and with whom we find ourselves? J.R.R. Tolkien created characters, like the loyal Sam Gamgee, whose personality traits were consistent across various times and places. The Italian playwright Luigi Pirandello had a different view. For him, personality was ever-changing, tailored to the particular role or situation. In one of Pirandello's plays, Lamberto Laudisi describes himself: "I am really what you take me to be; though, my dear madam, that does not prevent me from also being really what your husband, my sister, my niece, and Signora Cini take me to be—because they also are absolutely right!" To which Signora Sirelli responds, "In other words you are a different person for each of us."

"There is as much difference between us and ourselves, as between us and others."
Michel de Montaigne, *Essays*, 1588

The Person-Situation Controversy

Who, then, typifies human personality, Tolkien's consistent Sam Gamgee or Pirandello's inconsistent Laudisi? Both. Our behavior is influenced by the interaction of our inner disposition with our environment. Still, the question lingers: Which is more important? Are we *more* as Tolkien or as Pirandello imagined us to be?

Roughly speaking, the temporary, external influences on behavior are the focus of social psychology, and the enduring, inner influences are the focus of personality psychology. In actuality, behavior always depends on the interaction of persons with situations.

When we explore this *person-situation controversy*, we look for genuine personality traits that persist over time *and* across situations. Are some people dependably conscientious and others unreliable, some cheerful and others dour, some friendly and outgoing and others shy? If we are to consider friendliness a trait, friendly people must act friendly at different times and places. Do they?

In considering research that has followed lives through time, some scholars (especially those who study infants) are impressed with personality change; others are struck by personality stability during adulthood. As **FIGURE 42.2** illustrates, data from 152 long-term studies reveal that personality trait scores are positively correlated with scores obtained seven years later, and that as people grow older their personality stabilizes. Interests may change—the avid collector of tropical fish may become an avid gardener. Careers may

Change and consistency can co-exist. If all people were to become somewhat less shy with age, there would be personality change, but also relative stability and predictability.

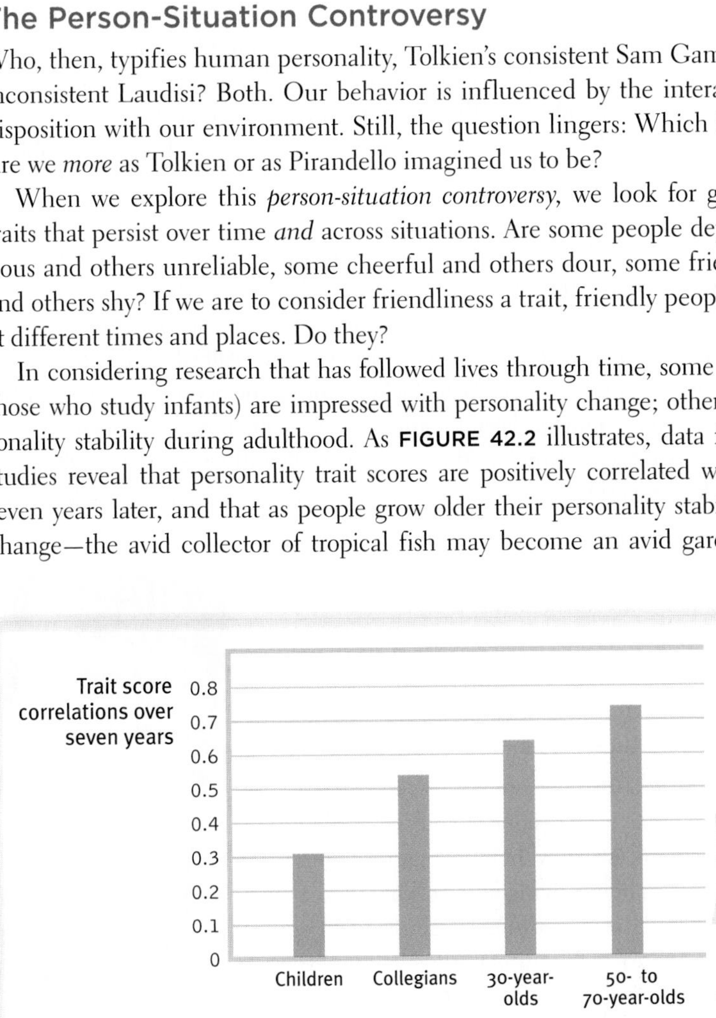

FIGURE 42.2
Personality stability With age, personality traits become more stable, as reflected in the stronger correlation of trait scores with follow-up scores seven years later. (Data from Roberts & DelVecchio, 2000.)

© The New Yorker Collection, 1984, W. Miller from cartoonbank.com. All Rights Reserved.

"Mr. Coughlin over there was the founder of one of the first motorcycle gangs."

change—the determined salesperson may become a determined social worker. Relationships may change—the hostile spouse may start over with a new partner. But most people recognize their traits as their own, note Robert McCrae and Paul Costa (1994), "and it is well that they do. A person's recognition of the inevitability of his or her one and only personality is . . . the culminating wisdom of a lifetime."

So most people—including most psychologists—would probably side with Tolkien's assumption of stability of personality traits. Moreover, our traits are socially significant. They influence our health, our thinking, and our job performance (Deary & Matthews, 1993; Hogan, 1998). Studies that follow lives through time show that personality traits rival socioeconomic status and cognitive ability as predictors of mortality, divorce, and occupational attainment (Roberts et al., 2007).

Although our personality *traits* may be both stable and potent, the consistency of our specific *behaviors* from one situation to the next is another matter. As Walter Mischel (1968, 2009) has pointed out, people do not act with predictable consistency. Mischel's studies of college students' conscientiousness revealed but a modest relationship between a student's being conscientious on one occasion (say, showing up for class on time) and being similarly conscientious on another occasion (say, turning in assignments on time). Pirandello would not have been surprised. If you've noticed how outgoing you are in some situations and how reserved you are in others, perhaps you're not surprised either (though for certain traits, Mischel reports, you may accurately assess yourself as more consistent).

© The New Yorker Collection, 2006, Victoria Roberts from cartoonbank.com. All Rights Reserved.

"I'm going to France—I'm a different person in France."

This inconsistency in behaviors also makes personality test scores weak predictors of behaviors. People's scores on an extraversion test, for example, do not neatly predict how sociable they actually will be on any given occasion. If we remember such results, says Mischel, we will be more cautious about labeling and pigeonholing individuals. Years in advance, science can tell us the phase of the Moon for any given date. A day in advance, meteorologists can often predict the weather. But we are much further from being able to predict how *you* will feel and act tomorrow.

However, people's *average* outgoingness, happiness, or carelessness over many situations is predictable (Epstein, 1983a,b). When rating someone's shyness or agreeableness, this consistency enables people who know someone well to agree on their ratings (Kenrick & Funder, 1988). By collecting snippets of people's daily experience via body-worn recording devices, Matthias Mehl and his colleagues (2006) confirmed that extraverts really do talk more. (I have repeatedly vowed to cut back on my jabbering and joking during my noontime pickup basketball games with friends. Alas, moments later, the irrepressible chatterbox inevitably reoccupies my body.) As our best friends can verify, we do have genetically influenced personality traits. And those traits even lurk, report Samuel Gosling and his colleagues in a series of studies, in our

- ***music preferences.*** Classical, jazz, blues, and folk music lovers tend to be open to experience and verbally intelligent; country, pop, and religious music lovers tend to be cheerful, outgoing, and conscientious (Rentfrow & Gosling, 2003, 2006). On first meeting, students often disclose their music preferences to each other; in doing so, they are swapping information about their personalities.
- ***dorm rooms and offices.*** Our personal spaces display our identity and leave a behavioral residue (in our scattered laundry or neat desktop). And that helps explain why just a few minutes' inspection of our living and working spaces can enable someone to assess with reasonable accuracy our conscientiousness, our openness to new experiences, and even our emotional stability (Gosling et al., 2002, 2008).

Alex Segre/Alamy

- ***personal websites.*** Is a personal website or a Facebook profile also a canvas for self-expression? Or is it an opportunity for people to present themselves in false or misleading ways? It's more the former (Back et al., 2010; Gosling et al., 2007; Marcus et al., 2006). Visitors to personal websites quickly gain important clues to the creator's extraversion, conscientiousness, and openness to experience. Even mere pictures of people, and their associated clothes, expressions, and postures, can give clues to personality (Naumann et al., 2009).
- ***e-mail.*** If you have ever felt you could detect someone's personality from the writing voice in their e-mail, you are right!! (What a cool, exciting finding!!!) People's ratings of others' personalities based solely on their e-mails (or blogs) correlate with actual personality scores on measures such as extraversion and neuroticism (Gill et al., 2006; Oberlander & Gill, 2006; Yarkoni, 2010). Extraverts, for example, use more adjectives.

Room with a cue Even at "zero acquaintance," people can discern something of others' personality from glimpsing their website, dorm room, or office. So, what is your read on University of Texas researcher Samuel Gosling?

John Langford Photography

In unfamiliar, formal situations—perhaps as a guest in the home of a person from another culture—our traits remain hidden as we carefully attend to social cues. In familiar, informal situations—just hanging out with friends—we feel less constrained, allowing our traits to emerge (Buss, 1989). In these informal situations, our expressive styles—our animation, manner of speaking, and gestures—are impressively consistent. That's why those very thin slices of someone's behavior—even just three 2-second clips of a teacher—can be revealing (Ambady & Rosenthal, 1992, 1993).

Some people are naturally expressive (and therefore talented at pantomime and charades); others are less expressive (and therefore better poker players). To evaluate people's voluntary control over their expressiveness, Bella DePaulo and her colleagues (1992) asked people to *act* as expressive or inhibited as possible while stating opinions. Their remarkable findings: Inexpressive people, even when feigning expressiveness, were less expressive than expressive people acting naturally. Similarly, expressive people, even when trying to seem inhibited, were less inhibited than inexpressive people acting naturally. It's hard to be someone you're not, or not to be who you are.

To sum up, we can say that at any moment the immediate situation powerfully influences a person's behavior. Social psychologists have assumed, albeit without much evidence, that this is especially so when a "strong situation" makes clear demands (Cooper & Withey, 2009). We can better predict drivers' behavior at traffic lights from knowing the color of the lights than from knowing the drivers' personalities. Thus, professors may perceive certain students as subdued (based on their classroom behavior), but friends may perceive them as pretty wild (based on their party behavior). Averaging our behavior across many occasions does, however, reveal distinct personality traits. Traits exist. We differ. And our differences matter.

RETRIEVAL PRACTICE

- How well do personality test scores predict our behavior? Explain.

ANSWER: Our scores on personality tests predict our *average* behavior across many situations much better than they predict our specific behavior in any given situation.

Social-Cognitive Theories

42-5 Who first proposed the social-cognitive perspective, and how do these theorists view personality development?

Today's psychological science views individuals as biopsychosocial organisms. The **social-cognitive perspective** on personality proposed by Albert Bandura (1986, 2006, 2008) emphasizes the interaction of our traits with our situations. Much as nature and nurture always work together, so do individuals and their situations.

social-cognitive perspective views behavior as influenced by the interaction between people's traits (including their thinking) and their social context.

reciprocal determinism the interacting influences of behavior, internal cognition, and environment.

Social-cognitive theorists believe we learn many of our behaviors either through conditioning or by observing and imitating others. (That's the "social" part.) They also emphasize the importance of mental processes: What we *think* about our situations affects our behavior. (That's the "cognitive" part.) Instead of focusing solely on how our environment *controls* us (behaviorism), social-cognitive theorists focus on how we and our environment *interact:* How do we interpret and respond to external events? How do our schemas, our memories, and our expectations influence our behavior patterns?

Reciprocal Influences

Bandura (1986, 2006) views the person-environment interaction as **reciprocal determinism.** "Behavior, internal personal factors, and environmental influences," he said, "all operate as interlocking determinants of each other" (**FIGURE 42.3**). For example, children's TV-viewing habits (past behavior) influence their viewing preferences (internal factor), which influence how television (environmental factor) affects their current behavior. The influences are mutual.

Consider three specific ways in which individuals and environments interact:

1. ***Different people choose different environments.*** The school you attend, the reading you do, the TV programs you watch, the music you listen to, the friends you associate with—all are part of an environment you have chosen, based partly on your dispositions (Funder, 2009; Ickes et al., 1997). You choose your environment and it then shapes you.
2. ***Our personalities shape how we interpret and react to events.*** Anxious people, for example, are attuned to potentially threatening events (Eysenck et al., 1987). Thus, they perceive the world as threatening, and they react accordingly.
3. ***Our personalities help create situations to which we react.*** Many experiments reveal that how we view and treat people influences how they in turn treat us. If we expect someone to be angry with us, we may give the person a cold shoulder, touching off the very anger we expect. If we have an easygoing, positive disposition, we will likely enjoy close, supportive friendships (Donnellan et al., 2005; Kendler, 1997).

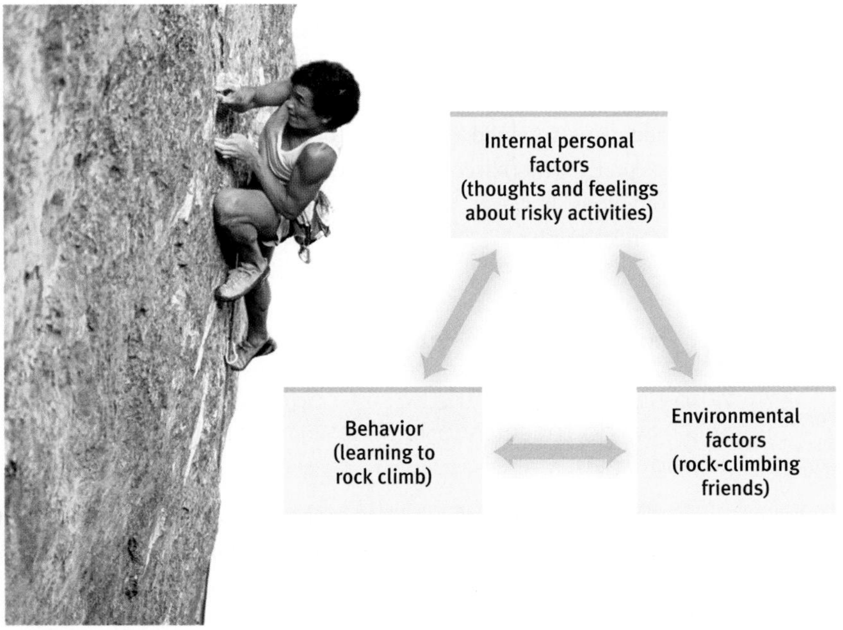

FIGURE 42.3
Reciprocal determinism The social-cognitive perspective proposes that our personalities are shaped by the interaction of our personal traits (including our thoughts and feelings), our environment, and our behaviors.

In such ways, we are both the products and the architects of our environments.

If all this has a familiar ring, it may be because it parallels and reinforces a pervasive theme in psychology and in this book: *Behavior emerges from the interplay of external and internal influences.* Boiling water turns an egg hard and a potato soft. A threatening environment turns one person into a hero, another into a scoundrel. Extraverts enjoy greater well-being in an extraverted culture than an introverted one (Fulmer et al., 2010). *At every moment,* our behavior is influenced by our biology, our social and cultural experiences, and our cognition and dispositions (**FIGURE 42.4**).

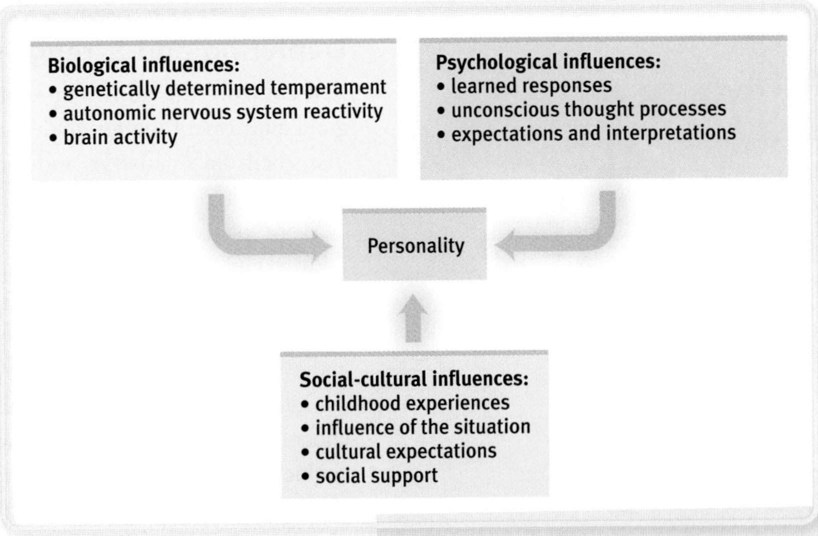

FIGURE 42.4
The biopsychosocial approach to the study of personality As with other psychological phenomena, personality is fruitfully studied at multiple levels.

RETRIEVAL PRACTICE

- Albert Bandura proposed the ___________-___________ perspective on personality, which emphasizes the interaction of people with their environment. To describe the interacting influences of behavior, thoughts, and environment, he used the term ___________ ___________.

ANSWERS: social-cognitive; reciprocal determinism

Personal Control

In studying how we interact with our environment, social-cognitive psychologists emphasize our sense of **personal control**—whether we learn to see ourselves as controlling, or as controlled by, our environment. Psychologists have two basic ways to study the effect of personal control (or any personality factor). One: *correlate* people's feelings of control with their behaviors and achievements. Two: *experiment,* by raising or lowering people's sense of control and noting the effects.

Internal Versus External Locus of Control

Consider your own feelings of control. Do you believe that your life is beyond your control? That the world is run by a few powerful people? That getting a good job depends mainly on being in the right place at the right time? Or do you more strongly believe that what happens to you is your own doing? That the average person can influence government decisions? That being a success is a matter of hard work?

Hundreds of studies have compared people who differ in their perceptions of control. On the one side are those who have what psychologist Julian Rotter called an **external locus of control**—the perception that chance or outside forces determine their fate. On the other are those who perceive an **internal locus of control,** who believe that they control their own destiny. In study after study, "internals" achieve more in school and work, act more independently, enjoy better health, and feel less depressed than do "externals" (Lefcourt, 1982; Ng et al., 2006). Moreover, they are better at delaying gratification and coping with various stressors, including marital problems (Miller & Monge, 1986). One study followed 7551 British people for two decades. Those who expressed a more internal locus of control at age 10 exhibited less obesity, hypertension, and distress at age 30 (Gale et al., 2008). Other studies find that people who believe in free will, or that willpower is controllable, learn better, perform better at work, and are more helpful (Baumeister & Tierney, 2011; Job et al., 2010; Stillman, 2010).

personal control the extent to which we perceive control over our environment.

external locus of control the perception that chance or outside forces beyond our personal control determine our fate.

internal locus of control the perception that you control your own fate.

© Michael Schmitt/Getty Images

Exercising self-control Physical exercise helps us practice self-regulation, which then increases self-control in other areas of our lives.

Depleting and Strengthening Self-Control

Self-control—the ability to control impulses and delay gratification—in turn predicts good adjustment, better grades, and social success (Tangney et al., 2004). Students who plan their day's activities and then live out their day as planned are also at low risk for depression (Nezlek, 2001).

None of us experiences unvarying self-control. Like a muscle, self-control temporarily weakens after an exertion, replenishes with rest, and becomes stronger with exercise (Baumeister & Exline, 2000; Hagger et al., 2010; Vohs & Baumeister, 2011). Exercising willpower temporarily depletes the mental energy needed for self-control on other tasks, and even depletes the blood sugar and neural activity associated with mental focus (Inzlicht & Gutsell, 2007). In one experiment, hungry people who had resisted the temptation to eat chocolate chip cookies gave up sooner on a tedious task than those who had not resisted the cookies. People also become less restrained in their aggressive responses to provocation and in their sexuality after expending willpower on laboratory tasks, such as stifling prejudice or saying the color of words (for example, "red" even if the red-colored word was *green*) (DeWall et al., 2007; Gaillot & Baumeister, 2007). But giving people energy-boosting sugar (in a naturally rather than an artificially sweetened lemonade) strengthens the research participants' effortful thinking (Masicampo & Baumeister, 2008).

In the long run, self-control requires attention and energy. People who practice self-regulation through physical exercise and time-managed study programs develop their self-regulation capacity. Their strengthened self-control is seen both in their performance on laboratory tasks and in their improved self-management of eating, drinking, smoking, and household chores (Oaten & Cheng, 2006a,b). Develop your self-discipline in one area of your life and your strengthened self-control may spill over into other areas as well. The bottom line: We can grow our willpower muscles—our capacity for self-regulation. But doing so requires some (dare I say it?) willpower.

Learned Helplessness Versus Personal Control

People who feel helpless and oppressed often perceive control as external. This perception then deepens their feelings of resignation, as experimenter Martin Seligman (1975, 1991) found. Dogs strapped in a harness and given repeated shocks, with no opportunity to avoid them, learned a sense of helplessness. Later placed in another situation where they *could* escape the punishment by simply leaping a hurdle, the dogs cowered as if without hope. In contrast, animals able to escape the first shocks learned personal control and easily escaped the shocks in the new situation.

It's not just animals. When repeatedly faced with traumatic events over which they have no control, people come to feel helpless, hopeless, and depressed. Psychologists call this passive resignation **learned helplessness** (**FIGURE 42.5**).

FIGURE 42.5
Learned helplessness When animals and people experience no control over repeated bad events, they often learn helplessness.

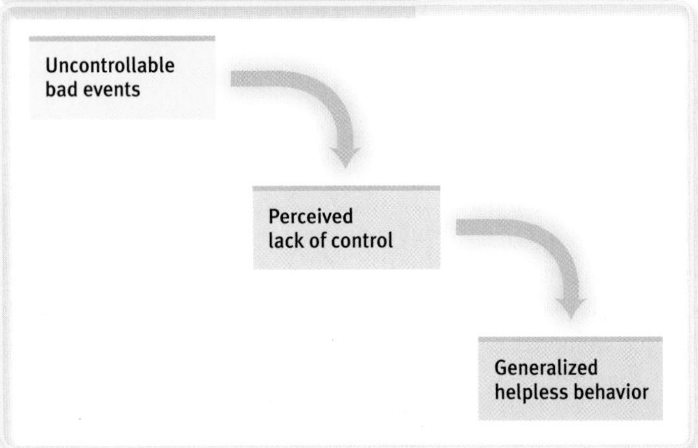

Part of the shock we feel in an unfamiliar culture comes from a diminished sense of control when unsure how others will respond (Triandis, 1994). Similarly, people given little control over their world in prisons, factories, colleges, and nursing homes experience lower morale and increased stress. Measures that increase control—allowing prisoners to move chairs and control room lights and the TV, having workers participate in decision making, offering nursing home patients choices about their environment—noticeably improve health and morale (Humphrey et al., 2007; Wang et al., 2010). When Gallup pollsters asked workers whether they were allowed to personalize their workspace, those who said they could were 55 percent more likely to report high work engagement (Krueger & Killham, 2006).

In one famous study of nursing home patients, 93 percent of those encouraged to exert more control became more alert, active, and happy (Rodin, 1986). As researcher Ellen Langer (1983, p. 291) concluded, "Perceived control is basic to human functioning." No wonder so many people like their iPads and DVRs, which give them control of the content and timing of their entertainment.

The verdict of these studies is reassuring: Under conditions of personal freedom and empowerment, people thrive. Small wonder that the citizens of stable democracies report higher levels of happiness, and others have become happier with democratization (Inglehart, 1990, 2009; Ott, 2010). Shortly before the democratic revolution in the former East Germany, psychologists Gabriele Oettingen and Martin Seligman (1990) studied the telltale body language of working-class men in East and West Berlin bars. Compared with their counterparts on the other side of the Wall, the empowered West Berliners much more often laughed, sat upright rather than slumped, and had upward- rather than downward-turned mouths.

Some freedom and control is better than none, notes Barry Schwartz (2000, 2004). But does ever-increasing choice breed ever-happier lives? Actually not. Schwartz notes that the "excess of freedom" in today's Western cultures contributes to decreasing life satisfaction, increased depression, and sometimes decisional paralysis. Increased consumer choices, as when buying a car or phone, are not an unmixed blessing. After choosing among 30 brands of jam or chocolate, people express less satisfaction than those choosing among a half-dozen options (Iyengar & Lepper, 2000). In the middle of the last century, an average supermarket carried 3750 items, notes Sheena Iyengar (2010), while today's Walmart and other big-box stores offer more than 100,000, and Amazon offers 24 million books and millions of other products. This *tyranny of choice* brings information overload and a greater likelihood that we will feel regret over some of the unchosen options.

self-control the ability to control impulses and delay short-term gratification for greater long-term rewards.

learned helplessness the hopelessness and passive resignation an animal or human learns when unable to avoid repeated aversive events.

Peter Turnley/Corbis

"Happy are those who choose their own path" These happy East Berliners, crossing over to West Berlin after the wall came down in 1989, seemed to personify this sentiment from the Roman philosopher Seneca. Surveys over time have confirmed increased life satisfaction for those in the former East Germany (Cummins et al., 2009).

Optimism Versus Pessimism

One measure of how helpless or effective you feel is where you stand on optimism-pessimism. How do you characteristically explain negative and positive events? Perhaps you have known students whose *attributional style* is pessimistic—who attribute poor performance to their lack of ability ("I can't do this") or to situations enduringly beyond their control ("There is nothing I can do about it"). Such students are more likely to continue getting low grades than are students who adopt the more hopeful attitude that effort, good study habits, and self-discipline can make a difference (Noel et al., 1987; Peterson & Barrett, 1987). Mere fantasies do not fuel motivation and success. Realistic positive expectations do (Oettingen & Mayer, 2002).

Attributional style also matters when dating couples wrestle with conflicts. Optimists and their partners see each other as engaging constructively, and they then tend to feel more supported and satisfied with the resolution and with their relationship (Srivastava et al., 2006). Expect good things from others, and often you will get what you expect. Such studies helped point Seligman toward proposing a more positive psychology (see Close-Up: Toward a More Positive Psychology on the next page).

Excessive Optimism Positive thinking in the face of adversity can pay dividends, but so, too, can a dash of realism (Schneider, 2001). Realistic anxiety over possible future failures can fuel energetic efforts to avoid the dreaded fate (Goodhart, 1986; Norem, 2001; Showers, 1992). Concerned about failing an upcoming exam, students may study thoroughly and outperform their equally able but more confident peers. Asian-American students express somewhat greater pessimism than their European-American counterparts, which Edward Chang (2001) suspects helps explain their often impressive academic achievements. Success requires enough optimism to provide hope and enough pessimism to prevent complacency. We want our airline pilots to be mindful of worst-possible outcomes.

"We just haven't been flapping them hard enough."

© The New Yorker Collection, 1995, S. Gross from cartoonbank.com. All Rights Reserved.

Positive expectations often motivate eventual success.

CLOSE-UP

Toward a More Positive Psychology

During its first century, psychology understandably focused much of its attention on understanding and alleviating negative states. Psychologists have studied abuse and anxiety, depression and disease, prejudice and poverty. Articles on selected negative emotions since 1887 have outnumbered those on positive emotions by 17 to 1.

In ages past, notes American Psychological Association past-president Martin Seligman (2002), times of relative peace and prosperity have enabled cultures to turn their attention from repairing weakness and damage to promoting "the highest qualities of life." Prosperous fifth-century Athens nurtured philosophy and democracy. Flourishing fifteenth-century Florence nurtured great art. Victorian England, flush with the bounty of the British Empire, nurtured honor, discipline, and duty. In this millennium, Seligman believes, thriving Western cultures have a parallel opportunity to create, as a "humane, scientific monument," a more **positive psychology**—a psychology concerned not only with weakness and damage but also with strength and virtue. Thanks to his own leadership, the new positive psychology movement has gained strength, with supporters in 77 countries from Croatia to China (IPPA, 2009, 2010; Seligman, 2004, 2011).

Positive psychology shares with humanistic psychology an interest in advancing human fulfillment, but its methodology is scientific. Positive psychology science is exploring

- *positive well-being*—which assesses exercises and interventions aimed at increasing happiness (Schueller, 2010; Sin & Lyubomirsky, 2009),
- *positive health*—which studies how positive emotions enhance and sustain physical well-being (Seligman, 2008; Seligman et al., 2011),
- *positive neuroscience*—which explores the biological foundations of positive emotions, resilience, and social behavior (www.posneuroscience.org), and
- *positive education*—which evaluates educational efforts to increase students' engagement, resilience, character strengths, optimism, and sense of meaning (Seligman et al., 2009).

"Positive psychology," say Seligman and colleagues (2005), "is an umbrella term for the study of positive emotions, positive character traits, and enabling institutions." Taken together, satisfaction with the past, happiness with the present, and optimism about the future define the movement's first pillar: *positive emotions.* Happiness, Seligman argues, is a by-product of a pleasant, engaged, and meaningful life.

Martin E. P. Seligman "The main purpose of a positive psychology is to measure, understand, and then build the human strengths and the civic virtues."

Courtesy of Martin E. P. Seligman, Ph.D. Director, Positive Psychology Center/ University of Pennsylvania

Positive psychology is about building not just a pleasant life, says Seligman, but also a good life that engages one's skills, and a meaningful life that points beyond oneself. Thus, the second pillar, *positive character,* focuses on exploring and enhancing creativity, courage, compassion, integrity, self-control, leadership, wisdom, and spirituality.

The third pillar, *positive groups, communities,* and *cultures,* seeks to foster a positive social ecology. This includes healthy families, communal neighborhoods, effective schools, socially responsible media, and civil dialogue.

Will psychology have a more positive mission in this century? Without slighting the need to repair damage and cure disease, positive psychology's proponents hope so. With *American Psychologist* and *British Psychologist* special issues devoted to positive psychology; with many new books; with networked scientists working in worldwide research groups; and with prizes, research awards, summer institutes, and a graduate program promoting positive psychology scholarship, these psychologists have reason to be positive.

positive psychology the scientific study of optimal human functioning; aims to discover and promote strengths and virtues that enable individuals and communities to thrive.

Excessive optimism can blind us to real risks. Neil Weinstein (1980, 1982, 1996) has shown how our natural positive-thinking bias can promote "an unrealistic optimism about future life events." Most late adolescents see themselves as much less vulnerable than their peers to the HIV virus that causes AIDS (Abrams, 1991). Most college students perceive themselves as less likely than their average classmate to develop drinking problems, drop out of school, have a heart attack by age 40, or go deeply into debt on their high-interest credit cards (Yang et al., 2006). If overconfident of our ability to control an impulse such as the urge to smoke, we are more likely to expose ourselves to temptations—and to fail (Nordgren et al., 2009). Those who optimistically deny the power and effects of smoking, venture into ill-fated relationships, and outwit themselves in dozens of other ways remind us that blind optimism can be self-defeating.

People also display illusory optimism about their groups. Throughout a National Football League season, fans of all teams correctly guessed that other teams would win about 50 percent of their games. But they incorrectly guessed, on average (across teams and weeks), that their own team stood about a 2 in 3 chance of winning (Massey et al., 2011). This optimistic and illogical bias persisted despite their team's experience and monetary incentives for accuracy.

Our natural positive-thinking bias does seem to vanish, however, when we are bracing ourselves for feedback, such as exam results (Carroll et al., 2006). (Have you ever noticed that, as a game nears its end, the outcome seems more in doubt when your team is ahead than when it is behind?) Positive illusions also vanish after a traumatic personal experience—as they did for victims of a catastrophic California earthquake, who had to give up their illusions of being less vulnerable than others to earthquakes (Helweg-Larsen, 1999).

Blindness to One's Own Incompetence Ironically, people often are most overconfident when most incompetent. That, say Justin Kruger and David Dunning (1999), is because it often takes competence to recognize competence. They found that most students scoring at the low end of grammar and logic tests believed they had scored in the top half. If you do not know what good grammar is, you may be unaware that your grammar is poor. This "ignorance of one's own incompetence" phenomenon has a parallel, as I can confirm, in hard-of-hearing people's difficulty recognizing their own hearing loss. We're not so much "in denial" as we are simply unaware of what we don't hear. If I fail to hear my friend calling my name, the friend notices my inattention. But for me it's a nonevent. I hear what I hear—which, to me, seems pretty normal.

"The living-room [Scrabble] player is lucky. . . . He has no idea how miserably he fails with almost every turn, how many possible words or optimal plays slip by unnoticed."
Stefan Fatsis, *Word Freak,* 2001

The difficulty in recognizing one's own incompetence helps explain why so many low-scoring students are dumbfounded after doing badly on an exam. If you don't know all the Scrabble word possibilities you've overlooked, you may feel pretty smart—until someone points them out. As Deanna Caputo and Dunning (2005) demonstrate in experiments that re-create this phenomenon, our ignorance of what we don't know helps sustain our confidence in our own abilities. Once part of our self-concept, our self-assessments also influence how we perceive our performance. Thinking we're good at something drives how we perceive ourselves doing (Critcher & Dunning, 2009).

To judge one's competence and predict one's future performance, it pays to invite others' assessments, notes Dunning (2006). Based on studies in which both individuals and their acquaintances predict their future, we can hazard some advice: If you're a junior doctor and want to predict how well you will do on a surgical skills exam, don't rate yourself—ask your peers for their candid prediction. If you're a Naval officer and need to assess your leadership ability—don't rate yourself, ask your fellow officers. And if you're in love and want to predict whether it will last, don't listen to your heart—ask your roommate.

© 1986 by G. B. Trudeau. Distributed by Universal Press Syndicate.

Assessing Behavior in Situations

42-6 How do social-cognitive researchers explore behavior, and what criticism have they faced?

Social-cognitive psychologists explore how people interact with situations. To predict behavior, they often observe behavior in realistic situations.

One ambitious example was the U.S. Army's World War II strategy for assessing candidates for spy missions. Rather than using paper-and-pencil tests, Army psychologists subjected the candidates to simulated undercover conditions. They tested their ability to handle stress, solve problems, maintain leadership, and withstand intense interrogation without blowing their cover. Although time-consuming and expensive, this assessment of behavior in a realistic situation helped predict later success on actual spy missions (OSS Assessment Staff, 1948). Modern studies indicate that assessment center exercises are more revealing of visible dimensions, such as communication ability, than others, such as inner achievement drive (Bowler & Woehr, 2006).

AP Photo/Jennifer Szymaszek

Assessing behavior in situations Reality TV shows, such as Donald Trump's *The Apprentice,* may take "show me" job interviews to the extreme, but they do illustrate a valid point. Seeing how a potential employee behaves in a job-relevant situation helps predict job performance.

Military and educational organizations and many Fortune 500 companies are adopting assessment center strategies (Bray et al., 1991, 1997; Eurich et al., 2009). AT&T has observed prospective managers doing simulated managerial work. Many colleges assess students' potential via internships and student teaching and assess potential faculty members' teaching abilities by observing them teach. Armies assess their soldiers by observing them during military exercises. Most American cities with populations of 50,000 or more have used assessment centers in evaluating police and fire officers (Lowry, 1997).

These procedures exploit the principle that the best means of predicting future behavior is neither a personality test nor an interviewer's intuition. Rather, it is *the person's past behavior patterns in similar situations* (Mischel, 1981; Ouellette & Wood, 1998; Schmidt & Hunter, 1998). As long as the situation and the person remain much the same, the best predictor of future job performance is past job performance; the best predictor of future grades is past grades; the best predictor of future aggressiveness is past aggressiveness; the best predictor of drug use in young adulthood is drug use in high school. If you can't check the person's past behavior, the next-best thing is to create an assessment situation that simulates the task so you can see how the person handles it (Lievens et al., 2009; Meriac et al., 2008).

A *New York Times* analysis of 100 rampage murders over the last half-century revealed that 55 of the killers had regularly exploded in anger and 63 had threatened violence (Goodstein & Glaberson, 2000). Most didn't, out of the blue, "just snap."

Evaluating Social-Cognitive Theories

Social-cognitive theories of personality sensitize researchers to how situations affect, and are affected by, individuals. More than other personality theories (see **TABLE 42.2**), they build from psychological research on learning and cognition.

Critics charge that social-cognitive theories focus so much on the situation that they fail to appreciate the person's inner traits. Where is the person in this view of personality, ask the dissenters, and where are human emotions? True, the situation does guide our behavior. But, say the critics, in many instances our unconscious motives, our emotions, and our pervasive traits shine through. Personality traits have been shown to predict behavior at work, love, and play. Our biologically influenced traits really do matter. Consider Percy Ray Pridgen and Charles Gill. Each faced the same situation: They had jointly won a $90 million lottery jackpot (Harriston, 1993). When Pridgen learned of the winning numbers, he began trembling uncontrollably, huddled with a friend behind a bathroom door while confirming the win, then sobbed. When Gill heard the news, he told his wife and then went to sleep.

group toward bad decisions, so open debate often shapes good ones. This is especially so with diverse groups, whose varied perspectives often enable creative or superior outcomes (Nemeth & Ormiston, 2007; Page, 2007). None of us is as smart as all of us.

"If you have an apple and I have an apple and we exchange apples then you and I will still each have one apple. But if you have an idea and I have an idea and we exchange these ideas, then each of us will have two ideas."

Attributed to dramatist George Bernard Shaw, 1856–1950

The Power of Individuals

In affirming the power of social influence, we must not overlook the power of individuals. *Social control* (the power of the situation) and *personal control* (the power of the individual) interact. People aren't billiard balls. When feeling coerced, we may react by doing the opposite of what is expected, thereby reasserting our sense of freedom (Brehm & Brehm, 1981).

Committed individuals can sway the majority and make social history. Were this not so, communism would have remained an obscure theory, Christianity would be a small Middle Eastern sect, and Rosa Parks' refusal to sit at the back of the bus would not have ignited the U.S. civil rights movement. Technological history, too, is often made by innovative minorities who overcome the majority's resistance to change. To many, the railroad was a nonsensical idea; some farmers even feared that train noise would prevent hens from laying eggs. People derided Robert Fulton's steamboat as "Fulton's Folly." As Fulton later said, "Never did a single encouraging remark, a bright hope, a warm wish, cross my path." Much the same reaction greeted the printing press, the telegraph, the incandescent lamp, and the typewriter (Cantril & Bumstead, 1960).

The power of one or two individuals to sway majorities is *minority influence* (Moscovici, 1985). In studies of groups in which one or two individuals consistently express a controversial attitude or an unusual perceptual judgment, one finding repeatedly stands out: When you are the minority, you are far more likely to sway the majority if you hold firmly to your position and don't waffle. This tactic won't make you popular, but it may make you influential, especially if your self-confidence stimulates others to consider *why* you react as you do. Even when a minority's influence is not yet visible, people may privately develop sympathy for the minority position and rethink their views (Wood et al., 1994). The powers of social influence are enormous, but so are the powers of the committed individual.

akg-images/Newscom

Gandhi As the life of Hindu nationalist and spiritual leader Mahatma Gandhi powerfully testifies, a consistent and persistent minority voice can sometimes sway the majority. Gandhi's nonviolent appeals and fasts were instrumental in winning India's independence from Britain in 1947.

RETRIEVAL PRACTICE

- What is social facilitation, and is it more likely to occur with a well-learned or a brand-new task? Why?

ANSWER: This improved performance in the presence of others is most likely to occur with a well-learned task, because the added arousal caused by an audience tends to strengthen the most likely response. This also predicts poorer performance on a difficult task in others' presence.

- People tend to exert less effort when working with a group than they would alone, which is called __________ __________.

ANSWER: social loafing

- You are organizing a meeting of fiercely competitive political candidates. To add to the fun, friends have suggested handing out masks of the candidates' faces for supporters to wear. What phenomenon might these masks engage?

ANSWER: The anonymity provided by the masks, combined with the arousal of the contentious setting, might create *deindividuation* (lessened self-awareness and self-restraint).

- When like-minded groups discuss a topic, and the result is the strengthening of the prevailing opinion, this is called __________ __________.

ANSWER: group polarization

- When a group's desire for harmony overrides its realistic analysis of other options, __________ has occurred.

ANSWER: groupthink

MODULE REVIEW

Social Influence

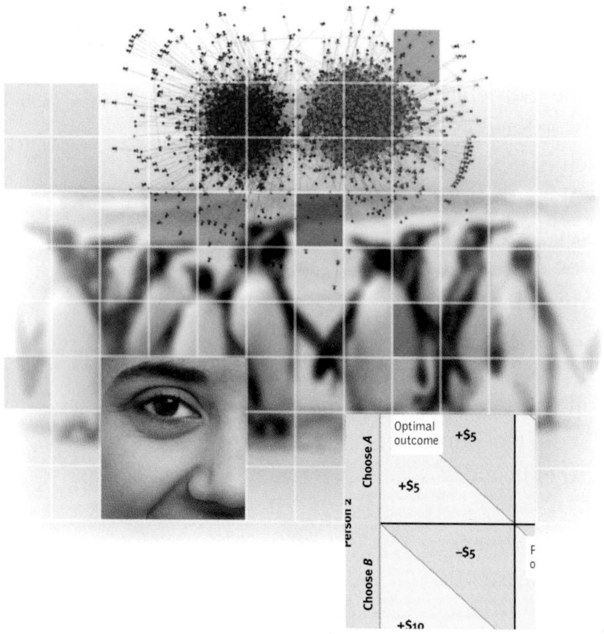

Learning Objectives

RETRIEVAL PRACTICE Take a moment to answer each of these Learning Objective Questions (repeated here from within the module). Then turn to Appendix B, Complete Module Reviews, to check your answers. Research suggests that trying to answer these questions on your own will improve your long-term retention (McDaniel et al., 2009).

44-1: What is automatic mimicry, and how do conformity experiments reveal the power of social influence?

44-2: What did Milgram's obedience experiments teach us about the power of social influence?

44-3: What have we learned from the Asch and Milgram studies?

44-4: How is our behavior affected by the presence of others?

44-5: What are group polarization and groupthink, and how much power do we have as individuals?

Terms and Concepts to Remember

RETRIEVAL PRACTICE Test yourself on these terms by trying to write down the definition before flipping back to the referenced page to check your answer.

conformity, p. 580
normative social influence, p. 581
informational social influence, p. 581
social facilitation, p. 587
social loafing, p. 587
deindividuation, p. 588
group polarization, p. 589
groupthink, p. 590

RETRIEVAL PRACTICE Gain an advantage, and benefit from immediate feedback, with the interactive self-testing resources at www.worthpublishers.com/myers.

MODULE 45

Antisocial Relations

- Prejudice
- Aggression

Social psychology studies how we think about and influence one another, and also how we *relate* to one another. What causes us to harm or to help or to fall in love? How can we move a destructive conflict toward a just peace? In this module we ponder insights into *antisocial* relations gleaned by researchers who have studied prejudice and aggression.

prejudice an unjustifiable and usually negative attitude toward a group and its members. Prejudice generally involves stereotyped beliefs, negative feelings, and a predisposition to discriminatory action.

stereotype a generalized (sometimes accurate but often overgeneralized) belief about a group of people.

discrimination unjustifiable negative behavior toward a group and its members.

Prejudice

45-1 What is prejudice? What are its social and emotional roots?

Prejudice means "prejudgment." It is an unjustifiable and usually negative attitude toward a group—often a different cultural, ethnic, or gender group. Like all attitudes, prejudice is a three-part mixture of

- *beliefs* (in this case, called **stereotypes**).
- *emotions* (for example, hostility or fear).
- predispositions to *action* (to discriminate).

To *believe* that obese people are gluttonous, to *feel* dislike for an obese person, and to be hesitant to hire or date an obese person is to be prejudiced. Prejudice is a negative *attitude*. **Discrimination** is a negative *behavior.*

How Prejudiced Are People?

To assess prejudice, we can observe what people say and what they do. Americans' expressed gender and racial attitudes have changed dramatically in the last half-century. The one-third of Americans who in 1937 told Gallup pollsters that they would vote for a qualified woman whom their party nominated for president soared to 89 percent in 2007 (Gallup Brain, 2008; Jones & Moore, 2003). Nearly everyone now agrees that women and men should receive the same pay for the same job, and that children of all races should attend the same schools.

Support for all forms of racial contact, including interracial dating (**FIGURE 45.1**), has also dramatically increased. Among 18- to 29-year-old Americans, 9 in 10 now say they would be fine with a family member marrying someone of a different race (Pew, 2010).

Percentage of 2008 American marriages to someone whose race or ethnicity differed from one's own:

Whites	9%
Blacks	16%
Hispanics	26%
Asians	31%

Source: Passel et al., 2010

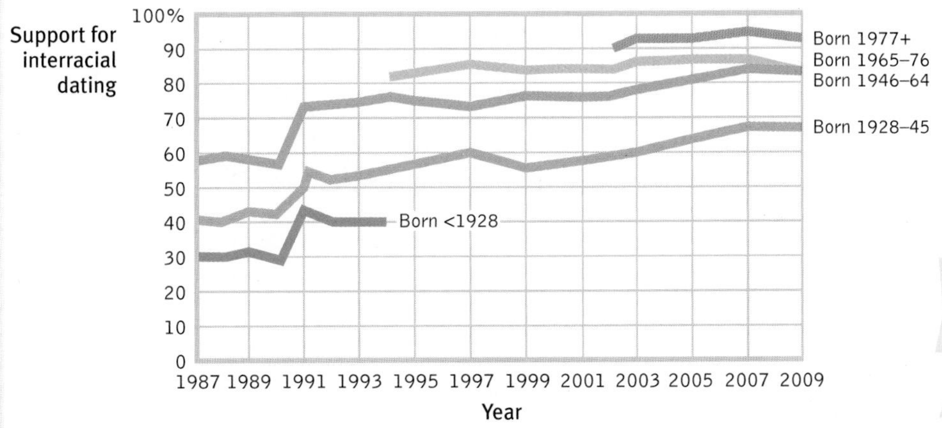

FIGURE 45.1 **Prejudice over time** Americans' approval of interracial dating has soared over the past quarter-century (Pew, 2010).

Yet as *overt* prejudice wanes, *subtle* prejudice lingers. Despite increased verbal support for interracial marriage, many people admit that in socially intimate settings (dating, dancing, marrying) they would feel uncomfortable with someone of another race. And many people who *say* they would feel upset with someone making racist slurs actually respond indifferently when hearing such racism (Kawakami et al., 2009). In Western Europe, where many "guest workers" and refugees settled at the end of the twentieth century, "modern prejudice"—rejecting immigrant minorities as job applicants for supposedly nonracial reasons—has been replacing blatant prejudice (Jackson et al., 2001; Lester, 2004; Pettigrew, 1998, 2006). A slew of recent experiments illustrates that prejudice can be not only subtle but also automatic and unconscious (see Close-Up: Automatic Prejudice).

Nevertheless, overt prejudice persists in many places. In the aftermath of 9/11 and the Iraq and Afghanistan wars, 4 in 10 Americans acknowledged "some feelings of prejudice against Muslims," and about half of non-Muslims in Western Europe and the United States perceived Muslims as "violent" (Saad, 2006; Wike & Grim, 2007). With Americans feeling threatened by Arabs, and as opposition to Islamic mosques and immigration flared in 2010, one observer noted that "Muslims are one of the last minorities in the United States that it is still possible to demean openly" (Kristof, 2010; Lyons et al., 2010). Muslims reciprocated the negativity, with most in Jordan, Egypt, Turkey, and Britain seeing Westerners as "greedy" and "immoral."

"Unhappily, the world has yet to learn how to live with diversity."
Pope John Paul II, Address to the United Nations, 1995

In most places in the world, gays and lesbians cannot comfortably acknowledge who they are and whom they love. Gender prejudice and discrimination persist, too. Despite gender equality in intelligence scores, people have tended to perceive their fathers as more intelligent than their mothers (Furnham & Rawles, 1995). In Saudi Arabia, women are not allowed to drive. In Western countries, we pay more to those (usually men) who care for our streets than to those (usually women) who care for our children. Worldwide, women are more likely to live in poverty (Lipps, 1999), and they are two-thirds of illiterate adults (CIA, 2010).

Female infants are no longer left out on a hillside to die of exposure, as was the practice in ancient Greece. Yet natural female mortality and the normal male-to-female newborn ratio (105-to-100) hardly explain the world's estimated 163 million (say that number slowly) "missing women" (Hvistendahl, 2011). In many places, sons are valued more than daughters. With testing that enables sex-selective abortions, several south Asian countries have experienced a shortfall in female births (**FIGURE 45.3**). Although China has declared that sex-selective abortions—gender genocide—are now a criminal offense, the country's newborn sex ratio is still 118 boys for every 100 girls (Hvistendahl, 2009, 2010, 2011), and 95 percent of the children in

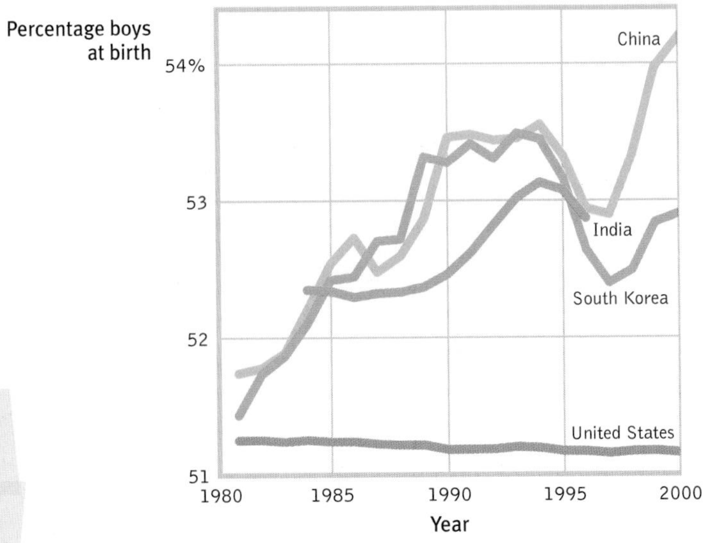

FIGURE 45.3
Missing girls In several Asian countries, especially in China, which has mandated one-child families, boy babies are overrepresented (Abrevaya, 2009).

CLOSE-UP

Automatic Prejudice

As we have seen throughout this book, the human mind processes thoughts, memories, and attitudes on two different tracks. Sometimes that processing is *explicit*—on the radar screen of our awareness. To an even greater extent, it is *implicit*—below the radar, leaving us unaware of how our attitudes are influencing our behavior. Modern studies indicate that prejudice is often implicit, an automatic attitude that is an unthinking knee-jerk response. Consider these findings:

Implicit Racial Associations Using Implicit Association Tests, researchers have demonstrated that even people who deny harboring racial prejudice may carry negative associations (Greenwald et al., 1998, 2009). (By 2011, nearly 5 million people had taken the Implicit Association Test, as you can at implicit.harvard.edu.) For example, 9 in 10 White respondents took longer to identify pleasant words (such as peace and paradise) as "good" when presented with Black-sounding names (such as Latisha and Darnell) rather than White-sounding names (such as Katie and Ian). Moreover, people who more quickly associate good things with White names or faces also are the quickest to perceive anger and apparent threat in Black faces (Hugenberg & Bodenhausen, 2003).

Although the test is useful for studying automatic prejudice, critics caution against using it to assess or label individuals (Blanton et al., 2006, 2007, 2009). Defenders counter that implicit biases predict behaviors that range from simple acts of friendliness to the evaluation of work quality (Greenwald et al., 2009). In the 2008 U.S. presidential election, implicit as well as explicit prejudice predicted voters' support for candidate Barack Obama, whose election in turn served to reduce implicit prejudice (Bernstein et al., 2010; Payne et al., 2010).

Unconscious Patronization When White university women evaluated a flawed essay said to be written by a Black fellow student, they gave markedly higher ratings and never expressed the harsh criticisms they assigned to flawed essays supposedly written by White students (Harber, 1998). Did the evaluators calibrate their evaluations to their racial stereotypes, leading to less exacting standards and a patronizing attitude? In real-world evaluations, such low expectations and the resulting "inflated praise and insufficient criticism" could hinder minority student achievement, the researcher noted. (To preclude such bias, many teachers read essays while "blind" to their authors.)

Race-Influenced Perceptions Our expectations influence our perceptions. In 1999, Amadou Diallo was accosted as he approached his apartment house doorway by police officers looking for a rapist. When he pulled out his wallet, the officers, perceiving a gun, riddled his body with 19 bullets from 41 shots. Curious about this killing of an unarmed man, two research teams reenacted the situation (Correll et al., 2002, 2007; Greenwald et al., 2003). They asked viewers to press buttons quickly to "shoot" or not shoot men who suddenly appeared on screen. Some of the on-screen men held a gun. Others held a harmless object, such as a flashlight or bottle. People (both Blacks and Whites, in one study) more often shot Black men holding the harmless objects. Priming people with a flashed Black rather than White face also makes them more likely then to misperceive a flashed tool as a gun (**FIGURE 45.2**).

Reflexive Bodily Responses Even people who consciously express little prejudice may give off telltale signals as their body responds selectively to another's race. Neuroscientists can detect these signals when people look at White and Black faces. The viewers' implicit prejudice may show up in facial-muscle responses and in the activation of their emotion-processing amygdala (Cunningham et al., 2004; Eberhardt, 2005; Stanley et al., 2008).

If your own gut check reveals you sometimes have feelings you would rather not have about other people, remember this: It is what we *do* with our feelings that matters. By monitoring our feelings and actions, and by replacing old habits with new ones based on new friendships, we can work to free ourselves from prejudice.

FIGURE 45.2
Race primes perceptions In experiments by Keith Payne (2006), people viewed a White or Black face, immediately followed by a gun or hand tool, which was then followed by a visual mask. Participants were more likely to misperceive a tool as a gun when it was preceded by a Black rather than White face.

Chinese orphanages are girls (Webley, 2009). With under-age-20 males exceeding females by 32 million, many Chinese bachelors will be unable to find mates (Zhu et al., 2009).

In the United States, a striking sex-ratio bias appears among Chinese, Korean, and Asian Indian parents with a third child. Sons outnumber daughters by 50 percent after two previous girl births. Given a previous boy birth, or given Caucasian parents, there is no sex-ratio bias (Almond & Edlund, 2008).

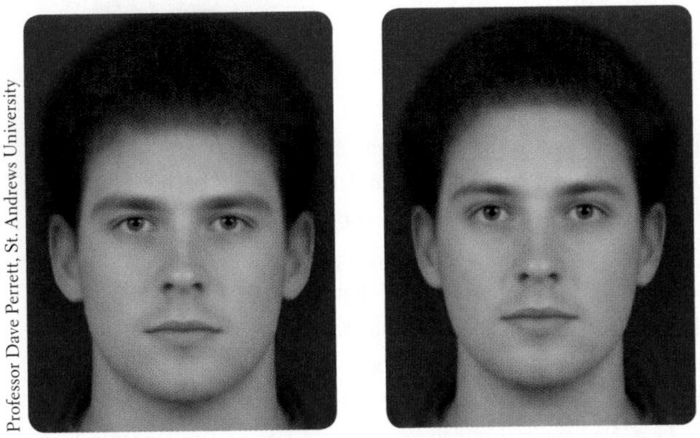

Professor Dave Perrett, St. Andrews University

(a) (b)

FIGURE 45.4
Who do you like best? Which one placed an ad seeking "a special lady to love and cherish forever"? (See answer below.)

Research suggests that subtly feminized features convey a likable image, which people tend to associate more with committed dads than with promiscuous cads. Thus, 66 percent of the women picked computer-generated face (b) in response to both of these questions.

Studies have shown, however, that most people *feel* more positively about women in general than they do about men (Eagly, 1994; Haddock & Zanna, 1994). Worldwide, people see women as having some traits (such as nurturance, sensitivity, and less aggressiveness) that most people prefer (Glick et al., 2004; Swim, 1994). That may explain why women tend to like women more than men like men (Rudman & Goodwin, 2004). And perhaps that is also why people prefer slightly feminized computer-generated faces—men's and women's—to slightly masculinized faces. Researcher David Perrett and his colleagues (1998) have speculated that a slightly feminized male face connotes kindness, cooperativeness, and other traits of a good father. When the British Broadcasting Corporation invited 18,000 women to guess which of the men in **FIGURE 45.4** was most likely to place a personal ad seeking a "special lady to love and cherish forever," which one do you think they picked?

Social Roots of Prejudice

Why does prejudice arise? Social inequalities and divisions are partly responsible.

Social Inequalities

When some people have money, power, and prestige and others do not, the "haves" usually develop attitudes that justify things as they are. The **just-world phenomenon** reflects an idea we commonly teach our children—that good is rewarded and evil is punished. From this it is but a short leap to assume that those who succeed must be good and those who suffer must be bad. Such reasoning enables the rich to see both their own wealth and the poor's misfortune as justly deserved.

Are women naturally unassertive but sensitive? This common perception suggests that women are well-suited for the caretaking tasks they have traditionally performed (Hoffman & Hurst, 1990). In an extreme case, slave "owners" perceived slaves as innately lazy, ignorant, and irresponsible—as having the very traits that justified enslaving them. Stereotypes rationalize inequalities.

© The New Yorker Collection, 1981, Robert Mankoff from cartoonbank.com. All Rights Reserved.

Victims of discrimination may react with either self-blame or anger (Allport, 1954). Either reaction can feed prejudice through the classic *blame-the-victim* dynamic. Do the circumstances of poverty breed a higher crime rate? If so, that higher crime rate can be used to justify discrimination against those who live in poverty.

Us and Them: Ingroup and Outgroup

We have inherited our Stone Age ancestors' need to belong, to live and love in groups. There was safety in solidarity (those who didn't band together left fewer descendants). Whether hunting, defending, or attacking, 10 hands were better than 2. Dividing the world into "us" and "them" entails racism and war, but it also provides the benefits of communal solidarity. Thus we cheer for our groups, kill for them, die for them. Indeed, we define who we are partly in terms of our groups. Through our *social identities* we associate ourselves with certain groups and contrast ourselves with others (Hogg, 1996, 2006; Turner, 1987, 2007). When Ian identifies himself as a man, an Aussie, a Labourite, a University of Sydney student, a Catholic, and a MacGregor, he knows who he is, and so do we.

Evolution prepared us, when encountering strangers, to make instant judgments: friend or foe? Those from our group, those who look like us, and also those who *sound* like us—with accents like our own—we instantly tend to like, from childhood onward (Gluszek & Dovidio, 2010; Kinzler et al., 2009). Mentally drawing a circle defines "us," the **ingroup**.

just-world phenomenon the tendency for people to believe the world is just and that people therefore get what they deserve and deserve what they get.

ingroup "Us"—people with whom we share a common identity.

outgroup "Them"—those perceived as different or apart from our ingroup.

ingroup bias the tendency to favor our own group.

scapegoat theory the theory that prejudice offers an outlet for anger by providing someone to blame.

Mike Hewitt/Getty Images

The ingroup Scotland's famed "Tartan Army" soccer fans, shown here during a match against archrival England, share a social identity that defines "us" (the Scottish ingroup) and "them" (the English outgroup).

But the social definition of who you are also states who you are not. People outside that circle are "them," the **outgroup.** An **ingroup bias**—a favoring of our own group—soon follows. Even arbitrarily creating us-them groups by tossing a coin creates this bias. In experiments, people have favored their own group when dividing any rewards (Tajfel, 1982; Wilder, 1981).

"For if [people were] to choose out of all the customs in the world [they would] end by preferring their own."

Greek historian Herodotus, 440 B.C.E.

The urge to distinguish enemies from friends predisposes prejudice against strangers (Whitley, 1999). To Greeks of the classical era, all non-Greeks were "barbarians." In our own era, most children believe their school is better than all other schools in town. Many high school students form cliques—jocks, goths, skaters, gangsters, freaks, geeks—and disparage those outside their own group. Even chimpanzees have been seen to wipe clean the spot where they were touched by a chimpanzee from another group (Goodall, 1986). They also display ingroup empathy, by yawning more after seeing ingroup (rather than outgroup) members yawn (Campbell & de Waal, 2011).

Ingroup bias explains the cognitive power of partisanship (Cooper, 2010; Douthat, 2010). In the United States in the late 1980s, most Democrats believed inflation had risen under Republican president Ronald Reagan (it had dropped). In 2010, most Republicans believed that taxes had increased under Democrat president Barak Obama (for most, they had decreased).

RETRIEVAL PRACTICE

- Why do sports fans tend to feel a sense of satisfaction when their archrival team loses?

ANSWER: Sports fans may feel a part of an *ingroup* that sets itself apart from an *outgroup* (fans of the archrival team). Ingroup bias tends to develop, leading to prejudice and the view that the outgroup "deserves" misfortune. So, the archrival team's loss may seem justified.

Emotional Roots of Prejudice

Prejudice springs not only from the divisions of society but also from the passions of the heart. **Scapegoat theory** notes that when things go wrong, finding someone to blame can provide a target for anger. Following 9/11, some outraged people lashed out at innocent Arab-Americans. Others called for eliminating Saddam Hussein, the Iraqi leader whom Americans had been grudgingly tolerating. "Fear and anger create aggression, and aggression against citizens of different ethnicity or race creates racism and, in turn, new forms of terrorism," noted Philip Zimbardo (2001). A decade after 9/11, anti-Muslim animosities still flared, with mosque burnings and efforts to block an Islamic community center near Ground Zero.

"If the Tiber reaches the walls, if the Nile does not rise to the fields, if the sky doesn't move or the Earth does, if there is famine, if there is plague, the cry is at once: 'The Christians to the lion!'"

Tertullian, *Apologeticus*, C.E. 197

Evidence for the scapegoat theory of prejudice comes from high prejudice among economically frustrated people, and from experiments in which a temporary frustration intensifies prejudice. Students who experience failure or are made to feel insecure often restore their self-esteem by disparaging a rival school or another person (Cialdini & Richardson, 1980; Crocker et al., 1987). To boost our own sense of status, it helps to have others to denigrate. That is why a rival's misfortune sometimes provides a twinge of pleasure. By contrast, those made to feel loved and supported become more open to and accepting of others who differ (Mikulincer & Shaver, 2001).

"The misfortunes of others are the taste of honey."

Japanese saying

other-race effect the tendency to recall faces of one's own race more accurately than faces of other races. Also called the *cross-race effect* and the *own-race bias.*

aggression any physical or verbal behavior intended to hurt or destroy.

Negative emotions nourish prejudice. When facing death, fearing threats, or experiencing frustration, people cling more tightly to their ingroup and their friends. As the terror of death heightens patriotism, it also produces loathing and aggression toward "them"—those who threaten our world (Pyszczynski et al., 2002, 2008). The few individuals who lack fear and its associated activity in the brain's emotion-processing amygdala—such as children with the genetic disorder Williams syndrome—also display a notable lack of racial stereotypes and prejudice (Santos et al., 2010).

Cognitive Roots of Prejudice

45-2 What are the cognitive roots of prejudice?

Prejudice springs from a culture's divisions, the heart's passions, and also from the mind's natural workings. Stereotyped beliefs are a by-product of how we cognitively simplify the world.

Forming Categories

© Dave Coverly

One way we simplify our world is to categorize. A chemist categorizes molecules as organic and inorganic. Therapists categorize psychological disorders. Human beings categorize people by race, with mixed-race people often assigned to their minority identity. Despite his mixed-race background and his rearing by a White mother and grandparents, President Obama is perceived by White Americans as Black. Researchers believe this happens because, after learning the features of a familiar racial group, the observer's selective attention is drawn to the distinctive features of the less-familiar minority. Jamin Halberstadt and his colleagues (2011) illustrated this learned-association effect by showing New Zealanders blended Chinese-Caucasian faces. Compared with Chinese participants, the Caucasian New Zealanders more readily classified ambiguous faces as Chinese (see **FIGURE 45.5**).

In categorizing people into groups, however, we often stereotype them. We recognize how greatly *we* differ from other individuals in *our* groups. But we overestimate the homogeneity of other groups. "They"—the members of some other group—seem to look and act alike, while "we" are more diverse (Bothwell et al., 1989). To those in one ethnic group, members of another often seem more alike than they really are in attitudes, personality, and appearance. Our greater recognition for own-race faces—called the **other-race effect** (also called the *cross-race effect* or *own-race bias*)—emerges during infancy, between 3 and 9 months of age (Gross, 2009; Kelly et al., 2007).

With effort and with experience, people get better at recognizing individual faces from another group (Hugenberg et al., 2010). People of European descent, for example, more accurately identify individual African faces if they have watched a great deal of basketball on television, exposing them to many African-heritage faces (Li et al., 1996). And the longer Chinese people have resided in a Western country, the less they exhibit the other-race effect (Hancock & Rhodes, 2008).

FIGURE 45.5
Categorizing mixed-race people When New Zealanders quickly classified 104 photos by race, those of European descent more often than those of Chinese descent classified the ambiguous middle two as Chinese (Halberstadt et al., 2011).

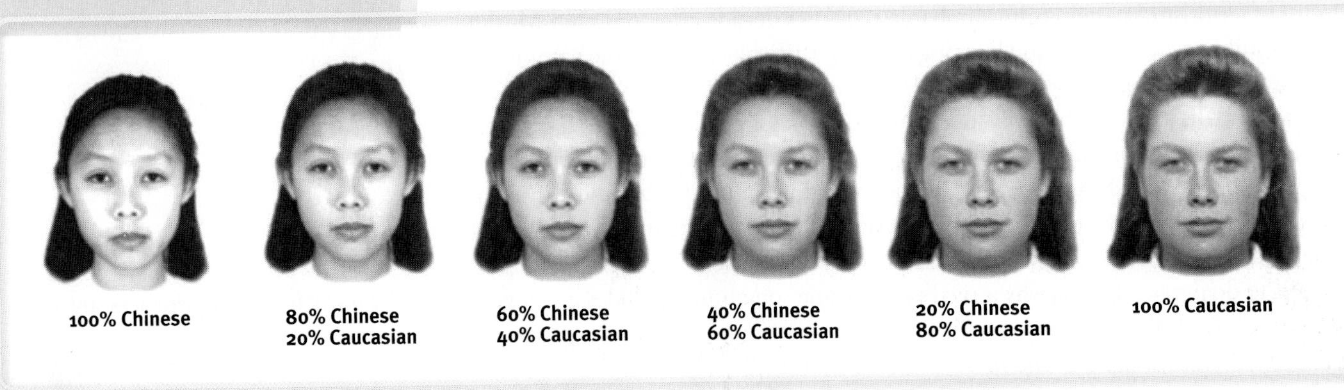

Dr. Jamin Halberstadt

Remembering Vivid Cases

We often judge the frequency of events by instances that readily come to mind. In a classic experiment, researchers showed two groups of University of Oregon students lists containing information about 50 men (Rothbart et al., 1978). The first group's list included 10 men arrested for *nonviolent* crimes, such as forgery. The second group's list included 10 men arrested for *violent* crimes, such as assault. Later, both groups were asked how many men on their list had committed *any* sort of crime. The second group overestimated the number. Vivid (violent) cases are more readily available to our memory and feed our stereotypes (**FIGURE 45.6**).

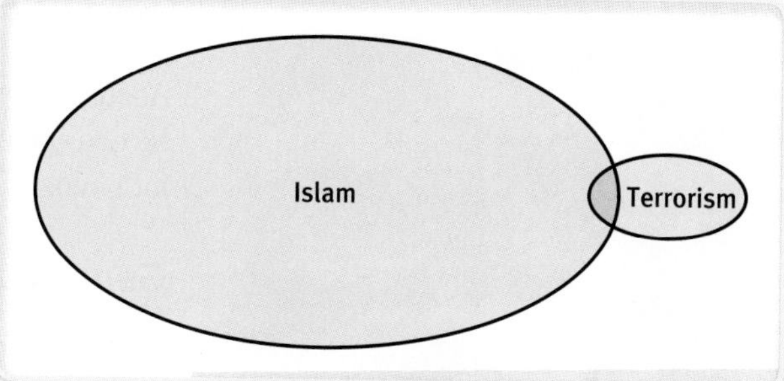

FIGURE 45.6
Vivid cases feed stereotypes The 9/11 Muslim terrorists created, in many minds, an exaggerated stereotype of Muslims as terror prone. Actually, reported a U.S. National Research Council panel on terrorism, when offering this inexact illustration, most terrorists are not Muslim and "the vast majority of Islamic people have no connection with and do not sympathize with terrorism" (Smelser & Mitchell, 2002).

Believing the World is Just As we noted earlier, people often justify their prejudices by blaming victims. If the world is just, "people must get what they deserve." As one German civilian is said to have remarked when visiting the Bergen-Belsen concentration camp shortly after World War II, "What terrible criminals these prisoners must have been to receive such treatment."

Hindsight bias is also at work here (Carli & Leonard, 1989). Have you ever heard people say that rape victims, abused spouses, or people with AIDS got what they deserved? In some countries, such as Pakistan, women who have been raped have sometimes been sentenced to severe punishment for having violated a law against adultery (Mydans, 2002). In one experiment illustrating the blame-the-victim phenomenon, people were given a detailed account of a date that ended with the woman being raped (Janoff-Bulman et al., 1985). They perceived the woman's behavior as at least partly to blame, and in hindsight, they thought, "She should have known better." (Blaming the victim also serves to reassure people that it couldn't happen to them.) Others, given the same account with the rape ending deleted, did not perceive the woman's behavior as inviting rape.

People also have a basic tendency to justify their culture's social systems (Jost et al., 2009; Kay et al, 2009). We're inclined to see the way things are as the way they ought to be. This natural conservatism makes it difficult to legislate major social changes, such as health care or climate-change policies. Once such policies are in place, our "system justification" tends to preserve them.

RETRIEVAL PRACTICE

- When prejudiced judgment causes us to find an undeserving person to blame for a problem, that person is called a ___________.

ANSWER: scapegoat

Aggression

45-3 How does psychology's definition of *aggression* differ from everyday usage? What biological factors make us more prone to hurt one another?

Prejudice hurts, but aggression often hurts more. In psychology, **aggression** is any physical or verbal behavior intended to hurt or destroy, whether done out of hostility or as a calculated means to an end. The assertive, persistent salesperson is not aggressive. Nor is the dentist who makes you wince with pain. But the person who passes along a vicious rumor about you, the person who verbally assaults you, and the attacker who mugs you for your money are aggressive.

Aggressive behavior emerges from the interaction of biology and experience. For a gun to fire, the trigger must be pulled; with some people, as with hair-trigger guns, it doesn't take much to trip an explosion. Let's look first at some biological factors that influence our thresholds for aggressive behavior, then at the psychological factors that pull the trigger.

In the last 40 years in the United States, well over 1 million people—more than all deaths in all wars in American history—have been killed by firearms in nonwar settings. Compared with people of the same sex, race, age, and neighborhood, those who keep a gun in the home (ironically, often for protection) are almost three times more likely to be murdered in the home—nearly always by a family member or close acquaintance. For every self-defense use of a gun in the home, there have been 4 unintentional shootings, 7 criminal assaults or homicides, and 11 attempted or completed suicides (Kellermann et al., 1993, 1997, 1998).

© The New Yorker Collection, 1995, D. Reilly from cartoonbank.com. All Rights Reserved.

"It's a guy thing."

The Biology of Aggression

Aggression varies too widely from culture to culture, era to era, and person to person to be considered an unlearned instinct. But biology does *influence* aggression. We can look for biological influences at three levels—genetic, neural, and biochemical.

Genetic Influences

Genes influence aggression. We know this because animals have been bred for aggressiveness—sometimes for sport, sometimes for research. The effect of genes also appears in human twin studies (Miles & Carey, 1997; Rowe et al., 1999). If one identical twin admits to "having a violent temper," the other twin will often independently admit the same. Fraternal twins are much less likely to respond similarly. Researchers continue to search for genetic markers in those who commit the most violence. (One is already well known and is carried by half the human race: the Y chromosome.)

Neural Influences

There is no one spot in the brain that controls aggression. Aggression is a complex behavior, and it occurs in particular contexts. But animal and human brains have neural systems that, given provocation, will either inhibit or facilitate aggressive behavior (Denson, 2011; Moyer, 1983). Consider:

- Researchers implanted a radio-controlled electrode in the brain of the domineering leader of a caged monkey colony. The electrode was in an area that, when stimulated, inhibits aggression. When researchers placed the control button for the electrode in the colony's cage, one small monkey learned to push it every time the boss became threatening.
- A neurosurgeon, seeking to diagnose a disorder, implanted an electrode in the amygdala of a mild-mannered woman. Because the brain has no sensory receptors, she was unable to feel the stimulation. But at the flick of a switch she snarled, "Take my blood pressure. Take it now," then stood up and began to strike the doctor.
- Studies of violent criminals have revealed diminished activity in the frontal lobes, which play an important role in controlling impulses. If the frontal lobes are damaged, inactive, disconnected, or not yet fully mature, aggression may be more likely (Amen et al., 1996; Davidson et al., 2000; Raine, 1999, 2005).

Biochemical Influences

Our genes engineer our individual nervous systems, which operate electrochemically. The hormone testosterone, for example, circulates in the bloodstream and influences the neural systems that control aggression. A raging bull will become a gentle Ferdinand when castration reduces its testosterone level. The same is true of mice. When injected with testosterone, gentle, castrated mice once again become aggressive.

Humans are less sensitive to hormonal changes. But as men age, their testosterone levels—and their aggressiveness—diminish. Hormonally charged, aggressive 17-year-olds mature into hormonally quieter and gentler 70-year-olds. Also, violent criminals tend to be muscular young males with higher-than-average testosterone levels, lower-than-average intelligence scores, and low levels of the neurotransmitter serotonin (Dabbs et al., 2001a; Pendick, 1994). Men more than women tend to have wide faces, a testosterone-linked trait, rather than roundish or long faces. And men's facial width is a predictor of their aggressiveness (Carré et al., 2009; Stirrat & Perrett, 2010).

"We could avoid two-thirds of all crime simply by putting all able-bodied young men in cryogenic sleep from the age of 12 through 28."

David T. Lykken, *The Antisocial Personalities*, 1995

High testosterone correlates with irritability, assertiveness, impulsiveness, and low tolerance for frustration—qualities that predispose somewhat more aggressive responses to provocation or competition for status (Dabbs et al., 2001b; Harris, 1999; McAndrew,

2009). Among both teenage boys and adult men, high testosterone levels correlate with delinquency, hard drug use, and aggressive-bullying responses to frustration (Berman et al., 1993; Dabbs & Morris, 1990; Olweus et al., 1988). Drugs that sharply reduce testosterone levels subdue men's aggressive tendencies.

Another drug that sometimes circulates in the bloodstream—alcohol—*unleashes* aggressive responses to frustration. In police data and prison surveys, as in experiments, aggression-prone people are more likely to drink, and they are more likely to become violent when intoxicated (White et al., 1993). People who have been drinking commit 4 in 10 violent crimes and 3 in 4 acts of spousal abuse (Karberg & James, 2005). Alcohol's effects are both biological and psychological (Bushman, 1993; Ito et al., 1996; Taylor & Chermack, 1993). Just *thinking* you've imbibed alcohol has some effect; but so, too, does unknowingly ingesting alcohol slipped into a drink. Unless people are distracted, alcohol tends to focus their attention on a provocation rather than on inhibitory cues (Giancola & Corman, 2007). Alcohol also inclines people to interpret ambiguous acts (such as a bump in a crowd) as provocations (Bègue et al., 2010).

Karl Ammannt/Getty Images

A lean, mean fighting machine—the testosterone-laden female hyena The hyena's unusual embryology pumps testosterone into female fetuses. The result is revved-up young female hyenas who seem born to fight.

Psychological and Social-Cultural Factors in Aggression

45-4 What psychological and social-cultural factors may trigger aggressive behavior?

Biological factors influence the ease with which aggression is triggered. But what psychological and social-cultural factors pull the trigger?

Aversive Events

Suffering sometimes builds character. In laboratory experiments, however, those made miserable have often made others miserable (Berkowitz, 1983, 1989). This phenomenon is called the **frustration-aggression principle**: Frustration creates anger, which can spark aggression. One analysis of 27,667 hit-by-pitch Major League Baseball incidents between 1960 and 2004 revealed this link (Timmerman, 2007). Pitchers were most likely to hit batters when

- they had been frustrated by the previous batter hitting a home run.
- the current batter had hit a home run the last time at bat.
- a teammate had been hit by a pitch in the previous half-inning.

Other aversive stimuli—hot temperatures, physical pain, personal insults, foul odors, cigarette smoke, crowding, and a host of others—can also evoke hostility. In laboratory experiments, when people get overheated, they think, feel, and act more aggressively. In baseball games, the number of hit batters rises with the temperature (Reifman et al., 1991; see **FIGURE 45.7** on the next page). And in the wider world, violent crime and spousal abuse rates have been higher during hotter years, seasons, months, and days (Anderson & Anderson, 1984). From the available data, Craig Anderson and his colleagues (2000, 2011) have projected that, other things being equal, global warming of 4 degrees Fahrenheit (about 2 degrees centigrade) would induce tens of thousands of additional assaults and murders—and that's before the added violence inducement from climate change-related drought, poverty, food insecurity, and migration.

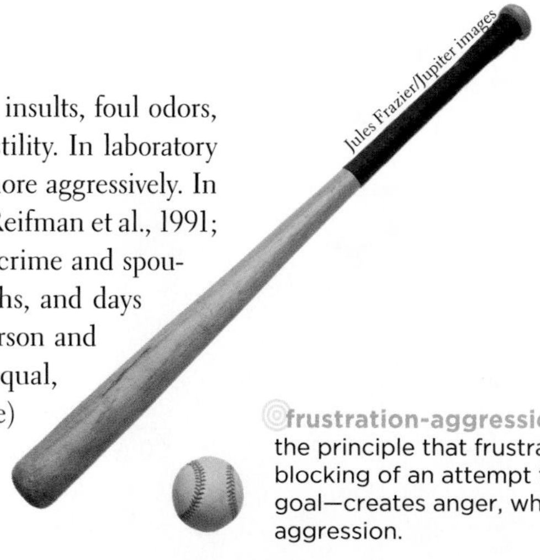

Jules Frazier/Jupiter images

frustration-aggression principle the principle that frustration—the blocking of an attempt to achieve some goal—creates anger, which can generate aggression.

FIGURE 45.7
Temperature and retaliation Richard Larrick and his colleagues (2011) looked for occurrences of batters hit by pitchers during 4,566,468 pitcher-batter matchups across 57,293 Major League Baseball games since 1952. The probability of a hit batter increased if one or more of the pitcher's teammates had been hit, and also with temperature.

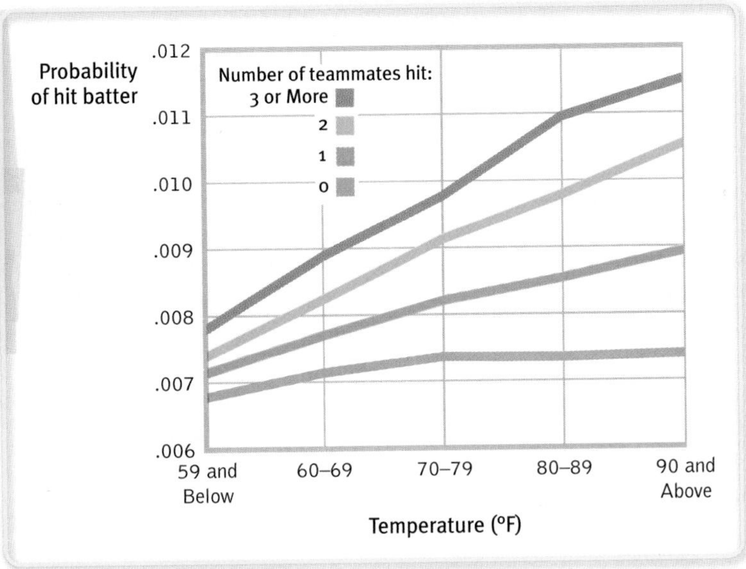

Reinforcement and Modeling

Aggression may be a natural response to aversive events, but learning can alter natural reactions. We learn when our behavior is reinforced, and we learn by watching others.

In situations where experience has taught us that aggression pays, we are likely to act aggressively again. Children whose aggression has successfully intimidated other children may become bullies. Animals that have successfully fought to get food or mates become increasingly ferocious. To foster a kinder, gentler world we had best model and reward sensitivity and cooperation from an early age, perhaps by training parents to discipline without modeling violence.

Parents of delinquent youngsters frequently cave in to (reward) their children's tears and temper tantrums. Then, exasperated, they discipline with beatings (Patterson et al., 1982, 1992).

Parent-training programs often advise parents to avoid modeling violence by screaming and hitting. Instead, parents should reinforce desirable behaviors and frame statements positively. ("When you finish loading the dishwasher you can go play," rather than "If you don't load the dishwasher, there'll be no playing.")

One *aggression-replacement program* worked with juvenile offenders and gang members and their parents. It taught both generations new ways to control anger, and more thoughtful approaches to moral reasoning (Goldstein et al., 1998). The result? The youths' re-arrest rates dropped.

Aggression-replacement program Part of the rehabilitation of these juvenile offenders at the Missouri Division of Youth Services' Rosa Parks Center involves learning anger management and peaceful ways to resolve disputes. Here they "circle up" to resolve a problem peacefully.

Tony Freeman/Photo Edit

Different cultures model, reinforce, and evoke different tendencies toward violence. For example, crime rates are higher (and average happiness is lower) in countries marked by a great disparity between rich and poor (Triandis, 1994). In the United States, cultures and families that experience minimal father care also have high violence rates (Triandis, 1994). Even after controlling for parental education, race, income, and teen motherhood, American male youths from father-absent homes have double their peers' incarceration rate (Harper & McLanahan, 2004).

Violence can also vary by culture within a country. Richard Nisbett and Dov Cohen (1996) analyzed violence among White Americans in southern towns settled by Scots-Irish herders whose tradition emphasized "manly honor," the use of arms to protect one's flock, and a history of coercive slavery. Compared with their White counterparts in New England towns settled by the more traditionally peaceful Puritan, Quaker, and Dutch farmer-artisans, the cultural descendants of those herders have triple the homicide rates and are more supportive of physically punishing children, of warfare initiatives, and of uncontrolled gun ownership. "Culture-of-honor" states also have higher rates of students bringing weapons to school and of school shootings (Brown et al., 2009).

social script culturally modeled guide for how to act in various situations.

Media Models for Violence

Parents are hardly the only aggression models. In the United States and elsewhere, TV, films, and video games offer supersized portions of violence. Repeatedly viewing on-screen violence teaches us **social scripts**—culturally provided mental files for how to act. When we find ourselves in new situations, uncertain how to behave, we rely on social scripts. After so many action films, youngsters may acquire a script that plays in their head when they face real-life conflicts. Challenged, they may "act like a man" by intimidating or eliminating the threat. Likewise, after viewing the multiple sexual innuendoes and acts found in most prime-time TV hours—often involving impulsive or short-term relationships—youths may acquire sexual scripts they later enact in real-life relationships (Kunkel et al., 2001; Sapolsky & Tabarlet, 1991).

Music lyrics also write social scripts. In one set of experiments, German university men administered hotter chili sauce to a woman and recalled more negative feelings and beliefs about women after listening to woman-hating song lyrics. Man-hating song lyrics had a similar effect on the aggressive behavior of women listeners (Fischer & Greitemeyer, 2006).

Sexual aggression is sometimes modeled in X-rated films and pornography. Content analyses have revealed that most X-rated films depict quick, casual sex between strangers, but sometimes also provide scenes of rape and sexual exploitation of women by men (Cowan et al., 1988; NCTV, 1987; Yang & Linz, 1990). These scenes often include enactments of the *rape myth*—the idea that some women invite or enjoy rape and get "swept away" while being "taken." (In actuality, rape is traumatic, and it frequently harms women's reproductive and psychological health [Golding, 1996].) Most rapists accept this myth (Brinson, 1992). So do many men and women who watch a great deal of TV: Compared with those who watch little television, heavy viewers are more accepting of the rape myth (Kahlor & Morrison, 2007).

Surveys of American and Australian teens, university students, and young adults reveal a huge gender difference in viewing habits: Viewing X-rated films and Internet pornography is several times higher among males than among females (Carroll et al., 2008; Flood, 2007; Wolak et al., 2007). Might sexually explicit media models in the $97 billion global pornography business contribute to sexually aggressive tendencies (D'Orlando, 2011)?

Most consumers of child and adult pornography commit no known sexual crimes (Seto, 2009). But they are more likely to accept the rape myth as reality (Kingston et al., 2009). Canadian and U.S. sex offenders acknowledge a greater-than-usual appetite for sexually explicit and sexually violent materials—materials typically labeled as pornography (Kingston et al., 2009; Marshall, 1989, 2000; Oddone-Paolucci et al., 2000). The Los Angeles Police Department, for example, reported that pornography was "conspicuously present" in 62 percent of its extrafamilial child sexual abuse cases during the 1980s (Bennett, 1991). High pornography consumption also has predicted greater sexual aggressiveness among university men, even after controlling for other predictors of antisocial behavior (Vega & Malamuth, 2007). But critics object. Since 1990, the reported U.S. rape rate has declined while pornography consumption has increased (Ferguson & Hartley, 2009). And aren't many sexual aggressors merely, as sex researcher John Money (1988) suspected, using pornography "as an alibi to explain to themselves what otherwise is inexplicable"?

People heavily exposed to televised crime see the world as more dangerous. People heavily exposed to pornography see the world as more sexual. Repeatedly watching X-rated films, even nonviolent films, has many effects (Kingston et al., 2009). One's own partner seems less attractive. Extramarital sex seems less troubling (Zillmann, 1989). A woman's friendliness seems more sexual. Sexual aggression seems less serious (Harris, 1994; Zillmann, 1989). These effects feed the ingredients of coercion against women.

In one experiment, undergraduates viewed six brief, sexually explicit films each week for six weeks (Zillmann & Bryant, 1984). A control group viewed nonerotic films during the same six-week period. Three weeks later, both groups read a newspaper report about a man convicted but not yet sentenced for raping a hitchhiker. When asked to suggest an appropriate prison term, viewers of the sexually explicit films recommended sentences half as long as those recommended by the control group.

Experiments cannot elicit actual sexual violence, but they can assess a man's willingness to hurt a woman. Often the research gauges the effect of violent versus nonviolent erotic films on men's willingness to deliver supposed electric shocks to women who had earlier provoked them. These experiments suggest that it's less the eroticism than the depictions of sexual *violence* (whether in R-rated slasher films or X-rated films) that most directly affect men's acceptance and performance of aggression against women. A statement by 21 social scientists, including many of the researchers who conducted these experiments, noted, "Pornography that portrays sexual aggression as pleasurable for the victim increases the acceptance of the use of coercion in sexual relations" (Surgeon General, 1986). Contrary to much popular opinion, viewing such depictions does not provide an outlet for bottled-up impulses. Rather, "in laboratory studies measuring short-term effects, exposure to violent pornography increases punitive behavior toward women."

To a lesser extent, nonviolent pornography can also influence aggression. In a series of studies, Nathaniel Lambert and his colleagues (2011) used various methods to explore pornography's effects on aggression against relationship partners. They found that pornography consumption predicted both self-reported aggression and laboratory noise blasts to their partner, and that abstaining from customary pornography consumption decreased aggression (while abstaining from their favorite food did not).

Neil Malamuth (1996) has shown that sexually coercive men typically are sexually promiscuous and hostile in their relationships with women (**FIGURE 45.8**). Several factors can create a predisposition to sexual violence (Malamuth et al., 1991, 1995). They include the media but also dominance motives, disinhibition by alcohol, and a history of child abuse. Still, if media depictions of violence can disinhibit and desensitize; if viewing sexual violence fosters hostile, domineering attitudes and behaviors; and if viewing pornography leads viewers to trivialize rape, devalue their partners, and engage in uncommitted sex, then media influence is not a minor issue.

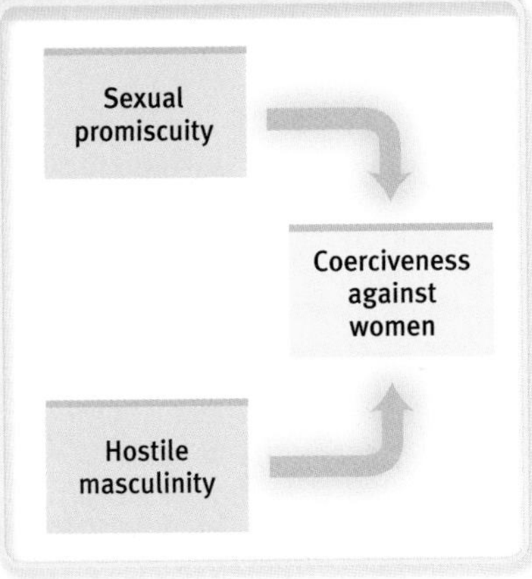

FIGURE 45.8
Men who sexually coerce women The recipe for coercion against women combines an impersonal approach to sex with a hostile masculinity. (Adapted from Malamuth, 1996.)

Might public consciousness be raised by making people aware of the information you have just been reading? In the 1940s, movies often depicted African-Americans as childlike superstitious buffoons, images we would not tolerate today. Many hope that entertainers, producers, and audiences might someday look back with embarrassment on the days when movies "entertained" us with scenes of sexual coercion, torture, and mutilation.

Do Violent Video Games Teach Social Scripts for Violence?

Violent video games became an issue for public debate after teenagers in more than a dozen places seemed to mimic the carnage in the shooter games they had so often played (Anderson, 2004a). In 2002, two Grand Rapids, Michigan, teens and a man in his early twenties spent part of a night drinking beer and playing Grand Theft Auto III. Using simulated cars, they ran down pedestrians, then beat them with fists, leaving a bloody body behind (Kolker, 2002). The same teens and man then went out for a real drive. Spotting a 38-year-old man on a bicycle, they ran him down with their car, got out, stomped and punched him, and returned home to play the game some more. (The victim, a father of three, died six days later.)

Observing TV violence tends to desensitize people to cruelty and prime them to respond aggressively when provoked. Does this *violence-viewing effect* extend to violent video games? Should parents worry about the ways actively role-playing aggression will affect their children? Experiments indicate that playing positive games has positive effects. For example, playing Lemmings, where a goal is to help others, increases real-life helping (Greitemeyer & Osswald, 2010). So, might a parallel effect occur after playing games that enact violence?

When combining data from 400 studies with 130,296 participants, Craig Anderson and his colleagues (2010) found such an effect: Playing violent video games increased aggression. The finding held for youth and for young adults; in North America, Japan, and Western Europe; and with each of three major research designs (correlational, experimental, and longitudinal). In a 2010 statement submitted for a U.S. Supreme Court case, Anderson was joined by more than 100 social scientists in explaining that "the psychological processes underlying such effects are well understood and include: imitation, observational learning, priming of cognitive, emotional, and behavioral scripts, physiological arousal, and emotional desensitization."

Consider some evidence:

- University men who spent the most hours playing violent video games tended to be the most physically aggressive (for example, more likely to acknowledge having hit or attacked someone else) (Anderson & Dill, 2000).
- People randomly assigned to play a game involving bloody murders with groaning victims (rather than to play nonviolent *Myst*) became more hostile. On a follow-up task, they also were more likely to blast intense noise at a fellow student.
- People with extensive experience in violent video gaming display desensitization to violence, as shown by blunted brain responses; they also are less likely to help an injured victim (Bartholow et al., 2006; Bushman & Anderson, 2009).
- After playing a violent rather than a neutral or prosocial video game, people become more likely to express dehumanized perceptions of immigrant outgroups (Greitemeyer & McLatchie, 2011).

Coincidence or cause? In 2011, Norwegian Anders Behring Breivik bombed government buildings in Oslo, and then went to a youth camp where he shot and killed 69 people, mostly teens. As a player of first-person shooter games, Breivik stirred debate when he commented that "I see MW2 [Modern Warfare 2] more as a part of my training-simulation than anything else." Did his violent game playing contribute to his violence, or was it a mere coincidental association? To explore such questions, psychologists experiment.

REUTERS/Andrew Berwick via www.freak.no/Handout

Young adolescents who play a lot of violent video games see the world as more hostile. Compared with nongaming kids, they get into more arguments and fights and get worse grades (Gentile, 2009). Ah, but is this merely because naturally hostile kids are drawn to such games? Apparently not. Comparisons of gamers and nongamers who scored low in hostility revealed a difference in the number of reported fights: 38 percent of the violent-game players had been in fights, versus only 4 percent of the nongamers. Over time, the nongamers became more likely to have fights only if they started playing the violent games (Anderson, 2004a). Another study, with German adolescents, found that today's violent game playing predicts future aggression, but today's aggression does not predict future game playing (Möller & Krahé, 2008). Some researchers believe that, due partly to the more active participation and rewarded violence of game play, violent video games have even greater effects on aggressive behavior and cognition than do violent television and movies (Anderson et al., 2007). The effects of violent gaming, some say, are comparable to the toxic effects of asbestos or second-hand smoke exposure (Bushman et al., 2010). "Playing violent video games probably will not turn your child into a psychopathic killer," acknowledges researcher Brad Bushman (2011), "but I would want to know how the child treats his or her parents, how they treat their siblings, how much compassion they have."

Others are unimpressed by violent-game-effect findings (Ferguson & Kilburn, 2010). They note that from 1996 to 2006, youth violence was declining while video game sales were increasing. Moreover, some point out that avid game players are quick and sharp: they develop speedy reaction times and enhanced visual skills (Dye et al., 2009; Green et al., 2010). The focused

©Microsoft Corporation.All Rights Reserved.

fun of game playing can satisfy basic needs for a sense of competence, control, and social connection (Przbylski et al., 2010). That helps explain why, in one experiment, elementary school boys randomly selected to receive a game system spent enormous amounts of time on it over the next four months, though with diminished time spent on schoolwork and with more academic problems (Weis & Cerankosky, 2010).

This much seems clear. We don't feel better if we "blow off steam" by venting our emotions. Instead, playing violent video games increases aggressive thoughts, emotions, and behaviors. As the Greek philosopher Aristotle observed, "We are what we repeatedly do."

Nevertheless, a 2011 Supreme Court decision overturned a California state law that banned the sale of violent video games to children (much like the bans on sales of sexually explicit materials to children). The First Amendment's free speech guarantee protects even offensive games, said the court's majority, which was unpersuaded by the evidence of harm. But the debate goes on. "What sense does it make to forbid selling to a 13-year-old a magazine with an image of a nude woman," wrote Justice Stephen Breyer, in a dissenting opinion, "while protecting the sale to that 13-year-old of an interactive video game in which he actively, but virtually, binds and gags the woman, then tortures and kills her?"

* * *

To sum up, significant behaviors, such as violence, usually have many determinants, making any single explanation an oversimplification. Asking what causes violence is therefore like asking what causes cancer. Asbestos exposure, for example, is indeed a cancer cause, albeit only one among many. Research reveals many different biological, psychological, and social-cultural influences on aggressive behavior. Like so much else, aggression is a biopsychosocial phenomenon (**FIGURE 45.9**).

It is also important to note that many people are leading gentle, even heroic lives amid personal and social stresses, reminding us again that individuals differ. The person matters. That people vary over time and place reminds us that environments also differ. Yesterday's plundering Vikings have become today's peace-promoting Scandinavians. Situations matter. Like all behavior, aggression arises from the interaction of persons and situations.

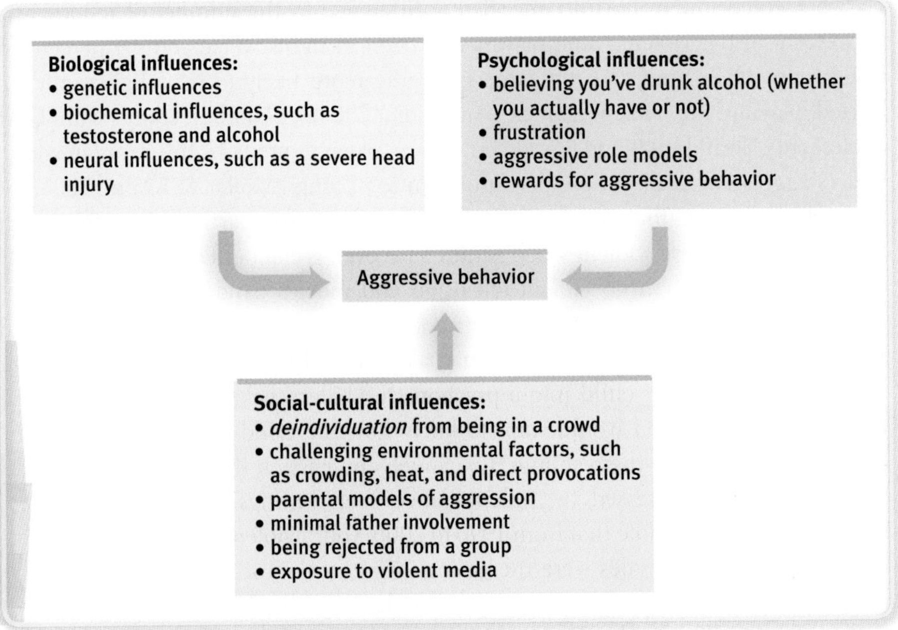

FIGURE 45.9
Biopsychosocial understanding of aggression Because many factors contribute to aggressive behavior, there are many ways to change such behavior, including learning anger management and communication skills, and avoiding violent media and video games.

RETRIEVAL PRACTICE

- What psychological, biological, and social-cultural influences interact to produce aggressive behaviors?

ANSWER: Our biology (our genes, neural systems, and biochemistry—including testosterone and alcohol levels) influences our tendencies to be aggressive. Psychological factors (such as frustration, previous rewards for aggressive acts, and observation of others' aggression) can trigger any aggressive tendencies we may have. Social influences, such as exposure to violent media or being ostracized from a group, and cultural influences, such as whether we've grown up in a "culture of honor" or had a father-absent home, can also affect our aggressive responses.

MODULE REVIEW

Antisocial Relations

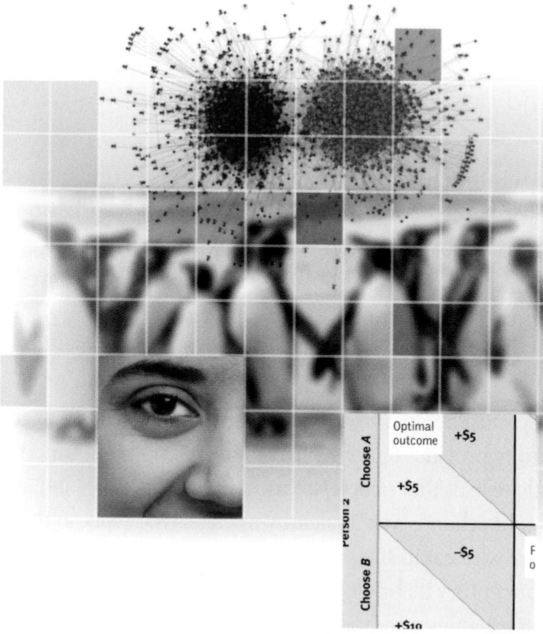

Learning Objectives

RETRIEVAL PRACTICE Take a moment to answer each of these Learning Objective Questions (repeated here from within the module). Then turn to Appendix B, Complete Module Reviews, to check your answers. Research suggests that trying to answer these questions on your own will improve your long-term retention (McDaniel et al., 2009).

45-1: What is prejudice? What are its social and emotional roots?

45-2: What are the cognitive roots of prejudice?

45-3: How does psychology's definition of *aggression* differ from everyday usage? What biological factors make us more prone to hurt one another?

45-4: What psychological and social-cultural factors may trigger aggressive behavior?

Terms and Concepts to Remember

RETRIEVAL PRACTICE Test yourself on these terms by trying to write down the definition before flipping back to the referenced page to check your answer.

prejudice, p. 593
stereotype, p. 593
discrimination, p. 593
just-world phenomenon, p. 596
ingroup, p. 596
outgroup, p. 597
ingroup bias, p. 597
scapegoat theory, p. 597
other-race effect, p. 598
aggression, p. 599
frustration-aggression principle, p. 601
social script, p. 603

RETRIEVAL PRACTICE Gain an advantage, and benefit from immediate feedback, with the interactive self-testing resources at www.worthpublishers.com/myers.

Prosocial Relations

- Attraction
- Altruism
- Peacemaking

Social psychology studies how we think about and influence one another, and also how we *relate* to one another. Social psychologists focus not only on the dark side of social relationships, but also on the bright side, by studying *prosocial* behavior—behavior that intends to help or benefit someone. Our positive behaviors toward others are evident from explorations of attraction, altruism, and peacemaking.

Rex USA

Familiarity breeds acceptance When this rare white penguin was born in the Sydney, Australia, zoo, his tuxedoed peers ostracized him. Zookeepers thought they would need to dye him black to gain acceptance. But after three weeks of contact, the other penguins came to accept him.

Attraction

Pause a moment and think about your relationships with two people—a close friend, and someone who has stirred your feelings of romantic love. What psychological chemistry binds us together in these special sorts of attachments that help us cope with all other relationships? Social psychology suggests some answers.

The Psychology of Attraction

46-1 Why do we befriend or fall in love with some people but not others?

We endlessly wonder how we can win others' affection and what makes our own affections flourish or fade. Does familiarity breed contempt, or does it intensify affection? Do birds of a feather flock together, or do opposites attract? Is beauty only skin deep, or does attractiveness matter greatly? To explore these questions, let's consider three ingredients of our liking for one another: proximity, attractiveness, and similarity.

Proximity

Before friendships become close, they must begin. *Proximity*—geographic nearness—is friendship's most powerful predictor. Proximity provides opportunities for aggression, but much more often it breeds liking. Study after study reveals that people are most inclined to like, and even to marry, those who live in the same neighborhood, who sit nearby in class, who work in the same office, who share the same parking lot, who eat in the same dining hall. Look around. Mating starts with meeting. (For a twenty-first-century technology that connects people not in physical proximity, see Close-Up: Online Matchmaking and Speed Dating.)

Proximity breeds liking partly because of the **mere exposure effect.** Repeated exposure to novel stimuli increases our liking for them. This applies to nonsense syllables, musical selections, geometric figures, Chinese characters, human faces, and the letters of our own name (Moreland & Zajonc, 1982; Nuttin, 1987; Zajonc, 2001). We are even somewhat more likely to marry someone whose first or last name resembles our own (Jones et al., 2004).

SHAUN CURRY/AFP/Getty Images

The mere exposure effect The mere exposure effect applies even to ourselves. Because the human face is not perfectly symmetrical, the face we see in the mirror is not the same face our friends see. Most of us prefer the familiar mirror image, while our friends like the reverse (Mita et al., 1977). The real British Prime Minister David Cameron is at left. The person he sees in the mirror each morning is shown at right, and that's the photo he would probably prefer.

So, within certain limits, familiarity breeds fondness (Bornstein, 1989, 1999). Researchers demonstrated this by having four equally attractive women silently attend a 200-student class for zero, 5, 10, or 15 class sessions (Moreland & Beach, 1992). At the end of the course, students were shown slides of each woman and asked to rate her attractiveness. The most attractive? The ones they'd seen most often. The phenomenon would come as no surprise to the young Taiwanese man who wrote more than 700 letters to his girlfriend, urging her to marry him. She did marry—the mail carrier (Steinberg, 1993).

No face is more familiar than your own. And that helps explain an interesting finding by Lisa DeBruine (2004): We like other people when their faces incorporate some morphed features of our own. When DeBruine (2002) had McMaster University students (both men and women) play a game with a supposed other player, they were more trusting and cooperative when the other person's image had some of their own facial features morphed into it. In me I trust. (See also **FIGURE 46.1.**)

CLOSE-UP

Online Matchmaking and Speed Dating

If you have not found a romantic partner in your immediate proximity, why not cast a wider net by joining the estimated 30 million people who each year try one of the some 1500 online dating services (Ellin, 2009)?

© Dave Coverly

Although published research on the effectiveness of Internet matchmaking services is sparse, this much seems well established: Some people, including occasional predators, dishonestly represent their age, attractiveness, occupation, or other details, and thus are not who they seem to be. Nevertheless, Katelyn McKenna and John Bargh and their colleagues have offered a surprising finding: Compared with relationships formed in person, Internet-formed friendships and romantic relationships are, on average, more likely to last beyond two years (Bargh et al. 2002, 2004; McKenna & Bargh, 1998, 2000; McKenna et al., 2002). In one of their studies, people disclosed more, with less posturing, to those whom they met online. When conversing online with someone for 20 minutes, they felt more liking for that person than they did for someone they had met and talked with face to face. This was true even when (unknown to them) it was the same person! Internet friendships often feel as real and important to people as in-person relationships. Small wonder that Harris Interactive (2010) found one leading online matchmaker enabling more than 500 U.S. marriages a day.

Speed dating pushes the search for romance into high gear. In a process pioneered by a matchmaking Jewish rabbi, people meet a succession of prospective partners, either in person or via webcam (Bower, 2009). After a 3- to 8-minute conversation, people move on to the next person. (In an in-person meeting, one partner—usually the woman—remains seated and the other circulates.) Those who want to meet again can arrange for future contacts. For many participants, 4 minutes is enough time to form a feeling about a conversational partner and to register whether the partner likes them (Eastwick & Finkel, 2008a,b).

Researchers have quickly realized that speed dating offers a unique opportunity for studying influences on our first impressions of potential romantic partners. Among recent findings are these:

- Men are more transparent. Observers (male or female) watching videos of speed-dating encounters can read a man's level of romantic interest more accurately than a woman's (Place et al., 2009).
- Given more options, people's choices become more superficial. Meeting lots of potential partners leads people to focus on more easily assessed characteristics, such as height and weight (Lenton & Francesconi, 2010). This was true even when researchers controlled for time spent with each partner.
- Men wish for future contact with more of their speed dates; women tend to be more choosy. But this gender difference disappears if the conventional roles are reversed, so that men stay seated while women circulate (Finkel & Eastwick, 2009).

For our ancestors, the mere exposure effect had survival value. What was familiar was generally safe and approachable. What was unfamiliar was more often dangerous and threatening. Evolution may therefore have hard-wired into us the tendency to bond with those who are familiar and to be wary of those who are unfamiliar (Zajonc, 1998). If so, gut-level prejudice against those who are culturally different could be a primitive, automatic emotional response (Devine, 1995). It's what we do with our knee-jerk prejudice that matters, say researchers. Do we let those feelings control our behavior? Or do we monitor our feelings and act in ways that reflect our conscious valuing of human equality?

mere exposure effect the phenomenon that repeated exposure to novel stimuli increases liking of them.

© Jeremy Bailenson and Nick Yee

Voter | George Bush | 60:40 Blend

FIGURE 46.1
I like the candidate who looks a bit like dear old me Jeremy Bailenson and his colleagues (2005) incorporated morphed features of voters' faces into the faces of 2004 U.S. presidential candidates George Bush and John Kerry. Without conscious awareness of their own incorporated features, the participants became more likely to favor the candidate whose face incorporated some of their own features.

© 1999 by Leigh Robin, Creators Syndicate, Inc.

When Neanderthals fall in love.

Physical Attractiveness

Once proximity affords us contact, what most affects our first impressions? The person's sincerity? Intelligence? Personality? Hundreds of experiments reveal that it is something far more superficial: physical appearance. This finding is unnerving for most of us who were taught that "beauty is only skin deep" and that "appearances can be deceiving."

In one early study, researchers randomly matched new University of Minnesota students for a Welcome Week dance (Walster et al., 1966). Before the dance, the researchers gave each student a battery of personality and aptitude tests, and they rated each student's level of physical attractiveness. On the night of the blind date, the couples danced and talked for more than two hours and then took a brief intermission to rate their dates. What determined whether they liked each other? Only one thing seemed to matter: appearance. Both the men and the women liked good-looking dates best. Women are more likely than men to say that another's looks don't affect them (Lippa, 2007). But studies show that a man's looks do affect women's behavior (Feingold, 1990; Sprecher, 1989; Woll, 1986). Speed-dating experiments confirm that attractiveness influences first impressions for both sexes (Belot & Francesconi, 2006; Finkel & Eastwick, 2008).

Physical attractiveness also predicts how often people date and how popular they feel. It affects initial impressions of people's personalities. We don't assume that attractive people are more compassionate, but we do perceive them as healthier, happier, more sensitive, more successful, and more socially skilled (Eagly et al., 1991; Feingold, 1992; Hatfield & Sprecher, 1986). Attractive, well-dressed people are more likely to make a favorable impression on potential employers, and they tend to be more successful in their jobs (Cash & Janda, 1984; Langlois et al., 2000; Solomon, 1987). Income analyses show a penalty for plainness or obesity and a premium for beauty (Engemann & Owyang, 2005).

An analysis of 100 top-grossing films since 1940 found that attractive characters were portrayed as morally superior to unattractive characters (Smith et al., 1999). But Hollywood modeling doesn't explain why, to judge from their gazing times, even babies prefer attractive over unattractive faces (Langlois et al., 1987). So do some blind people, as University of Birmingham professor John Hull (1990, p. 23) discovered after going blind. A colleague's remarks on a woman's beauty would strangely affect his feelings. He found this "deplorable. . . . What can it matter to me what sighted men think of women . . . yet I do care what sighted men think, and I do not seem able to throw off this prejudice."

"Personal beauty is a greater recommendation than any letter of introduction."

Aristotle, *Apothegems,* 330 B.C.E.

For those who find importance of looks unfair and unenlightened, two attractiveness findings may be reassuring. First, people's attractiveness is surprisingly unrelated to their self-esteem and happiness (Diener et al., 1995; Major et al., 1984). Unless we have just compared ourselves with superattractive people, few of us (thanks, perhaps, to the mere exposure effect) view ourselves as unattractive (Thornton & Moore, 1993). Second, strikingly attractive people are sometimes suspicious that praise for their work may simply be a reaction to their looks. Less attractive people are more likely to accept praise as sincere (Berscheid, 1981).

Percentage of Men and Women Who "Constantly Think About Their Looks"

	Men	Women
Canada	18%	20%
United States	17	27
Mexico	40	45
Venezuela	47	65

From Roper Starch survey, reported by McCool (1999).

Beauty is in the eye of the culture. Hoping to look attractive, people across the globe have pierced their noses, lengthened their necks, bound their feet, and dyed or painted their skin and hair. They have gorged themselves to achieve a full figure or liposuctioned fat to achieve a slim one, applied chemicals hoping to rid themselves of unwanted hair or to regrow wanted hair, strapped on leather garments to make their breasts seem smaller or surgically filled their breasts with silicone and put on Wonderbras to make them look bigger. Cultural ideals also change over time. For women in North America, the ultra-thin ideal of the Roaring Twenties gave way to the soft, voluptuous Marilyn Monroe ideal of the 1950s, only to be replaced by today's lean yet busty ideal.

New York Times columnist Maureen Dowd on liposuction (January 19, 2000): "Women in the 50's vacuumed. Women in the 00's are vacuumed. Our Hoovers have turned on us!"

If we're not born attractive, we may try to buy beauty. Americans now spend more on beauty supplies than on education and social services combined. Still not satisfied, millions undergo plastic surgery, teeth capping and whitening, Botox skin smoothing, and laser hair removal (ASPS, 2010).

combine their strength, pulling and pushing together. Having used isolation and competition to make strangers into enemies, Sherif used shared predicaments and goals to turn enemies into friends. What reduced conflict was not mere contact, but *cooperative* contact.

Syracuse Newspapers/The Image Works

Superordinate goals override differences Cooperative efforts to achieve shared goals are an effective way to break down social barriers.

A shared predicament likewise had a powerfully unifying effect in the weeks after 9/11. Patriotism soared as Americans felt "we" were under attack. Gallup-surveyed approval of "our President" shot up from 51 percent the week before the attack to a highest-ever 90 percent level 10 days after (Newport, 2002). In chat groups and everyday speech, even the word *we* (relative to *I*) surged in the immediate aftermath (Pennebaker, 2002).

At such times, cooperation can lead people to define a new, inclusive group that dissolves their former subgroups (Dovidio & Gaertner, 1999). To accomplish this, you might seat members of two groups not on opposite sides, but alternately around a table. Give them a new, shared name. Have them work together. Then watch "us" and "them" become "we." After 9/11, one 18-year-old New Jersey man described this shift in his own social identity: "I just thought of myself as Black. But now I feel like I'm an American, more than ever" (Sengupta, 2001). In a real experiment, White Americans who read a newspaper article about a terrorist threat against all Americans subsequently expressed reduced prejudice against Black Americans (Dovidio et al., 2004).

If cooperative contact between rival group members encourages positive attitudes, might this principle bring people together in multicultural schools? Could interracial friendships replace competitive classroom situations with cooperative ones? Could cooperative learning maintain or even enhance student achievement? Experiments with adolescents from 11 countries confirm that, in each case, the answer is *Yes* (Roseth et al., 2008). In the classroom as in the sports arena, members of interracial groups who work together on projects typically come to feel friendly toward one another. Knowing this, thousands of teachers have made interracial cooperative learning part of their classroom experience.

The power of cooperative activity to make friends of former enemies has led psychologists to urge increased international exchange and cooperation. As we engage in mutually beneficial trade, as we work to protect our common destiny on this fragile planet, and as we become more aware that our hopes and fears are shared, we can transform misperceptions that feed conflict into feelings of solidarity based on common interests.

Kofi Annan "Most of us have overlapping identities which unite us with very different groups. We *can* love what we are, without hating what—and who—we are *not*. We can thrive in our own tradition, even as we learn from others" (Nobel lecture, 2001).

Shawn Baldwin/Associated Press

Communication

When real-life conflicts become intense, a third-party mediator—a marriage counselor, labor mediator, diplomat, community volunteer—may facilitate much-needed communication (Rubin et al., 1994). Mediators help each party to voice its viewpoint and to understand the other's needs and goals. If successful, mediators can replace a competitive *win-lose* orientation with a cooperative *win-win* orientation that leads to a mutually beneficial resolution. A classic example: Two friends, after quarreling over an orange, agreed to split it. One squeezed his half for juice. The other used the peel from her half to flavor a cake. If only the two had understood each other's motives, they could have hit on the win-win solution of one having all the juice, the other all the peel.

Conciliation

Understanding and cooperative resolution are most needed, yet least likely, in times of anger or crisis (Bodenhausen et al., 1994; Tetlock, 1988). When conflicts intensify, images become more stereotyped, judgments more rigid, and communication more difficult, or

GRIT Graduated and Reciprocated Initiatives in Tension-Reduction—a strategy designed to decrease international tensions.

© The New Yorker Collection, 1983, W. Miller from cartoonbank.com. All Rights Reserved.

"To begin with, I would like to express my sincere thanks and deep appreciation for the opportunity to meet with you. While there are still profound differences between us, I think the very fact of my presence here today is a major breakthrough."

even impossible. Each party is likely to threaten, coerce, or retaliate. In the weeks before the Persian Gulf war, the first President George Bush threatened, in the full glare of publicity, to "kick Saddam's ass." Saddam Hussein communicated in kind, threatening to make Americans "swim in their own blood."

Under such conditions, is there an alternative to war or surrender? Social psychologist Charles Osgood (1962, 1980) advocated a strategy of *Graduated and Reciprocated Initiatives in Tension-Reduction*, nicknamed **GRIT.** In applying GRIT, one side first announces its recognition of mutual interests and its intent to reduce tensions. It then initiates one or more small, conciliatory acts. Without weakening one's retaliatory capability, this modest beginning opens the door for reciprocity by the other party. Should the enemy respond with hostility, one reciprocates in kind. But so, too, with any conciliatory response.

In laboratory experiments, small conciliatory gestures—a smile, a touch, a word of apology—have allowed both parties to begin edging down the tension ladder to a safer rung where communication and mutual understanding can begin (Lindskold et al., 1978, 1988). In a real-world international conflict, U.S. President John F. Kennedy's gesture of stopping atmospheric nuclear tests began a series of reciprocated conciliatory acts that culminated in the 1963 atmospheric test-ban treaty.

As working toward shared goals reminds us, we are more alike than different. Civilization advances not by conflict and cultural isolation, but by tapping the knowledge, the skills, and the arts that are each culture's legacy to the whole human race. Thanks to cultural sharing, every modern society is enriched by a cultural mix (Sowell, 1991). We have China to thank for paper and printing and for the magnetic compass that opened the great explorations. We have Egypt to thank for trigonometry. We have the Islamic world and India's Hindus to thank for our Arabic numerals. While celebrating and claiming these diverse cultural legacies, we can also welcome the enrichment of today's social diversity. We can view ourselves as instruments in a human orchestra. And we—this book's worldwide readers—can therefore each affirm our own culture's heritage while building bridges of communication, understanding, and cooperation across our cultural traditions.

RETRIEVAL PRACTICE

- What are some ways to reconcile conflicts and promote peace?

ANSWER: Peacemakers should encourage equal-status *contact*, cooperation to achieve *superordinate goals* (shared goals that override differences), understanding through communication, and reciprocated conciliatory gestures (each side gives a little).

MODULE REVIEW

Prosocial Relations

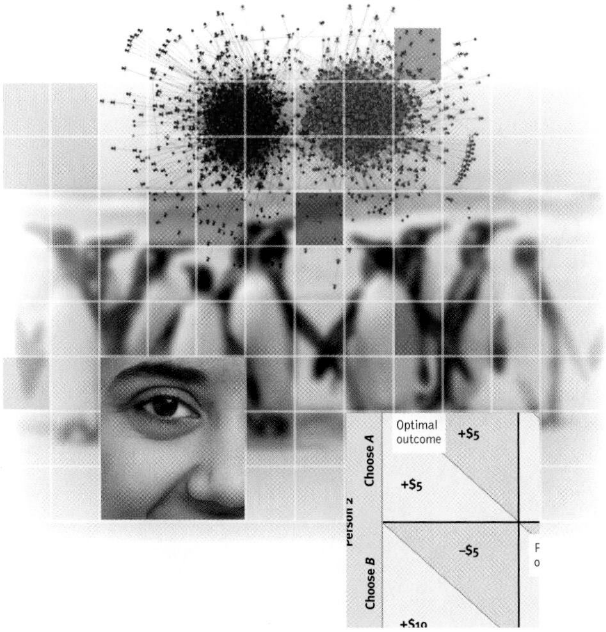

Learning Objectives

RETRIEVAL PRACTICE Take a moment to answer each of these Learning Objective Questions (repeated here from within the module). Then turn to Appendix B, Complete Module Reviews, to check your answers. Research suggests that trying to answer these questions on your own will improve your long-term retention (McDaniel et al., 2009).

46-1: Why do we befriend or fall in love with some people but not others?

46-2: How does romantic love typically change as time passes?

46-3: When are people most—and least—likely to help?

46-4: How do social exchange theory and social norms explain helping behavior?

46-5: How do social traps and mirror-image perceptions fuel social conflict?

46-6: How can we transform feelings of prejudice, aggression, and conflict into attitudes that promote peace?

Terms and Concepts to Remember

RETRIEVAL PRACTICE Test yourself on these terms by trying to write down the definition before flipping back to the referenced page to check your answer.

mere exposure effect, p. 608
passionate love, p. 613
companionate love, p. 613
equity, p. 614
self-disclosure, p. 614
altruism, p. 615
bystander effect, p. 616
social exchange theory, p. 617
reciprocity norm, p. 617
social-responsibility norm, p. 617
conflict, p. 618
social trap, p. 618
mirror-image perceptions, p. 619
superordinate goals, p. 620
GRIT, p. 622

RETRIEVAL PRACTICE Gain an advantage, and benefit from immediate feedback, with the interactive self-testing resources at www.worthpublishers.com/myers.

Psychological Disorders

MODULES

47 Introduction to Psychological Disorders

I felt the need to clean my room at home in Indianapolis every Sunday and would spend four to five hours at it. I would take every book out of the bookcase, dust and put it back. . . . I couldn't stop.

Marc, diagnosed with obsessive-compulsive disorder (from Summers, 1996)

Whenever I get depressed it's because I've lost a sense of self. I can't find reasons to like myself. I think I'm ugly. I think no one likes me.

Greta, diagnosed with depression (from Thorne, 1993, p. 21)

Voices, like the roar of a crowd, came. I felt like Jesus; I was being crucified.

Stuart, diagnosed with schizophrenia (from Emmons et al., 1997)

People are fascinated by the exceptional, the unusual, the abnormal. "The sun shines and warms and lights us and we have no curiosity to know why this is so," observed Ralph Waldo Emerson, "but we ask the reason of all evil, of pain, and hunger, and [unusual] people."

Why such fascination with disturbed people? Even when we are well, do we see in them something of ourselves? At various moments, all of us feel, think, or act the way disturbed people do much of the time. We, too, get anxious, depressed, withdrawn, suspicious, or deluded, just less intensely and more briefly. No

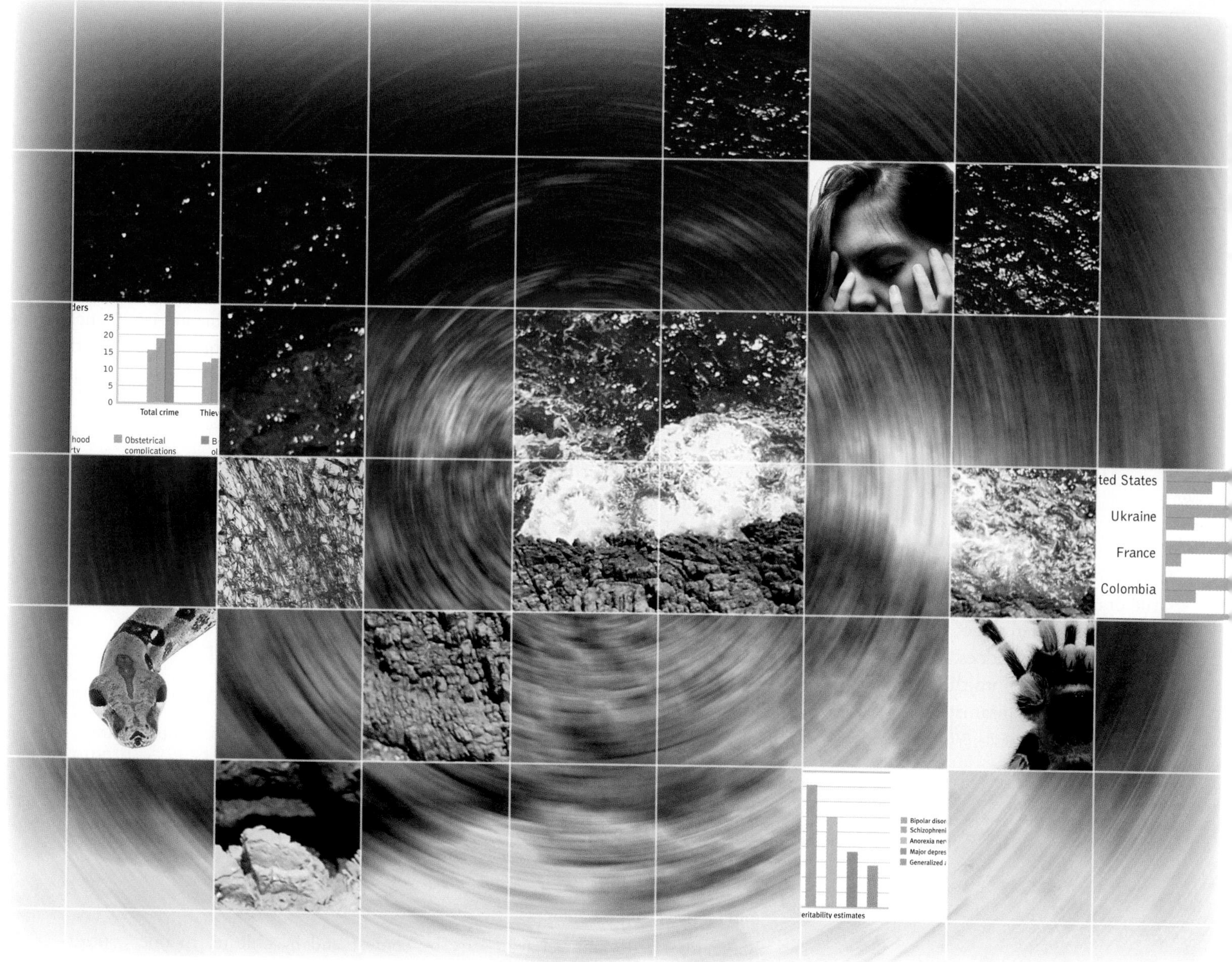

48 Anxiety Disorders | 49 Mood Disorders | 50 Schizophrenia | 51 Dissociative, Personality, and Eating Disorders

wonder studying psychological disorders sometimes evokes an eerie sense of self-recognition, one that illuminates our own personality. "To study the abnormal is the best way of understanding the normal," proposed William James (1842–1910).

Another reason for our curiosity is that so many of us have felt, either personally or through friends or family, the bewilderment and pain of a psychological disorder that may bring unexplained physical symptoms, irrational fears, or a feeling that life is not worth living. Indeed, as members of the human family, most of us will at some point encounter a person with a psychological disorder.

The World Health Organization (WHO, 2010) reports that, worldwide, some 450 million people suffer from mental or behavioral disorders. These disorders account for 15.4 percent of the years of life lost due to death or disability—scoring slightly below cardiovascular conditions and slightly above cancer (Murray & Lopez, 1996). Rates and symptoms of psychological disorders vary by culture, but no known society is free of two terrible maladies: depression and schizophrenia.

Module 47 provides an overview of psychological disorders, explaining the major perspectives, categories, and risks of labeling, and outlines the prevalence of various disorders. Modules 48 through 51 describe the symptoms and possible causes of several well-known disorders, including phobias, obsessive-compulsive disorder, depression, schizophrenia, the controversial dissociative identity disorder, and the more common eating disorders.

Introduction to Psychological Disorders

- Defining Psychological Disorders
- Understanding Psychological Disorders
- Classifying Psychological Disorders
- Labeling Psychological Disorders
- Rates of Psychological Disorders

"Who in the rainbow can draw the line where the violet tint ends and the orange tint begins? Distinctly we see the difference of the colors, but where exactly does the one first blendingly enter into the other? So with sanity and insanity."

Herman Melville, *Billy Budd, Sailor,* 1924

Most people would agree that someone who is too depressed to get out of bed for weeks at a time has a psychological disorder. But what about those who, having experienced a loss, are unable to resume their usual social activities? Where should we draw the line between sadness and depression? Between zany creativity and bizarre irrationality? Between normality and abnormality? Let's start with these questions:

- How should we *define* psychological disorders?
- How should we *understand* disorders—as sicknesses that need to be diagnosed and cured, or as natural responses to a troubling environment?
- How should we *classify* psychological disorders? And can we do so in a way that allows us to help people without stigmatizing them with *labels?*
- How *prevalent* are these disorders, and who is likely to experience them?

Defining Psychological Disorders

47-1 How should we draw the line between normality and disorder?

Mental health workers view **psychological disorders** as patterns of thoughts, feelings, or actions that are deviant, distressful, and dysfunctional (Comer, 2004; Stein et al., 2010).

Being different *(deviant)* from most other people in one's culture is *part* of what it takes to define a psychological disorder. As the reclusive poet Emily Dickinson observed in 1862,

Assent—and you are sane—
Demur—you're straightaway dangerous—
and handled with a Chain.

Standards for deviant behavior vary by context and by culture. In one context—wartime—mass killing may be viewed as normal and even heroic. In some contexts, people are presumed deranged when they hear voices. But in cultures practicing ancestor worship, reasonable-seeming people may claim to talk with the dead (Friedrich, 1987).

Standards for deviance also vary with time. From 1952 through December 9, 1973, homosexuality was classified as an illness. By day's end on December 10, it was not. The American Psychiatric Association had dropped homosexuality as a disorder because more and more of its members no longer viewed it as a psychological problem. (Later research revealed that the stigma and stresses that often accompany homosexuality, however, increase the risk of mental health problems [Hatzenbuehler et al., 2009; Meyer, 2003].) In this new century, controversy swirls over the frequent diagnosing of children with *attention-deficit hyperactivity disorder* (see Thinking Critically About: ADHD—Normal High Energy or Genuine Disorder?).

But there is more to a disorder than being deviant. Olympic gold medalists deviate from the norm in their physical abilities, and society honors them. Social deviance—which some

Culture and normality Young men of the West African Wodaabe tribe put on elaborate makeup and costumes to attract women. Young American men may buy flashy cars with loud stereos to do the same. Each culture may view the other's behavior as abnormal.

Carol Beckwith

© Image Source/Corbis

THINKING CRITICALLY ABOUT

ADHD—Normal High Energy or Genuine Disorder?

47-2 Why is there controversy over attention-deficit hyperactivity disorder?

Eight-year-old Todd has always been energetic. At home, he chatters away and darts from one activity to the next, rarely settling down to read a book or focus on a game. At play, he is reckless and overreacts when playmates bump into him or take one of his toys. At school, his exasperated teacher complains that fidgety Todd doesn't listen, follow instructions, or stay in his seat and do his lessons. As he matures to adulthood, Todd's hyperactivity likely will subside, but his inattentiveness may persist (Kessler et al., 2010).

If taken for a psychological evaluation, Todd may be diagnosed with **attention-deficit hyperactivity disorder (ADHD),** as are some 5 percent of children and 3 percent of adolescents who display at least one of its key symptoms (extreme inattention, hyperactivity, and impulsivity) (Polanczyk et al., 2007). Studies also find 2.5 percent of adults—though a diminishing number with age—exhibiting ADHD symptoms (Simon et al., 2009).

To skeptics, being distractible, fidgety, and impulsive sounds like a "disorder" caused by a single genetic variation: a Y chromosome. And sure enough, ADHD is diagnosed three times more often in boys than in girls. Does energetic child + boring school = ADHD overdiagnosis? Is the label being applied to healthy schoolchildren who, in more natural outdoor environments, would seem perfectly normal?

Skeptics think so. In the decade after 1987, they note, the proportion of American children being treated for ADHD nearly quadrupled (Olfson et al., 2003). How commonplace the diagnosis is depends in part on teacher referrals. Some teachers refer lots of kids for ADHD assessment, others none. ADHD rates have varied by a factor of 10 in different counties of New York State (Carlson, 2000). Although African-American youth display more ADHD symptoms than do Caucasian youth, they less often receive an ADHD diagnosis (Miller et al., 2009). Depending on where they live, children who are "a persistent pain in the neck in school" are often diagnosed with ADHD and given powerful prescription drugs, notes Peter Gray (2010). But the problem resides less in the child, he argues, than in today's abnormal environment that forces children to do what evolution has not prepared them to do—to sit for long hours in chairs.

On the other side of the debate are those who argue that the more frequent diagnoses of ADHD today reflect increased awareness of the disorder, especially in those areas where rates are highest. They acknowledge that diagnoses can be subjective and sometimes inconsistent—ADHD is not as objectively defined as is a broken arm. Nevertheless, declared the World Federation for Mental Health (2005), "there is strong agreement among the international scientific community that ADHD is a real neurobiological disorder whose existence should no longer be debated." In neuroimaging studies, ADHD has associations with abnormal brain-activity patterns, noted a consensus statement by 75 researchers (Barkley et al., 2002).

What, then, is known about ADHD's causes? It is not caused by too much sugar or poor schools. There is mixed evidence suggesting that extensive TV watching and video gaming are associated with reduced cognitive self-regulation and ADHD (Bailey et al., 2011; Courage & Setliff, 2010; Ferguson, 2011). ADHD often coexists with a learning disorder or with defiant and temper-prone behavior. ADHD is *heritable,* and research teams are sleuthing the culprit genes and abnormal neural pathways (Nikolas & Burt, 2010; Poelmans et al., 2011; Volkow et al., 2009; Williams et al., 2010). It is treatable with medications such as Ritalin and Adderall, which are considered stimulants but help calm hyperactivity and increase one's ability to sit and focus on a task—and to progress normally in school (Barbaresi et al., 2007). Psychological therapies, such as those focused on shaping behaviors in the classroom and at home, have also helped address the distress of ADHD (Fabiano et al., 2008).

The bottom line: Extreme inattention, hyperactivity, and impulsivity can derail social, academic, and vocational achievements, and these symptoms can be treated with medication and other treatment. But the debate continues over whether normal rambunctiousness is too often diagnosed as a psychiatric disorder, and whether there is a cost to the long-term use of stimulant drugs in treating ADHD.

attention-deficit hyperactivity disorder (ADHD) a psychological disorder marked by the appearance by age 7 of one or more of three key symptoms: extreme inattention, hyperactivity, and impulsivity.

political regimes use to diagnose and isolate their opponents—may bring dishonor. But to be considered disordered, deviant behavior usually causes the person *distress.* Marc, Greta, and Stuart were all clearly distressed by their behaviors.

Deviant and distressful behaviors are more likely to be considered disordered when also judged to be a *harmful dysfunction* (Wakefield, 1992, 2006). Marc's distracting obsessive behaviors, for example, interfered with his work and leisure. By this measuring stick, even typical behaviors, such as the occasional despondency many college students feel, may signal a psychological disorder *if* they become disabling. Dysfunction is key to defining a disorder: An intense fear of spiders may be deviant, but if it doesn't impair your life it is not a disorder.

psychological disorder deviant, distressful, and dysfunctional patterns of thoughts, feelings, or behaviors.

RETRIEVAL PRACTICE

- A lawyer is distressed by feeling the need to wash his hands 100 times a day. He has no time left to meet with clients, and his colleagues are wondering about his competence. His behavior would probably be labeled disordered, because he is (1) *distressed* about his behavior, and it is also (2) __________ from the behaviors of those around him, and (3) __________—interfering with his day-to-day life.

ANSWERS: deviant; dysfunctional

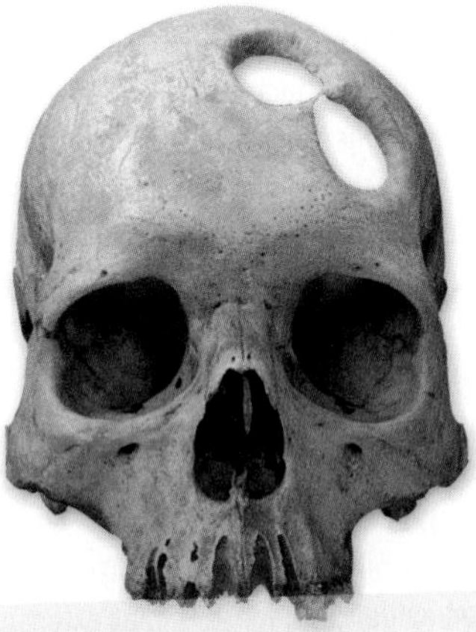

Yesterday's "therapy" In other times and places, psychologically disordered people sometimes received brutal treatments, including the trephination evident in this Stone Age skull. Drilling skull holes like these may have been an attempt to release evil spirits and cure those with mental disorders. Did this patient survive the "cure"?

John W. Verano

Understanding Psychological Disorders

47-3 How do the medical model and the biopsychosocial approach understand psychological disorders?

To explain puzzling behavior, people in earlier times often presumed the work of strange forces—the movements of the stars, god-like powers, or evil spirits. Had you lived during the Middle Ages, you might have said "The devil made him do it," and you might have approved of a cure to rid the evil force by exorcising the demon. Until the last two centuries, "mad" people were sometimes caged in zoo-like conditions or given "therapies" appropriate to a demon: beatings, burning, or castration. In other times, therapy included pulling teeth, removing lengths of intestines, cauterizing the clitoris, or giving transfusions of animal blood (Farina, 1982).

The Medical Model

In opposition to brutal treatments, reformers, including Philippe Pinel (1745–1826) in France, insisted that madness is not demon possession but a sickness of the mind caused by severe stresses and inhumane conditions. For Pinel and others, "moral treatment" included boosting patients' morale by unchaining them and talking with them, and by replacing brutality with gentleness, isolation with activity, and filth with clean air and sunshine. While such measures did not often cure patients, they were certainly more humane.

By the 1800s, the discovery that syphilis infects the brain and distorts the mind drove further gradual reform. Hospitals replaced asylums, and the medical world began searching for physical causes and treatments of mental disorders. Today, this **medical model** is

"Moral treatment" Under Philippe Pinel's influence, hospitals sometimes sponsored patient dances, often called "lunatic balls," depicted in this painting by George Bellows *(Dance in a Madhouse)*.

George Wesley Bellows, *Dance in a Madhouse*, 1907. © 1997 The Art Institute of Chicago recognizable in the terminology of the mental *health* movement: A mental *illness* (also called a psycho*pathology*) needs to be *diagnosed* on the basis of its *symptoms* and *treated* through *therapy*, which may include time in a psychiatric *hospital*.

medical model the concept that diseases, in this case psychological disorders, have physical causes that can be *diagnosed, treated,* and, in most cases, *cured,* often through treatment in a *hospital.*

The medical perspective has gained credibility from recent discoveries that genetically influenced abnormalities in brain structure and biochemistry contribute to many disorders. But as we will see, psychological factors, such as chronic or traumatic stress, also play an important role.

The Biopsychosocial Approach

Today's psychologists contend that *all* behavior, whether called normal or disordered, arises from the interaction of nature (genetic and physiological factors) and nurture (past and present experiences). To presume that a person is "mentally ill," they say, attributes the condition to a "sickness" that must be identified and cured. But difficulty in the person's environment, in the person's current interpretations of events, or in the person's bad habits and poor social skills may also be factors.

"It's no measure of health to be well adjusted to a profoundly sick society."

Krishnamurti, 1895–1986

Evidence of such effects comes from links between specific disorders and cultures (Beardsley, 1994; Castillo, 1997). Cultures differ in their sources of stress, and they produce different ways of coping. The eating disorders anorexia nervosa and bulimia nervosa, for example, have occurred mostly in Western cultures. In Malaysia, *amok* describes a sudden outburst of violent behavior (thus the phrase "run amok"). Latin America lays claim to *susto*, a condition marked by severe anxiety, restlessness, and a fear of black magic. *Taijin-kyofusho*, social anxiety about one's appearance combined with a readiness to blush and a fear of eye contact, appears in Japan, as does the extreme withdrawal of *hikikomori*. Such disorders may share an underlying dynamic (such as anxiety) while differing in the symptoms (an eating problem or a type of fear) manifested in a particular culture.

Increasingly, North American disorders, such as eating disorders, are, along with McDonald's and MTV, spreading across the globe (Watters, 2010).

But not all disorders are culture-bound. Depression and schizophrenia occur worldwide. From Asia to Africa and across the Americas, schizophrenia's symptoms often include irrationality and incoherent speech.

To assess the whole set of influences—genetic predispositions and physiological states, inner psychological dynamics, and social and cultural circumstances—the biopsychosocial model helps (**FIGURE 47.1**). This approach recognizes that mind and body are inseparable. Negative emotions contribute to physical illness, and physical abnormalities contribute to negative emotions. We are mind embodied and socially embedded.

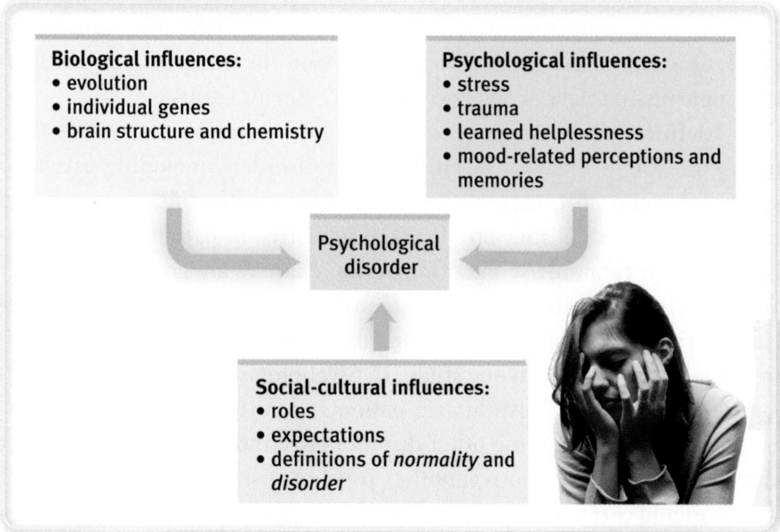

FIGURE 47.1
The biopsychosocial approach to psychological disorders Today's psychology studies how biological, psychological, and social-cultural factors interact to produce specific psychological disorders.

RETRIEVAL PRACTICE

- Are psychological disorders universal, or are they culture-specific? Explain with examples.

ANSWER: Some psychological disorders are culture-specific. For example, anorexia nervosa occurs mostly in Western cultures, and *taijin-kyofusho* appears largely in Japan. Other disorders, such as schizophrenia, occur in all cultures.

Classifying Psychological Disorders

47-4 How and why do clinicians classify psychological disorders?

In biology and the other sciences, classification creates order. To classify an animal as a "mammal" says a great deal—that it is warm-blooded, has hair or fur, and nourishes its young with milk. In psychiatry and psychology, too, classification orders and describes symptoms. To classify a person's disorder as "schizophrenia" suggests that the person talks incoherently; hallucinates or has delusions (bizarre beliefs); shows either little emotion or inappropriate emotion; or is socially withdrawn. "Schizophrenia" provides a handy shorthand for describing a complex cluster of disorders.

In psychiatry and psychology, diagnostic classification aims not only to describe a disorder but also to predict its future course, imply appropriate treatment, and stimulate research into its causes. Indeed, to study a disorder we must first name and describe it. A current authoritative scheme for classifying psychological disorders is the **DSM-IV-TR.** This volume is the American Psychiatric Association's *Diagnostic and Statistical Manual of Mental Disorders*, Fourth Edition, updated as a 2000 "text revision." In 2010, the American Psychiatric Association released the first draft of the upcoming DSM-5, a revision to appear in 2013 (Clay, 2011; www.DSM5.org; Miller & Holden, 2010). Some proposed changes are to the diagnostic labels. "Mental retardation," for example, is slated to become "intellectual developmental disorder." Some proposed categories, such as "hypersexual disorder," "hoarding disorder," and "binge-eating disorder" would be new. The eleventh edition of the World Health Organization's *International Classification of Diseases* (ICD-11), covering both medical and psychological disorders, is expected in 2014 (Clay, 2010).

A book of case illustrations accompanying the DSM-IV-TR provides several examples for Modules 47 through 51.

Despite its medical terminology *(diagnosing, symptoms, illness)*, most practitioners find the DSM-IV-TR a helpful and practical tool. It is also financially necessary: North American health insurance companies usually require an ICD/DSM diagnosis before they pay for therapy. One aim of the new DSM-5 is to support the integration of psychiatric diagnoses into mainstream medical practice (Kupfer & Regier, 2010).

The DSM-IV-TR defines a diagnostic process and 16 clinical syndromes (**TABLE 47.1**). Without presuming to explain their causes, it describes disorders, including *psychotic disorders*. To be helpful and useful, these categories and diagnostic guidelines must be reliable, and to a reasonable extent they are. If one psychiatrist or psychologist diagnoses someone as having, say, catatonic schizophrenia, the chances are good that another mental health worker will independently give the same diagnosis. Following these guidelines, clinicians answer a series of objective questions about observable behaviors, such as, "Is the person afraid to leave home?" In one study, 16 psychologists used this structured-interview procedure to diagnose 75 psychiatric patients as suffering from (1) depression, (2) generalized anxiety, or (3) some other disorder (Riskind et al., 1987). Without knowing the first psychologist's diagnosis, another psychologist viewed a videotape of each interview and offered a second opinion. For 83 percent of the patients, the two opinions agreed.

© 1992 by Sidney Harris.

"I'm always like this, and my family was wondering if you could prescribe a mild depressant."

TABLE 47.1

How Are Psychological Disorders Diagnosed?

Based on assessments, interviews, and observations, many clinicians diagnose by answering the following questions from the five levels, or axes, of the DSM-IV-TR.

Axis I Is a *Clinical Syndrome* present?
Using specifically defined criteria, clinicians may select none, one, or more syndromes from the following list:

- Disorders usually first diagnosed in infancy, childhood, and adolescence
- Delirium, dementia, amnesia, and other cognitive disorders
- Mental disorders due to a general medical condition
- Substance-related disorders
- Schizophrenia and other psychotic disorders
- Mood disorders
- Anxiety disorders
- Somatoform disorders (bodily symptoms without apparent physical causes)
- Factitious disorders (intentionally faked)
- Dissociative disorders
- Eating disorders
- Sexual disorders and gender identity disorder
- Sleep disorders
- Impulse-control disorders not classified elsewhere
- Adjustment disorders
- Other conditions that may be a focus of clinical attention

Axis II Is a *Personality Disorder* or *Mental Retardation [Intellectual Developmental Disorder]* present?
Clinicians may or may not also select one of these two conditions.

Axis III Is a *General Medical Condition,* such as diabetes, hypertension, or arthritis, also present?

Axis IV Are *Psychosocial* or *Environmental Problems,* such as school or housing issues, also present?

Axis V What is the *Global Assessment* of this person's functioning?
Clinicians assign a code from 0–100.

DSM-IV-TR the American Psychiatric Association's *Diagnostic and Statistical Manual of Mental Disorders,* Fourth Edition, with an updated "text revision"; a widely used system for classifying psychological disorders.

Reprinted with permission from *Diagnostic and Statistical Manual of Mental Disorders,* Fourth Edition, Text Revision. Copyright © 2000 by the American Psychiatric Association.

Some critics have faulted the manual for casting too wide a net and bringing "almost any kind of behavior within the compass of psychiatry" (Eysenck et al., 1983). Others note that as the number of disorder categories has swelled (today's nearly 300 disorders are quintuple those in the 1952 first edition), so has the number of adults who meet the criteria for at least one of them—26 percent in any year, according to the U.S. National Institute of Mental Health (2008), and 46 percent at some time in their lives (Kessler et al., 2005). Critics worry that the draft DSM-5 will extend the pathologizing of everyday life—for example, by turning bereavement grief into depression and boyish rambunctiousness into hyperactivity (Shorter, 2010). Others respond that depression and hyperactivity, though needing careful definition, are genuine disorders even, for example, those triggered by a major life stress such as a death when the grief does not go away (Kendler, 2011).

RETRIEVAL PRACTICE

- What is the biopsychosocial perspective, and why is it important in our understanding of psychological disorders?

ANSWER: Biological, psychological, and social-cultural influences combine to produce psychological disorders. This broad perspective helps us understand that our well-being is affected by our genes, brain functioning, inner thoughts and feelings, and the influences of our social and cultural environment.

Labeling Psychological Disorders

47-5 Why do some psychologists criticize the use of diagnostic labels?

The DSM has other critics who register a more fundamental complaint—that these labels are at best arbitrary and at worst value judgments masquerading as science. Once we label a person, we view that person differently (Farina, 1982). Labels create preconceptions that guide our perceptions and our interpretations.

In a now-classic study of the biasing power of labels, David Rosenhan (1973) and seven others went to hospital admissions offices, complaining of "hearing voices" saying *empty, hollow,* and *thud*. Apart from this complaint and giving false names and occupations, they answered questions truthfully. All eight normal people were misdiagnosed with disorders.

Should we be surprised? As one psychiatrist noted, if someone swallows blood, goes to an emergency room, and spits it up, should we fault the doctor for diagnosing a bleeding ulcer? Surely not. But what followed the diagnosis in the Rosenhan study was startling. Until being released an average of 19 days later, the "patients" exhibited no further symptoms such as hearing voices. Yet after analyzing their (quite normal) life histories, clinicians were able to "discover" the causes of their disorders, such as reacting with mixed emotions about a parent. Even the routine behavior of taking notes was misinterpreted as a symptom.

"One of the unpardonable sins, in the eyes of most people, is for a man to go about unlabeled. The world regards such a person as the police do an unmuzzled dog, not under proper control."

T. H. Huxley, *Evolution and Ethics,* 1893

Labels matter. When people in another experiment watched videotaped interviews, those told the interviewees were job applicants perceived them as normal (Langer et al., 1974, 1980). Those who thought they were watching psychiatric or cancer patients perceived them as "different from most people." Therapists who thought an interviewee was a psychiatric patient perceived him as "frightened of his own aggressive impulses," a "passive, dependent type," and so forth. A label can, as Rosenhan discovered, have "a life and an influence of its own."

"My sister suffers from a bipolar disorder and my nephew from schizoaffective disorder. There has, in fact, been a lot of depression and alcoholism in my family and, traditionally, no one ever spoke about it. It just wasn't done. The stigma is toxic."

Actress Glenn Close, "Mental Illness: The Stigma of Silence," 2009

Surveys in Europe and North America have demonstrated the stigmatizing power of labels (Page, 1977). Getting a job or finding a place to rent can be a challenge for those known to be just released from prison—or a mental hospital. But as we are coming to understand that many psychological disorders are diseases of the brain, not failures of character, the stigma seems to be lifting (Solomon, 1996). Public figures are feeling freer to "come out" and speak with candor about their struggles with disorders such as depression. And the more contact people have with individuals with disorders, the more accepting their attitudes are (Kolodziej & Johnson, 1996). People express greatest sympathy for people whose disorders are gender atypical—for men suffering depression (which is more common among women), or for women plagued by alcohol dependence (Wirth & Bodenhausen, 2009).

Accurate portrayal Popular movies, such as *Silence of the Lambs* and *Psycho,* have often portrayed those with psychological disorders as aggressive and dangerous. The TV show *Law & Order: Criminal Intent* has portrayed more typical suffering and personal disruption.

USA Network/Courtesy Everett Collection

Nevertheless, stereotypes linger in media portrayals of psychological disorders. Some are reasonably accurate and sympathetic. But too often people with disorders are portrayed as objects of humor or ridicule (*As Good as It Gets*), as homicidal maniacs (Hannibal Lecter in *Silence of the Lambs*), or as freaks (Nairn, 2007). Apart from the few who experience threatening delusions and hallucinated voices that command a violent act, and from those whose dysfunctionality includes substance abuse, mental disorders seldom lead to violence (Douglas et al., 2009; Elbogen & Johnson, 2009; Fazel et al., 2009, 2010). In real life, people with disorders are more likely to be the *victims* of violence than the perpetrators (Marley & Bulia, 2001). Indeed, reported the U.S. Surgeon General's Office (1999, p. 7), "There is very little risk of violence or harm to a stranger from casual contact with an individual who has a mental disorder." (Although most people with psychological disorders are not violent, those who are create a moral dilemma for society. For more on this topic, see Thinking Critically About: Insanity and Responsibility.)

THINKING CRITICALLY ABOUT

Insanity and Responsibility

AP/*Arizona Daily Star*, Mamta Popat

Jail or hospital? Jared Lee Loughner was charged with the 2011 Tucson, Arizona, shooting that killed six people and left over a dozen others injured, including U.S. Representative Gabrielle Giffords. Loughner had a history of mental health issues, including paranoid beliefs, and was diagnosed with schizophrenia. Usually, however, schizophrenia is associated with violence only when accompanied by substance abuse (Fazel et al., 2009).

"My brain . . . my genes . . . my bad upbringing made me do it." Such defenses were anticipated by Shakespeare's *Hamlet*. If I wrong someone when not myself, he explained, "then Hamlet does it not, Hamlet denies it. Who does it then? His madness." Such is the essence of a legal insanity defense, created in 1843 after a deluded Scotsman tried to shoot the prime minister (who he thought was persecuting him) but killed an assistant by mistake. Like U.S. President Ronald Reagan's near-assassin, John Hinckley, Scotsman Daniel M'Naughten was sent to a mental hospital rather than to prison.

In both cases, the public was outraged. "Hinckley Insane, Public Mad," declared one headline. They were mad again when a deranged Jeffrey Dahmer in 1991 admitted murdering 15 young men and eating parts of their bodies. They were mad in 1998 when 15-year-old Kip Kinkel, driven by "those voices in my head," killed his parents and two fellow Springfield, Oregon, students and wounded 25 others. They were mad in 2002 when Andrea Yates, after being taken off her antipsychotic medication, was tried in Texas for drowning her five children. And they were mad in 2011, when an irrational Jared Loughner gunned down a crowd of people, including survivor Congresswoman Gabrielle Giffords, in an Arizona supermarket parking lot. Most of these people were sent to jails, not hospitals, following their arrests (Hinkley was sent to a psychiatric hospital and later, after another trial, Yates was instead hospitalized). As Yates' fate illustrates, 99 percent of those whose insanity defense is accepted are nonetheless institutionalized, often for as long as those convicted of crimes (Lilienfeld & Arkowitz, 2011).

Most people with psychological disorders are not violent. But what should society do with those who are? Many people who have been executed or are now on death row have been limited by intellectual disability or motivated by delusional voices. The State of Arkansas forced one murderer with schizophrenia, Charles Singleton, to take two antipsychotic drugs—in order to make him mentally competent, so that he could then be put to death.

Which of Yates' two juries made the right decision? The first, which decided that people who commit such rare but terrible crimes should be held responsible? Or the second, which decided to blame the "madness" that clouds their vision? As we come to better understand the biological and environmental basis for all human behavior, from generosity to vandalism, when should we—and should we not—hold people accountable for their actions?

Not only can labels bias perceptions, they can also change reality. When teachers are told certain students are "gifted," when students expect someone to be "hostile," or when interviewers check to see whether someone is "extraverted," they may act in ways that elicit the very behavior expected (Snyder, 1984). Someone who was led to think you are nasty may treat you coldly, leading you to respond as a mean-spirited person would. Labels can serve as *self-fulfilling prophecies*.

But let us remember the *benefits* of diagnostic labels. Mental health professionals use labels to communicate about their cases, to comprehend the underlying causes, and to discern effective treatment programs. Diagnostic definitions also inform patients' self-understanding. And they are useful in research that explores the causes and treatments of disorder.

"What's the use of their having names," the Gnat said, "if they won't answer to them?"
"No use to *them*," said Alice; "but it's useful to the people that name them, I suppose."

Lewis Carroll, *Through the Looking-Glass*, 1871

RETRIEVAL PRACTICE

- What is the value, and what are the dangers, of labeling individuals with disorders?

ANSWER: Therapists and others use disorder labels to communicate with one another using a common language, and to share concepts during research. Insurance companies require a diagnosis (a label) before they will pay for therapy. The danger of labeling people is that they will begin to act as they have been labeled, and labels can create expectations that will change our behavior toward the people we label.

Rates of Psychological Disorders

47-6 How many people suffer, or have suffered, from a psychological disorder? Is poverty a risk factor?

Who is most vulnerable to psychological disorders? At what times of life? To answer such questions, various countries have conducted lengthy, structured interviews with representative samples of thousands of their citizens. After asking hundreds of questions that probed for symptoms—"Has there ever been a period of two weeks or more when you felt like you wanted to die?"—the researchers have estimated the current, prior-year, and lifetime prevalence of various disorders.

How many people have, or have had, a psychological disorder? More than most of us suppose:

- The U.S. National Institute of Mental Health (2008, based on Kessler et al., 2005) estimates that 26 percent of adult Americans "suffer from a diagnosable mental disorder in a given year" (**TABLE 47.2**).
- A twenty-first-century World Health Organization (2004a) study—based on 90-minute interviews of 60,463 people—estimated the number of prior-year mental disorders in 14 countries. As **FIGURE 47.2** displays, the lowest rate of reported mental disorders was in Shanghai, the highest rate in the United States. Moreover, immigrants to the United States from Mexico, Africa, and Asia average better mental health than their native U.S. counterparts (Breslau et al., 2007; Maldonado-Molina et al., 2011). For example, compared with people who have recently immigrated from Mexico, Mexican-Americans born in the United States are at greater risk of mental disorder—a phenomenon known as the *immigrant paradox* (Schwartz et al., 2010).

TABLE 47.2

Percentage of Americans Reporting Selected Psychological Disorders in the Past Year

Psychological Disorder	Percentage
Generalized anxiety	3.1
Social phobia	6.8
Phobia of specific object or situation	8.7
Mood disorder	9.5
Obsessive-compulsive disorder (OCD)	1.0
Schizophrenia	1.1
Post-traumatic stress disorder (PTSD)	3.5
Attention-deficit hyperactivity disorder (ADHD)	4.1
Any mental disorder	26.2

Source: National Institute of Mental Health, 2008.

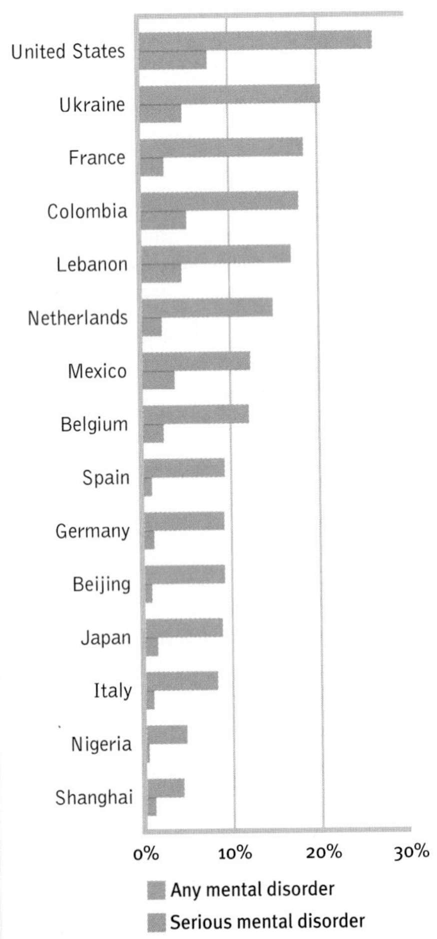

FIGURE 47.2 **Prior-year prevalence of disorders in selected areas** From World Health Organization (WHO, 2004a) interviews in 14 countries.

Who is most vulnerable to mental disorders? As we have seen, the answer varies with the disorder. One predictor of mental disorder, poverty, crosses ethnic and gender lines. The incidence of serious psychological disorders has been doubly high among those below the poverty line (CDC, 1992). Like so many other correlations, the poverty-disorder association raises a chicken-and-egg question: Does poverty cause disorders? Or do disorders cause poverty? It is both, though the answer varies with the disorder. Schizophrenia understandably leads to poverty. Yet the stresses and demoralization of poverty can also precipitate disorders, especially depression in women and substance abuse in men (Dohrenwend et al., 1992). In one natural experiment on the poverty-pathology link, researchers tracked rates of behavior problems in North Carolina Native American children as economic development enabled a dramatic reduction in their community's poverty rate. As the study began, children of poverty exhibited more deviant and aggressive behaviors. After four years, children whose families had moved above the poverty line exhibited a 40 percent decrease in the behavior problems, while those who continued in their previous positions below or above the poverty line exhibited no change (Costello et al., 2003).

TABLE 47.3

Risk and Protective Factors for Mental Disorders

Risk Factors	Protective Factors
Academic failure	Aerobic exercise
Birth complications	Community offering empowerment, opportunity, and security
Caring for chronically ill or patients with dementia	Economic independence
Child abuse and neglect	Effective parenting
Chronic insomnia	Feelings of mastery and control
Chronic pain	Feelings of security
Family disorganization or conflict	Literacy
Low birth weight	Positive attachment and early bonding
Low socioeconomic status	Positive parent-child relationships
Medical illness	Problem-solving skills
Neurochemical imbalance	Resilient coping with stress and adversity
Parental mental illness	Self-esteem
Parental substance abuse	Social and work skills
Personal loss and bereavement	Social support from family and friends
Poor work skills and habits	
Reading disabilities	
Sensory disabilities	
Social incompetence	
Stressful life events	
Substance abuse	
Trauma experiences	

Source: World Health Organization (WHO, 2004b,c).

As **TABLE 47.3** indicates, there is a wide range of risk and protective factors for mental disorders. At what times of life do disorders strike? Usually by early adulthood. "Over 75 percent of our sample with any disorder had experienced its first symptoms by age 24," reported Lee Robins and Darrel Regier (1991, p. 331). The symptoms of antisocial personality disorder and of phobias are among the earliest to appear, at a median age of 8 and 10, respectively. Symptoms of alcohol dependence, obsessive-compulsive disorder, bipolar disorder, and schizophrenia appear at a median age near 20. Major depression often hits somewhat later, at a median age of 25. Such findings make clear the need for research and treatment to help the growing number of people, especially teenagers and young adults, who suffer the bewilderment and pain of a psychological disorder.

Although mindful of the pain, we can also be encouraged by the many successful people—including Leonardo da Vinci, Isaac Newton, and Leo Tolstoy—who pursued brilliant careers while enduring psychological difficulties. So have 18 U.S. presidents, including the periodically depressed Abraham Lincoln, according to one psychiatric analysis of their biographies (Davidson et al., 2006). The bewilderment, fear, and sorrow caused by psychological disorders are real. But hope, too, is real.

RETRIEVAL PRACTICE

- What is the relationship between poverty and psychological disorders?

ANSWER: Poverty-related stresses can help trigger disorders, but disabling disorders can also contribute to poverty. Thus, poverty and disorder are often a chicken-and-egg situation, and it's hard to know which came first.

MODULE REVIEW

Introduction to Psychological Disorders

Learning Objectives

RETRIEVAL PRACTICE Take a moment to answer each of these Learning Objective Questions (repeated here from within the module). Then turn to Appendix B, Complete Module Reviews, to check your answers. Research suggests that trying to answer these questions on your own will improve your long-term retention (McDaniel et al., 2009).

47-1: How should we draw the line between normality and disorder?

47-2: Why is there controversy over attention-deficit hyperactivity disorder?

47-3: How do the medical model and the biopsychosocial approach understand psychological disorders?

47-4: How and why do clinicians classify psychological disorders?

47-5: Why do some psychologists criticize the use of diagnostic labels?

47-6: How many people suffer, or have suffered, from a psychological disorder? Is poverty a risk factor?

Terms and Concepts to Remember

RETRIEVAL PRACTICE Test yourself on these terms by trying to write down the definition before flipping back to the referenced page to check your answer.

psychological disorder, p. 626
attention-deficit hyperactivity disorder (ADHD), p. 627
medical model, p. 628
DSM-IV-TR, p. 630

RETRIEVAL PRACTICE Gain an advantage, and benefit from immediate feedback, with the interactive self-testing resources at www.worthpublishers.com/myers.

Anxiety Disorders

- Generalized Anxiety Disorder
- Panic Disorder
- Phobias
- Obsessive-Compulsive Disorder
- Post-Traumatic Stress Disorder
- Understanding Anxiety Disorders

48-1 What are the different anxiety disorders?

Anxiety is part of life. Speaking in front of a class, peering down from a ladder, or waiting to play in a big game, any one of us might feel anxious. At times we may feel enough anxiety to avoid making eye contact or talking with someone—"shyness," we call it. Fortunately for most of us, our uneasiness is not intense and persistent.

Some of us, however, are more prone to notice and remember threats (Mitte, 2008). This tendency may place us at risk for one of the **anxiety disorders,** marked by distressing, persistent anxiety or dysfunctional anxiety-inducing behaviors. Let's consider these five:

- ***Generalized anxiety disorder,*** in which a person is unexplainably and continually tense and uneasy
- ***Panic disorder,*** in which a person experiences sudden episodes of intense dread
- ***Phobias,*** in which a person is intensely and irrationally afraid of a specific object, activity, or situation
- ***Obsessive-compulsive disorder,*** in which a person is troubled by repetitive thoughts and/or actions
- ***Post-traumatic stress disorder,*** in which a person has lingering memories, nightmares, and other symptoms for weeks after a severely threatening, uncontrollable event

Snapshots

Obsessing about obsessive-compulsive disorder

Generalized Anxiety Disorder

For the past two years, Tom, a 27-year-old electrician, has been bothered by dizziness, sweating palms, heart palpitations, and ringing in his ears. He feels edgy and sometimes finds himself shaking. With reasonable success, he hides his symptoms from his family and co-workers. But he allows himself few other social contacts, and occasionally he has to leave work. His family doctor and a neurologist can find no physical problem.

Tom's unfocused, out-of-control, negative feelings suggest a **generalized anxiety disorder,** which is marked by pathological worry. The symptoms of this disorder are commonplace; their persistence, for six months or more, is not. People with this condition—two-thirds are women (McLean & Anderson, 2009)—worry continually, and they are often jittery, agitated, and sleep-deprived. Concentration is difficult as attention switches from worry to worry, and their tension and apprehension may leak out through furrowed brows, twitching eyelids, trembling, perspiration, or fidgeting.

One of generalized anxiety disorder's worst characteristics is that the person may not be able to identify, and therefore deal with or avoid, its cause. To use Sigmund Freud's term, the anxiety is *free-floating.* Generalized anxiety disorder is often accompanied by depressed mood, but even without depression it tends to be disabling (Hunt et al., 2004; Moffitt et al., 2007b). Moreover, it may lead to physical problems, such as high blood pressure.

Many people with generalized anxiety disorder were maltreated and inhibited as children (Moffitt et al., 2007a). As time passes, however, emotions tend to mellow, and by age 50, generalized anxiety disorder becomes fairly rare (Rubio & López-Ibor, 2007).

anxiety disorders psychological disorders characterized by distressing, persistent anxiety or maladaptive behaviors that reduce anxiety.

generalized anxiety disorder an anxiety disorder in which a person is continually tense, apprehensive, and in a state of autonomic nervous system arousal.

panic disorder an anxiety disorder marked by unpredictable, minutes-long episodes of intense dread in which a person experiences terror and accompanying chest pain, choking, or other frightening sensations.

Panic Disorder

Panic disorder is an anxiety tornado. It strikes suddenly, wreaks havoc, and disappears. For the 1 person in 75 with this disorder, anxiety suddenly escalates into a terrifying *panic attack*—a minutes-long episode of intense fear that something horrible is about to happen.

phobia an anxiety disorder marked by a persistent, irrational fear and avoidance of a specific object, activity, or situation.

obsessive-compulsive disorder (OCD) an anxiety disorder characterized by unwanted repetitive thoughts (obsessions) and/or actions (compulsions).

post-traumatic stress disorder (PTSD) an anxiety disorder characterized by haunting memories, nightmares, social withdrawal, jumpy anxiety, and/or insomnia that lingers for four weeks or more after a traumatic experience.

Heart palpitations, shortness of breath, choking sensations, trembling, or dizziness typically accompany the panic, which may be misperceived as a heart attack or other serious physical ailment. Smokers have at least a doubled risk of panic disorder (Zvolensky & Bernstein, 2005). Because nicotine is a stimulant, lighting up doesn't lighten up.

One woman recalled suddenly feeling "hot and as though I couldn't breathe. My heart was racing and I started to sweat and tremble and I was sure I was going to faint. Then my fingers started to feel numb and tingly and things seemed unreal. It was so bad I wondered if I was dying and asked my husband to take me to the emergency room. By the time we got there (about 10 minutes) the worst of the attack was over and I just felt washed out" (Greist et al., 1986).

Phobias

Phobias are anxiety disorders in which an irrational fear causes the person to avoid some object, activity, or situation. Many people accept their phobias and live with them, but others are incapacitated by their efforts to avoid the feared situation. Marilyn, an otherwise healthy and happy 28-year-old, fears thunderstorms so intensely that she feels anxious as soon as a weather forecaster mentions possible storms later in the week. If her husband is away and a storm is forecast, she may stay with a close relative. During a storm, she hides from windows and buries her head to avoid seeing the lightning.

Other *specific phobias* may focus on animals, insects, heights, blood, or close spaces (**FIGURE 48.1**). People avoid the stimulus that arouses the fear, hiding during thunderstorms or avoiding high places.

Not all phobias have such specific triggers. *Social phobia* is shyness taken to an extreme. Those with a social phobia, an intense fear of being scrutinized by others, avoid potentially embarrassing social situations, such as speaking up, eating out, or going to parties—or will sweat or tremble when doing so.

Much as fretting over insomnia may, ironically, cause insomnia, so worries about anxiety—perhaps fearing another panic attack, or fearing anxiety-caused sweating in public—can amplify anxiety symptoms (Olatunji & Wolitzky-Taylor, 2009). People who have experienced several panic attacks may come to avoid situations where the panic has struck before. If the fear is intense enough, it may become *agoraphobia*, fear or avoidance of situations in which escape might be difficult or help unavailable when panic strikes. Given such fear, people may avoid being outside the home, in a crowd, on a bus, or on an elevator.

After spending five years sailing the world, Charles Darwin began suffering panic disorder at age 28. Because of the attacks, he moved to the country, avoided social gatherings, and traveled only in his wife's company. But the relative seclusion did free him to focus on developing his evolutionary theory. "Even ill health," he reflected, "has saved me from the distraction of society and its amusements" (quoted in Ma, 1997).

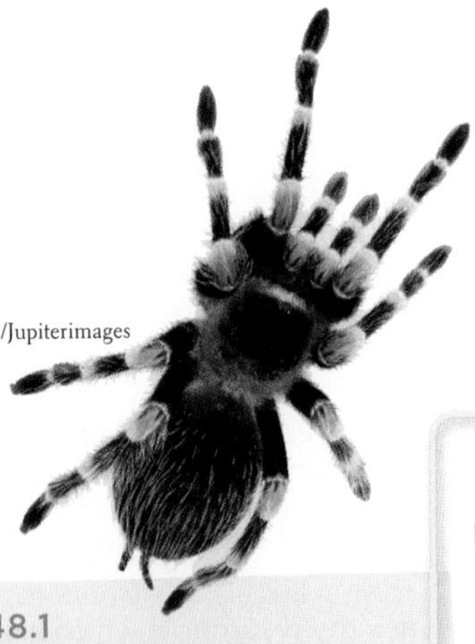

Martin Harvey/Jupiterimages

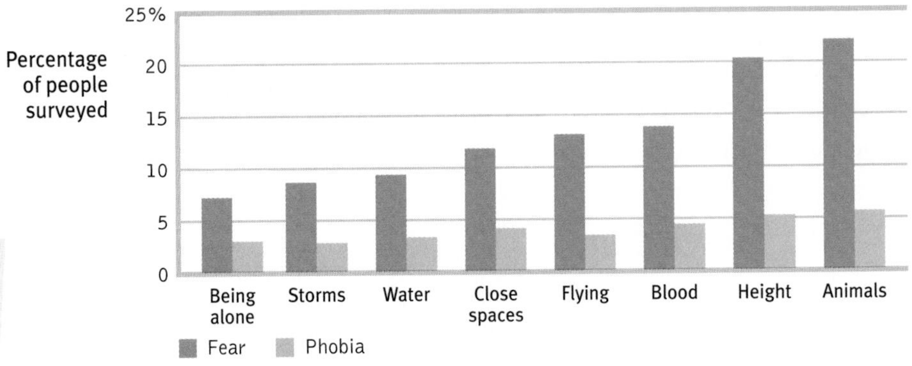

FIGURE 48.1
Some common and uncommon specific fears This national interview study identified the commonality of various specific fears. A strong fear becomes a phobia if it provokes a compelling but irrational desire to avoid the dreaded object or situation. (From Curtis et al., 1998.)

Obsessive-Compulsive Disorder

As with generalized anxiety and phobias, we can see aspects of **obsessive-compulsive disorder (OCD)** in our everyday behavior. We all may at times be obsessed with senseless or offensive thoughts that will not go away. Or we may engage in compulsive behaviors, perhaps lining up books and pencils "just so" before studying.

Obsessive thoughts and compulsive behaviors cross the fine line between normality and disorder when they persistently interfere with everyday living and cause distress. Checking to see you locked the door is normal; checking 10 times is not. Washing your hands is normal; washing so often that your skin becomes raw is not. (**TABLE 48.1** offers more examples.) At some time during their lives, often during their late teens or twenties, 2 to 3 percent of people cross that line from normal preoccupations and fussiness to debilitating disorder (Karno et al., 1988). Although the person knows them to be irrational, the anxiety-fueled obsessive thoughts become so haunting, the compulsive rituals so senselessly time-consuming, that effective functioning becomes impossible.

The New Yorker Collection, 2010, Joe Dator, from cartoonbank.com. All Rights Reserved

"Spin your partner round and round, then spin your partner round again, spin her round six more times, now touch the light switch near the door."

TABLE 48.1

Common Obsessions and Compulsions Among Children and Adolescents With Obsessive-Compulsive Disorder

Thought or Behavior	Percentage Reporting Symptom
Obsessions (repetitive *thoughts*)	
Concern with dirt, germs, or toxins	40
Something terrible happening (fire, death, illness)	24
Symmetry, order, or exactness	17
Compulsions (repetitive *behaviors*)	
Excessive hand washing, bathing, toothbrushing, or grooming	85
Repeating rituals (in/out of a door, up/down from a chair)	51
Checking doors, locks, appliances, car brakes, homework	46

Source: Adapted from Rapoport, 1989.

OCD is more common among teens and young adults than among older people (Samuels & Nestadt, 1997). A 40-year follow-up study of 144 Swedish people diagnosed with the disorder found that, for most, the obsessions and compulsions had gradually lessened, though only 1 in 5 had completely recovered (Skoog & Skoog, 1999).

Don't Touch Me As the title of his 2009 memoir indicates, comedian and TV host Howie Mandel has used humor to deal with the reality of mental disorders. Obsessive-compulsive disorder and a germ phobia prompted him to shave his head to "feel cleaner."

© Mario Anzvoni/Reuters/Corbis

Post-Traumatic Stress Disorder

As an Iraq war soldier, Jesse "saw the murder of children, women. It was just horrible for anyone to experience." After calling in a helicopter strike on one house where he had seen ammunition crates carried in, he heard the screams of children from within. "I didn't know there were kids there," he recalls. Back home in Texas, he suffered "real bad flashbacks" (Welch, 2005).

Our memories exist in part to protect us in the future. So there is biological wisdom in not being able to forget our most emotional or traumatic experiences—our greatest embarrassments, our worst accidents, our most horrid experiences. But sometimes, for some of us, the unforgettable takes over our lives. The complaints of battle-scarred veterans such as Jesse—recurring haunting memories and nightmares, a numbed social withdrawal, jumpy anxiety, insomnia—are typical of what once was called "shellshock" or "battle fatigue" and now is called **post-traumatic stress disorder (PTSD)** (Babson &

Bringing the war home During his three deployments to Iraq, this Marine Staff Sergeant suffered traumatic brain injury. After his return home, he was diagnosed with post-traumatic stress disorder. He regularly travels two hours each way with his wife to Bethesda Naval Hospital for psychiatric and medical appointments.

Feldner, 2010; Yufik & Simms, 2010). What defines and explains PTSD is less the event itself than the severity and persistence of the trauma memory (Rubin et al., 2008).

PTSD symptoms have also been reported by survivors of accidents, disasters, and violent and sexual assaults (including an estimated two-thirds of prostitutes) (Brewin et al., 1999; Farley et al., 1998; Taylor et al., 1998). A month after the 9/11 terrorist attacks, a survey of Manhattan residents indicated that 8.5 percent were suffering PTSD, most as a result of the attack (Galea et al., 2002). Among those living near the World Trade Center, 20 percent reported such telltale signs as nightmares, severe anxiety, and fear of public places (Susser et al., 2002).

To pin down the frequency of this disorder, the U.S. Centers for Disease Control (1988) compared 7000 Vietnam combat veterans with 7000 noncombat veterans who served during the same years. On average, according to a reanalysis, 19 percent of all Vietnam veterans reported PTSD symptoms. The rate varied from 10 percent among those who had never seen combat to 32 percent among those who had experienced heavy combat (Dohrenwend et al., 2006). Similar variations in rates have been found among more recent combat veterans and among people who have experienced a natural disaster or have been kidnapped, held captive, tortured, or raped (Brewin et al., 2000; Brody, 2000; Kessler, 2000; Stone, 2005; Yaffe et al., 2010).

The toll seems at least as high for veterans of the Iraq war, where 1 in 6 U.S. combat infantry personnel has reported symptoms of PTSD, depression, or severe anxiety in the months after returning home (Hoge et al., 2006, 2007). In one study of 103,788 veterans returning from Iraq and Afghanistan, 1 in 4 was diagnosed with a psychological disorder, most frequently PTSD (Seal et al., 2007).

So what determines whether a person suffers PTSD after a traumatic event? Research indicates that the greater one's emotional distress during a trauma, the higher the risk for post-traumatic symptoms (Ozer et al., 2003). Among New Yorkers who witnessed the 9/11 attacks, PTSD was doubled for survivors who were inside rather than outside the World Trade Center (Bonanno et al., 2006). And the more frequent an assault experience, the more adverse the long-term outcomes tend to be (Golding, 1999). In the 30 years after the Vietnam war, veterans who came home with a PTSD diagnosis had twice the normal likelihood of dying (Crawford et al., 2009).

A sensitive limbic system seems to increase vulnerability, by flooding the body with stress hormones again and again as images of the traumatic experience erupt into consciousness (Kosslyn, 2005; Ozer & Weiss, 2004). Brain scans of PTSD patients suffering memory flashbacks reveal an aberrant and persistent right temporal lobe activation (Engdahl et al., 2010). Genes may also play a role. Some combat-exposed men have identical twins who did not experience combat. But these nonexposed co-twins tend to share their brother's risk for cognitive difficulties, such as unfocused attention. Such findings suggest that some PTSD symptoms may actually be genetically predisposed (Gilbertson et al., 2006).

Some psychologists believe that PTSD has been overdiagnosed, due partly to a broadening definition of *trauma* (Dobbs, 2009; McNally, 2003). PTSD is actually infrequent, say those critics, and well-intentioned attempts to have people relive the trauma may exacerbate their emotions and pathologize normal stress reactions (Wakefield & Spitzer, 2002). "Debriefing" survivors right after a trauma by getting them to revisit the experience and vent emotions has actually proven generally ineffective and sometimes harmful (Bonanno et al., 2010).

Researchers have noted the impressive *survivor resiliency* of those who do *not* develop PTSD (Bonanno et al., 2010). About half of adults experience at least one traumatic event in their lifetime, but only about 1 in 10 women and 1 in 20 men develop PTSD (Olff et al., 2007; Ozer & Weiss, 2004; Tolin & Foa, 2006). More than 9 in 10 New Yorkers, although stunned and grief-stricken by 9/11, did *not* respond pathologically. By the following January, the stress symptoms of the rest had mostly subsided (Galea et al., 2002). Similarly, most combat-stressed veterans and most political dissidents who survive dozens of episodes of torture do not later exhibit PTSD (Mineka & Zinbarg, 1996). Likewise, the Holocaust survivors in 71 studies "showed remarkable resilience." Despite some lingering stress symptoms, most experienced essentially normal physical health and cognitive functioning (Barel et al., 2010).

Psychologist Peter Suedfeld (1998, 2000; Cassel & Suedfeld, 2006), who as a boy survived the Holocaust under deprived conditions while his mother died in Auschwitz, has documented the *resilience* of Holocaust survivors, most of whom have lived productive lives. "It is not always true that 'What doesn't kill you makes you stronger,' but it is often true," he reports. And "what doesn't kill you may reveal to you just how strong you really are."

A $125 million, five-year U.S. Army program is currently assessing the well-being of 800,000 soldiers and training them in emotional resilience (Stix, 2011).

Indeed, suffering can lead to "benefit finding" (Aspinwall & Tedeschi, 2010a,b; Helgeson et al., 2006), and to what Richard Tedeschi and Lawrence Calhoun (2004) call **post-traumatic growth.** Tedeschi and Calhoun have found that the struggle with challenging crises, such as facing cancer, often leads people later to report an increased appreciation for life, more meaningful relationships, increased personal strength, changed priorities, and a richer spiritual life. This idea—that suffering has transformative power—is also found in Judaism, Christianity, Hinduism, Buddhism, and Islam. The idea is confirmed by research with ordinary people. Compared with those with traumatic life histories and with those unchallenged by any significant adversity, people whose life history includes *some* adversity tend to enjoy better mental health and well-being (Seery et al., 2010). Out of even our worst experiences some good can come. Like the body, the mind has great recuperative powers and may grow stronger with exertion.

"'Tis an ill wind that blows no good."
English proverb

RETRIEVAL PRACTICE

- Unfocused tension, apprehension, and arousal is called ________ ________ disorder. If a person is focusing anxiety on specific feared objects or situations, that person may have a(n) ________. Those who express anxiety through unwanted repetitive thoughts or actions may have a(n) ________-________ disorder. Anxiety accompanied by recurring memories and nightmares, social withdrawal, and insomnia for weeks after a traumatic event may be diagnosed as ________-________ ________ disorder. Those who experience unpredictable periods of terror and intense dread, accompanied by frightening physical sensations, may be diagnosed with a(n) ________ disorder.

ANSWERS: generalized anxiety; phobia; obsessive-compulsive; post-traumatic stress; panic

Understanding Anxiety Disorders

48-2 How do the learning and biological perspectives explain anxiety disorders?

Anxiety is both a feeling and a cognition, a doubt-laden appraisal of one's safety or social skill. How do these anxious feelings and cognitions arise? Freud's psychoanalytic theory proposed that, beginning in childhood, people *repress* intolerable impulses, ideas, and feelings and that this submerged mental energy sometimes produces mystifying symptoms, such as anxiety. Today's psychologists have turned to two contemporary perspectives—learning and biological.

The Learning Perspective

Fear Conditioning

When bad events happen unpredictably and uncontrollably, anxiety often develops (Field, 2006; Mineka & Oehlberg, 2008). Decades of research on conditioning show that dogs learn to fear neutral stimuli associated with shock and that infants come to fear furry objects associated with frightening noises. Using classical conditioning, researchers have also created chronically anxious, ulcer-prone rats by giving them unpredictable electric shocks (Schwartz, 1984). Like assault victims who report feeling anxious when returning to the scene of the

post-traumatic growth positive psychological changes as a result of struggling with extremely challenging circumstances and life crises.

crime, the rats become apprehensive in their lab environment. This link between conditioned fear and general anxiety helps explain why anxious people are hyperattentive to possible threats, and how panic-prone people come to associate anxiety with certain cues (Bar-Haim et al., 2007; Bouton et al., 2001). In one survey, 58 percent of those with social phobia experienced their disorder after a traumatic event (Ost & Hugdahl, 1981).

Through conditioning, the short list of naturally painful and frightening events can multiply into a long list of human fears. My car was once struck by another whose driver missed a stop sign. For months afterward, I felt a twinge of unease when any car approached from a side street. Marilyn's phobia of thunderstorms (a phobia also shared by recording artist Madonna) may have been similarly conditioned during a terrifying or painful experience associated with a thunderstorm.

Two specific learning processes can contribute to such anxiety. The first, *stimulus generalization*, occurs, for example, when a person attacked by a fierce dog later develops a fear of *all* dogs. The second learning process, *reinforcement*, helps maintain our phobias and compulsions after they arise. Avoiding or escaping the feared situation reduces anxiety, thus reinforcing the phobic behavior. Feeling anxious or fearing a panic attack, a person may go inside and be reinforced by feeling calmer (Antony et al., 1992). Compulsive behaviors operate similarly. If washing your hands relieves your feelings of anxiety, you may wash your hands again when those feelings return.

Hemera Technologies/Jupiterimages

Observational Learning

We may also learn fear through observational learning—by observing others' fears. Susan Mineka (1985, 2002) sought to explain why nearly all monkeys reared in the wild fear snakes, yet lab-reared monkeys do not. Surely, most wild monkeys do not actually suffer snake bites. Do they learn their fear through observation? To find out, Mineka experimented with six monkeys reared in the wild (all strongly fearful of snakes) and their lab-reared offspring (virtually none of which feared snakes). After repeatedly observing their parents or peers refusing to reach for food in the presence of a snake, the younger monkeys developed a similar strong fear of snakes. When retested three months later, their learned fear persisted. Humans likewise learn fears by observing others (Olsson et al., 2007).

Cognition

Observational learning is not the only cognitive influence on anxiety. Our interpretations and irrational beliefs also make for anxiety. Whether we interpret the creaky sound in the old house simply as the wind or as a possible knife-wielding intruder determines whether we panic. People with anxiety disorder also tend to be *hypervigilant*. A pounding heart becomes a sign of a heart attack. A lone spider near the bed becomes a likely infestation. An everyday disagreement with a mate or boss spells possible doom for the relationship. Anxiety is especially common when people cannot switch off such intrusive thoughts and perceive a loss of control and a sense of helplessness (Franklin & Foa, 2011).

The Biological Perspective

There is, however, more to anxiety than conditioning, observational learning, and cognition. The biological perspective can help us understand why few people develop lasting phobias after suffering traumas, why we learn some fears more readily, and why some individuals are more vulnerable.

Natural Selection

We humans seem biologically prepared to fear threats faced by our ancestors. Our phobias focus on such specific fears: spiders, snakes, and other animals; close spaces and heights; storms and darkness. (Those fearless about these occasional threats were less

- ***With each new generation, depression is striking earlier (now often in the late teens) and affecting more people, with the highest rates in developed countries among young adults.*** This is true in Canada, the United States, England, France, Germany, Italy, Lebanon, New Zealand, Puerto Rico, and Taiwan (Collishaw et al., 2007; Cross-National Collaborative Group, 1992; Kessler et al., 2010; Twenge et al., 2008). In one study, 12 percent of Australian adolescents reported symptoms of depression (Sawyer et al., 2000). Most hid it from their parents; almost 90 percent of those parents perceived their depressed teen as *not* suffering depression. In North America, today's young adults are three times more likely than their grandparents to report having recently—or ever—suffered depression (despite the grandparents' many more years of being at risk). The increase appears partly authentic, but it may also reflect today's young adults' greater willingness to disclose depression.

"I see depression as the plague of the modern era."

Lewis Judd, former chief, National Institute of Mental Health, 2000

Today's researchers propose biological and cognitive explanations of depression, often combined in a biopsychosocial perspective.

The Biological Perspective

Genetic Influences

Mood disorders run in families. As one researcher noted, emotions are "postcards from our genes" (Plotkin, 1994). The risk of major depression and bipolar disorder increases if you have a parent or sibling with the disorder (Sullivan et al., 2000). If one identical twin is diagnosed with major depressive disorder, the chances are about 1 in 2 that at some time the other twin will be, too. If one identical twin has bipolar disorder, the chances are 7 in 10 that the other twin will at some point be diagnosed similarly. Among fraternal twins, the corresponding odds are just under 2 in 10 (Tsuang & Faraone, 1990). The greater similarity among identical twins holds even among twins reared apart (DiLalla et al., 1996). Summarizing the major twin studies (see **FIGURE 49.2**), one research team estimated the heritability (extent to which individual differences are attributable to genes) of major depression at 37 percent.

Moreover, adopted people who suffer a mood disorder often have close biological relatives who suffer mood disorders, become dependent on alcohol, or commit suicide (Wender et al., 1986). (Close-Up: Suicide and Self-Injury reports other research findings on the next page.)

To tease out the genes that put people at risk for depression, some researchers have turned to *linkage analysis*. After finding families in which the disorder appears across several generations, geneticists examine DNA from affected and unaffected family members, looking for differences. Linkage analysis points us to a chromosome neighborhood,

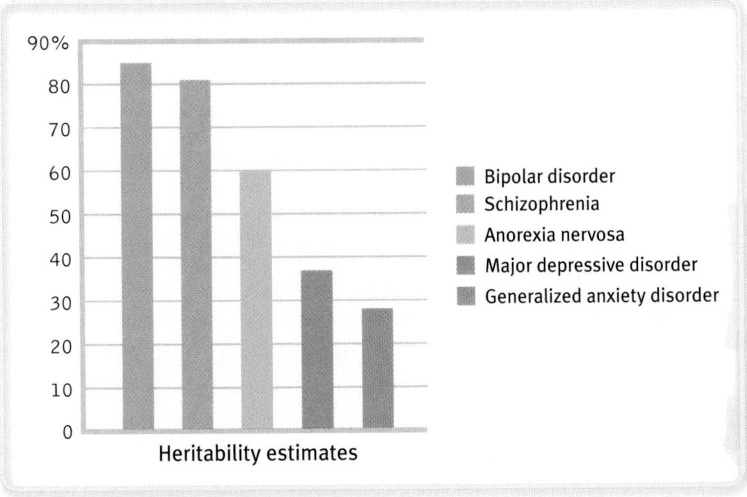

FIGURE 49.2
The heritability of various psychological disorders Researchers Joseph Bienvenu, Dimitry Davydow, and Kenneth Kendler (2011) aggregated data from studies of identical and fraternal twins to estimate the heritability of bipolar disorder, schizophrenia, anorexia nervosa, major depressive disorder, and generalized anxiety disorder.

CLOSE-UP

Suicide and Self-Injury

49-3 What factors affect suicide and self-injuring, and what are some of the important warning signs to watch for in suicide prevention efforts?

"But life, being weary of these worldly bars, Never lacks power to dismiss itself."

William Shakespeare, *Julius Caesar,* 1599

Each year nearly 1 million despairing people worldwide will elect a permanent solution to what might have been a temporary problem. Comparing the suicide rates of different groups, researchers have found

- ***national differences:*** Britain's, Italy's, and Spain's suicide rates are little more than half those of Canada, Australia, and the United States. Austria's and Finland's are about double (WHO, 2011). Within Europe, people in the most suicide-prone country (Belarus) have been 16 times more likely to kill themselves than those in the least (Georgia).
- ***racial differences:*** Within the United States, Whites kill themselves twice as often as Blacks (AAS, 2010).
- ***gender differences:*** Women are much more likely than men to attempt suicide (WHO, 2011). But men are two to four times more likely (depending on the country) to actually end their lives. Men use more lethal methods, such as firing a bullet into the head, the method of choice in 6 of 10 U.S. suicides.
- ***age differences and trends:*** In late adulthood, rates increase, peaking in middle age and beyond. In the last half of the twentieth century, the global rate of annual suicide deaths nearly doubled (WHO, 2008).
- ***other group differences:*** Suicide rates are much higher among the rich, the nonreligious, and those who are single, widowed, or divorced (Hoyer & Lund, 1993; Stack, 1992; Stengel, 1981). When facing an unsupportive environment, including family or peer rejection, gay and lesbian youth are at increased risk of attempting suicide (Goldfried, 2001; Haas et al., 2011; Hatzenbuehler, 2011).
- ***day of the week:*** 25 percent of suicides occur on Wednesdays (Kposowa & D'Auria, 2009).

The risk of suicide is at least five times greater for those who have been depressed than for the general population (Bostwick & Pankratz, 2000). People seldom commit suicide while in the depths of depression, when energy and initiative are lacking. The risk increases when they begin to rebound and become capable of following through. Compared with people who suffer no disorder, those with alcohol dependence are roughly 100 times more likely to commit suicide; some 3 percent of them do (Murphy & Wetzel, 1990; Sher, 2006).

Because suicide is so often an impulsive act, environmental barriers (such as jump barriers on high bridges and the unavailability of loaded guns) can reduce suicides (Anderson, 2008). Although common sense might suggest that a determined person would simply find another way to complete the act, such restrictions give time for self-destructive impulses to subside.

Social suggestion may trigger suicide. Following highly publicized suicides and TV programs featuring suicide, known suicides increase. So do fatal auto and private airplane "accidents." One six-year study tracked suicide cases among all 1.2 million people who lived in metropolitan Stockholm at any time during the 1990s (Hedström et al., 2008). Men exposed to a family suicide were 8 times more likely to commit suicide than were nonexposed men. Although that phenomenon may be partly attributable to family genes, shared genetic predispositions do not explain why men exposed to a co-worker's suicide were 3.5 times more likely to commit suicide, compared with nonexposed men.

Suicide is not necessarily an act of hostility or revenge. The elderly sometimes choose death as an alternative to current or future suffering. In people of all ages, suicide may be a way of switching off unendurable pain and relieving a perceived burden on family members. "People desire death when two fundamental needs are frustrated to the point of extinction," notes Thomas Joiner (2006, p. 47): "The need to belong with or connect to others, and the need to feel effective with or to influence others." Suicidal urges typically arise when people feel disconnected from others, and a burden to them (Joiner, 2010), or when they feel defeated and trapped by an inescapable situation (Taylor et al., 2011). Thus, suicide rates increase a bit during economic recessions (Luo et al., 2011). Suicidal thoughts also may increase when people are driven to reach a goal or standard—to become thin or straight or rich—and find it unattainable (Chatard & Selimbegovi, 2011).

In hindsight, families and friends may recall signs they believe should have forewarned them—verbal hints, giving possessions away, or withdrawal and preoccupation with death. To judge from surveys of 84,850 people across 17 nations, about 9 percent of people at some point in their lives have thought seriously of suicide. About 30 percent of these

note behavior genetics researchers Robert Plomin and Peter McGuffin (2003); "a house-to-house search is then needed to find the culprit gene." Such studies are reinforcing the view that depression is a complex condition. Many genes work together, producing a mosaic of small effects that interact with other factors to put some people at greater risk. If the culprit gene variations can be identified—with chromosome 3 genes implicated in separate British and American studies (Breen et al., 2011; Pergadia et al., 2011)—they may open the door to more effective drug therapy.

(3 percent of people) actually attempt it (Nock et al., 2008). For only about 1 in 25 does the attempt become their final act (AAS, 2009). Of those who die, one-third had tried to kill themselves previously. Most discussed it beforehand. So, if a friend talks suicide to you, it's important to listen and to direct the person to professional help. Anyone who threatens suicide is at least sending a signal of feeling desperate or despondent.

Non-Suicidal Self-Injury

Suicide is not the only way to send a message or deal with distress. Some people, especially adolescents and young adults, may engage in *non-suicidal self-injury (NSSI)* (**FIGURE 49.3**). Such behavior includes cutting or burning the skin, hitting oneself, pulling hair out, inserting objects under the nails or skin, and self-administered tattooing (Fikke et al., 2011).

Why do people hurt themselves? Those who do so tend to be less able to tolerate emotional distress, are extremely self-critical, and often have poor communication and problem-solving skills (Nock, 2010). They engage in NSSI to

- gain relief from intense negative thoughts through the distraction of pain,
- ask for help and gain attention,
- relieve guilt by self-punishment, or
- get others to change their negative behavior (bullying, criticism), or to fit in with a peer group.

Does NSSI lead to suicide? Usually not. Those who engage in NSSI are typically *suicide gesturers,* not *suicide attempters* (Nock & Kessler, 2006). Suicide gesturers engage in NSSI as a desperate but non-life-threatening form of communication or when they are feeling overwhelmed. But NSSI has been shown to be a risk factor for future suicide attempts (Wilkinson & Goodyer, 2011). If people do not find help, their non-suicidal behavior may escalate to thinking about suicide and finally, to attempted suicide.

FIGURE 49.3

Rates of nonfatal self-injury in the U.S. Self-injury rates peak higher for females than for males (CDC, 2009).

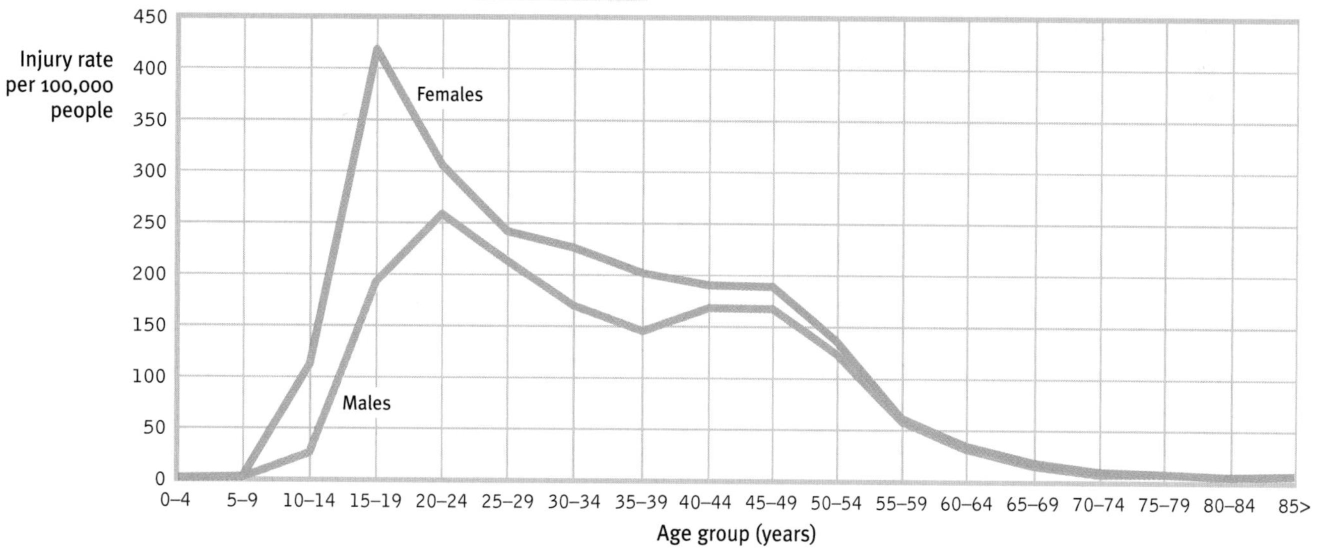

The Depressed Brain

Using modern technology, researchers are also gaining insight into brain activity during depressed and manic states, and into the effects of certain neurotransmitters during these states. One study gave 13 elite Canadian swimmers the wrenching experience of watching a video of the swim in which they failed to make the Olympic team or failed at the Olympic games (Davis et al., 2008). Functional MRI scans showed the disappointed swimmers experiencing brain-activity patterns akin to those of patients with depressed moods.

Courtesy of Lewis Baxter nd Michael E. Phelps, UCLA School of Medicine

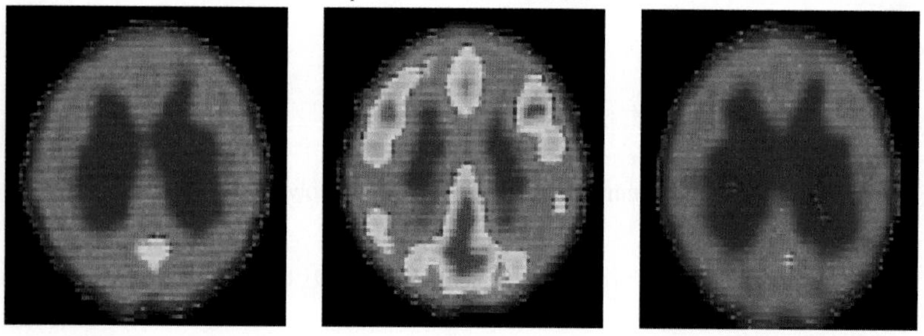

FIGURE 49.4
The ups and downs of bipolar disorder These top-facing PET scans show that brain energy consumption rises and falls with the patient's emotional switches. Red areas are where the brain rapidly consumes glucose.

Many studies have found diminished brain activity during slowed-down depressive states, and more activity during periods of mania (**FIGURE 49.4**). The left frontal lobe and an adjacent brain reward center are active during positive emotions, but less active during depressed states (Davidson et al., 2002; Heller et al., 2009). In one study of people with severe depression, MRI scans also found their frontal lobes 7 percent smaller than normal (Coffey et al., 1993). Other studies show that the *hippocampus,* the memory-processing center linked with the brain's emotional circuitry, is vulnerable to stress-related damage.

Bipolar disorder likewise correlates with brain structure. Neuroscientists have found structural differences, such as decreased axonal white matter or enlarged fluid-filled ventricles, in the brains of people with bipolar disorder (Kempton et al., 2008; van der Schot et al., 2009).

Neurotransmitter systems influence mood disorders. *Norepinephrine,* which increases arousal and boosts mood, is scarce during depression and overabundant during mania. (Drugs that alleviate mania reduce norepinephrine.) Many people with a history of depression also have a history of habitual smoking, and smoking increases one's risk for future depression (Pasco et al. 2008). This may indicate an attempt to self-medicate with inhaled nicotine, which can temporarily increase norepinephrine and boost mood (HMHL, 2002).

Researchers are also exploring a second neurotransmitter, *serotonin* (Carver et al., 2008). One well-publicized study of New Zealand young adults found that the recipe for depression combined two necessary ingredients—significant life stress plus a variation on a serotonin-controlling gene (Caspi et al., 2003; Moffitt et al., 2006). Depression arose from the interaction of an adverse environment plus a genetic susceptibility, but not from either alone. But stay tuned: The story of gene-environment interactions is still being written, as other researchers debate the reliability of this result (Caspi et al., 2010; Karg et al., 2011; Munafò et al., 2009; Risch et al., 2009; Uher & McGuffin, 2010).

Drugs that relieve depression tend to increase norepinephrine or serotonin supplies by blocking either their reuptake (as Prozac, Zoloft, and Paxil do with serotonin) or their chemical breakdown. Repetitive physical exercise, such as jogging, reduces depression as it increases serotonin (Ilardi et al., 2009; Jacobs, 1994). Boosting serotonin may promote recovery from depression by stimulating hippocampus neuron growth (Airan et al., 2007; Jacobs et al., 2000).

What's good for the heart is also good for the brain and mind. People who eat a heart-healthy "Mediterranean diet" (heavy on vegetables, fish, and olive oil) have a comparatively low risk of developing heart disease, late-life cognitive decline, and depression—all of which are associated with inflammation (Dowlati et al., 2010; Sánchez-Villegas et al., 2009; Tangney et al., 2011). Excessive alcohol use also correlates with depression—mostly because alcohol misuse *leads to* depression (Fergusson et al., 2009).

The Social-Cognitive Perspective

Depression is a whole-body disorder. Biological influences contribute to depression but don't fully explain it. The social-cognitive perspective explores the roles of thinking and acting.

Depressed people view life through the dark glasses of low self-esteem (Orth et al., 2009). Their intensely negative assumptions about themselves, their situation, and their future lead them to magnify bad experiences and minimize good ones. Listen to Norman, a Canadian college professor, recalling his depression:

> I [despaired] of ever being human again. I honestly felt subhuman, lower than the lowest vermin. Furthermore, I was self-deprecatory and could not understand why anyone would want to associate with me, let alone love me. . . . I was positive that I was a fraud and a phony and that I didn't deserve my Ph.D. I didn't deserve to have tenure; I didn't deserve to be a Full Professor. . . . I didn't deserve the research grants I had been awarded; I couldn't understand how I had written books and journal articles. . . . I must have conned a lot of people. (Endler, 1982, pp. 45–49)

Research reveals how *self-defeating beliefs* and a *negative explanatory style* feed depression's vicious cycle.

Michael Marsland

Susan Nolen-Hoeksema "This epidemic of morbid meditation is a disease that women suffer much more than men. Women can ruminate about anything and everything—our appearance, our families, our career, our health." (*Women Who Think Too Much: How to Break Free of Overthinking and Reclaim Your Life*, 2003)

Negative Thoughts and Negative Moods Interact

Self-defeating beliefs may arise from *learned helplessness*. Both dogs and humans act depressed, passive, and withdrawn after experiencing uncontrollable painful events. Learned helplessness is more common in women than in men, and women may respond more strongly to stress (Hankin & Abramson, 2001; Mazure et al., 2002; Nolen-Hoeksema, 2001, 2003). For example, 38 percent of women and 17 percent of men entering American colleges and universities report feeling at least occasionally "overwhelmed by all I have to do" (Pryor et al., 2006). (Men report spending more of their time in "light anxiety" activities such as sports, TV watching, and partying, possibly avoiding activities that might make them feel overwhelmed.) This may help explain why, beginning in their early teens, women are nearly twice as vulnerable to depression. Susan Nolen-Hoeksema (2003) believes women's higher risk of depression may also be related to what she describes as their tendency to *overthink*, to ruminate. Rumination—staying focused on a problem (thanks to the continuous firing of a frontal lobe area that sustains attention)—can be adaptive (Altamirano et al., 2010; Andrews & Thomson, 2009a,b). But when it is relentless, self-focused rumination diverts us from thinking about other life tasks and produces a negative emotional inertia (Kuppens et al., 2010).

But why do life's unavoidable failures lead only some people to become depressed? The answer lies partly in their *explanatory style*—who or what they blame for their failures. Think of how you might feel if you failed a test. If you can externalize the blame ("What an unfair test!"), you are more likely to feel angry. If you blame yourself, you probably will feel stupid and depressed.

> "I have learned to accept my mistakes by referring them to a personal history which was not of my making."
>
> B. F. Skinner (1983)

So it is with depressed people, who tend to explain bad events in terms that are *stable* ("It's going to last forever"), *global* ("It's going to affect everything I do"), and *internal* ("It's all my fault") (**FIGURE 49.5** on the next page). Depression-prone people respond to bad events in an especially self-focused, self-blaming way (Mor & Winquist, 2002; Pyszczynski et al., 1991; Wood et al., 1990a,b). Their self-esteem fluctuates more rapidly up with boosts and down with threats (Butler et al., 1994).

The result of these pessimistic, overgeneralized, self-blaming attributions may be a depressing sense of hopelessness (Abramson et al., 1989; Panzarella et al., 2006). As Martin Seligman has noted, "A recipe for severe depression is preexisting pessimism encountering failure" (1991, p. 78). What then might we expect of new college students who are not depressed but do exhibit a pessimistic explanatory style? Lauren Alloy and her collaborators (1999) monitored Temple University and University of Wisconsin students every 6 weeks for 2.5 years. Among those identified as having a pessimistic thinking style, 17 percent had a first episode of major depression, as did only 1 percent of those who began college with an optimistic thinking style.

The New Yorker Collection, 2009, William Haefeli, from cartoonbank.com. All Rights Reserved

"You should never engage in unsupervised introspection."

Seligman (1991, 1995) contends that depression is common among young Westerners because the rise of individualism and the decline of commitment to religion and family have forced young people to take personal responsibility for failure or rejection. In non-Western cultures, where close-knit relationships and cooperation are the norm, major depression is less common and less tied to self-blame over personal failure (WHO, 2004a).

FIGURE 49.5
Explanatory style and depression After a negative experience, a depression-prone person may respond with a negative explanatory style.

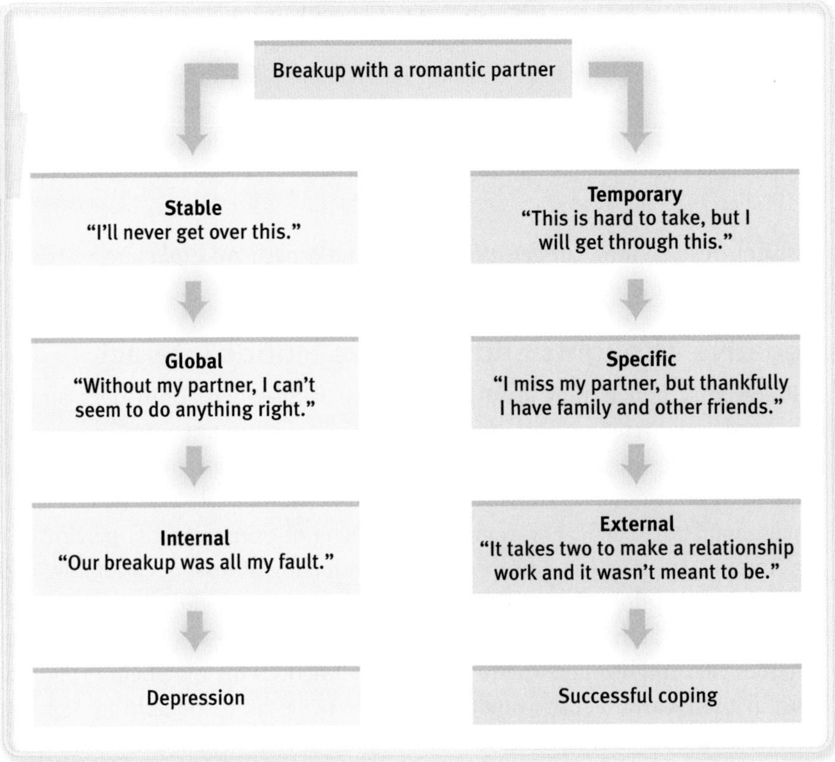

"Man never reasons so much and becomes so introspective as when he suffers, since he is anxious to get at the cause of his sufferings."
Luigi Pirandello, *Six Characters in Search of an Author*, 1922

In Japan, for example, depressed people instead tend to report feeling shame over letting others down (Draguns, 1990a).

There is, however, a chicken-and-egg problem with the social-cognitive explanation of depression. Self-defeating beliefs, negative attributions, and self-blame *coincide* with a depressed mood and are *indicators* of depression. But do they *cause* depression, any more than a speedometer's reading causes a car's speed? Before or after being depressed, people's thoughts are less negative. Perhaps this is because, in a phenomenon known as *state-dependent memory*, a depressed mood triggers negative thoughts. If you temporarily put people in a bad or sad mood, their memories, judgments, and expectations suddenly become more pessimistic.

Depression's Vicious Cycle

Depression, as we have seen, is often brought on by stressful experiences—losing a job, getting divorced or rejected, suffering physical trauma—by anything that disrupts our sense of who we are and why we are worthy human beings. This disruption in turn leads to brooding, which amplifies negative feelings. But being withdrawn, self-focused, and complaining can by itself elicit rejection (Furr & Funder, 1998; Gotlib & Hammen, 1992). In one study, researchers Stephen Strack and James Coyne (1983) noted that "depressed persons induced hostility, depression, and anxiety in others and got rejected. Their guesses that they were not accepted were not a matter of cognitive distortion." Indeed, people in the throes of depression are at high risk for divorce, job loss, and other stressful life events. Weary of the person's fatigue, hopeless attitude, and lethargy, a spouse may threaten to leave or a boss may begin to question the person's competence. (This provides another example of genetic-environmental interaction: People genetically predisposed to depression more often experience depressing events.) The losses and stress only serve to compound the original depression. Rejection and depression feed each other. Misery may love another's company, but company does not love another's misery.

"Some cause happiness wherever they go; others, whenever they go."
Irish writer Oscar Wilde (1854–1900)

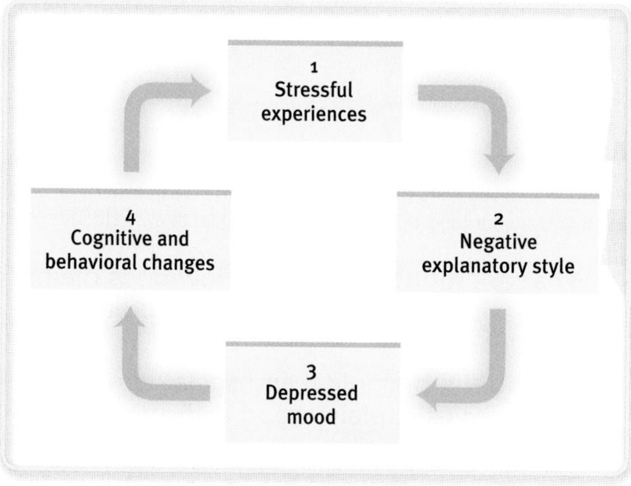

FIGURE 49.6
The vicious cycle of depressed thinking Cognitive therapists attempt to break this cycle by changing the way depressed people process events. Psychiatrists attempt to alter with medication the biological roots of persistently depressed moods.

We can now assemble some of the pieces of the depression puzzle (**FIGURE 49.6**): (1) Negative, stressful events interpreted through (2) a ruminating, pessimistic explanatory style create (3) a hopeless, depressed state that (4) hampers the way the person thinks and acts. This, in turn, fuels (1) negative, stressful experiences such as rejection.

None of us is immune to the dejection, diminished self-esteem, and negative thinking brought on by rejection or defeat. As Edward Hirt and his colleagues (1992) demonstrated, even small losses can temporarily sour our thinking. They studied some avid Indiana University basketball fans who seemed to regard the team as an extension of themselves. After the fans watched their team lose or win, the researchers asked them to predict the team's future performance and their own. After a loss, the morose fans offered bleaker assessments not only of the team's future but also of their own likely performance at throwing darts, solving anagrams, and getting a date. When things aren't going our way, it may seem as though they never will.

It is a cycle we can all recognize. Bad moods feed on themselves: When we *feel* down, we *think* negatively and remember bad experiences. On the brighter side, we can break the cycle of depression at any of these points—by moving to a different environment, by reversing our self-blame and negative attributions, by turning our attention outward, or by engaging in more pleasant activities and more competent behavior.

Winston Churchill called depression a "black dog" that periodically hounded him. Poet Emily Dickinson was so afraid of bursting into tears in public that she spent much of her adult life in seclusion (Patterson, 1951). As each of these lives reminds us, people can and do struggle through depression. Most regain their capacity to love, to work, and even to succeed at the highest levels.

RETRIEVAL PRACTICE

- What does it mean to say that "depression is a whole-body disorder"?

ANSWER: Many factors contribute to depression, including the biological influences of genetics and brain function. Social-cognitive factors also matter, including the interaction of explanatory style, mood, our responses to stressful experiences, and changes in our patterns of thinking and behaving. The whole body is involved.

MODULE REVIEW

Mood Disorders

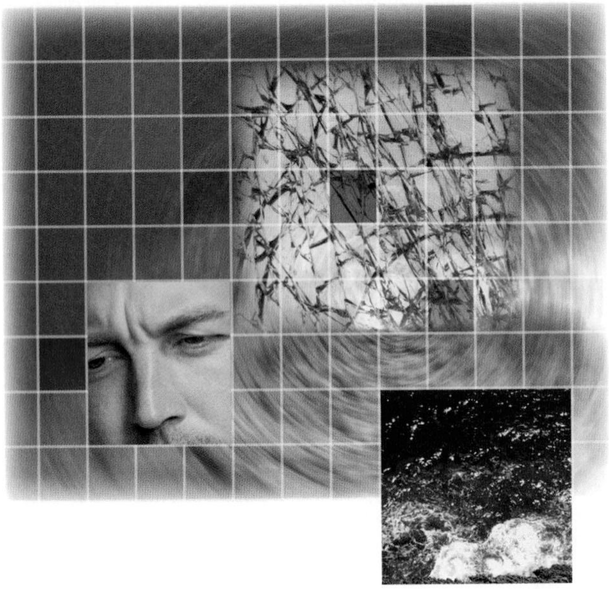

Learning Objectives

RETRIEVAL PRACTICE Take a moment to answer each of these Learning Objective Questions (repeated here from within the module). Then turn to Appendix B, Complete Module Reviews, to check your answers. Research suggests that trying to answer these questions on your own will improve your long-term retention (McDaniel et al., 2009).

49-1: What are mood disorders? How does major depressive disorder differ from bipolar disorder?

49-2: How do the biological and social-cognitive perspectives explain mood disorders?

49-3: What factors affect suicide and self-injuring, and what are some of the important warning signs to watch for in suicide prevention efforts?

Terms and Concepts to Remember

RETRIEVAL PRACTICE Test yourself on these terms by trying to write down the definition before flipping back to the referenced page to check your answer.

mood disorders, p. 645
major depressive disorder, p. 646
mania, p. 646
bipolar disorder, p. 646

RETRIEVAL PRACTICE Gain an advantage, and benefit from immediate feedback, with the interactive self-testing resources at www.worthpublishers.com/myers.

MODULE 50

Schizophrenia

- Symptoms of Schizophrenia
- Onset and Development of Schizophrenia
- Understanding Schizophrenia

Chronic schizophrenia is the cancer of psychological disorders. Nearly 1 in 100 people (about 60 percent men) will develop schizophrenia, joining the estimated 24 million across the world who suffer from one of humanity's most dreaded disorders (Abel et al., 2010; WHO, 2011).

Symptoms of Schizophrenia

50-1 What patterns of thinking, perceiving, feeling, and behaving characterize schizophrenia?

Literally translated, **schizophrenia** means "split mind." It refers *not* to a multiple-personality split but rather to a split from reality that shows itself in disorganized thinking, disturbed perceptions, and inappropriate emotions and actions. As such, it is the chief example of a **psychosis,** a disorder marked by irrationality and lost contact with reality.

schizophrenia a group of severe disorders characterized by disorganized and delusional thinking, disturbed perceptions, and inappropriate emotions and behaviors.

psychosis a psychological disorder in which a person loses contact with reality, experiencing irrational ideas and distorted perceptions.

delusions false beliefs, often of persecution or grandeur, that may accompany psychotic disorders.

Disorganized Thinking

Imagine trying to communicate with Maxine, a young woman whose thoughts spill out in no logical order. Her biographer, Susan Sheehan (1982, p. 25), observed her saying aloud to no one in particular, "This morning, when I was at Hillside [Hospital], I was making a movie. I was surrounded by movie stars. . . . I'm Mary Poppins. Is this room painted blue to get me upset? My grandmother died four weeks after my eighteenth birthday."

As this strange monologue illustrates, the thinking of a person with schizophrenia is fragmented, bizarre, and often distorted by false beliefs called **delusions** ("I'm Mary Poppins"). Those with *paranoid* tendencies are particularly prone to delusions of persecution. Even within sentences, jumbled ideas may create what is called *word salad.* One young man begged for "a little more allegro in the treatment," and suggested that "liberationary movement with a view to the widening of the horizon" will "ergo extort some wit in lectures."

Disorganized thoughts may result from a breakdown in *selective attention.* We normally have a remarkable capacity for giving our undivided attention to one set of sensory stimuli while filtering out others. Those with schizophrenia cannot do this. Thus, irrelevant, minute stimuli, such as the grooves on a brick or the inflections of a voice, may distract their attention from a bigger event or a speaker's meaning. As one former patient recalled, "What had happened to me . . . was a breakdown in the filter, and a hodge-podge of unrelated stimuli were distracting me from things which should have had my undivided attention" (MacDonald, 1960, p. 218). This selective-attention difficulty is but one of dozens of cognitive differences associated with schizophrenia (Reichenberg & Harvey, 2007).

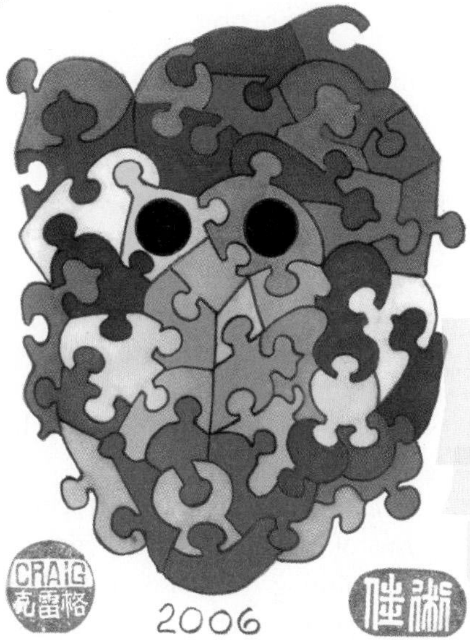

Art by someone diagnosed with schizophrenia Commenting on the kind of artwork shown here (from Craig Geiser's 2010 art exhibit in Michigan), poet and art critic John Ashbery wrote: "The lure of the work is strong, but so is the terror of the unanswerable riddles it proposes."

Craig Geiser

Disturbed Perceptions

A person with schizophrenia may have *hallucinations* (sensory experiences without sensory stimulation). They may see, feel, taste, or smell things that are not there. Most often, however, the hallucinations are auditory, frequently voices making insulting remarks or giving orders. The voices may tell the patient that she is bad or that she must burn herself with a cigarette lighter. Imagine your own reaction if a dream broke into your waking consciousness. When the unreal seems real, the resulting perceptions are at best bizarre, at worst terrifying.

"When someone asks me to explain schizophrenia I tell them, you know how sometimes in your dreams you are in them yourself and some of them feel like real nightmares? My schizophrenia was like I was walking through a dream. But everything around me was real. At times, today's world seems so boring and I wonder if I would like to step back into the schizophrenic dream, but then I remember all the scary and horrifying experiences."

Stuart Emmons, with Craig Geiser, Kalman J. Kaplan, and Martin Harrow, *Living With Schizophrenia,* 1997

Inappropriate Emotions and Actions

The expressed emotions of schizophrenia are often utterly inappropriate, split off from reality (Kring & Caponigro, 2010). Maxine laughed after recalling her grandmother's death. On other occasions, she cried when others laughed, or became angry for no apparent reason. Others with schizophrenia lapse into an emotionless state of *flat affect.* Most also have difficulty perceiving facial emotions and reading others' states of mind (Green & Horan, 2010; Kohler et al., 2010).

Motor behavior may also be inappropriate. Some perform senseless, compulsive acts, such as continually rocking or rubbing an arm. Others, who exhibit *catatonia,* may remain motionless for hours and then become agitated.

As you can imagine, such disorganized thinking, disturbed perceptions, and inappropriate emotions and actions profoundly disrupt social relationships and make it difficult to hold a job. During their most severe periods, those with schizophrenia live in a private inner world, preoccupied with illogical ideas and unreal images. Given a supportive environment and medication, over 40 percent of schizophrenia patients will have periods of a year or more of normal life experience (Jobe & Harrow, 2010). Many others remain socially withdrawn and isolated or rejected throughout much of their lives (Hooley, 2010).

Onset and Development of Schizophrenia

50-2 What are the schizophrenia subtypes? How do chronic and acute schizophrenia differ?

Schizophrenia typically strikes as young people are maturing into adulthood. It knows no national boundaries, and it affects both males and females—though men tend to be struck earlier, more severely, and slightly more often (Aleman et al., 2003; Picchioni & Murray, 2007). Studies of Swedish and Danish male populations reveal that thin young men, and those who were not breast-fed, are more vulnerable (Sørensen et al., 2005, 2006; Zammit et al., 2007).

For some, schizophrenia will appear suddenly, seemingly as a reaction to stress. For others, as was the case with Maxine, schizophrenia develops gradually, emerging from a long history of social inadequacy and poor school performance (MacCabe et al., 2008). No wonder those predisposed to schizophrenia often end up in the lower socioeconomic levels, or even homeless.

We have thus far described schizophrenia as if it were a single disorder. Actually, it is a cluster of disorders. The subtypes share some common features, but they also have some distinguishing symptoms (**TABLE 50.1**). Schizophrenia patients with *positive symptoms* may experience hallucinations, talk in disorganized and deluded ways, and exhibit inappropriate laughter, tears, or rage. Those with *negative symptoms* have toneless voices,

TABLE 50.1

Subtypes of Schizophrenia

Subtype	Symptoms
Paranoid	Preoccupation with delusions or hallucinations, often with themes of persecution or grandiosity
Disorganized	Disorganized speech or behavior, or flat or inappropriate emotion
Catatonic	Immobility (or excessive, purposeless movement), extreme negativism, and/or parrot-like repeating of another's speech or movements
Undifferentiated	Many and varied symptoms
Residual	Withdrawal, after hallucinations and delusions have disappeared

expressionless faces, or mute and rigid bodies. Thus, positive symptoms are the *presence* of inappropriate behaviors, and negative symptoms are the *absence* of appropriate behaviors. Because schizophrenia is a cluster of disorders, these varied symptoms could have more than one cause.

One rule holds true around the world: When schizophrenia is a slow-developing process (called *chronic*, or *process, schizophrenia*), recovery is doubtful (WHO, 1979). Those with chronic schizophrenia often exhibit the persistent and incapacitating negative symptom of withdrawal (Kirkpatrick et al., 2006). Men, whose schizophrenia develops on average four years earlier than women's, more often exhibit negative symptoms and chronic schizophrenia (Räsänen et al., 2000). When previously well-adjusted people develop schizophrenia rapidly (called *acute*, or *reactive schizophrenia*) following particular life stresses, recovery is much more likely. They more often have the positive symptoms that are more likely to respond to drug therapy (Fenton & McGlashan, 1991, 1994; Fowles, 1992).

Understanding Schizophrenia

Schizophrenia is not only the most dreaded psychological disorder but also one of the most heavily researched. Most of the new research studies link it with brain abnormalities and genetic predispositions. Schizophrenia is a disease of the brain manifest in symptoms of the mind.

Brain Abnormalities

50-3 How do brain abnormalities and viral infections help explain schizophrenia?

Might imbalances in brain chemistry underlie schizophrenia? Scientists have long known that strange behavior can have strange chemical causes. The saying "mad as a hatter" refers to the psychological deterioration of British hatmakers whose brains, it was later discovered, were slowly poisoned as they moistened the brims of mercury-laden felt hats with their tongue and lips (Smith, 1983). Similarly, scientists are clarifying the mechanism by which chemicals such as LSD produce hallucinations. These discoveries hint that schizophrenia symptoms might have a biochemical key.

Dopamine Overactivity

Researchers discovered one such key when they examined schizophrenia patients' brains after death and found an excess of receptors for the neurotransmitter *dopamine*—a sixfold excess for the so-called D4 dopamine receptor (Seeman et al., 1993; Wong et al., 1986).

They now speculate that such a hyper-responsive dopamine system may intensify brain signals in schizophrenia, creating positive symptoms such as hallucinations and paranoia (Grace, 2010). As we might therefore expect, drugs that block dopamine receptors often lessen these symptoms; drugs that increase dopamine levels, such as amphetamines and cocaine, sometimes intensify them (Seeman, 2007; Swerdlow & Koob, 1987).

Abnormal Brain Activity and Anatomy

Modern brain-scanning techniques reveal that many people with chronic schizophrenia have abnormal activity in multiple brain areas. Some have abnormally low brain activity in the frontal lobes, which are critical for reasoning, planning, and problem solving (Morey et al., 2005; Pettegrew et al., 1993; Resnick, 1992). People diagnosed with schizophrenia also display a noticeable decline in the brain waves that reflect synchronized neural firing in the frontal lobes (Spencer et al., 2004; Symond et al., 2005). Out-of-sync neurons may disrupt the integrated functioning of neural networks, possibly contributing to schizophrenia symptoms.

Most schizophrenia patients smoke, often heavily. Nicotine apparently stimulates certain brain receptors, which helps focus attention (Diaz et al., 2008; Javitt & Coyle, 2004).

One study took PET scans of brain activity while people were hallucinating (Silbersweig et al., 1995). When participants heard a voice or saw something, their brain became vigorously active in several core regions, including the thalamus, a structure deep in the brain that filters incoming sensory signals and transmits them to the cortex. Another PET scan study of people with paranoia found increased activity in the amygdala, a fear-processing center (Epstein et al., 1998).

Many studies have found enlarged, fluid-filled areas and a corresponding shrinkage and thinning of cerebral tissue in people with schizophrenia (Goldman et al., 2009; Wright et al., 2000). Some studies have even found such abnormalities in the brains of people who would *later* develop this disorder and in their close relatives (Karlsgodt et al., 2010). The greater the brain shrinkage, the more severe the thought disorder (Collinson et al., 2003; Nelson et al., 1998; Shenton, 1992). One smaller-than-normal area is the cortex. Another is the corpus callosum connection between the two hemispheres (Arnone et al., 2008). Another is the thalamus, which may explain why people with schizophrenia have difficulty filtering sensory input and focusing attention (Andreasen et al., 1994; Ellison-Wright et al., 2008). The bottom line of various studies is that schizophrenia involves not one isolated brain abnormality but problems with several brain regions and their interconnections (Andreasen, 1997, 2001).

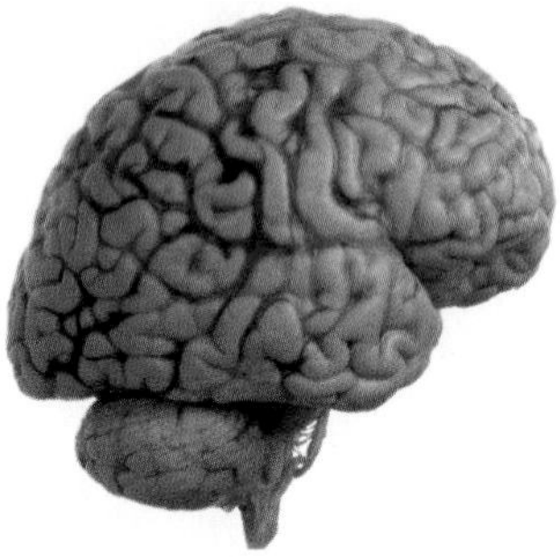

Ralph Hutchings/Visuals Unlimited, Inc.

Naturally, scientists wonder what causes these abnormalities. Some point to mishaps during prenatal development or delivery (Fatemi & Folsom, 2009; Walker et al., 2010). Risk factors for schizophrenia include low birth weight, maternal diabetes, older paternal age, and oxygen deprivation during delivery (King et al., 2010). Famine may also increase risks. People conceived during the peak of the Dutch wartime famine later displayed a doubled rate of schizophrenia, as did those conceived during the famine that occurred from 1959 to 1961 in eastern China (St. Clair et al., 2005; Susser et al., 1996).

Studying the neurophysiology of schizophrenia Psychiatrist E. Fuller Torrey is collecting the brains of hundreds of those who died as young adults and suffered disorders such as schizophrenia and bipolar disorder. Torrey is making tissue samples available to researchers worldwide.

Chris Usher

Maternal Virus During Midpregnancy

Consider another possible culprit: a midpregnancy viral infection that impairs fetal brain development (Patterson, 2007). Can you imagine some ways to test this fetal-virus idea? Scientists have asked the following:

- *Are people at increased risk of schizophrenia if, during the middle of their fetal development, their country experienced a flu epidemic?* The repeated answer is *Yes* (Mednick et al., 1994; Murray et al., 1992; Wright et al., 1995).
- *Are people born in densely populated areas, where viral diseases spread more readily, at greater risk for schizophrenia?* The answer, confirmed in a study of 1.75 million Danes, is *Yes* (Jablensky, 1999; Mortensen, 1999).
- *Are those born during the winter and spring months—after the fall-winter flu season—also at increased risk?* Although the increase is small, just 5 to 8 percent, the answer is again *Yes* (Fox, 2010; Torrey et al., 1997, 2002).
- *In the Southern Hemisphere, where the seasons are the reverse of the Northern Hemisphere, are the months of above-average schizophrenia births similarly reversed?* Again, the answer is *Yes*, though somewhat less so. In Australia, for example, people born between August and October are at greater risk—*unless* they migrated from the Northern Hemisphere, in which case their risk is greater if they were born between January and March (McGrath et al., 1995, 1999).
- *Are mothers who report being sick with influenza during pregnancy more likely to bear children who develop schizophrenia?* In one study of nearly 8000 women, the answer was *Yes*. The schizophrenia risk increased from the customary 1 percent to about 2 percent—but only when infections occurred during the second trimester (Brown et al., 2000). Maternal influenza infection during pregnancy also affects brain development in monkeys (Short et al., 2010).
- *Does blood drawn from pregnant women whose offspring develop schizophrenia show higher-than-normal levels of antibodies that suggest a viral infection?* In one study of 27 women whose children later developed schizophrenia, the answer was *Yes* (Buka et al., 2001). And the answer was again *Yes* in a huge California study, which collected blood samples from some 20,000 pregnant women during the 1950s and 1960s (Brown et al., 2004). Another study found traces of a specific retrovirus (HERV) in nearly half of people with schizophrenia and virtually none in healthy people (Perron et al., 2008).

These converging lines of evidence suggest that fetal-virus infections play a contributing role in the development of schizophrenia. They also strengthen the recommendation that "women who will be more than three months pregnant during the flu season" have a flu shot (CDC, 2003).

Why might a second-trimester maternal flu bout put fetuses at risk? Is it the virus itself? The mother's immune response to it? Medications taken? (Wyatt et al., 2001). Does the infection weaken the brain's supportive glial cells, leading to reduced synaptic connections (Moises et al., 2002)? In time, answers may become available.

Genetic Factors

50-4 Are there genetic influences on schizophrenia? What factors may be early warning signs of schizophrenia in children?

Fetal-virus infections do appear to increase the odds that a child will develop schizophrenia. But this theory cannot tell us why only 2 percent of women who catch the flu during their second trimester of pregnancy bear children who develop schizophrenia. Might people also inherit a predisposition to this disorder? The evidence strongly suggests that, *Yes*, some

FIGURE 50.1
Risk of developing schizophrenia The lifetime risk of developing schizophrenia varies with one's genetic relatedness to someone having this disorder. Across countries, barely more than 1 in 10 fraternal twins, but some 5 in 10 identical twins, share a schizophrenia diagnosis. (Adapted from Gottesman, 2001.)

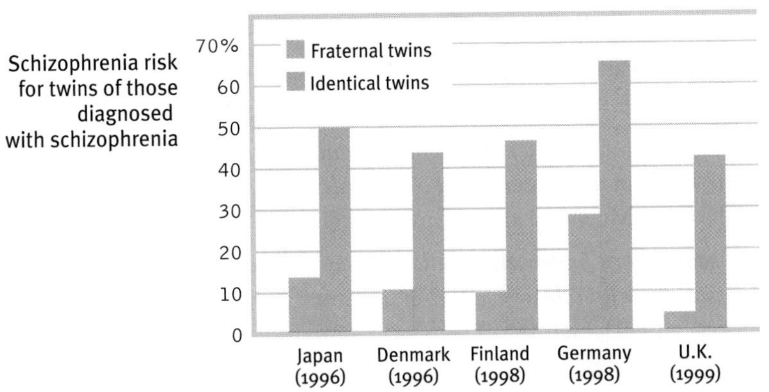

do. The nearly 1-in-100 odds of any person's being diagnosed with schizophrenia become about 1 in 10 among those whose sibling or parent has the disorder, and close to 1 in 2 if the affected sibling is an identical twin (**FIGURE 50.1**). Although only a dozen or so such cases are on record, the co-twin of an identical twin with schizophrenia retains that 1-in-2 chance even when the twins are reared apart (Plomin et al., 1997).

Remember, though, that identical twins also share a prenatal environment. About two-thirds also share a placenta and the blood it supplies; the other one-third have two single placentas. If an identical twin has schizophrenia, the co-twin's chances of being similarly afflicted are 6 in 10 if they shared a placenta. If they had separate placentas, as do fraternal twins, the chances are only 1 in 10 (Davis et al., 1995a,b; Phelps et al., 1997). Twins who share a placenta are more likely to experience the same prenatal viruses. So it is possible that shared germs as well as shared genes produce identical twin similarities.

Adoption studies, however, confirm that the genetic link is real (Gottesman, 1991). Children adopted by someone who develops schizophrenia seldom "catch" the disorder. Rather, adopted children have an elevated risk if a *biological* parent is diagnosed with schizophrenia.

With the genetic factor established, researchers are now sleuthing specific genes that, in some combination, might predispose schizophrenia-inducing brain abnormalities (Levinson et al., 2011; Mitchell & Porteous, 2011; Vacic et al., 2011; Wang et al., 2010). (It is not our genes but our brains that directly control our behavior.) Some of these genes influence the effects of dopamine and other neurotransmitters in the brain. Others affect the production of *myelin*, a fatty substance that coats the axons of nerve cells and lets impulses travel at high speed through neural networks.

Although the genetic contribution to schizophrenia is beyond question, the genetic formula is not as straightforward as the inheritance of eye color. Genome studies of thousands of individuals with and without schizophrenia indicate that schizophrenia is influenced by many genes, each with very small effects (International Schizophrenia Consortium, 2009; Pogue-Geile & Yokley, 2010). And genes are not always "turned on": *Epigenetic* (literally "in addition to genetic") factors influence gene expression. Like hot water activating the tea bag, environmental factors such as viral infections, nutritional deprivation, and maternal stress can "turn on" the genes that predispose schizophrenia. Identical twins' differing histories in the womb and beyond explain why only one of them may show differing gene expressions (Walker et al., 2010). As we have so often seen, nature and nurture interact. Neither hand claps alone.

Thanks to our expanding understanding of genetic and brain influences on maladies such as schizophrenia, the general public more and more attributes psychiatric disorders to biological factors (Pescosolido

Schizophrenia in identical twins When twins differ, only the one afflicted with schizophrenia typically has enlarged, fluid-filled cranial cavities (right) (Suddath et al., 1990). The difference between the twins implies some nongenetic factor, such as a virus, is also at work.

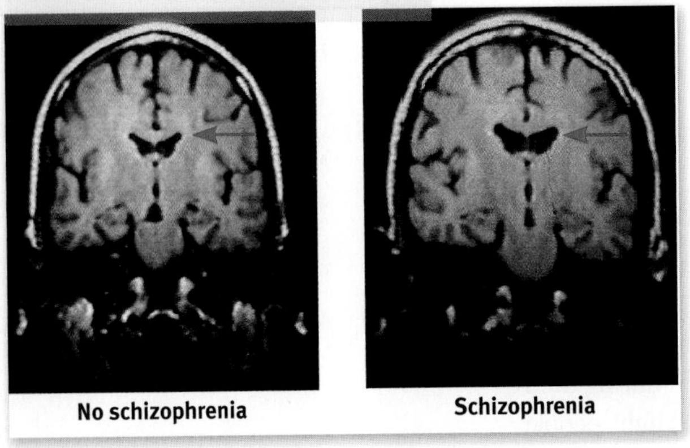

Both photos: Courtesy of Daniel R. Weinberger, M.D., NIH-NIMH/NSC

et al., 2010). In 2007, one privately funded new research center announced its ambitious aim: "To unambiguously diagnose patients with psychiatric disorders based on their DNA sequence in 10 years' time" (Holden, 2007). In 2010, $120 million in start-up funding launched a bold new effort to study the neuroscience and genetics of schizophrenia and other psychiatric disorders (Kaiser, 2010). So, can scientists develop genetic tests that reveal who is at risk? If so, will people in the future subject their embryos to genetic testing (and gene repair or abortion) if they are at risk for this or some other psychological or physical malady? Might they take their egg and sperm to a genetics lab for screening before combining them to produce an embryo? Or will children be tested for genetic risks and given appropriate preventive treatments? In this brave new twenty-first-century world, such questions await answers.

Courtesy of Genain family

The Genain quadruplets The odds of any four people picked at random all being diagnosed with schizophrenia are 1 in 100 million. But genetically identical sisters Nora, Iris, Myra, and Hester Genain all have the disease. Two of the sisters have more severe forms of the disorder than the others, suggesting the influence of environmental as well as biological factors.

Psychological Factors

If prenatal viruses and genetic predispositions do not, by themselves, cause schizophrenia, neither do family or social factors alone. It remains true, as Susan Nicol and Irving Gottesman (1983) noted almost three decades ago, that "no environmental causes have been discovered that will invariably, or even with moderate probability, produce schizophrenia in persons who are not related to" a person with schizophrenia.

Hoping to identify environmental triggers of schizophrenia, several investigators are following the development of "high-risk" children, such as those born to a parent with schizophrenia or exposed to prenatal risks (Freedman et al., 1998; Olin & Mednick, 1996; Susser, 1999). One study followed 163 teens and early-twenties adults who had two relatives with schizophrenia. During the 2.5-year study, the 20 percent who developed schizophrenia displayed some tendency to withdraw socially and behave oddly before the onset of the disorder (Johnstone et al., 2005). By comparing the experiences of high-risk and low-risk children who do versus do not develop schizophrenia, researchers have so far pinpointed the following possible early warning signs:

- A mother whose schizophrenia was severe and long-lasting
- Birth complications, often involving oxygen deprivation and low birth weight
- Separation from parents
- Short attention span and poor muscle coordination
- Disruptive or withdrawn behavior
- Emotional unpredictability
- Poor peer relations and solo play

* * *

Most of us can relate more easily to the ups and downs of mood disorders than to the strange thoughts, perceptions, and behaviors of schizophrenia. Sometimes our thoughts do jump around, but in the absence of disorder we do not talk nonsensically. Occasionally we feel unjustly suspicious of someone, but we do not fear that the world is plotting against us. Often our perceptions err, but rarely do we see or hear things that are not there. We have felt regret after laughing at someone's misfortune, but we rarely giggle in response to bad news. At times we just want to be alone, but we do not live in social isolation. However, millions of people around the world do talk strangely, suffer delusions, hear nonexistent voices, see things that are not there, laugh or cry at inappropriate times, or withdraw into private imaginary worlds. The quest to solve the cruel puzzle of schizophrenia therefore continues, and more vigorously than ever.

RETRIEVAL PRACTICE

- A person with schizophrenia who has __________ (positive/negative) symptoms may have an expressionless face and toneless voice. These symptoms are most common with __________ (chronic/acute) schizophrenia and are not likely to respond to drug therapy. Those with __________ (positive/negative) symptoms are likely to experience delusions and to be diagnosed with __________ (chronic/acute) schizophrenia, which is much more likely to respond to drug therapy.

ANSWERS: negative; chronic; positive; acute

- What factors contribute to the onset and development of schizophrenia?

ANSWER: Biological factors include abnormalities in brain structure and function, prenatal exposure to a maternal virus, and genetic factors. However, schizophrenia is more likely to develop given a high-risk environment.

MODULE REVIEW

Schizophrenia

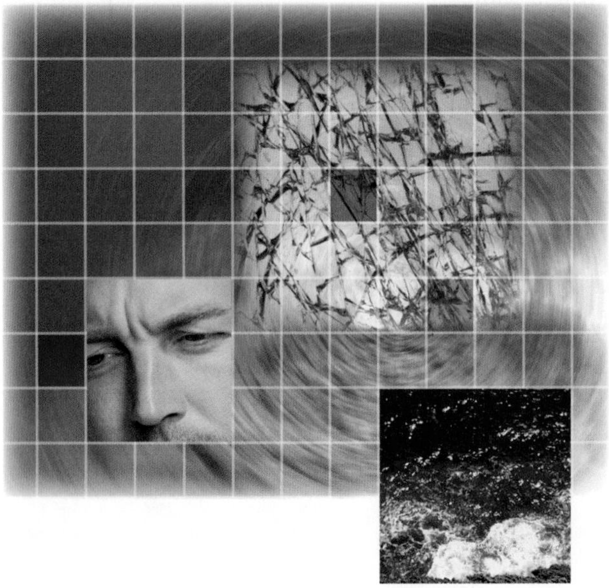

Learning Objectives

RETRIEVAL PRACTICE Take a moment to answer each of these Learning Objective Questions (repeated here from within the module). Then turn to Appendix B, Complete Module Reviews, to check your answers. Research suggests that trying to answer these questions on your own will improve your long-term retention (McDaniel et al., 2009).

50-1: What patterns of thinking, perceiving, feeling, and behaving characterize schizophrenia?

50-2: What are the schizophrenia subtypes? How do chronic and acute schizophrenia differ?

50-3: How do brain abnormalities and viral infections help explain schizophrenia?

50-4: Are there genetic influences on schizophrenia? What factors may be early warning signs of schizophrenia in children?

Terms and Concepts to Remember

RETRIEVAL PRACTICE Test yourself on these terms by trying to write down the definition before flipping back to the referenced page to check your answer.

schizophrenia, p. 657
psychosis, p. 657
delusions, p. 657

MODULE 51

Dissociative, Personality, and Eating Disorders

- Dissociative Disorders
- Personality Disorders
- Eating Disorders

Dissociative Disorders

51-1 What are dissociative disorders, and why are they controversial?

Among the most bewildering disorders are the rare **dissociative disorders.** These are disorders of consciousness, in which a person appears to experience a sudden loss of memory or change in identity, often in response to an overwhelmingly stressful situation. One Vietnam veteran who was haunted by his comrades' deaths, and who had left his World Trade Center office shortly before the 9/11 attack, disappeared en route to work one day and was discovered six months later in a Chicago homeless shelter, reportedly with no memory of his identity or family (Stone, 2006). In such "fugue state" cases, the person's conscious awareness is said to *dissociate* (become separated) from painful memories, thoughts, and feelings. (Note that this explanation presumes the existence of repressed memories, which have been questioned by memory researchers.)

Dissociation itself is not so rare. Now and then, many people may have a sense of being unreal, of being separated from their body, of watching themselves as if in a movie. Sometimes we may say, "I was not myself at the time." Perhaps you can recall getting up to go somewhere and ending up at some unintended location while your mind was preoccupied elsewhere. Or perhaps you can play a well-practiced tune on a guitar or piano while talking to someone. Facing trauma, dissociative detachment may actually protect a person from being overwhelmed by emotion.

Dissociative Identity Disorder

A massive dissociation of self from ordinary consciousness characterizes those with **dissociative identity disorder (DID),** in which two or more distinct identities are said to alternately control the person's behavior. Each personality has its own voice and mannerisms. Thus, the person may be prim and proper one moment, loud and flirtatious the next. Typically, the original personality denies any awareness of the other(s).

Mary Evans/C20TH FOX/TWENTIETH CENTURY FOX/Ronald Grant/Everett Collection

Multiple personalities Chris Sizemore's story, told in the book and movie, *The Three Faces of Eve,* gave early visibility to what is now called *dissociative identity disorder.*

dissociative disorders disorders in which conscious awareness becomes separated (dissociated) from previous memories, thoughts, and feelings.

dissociative identity disorder (DID) a rare dissociative disorder in which a person exhibits two or more distinct and alternating personalities. Formerly called *multiple personality disorder.*

AP/Wide World Photos

The "Hillside Strangler" Kenneth Bianchi is shown here at his trial.

People diagnosed with DID (formerly called *multiple personality disorder*) are usually not violent, but cases have been reported of dissociations into a "good" and a "bad" (or aggressive) personality—a modest version of the Dr. Jekyll/Mr. Hyde split immortalized in Robert Louis Stevenson's story. One unusual case involved Kenneth Bianchi, accused in the "Hillside Strangler" rapes and murders of 10 California women. During a hypnosis session with Bianchi, psychologist John Watkins (1984) "called forth" a hidden personality: "I've talked a bit to Ken, but I think that perhaps there might be another part of Ken that . . . maybe feels somewhat differently from the part that I've talked to. . . . Would you talk with me, Part, by saying, 'I'm here'?" Bianchi answered "Yes" and then claimed to be "Steve."

Speaking as Steve, Bianchi stated that he hated Ken because Ken was nice and that he (Steve), aided by a cousin, had murdered women. He also claimed Ken knew nothing about Steve's existence and was innocent of the murders. Was Bianchi's second personality a ruse, simply a way of disavowing responsibility for his actions? Indeed, Bianchi—a practiced liar who had read about multiple personality in psychology books—was later convicted.

Understanding Dissociative Identity Disorder

Skeptics question whether DID is a genuine disorder or an extension of our normal capacity for personality shifts. Nicholas Spanos (1986, 1994, 1996) asked college students to pretend they were accused murderers being examined by a psychiatrist. Given the same hypnotic treatment Bianchi received, most spontaneously expressed a second personality. This discovery made Spanos wonder: Are dissociative identities simply a more extreme version of our capacity to vary the "selves" we present—as when we display a goofy, loud self while hanging out with friends, and a subdued, respectful self around grandparents? Are clinicians who discover multiple personalities merely triggering role playing by fantasy-prone people? Do these patients, like actors who commonly report "losing themselves" in their roles, then convince themselves of the authenticity of their own role enactments? Spanos was no stranger to this line of thinking. In a related research area, he had also raised these questions about the hypnotic state. Given that most DID patients are highly hypnotizable, whatever explains one condition—dissociation or role playing—may help explain the other.

"Pretense may become reality."
Chinese proverb

Skeptics also find it suspicious that the disorder is so localized in time and space. Between 1930 and 1960, the number of DID diagnoses in North America was 2 per decade. In the 1980s, when the *Diagnostic and Statistical Manual* contained the first formal code for this disorder, the number of reported cases had exploded to more than 20,000 (McHugh, 1995a). The average number of displayed personalities also mushroomed—from 3 to 12 per patient (Goff & Simms, 1993). Outside North America, the disorder is much less prevalent, although in other cultures some people are said to be "possessed" by an alien spirit (Aldridge-Morris, 1989; Kluft, 1991). In Britain, DID—which some have considered "a wacky American fad" (Cohen, 1995)—is rare. In India and Japan, it is essentially nonexistent (or at least unreported).

Such findings, skeptics say, point to a cultural phenomenon—a disorder created by therapists in a particular social context (Merskey, 1992). Rather than being provoked by trauma, dissociative symptoms tend to be exhibited by suggestible, fantasy-prone people (Giesbrecht et al., 2008, 2010). Patients do not enter therapy saying "Allow me to introduce myselves." Rather, note these skeptics, some therapists go fishing for multiple personalities: "Have you ever felt like another part of you does things you can't control? Does this part of you have a name? Can I talk to the angry part of you?" Once patients permit a therapist to talk, by name, "to the part of you that says those angry things," they begin acting out the fantasy. Like actors who lose themselves in their roles, vulnerable patients may "become" the parts they are acting out. The result may be the experience of another self.

© The New Yorker Collection, 2001, Leo Cullum from cartoonbank.com. All Rights Reserved.

"Would it be possible to speak with the personality that pays the bills?"

Other researchers and clinicians believe DID is a real disorder. They find support for this view in the distinct brain and body states associated with differing personalities (Putnam, 1991). Handedness, for example, sometimes switches with personality

(Henninger, 1992). Ophthalmologists have detected shifting visual acuity and eye-muscle balance as patients switched personalities, changes that did not occur among control group members trying to simulate DID (Miller et al., 1991). Dissociative disorder patients also have exhibited heightened activity in brain areas associated with the control and inhibition of traumatic memories (Elzinga et al., 2007).

Researchers and clinicians have interpreted DID symptoms from psychodynamic and learning perspectives. Both views agree that the symptoms are ways of dealing with anxiety. Psychodynamic theorists see them as defenses against the anxiety caused by the eruption of unacceptable impulses; a wanton second personality enables the discharge of forbidden impulses. Learning theorists see dissociative disorders as behaviors reinforced by anxiety reduction.

Other clinicians include dissociative disorders under the umbrella of post-traumatic disorders—a natural, protective response to "histories of childhood trauma" (Putnam, 1995; Spiegel, 2008). Many DID patients recall suffering physical, sexual, or emotional abuse as children (Gleaves, 1996; Lilienfeld et al., 1999). In one study of 12 murderers diagnosed with DID, 11 had suffered severe, torturous child abuse (Lewis et al., 1997). One was set afire by his parents. Another was used in child pornography and was scarred from being made to sit on a stove burner. Some critics wonder, however, whether vivid imagination or therapist suggestion contributes to such recollections (Kihlstrom, 2005).

So the debate continues. On one side are those who believe multiple personalities are the desperate efforts of the traumatized to detach from a horrific existence. On the other are the skeptics who think DID is a condition contrived by fantasy-prone, emotionally vulnerable people, and constructed out of the therapist-patient interaction. If the skeptics' view wins, predicted psychiatrist Paul McHugh (1995b), "this epidemic will end in the way that the witch craze ended in Salem. The [multiple personality phenomenon] will be seen as manufactured."

personality disorders psychological disorders characterized by inflexible and enduring behavior patterns that impair social functioning.

"Though this be madness, yet there is method in 't."

William Shakespeare, *Hamlet*, 1600

RETRIEVAL PRACTICE

- The psychodynamic and learning perspectives agree that dissociative identity disorder symptoms are ways of dealing with anxiety. How do their explanations differ?

ANSWER: The psychodynamic explanation of DID symptoms is that they are defenses against anxiety generated by unacceptable urges. The learning perspective attempts to explain these symptoms as behaviors that have been reinforced by relieving anxiety in the past.

Personality Disorders

51-2 What are the three clusters of personality disorders? What behaviors and brain activity characterize the antisocial personality?

Some dysfunctional behavior patterns impair people's social functioning without depression or delusions. Among them are **personality disorders**—disruptive, inflexible, and enduring behavior patterns that impair one's social functioning. Anxiety is a feature of one cluster of these disorders, such as a fearful sensitivity to rejection that predisposes the withdrawn *avoidant personality disorder.* A second cluster expresses eccentric or odd behaviors, such as the emotionless disengagement of the *schizoid personality disorder.* A third cluster exhibits dramatic or impulsive behaviors, such as the attention-getting *histrionic personality disorder* and the self-focused and self-inflating *narcissistic personality disorder.* The personality disorders categories are not sharply distinguished, however, and some are slated to be revised or eliminated in the next DSM revision (Holden, 2010).

EPA/Jeff Tuttle/Landov

No remorse Dennis Rader, known as the "BTK killer" in Kansas, was convicted in 2005 of killing 10 people over a 30-year span. Rader exhibited the extreme lack of conscience that marks antisocial personality disorder.

Many criminals, like this one, exhibit a sense of conscience and responsibility in other areas of their life, and thus do not exhibit antisocial personality disorder.

© The New Yorker Collection, 2007, Leo Cullum from cartoonbank.com. All Rights Reserved.

"Thursday is out. I have jury duty."

Antisocial Personality Disorder

The most troubling and heavily researched personality disorder is the **antisocial personality disorder.** The person (sometimes called a *sociopath* or a *psychopath*) is typically a male whose lack of conscience becomes plain before age 15, as he begins to lie, steal, fight, or display unrestrained sexual behavior (Cale & Lilienfeld, 2002). About half of such children become antisocial adults—unable to keep a job, irresponsible as a spouse and parent, and assaultive or otherwise criminal (Farrington, 1991). When the antisocial personality combines a keen intelligence with amorality, the result may be a charming and clever con artist, a ruthless corporate executive (*Snakes in Suits* is a book on antisocial behavior in business)—or worse.

Despite their remorseless and sometimes criminal behavior, criminality is not an essential component of antisocial behavior (Skeem & Cooke, 2010). Moreover, many criminals do not fit the description of antisocial personality disorder. Why? Because they actually show responsible concern for their friends and family members.

Antisocial personalities behave impulsively, and then feel and fear little (Fowles & Dindo, 2009). The results sometimes are horrifying, as they were in the case of Henry Lee Lucas. He killed his first victim when he was 13. He felt little regret then or later. He confessed that, during his 32 years of crime, he had brutally beaten, suffocated, stabbed, shot, or mutilated some 360 women, men, and children. For the last 6 years of his reign of terror, Lucas teamed with Elwood Toole, who reportedly slaughtered about 50 people he "didn't think was worth living anyhow" (Darrach & Norris, 1984).

Understanding Antisocial Personality Disorder

Antisocial personality disorder is woven of both biological and psychological strands. No single gene codes for a complex behavior such as crime, but twin and adoption studies reveal that biological relatives of those with antisocial and unemotional tendencies are at increased risk for antisocial behavior (Larsson et al., 2007; Livesley & Jang, 2008). Molecular geneticists have identified some specific genes that are more common in those with antisocial personality disorder (Gunter et al., 2010). The genetic vulnerability of people with antisocial and unemotional tendencies appears as a fearless approach to life. Awaiting aversive events, such as electric shocks or loud noises, they show little autonomic nervous system arousal (Hare, 1975; van Goozen et al., 2007). Long-term studies have shown that their levels of stress hormones were lower than average when they were youngsters, before committing any crime (**FIGURE 51.1**). Three-year-olds who are slow to develop conditioned fears are later more likely to commit a crime (Gao et al., 2010).

FIGURE 51.1
Cold-blooded arousability and risk of crime Levels of the stress hormone adrenaline were measured in two groups of 13-year-old Swedish boys. In both stressful and nonstressful situations, those who would later be convicted of a crime as 18- to 26-year-olds showed relatively low arousal. (From Magnusson, 1990.)

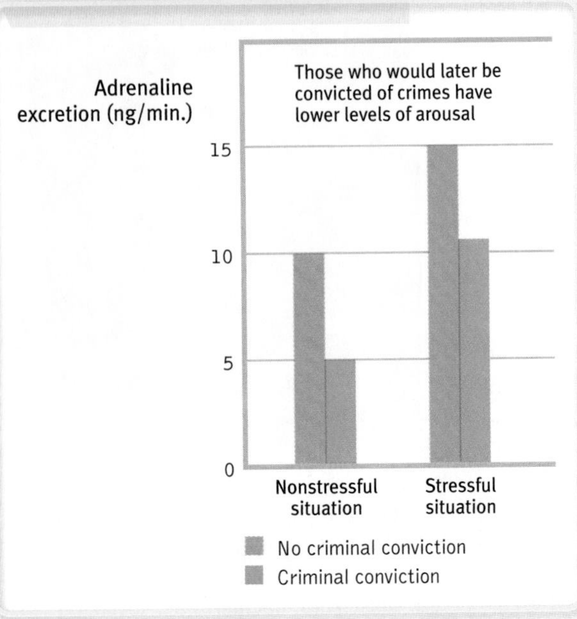

Other studies have found that preschool boys who later became aggressive or antisocial adolescents tended to be impulsive, uninhibited, unconcerned with social rewards, and low in anxiety (Caspi et al., 1996; Tremblay et al., 1994). If channeled in more productive directions, such fearlessness may lead to courageous heroism, adventurism, or star-level athleticism (Poulton & Milne, 2002). Lacking a sense of social responsibility, the same disposition may produce a cool con artist or killer (Lykken, 1995). The genes that put people at risk for antisocial behavior also put people at risk for dependence on alcohol and other drugs, which helps explain why these disorders often appear in combination (Dick, 2007).

Genetic influences, often in combination with child abuse, help wire the brain (Dodge, 2009). Adrian Raine (1999, 2005) compared PET scans of 41 murderers' brains with those from people of similar age and sex. Raine found

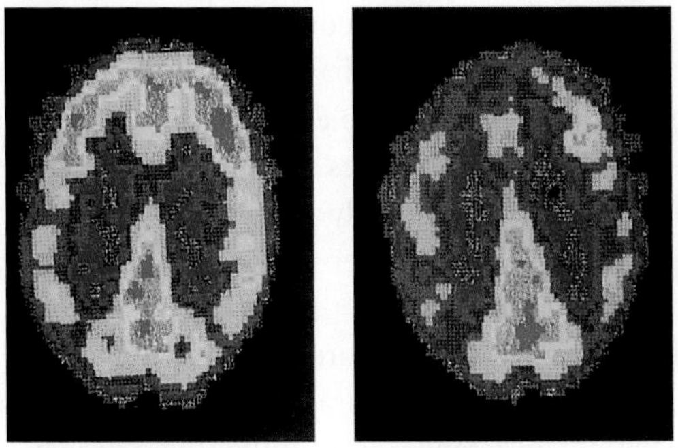

Courtesy of Adrian Raine, University of Southern California

FIGURE 51.2
Murderous minds These top-facing PET scans illustrate reduced activation (less red and yellow) in a murderer's frontal cortex—a brain area that helps brake impulsive, aggressive behavior. (From Raine, 1999.)

reduced activity in the murderers' frontal lobes, an area of the cortex that helps control impulses (**FIGURE 51.2**). This reduction was especially apparent in those who murdered impulsively. In a follow-up study, Raine and his team (2000) found that violent repeat offenders had 11 percent less frontal lobe tissue than normal. This helps explain why people with antisocial personality disorder exhibit marked deficits in frontal lobe cognitive functions, such as planning, organization, and inhibition (Morgan & Lilienfeld, 2000). Compared with people who feel and display empathy, their brains also respond less to facial displays of others' distress (Deeley et al., 2006).

antisocial personality disorder a personality disorder in which a person (usually a man) exhibits a lack of conscience for wrongdoing, even toward friends and family members. May be aggressive and ruthless or a clever con artist.

A biologically based fearlessness, as well as early environment, helps explain the reunion of long-separated sisters Joyce Lott, 27, and Mary Jones, 29—in a South Carolina prison where both were sent on drug charges. After a newspaper story about their reunion, their long-lost half-brother Frank Strickland called. He explained it would be a while before he could come see them—because he, too, was in jail, on drug, burglary, and larceny charges (Shepherd et al., 1990).

Genetics alone is hardly the whole story of antisocial crime, however. A study of criminal tendencies among young Danish men illustrates the usefulness of a complete biopsychosocial perspective. Another Adrian Raine-led study (1996) checked criminal records on nearly 400 men at ages 20 to 22, knowing that these men either had experienced biological risk factors at birth (such as premature birth) or came from family backgrounds marked by poverty and family instability. The researchers then compared each of these two groups with a third *biosocial* group whose lives were marked by *both* the biological and social risk factors. The biosocial group had double the risk of committing crime (**FIGURE 51.3**). Similar findings emerged from a famous study

Does a full Moon trigger "madness" in some people? James Rotton and I. W. Kelly (1985) examined data from 37 studies that related lunar phase to crime, homicides, crisis calls, and mental hospital admissions. Their conclusion: There is virtually no evidence of "Moon madness." Nor does lunar phase correlate with suicides, assaults, emergency room visits, or traffic disasters (Martin et al., 1992; Raison et al., 1999).

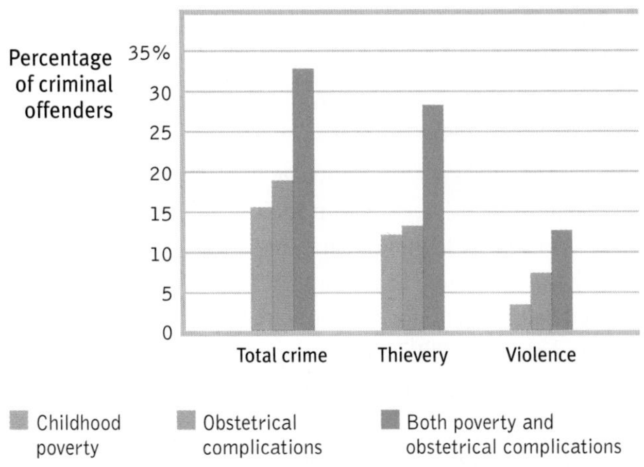

FIGURE 51.3
Biopsychosocial roots of crime Danish male babies whose backgrounds were marked both by obstetrical complications and social stresses associated with poverty were twice as likely to be criminal offenders by ages 20 to 22 as those in either the biological or social risk groups. (From Raine et al., 1996.)

that followed 1037 children for a quarter-century: Two combined factors—childhood maltreatment and a gene that altered neurotransmitter balance—predicted antisocial problems (Caspi et al., 2002). Neither "bad" genes alone nor a "bad" environment alone predisposed later antisocial behavior. Rather, genes predisposed some children to be more sensitive to maltreatment. Within "genetically vulnerable segments of the population," environmental influences matter—for better or for worse (Belsky et al., 2007; Moffitt, 2005).

With antisocial behavior, as with so much else, nature and nurture interact and together leave their marks on the brain. To explore the neural basis of antisocial disorder, neuroscientists are identifying brain activity differences in criminals who display antisocial personality disorder. Shown emotionally evocative photographs, such as a man holding a knife to a woman's throat, they display blunted heart rate and perspiration responses, and less activity in brain areas that typically respond to emotional stimuli (Harenski et al., 2010; Kiehl & Buckholtz, 2010). They also display a hyper-reactive dopamine reward system that predisposes their impulsive drive to do something rewarding, despite the consequences (Buckholtz et al., 2010). Such data provide another reminder: Everything psychological is also biological.

RETRIEVAL PRACTICE

- How do biological and psychological factors contribute to antisocial personality disorder?

ANSWER: Twin and adoption studies show that biological relatives of people with this disorder are at increased risk for antisocial behavior. Negative environmental factors, such as poverty or childhood abuse, may channel genetic traits such as fearlessness in more dangerous directions—toward aggression and away from social responsibility.

Eating Disorders

51-3 How do anorexia nervosa, bulimia nervosa, and binge-eating disorder demonstrate the influence of psychological forces?

Our bodies are naturally disposed to maintain a normal weight, including stored energy reserves for times when food becomes unavailable. Yet sometimes psychological influences overwhelm biological wisdom. This becomes painfully clear in three eating disorders.

- **Anorexia nervosa** typically begins as a weight-loss diet. People with anorexia—usually adolescents and 9 out of 10 times females—drop significantly (typically 15 percent or more) below normal weight. Yet they feel fat, fear gaining weight, remain obsessed with losing weight, and sometimes exercise excessively. About half of those with anorexia display a binge-purge-depression cycle.
- **Bulimia nervosa** may also be triggered by a weight-loss diet, broken by gorging on forbidden foods. Binge-purge eaters—mostly women in their late teens or early twenties—eat the way some people with alcohol dependence drink—in spurts, sometimes influenced by friends who are bingeing (Crandall, 1988). In a cycle of repeating episodes, overeating is followed by compensatory purging (through vomiting or laxative use) or fasting (Wonderlich et al., 2007). Preoccupied with food (craving sweet and high-fat foods), and fearful of becoming overweight, binge-purge eaters experience bouts of depression and anxiety during and following binges (Hinz & Williamson, 1987; Johnson et al., 2002). Unlike anorexia, bulimia is marked by weight fluctuations within or above normal ranges, making the condition easy to hide.

anorexia nervosa an eating disorder in which a person (usually an adolescent female) maintains a starvation diet despite being significantly (15 percent or more) underweight.

bulimia nervosa an eating disorder in which a person alternates binge eating (usually of high-calorie foods) with purging (by vomiting or laxative use) or fasting.

binge-eating disorder significant binge-eating episodes, followed by distress, disgust, or guilt, but without the compensatory purging or fasting that marks bulimia nervosa.

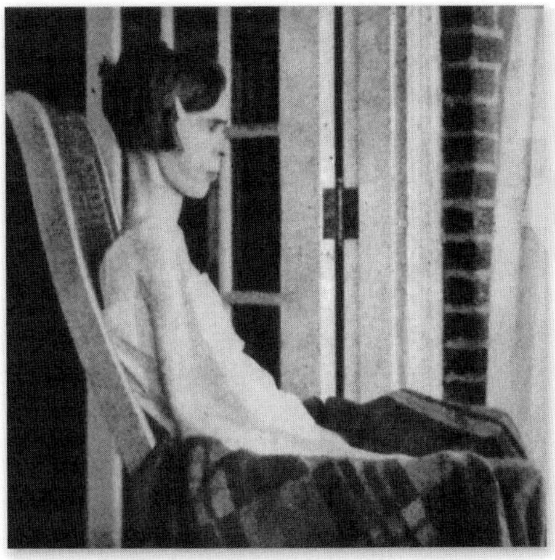

Reprinted by permission of *The New England Journal of Medicine*, 207, (Oct. 5, 1932), 613–617.

Dying to be thin Anorexia was identified and named in the 1870s, when it appeared among affluent adolescent girls (Brumberg, 2000). This 1930s photo illustrates the physical condition.

- Those who do significant binge eating, followed by remorse—but do not purge or fast—are said to have **binge-eating disorder.**

A national study funded by the U.S. National Institute of Mental Health reported that, at some point during their lifetime, 0.6 percent of people meet the criteria for anorexia, 1 percent for bulimia, and 2.8 percent for binge-eating disorder (Hudson et al., 2007). So, how can we explain these disorders?

Eating disorders do *not* provide (as some have speculated) a telltale sign of childhood sexual abuse (Smolak & Murnen, 2002; Stice, 2002). The family environment may provide a fertile ground for the growth of eating disorders in other ways, however.

- Mothers of girls with eating disorders tend to focus on their own weight and on their daughters' weight and appearance (Pike & Rodin, 1991).
- Families of bulimia patients have a higher-than-usual incidence of childhood obesity and negative self-evaluation (Jacobi et al., 2004).
- Families of anorexia patients tend to be competitive, high-achieving, and protective (Pate et al., 1992; Yates, 1989, 1990).

© Julie Ridge/iStockphoto

A too-fat body image underlies anorexia.

Those with eating disorders often have low self-evaluations, set perfectionist standards, fret about falling short of expectations, and are intensely concerned with how others perceive them (Pieters et al., 2007; Polivy & Herman, 2002; Sherry & Hall, 2009). Some of these factors also predict teen boys' pursuit of unrealistic muscularity (Ricciardelli & McCabe, 2004).

Genetics also influence susceptibility to eating disorders. Twins are more likely to share the disorder if they are identical rather than fraternal (Culbert et al., 2009; Klump et al., 2009; Root et al., 2010). Scientists are now searching for culprit genes, which may influence the body's available serotonin and estrogen (Klump & Culbert, 2007).

But these disorders also have cultural and gender components. Ideal shapes vary across culture and time. In impoverished areas of the world, including much of Africa—where plumpness means prosperity and thinness can signal poverty or illness—bigger seems better (Knickmeyer, 2001; Swami et al., 2010). Bigger does not seem better in Western cultures, where, according to 222 studies of 141,000 people, the rise in eating disorders over the last 50 years has coincided with a dramatic increase in women having a poor body image (Feingold & Mazzella, 1998).

Those most vulnerable to eating disorders are also those (usually women or gay men) who most idealize thinness and have the greatest body dissatisfaction (Feldman & Meyer, 2010; Kane, 2010; Stice et al., 2010). Should it surprise us, then, that when women

"Skeletons on Parade" A newspaper article used this headline in criticizing super-thin models. Do such models make self-starvation fashionable?

Reuters/Philippe Wojazer

view real and doctored images of unnaturally thin models and celebrities, they often feel ashamed, depressed, and dissatisfied with their own bodies—the very attitudes that predispose eating disorders (Grabe et al., 2008; Myers & Crowther, 2009; Tiggeman & Miller, 2010)? Eric Stice and his colleagues (2001) tested this modeling idea by giving some adolescent girls (but not others) a 15-month subscription to an American teen-fashion magazine. Compared with their counterparts who had not received the magazine, vulnerable girls—defined as those who were already dissatisfied, idealizing thinness, and lacking social support—exhibited increased body dissatisfaction and eating disorder tendencies. But even ultra-thin models do not reflect the impossible standard of the classic Barbie doll, who had, when adjusted to a height of 5 feet 7 inches, a 32–16–29 figure (in centimeters, 82–41–73) (Norton et al., 1996).

"Why do women have such low self-esteem? There are many complex psychological and societal reasons, by which I mean Barbie."

Dave Barry, 1999

It seems clear that the sickness of today's eating disorders lies in part within our weight-obsessed culture—a culture that says, in countless ways, "Fat is bad," that motivates millions of women to be "always dieting," and that encourages eating binges by pressuring women to live in a constant state of semistarvation. If cultural learning contributes to eating behavior, then might prevention programs increase acceptance of one's body? Reviews of prevention studies answer *Yes*, and especially if the programs are interactive and focused on girls over age 15 (Stice et al., 2007; Vocks et al., 2010).

RETRIEVAL PRACTICE

- People with __________ (anorexia nervosa/bulimia nervosa) continue to want to lose weight even when they are underweight. Those with __________ (anorexia nervosa/bulimia nervosa) tend to have weight that fluctuates within or above normal ranges.

ANSWERS: anorexia nervosa; bulimia nervosa

into her angry impulses and her defenses against anger. An interpersonal therapist would concur, but would also engage her thinking on more immediate issues—how she could balance work and home, resolve the dispute with her husband, and express her emotions more effectively (Markowitz et al., 1998).

psychodynamic therapy therapy deriving from the psychoanalytic tradition that views individuals as responding to unconscious forces and childhood experiences, and that seeks to enhance self-insight.

insight therapies a variety of therapies that aim to improve psychological functioning by increasing a person's awareness of underlying motives and defenses.

client-centered therapy a humanistic therapy, developed by Carl Rogers, in which the therapist uses techniques such as active listening within a genuine, accepting, empathic environment to facilitate clients' growth. (Also called *person-centered therapy.*)

active listening empathic listening in which the listener echoes, restates, and clarifies. A feature of Rogers' client-centered therapy.

Humanistic Therapies

52-3 What are the basic themes of humanistic therapy? What are the specific goals and techniques of Rogers' client-centered approach?

The *humanistic* perspective has emphasized people's inherent potential for self-fulfillment. Like psychodynamic therapies, humanistic therapies have attempted to reduce growth-impeding inner conflicts by providing clients with new insights. Indeed, the psychodynamic and humanistic therapies are often referred to as **insight therapies.** But humanistic therapists differ from psychoanalytic therapists in many other ways:

- *Humanistic therapists aim to boost people's self-fulfillment by helping them grow in self-awareness and self-acceptance.*
- *Promoting this growth, not curing illness, is the focus of therapy.* Thus, those in therapy became "clients" or just "persons" rather than "patients" (a change many other therapists have adopted).
- *The path to growth is taking immediate responsibility for one's feelings and actions, rather than uncovering hidden determinants.*
- *Conscious thoughts are more important than the unconscious.*
- *The present and future are more important than the past.* The goal is to explore feelings as they occur, rather than achieve insights into the childhood origins of the feelings.

Carl Rogers (1902–1987) developed the widely used humanistic technique he called **client-centered therapy,** which focuses on the person's conscious self-perceptions. In this *nondirective therapy,* the therapist listens, without judging or interpreting, and seeks to refrain from directing the client toward certain insights.

Believing that most people possess the resources for growth, Rogers (1961, 1980) encouraged therapists to exhibit *genuineness, acceptance,* and *empathy.* When therapists drop their facades and genuinely express their true feelings, when they enable their clients to feel unconditionally accepted, and when they empathically sense and reflect their clients' feelings, the clients may deepen their self-understanding and self-acceptance (Hill & Nakayama, 2000). As Rogers (1980, p. 10) explained,

> Hearing has consequences. When I truly hear a person and the meanings that are important to him at that moment, hearing not simply his words, but him, and when I let him know that I have heard his own private personal meanings, many things happen. There is first of all a grateful look. He feels released. He wants to tell me more about his world. He surges forth in a new sense of freedom. He becomes more open to the process of change.
>
> I have often noticed that the more deeply I hear the meanings of the person, the more there is that happens. Almost always, when a person realizes he has been deeply heard, his eyes moisten. I think in some real sense he is weeping for joy. It is as though he were saying, "Thank God, somebody heard me. Someone knows what it's like to be me."

"Hearing" refers to Rogers' technique of **active listening**—echoing, restating, and seeking clarification of what the person expresses (verbally or nonverbally) and acknowledging the expressed feelings. Active listening is now an accepted part of therapeutic counseling

"We have two ears and one mouth that we may listen the more and talk the less."

Zeno, 335–263 B.C.E., *Diogenes Laertius*

practices in many schools, colleges, and clinics. The counselor listens attentively and interrupts only to restate and confirm feelings, to accept what is being expressed, or to seek clarification. The following brief excerpt between Rogers and a male client illustrates how he sought to provide a psychological mirror that would help clients see themselves more clearly.

Rogers: Feeling that now, hm? That you're just no good to yourself, no good to anybody. Never will be any good to anybody. Just that you're completely worthless, huh?—Those really are lousy feelings. Just feel that you're no good at all, hm?

Client: Yeah. *(Muttering in low, discouraged voice)* That's what this guy I went to town with just the other day told me.

Rogers: This guy that you went to town with really told you that you were no good? Is that what you're saying? Did I get that right?

Client: M-hm.

Rogers: I guess the meaning of that if I get it right is that here's somebody that—meant something to you and what does he think of you? Why, he's told you that he thinks you're no good at all. And that just really knocks the props out from under you. *(Client weeps quietly.)* It just brings the tears. *(Silence of 20 seconds)*

Client: *(Rather defiantly)* I don't care though.

Rogers: You tell yourself you don't care at all, but somehow I guess some part of you cares because some part of you weeps over it.

(Meador & Rogers, 1984, p. 167)

Can a therapist be a perfect mirror, without selecting and interpreting what is reflected? Rogers conceded that one cannot be *totally* nondirective. Nevertheless, he believed that the therapist's most important contribution is to accept and understand the client. Given a nonjudgmental, grace-filled environment that provides **unconditional positive regard,** people may accept even their worst traits and feel valued and whole.

If you want to listen more actively in your own relationships, three Rogerian hints may help:

1. ***Paraphrase.*** Rather than saying "I know how you feel," check your understandings by summarizing the person's words in your own words.
2. ***Invite clarification.*** "What might be an example of that?" may encourage the person to say more.
3. ***Reflect feelings.*** "It sounds frustrating" might mirror what you're sensing from the person's body language and intensity.

Michael Rougier/Life Magazine © Time Warner, Inc.

Active listening Carl Rogers (right) empathized with a client during this group therapy session.

Behavior Therapies

52-4 How does the basic assumption of behavior therapy differ from those of psychodynamic and humanistic therapies? What techniques are used in exposure therapies and aversive conditioning?

Science Cartoons Plus

The insight therapies assume that many psychological problems diminish as self-awareness grows. Psychodynamic therapists expect problems to subside as people gain insight into their unresolved and unconscious tensions. Humanistic therapists expect problems to diminish as people get in touch with their feelings. Proponents of **behavior therapy**, however, doubt the healing power of self-awareness. (You can become aware of why you are highly anxious during exams and still be anxious.) They assume that problem behaviors *are* the problems, and the application of learning principles can eliminate them. Rather than delving deeply below the surface looking for inner causes, behavior therapists view maladaptive symptoms—such as phobias or sexual disorders—as learned behaviors that can be replaced by constructive behaviors.

Classical Conditioning Techniques

One cluster of behavior therapies derives from principles developed in Ivan Pavlov's early twentieth-century conditioning experiments. As Pavlov and others showed, we learn various behaviors and emotions through *classical conditioning*. Could maladaptive symptoms be examples of conditioned responses? If so, might reconditioning be a solution? Learning theorist O. H. Mowrer thought so and developed a successful conditioning therapy for chronic bed-wetters. The child sleeps on a liquid-sensitive pad connected to an alarm. Moisture on the pad triggers the alarm, waking the child. With sufficient repetition, this association of bladder relaxation with waking up stops the bed-wetting. In three out of four cases the treatment is effective, and the success provides a boost to the child's self-image (Christophersen & Edwards, 1992; Houts et al., 1994).

Another example: If a claustrophobic fear of elevators is a learned aversion to the stimulus of being in a confined space, then might one unlearn that association by undergoing another round of conditioning to replace the fear response? **Counterconditioning** pairs the trigger stimulus (in this case, the enclosed space of the elevator) with a new response (relaxation) that is incompatible with fear. Indeed, behavior therapists have successfully counterconditioned people with such fears. Two specific counterconditioning techniques—*exposure therapy* and *aversive conditioning*—replace unwanted responses.

RETRIEVAL PRACTICE

- What might a psychodynamic therapist say about Mowrer's therapy for bed-wetting? How might a behavior therapist reply?

ANSWER: A psychodynamic therapist might be more interested in helping the child develop insight about the underlying problems that have caused the bed-wetting response. A behavior therapist would be more likely to agree with Mowrer that the bed-wetting symptom *is* the problem, and that counterconditioning the unwanted behavior would indeed bring emotional relief.

Exposure Therapies

Picture this scene reported in 1924 by behaviorist psychologist Mary Cover Jones: Three-year-old Peter is petrified of rabbits and other furry objects. Jones plans to replace Peter's fear of rabbits with a conditioned response incompatible with fear. Her strategy is to associate the fear-evoking rabbit with the pleasurable, relaxed response associated with eating.

As Peter begins his midafternoon snack, Jones introduces a caged rabbit on the other side of the huge room. Peter, eagerly munching away on his crackers and drinking his milk, hardly notices. On succeeding days, she gradually moves the rabbit closer and closer. Within two months, Peter is tolerating the rabbit in his lap, even stroking it while he eats. Moreover, his fear of other furry objects subsides as well, having been *countered*, or replaced, by a relaxed state that cannot coexist with fear (Fisher, 1984; Jones, 1924).

Kim Reinick/Shutterstock

unconditional positive regard a caring, accepting, nonjudgmental attitude, which Carl Rogers believed would help clients to develop self-awareness and self-acceptance.

behavior therapy therapy that applies learning principles to the elimination of unwanted behaviors.

counterconditioning a behavior therapy procedure that uses classical conditioning to evoke new responses to stimuli that are triggering unwanted behaviors; includes *exposure therapies* and *aversive conditioning*.

Unfortunately for those who might have been helped by her counterconditioning procedures, Jones' story of Peter and the rabbit did not immediately become part of psychology's lore. It was more than 30 years later that psychiatrist Joseph Wolpe (1958; Wolpe & Plaud, 1997) refined Jones' technique into what are now the most widely used types of behavior therapies: **exposure therapies,** which expose people to what they normally avoid or escape (behaviors that get reinforced by reduced anxiety). Exposure therapies have them face their fear, and thus overcome their fear of the fear response itself. As people can habituate to the sound of a train passing their new apartment, so, with repeated exposure, can they become less anxiously responsive to things that once petrified them (Rosa-Alcázar et al., 2008; Wolitzky-Taylor et al., 2008).

One widely used exposure therapy is **systematic desensitization.** Wolpe assumed, as did Jones, that you cannot be simultaneously anxious and relaxed. Therefore, if you can repeatedly relax when facing anxiety-provoking stimuli, you can gradually eliminate your anxiety. The trick is to proceed gradually. Let's see how this might work with a common phobia. Imagine yourself afraid of public speaking. A behavior therapist might first ask for your help in constructing a hierarchy of anxiety-triggering speaking situations. Yours might range from mildly anxiety-provoking situations, perhaps speaking up in a small group of friends, to panic-provoking situations, such as having to address a large audience.

Next, using *progressive relaxation*, the therapist would train you to relax one muscle group after another, until you achieve a blissful state of complete relaxation and comfort. Then the therapist would ask you to imagine, with your eyes closed, a mildly anxiety-arousing situation: You are having coffee with a group of friends and are trying to decide whether to speak up. If imagining the scene causes you to feel any anxiety, you would signal your tension by raising your finger, and the therapist would instruct you to switch off the mental image and go back to deep relaxation. This imagined scene is repeatedly paired with relaxation until you feel no trace of anxiety.

The therapist would progress up the constructed anxiety hierarchy, using the relaxed state to desensitize you to each imagined situation. After several sessions, you move to actual situations and practice what you had only imagined before, beginning with relatively easy tasks and gradually moving to more anxiety-filled ones. Conquering your anxiety in an actual situation, not just in your imagination, raises your self-confidence (Foa & Kozak, 1986; Williams, 1987). Eventually, you may even become a confident public speaker.

When an anxiety-arousing situation is too expensive, difficult, or embarrassing to re-create, **virtual reality exposure therapy** offers an efficient middle ground. Wearing a head-mounted display unit that projects a three-dimensional virtual world, you would view a lifelike series of scenes that would be tailored to your particular fear and shift as your head turned. Experiments led by several research teams have treated many different people with many different fears—flying, heights, particular animals, and public speaking (Parsons & Rizzo, 2008). People who fear flying, for example, can peer out a virtual window of a simulated plane, feel vibrations, and hear the engine roar as the plane taxis down the runway and takes off. In studies comparing control groups with people experiencing virtual reality exposure therapy, the therapy has provided greater relief from real-life fear (Hoffman, 2004; Krijn et al., 2004).

Developments in virtual reality therapy suggest the likelihood of increasingly sophisticated simulated worlds in which people,

Virtual reality exposure therapy Virtual reality technology exposes people to vivid simulations of feared stimuli. The head-mounted display unit projects a three-dimensional, lifelike series of scenes. As the client's head turns, motion sensors adjust the scene.

Bob Mahoney /The Image Works

Bob Mahoney /The Image Works

using avatars (computer representations of themselves), try out new behaviors in virtual environments (Gorini, 2007). For example, someone with a social phobia might visit virtual parties or group discussions, which others join over time.

Aversive Conditioning

In systematic desensitization, the goal is substituting a positive (relaxed) response for a negative (fearful) response to a *harmless* stimulus. In **aversive conditioning,** the goal is substituting a negative (aversive) response for a positive response to a *harmful* stimulus (such as alcohol). Thus, aversive conditioning is the reverse of systematic desensitization—it seeks to condition an aversion to something the person *should* avoid.

The procedure is simple: It associates the unwanted behavior with unpleasant feelings. To treat nail biting, one can paint the fingernails with a nasty-tasting nail polish (Baskind, 1997). To treat alcohol dependence, an aversion therapist offers the client appealing drinks laced with a drug that produces severe nausea. By linking alcohol with violent nausea, the therapist seeks to transform the person's reaction to alcohol from positive to negative (**FIGURE 52.1**).

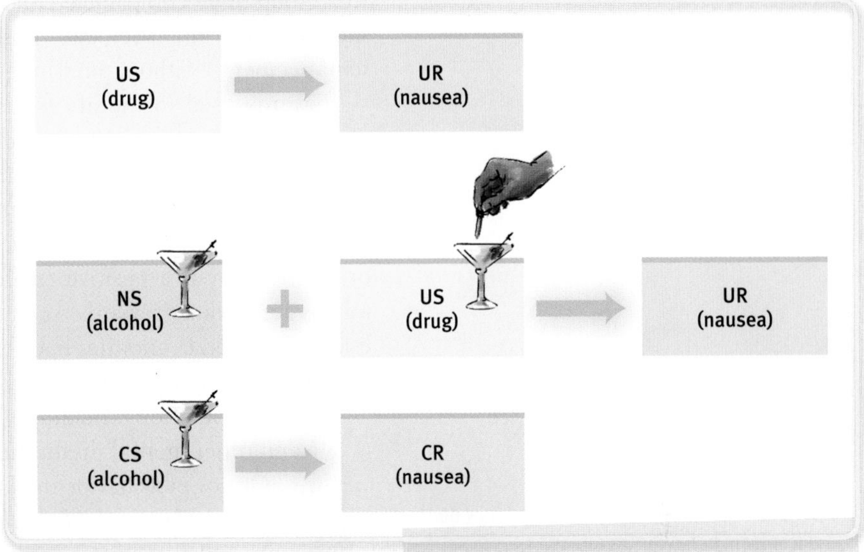

FIGURE 52.1
Aversion therapy for alcohol dependence After repeatedly imbibing an alcoholic drink mixed with a drug that produces severe nausea, some people with a history of alcohol abuse develop at least a temporary conditioned aversion to alcohol. (Classical conditioning terms: US is *unconditioned stimulus,* UR is *unconditioned response,* NS is *neutral stimulus,* CS is *conditioned stimulus,* and CR is *conditioned response.*)

Does aversive conditioning work? In the short run it may. Arthur Wiens and Carol Menustik (1983) studied 685 patients with alcohol dependence who completed an aversion therapy program at a Portland, Oregon, hospital. One year later, after returning for several booster treatments of alcohol-sickness pairings, 63 percent were still successfully abstaining. But after three years, only 33 percent had remained abstinent.

The problem is that in therapy (as in research), cognition influences conditioning. People know that outside the therapist's office they can drink without fear of nausea. Their ability to discriminate between the aversive conditioning situation and all other situations can limit the treatment's effectiveness. Thus, therapists often use aversive conditioning in combination with other treatments.

Operant Conditioning

52-5 What is the main premise of therapy based on operant conditioning principles, and what are the views of its proponents and critics?

The work of B. F. Skinner and others teaches us a basic principle of *operant conditioning:* Voluntary behaviors are strongly influenced by their consequences. Knowing this, behavior therapists can practice *behavior modification*—reinforcing desired behaviors, and withholding reinforcement for undesired behaviors. Using operant conditioning to solve specific behavior problems has raised hopes for some otherwise hopeless cases. Children with intellectual disabilities have been taught to care for themselves. Socially withdrawn children with autism have learned to interact. People with schizophrenia have been helped to behave more rationally in their hospital ward. In such cases, therapists use positive reinforcers to shape behavior in a step-by-step manner, rewarding closer and closer approximations of the desired behavior.

In extreme cases, treatment must be intensive. One study worked with 19 withdrawn, uncommunicative 3-year-olds with autism. Each participated in a 2-year program in which their parents spent 40 hours a week attempting to shape their behavior (Lovaas, 1987).

exposure therapies behavioral techniques, such as *systematic desensitization* and *virtual reality exposure therapy,* that treat anxieties by exposing people (in imagination or actual situations) to the things they fear and avoid.

systematic desensitization a type of exposure therapy that associates a pleasant relaxed state with gradually increasing anxiety-triggering stimuli. Commonly used to treat phobias.

virtual reality exposure therapy an anxiety treatment that progressively exposes people to electronic simulations of their greatest fears, such as airplane flying, spiders, or public speaking.

aversive conditioning a type of counterconditioning that associates an unpleasant state (such as nausea) with an unwanted behavior (such as drinking alcohol).

The combination of positively reinforcing desired behaviors, and ignoring or punishing aggressive and self-abusive behaviors, worked wonders for some. By first grade, 9 of the 19 children were functioning successfully in school and exhibiting normal intelligence. In a group of 40 comparable children not undergoing this effortful treatment, only one showed similar improvement. (Ensuing studies focused on the effective aspect—positive reinforcement—without punishment.)

Rewards used to modify behavior vary. For some people, the reinforcing power of attention or praise is sufficient. Others require concrete rewards, such as food. In institutional settings, therapists may create a **token economy.** When people display appropriate behavior, such as getting out of bed, washing, dressing, eating, talking coherently, cleaning up their rooms, or playing cooperatively, they receive a token or plastic coin as a positive reinforcer. Later, they can exchange their accumulated tokens for various rewards, such as candy, TV time, trips to town, or better living quarters. Token economies have been successfully applied in various settings (homes, classrooms, hospitals, institutions for juvenile offenders) and among members of various populations (including disturbed children and people with schizophrenia and other mental disabilities).

Critics of behavior modification express two concerns. The first is practical: *How durable are the behaviors?* Will people become so dependent on extrinsic rewards that the appropriate behaviors will stop when the reinforcers stop? Proponents of behavior modification believe the behaviors will endure if therapists wean patients from the tokens by shifting them toward other, real-life rewards, such as social approval. They also point out that the appropriate behaviors themselves can be intrinsically rewarding. For example, as a withdrawn person becomes more socially competent, the intrinsic satisfactions of social interaction may help the person maintain the behavior.

The second concern is ethical: *Is it right for one human to control another's behavior?* Those who set up token economies deprive people of something they desire and decide which behaviors to reinforce. To critics, this whole process has an authoritarian taint. Advocates reply that some patients request the therapy. Moreover, control already exists; rewards and punishers are already maintaining destructive behavior patterns. So why not reinforce adaptive behavior instead? Treatment with positive rewards is more humane than being institutionalized or punished, advocates argue, and the right to effective treatment and an improved life justifies temporary deprivation.

RETRIEVAL PRACTICE

- What are the *insight therapies,* and how do they differ from behavior therapies?

ANSWER: The *insight therapies*—psychodynamic and humanistic therapies—seek to relieve problems by providing an understanding of their origins. Behavior therapies assume the problem behavior *is* the problem and treat it directly, paying less attention to its origins.

- Some maladaptive behaviors are learned. What hope does this fact provide?

ANSWER: If a behavior can be learned, it can be *un*learned, and replaced by other more adaptive responses.

- Exposure therapies and aversive conditioning are applications of __________ conditioning. Token economies are an application of __________ conditioning.

ANSWERS: classical; operant

Cognitive Therapies

52-6 What are the goals and techniques of cognitive therapy and of cognitive-behavioral therapy?

We have seen how behavior therapists treat specific fears and problem behaviors. But how do they deal with major depression? Or with generalized anxiety, in which anxiety has no focus and developing a hierarchy of anxiety-triggering situations is difficult? Behavior therapists treating these less clearly defined psychological problems have had help from the same *cognitive revolution* that has profoundly changed other areas of psychology during the last half-century.

The **cognitive therapies** assume that our thinking colors our feelings (**FIGURE 52.2**). Between the event and our response lies the mind. Self-blaming and overgeneralized explanations of bad events are often an integral part of the vicious cycle of depression. The depressed person interprets a suggestion as criticism, disagreement as dislike, praise as flattery, friendliness as pity. Ruminating on such thoughts sustains the negative thinking. If

token economy an operant conditioning procedure in which people earn a token of some sort for exhibiting a desired behavior and can later exchange the tokens for various privileges or treats.

cognitive therapy therapy that teaches people new, more adaptive ways of thinking; based on the assumption that thoughts intervene between events and our emotional reactions.

Lara Jo Regan/Gamma Liaison

Cognitive therapy for eating disorders aided by journaling Cognitive therapists guide people toward new ways of explaining their good and bad experiences. By recording positive events and how she has enabled them, this woman may become more mindful of her self-control and more optimistic.

such thinking patterns can be learned, then surely they can be replaced. Cognitive therapists therefore try in various ways to teach people new, more constructive ways of thinking. If people are miserable, they can be helped to change their minds.

"Life does not consist mainly, or even largely, of facts and happenings. It consists mainly of the storm of thoughts that are forever blowing through one's mind."

Mark Twain, 1835–1910

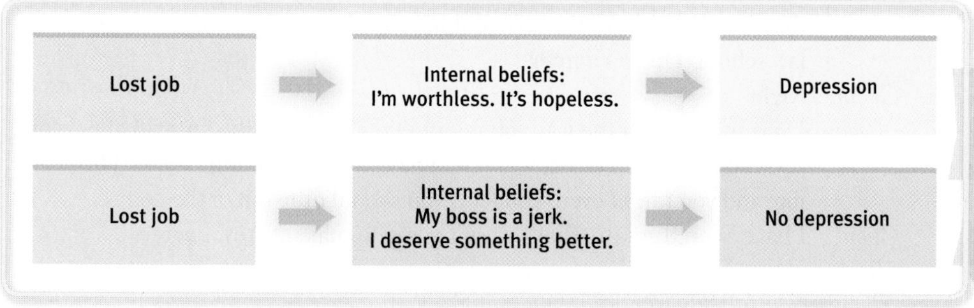

FIGURE 52.2

A cognitive perspective on psychological disorders The person's emotional reactions are produced not directly by the event but by the person's thoughts in response to the event.

Rational-Emotive Behavior Therapy

According to Albert Ellis (1962, 1987, 1993), the creator of **rational-emotive behavior therapy (REBT)**, many problems arise from irrational thinking. For example, he described a disturbed woman and suggested how therapy might challenge her illogical, self-defeating assumptions (Ellis, 2011, pp. 198–199):

> [She] does not merely believe it is undesirable if her lover rejects her. She tends to believe, also, that (a) it is awful; (b) she cannot stand it; (c) she should not, *must* not be rejected; (d) she will never be accepted by any desirable partner; (e) she is a worthless person because one lover has rejected her; and (f) she deserves to be rejected for being so worthless. Such common covert hypotheses are illogical, unrealistic, and destructive. . . . They can be easily elicited and demolished by any scientist worth his or her salt; and the rational-emotive therapist is exactly that: an exposing and nonsense-annihilating scientist.

Change people's thinking by revealing the "absurdity" of their self-defeating ideas, the tart-tongued Ellis believed, and you will change their self-defeating feelings and enable healthier behaviors.

rational-emotive behavior therapy (REBT) a confrontational cognitive therapy, developed by Albert Ellis, that vigorously challenges people's illogical, self-defeating attitudes and assumptions.

Aaron Beck's Therapy for Depression

Cognitive therapist Aaron Beck also believes that changing people's thinking can change their functioning, though he has a gentler approach. Originally trained in Freudian techniques, Beck analyzed the dreams of depressed people. He found recurring negative themes of loss, rejection, and abandonment that extended into their waking thoughts. Such negativity even extends into therapy, as clients recall and rehearse their failings and worst impulses (Kelly, 2000). With cognitive therapy, Beck and his colleagues (1979) have sought to reverse clients' *catastrophizing* beliefs about themselves, their situations, and their futures. Gentle questioning seeks to reveal irrational thinking, and then to persuade people to remove the dark glasses through which they view life (Beck et al., 1979, pp. 145–146):

Client: I agree with the descriptions of me but I guess I don't agree that the way I think makes me depressed.

Beck: How do you understand it?

Client: I get depressed when things go wrong. Like when I fail a test.

Beck: How can failing a test make you depressed?

Client: Well, if I fail I'll never get into law school.

Beck: So failing the test means a lot to you. But if failing a test could drive people into clinical depression, wouldn't you expect everyone who failed the test to have a depression? . . . Did everyone who failed get depressed enough to require treatment?

Client: No, but it depends on how important the test was to the person.

Beck: Right, and who decides the importance?

Client: I do.

Beck: And so, what we have to examine is your way of viewing the test (or the way that you think about the test) and how it affects your chances of getting into law school. Do you agree?

Client: Right.

Beck: Do you agree that the way you interpret the results of the test will affect you? You might feel depressed, you might have trouble sleeping, not feel like eating, and you might even wonder if you should drop out of the course.

Client: I have been thinking that I wasn't going to make it. Yes, I agree.

Beck: Now what did failing mean?

Client: *(tearful)* That I couldn't get into law school.

Beck: And what does that mean to you?

Client: That I'm just not smart enough.

Beck: Anything else?

Client: That I can never be happy.

Beck: And how do these thoughts make you feel?

Client: Very unhappy.

Beck: So it is the meaning of failing a test that makes you very unhappy. In fact, believing that you can never be happy is a powerful factor in producing unhappiness. So, you get yourself into a trap—by definition, failure to get into law school equals "I can never be happy."

We often think in words. Therefore, getting people to change what they say to themselves is an effective way to change their thinking. Perhaps you can identify with the anxious students who, before an exam, make matters worse with self-defeating thoughts: "This exam's probably going to be impossible. All these other students seem so relaxed and confident.

PEANUTS

Drawing by Charles Schulz; © 1956 Reprinted by permission of United Feature Syndicate, Inc.

TABLE 52.1

Selected Cognitive Therapy Techniques

Aim of Technique	Technique	Therapists' Directives
Reveal beliefs	Question your interpretations	Explore your beliefs, revealing faulty assumptions such as "I must be liked by everyone."
	Rank thoughts and emotions	Gain perspective by ranking your thoughts and emotions from mildly to extremely upsetting.
Test beliefs	Examine consequences	Explore difficult situations, assessing possible consequences and challenging faulty reasoning.
	Decatastrophize thinking	Work through the actual worst-case consequences of the situation you face (it is often not as bad as imagined). Then determine how to cope with the real situation you face.
Change beliefs	Take appropriate responsibility	Challenge total self-blame and negative thinking, noting aspects for which you may be truly responsible, as well as aspects that aren't your responsibility.
	Resist extremes	Develop new ways of thinking and feeling to replace maladaptive habits. For example, change from thinking "I am a total failure" to "I got a failing grade on that paper, and I can make these changes to succeed next time."

I wish I were better prepared. Anyhow, I'm so nervous I'll forget everything." To change such negative self-talk, Donald Meichenbaum (1977, 1985) offered *stress inoculation training:* teaching people to restructure their thinking in stressful situations. Sometimes it may be enough simply to say more positive things to oneself: "Relax. The exam may be hard, but it will be hard for everyone else, too. I studied harder than most people. Besides, I don't need a perfect score to get a good grade." After being trained to dispute their negative thoughts, depression-prone children and college students exhibit a halved rate of future depression (Seligman, 2002). To a great extent, it *is* the thought that counts. **TABLE 52.1** provides a sampling of techniques commonly used in cognitive therapy.

Cognitive-Behavioral Therapy

Cognitive-behavioral therapy, a widely practiced integrative therapy, aims not only to alter the way people think (cognitive therapy), but also to alter the way they act (behavior therapy). It seeks to make people aware of their irrational negative thinking, to replace it with new ways of thinking, and to *practice* the more positive approach in everyday settings. Behavioral change is typically addressed first, followed by sessions on cognitive change; the therapy concludes with a focus on maintaining both and preventing relapses.

"The trouble with most therapy is that it helps you to feel better. But you don't get better. You have to back it up with action, action, action."
Therapist Albert Ellis (1913–2007)

Anxiety and mood disorders share a common problem: emotion regulation (Aldao & Nolen-Hoeksema, 2010). An effective treatment program for these emotional disorders trains people both to replace their catastrophizing thinking with more realistic appraisals, and, as homework, to practice behaviors that are incompatible with their problem (Kazantzis et al., 2010a,b; Moses & Barlow, 2006). A person might, for example, keep a log of daily situations associated with negative and positive emotions, and engage more in activities that lead to feeling good. Or those who fear social situations might be assigned to practice approaching people.

In one study, people with obsessive-compulsive behaviors learned to relabel their compulsive thoughts (Schwartz et al., 1996). Feeling the urge to wash their hands again, they would tell themselves, "I'm having a compulsive urge," and attribute it to their brain's abnormal activity, as previously viewed in their PET scans. Instead of giving in to the urge, they would then spend 15 minutes in an enjoyable, alternative behavior, such as practicing an instrument, taking a walk, or gardening. This helped "unstick" the brain by shifting attention and engaging other brain areas. For two or three months, the weekly

cognitive-behavioral therapy a popular integrative therapy that combines cognitive therapy (changing self-defeating thinking) with behavior therapy (changing behavior).

therapy sessions continued, with relabeling and refocusing practice at home. By the study's end, most participants' symptoms had diminished and their PET scans revealed normalized brain activity. Many other studies confirm cognitive-behavioral therapy's effectiveness for those suffering anxiety, depression, or anorexia nervosa (Covin et al., 2008; Mitte, 2005; Norton & Price, 2007). Studies have also found that cognitive-behavioral skills can be effectively taught and therapy conducted over the Internet (Barak et al., 2008; Kessler et al., 2009; Marks & Cavanaugh, 2009; Stross, 2011).

RETRIEVAL PRACTICE

- How do the humanistic and cognitive therapies differ?

ANSWER: By reflecting clients' feelings in a nondirective setting, the *humanistic therapies* attempt to foster personal growth by helping clients become more self-aware and self-accepting. By making clients aware of self-defeating patterns of thinking, *cognitive therapies* guide people toward more adaptive ways of thinking about themselves and their world.

- The confrontational REBT (rational-emotive behavior therapy) was developed by ____________ ____________. A gentler cognitive therapy for depression was developed by ____________ ____________.

ANSWERS: Albert Ellis; Aaron Beck

- What is cognitive-behavioral therapy, and what sorts of problems does this therapy best address?

ANSWER: This integrative therapy helps people change self-defeating thinking and behavior. It has been shown to be effective for those with anxiety disorders, mood disorders, and anorexia nervosa.

Group and Family Therapies

52-7 What are the aims and benefits of group and family therapy?

Group Therapy

Except for traditional psychoanalysis, most therapies may also occur in small groups. **Group therapy** does not provide the same degree of therapist involvement with each client. However, it offers benefits:

- *It saves therapists' time and clients' money,* often with no less effectiveness than individual therapy (Fuhriman & Burlingame, 1994).
- *It offers a social laboratory for exploring social behaviors and developing social skills.* Therapists frequently suggest group therapy for people experiencing frequent conflicts or whose behavior distresses others. For up to 90 minutes weekly, the therapist guides people's interactions as they discuss issues and try out new behaviors.
- *It enables people to see that others share their problems.* It can be a relief to discover that you are not alone—to learn that others, despite their composure, experience some of the same troublesome feelings and behaviors.
- *It provides feedback as clients try out new ways of behaving.* Hearing that you look poised, even though you feel anxious and self-conscious, can be very reassuring.

group therapy therapy conducted with groups rather than individuals, permitting therapeutic benefits from group interaction.

family therapy therapy that treats the family as a system. Views an individual's unwanted behaviors as influenced by, or directed at, other family members.

Family Therapy

One special type of group interaction, **family therapy,** assumes that no person is an island: We live and grow in relation to others, especially our families. We struggle to differentiate ourselves from our families, but we also need to connect with them

Michael Newman/PhotoEdit

Family therapy This type of therapy often acts as a preventive mental health strategy. The therapist helps family members understand how their ways of relating to one another create problems. The treatment's emphasis is not on changing the individuals but on changing their relationships and interactions.

emotionally. Some of our problem behaviors arise from the tension between these two tendencies, which can create family stress.

Unlike most psychotherapy, which focuses on what happens inside the person's own skin, family therapists work with multiple family members to heal relationships and to mobilize family resources. They tend to view the family as a system in which each person's actions trigger reactions from others, and they help family members discover their role within their family's social system. A child's rebellion, for example, affects and is affected by other family tensions. Therapists also attempt—usually with some success, research suggests—to open up communication within the family or to help family members discover new ways of preventing or resolving conflicts (Hazelrigg et al., 1987; Shadish et al., 1993).

Self-Help Groups

Many people also participate in self-help and support groups (Yalom, 1985). One analysis of online support groups and more than 14,000 self-help groups reported that most support groups focus on stigmatized or hard-to-discuss illnesses (Davison et al., 2000). AIDS patients, for example, are 250 times more likely than hypertension patients to be in support groups. Those struggling with anorexia and alcohol dependence often join groups; those with migraines and ulcers usually do not. People with hearing loss have national organizations with local chapters; people with vision loss more often cope on their own.

With more than 2 million members worldwide, AA is said to be "the largest organization on Earth that nobody wanted to join" (Finlay, 2000).

The grandparent of support groups, Alcoholics Anonymous (AA), reports having more than 2 million members in 114,000 groups worldwide. Its famous 12-step program, emulated by many other self-help groups, asks members to admit their powerlessness, to seek help from a higher power and from one another, and (the twelfth step) to take the message to others in need of it. In one eight-year, $27 million investigation, AA participants reduced their drinking sharply, although so did those assigned to cognitive-behavioral therapy or to "motivational therapy" (Project Match, 1997). Other studies have similarly found that 12-step programs such as AA have helped reduce alcohol dependence comparably to other treatment interventions (Ferri et al., 2006; Moos & Moos, 2005). The more meetings members attend, the greater their alcohol abstinence (Moos & Moos, 2006). In one study of 2300 veterans who sought treatment for alcohol dependence, a high level of AA involvement was followed by diminished alcohol problems (McKellar et al., 2003).

In an individualistic age, with more and more people living alone or feeling isolated, the popularity of support groups—for the addicted, the bereaved, the divorced, or simply

TABLE 52.2

Comparing Modern Psychotherapies

Therapy	Presumed Problem	Therapy Aim	Therapy Technique
Psychodynamic	Unconscious conflicts from childhood experiences	Reduce anxiety through self-insight.	Interpret patients' memories and feelings.
Client-centered	Barriers to self-understanding and self-acceptance	Enable growth via unconditional positive regard, genuineness, and empathy.	Listen actively and reflect.
Behavior	Dysfunctional behaviors	Relearn adaptive behaviors; extinguish problem ones.	Use classical conditioning (via exposure or aversion therapy) or operant conditioning (as in token economies).
Cognitive	Negative, self-defeating thinking	Promote healthier thinking and self-talk.	Train people to dispute negative thoughts and attributions.
Cognitive-behavioral	Self-harmful thoughts and behaviors	Promote healthier thinking and adaptive behaviors.	Train people to counter self-harmful thoughts and behaviors.
Group and family	Stressful relationships	Heal relationships.	Develop an understanding of family and other social systems, explore roles, and improve communication.

those seeking fellowship and growth—seems to reflect a longing for community and connectedness. More than 100 million Americans belong to small religious, interest, or self-help groups that meet regularly—and 9 in 10 report that group members "support each other emotionally" (Gallup, 1994).

* * *

For a synopsis of the modern forms of psychotherapy we've been discussing, see **TABLE 52.2.**

RETRIEVAL PRACTICE

- Which of the following is NOT a benefit of group therapy?

  a. more focused attention from the therapist
  b. less expensive
  c. social feedback
  d. reassurance that others share troubles

  ANSWER: a

- Which therapeutic technique focuses more on the present and future than the past, and involves unconditional positive regard and active listening?

  ANSWER: humanistic therapy—specifically Carl Rogers' client-centered therapy

MODULE REVIEW

The Psychological Therapies

Learning Objectives

RETRIEVAL PRACTICE Take a moment to answer each of these Learning Objective Questions (repeated here from within the module). Then turn to Appendix B, Complete Module Reviews, to check your answers. Research suggests that trying to answer these questions on your own will improve your long-term retention (McDaniel et al., 2009).

52-1: How do *psychotherapy, biomedical therapy,* and an *eclectic approach* to therapy differ?

52-2: What are the goals and techniques of psychoanalysis, and how have they been adapted in psychodynamic therapy?

52-3: What are the basic themes of humanistic therapy? What are the specific goals and techniques of Rogers' client-centered approach?

52-4: How does the basic assumption of behavior therapy differ from those of psychodynamic and humanistic therapies? What techniques are used in exposure therapies and aversive conditioning?

52-5: What is the main premise of therapy based on operant conditioning principles, and what are the views of its proponents and critics?

52-6: What are the goals and techniques of cognitive therapy and of cognitive-behavioral therapy?

52-7: What are the aims and benefits of group and family therapy?

Terms and Concepts to Remember

RETRIEVAL PRACTICE Test yourself on these terms by trying to write down the definition before flipping back to the referenced page to check your answer.

psychotherapy, p. 676
biomedical therapy, p. 676
eclectic approach, p. 676
psychoanalysis, p. 677
resistance, p. 677
interpretation, p. 677
transference, p. 677
psychodynamic therapy, p. 678
insight therapies, p. 679
client-centered therapy, p. 679
active listening, p. 679
unconditional positive regard, p. 680
behavior therapy, p. 681
counterconditioning, p. 681
exposure therapies, p. 682
systematic desensitization, p. 682
virtual reality exposure therapy, p. 682
aversive conditioning, p. 683
token economy, p. 684
cognitive therapy, p. 684
rational-emotive behavior therapy (REBT), p. 685
cognitive-behavioral therapy, p. 687
group therapy, p. 688
family therapy, p. 688

RETRIEVAL PRACTICE Gain an advantage, and benefit from immediate feedback, with the interactive self-testing resources at www.worthpublishers.com/myers.

MODULE 53

Evaluating Psychotherapies

- Is Psychotherapy Effective?
- The Relative Effectiveness of Different Psychotherapies
- Evaluating Alternative Therapies
- Commonalities Among Psychotherapies
- Culture, Gender, and Values in Psychotherapy
- Preventing Psychological Disorders

Advice columnists frequently urge their troubled letter writers to get professional help: "Don't give up. Find a therapist who can help you. Make an appointment."

Many Americans share this confidence in **psychotherapy's** effectiveness. Before 1950, psychiatrists were the primary providers of mental health care. Today's providers include clinical and counseling psychologists; clinical social workers; clergy, marital, and school counselors; and psychiatric nurses. With such an enormous outlay of time as well as money, effort, and hope, it is important to ask: Are the millions of people worldwide justified in placing their hopes in psychotherapy?

psychotherapy treatment involving psychological techniques; consists of interactions between a trained therapist and someone seeking to overcome psychological difficulties or achieve personal growth.

Is Psychotherapy Effective?

53-1 Does psychotherapy work? Who decides?

The question, though simply put, is not simple to answer. Measuring therapy's effectiveness is not like taking your body's temperature to see if your fever has gone away. If you and I were to undergo psychotherapy, how would we assess its effectiveness? By how we feel about our progress? By how our therapist feels about it? By how our friends and family feel about it? By how our behavior has changed?

Clients' Perceptions

If clients' testimonials were the only measuring stick, we could strongly affirm the effectiveness of psychotherapy. When 2900 *Consumer Reports* readers (1995; Kotkin et al., 1996; Seligman, 1995) related their experiences with mental health professionals, 89 percent said they were at least "fairly well satisfied." Among those who recalled feeling *fair* or *very poor* when beginning therapy, 9 in 10 now were feeling *very good, good,* or at least *so-so*. We have their word for it—and who should know better?

We should not dismiss these testimonials lightly. But for several reasons, client testimonials do not persuade psychotherapy's skeptics:

- ***People often enter therapy in crisis.*** When, with the normal ebb and flow of events, the crisis passes, people may attribute their improvement to the therapy.
- ***Clients may need to believe the therapy was worth the effort.*** To admit investing time and money in something ineffective is like admitting to having one's car serviced repeatedly by a mechanic who never fixes it. Self-justification is a powerful human motive.
- ***Clients generally speak kindly of their therapists.*** Even if the problems remain, say the critics, clients "work hard to find something positive to say. The therapist had been very understanding, the client had gained a new perspective, he learned to communicate better, his mind was eased, anything at all so as not to have to say treatment was a failure" (Zilbergeld, 1983, p. 117).

As research findings continue to document, we are prone to selective and biased recall and to making judgments that confirm our beliefs. Consider the testimonials gathered in a massive experiment with over 500 Massachusetts boys, aged 5 to 13 years, many of whom seemed bound for delinquency. By the toss of a coin, half the boys were assigned to a 5-year treatment program. The treated boys were visited by counselors twice a month. They participated in community programs, and they received academic tutoring, medical attention, and family assistance as needed. Some 30 years later, Joan McCord (1978, 1979) located

485 participants, sent them questionnaires, and checked public records from courts, mental hospitals, and other sources. Was the treatment successful?

Client testimonials yielded encouraging results, even glowing reports. Some men noted that, had it not been for their counselors, "I would probably be in jail," "My life would have gone the other way," or "I think I would have ended up in a life of crime." Court records offered apparent support: Even among the "difficult" boys in the treatment group, 66 percent had no official juvenile crime record.

But keep in mind psychology's most powerful tool for sorting reality from wishful thinking: the *control group*. For every boy in the treatment group, there was a similar boy in a control group, receiving no counseling. Of these untreated men, *70 percent* had no juvenile record. On several other measures, such as a record of having committed a second crime, alcohol dependence, death rate, and job satisfaction, the untreated men exhibited slightly *fewer* problems. The glowing testimonials of those treated had been unintentionally deceiving.

Trauma These women are mourning the tragic loss of lives and homes in the 2010 earthquake in China. Those who suffer through such trauma may benefit from counseling, though many people recover on their own, or with the help of supportive relationships with family and friends. "Life itself still remains a very effective therapist," noted psychodynamic therapist Karen Horney (*Our Inner Conflicts,* 1945).

Feng Li/Getty Images

Clinicians' Perceptions

Do clinicians' perceptions give us any more reason to celebrate? Case studies of successful treatment abound. The problem is that clients justify entering psychotherapy by emphasizing their unhappiness and justify leaving by emphasizing their well-being. Therapists treasure compliments from clients as they say good-bye or later express their gratitude, but they hear little from clients who experience only temporary relief and seek out new therapists for their recurring problems. Thus, the same person—with the same recurring anxieties, depression, or marital difficulty—may be a "success" story in several therapists' files.

Because people enter therapy when they are extremely unhappy, and usually leave when they are less extremely unhappy, most therapists, like most clients, testify to therapy's success—regardless of the treatment (see Thinking Critically About: "Regressing" From Unusual to Usual).

THINKING CRITICALLY ABOUT

"Regressing" From Unusual to Usual

Clients' and therapists' perceptions of therapy's effectiveness are vulnerable to inflation from two phenomena. One is the *placebo effect*—the power of belief in a treatment. If you think a treatment is going to be effective, it just may be (thanks to the healing power of your positive expectation).

The second phenomenon is **regression toward the mean**—the tendency for unusual events (or emotions) to "regress" (return) to their average state. Thus, extraordinary happenings (feeling low) tend to be followed by more ordinary ones (a return to our more usual state). Indeed, when things hit bottom, whatever we try—going to a psychotherapist, starting yoga, doing aerobic exercise—is more likely to be followed by improvement than by further descent.

The point may seem obvious, yet we regularly miss it: We sometimes attribute what may be a normal regression (the expected return to normal) to something we have done. Consider:

"Once you become sensitized to it, you see regression everywhere."

Psychologist Daniel Kahneman (1985)

- Students who score much lower or higher on an exam than they usually do are likely, when retested, to return toward their average.
- Unusual ESP subjects who defy chance when first tested nearly always lose their "psychic powers" when retested (a phenomenon parapsychologists have called the *decline effect*).
- Coaches often yell at their players after an unusually bad first half. They may then feel rewarded for having done so when the team's performance improves (returns to normal) during the second half.

In each case, the cause-effect link may be genuine. Each may, however, be an instance of the natural tendency for behavior to regress from the unusual to the more usual. And this defines the task for therapy-efficacy research: Does the client's improvement following a particular therapy exceed what could be expected from the placebo and regression effects alone, shown by comparison with control groups?

regression toward the mean the tendency for extreme or unusual scores to fall back (regress) toward their average.

meta-analysis a procedure for statistically combining the results of many different research studies.

Outcome Research

How, then, can we objectively measure the effectiveness of psychotherapy if neither clients nor clinicians can tell us? How can we determine which people and problems are best helped, and by what type of psychotherapy?

In search of answers, psychologists have turned to controlled research studies. Similar research in the 1800s transformed the field of medicine. Physicians, skeptical of many of the fashionable treatments (bleeding, purging, infusions of plant and metal substances), began to realize that many patients got better on their own, without these treatments, and that others died despite them. Sorting fact from superstition required observing patients with and without a particular treatment. Typhoid fever patients, for example, often improved after being bled, convincing most physicians that the treatment worked. Not until a control group was given mere bed rest—and 70 percent were observed to improve after five weeks of fever—did physicians learn, to their shock, that the bleeding was worthless (Thomas, 1992).

In psychology, the opening challenge to the effectiveness of psychotherapy was issued by British psychologist Hans Eysenck (1952). Launching a spirited debate, he summarized studies showing that two-thirds of those receiving psychotherapy for nonpsychotic disorders improved markedly. To this day, no one disputes that optimistic estimate.

Why, then, are we still debating psychotherapy's effectiveness? Because Eysenck also reported similar improvement among *untreated* persons, such as those who were on waiting lists. With or without psychotherapy, he said, roughly two-thirds improved noticeably. Time was a great healer.

Later research revealed shortcomings in Eysenck's analyses; his sample was small (only 24 studies of psychotherapy outcomes in 1952). Today, hundreds of studies are available. The best are *randomized clinical trials,* in which researchers randomly assign people on a waiting list to therapy or to no therapy, and later evaluate everyone, using tests and assessments by others who don't know whether therapy was given. The results of many such studies are then digested by means of a **meta-analysis,** a statistical procedure that combines the conclusions of a large number of different studies. Simply said, meta-analyses give us the bottom-line results of lots of studies.

Psychotherapists welcomed the first meta-analysis of some 475 psychotherapy outcome studies (Smith et al., 1980). It showed that the average therapy client ends up better off than 80 percent of the untreated individuals on waiting lists (**FIGURE 53.1**). The claim is modest—by definition, about 50 percent of untreated people also are better off than the

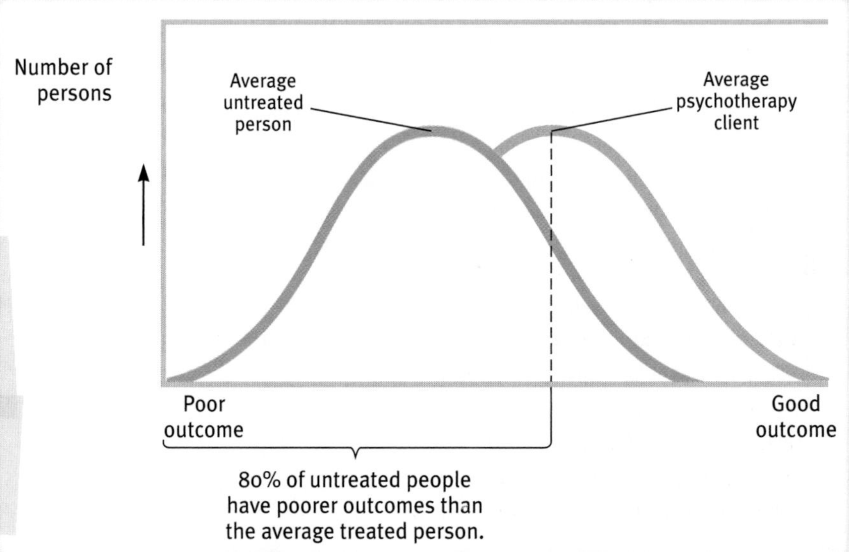

FIGURE 53.1
Treatment versus no treatment
These two normal distribution curves based on data from 475 studies show the improvement of untreated people and psychotherapy clients. The outcome for the average therapy client surpassed that for 80 percent of the untreated people. (Adapted from Smith et al., 1980.)

average untreated person. Nevertheless, Mary Lee Smith and her colleagues exulted that "psychotherapy benefits people of all ages as reliably as schooling educates them, medicine cures them, or business turns a profit" (p. 183).

Dozens of subsequent summaries have now examined this question. Their verdict echoes the results of the earlier outcome studies: *Those not undergoing therapy often improve, but those undergoing therapy are more likely to improve more quickly, and with less risk of relapse.*

Is psychotherapy also cost-effective? Again, the answer is *Yes.* Studies show that when people seek psychological treatment, their search for other medical treatment drops—by 16 percent in one digest of 91 studies (Chiles et al., 1999). Given the staggering annual cost of psychological disorders and substance abuse—including crime, accidents, lost work, and treatment—psychotherapy is a good investment, much like money spent on prenatal and well-baby care. Both *reduce* long-term costs. Boosting employees' psychological well-being, for example, can lower medical costs, improve work efficiency, and diminish absenteeism.

But note that the claim—that psychotherapy, *on average,* is somewhat effective—refers to no one therapy in particular. It is like reassuring lung-cancer patients that "on average," medical treatment of health problems is effective. What people want to know is the effectiveness of a *particular* treatment for their specific problems.

RETRIEVAL PRACTICE

- How do (a) the *placebo effect* and (b) *regression toward the mean* bias clients' and clinicians' appraisals of the effectiveness of psychotherapies?

ANSWERS: (a) The *placebo effect* is the healing power of *belief* in a treatment. Patients and therapists who expect a treatment to be effective may believe it was. (b) Given the natural tendency of extraordinary happenings to *regress* back to ordinary ones, patients and clinicians may attribute a normal regression to successful treatment.

The Relative Effectiveness of Different Psychotherapies

53-2 Are some psychotherapies more effective than others for specific disorders?

So what can we tell people considering psychotherapy, and those paying for it, about *which* psychotherapy will be most effective for their problem? The statistical summaries and surveys fail to pinpoint any one type of therapy as generally superior (Smith et al., 1977, 1980). Clients seemed equally satisfied, *Consumer Reports* concluded, whether treated by a psychiatrist, psychologist, or social worker; whether seen in a group or individual context; whether the therapist had extensive or relatively limited training and experience (Seligman, 1995). Other studies concur. There is little if any connection between clinicians' experience, training, supervision, and licensing and their clients' outcomes (Luborsky et al., 2002; Wampold, 2007).

"Whatever differences in treatment efficacy exist, they appear to be extremely small, at best."

Bruce Wampold et al. (1997)

So, was the dodo bird in *Alice in Wonderland* right: "Everyone has won and all must have prizes"? Not quite. Some forms of therapy get prizes for particular problems, though there is often an overlapping—or *comorbidity*—of disorders. Behavioral conditioning therapies, for example, have achieved especially favorable results with specific behavior problems, such as bed-wetting, phobias, compulsions, marital problems, and sexual disorders (Baker et al., 2008; Hunsley & DiGiulio, 2002; Shadish & Baldwin, 2005). Psychodynamic therapy has had success with depression and anxiety (Driessen et al., 2010; Leichsenring & Rabung, 2008; Shedler, 2010b). And new studies confirm cognitive and cognitive-behavioral therapy's effectiveness (some say superiority) in coping with anxiety, post-traumatic stress disorder, and depression (Baker et al., 2008; De Los Reyes & Kazdin, 2009; Stewart & Chambliss, 2009; Tolin, 2010).

"Different sores have different salves."

English proverb

Moreover, we can say that therapy is most effective when the problem is clear-cut (Singer, 1981; Westen & Morrison, 2001). Those who experience phobias or panic, who are unassertive, or who are frustrated by sexual performance problems can hope for improvement. Those with less-focused problems, such as depression and anxiety, usually benefit in the short term but often relapse later. And those with the negative symptoms of chronic schizophrenia or a desire to change their entire personality are unlikely to benefit from psychotherapy alone (Pfammatter et al., 2006; Zilbergeld, 1983). The more specific the problem, the greater the hope.

But no prizes—and little or no scientific support—go to certain other therapies (Arkowitz & Lilienfeld, 2006). We would all therefore be wise to avoid energy therapies that propose to manipulate people's invisible energy fields, recovered-memory therapies that aim to unearth "repressed memories" of early child abuse, and rebirthing therapies that engage people in reenacting the supposed trauma of their birth.

As with some medical treatments, it's possible for psychological treatments not only to be ineffective but harmful—by making people worse or preventing their getting better (Barlow, 2010; Castonguay et al., 2010; Dimidjian & Hollon, 2010). The National Science and Technology Council cites the Scared Straight program (seeking to deter children and youth from crime) as an example of well-intentioned programs that have proved ineffective or even harmful. The evaluation question—which therapies get prizes and which do not?—lies at the heart of what some call psychology's civil war. To what extent should science guide both clinical practice and the willingness of health care providers and insurers to pay for psychotherapy?

FIGURE 53.2
Evidence-based clinical decision making The ideal clinical decision making is a three-legged stool, upheld by research evidence, clinical expertise, and knowledge of the patient.

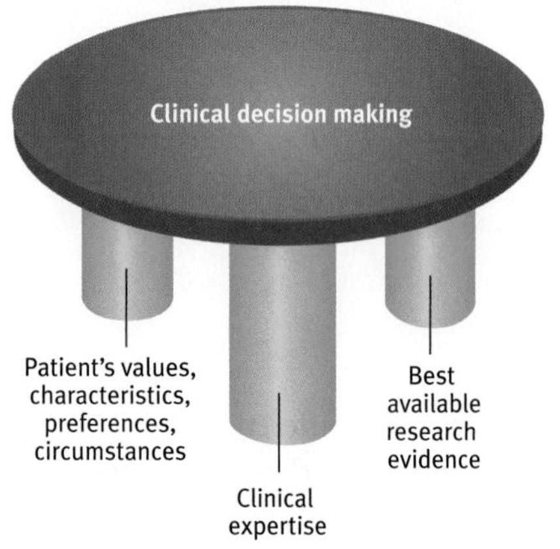

On the one side are research psychologists using scientific methods to extend the list of well-defined and validated therapies for various disorders. They decry clinicians who "give more weight to their personal experiences" (Baker et al., 2008). On the other side are nonscientist therapists who view their practice as more art than science, saying that people are too complex and therapy too intuitive to describe in a manual or test in an experiment. Between these two factions stand the science-oriented clinicians, who aim to base practice on evidence and make mental health professionals accountable for effectiveness.

To encourage **evidence-based practice** in psychology, the American Psychological Association and others (2006; Baker et al., 2008; Levant & Hasan, 2008) have followed the Institute of Medicine's lead, advocating that clinicians integrate the best available research with clinical expertise and with patient preferences and characteristics. Available therapies "should be rigorously evaluated" and then applied by clinicians who are mindful of their skills and of each patient's unique situation (**FIGURE 53.2**). Increasingly, insurer and government support for mental health services requires evidence-based practice. In 2007, for example, Britain's National Health Service announced that it would pour the equivalent of $600 million into training new mental health workers in evidence-based practices (such as cognitive-behavioral therapy) and to disseminating information about such treatments (DeAngelis, 2008).

RETRIEVAL PRACTICE

- Therapy is more likely to be helpful for those with the ________ (most/least) defined problems.

ANSWER: most

Evaluating Alternative Therapies

53-3 How do alternative therapies fare under scientific scrutiny?

The tendency of many abnormal states of mind to regress to normal, combined with the placebo effect, creates fertile soil for pseudotherapies. Bolstered by anecdotes, heralded by the media, and broadcast on the Internet, alternative therapies can spread like wildfire. In one national survey, 57 percent of those with a history of anxiety attacks and 54 percent of those with a history of depression had used alternative treatments, such as herbal medicine, massage, and spiritual healing (Kessler et al., 2001).

Testimonials aside, what does the evidence say? This is a tough question, because there is no evidence for or against most of them, though their proponents often feel personal experience is evidence enough. Some, however, have been the subject of controlled research. Let's consider two of them. As we do, remember that sifting sense from nonsense requires the scientific attitude: being skeptical but not cynical, open to surprises but not gullible.

evidence-based practice clinical decision making that integrates the best available research with clinical expertise and patient characteristics and preferences.

Eye Movement Desensitization and Reprocessing (EMDR)

EMDR (eye movement desensitization and reprocessing) is a therapy adored by thousands and dismissed by thousands more as a sham—"an excellent vehicle for illustrating the differences between scientific and pseudoscientific therapy techniques," suggested James Herbert and seven others (2000). Francine Shapiro (1989, 2007) developed EMDR while walking in a park and observing that anxious thoughts vanished as her eyes spontaneously darted about. Offering her novel anxiety treatment to others, she had people imagine traumatic scenes while she triggered eye movements by waving her finger in front of their eyes, supposedly enabling them to unlock and reprocess previously frozen memories. Tens of thousands of mental health professionals from more than 75 countries have since undergone training (EMDR, 2011). Not since the similarly charismatic Franz Anton Mesmer introduced *animal magnetism* (hypnosis) more than two centuries ago (also after feeling inspired by an outdoor experience) has a new therapy attracted so many devotees so quickly.

Does it work? For 84 to 100 percent of single-trauma victims participating in four studies, the answer is *Yes,* reports Shapiro (1999, 2002). Moreover, the treatment need take no more than three 90-minute sessions. The Society of Clinical Psychology task force on empirically validated treatments acknowledges that EMDR is "probably efficacious" for the treatment of nonmilitary post-traumatic stress disorder (Chambless et al., 1997; see also Bisson & Andrew, 2007; Rodenburg et al., 2009; Seidler & Wagner, 2006).

Why, wonder the skeptics, would rapidly moving one's eyes while recalling traumas be therapeutic? Some argue that eye movements serve to relax or distract patients, thus allowing the memory-associated emotions to extinguish (Gunter & Bodner, 2008). Others believe that eye movements in themselves are *not* the therapeutic ingredient. Trials in which people imagined traumatic scenes and tapped a finger, or just stared straight ahead while the therapist's finger wagged, have produced therapeutic results (Devilly, 2003). EMDR does work better than doing nothing, acknowledge the skeptics (Lilienfeld & Arkowitz, 2007), but many suspect that what is therapeutic is the combination of exposure therapy—repeatedly associating with traumatic memories a safe and reassuring context that provides some emotional distance from the experience—and a robust placebo effect. Had Mesmer's pseudotherapy been compared with no treatment at all, it, too (thanks to the healing power of positive belief), might have been found "probably efficacious," observed Richard McNally (1999).

"Studies indicate that EMDR is just as effective with fixed eyes. If that conclusion is right, what's useful in the therapy (chiefly behavioral desensitization) is not new, and what's new is superfluous."

Harvard Mental Health Letter, 2002

Light Exposure Therapy

Have you ever found yourself oversleeping, gaining weight, and feeling lethargic during the dark mornings and overcast days of winter? There likely was a survival advantage to your distant ancestors' slowing down and conserving energy during the dark days of winter. For some people, however, especially women and those living far from the equator, the wintertime blahs constitute a form of depression known as *seasonal affective disorder,* for which the appropriate acronym is SAD. To counteract these dark spirits, National Institute of Mental Health researchers in the early 1980s had an idea: Give SAD people a timed daily dose of intense light. Sure enough, people reported they felt better.

© Kathryn LeMieux, distributed by King Features Syndicate

© Bryan & Cherry Alexander Photography/Alamy

Light therapy To counteract winter depression, some people spend time each morning exposed to intense light that mimics natural outdoor light. These Norwegian high school students receive regular light therapy at school during the winter months. In the United States, light boxes to counteract SAD are available from health supply and lighting stores.

Was this a bright idea, or another dim-witted example of the placebo effect? Research sheds some light. One study exposed some people with SAD to 90 minutes of bright light and others to a sham placebo treatment—a hissing "negative ion generator" about which the staff expressed similar enthusiasm (but which was not even turned on). After four weeks, 61 percent of those exposed to morning light had greatly improved, as had 50 percent of those exposed to evening light and 32 percent of those exposed to the placebo (Eastman et al., 1998). Other studies have found that 30 minutes of exposure to 10,000-lux white fluorescent light produced relief for more than half the people receiving morning light therapy (Flory et al., 2010; Terman et al., 1998, 2001). From 20 carefully controlled trials we have a verdict (Golden et al., 2005; Wirz-Justice, 2009): Morning bright light does indeed dim SAD symptoms for many people. Moreover, it does so as effectively as taking antidepressant drugs or undergoing cognitive-behavioral therapy (Lam et al., 2006; Rohan et al., 2007). The effects are clear in brain scans; light therapy sparks activity in a brain region that influences the body's arousal and hormones (Ishida et al., 2005).

RETRIEVAL PRACTICE

- Which of the following alternative therapies HAS shown promise as an effective treatment?

  a. light therapy
  b. rebirthing therapies
  c. recovered-memory therapies
  d. energy therapies

  ANSWER: a

- What is evidence-based clinical decision making?

  ANSWER: Using this approach, therapists make decisions about treatment based on research evidence, clinical expertise, and knowledge of the client.

Commonalities Among Psychotherapies

53-4 What three elements are shared by all forms of psychotherapy?

Why have studies found little correlation between therapists' training and experience and clients' outcomes? In search of some answers, Jerome Frank (1982), Marvin Goldfried (Goldfried & Padawer, 1982), Hans Strupp (1986), and Bruce Wampold (2001, 2007) have studied the common ingredients of various therapies. They suggest they all offer at least three benefits:

- ***Hope for demoralized people*** People seeking therapy typically feel anxious, depressed, devoid of self-esteem, and incapable of turning things around. What any therapy offers is the expectation that, with commitment from the therapy seeker, things can and will get better. This belief, apart from any therapeutic technique, may function as a placebo, improving morale, creating feelings of self-efficacy, and diminishing symptoms (Prioleau et al., 1983).
- ***A new perspective*** Every therapy also offers people a plausible explanation of their symptoms and an alternative way of looking at themselves or responding to their world. Armed with a believable fresh perspective, they may approach life with a new attitude, open to making changes in their behaviors and their views of themselves.
- ***An empathic, trusting, caring relationship*** To say that therapy outcome is unrelated to training and experience is not to say all *therapists* are equally effective. No matter what therapeutic technique they use, effective therapists are empathic people who seek to understand another's experience; who communicate their care and concern to the client; and who earn the client's trust through respectful listening, reassurance, and advice. Marvin Goldfried and his associates (1998) found these qualities in recorded therapy sessions from 36 recognized master therapists. Some were cognitive-behavioral therapists, others were psychodynamic therapists. Regardless, the striking finding was how *similar* they were. At key moments, the empathic therapists of both persuasions would help clients evaluate themselves, link one aspect of their life with another, and gain insight into their interactions with others.

therapeutic alliance a bond of trust and mutual understanding between a therapist and client, who work together constructively to overcome the client's problem.

The emotional bond between therapist and client—the **therapeutic alliance**—is a key aspect of effective therapy (Klein et al., 2003; Wampold, 2001). One U.S. National Institute of Mental Health depression-treatment study confirmed that the most effective therapists were those who were perceived as most empathic and caring and who established the closest therapeutic bonds with their clients (Blatt et al., 1996). That all therapies offer hope through a fresh perspective offered by a caring person is what also enables paraprofessionals (briefly trained caregivers) to assist so many troubled people so effectively (Christensen & Jacobson, 1994).

These three common elements are also part of what the growing numbers of self-help and support groups offer their members. And they are part of what traditional healers have offered (Jackson, 1992). Healers everywhere—special people to whom others disclose their suffering, whether psychiatrists, witch doctors, or shamans—have listened in order to understand and to empathize, reassure, advise, console, interpret, or explain (Torrey, 1986). Such qualities may explain why people who feel supported by close relationships—who enjoy the fellowship and friendship of caring people—are less likely to need or seek therapy (Frank, 1982; O'Connor & Brown, 1984).

David Buffington/Getty Images

A caring relationship Effective therapists form a bond of trust with their clients.

* * *

To recap, people who seek help usually improve. So do many of those who do not undergo psychotherapy, and that is a tribute to our human resourcefulness and our capacity to care for one another. Nevertheless, though the therapist's orientation and experience appear not to matter much, people who receive some psychotherapy usually improve more than those who do not. People with clear-cut, specific problems tend to improve the most.

RETRIEVAL PRACTICE

- Those who undergo psychotherapy are ________ (more/less) likely to show improvement than those who do not undergo psychotherapy.

ANSWER: more

Culture, Gender, and Values in Psychotherapy

53-5 How do culture, gender, and values influence the therapist-client relationship?

All therapies offer hope, and nearly all therapists attempt to enhance their clients' sensitivity, openness, personal responsibility, and sense of purpose (Jensen & Bergin, 1988). But in matters of diversity, therapists differ from one another and may differ from their clients (Delaney et al., 2007; Kelly, 1990).

These differences can become significant when a therapist from one culture or gender meets a client from another. In North America, Europe, and Australia, for example, most therapists reflect their culture's individualism, which often gives priority to personal desires and identity, particularly for men. Clients who are immigrants from Asian countries, where people are mindful of others' expectations, may have trouble relating to therapies that require them to think only of their own well-being. And women seeking therapy who are from a collectivist culture might be doubly discomfited. Such differences help explain minority populations' reluctance to use mental health services and tendency to prematurely terminate therapy (Chen et al., 2009; Sue, 2006). In one experiment, Asian-American clients matched with counselors who shared their cultural values (rather than mismatched with those who did not) perceived more counselor empathy and felt a stronger alliance with the counselor (Kim et al., 2005). Recognizing that therapists and clients may differ in their values, communication styles, and language, American Psychological Association–accredited therapy training programs now provide training in cultural sensitivity and recruit members of underrepresented cultural groups.

Another area of potential value conflict is religion. Highly religious people may prefer and benefit from religiously similar therapists (Masters, 2010; Smith et al., 2007; Wade et al., 2006). They may have trouble establishing an emotional bond with a therapist who does not share their values.

Albert Ellis, who advocated the aggressive *rational-emotive behavior therapy (REBT)*, and Allen Bergin, co-editor of the *Handbook of Psychotherapy and Behavior Change*, illustrated how sharply therapists can differ, and how those differences can affect their view of a healthy person. Ellis (1980) assumed that "no one and nothing is supreme," that "self-gratification" should be encouraged, and that "unequivocal love, commitment, service, and . . . fidelity to any interpersonal commitment, especially marriage, leads to harmful consequences." Bergin (1980) assumed the opposite—that "because God is supreme, humility and the acceptance of divine authority are virtues," that "self-control and committed love and self-sacrifice are to be encouraged," and that "infidelity to any interpersonal commitment, especially marriage, leads to harmful consequences."

Bergin and Ellis disagreed more radically than most therapists on what values are healthiest. In so doing, however, they agreed on a more general point: Psychotherapists' personal beliefs influence their practice. Because clients tend to adopt their therapists' values (Worthington et al., 1996), some psychologists believe therapists should divulge those values more openly. (For those thinking about seeking therapy, Close-Up: A Consumer's Guide to Psychotherapists offers some tips on when to seek help and how to start searching for a therapist who shares your perspective and goals.)

CLOSE-UP

A Consumer's Guide to Psychotherapists

53-6 What should a person look for when selecting a therapist?

Life for everyone is marked by a mix of serenity and stress, blessing and bereavement, good moods and bad. So, when should we seek a mental health professional's help? The American Psychological Association offers these common trouble signals:

- Feelings of hopelessness
- Deep and lasting depression
- Self-destructive behavior, such as alcohol and drug abuse
- Disruptive fears
- Sudden mood shifts
- Thoughts of suicide
- Compulsive rituals, such as hand washing
- Sexual difficulties
- Hearing voices or seeing things that others don't experience

In looking for a therapist, you may want to have a preliminary consultation with two or three. College health centers are generally good starting points, and may offer some free services. You can describe your problem and learn each therapist's treatment approach. You can ask questions about the therapist's values, credentials (**TABLE 53.1**), and fees. And you can assess your own feelings about each of them. The emotional bond between therapist and client is perhaps the most important factor in effective therapy.

TABLE 53.1

Therapists and Their Training

Type	Description
Clinical psychologists	Most are psychologists with a Ph.D. (includes research training) or Psy.D. (focuses on therapy) supplemented by a supervised internship and, often, postdoctoral training. About half work in agencies and institutions, half in private practice.
Psychiatrists	Psychiatrists are physicians who specialize in the treatment of psychological disorders. Not all psychiatrists have had extensive training in psychotherapy, but as M.D.s or D.O.s they can prescribe medications. Thus, they tend to see those with the most serious problems. Many have their own private practice.
Clinical or psychiatric social workers	A two-year master of social work graduate program plus postgraduate supervision prepares some social workers to offer psychotherapy, mostly to people with everyday personal and family problems. About half have earned the National Association of Social Workers' designation of clinical social worker.
Counselors	Marriage and family counselors specialize in problems arising from family relations. Clergy provide counseling to countless people. Abuse counselors work with substance abusers and with spouse and child abusers and their victims. Mental health and other counselors may be required to have a two-year master's degree.

Preventing Psychological Disorders

53-7 What is the rationale for preventive mental health programs?

Psychological research has shown that lifestyle change can help *reverse* some of the symptoms of psychological disorders. Might such change also *prevent* some disorders by building individuals' **resilience**—an ability to cope with stress and recover from adversity? Faced with unforeseen trauma, most adults exhibit resilience. This was true of New Yorkers in the aftermath of 9/11, especially those who enjoyed supportive close relationships and who had not recently experienced other stressful events (Bonanno et al., 2007). More than 9 in 10 New Yorkers, although stunned and grief-stricken by 9/11, did *not* have a dysfunctional stress reaction. By the following January, the stress symptoms of those who did were mostly gone (Person et al., 2006). Even in groups of combat-stressed veterans and political rebels who have survived dozens of episodes of torture, most do not later exhibit PTSD (Mineka & Zinbarg, 1996).

resilience the personal strength that helps most people cope with stress and recover from adversity and even trauma.

Psychotherapies and *biomedical therapies* tend to locate the cause of psychological disorders within the person with the disorder. We infer that people who act cruelly must be cruel and that people who act "crazy" must be "sick." We attach labels to such people, thereby distinguishing them from "normal" folks. It follows, then, that we try to treat "abnormal" people by giving them insight into their problems, by changing their thinking, by helping them gain control with drugs.

There is an alternative viewpoint: We could interpret many psychological disorders as understandable responses to a disturbing and stressful society. According to this view, it is not just the person who needs treatment, but also the person's social context. Better to prevent a problem by reforming a sick situation and by developing people's coping competencies than to wait for a problem to arise and then treat it.

A story about the rescue of a drowning person from a rushing river illustrates this viewpoint: Having successfully administered first aid to the first victim, the rescuer spots another struggling person and pulls her out, too. After a half-dozen repetitions, the rescuer suddenly turns and starts running away while the river sweeps yet another floundering person into view. "Aren't you going to rescue that fellow?" asks a bystander. "Heck no," the rescuer replies. "I'm going upstream to find out what's pushing all these people in."

"It is better to prevent than to cure."
Peruvian folk wisdom

Preventive mental health is upstream work. It seeks to prevent psychological casualties by identifying and alleviating the conditions that cause them. As George Albee (1986) pointed out, there is abundant evidence that poverty, meaningless work, constant criticism, unemployment, racism, and sexism undermine people's sense of competence, personal control, and self-esteem. Such stresses increase their risk of depression, alcohol dependence, and suicide.

We who care about preventing psychological casualties should, Albee contended, support programs that alleviate these demoralizing situations. We eliminated smallpox not by treating the afflicted but by inoculating the unafflicted. We conquered yellow fever by controlling mosquitoes. Preventing psychological problems means empowering those who have learned an attitude of helplessness, changing environments that breed loneliness, renewing the disintegrating family, promoting communication training for couples, and bolstering parents' and teachers' skills. "Everything aimed at improving the human condition, at making life more fulfilling and meaningful, may be considered part of primary prevention of mental or emotional disturbance" (Kessler & Albee, 1975, p. 557). That includes the cognitive training that promotes positive thinking in children at risk for depression (Brunwasser et al., 2009; Gillham et al., 2006; Stice et al., 2009). A 2009 National Research Council and Institute of Medicine report—*Preventing Mental, Emotional, and Behavioral Disorders Among Young People*—offers encouragement. It documents that intervention efforts often based on cognitive-behavioral therapy principles significantly boost child and adolescent flourishing. Through such preventive efforts and healthy lifestyles, fewer of us will fall into the rushing river of psychological disorders.

"Mental disorders arise from physical ones, and likewise physical disorders arise from mental ones."
The Mahabharata, 200 B.C.E.

RETRIEVAL PRACTICE

- What is the difference between preventive mental health and psychological or biomedical therapy?

ANSWER: Psychological and biomedical therapies attempt to relieve people's suffering from psychological disorders. Preventive mental health attempts to prevent suffering by identifying and eliminating the conditions that cause disorders.

MODULE REVIEW

Evaluating Psychotherapies

Learning Objectives

RETRIEVAL PRACTICE Take a moment to answer each of these Learning Objective Questions (repeated here from within the module). Then turn to Appendix B, Complete Module Reviews, to check your answers. Research suggests that trying to answer these questions on your own will improve your long-term retention (McDaniel et al., 2009).

53-1: Does psychotherapy work? Who decides?

53-2: Are some psychotherapies more effective than others for specific disorders?

53-3: How do alternative therapies fare under scientific scrutiny?

53-4: What three elements are shared by all forms of psychotherapy?

53-5: How do culture, gender, and values influence the therapist-client relationship?

53-6: What should a person look for when selecting a therapist?

53-7: What is the rationale for preventive mental health programs?

Terms and Concepts to Remember

RETRIEVAL PRACTICE Test yourself on these terms by trying to write down the definition before flipping back to the referenced page to check your answer.

psychotherapy, p. 692
regression toward the mean, p. 693
meta-analysis, p. 694
evidence-based practice, p. 696
therapeutic alliance, p. 699
resilience, p. 701

RETRIEVAL PRACTICE Gain an advantage, and benefit from immediate feedback, with the interactive self-testing resources at www.worthpublishers.com/myers.

MODULE 54

The Biomedical Therapies

- Drug Therapies
- Brain Stimulation
- Psychosurgery
- Therapeutic Lifestyle Change

One way to treat psychological disorders is with *psychotherapy,* in which a trained therapist uses psychological techniques to assist someone seeking to overcome difficulties or achieve personal growth. The other, often used with serious disorders, is **biomedical therapy**—physically changing the brain's functioning by altering its chemistry with drugs, or affecting its circuitry with electroconvulsive shock, magnetic impulses, or psychosurgery. Psychologists can provide psychological therapies. But with a few exceptions, only psychiatrists (as medical doctors) offer biomedical therapies.

Drug or placebo effect? For many people, depression lifts while taking an antidepressant drug. But people given a placebo may experience the same effect. Double-blind clinical trials suggest that, especially for those with severe depression, antidepressant drugs do have at least a modest clinical effect.

© The New Yorker Collection, 2007, Edward Koren from cartoonbank.com. All Rights Reserved.

"Our psychopharmacologist is a genius."

Drug Therapies

54-1 What are the drug therapies? How do double-blind studies help researchers evaluate a drug's effectiveness?

By far the most widely used biomedical treatments today are the drug therapies. Since the 1950s, discoveries in **psychopharmacology** (the study of drug effects on mind and behavior) have revolutionized the treatment of people with severe disorders, liberating hundreds of thousands from hospital confinement. Thanks to drug therapy—and to efforts to minimize involuntary hospitalization and to support people with community mental health programs—the resident population of mental hospitals is a small fraction of what it was a half-century ago. For some unable to care for themselves, however, release from hospitals has meant homelessness, not liberation.

Almost any new treatment, including drug therapy, is greeted by an initial wave of enthusiasm as many people apparently improve. But that enthusiasm often diminishes after researchers subtract the rates of (1) normal recovery among untreated persons and (2) recovery due to the *placebo effect,* which arises from the positive expectations of patients and mental health workers alike. So, to evaluate the effectiveness of any new drug, researchers give half the patients the drug, and the other half a similar-appearing placebo. Because neither the staff nor the patients know who gets which, this is called a *double-blind procedure.* The good news: In double-blind studies, some drugs have proven useful.

Antipsychotic Drugs

The revolution in drug therapy for psychological disorders began with the accidental discovery that certain drugs, used for other medical purposes, calmed patients with *psychoses* (disorders in which hallucinations or delusions indicate some loss of contact with reality). These **antipsychotic drugs,** such as chlorpromazine (sold as Thorazine), dampened responsiveness to irrelevant stimuli. Thus, they provided the most help to patients experiencing positive symptoms of schizophrenia, such as auditory hallucinations and paranoia (Lehman et al., 1998; Lenzenweger et al., 1989).

The molecules of most conventional antipsychotic drugs are similar enough to molecules of the neurotransmitter dopamine to occupy its receptor sites and block its activity. This finding reinforces the idea that an overactive dopamine system contributes to schizophrenia.

Perhaps you can guess an occasional side effect of L-dopa, a drug that raises dopamine levels for Parkinson's patients: hallucinations.

Antipsychotics also have powerful side effects. Some produce sluggishness, tremors, and twitches similar to those of Parkinson's disease (Kaplan & Saddock, 1989). Long-term use of antipsychotics can produce *tardive dyskinesia,* with involuntary movements of the facial muscles (such as grimacing), tongue, and limbs. Although not more effective in controlling schizophrenia symptoms, many of the newer-generation antipsychotics, such as risperidone (Risperdal) and olanzapine (Zyprexa), have fewer of these effects. These drugs may, however, increase the risk of obesity and diabetes (Buchanan et al., 2010; Tiihonen et al., 2009).

Antipsychotics, combined with life-skills programs and family support, have given new hope to many people with schizophrenia (Guo, 2010). Hundreds of thousands of patients have left the wards of mental hospitals and returned to work and to near-normal lives (Leucht et al., 2003).

biomedical therapy prescribed medications or procedures that act directly on the person's physiology.

psychopharmacology the study of the effects of drugs on mind and behavior.

antipsychotic drugs drugs used to treat schizophrenia and other forms of severe thought disorder.

antianxiety drugs drugs used to control anxiety and agitation.

antidepressant drugs drugs used to treat depression and some anxiety disorders. Different types work by altering the availability of various neurotransmitters.

Antianxiety Drugs

Like alcohol, **antianxiety drugs,** such as Xanax or Ativan, depress central nervous system activity (and so should not be used in combination with alcohol). Antianxiety drugs are often used in combination with psychological therapy. One antianxiety drug, the antibiotic D-cycloserine, acts upon a receptor that, in combination with behavioral treatments, facilitates the extinction of learned fears. Experiments indicate that the drug enhances the benefits of exposure therapy and helps relieve the symptoms of post-traumatic stress disorder and obsessive-compulsive disorder (Davis, 2005; Kushner et al., 2007).

A criticism sometimes made of antianxiety drugs is that they reduce symptoms without resolving underlying problems. "Popping a Xanax" at the first sign of tension can produce psychological dependence; the immediate relief reinforces a person's tendency to take drugs when anxious. Antianxiety drugs can also cause physiological dependence. After heavy use, people who stop taking them may experience increased anxiety, insomnia, and other withdrawal symptoms.

Over the dozen years at the end of the twentieth century, the rate of outpatient treatment for anxiety disorders nearly doubled. The proportion of psychiatric patients receiving medication during that time increased from 52 to 70 percent (Olfson et al., 2004). And the new standard drug treatment for anxiety disorders? Antidepressants.

Antidepressant Drugs

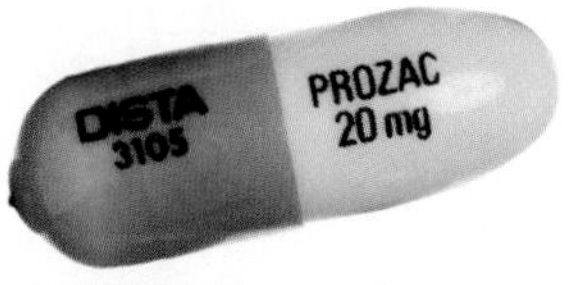

© John Greim/Agerotostock

The **antidepressants** were named for their ability to lift people up from a state of depression, and this was their main use until recently. The label is a bit of a misnomer now that these drugs are increasingly being used to successfully treat anxiety disorders such as obsessive-compulsive disorder. They work by increasing the availability of norepinephrine or serotonin, neurotransmitters that elevate arousal and mood and appear scarce during depression. Fluoxetine, which tens of millions of users worldwide have known as Prozac, partially blocks the reabsorption and removal of serotonin from synapses (**FIGURE 54.1** on the next page). Because they slow the synaptic vacuuming up of serotonin, Prozac and its cousins Zoloft and Paxil are called *selective-serotonin-reuptake-inhibitors (SSRIs).* (Given their use in treating other disorders, from anxiety to strokes, some professionals refer to "SSRI drugs" rather than "antidepressants" [Kramer, 2011].) Other antidepressant drugs work by blocking the reabsorption or breakdown of both norepinephrine and serotonin. Though effective, these dual-action drugs have more potential side effects, such as dry mouth, weight gain, hypertension, or dizzy spells (Anderson, 2000; Mulrow, 1999). Administering them by means of a patch, bypassing the intestines and liver, helps reduce such side effects (Bodkin & Amsterdam, 2002).

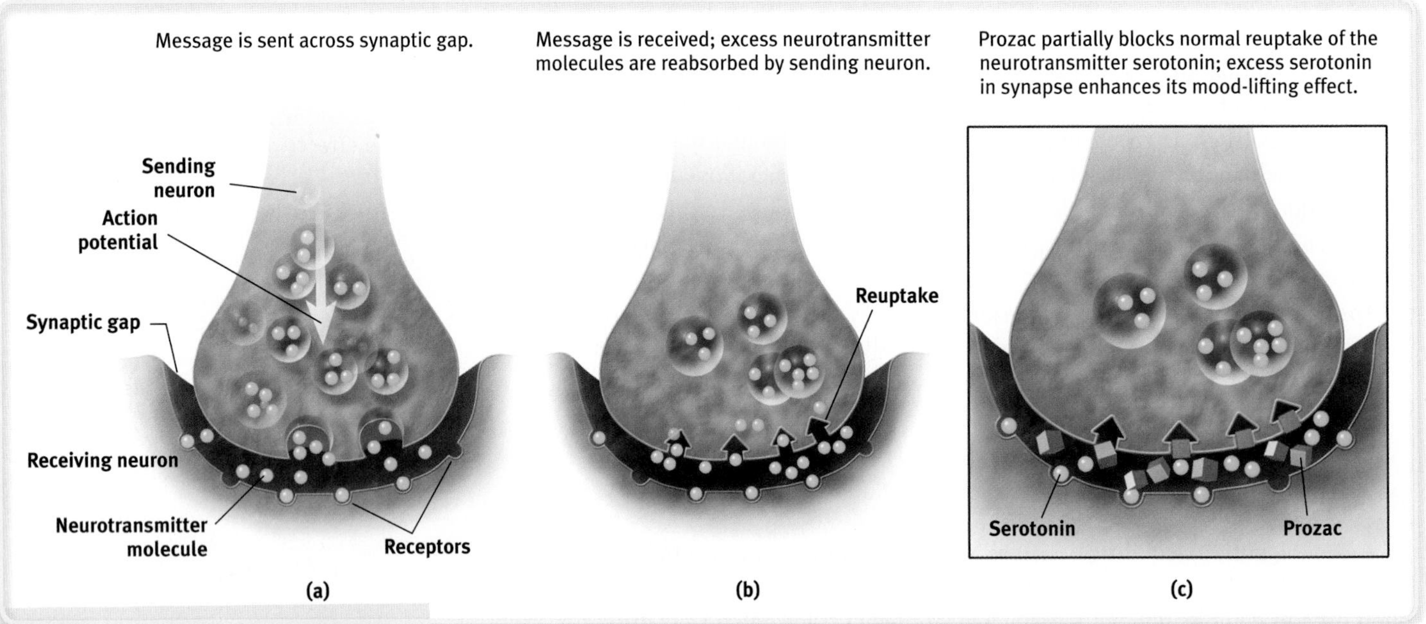

FIGURE 54.1
Biology of antidepressants Shown here is the action of Prozac, which partially blocks the reuptake of serotonin.

After the introduction of SSRI drugs, the percentage of patients receiving medication for depression jumped dramatically, from 70 percent in 1987, the year before SSRIs were introduced, to 89 percent in 2001 (Olfson et al., 2003; Stafford et al., 2001). From 1996 to 2005, the number of Americans prescribed antidepressant drugs doubled, from 13 to 27 million (Olfson & Marcus, 2009). Between 2002 and 2007 in Australia, antidepressant drug use increased 41 percent (Hollingworth et al., 2010).

Be advised: Patients with depression who begin taking antidepressants do not wake up the next day singing "Oh, what a beautiful morning!" Although the drugs begin to influence neurotransmission within hours, their full psychological effect often requires four weeks (and may involve a side effect of diminished sexual desire). One possible reason for the delay is that increased serotonin promotes *neurogenesis*—the birth of new brain cells, perhaps reversing stress-induced loss of neurons (Becker & Wojtowicz, 2007; Jacobs, 2004).

© The New Yorker Collection, 2000, P. C. Vey from cartoonbank.com. All Rights Reserved.

"If this doesn't help you don't worry, it's a placebo."

Antidepressant drugs are not the only way to give the body a lift. Aerobic exercise, which calms people who feel anxious and energizes those who feel depressed, does about as much good for some people with mild to moderate depression, and has additional positive side effects (more on this topic later in this module). Cognitive therapy, by helping people reverse their habitual negative thinking style, can boost the drug-aided relief from depression and reduce the post-treatment risk of relapse (Hollon et al., 2002; Keller et al., 2000; Vittengl et al., 2007). Better yet, some studies suggest, is to attack depression (and anxiety) from both below and above (Cuijpers et al., 2010; Walkup et al., 2008). Use antidepressant drugs (which work, bottom-up, on the emotion-forming limbic system) in conjunction with cognitive-behavioral therapy (which works, top-down, starting with changed frontal lobe activity).

Everyone agrees that people with depression often improve after a month on antidepressants. But after allowing for natural recovery (the return to normal called *spontaneous recovery*) and the placebo effect, how big is the drug effect? Not big, report Irving Kirsch and his colleagues (1998, 2002, 2010). Their analyses of double-blind clinical trials indicate that placebos accounted for about 75 percent of the active drug's effect. In a follow-up review that included unpublished clinical trials, the antidepressant drug effect was again modest (Kirsch et al., 2008). The placebo effect was less for those with severe depression, which made the added benefit of the drug somewhat greater for them. "Given these results, there seems little reason to prescribe antidepressant medication to any but the most severely depressed patients, unless alternative treatments have failed,"

"No twisted thought without a twisted molecule."

Attributed to psychologist Ralph Gerard

12-7: How do gender roles and gender typing influence gender development?

Gender roles, the behaviors a culture expects from its males and females, vary across place and time. *Social learning theory* proposes that we learn *gender identity*—our sense of being male or female—as we learn other things: through reinforcement, punishment, and observation. Critics argue that cognition also plays a role because modeling and rewards cannot explain *gender typing*. *Transgender* people's gender identity or expression differs from their birth sex.

12-8: What is included in the biopsychosocial approach to development?

Individual development results from the interaction of biological, psychological, and social-cultural influences. Biological influences include our shared human genome; individual variations; prenatal environment; and sex-related genes, hormones, and physiology. Psychological influences include gene-environment interactions; the effect of early experiences on neural networks; responses evoked by our own characteristics, such as gender and temperament; and personal beliefs, feelings, and expectations. Social-cultural influences include parental and peer influences; cultural traditions and values; and cultural gender norms.

Developing Through the Life Span

MODULE 13: Developmental Issues, Prenatal Development, and the Newborn

13-1: What three issues have engaged developmental psychologists?

Developmental psychologists study physical, mental, and social changes throughout the life span. They focus on three issues: nature and nurture (the interaction between our genetic inheritance and our experiences); continuity and stages (whether development is gradual and continuous or a series of relatively abrupt changes); and stability and change (whether our traits endure or change as we age).

13-2: What is the course of prenatal development, and how do teratogens affect that development?

The life cycle begins at conception, when one sperm cell unites with an egg to form a *zygote*. The zygote's inner cells become the *embryo*, and in the next 6 weeks, body organs begin to form and function. By 9 weeks, the *fetus* is recognizably human.

Teratogens are potentially harmful agents that can pass through the placental screen and harm the developing embryo or fetus, as happens with *fetal alcohol syndrome*.

13-3: What are some newborn abilities, and how do researchers explore infants' mental abilities?

Babies are born with sensory equipment and reflexes that facilitate their survival and their social interactions with adults. For example, they quickly learn to discriminate their mother's smell and sound. Researchers use techniques that test *habituation*, such as the novelty-preference procedure, to explore infants' abilities.

MODULE 14: Infancy and Childhood

14-1: During infancy and childhood, how do the brain and motor skills develop?

The brain's nerve cells are sculpted by heredity and experience. Their interconnections multiply rapidly after birth, a process that continues until puberty, when a pruning process begins shutting down unused connections. Complex motor skills—sitting, standing, walking—develop in a predictable sequence, though the timing of that sequence is a function of individual *maturation* and culture. We have no conscious memories of events occurring before about age 3½, in part because major brain areas have not yet matured.

14-2: From the perspectives of Piaget, Vygotsky, and today's researchers, how does a child's mind develop?

In his theory of *cognitive* development, Jean Piaget proposed that children actively construct and modify their understanding of the world through the processes of *assimilation* and *accommodation*. They form *schemas* that help them organize their experiences. Progressing from the simplicity of the *sensorimotor stage* of the first two years, in which they develop *object permanence*, children move to more complex ways of thinking. In the *preoperational stage* (about age 2 to about 6 or 7), they develop a *theory of mind*, but they are *egocentric* and unable to perform simple logical operations. At about age 7, they enter the *concrete operational stage* and are able to comprehend the principle of *conservation*. By about age 12, children enter the *formal operational stage* and can reason systematically.

Research supports the sequence Piaget proposed, but it also shows that young children are more capable, and their development more continuous, than he believed.

Lev Vygotsky's studies of child development focused on the ways a child's mind grows by interacting with the social environment. In his view, parents and caretakers provide temporary scaffolds enabling children to step to higher levels of learning.

14-3: How do parent-infant attachment bonds form?

At about 8 months, soon after object permanence develops, children separated from their caregivers display *stranger anxiety*. Infants form *attachments* not simply because parents gratify biological needs but, more important, because they are comfortable, familiar, and responsive. Ducks and other animals have a more rigid attachment process, called *imprinting*, that occurs during a *critical period*.

14-4: How have psychologists studied attachment differences, and what have they learned?

Attachment has been studied in strange situation experiments, which show that some children are securely attached and others are insecurely attached. Infants' differing attachment styles reflect both their individual temperament and the responsiveness of their parents and child-care providers. Adult relationships seem to reflect the attachment styles of early childhood, lending support to Erik Erikson's idea that *basic trust* is formed in infancy by our experiences with responsive caregivers.

14-5: Does childhood neglect, abuse, or family disruption affect children's attachments?

Children are very resilient, but those who are moved repeatedly, severely neglected by their parents, or otherwise prevented from forming attachments at an early age may be at risk for attachment problems.

14-6: How does day care affect children?

Quality day care, with responsive adults interacting with children in a safe and stimulating environment, does not appear to harm children's thinking and language skills. Some studies have linked extensive time in day care with increased aggressiveness and defiance, but other factors—the child's temperament, the parents' sensitivity, and the family's economic and educational levels and culture—also matter.

14-7: How do children's self-concepts develop?

Self-concept, an understanding and evaluation of who we are, emerges gradually. At 15 to 18 months, children recognize themselves in a mirror. By school age, they can describe many of their own traits, and by age 8 to 10 their self-image is stable.

14-8: What are three parenting styles, and how do children's traits relate to them?

Parenting styles—authoritarian, permissive, and authoritative—reflect varying degrees of control. Children with high self-esteem tend to have authoritative parents and to be self-reliant and socially competent, but the direction of cause and effect in this relationship is not clear.

MODULE 15: Adolescence

15-1: How is adolescence defined, and what physical changes mark this period?

Adolescence is the transition period from childhood to adulthood, extending from *puberty* to social independence. During puberty, both *primary* and *secondary sex characteristics* develop dramatically. Boys seem to benefit from "early" maturation, girls from "late" maturation. The brain's frontal lobes mature and myelin growth increases during adolescence and the early twenties, enabling improved judgment, impulse control, and long-term planning.

15-2: How did Piaget, Kohlberg, and later researchers describe adolescent cognitive and moral development?

Piaget theorized that adolescents develop a capacity for formal operations and that this development is the foundation for moral judgment. Lawrence Kohlberg proposed a stage theory of moral reasoning, from a preconventional morality of self-interest, to a conventional morality concerned with upholding laws and social rules, to (in some people) a postconventional morality of universal ethical principles. Other researchers believe that morality lies in moral intuition and moral action as well as thinking. Some critics argue that Kohlberg's postconventional level represents morality from the perspective of individualist, middle-class people.

15-3: What are the social tasks and challenges of adolescence?

Erikson theorized that each life stage has its own psychosocial task, and that a chief task of adolescence is solidifying one's sense of self—one's *identity*. This often means "trying on" a number of different roles. *Social identity* is the part of the self-concept that comes from a person's group memberships.

15-4: How do parents and peers influence adolescents?

During adolescence, parental influence diminishes and peer influence increases. Adolescents adopt their peers' ways of dressing, acting, and communicating. Parents have more influence in religion, politics, and college and career choices.

15-5: What is emerging adulthood?

The transition from adolescence to adulthood is now taking longer. *Emerging adulthood* is the period from age 18 to the mid-twenties, when many young people are not yet fully independent. But observers note that this stage is found mostly in today's Western cultures.

MODULE 16: Adulthood

16-1: What physical changes occur during middle and late adulthood?

Muscular strength, reaction time, sensory abilities, and cardiac output begin to decline in the late twenties and continue to decline throughout middle adulthood (roughly age 40 to 65) and late adulthood (the years after 65). Women's period of fertility ends with *menopause* around age 50; men have no similar age-related sharp drop in hormone levels or fertility. In late adulthood, the immune system weakens, increasing susceptibility to life-threatening illnesses. Chromosome tips (telomeres) wear down, reducing the chances of normal genetic replication. But for some, longevity-supporting genes, low stress, and good health habits enable better health in later life.

16-2: How does memory change with age?

As the years pass, recall begins to decline, especially for meaningless information, but recognition memory remains strong. Older adults rely more on time management and memory cues to remember time-based and habitual tasks. Dementia and Alzheimer's disease are brain ailments, not normal parts of aging. Developmental researchers study age-related changes (such as memory) with *cross-sectional studies* (comparing people of different ages) and *longitudinal studies* (retesting the same people over a period of years). "Terminal decline" describes the cognitive decline in the final few years of life.

16-3: What themes and influences mark our social journey from early adulthood to death?

Adults do not progress through an orderly sequence of age-related social stages. Chance events can determine life choices. The *social clock* is a culture's preferred timing for social events, such as marriage, parenthood, and retirement. Adulthood's dominant themes are love and work, which Erikson called intimacy and generativity.

16-4: Do self-confidence and life satisfaction vary with life stages?

Self-confidence tends to strengthen across the life span. Surveys show that life satisfaction is unrelated to age. Positive emotions increase after midlife and negative ones decrease.

16-5: A loved one's death triggers what range of reactions?

People do not grieve in predictable stages, as was once supposed. Strong expressions of emotion do not purge grief, and bereavement therapy is not significantly more effective than grieving without such aid. Erikson viewed the late-adulthood psychosocial task as developing a sense of integrity (versus despair).

▶Sensation and Perception

MODULE 17: Basic Principles of Sensation and Perception

17-1: What are *sensation* and *perception*? What do we mean by *bottom-up processing* and *top-down processing*?

Sensation is the process by which our sensory receptors and nervous system receive and represent stimulus energies from our environment. *Perception* is the process of organizing and interpreting this information, enabling recognition of meaningful events. Sensation and perception are actually parts of one continuous process. *Bottom-up processing* is sensory analysis that begins at the entry level, with information flowing from the sensory receptors to the brain. *Top-down processing* is information processing guided by high-level mental processes, as when we construct perceptions by filtering information through our experience and expectations.

17-2: What three steps are basic to all our sensory systems?

Our senses (1) receive sensory stimulation (often using specialized receptor cells); (2) transform that stimulation into neural impulses; and (3) deliver the neural information to the brain. *Transduction* is the process of converting one form of energy into another. Researchers in *psychophysics* study the relationships between stimuli's physical characteristics and our psychological experience of them.

17-3: What are the absolute and difference thresholds, and do stimuli below the absolute threshold have any influence on us?

Our *absolute threshold* for any stimulus is the minimum stimulation necessary for us to be consciously aware of it 50 percent of the time. *Signal detection theory* predicts how and when we will detect a faint stimulus amid background noise. Individual absolute thresholds vary, depending on the strength of the signal and also on our experience, expectations, motivation, and alertness. Our *difference threshold* (also called *just noticeable difference*, or *jnd*) is the difference we can discern between two stimuli 50 percent of the time. *Weber's law* states that two stimuli must differ by a constant proportion (not a constant amount) to be perceived as different.

Priming shows that we can process some information from stimuli below our absolute threshold for conscious awareness. But the effect is too fleeting to enable people to exploit us with *subliminal* messages.

17-4: What is the function of sensory adaptation?

Sensory adaptation (our diminished sensitivity to constant or routine odors, sounds, and touches) focuses our attention on informative changes in our environment.

17-5: How do our expectations, contexts, emotions, and motivation influence our perceptions?

Perceptual set is a mental predisposition that functions as a lens through which we perceive the world. Our learned concepts (schemas) prime us to organize and interpret ambiguous stimuli in certain ways. Our physical and emotional context, as well as our motivation, can create expectations and color our interpretation of events and behaviors.

MODULE 18: Vision and Perceptual Organization and Interpretation

18-1: What is the energy that we see as visible light, and how does the eye transform light energy into neural messages?

After entering the eye and being focused by a *lens*, light energy particles (from a thin slice of the broad spectrum of electromagnetic energy) strike the eye's inner surface, the *retina*. The retina's light-sensitive *rods* and color-sensitive *cones* convert the light energy into neural impulses. The *hue* we perceive in a light depends on its *wavelength*, and its brightness depends on its *intensity*.

18-2: How do the eye and the brain process visual information?

After processing by bipolar and ganglion cells in the eyes' retina, neural impulses travel through the *optic nerve*, to the thalamus, and on to the visual cortex. In the visual cortex, *feature detectors* respond to specific features of the visual stimulus. Supercell clusters in other critical areas respond to more complex patterns. Through *parallel processing*, the brain handles many aspects of vision (color, movement, form, and depth) simultaneously. Other neural teams integrate the results, comparing them with stored information and enabling perceptions.

18-3: What theories help us understand color vision?

The Young-Helmholtz trichromatic (three-color) theory proposed that the retina contains three types of color receptors. Contemporary research has found three types of cones, each most sensitive to the wavelengths of one of the three primary colors of light (red, green, or blue).

Hering's *opponent-process theory* proposed three additional color processes (red-versus-green, blue-versus-yellow, black-versus-white). Contemporary research has confirmed that, en route to the brain, neurons in the retina and the thalamus code the color-related information from the cones into pairs of opponent colors.

These two theories, and the research supporting them, show that color processing occurs in two stages.

18-4: How did the Gestalt psychologists understand perceptual organization, and how do figure-ground and grouping principles contribute to our perceptions?

Gestalt psychologists searched for rules by which the brain organizes fragments of sensory data into *gestalts* (from the German word for "whole"), or meaningful forms. In pointing out that the whole may exceed the sum of its parts, they noted that we filter sensory information and construct our perceptions.

To recognize an object, we must first perceive it (see it as a *figure*) as distinct from its surroundings (the *ground*). We bring order and form to stimuli by organizing them into meaningful *groups*, following such rules as proximity, continuity, and closure.

18-5: How do we use binocular and monocular cues to perceive the world in three dimensions and perceive motion?

Depth perception is our ability to see objects in three dimensions and judge distance. The *visual cliff* and other research demonstrate that many species perceive the world in three dimensions at, or very soon after, birth. *Binocular cues*, such as *retinal disparity*, are depth cues that rely on information from both eyes. *Monocular cues* (such as relative size, interposition, relative height, relative motion, linear perspective, and light and shadow) let us judge depth using information transmitted by only one eye.

As objects move, we assume that shrinking objects are retreating and enlarging objects are approaching. A quick succession of images on the retina can create an illusion of movement, as in stroboscopic movement or the *phi phenomenon*.

18-6: How do perceptual constancies help us organize our sensations into meaningful perceptions?

Perceptual constancy enables us to perceive objects as stable despite the changing image they cast on our retinas. *Color constancy* is our ability to perceive consistent color in objects, even though the lighting and wavelengths shift. Brightness (or lightness) constancy is our ability to perceive an object as having a constant lightness even when its illumination—the light cast upon it—changes. Our brain constructs our experience of an object's color or brightness through comparisons with other surrounding objects.

Shape constancy is our ability to perceive familiar objects (such as an opening door) as unchanging in shape. Size constancy is perceiving objects as unchanging in size despite their changing retinal images. Knowing an object's size gives us clues to its distance; knowing its distance gives clues about its size, but we sometimes misread monocular distance cues and reach the wrong conclusions, as in the Moon illusion.

18-7: What does research on restored vision, sensory restriction, and perceptual adaptation reveal about the effects of experience on perception?

Experience guides our perceptual interpretations. People blind from birth who gained sight after surgery lack the experience to visually recognize shapes, forms, and complete faces.

Sensory restriction research indicates that there is a critical period for some aspects of sensory and perceptual development. Without early stimulation, the brain's neural organization does not develop normally.

People given glasses that shift the world slightly to the left or right, or even upside-down, experience *perceptual adaptation*. They are initially disoriented, but they manage to adapt to their new context.

18-8: What are the claims of ESP, and what have most research psychologists concluded after putting these claims to the test?

Parapsychology is the study of paranormal phenomena, including *extrasensory perception (ESP)* and psychokinesis. The three most testable forms of ESP are telepathy (mind-to-mind communication), clairvoyance (perceiving remote events), and precognition (perceiving future events).

Skeptics argue that (1) to believe in ESP, you must believe the brain is capable of perceiving without sensory input, and (2) researchers have been unable to replicate ESP phenomena under controlled conditions.

MODULE 19: The Nonvisual Senses

19-1: What are the characteristics of air pressure waves that we hear as sound, and how does the ear transform sound energy into neural messages?

Sound waves are bands of compressed and expanded air. Our ears detect these changes in air pressure and transform them into neural impulses, which the brain decodes as sound. Sound waves vary in amplitude, which we perceive as differing loudness, and in *frequency*, which we experience as differing *pitch*.

The outer ear is the visible portion of the ear. The *middle ear* is the chamber between the eardrum and *cochlea*. The *inner ear* consists of the cochlea, semicircular canals, and vestibular sacs. Through a mechanical chain of events, sound waves traveling through the auditory canal cause tiny vibrations in the eardrum. The bones of the middle ear amplify the vibrations and relay them to the fluid-filled cochlea. Rippling of the basilar membrane, caused by pressure changes in the cochlear fluid, causes movement of the tiny hair cells, triggering neural messages to be sent (via the thalamus) to the auditory cortex in the brain.

Sensorineural hearing loss (or nerve deafness) results from damage to the cochlea's hair cells or their associated nerves. *Conduction hearing loss* results from damage to the mechanical system that transmits sound waves to the cochlea. *Cochlear implants* can restore hearing for some people, but their use is controversial.

19-2: What theories help us understand pitch perception?

Place theory explains how we hear high-pitched sounds, and *frequency theory* explains how we hear low-pitched sounds. (A combination of the two theories explains how we hear pitches in the middle range.) *Place theory* proposes that our brain interprets a particular pitch by decoding the place where a sound wave stimulates the cochlea's basilar membrane.

Frequency theory proposes that the brain deciphers the frequency of the neural impulses traveling up the auditory nerve to the brain.

19-3: How do we locate sounds?

Sound waves strike one ear sooner and more intensely than the other. The brain analyzes the minute differences in the sounds received by the two ears and computes the sound's source.

19-4: How do we sense touch?

Our sense of touch is actually several senses—pressure, warmth, cold, and pain—that combine to produce other sensations, such as "hot."

19-5: How can we best understand and control pain?

Pain reflects bottom-up sensations (such as input from nociceptors, the sensory receptors that detect hurtful temperatures, pressure, or chemicals) and top-down processes (such as experience, attention, and culture). One theory of pain is that a *"gate"* in the spinal cord either opens to permit pain signals traveling up small nerve fibers to reach the brain, or closes to prevent their passage.

The biopsychosocial perspective views our perception of pain as the sum of biological, psychological, and social-cultural influences. Pain treatments often combine physical and psychological elements, including placebos and distractions.

19-6: How do we experience taste and smell, and how do they interact?

Taste and smell are chemical senses. Taste is a composite of five basic sensations—sweet, sour, salty, bitter, and umami—and of the aromas that interact with information from the taste receptor cells of the taste buds.

There are no basic sensations for smell. We have some 5 million olfactory receptor cells, with about 350 different receptor proteins. Odor molecules trigger combinations of receptors, in patterns that the olfactory cortex interprets. The receptor cells send messages to the brain's olfactory bulb, then to the temporal lobe, and to parts of the limbic system.

The influence of smell on our sense of taste is an example of *sensory interaction. Embodied cognition* is the influence of bodily sensations, gestures, and other states on cognitive preferences and judgments.

19-7: How do we sense our body's position and movement?

Through *kinesthesis,* we sense the position and movement of our body parts. We monitor our body's position and movement, and maintain our balance with our *vestibular sense.*

▶Learning

MODULE 20: Basic Learning Concepts and Classical Conditioning

20-1: What is learning, and what are some basic forms of learning?

Learning is the process of acquiring new and relatively enduring information or behaviors. In *associative learning,* we learn that certain events occur together. In classical conditioning, we learn to associate two or more stimuli (a *stimulus* is any event or situation that evokes a response). In operant conditioning, we learn to associate a response and its consequences. Through *cognitive learning,* we acquire mental information that guides our behavior. For example, in observational learning, we learn new behaviors by observing events and watching others.

20-2: What are the basic components of classical conditioning, and what was behaviorism's view of learning?

Classical conditioning is a type of learning in which an organism comes to associate stimuli. In classical conditioning, an *NS* is a stimulus that elicits no response before conditioning. A *UR* is an event that occurs naturally (such as salivation), in response to some stimulus. A *US* is something that naturally and automatically (without learning) triggers the unlearned response (as food in the mouth triggers salivation). A *CS* is a previously neutral stimulus (such as a tone) that, after association with a US (such as food) comes to trigger a CR. A *CR* is the learned response (salivating) to the originally neutral (but now conditioned) stimulus.

Ivan Pavlov's work on classical conditioning laid the foundation for *behaviorism,* the view that psychology should be an objective science that studies behavior without reference to mental processes. The behaviorists believed that the basic laws of learning are the same for all species, including humans.

20-3: In classical conditioning, what are the processes of acquisition, extinction, spontaneous recovery, generalization, and discrimination?

In classical conditioning, *acquisition* is associating an NS with the US so that the NS begins triggering the CR. Acquisition occurs most readily when the NS is presented just before (ideally, about a half-second before) a US, preparing the organism for the upcoming event. This finding supports the view that classical conditioning is biologically adaptive. Through higher-order conditioning, a new NS can become a new CS.

Extinction is diminished responding when the CS no longer signals an impending US. *Spontaneous recovery* is the appearance of a formerly extinguished response, following a rest period. *Generalization* is the tendency to respond to stimuli that are similar to a CS. *Discrimination* is the learned ability to distinguish between a CS and other irrelevant stimuli.

20-4: Why does Pavlov's work remain so important, and what have been some applications of his work to human health and well-being?

Pavlov taught us that significant psychological phenomena can be studied objectively, and that classical conditioning is a basic form of learning that applies to all species.

Classical conditioning techniques are used to improve human health and well-being in many areas, including behavioral therapy for some types of psychological disorders. The body's immune system may also respond to classical conditioning.

MODULE 21: Operant Conditioning

21-1: What is operant conditioning, and how is operant behavior reinforced and shaped?

In *operant conditioning,* behaviors followed by reinforcers increase; those followed by punishers often decrease. Expanding on Edward Thorndike's *law of effect,* B. F. Skinner and others found that the behavior of rats or pigeons placed in an *operant chamber* (Skinner box) can be *shaped* by using reinforcers to guide closer and closer approximations of the desired behavior.

21-2: How do positive and negative reinforcement differ, and what are the basic types of reinforcers?

Reinforcement is any consequence that strengthens behavior. *Positive reinforcement* adds a desirable stimulus to increase the frequency of a behavior. *Negative reinforcement* removes an aversive stimulus to increase the frequency of a behavior.

Primary reinforcers (such as receiving food when hungry or having nausea end during an illness) are innately satisfying—no learning is required. *Conditioned* (or secondary) *reinforcers* (such as cash) are satisfying because we have learned to associate them with more basic rewards (such as the food or medicine we buy with them). Immediate reinforcers (such as a purchased treat) offer immediate payback; delayed reinforcers (such as a weekly paycheck) require the ability to delay gratification.

21-3: How do different reinforcement schedules affect behavior?

A *reinforcement schedule* defines how often a response will be reinforced. In *continuous reinforcement* (reinforcing desired responses every time they occur), learning is rapid, but so is extinction if rewards cease. In *partial (intermittent) reinforcement* (reinforcing responses only sometimes), initial learning is slower, but the behavior is much more resistant to extinction. *Fixed-ratio schedules* reinforce behaviors after a set number of responses; *variable-ratio schedules,* after an unpredictable number. *Fixed-interval schedules* reinforce behaviors after set time periods; *variable-interval schedules,* after unpredictable time periods.

21-4: How does punishment differ from negative reinforcement, and how does punishment affect behavior?

Punishment administers an undesirable consequence (such as spanking) or withdraws something desirable (such as taking away a favorite toy) in an attempt to decrease the frequency of a behavior (a child's disobedience). Negative reinforcement (taking an aspirin) removes an aversive stimulus (a headache). This desired consequence (freedom from pain) increases the likelihood that the behavior (taking aspirin to end pain) will be repeated.

Punishment can have undesirable side effects, such as suppressing rather than changing unwanted behaviors; teaching aggression; creating fear; encouraging discrimination (so that the undesirable behavior appears when the punisher is not present); and fostering depression and feelings of helplessness.

21-5: Why did Skinner's ideas provoke controversy, and how might his operant conditioning principles be applied at school, in sports, at work, and at home?

Critics of Skinner's principles believed the approach dehumanized people by neglecting their personal freedom and seeking to control their actions. Skinner replied that people's actions are already controlled by external consequences, and that reinforcement is more humane than punishment as a means for controlling behavior.

At school, teachers can use shaping techniques to guide students' behaviors, and they can use interactive software and websites to provide immediate feedback. In sports, coaches can build players' skills and self-confidence by rewarding small improvements. At work, managers can boost productivity and morale by rewarding well-defined and achievable behaviors. At home, parents can reward desired behaviors but not undesirable ones. We can shape our own behaviors by stating our goals, monitoring the frequency of desired behaviors, reinforcing desired behaviors, and gradually reducing rewards as behaviors become habitual.

21-6: How does operant conditioning differ from classical conditioning?

In operant conditioning, an organism learns associations between its own behavior and resulting events; this form of conditioning involves *operant behavior* (behavior that operates on the environment, producing rewarding or punishing consequences). In classical conditioning, the organism forms associations between stimuli—events it does not control; this form of conditioning involves *respondent behavior* (automatic responses to some stimulus).

MODULE 22: Effects of Biology and Cognition, and Learning by Observation

22-1: How do biological constraints affect classical and operant conditioning?

Classical conditioning principles, we now know, are constrained by biological predispositions, so that learning some associations is easier than learning others. Learning is adaptive: Each species learns behaviors that aid its survival. Biological constraints also place limits on operant conditioning. Training that attempts to override biological constraints will probably not endure because animals will revert to predisposed patterns.

22-2: How do cognitive processes affect classical and operant conditioning?

In classical conditioning, animals may learn when to expect a US and may be aware of the link between stimuli and responses. In operant conditioning, *cognitive mapping* and *latent learning* research demonstrate the importance of cognitive processes in learning. Other research shows that excessive rewards (driving *extrinsic motivation*) can undermine *intrinsic motivation.*

22-3: What is observational learning, and how do some scientists believe it is enabled by mirror neurons?

In *observational learning,* as we observe and imitate others we learn to anticipate a behavior's consequences because we experience vicarious reinforcement or vicarious punishment.

Our brain's frontal lobes have a demonstrated ability to mirror the activity of another's brain. The same areas fire when we perform certain actions (such as responding to pain or moving our mouth to form words), as when we observe someone else performing those actions.

22-4: What is the impact of prosocial modeling and of antisocial modeling?

Children tend to imitate what a model does and says, whether the behavior being *modeled* is *prosocial* (positive, constructive, and helpful) or antisocial. If a model's actions and words are inconsistent, children may imitate the hypocrisy they observe.

▶Memory

MODULE 23: Studying and Building Memories

23-1: What is memory?

Memory is learning that has persisted over time, through the storage and retrieval of information. Evidence of memory may be *recalling* information, *recognizing* it, or *relearning* it more easily on a later attempt.

23-2: What are three measures of retention?

Three measures of retention are recalling information, recognizing it, or relearning it more easily on a later attempt.

23-3: How do psychologists describe the human memory system?

Psychologists use memory models to think and communicate about memory. Information-processing models involve three processes: *encoding, storage,* and *retrieval.* The connectionism information-processing model views memories as products of interconnected neural networks. The three processing stages in the Atkinson-Shiffrin model are *sensory memory, short-term memory,* and *long-term memory.* More recent research has updated this model to include two important concepts: (1) *working memory,* to stress the active processing occurring in the second memory stage; and (2) automatic processing, to address the processing of information outside of conscious awareness.

23-4: How are explicit and implicit memories distinguished?

Through parallel processing, the human brain processes many things simultaneously, on dual tracks. *Explicit* (declarative) *memories*—our conscious memories of facts and

31-4: How and why do racial and ethnic groups differ in mental ability scores?

As a group, American Whites have scored higher than their Hispanic and Black counterparts; this gap was wider a half-century ago than it is now. The evidence suggests that environmental differences are largely, perhaps entirely responsible for these group differences.

31-5: Are intelligence tests inappropriately biased?

Aptitude tests aim to predict how well a test-taker will perform in a given situation. So they are necessarily "biased" in the sense that they are sensitive to performance differences caused by cultural experience. By "inappropriately biased," psychologists mean that a test predicts less accurately for one group than for another. In this sense, most experts consider the major aptitude tests unbiased. *Stereotype threat,* a self-confirming concern that one will be evaluated based on a negative stereotype, affects performance on all kinds of tests.

▶Motivation and Work

MODULE 32: Basic Motivational Concepts and Hunger

32-1: How do psychologists define *motivation?* From what perspectives do they view motivated behavior?

Motivation is a need or desire that energizes and directs behavior. The *instinct*/evolutionary perspective explores genetic influences on complex behaviors. *Drive-reduction theory* explores how physiological needs create aroused tension states (drives) that direct us to satisfy those needs. Drive-reduction's goal is *homeostasis,* maintaining a steady internal state. Arousal theory proposes that some behaviors (such as those driven by curiosity) do not reduce physiological needs but rather are prompted by a search for an optimum level of arousal. Abraham Maslow's *hierarchy of needs* proposes a pyramid of human needs, from basic needs such as hunger and thirst up to higher-level needs such as actualization and transcendence.

32-2: What physiological factors produce hunger?

Hunger's pangs correspond to the stomach's contractions, but hunger also has other causes. Neural areas in the brain, some within the hypothalamus, monitor blood chemistry (including level of glucose) and incoming information about the body's state. Appetite hormones include insulin (controls blood *glucose*); ghrelin (secreted by an empty stomach); orexin (secreted by the hypothalamus); leptin (secreted by fat cells); and PYY (secreted by the digestive tract). *Basal metabolic rate* is the body's resting rate of energy expenditure. The body may have a *set point* (a biologically fixed tendency to maintain an optimum weight) or a looser settling point (also influenced by the environment).

32-3: What psychological, cultural, and situational factors influence hunger?

Hunger also reflects our memory of when we last ate and our expectation of when we should eat again. Humans as a species prefer certain tastes (such as sweet and salty), but our individual preferences are also influenced by conditioning, culture, and situation. Some taste preferences, such as the avoidance of new foods, or of foods that have made us ill, have survival value.

32-4: What factors predispose some people to become and remain obese?

Genes and environment interact to produce obesity. Environmental influences include lack of exercise, an abundance of high-calorie food, and social influence. Obesity contributes to depression, especially among women, and depression fosters obesity.

Twin and adoption studies indicate that body weight is also genetically influenced (in resting metabolism, body mass, and presence of the FTO gene).

Those wishing to lose weight are advised to make a lifelong change in habits: minimize exposure to tempting food cues; boost energy expenditure through exercise; eat healthy, portioned foods; space meals throughout the day; beware of the binge; get enough sleep; and forgive the occasional lapse.

MODULE 33: Sexual Motivation and the Need to Belong

33-1: What physiological factors affect human sexual behavior, and what disorders disrupt the sexual response cycle?

William Masters and Virginia Johnson described four stages in the human *sexual response cycle:* excitement, plateau, orgasm (which seems to involve similar feelings and brain activity in males and females), and resolution. In the resolution phase, males experience a *refractory period,* during which renewed arousal and orgasm are impossible.

Sexual disorders are problems that consistently impair sexual arousal or functioning. They can often be successfully treated by behaviorally oriented therapy or drug therapy.

33-2: How do hormones, and external and internal stimuli, influence human sexual motivation?

The female *estrogen* and male *testosterone* hormones influence human sexual behavior less directly than they influence sexual behavior in other species. Women's sexuality is more responsive to testosterone level than to estrogen level. Short-term shifts in testosterone level are normal in men, partly in response to stimulation.

External stimuli can trigger sexual arousal in both men and women, although the activated brain areas differ somewhat. Men respond more specifically to sexual depictions involving their preferred sex. Sexually explicit material may lead people to perceive their partners as comparatively less appealing and to devalue their relationships. Imagined stimuli (dreams and fantasies) also influence sexual arousal.

33-3: What factors influence teen pregnancy and risk of sexually transmitted infections?

Rates of teen intercourse vary from culture to culture and era to era. Factors contributing to teen pregnancy include minimal communication about birth control with parents, partners, and peers; guilt related to sexual activity; alcohol use; and mass media norms of unprotected and impulsive sexuality. STIs—sexually transmitted infections—have spread rapidly. Attempts to protect teens through comprehensive sex-education programs include contraceptive and abstinence education. High intelligence, religious engagement, father presence, and participation in service learning programs have been predictors of teen sexual restraint.

33-4: What has research taught us about sexual orientation?

Surveys can tell us how many people (about 3 percent) are attracted to their own sex, but statistics cannot decide issues of human rights. *Sexual orientation* is not an indicator of mental health. There is no evidence that environmental influences determine sexual orientation. Evidence for biological influences includes the presence of same-sex attraction in many animal species; straight-gay differences in body and brain characteristics; higher rates in certain families and in identical twins; exposure to certain hormones during critical periods of prenatal development; and the fraternal birth-order effect.

33-5: Is scientific research on sexual motivation value free?

Scientific research on sexual motivation does not attempt to define the personal meaning of sex in our lives, but sex research and education are not value-free.

33-6: What evidence points to our human need to belong?

Our need to affiliate or belong—to feel connected and identified with others—had survival value for our ancestors, which may explain why humans in every society live in groups. Because of their need to belong, people suffer when socially excluded, and they may engage in self-defeating behaviors (performing below their ability) or in antisocial behaviors. Feeling loved activates brain reward centers.

33-7: How does social networking influence us?

We connect with others through social networking, strengthening our relationships with those we already know. When networking, people tend toward increased self-disclosure. Working out strategies for self-control and disciplined usage can help people maintain a healthy balance between social connections and school and work performance.

MODULE 34: Motivation at Work

34-1: What is "flow," and what are the three subfields of industrial-organizational psychology?

Flow is a completely involved, focused state of consciousness with diminished awareness of self and time. It results from fully engaging one's skills. *Industrial-organizational psychology's* three subfields are personnel, organizational, and human factors psychology.

34-2: How do personnel psychologists help organizations with employee selection, work placement, and performance appraisal?

Personnel psychologists work with organizations to devise selection methods for new employees; recruit and evaluate applicants; design and evaluate training programs; identify people's strengths; analyze job content; and appraise individual and organizational performance. Subjective interviews foster the interviewer illusion; *structured interviews* pinpoint job-relevant strengths and are better predictors of performance. Checklists, graphic rating scales, and behavior rating scales are useful performance appraisal methods.

34-3: What is achievement motivation? What is the role of organizational psychologists?

Achievement motivation is the desire for significant accomplishment; for mastery of skills and ideas; and for rapidly attaining a high standard. *Organizational psychologists* examine influences on worker satisfaction and productivity and facilitate organizational change. Employee satisfaction and engagement tend to correlate with organizational success.

34-4: What are some effective leadership techniques?

Effective leaders harness job-relevant strengths; set specific challenging goals; and choose an appropriate leadership style. Leadership style may be goal-oriented *(task leadership)*, or group-oriented *(social leadership)*, or some combination of the two.

34-5: How do human factors psychologists work to create user-friendly machines and work settings?

Human factors psychologists contribute to human safety and improved design by encouraging developers and designers to consider human perceptual abilities, to avoid the curse of knowledge, and to test users to reveal perception-based problems.

Emotions, Stress, and Health

MODULE 35: Introduction to Emotion

35-1: How do arousal and expressive behaviors interact in emotion?

Emotions are psychological responses of the whole organism involving an interplay among physiological arousal, expressive behaviors, and conscious experience.

Theories of emotion generally address two major questions: (1) Does physiological arousal come before or after emotional feelings, and (2) how do cognition and feeling interact? The *James-Lange theory* maintains that emotional feelings follow our body's response to emotion-inducing stimuli. The *Cannon-Bard theory* proposes that our body responds to emotion at the same time that we experience the emotion (one does not cause the other).

35-2: To experience emotions, must we consciously interpret and label them?

The Schachter-Singer *two-factor theory* holds that our emotions have two ingredients, physical arousal and a cognitive label, and the cognitive labels we put on our states of arousal are an essential ingredient of emotion. Lazarus agreed that many important emotions arise from our interpretations or inferences. Zajonc and LeDoux, however, believe that some simple emotional responses occur instantly, not only outside our conscious awareness, but before any cognitive processing occurs. This interplay between emotion and cognition illustrates our dual-track mind.

35-3: What is the link between emotional arousal and the autonomic nervous system? How does arousal affect performance?

The arousal component of emotion is regulated by the autonomic nervous system's sympathetic (arousing) and parasympathetic (calming) divisions. Performance peaks at lower levels of arousal for difficult tasks, and at higher levels for easy or well-learned tasks.

35-4: Do different emotions activate different physiological and brain-pattern responses?

Emotions may be similarly arousing, but some subtle physiological responses, such as facial muscle movements, distinguish them. More meaningful differences have been found in activity in the brain's pathways and cortical areas and in hormone secretion associated with different emotions.

35-5: How effective are polygraphs in using body states to detect lies?

Polygraphs, which measure several physiological indicators of emotion, are not accurate enough to justify widespread use in business and law enforcement. The use of guilty knowledge questions and new forms of technology may produce better indications of lying.

MODULE 36: Expressed Emotion

36-1: How do we communicate nonverbally?

Much of our communication is through body movements, facial expressions, and voice tones. Even seconds-long filmed slices of behavior can reveal feelings.

36-2: How do the genders differ in their ability to communicate nonverbally?

Women tend to read emotional cues more easily and to be more empathic than men.

36-3: Are nonverbal expressions of emotion universally understood?

The meaning of gestures varies with culture, but facial expressions, such as those of happiness and fear, are common the world over. Cultures also differ in the amount of emotion they express.

36-4: Do our facial expressions influence our feelings?

Research on the *facial feedback effect* shows that our facial expressions can trigger emotional feelings and signal the body to respond accordingly. We also mimic others' expressions, which helps us empathize.

MODULE 37: Experienced Emotion

37-1: What are some basic emotions, and what two dimensions help differentiate them?

Carroll Izard's 10 basic emotions are joy, interest-excitement, surprise, sadness, anger, disgust, contempt, fear, shame, and guilt. The two dimensions of emotion are positive-versus-negative valence, and low-versus-high arousal.

37-2: What are the causes and consequences of anger?

Anger is most often evoked by misdeeds that we interpret as willful, unjustified, and avoidable. But smaller frustrations and blameless annoyances can also trigger anger. Emotional *catharsis* may be temporarily calming, but in the long run it does not reduce anger. Rehearsing anger can make us more angry. Controlled assertions of feelings may resolve conflicts, and forgiveness may rid us of angry feelings.

37-3: What are the causes and consequences of happiness?

A good mood brightens people's perceptions of the world and makes them more willing to help others (the *feel-good, do-good phenomenon*). The moods triggered by good or bad events seldom last beyond that day. Even significant good events, such as sudden wealth, seldom increase happiness for long. Happiness is relative to our own experiences (the *adaptation-level phenomenon*) and to others' success (the *relative deprivation* principle). Some individuals seem genetically predisposed to be happier than others. Cultures, which vary in the traits they value and the behaviors they expect and reward, also influence personal levels of happiness.

MODULE 38: Stress and Health

38-1: What events provoke stress responses, and how do we respond and adapt to stress?

Stress is the process by which we appraise and respond to stressors (catastrophic events, significant life changes, and daily hassles) that challenge or threaten us. Walter Cannon viewed the stress response as a "fight-or-flight" system. Later researchers identified an additional stress-response system in which the adrenal glands secrete glucocorticoid stress hormones. Hans Selye proposed a general three-phase (alarm-resistance-exhaustion) *general adaptation syndrome (GAS)*. Prolonged stress can damage neurons, hastening cell death. Facing stress, women may have a *tend-and-befriend* response; men may withdraw socially, turn to alcohol, or become aggressive.

38-2: How does stress make us more vulnerable to disease?

Psychoneuroimmunologists study mind-body interactions, including stress-related physical illnesses, such as hypertension and some headaches. Stress diverts energy from the immune system, inhibiting the activities of its B and T *lymphocytes*, macrophages, and NK cells. Stress does not cause diseases such as AIDS and cancer, but by altering our immune functioning it may make us more vulnerable to them and influence their progression.

38-3: Why are some of us more prone than others to coronary heart disease?

Coronary heart disease, North America's number one cause of death, has been linked with the reactive, anger-prone *Type* A personality. Compared with relaxed, easygoing *Type B* personalities, Type A people secrete more of the hormones that accelerate the buildup of plaque on the heart's artery walls. Chronic stress also contributes to persistent inflammation, which heightens the risk of clogged arteries and depression.

MODULE 39: Promoting Health

39-1: In what ways do people cope with stress, and how does a perceived lack of control affect health?

Problem-focused coping attempts to change the stressor or the way we interact with it. *Emotion-focused coping* aims to avoid or ignore stressors and attend to emotional needs related to stress reactions. A perceived loss of control provokes an outpouring of hormones that put people's health at risk.

39-2: What are the links among basic outlook on life, social support, stress, and health?

Studies of people with an optimistic outlook show that their blood pressure does not increase as sharply in response to stress, their recovery from heart bypass surgery is faster, and their life expectancy is longer, compared with their pessimistic counterparts. Social support promotes health by calming us, reducing blood pressure and stress hormones, and by fostering stronger immune functioning.

39-3: How effective is aerobic exercise as a way to manage stress and improve well-being?

Aerobic exercise is sustained, oxygen-consuming activity that increases heart and lung fitness. It increases arousal, leads to muscle relaxation and sounder sleep, triggers production of neurotransmitters, and enhances self-image. It can relieve depression and, in later life, is associated with better cognitive functioning and longer life.

39-4: In what ways might relaxation and meditation influence stress and health?

Relaxation and meditation have been shown to reduce stress by relaxing muscles, lowering blood pressure, improving immune functioning, and lessening anxiety and depression.

39-5: What is the faith factor, and what are some possible explanations for this link?

The faith factor is the finding that religiously active people tend to live longer than those who are not religiously active. Possible explanations may include the effect of intervening variables, such as the healthy behaviors, social support, or positive emotions often found among people who regularly attend religious services.

39-6: What is complementary and alternative medicine, and how is it best assessed through scientific research?

Complementary and alternative medicine (*CAM*) comprises health care treatments intended to serve as supplements or alternatives to conventional medicine; they are not widely taught in medical schools, used in hospitals, or reimbursed by insurance companies. To isolate real CAM treatment effects from placebo effects and spontaneous recovery influences, researchers experiment, randomly assigning people to experimental and control conditions.

▶Personality

Personality is an individual's characteristic pattern of thinking, feeling, and acting.

MODULE 40: Psychodynamic Theories

Psychodynamic theories view personality from the perspective that behavior is a dynamic interaction between the conscious and unconscious mind. The theories trace their origin to Sigmund Freud's theory of *psychoanalysis*.

40-1: How did Sigmund Freud's treatment of psychological disorders lead to his view of the unconscious mind?

In treating patients whose disorders had no clear physical explanation, Freud concluded that these problems reflected unacceptable thoughts and feelings, hidden away in the *unconscious* mind. To explore this hidden part of a patient's mind, Freud used *free association* and dream analysis.

40-2: What was Freud's view of personality?

Freud believed that personality results from conflict arising from the interaction among the mind's three systems: the *id* (pleasure-seeking impulses), *ego* (reality-oriented executive), and *superego* (internalized set of ideals, or conscience).

40-3: What developmental stages did Freud propose?

He believed children pass through five *psychosexual stages* (oral, anal, phallic, latency, and genital). Unresolved conflicts at any stage can leave a person's pleasure-seeking impulses *fixated* (stalled) at that stage.

40-4: How did Freud think people defended themselves against anxiety?

For Freud, anxiety was the product of tensions between the demands of the id and superego. The ego copes by using unconscious *defense mechanisms*, such as *repression*, which he viewed as the basic mechanism underlying and enabling all the others.

40-5: Which of Freud's ideas did his followers accept or reject?

Freud's early followers, the neo-Freudians, accepted many of his ideas. They differed in placing more emphasis on the conscious mind and in stressing social motives more than sex or aggression. Contemporary psychodynamic theorists and therapists reject Freud's emphasis on sexual motivation. They stress, with support from modern research findings, the view that much of our mental life is unconscious, and they believe that our childhood experiences influence our adult personality and attachment patterns.

40-6: What are projective tests, how are they used, and what are some criticisms of them?

Projective tests attempt to assess personality by showing people vague stimuli with many possible interpretations; answers reveal unconscious motives. One such test, the *Rorschach inkblot test,* has low reliability and validity.

40-7: How do contemporary psychologists view Freud's psychoanalysis?

They give Freud credit for drawing attention to the vast unconscious, to the struggle to cope with our sexuality, to the conflict between biological impulses and social restraints, and for some forms of defense mechanisms (false consensus effect/projection; reaction formation), and unconscious *terror-management* defenses. But his concept of repression, and his view of the unconscious as a collection of repressed and unacceptable thoughts, wishes, feelings, and memories, have not survived scientific scrutiny. Freud offered after-the-fact explanations, which are hard to test scientifically. Research does not support many of Freud's specific ideas, such as the view that development is fixed in childhood. (We now know it is lifelong.)

40-8: How has modern research developed our understanding of the unconscious?

Current research confirms that we do not have full access to all that goes on in our mind, but the current view of the unconscious is not that of a hidden storehouse filled with repressed feelings and thoughts. Rather, researchers see the unconscious as a separate and parallel track of information processing that occurs outside our awareness, such as schemas that control our perceptions; priming; implicit memories of learned skills; instantly activated emotions; and self-concepts and stereotypes that filter information about ourselves and others.

MODULE 41: Humanistic Theories

41-1: How did humanistic psychologists view personality, and what was their goal in studying personality?

The *humanistic psychologists'* view of personality focused on the potential for healthy personal growth and people's striving for self-determination and self-realization. Abraham Maslow proposed that human motivations form a hierarchy of needs; if basic needs are fulfilled, people will strive toward *self-actualization* and self-transcendence. Carl Rogers believed that the ingredients of a growth-promoting environment are genuineness, acceptance (including *unconditional positive regard*), and empathy. *Self-concept* was a central feature of personality for both Maslow and Rogers.

41-2: How did humanistic psychologists assess a person's sense of self?

Some rejected any standardized assessments and relied on interviews and conversations. Rogers sometimes used questionnaires in which people described their ideal and actual selves, which he later used to judge progress during therapy.

41-3: How have humanistic theories influenced psychology? What criticisms have they faced?

Humanistic psychology helped renew interest in the concept of self. Critics have said that humanistic psychology's concepts were vague and subjective, its values self-centered, and its assumptions naively optimistic.

MODULE 42: Trait Theories, Social-Cognitive Theories, and the Self

42-1: How do psychologists use traits to describe personality?

Trait theorists see personality as a stable and enduring pattern of behavior. They describe our differences rather than trying to explain them. Using factor analysis, they identify clusters of behavior tendencies that occur together. Genetic predispositions influence many traits.

42-2: What are personality inventories, and what are their strengths and weaknesses as trait-assessment tools?

Personality inventories (such as the *MMPI*) are questionnaires on which people respond to items designed to gauge a wide range of feelings and behaviors. Test items are *empirically derived*, and the tests are objectively scored. But people can fake their answers to create a good impression, and the ease of computerized testing may lead to misuse of the tests.

43-3: Which traits seem to provide the most useful information about personality variation?

The Big Five personality factors—conscientiousness, agreeableness, neuroticism, openness, and extraversion (CANOE)—currently offer the clearest picture of personality. These factors are stable and appear to be found in all cultures.

42-4: Does research support the consistency of personality traits over time and across situations?

A person's average traits persist over time and are predictable over many different situations. But traits cannot predict behavior in any one particular situation.

42-5: Who first proposed the social-cognitive perspective, and how do these theorists view personality development?

Albert Bandura first proposed the *social-cognitive perspective*, which views personality as the product of the interaction between a person's traits (including thinking) and the situation—the social context. Social-cognitive researchers apply principles of learning, cognition, and social behavior to personality. Reciprocal determinism is a term describing the interaction and mutual influence of behavior, internal personal factors, and environmental factors. By studying how people vary in their perceived *locus of control* (*external* or *internal*), researchers have found that a sense of *personal control* helps people to cope with life. Research on *learned helplessness* evolved into research on the effects of optimism and pessimism, which led to a broader *positive psychology*.

42-6: How do social-cognitive researchers explore behavior, and what criticism have they faced?

Social-cognitive researchers tend to believe that the best way to predict someone's behavior in a given situation is to observe that person's behavior in similar situations. They have been faulted for underemphasizing the importance of unconscious dynamics, emotions, and inner traits. Their response is that the social cognitive perspective builds on psychology's well-established concepts of learning and cognition and reminds us of the power of situations.

42-7: Why has psychology generated so much research on the self? How important is self-esteem to psychology and to human well-being?

The *self* is the center of personality, organizing our thoughts, feelings, and actions. Considering possible selves helps motivate us toward positive development, but focusing too intensely on ourselves can lead to the *spotlight effect*. High *self-esteem* (our feeling of self-worth) is beneficial, but unrealistically high self-esteem is dangerous (linked to aggressive behavior) and fragile.

42-8: What evidence reveals self-serving bias, and how do defensive and secure self-esteem differ?

Self-serving bias is our tendency to perceive ourselves favorably, as when viewing ourselves as better than average or when accepting credit for our successes but not blame for our failures. Defensive self-esteem is fragile, focuses on sustaining itself, and views failure or criticism as a threat. Secure self-esteem enables us to feel accepted for who we are.

▸Social Psychology

MODULE 43: Social Thinking

43-1: What do social psychologists study? How do we tend to explain others' behavior and our own?

Social psychologists focus on how we think about, influence, and relate to one another. They study the social influences that explain why the same person will act differently in different situations. When explaining others' behavior, we may commit the *fundamental attribution error* (underestimating the influence of the situation and overestimating the effects of personality). When explaining our own behavior, we more readily attribute it to the influence of the situation.

43-2: Does what we think affect what we do, or does what we do affect what we think?

Attitudes are feelings, often influenced by our beliefs, that predispose us to respond in certain ways. *Peripheral route persuasion* uses incidental cues (such as celebrity endorsement) to try to produce fast but relatively thoughtless changes in attitudes. *Central route persuasion* offers evidence and arguments to trigger thoughtful responses. When other influences are minimal, attitudes that are stable, specific, and easily recalled can affect our actions.

Actions can modify attitudes, as in the *foot-in-the-door phenomenon* (complying with a large request after having agreed to a small request) and *role* playing (acting a social part by following guidelines for expected behavior). When our attitudes don't fit with our actions, *cognitive dissonance theory* suggests that we will reduce tension by changing our attitudes to match our actions.

MODULE 44: Social Influence

44-1: What is automatic mimicry, and how do conformity experiments reveal the power of social influence?

Automatic mimicry (the chameleon effect), our tendency to unconsciously imitate others' expressions, postures, and voice tones, is a form of *conformity.*

Solomon Asch and others have found that we are most likely to adjust our behavior or thinking to coincide with a group standard when (a) we feel incompetent or insecure, (b) our group has at least three people, (c) everyone else agrees, (d) we admire the group's status and attractiveness, (e) we have not already committed to another response, (f) we know we are being observed, and (g) our culture encourages respect for social standards. We may conform to gain approval *(normative social influence)* or because we are willing to accept others' opinions as new information *(informational social influence).*

44-2: What did Milgram's obedience experiments teach us about the power of social influence?

Stanley Milgram's experiments—in which people obeyed orders even when they thought they were harming another person—demonstrated strong social influence. Obedience was highest when (a) the person giving orders was nearby and was perceived as a legitimate authority figure; (b) the research was supported by a prestigious institution; (c) the victim was depersonalized or at a distance; and (d) there were no role models for defiance.

44-3: What have we learned from the Asch and Milgram studies?

These experiments demonstrated that strong social influences can make people conform to falsehoods or give in to cruelty.

44-4: How is our behavior affected by the presence of others?

In *social facilitation*, the mere presence of others arouses us, improving our performance on easy or well-learned tasks but decreasing it on difficult ones. In *social loafing*, participating in a group project makes us feel less responsible, and we may free ride on others' efforts. When the presence of others both arouses us and makes us feel anonymous, we may experience *deindividuation*—loss of self-awareness and self-restraint.

44-5: What are group polarization and groupthink, and how much power do we have as individuals?

In *group polarization*, group discussions with like-minded others strengthens members' prevailing beliefs and attitudes. Internet communication magnifies this effect, for better and for worse. *Groupthink* is driven by a desire for harmony within a decision-making group, overriding realistic appraisal of alternatives.

The power of the individual and the power of the situation interact. A small minority that consistently expresses its views may sway the majority.

MODULE 45: Antisocial Relations

45-1: What is prejudice? What are its social and emotional roots?

Prejudice is an unjustifiable, usually negative attitude toward a group and its members. Prejudice's three components are beliefs (often *stereotypes*), emotions, and predispositions to action *(discrimination)*. Overt prejudice in North America has decreased over time, but implicit prejudice—an automatic, unthinking attitude—continues.

The social roots of prejudice include social inequalities and divisions. Higher-status groups often justify their privileged position with the *just-world phenomenon.* We tend to favor our own group (*ingroup bias*) as we divide ourselves into "us" (the *ingroup*) and "them" (the *outgroup*).

Prejudice can also be a tool for protecting our emotional well-being, as when we focus our anger by blaming events on a *scapegoat.*

45-2: What are the cognitive roots of prejudice?

The cognitive roots of prejudice grow from our natural ways of processing information: forming categories, remembering vivid cases, and believing that the world is just and our own and our culture's ways of doing things are the right ways.

45-3: How does psychology's definition of *aggression* differ from everyday usage? What biological factors make us more prone to hurt one another?

In psychology, *aggression* is any physical or verbal behavior intended to hurt or destroy. Biology influences our threshold for aggressive behaviors at three levels: genetic (inherited traits), neural (activity in key brain areas), and biochemical (such as alcohol or excess testosterone in the bloodstream). Aggression is a complex behavior resulting from the interaction of biology and experience.

45-4: What psychological and social-cultural factors may trigger aggressive behavior?

Frustration *(frustration-aggression principle)*, previous reinforcement for aggressive behavior, and observing an aggressive role model can all contribute to aggression. Media portrayals of violence provide *social scripts* that children learn to follow. Viewing sexual violence contributes to greater aggression toward women. Playing violent video games increases aggressive thoughts, emotions, and behaviors.

MODULE 46: Prosocial Relations

46-1: Why do we befriend or fall in love with some people but not others?

Proximity (geographical nearness) increases liking, in part because of the *mere exposure effect*—exposure to novel stimuli increases liking of those stimuli. Physical attractiveness increases social opportunities and improves the way we are perceived. Similarity of attitudes and interests greatly increases liking, especially as relationships develop. We also like those who like us.

46-2: How does romantic love typically change as time passes?

Intimate love relationships start with *passionate love*—an intensely aroused state. Over time, the strong affection of *companionate love* may develop, especially if enhanced by an *equitable* relationship and by intimate *self-disclosure*.

46-3: When are people most—and least—likely to help?

Altruism is unselfish regard for the well-being of others. We are most likely to help when we (a) notice an incident, (b) interpret it as an emergency, and (c) assume responsibility for helping. Other factors, including our mood and our similarity to the victim, also affect our willingness to help. We are least likely to help if other bystanders are present (the *bystander effect*).

46-4: How do social exchange theory and social norms explain helping behavior?

Social exchange theory is the view that we help others because it is in our own self-interest; in this view, the goal of social behavior is maximizing personal benefits and minimizing costs. Others believe that helping results from socialization, in which we are taught guidelines for expected behaviors in social situations, such as the *reciprocity norm* and the *social-responsibility norm*.

46-5: How do social traps and mirror-image perceptions fuel social conflict?

A *conflict* is a perceived incompatibility of actions, goals, or ideas. *Social traps* are situations in which people in conflict pursue their own individual self-interest, harming the collective well-being. Individuals and cultures in conflict also tend to form *mirror-image perceptions:* Each party views the opponent as untrustworthy and evil-intentioned, and itself as an ethical, peaceful victim.

46-6: How can we transform feelings of prejudice, aggression, and conflict into attitudes that promote peace?

Peace can result when individuals or groups work together to achieve *superordinate* (shared) *goals*. Research indicates that four processes—contact, cooperation, communication, and conciliation—help promote peace.

►Psychological Disorders

MODULE 47: Introduction to Psychological Disorders

47-1: How should we draw the line between normality and disorder?

Psychologists and psychiatrists define *psychological disorders* as deviant, distressful, and dysfunctional patterns of thoughts, feelings, or behaviors. The definition of deviant varies with context, culture, and time.

47-2: Why is there some controversy over attention-deficit hyperactivity disorder?

A child who by age 7 displays extreme inattention, hyperactivity, and impulsivity may be diagnosed with *attention-deficit hyperactivity disorder (ADHD)* and treated with medication and other therapy. The controversy centers on whether the growing number of ADHD cases reflects overdiagnosis or increased awareness of the disorder. Long-term effects of stimulant-drug treatment for ADHD are not yet known.

47-3: How do the medical model and the biopsychosocial approach understand psychological disorders?

The *medical model* assumes that psychological disorders are mental illnesses with physical causes that can be diagnosed, treated, and, in most cases, cured through therapy, sometimes in a hospital. The biopsychosocial perspective assumes that three sets of influences—biological (evolution, genetics, brain structure and chemistry), psychological (stress, trauma, learned helplessness, mood-related perceptions and memories), and social-cultural (roles, expectations, definitions of "normality" and "disorder")—interact to produce specific psychological disorders.

47-4: How and why do clinicians classify psychological disorders?

The American Psychiatric Association's *DSM-IV-TR (Diagnostic and Statistical Manual of Mental Disorders)* contains diagnostic labels and descriptions that provide a common language and shared concepts for communication and research. (DSM-5 will soon replace and update DSM-IV-TR.) Some critics believe the DSM editions have become too detailed and extensive. Most U.S. health insurance organizations require an ICD/DSM diagnosis before paying for therapy.

47-5: Why do some psychologists criticize the use of diagnostic labels?

Other critics view DSM diagnoses as arbitrary labels that create preconceptions, which bias perceptions of the labeled person's past and present behavior. One such label, "insanity," raises moral and ethical questions about whether society should hold people with disorders responsible for their violent actions. Most people with disorders are nonviolent and are more likely to be victims than attackers.

47-6: How many people suffer, or have suffered, from a psychological disorder? Is poverty a risk factor?

Psychological disorder rates vary, depending on the time and place of the survey. In one multinational survey, rates for any disorder ranged from less than 5 percent (Shanghai) to more than 25 percent (the United States). Poverty is a risk factor: Conditions and experiences associated with poverty contribute to the development of psychological disorders. But some disorders, such as schizophrenia, can drive people into poverty.

MODULE 48: Anxiety Disorders

48-1: What are the different anxiety disorders?

Anxious feelings and behaviors are classified as an *anxiety disorder* only when they form a pattern of distressing, persistent anxiety or maladaptive behaviors that reduce anxiety. People with *generalized anxiety disorder* feel persistently and uncontrollably tense and apprehensive, for no apparent reason. In the more extreme *panic disorder*, anxiety escalates into periodic episodes of intense dread. Those with a *phobia* may be irrationally afraid of a specific object or situation. Persistent and repetitive thoughts (obsessions) and actions (compulsions) characterize *obsessive-compulsive disorder*. Symptoms of *post-traumatic stress disorder* include four or more weeks of haunting memories, nightmares, social withdrawal, jumpy anxiety, and sleep problems following some traumatic experience.

48-2: How do the learning and biological perspectives explain anxiety disorders?

The learning perspective views anxiety disorders as a product of fear conditioning, stimulus generalization, fearful-behavior reinforcement, and observational learning of others' fears and cognitions (interpretations, irrational beliefs, and hypervigilance). The biological perspective considers the role that fears of life-threatening animals, objects or situations played in natural selection and evolution; genetic predispositions for high levels of emotional reactivity and neurotransmitter production; and abnormal responses in the brain's fear circuits.

MODULE 49: Mood Disorders

49-1: What are mood disorders? How does major depressive disorder differ from bipolar disorder?

Mood disorders are characterized by emotional extremes. A person with *major depressive disorder* experiences two or more weeks of seriously depressed moods and feelings of worthlessness, and takes little interest in, and derives little pleasure from, most activities.

A person with the less common condition of *bipolar disorder* experiences not only depression but also *mania*—episodes of hyperactive and wildly optimistic, impulsive behavior.

49-2: How do the biological and social-cognitive perspectives explain mood disorders?

The biological perspective on depression focuses on genetic predispositions and on abnormalities in brain structures and function (including those found in neurotransmitter systems). The social-cognitive perspective views depression as an ongoing cycle of stressful experiences (interpreted through negative beliefs, attributions, and memories) leading to negative moods and actions and fueling new stressful experiences.

49-3: What factors affect suicide and self-injuring, and what are some of the important warning signs to watch for in suicide prevention efforts?

Suicide rates differ by nation, race, gender, age group, income, religious involvement, marital status, and (for gay and lesbian youth) social support structure. Those with depression are more at risk for suicide than others are, but social suggestion, health status, and economic and social frustration are also contributing factors. Non-suicidal self-injury (NSSI) does not usually lead to suicide but may escalate to suicidal thoughts and acts if untreated. People who engage in NSSI do not tolerate stress well and tend to be self-critical, with poor communication and problem-solving skills. Environmental barriers (such as jump barriers) are effective in preventing suicides. Forewarnings of suicide may include verbal hints, giving away possessions, withdrawal, preoccupation with death, and discussing one's own suicide.

MODULE 50: Schizophrenia

50-1: What patterns of thinking, perceiving, feeling, and behaving characterize schizophrenia?

Schizophrenia is a group of disorders that typically strike during late adolescence, affect men more than women, and seem to occur in all cultures. Symptoms are disorganized and delusional thinking, disturbed perceptions, and inappropriate emotions and actions. *Delusions* are false beliefs; hallucinations are sensory experiences without sensory stimulation.

50-2: What are the schizophrenia subtypes? How do chronic and acute schizophrenia differ?

Schizophrenia symptoms may be positive (the presence of inappropriate behaviors) or negative (the absence of appropriate behaviors). Schizophrenia's subtypes are paranoid, disorganized, catatonic, undifferentiated, and residual. In chronic (or process) schizophrenia, the disorder develops gradually and recovery is doubtful. In acute (or reactive) schizophrenia, the onset is sudden, in reaction to stress, and the prospects for recovery are brighter.

50-3: How do brain abnormalities and viral infections help explain schizophrenia?

People with schizophrenia have increased dopamine receptors, which may intensify brain signals, creating positive symptoms such as hallucinations and paranoia. Brain abnormalities associated with schizophrenia include enlarged, fluid-filled cerebral cavities and corresponding decreases in the cortex. Brain scans reveal abnormal activity in the frontal lobes, thalamus, and amygdala. Interacting malfunctions in multiple brain regions and their connections may produce schizophrenia's symptoms. Possible contributing factors include viral infections or famine conditions during the mother's pregnancy; low weight or oxygen deprivation at birth; and maternal diabetes or older paternal age.

50-4: Are there genetic influences on schizophrenia? What factors may be early warning signs of schizophrenia in children?

Twin and adoption studies indicate that the predisposition to schizophrenia is inherited, and environmental factors influence gene expression to enable this disorder, which is found worldwide. No environmental causes invariably produce schizophrenia. Possible early warning signs of later development of schizophrenia include both biological factors (a mother with severe and long-lasting schizophrenia; oxygen deprivation and low weight at birth; short attention span and poor muscle coordination) as well as psychological factors (disruptive or withdrawn behavior; emotional unpredictability; poor peer relations and solo play).

MODULE 51: Dissociative, Personality, and Eating Disorders

51-1: What are dissociative disorders, and why are they controversial?

Dissociative disorders are conditions in which conscious awareness seems to become separated from previous memories, thoughts, and feelings. Skeptics note that *dissociative identity disorder,* formerly known as multiple personality disorder, increased dramatically in the late twentieth century, that it is rarely found outside North America, and that it may reflect role-playing by people who are vulnerable to therapists' suggestions. Others view this disorder as a manifestation of feelings of anxiety, or as a response learned when behaviors are reinforced by anxiety-reduction.

51-2: What are the three clusters of personality disorders? What behaviors and brain activity characterize the antisocial personality?

Personality disorders are disruptive, inflexible, and enduring behavior patterns that impair social functioning. This disorder forms three clusters, based on main characteristics: (1) anxiety; (2) eccentric or odd behaviors; and (3) dramatic or impulsive behaviors.

Antisocial personality disorder is characterized by a lack of conscience and, sometimes, by aggressive and fearless behavior. Genetic predispositions may interact with the environment to produce the altered brain activity associated with antisocial personality disorder.

51-3: How do anorexia nervosa, bulimia nervosa, and binge-eating disorder demonstrate the influence of psychological forces?

In these eating disorders, psychological factors may overwhelm the homeostatic drive to maintain a balanced internal state. Despite being significantly underweight, people with *anorexia nervosa* (usually adolescent females) continue to diet because they view themselves as fat. Those with *bulimia nervosa* (usually females in their teens and twenties) secretly binge and then compensate by purging, fasting, or excessive exercise. Those with *binge-eating disorder* binge but do not follow with purging, fasting, and exercise. Cultural pressures, low self-esteem, and negative emotions interact with stressful life experiences and genetics to produce eating disorders.

▶Therapy

MODULE 52: The Psychological Therapies

52-1: How do *psychotherapy, biomedical therapy,* and an *eclectic approach* to therapy differ?

Psychotherapy is treatment involving psychological techniques; it consists of interactions between a trained therapist and someone seeking to overcome psychological difficulties or achieve personal growth. The major psychotherapies derive from psychology's psychodynamic, humanistic, behavioral, and cognitive perspectives. *Biomedical therapy* treats psychological disorders with medications or procedures that act directly on a patient's physiology. An *eclectic approach* combines techniques from various forms of therapy.

52-2: What are the goals and techniques of psychoanalysis, and how have they been adapted in psychodynamic therapy?

Through *psychoanalysis,* Sigmund Freud tried to give people self-insight and relief from their disorders by bringing anxiety-laden feelings and thoughts into conscious awareness.

Techniques included using free association and *interpretation* of instances of *resistance* and *transference*. Contemporary *psychodynamic therapy* has been influenced by traditional psychoanalysis but is briefer, less expensive, and more focused on helping the client find relief from current symptoms. Therapists help clients understand past and present relationship themes. Interpersonal therapy is a brief 12- to 16-session form of psychodynamic therapy that has been effective in treating depression.

52-3: What are the basic themes of humanistic therapy? What are the specific goals and techniques of Rogers' client-centered approach?

Both psychoanalytic and humanistic therapists are *insight therapies*—they attempt to improve functioning by increasing clients' awareness of motives and defenses. Humanistic therapy's goals have included helping clients grow in self-awareness and self-acceptance; promoting personal growth rather than curing illness; helping clients take responsibility for their own growth; focusing on conscious thoughts rather than unconscious motivations; and seeing the present and future as more important than the past.

Carl Rogers' *client-centered therapy* proposed that therapists' most important contributions are to function as a psychological mirror through *active listening* and to provide a growth-fostering environment of *unconditional positive regard,* characterized by genuineness, acceptance, and empathy.

52-4: How does the basic assumption of behavior therapy differ from those of psychodynamic and humanistic therapies? What techniques are used in exposure therapies and aversive conditioning?

Behavior therapies are not insight therapies. Their goal is to apply learning principles to modify problem behaviors.

Classical conditioning techniques, including *exposure therapies* (such as *systematic desensitization* or *virtual reality exposure therapy*) and *aversive conditioning,* attempt to change behaviors through *counterconditioning*—evoking new responses to old stimuli that trigger unwanted behaviors.

52-5: What is the main premise of therapy based on operant conditioning principles, and what are the views of its proponents and critics?

Therapy based on operant conditioning principles uses behavior modification techniques to change unwanted behaviors through positively reinforcing desired behaviors and ignoring or punishing undesirable behaviors. Critics maintain that (1) techniques such as those used in *token economies* may produce behavior changes that disappear when rewards end, and (2) deciding which behaviors should change is authoritarian and unethical. Proponents argue that treatment with positive rewards is more humane than punishing people or institutionalizing them for undesired behaviors.

52-6: What are the goals and techniques of cognitive therapy and of cognitive-behavioral therapy?

The *cognitive therapies,* such as Aaron Beck's cognitive therapy for depression, assume that our thinking influences our feelings, and that the therapist's role is to change clients' self-defeating thinking by training them to view themselves in more positive ways. *Rational-emotive behavior therapy* is a confrontational cognitive therapy that actively challenges irrational beliefs. The widely researched and practiced *cognitive-behavioral therapy* combines cognitive therapy and behavior therapy by helping clients regularly act out their new ways of thinking and talking in their everyday life.

52-7: What are the aims and benefits of group and family therapy?

Group therapy sessions can help more people and costs less per person than individual therapy would. Clients may benefit from exploring feelings and developing social skills in a group situation, from learning that others have similar problems, and from getting feedback on new ways of behaving. *Family therapy* views a family as an interactive system and attempts to help members discover the roles they play and to learn to communicate more openly and directly.

MODULE 53: Evaluating Psychotherapies

53-1: Does psychotherapy work? Who decides?

Clients' and therapists' positive testimonials cannot prove that therapy is actually effective, and the placebo effect and *regression toward the mean* (the tendency for extreme or unusual scores to fall back toward their average) make it difficult to judge whether improvement occurred because of the treatment. Using *meta-analyses* to statistically combine the results of hundreds of randomized psychotherapy outcome studies, researchers have found that those not undergoing treatment often improve, but those undergoing psychotherapy are more likely to improve more quickly, and with less chance of relapse.

53-2: Are some psychotherapies more effective than others for specific disorders?

No one type of psychotherapy is generally superior to all others. Therapy is most effective for those with clear-cut, specific problems. Some therapies—such as behavior conditioning for treating phobias and compulsions—are more effective for specific disorders. Psychodynamic therapy has been effective for depression and anxiety, and cognitive and cognitive-behavioral therapies have been effective in coping with anxiety, PTSD, and depression. *Evidence-based practice* integrates the best available research with clinicians' expertise and patients' characteristics, preferences, and circumstances.

53-3: How do alternative therapies fare under scientific scrutiny?

Controlled research has not supported the claims of eye movement desensitization and reprocessing (EMDR) therapy. Light exposure therapy does seem to relieve the symptoms of seasonal affective disorder (SAD) by activating a brain region that influences arousal and hormones.

53-4: What three elements are shared by all forms of psychotherapy?

All psychotherapies offer new hope for demoralized people; a fresh perspective; and (if the therapist is effective) an empathic, trusting, and caring relationship. The emotional bond of trust and understanding between therapist and client—the *therapeutic alliance*—is an important element in effective therapy.

53-5: How do culture, gender, and values influence the therapist-client relationship?

Therapists differ in the values that influence their goals in therapy and their views of progress. These differences may create problems if therapists and clients differ in their cultural, gender, or religious perspectives.

53-6: What should a person look for when selecting a therapist?

A person seeking therapy may want to ask about the therapist's treatment approach, values, credentials, and fees. An important consideration is whether the therapy seeker feels comfortable and able to establish a bond with the therapist.

53-7: What is the rationale for preventive mental health programs?

Preventive mental health programs are based on the idea that many psychological disorders could be prevented by changing oppressive, esteem-destroying environments into more benevolent, nurturing environments that foster growth, self-confidence, and *resilience*.

MODULE 54: The Biomedical Therapies

54-1: What are the drug therapies? How do double-blind studies help researchers evaluate a drug's effectiveness?

Psychopharmacology, the study of drug effects on mind and behavior, has helped make drug therapy the most widely used *biomedical therapy*. *Antipsychotic drugs*, used

positive psychology the scientific study of human functioning, with the goals of discovering and promoting strengths and virtues that help individuals and communities to thrive. (p. 560)

positive reinforcement increasing behaviors by presenting positive reinforcers. A positive reinforcer is any stimulus that, when *presented* after a response, strengthens the response. (p. 288)

posthypnotic suggestion a suggestion, made during a hypnosis session, to be carried out after the subject is no longer hypnotized; used by some clinicians to help control undesired symptoms and behaviors. (p. 111)

post-traumatic growth positive psychological changes as a result of struggling with extremely challenging circumstances and life crises. (p. 641)

post-traumatic stress disorder (PTSD) an anxiety disorder characterized by haunting memories, nightmares, social withdrawal, jumpy anxiety, and/or insomnia that lingers for four weeks or more after a traumatic experience. (p. 639)

predictive validity the success with which a test predicts the behavior it is designed to predict; it is assessed by computing the correlation between test scores and the criterion behavior. (Also called *criterion-related validity*.) (p. 397)

prejudice an unjustifiable and usually negative attitude toward a group and its members. Prejudice generally involves stereotyped beliefs, negative feelings, and a predisposition to discriminatory action. (p. 593)

preoperational stage in Piaget's theory, the stage (from about 2 to about 6 or 7 years of age) during which a child learns to use language but does not yet comprehend the mental operations of concrete logic. (p. 182)

primary reinforcer an innately reinforcing stimulus, such as one that satisfies a biological need. (p. 289)

primary sex characteristics the body structures (ovaries, testes, and external genitalia) that make sexual reproduction possible. (p. 197)

priming the activation, often unconsciously, of certain associations, thus predisposing one's perception, memory, or response. (pp. 225, 330)

proactive interference the disruptive effect of prior learning on the recall of new information. (p. 338)

problem-focused coping attempting to alleviate stress directly—by changing the stressor or the way we interact with that stressor. (p. 517)

projective test a personality test, such as the Rorschach, that provides ambiguous stimuli designed to trigger projection of one's inner dynamics. (p. 538)

prosocial behavior positive, constructive, helpful behavior. The opposite of antisocial behavior. (p. 306)

prototype a mental image or best example of a category. Matching new items to a prototype provides a quick and easy method for sorting items into categories (as when comparing feathered creatures to a prototypical bird, such as a robin). (p. 352)

psychiatry a branch of medicine dealing with psychological disorders; practiced by physicians who sometimes provide medical (for example, drug) treatments as well as psychological therapy. (p. 11)

psychoactive drug a chemical substance that alters perceptions and moods. (p. 115)

psychoanalysis (1) Sigmund Freud's theory of personality that attributes thoughts and actions to unconscious motives and conflicts; (2) Freud's therapeutic technique used in treating psychological disorders. Freud believed that the patient's free associations, resistances, dreams, and transferences—and the therapist's interpretations of them—released previously repressed feelings, allowing the patient to gain self-insight. (pp. 532, 677)

psychodynamic theories view personality with a focus on the unconscious and the importance of childhood experiences. (p. 532)

psychodynamic therapy therapy deriving from the psychoanalytic tradition that views individuals as responding to unconscious forces and childhood experiences, and that seeks to enhance self-insight. (p. 678)

psychological dependence a psychological need to use a drug, such as to relieve negative emotions. (p. 115)

psychological disorder deviant, distressful, and dysfunctional patterns of thoughts, feelings, or behaviors. (p. 626)

psychology the science of behavior and mental processes. (p. 6)

psychoneuroimmunology the study of how psychological, neural, and endocrine processes together affect the immune system and resulting health. (p. 509)

psychopharmacology the study of the effects of drugs on mind and behavior. (p. 704)

psychophysics the study of relationships between the physical characteristics of stimuli, such as their intensity, and our psychological experience of them. (p. 225)

psychophysiological illness literally, "mind-body" illness; any stress-related physical illness, such as hypertension and some headaches. (p. 509)

psychosexual stages the childhood stages of development (oral, anal, phallic, latency, genital) during which, according to Freud, the id's pleasure-seeking energies focus on distinct erogenous zones. (p. 534)

psychosis a psychological disorder in which a person loses contact with reality, experiencing irrational ideas and distorted perceptions. (p. 657)

psychosurgery surgery that removes or destroys brain tissue in an effort to change behavior. (p. 710)

psychotherapy treatment involving psychological techniques; consists of interactions between a trained therapist and someone seeking to overcome psychological difficulties or achieve personal growth. (pp. 676, 692)

puberty the period of sexual maturation, during which a person becomes capable of reproducing. (p. 197)

punishment an event that tends to *decrease* the behavior that it follows. (p. 292)

pupil the adjustable opening in the center of the eye through which light enters. (p. 235)

random assignment assigning participants to experimental and control groups by chance, thus minimizing preexisting differences between those assigned to the different groups. (p. 35)

random sample a sample that fairly represents a population because each member has an equal chance of inclusion. (p. 31)

range the difference between the highest and lowest scores in a distribution. (p. 40)

rational-emotive behavior therapy (REBT) a confrontational cognitive therapy, developed by Albert Ellis, that vigorously challenges people's illogical, self-defeating attitudes and assumptions. (p. 685)

recall a measure of memory in which the person must retrieve information learned earlier, as on a fill-in-the-blank test. (p. 312)

reciprocal determinism the interacting influences of behavior, internal cognition, and environment. (p. 556)

reciprocity norm an expectation that people will help, not hurt, those who have helped them. (p. 617)

recognition a measure of memory in which the person need only identify items previously learned, as on a multiple-choice test. (p. 312)

reflex a simple, automatic response to a sensory stimulus, such as the knee-jerk response. (p. 56)

refractory period a resting period after orgasm, during which a man cannot achieve another orgasm. (p. 436)

regression toward the mean the tendency for extreme or unusual scores to fall back (regress) toward their average. (p. 693)

reinforcement in operant conditioning, any event that *strengthens* the behavior it follows. (p. 287)

reinforcement schedule a pattern that defines how often a desired response will be reinforced. (p. 290)

relative deprivation the perception that one is worse off relative to those with whom one compares oneself. (p. 499)

relearning a measure of memory that assesses the amount of time saved when learning material for a second time. (p. 312)

reliability the extent to which a test yields consistent results, as assessed by the consistency of scores on two halves of the test, or on retesting. (p. 397)

REM rebound the tendency for REM sleep to increase following REM sleep deprivation (created by repeated awakenings during REM sleep). (p. 109)

REM sleep rapid eye movement sleep; a recurring sleep stage during which vivid dreams commonly occur. Also known as *paradoxical sleep*, because the muscles are relaxed (except for minor twitches) but other body systems are active. (p. 93)

repetitive transcranial magnetic stimulation (rTMS) the application of repeated pulses of magnetic energy to the brain; used to stimulate or suppress brain activity. (p. 709)

replication repeating the essence of a research study, usually with different participants in different situations, to see whether the basic finding extends to other participants and circumstances. (p. 26)

repression in psychoanalytic theory, the basic defense mechanism that banishes anxiety-arousing thoughts, feelings, and memories from consciousness. (pp. 339, 536)

resilience the personal strength that helps most people cope with stress and recover from adversity and even trauma. (p. 701)

resistance in psychoanalysis, the blocking from consciousness of anxiety-laden material. (p. 677)

respondent behavior behavior that occurs as an automatic response to some stimulus. (pp. 277, 296)

reticular formation a nerve network that travels through the brainstem and plays an important role in controlling arousal. (p. 64)

retina the light-sensitive inner surface of the eye, containing the receptor rods and cones plus layers of neurons that begin the processing of visual information. (p. 235)

retinal disparity a binocular cue for perceiving depth: By comparing images from the retinas in the two eyes, the brain computes distance—the greater the disparity (difference) between the two images, the closer the object. (p. 245)

retrieval the process of getting information out of memory storage. (p. 314)

retroactive interference the disruptive effect of new learning on the recall of old information. (p. 338)

retrograde amnesia an inability to retrieve information from one's past. (p. 335)

reuptake a neurotransmitter's reabsorption by the sending neuron. (p. 51)

rods retinal receptors that detect black, white, and gray; necessary for peripheral and twilight vision, when cones don't respond. (p. 236)

role a set of expectations (norms) about a social position, defining how those in the position ought to behave. (pp. 162, 575)

Rorschach inkblot test the most widely used projective test, a set of 10 inkblots, designed by Hermann Rorschach; seeks to identify people's inner feelings by analyzing their interpretations of the blots. (p. 538)

savant syndrome a condition in which a person otherwise limited in mental ability has an exceptional specific skill, such as in computation or drawing. (p. 383)

scapegoat theory the theory that prejudice offers an outlet for anger by providing someone to blame. (p. 597)

scatterplot a graphed cluster of dots, each of which represents the values of two variables. The slope of the points suggests the direction of the relationship between the two variables. The amount of scatter suggests the strength of the correlation (little scatter indicates high correlation). (p. 31)

schema a concept or framework that organizes and interprets information. (p. 179)

schizophrenia a group of severe disorders characterized by disorganized and delusional thinking, disturbed perceptions, and inappropriate emotions and behaviors. (p. 657)

secondary sex characteristics nonreproductive sexual characteristics, such as female breasts and hips, male voice quality, and body hair. (p. 197)

selective attention the focusing of conscious awareness on a particular stimulus. (p. 88)

self in contemporary psychology, assumed to be the center of personality, the organizer of our thoughts, feelings, and actions. (p. 564)

self-actualization according to Maslow, one of the ultimate psychological needs that arises after basic physical and psychological needs are met and self-esteem is achieved; the motivation to fulfill one's potential. (p. 543)

self-concept all our thoughts and feelings about ourselves, in answer to the question, "Who am I?" (pp. 193, 554)

self-control the ability to control impulses and delay short-term gratification for greater long-term rewards. (p. 558)

self-disclosure revealing intimate aspects of oneself to others. (p. 614)

self-esteem one's feelings of high or low self-worth. (p. 564)

self-serving bias a readiness to perceive oneself favorably. (p. 565)

sensation the process by which our sensory receptors and nervous system receive and represent stimulus energies from our environment. (p. 224)

sensorimotor stage in Piaget's theory, the stage (from birth to about 2 years of age) during which infants know the world mostly in terms of their sensory impressions and motor activities. (p. 180)

sensorineural hearing loss hearing loss caused by damage to the cochlea's receptor cells or to the auditory nerves; also called *nerve deafness.* (p. 258)

sensory adaptation diminished sensitivity as a consequence of constant stimulation. (p. 228)

sensory cortex area at the front of the parietal lobes that registers and processes body touch and movement sensations. (p. 73)

sensory interaction the principle that one sense may influence another, as when the smell of food influences its taste. (p. 267)

sensory memory the immediate, very brief recording of sensory information in the memory system. (p. 315)

sensory neurons neurons that carry incoming information from the sensory receptors to the brain and spinal cord. (p. 54)

serial position effect our tendency to recall best the last and first items in a list. (p. 332)

set point the point at which an individual's "weight thermostat" is supposedly set. When the body falls below this weight, an increase in hunger and a lowered metabolic rate may act to restore the lost weight. (p. 423)

sexual disorder a problem that consistently impairs sexual arousal or functioning. (p. 436)

sexual orientation an enduring sexual attraction toward members of either one's own sex (homosexual orientation) or the other sex (heterosexual orientation). (p. 442)

sexual response cycle the four stages of sexual responding described by Masters and Johnson—excitement, plateau, orgasm, and resolution. (p. 435)

shallow processing encoding on a basic level based on structure or appearance of words. (p. 320)

shaping an operant conditioning procedure in which reinforcers guide behavior toward closer and closer approximations of the desired behavior. (p. 276)

short-term memory activated memory that holds a few items briefly, such as the seven digits of a phone number while dialing, before the information is stored or forgotten. (p. 315)

signal detection theory a theory predicting how and when we detect the presence of a faint stimulus *(signal)* amid background stimulation *(noise)*. Assumes there is no single absolute threshold and that detection depends partly on a person's experience, expectations, motivation, and alertness. (p. 225)

sleep periodic, natural, easily reversible loss of consciousness—as distinct from unconsciousness resulting from a coma, general anesthesia, or hibernation. (Adapted from Dement, 1999.) (p. 93)

sleep apnea a sleep disorder characterized by temporary cessations of breathing during sleep and repeated momentary awakenings. (p. 104)

social clock the culturally preferred timing of social events such as marriage, parenthood, and retirement. (p. 215)

social exchange theory the theory that our social behavior is an exchange process, the aim of which is to maximize benefits and minimize costs. (p. 617)

social facilitation stronger responses on simple or well-learned tasks in the presence of others. (p. 587)

social identity the "we" aspect of our self-concept; the part of our answer to "Who am I?" that comes from our group memberships. (p. 203)

social leadership group-oriented leadership that builds teamwork, mediates conflict, and offers support. (p. 467)

social learning theory the theory that we learn social behavior by observing and imitating and by being rewarded or punished. (p. 162)

social loafing the tendency for people in a group to exert less effort when pooling their efforts toward attaining a common goal than when individually accountable. (p. 587)

social psychology the scientific study of how we think about, influence, and relate to one another. (p. 572)

social script culturally modeled guide for how to act in various situations. (p. 603)

social trap a situation in which the conflicting parties, by each rationally pursuing their self-interest, become caught in mutually destructive behavior. (p. 618)

social-cognitive perspective views behavior as influenced by the interaction between people's traits (including their thinking) and their social context. (p. 555)

social-responsibility norm an expectation that people will help those dependent upon them. (p. 617)

somatic nervous system the division of the peripheral nervous system that controls the body's skeletal muscles. Also called the *skeletal nervous system.* (p. 54)

source amnesia attributing to the wrong source an event we have experienced, heard about, read about, or imagined. (Also called *source misattribution.*) Source amnesia, along with the misinformation effect, is at the heart of many false memories. (p. 343)

spacing effect the tendency for distributed study or practice to yield better long-term retention than is achieved through massed study or practice. (p. 319)

split brain a condition resulting from surgery that isolates the brain's two hemispheres by cutting the fibers (mainly those of the corpus callosum) connecting them. (p. 77)

spontaneous recovery the reappearance, after a pause, of an extinguished conditioned response. (p. 281)

spotlight effect overestimating others' noticing and evaluating our appearance, performance, and blunders (as if we presume a spotlight shines on us). (p. 564)

SQ3R a study method incorporating five steps: Survey, Question, Read, Retrieve, Review. (p. 12)

standard deviation a computed measure of how much scores vary around the mean score. (p. 40)

standardization defining meaningful scores by comparison with the performance of a pretested group. (p. 395)

Stanford-Binet the widely used American revision (by Terman at Stanford University) of Binet's original intelligence test. (p. 393)

statistical significance a statistical statement of how likely it is that an obtained result occurred by chance. (p. 42)

stereotype a generalized (sometimes accurate but often overgeneralized) belief about a group of people. (p. 593)

stereotype threat a self-confirming concern that one will be evaluated based on a negative stereotype. (p. 414)

stimulants drugs (such as caffeine, nicotine, and the more powerful amphetamines, cocaine, Ecstasy, and methamphetamine) that excite neural activity and speed up body functions. (p. 119)

stimulus any event or situation that evokes a response. (pp. 277, 286)

storage the retention of encoded information over time. (p. 314)

stranger anxiety the fear of strangers that infants commonly display, beginning by about 8 months of age. (p. 187)

stress the process by which we perceive and respond to certain events, called *stressors*, that we appraise as threatening or challenging. (p. 504)

structured interviews interview process that asks the same job-relevant questions of all applicants, each of whom is rated on established scales. (p. 461)

subjective well-being self-perceived happiness or satisfaction with life. Used along with measures of objective well-being (for example, physical and economic indicators) to evaluate people's quality of life. (p. 495)

subliminal below one's absolute threshold for conscious awareness. (p. 225)

superego the part of personality that, according to Freud, represents internalized ideals and provides standards for judgment (the conscience) and for future aspirations. (p. 534)

superordinate goals shared goals that override differences among people and require their cooperation. (p. 620)

survey a technique for ascertaining the self-reported attitudes or behaviors of a particular group, usually by questioning a representative, random sample of the group. (p. 30)

sympathetic nervous system the division of the autonomic nervous system that arouses the body, mobilizing its energy in stressful situations. (p. 54)

synapse [SIN-aps] the junction between the axon tip of the sending neuron and the dendrite or cell body of the receiving neuron. The tiny gap at this junction is called the *synaptic gap* or *synaptic cleft*. (p. 50)

systematic desensitization a type of exposure therapy that associates a pleasant relaxed state with gradually increasing anxiety-triggering stimuli. Commonly used to treat phobias. (p. 682)

task leadership goal-oriented leadership that sets standards, organizes work, and focuses attention on goals. (p. 467)

telegraphic speech early speech stage in which a child speaks like a telegram—"go car"—using mostly nouns and verbs. (p. 368)

temperament a person's characteristic emotional reactivity and intensity. (p. 137)

temporal lobes portion of the cerebral cortex lying roughly above the ears; includes the auditory areas, each receiving information primarily from the opposite ear. (p. 69)

tend and befriend under stress, people (especially women) often provide support to others (tend) and bond with and seek support from others (befriend). (p. 508)

teratogens (literally, "monster maker") agents, such as chemicals and viruses, that can reach the embryo or fetus during prenatal development and cause harm. (p. 174)

terror-management theory a theory of death-related anxiety; explores people's emotional and behavioral responses to reminders of their impending death. (p. 541)

testing effect enhanced memory after retrieving, rather than simply reading, information. Also sometimes referred to as a *retrieval practice effect* or *test-enhanced learning*. (pp. 12, 320)

testosterone the most important of the male sex hormones. Both males and females have it, but the additional testosterone in males stimulates the growth of the male sex organs in the fetus and the development of the male sex characteristics during puberty. (pp. 160, 436)

thalamus [THAL-uh-muss] the brain's sensory switchboard, located on top of the brainstem; it directs messages to the sensory receiving areas in the cortex and transmits replies to the cerebellum and medulla. (p. 64)

THC the major active ingredient in marijuana; triggers a variety of effects, including mild hallucinations. (p. 124)

theory an explanation using an integrated set of principles that organizes observations and predicts behaviors or events. (p. 26)

theory of mind people's ideas about their own and others' mental states—about their feelings, perceptions, and thoughts, and the behaviors these might predict. (p. 183)

therapeutic alliance a bond of trust and mutual understanding between a therapist and client, who work together constructively to overcome the client's problem. (p. 699)

threshold the level of stimulation required to trigger a neural impulse. (p. 49)

token economy an operant conditioning procedure in which people earn a token of some sort for exhibiting a desired behavior and can later exchange the tokens for various privileges or treats. (p. 684)

tolerance the diminishing effect with regular use of the same dose of a drug, requiring the user to take larger and larger doses before experiencing the drug's effect. (p. 115)

top-down processing information processing guided by higher-level mental processes, as when we construct perceptions drawing on our experience and expectations. (p. 224)

trait a characteristic pattern of behavior or a disposition to feel and act, as assessed by self-report inventories and peer reports. (p. 547)

transduction conversion of one form of energy into another. In sensation, the transforming of stimulus energies, such as sights, sounds, and smells, into neural impulses our brain can interpret. (p. 224)

transference in psychoanalysis, the patient's transfer to the analyst of emotions linked with other relationships (such as love or hatred for a parent). (p. 677)

transgender an umbrella term describing people whose gender identity or expression differs from that associated with their birth sex. (p. 163)

two-factor theory the Schachter-Singer theory that to experience emotion one must (1) be physically aroused and (2) cognitively label the arousal. (p. 475)

two-word stage beginning about age 2, the stage in speech development during which a child speaks mostly in two-word statements. (p. 368)

Type A Friedman and Rosenman's term for competitive, hard-driving, impatient, verbally aggressive, and anger-prone people. (p. 513)

Type B Friedman and Rosenman's term for easygoing, relaxed people. (p. 513)

unconditional positive regard a caring, accepting, nonjudgmental attitude, which Carl Rogers believed would help clients to develop self-awareness and self-acceptance. (pp. 544, 680)

unconditioned response (UR) in classical conditioning, an unlearned, naturally occurring response (such as salivation) to an unconditioned stimulus (US) (such as food in the mouth). (p. 279)

unconditioned stimulus (US) in classical conditioning, a stimulus that unconditionally—naturally and automatically—triggers a response (UR). (p. 279)

unconscious according to Freud, a reservoir of mostly unacceptable thoughts, wishes, feelings, and memories. According to contemporary psychologists, information processing of which we are unaware. (p. 533)

validity the extent to which a test measures or predicts what it is supposed to. (See also *content validity* and *predictive validity*.) (p. 397)

variable-interval schedule in operant conditioning, a reinforcement schedule that reinforces a response at unpredictable time intervals. (p. 291)

variable-ratio schedule in operant conditioning, a reinforcement schedule that reinforces a response after an unpredictable number of responses. (p. 291)

vestibular sense the sense of body movement and position, including the sense of balance. (p. 272)

virtual reality exposure therapy an anxiety treatment that progressively exposes people to electronic simulations of their greatest fears, such as airplane flying, spiders, or public speaking. (p. 682)

visual cliff a laboratory device for testing depth perception in infants and young animals. (p. 244)

wavelength the distance from the peak of one light or sound wave to the peak of the next. Electromagnetic wavelengths vary from the short blips of cosmic rays to the long pulses of radio transmission. (p. 235)

Weber's law the principle that, to be perceived as different, two stimuli must differ by a given percentage (rather than a given amount). (p. 227)

Wechsler Adult Intelligence Scale (WAIS) the WAIS is the most widely used intelligence test; contains verbal and performance (nonverbal) subtests. (p. 394)

Wernicke's area controls language reception—a brain area involved in language comprehension and expression; usually in the left temporal lobe. (p. 372)

withdrawal the discomfort and distress that follow discontinuing the use of an addictive drug. (p. 115)

working memory a newer understanding of short-term memory that focuses on conscious, active processing of incoming auditory and visual-spatial information, and of information retrieved from long-term memory. (p. 315)

X chromosome the sex chromosome found in both men and women. Females have two X chromosomes; males have one. An X chromosome from each parent produces a female child. (p. 160)

Y chromosome the sex chromosome found only in males. When paired with an X chromosome from the mother, it produces a male child. (p. 160)

Young-Helmholtz trichromatic (three-color) theory the theory that the retina contains three different color receptors—one most sensitive to red, one to green, one to blue—which, when stimulated in combination, can produce the perception of any color. (p. 241)

zygote the fertilized egg; it enters a 2-week period of rapid cell division and develops into an embryo. (p. 173)

References

AAS. (2009, April 25). *USA suicide: 2006 final data.* Prepared for the American Association of Suicidology by J. L. McIntosh (www.suicidology.org). (p. 651)

AAS. (2010, May 23). *U.S.A. suicide: 2007 official final data.* Prepared for the American Association of Suicidology by J. L. McIntosh (www.suicidology.org). (p. 650)

Abbey, A. (1987). Misperceptions of friendly behavior as sexual interest: A survey of naturally occurring incidents. *Psychology of Women Quarterly, 11,* 173–194. (p. 145)

Abel, E. L., & Kruger, M. L. (2010). Smile intensity in photographs predicts longevity. *Psychological Science, 21,* 542–544. (p. 514)

Abel, K. M., Drake, R., & Goldstein, J. M. (2010). Sex differences in schizophrenia. *International Review of Psychiatry, 22,* 417–428. (p. 657)

Abrams, D. B. (1991). AIDS: What young people believe and what they do. Paper presented at the British Association for the Advancement of Science conference. (p. 560)

Abrams, D. B., & Wilson, G. T. (1983). Alcohol, sexual arousal, and self-control. *Journal of Personality and Social Psychology, 45,* 188–198. (p. 118)

Abrams, L. (2008). Tip-of-the-tongue states yield language insights. *American Scientist, 96,* 234–239. (p. 337)

Abrams, M. (2002, June). Sight unseen—Restoring a blind man's vision is now a real possibility through stem-cell surgery. But even perfect eyes cannot see unless the brain has been taught to use them. *Discover, 23,* 54–60. (p. 250)

Abramson, L. Y., Metalsky, G. I., & Alloy, L. B. (1989). Hopelessness depression: A theory-based subtype. *Psychological Review, 96,* 358–372. (p. 653)

Abrevaya, J. (2009). Are there missing girls in the United States? Evidence from birth data. *American Economic Journal: Applied Economics, 1*(2), 1–34. (p. 594)

Acevedo, B. P., & Aron, A. (2009). Does a long-term relationship kill romantic love? *Review of General Psychology, 13,* 59–65. (p. 613)

ACHA. (2009). *American College Health Association-National College Health Assessment II: Reference group executive summary Fall 2008.* Baltimore: American College Health Association. (p. 645)

Ackerman, D. (2004). *An alchemy of mind: The marvel and mystery of the brain.* New York: Scribner. (p. 50)

Ackerman, J. M., Nocera, C. C., & Bargh, J. A. (2010). Incidental haptic sensations influence social judgments and decisions. *Science, 328,* 1712–1715. (p. 268)

ACMD. (2009). *MDMA ('ecstasy'): A review of its harms and classification under the misuse of drugs act 1971.* London: Home Office; Advisory Council on the Misuse of Drugs. (pp. 121, 122)

Adelmann, P. K., Antonucci, T. C., Crohan, S. F., & Coleman, L. M. (1989). Empty nest, cohort, and employment in the well-being of midlife women. *Sex Roles, 20,* 173–189. (p. 217)

Adelson, R. (2004, August). Detecting deception. *APA Monitor,* pp. 70–73. (p. 482)

Ader, R., & Cohen, N. (1985). CNS-immune system interactions: Conditioning phenomena. *Behavioral and Brain Sciences, 8,* 379–394. (p. 284)

Affleck, G., Tennen, H., Urrows, S., & Higgins, P. (1994). Person and contextual features of daily stress reactivity: Individual differences in relations of undesirable daily events with mood disturbance and chronic pain intensity. *Journal of Personality and Social Psychology, 66,* 329–340. (p. 496)

Agrawal, Y., Platz, E. A., & Niparko, J. K. (2008). Prevalence of hearing loss and differences by demographic characteristics among US adults: Data from the *National Health and Nutrition Examination Survey, 1999–2004. Archives of Internal Medicine, 168,* 1522–1530. (p. 371)

Agrillo, C. (2011). Near-death experience: Out-of-body and out-of-brain? *Review of General Psychology, 15,* 1–10. (p. 124)

Ai, A. L., Park, C. L., Huang, B., Rodgers, W., & Tice, T. N. (2007). Psychosocial mediation of religious coping styles: A study of short-term psychological distress following cardiac surgery. *Personality and Social Psychology Bulletin, 33,* 867–882. (p. 527)

Aiello, J. R., Thompson, D. D., & Brodzinsky, D. M. (1983). How funny is crowding anyway? Effects of room size, group size, and the introduction of humor. *Basic and Applied Social Psychology, 4,* 193–207. (p. 587)

Aimone, J. B., Jessberger, S., & Gage, F. H. (2010, last modified February 5). Adult neurogenesis. *Scholarpedia* (www.scholarpedia.org). (p. 76)

Ainsworth, M. D. S. (1973). The development of infant-mother attachment. In B. Caldwell & H. Ricciuti (Eds.), *Review of child development research* (Vol. 3). Chicago: University of Chicago Press. (p. 189)

Ainsworth, M. D. S. (1979). Infant-mother attachment. *American Psychologist, 34,* 932–937. (p. 189)

Ainsworth, M. D. S. (1989). Attachments beyond infancy. *American Psychologist, 44,* 709–716. (p. 189)

Airan, R. D., Meltzer, L. A., Roy, M., Gong, Y., Chen, H., & Deisseroth, K. (2007). High-speed imaging reveals neurophysiological links to behavior in an animal model of depression. *Science, 317,* 819–823. (p. 652)

Åkerstedt, T., Kecklund, G., & Axelsson, J. (2007). Impaired sleep after bedtime stress and worries. *Biological Psychology, 76,* 170–173. (p. 104)

Alanko, K., Santtila, P., Harlaar, N., Witting, K., Varjonen, M., Jern, P., Johansson, A., von der Pahlen, B., & Sandnabba, N. K. (2010). Common genetic effects of gender atypical behavior in childhood and sexual orientation in adulthood: A study of Finnish twins. *Archives of Sexual Behavior, 39,* 81–92. (p. 445)

Albee, G. W. (1986). Toward a just society: Lessons from observations on the primary prevention of psychopathology. *American Psychologist, 41,* 891–898. (p. 702)

Alcock, J. (2011, March/April). Back from the future: Parapsychology and the Bem affair. *Skeptical Inquirer,* pp. 31–39. (p. 255)

Aldao, A., & Nolen-Hoeksema, S. (2010). Emotion-regulation strategies across psychopathology: A meta-analytic review. *Clinical Psychology Review, 30,* 217–237. (p. 687)

Aldrich, M. S. (1989). Automobile accidents in patients with sleep disorders. *Sleep, 12,* 487–494. (p. 103)

Aldridge-Morris, R. (1989). *Multiple personality: An exercise in deception.* Hillsdale, NJ: Erlbaum. (p. 666)

Aleman, A., Kahn, R. S., & Selten, J-P. (2003). Sex differences in the risk of schizophrenia: Evidence from meta-analysis. *Archives of General Psychiatry, 60,* 565–571. (p. 658)

Alexander, L., & Tredoux, C. (2010). The spaces between us: A spatial analysis of informal segregation. *Journal of Social Issues, 66,* 367–386. (p. 620)

Allard, F., & Burnett, N. (1985). Skill in sport. *Canadian Journal of Psychology, 39,* 294–312. (p. 318)

Allen, J. B., Repinski, D. J., Ballard, J. C., & Griffin, B. W. (1996). Beliefs about the etiology of homosexuality may influence attitudes toward homosexuals. Paper presented to the American Psychological Society convention. (p. 448)

Allen, K. (2003). Are pets a healthy pleasure? The influence of pets on blood pressure. *Current Directions in Psychological Science, 12,* 236–239. (p. 520)

Allen, M. W., Gupta, R., & Monnier, A. (2008). The interactive effect of cultural symbols and human values on taste evaluation. *Journal of Consumer Research, 35,* 294–308. (p. 267)

Allesøe, K., Hundrup, V. A., Thomsen, J. F., & Osler, M. (2010). Psychosocial work environment and risk of ischaemic heart disease in women: The Danish Nurse Cohort Study. *Occupational and Environmental Medicine, 67,* 318–322. (p. 514)

Alloy, L. B., Abramson, L. Y., Whitehouse, W. G., Hogan, M. E., Tashman, N. A., Steinberg, D. L., Rose, D. T., & Donovan, P. (1999). Depressogenic cognitive styles: Predictive validity, information processing and personality characteristics, and developmental origins. *Behaviour Research and Therapy, 37,* 503–531. (p. 653)

Allport, G. W. (1954). *The nature of prejudice.* New York: Addison-Wesley. (pp. 28, 586)

Allport, G. W., & Odbert, H. S. (1936). Trait-names: A psycho-lexical study. *Psychological Monographs, 47*(1). (p. 548)

Almås, I., Cappelen, A. W., Sørensen, E. Ø., & Tungodden, B. (2010). Fairness and the development of inequality acceptance. *Science, 328,* 1176–1178. (p. 200)

Almond, D., & Edlund, L. (2008). Son-biased sex ratios in the 2000 United States Census. *PNAS, 105,* 5681–5682. (p. 595)

Altamirano, L. J., Miyake, A., & Whitmer, A. J. (2010). When mental inflexibility facilitates executive control: Beneficial side effects of ruminative tendencies on goal maintenance. *Psychological Science, 21,* 1377–1382. (p. 653)

Altman, L. K. (2004, November 24). Female cases of HIV found rising worldwide. *New York Times* (www.nytimes.com). (p. 511)

Alwin, D. F. (1990). Historical changes in parental orientations to children. In N. Mandell (Ed.), *Sociological studies of child development* (Vol. 3). Greenwich, CT: JAI Press. (p. 155)

Amabile, T. M. (1983). *The social psychology of creativity.* New York: Springer-Verlag. (p. 565)

Amabile, T. M., & Hennessey, B. A. (1992). The motivation for creativity in children. In A. K. Boggiano & T. S. Pittman (Eds.), *Achievement and motivation: A social-developmental perspective.* New York: Cambridge University Press. (p. 387)

Amato, P. R., Booth, A., Johnson, D. R., & Rogers, S. J. (2007). *Alone together: How marriage in America is changing.* Cambridge, MA: Harvard University Press. (p. 162)

Ambady, N., & Bharucha, J. (2009). Culture and the brain. *Current Directions in Psychological Science, 18,* 342–345. (p. 155)

Ambady, N., Hallahan, M., & Rosenthal, R. (1995). On judging and being judged accurately in zero-acquaintance situations. *Journal of Personality and Social Psychology, 69,* 518–529. (p. 485)

Ambady, N., & Rosenthal, R. (1992). Thin slices of expressive behavior as predictors of interpersonal consequences: A meta-analysis. *Psychological Bulletin, 111,* 256–274. (p. 555)

Ambady, N., & Rosenthal, R. (1993). Half a minute: Predicting teacher evaluations from thin slices of nonverbal behavior and physical attractiveness. *Journal of Personality and Social Psychology, 64,* 431–441. (p. 555)

Ambrose, C. T. (2010). The widening gyrus. *American Scientist, 98,* 270–274. (p. 149)

Amedi, A., Floel, A., Knect, S., Zohary, E., & Cohen, L. (2004). Transcranial magnetic stimulation of the occipital pole interferes with verbal processing in blind subjects. *Nature Neuroscience, 7,* 1266–1270. (p. 75)

Amedi, A., Merabet, L. B., Bermpohl, F., & Pascual-Leone, A. (2005). The occipital cortex in the blind: Lessons about plasticity and vision. *Current Directions in Psychological Science, 14,* 306–311. (p. 75)

Amedi, A., Raz, N., Pianka, P., Malach, R., & Zohary, E. (2003). Early visual cortex activation correlates with superior verbal memory performance in the blind. *Nature Neuroscience, 6,* 758–766. (p. 371)

Amen, D. G., Stubblefield, M., Carmichael, B., & Thisted, R. (1996). Brain SPECT findings and aggressiveness. *Annals of Clinical Psychiatry, 8,* 129–137. (p. 600)

American Academy of Pediatrics. (2009). Policy statement—media violence. *Pediatrics, 124,* 1495–1503. (p. 308)

American Enterprise. (1992, January/February). Women, men, marriages & ministers. p. 106. (p. 155)

American Psychological Association. (2006). Evidence-based practice in psychology (from APA Presidential Task Force on Evidence-Based Practice). *American Psychologist, 61,* 271–285. (p. 696)

American Psychological Association. (2007). *Answers to your questions about sexual orientation and homosexuality.* (www.apa.org. Accessed December 6, 2007). (p. 443)

Ames, D. R. (2008). In search of the right touch: Interpersonal assertiveness in organizational life. *Current Directions in Psychological Science, 17,* 381–385. (p. 467)

Andersen, R. A. (2005, October). Dialogue: A locksmith for the mind. *Discover* (www.discovermagazine.com). (p. 71)

Andersen, R. A., Burdick, J. W., Musallam, S., Pesaran, B., & Cham, J. G. (2004). Cognitive neural prosthetics. *Trends in Cognitive Sciences, 8,* 486–493. (p. 71)

Andersen, R. A., Hwang, E. J., & Mulliken, G. H. (2010). Cognitive neural prosthetics. *Annual Review of Psychology, 61,* 169–190. (p. 72)

Andersen, S. M. (1998). *Service learning: A national strategy for youth development.* A position paper issued by the Task Force on Education Policy. Washington, DC: Institute for Communitarian Policy Studies, George Washington University. (p. 202)

Andersen, S. M., & Saribay, S. A. (2005). The relational self and transference: Evoking motives, self-regulation, and emotions through activation of mental representations of significant others. In M. W. Baldwin (Ed.), *Interpersonal cognition.* New York: Guilford. (p. 330)

Anderson, A. K., & Phelps, E. A. (2000). Expression without recognition: Contributions of the human amygdala to emotional communication. *Psychological Science, 11,* 106–111. (p. 65)

Anderson, B. L. (2002). Biobehavioral outcomes following psychological interventions for cancer patients. *Journal of Consulting and Clinical Psychology, 70,* 590–610. (p. 512)

Anderson, C. A. (2004). An update on the effects of playing violent video games. *Journal of Adolescence, 27,* 113–122. (pp. 604, 605)

Anderson, C. A., & Anderson, D. C. (1984). Ambient temperature and violent crime: Tests of the linear and curvilinear hypotheses. *Journal of Personality and Social Psychology, 46,* 91–97. (p. 601)

Anderson, C. A., Anderson, K. B., Dorr, N., DeNeve, K. M., & Flanagan, M. (2000). Temperature and aggression. In M. P. Zanna (Ed.), *Advances in Experimental Social Psychology.* San Diego: Academic Press. (p. 601)

Anderson, C. A., & Delisi, M. (2011). Implications of global climate change for violence in developed and developing countries. In J. Forgas, A. Kruglanski., & K. Williams (eds.), *The psychology of social conflict and aggression.* New York: Psychology Press. (p. 601)

Anderson, C. A., & Dill, K. E. (2000). Video games and aggressive thoughts, feelings, and behavior in the laboratory and in life. *Journal of Personality and Social Psychology, 78,* 772–790. (p. 605)

Anderson, C. A., & Gentile, D. A. (2008). Media violence, aggression, and public policy. In E. Borgida & S. Fiske (Eds.), *Beyond common sense: Psychological science in the courtroom.* Malden, MA: Blackwell. (p. 308)

Anderson, C. A., Gentile, D. A., & Buckley, K. E. (2007). *Violent video game effects on children and adolescents: Theory, research, and public policy.* New York: Oxford University Press. (pp. 324, 605)

Anderson, C. A., Lindsay, J. J., & Bushman, B. J. (1999). Research in the psychological laboratory: Truth or triviality? *Current Directions in Psychological Science, 8,* 3–9. (p. 21)

Anderson, C. A., Shibuya, A., Ihori, N., Swing, E. L., Bushman, B. J., Sakamoto, A., Rothstein, H. R., & Saleem, M. (2010). Violent video game effects on aggression, empathy, and prosocial behavior in Eastern and Western countries: A meta-analytic review. *Psychological Bulletin, 136,* 151–173. (pp. 363, 605)

Anderson, I. M. (2000). Selective serotonin reuptake inhibitors versus tricyclic antidepressants: A meta-analysis of efficacy and tolerability. *Journal of Affective Disorders, 58,* 19–36. (p. 705)

Anderson, J. R., Myowa-Yamakoshi, M., & Matsuzawa, T. (2004). Contagious yawning in chimpanzees. *Biology Letters, 271,* S468–S470. (p. 579)

Anderson, R. C., Pichert, J. W., Goetz, E. T., Schallert, D. L., Stevens, K. V., & Trollip, S. R. (1976). Instantiation of general terms. *Journal of Verbal Learning and Verbal Behavior, 15,* 667–679. (p. 338)

Anderson, S. (2008, July 6). The urge to end it. *New York Times* (www.nytimes.com). (p. 650)

Anderson, S. E., Dallal, G. E., & Must, A. (2003). Relative weight and race influence average age at menarche: Results from two nationally representative surveys of U.S. girls studied 25 years apart. *Pediatrics, 111,* 844–850. (p. 198)

Anderson, S. R. (2004). *Doctor Dolittle's delusion: Animals and the uniqueness of human language.* New Haven: Yale University Press. (p. 374)

Anderson, U. S., Stoinski, T. S., Bloomsmith, M. A., Marr, M. J., Anderson, D., & Maple, T. L. (2005). Relative numerous judgment and summation in young and old western lowland gorillas. *Journal of Comparative Psychology, 119,* 285–295. (p. 399)

Andreasen, N. C. (1997). Linking mind and brain in the study of mental illnesses: A project for a scientific psychopathology. *Science, 275,* 1586–1593. (p. 660)

Andreasen, N. C. (2001). *Brave new brain: Conquering mental illness in the era of the genome.* New York: Oxford University Press. (p. 660)

Andreasen, N. C., Arndt, S., Swayze, V., II, Cizadlo, T., & Flaum, M. (1994). Thalamic abnormalities in schizophrenia visualized through magnetic resonance image averaging. *Science, 266,* 294–298. (p. 660)

Andrews, P. W., & Thomson, J. A., Jr. (2009a). The bright side of being blue: Depression as an adaptation for analyzing complex problems. *Psychological Review, 116,* 620–654. (pp. 645, 653)

Andrews, P. W., & Thomson, Jr., J. A. (2009b, January/February). Depression's evolutionary roots. *Scientific American Mind,* pp. 57–61. (pp. 645, 653)

Angell, M., & Kassirer, J. P. (1998). Alternative medicine: The risks of untested and unregulated remedies. *New England Journal of Medicine, 17,* 839–841. (p. 526)

Angelsen, N. K., Vik, T., Jacobsen, G., & Bakketeig, L. S. (2001). Breast feeding and cognitive development at age 1 and 5 years. *Archives of Disease in Childhood, 85,* 183–188. (p. 34)

Caspi, A., Moffitt, T. E., Newman, D. L., & Silva, P. A. (1996). Behavioral observations at age 3 years predict adult psychiatric disorders: Longitudinal evidence from a birth cohort. *Archives of General Psychiatry, 53,* 1033–1039. (p. 668)

Cassel, L., & Suedfeld, P. (2006). Salutogenesis and autobiographical disclosure among Holocaust survivors. *The Journal of Positive Psychology, 1,* 212–225. (p. 641)

Cassidy, J., & Shaver, P. R. (1999). *Handbook of attachment.* New York: Guilford. (p. 188)

Castillo, R. J. (1997). *Culture and mental illness: A client-centered approach.* Pacific Grove, CA: Brooks/Cole. (p. 629)

Castonguay, L. G., Boswell, J. F., Constantino, M. J., Goldfried, M. R., & Hill, C. E. (2010). Training implications of harmful effects of psychological treatments. *American Psychologist, 65,* 34–49. (p. 696)

Cattell, R. B. (1963). Theory of fluid and crystallized intelligence: A critical experiment. *Journal of Educational Psychology, 54,* 1–22. (p. 399)

Cavalli-Sforza, L., Menozzi, P., & Piazza, A. (1994). *The history and geography of human genes.* Princeton, NJ: Princeton University Press. (pp. 411, 412)

Cavigelli, S. A., & McClintock, M. K. (2003). Fear of novelty in infant rats predicts adult corticosterone dynamics and an early death. *Proceedings of the National Academy of Sciences, 100,* 16131–16136. (p. 508)

Cawley, B. D., Keeping, L. M., & Levy, P. E. (1998). Participation in the performance appraisal process and employee reactions: A meta-analytic review of field investigations. *Journal of Applied Psychology, 83,* 615–633. (p. 467)

CDC. (2003). *Who should get a flu shot (influenza vaccine).* National Center for Infectious Diseases (http: //www.cdc.gov/ncidod/diseases/flu/who.htm). (p. 661)

CDC. (2009). *Self-harm, all injury causes, nonfatal injuries and rates per 100,000.* National Center for Injury Prevention and Control. http: //webappa.cdc.gov/cgi-bin/broker.exe. (p. 651)

CDC. (2009, December 18). Prevalence of autism spectrum disorders—Autism and developments disabilities monitoring network, United States, 2006 (corresponding author: Catherine Rice). *MMWR,* 58(SS10), 1–20. (www.cdc.gov). (p. 184)

CDC. (2010, June 4). Youth risk behavior surveillance—United States, 2009. *Morbidity and Mortality Weekly,* 59SS05, 1–142 (by D. K. Eaton & 13 others). (p. 439)

CDC. (2011, accessed April 20). *Who's at risk? Tobacco use—smoking.* Centers for Disease Control and Prevention (cdc.gov/vitalsigns/TobaccoUse/Smoking/Risk.html). (p. 128)

Ceci, S. J. (1993). Cognitive and social factors in children's testimony. Master lecture, American Psychological Association convention. (pp. 344, 345)

Ceci, S. J., & Bruck, M. (1993). Child witnesses: Translating research into policy. *Social Policy Report* (Society for Research in Child Development), 7(3), 1–30. (p. 344)

Ceci, S. J., & Bruck, M. (1995). *Jeopardy in the courtroom: A scientific analysis of children's testimony.* Washington, DC: American Psychological Association. (p. 344)

Ceci, S. J., Huffman, M. L. C., Smith, E., & Loftus, E. F. (1994). Repeatedly thinking about a non-event: Source misattributions among preschoolers. *Consciousness and Cognition,* 3, 388–407. (p. 344)

Ceci, S. J., & Kanaya, T. (2010)., "Apples and oranges are both round": Furthering the discussion on the Flynn effect. *Journal of Psychoeducational Assessment, 28,* 441–447. (p. 396)

Ceci, S. J., & Williams, W. M. (1997). Schooling, intelligence, and income. *American Psychologist, 52,* 1051–1058. (p. 408)

Ceci, S. J., & Williams, W. M. (2010). Sex differences in math-intensive fields. *Current Directions in Psychological Science, 19,* 275–279. (p. 410)

Ceci, S. J., & Williams, W. M. (2011). Understanding current causes of women's underrepresentation in science. *Proceedings of the National Academy of Sciences, 108.* 3157–3162. (p. 410)

Centers for Disease Control. (1992, September 16). Serious mental illness and disability in the adult household population: United States, 1989. *Advance Data* No. 218 from *Vital and Health Statistics,* National Center for Health Statistics. (p. 634)

Centers for Disease Control Vietnam Experience Study. (1988). Health status of Vietnam veterans. *Journal of the American Medical Association, 259,* 2701–2709. (p. 640)

Centerwall, B. S. (1989). Exposure to television as a risk factor for violence. *American Journal of Epidemiology, 129,* 643–652. (p. 308)

Cepeda, N. J., Pashler, H., Vul, E., Wixted, J. T., & Rohrer, D. (2006). Distributed practice in verbal recall tasks: A review and quantitative synthesis. *Psychological Bulletin, 132,* 354–380. (p. 319)

Cepeda, N. J., Vul, E., Rohrer, D., Wixed, J. T., & Pashler, H. (2008). Spacing effects in learning: A temporal ridgeline of optimal retention. *Psychological Science, 19,* 1095–1102. (p. 320)

Cerella, J. (1985). Information processing rates in the elderly. *Psychological Bulletin, 98,* 67–83. (p. 211)

CFI. (2003, July). *International developments. Report.* Amherst, NY: Center for Inquiry International. (p. 255)

Chabris, C. F., & Simons, D. (2010). *The invisible gorilla: And other ways our intuitions deceive us.* New York: Crown. (p. 90)

Chambless, D. L., Baker, M. J., Baucom, D. H., Beutler, L. E., Calhoun, K. S., Crits-Christoph, P., Daiuto, A., DeRubeis, R., Detweiler, J., Haaga, D. A. F., Johnson, S. B., McCurry, S., Mueser, K. T., Pope, K. S., Sanderson, W. C., Shoham, V., Stickle, T., Williams, D. A., & Woody, S. R. (1997). Update on empirically validated therapies, II. *The Clinical Psychologist, 51*(1), 3–16. (p. 697)

Chamove, A. S. (1980). Nongenetic induction of acquired levels of aggression. *Journal of Abnormal Psychology, 89,* 469–488. (p. 307)

Champagne, F. A. (2010). Early adversity and developmental outcomes: Interaction between genetics, epigenetics, and social experiences across the life span. *Perspectives on Psychological Science, 5,* 564–574. (p. 140)

Champagne, F. A., Francis, D. D., Mar, A, & Meaney, M. J. (2003). Naturally-occurring variations in maternal care in the rat as a mediating influence for the effects of environment on the development of individual differences in stress reactivity. *Physiology & Behavior, 79,* 359–371. (p. 140)

Champagne, F. A., & Mashoodh, R. (2009). Genes in context: Gene-environment interplay and the origins of individual differences in behavior. *Current Directions in Psychological Science, 18,* 127–131. (p. 140)

Chance News. (1997, 25 November). More on the frequency of letters in texts. Dart. Chance@Dartmouth.edu. (p. 31)

Chandler, J., & Schwarz, N. (2009). How extending your middle finger affects your perception of others: learned movements influence concept accessibility. *Journal of Experimental Social Psychology, 45,* 123–128. (p. 490)

Chandra, A., Mosher, W. D., & Copen, C. (2011, March). Sexual behavior, sexual attraction, and sexual identity in the United States: Data from the 2006–2008 National Survey of Family Growth. *National Health Statistics Reports,* Number 36 (Centers for Disease Control and Prevention). (p. 442)

Chang, E. C. (2001). Cultural influences on optimism and pessimism: Differences in Western and Eastern construals of the self. In E. C. Chang (Ed.), *Optimism and pessimism.* Washington, DC: APA Books. (p. 559)

Chang, P. P., Ford, D. E., Meoni, L. A., Wang, N-Y., & Klag, M. J. (2002). Anger in young men and subsequent premature cardiovascular disease: The precursors study. *Archives of Internal Medicine, 162,* 901–906. (p. 513)

Chaplin, W. F., Phillips, J. B., Brown, J. D., Clanton, N. R., & Stein, J. L. (2000). Handshaking, gender, personality, and first impressions. *Journal of Personality and Social Psychology, 79,* 110–117. (p. 484)

Charness, N., & Boot, W. R. (2009). Aging and information technology use. *Current Directions in Psychological Science, 18,* 253–258. (p. 400)

Charpak, G., & Broch, H. (2004). *Debunked! ESP, telekinesis, and other pseudoscience.* Baltimore, MD: Johns Hopkins University Press. (p. 254)

Chartrand, T. L., & Bargh, J. A. (1999). The chameleon effect: The perception-behavior link and social interaction. *Journal of Personality and Social Psychology, 76,* 893–910. (p. 579)

Chatard, A., & Selimbegović, L. (2011). When self-destructive thoughts flash through the mind: Failure to meet standards affects the accessibility of suicide-related thoughts. *Journal of Personality and Social Psychology, 100,* 587–605. (p. 650)

Chater, N., Reali, F., & Christiansen, M. H. (2009). Restrictions on biological adaptation in language evolution. *PNAS, 106,* 1015–1020. (p. 369)

Cheek, J. M., & Melchior, L. A. (1990). Shyness, self-esteem, and self-consciousness. In H. Leitenberg (Ed.), *Handbook of social and evaluation anxiety.* New York: Plenum. (p. 154)

Cheit, R. E. (1998). Consider this, skeptics of recovered memory. *Ethics & Behavior, 8,* 141–160. (p. 540)

Chen, A. W., Kazanjian, A., & Wong, H. (2009). Why do Chinese Canadians not consult mental health services: Health status, language or culture? *Transcultural Psychiatry, 46,* 623–640. (p. 700)

Chen, E. (2004). Why socioeconomic status affects the health of children: A psychosocial perspective. *Current Directions in Psychological Science, 13,* 112–115. (p. 518)

Chen, S-Y., & Fu, Y-C. (2008). Internet use and academic achievement: Gender differences in early adolescence. *Adolescence, 44,* 797–812. (p. 455)

Chen, X., Beydoun, M. A., & Wang, Y. (2008). Is sleep duration associated with childhood obesity? A systematic review and meta-analysis. *Obesity, 16,* 265–274. (p. 102)

Cheng, M. (2006, November 16). Europeans OK anti-obesity charter. *Associated Press.* (p. 432)

Cherkas, L. F., Hunkin, J. L., Kato, B. S., Richards, J. B., Gardner, J. P., Surdulescu, G. L., Kimura, M., Lu, X., Spector, T. D., & Aviv, A. (2008). The association between physical activity in leisure time and leukocyte telomere length. *Archives of Internal Medicine, 168,* 154–158. (p. 212)

Cherniss, C. (2010a). Emotional intelligence: Toward clarification of a concept. *Industrial and Organizational Psychology,* 3, 110–126. (p. 389)

Cherniss, C. (2010b). Emotional intelligence: New insights and further clarifications. *Industrial and Organizational Psycvhology,* 3, 183–191. (p. 389)

Chess, S., & Thomas, A. (1987). *Know your child: An authoritative guide for today's parents.* New York: Basic Books. (pp. 137, 190)

Cheung, B. Y., Chudek, M., & Heine, S. J. (2011). Evidence for a sensitive period for acculturation: Younger immigrants report acculturating at a faster rate. *Psychological Science, 22,* 147–152. (p. 369)

Chiao, J. Y. (2009). Cultural neuroscience: A once and future discipline. *Progress in Brain Research, 178,* 287–304. (p. 155)

Chiao, J. Y. & Blizinsky, K. D. (2010). Culture-gene coevolution of individualism-collectivism and the serotonin transporter gene (5-HTTLPR). *Proceedings of the Royal Society B: Biological Sciences, 277,* 529–537. (p. 155)

Chida, Y., & Hamer, M. (2008). Chronic psychosocial factors and acute physiological responses to laboratory-induced stress in healthy populations: A quantitative review of 30 years of investigations. *Psychological Bulletin, 134,* 829–885. (p. 513)

Chida, Y., Hamer, M., Wardle, J., & Steptoe, A. (2008). Do stress-related psychosocial factors contribute to cancer incidence and survival? *Nature Reviews: Clinical Oncology, 5,* 466–475. (p. 512)

Chida, Y., & Steptoe, A. (2009). The association of anger and hostility with future coronary heart disease: A meta-analytic review of prospective evidence. *Journal of the American College of Cardiology, 17,* 936–946. (p. 513)

Chida, Y., Steptoe, A., & Powell, L. H. (2009). Religiosity/spirituality and mortality. *Psychotherapy and Psychosomatics, 78,* 81–90. (p. 527)

Chiles, J. A., Lambert, M. J., & Hatch, A. L. (1999). The impact of psychological interventions on medical cost offset: A meta-analytic review. *Clinical Psychology: Science and Practice, 6,* 204–220. (p. 695)

Chisolm, T. H., Johnson, C. E., Danhauer, J. L., Portz, L. J. P., Abrams, H. B., Lesner, S., McCarthy, P. A., & Newman, C. W. (2007). A systematic review of health-related quality of life and hearing aids: Final report of the American Academy of Audiology Task Force on the Health-Related Quality of Life Benefits of Amplification in Adults. *Journal of the American Academy of Audiology, 18,* 151–183. (p. 371)

Chivers, M. L. (2005). A brief review and discussion of sex differences in the specificity of sexual arousal. *Sexual and Relationship Therapy, 20,* 377–390. (p. 443)

Chivers, M. L., Seto, M. C., & Blanchard, R. (2007). Gender and sexual orientation differences in sexual response to sexual activities versus gender of actors in sexual films. *Journal of Personality and Social Psychology, 93,* 1108–1121. (p. 444)

Chivers, M. L., Seto, M. C., Lalumière, M. L., Laan, E., & Grimbos, T. (2010). Agreement of self-reported and genital measures of sexual arousal in men and women: A meta-analysis. *Archives of Sexual Behavior, 39,* 5–56. (p. 438)

Choi, C. Q. (2008, March). Do you need only half your brain? *Scientific American,* p. 104. (p. 75)

Choi, I., & Choi, Y. (2002). Culture and self-concept flexibility. *Personality and Social Psychology Bulletin, 28,* 1508–1517. (p. 153)

Chomsky, N. (1972). *Language and mind.* New York: Harcourt Brace. (p. 373)

Christakis, N. A., & Fowler, J. H. (2007). The spread of obesity in a large social network over 32 years. *New England Journal of Medicine, 357,* 370–379. (p. 431)

Christakis, N. A., & Fowler, J. H. (2008, May). The collective dynamics of smoking in a large social network. *New England Journal of Medicine,* 358(21), 2249–2258. (p. 128)

Christakis, N. A., & Fowler, J. H. (2009). *Connected: The surprising power of social networks and how they shape our lives.* New York: Little, Brown. (pp. 521, 579)

Christensen, A., & Jacobson, N. S. (1994). Who (or what) can do psychotherapy: The status and challenge of nonprofessional therapies. *Psychological Science, 5,* 8–14. (p. 699)

Christophersen, E. R., & Edwards, K. J. (1992). Treatment of elimination disorders: State of the art 1991. *Applied & Preventive Psychology, 1,* 15–22. (p. 681)

Chua, H. F., Boland, J. E., & Nisbett, R. E. (2005). Cultural variation in eye movements during scene perception. *Proceedings of the National Academy of Sciences, 102,* 12629–12633. (p. 572)

Chugani, H. T., & Phelps, M. E. (1986). Maturational changes in cerebral function in infants determined by 18FDG positron emission tomography. *Science, 231,* 840–843. (p. 177)

Church, T. S., Thomas, D. M., Tudor-Locke, C., Katzmarzyk, P. T., Earnest, C. P., Rodarte, R. Q., Martin, C. K., Blair, S. N., & Bouchard, C. (2011). Trends over 5 decades in U.S. occupation-related physical activity and their associations with obesity. *PLoS ONE, 6(5),* e19657. (p. 432)

CIA. (2010). *The World Fact Book:* Literacy. Washington, D.C.: CIA (https://www.cia.gov/library/publications/the-world-factbook/fields/2103.html). (p. 594)

CIA. (2010, accessed August 23). Field testing: Life expectancy at birth. *CIA Fact Book* (www.cia.gov). (p. 209)

Cialdini, R. B. (1993). *Influence: Science and practice* (3rd ed.). New York: HarperCollins. (p. 575)

Cialdini, R. B., & Richardson, K. D. (1980). Two indirect tactics of image management: Basking and blasting. *Journal of Personality and Social Psychology, 39,* 406–415. (p. 597)

Ciarrochi, J., Forgas, J. P., & Mayer, J. D. (2006). *Emotional intelligence in everyday life* (2nd ed.). New York: Psychology Press. (p. 389)

Cin, S. D., Gibson, B., Zanna, M. P., Shumate, R., & Fong, G. T. (2007). Smoking in movies, implicit associations of smoking with the self, and intentions to smoke. *Psychological Science, 18,* 559–563. (p. 119)

Clack, B., Dixon, J., & Tredoux, C. (2005). Eating together apart: Patterns of segregation in a multi-ethnic cafeteria. *Journal of Community and Applied Social Psychology, 15,* 1–16. (p. 620)

Clancy, S. A. (2005). *Abducted: How people come to believe they were kidnapped by aliens.* Cambridge, MA: Harvard University Press. (p. 95)

Clancy, S. A. (2010). *The trauma myth: The truth about the sexual abuse of children—and its aftermath.* New York: Basic Books. (p. 191)

Clancy, S. A., Schacter, D. L., McNally, R. J., & Pitman, R. K. (2000). False recognition in women reporting recovered memories of sexual abuse. *Psychological Science, 11,* 26–31. (p. 347)

Clark, A., Seidler, A., & Miller, M. (2001). Inverse association between sense of humor and coronary heart disease. *International Journal of Cardiology, 80,* 87–88. (p. 519)

Clark, K. B., & Clark, M. P. (1947). Racial identification and preference in Negro children. In T. M. Newcomb & E. L. Hartley (Eds.), *Readings in social psychology.* New York: Holt. (p. 24)

Clay, R. A. (2010, July/August). Defining disease worldwide. *Monitor on Psychology,* pp. 54–57. (p. 630)

Clay, R. A. (2011, January). Revising the DSM. *Monitor on Psychology,* pp. 54–55. (p. 630)

Cleary, A. M. (2008). Recognition memory, familiarity, and déjà vu experiences. *Current Directions in Psychological Science, 17,* 353–357. (p. 343)

Clifton, J., & Morales, L. (2011, February 2). Egyptians', Tunisians' wellbeing plummets despite GDP gains. *Gallup* (www.gallup.com). (p. 502)

Coan, J. A., Schaefer, H. S., & Davidson, R. J. (2006). Lending a hand: Social regulation of the neural response to threat. *Psychological Science, 17,* 1032–1039. (p. 519)

Coelho, C. M., & Purkis, H. (2009). The origins of specific phobias: Influential theories and current perspectives. *Review of General Psychology, 13,* 335–348. (p. 643)

Coffey, C. E., Wilkinson, W. E., Weiner, R. D., Parashos, I. A., Djang, W. T., Webb, M. C., Figiel, G. S., & Spritzer, C. E. (1993). Quantitative cerebral anatomy in depression: A controlled magnetic resonance imaging study. *Archives of General Psychiatry, 50,* 7–16. (p. 652)

Cogan, J. C., & Ernsberger, P. (1999). Dieting, weight, and health: Reconceptualizing research and policy. *Journal of Social Issues, 55,* 187–205. (p. 433)

Cohen, A. B. (2009). Many forms of culture. *American Psychologist, 64,* 194–204. (pp. 151, 154)

Cohen, D. (1995, June 17). Now we are one, or two, or three. *New Scientist,* pp. 14–15. (p. 666)

Cohen, G. L., Garcia, J., Apfel, N., & Master, A. (2006). Reducing the racial achievement gap: A social-psychological intervention. *Science, 313,* 1307–1310. (p. 414)

Cohen, G. L., Garcia, J., Purdie-Vaughns, V., Apfel, N., Brzustoski, P. (2009). Recursive processes in self-affirmation: Intervening to close the minority achievement gap. *Science, 324,* 400–403. (p. 414)

Cohen, K. M. (2002). Relationships among childhood sex-atypical behavior, spatial ability, handedness, and sexual orientation in men. *Archives of Sexual Behavior, 31,* 129–143. (p. 447)

Cohen, N. (2011, January 30). Define gender gap? Look up Wikipedia's contributor list. *New York Times* (www.nytimes.com). (p. 159)

Cohen, P. (2007, November 15). Freud is widely taught at universities, except in the psychology department. *New York Times* (www.nytimes.com). (p. 532)

Empson, J. A. C., & Clarke, P. R. F. (1970). Rapid eye movements and remembering. *Nature, 227,* 287–288. (p. 107)

Endler, N. S. (1982). *Holiday of darkness: A psychologist's personal journey out of his depression.* New York: Wiley. (pp. 653, 709)

Engdahl, B., Leuthold, A. C., Tan, H-R. M., Lewis, S. M., Winskowski, A. M., & Georgopoulos, A. P. (2010). Post-traumatic stress disorder: A right temporal lobe syndrome? *Journal of Neural Engineering, 7,* 066005. (p. 640)

Engemann, K. M., & Owyang, M. T. (2005, April). So much for that merit raise: The link between wages and appearance. *Regional Economist* (www.stlouisfed.org). (p. 610)

Engen, T. (1987). Remembering odors and their names. *American Scientist, 75,* 497–503. (p. 271)

Engle, R. W. (2002). Working memory capacity as executive attention. *Current Directions in Psychological Science, 11,* 19–23. (p. 315)

Epel, E. S. (2009). Telomeres in a life-span perspective: A new "psychobiomarker"? *Current Directions in Psychological Science, 18,* 6–9. (p. 209)

Epel, E. S., Blackburn, E. H., Lin, J., Dhabhar, F. S., Adler, N. E., Morrow, J. D., & Cawthon, R. M. (2004). Accelerated telomere shortening in response to life stress. *Proceedings of the National Academy of Sciences, 101,* 17312–17315. (p. 508)

Epley, N., & Dunning, D. (2000). Feeling "holier than thou": Are self-serving assessments produced by errors in self- or social prediction? *Journal of Personality and Social Psychology, 79,* 861–875. (p. 566)

Epley, N., Keysar, B., Van Boven, L., & Gilovich, T. (2004). Perspective taking as egocentric anchoring and adjustment. *Journal of Personality and Social Psychology, 87,* 327–339. (p. 182)

EPOCH. (2000). Legal reforms: Corporal punishment of children in the family. (www.stophitting.com/laws/legalReform.php). (p. 292)

Epstein, J., Stern, E., & Silbersweig, D. (1998). Mesolimbic activity associated with psychosis in schizophrenia: Symptom-specific PET studies. In J. F. McGinty (Ed.), *Advancing from the ventral striatum to the extended amygdala: Implications for neuropsychiatry and drug use: In honor of Lennart Heimer. Annals of the New York Academy of Sciences, 877,* 562–574. (p. 660)

Epstein, L. H., Dearing, K. K., Roba, L. G., & Finkelstein, E. (2010). The influence of taxes and subsidies on energy purchased in an experimental purchasing study. *Psychological Science, 21,* 406–414. (p. 432)

Epstein, S. (1983a). Aggregation and beyond: Some basic issues on the prediction of behavior. *Journal of Personality, 51,* 360–392. (p. 554)

Epstein, S. (1983b). The stability of behavior across time and situations. In R. Zucker, J. Aronoff, & A. I. Rabin (Eds.), *Personality and the prediction of behavior.* San Diego: Academic Press. (p. 554)

Epstein, S., & Meier, P. (1989). Constructive thinking: A broad coping variable with specific components. *Journal of Personality and Social Psychology, 57,* 332–350. (p. 389)

Erdberg, P. (1990). Rorschach assessment. In G. Goldstein & M. Hersen (Eds.), *Handbook of psychological assessment* (2nd ed.). New York: Pergamon. (p. 538)

Erdelyi, M. H. (1985). *Psychoanalysis: Freud's cognitive psychology.* New York: Freeman. (p. 540)

Erdelyi, M. H. (1988). Repression, reconstruction, and defense: History and integration of the psychoanalytic and experimental frameworks. In J. Singer (Ed.), *Repression: Defense mechanism and cognitive style.* Chicago: University of Chicago Press. (p. 540)

Erdelyi, M. H. (2006). The unified theory of repression. *Behavioral and Brain Sciences, 29,* 499–551. (p. 540)

Erel, O., & Burman, B. (1995). Interrelatedness of marital relations and parent-child relations: A meta-analytic review. *Psychological Bulletin, 118,* 108–132. (p. 217)

Erickson, K. I. (2009). Aerobic fitness is associated with hippocampal volume in elderly humans. *Hippocampus, 19,* 1030–1039. (p. 212)

Erickson, K. I. & 9 others. (2010). Physical activity predicts gray matter volume in late adulthood: The Cardiovascular Health Study. *Neurology, 75,* 1415–1422. (p. 211)

Erickson, M. F., & Aird, E. G. (2005). *The motherhood study: Fresh insights on mothers' attitudes and concerns.* New York: The Motherhood Project, Institute for American Values. (p. 217)

Ericsson, K. A. (2001). Attaining excellence through deliberate practice: Insights from the study of expert performance. In M. Ferrari (Ed.), *The pursuit of excellence in education.* Hillsdale, NJ: Erlbaum. (p. 463)

Ericsson, K. A. (2002). Attaining excellence through deliberate practice: Insights from the study of expert performance. In C. Desforges & R. Fox (Eds.), *Teaching and learning: The essential readings.* Malden, MA: Blackwell Publishers. (p. 385)

Ericsson, K. A. (2006). The influence of experience and deliberate practice on the development of superior expert performance. In K. A. Ericsson, N. Charness, P. J. Feltovich, & R. R. Hoffman (Eds.), *The Cambridge handbook of expertise and expert performance.* Cambridge: Cambridge University Press. (p. 463)

Ericsson, K. A. (2007). Deliberate practice and the modifiability of body and mind: Toward a science of the structure and acquisition of expert and elite performance. *International Journal of Sport Psychology, 38,* 4–34. (pp. 385, 463)

Ericsson, K. A., Krampe, R. T., & Tesch-Römer, C. (1993). The role of deliberate practice in the acquisition of expert performance. *Psychological Review, 100,* 363–406. (p. 100)

Ericsson, K. A., Roring, R. W., & Nandagopal, K. (2007). Giftedness and evidence for reproducibly superior performance: An account based on the expert performance framework. *High Ability Studies, 18,* 3–56. (pp. 385, 408)

Erikson, E. H. (1963). *Childhood and society.* New York: Norton. (p. 202)

Erikson, E. H. (1983, June). A conversation with Erikson (by E. Hall). *Psychology Today,* pp. 22–30. (p. 191)

Ertmer, D. J., Young, N. M., & Nathani, S. (2007). Profiles of focal development in young cochlear implant recipients. *Journal of Speech, Language, and Hearing Research, 50,* 393–407. (p. 368)

Escobar-Chaves, S. L., Tortolero, S. R., Markham, C. M., Low, B. J., Eitel, P., & Thickstun, P. (2005). Impact of the media on adolescent sexual attitudes and behaviors. *Pediatrics, 116,* 303–326. (p. 440)

Escobedo, J. R., & Adolphs, R. (2010). Becoming a better person: Temporal remoteness biases autobiographical memories for moral events. *Emotion, 10,* 511–518. (p. 568)

Eskine, K. J., Kacinik, N. A., & Prinz, J. J. (2011). A bad taste in the mouth: Gustatory disgust influences moral judgment. *Psychological Science, 22,* 295–299. (p. 201)

ESPAD. (2003). *Summary of the 2003 findings.* European School Survey Project on Alcohol and Other Drugs. (www.espad.org). (p. 127)

Esser, J. K., & Lindoerfer, J. S. (1989). Groupthink and the space shuttle Challenger accident: Toward a quantitative case analysis. *Journal of Behavioral Decision Making, 2,* 167–177. (p. 590)

Esterson, A. (2001). The mythologizing of psychoanalytic history: Deception and self-deception in Freud's accounts of the seduction theory episode. *History of Psychiatry, 12,* 329–352. (p. 539)

Etkin, A., & Wager, T. D. (2007). Functional neuroimaging of anxiety: A meta-analysis of emotional processing in PTSD, social anxiety disorder, and specific phobia. *American Journal of Psychiatry, 164,* 1476–1488. (p. 643)

Eurich, T. L., Krause, D. E., Cigularov, K., & Thornton, G. C., III. (2009). Assessment centers: Current practices in the United States. *Journal of Business Psychology, 24,* 387–407. (p. 562)

Euston, D. R., Tatsuno, M., & McNaughton, B. L. (2007). Fast-forward playback of recent memory sequences in prefrontal cortex during sleep. *Science, 318,* 1147–1150. (p. 324)

Evans, C. R., & Dion, K. L. (1991). Group cohesion and performance: A meta-analysis. *Small Group Research, 22,* 175–186. (p. 467)

Evans, G. W., Palsane, M. N., & Carrere, S. (1987). Type A behavior and occupational stress: A cross-cultural study of blue-collar workers. *Journal of Personality and Social Psychology, 52,* 1002–1007. (p. 513)

Evans, N., & Levinson, S. C. (2009). The myth of language universals: Language diversity and its importance for cognitive science. *Behavioral and Brain Sciences, 32,* 429–492. (p. 368)

Everson, S. A., Goldberg, D. E., Kaplan, G. A., Cohen, R. D., Pukkala, E., Tuomilehto, J., & Salonen, J. T. (1996). Hopelessness and risk of mortality and incidence of myocardial infarction and cancer. *Psychosomatic Medicine, 58,* 113–121. (p. 519)

Exner, J. E. (2003). *The Rorschach: A comprehensive system* (4th ed.). Hoboken, NJ: Wiley. (p. 538)

Eysenck, H. J. (1952). The effects of psychotherapy: An evaluation. *Journal of Consulting Psychology, 16,* 319–324. (p. 694)

Eysenck, H. J. (1990, April 30). An improvement on personality inventory. *Current Contents: Social and Behavioral Sciences,* 22(18), 20. (p. 548)

Eysenck, H. J. (1992). Four ways five factors are *not* basic. *Personality and Individual Differences, 13,* 667–673. (p. 548)

Eysenck, H. J., & Grossarth-Maticek, R. (1991). Creative novation behaviour therapy as a prophylactic treatment for cancer and coronary heart disease: Part II—Effects of treatment. *Behaviour Research and Therapy, 29,* 17–31. (p. 523)

Eysenck, H. J., Wakefield, J. A., Jr., & Friedman, A. F. (1983). Diagnosis and clinical assessment: The DSM-III. *Annual Review of Psychology, 34,* 167–193. (p. 631)

Eysenck, M. W., MacLeod, C., & Mathews, A. (1987). Cognitive functioning and anxiety. *Psychological Research, 49,* 189–195. (p. 556)

Eysenck, S. B. G., & Eysenck, H. J. (1963). The validity of questionnaire and rating assessments of extraversion and neuroticism, and their factorial stability. *British Journal of Psychology, 54,* 51–62. (p. 548)

Faber, N. (1987, July). Personal glimpse. *Reader's Digest,* p. 34. (p. 387)

Fabiano, G. A., Pelham, Jr., W. E., Coles, E. K., Gnagy, E. M., Chronis-Tuscano, A., & O'Connor, B. C. (2008). A meta-analysis of behavioral treatments for attention-deficit/hyperactivity disorder. *Clinical Psychology Review, 29,* 129–140. (p. 627)

Fagan, J. F., & Holland, C. R. (2007). Equal opportunity and racial differences in IQ. *Intelligence, 30,* 361–387. (pp. 412, 413)

Falk, C. F., Heine, S. J., Yuki, M., & Takemura, K. (2009). Why do Westerners self-enhance more than East Asians? *European Journal of Personality, 23,* 183–203. (p. 566)

Falk, R., Falk, R., & Ayton, P. (2009). Subjective patterns of randomness and choice: Some consequences of collective responses. *Journal of Experimental Psychology: Human Perception and Performance, 35,* 203–224. (p. 17)

Fanti, K. A., Vanman, E., Henrich, C. C., & Avraamides, M. N. (2009). Desensitization to media violence over a short period of time. *Aggressive Behavior, 35,* 179–187. (p. 308)

FAO. (2010). *2010 hunger report.* Food and Agriculture Organization of the United Nations (www.fao.org). (p. 431)

Farah, M. J., Rabinowitz, C., Quinn, G. E., & Liu, G. T. (2000). Early commitment of neural substrates for face recognition. *Cognitive Neuropsychology, 17,* 117–124. (p. 75)

Farina, A. (1982). The stigma of mental disorders. In A. G. Miller (Ed.), *In the eye of the beholder.* New York: Praeger. (pp. 628, 632)

Farley, M., Baral, I., Kiremire, M., & Sezgin, U. (1998). Prostitution in five countries: Violence and post-traumatic stress disorder. *Feminism and Psychology, 8,* 405–426. (p. 640)

Farrington, D. P. (1991). Antisocial personality from childhood to adulthood. *The Psychologist: Bulletin of the British Psychological Society, 4,* 389–394. (p. 668)

Fatemi, S. H., & Folsom, T. D. (2009). The neurodevelopmental hypothesis of schizophrenia, revisted. *Schizophrenia Bulletin, 35,* 528–548. (p. 660)

Fazel, S., Langstrom, N., Hjern, A., Grann, M., & Lichtenstein, P. (2009). Schizophrenia, substance abuse, and violent crime. *JAMA, 301,* 2016–2023. (pp. 632, 633)

Fazel, S, Lichtenstein, P, Grann, M, Goodwin, G. M., & Långström, N. (2010). bipolar disorder and violent crime: new evidence from population-based longitudinal studies and systematic review. *Archives of General Psychiatry, 67,* 931–938. (p. 632)

FBI. (2009). *Uniform Crime Reports.* Table 3. Washington, DC: Federal Bureau of Investigation. (p. 158)

Feder, H. H. (1984). Hormones and sexual behavior. *Annual Review of Psychology, 35,* 165–200. (p. 436)

Feeney, D. M. (1987). Human rights and animal welfare. *American Psychologist, 42,* 593–599. (p. 23)

Feeney, J. A., & Noller, P. (1990). Attachment style as a predictor of adult romantic relationships. *Journal of Personality and Social Psychology, 58,* 281–291. (p. 191)

Feigenson, L., Carey, S., & Spelke, E. (2002). Infants' discrimination of number vs. continuous extent. *Cognitive Psychology, 44,* 33–66. (p. 182)

Feingold, A. (1990). Gender differences in effects of physical attractiveness on romantic attraction: A comparison across five research paradigms. *Journal of Personality and Social Psychology, 59,* 981–993. (p. 610)

Feingold, A. (1992). Good-looking people are not what we think. *Psychological Bulletin, 111,* 304–341. (p. 610)

Feingold, A., & Mazzella, R. (1998). Gender differences in body image are increasing. *Psychological Science, 9,* 190–195. (p. 671)

Feinstein, J. S., Duff, M. C., & Tranel, D. (2010, April 27). Sustained experiences of emotion after loss of memory in patients with amnesia. *Proceedings of the National Academy of Sciences, 107,* 7674–7679. (p. 326)

Feldman, M. B., & Meyer, I. H. (2010). Comorbidity and age of onset of eating disorders in gay men, lesbians, and bisexuals. *Psychiatry research, 180,* 126–131. (p. 671)

Fellinger, J., Holzinger, D., Gerich, J., & Goldberg, D. (2007). Mental distress and quality of life in the hard of hearing. *Acta Psychiatrica Scandinavica, 115,* 243–245. (p. 371)

Fellowes, D., Barnes, K., & Wilkinson, S. (2004). Aromatherapy and massage for symptom relief in patients with cancer. *The Cochrane Library, 3,* Oxford, England: Update Software. (p. 526)

Feng, J., Spence, I., & Pratt, J. (2007). Playing an action video game reduces gender differences in spatial cognition. *Psychological Science, 18,* 850–855. (p. 409)

Fenton, W. S., & McGlashan, T. H. (1991). Natural history of schizophrenia subtypes: II. Positive and negative symptoms and long-term course. *Archives of General Psychiatry, 48,* 978–986. (p. 659)

Fenton, W. S., & McGlashan, T. H. (1994). Antecedents, symptom progression, and long-term outcome of the deficit syndrome in schizophrenia. *American Journal of Psychiatry, 151,* 351–356. (p. 659)

Ferguson, C. (2009, June 14). Not every child is secretly a genius. *The Chronicle Review* (http://chronicle.com/article/Not-Every-Child-Is-Secretly/48001). (p. 384)

Ferguson, C. J. (2010). A meta-analysis of normal and disordered personality across the life span. *Journal of Personality and Social Psychology, 98,* 659–667. (pp. 171, 627)

Ferguson, C. J., & Hartley, R. D. (2009). The pleasure is momentary . . . the expense damnable? The influence of pornography on rape and sexual assault. *Aggression and Violent Behavior, 14,* 323–329. (p. 603)

Ferguson, C. J., & Kilburn, J. (2010). Much ado about nothing: The misestimation and overinterpretation of violent video game effects in Eastern and Western nations: Common on Anderson et al. (2010). *Psychological Bulletin, 136,* 174–178. (p. 605)

Ferguson, E. D. (1989). Adler's motivational theory: An historical perspective on belonging and the fundamental human striving. *Journal of Individual Psychology, 45,* 354–361. (p. 449)

Ferguson, E. D. (2001). Adler and Dreikurs: Cognitive-social dynamic innovators. *Journal of Individual Psychology, 57,* 324–341. (p. 449)

Ferguson, E. D. (2003). Social processes, personal goals, and their intertwining: Their importance in Adlerian theory and practice. *Journal of Individual Psychology, 59,* 136–144. (p. 537)

Ferguson, E. D. (2010). Editor's notes: Adler's innovative contributions regarding the need to belong. *Journal of Individual Psychology, 66*(1), 1–7. (p. 449)

Ferguson, M. J., & Zayas, V. (2009). Automatic evaluation. *Current Directions in Psychological Science, 18,* 362–366. (p. 226)

Fergusson, D. M., Boden, J. M., & Horwood, L. J. (2009). Tests of causal links between alcohol abuse or dependence and major depression. *Archives of General Psychiatry, 66,* 260–266. (p. 652)

Fergusson, D. M., & Woodward, L. G. (2002). Mental health, educational, and social role outcomes of adolescents with depression. *Archives of General Psychiatry, 59,* 225–231. (p. 648)

Fernandez-Dols, J-M., & Ruiz-Belda, M-A. (1995). Are smiles a sign of happiness? Gold medal winners at the Olympic Games. *Journal of Personality and Social Psychology, 69,* 1113–1119. (p. 488)

Fernyhough, C. (2008). Getting Vygotskian about theory of mind: Mediation, dialogue, and the development of social understanding. *Developmental Review, 28,* 225–262. (p. 186)

Ferri, M., Amato, L., & Davoli, M. (2006). Alcoholics Anonymous and other 12-step programmes for alcohol dependence. *Cochrane Database of Systematic Reviews,* Issue 3. Art. No.: CD005032. (p. 689)

Ferriman, K., Lubinski, D., & Benbow, C. P. (2009). Work preferences, life values, and personal views of top math/science graduate students and the profoundly gifted: Developmental changes and gender differences during emerging adulthood and parenthood. *Journal of Personality and Social Psychology, 97,* 517–522. (p. 160)

Ferris, C. F. (1996, March). The rage of innocents. *The Sciences,* pp. 22–26. (p. 192)

Festinger, L. (1957). *A theory of cognitive dissonance.* Stanford: Stanford University Press. (p. 576)

Feynman, R. (1997). Quoted by E. Hutchings (Ed.), *"Surely you're joking, Mr. Feynman."* New York: Norton. (p. 15)

Fiedler, F. E. (1981). Leadership effectiveness. *American Behavioral Scientist, 24,* 619–632. (p. 467)

Fiedler, F. E. (1987, September). When to lead, when to stand back. *Psychology Today,* pp. 26–27. (p. 467)

Fiedler, K., Nickel, S., Muehlfriedel, T., & Unkelbach, C. (2001). Is mood congruency an effect of genuine memory or response bias? *Journal of Experimental Social Psychology, 37,* 201–214. (p. 332)

Field, A. P. (2006). I don't like it because it eats sprouts: Conditioning preferences in children. *Behaviour Research and Therapy, 44,* 439–455. (p. 301)

Field, A. P. (2006). Is conditioning a useful framework for understanding the development and treatment of phobias? *Clinical Psychology Review, 26,* 857–875. (p. 641)

Field, T. (1996). Attachment and separation in young children. *Annual Review of Psychology, 47,* 541–561. (p. 193)

Field, T., Diego, M., & Hernandez-Reif, M. (2007). Massage therapy research. *Developmental Review, 27,* 75–89. (p. 149)

Field, T., Hernandez-Reif, M., Feijo, L., & Freedman, J. (2006). Prenatal, perinatal and neonatal stimulation: A survey of neonatal nurseries. *Infant Behavior & Development, 29,* 24–31. (p. 149)

Fields, R. D. (2004, April). The other half of the brain. *Scientific American,* pp. 54–61. (p. 69)

Fields, R. D. (2005, February). Making memories stick. *Scientific American,* pp. 75–81. (p. 327)

Fields, R. D. (2008, March). White matter. *Scientific American,* pp. 54–61. (p. 48)

Fields, R. D. (2009). *The other brain: From dementia to schizophrenia, how new discoveries about the brain are revolutionizing medicine and science.* New York: Simon & Schuster. (p. 69)

Fikke, L. T., Melinder, A., & Landrø, N. I. (2011). Executive functions are impaired in adolescents engaging in non-suicidal self-injury. *Psychological Medicine, 41,* 601–610. (p. 651)

Fincham, F. D., & Bradbury, T. N. (1993). Marital satisfaction, depression, and attributions: A longitudinal analysis. *Journal of Personality and Social Psychology, 64,* 442–452. (p. 573)

Finchilescu, G., & Tredoux, C. (eds.) (2010). Intergroup relations in post apartheid South Africa: Change, and obstacles to change. *Journal of Social Issues, 66,* 223–236. (p. 620)

Fingelkurts, A. A., & Fingelkurts, A. A. (2009). Is our brain hardwired to produce God, or is our brain hardwire to perceive God? A systematic review on the role of the brain in mediating religious experience. *Cognitive Processes, 10,* 293–326. (pp. 62, 75)

Fingerman, K. L., & Charles, S. T. (2010). It takes two to tango: Why older people have the best relationships. *Current Directions in Psychological Science, 19,* 172–176. (p. 218)

Fink, G. R., Markowitsch, H. J., Reinkemeier, M., Bruckbauer, T., Kessler, J., & Heiss, W-D. (1996). Cerebral representation of one's own past: Neural =networks involved in autobiographical memory. *Journal of Neuroscience, 16,* 4275–4282. (p. 323)

Fink, M. (2009). *Electroconvulsive therapy: A guide for professionals and their patients.* New York: Oxford University Press. (p. 708)

Finkel, E. J., & Eastwick, P. W. (2008). Speed-dating. *Current Directions in Psychological Science, 17,* 193–197. (p. 610)

Finkel, E. J., & Eastwick, P. W. (2009). Arbitrary social norms influence sex differences in romantic selectivity. *Psychological Science 20,* 1290–1295. (p. 609)

Finlay, S. W. (2000). Influence of Carl Jung and William James on the origin of alcoholics anonymous. *Review of General Psychology, 4,* 3–12. (p. 689)

Finney, E. M., Fine, I., & Dobkins, K. R. (2001). Visual stimuli activate auditory cortex in the deaf. *Nature Neuroscience, 4,* 1171–1173. (p. 371)

Finzi, E., & Wasserman, E. (2006). Treatment of depression with botulinum toxin A: A case series. *Dermatological Surgery, 32,* 645–650. (p. 490)

Fiore, M. C. & 23 others. (2008). *Treating tobacco use and dependence: 2008 update. Clinical practice guideline.* Rockville, MD: U.S. Department of Health and Human Services, Public Health Service. (p. 121)

Fiori, M. (2009). A new look at emotional intelligence: A dual-process framework. *Personality and Social Psychology Review, 13,* 21–44. (p. 389)

Fischer, P., & Greitemeyer, T. (2006). Music and aggression: The impact of sexual-aggressive song lyrics on aggression-related thoughts, emotions, and behavior toward the same and the opposite sex. *Personality and Social Psychology Bulletin, 32,* 1165–1176. (p. 603)

Fischhoff, B. (1982). Debiasing. In D. Kahneman, P. Slovic, & A. Tversky (Eds.), *Judgment under uncertainty: Heuristics and biases.* New York: Cambridge University Press. (p. 357)

Fischhoff, B., Slovic, P., & Lichtenstein, S. (1977). Knowing with certainty: The appropriateness of extreme confidence. *Journal of Experimental Psychology: Human Perception and Performance, 3,* 552–564. (p. 357)

Fischtein, D. S., Herold, E. S., & Desmarais, S. (2007). How much does gender explain in sexual attitudes and behaviors? A survey of Canadian adults. *Archives of Sexual Behavior, 36,* 451–461. (p. 145)

Fishbach, A., Dhar, R., & Zhang, Y. (2006). Subgoals as substitutes or complements: The role of goal accessibility. *Journal of Personality and Social Psychology, 91,* 232–242. (p. 467)

Fisher, H. E. (1993, March/April). After all, maybe it's biology. *Psychology Today,* pp. 40–45. (p. 216)

Fisher, H. E., Aron, A., Mashek, D., Li, H., & Brown, L. L. (2002). Defining the brain systems of lust, romantic attraction, and attachment. *Archives of Sexual Behavior, 31,* 413–419. (p. 435)

Fisher, H. T. (1984). Little Albert and Little Peter. *Bulletin of the British Psychological Society, 37,* 269. (p. 681)

Fisher, K., Egerton, M., Gershuny, J. I., & Robinson, J. P. (2006). Gender convergence in the American Heritage Time Use Study (AHTUS). *Social Indicators Research, 82,* 1–33. (p. 162)

Flegal, K. M., Carroll, M. D., Ogden, C. L., & Curtin, L. R. (2010). Prevalence and trends in obesity among US adults, 1999–2008. *JAMA, 303,* 235–241. (p. 428)

Fleming, I., Baum, A., & Weiss, L. (1987). Social density and perceived control as mediator of crowding stress in high-density residential neighborhoods. *Journal of Personality and Social Psychology, 52,* 899–906. (p. 518)

Fleming, J. H. (2001, Winter/Spring). Introduction to the special issue on linkage analysis. *The Gallup Research Journal,* pp. i-vi. (p. 466)

Fleming, J. H., & Scott, B. A. (1991). The costs of confession: The Persian Gulf War POW tapes in historical and theoretical perspective. *Contemporary Social Psychology, 15,* 127–138. (p. 487)

Fletcher, G. J. O., Fitness, J., & Blampied, N. M. (1990). The link between attributions and happiness in close relationships: The roles of depression and explanatory style. *Journal of Social and Clinical Psychology, 9,* 243–255. (p. 573)

Flier, J. S., & Maratos-Flier, E. (2007, September). What fuels fat. *Scientific American,* pp. 72–81. (p. 430)

Flood, M. (2007). Exposure to pornography among youth in Australia. *Journal of Sociology, 43,* 45–60. (p. 603)

Flora, S. R. (2004). *The power of reinforcement.* Albany, NJ: SUNY Press. (p. 294)

Flora, S. R., & Bobby, S. E. (2008, September/October). The bipolar bamboozle. *Skeptical Inquirer,* pp. 41–45. (p. 646)

Flory, R., Ametepe, J., & Bowers, B. (2010). A randomized, place-controlled trial of bright light and high-density negative air ions for treatment of Season Affective Disorder. *Psychiatry Research, 177,* 101–108. (p. 698)

Floud, R., Fogel, R. W., Harris, B., Hong, S. C. (2011). *The changing body: Health, nutrition, and human development in the western world since 1700.* New York: Cambridge University Press. (p. 411)

Flouri, E., & Buchanan, A. (2004). Early father's and mother's involvement and child's later educational outcomes. *British Journal of Educational Psychology, 74,* 141–153. (p. 190)

Flynn, J. R. (1987). Massive IQ gains in 14 nations: What IQ tests really measure. *Psychological Bulletin, 101,* 171–191. (p. 396)

Flynn, J. R. (2009). Requiem for nutrition as the cause of IQ gains: Raven's gains in Britain 1938–2008. *Economics and Human Biology, 7,* 18–27. (p. 396)

Flynn, J. R. (2009). *What is intelligence? Beyond the Flynn effect* (expanded edition). Cambridge: Cambridge University Press. (p. 396)

Flynn, J. R. (2010). Problems with IQ gains: The huge vocabulary gap. *Journal of Psychoeducational Assessment, 28,* 412–433. (p. 396)

Foa, E. B., & Kozak, M. J. (1986). Emotional processing of fear: Exposure to corrective information. *Psychological Bulletin, 99,* 20–35. (p. 682)

Fodor, J. D. (1999). Let your brain alone. *London Review of Books, 21* (www.lrb.co.uk). (p. 60)

Food and Drug Administration (2011). FDA Executive Summary. Prepared for the January 27–28, 2011 meeting of the Neurological Devices Panel (www.fda.gov). (p. 708)

Ford, E. S. (2002). Does exercise reduce inflammation? Physical activity and B-reactive protein among U.S. adults. *Epidemiology, 13,* 561–569. (p. 521)

Foree, D. D., & LoLordo, V. M. (1973). Attention in the pigeon: Differential effects of food-getting versus shock-avoidance procedures. *Journal of Comparative and Physiological Psychology, 85,* 551–558. (p. 301)

Forer, B. R. (1949). The fallacy of personal validation: A classroom demonstration of gullibility. *Journal of Abnormal and Social Psychology, 44,* 118–123. (p. 551)

Forgas, J. P. (2008b). Affect and cognition. *Perspectives on Psychological Science, 3,* 94–101. (p. 495)

Forgas, J. P. (2009, November/December). Think negative! *Australian Science,* pp. 14–17. (p. 645)

Forgas, J. P., Bower, G. H., & Krantz, S. E. (1984). The influence of mood on perceptions of social interactions. *Journal of Experimental Social Psychology, 20,* 497–513. (p. 332)

Forhan, S. E., Gottlieb, S. L., Sternberg, M. R., Xu, F., Datta, D., Berman, S., & Markowitz, L. (2008). Prevalence of sexually transmitted infections and bacterial vaginosis among female adolescents in the United States: Data from the National Health and Nutrition Examination Survey (NHANES) 2003–2004. Paper presented to the 2008 National STD Prevention Conference, Chicago, Illinois. (p. 440)

Forman, D. R., Aksan, N., & Kochanska, G. (2004). Toddlers' responsive imitation predicts preschool-age conscience. *Psychological Science, 15,* 699–704. (p. 306)

Fortenberry, J. D., Schick, V., Herbenick, D., Sanders, S. A., Dodge, B., & Reece, M. (2010). Sexual behaviors and condom use at last vaginal intercourse: A national sample of adolescents ages 14 to 17 years. *Journal of Sexual Medicine, 7*(Suppl. 5): 305–314. (p. 439)

Foss, D. J., & Hakes, D. T. (1978). *Psycholinguistics: An introduction to the psychology of language.* Englewood Cliffs, NJ: Prentice-Hall. (p. 539)

Foulkes, D. (1999). *Children's dreaming and the development of consciousness.* Cambridge, MA: Harvard University Press. (p. 108)

Fournier, J. C., DeRubeis, R. J., Hollon, S. D., Dimidjian, S., Amsterdam, J. D., Shelton, R. C., & Fawcett, J. (2010). Antidepressant drug effects and depression severity: A patient-level meta-analysis. *Journal of the American Medical Association, 303,* 47–53. (p. 707)

Fouts, R. S. (1992). Transmission of a human gestural language in a chimpanzee mother-infant relationship. *Friends of Washoe, 12/13,* pp. 2–8. (p. 374)

Fouts, R. S. (1997). *Next of kin: What chimpanzees have taught me about who we are.* New York: Morrow. (p. 374)

Fowler, M. J., Sullivan, M. J., & Ekstrand, B. R. (1973). Sleep and memory. *Science, 179,* 302–304. (p. 338)

Fowles, D. C. (1992). Schizophrenia: Diathesis-stress revisited. *Annual Review of Psychology, 43,* 303–336. (p. 659)

Fowles, D. C., & Dindo, L. (2009). Temperament and psychopathy: A dual-pathway model. *Current Directions in Psychological Science, 18,* 179–183. (p. 668)

Fox, D. (2010, June). The insanity virus. *Discover,* pp. 58–64. (p. 661)

Fox, J. L. (1984). The brain's dynamic way of keeping in touch. *Science, 225,* 820–821. (p. 76)

Fox, N. A., Hane, A. E., & Pine, D. S. (2007). Plasticity for affective neurocircuitry. *Current Directions in Psychological Science, 16,* 1–5. (p. 138)

Fozard, J. L., & Popkin, S. J. (1978). Optimizing adult development: Ends and means of an applied psychology of aging. *American Psychologist, 33,* 975–989. (p. 211)

Fracassini, C. (2000, August 27). Holidaymakers led by the nose in sales quest. *Scotland on Sunday.* (p. 271)

Fraley, R. C. (2002). Attachment stability from infancy to adulthood: Meta-analysis and dynamic modeling of developmental mechanisms. *Personality and Social Psychology Review, 6,* 123–151. (p. 191)

Frank, J. D. (1982). Therapeutic components shared by all psychotherapies. In J. H. Harvey & M. M. Parks (Eds.), *The Master Lecture Series: Vol. 1. Psychotherapy research and behavior change.* Washington, DC: American Psychological Association. (pp. 698, 699)

Frank, R. (1999). *Luxury fever: Why money fails to satisfy in an era of excess.* New York: Free Press. (p. 153)

Frankel, A., Strange, D. R., & Schoonover, R. (1983). CRAP: Consumer rated assessment procedure. In G. H. Scherr & R. Liebmann-Smith (Eds.), *The best of The Journal of Irreproducible Results.* New York: Workman Publishing. (p. 549)

Frankenburg, W., Dodds, J., Archer, P., Shapiro, H., & Bresnick, B. (1992). The Denver II: A major revision and restandardization of the Denver Developmental Screening Test. *Pediatrics, 89,* 91–97. (p. 178)

Franklin, M., & Foa, E. B. (2011). Treatment of obsessive-compulsive disorder. *Annual Review of Clinical Psychology, 7,* 229–243. (p. 642)

Franz, E. A., Waldie, K. E., & Smith, M. J. (2000). The effect of callosotomy on novel versus familiar bimanual actions: A neural dissociation between controlled and automatic processes? *Psychological Science, 11,* 82–85. (p. 78)

Frasure-Smith, N., & Lespérance, F. (2005). Depression and coronary heart disease: Complex synergism of mind, body, and environment. *Current Directions in Psychological Science, 14,* 39–43. (p. 514)

Frattaroli, J. (2006). Experimental disclosure and its moderators: A meta-analysis. *Psychological Bulletin, 132,* 823–865. (p. 520)

Frayling, T. M., & 41 others. (2007, April 12). A common variant in the *FTO* gene is associated with body mass index and predisposes to childhood and adult obesity. *Science, 316,* 889–894. (p. 430)

Fredrickson, B. L. (2006). The broaden-and-build theory of positive emotions. In M. Csikszentmihalyi & I. S. Csikszentmihalyi (Eds.), *A life worth living: Contributions to positive psychology.* New York: Oxford University Press. (p. 495)

Freedman, D. H. (2011, February). How to fix the obesity crisis. *Scientific American,* pp. 40–47. (p. 433)

Freedman, D. J., Riesenhuber, M., Poggio, T., & Miller, E. K. (2001). Categorical representation of visual stimuli in the primate prefrontal cortex. *Science, 291,* 312–316. (p. 362)

Freedman, J. L. (1988). Television violence and aggression: What the evidence shows. In S. Oskamp (Ed.), *Television as a social issue.* Newbury Park, CA: Sage. (p. 308)

Freedman, J. L., & Fraser, S. C. (1966). Compliance without pressure: The foot-in-the-door technique. *Journal of Personality and Social Psychology, 4,* 195–202. (p. 575)

Freedman, J. L., & Perlick, D. (1979). Crowding, contagion, and laughter. *Journal of Experimental Social Psychology, 15,* 295–303. (p. 587)

Freedman, L. R., Rock, D., Roberts, S. A., Cornblatt, B. A., & Erlenmeyer-Kimling, L. (1998). The New York high-risk project: Attention, anhedonia and social outcome. *Schizophrenia Research, 30,* 1–9. (p. 663)

Freeman, E. C., & Twenge, J. M. (2010, January). Using MySpace increases the endorsement of narcissistic personality traits. Poster presented at the annual conference of the Society for Personality and Social Psychology, Las Vegas, NV. (p. 454)

Freeman, J. B., Johnson, K. L., Ambady, N., & Role, N. O. (2010). Sexual orientation perception involves gendered facial cues. *Personality and Social Psychology Bulletin, 36,* 1318–1331. (p. 447)

Freeman, W. J. (1991, February). The physiology of perception. *Scientific American,* pp. 78–85. (p. 257)

Freud, S. (1931; reprinted 1961). Female sexuality. In J. Strachey (Trans.), *The standard edition of the complete psychological works of Sigmund Freud.* London: Hogarth Press. (p. 532)

Freud, S. (1935: reprinted 1960). *A general introduction to psychoanalysis.* New York: Washington Square Press. (p. 215)

Frey, M. C., & Detterman, D. K. (2004). Scholastic assessment or g? The relationship between the Scholastic Assessment Test and general cognitive ability. *Psychological Science, 15,* 373–378. (p. 394)

Freyd, J. J., DePrince, A. P., & Gleaves, D. H. (2007). The state of betrayal trauma theory: Reply to McNally—Conceptual issues and future directions. *Memory, 15,* 295–311. (p. 346)

Freyd, J. J., Putnam, F. W., Lyon, T. D., Becker-Blease, K. A., Cheit, R. E., Siegel, N. B., & Pezdek, K. (2005). The science of child sexual abuse. *Science, 308,* 501. (p. 192)

Friedman, M., & Ulmer, D. (1984). *Treating Type A behavior—and your heart.* New York: Knopf. (pp. 512, 524)

Friedman, R., & James, J. W. (2008). The myth of the sages of dying, death and grief. *Skeptic, 14*(2), 37–41. (p. 220)

Friedman, S. L., & Boyle, D. E. (2008). Attachment in US children experiencing nonmaternal care in the early 1990s. *Attachment & Human Development, 10,* 225–261. (p. 192)

Friedrich, O. (1987, December 7). New age harmonies. *Time,* pp. 62–72. (p. 626)

Frijda, N. H. (1988). The laws of emotion. *American Psychologist, 43,* 349–358. (p. 499)

Frisch, M., & Zdravkovic, S. (2010). Body size at birth and same-sex marriage in young adulthood. *Archives of Sexual Behavior, 39,* 117–123. (p. 446)

Frith, U., & Frith, C. (2001). The biological basis of social interaction. *Current Directions in Psychological Science, 10,* 151–155. (p. 184)

Fritz, T., Jentschke, S., Gosselin, N., Sammler, D., Peretz, I., Turner, R., Friederici, A., & Koelsch, S. (2009). Universal recognition of three basic emotions in music. *Current Biology, 19,* 573–576. (p. 488)

Fromkin, V., & Rodman, R. (1983). *An introduction to language* (3rd ed.). New York: Holt, Rinehart & Winston. (p. 368)

Fry, A. F., & Hale, S. (1996). Processing speed, working memory, and fluid intelligence: Evidence for a developmental cascade. *Psychological Science, 7,* 237–241. (p. 211)

Fry, R., & Cohn, D. (2010, January 19). Women, men and the new economics of marriage. Pew Research Center (pewresearch.org). (p. 162)

Fryar, C., Hirsch, R., Porter, K. S., Kottiri, B., Brody, D. J., & Louis, T. (2007, June 28). Drug use and sexual behavior reported by adults: United States, 1999–2002. *Advance Data: From Vital and Health Statistics,* Number 384 (Centers for Disease Control and Prevention). (p. 436)

Fuhriman, A., & Burlingame, G. M. (1994). Group psychotherapy: Research and practice. In A. Fuhriman & G. M. Burlingame (Eds.), *Handbook of group psychotherapy.* New York: Wiley. (p. 688)

Fujiki, N., Yoshida, Y., Ripley, B., Mignot, E., & Nishino, S. (2003). Effects of IV and ICV hypocretin-1 (Orexin A) in hypocretin receptor-2 gene mutated narcoleptic dogs and IV hypocretin-1 replacement therapy in a hypocretin-ligand-deficient narcoleptic dog. *Sleep, 26,* 953–959. (p. 104)

Fuller, M. J., & Downs, A. C. (1990). Spermarche is a salient biological marker in men's development. Poster presented at the American Psychological Society convention. (p. 198)

Fulmer, C. A., Gelfand, M. J., Kruglanski, A. W., Kim-Prieto, C., Diener, E., Pierro, A., & Higgins, E. T. (2010). On "feeling right" in cultural contexts: how person-culture match affects self-esteem and subjective well-being. *Psychological Science, 21,* 1563–1569. (p. 557)

Fulmer, I. S., Gerhart, B., & Scott, K. S. (2003). Are the 100 best better? An empirical investigation of the relationship between being a "great place to work" and firm performance. *Personnel Psychology, 56,* 965–993. (p. 465)

Funder, D. C. (2001). Personality. *Annual Review of Psychology, 52,* 197–221. (p. 551)

Funder, D. C. (2009). Persons, behaviors and situations: An agenda for personality psychology in the postwar era. *Journal of Research in Personality, 43,* 155–162. (p. 556)

Funder, D. C., & Block, J. (1989). The role of ego-control, ego-resiliency, and IQ in delay of gratification in adolescence. *Journal of Personality and Social Psychology, 57,* 1041–1050. (p. 202)

Furlow, F. B., & Thornhill, R. (1996, January/February). The orgasm wars. *Psychology Today,* pp. 42–46. (p. 435)

Furnham, A. (1982). Explanations for unemployment in Britain. *European Journal of Social Psychology, 12,* 335–352. (p. 573)

Furnham, A., & Baguma, P. (1994). Cross-cultural differences in the evaluation of male and female body shapes. *International Journal of Eating Disorders, 15,* 81–89. (p. 427)

Furnham, A., & Rawles, R. (1995). Sex differences in the estimation of intelligence. *Journal of Social Behavior and Personality, 10,* 741–748. (p. 594)

Furr, R. M., & Funder, D. C. (1998). A multimodal analysis of personal negativity. *Journal of Personality and Social Psychology, 74,* 1580–1591. (p. 654)

Furukawa, T. A., Yoshimura, R., Harai, H., Imaizumi, T., Takeuchi, H., Kitamua, T., & Takahashi, K. (2009). How many well vs. unwell days can you expect over 10 years, once you become depressed? *Acta Psychiatrica Scandinavica, 119,* 290–297. (p. 648)

Gable, S. L., Gonzaga, G. C., & Strachman, A. (2006). Will you be there for me when things go right? Supportive responses to positive event disclosures. *Journal of Personality and Social Psychology, 91,* 904–917. (p. 217)

Gabrieli, J. D. E., Desmond, J. E., Demb, J. E., Wagner, A. D., Stone, M. V., Vaidya, C. J., & Glover, G. H. (1996). Functional magnetic resonance imaging of semantic memory processes in the frontal lobes. *Psychological Science, 7,* 278–283. (p. 323)

Gaillard, R., Dehaene, S., Adam, C., Clémenceau, S., Hasboun, D., Baulac, M., Cohen, L., & Naccache, L. (2009). Converging intracranial markers of conscious access. *PLoS Biology, 7*(e): e1000061. (p. 85)

Gaillot, M. T., & Baumeister, R. F. (2007). Self-regulation and sexual restraint: Dispositionally and temporarily poor self-regulatory abilities contribute to failures at restraining sexual behavior. *Personality and Social Psychology Bulletin, 33,* 173–186. (p. 558)

Galak, J., & Nelson, L. D. (2010). A replication of the procedures from Bem (2010, Study 8) and a Failure to Replicate the Same Results. ssrn.com/abstract=1699970. Also personal correspondence, February 10, 2011. (p. 255)

Galambos, N. L. (1992). Parent-adolescent relations. *Current Directions in Psychological Science, 1,* 146–149. (p. 205)

Galanter, E. (1962). Contemporary psychophysics. In R. Brown, E. Galanter, E. H. Hess, & G. Mandler (Eds.), *New directions in psychology.* New York: Holt Rinehart & Winston. (p. 225)

Galati, D., Scherer, K. R., & Ricci-Bitti, P. E. (1997). Voluntary facial expression of emotion: Comparing congenitally blind with normally sighted encoders. *Journal of Personality and Social Psychology, 73,* 1363–1379. (p. 488)

Galdi, S., Arcuri, L., & Gawronski, B. (2008). Automatic mental associations predict future choices of undecided decision-makers. *Science, 321,* 1100–1102. (p. 361)

Gale, C. R., Batty, G. D., & Deary, I. J. (2008). Locus of control at age 10 years and health outcomes and behaviors at age 30 years: The 1970 British Cohort Study. *Psychosomatic Medicine, 70,* 397–403. (p. 557)

Galea, S., Boscarino, J., Resnick, H., & Vlahov, D. (2002). Mental health in New York City after the September 11 terrorist attacks: Results from two population surveys. In R. W. Manderscheid & M. J. Henderson (Eds.), *Mental-Health, United States, 2001.* Washington, DC: U.S. Government Printing Office. (p. 640)

Galinsky, E., Aumann, K., & Bond, J. T. (2008). *Times are changing: Gender and generation at work and at home.* Work and Families Institute (www.familiesandwork.org). (p. 565)

Gallese, V., Gernsbacher, M. A., Heyes, C., Hickok, G., & Iacoboni, M. (2011). Mirror neuron forum. *Perspectives on Psychological Science, 6,* 369–407. (p. 185)

Gallo, W. T., Teng, H. M., Falba, T. A., Kasl, S. V., Krumholz, H. M., & Bradley, E. H. (2006). The impact of late career job loss on myocardial infarction and stroke: A 10 year follow up using the health and retirement survey. *Occupational and Environmental Medicine, 63,* 683–687. (pp. 505, 514)

Gallup. (2010, accessed June 28). Gallup daily: U.S. mood. Based on the Gallup-Healthways well-being index. www.gallup.com (p. 30)

Gallup Brain. (2008, accessed February 20). Woman for president: Question qn2f, March, 2007 wave. Brain.Gallup.com. (p. 593)

Gallup Organization. (2003, July 8). American public opinion about Iraq. *Gallup Poll News Service* (www.gallup.com). (p. 577)

Gallup Organization. (2004, August 16). 65% of Americans receive NO praise or recognition in the workplace. E-mail from Tom Rath: bucketbook@gallup.com. (p. 466)

Gallup, G. G., Jr. (1970). Chimpanzees: Self-recognition. *Science, 167,* 86–87. (p. 194)

Gallup, G. G., Jr., & Frederick, D. A. (2010). The science of sex appeal: An evolutionary perspective. *Review of General Psychology, 14,* 240–250. (p. 611)

Gallup, G. G., Jr., & Suarez, S. D. (1986). Self-awareness and the emergence of mind in humans and other primates. In J. Suls & A. G. Greenwald (Eds.), *Psychological perspectives on the self* (Vol. 3.). Hillsdale, NJ: Erlbaum. (p. 194)

Gallup, G. H. (1972). *The Gallup poll: Public opinion 1935–1971* (Vol. 3). New York: Random House. (p. 619)

Gallup, G. H., Jr. (1994, October). Millions finding care and support in small groups. *Emerging Trends,* pp. 2–5. (p. 690)

Gallup, G. H., Jr. (2002, April 30). Education and youth. *Gallup Tuesday Briefing* (www.gallup.com/poll/tb/educaYouth/20020430.asp). (p. 307)

Gangestad, S. W., & Simpson, J. A. (2000). The evolution of human mating: Trade-offs and strategic pluralism. *Behavioral and Brain Sciences, 23,* 573–587. (p. 145)

Gangestad, S. W., Thornhill, R., & Garver-Apgar, C. E. (2010). Men's facial masculinity predicts changes in their female partners' sexual interests across the ovulatory cycle, whereas men's intelligence does not. *Evolution and Human Behavior, 31,* 412–424. (p. 611)

Gangwisch, J. E., Babiss, L. A., Malaspina, D., Turner, J. B., Zammit, G. K., & Posner, K. (2010). Earlier parental set bedtimes as a protective factor against depression and suicidal ideation. *Sleep, 33,* 97–106. (p. 101)

Gao, Y., Raine, A., Venables, P. H., Dawson, M. E., & Mednick, S. A. (2010). Association of poor child fear conditioning and adult crime. *American Journal of Psychiatry, 167,* 56–60. (p. 668)

Garber, K. (2007). Autism's cause may reside in abnormalities at the synapse. *Science, 317,* 190–191. (p. 185)

Garcia, J., & Gustavson, A. R. (1997, January). Carl R. Gustavson (1946–1996): Pioneering wildlife psychologist. *APS Observer,* pp. 34–35. (p. 299)

Garcia, J., & Koelling, R. A. (1966). Relation of cue to consequence in avoidance learning. *Psychonomic Science, 4,* 123–124. (p. 299)

Gardner, H. (1983). *Frames of mind: The theory of multiple intelligences.* New York: Basic Books. (p. 383)

Gardner, H. (1998, March 19). An intelligent way to progress. *The Independent* (London), p. E4. (p. 383)

Gardner, H. (1998, November 5). Do parents count? *New York Review of Books* (www.nybooks.com). (p. 150)

Gardner, H. (1999). *Multiple views of multiple intelligence.* New York: Basic Books. (p. 389)

Gardner, H. (1999, February). Who owns intelligence? *Atlantic Monthly,* pp. 67–76. (p. 394)

Gardner, H. (2006). *The development and education of the mind: The selected works of Howard Gardner.* New York: Routledge/Taylor & Francis. (p. 383)

Gardner, J., & Oswald, A. J. (2007). Money and mental well-being: A longitudinal study of medium–sized lottery wins. *Journal of Health Economics, 6,* 49–60. (p. 499)

Gardner, M. (2006, January/February). The memory wars, part one. *Skeptical Inquirer, 30,* 28–31. (p. 345)

Gardner, R. A., & Gardner, B. I. (1969). Teaching sign language to a chimpanzee. *Science, 165,* 664–672. (p. 373)

Gardner, R. M., & Tockerman, Y. R. (1994). A computer-TV video methodology for investigating the influence of somatotype on perceived personality traits. *Journal of Social Behavior and Personality, 9,* 555–563. (p. 429)

Garfield, C. (1986). *Peak Performers: The new heroes of American Business.* New York: Morrow. (p. 378)

Garnets, L. D., & Kimmel, D. (1990). Lesbian and gay dimensions in the psychological study of human diversity. Master lecture, American Psychological Association convention. (p. 442)

Garon, N., Bryson, S. E., & Smith, I. M. (2008). Executive function in preschoolers: A review using an integrative framework. *Psychological Bulletin, 134,* 31–60. (p. 177)

Garrett, B. L. (2008). Judging innocence. *Columbia Law Review, 108,* 55–142. (p. 344)

Garry, M., Loftus, E. F., & Brown, S. W. (1994). Memory: A river runs through it. *Consciousness and Cognition,* 3, 438–451. (p. 540)

Garry, M., Manning, C. G., Loftus, E. F., & Sherman, S. J. (1996). Imagination inflation: Imagining a childhood event inflates confidence that it occurred. *Psychonomic Bulletin & Review,* 3, 208–214. (p. 342)

Gartrell, N., & Bos, H. (2010). U.S. national longitudinal lesbian family study: Psychological adjustment of 17-year-old adolescents. *Pediatrics, 126,* 28–36. (p. 444)

Gatchel, R. J., Peng, Y. B., Peters, M. L., Fuchs, P. N., & Turk, D. C. (2007). The biopsychosocial approach to chronic pain: Scientific advances and future directions. *Psychological Bulletin,* 133, 581–624. (p. 263)

Gates, W. (1998, July 20). Charity begins when I'm ready (interview). *Fortune* (www.pathfinder.com/fortune/1998/980720/bil7.html). (p. 385)

Gawande, A. (1998, September 21). The pain perplex. *The New Yorker,* pp. 86–94. (p. 265)

Gawin, F. H. (1991). Cocaine addiction: Psychology and neurophysiology. *Science, 251,* 1580–1586. (p. 121)

Gazzaniga, M. S. (1967, August). The split brain in man. *Scientific American,* pp. 24–29. (p. 77)

Gazzaniga, M. S. (1983). Right hemisphere language following brain bisection: A 20–year perspective. *American Psychologist,* 38, 525–537. (p. 78)

Gazzaniga, M. S. (1988). Organization of the human brain. *Science, 245,* 947–952. (pp. 78, 116)

Gazzaniga, M. S. (2011, April). Neuroscience in the courtroom. *Scientific American,* pp. 54–59. (p. 482)

Ge, X., & Natsuaki, M. N. (2009). In search of explanations for early pubertal timing effects on developmental psychopathology. *Current Directions in Psychological Science, 18,* 327–441. (p. 199)

Geary, D. C. (1995). Sexual selection and sex differences in spatial cognition. *Learning and Individual Differences, 7,* 289–301. (p. 409)

Geary, D. C. (1996). Sexual selection and sex differences in mathematical abilities. *Behavioral and Brain Sciences, 19,* 229–247. (p. 409)

Geary, D. C. (1998). *Male, female: The evolution of human sex differences.* Washington, DC: American Psychological Association. (p. 145)

Geary, D. C. (2010). *Male, female: The evolution of human sex differences* (second edition). Washington, DC: American Psychological Association. (p. 160)

Geary, D. C., Salthouse, T. A., Chen, G-P., & Fan, L. (1996). Are East Asian versus American differences in arithmetical ability a recent phenomenon? *Developmental Psychology,* 32, 254–262. (p. 412)

Geen, R. G., & Quanty, M. B. (1977). The catharsis of aggression: An evaluation of a hypothesis. In L. Berkowitz (Ed.), *Advances in experimental social psychology* (Vol. 10). New York: Academic Press. (p. 494)

Geen, R. G., & Thomas, S. L. (1986). The immediate effects of media violence on behavior. *Journal of Social Issues,* 42(3), 7–28. (p. 308)

Gehring, W. J., Wimke, J., & Nisenson, L. G. (2000). Action monitoring dysfunction in obsessive-compulsive disorder. *Psychological Science,* 11(1), 1–6. (p. 643)

Geier, A. B., Rozin, P., & Doros, G. (2006). Unit bias: A new heuristic that helps explain the effects of portion size on food intake. *Psychological Science, 17,* 521–525. (p. 426)

Gelman, D. (1989, May 15). Voyages to the unknown. *Newsweek,* pp. 66–69. (p. 488)

Genesee, F., & Gándara, P. (1999). Bilingual education programs: A cross-national perspective. *Journal of Social Issues, 55,* 665–685. (p. 377)

Genevro, J. L. (2003). *Report on bereavement and grief research.* Washington, DC: Center for the Advancement of Health. (p. 220)

Gentile, B., Grabe, S., Dolan-Pascoe, B., Wells, B. E., & Maitino, A. (2009). Gender differences in domain-specific self-esteem: A meta-analysis. *Journal of General Psychology, 13,* 34–45. (p. 157)

Gentile, B., Twenge, J. M., & Campbell, W. K. (2010). Birth cohort differences in self-esteem, 1988–2008: A cross-temporal meta-analysis. *Review of General Psychology, 14,* 261–268. (p. 567)

Gentile, D. (2009). Pathological video-game use among youth ages 8 to 18: A national study. *Psychological Science, 20,* 594–602. (pp. 116, 605)

Gentile, D. A., Lynch, P. J., Linder, J. R., & Walsh, D. A. (2004). The effects of violent video game habits on adolescent hostility, aggressive behaviors, and school performance. *Journal of Adolescence, 27,* 5–22. (p. 308)

George, L. K., Ellison, C. G., & Larson, D. B. (2002). Explaining the relationships between religious involvement and health. *Psychological Inquiry, 13,* 190–200. (p. 527)

George, M. S. (2003, September). Stimulating the brain. *Scientific American,* pp. 67–73. (p. 709)

George, M. S. & 12 others. (2010). Daily left prefrontal transcranial magnetic stimulation therapy for major depressive disorder: A sham-controlled randomized trial. *Archives of General Psychiatry, 67,* 507–516. (p. 709)

Geraerts, E., Bernstein, D. M., Merckelbach, H., Linders, C., Raymaekers, L., & Loftus, E. F. (2008). Lasting false beliefs and their behavioral consequences. *Psychological Science, 19,* 749–753. (p. 342)

Geraerts, E., Schooler, J. W., Merckelbach, H., Jelicic, M., Hauer, B. J. A., & Ambadar, Z. (2007). The reality of recovered memories: Corroborating continuous and discontinuous memories of childhood sexual abuse. *Psychological Science, 18,* 564–568. (p. 346)

Gerhart, K. A., Koziol-McLain, J., Lowenstein, S. R., & Whiteneck, G. G. (1994). Quality of life following spinal cord injury: Knowledge and attitudes of emergency care providers. *Annals of Emergency Medicine,* 23, 807–812. (p. 497)

Gernsbacher, M. A., Dawson, M., & Goldsmith, H. H. (2005). Three reasons not to believe in an autism epidemic. *Current Directions in Psychological Science, 14,* 55–58. (p. 184)

Gerrard, M., & Luus, C. A. E. (1995). Judgments of vulnerability to pregnancy: The role of risk factors and individual differences. *Personality and Social Psychology Bulletin, 21,* 160–171. (p. 439)

Gershoff, E. T. (2002). Parental corporal punishment and associated child behaviors and experiences: A meta-analytic and theoretical review. *Psychological Bulletin, 128,* 539–579. (p. 292)

Gershoff, E. T., Grogan-Kaylor, A., Lansford, J. E., Chang, L., Zelli, A., Deater-Deckard, K., & Dodge, K. A. (2010). Parent discipline practices in an international sample: Associations with child behaviors and moderation by perceived normativeness. *Child Development, 81,* 487–502. (p. 292)

Gerstorf, D., Ram, N., Röcke, C., Lindenberger, U., & Smith, J. (2008). Decline in life satisfaction in old age: Longitudinal evidence for links to distance-to-death. *Psychology and Aging,* 23, 154–168. (p. 218)

Gertner, J. (2010, May 10). The rise and fall of the G.D.P. *New York Times* (www.nytimes.com). (p. 502)

Geschwind, N. (1979, September). Specializations of the human brain. *Scientific American, 241,* 180–199. (p. 372)

Geschwind, N., & Behan, P. O. (1984). Laterality, hormones, and immunity. In N. Geschwind & A. M. Galaburda (Eds.), *Cerebral dominance: The biological foundations.* Cambridge, MA: Harvard University Press. (p. 80)

Gfeller, J. D., Lynn, S. J., & Pribble, W. E. (1987). Enhancing hypnotic susceptibility: Interpersonal and rapport factors. *Journal of Personality and Social Psychology, 52,* 586–595. (p. 112)

Giancola, P. R., & Corman, M. D. (2007). Alcohol and aggression: A test of the attention-allocation model. *Psychological Science, 18,* 649–655. (p. 601)

Giancola, P. R., Josephs, R. A., Parrott, D. J., & Duke, A. A. (2010). Alcohol myopia revisited: Clarifying aggression and other acts of disinhibition through a distorted lens. *Perspectives on Psychological Science, 5,* 265–278. (p. 118)

Gibbons, F. X. (1986). Social comparison and depression: Company's effect on misery. *Journal of Personality and Social Psychology, 51,* 140–148. (p. 500)

Gibbs, W. W. (1996, June). Mind readings. *Scientific American,* pp. 34–36. (p. 70)

Gibson, E. J., & Walk, R. D. (1960, April). The "visual cliff." *Scientific American,* pp. 64–71. (p. 244)

Gibson, H. B. (1995, April). Recovered memories. *The Psychologist,* pp. 153–154. (p. 111)

Gibson, J. L., & Claassen, C. (2010). Racial reconciliation in South Africa: Interracial contact. *Journal of Social Issues, 66,* 255–272. (p. 620)

Gick, B., & Derrick, D. (2009). Aero-tactile integration in speech perception. *Nature, 462,* 502–504. (p. 268)

Giesbrecht, T., Lynn, S. J., Lilienfeld, S. O., & Merckelbach, H. (2008). Cognitive processes in dissociation: An analysis of core theoretical assumptions. *Psychological Bulletin, 134,* 617–647. (p. 666)

Giesbrecht, T., Lynn, S. J., Lilienfeld, S. O., & Merckelbach, H. (2010). Cognitive processes, trauma, and dissociation—Misconceptions and misrepresentations: Reply to Bremmer (2010). *Psychological Bulletin, 136,* 7–11. (p. 666)

Gigerenzer, G. (2004). Dread risk, September 11, and fatal traffic accidents. *Psychological Science, 15,* 286–287. (p. 358)

Gigerenzer, G. (2006). Out of the frying pan into the fire: Behavioral reactions to terrorist attacks. *Risk Analysis, 26,* 347–351. (p. 358)

Gigerenzer, G. (2010). *Rationality for mortals: How people cope with uncertainty.* New York: Oxford University Press. (p. 38)

Gigerenzer, G., Gaissmaier, W., Kurz-Milcke, E., Schwartz, L. M., & Woloshin, S. (2008). Helping doctors and patients make sense of health statistics. *Psychological Science in the Public Interest, 8,* 53–96. (p. 38)

Gigerenzer, G., Gaissmaier, W., Kurz-Milcke, E., Schwartz, L. M., & Woloshin, S. (2009, April/May). Knowing your chances. *Scientific American Mind,* pp. 44–51. (p. 38)

Gilbert, D. T. (2006). *Stumbling on happiness.* New York: Knopf. (pp. 217, 340, 354, 476, 566)

Gilbert, D. T., Pelham, B. W., & Krull, D. S. (2003). The psychology of good ideas. *Psychological Inquiry, 14,* 258–260. (p. 16)

Gilbert, D. T., Pinel, E. C., Wilson, T. D., Blumberg, S. J., & Wheatley, T. P. (1998). Immune neglect: A source of durability bias in affective forecasting. *Journal of Personality and Social Psychology, 75,* 617–638. (p. 496)

Gilbertson, M. W., Paulus, L. A., Williston, S. K., Gurvits, T. V., Lasko, N. B., Pitman, R. K., & Orr, S. P. (2006). Neurocognitive function in monozygotic twins discordant for combat exposure: Relationship to posttraumatic stress disorder. *Journal of Abnormal Psychology, 115,* 484–495. (p. 640)

Giles, D. E., Dahl, R. E., & Coble, P. A. (1994). Childbearing, developmental, and familial aspects of sleep. In J. M. Oldham & M. B. Riba (Eds.), *Review of psychiatry* (Vol. 13). Washington, DC: American Psychiatric Press. (p. 105)

Gilestro, G. F., Tononi, G., & Cirelli, C. (2009). Widespread changes in synaptic markers as a function of sleep and wakefulness in *Drosophila. Science, 324,* 109–112. (p. 98)

Gill, A. J., Oberlander, J., & Austin, E. (2006). Rating e-mail personality at zero acquaintance. *Personality and Individual Differences, 40,* 497–507. (p. 555)

Gillham, J. E., Hamilton, J., Freres, D. R., Patton, K. & Gallop, R. (2006). Preventing depression among early adolescents in the primary care setting: A randomized controlled study of the Penn Resiliency Program. *Journal of Abnormal Child Psychology, 34,* 195–211. (p. 702)

Gilovich, T., & Medvec, V. H. (1995). The experience of regret: What, when, and why. *Psychological Review, 102,* 379–395. (p. 218)

Gilovich, T., Vallone, R., & Tversky, A. (1985). The hot hand in basketball: On the misperception of random sequences. *Cognitive Psychology, 17,* 295–314. (p. 18)

Gilovich, T. D. (1996). The spotlight effect: Exaggerated impressions of the self as a social stimulus. Unpublished manuscript, Cornell University. (p. 564)

Gilovich, T. D., Kruger, J., & Medvec, V. H. (2002). The spotlight effect revisited: Overestimating the manifest variability of our actions and appearance. *Journal of Experimental Social Psychology, 38,* 93–99. (p. 564)

Gilovich, T. D., & Savitsky, K. (1999). The spotlight effect and the illusion of transparency: Egocentric assessments of how we are seen by others. *Current Directions in Psychological Science, 8,* 165–168. (p. 564)

Giltay, E. J., Geleijnse, J. M., Zitman, F. G., Buijsse, B., & Kromhout, D. (2007). Lifestyle and dietary correlates of dispositional optimism in men: The Zutphen Elderly Study. *Journal of Psychosomatic Research, 63,* 483–490. (p. 518)

Giltay, E. J., Geleijnse, J. M., Zitman, F. G., Hoekstra, T., & Schouten, E. G. (2004). Dispositional optimism and all-cause and cardiovascular mortality in a prospective cohort of elderly Dutch men and women. *Archives of General Psychiatry, 61,* 1126–1135. (p. 518)

Gingerich, O. (1999, February 6). Is there a role for natural theology today? *The Real Issue* (www.origins.org/real/n9501/natural.html). (p. 166)

Gingerich, O. (2006). *God's universe.* Cambridge, MA: Belknap Press of Harvard University Press. (p. xlii)

Giuliano, T. A., Barnes, L. C., Fiala, S. E., & Davis D. M. (1998a). An empirical investigation of male answer syndrome. Paper presented at the Southwestern Psychological Association convention. (p. 158)

Giuliano, T. A., Fiala, S. E., Davis, D. M., Barnes, L. C., & Patrick, E. C. (1998b). The reluctance to admit "I don't know": Exploring "male answer syndrome." Paper presented to the American Psychological Society convention. (p. 158)

Gladue, B. A. (1990). Hormones and neuroendocrine factors in atypical human sexual behavior. In J. R. Feierman (Ed.), *Pedophilia: Biosocial dimensions.* New York: Springer-Verlag. (p. 446)

Gladue, B. A. (1994). The biopsychology of sexual orientation. *Current Directions in Psychological Science, 3,* 150–154. (p. 447)

Gladwell, M. (2000, May 9). The new-boy network: What do job interviews really tell us? *New Yorker,* pp. 68–86. (p. 462)

Gladwell, M. (2005). *Blink: The power of thinking without thinking.* New York: Little, Brown. (p. 612)

Glasman, L. R., & Albarracin, D. (2006). Forming attitudes that predict future behavior: A meta-analysis of the attitude-behavior relation. *Psychological Bulletin, 132,* 778–822. (p. 574)

Glass, R. I. (2004). Perceived threats and real killers. *Science, 304,* 927. (p. 359)

Glass, R. M. (2001). Electroconvulsive therapy: Time to bring it out of the shadows. *Journal of the American Medical Association, 285,* 1346–1348. (p. 708)

Gleason, K. A., Jensen-Campbell, L. A., & Ickes, W. (2009). The role of empathic accuracy in adolescents' peer relations and adjustment. *Personality and Social Psychology Bulletin, 35,* 997–1011. (p. 486)

Gleaves, D. H. (1996). The sociocognitive model of dissociative identity disorder: A reexamination of the evidence. *Psychological Bulletin, 120,* 42–59. (p. 667)

Glick, P., & 15 others. (2004). Bad but bold: Ambivalent attitudes toward men predict gender inequality in 16 nations. *Journal of Personality and Social Psychology, 86,* 713–728. (p. 596)

Glick, P., Gottesman, D., & Jolton, J. (1989). The fault is not in the stars: Susceptibility of skeptics and believers in astrology to the Barnum effect. *Personality and Social Psychology Bulletin, 15,* 572–583. (p. 551)

Gluszek, A., & Dovidio, J. F. (2010). The way *they* speak: A social psychological perspective on the stigma of nonnative accents in communication. *Personality and Social Psychology Review, 14,* 214–237. (p. 596)

Godden, D. R., & Baddeley, A. D. (1975). Context-dependent memory in two natural environments: On land and underwater. *British Journal of Psychology, 66,* 325–331. (p. 331)

Goel, V., & Dolan, R. J. (2001). The functional anatomy of humor: Segregating cognitive and affective components. *Nature Neuroscience, 4,* 237–238. (p. 373)

Goff, D. C., & Simms, C. A. (1993). Has multiple personality disorder remained consistent over time? *Journal of Nervous and Mental Disease, 181,* 595–600. (p. 666)

Golan, O., Ashwin, E., Granader, Y., McClintock, S., Day, K., Leggett, V., & Baron-Cohen, S. (2010). Enhancing emotion recognition in children with autism spectrum conditions: An intervention using animated vehicles with real emotional faces. *Journal of Autism Development and Disorders, 40,* 269–279. (p. 185)

Gold, M., & Yanof, D. S. (1985). Mothers, daughters, and girlfriends. *Journal of Personality and Social Psychology, 49,* 654–659. (p. 205)

Goldberg, J. (2007, accessed May 31). *Quivering bundles that let us hear.* Howard Hughes Medical Institute (www.hhmi.org/senses/c120.html). (p. 258)

Goldberg, W. A., Prause, J., Lucas-Thompson, R., & Himsel, A. (2008). Maternal employment and children's achievement in context: A meta-analysis of four decades of research. *Psychological Bulletin, 134,* 77–108. (p. 192)

Golden, R. N., Gaynes, B. N., Ekstrom, R. D., Hamer, R. M., Jacobsen, F. M., Suppes, T., Wisner, K. L., & Nemeroff, C. B. (2005). The efficacy of light therapy in the treatment of mood disorders: A review and meta-analysis of the evidence. *American Journal of Psychiatry, 162,* 656–662. (p. 698)

Goldfried, M. R. (2001). Integrating gay, lesbian, and bisexual issues into mainstream psychology. *American Psychologist, 56,* 977–988. (p. 650)

Goldfried, M. R., & Padawer, W. (1982). Current status and future directions in psychotherapy. In M. R. Goldfried (Ed.), *Converging themes in psychotherapy: Trends in psychodynamic, humanistic, and behavioral practice.* New York: Springer. (p. 698)

Goldfried, M. R., Raue, P. J., & Castonguay, L. G. (1998). The therapeutic focus in significant sessions of master therapists: A comparison of cognitive-behavioral and psychodynamic-interpersonal interventions. *Journal of Consulting and Clinical Psychology, 66,* 803–810. (p. 699)

Golding, J. M. (1996). Sexual assault history and women's reproductive and sexual health. *Psychology of Women Quarterly, 20,* 101–121. (p. 603)

Golding, J. M. (1999). Sexual-assault history and the long-term physical health problems: Evidence from clinical and population epidemiology. *Current Directions in Psychological Science, 8,* 191–194. (p. 640)

Goldin-Meadow, S., & Beilock, S. L. (2010). Action's influence on thought: The case of gesture. *Perspectives on Psychological Science, 5,* 664–674. (p. 490)

Goldman, A. L., Pezawas, L., Mattay, V. S., Fischl, B., Verchinski, B. A., Chen, Q., Weinberger, D. R., & Meyer-Lindenberg, A. (2009). Widespread reductions of cortical thickness in schizophrenia and spectrum disorders and evidence of heritability. *Archives of General Psychiatry, 66,* 467–477. (p. 660)

Goldstein, A. P., Glick, B., & Gibbs, J. C. (1998). *Aggression replacement training: A comprehensive intervention for aggressive youth* (rev. ed.). Champaign, IL: Research Press. (p. 602)

Goldstein, I. (2000, August). Male sexual circuitry. *Scientific American*, pp. 70–75. (p. 57)

Goldstein, I., Lue, T. F., Padma-Nathan, H., Rosen, R. C., Steers, W. D., & Wicker, P. A. (1998). Oral sildenafil in the treatment of erectile dysfunction. *New England Journal of Medicine, 338*, 1397–1404. (p. 36)

Goleman, D. (1980, February). 1,528 little geniuses and how they grew. *Psychology Today*, pp. 28–53. (p. 463)

Goleman, D. (2006). *Social intelligence*. New York: Bantam Books. (p. 388)

Gonsalkorale, K., & Williams, K. D. (2006). The KKK would not let me play: Ostracism even by a despised outgroup hurts. *European Journal of Social Psychology, 36*, 1–11. (p. 452)

Gonsalves, B., Reber, P. J., Gitelman, D. R., Parrish, T. B., Mesulam, M.-M., & Paller, K. A. (2004). Neural evidence that vivid imagining can lead to false remembering. *Psychological Science, 15*, 655–659. (p. 342)

González-Vallejo, C., Lassiter, G. D., Bellezza, F. S., & Lindberg, M. J. (2008). "Save angels perhaps": A critical examination of unconscious thought theory and the deliberation-without-attention effect. *Review of General Psychology, 12*, 282–296. (p. 360)

Goodall, J. (1968). The behaviour of free-living chimpanzees in the Gombe Stream Reserve. *Animal Behaviour Monographs, 1*, 161–311. (p. 150)

Goodall, J. (1986). *The chimpanzees of Gombe: Patterns of behavior*. Cambridge, MA: Harvard University Press. (p. 597)

Goodall, J. (1998). Learning from the chimpanzees: A message humans can understand. *Science, 282*, 2184–2185. (p. 28)

Goode, E. (1999, April 13). If things taste bad, 'phantoms' may be at work. *New York Times* (www.nytimes.com). (p. 264)

Goodhart, D. E. (1986). The effects of positive and negative thinking on performance in an achievement situation. *Journal of Personality and Social Psychology, 51*, 117–124. (p. 559)

Goodman, G. S. (2006). Children's eyewitness memory: A modern history and contemporary commentary. *Journal of Social Issues, 62*, 811–832. (p. 345)

Goodman, G. S., Ghetti, S., Quas, J. A., Edelstein, R. S., Alexander, K. W., Redlich, A. D., Cordon, I. M., & Jones, D. P. H. (2003). A prospective study of memory for child sexual abuse: New findings relevant to the repressed-memory controversy. *Psychological Science, 14*, 113–118. (p. 346)

Goodstein, L., & Glaberson, W. (2000, April 9). The well-marked roads to homicidal rage. *New York Times* (www.nytimes.com). (p. 562)

Goodwin, P. Y., Mosher, W. D., & Chandra, A. (2010). Marriage and cohabitation in the United States: A statistical portrait based on Cycle 6 (2002) of the National Survey of Family Growth. National Center for Health Statistics. *Vital Health Statistics, 23*(28). (p. 216)

Gopnik, A., & Meltzoff, A. N. (1986). Relations between semantic and cognitive development in the one-word stage: The specificity hypothesis. *Child Development, 57*, 1040–1053. (p. 377)

Goranson, R. E. (1978). *The hindsight effect in problem solving*. Unpublished manuscript, cited by G. Wood (1984), Research methodology: A decision-making perspective. In A. M. Rogers & C. J. Scheirer (Eds.), *The G. Stanley Hall Lecture Series* (Vol. 4). Washington, DC. (p. 17)

Gorchoff, S. M., John, O. P., & Helson, R. (2008). Contextualizing change in marital satisfaction during middle age. *Psychological Science, 19*, 1194–1200. (p. 217)

Gordon, P. (2004). Numerical cognition without words: Evidence from Amazonia. *Science, 306*, 496–499. (p. 376)

Gore-Felton, C., Koopman, C., Thoresen, C., Arnow, B., Bridges, E., & Spiegel, D. (2000). Psychologists' beliefs and clinical characteristics: Judging the veracity of childhood sexual abuse memories. *Professional Psychology: Research and Practice, 31*, 372–377. (p. 346)

Gorini, A. (2007). Virtual worlds, real healing. *Science, 318*, 1549. (p. 683)

Gortmaker, S. L., Must, A., Perrin, J. M., Sobol, A. M., & Dietz, W. H. (1993). Social and economic consequences of overweight in adolescence and young adulthood. *New England Journal of Medicine, 329*, 1008–1012. (p. 429)

Gosling, S. D. (2008). *Snoop: what your stuff says about you*. New York: Basic Books. (p. 554)

Gosling, S. D., Gladdis, S., & Vazire, S. (2007). Personality impressions based on Facebook profiles. Paper presented to the Society for Personality and Social Psychology meeting. (p. 555)

Gosling, S. D., Ko, S. J., Mannarelli, T., & Morris, M. E. (2002). A room with a cue: Personality judgments based on offices and bedrooms. *Journal of Personality and Social Psychology, 82*, 379–398. (p. 554)

Gosling, S. D., Kwan, V. S. Y., & John, O. P. (2003). A dog's got personality: A cross-species comparative approach to personality judgments in dogs and humans. *Journal of Personality and Social Psychology, 85*, 1161–1169. (p. 549)

Gotlib, I. H., & Hammen, C. L. (1992). *Psychological aspects of depression: Toward a cognitive-interpersonal integration*. New York: Wiley. (p. 654)

Gottesman, I. I. (1991). *Schizophrenia genesis: The origins of madness*. New York: Freeman. (p. 662)

Gottesman, I. I. (2001). Psychopathology through a life span—genetic prism. *American Psychologist, 56*, 867–881. (p. 662)

Gottfredson, L. S. (2002a). Where and why g matters: Not a mystery. *Human Performance, 15*, 25–46. (p. 384)

Gottfredson, L. S. (2002b). g: Highly general and highly practical. In R. J. Sternberg & E. L. Grigorenko (Eds.), *The general factor of intelligence: How general is it?* Mahwah, NJ: Erlbaum. (p. 384)

Gottfredson, L. S. (2003a). Dissecting practical intelligence theory: Its claims and evidence. *Intelligence, 31*, 343–397. (p. 384)

Gottfredson, L. S. (2003b). On Sternberg's "Reply to Gottfredson." *Intelligence, 31*, 415–424. (p. 384)

Gottfried, J. A., O'Doherty, J., & Dolan, R. J. (2003). Encoding predictive reward value in human amygdala and orbitofrontal cortex. *Science, 301*, 1104–1108. (p. 279)

Gottman, J. (2007). *Why marriages succeed or fail—2007 publication*. London: Bloomsbury. (p. 614)

Gottman, J., with Silver, N. (1994). *Why marriages succeed or fail*. New York: Simon & Schuster. (p. 216)

Gougoux, F., Zatorre, R., Lassonde, M., Voss, P., & Lepore, F. (2005). A functional neuroimaging study of sound localization: Visual cortex activity predicts performance in early-blind individuals. *PloS Biology*, 3(2), e27. (p. 371)

Gould, E. (2007). How widespread is adult neurogenesis in mammals? *Nature Neuroscience, 8*, 481–488. (p. 76)

Gould, S. J. (1981). *The mismeasure of man*. New York: Norton. (p. 393)

Gould, S. J. (1997, June 12). Darwinian fundamentalism. *The New York Review of Books, XLIV*(10), 34–37. (p. 146)

Gow, A. J., Johnson, W., Pattie, A., Brett, C. E., Roberts, B., Starr, J. M., & Deary, I. J. (2011). Stability and change in intelligence from age 11 to ages 70, 79, and 87: The Lothian birth cohorts of 1921 and 1936. *Psychology and Aging, 26*, 232–240. (p. 401)

Grabe, S., Ward, L. M., & Hyde, J. S. (2008). The role of the media in body image concerns among women: A meta-analysis of experimental and correlational studies. *Psychological Bulletin, 134*, 460–476. (p. 672)

Grace, A. A. (2010). Ventral hippocampus, interneurons, and schizophrenia: A new understanding of the pathophysiology of schizophrenia and its implications for treatment and prevention. *Current Directions in Psychological Science, 19*, 232–237. (p. 660)

Grady, C. L., McIntosh, A. R., Horwitz, B., Maisog, J. M., Ungeleider, L. G., Mentis, M. J., Pietrini, P., Schapiro, M. B., & Haxby, J. V. (1995). Age-related reductions in human recognition memory due to impaired encoding. *Science, 269*, 218–221. (p. 335)

Graf, P. (1990). Life-span changes in implicit and explicit memory. *Bulletin of the Psychonomic Society, 28*, 353–358. (p. 214)

Graham, J. E., Christian, L. M., & Kiecolt-Glaser, J. K. (2006). Marriage, health, and immune function. In S. R. H. Beach & others (Eds.), *Relational processes and DSM-V: Neuroscience, assessment, prevention, and treatment*. Washington, DC: American Psychiatric Association. (p. 519)

Granqvist, P., Mikulincer, M., & Shaver, P. R. (2010). Religion as attachment: Normative processes and individual differences. *Personality and Social Psychology Review, 14*, 49–59. (p. 188)

Grant, N., Wardle, J., & Steptoe, A. (2009). The relationship between life satisfaction and health behavior: A cross-cultural analysis of young adults. *International Journal of Behavioral Medicine, 16*, 259–268. (p. 522)

Gray, P. (2010, July 7). ADHD and school: The problem of assessing normaly in an abnormal environment. *Psychology Today Blog* (www.psychologytoday.com). (p. 627)

Gray, P. B., Anderson, K. G. (2010). *Fatherhood: Evolution and human paternal behavior*. Cambridge, MA: Harvard University Press. (p. 146)

Gray, P. B., Yang, C-F. J., & Pope, Jr., H. G. (2006). Fathers have lower salivary testosterone levels than unmarried men and married non-fathers in Beijing, China. *Proceedings of the Royal Society, 273*, 333–339. (p. 437)

Gray-Little, B., & Burks, N. (1983). Power and satisfaction in marriage: A review and critique. *Psychological Bulletin, 93*, 513–538. (p. 614)

Green, B. (2002). Listening to leaders: Feedback on 360-degree feedback one year later. *Organizational Development Journal, 20*, 8–16. (p. 462)

Green, C. S., Pouget, A., & Bavelier, D. (2010). Improved probabilistic inference, as a general learning mechanism with action video games. *Current Biology, 20,* 1573–1579. (p. 605)

Green, J. D., Sedikides, C., & Gregg, A. P. (2008). Forgotten but not gone: The recall and recognition of self-threatening memories. *Journal of Experimental Social Psychology, 44,* 547–561. (p. 540)

Green, J. T., & Woodruff-Pak, D. S. (2000). Eyeblink classical conditioning: Hippocampal formation is for neutral stimulus associations as cerebellum is for association-response. *Psychological Bulletin, 126,* 138–158. (p. 325)

Green, M. F., & Horan, W. P. (2010). Social cognition in schizophrenia. *Current Directions in Psychological Science, 19,* 243–248. (p. 658)

Greenberg, J. (2008). Understanding the vital human quest for self-esteem. *Perspectives on Psychological Science, 3,* 48–55. (p. 564)

Greenberg, J., Solomon, S., & Pyszczynski, T. (1997). Terror management theory of self-esteem and cultural worldviews: Empirical assessments and conceptual refinements. *Advances in Social Psychology, 29,* 61–142. (p. 541)

Greene, J. (2010). *Remarks to An Edge conference: The new science of morality.* www.edge.org. (p. 202)

Greene, J., Sommerville, R. B., Nystrom, L. E., Darley, J. M., & Cohen, J. D. (2001). An fMRI investigation of emotional engagement in moral judgment. *Science, 293,* 2105. (p. 202)

Greenwald, A. G. (1992). Subliminal semantic activation and subliminal snake oil. Paper presented to the American Psychological Association Convention, Washington, DC. (p. 227)

Greenwald, A. G., McGhee, D. E., & Schwartz, J. L. K. (1998). Measuring individual differences in implicit cognition: The implicit association test. *Journal of Personality and Social Psychology, 74,* 1464–1480. (p. 595)

Greenwald, A. G., Oakes, M. A., & Hoffman, H. (2003). Targets of discrimination: Effects of race on responses to weapons holders. *Journal of Experimental Social Psychology, 39,* 399. (p. 595)

Greenwald, A. G., Poehlman, T. A., Uhlmann, E. L., & Banaji, M. R. (2009). Understanding and using the implicit association test: III. Meta-analysis of the predictive validity. *Journal of Personality and Social Psychology, 97,* 17–41. (p. 595)

Greenwald, A. G., Spangenberg, E. R., Pratkanis, A. R., & Eskenazi, J. (1991). Double-blind tests of subliminal self-help audiotapes. *Psychological Science, 2,* 119–122. (p. 227)

Greer, G. (1984, April). The uses of chastity and other paths to sexual pleasures. *MS,* pp. 53–60, 96. (p. 438)

Gregory, A. M., Rijksdijk, F. V., Lau, J. Y., Dahl, R. E., & Eley, T. C. (2009). The direction of longitudinal associations between sleep problems and depression symptoms: A study of twins aged 8 and 10 years. *Sleep, 32,* 189–199. (p. 101)

Gregory, R. L. (1978). *Eye and brain: The psychology of seeing* (3rd ed.). New York: McGraw-Hill. (p. 250)

Gregory, R. L., & Gombrich, E. H. (Eds.). (1973). *Illusion in nature and art.* New York: Charles Scribner's Sons. (p. 231)

Greif, E. B., & Ulman, K. J. (1982). The psychological impact of menarche on early adolescent females: A review of the literature. *Child Development, 53,* 1413–1430. (p. 198)

Greist, J. H., Jefferson, J. W., & Marks, I. M. (1986). *Anxiety and its treatment: Help is available.* Washington, DC: American Psychiatric Press. (p. 638)

Greitemeyer, T., & McLatchie, N. (2011). Denying humanness to others: A newly discovered mechanism by which violent video games increase aggressive behavior. *Psychological Science, 22,* 655–659. (p. 605)

Greitemeyer, T., & Osswald, S. (2010). Effects of prosocial video games on prosocial behavior. *Journal of Personality and Social Psychology, 98,* 211–221. (p. 605)

Grello, C. M., Welsh, D. P., & Harper, M. S. (2006). No strings attached: The nature of casual sex in college students. *Journal of Sex Research, 43,* 255–267. (p. 117)

Greyson, B. (2010). Implications of near-death experiences for a postmaterialist psychology. *Review of Religion and Spirituality, 2,* 37–45. (p. 124)

Grèzes, J., & Decety, J. (2001). Function anatomy of execution, mental simulation, observation, and verb generation of actions: A meta-analysis. *Human Brain Mapping, 12,* 1–19. (p. 378)

Griffiths, M. (2001). Sex on the Internet: Observations and implications for Internet sex addiction. *Journal of Sex Research, 38,* 333–342. (p. 116)

Grilo, C. M., & Pogue-Geile, M. F. (1991). The nature of environmental influences on weight and obesity: A behavior genetic analysis. *Psychological Bulletin, 110,* 520–537. (p. 430)

Grinker, R. R. (2007). *Unstrange minds: Remapping the world of autism.* New York: Basic Books. (p. 184)

Grobstein, C. (1979, June). External human fertilization. *Scientific American,* pp. 57–67. (p. 173)

Grogan-Kaylor, A. (2004). The effect of corporal punishment on antisocial behavior in children. *Social Work Research, 28,* 153–162. (p. 293)

Groothuis, T. G. G., & Carere, C. (2005). Avian personalities: Characterization and epigenesis. *Neuroscience and Biobehavioral Reviews, 29,* 137–150. (p. 549)

Gross, A. E., & Crofton, C. (1977). What is good is beautiful. *Sociometry, 40,* 85–90. (p. 612)

Gross, T. F. (2009). Own-ethnicity bias in the recognition of Black, East Asian, Hispanic, and White faces. *Basic and Applied Social Psychology, 31,* 128–135. (p. 598)

Grossberg, S. (1995). The attentive brain. *American Scientist, 83,* 438–449. (p. 231)

Grossmann, I., Na, J., Varnum, M. E. W., Park, D. C., Kitayama, S., & Nisbett, R. E. (2010). Reasoning about social conflicts improves into old age. *PNAS, 107,* 7246–7250. (p. 399)

Gruder, C. L. (1977). Choice of comparison persons in evaluating oneself. In J. M. Suls & R. L. Miller (Eds.), *Social comparison processes.* New York: Hemisphere. (p. 500)

Guenther, C. L., & Alicke, M. D. (2010). Deconstructing the better-than-average effect. *Journal of Personality and Social Psychology, 99,* 755–770. (p. 566)

Guerin, B. (1986). Mere presence effects in humans: A review. *Journal of Personality and Social Psychology, 22,* 38–77. (p. 587)

Guerin, B. (2003). Language use as social strategy: A review and an analytic framework for the social sciences. *Review of General Psychology, 7,* 251–298. (p. 365)

Guiso, L., Monte, F., Sapienza, P., & Zingales, L. (2008). Culture, gender, and math. *Science, 320,* 1164–1165. (p. 410)

Gunstad, J., Strain, G., Devlin, M. J., Wing, R., Cohen, R. A., Paul, R. H., Crosby, R. D., & Mitchell, J. E. (2011). Improved memory function 12 weeks after bariatric surgery. *Surgery for Obesity and Related Diseases, 7,* 465–472. (p. 428)

Gunter, R. W., & Bodner, G. E. (2008). How eye movements affect unpleasant memories: Support for a working-memory account. *Behaviour Research and Therapy, 46,* 913–931. (p. 697)

Gunter, T. D., Vaughn, M. G., & Philibert, R. A. (2010). Behavioral genetics in antisocial spectrum disorders and psychopathy: A review of the recent literature. *Behavioral Sciences and the Law, 28,* 148–173. (p. 668)

Güntürkün, O. (2003). Adult persistence of head-turning asymmetry. *Nature, 421,* 711. (p. 80)

Guo, X. & 19 others. (2010). Effect of antipsychotic medication alone vs combined with psychosocial intervention on outcomes of early-stage schizophrenia. *Archives of General Psychiatry, 67,* 895–904. (p. 705)

Gustavson, C. R., Garcia, J., Hankins, W. G., & Rusiniak, K. W. (1974). Coyote predation control by aversive conditioning. *Science, 184,* 581–583. (p. 299)

Gustavson, C. R., Kelly, D. J., & Sweeney, M. (1976). Prey-lithium aversions I: Coyotes and wolves. *Behavioral Biology, 17,* 61–72. (p. 299)

Guttmacher Institute. (1994). *Sex and America's teenagers.* New York: Alan Guttmacher Institute. (pp. 206, 440)

Guttmacher Institute. (2000). *Fulfilling the promise: Public policy and U.S. family planning clinics.* New York: Alan Guttmacher Institute. (p. 206)

H., Sally. (1979, August). Videotape recording number T–3, Fortunoff Video Archive of Holocaust Testimonies. New Haven, CT: Yale University Library. (p. 540)

Haas, A. P. & 25 others. (2011). Suicide and suicide risk in lesbian, gay, bisexual, and transgender populations: Review and recommendations. *Journal of Homosexuality, 58,* 10–51. (p. 650)

Haase, C. M., Tomasik, M. JH., & Silbereisen, R. K. (2008). Premature behavioral autonomy: Correlates in late adolescence and young adulthood. *European Psychologist, 13,* 255–266. (p. 195)

Haber, R. N. (1970, May). How we remember what we see. *Scientific American,* pp. 104–112. (p. 312)

Haddock, G., & Zanna, M. P. (1994). Preferring "housewives" to "feminists." *Psychology of Women Quarterly, 18,* 25–52. (p. 596)

Hagger, M. S., Wood, C., Stiff, C., & Chatzisarantis, N. L. D. (2010). Ego depletion and the strength model of self-control: A meta-analysis. *Psychological Bulletin, 136,* 495–525. (p. 558)

Haidt, J. (2000). The positive emotion of elevation. *Prevention and Treatment, 3,* article 3 (journals.apa.org/prevention/volume3). (p. 201)

Haidt, J. (2002). The moral emotions. In R. J. Davidson, K. Scherer, & H. H. Goldsmith (Eds.), *Handbook of affective sciences.* New York: Oxford University Press. (p. 201)

Haidt, J. (2006). *The happiness hypothesis: Finding modern truth in ancient wisdom.* New York: Basic Books. (p. 201)

Haidt, J. (2010). Moral psychology must not be based on faith and hope: Commentary on Narvaez. *Perspectives on Psychological Science, 5,* 182–184. (p. 201)

Haier, R. J. (2009, November/December). What does a smart brain look like? *Scientific American Mind,* pp. 26–33. (p. 390)

Haier, R. J., Colom, R., Schroeder, D. H., Condon, C. A., Tang, C., Eaves, E., & Head, K. (2009). Gray matter and intelligence factors: Is there a neuro-g? *Intelligence, 37,* 136–144. (p. 390)

Hakuta, K., Bialystok, E., & Wiley, E. (2003). Critical evidence: A test of the critical-period hypothesis for second-language acquisition. *Psychological Science, 14,* 31–38. (p. 369)

Halberstadt, J. B., Niedenthal, P. M., & Kushner, J. (1995). Resolution of lexical ambiguity by emotional state. *Psychological Science, 6,* 278–281. (p. 232)

Halberstadt, J., Sherman, S. J., & Sherman, J. W. (2011). Why Barack Obama is black. *Psychological Science, 22,* 29–33. (p. 598)

Haldeman, D. C. (1994). The practice and ethics of sexual orientation conversion therapy. *Journal of Consulting and Clinical Psychology, 62,* 221–227. (p. 443)

Haldeman, D. C. (2002). Gay rights, patient rights: The implications of sexual orientation conversion therapy. *Professional Psychology: Research and Practice, 33,* 260–264. (p. 443)

Hall, C. S., Dornhoff, W., Blick, K. A., & Weesner, K. E. (1982). The dreams of college men and women in 1950 and 1980: A comparison of dream contents and sex differences. *Sleep, 5,* 188–194. (p. 105)

Hall, C. S., & Lindzey, G. (1978). *Theories of personality* (2nd ed.). New York: Wiley. (p. 539)

Hall, G. (1997). Context aversion, Pavlovian conditioning, and the psychological side effects of chemotherapy. *European Psychologist, 2,* 118–124. (p. 300)

Hall, G. S. (1904). *Adolescence: Its psychology and its relations to physiology, anthropology, sex, crime, religion and education (Vol. I).* New York: Appleton-Century-Crofts. (p. 197)

Hall, J. A. (1984). *Nonverbal sex differences: Communication accuracy and expressive style.* Baltimore: Johns Hopkins University Press. (p. 485)

Hall, J. A. (1987). On explaining gender differences: The case of nonverbal communication. In P. Shaver & C. Hendrick (Eds.), *Review of Personality and Social Psychology, 7,* 177–200. (p. 485)

Hall, J. A. Y., & Kimura, D. (1994). Dermatoglyphic assymetry and sexual orientation in men. *Behavioral Neuroscience, 108,* 1203–1206. (p. 447)

Hall, J. G. (2003). Twinning. *Lancet, 362,* 735–743. (p. 134)

Hall, L., Johansson, P., Tärning, B., Sikström, S., & Deutgen, T. (2010). Magic at the marketplace: Choice blindness for the taste of jam and the smell of tea. *Cognition, 117,* 54–61. (p. 90)

Hall, S. S. (2004, May). The good egg. *Discover,* pp. 30–39. (p. 173)

Hall, W. (2006). The mental health risks of adolescent cannabis use. *PloS Medicine,* 3(2), e39. (p. 124)

Halpern, D. F. (2000). *Sex-related ability differences: Changing perspectives, changing minds.* Mahwah, NJ: Erlbaum. (pp. 409, 441)

Halpern, D. F., Benbow, C. P., Geary, D. C., Gur, R. C., Hyde, J. S., & Gernsbacher, M. A. (2007). The science of sex differences in science and mathematics. *Psychological Science in the Public Interest, 8,* 1–51. (p. 409)

Halsey, A., III. (2010, January 26). U.S. bans truckers, bus drivers from texting while driving. *Washington Post* (www.washingtonpost.com). (p. 88)

Hamann, S., Herman, R. A., Nolan, C. L., & Wallen, K. (2004). Men and women differ in amygdala response to visual sexual stimuli. *Nature Neuroscience, 7,* 411–416. (p. 438)

Hamilton, R. H. (2000, November). Increased prevalence of absolute pitch in blind musicians (Abstract 739.13). Society for Neuroscience meeting, New Orleans. (p. 371)

Hammack, P. L., (2005). The life course development of human sexual orientation: An integrative paradigm. *Human Development, 48,* 267–290. (pp. 442, 445)

Hammer, E. (2003). How lucky you are to be a psychology major. *Eye on Psi Chi,* 4–5. (p. A-5)

Hammersmith, S. K. (1982, August). Sexual preference: An empirical study from the Alfred C. Kinsey Institute for Sex Research. Paper presented at the meeting of the American Psychological Association, Washington, DC. (p. 444)

Hammond, D. C. (2008). Hypnosis as sole anesthesia for major surgeries: Historical and contemporary perspectives. *American Journal of Clinical Hypnosis, 51,* 101–121. (p. 112)

Hampson, R. (2000, April 10). In the end, people just need more room. *USA Today,* p. 19A. (p. 432)

Han, J. H., Kushner, S. A., Yiu, A. P., Hsiang, H. L., Buch, T., Waisman, A., Bontempi, B., Neve, R. L., Frankland, P. W., & Josselyn, S. A. (2009, March 13). Selective erasure of a fear memory. *Science, 323,* 1492–1496. (p. 328)

Han, S. (2008, January). Bloom and grow: My view of psychological research in China. *Observer,* pp. 21–22. (p. 6)

Hancock, K. J., & Rhodes, G. (2008). Contact, configural coding and the other-race effect in face recognition. *British Journal of Psychology, 99,* 45–56. (p. 598)

Hankin, B. L., & Abramson, L. Y. (2001). Development of gender differences in depression: An elaborated cognitive vulnerability-transactional stress theory. *Psychological Bulletin, 127,* 773–796. (p. 653)

Hansen, C. H., & Hansen, R. D. (1988). Finding the face-in-the-crowd: An anger superiority effect. *Journal of Personality and Social Psychology, 54,* 917–924. (p. 484)

Harbaugh, W. T., Mayr, U., & Burghart, D. R. (2007). Neural responses to taxation and voluntary giving reveal motives for charitable donations. *Science, 316,* 1622–1625. (p. 616)

Harber, K. D. (1998), Feedback to minorities: Evidence of a positive bias. *Journal of Personality and Social Psychology, 74,* 622–628. (p. 595)

Hardeveld, H. S., De Graaf, R., Nolen, W. A., & Beckman, A. T. F. (2010). Prevalence and predictors of recurrence of major depressive disorder in the adult population. *Acta Psychiatrica Scandinavia, 122,* 184–191. (p. 648)

Hardisty, D. J., Johnson, E. J., & Weber, E. U. (2010). A dirty word or a dirty world? Attribute framing, political affiliation, and query theory. *Psychological Science, 21,* 86–92. (p. 360)

Hardt, O., Einarsson, E. O., & Nader, K. (2010). A bridge over troubled water: Reconsolidation as a link between cognitive and neuroscientific memory research traditions. *Annual Review of Psychology, 61,* 141–167. (p. 340)

Hare, R. D. (1975). Psychophysiological studies of psychopathy. In D. C. Fowles (Ed.), *Clinical applications of psychophysiology.* New York: Columbia University Press. (p. 668)

Harenski, C. L., Harenski, K. A., Shane, M. W., & Kiehl, K. A. (2010). Aberrant neural processing of moral violations in criminal psychopaths. *Journal of Abnormal Psychology, 119,* 863–874. (p. 670)

Harker, L. A., & Keltner, D. (2001). Expressions of positive emotion in women's college yearbook pictures and their relationship to personality and life outcomes across adulthood. *Journal of Personality and Social Psychology, 80,* 112–124. (p. 495)

Harkins, S. G., & Szymanski, K. (1989). Social loafing and group evaluation. *Journal of Personality and Social Psychology, 56,* 934–941. (p. 588)

Harlow, H. F., Harlow, M. K., & Suomi, S. J. (1971). From thought to therapy: Lessons from a primate laboratory. *American Scientist, 59,* 538–549. (p. 188)

Harmon-Jones, E., Abramson, L. Y., Sigelman, J., Bohlig, A., Hogan, M. E., & Harmon-Jones, C. (2002). Proneness to hypomania/mania symptoms or depression symptoms and asymmetrical frontal cortical responses to an anger-evoking event. *Journal of Personality and Social Psychology, 82,* 610–618. (p. 480)

Harper, C., & McLanahan, S. (2004). Father absence and youth incarceration. *Journal of Research on Adolescence, 14,* 369–397. (p. 602)

Harper's. (2009, November). Harper's index. *Harper's,* p. 13. (p. 611)

Harper's Index. (2010, September). India mobile phones, p. 11. (p. 453)

Harris, B. (1979). Whatever happened to Little Albert? *American Psychologist, 34,* 151–160. (p. 284)

Harris, J. A. (1999). Review and methodological considerations in research on testosterone and aggression. *Aggression and Violent Behavior, 4,* 273–291. (p. 600)

Harris, J. R. (1998). *The nurture assumption.* New York: Free Press. (pp. 150, 190)

Harris, J. R. (2000). Beyond the nurture assumption: Testing hypotheses about the child's environment. In J. G. Borkowski & S. L. Ramey (Eds.), *Parenting and the child's world: Influences on academic, intellectual, and social-emotional development.* Washington, DC: APA Books. (p. 150)

Harris, J. R. (2006). *No two are alike: Human nature and human individuality.* New York: Norton. (p. 135)

Harris, J. R. (2007, August 8). Do pals matter more than parents? *The Times* (www.timesonline.co.uk). (p. 150)

Harris, R. J. (1994). The impact of sexually explicit media. In J. Brant & D. Zillmann (Eds.), *Media effects: Advances in theory and research.* Hillsdale, NJ: Erlbaum. (p. 603)

Harris Interactive. (2010). 2009 eHarmony® marriage metrics study: Methodological notes. www.eharmony.com/harrisinteractivepoll. (p. 609)

Harriston, K. A. (1993, December 24). 1 shakes, 1 snoozes: Both win $45 million. *Washington Post* release (in *Tacoma News Tribune,* pp. A1, A2). (p. 562)

Harter, J. K., Schmidt, F. L., Asplund, J. W., Killham, E. A., & Agrawal, S. (2010). Causal impact of employee work perceptions on the bottom line of organizations. *Perspectives on Psychological Science, 5,* 378–389. (p. 466)

Harter, J. K., Schmidt, F. L., & Hayes, T. L. (2002). Business-unit-level relationship between employee satisfaction, employee engagement, and business outcomes: A meta-analysis. *Journal of Applied Psychology, 87,* 268–279. (p. 465)

Hartmann, E. (1981, April). The strangest sleep disorder. *Psychology Today,* pp. 14, 16, 18. (p. 104)

Hartwig, M., & Bond, C. F., Jr. (2011). Why do lie-catchers fail? A lens model meta-analysis of human lie judgments. *Psychological Bulletin, 137,* 643–659. (p. 485)

Harvard Mental Health Letter. (2002, February). EMDR (Eye movement and reprocessing). *Harvard Mental Health Letter, 18,* 4–5. (p. 697)

Haslam, N., & Levy, S. R. (2006). Essentialist beliefs about homosexuality: Structure and implications for prejudice. *Personality and Social Psychology Bulletin, 32,* 471–485. (p. 448)

Haslam, S. A., & Reicher, S. (2007). Beyond the banality of evil: Three dynamics of an interactionist social psychology of tyranny. *Personality and Social Psychology Bulletin, 33,* 615–622. (p. 576)

Hassan, B., & Rahman, Q. (2007). Selective sexual orientation-related differences in object location memory. *Behavioral Neuroscience, 121,* 625–633. (p. 448)

Hatfield, E. (1988). Passionate and companionate love. In R. J. Sternberg & M. L. Barnes (Eds.), *The psychology of love.* New Haven, CT: Yale University Press. (p. 613)

Hatfield, E., & Sprecher, S. (1986). *Mirror, mirror . . . The importance of looks in everyday life.* Albany: State University of New York Press. (p. 610)

Hatfield, J., Faunce, G. J., & Job, R. F. S. (2006). Avoiding confusion surrounding the phrase "correlation does not imply causation." *Teaching of Psychology, 33,* 49–51. (p. 34)

Hathaway, S. R. (1960). *An MMPI Handbook* (Vol. 1, Foreword). Minneapolis: University of Minnesota Press (rev. ed.) (p. 1972). (p. 549)

Hatzenbuehler, M. L. (2011). The social environment and suicide attempts in lesbian, gay, and bisexual youth. *Pediatrics, 127,* 896–903. (p. 650)

Hatzenbuehler, M. L., Nolen-Hoeksema, S., & Dovidio, J. (2009). How does stigma "get under the skin?" The mediating role of emotion regulation. *Psychological Science, 20,* 1282–1289. (p. 626)

Hauser, M. (2006). *Moral minds: How nature designed our universal sense of right and wrong.* New York: Ecco. (p. 143)

Hauser, M. (2009). It seems biology (not religion) equals morality. The Edge (www.edge.org). (p. 143)

Hauser, M. D., Chomsky, N., & Fitch, W. T. (2002). The faculty of language: What is it, who has it, and how did it evolve? *Science, 298,* 1569–1579. (p. 366)

Havas, D. A., Glenberg, A. M., Gutowski, K. A., Lucarelli, M. J., & Davidson, R. J. (2010). Cosmetic use of Botulinum Toxin-A affects processing of emotional language. *Psychological Science, 21,* 895–900. (p. 490)

Havas, D. A., Glenberg, A. M., & Rink, M. (2007). Emotion simulation during language comprehension. *Psychonomic Bulletin & Review, 14,* 436–441. (p. 490)

Haworth, C. M. A. & 23 others. (2010). The heritability of general cognitive ability increases linearly from childhood to young adulthood. *Molecular Psychiatry, 15,* 1112–1120. (p. 406)

Haxby, J. V. (2001, July 7). Quoted by B. Bower, Faces of perception. *Science News,* pp. 10–12. See also J. V. Haxby, M. I. Gobbini, M. L. Furey, A. Ishai, J. L. Schouten & P. Pietrini, Distributed and overlapping representations of faces and objects in ventral temporal cortex. *Science, 293,* 2425–2430. (p. 239)

Haynes, J-D., & Rees, G. (2005). Predicting the orientation of invisible stimuli from activity in human primary visual cortex. *Nature Neuroscience, 8,* 686–691. (p. 226)

Haynes, J-D., & Rees, G. (2006). Decoding mental states from brain activity in humans. *Nature Reviews Neuroscience, 7,* 523–534. (p. 226)

Hazan, C., & Shaver, P. R. (1994). Attachment as an organizational framework for research on close relationships. *Psychological Inquiry, 5,* 1–22. (p. 192)

Hazelrigg, M. D., Cooper, H. M., & Borduin, C. M. (1987). Evaluating the effectiveness of family therapies: An integrative review and analysis. *Psychological Bulletin, 101,* 428–442. (p. 689)

He, Y., Jones, C. R., Fujiki, N., Xu, Y., Guo, B., Holder, J. L., Jr., Rossner, M. J., Nishino, S., & Fu, Y-H. (2009). The transcriptional repressor DEC2 regulates sleep length in mammals. *Science, 325,* 866–870. (p. 97)

Head Start. (2010). Head Start program fact sheet. Office of Head Start, U. S. Department of Health and Human Services (www.acf.hhs.gov/programs/ohs/about/fy2010.html). (p. 408)

Headey, B., Muffels, R., & Wagner, G. G. (2010). Long-running German panel survey shows that personal and economic choices, not just genes, matter for happiness. *PNAS,107,* 17922–17926. (p. 500)

Heatherton, T. F., & Sargent, J. D. (2009). Does watching smoking in movies promote teenage smoking? *Current Directions in Psychological Science, 18,* 63–67. (p. 127)

Heavey, C. L., & Hurlburt, R. T. (2008). The phenomena of inner experience. *Consciousness and Cognition, 17,* 798–810. (pp. 29, 376)

Hedström, P., Liu, K-Y., & Nordvik, M. K. (2008). Interaction domains and suicides: A population-based panel study of suicides in the Stockholm metropolitan area, 1991–1999. *Social Forces, 2,* 713–740. (p. 650)

Heider, F. (1958). *The psychology of interpersonal relations.* New York: Wiley. (p. 572)

Heiman, J. R. (1975, April). The physiology of erotica: Women's sexual arousal. *Psychology Today,* pp. 90–94. (p. 438)

Heine, S. J., & Buchtel, E. E. (2009). Personality: The universal and the culturally specific. *Annual Review of Psychology, 60,* 369–394. (pp. 155, 551)

Heine, S. J., & Hamamura, T. (2007). In search of East Asian self-enhancement. *Personality and Social Psychology Review, 11,* 4–27. (p. 566)

Heine, S. J., & Ruby, M. B. (2010). Cultural psychology. *Wiley Interdisciplinary Reviews: Cognitive Science, 1,* 254–266. (p. 572)

Hejmadi, A., Davidson, R. J., & Rozin, P. (2000). Exploring Hindu Indian emotion expressions: Evidence for accurate recognition by Americans and Indians. *Psychological Science, 11,* 183–187. (p. 484)

Helfland, D. (2011, January 7). An assault on rationality. *New York Times* (www.nytimes.com). (p. 255)

Helgeson, V. S., Reynolds, K. A., & Tomich, P. L. (2006). A meta-analytic review of benefit finding and growth. *Journal of Consulting and Clinical Psychology, 74,* 797–816. (p. 641)

Heller, A. S., Johnstone, T., Schackman, A. J., Light, S. N., Peterson, M. J., Kolden, G. G., Kalin, N. H., & Davidson, R. J. (2009). Reduced capacity to sustain positive emotion in major depression reflects diminished maintenance of fronto-striatal brain activation. *PNAS, 106,* 22445–22450. (p. 652)

Heller, W. (1990, May/June). Of one mind: Second thoughts about the brain's dual nature. *The Sciences,* pp. 38–44. (p. 79)

Helmreich, W. B. (1992). *Against all odds: Holocaust survivors and the successful lives they made in America.* New York: Simon & Schuster. (pp. 191, 540)

Helmreich, W. B. (1994). Personal correspondence. Department of Sociology, City University of New York. (p. 540)

Helms, J. E., Jernigan, M., & Mascher, J. (2005). The meaning of race in psychology and how to change it: A methodological perspective. *American Psychologist, 60,* 27–36. (p. 412)

Helmuth, L. (2001). Boosting brain activity from the outside in. *Science, 292,* 1284–1286. (p. 709)

Helton, W. S. (2008). Expertise acquisition as sustained learning in humans and other animals: Commonalities across species. *Animal Cognition, 11,* 99–107. (p. 385)

Helweg-Larsen, M. (1999). (The lack of) optimistic biases in response to the 1994 Northridge earthquake: The role of personal experience. *Basic and Applied Social Psychology, 21,* 119–129. (p. 561)

Hembree, R. (1988). Correlates, causes, effects, and treatment of test anxiety. *Review of Educational Research, 58,* 47–77. (p. 480)

Hemenover, S. H. (2003). The good, the bad, and the healthy: Impacts of emotional disclosure of trauma on resilient self-concept and psychological distress. *Personality and Social Psychology Bulletin, 29,* 1236–1244. (p. 521)

Henderlong, J., & Lepper, M. R. (2002). The effects of praise on children's intrinsic motivation: A review and synthesis. *Psychological Bulletin, 128,* 774–795. (p. 303)

Henderson, J. M. (2007). Regarding scenes. *Current Directions in Psychological Science, 16,* 219–222. (p. 228)

Henig, R. M. (2010, August 18). What is it about 20-somethings? *New York Times* (www.nytimes.com). (p. 206)

Henkel, L. A., Franklin, N., & Johnson, M. K. (2000, March). Cross-modal source monitoring confusions between perceived and imagined events. *Journal of Experimental Psychology: Learning, Memory, & Cognition, 26,* 321–335. (p. 343)

Henley, N. M. (1989). Molehill or mountain? What we know and don't know about sex bias in language. In M. Crawford & M. Gentry (Eds.), *Gender and thought: Psychological perspectives.* New York: Springer-Verlag. (p. 377)

Hennenlotter, A., Dresel, C., Castrop, F., Ceballos Baumann, A., Wohschlager, A., & Haslinger, B. (2008). The link between facial feedback and neural activity within central circuitries of emotion: New insights from Botulinum Toxin-induced denervation of frown muscles. *Cerebral Cortex, 19,* 537–542. (p. 490)

Hennessey, B. A., & Amabile, T. M. (2010). Creativity. *Annual Review of Psychology, 61*, 569–598. (pp. 387, 468)

Henninger, P. (1992). Conditional handedness: Handedness changes in multiple personality disordered subject reflect shift in hemispheric dominance. *Consciousness and Cognition, 1*, 265–287. (p. 667)

Henrich, J., Heine, S. J., & Norenzayan, A. (2010). The weirdest people in the world? *Behavioral and Brain Sciences, 33*, 61–135. (p. 21)

Henry, J. D., MacLeod, M. S., Phillips, L. H., & Crawford, J. R. (2004). A meta-analytic review of prospective memory and aging. *Psychology and Aging, 19*, 27–39. (p. 214)

Hepper, P. (2005). Unravelling our beginnings. *The Psychologist, 18*, 474–477. (p. 174)

Hepper, P. G., Shahidullah, S., & White, R. (1990). Origins of fetal handedness. *Nature, 347*, 431. (p. 80)

Hepper, P. G., Wells, D. L., & Lynch, C. (2004). Prenatal thumb sucking is related to postnatal handedness. *Neuropsychologia, 43*, 313–315. (p. 80)

Herbenick, D., Reece, M., Schick, V., Sanders, S. A., Dodge, B., & Fortenberry, J. D. (2010). Sexual behaviors, relationships, and perceived health among adult women in the United States: Results from a national probability sample. *Journal of Sexual Medicine, 7* (suppl 5), 277–290. (p. 209)

Herbenick, D., Reece, M., Schick, V., Sanders, S. A., Dodge, B., & Fortenberry, J. D. (2010). Sexual behavior in the United States: Results from a national probability sample of men and women ages 14–94. *Journal of Sexual Medicine, 7*(suppl. 5): 255–265. (p. 442)

Herbert, J. D., Lilienfeld, S. O., Lohr, J. M., Montgomery, R. W., O'Donohue, W. T., Rosen, G. M., & Tolin, D. F. (2000). Science and pseudoscience in the development of eye movement desensitization and reprocessing: Implications for clinical psychology. *Clinical Psychology Review, 20*, 945–971. (p. 697)

Herek, G. M. (2006). Legal recognition of same-sex relationships in the United States: A social science perspective. *American Psychologist, 61*, 607–621. (p. 443)

Herman, C. P., & Polivy, J. (1980). Restrained eating. In A. J. Stunkard (Ed.), *Obesity*. Philadelphia: Saunders. (p. 433)

Herman, C. P., Roth, D. A., & Polivy, J. (2003). Effects of the presence of others on food intake: A normative interpretation. *Psychological Bulletin, 129*, 873–886. (p. 426)

Herman-Giddens, M. E., Wang, L., & Koch, G. (2001). Secondary sexual characteristics in boys: Estimates from the National Health and Nutrition Examination Survey III, 1988–1994. *Archives of Pediatrics and Adolescent Medicine, 155*, 1022–1028. (p. 198)

Hernandez, A. E., & Li, P. (2007). Age of acquisition: Its neural and computational mechanisms. *Psychological Bulletin, 133*, 638–650. (p. 369)

Herrmann, E., Call, J., Hernández-Lloreda, M. V., Hare, B., & Tomasello, M. (2007). Humans have evolved specialized skills of social cognition: The cultural intelligence hypothesis. *Science, 317*, 1360–1365. (p. 305)

Herrmann, E., Hernández-Lloreda, V., Call, J., Hare, B., & Tomasello, M. (2010). The structure of individual differences in the cognitive abilities of children and chimpanzees. *Psychological Science, 21*, 102–110. (p. 375)

Herrnstein, R. J., & Loveland, D. H. (1964). Complex visual concept in the pigeon. *Science, 146*, 549–551. (p. 287)

Herrnstein, R. J., & Murray, C. A. (1994). *The bell curve: Intelligence and class structure in American life*. New York: Free Press. (p. 411)

Hershenson, M. (1989). *The moon illusion*. Hillsdale, NJ: Erlbaum. (p. 249)

Hertel, G., Schroer, J., Batinic, B., & Naumann, S. (2008). Do shy people prefer to send e-mail: Personality effects on communication media preferences in threatening and nonthreatening situations. *Social Psychology, 39*, 231–243. (p. 552)

Hertenstein, M. J., Hansel, C., Butts, S., Hile, S. (2009). Smile intensity in photographs predicts divorce later in life. *Motivation & Emotion, 33*, 99–105. (p. 171)

Hertenstein, M. J., Keltner, D., App, B. Bulleit, B., & Jaskolka, A. (2006). Touch communicates distinct emotions. *Emotion, 6*, 528–533. (pp. 188, 262)

Herz, R. S. (2001). Ah sweet skunk! Why we like or dislike what we smell. *Cerebrum, 3*(4), 31–47. (p. 270)

Herz, R. S., Beland, S. L., & Hellerstein, M. (2004). Changing odor hedonic perception through emotional associations in humans. *International Journal of Comparative Psychology, 17*, 315–339. (p. 271)

Herzog, H. (2010). *Some we love, some we hate, some we eat: Why it's so hard to think straight about animals*. New York: Harper. (p. 520)

Hess, E. H. (1956, July). Space perception in the chick. *Scientific American*, pp. 71–80. (p. 251)

Hess, U., & Thibault, P. (2009). Darwin and emotion expression. *American Psychologist, 64*, 120–128. (p. 488)

Hetherington, M. M., Anderson, A. S., Norton, G. N. M., & Newson, L. (2006). Situational effects on meal intake: A comparison of eating alone and eating with others. *Physiology and Behavior, 88*, 498–505. (p. 426)

Hettema, J. M., Neale, M. C., & Kendler, K. S. (2001). A review and meta-analysis of the genetic epidemiology of anxiety disorders. *American Journal of Psychiatry, 158*, 1568–1578. (p. 643)

Hickok, G., Bellugi, U., & Klima, E. S. (2001, June). Sign language in the brain. *Scientific American*, pp. 58–65. (p. 79)

Higgins, E. S., & George, M. S. (2007). *The neuroscience of clinical psychiatry: The pathophysiology of behavior and mental illness*. Hagerstown, MD: Lippincott, Williams, & Wilkins. (p. 53)

Hilgard, E. R. (1986). *Divided consciousness: Multiple controls in human thought and action*. New York: Wiley. (p. 113)

Hilgard, E. R. (1992). Dissociation and theories of hypnosis. In E. Fromm & M. R. Nash (Eds.), *Contemporary hypnosis research*. New York: Guilford. (p. 113)

Hill, C. E., & Nakayama, E. Y. (2000). Client-centered therapy: Where has it been and where is it going? A comment on Hathaway. *Journal of Clinical Psychology, 56*, 961–875. (p. 679)

Hines, M. (2004). *Brain gender*. New York: Oxford University Press. (p. 160)

Hines, M., & Green, R. (1991). Human hormonal and neural correlates of sex-typed behaviors. *Review of Psychiatry, 10*, 536–555. (p. 161)

Hingson, R. W., Heeren, T., & Winter, M. R. (2006). Age at drinking onset and alcohol dependence. *Archives of Pediatrics & Adolescent Medicine, 160*, 739–746. (p. 127)

Hintzman, D. L. (1978). *The psychology of learning and memory*. San Francisco: Freeman. (p. 318)

Hinz, L. D., & Williamson, D. A. (1987). Bulimia and depression: A review of the affective variant hypothesis. *Psychological Bulletin, 102*, 150–158. (p. 670)

Hirt, E. R., Zillmann, D., Erickson, G. A., & Kennedy, C. (1992). Costs and benefits of allegiance: Changes in fans' self-ascribed competencies after team victory versus defeat. *Journal of Personality and Social Psychology, 63*, 724–738. (p. 655)

Hjelmborg, J. v. B., Fagnani, C., Silventoinen, K., McGue, M., Korkeila, M., Christensen, K., Rissanen, A., & Kaprio, J. (2008). Genetic influences on growth traits of BMI: A longitudinal study of adult twins. *Obesity, 16*, 847–852. (p. 430)

HMHL. (2002, August). Smoking and depression. *Harvard Mental Health Letter*, Harvard Medical School, pp. 6–7. (p. 652)

HMHL. (2002, January). Disaster and trauma. *Harvard Mental Health Letter*, Harvard Medical School pp. 1–5. (p. 505)

HMHL. (2007, February). Electroconvulsive therapy. *Harvard Mental Health Letter*, Harvard Medical School, pp. 1–4. (p. 708)

Hobaiter, C., & Byrne, R. W. (2011). The gestural repertoire of the wild chimpanzee. *Animal Cognition*, DOI: 10.1007/s10071-011-0409-2. (p. 374)

Hobson, J. A. (1995, September). Quoted by C. H. Colt, The power of dreams. *Life*, pp. 36–49. (p. 107)

Hobson, J. A. (2003). *Dreaming: An introduction to the science of sleep*. New York: Oxford. (p. 107)

Hobson, J. A. (2004). *13 dreams Freud never had: The new mind science*. New York: Pi Press. (p. 107)

Hobson, J. A. (2009). REM sleep and dreaming: Towards a theory of protoconsciousness. *Nature Reviews, 10*, 803–814. (p. 107)

Hochberg, L. R., Serruya, M. D., Friehs, G. M., Mukand, J. A., Saleh, M., Caplan, A. H., Branner, A., Chen, D., Penn, R. D., & Donoghue, J. P. (2006). Neuronal ensemble control of prosthetic devices by a human with tetraplegia. *Nature, 442*, 164–171. (p. 72)

Hodgkinson, V. A., & Weitzman, M. S. (1992). *Giving and volunteering in the United States*. Washington, DC: Independent Sector. (p. 617)

Hoebel, B. G., & Teitelbaum, P. (1966). Effects of forcefeeding and starvation on food intake and body weight in a rat with ventromedial hypothalamic lesions. *Journal of Comparative and Physiological Psychology, 61*, 189–193. (p. 423)

Hoeft, F., Watson, C. L., Kesler, S. R., Bettinger, K. E., & Reiss, A. L. (2008). Gender differences in the mesocorticolimbic system during computer game-play. *Journal of Psychiatric Research, 42*, 253–258. (p. 116)

Hoffman, C., & Hurst, N. (1990). Gender stereotypes: Perception or rationalization? *Journal of Personality and Social Psychology, 58*, 197–208. (p. 596)

Hoffman, D. D. (1998). *Visual intelligence: How we create what we see*. New York: Norton. (p. 240)

Hoffman, H. G. (2004, August). Virtual-reality therapy. *Scientific American*, pp. 58–65. (pp. 266, 682)

Hofmann, S. G., Sawyer, A. T., Witt, A. A., & Oh, D. (2010). The effect of mindfulness-based therapy on anxiety and depression: A meta-analytic review. *Journal of Consulting and Clinical Psychology, 78,* 169–183. (p. 525)

Hofmann, W., De Houwer, J., Perugini, M., Baeyens, F., & Crombez, G. (2010). Evaluative conditioning in humans: A meta-analysis. *Psychological Bulletin, 136,* 390–421. (p. 301)

Hofstadter, D. (2011, January 7). A cutoff for craziness. *New York Times* (www.nytimes.com). (p. 255)

Hogan, J. (1995, November). Get smart, take a test. *Scientific American,* pp. 12, 14. (p. 396)

Hogan, R. (1998). Reinventing personality. *Journal of Social and Clinical Psychology, 17,* 1–10. (p. 554)

Hoge, C. W., & Castro, C. A. (2006). Post-traumatic stress disorder in UK and U.S. forces deployed to Iraq. *Lancet, 368,* 837. (p. 640)

Hoge, C. W., Terhakopian, A., Castro, C. A., Messer, S. C., & Engel, C. C. (2007). Association of posttraumatic stress disorder with somatic symptoms, health care visits, and absenteeism among Iraq War veterans. *American Journal of Psychiatry, 164,* 150–153. (p. 640)

Hogg, M. A. (1996). Intragroup processes, group structure and social identity. In W. P. Robinson (Ed.), *Social groups and identities: Developing the legacy of Henri Tajfel.* Oxford: Butterworth Heinemann. (p. 596)

Hogg, M. A. (2006). Social identity theory. In P. J. Burke (Ed.), *Contemporary social psychological theories.* Stanford, CA: Stanford University Press. (p. 596)

Hohmann, G. W. (1966). Some effects of spinal cord lesions on experienced emotional feelings. *Psychophysiology, 3,* 143–156. (p. 474)

Hokanson, J. E., & Edelman, R. (1966). Effects of three social responses on vascular processes. *Journal of Personality and Social Psychology, 3,* 442–447. (p. 494)

Holahan, C. K., & Sears, R. R. (1995). *The gifted group in later maturity.* Stanford, CA: Stanford University Press. (p. 403)

Holden, C. (1980a). Identical twins reared apart. *Science, 207,* 1323–1325. (p. 135)

Holden, C. (1980b, November). Twins reunited. *Science, 80,* 55–59. (p. 135)

Holden, C. (2007). Mental illness: The next frontier. *Science, 317,* 23. (p. 663)

Holden, C. (2008). Parsing the genetics of behavior. *Science, 322,* 892–895. (p. 138)

Holden, C. (2010). Behavioral addictions debut in proposed DSM-V. *Science, 327,* 935. (p. 667)

Holden, C. (2010). Experts map the terrain of mood disorders. *Science, 327,* p. 1068. (p. 645)

Holden, G. W., & Miller, P. C. (1999). Enduring and different: A meta-analysis of the similarity in parents' child rearing. *Psychological Bulletin, 125,* 223–254. (p. 195)

Holliday, R. E., & Albon, A. J. (2004). Minimizing misinformation effects in young children with cognitive interview mnemonics. *Applied Cognitive Psychology, 18,* 263–281. (p. 345)

Hollingworth, P. (2011). Common variants at ABCA7, MS4A6A/MS4A43, EPHA1, CD33 and CD2AP are associated with Alzheimer's disease. *Nature, 43,* 429–435. (p. 212)

Hollingworth, S. A., Burgess, P. M., & Whiteford, H. A. (2010). Affective and anxiety disorders: Prevalence, treatment and antidepressant medication use. *Australian and New Zealand Journal of Psychiatry, 44,* 513–519. (p. 706)

Hollis, K. L. (1997). Contemporary research on Pavlovian conditioning: A "new" functional analysis. *American Psychologist, 52,* 956–965. (p. 280)

Hollon, S. D., Thase, M. E., & Markowitz, J. C. (2002). Treatment and prevention of depression. *Psychological Science in the Public Interest, 3,* 39–77. (p. 706)

Holstege, G., Georgiadis, J. R., Paans, A. M. J., Meiners, L. C., van der Graaf, F. H. C. E., & Reinders, A. A. T. S. (2003a). Brain activation during male ejaculation. *Journal of Neuroscience, 23,* 9185–9193. (p. 435)

Holstege, G., Reinders, A. A. T., Paans, A. M. J., Meiners, L. C., Pruim, J., & Georgiadis, J. R. (2003b). *Brain activation during female sexual orgasm. Program No. 727.7.* Washington, DC: Society for Neuroscience. (p. 435)

Holt, L. (2002, August). Reported in "Sounds of speech," p. 26, and in personal correspondence, July 18, 2002. (p. 366)

Holtgraves, T. (2011). Text messaging, personality, and the social context. *Journal of Research in Personality, 45,* 92–99. (p. 552)

Holt-Lunstad, J., Smith, T. B., & Layton, J. B. (2010). Social relationships and mortality risk: A meta-analytic review. *PLoS Medicine, 7* (www.plosmedicine.org: e1000316). (p. 519)

Homer, B. D., Solomon, T. M., Moeller, R. W., Mascia, A., DeRaleau, L., & Halkitis, P. N. (2008). Methamphetamine abuse and impairment of social functioning: A review of the underlying neurophysiological causes and behavioral implications. *Psychological Bulletin, 134,* 301–310. (p. 122)

Hooley, J. M. (2010). Social factors in schizophrenia. *Current Directions in Psychological Science, 19,* 238–242. (p. 658)

Hooper, J., & Teresi, D. (1986). *The three-pound universe.* New York: Macmillan. (p. 66)

Hopkins, E. D., & Cantalupo, C. (2008). Theoretical speculations on the evolutionary origins of hemispheric specialization. *Current Directions in Psychological Science, 17,* 233–237. (p. 79)

Hopkins, W. D. (2006). Comparative and familial analysis of handedness in great apes. *Psychological Bulletin, 132,* 538–559. (p. 80)

Hopper, L. M., Lambeth, S. P., Schapiro, S. J., & Whiten, A. (2008). Observational learning in chimpanzees and children studied through 'ghost' conditions. *Proceedings of the Royal Society, 275,* 835–840. (p. 305)

Hopwood, C. J., Donnellan, M. B., Blonigen, D. M., Krueger, R. F., McGue, M., Iacono, W. G., & Burt, S. A. (2011). Genetic and environmental influences on personality trait stability and growth during the transition to adulthood: A three-wave longitudinal study. *Journal of Personality and Social Psychology, 100,* 545–556. (p. 171)

Hor, H., & Tafti, M. (2009). How much sleep do we need? *Science, 325,* 825–826. (p. 97)

Horn, J. L. (1982). The aging of human abilities. In J. Wolman (Ed.), *Handbook of developmental psychology.* Englewood Cliffs, NJ: Prentice-Hall. (p. 399)

Horner, V., Whiten, A., Flynn, E., & de Waal, F. B. M. (2006). Faithful replication of foraging techniques along cultural transmission chains by chimpanzees and children. *Proceedings of the National Academy of Sciences, 103,* 13878–13883. (p. 362)

Horwood, L. J., & Fergusson, D. M. (1998). Breastfeeding and later cognitive and academic outcomes. *Pediatrics, 101*(1). (p. 33)

Hostetter, A. B. (2011). When do gestures communicate? A meta-analysis. *Psychological Bulletin, 137,* 297–315. (p. 374)

Hou, W-H., Chiang, P-T, Hsu, T-Y, Chiu, S-Y, & Yen, Y-C. (2010). Treatment effects of massage therapy in depressed people: A meta-analysis. *Journal of Clinical Psychiatry, 71,* 894–901. (p. 709)

House, R. J., & Singh, J. V. (1987). Organizational behavior: Some new directions for I/O psychology. *Annual Review of Psychology, 38,* 669–718. (p. 467)

Houser-Marko, L., & Sheldon, K. M. (2008). Eyes on the prize or nose to the grindstone? The effects of level of goal evaluation on mood and motivation. *Personality and Social Psychology Bulletin, 34,* 1556–1569. (p. 467)

Houts, A. C., Berman, J. S., & Abramson, H. (1994). Effectiveness of psychological and pharmacological treatments for nocturnal enuresis. *Journal of Consulting and Clinical Psychology, 62,* 737–745. (p. 681)

Houts, R. M., Caspi, A., Pianta, R. C., Arseneault, L., & Moffitt, T. E. (2010). The challenging pupil in the classroom: The effect of the child on the teacher. *Psychological Science, 21,* 1802–1810. (p. 171)

Hovatta, I., Tennant, R. S., Helton, R., Marr, R. A., Singer, O., Redwine, J. M., Ellison, J. A., Schadt, E. E., Verma, I. M., Lockhart, D. J., & Barlow, C. (2005). Glyoxalase 1 and glutathione reductase 1 regulate anxiety in mice. *Nature, 438,* 662–666. (p. 643)

Howe, M. L. (1997). Children's memory for traumatic experiences. *Learning and Individual Differences, 9,* 153–174. (p. 345)

Howell, A. J. (2009). Flourishing: Achievement-related correlates of students' well-being. *Journal of Positive Psychology, 4,* 1–13. (p. 408)

Howell, R. T., & Howell, C. J. (2008). The relation of economic status to subjective well-being in developing countries: A meta-analysis. *Psychological Bulletin, 134,* 536–560. (p. 497)

Hoyer, G., & Lund, E. (1993). Suicide among women related to number of children in marriage. *Archives of General Psychiatry, 50,* 134–137. (p. 650)

Hsee, C. K., Yang, A. X., & Wang, L. (2010). Idleness aversion and the need for justifiable busyness. *Psychological Science, 21,* 926–930. (p. 457)

Hu, X-Z., Lipsky, R. H., Zhu, G., Akhtar, L. A., Taubman, J., Greenberg, B. D., Xu, K., Arnold, P. D., Richter, M. A., Kennedy, J. L., Murphy, D. L., & Goldman, D. (2006). Serotonin transporter promoter gain-of-function genotypes are linked to obsessive-compulsive disorder. *American Journal of Human Genetics, 78,* 815–826. (p. 643)

Huang, C. (2010). Mean-level change in self-esteem from childhood through adulthood meta-analysis of longitudinal studies. *Review of General Psychology, 14,* 251–260. (p. 218)

Huang, X., Iun, J., Liu, A., & Gong, Y. (2010). Does participative leadership enhance work performance by inducing empowerment or trust? The differential effects on managerial and non-managerial subordinates. *Journal of Organizational Behavior, 31,* 122–143. (p. 468)

Huart, J., Corneille, O., & Becquart, E. (2005). Face-based categorization, context-based categorization, and distortions in the recollection of gender ambiguous faces. *Journal of Experimental Social Psychology, 41,* 598–608. (p. 352)

Hubbard, E. M., Arman, A. C., Ramachandran, V. S., & Boynton, G. M. (2005). Individual differences among grapheme-color synesthetes: Brain-behavior correlations. *Neuron, 45,* 975–985. (p. 269)

Hubel, D. H. (1979, September). The brain. *Scientific American,* pp. 45–53. (p. 228)

Hubel, D. H., & Wiesel, T. N. (1979, September). Brian mechanisms of vision. *Scientific American,* pp. 150–162. (p. 238)

Hublin, C., Kaprio, J., Partinen, M., Heikkila, K., & Koskenvuo, M. (1997). Prevalence and genetics of sleepwalking—A population-based twin study. *Neurology, 48,* 177–181. (p. 105)

Hublin, C., Kaprio, J., Partinen, M., & Koskenvuo, M. (1998). Sleeptalking in twins: Epidemiology and psychiatric comorbidity. *Behavior Genetics, 28,* 289–298. (p. 105)

Hucker, S. J., & Bain, J. (1990). Androgenic hormones and sexual assault. In W. Marshall, R. Law, & H. Barbaree (Eds.), *The handbook on sexual assault.* New York: Plenum. (p. 437)

Hudson, J. I., Hiripi, E., Pope, H. G., & Kessler, R. C. (2007). The prevalence and correlates of eating disorders in the National Comorbidity Survey Replication. *Biological Psychiatry, 61,* 348–358. (p. 671)

Huey, E. D., Krueger, F., & Grafman, J. (2006). Representations in the human prefrontal cortex. *Current Directions in Psychological Science, 15,* 167–171. (p. 74)

Huffcutt, A. I., Conway, J. M., Roth, P. L., & Stone, N. J. (2001). Identification and meta-analytic assessment of psychological constructs measured in employment interviews. *Journal of Applied Psychology, 86,* 897–913. (p. 462)

Hugenberg, K., & Bodenhausen, G. V. (2003). Facing prejudice: Implicit prejudice and the perception of facial threat. *Psychological Science, 14,* 640–643. (p. 595)

Hugenberg, K., Young, S. G., Bernstein, M. J., & Sacco, D. F. (2010). The categorization-individuation model: An integrative account of the other-race recognition deficit. *Psychological Review, 117,* 1168–1187. (p. 598)

Hughes, J. R. (2010). Craving among long-abstinent smokers: An Internet survey. *Nicotine & Tobacco Research, 12,* 459–462. (p. 121)

Hugick, L. (1989, July). Women play the leading role in keeping modern families close. *Gallup Report, No. 286,* p. 27–34. (p. 159)

Huizink, A. C., & Mulder, E. J. (2006). Maternal smoking, drinking or cannabis use during pregnancy and neurobehavioral and cognitive functioning in human offspring. *Neuroscience and Biobehavioral Reviews, 30,* 24–41. (p. 124)

Hulbert, A. (2005, November 20). The prodigy puzzle. *New York Times Magazine* (www.nytimes.com). (p. 403)

Hull, H. R., Morrow, M. L., Dinger, M. K., Han, J. L., & Fields, D. A. (2007, November 20). Characterization of body weight and composition changes during the sophomore year of college. *BMC Women's Health, 7,* 21 (biomedcentral.com). (p. 102)

Hull, J. G., & Bond, C. F., Jr. (1986). Social and behavioral consequences of alcohol consumption and expectancy: A meta-analysis. *Psychological Bulletin, 99,* 347–360. (p. 118)

Hull, J. M. (1990). *Touching the rock: An experience of blindness.* New York: Vintage Books. (pp. 330, 610)

Hülsheger, U. R., Anderson, N., & Salgado, J. F. (2009). Team-level predictors of innovation at work: A comprehensive meta-analysis spanning three decades of research. *Journal of Applied Psychology, 94,* 1128–1145. (p. 388)

Hummer, R. A., Rogers, R. G., Nam, C. B., & Ellison, C. G. (1999). Religious involvement and U.S. adult mortality. *Demography, 36,* 273–285. (p. 527)

Humphrey, S. E., Nahrgang, J. D., & Morgeson, F. P. (2007). Integrating motivational, social, and contextual work design features: A meta-analytic summary and theoretical extension of the work design literature. *Journal of Applied Psychology, 92,* 1332–1356. (p. 558)

Humphreys, L. G., & Davey, T. C. (1988). Continuity in intellectual growth from 12 months to 9 years. *Intelligence, 12,* 183–197. (p. 400)

Hunsberger, J. G., Newton, S. S., Bennett, A. H., Duman, C. H., Russell, D. S., Salton, S. R., & Duman, R. S. (2007). Antidepressant actions of the exercise-regulated gene VGF. *Nature Medicine, 13,* 1476–1482. (p. 523)

Hunsley, J., & Di Giulio, G. (2002). Dodo bird, phoenix, or urban legend? The question of psychotherapy equivalence. *Scientific Review of Mental Health Practice, 1,* 11–22. (p. 695)

Hunt, C., Slade, T., & Andrews, G. (2004). Generalized anxiety disorder and major depressive disorder comorbidity in the National Survey of Mental Health and Well-Being. *Depression and Anxiety, 20,* 23–31. (p. 637)

Hunt, E. (1983). On the nature of intelligence. *Science, 219,* 141–146. (p. 390)

Hunt, E., & Carlson, J. (2007). Considerations relating to the study of group differences in intelligence. *Perspectives on Psychological Science, 2,* 194–213. (pp. 412, 413)

Hunt, J. M. (1982). Toward equalizing the developmental opportunities of infants and preschool children. *Journal of Social Issues,* 38(4), 163–191. (p. 407)

Hunt, M. (1974). *Sexual behavior in the 1970s.* Chicago: Playboy Press. (p. 439)

Hunt, M. (1990). *The compassionate beast: What science is discovering about the humane side of humankind.* New York: William Morrow. (p. 12)

Hunt, M. (1993). *The story of psychology.* New York: Doubleday. (pp. 3, 6, 46, 203, 284, 403, 535)

Hunter, S., & Sundel, M. (Eds.). (1989). *Midlife myths: Issues, findings, and practice implications.* Newbury Park, CA: Sage. (p. 215)

Hurlburt, R. T., & Akhter, S. A. (2008). Unsymbolized thinking. *Consciousness and Cognition, 17,* 1364–1374. (p. 376)

Hurst, M. (2008, April 22). Who gets any sleep these days? Sleep patterns of Canadians. *Canadian Social Trends.* Statistics Canada Catalogue No. 11–008. (p. 97)

Huston, A. C., Donnerstein, E., Fairchild, H., Feshbach, N. D., Katz, P. A., & Murray, J. P. (1992). *Big world, small screen: The role of television in American society.* Lincoln: University of Nebraska Press. (p. 307)

Hutchinson, R. (2006). *Calum's road.* Edinburgh: Burlinn Limited. (p. 463)

Hvistendahl, M. (2009). Making every baby girl count. *Science, 323,* 1164–1166. (p. 594)

Hvistendahl, M. (2010). Has China outgrown the one-child policy? *Science, 329,* 1458–1461. (p. 594)

Hvistendahl, M. (2011). China's population growing slowly, changing fast. *Science, 332,* 650–651. (p. 594)

Hyde, J. S. (2005). The gender similarities hypothesis. *American Psychologist, 60,* 581–592. (pp. 144, 157)

Hyde, J. S., & Mertz, J. E. (2009). Gender, culture, and mathematics performance. *Proceedings of the National Academy of Sciences, 106,* 8801–8807. (p. 409)

Hyde, J. S., Mezulis, A. H., & Abramson, L. Y. (2008). The ABCs of depression: Integrating affective, biological, and cognitive models to explain the emergence of the gender difference in depression. *Psychological Review, 115,* 291–313. (p. 647)

Hyman, I. E., Jr., Boss, S. M., Wise, B. M., McKenzie, K. E., & Caggiano, J. M. (2010). Did you see the unicycling clown? Inattentional blindness while walking and talking on a cell phone. *Applied Cognitive Psychology,* in press. (p. 89)

Hyman, R. (1981). Cold reading: How to convince strangers that you know all about them. In K. Frazier (Ed.), *Paranormal borderlands of science.* Buffalo, NY: Prometheus. (p. 551)

Hyman, R. (2010). Meta-analysis that conceals more than it reveals: Comment on Storm et al. (2010). *Psychological Bulletin, 136,* 486–490. (p. 254)

Iacoboni, M. (2008). *Mirroring people: The new science of how we connect with others.* New York: Farrar, Straus & Giroux. (pp. 304, 305)

Iacoboni, M. (2009). Imitation, empathy, and mirror neurons. *Annual Review of psychology, 60,* 653–670. (pp. 304, 305)

IAP. (2006, June 21). IAP statement on the teaching of evolution. *The Interacademy Panel on International Issues* (www.interacademies.net/iap). (p. 165)

Ickes, W., Snyder, M., & Garcia, S. (1997). Personality influences on the choice of situations. In R. Hogan, J. Johnson, & S. Briggs (Eds.). *Handbook of personality psychology.* San Diego, CA: Academic Press. (p. 556)

Idson, L. C., & Mischel, W. (2001). The personality of familiar and significant people: The lay perceiver as a social-cognitive theorist. *Journal of Personality and Social Psychology, 80,* 585–596. (p. 573)

IJzerman, H., & Semin, G. R. (2009). The thermometer of social relations: Mapping social proximity on temperature. *Psychological Science, 20,* 1214–1220. (p. 268)

Ikonomidou, C., Bittigau, P., Ishimaru, M. J., Wozniak, D. F., Koch, C., Genz, K., Price, M. T., Stefovska, V., Hoerster, F., Tenkova, T., Dikranian, K., & Olney, J. W. (2000). Ethanol-induced apoptotic neurodegeneration and fetal alcohol syndrome. *Science, 287,* 1056–1060. (p. 174)

Ilardi, S. S. (2009). *The depression cure: The six-step program to beat depression without drugs.* Cambridge, MA: De Capo Lifelong Books. (pp. 652, 711)

Inbar, Y., Cone, J., & Gilovich, T. (2010). People's intuitions about intuitive insight and intuitive choice. *Journal of Personality and Social Psychology, 99,* 232–247. (p. 360)

Inbar, Y., Pizarro, D., & Bloom, P. (2011). Disgusting smells cause decreased liking of gay men. Unpublished manuscript, Tillburg University. (p. 271)

Independent Sector. (2002). *Faith and philanthropy: The connection between charitable giving behavior and giving to religion.* Washington, DC: Author. (p. 617)

Ingham, A. G., Levinger, G., Graves, J., & Peckham, V. (1974). The Ringelmann effect: Studies of group size and group performance. *Journal of Experimental Social Psychology, 10,* 371–384. (p. 587)

Inglehart, R. (1990). *Culture shift in advanced industrial society.* Princeton, NJ: Princeton University Press. (p. 451)

Inglehart, R. (2008). Cultural change and democracy in Latin America. In F. Hagopian (Ed.), *Contemporary Catholicism, religious pluralism and democracy in Latin America.* South Bend, IN: Notre Dame University Press, 67–95. (p. 497)

Inglehart, R. (2009). Cultural change and democracy in Latin America. In F. Hagopian (Ed.), *Contemporary Catholicism, religious pluralism and democracy in Latin America.* South Bend, IN: University of Notre Dame University Press. (p. 559)

Inman, M. L., & Baron, R. S. (1996). Influence of prototypes on perceptions of prejudice. *Journal of Personality and Social Psychology, 70,* 727–739. (p. 353)

Insana, R. (2005, February 21). Coach says honey gets better results than vinegar (interview with Larry Brown). *USA Today,* p. 4B. (p. 467)

Insel, T. R. (2010, April). Faulty circuits. *Scientific American,* pp. 44–51. (p. 643)

International Schizophrenia Consortium. (2009). Common polygenic variation contributes to risk of schizophrenia and bipolar disorder. *Nature, 460,* 748–752. (p. 662)

Inzlicht, M., & Ben-Zeev, T. (2000). A threatening intellectual environment: Why females are susceptible to experiencing problem-solving deficits in the presence of males. *Psychological Science, 11,* 365–371. (p. 414)

Inzlicht, M., & Gutsell, J. N. (2007). Running on empty: Neural signals for self-control failure. *Psychological Science, 18,* 933–937. (p. 558)

Inzlicht, M., & Kang, S. K. (2010). Stereotype threat spillover: How coping with threats to social identity affects aggression, eating, decision making, and attention. *Journal of Personality and Social Psychology, 99,* 467–481. (p. 414)

Inzlicht, M., McGregor, I., Hirsh, J. C., & Nash, K. (2009). Neural markers of religious conviction. *Psychological Science, 20,* 385–392. (p. 62)

IPPA. (2009, January 22). Membership letter. International Positive Psychology Association. (p. 560)

IPPA. (2010, August). International conference on positive psychology and education in China, by S. Choong. *The IPPA Newsletter,* International Positive Psychology Association. (p. 560)

Ipsos. (2010a, June 29). Online Canadians report a large 35% decline in the amount of email received. www.ipsos-na.com. (pp. 30, 453)

Ipsos. (2010b, April 8). One in five (20%) global citizens believe that alien being have come down to earth and walk amongst us in our communities disguised as humans. www.ipsos-na.com. (p. 30)

IPU. (2011). Women in national parliaments: Situation as of 31 November 2011. International Parliamentary Union (www.ipu.org). (p. 158)

Ireland, M. E., & Pennebaker, J. W. (2010). Language style matching in writing: Synchrony in essays, correspondence, and poetry. *Journal of Personality and Social Psychology,* 99, 549–571. (pp. 306, 579)

Ironson, G., Solomon, G. F., Balbin, E. G., O'Cleirigh, C., George, A., Kumar, M., Larson, D., & Woods, T. E. (2002). The Ironson-Woods spiritual/religiousness index is associated with long survival, health behaviors, less distress, and low cortisol in people with HIV/AIDS. *Annals of Behavioral Medicine, 24,* 34–48. (p. 528)

Irwin, M. R., Cole, J. C., & Nicassio, P. M. (2006). Comparative meta-analysis of behavioral interventions for insomnia and their efficacy in middle-aged adults and in older adults 55+ years of age. *Health Psychology, 25,* 3–14. (p. 103)

Isaacson, W. (2009, Spring). Einstein's final quest. In Character. http://incharacter.org/features/einsteins-final-quest. (p. 415)

Ishida, A., Mutoh, T., Ueyama, T., Brando, H., Masubuchi, S., Nakahara, D., Tsujimoto, G., & Okamura, H. (2005). Light activates the adrenal gland: Timing of gene expression and glucocorticoid release. *Cell Metabolism, 2,* 297–307. (p. 698)

Iso, H., Simoda, S., & Matsuyama, T. (2007). Environmental change during postnatal development alters behaviour. *Behavioural Brain Research, 179,* 90–98. (p. 76)

Ito, T. A., Miller, N., & Pollock, V. E. (1996). Alcohol and aggression: A meta-analysis on the moderating effects of inhibitory cues, triggering events, and self-focused attention. *Psychological Bulletin, 120,* 60–82. (p. 601)

ITU. (2010). The world in 2010: ICT facts and figures. International Telecommunication Union (www.itu.int/ict). (p. 453)

Iversen, L. L. (2000). *The science of marijuana.* New York: Oxford. (p. 124)

Iyengar, S. (2010). *The art of choosing.* New York: Twelve Publishers. (p. 559)

Iyengar, S. S., & Lepper, M. R. (2000). When choice is demotivating: Can one desire too much of a good thing? *Journal of Personality and Social Psychology, 79,* 995–1006. (p. 559)

Izard, C. E. (1977). *Human emotions.* New York: Plenum Press. (pp. 487, 492)

Izard, C. E. (1994). Innate and universal facial expressions: Evidence from developmental and cross-cultural research. *Psychological Bulletin, 114,* 288–299. (p. 487)

Jablensky, A. (1999). Schizophrenia: Epidemiology. *Current Opinion in Psychiatry, 12,* 19–28. (p. 661)

Jackson, G. (2009). Sexual response in cardiovascular disease. *Journal of Sex Research, 46,* 233–236. (p. 435)

Jackson, J. M., & Williams, K. D. (1988). *Social loafing: A review and theoretical analysis.* Unpublished manuscript, Fordham University. (p. 587)

Jackson, J. S., Brown, K. T., Brown, T. N., & Marks, B. (2001). Contemporary immigration policy orientations among dominant-group members in western Europe. *Journal of Social Issues, 57,* 431–456. (p. 594)

Jackson, L. A., & Gerard, D. A. (1996). Diurnal types, the "Big Five" personality factors and other personal characteristics. *Journal of Social Behavior and Personality, 11,* 273–283. (p. 552)

Jackson, S. W. (1992). The listening healer in the history of psychological healing. *American Journal Psychiatry, 149,* 1623–1632. (p. 699)

Jacobi, C., Hayward, C., deZwaan, M., Kraemer, H. C., & Agras, W. S. (2004). Coming to terms with risk factors for eating disorders: Application of risk terminology and suggestions for a general taxonomy. *Psychological Bulletin, 130,* 19–65. (p. 671)

Jacobs, B. L. (1994). Serotonin, motor activity, and depression-related disorders. *American Scientist, 82,* 456–463. (pp. 523, 652)

Jacobs, B. L. (2004). Depression: The brain finally gets into the act. *Current Directions in Psychological Science, 13,* 103–106. (p. 706)

Jacobs, B., L., van Praag, H., & Gage, F. H. (2000). Adult brain neurogenesis and psychiatry: A novel theory of depression. *Molecular Psychiatry, 5,* 262–269. (p. 652)

Jacoby, L. L., Bishara, A. J., Hessels, S., & Toth, J. P. (2005). Aging, subjective experience, and cognitive control: Dramatic false remembering by older adults. *Journal of Experimental Psychology: General, 154,* 131–148. (p. 345)

Jacoby, L. L., & Rhodes, M. G. (2006). False remembering in the aged. *Current Directions in Psychological Science, 15,* 49–53. (p. 345)

Jacques, C., & Rossion, B. (2006). The speed of individual face categorization. *Psychological Science, 17,* 485–492. (p. 223)

Jacques-Tiura, A. J., Abbey, A., Parkhill, M. R., & Zawacki, T. (2007). Why do some men misperceive women's sexual intentions more frequently than others do? An application of the confluence model. *Personality and Social Psychology Bulletin,* 33, 1467–1480. (p. 573)

James, K. (1986). Priming and social categorizational factors: Impact on awareness of emergency situations. *Personality and Social Psychology Bulletin, 12,* 462–467. (p. 330)

James, W. (1890). *The principles of psychology* (Vol. 2). New York: Holt. (pp. 57, 113, 262, 334, 347, 474, 489, 577)

Jameson, D. (1985). Opponent-colors theory in light of physiological findings. In D. Ottoson & S. Zeki (Eds.), *Central and peripheral mechanisms of color vision.* New York: Macmillan. (p. 247)

Jamieson, J. P. (2010). The home field advantage in athletics: A meta-analysis. *Journal of Applied Social Psychology, 40,* 1819–1848. (p. 587)

Jamison, K. R. (1993). *Touched with fire: Manic-depressive illness and the artistic temperament.* New York: Free Press. (p. 647)

Jamison, K. R. (1995). *An unquiet mind.* New York: Knopf. (pp. 647, 674)

Janis, I. L. (1982). *Groupthink: Psychological studies of policy decisions and fiascoes.* Boston: Houghton Mifflin. (p. 590)

Janis, I. L. (1986). Problems of international crisis management in the nuclear age. *Journal of Social Issues, 42*(2), 201–220. (p. 355)

Janoff-Bulman, R., Timko, C., & Carli, L. L. (1985). Cognitive biases in blaming the victim. *Journal of Experimental Social Psychology, 21,* 161–177. (p. 599)

Jaremka, L. M., Gabriel, S., & Carvallo, M. (2011). What makes us feel the best also makes us feel the worst: The emotional impact of independent and interdependent experiences. *Self and Identity, 10,* 44–63. (p. 451)

Jarrett, B., Bloch, G. J., Bennett, D., Bleazard, B., & Hedges, D. (2010). The influence of body mass index, age and gender on current illness: A cross-sectional study. *International Journal of Obesity, 34,* 429–436. (p. 428)

Javitt, D. C., & Coyle, J. T. (2004, January). Decoding schizophrenia. *Scientific American,* pp. 48–55. (p. 660)

Jemmott, J. B., III, Jemmott, L. S., & Fong, G. (2010). Efficacy of a theory-based abstinence-only intervention over 24 months. *Archives of Pediatric and Adolescent Medicine, 164,* 152–159. (p. 441)

Jenkins, J. G., & Dallenbach, K. M. (1924). Obliviscence during sleep and waking. *American Journal of Psychology, 35,* 605–612. (pp. 338, 339)

Jenkins, J. M., & Astington, J. W. (1996). Cognitive factors and family structure associated with theory of mind development in young children. *Developmental Psychology,* 32, 70–78. (p. 183)

Jensen, A. R. (1980). *Bias in mental testing.* New York: Free Press. (p. 397)

Jensen, A. R. (1983, August). The nature of the Black-White difference on various psychometric tests: Spearman's hypothesis. Paper presented at the meeting of the American Psychological Association, Anaheim, CA. (p. 413)

Jensen, A. R. (1989). New findings on the intellectually gifted. *New Horizons, 30,* 73–80. (pp. 390, 413)

Jensen, J. P., & Bergin, A. E. (1988). Mental health values of professional therapists: A national interdisciplinary survey. *Professional Psychology: Research and Practice, 19,* 290–297. (p. 700)

Jensen, M. P. (2008). The neurophysiology of pain perception and hypnotic analgesia: Implications for clinical practice. *American Journal of Clinical Hypnosis, 51,* 123–147. (p. 111)

Jepson, C., Krantz, D. H., & Nisbett, R. E. (1983). Inductive reasoning: Competence or skill. *The Behavioral and Brain Sciences,* 3, 494–501. (p. 42)

Jessberger, S., Aimone, J. B., & Gage, F. H. (2008). *Neurogenesis. In learning and memory: A comprehensive reference.* Oxford: Elsevier. (p. 76)

Jiang, Y., Costello, P., Fang, F., Huang, M., He, S. (2006). A gender- and sexual orientation-dependent spatial attentional effect of invisible things. *Proceedings of the National Academy of Sciences, 103,* 17048–17052. (pp. 226, 443)

Job, V., Dweck, C.S., & Walton, G.M. (2010). Ego depletion–Is it all in your head?: Implicit theories about willpower affect self-regulation. *Psychological Science, 21.* Published online at: http://pss.sagepub.com/content/early/2010/09/28/0956797610384745. (p. 557)

Jobe, T. H., & Harrow, M. (2010). Schizophrenia course, long-term outcome, recovery, and prognosis. *Current Directions in Psychological Science, 19,* 220–225. (p. 658)

Johnson, C. B., Stockdale, M. S., & Saal, F. E. (1991). Persistence of men's misperceptions of friendly cues across a variety of interpersonal encounters. *Psychology of Women Quarterly, 15,* 463–475. (p. 145)

Johnson, D. F. (1997). Margaret Floy Washburn. *Psychology of Women Newsletter,* pp. 17, 22. (p. 4)

Johnson, D. L., Wiebe, J. S., Gold, S. M., Andreasen, N. C., Hichwa, R. D., Watkins, G. L., & Ponto, L. L. B. (1999). Cerebral blood flow and personality: A positron emission tomography study. *American Journal of Psychiatry, 156,* 252–257. (p. 548)

Johnson, E. J., & Goldstein, D. (2003). Do defaults save lives? *Science, 302,* 1338–1339. (p. 359)

Johnson, J. A. (2007, June 26). Not so situational. Commentary on the SPSP listserv (spsp-discuss@stolaf.edu). (p. 576)

Johnson, J. G., Cohen, P., Kotler, L., Kasen, S., & Brook, J. S. (2002). Psychiatric disorders associated with risk for the development of eating disorders during adolescence and early adulthood. *Journal of Consulting and Clinical Psychology, 70,* 1119–1128. (p. 670)

Johnson, J. S., & Newport, E. L. (1991). Critical period affects on universal properties of language: The status of subjacency in the acquisition of a second language. *Cognition, 39,* 215–258. (pp. 369, 370)

Johnson, M. H. (1992). Imprinting and the development of face recognition: From chick to man. *Current Directions in Psychological Science, 1,* 52–55. (p. 189)

Johnson, M. H., & Morton, J. (1991). *Biology and cognitive development: The case of face recognition.* Oxford: Blackwell Publishing. (p. 175)

Johnson, R. E., Chang, C-H., & Lord, R. G. (2006). Moving from cognition to behavior: What the research says. *Psychological Bulletin, 132,* 381–415. (p. 467)

Johnson, S. C., & 13 others. (2006). Activation of brain regions vulnerable to Alzheimer's disease: The effect of mild cognitive impairment. *Neurobiology of Aging, 27,* 1604–1612. (p. 213)

Johnson, W. (2010). Understanding the genetics of intelligence: Can height help? Can corn oil? *Current Directions in Psychological Science, 19,* 177–182. (p. 405)

Johnson, W., Carothers, A., & Deary, I. J. (2008). Sex differences in variability in general intelligence: A new look at the old question. *Perspectives on Psychological Science, 3,* 518–531. (pp. 384, 409)

Johnson, W., Gow, A. J., Corley, J., Starr, J. M., & Deary, I. J. (2010). Location in cognitive and residential space at age 70 reflects a lifelong trait over parental and environmental circumstances: The Lothian Birth Cohort 1936. *Intelligence, 38,* 403–411. (p. 401)

Johnson, W., Turkheimer, E., Gottesman, I. I., & Bouchard, Jr., T. J. (2009). Beyond heritability: Twin studies in behavioral research. *Current Directions in Psychological Science, 18,* 217–220. (pp. 134, 139, 405)

Johnston, L. D., O'Malley, P. M., Bachman, J. G., & Schulenberg, J. E. (2007). *Monitoring the Future national results on adolescent drug use: Overview of key findings, 2006.* Bethesda, MD: National Institute on Drug Abuse. (p. 127)

Johnston, L. D., O'Malley, P. M., Bachman, J. G., & Schulenberg, J. E. (2011). *Monitoring the future national results on adolescent drug use: Overview of key findings, 2010.* Ann Arbor, MI: Institute for Social Research, University of Michigan. (pp. 121, 126)

Johnstone, E. C., Ebmeier, K. P., Miller, P., Owens, D. G. C., & Lawrie, S. M. (2005). Predicting schizophrenia: Findings from the Edinburgh High-Risk Study. *British Journal of Psychiatry, 186,* 18–25. (p. 663)

Joiner, T. (2006). *Why people die by suicide.* Cambridge, MA: Harvard University Press. (p. 650)

Joiner, T. E., Jr. (2010). *Myths about suicide.* Cambridge, MA: Harvard University Press. (p. 650)

Jokela, M., Elovainio, M., Archana, S-M., & Kivimäki, M. (2009). IQ, socioeconomic status, and early death: The US National Longitudinal Survey of Youth. *Psychosomatic Medicine, 71,* 322–328. (p. 518)

Jolly, A. (2007). The social origin of mind. *Science, 317,* 1326. (p. 363)

Jonas, E., & Fischer, P. (2006). Terror management and religion: Evidence that intrinsic religiousness mitigates worldview defense following mortality salience. *Journal of Personality and Social Psychology, 91,* 553–567. (p. 541)

Jones, A. C., & Gosling, S. D. (2005). Temperament and personality in dogs (*Canis familiaris*): A review and evaluation of past research. *Applied Animal Behaviour Science, 95,* 1–53. (p. 549)

Jones, J. M. (2007, July 25). Latest Gallup update shows cigarette smoking near historical lows. *Gallup Poll News Service* (poll.gallup.com). (p. 121)

Jones, J. M. (2009, November 20). In U.S., more would like lose weight than are trying to. www.gallup.com. (p. 432)

Jones, J. M., & Moore, D. W. (2003, June 17). Generational differences in support for a woman president. The Gallup Organization (www.gallup.com). (p. 593)

Jones, J. T., Pelham, B. W., Carvallo, M., & Mirenberg, M. C. (2004). How do I love thee? Let me count the Js: Implicit egotism and interpersonal attraction. *Journal of Personality and Social Psychology, 87,* 665–683. (p. 608)

Jones, L. (2000, December). Skeptics New Year quiz. *Skeptical Briefs,* p. 11. (p. 551)

Jones, M. C. (1924). A laboratory study of fear: The case of Peter. *Journal of Genetic Psychology, 31,* 308–315. (p. 681)

Jones, M. V., Paull, G. C., & Erskine, J. (2002). The impact of a team's aggressive reputation on the decisions of association football referees. *Journal of Sports Sciences, 20,* 991–1000. (p. 232)

Jones, S. S. (2007). Imitation in infancy: The development of mimicry. *Psychological Science, 18,* 593–599. (p. 305)

Jones, S. S., Collins, K., & Hong, H-W. (1991). An audience effect on smile production in 10–month-old infants. *Psychological Science, 2,* 45–49. (p. 488)

Jones, W. H., Carpenter, B. N., & Quintana, D. (1985). Personality and interpersonal predictors of loneliness in two cultures. *Journal of Personality and Social Psychology, 48,* 1503–1511. (p. 22)

Jordan, A. H., Monin, B., Dweck, C. S., Lovett, B. J., John, O. P., & Gross, J. J. (2011). Misery has more company than people think: Underestimating the prevalence of others' negative emotions. *Personality and Social Psychology Bulletin, 37,* 120–135. (p. 645)

Jose, A., O'Leary, D., & Moyer, A. (2010). Does premarital cohabitation predict subsequent marital stability and marital quality? A meta-analysis. *Journal of Marriage and Family, 72,* 105–116. (p. 216)

Joseph, D. L., & Newman, D. A. (2010). Emotional intelligence: An integrative meta-analysis and cascading model. *Journal of Applied Psychology, 95,* 54–78. (p. 389)

Joseph, J. (2001). Separated twins and the genetics of personality differences: A critique. *American Journal of Psychology, 114,* 1–30. (p. 136)

Jost, J. T., Kay, A. C., & Thorisdottir, H. (eds.) (2009). *Social and psychological bases of ideology and system justification.* New York: Oxford University Press. (p. 599)

Jovanovic, T., Blanding, N. Q., Norrholm, S. D., Duncan, E., Bradley, B., & Ressler, K. J. (2009). Childhood abuse is associated with increased startle reactivity in adulthood. *Depression and Anxiety, 26,* 1018–1026. (p. 192)

Judge, T. A., Thoresen, C. J., Bono, J. E., & Patton, G. K. (2001). The job satisfaction/job performance relationship: A qualitative and quantitative review. *Psychological Bulletin, 127,* 376–407. (p. 465)

Jung-Beeman, M., Bowden, E. M., Haberman, J., Frymiare, J. L., Arambel-Liu, S., Greenblatt, R., Reber, P. J., & Kounios, J. (2004). Neural activity when people solve verbal problems with insight. *PloS Biology* 2(4), e111. (p. 354)

Jung, R. E., & Haier, R. J. (2007). The Parieto-Frontal Integration Theory (P-FIT) of intelligence: Converging neuroimaging evidence. *Behavioral and Brain Sciences, 30,* 135–187. (p. 390)

Just, M. A., Keller, T. A., & Cynkar, J. (2008). A decrease in brain activation associated with driving when listening to someone speak. *Brain Research, 1205,* 70–80. (p. 88)

Kagan, J. (1976). Emergent themes in human development. *American Scientist, 64,* 186–196. (p. 190)

Kagan, J. (1984). *The nature of the child.* New York: Basic Books. (p. 187)

Kagan, J. (1995). On attachment. *Harvard Review of Psychiatry, 3,* 104–106. (p. 189)

Kagan, J. (1998). *Three seductive ideas.* Cambridge, MA: Harvard University Press. (pp. 81, 171)

Kagan, J., Arcus, D., Snidman, N., Feng, W. Y., Hendler, J., & Greene, S. (1994). Reactivity in infants: A cross-national comparison. *Developmental Psychology, 30,* 342–345. (p. 137)

Kagan, J., Lapidus, D. R., & Moore, M. (December, 1978). Infant antecedents of cognitive functioning: A longitudinal study. *Child Development, 49*(4), 1005–1023. (p. 171)

Kagan, J., & Snidman, N. (2004). *The long shadow of temperament.* Cambridge, MA: Belknap Press. (p. 138)

Kagan, J., Snidman, N., & Arcus, D. M. (1992). Initial reactions to unfamiliarity. *Current Directions in Psychological Science, 1,* 171–174. (p. 137)

Kahlor, L., & Morrison, D. (2007). Television viewing and rape myth acceptance among college women. *Sex Roles, 56,* 729–739. (p. 603)

Kahneman, D. (1985, June). Quoted by K. McKean, Decisions, decisions. *Discover,* pp. 22–31. (p. 693)

Kahneman, D. (1999). Assessments of objective happiness: A bottom-up approach. In D. Kahneman, E. Diener, & N. Schwartz (Eds.), *Understanding well-being: Scientific perspectives on enjoyment and suffering.* New York: Russell Sage Foundation. (p. 265)

Kahneman, D. (2005, January 13). What were they thinking? Q&A with Daniel Kahneman. *Gallup Management Journal* (gmj.gallup.com). (p. 355)

Kahneman, D. (2005, February 10). Are you happy now? *Gallup Management Journal* interview (www.gmj.gallup.com). (p. 497)

Kahneman, D., & Deaton, A. (2010). High income improves evaluation of life but not emotional well-being. *Proceedings of the National Academy of Sciences, 107,* 16489–16493. (p. 497)

Kahneman, D., Fredrickson, B. L., Schreiber, C. A., & Redelmeier, D. A. (1993). When more pain is preferred to less: Adding a better end. *Psychological Science, 4,* 401–405. (p. 265)

Kahneman, D., Krueger, A. B., Schkade, D. A., Schwarz, N., & Stone, A. A. (2004). A survey method for characterizing daily life experience: The day reconstruction method. *Science, 306,* 1776–1780. (pp. 100, 496)

Kahneman, D., & Renshon, J. (2007, January/February). Why hawks win. *Foreign Policy* (www.foreignpolicy.com). (p. 566)

Kail, R. (1991). Developmental change in speed of processing during childhood and adolescence. *Psychological Bulletin, 109,* 490–501. (p. 211)

Kail, R., & Hall, L. K. (2001). Distinguishing short-term memory from working memory. *Memory & Cognition, 29,* 1–9. (p. 315)

Kaiser. (2001). Inside-out: A report on the experiences of lesbians, gays and bisexuals in America and the public's views on issues and policies related to sexual orientation. The Henry J. Kaiser Foundation (www.kff.org). (p. 448)

Kaiser. (2010, January). Generation M^2: Media in the lives of 8- to 18-year-olds (by V. J. Rideout, U. G. Foeher, & D. F. Roberts). Menlo Park, CA: Henry J. Kaiser Family Foundation. (pp. 33, 453, 455, 663)

Kamarck, T., & Jennings, J. R. (1991). Biobehavioral factors in sudden cardiac death. *Psychological Bulletin, 109,* 42–75. (p. 513)

Kamel, N. S., & Gammack, J. K. (2006). Insomnia in the elderly: Cause, approach, and treatment. *American Journal of Medicine, 119,* 463–469. (p. 96)

Kamil, A. C., & Cheng, K. (2001). Way-finding and landmarks: The multiple-bearings hypothesis. *Journal of Experimental Biology, 204,* 103–113. (p. 324)

Kaminski, J., Cali, J., & Fischer, J. (2004). Word learning in a domestic dog: Evidence for "fast mapping." *Science, 304,* 1682–1683. (p. 374)

Kanaya, T., Scullin, M. H., & Ceci, S. J. (2003). The Flynn effect and U.S. policies: The impact of rising IQ scores on American society via mental retardation diagnoses. *American Psychologist, 58,* 778–790. (p. 402)

Kanazawa, S. (2004). General intelligence as a domain-specific adaptation. *Psychological Review, 111,* 512–523. (p. 382)

Kanazawa, S. (2010). Evolutionary psychology and intelligence research. *American Psychologist, 65,* 279–289. (p. 382)

Kandel, D. B., & Raveis, V. H. (1989). Cessation of illicit drug use in young adulthood. *Archives of General Psychiatry, 46,* 109–116. (p. 128)

Kandel, E. R., & Schwartz, J. H. (1982). Molecular biology of learning: Modulation of transmitter release. *Science, 218,* 433–443. (p. 327)

Kandler, C., Bleidorn, W., Riemann, R., Spinath, F. M., Thiel, W., & Angleitner, A. (2010). Sources of cumulative continuity in personality: A longitudinal multiple-rater twin study. *Journal of Personality and Social Psychology, 98,* 995–1008. (p. 171)

Kane, G. D. (2010). Revisiting gay men's body image issues: Exposing the fault lines. *Review of General Psychology, 14,* 311–317. (p. 671)

Kane, M. J., Brown, L. H., McVay, J. C., Silvia, P. J., Myin-Germeys, I., & Kwapil, T. R. (2007). For whom the mind wanders, and when: An experience-sampling study of working memory and executive control in daily life. *Psychological Science, 18,* 614–621. (p. 318)

Kaplan, H. I., & Saddock, B. J. (Eds.). (1989). *Comprehensive textbook of psychiatry, V.* Baltimore, MD: Williams and Wilkins. (p. 705)

Kaplan, R. M., & Kronick, R. G. (2006). Marital status and longevity in the United States population. *Journal of Epidemiology and Community Health, 60,* 760–765. (p. 519)

Kaplan, S., Bradley, J. C., Luchman, J. N., & Haynes, D. (2009). On the role of positive and negative affectivity in job performance: A meta-analytic investigation. *Journal of Applied Psychology, 94,* 162–176. (p. 465)

Kapogiannis, D., Barbey, A. K., Sue, M., Zamboni, G., Krueger, F., & Grafman, J. (2009). Cognitive and neural foundations of religious belief. *PNAS, 106,* 4876–4881. (p. 62)

Kaprio, J., Koskenvuo, M., & Rita, H. (1987). Mortality after bereavement: A prospective study of 95,647 widowed persons. *American Journal of Public Health, 77,* 283–287. (p. 506)

Kaptchuk, T. J., Stason, W. B., Davis, R. B., Legedza, A. R. T., Schnyer, R. N., Kerr, C. E., Stone, D. A., Nam, B. H., Kirsch, I., & Goldman, R. H. (2006). Sham device v inert pill: Randomised controlled trial of two placebo treatments. *British Medical Journal, 332,* 391–397. (p. 266)

Karacan, I., Aslan, C., & Hirshkowitz, M. (1983). Erectile mechanisms in man. *Science, 220,* 1080–1082. (p. 95)

Karacan, I., Goodenough, D. R., Shapiro, A., & Starker, S. (1966). Erection cycle during sleep in relation to dream anxiety. *Archives of General Psychiatry, 15,* 183–189. (p. 95)

Karau, S. J., & Williams, K. D. (1993). Social loafing: A meta-analytic review and theoretical integration. *Journal of Personality and Social Psychology, 65,* 681–706. (p. 588)

Karberg, J. C., & James, D. J. (2005, July). Substance dependence, abuse, and treatment of jail inmates, 2002. *Bureau of Justice Statistics Special Report* (NCJ 209588). (p. 601)

Karg, K., Burmeister, M., Shedden, K., & Sen, S. (2011). The serotonin transporter promoters variant (*5-HTTLPR*), stress, and depression meta-analysis revised: Evidence of genetic moderation. *Archives of General Psychiatry, 68,* 444–454. (p. 652)

Kark, J. D., Shemi, G., Friedlander, Y., Martin, O., Manor, O., & Blondheim, S. H. (1996). Does religious observance promote health? Mortality in secular vs. religious kibbutzim in Israel. *American Journal of Public Health, 86,* 341–346. (p. 525)

Karlsgodt, K. H., Sun, D., & Cannon, T. D. (2010). Structural and functional brain abnormalities in schizophrenia. *Current Directions in Psychological Science, 19,* 226–231. (p. 660)

Karni, A., Meyer, G., Rey-Hipolito, C., Jezzard, P., Adams, M. M., Turner, R., & Ungerleider, L. G. (1998). The acquisition of skilled motor performance: Fast and slow experience-driven changes in primary motor cortex. *Proceedings of the National Academy of Sciences, 95,* 861–868. (p. 149)

Karni, A., & Sagi, D. (1994). Dependence on REM sleep for overnight improvement of perceptual skills. *Science, 265,* 679–682. (p. 107)

Karno, M., Golding, J. M., Sorenson, S. B., & Burnam, A. (1988). The epidemiology of obsessive-compulsive disorder in five US communities. *Archives of General Psychiatry, 45,* 1094–1099. (p. 639)

Karpicke, J. D., & Roediger, H. L., III. (2008). The critical importance of retrieval for learning. *Science, 319,* 966–968. (p. 12)

Karremans, J. C., Frankenhis, W. E., & Arons, S. (2010). Blind men prefer a low waist-to-hip ratio. *Evolution and Human Behavior, 31,* 182–186. (p. 611)

Karremans, J. C., Stroebe, W., & Claus, J. (2006). Beyond Vicary's fantasies: The impact of subliminal priming and brand choice. *Journal of Experimental Social Psychology, 42,* 792–798. (p. 227)

Kasen, S., Chen, H., Sneed, J., Crawford, T., & Cohen, P. (2006). Social role and birth cohort influences on gender-linked personality traits in women: A 20-year longitudinal analysis. *Journal of Personality and Social Psychology, 91,* 944–958. (p. 160)

Kashima, Y., Siegal, M., Tanaka, K., & Kashima, E. S. (1992). Do people believe behaviours are consistent with attitudes? Towards a cultural psychology of attribution processes. *British Journal of Social Psychology, 31,* 111–124. (p. 153)

Kashubeck-West, S., & Meyer, J. (2009). The well-being of women who are late deafened. *Journal of Counseling Psychology, 55,* 463–472. (p. 371)

Kasser, T. (2002). *The high price of materialism.* Cambridge, MA: MIT Press. (p. 499)

Kasser, T. (2011). Cultural values and the well-being of future generations: A cross-national study. *Journal of Cross-Cultural Psychology, 42, 42,* 206–215. (p. 499)

Katz-Wise, S. L., Priess, H. A., & Hyde, J. S. (2010). Gender-role attitudes and behavior across the transition to parenthood. *Developmental Psychology, 46,* 18–28. (p. 160)

Kaufman, J., & Zigler, E. (1987). Do abused children become abusive parents? *American Journal of Orthopsychiatry, 57,* 186–192. (p. 192)

Kaufman, J. C., & Baer, J. (2002). I bask in dreams of suicide: Mental illness, poetry, and women. *Review of General Psychology, 6,* 271–286. (p. 647)

Kaufman, L., & Kaufman, J. H. (2000). Explaining the moon illusion. *Proceedings of the National Academy of Sciences, 97,* 500–505. (p. 249)

Kawakami, K., Dunn, E., Karmali, F., & Dovidio, J. F. (2009). Mispredicting affective and behavioral responses to racism. *Science, 323,* 276–278. (p. 594)

Kay, A. C., Baucher, D., Peach, J. M., Laurin, K., Friesen, J., Zanna, M. P., & Spencer, S. J. (2009). Inequality, discrimination, and the power of the status quo: Direct evidence for a motivation to see the way things are as the way they should be. *Journal of Personality and social Psychology, 97,* 421–434. (p. 599)

Kayser, C. (2007, April/May). Listening with your eyes. *Scientific American Mind,* pp. 24–29. (p. 268)

Kayser, D. N., Elliot, A. J., & Felman, R. (2010). Rea and romantic behavior in men viewing women. *European Journal of Social Psychology, 40,* 901–908. (p. 300)

Kazantzis, N., & Dattilio, F. M. (2010b). Definitions of homework, types of homework and ratings of the importance of homework among psychologists with cognitive behavior therapy and psychoanalytic theoretical orientations. *Journal of Clinical Psychology, 66,* 758–773. (p. 687)

Kazantzis, N., Whittington, C., & Dattilio, F. M. (2010a). Meta-analysis of homework effects in cognitive and behavioral therapy: A replication and extension. *Clinical Psychology: Science and Practice, 17,* 144–156. (p. 687)

Kazdin, A. E., & Benjet, C. (2003). Spanking children: Evidence and issues. *Current Directions in Psychological Science, 12,* 99–103. (p. 292)

Keesey, R. E., & Corbett, S. W. (1983). Metabolic defense of the body weight set-point. In A. J. Stunkard & E. Stellar (Eds.), *Eating and its disorders.* New York: Raven Press. (p. 423)

Keith, S. W., & 19 others. (2006). Putative contributors to the secular increase in obesity: Exploring the roads less traveled. *International Journal of Obesity, 30,* 1585–1594. (p. 431)

Keller, J. (2007, March 9). As football players get bigger, more of them risk a dangerous sleep disorder. *Chronicle of Higher Education,* pp. A43–A44. (p. 104)

Keller, M. B., McCullough, J. P., Klein, D. N., Arnow, B., Dunner, D. L., Gelenberg, A. J., Markowitz, J. C., Nemeroff, C. B., Russell, J. M., Thase, M. E., Trivedi, M. H., & Zajecka J. (2000). A comparison of nefazodone, the cognitive behavioral-analysis system of psychotherapy, and their combination for the treatment of chronic depression. *New England Journal of Medicine, 342,* 1462–1470. (p. 706)

Kellerman, J., Lewis, J., & Laird, J. D. (1989). Looking and loving: The effects of mutual gaze on feelings of romantic love. *Journal of Research in Personality, 23,* 145–161. (p. 484)

Kellermann, A. L. (1997). Comment: Gunsmoke—changing public attitudes toward smoking and firearms. *American Journal of Public Health, 87,* 910–913. (p. 599)

Kellermann, A. L., Rivara, F. P., Rushforth, N. B., Banton, H. G., Feay, D. T., Francisco, J. T., Locci, A. B., Prodzinski, J., Hackman, B. B., & Somes, G. (1993). Gun ownership as a risk factor for homicide in the home. *New England Journal of Medicine, 329,* 1084–1091. (p. 599)

Kellermann, A. L., Somes, G., Rivara, F. P., Lee, R. K., & Banton, J. G. (1998). Injuries and deaths due to firearms in the home. *Journal of Trauma, 45,* 263–267. (p. 599)

Kelling, S. T., & Halpern, B. P. (1983). Taste flashes: Reaction times, intensity, and quality. *Science, 219,* 412–414. (p. 267)

Kellner, C. H., & 16 others. (2006). Continuation electroconvulsive therapy vs. pharmacotherapy for relapse prevention in major depression: A multisite study from the Consortium for Research in Electroconvulsive Therapy (CORE). *Archives of General Psychiatry, 63,* 1337–1344. (p. 708)

Kelly, A. E. (2000). Helping construct desirable identities: A self-presentational view of psychotherapy. *Psychological Bulletin, 126,* 475–494. (p. 686)

Kelly, D. J., Quinn, P. C., Slater, A. M., Lee, K., Ge, L., & Pascalis, O. (2007). The other-race effect develops during infancy: Evidence of perceptual narrowing. *Psychological Science, 18,* 1084–1089. (p. 598)

Kelly, I. W. (1997). Modern astrology: A critique. *Psychological Reports, 81,* 1035–1066. (p. 550)

Kelly, I. W. (1998). Why astrology doesn't work. *Psychological Reports, 82,* 527–546. (p. 550)

Kelly, S. D., Özyürek, A., & Maris, E. (2010). Two sides of the same coin: Speech and gesture mutually interact to enhance comprehension. *Psychological Science, 21,* 260–267. (p. 374)

Kelly, T. A. (1990). The role of values in psychotherapy: A critical review of process and outcome effects. *Clinical Psychology Review, 10,* 171–186. (p. 700)

Kempe, R. S., & Kempe, C. C. (1978). *Child abuse.* Cambridge, MA: Harvard University Press. (p. 192)

Kempton, M. J., Geddes, J. R., Ettinger, U., Williams, S. C. R., & Grasby, P. M. (2008). Meta-analysis, database, and meta-regression of 98 structural imaging studies in bipolar disorder. *Archives of General Psychiatry, 65,* 1017–1032. (p. 652)

Kendall-Tackett, K. A. (Ed.). (2004). *Health consequences of abuse in the family: A clinical guide for evidence-based practice.* Washington, DC: American Psychological Association. (p. 192)

Kendall-Tackett, K. A., Williams, L. M., & Finkelhor, D. (1993). Impact of sexual abuse on children: A review and synthesis of recent empirical studies. *Psychological Bulletin, 113,* 164–180. (pp. 192, 346)

Kendler, K. S. (1996). Parenting: A genetic-epidemiologic perspective. *The American Journal of Psychiatry, 153,* 11–20. (p. 195)

Kendler, K. S. (1997). Social support: A genetic-epidemiologic analysis. *American Journal of Psychiatry, 154,* 1398–1404. (p. 556)

Kendler, K. S. (1998, January). Major depression and the environment: A psychiatric genetic perspective. *Pharmacopsychiatry, 31*(1), 5–9. (p. 648)

Kendler, K. S. (2011). A statement from Kenneth S. Kendler, M.D., on the proposal to eliminate the grief exclusion criterion from major depression. www.dsm5.org. (p. 631)

Kendler, K. S., Gardner, C. O., & Prescott, C. A. (2006). Toward a comprehensive developmental model for major depression in men. *American Journal of Psychiatry, 163,*115–124. (p. 648)

Kendler, K. S., Jacobson, K. C., Myers, J., & Prescott, C. A. (2002a). Sex differences in genetic and environmental risk factors for irrational fears and phobias. *Psychological Medicine, 32,* 209–217. (p. 643)

Kendler, K. S., Karkowski, L. M., & Prescott, C. A. (1999). Fears and phobias: Reliability and heritability. *Psychological Medicine, 29,* 539–553. (p. 643)

Kendler, K. S., Myers, J., & Prescott, C. A. (2002b). The etiology of phobias: An evaluation of the stress-diathesis model. *Archives of General Psychiatry, 59,* 242–248. (p. 643)

Kendler, K. S., Myers, J., & Zisook, S. (2008). Does bereavement-related major depression differ from major depression associated with other stressful life events? *American Journal of Psychiatry, 165,* 1449–1455. (p. 648)

Kendler, K. S., Neale, M. C., Kessler, R. C., Heath, A. C., & Eaves, L. J. (1992). Generalized anxiety disorder in women: A population-based twin study. *Archives of General Psychiatry, 49,* 267–272. (p. 643)

Kendler, K. S., Neale, M. C., Thornton, L. M., Aggen, S. H., Gilman, S. E., & Kessler, R. C. (2002). Cannabis use in the last year in a U.S. national sample of twin and sibling pairs. *Psychological Medicine, 32,* 551–554. (p. 126)

Kendler, K. S., Thornton, L. M., & Gardner, C. O. (2001). Genetic risk, number of previous depressive episodes, and stressful life events in predicting onset of major depression. *American Journal of Psychiatry, 158,* 582–586. (p. 648)

Kennedy, S., & Over, R. (1990). Psychophysiological assessment of male sexual arousal following spinal cord injury. *Archives of Sexual Behavior, 19,* 15–27. (p. 57)

Kennedy, S. H., Giacobbe, P., Rizvi, S. J., Placenza, F. M., Nishikawa, Y., Mayberg, H. S., & Lozano, A. M. (2011). Deep brain stimulation for treatment-resistant depression: Follow-up after 3 to 6 years. *American Journal of Psychiatry, 168,* 502–510. (p. 710)

Kenrick, D. T., & Funder, D. C. (1988). Profiting from controversy: Lessons from the person-situation debate. *American Psychologist, 43,* 23–34. (p. 554)

Kenrick, D. T., Griskevicious, V., Neuberg, S. L., & Schaller, M. (2010). Renovating the pyramid of needs: Contemporary extensions build upon ancient foundations. *Perspectives on Psychological Science, 5,* 292–314. (p. 421)

Kenrick, D. T., & Gutierres, S. E. (1980). Contrast effects and judgments of physical attractiveness: When beauty becomes a social problem. *Journal of Personality and Social Psychology, 38,* 131–140. (p. 438)

Kenrick, D. T., Gutierres, S. E., & Goldberg, L. L. (1989). Influence of popular erotica on judgments of strangers and mates. *Journal of Experimental Social Psychology, 25,* 159–167. (p. 438)

Kenrick, D. T., Nieuweboer, S., & Buunk, A. P. (2009). Universal mechanisms and cultural diversity: Replacing the blank slate with a coloring book. In M. Schaller, A. Norenzayan, S. Heine, A. Norenzayan, T. Yamagishi, & T. Kameda (eds.), *Evolution, culture, and the human mind.* Mahwah, NJ: Lawrence Erlbaum. (pp. 145, 148)

Kensinger, E. A. (2007). Negative emotion enhances memory accuracy: Behavioral and neuroimaging evidence. *Current Directions in Psychological Science, 16,* 213–218. (p. 326)

Keough, K. A., Zimbardo, P. G., & Boyd, J. N. (1999). Who's smoking, drinking, and using drugs? Time perspective as a predictor of substance use. *Basic and Applied Social Psychology, 2,* 149–164. (p. 534)

Kernis, M. H. (2003). Toward a conceptualization of optimal self-esteem. *Psychological Inquiry, 14,* 1–26. (p. 568)

Kerr, N. L., & Bruun, S. E. (1983). Dispensability of member effort and group motivation losses: Free-rider effects. *Journal of Personality and Social Psychology, 44,* 78–94. (p. 588)

Kerr, R. A. (2009). Amid worrisome signs of warming, 'climate fatigue' sets in. *Science,* 326, 926–928. (p. 574)

Kessing, L. V., Forman, J. L., & Andersen, P. K. (2010). Does lithium protect against dementia? *Bipolar Disorders, 12,* 87–94. (p. 707)

Kessler, D., Lewis, G., Kaur, S., Wiles, N., King, M., Welch, S., Sharp, D. J., Araya, R., Hollinghurst, & Peters, T. J. (2009). Therapist-delivered Internet psychotherapy for depression primary care: A randomized controlled trial. *The Lancet, 374,* 628–634. (p. 688)

Kessler, M., & Albee, G. (1975). Primary prevention. *Annual Review of Psychology, 26,* 557–591. (p. 702)

Kessler, R. C. (2000). Posttraumatic stress disorder: The burden to the individual and to society. *Journal of Clinical Psychiatry, 61*(suppl. 5), 4–12. (p. 640)

Kessler, R. C. & 12 others. (2010). Structure and diagnosis of adult attention-deficit/hyperactivity disorder: Analysis of expanded symptom criteria from the adult ADHD Clinical Diagnostic Scale. *Archives of General Psychiatry, 67,* 1168–1178. (p. 627)

Kessler, R. C. & 22 others. (2010). Age differences in the prevalence and co-morbidity of DSM-IV major depressive episodes: Results from the WHO World Mental Health Survey Initiative. *Depression and Anxiety, 27,* 351–364. (p. 649)

Kessler, R. C., Akiskal, H. S., Ames, M., Birnbaum, H., Greenberg, P., Hirschfeld, R. M. A., Jin, R., Merikangas, K. R., Simon, G. E., & Wang, P. S. (2006). Prevalence and effects of mood disorders on work performance in a nationally representative sample of U.S. workers. *American Journal of Psychiatry, 163,* 1561–1568. (p. 647)

Kessler, R. C., Berglund, P., Demler, O., Jin, R., Merikangos, K. R., & Walters, E. E. (2005). Lifetime prevalence and age-of-onset distributions of DSM-IV disorders in the National Comorbidity Survey Replication. *Archives of General Psychiatry, 62,* 593–602. (pp. 631, 634)

Kessler, R. C., Foster, C., Joseph, J., Ostrow, D., Wortman, C., Phair, J., & Chmiel, J. (1991). Stressful life events and symptom onset in HIV infection. *American Journal of Psychiatry, 148,* 733–738. (p. 512)

Kessler, R. C., Soukup, J., Davis, R. B., Foster, D. F., Wilkey, S. A., Van Rompay, M. I., & Eisenberg, D. M. (2001). The use of complementary and alternative therapies to treat anxiety and depression in the United States. *American Journal of Psychiatry, 158,* 289–294. (p. 696)

Keynes, M. (1980, December 20/27). Handel's illnesses. *Lancet,* pp. 1354–1355. (p. 647)

Keys, A., Brozek, J., Henschel, A., Mickelsen, O., & Taylor, H. L. (1950). *The biology of human starvation.* Minneapolis: University of Minnesota Press. (p. 421)

Kiecolt-Glaser, J. K. (2009). Psychoneuroimmunology: Psychology's gateway to the biomedical future. *Perspectives on Psychological Science, 4,* 367–369. (p. 509)

Kiecolt-Glaser, J. K., & Glaser, R. (1995). Psychoneuroimmunology and health consequences: Data and shared mechanisms. *Psychosomatic Medicine, 57,* 269–274. (p. 511)

Kiecolt-Glaser, J. K., Loving, T. J., Stowell, J. R., Malarkey, W. B., Lemeshow, S., Dickinson, S. L., & Glaser, R. (2005). Hostile marital interactions, proinflammatory cytokine production, and wound healing. *Archives of General Psychiatry, 62,* 1377–1384. (p. 510)

Kiecolt-Glaser, J. K., Page, G. G., Marucha, P. T., MacCallum, R. C., & Glaser, R. (1998). Psychological influences on surgical recovery: Perspectives from psychoneuroimmunology. *American Psychologist, 53,* 1209–1218. (p. 510)

Kiehl, K. A., & Buckholtz, J. W. (2010, September/October). Inside the mind of a psychopath. *Scientific American Mind,* pp. 22–29. (p. 670)

Kihlstrom, J. F. (2005). Dissociative disorders. *Annual Review of Clinical Psychology, 1,* 227–253. (p. 667)

Kihlstrom, J. F. (2006). Repression: A unified theory of a will-o'-the-wisp. *Behavioral and Brain Sciences, 29,* 523. (p. 540)

Killingsworth, M. A., & Gilbert, D. T. (2010). A wandering mind is an unhappy mind. *Science, 330,* 932. (pp. 454, 457)

Kim, B. S. K., Ng, G. F., & Ahn, A. J. (2005). Effects of client expectation for counseling success, client-counselor worldview match, and client adherence to Asian and European American cultural values on counseling process with Asian Americans. *Journal of Counseling Psychology, 52,* 67–76. (p. 700)

Kim, G., & Tong, A. (2010, February 23). Airline passengers have grown, seats haven't. *Sacramento Bee* (reprinted by *Grand Rapids Press,* pp. B1, B3). (p. 432)

Kim, H., & Markus, H. R. (1999). Deviance or uniqueness, harmony or conformity? A cultural analysis. *Journal of Personality and Social Psychology, 77,* 785–800. (p. 154)

Kimata, H. (2001). Effect of humor on allergen-induced wheal reactions. *Journal of the American Medical Association, 285,* 737. (p. 519)

Kimble, G. A. (1981). *Biological and cognitive constraints on learning.* Washington, DC: American Psychological Association. (p. 298)

Kindt, M., Soeter, M., & Vervliet, B. (2009). Beyond extinction: erasing human fear responses and preventing the return of fear. *Nature Neuroscience, 12,* 256–258. (p. 644)

King, M., & Bartlett, A. (2006). What same sex civil partnerships may mean for health. *Journal of Epidemiology and Community Health, 60,* 188–191. (p. 443)

King, R. N., & Koehler, D. J. (2000). Illusory correlations in graphological interference. *Journal of Experimental Psychology: Applied, 6,* 336–348. (p. 550)

King, S., St-Hilaire, A., & Heidkamp, D. (2010). Prenatal factors in schizophrenia. *Current Directions in Psychological Science, 19,* 209–213. (p. 660)

Kingston, D. W., Malamuth, N. M., Fedoroff, N. M., & Marshall, W. L. (2009). The importance of individual differences in pornography use: Theoretical perspectives and implications for treating sexual offenders. *Journal of Sex Research, 46,* 216–232. (p. 603)

Kinnier, R. T., & Metha, A. T. (1989). Regrets and priorities at three stages of life. *Counseling and Values,* 33, 182–193. (p. 218)

Kinzler, K. D., Shutts, K., Dejesus, J., & Spelke, E. S. (2009). Accent trumps race in guiding children's social preferences. *Social Cognition, 27,* 623–634. (p. 596)

Kirby, D. (2002). Effective approaches to reducing adolescent unprotected sex, pregnancy, and childbearing. *Journal of Sex Research, 39,* 51–57. (p. 441)

Kirkpatrick, B., Fenton, W. S., Carpenter, W. T., Jr., & Marder, S. R. (2006). The NIMH-MATRICS consensus statement on negative symptoms. *Schizophrenia Bulletin,* 32, 214–219. (p. 659)

Kirkpatrick, L. (1999). Attachment and religious representations and behavior. In J. Cassidy & P. R. Shaver (Eds.), *Handbook of attachment.* New York: Guilford. (p. 188)

Kirkpatrick, R. M., McGue, M., & Iacono, W. G. (2009). Shared-environmental contributions to high cognitive ability. *Behavior Genetics,* 39, 406–416. (p. 406)

Kirsch, I. (1996). Hypnotic enhancement of cognitive-behavioral weight loss treatments: Another meta-reanalysis. *Journal of Consulting and Clinical Psychology, 64,* 517–519. (p. 111)

Kirsch, I. (2010). *The emperor's new drugs: Exploding the antidepressant myth.* New York: Basic Books. (pp. 35, 706)

Kirsch, I., & Braffman, W. (2001). Imaginative suggestibility and hypnotizability. *Current Directions in Psychological Science, 10,* 57–61. (p. 110)

Kirsch, I., Deacon, B. J., Huedo-Medina, T. B., Scoboria, A., Moore, T. J., & Johnson, B. T. (2008). Initial severity and antidepressant benefits: A meta-analysis of data submitted to the Food and Drug Administration. *Public Library of Science Medicine, 5,* e45. (p. 706)

Kirsch, I., & Lynn, S. J. (1995). The altered state of hypnosis. *American Psychologist, 50,* 846–858. (p. 111)

Kirsch, I., Moore, T. J., Scoboria, A., & Nicholls, S. S. (2002, July 15). New study finds little difference between effects of antidepressants and placebo. *Prevention and Treatment* (journals.apa.org/prevention). (p. 706)

Kirsch, I., & Sapirstein, G. (1998). Listening to Prozac but hearing placebo: A meta-analysis of antidepressant medication. *Prevention and Treatment, 1,* posted June 26 at (journals.apa.org/prevention/volume1). (p. 706)

Kisley, M. A., Wood, S., & Burrows, C. L. (2007). Looking at the sunny side of life: Age-related change in an event-related potential measure of the negativity bias. *Psychological Science, 18,* 838–843. (p. 218)

Kisor, H. (1990). *What's that pig outdoors.* New York: Hill and Wang. (p. 371)

Kitayama, S., Conway, III, L. G., Pietromonaci, P. R., Park, H., & Plaut, V. C. (2010). Ethos of independence across regions in the United States: The production-adoption model of cultural change. *American Psychologist, 65,* 559–574. (p. 155)

Kitayama, S., Ishii, K., Imada, T., Takemura, K., & Ramaswamy, J. (2006). Voluntary settlement and the spirit of independence: Evidence from Japan's "northern frontier." *Journal of Personality and Social Psychology, 91,* 369–384. (p. 154)

Kitayama, S., Park, H., Sevincer, A. T., Karasawa, M., & Uskul, A. K. (2009). A cultural task analysis of implicit independence: Comparing North America, Western Europe, and East Asia. *Journal of Personality and Social Psychology, 97,* 236–255. (pp. 155, 572)

Kitts, R. L. (2005). Gay adolescents and suicide: Understanding the association. *Adolescence, 40,* 621–628. (p. 443)

Kivimaki, M., Leino-Arjas, P., Luukkonen, R., Rihimaki, H., & Kirjonen, J. (2002). Work stress and risk of cardiovascular mortality: Prospective cohort study of industrial employees. *British Medical Journal, 325,* 857. (p. 518)

Klayman, J., & Ha, Y-W. (1987). Confirmation, disconfirmation, and information in hypothesis testing. *Psychological Review, 94,* 211–228. (p. 353)

Klein, D. N. (2010). Chronic depression: Diagnosis and classification. *Current Directions in Psychological Science, 19,* 96–100. (p. 648)

Klein, D. N., & 16 others. (2003). Therapeutic alliance in depression treatment: Controlling for prior change and patient characteristics. *Journal of Consulting and Clinical Psychology, 71,* 997–1006. (p. 699)

Kleinke, C. L. (1986). Gaze and eye contact: A research review. *Psychological Bulletin, 1000,* 78–100. (p. 484)

Kleinmuntz, B., & Szucko, J. J. (1984). A field study of the fallibility of polygraph lie detection. *Nature, 308,* 449–450. (p. 481)

Kleitman, N. (1960, November). Patterns of dreaming. *Scientific American,* pp. 82–88. (p. 93)

Klemm, W. R. (1990). Historical and introductory perspectives on brainstem-mediated behaviors. In W. R. Klemm & R. P. Vertes (Eds.), *Brainstem mechanisms of behavior.* New York: Wiley. (p. 63)

Klimstra, T. A., Hale, III, W. W., Raaijmakers, Q. A. W., Branje, S. J. T., & Meeus, W. H. J. (2009). Maturation of personality in adolescence. *Journal of Personality and Social Psychology, 96,* 898–912. (p. 204)

Kline, D., & Schieber, F. (1985). Vision and aging. In J. E. Birren & K. W. Schaie (Eds.), *Handbook of the psychology of aging.* New York: Van Nostrand Reinhold. (p. 210)

Klinke, R., Kral, A., Heid, S., Tillein, J., & Hartmann, R. (1999). Recruitment of the auditory cortex in congenitally deaf cats by long-term cochlear electrostimulation. *Science, 285,* 1729–1733. (p. 260)

Kluft, R. P. (1991). Multiple personality disorder. In A. Tasman & S. M. Goldfinger (Eds.), *Review of Psychiatry* (Vol. 10). Washington, DC: American Psychiatric Press. (p. 666)

Klump, K. L., & Culbert, K. M. (2007). Molecular genetic studies of eating disorders: Current status and future directions. *Current Directions in Psychological Science, 16,* 37–41. (p. 671)

Klump, K. L., Suisman, J. L., Burt, S. A., McGue, M., & Iacono, W. G. (2009). Genetic and environmental influences on disordered eating: An adoption study. *Journal of Abnormal Psychology, 118,* 797–805. (p. 671)

Knapp, S., & VandeCreek, L. (2000, August). Recovered memories of childhood abuse: Is there an underlying professional consensus? *Professional Psychology: Research and Practice, 31,* 365–371. (p. 346)

Knäuper, B., Kornik, R., Atkinson, K., Guberman, C., & Aydin, C. (2005). Motivation influences the underestimation of cumulative risk. *Personality and Social Psychology Bulletin, 31,* 1511–1523. (p. 441)

Knickmeyer, E. (2001, August 7). In Africa, big is definitely better. *Seattle Times,* p. A7. (p. 671)

Knight, R. T. (2007). Neural networks debunk phrenology. *Science, 316,* 1578–1579. (p. 75)

Knight, W. (2004, August 2). Animated face helps deaf with phone chat. NewScientist.com. (p. 268)

Knoblich, G., & Oellinger, M. (2006, October/November). The Eureka moment. *Scientific American Mind,* pp. 38–43. (p. 353)

Knutson, K. L., Spiegel, K., Penev, P., & Van Cauter, E. (2007). The metabolic consequences of sleep deprivation. *Sleep Medicine Reviews, 11,* 163–178. (p. 102)

Ko, C-K., Yen, J-Y., Chen, C-C., Chen, S-H., & Yen, C-F. (2005). Proposed diagnostic criteria of Internet addiction for adolescents. *Journal of Nervous and Mental Disease, 193,* 728–733. (p. 116)

Koch, C., & Greenfield, S. (2007, October). How does consciousness happen? *Scientific American,* pp. 76–83. (p. 85)

Koenen, K. C., Moffitt, T. E., Roberts, A. L., Martin, L. T., Kubzansky, L., Harrington, H., Poulton, R., & Caspi, A. (2009). Childhood IQ and adult mental disorders: A test of the cognitive reserve hypothesis. *American Journal of Psychiatry, 166,* 50–57. (p. 403)

Koenig, H. G., King, D. E., & Carson, V. B. (2011). *Handbook of religion and health.* New York: Oxford University Press. (p. 525)

Koenig, H. G., & Larson, D. B. (1998). Use of hospital services, religious attendance, and religious affiliation. *Southern Medical Journal, 91,* 925–932. (p. 528)

Koenig, L. B., McGue, M., Krueger, R. F., & Bouchard, T. J., Jr. (2005). Genetic and environmental influences on religiousness: Findings for retrospective and current religiousness ratings. *Journal of Personality, 73,* 471–488. (p. 137)

Koenig, L. B., & Vaillant, G. E. (2009). A prospective study of church attendance and health over the lifespan. *Health Psychology, 28,* 117–124. (p. 527)

Koenigs, M., Young, L., Adolphs, R., Tranel, D., Cushman, F., Hauser, M., & Damasio, A. (2007). Damage to the prefrontal cortex increases utilitarian moral judgements. *Nature, 446,* 908–911. (p. 74)

Koestner, R., Lekes, N., Powers, T. A., & Chicoine, E. (2002). Attaining personal goals: Self-concordance plus implementation intentions equals success. *Journal of Personality and Social Psychology, 83,* 231–244. (p. 467)

Kohlberg, L. (1981). *The philosophy of moral development: Essays on moral development* (Vol. I). San Francisco: Harper & Row. (p. 200)

Kohlberg, L. (1984). *The psychology of moral development: Essays on moral development* (Vol. II). San Francisco: Harper & Row. (p. 200)

Kohler, C. G., Walker, J. B., Martin, E. A., Healey, K. M., & Moberg, P. J. (2010). Facial emotion perception in schizophrenia: A meta-analytic review. *Schizophrenia Bulletin, 36,* 1009–1019. (p. 658)

Kohler, I. (1962, May). Experiments with goggles. *Scientific American,* pp. 62–72. (p. 251)

Köhler, W. (1925; reprinted 1957). *The mentality of apes.* London: Pelican. (p. 362)

Kohn, P. M., & Macdonald, J. E. (1992). The survey of recent life experiences: A decontaminated hassles scale for adults. *Journal of Behavioral Medicine, 15,* 221–236. (p. 507)

Kolassa, I-T., & Elbert, T. (2007). Structural and functional neuroplasticity in relation to traumatic stress. *Current Directions in Psychological Science, 16,* 321–325. (p. 643)

Kolata, G. (1987). Metabolic catch-22 of exercise regimens. *Science, 236,* 146–147. (p. 433)

Kolata, G. (2010, January 21). I.O.C. panel calls for treatment in sex ambiguity cases. *New York Times* (www.nytimes.com). (p. 161)

Kolata, G. (2010, July 16). Drug trials test bold plan to slow Alzheimer's. *New York Times* (www.nytimes.com). (p. 212)

Kolb, B. (1989). Brain development, plasticity, and behavior. *American Psychologist, 44,* 1203–1212. (p. 75)

Kolb, B., & Whishaw, I. Q. (1998). Brain plasticity and behavior. *Annual Review of Psychology, 49,* 43–64. (p. 149)

Kolb, B., & Whishaw, I. Q. (2006). *An introduction to brain and behavior,* 2nd edition. New York: Worth Publishers. (p. 387)

Kolivas, E. D., & Gross, A. M. (2007). Assessing sexual aggression: Addressing the gap between rape victimization and perpetration prevalence rates. *Aggression and Violent Behavior, 12,* 315–328. (p. 145)

Kolker, K. (2002, December 8). Video violence disturbs some: Others scoff at influence. *Grand Rapids Press,* pp. A1, A12. (p. 604)

Kolodziej, M. E., & Johnson, B. T. (1996). Interpersonal contact and acceptance of persons with psychiatric disorders: A research synthesis. *Journal of Consulting and Clinical Psychology, 64,* 1387–1396. (p. 632)

Koltko-Rivera, M. E. (2006). Rediscovering the later version of Maslow's hierarchy of needs: Self-transcendence and opportunities for theory, research, and unification. *Review of General Psychology, 10,* 302–317. (p. 421)

Konkle, T., Brady, T. F., Alvarez, G. A., & Oliva, A. (2010). Conceptual distinctiveness supports detailed visual long-term memory for real-world objects. *Journal of Experimental Psychology: General, 139,* 558–578. (p. 312)

Konrath, S. H., O'Brien E. H., & Hsing, C. (2011). Changes in dispositional empathy in American college students over time: A meta-analysis. *Personality and Social Psychology Review, 15,* 180–198. (p. 567)

Kontula, O., & Haavio-Mannila, E. (2009). The impact of aging on human sexual activity and sexual desire. *Journal of Sex Research, 46,* 46–56. (p. 209)

Koole, S. L., Greenberg, J., & Pyszczynski, T. (2006). Introducing science to the psychology of the soul. *Current Directions in Psychological Science, 15,* 212–216. (p. 541)

Kornell, N., & Bjork, R. A. (2008). Learning concepts and categories: Is spacing the "enemy of induction?" *Psychological Science, 19,* 585–592. (p. 13)

Kosfeld, M., Heinrichs, M., Zak, P. J., Fischbacher, U., & Fehr, E. (2005). Oxytocin increases trust in humans. *Nature, 435,* 673–676. (p. 58)

Kosslyn, S. M. (2005). Reflective thinking and mental imagery: A perspective on the development of posttraumatic stress disorder. *Development and Psychopathology, 17,* 851–863. (p. 640)

Kosslyn, S. M., & Koenig, O. (1992). *Wet mind: The new cognitive neuroscience.* New York: Free Press. (p. 56)

Kosslyn, S. M., Thompson, W. L., Costantini-Ferrando, M. F., Alpert, N. M., & Spiegel, D. (2000). Hypnotic visual illusion alters color processing in the brain. *American Journal of Psychiatry, 157,* 1279–1284. (p. 113)

Kotchick, B. A., Shaffer, A., & Forehand, R. (2001). Adolescent sexual risk behavior: A multi-system perspective. *Clinical Psychology Review, 21,* 493–519. (p. 439)

Koten, J. W., Jr., Wood, G., Hagoort, P., Goebel, R., Propping, P., Willmes, K., & Boomsma, D. I. (2009). Genetic contribution to variation in cognitive function: An fMRI study in twins. *Science, 323,* 1737–1740. (p. 405)

Kotkin, M., Daviet, C., & Gurin, J. (1996). The *Consumer Reports* mental health survey. *American Psychologist, 51,* 1080–1082. (p. 692)

Kounios, J., & Beeman, M. (2009). The *Aha!* moment: The cognitive neuroscience of insight. *Current Directions in Psychological Science, 18,* 210–215. (p. 353)

Kovács, Á., & Mehler, J. (2009). Cognitive gains in 7-month-old bilingual infants. *Proceedings of the National Academy of Sciences, 106,* 6556–6560. (p. 377)

Kovács, Á. M., Téglás, E., & Endress, A. D. (2010). The social sense: Susceptibility to others' beliefs in human infants and adults. *Science, 330,* 1830–1834. (p. 183)

Kposowa, A. J., & D'Auria, S. (2009). Association of temporal factors and suicides in the United States, 2000–2004. *Social Psychiatry and Psychiatric Epidemiology, 45,* 433–445. (p. 650)

Kraft, C. (1978). A psychophysical approach to air safety: Simulator studies of visual illusions in night approaches. In H. L. Pick, H. W. Leibowitz, J. E. Singer, A. Steinschneider, & H. W. Stevenson (Eds.), *Psychology: From research to practice.* New York: Plenum Press. (pp. 469, 470)

Kraft, R. N. (2002). *Memory perceived: Recalling the Holocaust.* Westport, CT: Praeger. (p. 347)

Kramer, A. (2010). Personal corrspondence. (p. 496)

Kramer, A. F., & Erickson, K. I. (2007). Capitalizing on cortical plasticity: Influence of physical activity on cognition and brain function. *Trends in Cognitive Sciences, 11,* 342–348. (p. 521)

Kramer, M. S., & 17 others. (2008). Breastfeeding and child cognitive development: New evidence from a large randomized trial. *Archives of General Psychiatry, 65,* 578–584. (p. 35)

Kramer, P. D. (2011, July 9). In defense of antidepressants. *New York Times* (www.nytimes.com). (p. 705)

Kranz, F., & Ishai, A. (2006). Face perception is modulated by sexual preference. *Current Biology, 16,* 63–68. (p. 445)

Kraul, C. (2010, October 12). Chief engineer knew it would take a miracle. *Los Angeles Times* (www.latimes.com). (p. 253)

Kraus, N., Malmfors, T., & Slovic, P. (1992). Intuitive toxicology: Expert and lay judgments of chemical risks. *Risk Analysis, 12,* 215–232. (p. 359)

Kraut, R., Patterson, M., Lundmark, V., Kiesler, S., Mukopadhyay, T., & Scherlis, W. (1998). Internet paradox: A social technology that reduces social involvement and psychological well being? *American Psychologist, 53,* 1017–1031. (p. 453)

Kraut, R. E., & Johnston, R. E. (1979). Social and emotional messages of smiling: An ethological approach. *Journal of Personality and Social Psychology, 37,* 1539–1553. (p. 488)

KRC Research & Consulting. (2001, August 7). Memory isn't quite what it used to be (survey for General Nutrition Centers). *USA Today,* p. D1. (p. 213)

Krebs, D. L., & Van Hesteren, F. (1994). The development of altruism: Toward an integrative model. *Developmental Review, 14,* 103–158. (p. 202)

Krijn, M., Emmelkamp, P. M. G., Olafsson, R. P., & Biemond, R. (2004). Virtual reality exposure therapy of anxiety disorders: A review. *Clinical Psychology Review, 24,* 259–281. (p. 682)

Kring, A. M., & Caponigro, J. M. (2010). Emotion in schizophrenia: Where feeling meets thinking. *Current Directions in Psychological Science, 19,* 255–259. (p. 658)

Kring, A. M., & Gordon, A. H. (1998). Sex differences in emotion: Expression, experience, and physiology. *Journal of Personality and Social Psychology, 74,* 686–703. (pp. 486, 487)

Kristensen, P., & Bjerkedal, T. (2007). Explaining the relation between birth order and intelligence. *Science, 316,* 1717. (p. 42)

Kristof, N. D. (2004, July 21). Saying no to killers. *New York Times* (www.nytimes.com). (p. 615)

Kristof, N. D. (2010, September 18). Message to Muslims: I'm sorry. *New York Times* (www.nytimes.com). (p. 594)

Króliczak, G., Heard, P., Goodale, M. A., & Gregory, R. L. (2006). Dissociation of perception and action unmasked by the hollow-face illusion. *Brain Research, 1080,* 9–16. (p. 86)

Krosnick, J. A. (2010, June 8). The climate majority. *New York Times* (www.nytimes.com). (p. 360)

Kross, E., Berman, M. G., Mischel, W., Smith, E. E., & Wager, T. D. (2011). Social rejection shares somatosensory representations with physical pain. *PNAS, 108,* 6270–6275. (p. 452)

Kruger, J., & Dunning, D. (1999). Unskilled and unaware of it: How difficulties in recognizing one's own incompetence lead to inflated self-assessments. *Journal of Personality and Social Psychology, 77,* 1121–1134. (p. 561)

Kruger, J., Epley, N., Parker, J., & Ng, Z-W. (2005). Egocentrism over e-mail: Can we communicate as well as we think? *Journal of Personality and Social Psychology, 89,* 925–936. (pp. 182, 485)

Krueger, J., & Killham, E. (2005, December 8). At work, feeling good matters. *Gallup Management Journal* (www.gmj.gallup.com). (p. 466)

Krueger, J., & Killham, E. (2006, March 9). Why Dilbert is right. Uncomfortable work environments make for disgruntled employees—just like the cartoon says. *Gallup Management Journal* (www.gmj.gallup.com). (p. 558)

Krupa, D. J., Thompson, J. K., & Thompson, R. F. (1993). Localization of a memory trace in the mammalian brain. *Science, 260,* 989–991. (p. 325)

Krützen, M., Mann, J., Heithaus, M. R., Connor, R. C., Bejder, L., & Sherwin, W. B. (2005). Cultural transmission of tool use in bottlenose dolphins. *Proceedings of the National Academy of Sciences, 102,* 8939–8943. (p. 363)

Kubey, R., & Csikszentmihalyi, M. (2002, February). Television addiction is no mere metaphor. *Scientific American,* pp. 74–80. (p. 307)

Kübler, A., Winter, S., Ludolph, A. C., Hautzinger, M., & Birbaumer, N. (2005). Severity of depressive symptoms and quality of life in patients with amyotrophic lateral sclerosis. *Neurorehabilitation and Neural Repair, 19*(3), 182–193. (p. 497)

Kubzansky, L. D., Koenen, K. C., Jones, C., & Eaton, W. W. (2009). A prospective study of posttraumatic stress disorder symptoms and coronary heart disease in women. *Health Psychology, 28,* 125–130. (p. 514)

Kubzansky, L. D., Sparrow, D., Vokanas, P., & Kawachi, I. (2001). Is the glass half empty or half full? A prospective study of optimism and coronary heart disease in the normative aging study. *Psychosomatic Medicine, 63,* 910–916. (p. 513)

Kuhl, B. A., Dudukovic, N. M., Kahn, I., & Wagner, A. D. (2007). Decreased demands on cognitive control reveal the neural processing benefits of forgetting. *Nature Neuroscience, 10,* 908–914. (p. 338)

Kuhl, P. K., & Meltzoff, A. N. (1982). The bimodal perception of speech in infancy. *Science, 218,* 1138–1141. (p. 367)

Kuhn, D. (2006). Do cognitive changes accompany developments in the adolescent brain? *Perspectives on Psychological Science, 1,* 59–67. (p. 199)

Kujala, U. M., Kaprio, J., Sarna, S., & Koskenvuo, M. (1998). Relationship of leisure-time physical activity and mortality: The Finnish twin cohort. *Journal of the American Medical Association, 279,* 440–444. (p. 521)

Kuncel, N. R., & Hezlett, S. A. (2007). Standardized tests predict graduate students' success. *Science, 315,* 1080–1081. (p. 397)

Kuncel, N. R., & Hezlett, S. A. (2010). Fact and fiction in cognitive ability testing for admissions and hiring decisions. *Current Directions in Psychological Science, 19,* 339–345. (p. 385)

Kunkel, D. (2001, February 4). *Sex on TV.* Menlo Park, CA: Henry J. Kaiser Family Foundation (www.kff.org). (p. 440)

Kunkel, D., Cope-Farrar, K., Biely, E., Farinola, W. J. M., & Donnerstein, E. (2001). *Sex on TV (2): A biennial report to the Kaiser Family Foundation.* Menlo Park, CA: Kaiser Family Foundation. (p. 603)

Kuntsche, E., Knibbe, R., Gmel, G., & Engels, R. (2005). Why do young people drink? A review of drinking motives. *Clinical Psychology Review, 25,* 841–861. (p. 127)

Kupfer, D. J., & Regier, D. A. (2010). Why all of medicine should care about DSM-5. *JAMA, 303,* 1974–1975. (p. 630)

Kuppens, P., Allen, N. B., & Sheeber, L. B. (2010). Emotional inertia and psychological maladjustment. *Psychological Science, 21,* 984–991. (p. 653)

Kupper, N., & Denollet, J. (2007). Type D personality as a prognostic factor in heart disease: Assessment and mediating mechanisms. *Journal of Personality Assessment, 89,* 265–276. (p. 513)

Kurdek, L. A. (2005). What do we know about gay and lesbian couples? *Current Directions in Psychological Science, 14,* 251–254. (p. 443)

Kushner, M. G., Kim, S. W., Conahue, C., Thuras, P., Adson, D., Kotlyar, M., McCabe, J., Peterson, J., & Foa, E. B. (2007). D-cycloserine augmented exposure therapy for obsessive-compulsive disorder. *Biological Psychiatry, 62,* 835–838. (p. 705)

Kutas, M. (1990). Event-related brain potential (ERP) studies of cognition during sleep: Is it more than a dream? In R. R. Bootzin, J. F. Kihlstrom, & D. Schacter (Eds.), *Sleep and cognition.* Washington, DC: American Psychological Association. (p. 92)

Kutcher, E. J., & Bragger, J. D. (2004). Selection interviews of overweight job applicants: Can structure reduce the bias? *Journal of Applied Social Psychology, 34,* 1993–2022. (p. 461)

L'Engle, M. (1972). *A Circle of Quiet.* New York: HarperCollins. (p. 647)

L'Engle, M. (1973). *A Wind in the Door, 87.* New York: Farrar, Straus and Giroux. (p. 15)

Labouvie-Vief, G., & Schell, D. A. (1982). Learning and memory in later life. In B. B. Wolman (Ed.), *Handbook of developmental psychology.* Englewood Cliffs, NJ: Prentice-Hall. (p. 214)

Lac, A., & Crano, W. D. (2009). Monitoring matters: Meta-analytic review reveals the reliable linkage of parental monitoring with adolescent marijuana use. *Perspectives on Psychological Science, 4,* 578–586. (p. 127)

Lacey, H. P., Smith, D. M., & Ubel, P. A. (2006). Hope I die before I get old: Mispredicting happiness across the lifespan. *Journal of Happiness Studies, 7,* 167–182. (p. 218)

Lacey, M. (2010, December 11). He found bag of cash, but did the unexpected. *New York Times* (www.nytimes.com). (p. 617)

Lachman, M. E. (2004). Development in midlife. *Annual Review of Psychology, 55,* 305–331. (p. 215)

Ladd, G. T. (1887). *Elements of physiological psychology.* New York: Scribner's. (p. 84)

Lafleur, D. L., Pittenger, C., Kelmendi, B., Gardner, T., Wasylink, S., Malison, R. T., Sanacora, G., Krystal, J. H., & Coric, V. (2006). N-acetylcysteine augmentation in serotonin reuptake inhibitor refractory obsessive-compulsive disorder. *Psychopharmacology, 184,* 254–256. (p. 643)

Laird, J. D. (1974). Self-attribution of emotion: The effects of expressive behavior on the quality of emotional experience. *Journal of Personality and Social Psychology, 29,* 475–486. (p. 489)

Laird, J. D. (1984). The real role of facial response in the experience of emotion: A reply to Tourangeau and Ellsworth, and others. *Journal of Personality and Social Psychology, 47,* 909–917. (p. 489)

Laird, J. D., Cuniff, M., Sheehan, K., Shulman, D., & Strum, G. (1989). Emotion specific effects of facial expressions on memory for life events. *Journal of Social Behavior and Personality, 4,* 87–98. (p. 489)

Lally, P., Van Jaarsveld, C. H. M., Potts, H. W. W., & Wardle, J. (2010). How are habits formed: Modelling habit formation in the real world. *European Journal of Social Psychology, 40,* 998–1009. (p. 276)

Lalumière, M. L., Blanchard, R., & Zucker, K. J. (2000). Sexual orientation and handedness in men and women: A meta-analysis. *Psychological Bulletin, 126,* 575–592. (p. 447)

Lam, R. W., Levitt, A. J., Levitan, R. D., Enns, M. W., Morehouse, R., Michalak, E. E., & Tam, E. M. (2006). The Can-SAD study: A randomized controlled trial of the effectiveness of light therapy and fluoxetine in patients with winter seasonal affective disorder. *American Journal of Psychiatry, 163,* 805–812. (p. 698)

Lambert, N. M., DeWall, C. N., Bushman, B. J., Tillman, T. F., Fincham, F. D., Pond, Jr., R. S., & Gwinn, A. M. (2011). Lashing out in lust: Effect of pornography on nonsexual, physical aggression against relationship partners. Paper presentation at the Society for Personality and Social Psychology convention. (p. 604)

Lambert, W. E. (1992). Challenging established views on social issues: The power and limitations of research. *American Psychologist, 47,* 533–542. (p. 377)

Lambert, W. E., Genesee, F., Holobow, N., & Chartrand, L. (1993). Bilingual education for majority English-speaking children. *European Journal of Psychology of Education, 8,* 3–22. (p. 377)

Lambird, K. H., & Mann, T. (2006). When do ego threats lead to self-regulation failure? Negative consequences of defensive high self-esteem. *Personality and Social Psychology Bulletin, 32,* 1177–1187. (p. 568)

Landauer, T. (2001, September). Quoted by R. Herbert, You must remember this. *APS Observer,* p. 11. (p. 347)

Landauer, T. K., & Whiting, J. W. M. (1979). Correlates and consequences of stress in infancy. In R. Munroe, B. Munroe, & B. Whiting (Eds.), *Handbook of cross-cultural human development.* New York: Garland. (p. 505)

Landry, M. J. (2002). MDMA: A review of epidemiologic data. *Journal of Psychoactive Drugs, 34,* 163–169. (p. 122)

Langer, E. J. (1983). *The psychology of control.* Beverly Hills, CA: Sage. (p. 559)

Langer, E. J., & Abelson, R. P. (1974). A patient by any other name . . .: Clinician group differences in labeling bias. *Journal of Consulting and Clinical Psychology, 42,* 4–9. (p. 632)

Langer, E. J., & Imber, L. (1980). The role of mindlessness in the perception of deviance. *Journal of Personality and Social Psychology, 39,* 360–367. (p. 632)

Langleben, D. D., & Dattilio, F. M. (2008). Commentary: The future of forensic functional brain imaging. *Journal of the American Academy of Psychiatry and the Law, 36,* 502–504. (p. 482)

Langleben, D. D., Dattilio, F. M., & Gutheil, T. G. (2006). True lies: Delusions and lie-detection technology. *Journal of Psychiatry and Law, 34,* 351–370. (p. 482)

Langlois, J. H., Kalakanis, L., Rubenstein, A. J., Larson, A., Hallam, M., & Smoot, M. (2000). Maxims or myths of beauty? A meta-analytic and theoretical review. *Psychological Bulletin, 126,* 390–423. (pp. 610, 611)

Langlois, J. H., & Roggman, L. A. (1990). Attractive faces are only average. *Psychological Science, 1,* 115–121. (p. 611)

Langlois, J. H., Roggman, L. A., Casey, R. J., Ritter, J. M., Rieser-Danner, L. A., & Jenkins, V. Y. (1987). Infant preferences for attractive faces: Rudiments of a stereotype? *Developmental Psychology, 23,* 363–369. (p. 610)

Langström, N. H., Rahman, Q., Carlström, E., & Lichtenstein, P. (2008). Genetic and environmental effects on same-sex sexual behavior: A population study of twins in Sweden. *Archives of Sexual Behavior.* (p. 446)

Langström, N. H., Rahman, Q., Carlstöm, E., & Lichtenstein, P. (2010). Genetic and environmental effects on same-sex sexual behavior: A population study of twins in Sweden. *Archives of Sexual Behavior, 39,* 75–80. (p. 446)

Lankford, A. (2009). Promoting aggression and violence at Abu Ghraib: The U.S. military's transformation of ordinary people into torturers. *Aggression and Violent Behavior, 14,* 388–395. (p. 586)

Larkin, K., Resko, J. A., Stormshak, F., Stellflug, J. N., & Roselli, C. E. (2002). Neuroanatomical correlates of sex and sexual partner preference in sheep. Paper presented at Society for Neuroscience convention. (p. 445)

Larrick, R. P., Timmerman, T. A., & Carton, A. M., & Abrevaya, J. (2011). Temper, temperature, and temptation: Heat-related retaliation in baseball. *Psychological Science, 22,* 423–428. (p. 602)

Larsen, R. J., & Diener, E. (1987). Affect intensity as an individual difference characteristic: A review. *Journal of Research in Personality, 21,* 1–39. (pp. 138, 478)

Larson, R. W., & Verma, S. (1999). How children and adolescents spend time across the world: Work, play, and developmental opportunities. *Psychological Bulletin, 125,* 701–736. (p. 412)

Larsson, H., Tuvblad, C., Rijsdijk, F. V., Andershed, H., Grann, M., & Lichetenstein, P. (2007). A common genetic factor explains the association between psychopathic personality and antisocial behavior. *Psychological Medicine, 37,* 15–26. (p. 668)

Larzelere, R. E. (2000). Child outcomes of non-abusive and customary physical punishment by parents: An updated literature review. *Clinical Child and Family Psychology Review, 3,* 199–221. (p. 293)

Larzelere, R. E., & Kuhn, B. R. (2005). Comparing child outcomes of physical punishment and alternative disciplinary tactics: A meta-analysis. *Clinical Child and Family Psychology Review, 8,* 1–37. (p. 293)

Larzelere, R. E., Kuhn, B. R., & Johnson, B. (2004). The intervention selection bias: An underrecognized confound in intervention research. *Psychological Bulletin, 130,* 289–303. (p. 293)

Lashley, K. S. (1950). In search of the engram. In *Symposium of the Society for Experimental Biology* (Vol. 4). New York: Cambridge University Press. (p. 323)

Lassiter, G. D., & Irvine, A. A. (1986). Video-taped confessions: The impact of camera point of view on judgments of coercion. *Journal of Personality and Social Psychology, 16,* 268–276. (p. 573)

Lassiter, G. D., Lindberg, M. JH., Gonzáles-Vallego, C., Bellezza, F. S., & Phillips, N. D. (2009). The deliberation-without-attention effect: Evidence for an artifactual interpretation. *Psychological Science, 20,* 671–675. (p. 360)

Latané, B. (1981). The psychology of social impact. *American Psychologist, 36,* 343–356. (p. 587)

Latané, B., & Dabbs, J. M., Jr. (1975). Sex, group size and helping in three cities. *Sociometry, 38,* 180–194. (p. 616)

Latham, G. P., & Locke, E. A. (2007). New developments in and directions for goal-setting research. *European Psychologist, 12,* 290–300. (p. 467)

Laudenslager, M. L., & Reite, M. L. (1984). Losses and separations: Immunological consequences and health implications. *Review of Personality and Social Psychology, 5,* 285–312. (p. 517)

Laumann, E. O., Gagnon, J. H., Michael, R. T., & Michaels, S. (1994). *The social organization of sexuality: Sexual practices in the United States.* Chicago: University of Chicago Press. (p. 145)

Laws, K. R., & Kokkalis, J. (2007). Ecstasy (MDMA) and memory function: A meta-analytic update. *Human Psychopharmacology: Clinical and Experimental, 22,* 381–388. (p. 123)

Lazaruk, W. (2007). Linguistic, academic, and cognitive benefits of French immersion. *Canadian Modern Language Review, 63,* 605–628. (p. 377)

Lazarus, R. S. (1991). Progress on a cognitive-motivational-relational theory of emotion. *American Psychologist, 46,* 352–367. (p. 477)

Lazarus. R. S. (1998). *Fifty years of the research and theory of R. S. Lazarus: An analysis of historical and perennial issues.* Mahwah, NJ: Erlbaum. (pp. 477, 505)

Lazer, D. & 14 others. (2009). Computational social science. *Science, 323,* 721–723. (p. 590)

Lea, S. E. G. (2000). Towards an ethical use of animals. *The Psychologist, 13,* 556–557. (p. 23)

Leal, S., & Vrij, A. (2008). Blinking during and after lying. *Journal of Nonverbal Behavior, 32,* 187–194. (p. 482)

Leaper, C., & Ayres, M. M. (2007). A meta-analytic review of gender variations in adults' language use: Talkativeness, affiliative speech, and assertive speech. *Personality and Social Psychology Review, 11,* 328–363. (p. 158)

Leary, M. R. (1999). The social and psychological importance of self-esteem. In R. M. Kowalski & M. R. Leary (Eds.), *The social psychology of emotional and behavioral problems.* Washington, DC: APA Books. (p. 564)

Leary, M. R., Haupt, A. L., Strausser, K. S., & Chokel, J. T. (1998). Calibrating the sociometer: The relationship between interpersonal appraisals and state self-esteem. *Journal of Personality and Social Psychology, 74,* 1290–1299. (p. 450)

Leask, S. J., & Beaton, A. A. (2007). Handedness in Great Britain. *Laterality, 12,* 559–572. (p. 80)

LeDoux, J. (1996). *The emotional brain: The mysterious underpinnings of emotional life.* New York: Simon & Schuster. (p. 325)

LeDoux, J. (2009, July/August). Quoted by K. McGowan, Out of the past. *Discover,* pp. 28–37. (p. 340)

LeDoux, J. E. (2002). *The synaptic self.* London: Macmillan. (pp. 149, 476)

LeDoux, J. E., & Armony, J. (1999). Can neurobiology tell us anything about human feelings? In D. Kahneman, E. Diener, & N. Schwartz (Eds.), *Well-being: The foundations of hedonic psychology.* New York: Sage. (p. 477)

Lee, J. D. (2008). Fifty years of driving safety research. *Human Factors, 50,* 521–528. (p. 469)

Lee, J. D. (2009). Can technology get your eyes back on the road? *Science, 324,* 344–346. (p. 89)

Lee, L., Frederick, S., & Ariely, D. (2006). Try it, you'll like it: The influence of expectation, consumption, and revelation on preferences for beer. *Psychological Science, 17,* 1054–1058. (p. 230)

Lee, P. S. N., Leung, L., Lo, V., Xiong, C., & Wu, T. (2011). Internet communication versus face-to-face interaction in quality of life. *Social Indicators Research, 100,* 375–389. (p. 454)

Lee, S. W. S., Schwarz, N., Taubman, D., & Hou, M. (2010). Sneezing in times of a flue pandemic: Public sneezing increases perception of unrelated risks and shifts preferences for federal spending. *Psychological Science, 21,* 375–377. (p. 356)

Lefcourt, H. M. (1982). *Locus of control: Current trends in theory and research.* Hillsdale, NJ: Erlbaum. (p. 557)

Legrand, L. N., Iacono, W. G., & McGue, M. (2005). Predicting addiction. *American Scientist, 93,* 140–147. (p. 127)

Lehavot, K., & Lambert, A. J. (2007). Toward a greater understanding of antigay prejudice: On the role of sexual orientation and gender role violation. *Basic and Applied Social Psychology, 29,* 279–292. (p. 612)

Lehman, A. F., Steinwachs, D. M., Dixon, L. B., Goldman, H. H., Osher, F., Postrado, L., Scott, J. E., Thompson, J. W., Fahey, M., Fischer, P., Kasper, J. A., Lyles, A., Skinner, E. A., Buchanan, R., Carpenter, W. T., Jr., Levine, J., McGlynn, E. A., Rosenheck, R., & Zito, J. (1998). Translating research into practice: The schizophrenic patient outcomes research team (PORT) treatment recommendations. *Schizophrenia Bulletin, 24,* 1–10. (p. 704)

Lehman, D. R., Wortman, C. B., & Williams, A. F. (1987). Long-term effects of losing a spouse or child in a motor vehicle crash. *Journal of Personality and Social Psychology, 52,* 218–231. (p. 220)

Leichsenring, F., & Rabung, S. (2008). Effectiveness of long-term psychodynamic psychotherapy: A meta-analysis. *JAMA, 300,* 1551–1565. (p. 695)

Leitenberg, H., & Henning, K. (1995). Sexual fantasy. *Psychological Bulletin, 117,* 469–496. (pp. 437, 439)

Lemonick, M. D. (2002, June 3). Lean and hungrier. *Time,* p. 54. (p. 423)

Lenhart, A. (2010, April 20). Teens, cell phones and texting. Pew Internet and American Life Project. Pew Research Center (www.pewresearch.org). (pp. 159, 453)

Lennox, B. R., Bert, S., Park, G., Jones, P. B., & Morris, P. G. (1999). Spatial and temporal mapping of neural activity associated with auditory hallucinations. *Lancet, 353,* 644. (p. 73)

Lenton, A. P., & Francesconi, M. (2010). How humans cognitively manage an abundance of mate options. *Psychological Science, 21,* 528–533. (p. 609)

Lenzenweger, M. F., Dworkin, R. H., & Wethington, E. (1989). Models of positive and negative symptoms in schizophrenia: An empirical evaluation of latent structures. *Journal of Abnormal Psychology, 98,* 62–70. (p. 704)

Leonhard, C., & Randler, C. (2009). In sync with the family: Children and partners influence the sleep-wake circadian rhythm and social habits of women. *Chronobiology International, 26,* 510–525. (p. 93)

Leserman, J., Jackson, E. D., Petitto, J. M., Golden, R. N., Silva, S. G., Perkins, D. O., Cai, J., Folds, J. D., & Evans, D. L. (1999). Progression to AIDS: The effects of stress, depressive symptoms, and social support. *Psychosomatic Medicine, 61,* 397–406. (p. 511)

Lessard, N., Pare, M., Lepore, F., & Lassonde, M. (1998). Early-blind human subjects localize sound sources better than sighted subjects. *Nature, 395,* 278–280. (p. 371)

Lester, W. (2004, May 26). AP polls: Nations value immigrant workers. *Associated Press* release. (p. 594)

Leucht, S., Barnes, T. R. E., Kissling, W., Engel, R. R., Correll, C., & Kane, J. M. (2003). Relapse prevention in schizophrenia with new-generation antipsychotics: A systematic review and exploratory meta-analysis of randomized, controlled trials. *American Journal of Psychiatry, 160,* 1209–1222. (p. 705)

Leung, A. K-Y., Maddux, W. W., Galinsky, A. D., & Chiu, C-Y. (2008). Multicultural experience enhances creativity: The when and how. *American Psychologist, 63,* 169–181. (p. 388)

Leuthardt, E. C., Schalk, G., Roland, J., Rouse, A., & Moran, D.W. (2009). Evolution of brain-computer interfaces: Going beyond classic motor physiology. *Neurosurgical Focus, 27,* p. E4. (p. 71)

Levant, R. F., & Hasan, N. T. (2008). Evidence-based practice in psychology. *Professional Psychology: Research and Practice, 39,* 658–662. (p. 696)

LeVay, S. (1991). A difference in hypothalamic structure between heterosexual and homosexual men. *Science, 253,* 1034–1037. (p. 445)

LeVay, S. (1994, March). Quoted in D. Nimmons, Sex and the brain. *Discover,* p. 64–71. (p. 445)

LeVay, S. (2011). *Gay, straight, and the reason why: The science of sexual orientation.* New York: Oxford University Press. (p. 446)

Levenson, R. W. (1992). Autonomic nervous system differences among emotions. *Psychological Science, 3,* 23–27. (p. 480)

Levin, R., & Nielsen, T. A. (2007). Disturbed dreaming, posttraumatic stress disorder, and affect distress: A review and neurocognitive model. *Psychological Bulletin, 133,* 482–528. (p. 106)

Levine, J. A., Eberhardt, N. L., & Jensen, M. D. (1999). Role of nonexercise activity thermogenesis in resistance to fat gain in humans. *Science, 283,* 212–214. (p. 430)

Levine, J. A., Lanningham-Foster, L. M., McCrady, S. K., Krizan, A. C., Olson, L. R., Kane, P. H., Jensen, M. D., & Clark, M. M. (2005). Interindividual variation in posture allocation: Possible role in human obesity. *Science, 307,* 584–586. (p. 430)

Levine, R., Sato, S., Hashimoto, T., & Verma, J. (1995). Love and marriage in eleven cultures. *Journal of Cross-Cultural Psychology, 26,* 554–571. (p. 614)

Levine, R. V., & Norenzayan, A. (1999). The pace of life in 31 countries. *Journal of Cross-Cultural Psychology, 30,* 178–205. (pp. 29, 152)

Levinson, D. F. & 23 others. (2011). Copy number variants in schizophrenia: Confirmation of five previous findings and new evidence for 3q29 microdeletions and VIPR2 duplications. *American Journal of Psychiatry, 168,* 302–316. (p. 662)

Levy, B., & Langer, E. (1992). Avoidance of the memory loss stereotype: Enhanced memory among the elderly deaf. Paper presented at American Psychological Association convention, Washington, DC. (p. 371)

Levy, P. E. (2003). Industrial/organizational psychology: Understanding the workplace. Boston: Houghton Mifflin. (p. 462)

Lewald, J. (2007). More accurate sound localisation induced by short-term light deprivation. *Neuropsychologia, 45,* 1215–1222. (p. 371)

Lewandowski, G. W., Jr., Aron, A., & Gee, J. (2007). Personality goes a long way: The malleability of opposite-sex physical attractiveness. *Personality Relationships, 14,* 571–585. (p. 611)

Lewicki, P. (1985). Nonconscious biasing effects of single instances on subsequent judgments. *Journal of Personality and Social Psychology, 48,* 563–574. (p. 330)

Lewinsohn, P. M., Hoberman, H., Teri, L., & Hautzinger, M. (1985). An integrative theory of depression. In S. Reiss & R. Bootzin (Eds.), *Theoretical issues in behavior therapy.* Orlando, FL: Academic Press. (p. 647)

Lewinsohn, P. M., Petit, J., Joiner, T. E., Jr., & Seeley, J. R. (2003). The symptomatic expression of major depressive disorder in adolescents and young adults. *Journal of Abnormal Psychology, 112,* 244–252. (p. 647)

Lewinsohn, P. M., Rohde, P., & Seeley, J. R. (1998). Major depressive disorder in older adolescents: Prevalence, risk factors, and clinical implications. *Clinical Psychology Review, 18,* 765–794. (p. 647)

Lewinsohn, P. M., & Rosenbaum, M. (1987). Recall of parental behavior by acute depressives, remitted depressives, and nondepressives. *Journal of Personality and Social Psychology, 52,* 611–619. (p. 332)

Lewis, C. S. (1960). *Mere Christianity.* New York: Macmillan. (p. 4)

Lewis, D. O., Pincus, J. H., Bard, B., Richardson, E., Prichep, L. S., Feldman, M., & Yeager, C. (1988). Neuropsychiatric, psychoeducational, and family characteristics of 14 juveniles condemned to death in the United States. *American Journal of Psychiatry, 145,* 584–589. (p. 192)

Lewis, D. O., Yeager, C. A., Swica, Y., Pincus, J. H., & Lewis, M. (1997). Objective documentation of child abuse and dissociation in 12 murderers with dissociative identity disorder. *American Journal of Psychiatry, 154,* 1703–1710. (p. 667)

Lewis, M. (1992). Commentary. *Human Development, 35,* 44–51. (p. 332)

Lewontin, R. (1976). Race and intelligence. In N. J. Block & G. Dworkin (Eds.), *The IQ controversy: Critical readings.* New York: Pantheon. (p. 411)

Lewontin, R. (1982). *Human diversity.* New York: Scientific American Library. (p. 142)

Li, J., Laursen, T. M., Precht, D. H., Olsen, J., & Mortensen, P. B. (2005). Hospitalization for mental illness among parents after the death of a child. *New England Journal of Medicine,* 352, 1190–1196. (p. 220)

Li, J. C., Dunning, D., & Malpass, R. L. (1996). Cross-racial identification among European-Americans basketball fandom and the contact hypothesis. Unpublished manuscript, Cornell University. (p. 598)

Li, N., & DiCarlo, J. J. (2008). Unsupervised natural experience rapidly alters invariant object representation in visual cortex. *Science, 321,* 1502–1506. (p. 248)

Li, Y., Johnson, E. J., & Zaval, L. (2011). Local warming: Daily temperature change influences belief in global warming. *Psychological Science, 22,* 454–459. (p. 356)

Li, Z. H., Jiang, D., Pepler, D., & Craig, W. (2010). Adolescent romantic relationships in China and Canada: A cross-national comparison. *International Journal of Behavioral Development, 34,* 113–120. (p. 204)

Liang, K. Y., Mintun, M. A., Fagan, A. M., Goate, A.M., Bugg, J.M., Holtzman, D. M., Morris, J. C., & Head, D. (2010). Exercise and Alzheimer's disease biomarkers in cognitively normal older adults. *Annals of Neurology, 68,* 311–318. (p. 211)

Liberman, P., & Pizarro, D. (2010, October 23). All politics is olfactory. *New York Times* (www.nytimes.com). (p. 271)

Liberman, V., Boehm, J. K., Lyubomirsky, S., & Ross, L. D. (2009). Happiness and memory: Affective significance of endowment and contrast. *Emotion, 9,* 666–680. (p. 495)

Libertus, M. E., & Brannon, E. M. (2009). Behavioral and neural basis of number sense in infancy. *Current Directions in Psychological Science, 18,* 346–351. (p. 182)

Libet, B. (1985). Unconscious cerebral initiative and the role of conscious will in voluntary action. *Behavioral and Brain Sciences, 12,* 181–187. (p. 87)

Libet, B. (2004). *Mind time: The temporal factor in consciousness.* Cambridge, MA: Harvard University Press. (p. 87)

Licata, A., Taylor, S., Berman, M., & Cranston, J. (1993). Effects of cocaine on human aggression. *Pharmacology Biochemistry and Behavior, 45,* 549–552. (p. 121)

Lichtenstein, E., Zhu, S-H., & Tedeschi, G. J. (2010). Smoking cessation quitlines: An underrecognized intervention success story. *American Psychologist, 65,* 252–261. (p. 185)

Lichtenstein, P., Calström, E., Råstam, M., Gillberg, C., & Anckarsäter, H. (2010). The genetics of autim spectrum disorders and related neuropsychiatric disorders in childhood. *American Journal of Psychiatry, 167,* 1357–1363. (p. 121)

Lieberman, M. D., & Eisenberger, M. I. (2009). Pains and pleasures of social life. *Science,* 323, 890–893. (p. 452)

Lieberman, M. D., Eisenberger, N. L., Crockett, M. J., Tom, S. M., Pfeifer, J. H., & Way, B. M. (2007). Putting feelings into words: Affect labeling disrupts amygdala activity in response to affective stimuli. *Psychological Science, 18,* 421–428. (p. 520)

Lievens, F., Dilchert, S., & Ones, D. S. (2009). The importance of exercise and dimension factors in assessment centers: Simultaneous examinations of construct-related and criterion-related validity. *Human Performance, 22,* 375–390. (p. 562)

Lilienfeld, S. O. (2009, Winter). Tips for spotting psychological pseudoscience: A student-friendly guide. *Eye of Psi Chi,* pp. 23–26. (p. 254)

Lilienfeld, S. O., & Arkowitz, H. (2007, April/May). Autism: An epidemic. *Scientific American Mind,* pp. 82–83. (p. 184)

Lilienfeld, S. O., & Arkowitz, H. (2007, December, 2006/January, 2007). Taking a closer look: Can moving your eyes back and forth help to ease anxiety? *Scientific American Mind,* pp. 80–81. (p. 697)

Lilienfeld, S. O., & Arkowitz, H. (2011, January/February). The insanity verdict on trial. *Scientific American,* pp. 64–65. (p. 633)

Lilienfeld, S. O., Lynn, S. J., Kirsch, I., Chaves, J. F., Sarbin, T. R., Ganaway, G. K., & Powell, R. A. (1999). Dissociative identity disorder and the sociocognitive model: Recalling the lessons of the past. *Psychological Bulletin, 125,* 507–523. (p. 667)

Lilienfeld, S. O., Wood, J. M., & Garb, H. N. (2001, May). What's wrong with this picture? *Scientific American,* pp. 81–87. (p. 538)

Lim, J., & Dinges, D. F. (2010). A meta-analysis of the impact of short-term sleep deprivation on cognitive variables. *Psychological Bulletin, 136,* 375–389. (p. 102)

Lindberg, S. M., Hyde, J. S., Linn, M. C., & Petersen, J. L. (2010). New trends in gender and mathematics performance: A meta-analysis. *Psychological Bulletin, 136,* 1125–1135. (p. 409)

Linde, K., & 10 others. (2005). Acupuncture for patients with migraine: A randomized controlled trial. *Journal of the American Medical Association, 293,* 2118–2125. (p. 526)

Linder, D. (1982). Social trap analogs: The tragedy of the commons in the laboratory. In V. J. Derlega & J. Grzelak (Eds.), *Cooperative and helping behavior: Theories and research.* New York: Academic Press. (p. 619)

Lindner, I., Echterhoff, G., Davidson, P. S. R., & Brand, M. (2010). Observation inflation: Your actions become mine. *Psychological Science, 21,* 1291–1299. (p. 306)

Lindskold, S. (1978). Trust development, the GRIT proposal, and the effects of conciliatory acts on conflict and cooperation. *Psychological Bulletin, 85,* 772–793. (p. 622)

Lindskold, S., & Han, G. (1988). GRIT as a foundation for integrative bargaining. *Personality and Social Psychology Bulletin, 14,* 335–345. (p. 622)

Lindson, N., Aveyard, P., & Hughes, J. R. (2010). Reduction versus abrupt cessation in smokers who want to quit (review). *Cochrane Collaboration* (Cochrane Library, Issue 3; www.thecochranelibrary.com). (p. 121)

Linville, P. W., Fischer, G. W., & Fischhoff, B. (1992). AIDS risk perceptions and decision biases. In J. B. Pryor & G. D. Reeder (Eds.), *The social psychology of HIV infection.* Hillsdale, NJ: Erlbaum. (p. 359)

Lippa, R. A. (2002). Gender-related traits of heterosexual and homosexual men and women. *Archives of Sexual Behavior, 31,* 83–98. (p. 444)

Lippa, R. A. (2005). *Gender, nature, and nurture* (2nd ed.). Mahwah, NJ: Erlbaum. (p. 159)

Lippa, R. A. (2006). Is high sex drive associated with increased sexual attraction to both sexes? It depends on whether you are male or female. *Psychological Science, 17,* 46–52. (p. 443)

Lippa, R. A. (2006). The gender reality hypothesis. *American Psychologist, 61,* 639–640. (p. 159)

Lippa, R. A. (2007a). The relation between sex drive and sexual attraction to men and women: A cross-national study of heterosexual, bisexual, and homosexual men and women. *Archives of Sexual Behavior,* 36, 209–222. (pp. 443, 448, 610)

Lippa, R. A. (2007b). The preferred traits of mates in a cross-national study of heterosexual and homosexual men and women: An examination of biological and cultural influences. *Archives of Sexual Behavior,* 36, 193–208. (p. 448)

Lippa, R. A. (2008) Sex differences and sexual orientation differences in personality: Findings from the BBC Internet survey. *Archives of Sexual Behavior, Special Issue; Biological research on sex-dimorphic behavior and sexual orientation,* 37(1), 173–187. (pp. 144, 159, 448)

Lippa, R. A. (2009). Sex differences in sex drive, sociosexuality, and height across 53 nations: Testing evolutionary and social structural theories. *Archives of Sexual Behavior,* 38, 631–651. (p. 144)

Lippa, R. A., Patterson, T. M., & Marelich, W. D. (2010). Looking at and longing for male and female "swimsuit models": Men are much more category-specific than women. *Social Psychological and Personality Science, 1,* 238–245. (p. 444)

Lipps, H. M. (1999). *A new psychology of women: Gender, culture, and ethnicity.* Mountain View, CA: Mayfield Publishing. (p. 594)

Lipsey, M. W., & Wilson, D. B. (1993). The efficacy of psychological, educational, and behavioral treatment: Confirmation from meta-analyses. *American Psychologist, 48,* 1181–1209. (p. 403)

Lipsitt, L. P. (2003). Crib death: A biobehavioral phenomenon? *Current Directions in Psychological Science, 12,* 164–170. (p. 178)

Little, A. C., Jones, B. C., & DeBruine, L. M. (2008). Preferences for variation in masculinity in real male faces change across the menstrual cycle: Women prefer more masculine faces when they are more fertile. *Personality and Individual Differences, 45,* 478–482. (p. 436)

Liu, H. (2009). Till Death Do Us Part: Marital Status and Mortality Trends, 1986–2000. *Journal of Marriage and Family, 71,* 1158–1173. (p. 519)

Liu, Y., Balaraman, Y., Wang, G., Nephew, K. P., & Zhou, F. C. (2010). Alcohol exposure alters DNA methylation profiles in mouse embryos at early neurulation. *Epigentics, 4,* 500–511. (p. 174)

Livesley, W. J., & Jang, K. L. (2008). The behavioral genetics of personality disorder. *Annual Review of Clinical Psychology, 4,* 247–274. (p. 668)

Livingstone, M., & Hubel, D. (1988). Segregation of form, color, movement, and depth: Anatomy, physiology, and perception. *Science, 240,* 740–749. (p. 239)

LoBue, V., & DeLoache, J. S. (2008). Detecting the snake in the grass: Attention to fear-relevant stimuli by adults and young children. *Psychological Science, 19,* 284–289. (p. 643)

Loehlin, J. C., Horn, J. M., & Ernst, J. L. (2007). Genetic and environmental influences on adult life outcomes: Evidence from the Texas adoption project. *Behavior Genetics, 37,* 463–476. (p. 137)

Loehlin, J. C., McCrae, R. R., & Costa, P. T., Jr. (1998). Heritabilities of common and measure-specific components of the Big Five personality factors. *Journal of Research in Personality,* 32, 431–453. (p. 552)

Loehlin, J. C., & Nichols, R. C. (1976). *Heredity, environment, and personality.* Austin: University of Texas Press. (p. 134)

Loftus, E. F. (1980). *Memory: Surprising new insights into how we remember and why we forget.* Reading, MA: Addison-Wesley. (p. 110)

Loftus, E. F. (2001, November). Imagining the past. *The Psychologist, 14,* 584–587. (p. 342)

Loftus, E. F., & Ketcham, K. (1994). *The myth of repressed memory.* New York: St. Martin's Press. (pp. 105, 323)

Loftus, E. F., Levidow, B., & Duensing, S. (1992). Who remembers best? Individual differences in memory for events that occurred in a science museum. *Applied Cognitive Psychology, 6,* 93–107. (p. 341)

Loftus, E. F., & Loftus, G. R. (1980). On the permanence of stored information in the human brain. *American Psychologist,* 35, 409–420. (p. 323)

Loftus, E. F., & Palmer, J. C. (October, 1974). Reconstruction of automobile destruction: An example of the interaction between language and memory. *Journal of Verbal Learning & Verbal Behavior, 13(5),* 585–589. (p. 341)

Logan, T. K., Walker, R., Cole, J., & Leukefeld, C. (2002). Victimization and substance abuse among women: Contributing factors, interventions, and implications. *Review of General Psychology, 6,* 325–397. (p. 127)

Logue, A. W. (1998a). Laboratory research on self-control: Applications to administration. *Review of General Psychology, 2,* 221–238. (p. 289)

Logue, A. W. (1998b). Self-control. In W. T. O'Donohue (Ed.), *Learning and behavior therapy.* Boston, MA: Allyn & Bacon. (p. 289)

Lomber, S. G., Meredith, M. A., & Krai, A. (2010). Cross-modal plasticity in specific auditory cortices underlies visual compensations in the deaf. *Nature Neuroscience, 13,* 1421–1427. (p. 371)

London, P. (1970). The rescuers: Motivational hypotheses about Christians who saved Jews from the Nazis. In J. Macaulay & L. Berkowitz (Eds.), *Altruism and helping behavior.* New York: Academic Press. (p. 306)

Looy, H. (2001). Sex differences: Evolved, constructed, and designed. *Journal of Psychology and Theology, 29,* 301–313. (p. 146)

Lopes, P. N., Brackett, M. A., Nezlek, J. B., Schutz, A., Sellin, II, & Salovey, P. (2004). Emotional intelligence and social interaction. *Personality and Social Psychology Bulletin, 30,* 1018–1034. (p. 389)

Lopez, D. J. (2002, January/February). Snaring the fowler: Mark Twain debunks phrenology. *Skeptical Inquirer* (www.csicop.org). (p. 47)

López-Ibor, J. J., López-Ibor, M-I., & Pastrana, J. I. (2008). Transcranial magnetic stimulation. *Current Opinion in Psychiatry, 21,* 640–644. (p. 709)

Lord, C. G., Lepper, M. R., & Preston, E. (1984). Considering the opposite: A corrective strategy for social judgment. *Journal of Personality and Social Psychology, 47,* 1231–1247. (p. 357)

Lord, C. G., Ross, L., & Lepper, M. (1979). Biased assimilation and attitude polarization: The effects of prior theories on subsequently considered evidence. *Journal of Personality and Social Psychology, 37,* 2098–2109. (p. 357)

Lorenz, K. (1937). The companion in the bird's world. *Auk, 54,* 245–273. (p. 188)

Louie, K., & Wilson, M. A. (2001). Temporally structured replay of awake hippocampal ensemble activity during rapid eye movement sleep. *Neuron, 29,* 145–156. (p. 107)

Lourenco, O., & Machado, A. (1996). In defense of Piaget's theory: A reply to 10 common criticisms. *Psychological Review, 103,* 143–164. (p. 187)

Lovaas, O. I. (1987). Behavioral treatment and normal educational and intellectual functioning in young autistic children. *Journal of Consulting and Clinical Psychology, 55,* 3–9. (p. 683)

Lowry, P. E. (1997). The assessment center process: New directions. *Journal of Social Behavior and Personality, 12,* 53–62. (p. 562)

Lu, Z-L., Williamson, S. J., & Kaufman, L. (1992). Behavioral lifetime of human auditory sensory memory predicted by physiological measures. *Science, 258,* 1668–1670. (p. 317)

Lubinski, D. (2009a). Cognitive epidemiology: with emphasis on untangling cognitive ability and socioeconomic status. *Intelligence, 37,* 625–633. (p. 403)

Lubinski, D. (2009b). Exceptional cognitive ability: The phenotype. *Behavioral Genetics, 39,* 350–358. (p. 403)

Lubinski, D., & Benbow, C. P. (2000). States of excellence. *American Psychologist,* 137–150. (p. 403)

Luborsky, L., Rosenthal, R., Diguer, L., Andrusyna, T. P., Berman, J. S., Levitt, J. T., Seligman, D. A., & Krause, E. D. (2002). The dodo bird verdict is alive and well—mostly. *Clinical Psychology: Science and Practice, 9,* 2–34. (p. 695)

Lucas, R. E. (2007a). Adaptation and the set-point model of subjective well-being. *Current Directions in Psychological Science, 16,* 75–79. (p. 497)

Lucas, R. E. (2007b). Long-term disability is associated with lasting changes in subjective well-being: Evidence from two nationally representative longitudinal studies. *Journal of Personality and Social Psychology, 92,* 717–730. (p. 497)

Lucas, R. E. (2008). Personality and subjective well-being. In M. Eid & R. Larsen (Eds.), *The science of subjective well-being.* New York: Guilford. (p. 501)

Lucas, R. E., Clark, A. E., Georgellis, Y., & Diener, E. (2003). Re-examining adaptation and the setpoint model of happiness: Reactions to changes in marital status. *Journal of Personality and Social Psychology, 84,* 527–539. (p. 220)

Lucas, R. E., Clark, A. E., Georgellis, Y., & Diener, E. (2004). Unemployment alters the set point for life satisfaction. *Psychological Science, 15,* 8–13. (p. 500)

Lucas, R. E., & Donnellan, M. B. (2007). How stable is happiness? Using the STARTS model to estimate the stability of life satisfaction. *Journal of Research in Personality, 41,* 1091–1098. (p. 501)

Lucas, R. E., & Donnellan, M. B. (2009). Age differences in personality: Evidence from a nationally representative Australian sample. *Developmental Psychology, 45,* 1353–1363. (p. 172)

Lucas, R. E., & Schimmack, U. (2009). Income and well-being: How big is the gap between the rich and the poor? *Journal of Research in Personality, 43,* 75–78. (p. 497)

Lucas-Thompson, R. G., Goldberg, W. A., & Prause, J. (2010). Maternal work early in the lives of children and its distal associations with achievement and behavior problems: A meta-analysis. *Psychological Bulletin, 136,* 915–942. (p. 192)

Lucero, S. M., Kusner, K. G., & Speace, E. A. (2008, May 24). Religousness and adolescent sexual behavior: A meta-analytic review. Paper presented at Association for Psychological Science Convention. (p. 441)

Luciano, M., Gow, A. J., Harris, S. E., Hayward, C., Allerhand, M., Starr, J. M., Visscher, P. M., & Deary, I. J. (2009). Cognitive ability at age 11 and 70 years, information processing speed, and *APOE* variation: The Lothian birth cohort 1936 study. *Psychology and Aging, 24,* 129–138. (p. 212)

Luciano, M., Posthuma, D., Wright, M. J., de Geus, E. J. C., Smith, G. A., Geffen, G. M., Boomsma, D. I., & Martin, N. G. (2005). Perceptual speed does not cause intelligence, and intelligence does not cause perceptual speed. *Biological Psychology, 70,* 1–8. (p. 391)

Ludwig, A. M. (1995). *The price of greatness: Resolving the creativity and madness controversy.* New York: Guilford Press. (pp. 444, 647)

Lui, M., & Rosenfeld, J. P. (2009). The application of subliminal priming in lie detection: Scenario for identification of members of a terrorist ring. *Psycholphysiology, 46,* 889–903. (p. 482)

Lumeng, J. C., Forrest, P., Appugliese, D. P., Kaciroti, N., Corwyn, R. F., Bradley, R. H. (2010). Weight status as a predictor of being bullied in third through sixth grades. *Pediatrics, 125,* e1301–7. (p. 429)

Luo, F., Florence, C. S., Quispe-Agnoli, M., Ouyang, L., & Crosby, A. E. (2011). Impact of business cycles on US suicide rates, 1928–2007. *American Journal of Public Health, 101,* 1139–1146. (p. 650)

Luo, M. (2011, January 25). In firearms research, cause is often the missing element. *New York Times* (www.nytimes.com). (p. 33)

Luppino, F. S., de Wit, L. M., Bouvy, P. F., Stijnen, T., Cuijpers, P., Penninx, W. J. H., & Zitman, F. G. (2010). Overweight, obesity, and depression. *Archives of General Psychiatry, 67,* 220–229. (p. 429)

Luria, A. M. (1968). In L. Solotaroff (Trans.), *The mind of a mnemonist.* New York: Basic Books. (p. 312)

Lustig, C., & Buckner, R. L. (2004). Preserved neural correlates of priming in old age and dementia. *Neuron, 42,* 865–875. (p. 335)

Lutfey, K. E., Link, C. L., Rosen, R. C., Wiegel, M., & McKinlay, J. B. (2009). Prevalence and correlates of sexual activity and function in women: Results from the Boston Area Community Health (BACH) survey. *Archives of Sexual Behavior, 38,* 514–527. (p. 436)

Lutgendorf, S. K., Russell, D., Ullrich, P., Harris, T. B., & Wallace, R. (2004). Religious participation, interleukin-6, and mortality in older adults. *Health Psychology, 23,* 465–475. (p. 528)

Lyall, S. (2005, November 29). What's the buzz? Rowdy teenagers don't want to hear it. *New York Times* (www.nytimes.com). (p. 210)

Lykins, A. D., Meana, M., & Strauss, G. P. (2008). Sex differences in visual attention to erotic and non-erotic stimuli. *Archives of Sexual Behavior, 37,* 219–228. (p. 443)

Lykken, D. T. (1991). Science, lies, and controversy: An epitaph for the polygraph. Invited address upon receipt of the Senior Career Award for Distinguished Contribution to Psychology in the Public Interest, American Psychological Association convention. (p. 481)

Lykken, D. T. (1995). *The antisocial personalities.* Hillsdale, NJ: Erlbaum. (pp. 600, 668)

Lykken, D. T. (1999). *Happiness: The Nature and Nurture of Joy and Contentment.* New York: Golden Books. (p. 405)

Lykken, D. T. (1999). *Happiness.* New York: Golden Books. (p. 399)

Lykken, D. T. (2001). Happiness—stuck with what you've got? *The Psychologist, 14,* 470–473. (p. 137)

Lykken, D. T., & Tellegen, A. (1996). Happiness is a stochastic phenomenon. *Psychological Science, 7,* 186–189. (p. 501)

Lynch, G. (2002). Memory enhancement: The search for mechanism-based drugs. *Nature Neuroscience, 5* (suppl.), 1035–1038. (p. 327)

Lynch, G., & Staubli, U. (1991). Possible contributions of long-term potentiation to the encoding and organization of memory. *Brain Research Reviews, 16,* 204–206. (p. 327)

Lynn, M. (1988). The effects of alcohol consumption on restaurant tipping. *Personality and Social Psychology Bulletin, 14,* 87–91. (p. 117)

Lynn, R. (2008). *The global bell curve: Race, IQ and inequality worldwide.* Augusta, GA: Washington Summit Publishers. (p. 411)

Lynn, R. (2009). What has caused the Flynn effect? Secular increases in the development quotients of infants. *Intelligence, 37,* 16–24. (p. 396)

Lynn, R., & Harvey, J. (2008). The decline of the world's intelligence. *Intelligence, 36,* 112–120. (p. 397)

Lynn, S. J., Rhue, J. W., & Weekes, J. R. (1990). Hypnotic involuntariness: A social cognitive analysis. *Psychological Review, 97,* 169–184. (p. 112)

Lynne, S. D., Graber, J. A., Nichols, T. R., Brooks-Gunn, J., & Botvin, G. J. (2007). Links between pubertal timing, peer influences, and externalizing behaviors among urban students followed through middle school. *Journal of Adolescent Health, 40,* 181.e7–181.e13. (p. 199)

Lyons, D. E., Young, A. G., Keil, F. C. (2007). The hidden structure of overimitation. *PNAS, 104,* 19751–10756. (p. 305)

Lyons, L. (2004, February 3). Growing up lonely: Examining teen alienation. *Gallup Poll Tuesday Briefing* (www.gallup.com). (p. 204)

Lyons, L. (2005, January 4). Teens stay true to parents' political perspectives. *Gallup Poll News Service* (www.gallup.com). (p. 205)

Lyons, P. A., Kenworthy, J. B., & Popan, J. R. (2010). Ingroup identification and group-level narcissism as predictors of U.S. citizens' attitudes and behavior toward Arab immigrants. *Personality and Social Psychology Bulletin, 36,* 1267–1280. (p. 594)

Lytton, H., & Romney, D. M. (1991). Parents' differential socialization of boys and girls: A meta-analysis. *Psychological Bulletin, 109,* 267–296. (p. 163)

Lyubomirsky, S. (2001). Why are some people happier than others? The role of cognitive and motivational processes in well-being. *American Psychologist, 56,* 239–249. (p. 499)

Lyubomirsky, S., Sousa, L., & Dickerhoof, R. (2006). The costs and benefits of writing, talking, and thinking about life's triumphs and defeats. *Journal of Personality and Social Psychology, 90*(4), 690–708. (p. 521)

Ma, L. (1997, September). On the origin of Darwin's ills. *Discover,* p. 27. (p. 638)

Maas, J. B. (1999). *Power sleep. The revolutionary program that prepares your mind and body for peak performance.* New York: HarperCollins. (p. 102)

Maas, J. B., & Robbins, R. S. (2010). *Sleep for success: Everything you must know about sleep but are too tired to ask.* Bloomington, IN: Author House. (p. 100)

Maass, A., D'Ettole, C., & Cadinu, M. (2008). Checkmate? The role of gender stereotypes in the ultimate intellectual sport. *European Journal of Social Psychology, 38,* 231–245. (p. 414)

Maass, A., Karasawa, M., Politi, F., & Suga, S. (2006). Do verbs and adjectives play different roles in different cultures? A cross-linguistic analysis of person representation. *Journal of Personality and Social Psychology, 90,* 734–750. (p. 155)

Maass, A., & Russo, A. (2003). Directional bias in the mental representation of spatial events: Nature or culture? *Psychological Science, 14,* 296–301. (p. 376)

Macaluso, E., Frith, C. D., & Driver, J. (2000). Modulation of human visual cortex by crossmodal spatial attention. *Science, 289,* 1206–1208. (p. 268)

Macan, T. H., & Dipboye, R. L. (1994). The effects of the application on processing of information from the employment interview. *Journal of Applied Social Psychology, 24,* 1291. (p. 461)

MacCabe, J. H., Lambe, M. P., Cnattingius, S., Torrång, A., Björk, C., Sham, P. C., David, A. S., Murray, R. M., & Hultman, C. M. (2008). Scholastic achievement at age 16 and risk of schizophrenia and other psychoses: A national cohort study. *Psychological Medicine, 38,* 1133–1140. (p. 658)

Maccoby, E. E. (1990). Gender and relationships: A developmental account. *American Psychologist, 45,* 513–520. (p. 158)

Maccoby, E. E. (1995). Divorce and custody: The rights, needs, and obligations of mothers, fathers, and children. *Nebraska Symposium on Motivation, 42,* 135–172. (p. 162)

Maccoby, E. E. (1998). *The paradox of gender.* Cambridge, MA: Harvard University Press. (p. 160)

Maccoby, E. E. (2002). Gender and group process: A developmental perspective. *Current Directions in Psychological Science, 11,* 54–58. (p. 589)

MacDonald, G., & Leary, M. R. (2005). Why does social exclusion hurt? The relationship between social and physical pain. *Psychological Bulletin, 131,* 202–223. (p. 452)

MacDonald, N. (1960). Living with schizophrenia. *Canadian Medical Association Journal, 82,* 218–221. (p. 657)

MacDonald, T. K., & Hynie, M. (2008). Ambivalence and unprotected sex: Failure to predict sexual activity and decreased condom use. *Journal of Applied Social Psychology, 38,* 1092–1107. (p. 439)

MacDonald, T. K., Zanna, M. P., & Fong, G. T. (1995). Decision making in altered states: Effects of alcohol on attitudes toward drinking and driving. *Journal of Personality and Social Psychology, 68,* 973–985. (p. 117)

MacFarlane, A. (1978, February). What a baby knows. *Human Nature,* pp. 74–81. (p. 175)

Macfarlane, J. W. (1964). Perspectives on personality consistency and change from the guidance study. *Vita Humana, 7,* 115–126. (p. 197)

Machin, S., & Pekkarinen, T. (2008). Global sex differences in test score variability. *Science, 322,* 1331–1332. (p. 409)

Maciejewski, P. K., Zhang, B., Block, S. D., & Prigerson, H. G. (2007). An empirical examination of the stage theory of grief. *Journal of the American Medical Association, 297,* 722–723. (p. 220)

Macmillan, M., & Lena, M. L. (2010). Rehabilitating Phineas Gage. *Neuropsychological Rehabilitation, 17,* 1–18. (p. 74)

MacNeilage, P. F., & Davis, B. L. (2000). On the origin of internal structure of word forms. *Science, 288,* 527–531. (p. 367)

MacNeilage, P. F., Rogers, L. J., & Vallortigara, G. (2009, July). Origins of the left and right brain. *Scientific American,* pp. 60–67. (pp. 79, 80)

Maddi, S. R., Harvey, R. H., Khoshaba, D. M., Fazel, M., & Resurreccion, N. (2009). Hardiness training facilitates performance in college. *Journal of Positive Psychology, 4,* 566–577. (p. 464)

Maddieson, I. (1984). *Patterns of sounds.* Cambridge: Cambridge University Press. (p. 366)

Maddux, W. W., & Galinsky, A. D. (2009). Cultural borders and mental barriers: The relationship between living abroad and creativity. *Journal of Personality and Social Psychology, 96,* 1047–1061. (p. 388)

Maddux, W. W., Adam, H., & Galinsky, A. D. (2010). When in Rome . . . learn why the Romans do what they do: How multicultural learning experiences facilitate creativity. *Personality and Social Psychology Bulletin, 36,* 731–741. (p. 388)

Maes, H. H. M., Neale, M. C., & Eaves, L. J. (1997). Genetic and environmental factors in relative body weight and human adiposity. *Behavior Genetics, 27,* 325–351. (p. 430)

Maestripieri, D. (2003). Similarities in affiliation and aggression between cross-fostered rhesus macaque females and their biological mothers. *Developmental Psychobiology, 43,* 321–327. (p. 137)

Maglaty, J. (2011, April 8). When did girls start wearing pink? *Smithsonian.com.* (p. 157)

Magnussen, S., Andersson, J., Cornoldi, C., De Beni, R., Endestad, T., Goodman, G. S., Helstrup, T., Koriat, A., Larsson, M., Melinder, A., Nilsson, L. G., Rönnberg, J., & Zimmer, H. (2006). What people believe about memory. *Memory, 4,* 595–613. (p. 340)

Magnusson, D. (1990). Personality research—challenges for the future. *European Journal of Personality, 4,* 1–17. (p. 668)

Maguire, E. A., Spiers, H. J., Good, C. D., Hartley, T., Frackowiak, R. S. J., & Burgess, N. (2003a). Navigation expertise and the human hippocampus: A structural brain imaging analysis. *Hippocampus, 13,* 250–259. (p. 324)

Maguire, E. A., Valentine, E. R., Wilding, J. M., & Kapur, N. (2003b). Routes to remembering: The brains behind superior memory. *Nature Neuroscience, 6,* 90–95. (pp. 319, 324)

Mahowald, M. W., & Ettinger, M. G. (1990). Things that go bump in the night: The parsomias revisted. *Journal of Clinical Neurophysiology, 7,* 119–143. (p. 105)

Maier, S. F., Watkins, L. R., & Fleshner, M. (1994). Psychoneuroimmunology: The interface between behavior, brain, and immunity. *American Psychologist, 49,* 1004–1017. (p. 510)

Major, B., Carrington, P. I., & Carnevale, P. J. D. (1984). Physical attractiveness and self-esteem: Attribution for praise from an other-sex evaluator. *Personality and Social Psychology Bulletin, 10,* 43–50. (p. 610)

Major, B., Schmidlin, A. M., & Williams, L. (1990). Gender patterns in social touch: The impact of setting and age. *Journal of Personality and Social Psychology, 58,* 634–643. (p. 158)

Malamuth, N. M. (1996). Sexually explicit media, gender differences, and evolutionary theory. *Journal of Communication, 46,* 8–31. (p. 604)

Malamuth, N. M., & Check, J. V. P. (1981). The effects of media exposure on acceptance of violence against women: A field experiment. *Journal of Research in Personality, 15,* 436–446. (p. 438)

Malamuth, N. M., Linz, D., Heavey, C. L., Barnes, G., & Acker, M. (1995). Using the confluence model of sexual aggression to predict men's conflict with women: A 10-year follow-up study. *Journal of Personality and Social Psychology, 69,* 353–369. (p. 604)

Malamuth, N. M., Sockloskie, R. J., Koss, M. P., & Tanaka, J. S. (1991). Characteristics of aggressors against women: Testing a model using a national sample of college students. *Journal of Consulting and Clinical Psychology, 59,* 670–681. (p. 604)

Maldonado-Molina, M. M., Reingle, J. M., Jennings, W. G., & Prado, G. (2011). Drinking and driving among immigrant and US-born Hispanic young adults: Results from a longitudinal and nationally representative study. *Addictive Behavior, 36,* 381–388. (p. 634)

Malkiel, B. (2004). *A random walk down Wall Street* (8th ed.). New York: Norton. (p. 357)

Malkiel, B. (2007). *A random walk down Wall Street: The time-tested strategy for successful investing (revised and updated).* New York: Norton. (p. 18)

Malle, B. F. (2006). The actor-observer asymmetry in attribution: A (surprising) meta-analysis. *Psychological Bulletin, 132,* 895–919. (p. 573)

Malle, B. F., Knobe, J. M., & Nelson, S. E. (2007). Actor-observe asymmetries in explanations of behavior: New answers to an old question. *Journal of Personality and Social Psychology, 93,* 491–514. (p. 573)

Malmquist, C. P. (1986). Children who witness parental murder: Post-traumatic aspects. *Journal of the American Academy of Child Psychiatry, 25,* 320–325. (p. 540)

Malnic, B., Hirono, J., Sato, T., & Buck, L. B. (1999). Combinatorial receptor codes for odors. *Cell, 96,* 713–723. (p. 270)

Mampe, B., Friederici, A. D., Christophe, A., & Wermke, K. (2009). Newborns' cry melody is shaped by their native language. *Current Biology, 19,* 1–4. (p. 174)

Maner, J. K., DeWall, C. N, Baumeister, R. F., & Schaller, M. (2007). Does social exclusion motivate interpersonal reconnection? Resolving the "porcupine problem." *Journal of Personality and Social Psychology, 92,* 42–55. (p. 452)

Manson, J. E. (2002). Walking compared with vigorous exercise for the prevention of cardiovascular events in women. *New England Journal of Medicine, 347,* 716–725. (p. 521)

Maquet, P. (2001). The role of sleep in learning and memory. *Science, 294,* 1048–1052. (p. 107)

Maquet, P., Peters, J-M., Aerts, J., Delfiore, G., Degueldre, C., Luxen, A., & Franck, G. (1996). Functional neuroanatomy of human rapid-eye-movement sleep and dreaming. *Nature, 383,* 163–166. (p. 107)

Mar, R. A., & Oatley, K. (2008). The function of fiction is the abstraction and simulation of social experience. *Perspectives on Psychological Science, 3,* 173–192. (p. 306)

Marcus, B., Machilek, F., & Schütz, A. (2006). Personality in cyberspace: Personal web sites as media for personality expressions and impressions. *Journal of Personality and Social Psychology, 90,* 1014–1031. (p. 555)

Marcus, G. F., Vijayan, S., Rao, S. B., & Vishton, P. M. (1999). Rule learning by seven-month-old infants. *Science, 283,* 77–80. (p. 369)

Maren, S. (2007). The threatened brain. *Science, 317,* 1043–1044. (p. 643)

Margolis, M. L. (2000). Brahms' lullaby revisited: Did the composer have obstructive sleep apnea? *Chest, 118,* 210–213. (p. 104)

Marinak, B. A., & Gambrell, L. B. (2008). Intrinsic motivation and rewards: What sustains young children's engagement with text? *Literacy Research and Instruction, 47,* 9–26. (p. 303)

Markovizky, G., & Samid, Y. (2008). The process of immigrant adjustment: The role of time in determining psychological adjustment. *Journal of Cross-Cultural Psychology, 39,* 782–798. (p. 506)

Markowitsch, H. J. (1995). Which brain regions are critically involved in the retrieval of old episodic memory? *Brain Research Reviews, 21,* 117–127. (p. 323)

Markowitz, J. C., Svartberg, M., & Swartz, H. A. (1998). Is IPT time-limited psychodynamic psychotherapy? *Journal of Psychotherapy Practice and Research, 7,* 185–195. (p. 679)

Marks, I., & Cavanagh, K. (2009). Computer-aided psychological treatments: Evolving issues. *Annual Review of Clinical Psychology, 5,* 121–141. (p. 688)

Markus, G. B. (1986). Stability and change in political attitudes: Observe, recall, and "explain." *Political Behavior, 8,* 21–44. (p. 344)

Markus, H. R., & Kitayama, S. (1991). Culture and the self: Implications for cognition, emotion, and motivation. *Psychological Review, 98,* 224–253. (pp. 153, 376, 493)

Markus, H. R., & Nurius, P. (1986). Possible selves. *American Psychologist, 41,* 954–969. (p. 564)

Markus, H. R., Uchida, Y., Omoregie, H., Townsend, S. S. M., & Kitayama, S. (2006). Going for the gold: Models of agency in Japanese and American contexts. *Psychological Science, 17,* 103–112. (p. 155)

Marley, J., & Bulia, S. (2001). Crimes against people with mental illness: Types, perpetrators and influencing factors. *Social Work, 46,* 115–124. (p. 632)

Marmot, M. G., Bosma, H., Hemingway, H., Brunner, E., & Stansfeld, S. (1997). Contribution to job control and other risk factors to social variations in coronary heart disease incidents. *Lancet, 350,* 235–239. (p. 518)

Marsh, A. A., Elfenbein, H. A., & Ambady, N. (2003). Nonverbal "accents": Cultural differences in facial expressions of emotion. *Psychological Science, 14,* 373–376. (p. 487)

Marsh, H. W., & Craven, R. G. (2006). Reciprocal effects of self-concept and performance from a multidimensional perspective: Beyond seductive pleasure and unidimensional perspectives. *Perspectives on Psychological Science, 1,* 133–163. (p. 564)

Marsh, H. W., & Parker, J. W. (1984). Determinants of student self-concept: Is it better to be a relatively large fish in a small pond even if you don't learn to swim as well? *Journal of Personality and Social Psychology, 47,* 213–231. (p. 500)

Marshall, M. J. (2002). *Why spanking doesn't work.* Springville, UT: Bonneville Books. (p. 292)

Marshall, R. D., Bryant, R. A., Amsel, L., Suh, E. J., Cook, J. M., & Neria, Y. (2007). The psychology of ongoing threat: Relative risk appraisal, the September 11 attacks, and terrorism-related fears. *American Psychologist, 62,* 304–316. (p. 356)

Marshall, W. L. (1989). Pornography and sex offenders. In D. Zillmann & J. Bryant (Eds.), *Pornography: Research advances and policy considerations.* Hillsdale, NJ: Erlbaum. (p. 603)

Marshall, W. L. (2000). Revisiting the use of pornography by sexual offenders: Implications for theory and practice. *Journal of Sexual Aggression, 6,* 67–77. (p. 603)

Marteau, T. M. (1989). Framing of information: Its influences upon decisions of doctors and patients. *British Journal of Social Psychology, 28,* 89–94. (p. 358)

Marti, M. W., Robier, D. M., & Baron, R. S. (2000). Right before our eyes: The failure to recognize non-prototypical forms of prejudice. *Group Processes and Intergroup Relations, 3,* 403–418. 409–416. (p. 353)

Martin, C. K., Anton, S. D., Walden, H., Arnett, C., Greenway, F. L., & Williamson, D. A. (2007). Slower eating rate reduces the food intake of men, but not women: Implications for behavioural weight control. *Behaviour Research and Therapy, 45,* 2349–2359. (p. 433)

Martin, C. L., & Ruble, D. (2004). Children's search for gender cues. *Current Directions in Psychological Science, 13,* 67–70. (p. 163)

Martin, C. L., Ruble, D. N., & Szkrybalo, J. (2002). Cognitive theories of early gender development. *Psychological Bulletin, 128,* 903–933. (p. 163)

Martin, R. J., White, B. D., & Hulsey, M. G. (1991). The regulation of body weight. *American Scientist, 79,* 528–541. (p. 424)

Martin, R. M., Goodall, S. H., Gunnell, D., & Smith, G. D. (2007). Breast feeding in infancy and social mobility: 60-year follow-up of the Boyd Orr cohort. *Archives of Disease in Childhood, 92,* 317–321. (p. 34)

Martin, S. J., Kelly, I. W., & Saklofske, D. H. (1992). Suicide and lunar cycles: A critical review over 28 years. *Psychological Reports, 71,* 787–795. (p. 669)

Martino, S. C., Collins, R. L., Kanouse, D. E., Elliott, M., & Berry, S. H. (2005). Social cognitive processes mediating the relationship between exposure to television's sexual content and adolescents' sexual behavior. *Journal of Personality and Social Psychology, 89,* 914–924. (p. 440)

Martins, Y., Preti, G., Crabtree, C. R., & Wysocki, C. J. (2005). Preference for human body odors is influenced by gender and sexual orientation. *Psychological Science, 16,* 694–701. (p. 445)

Marx, D. M., Ko, S. J., & Friedman, R. A. (2009). The "Obama effect": How a salient role model reduces race-based performance differences. *Journal of Experimental Social Psychology, 45,* 953–956. (p. 414)

Masicampo, E. J., & Baumeister, R. F. (2008). Toward a physiology of dual-process reasoning and judgment: Lemonade, willpower, and the expensive rule-based analysis. *Psychological Science, 19,* 255–260. (p. 558)

Maslow, A. H. (1970). *Motivation and personality* (2nd ed.). New York: Harper & Row. (pp. 420, 543)

Maslow, A. H. (1971). *The farther reaches of human nature.* New York: Viking Press. (p. 420)

Mason, A. E., Sbarra, D. A., & Mehl, M. R. (2010). Thin-slicing divorce: Thirty seconds of information predict changes in psychological adjustment over 90 days. *Psychological Science, 21,* 1420–1422. (p. 485)

Mason, C., & Kandel, E. R. (1991). Central visual pathways. In E. R. Kandel, J. H. Schwartz, & T. M. Jessell (Eds.), *Principles of neural science* (3rd ed.). New York: Elsevier. (p. 54)

Mason, H. (2003, March 25). Wake up, sleepy teen. *Gallup Poll Tuesday Briefing* (www.gallup.com). (p. 101)

Mason, H. (2003, September 2). Americans, Britons at odds on animal testing. *Gallup Poll News Service* (http://www.gallup.com). (p. 23)

Mason, H. (2005, January 25). Who dreams, perchance to sleep? *Gallup Poll News Service* (www.gallup.com). (pp. 100, 101)

Mason, R. A., & Just, M. A. (2004). How the brain processes causal inferences in text. *Psychological Science, 15,* 1–7. (p. 79)

Masse, L. C., & Tremblay, R. E. (1997). Behavior of boys in kindergarten and the onset of substance use during adolescence. *Archives of General Psychiatry, 54,* 62–68. (p. 126)

Massey, C., Simmons, J. P., & Armor, D. A. (2011). Hope over experience: Desirability and the persistence of optimism. *Psychological Science, 22,* 274–281. (p. 561)

Massimini, M., Ferrarelli, F., Huber, R., Esser, S. K., Singh, H., & Tononi, G. (2005). Breakdown of cortical effective connectivity during sleep. *Science, 309,* 2228–2232. (p. 93)

Mast, M. S., & Hall, J. A. (2006). Women's advantage at remembering others' appearance: A systematic look at the why and when of a gender difference. *Personality and Social Psychology Bulletin, 32,* 353–364. (p. 611)

Masten, A. S. (2001). Ordinary magic: Resilience processes in development. *American Psychologist, 56,* 227–238. (p. 191)

Masters, K. S. (2010). The role of religion in therapy: Time for psychologists to have a little faith? *Cognitive and Behavioral Practice, 17,* 393–400. (p. 700)

Masters, W. H., & Johnson, V. E. (1966). *Human sexual response.* Boston: Little, Brown. (p. 435)

Mastroianni, G. R. (2002). Milgram and the Holocaust: A reexamination. *Journal of Theoretical and Philosophical Psychology, 22,* 158–173. (p. 584)

Mastroianni, G. R., & Reed, G. (2006). Apples, barrels, and Abu Ghraib. *Sociological Focus, 39,* 239–250. (p. 576)

Masuda, T., Ellsworth, P. C., Mesquita, B., Leu, J., Tanida, S., & Van de Veerdonk, E. (2008). Placing the face in context: Cultural differences in the perception of facial emotion. *Journal of Personality and Social Psychology, 94,* 365–381. (p. 489)

Mataix-Cols, D., Rosario-Campos, M. C., & Leckman, J. F. (2005). A multidimensional model of obsessive-compulsive disorder. *American Journal of Psychiatry, 162,* 228–238. (p. 643)

Mataix-Cols, D., Wooderson, S., Lawrence, N., Brammer, M. J., Speckens, A., & Phillips, M. L. (2004). Distinct neural correlates of washing, checking, and hoarding symptom dimensions in obsessive-compulsive disorder. *Archives of General Psychiatry, 61,* 564–576. (p. 643)

Mather, M., Canli, T., English, T., Whitfield, S., Wais, P., Ochsner, K., Gabrieli, J. D. E., & Carstensen, L. L. (2004). Amygdala responses to emotionally valenced stimuli in older and younger adults. *Psychological Science, 15,* 259–263. (p. 218)

Mather, M., Lighthall, N. R., Nga, L., & Gorlick, M. A. (2010). Sex differences in how stress affects brain activity during face viewing. *NeuroReport, 21,* 933–937. (p. 508)

Matsumoto, D. (1994). *People: Psychology from a cultural perspective.* Pacific Grove, CA: Brooks/Cole. (p. 376)

Matsumoto, D., & Ekman, P. (1989). American-Japanese cultural differences in intensity ratings of facial expressions of emotion. *Motivation and Emotion, 13,* 143–157. (p. 487)

Matsumoto, D., & Willingham, B. (2006). The thrill of victory and the agony of defeat: Spontaneous expressions of medal winners of the 2004 Athens Olympic Games. *Journal of Personality and Social Psychology, 91,* 568–581. (p. 488)

Matsumoto, D., & Willingham, B. (2009a). Spontaneous facial expressions of emotion of congenitally and noncongenitally blind individuals. *Journal of Personality and Social Psychology, 96,* 1–10. (p. 488)

Matsumoto, D., Willingham, B., & Olide, A. (2009b). Sequential dynamics of culturally moderated facial expressions of emotion. *Psychological Science, 20,* 1269–1275. (p. 489)

Matthews, K. A. (2005). Psychological perspectives on the development of coronary heart disease. *American Psychologist, 60,* 783–796. (p. 514)

Matthews, R. N., Domjan, M., Ramsey, M., & Crews, D. (2007). Learning effects on sperm competition and reproductive fitness. *Psychological Science, 18,* 758–762. (p. 280)

Maurer, D., & Maurer, C. (1988). *The world of the newborn.* New York: Basic Books. (p. 175)

Mauss, I. B., Shallcross, A. J., Troy, A. S., John, O. P., Ferrer, E., Wilhelm, F. H., & Gross, J. J. (2011). Don't hide your happiness! Positive emotion dissociation, social connectedness, and psychological functioning. *Journal of Personality and Social Psychology, 100,* 738–748. (p. 495)

May, C., & Hasher, L. (1998). Synchrony effects in inhibitory control over thought and action. *Journal of Experimental Psychology: Human Perception and Performance, 24,* 363–380. (p. 93)

May, P. A., & Gossage, J.P. (2001). Estimating the prevalence of fetal alcohol syndrome: A summary. *Alcohol Research and Health, 25,* 159–167. (p. 174)

Mayberg, H. S. (2006). Defining neurocircuits in depression: Strategies toward treatment selection based on neuroimaging phenotypes. *Psychiatric Annals, 36,* 259–268. (p. 709)

Mayberg, H. S. (2007). Defining the neural circuitry of depression: Toward a new nosology with therapeutic implications. *Biological Psychiatry, 61,* 729–730. (p. 709)

Mayberg, H. S. (2009). Targeted Modulation of Neural Circuits: A New Treatment Strategy for Depression. *Journal of Clinical Investigation, 119,* 717–25. (p. 709)

Mayberg, H. S., Lozano, A. M., Voon, V., McNeely, H. E., Seminowicz, D., Hamani, C., Schwalb, J. M., & Kennedy, S. H. (2005). Deep brain stimulation for treatment-resistant depression. *Neuron, 45,* 651–660. (p. 709)

Mayberry, R. I., Lock, E., & Kazmi, H. (2002). Linguistic ability and early language exposure. *Nature, 417,* 38. (p. 370)

Mayer, J. D., Salovey, P., & Caruso, D. (2002). *The Mayer-Salovey-Caruso emotional intelligence test (MSCEIT).* Toronto: Multi-Health Systems, Inc. (p. 389)

Mayer, J. D., Salovey, P., & Caruso, D. R. (2008). Emotional intelligence: New ability or eclectic traits? *American Psychologist, 63,* 503–517. (p. 389)

Mays, V. M., Cochran, S. D., & Barnes, N. W. (2007). Race, race-based discrimination, and health outcomes among African Americans. *Annual Review of Psychology, 58,* 201–225. (p. 507)

Mazure, C., Keita, G., & Blehar, M. (2002). *Summit on women and depression: Proceedings and recommendations.* Washington, DC: American Psychological Association (www.apa.org/pi/wpo/women&depression.pdf). (p. 653)

Mazzoni, G., & Memon, A. (2003). Imagination can create false autobiographical memories. *Psychological Science, 14,* 186–188. (p. 342)

Mazzoni, G., Scoboria, A., & Harvey, L. (2010). Nonbelieved memories. *Psychological Science, 21,* 1334–1340. (p. 342)

Mazzoni, G., & Vannucci, M. (2007). Hindsight bias, the misinformation effect, and false autobiographical memories. *Social Cognition, 25,* 203–220. (p. 344)

McAndrew, F. T. (2009). The interacting roles of testosterone and challenges to status in human male aggression. *Aggression and Violent Behavior, 14,* 330–335. (pp. 600, 601)

McAneny, L. (1996, September). Large majority think government conceals information about UFO's. *Gallup Poll Monthly,* pp. 23–26. (p. 343)

McBeath, M. K., Shaffer, D. M., & Kaiser, M. K. (1995). How baseball outfielders determine where to run to catch fly balls. *Science, 268,* 569–572. (p. 247)

McBurney, D. H. (1996). *How to think like a psychologist: Critical thinking in psychology.* Upper Saddle River, NJ: Prentice-Hall. (p. 73)

McBurney, D. H., & Collings, V. B. (1984). *Introduction to sensation and perception* (2nd ed.). Englewood Cliffs, NJ: Prentice-Hall. (pp. 248, 249)

McBurney, D. H., & Gent, J. F. (1979). On the nature of taste qualities. *Psychological Bulletin, 86,* 151–167. (p. 266)

McCain, N. L., Gray, D. P., Elswick, R. K., Jr., Robins, J. W., Tuck, I., Walter, J. M., Rausch, S. M., & Ketchum, J. M. (2008). A randomized clinical trial of alternative stress management interventions in persons with HIV infection. *Journal of Consulting and Clinical Psychology, 76,* 431–441. (p. 511)

McCann, I. L., & Holmes, D. S. (1984). Influence of aerobic exercise on depression. *Journal of Personality and Social Psychology, 46,* 1142–1147. (p. 522)

McCann, U. D., Eligulashvili, V., & Ricaurte, G. A. (2001). (+–)3,4–Methylenedioxymethamphetamine ('Ecstasy')-induced serotonin neurotoxicity: Clinical studies. *Neuropsychobiology, 42,* 11–16. (p. 123)

McCarthy, P. (1986, July). Scent: The tie that binds? *Psychology Today,* pp. 6, 10. (p. 269)

McCauley, C. R. (2002). Psychological issues in understanding terrorism and the response to terrorism. In C. E. Stout (Ed.), *The psychology of terrorism* (Vol. 3). Westport, CT: Praeger/Greenwood. (p. 589)

McCauley, C. R., & Segal, M. E. (1987). Social psychology of terrorist groups. In C. Hendrick (Ed.), *Group processes and intergroup relations.* Beverly Hills, CA: Sage. (p. 589)

McClendon, B. T., & Prentice-Dunn, S. (2001). Reducing skin cancer risk: An intervention based on protection motivation theory. *Journal of Health Psychology, 6,* 321–328. (p. 574)

McClintock, M. K., & Herdt, G. (1996, December). Rethinking puberty: The development of sexual attraction. *Current Directions in Psychological Science, 5*(6), 178–183. (p. 197)

McClure, M. J., Lydon, J. E., Baccus, J. R., & Baldwin, M. W. (2010). A signal detection analysis of chronic attachment anxiety at speed dating: Being unpopular is only the first part of the problem. *Personality and Social Psychology Bulletin, 36,* 1024–1036. (p. 225)

McConkey, K. M. (1995). Hypnosis, memory, and the ethics of uncertainty. *Australian Psychologist, 30,* 1–10. (p. 111)

McConnell, R. A. (1991). National Academy of Sciences opinion on parapsychology. *Journal of the American Society for Psychical Research, 85,* 333–365. (p. 253)

McCool, G. (1999, October 26). Mirror-gazing Venezuelans top of vanity stakes. *Toronto Star* (via web.lexis-nexis.com). (p. 610)

McCord, J. (1978). A thirty-year follow-up on treatment effects. *American Psychologist, 33,* 284–289. (p. 692)

McCord, J. (1979). Following up on Cambridge-Somerville. *American Psychologist, 34,* 727. (p. 692)

McCormick, C. M., & Witelson, S. F. (1991). A cognitive profile of homosexual men compared to heterosexual men and women. *Psychoneuroendocrinology, 16,* 459–473. (p. 447)

McCrae, R. R. (2009). The five-factor model of personality traits: Consensus and controversy. In P. J. Corr & G. Matthews, Gerald (eds.). *The Cambridge handbook of personality psychology.* New York: Cambridge University Press. (p. 551)

McCrae, R. R. (2011). Personality theories for the 21st century. *Teaching of Psychology, 38,* 209–214. (pp. 551, 552)

McCrae, R. R., & Costa, P. T., Jr. (1986). Clinical assessment can benefit from recent advances in personality psychology. *American Psychologist, 41,* 1001–1003. (p. 552)

McCrae, R. R., & Costa, P. T., Jr. (1994). The stability of personality: Observations and evaluations. *Current Directions in Psychological Science, 3,* 173–175. (p. 554)

McCrae, R. R., & Costa, P. T., Jr. (2008). The Five-Factor Theory of personality. In O. P. John, R. W., Robins, & L. A. Pervin (eds.), *Handbook of personality: Theory and research, 3rd edition.* New York: Guilford. (p. 552)

McCrae, R. R., Costa, P. T., Jr., Ostendorf, F., Angleitner, A., Hrebickova, M., Avia, M. D., Sanz, J., Sanchez-Bernardos, M. L., Kusdil, M. E., Woodfield, R., Saunders, P. R., & Smith, P. B. (2000). Nature over nurture: Temperament, personality, and life span development. *Journal of Personality and Social Psychology, 78,* 173–186. (p. 138)

McCrae, R. R., Scally, M., Terraccioani, A., Abecasis, G. R., & Costa, Jr., P. T. (2010). An alternative to the search for single polymorphisms: Toward molecular personality scales for the Five-Factor Model. *Journal of Personality and Social Psychology, 99,* 1014–1024. (p. 552)

McCrae, R. R., Terracciano, A., & Khoury, B. (2007). *Dolce far niente:* The positive psychology of personality stability and invariance. In A. D. Ong & M. H. Van Dulmen (Eds.), *Oxford handbook of methods in positive psychology.* New York: Oxford University Press. (p. 138)

McCrink, K., & Wynn, K. (2004). Large-number addition and subtraction by 9-month-old infants. *Psychological Science, 15,* 776–781. (p. 182)

McCullough, M. E., Hoyt, W. T., Larson, D. B., Koenig, H. G., & Thoresen, C. (2000). Religious involvement and mortality: A meta-analytic review. *Health Psychology, 19,* 211–222. (p. 527)

McCullough, M. E., & Laurenceau, J-P. (2005). Religiousness and the trajectory of self-rated health across adulthood. *Personality and Social Psychology Bulletin, 31,* 560–573. (p. 527)

McCullough, M. E., & Willoughby, B. L. B. (2009). Religion, self-regulation, and self-control: Associations, explanations, and implications. *Psychological Bulletin, 135,* 69–93. (p. 527)

McDaniel, M. A. (2005). Big-brained people are smarter: A meta-analysis of the relationship between in vivo brain volume and intelligence. *Intelligence, 33,* 337–346. (p. 390)

McDaniel, M. A., Howard, D. C., & Einstein, G. O. (2009). The read-recite-review study strategy: Effective and portable. *Psychological Science, 20,* 516–522. (pp. 12, 25, 42, 59, 68, 81, 91, 109, 114, 129, 147, 167, 176, 207, 221, 233, 256, 273, 285, 297, 309, 322, 329, 349, 364, 380, 391, 404, 415, 434, 456, 471, 483, 491, 503, 516, 529, 542, 546, 569, 578, 592, 607, 623, 636, 644, 656, 664, 673, 691, 703, 713)

McEvoy, S. P., Stevenson, M. R., McCartt, A. T., Woodward, M., Hawroth, C., Palamara, P., & Ceracelli, R. (2005). Role of mobile phones in motor vehicle crashes resulting in hospital attendance: A case-crossover study. *British Medical Journal, 33,* 428. (p. 89)

McEvoy, S. P., Stevenson, M. R., & Woodward, M. (2007). The contribution of passengers versus mobile phone use to motor vehicle crashes resulting in hospital attendance by the driver. *Accident Analysis and Prevention, 39,* 1170–1176. (p. 89)

McFadden, D. (2002). Masculinization effects in the auditory system. *Archives of Sexual Behavior, 31,* 99–111. (p. 446)

McFarland, C., & Ross, M. (1987). The relation between current impressions and memories of self and dating partners. *Psychological Bulletin, 13,* 228–238. (p. 344)

McGaugh, J. L. (1994). Quoted by B. Bower, Stress hormones hike emotional memories. *Science News, 146,* 262. (p. 326)

McGaugh, J. L. (2003). *Memory and emotion: The making of lasting memories.* New York: Columbia University Press. (p. 326)

McGhee, P. E. (June, 1976). Children's appreciation of humor: A test of the cognitive congruency principle. *Child Development, 47*(2), 420–426. (p. 183)

McGowan, P. O., Sasaki, A., D'Alessio, A. C., Dymov, S., Labonté, B., Szyl, M., Turecki, G., & Meaney, M. J. (2009). Epigenetic regulation of the glucocorticoid receptor in human brain associates with childhood abuse. *Nature Neuroscience, 12,* 342–348. (p. 140)

McGrath, J. J., & Welham, J. L. (1999). Season of birth and schizophrenia: A systematic review and meta-analysis of data from the Southern hemisphere. *Schizophrenia Research, 35,* 237–242. (p. 661)

McGrath, J. J., Welham, J., & Pemberton, M. (1995). Month of birth, hemisphere of birth and schizophrenia. *British Journal of Psychiatry, 167,* 783–785. (p. 661)

McGue, M. (2010). The end of behavioral genetics? *Behavioral Genetics, 40,* 284–296. (p. 141)

McGue, M., & Bouchard, T. J., Jr. (1998). Genetic and environmental influences on human behavioral differences. *Annual Review of Neuroscience, 21,* 1–24. (p. 136)

McGue, M., Bouchard, T. J., Jr., Iacono, W. G., & Lykken, D. T. (1993). Behavioral genetics of cognitive ability: A life-span perspective. In R. Plomin & G. E. McClearn (Eds.), *Nature, nurture and psychology.* Washington, DC: American Psychological Association. (p. 406)

McGue, M., & Lykken, D. T. (1992). Genetic influence on risk of divorce. *Psychological Science, 3,* 368–373. (p. 134)

McGuire, W. J. (1986). The myth of massive media impact: Savings and salvagings. In G. Comstock (Ed.), *Public communication and behavior.* Orlando, FL: Academic Press. (p. 308)

McGurk, H., & MacDonald, J. (1976). Hearing lips and seeing voices. *Nature, 264,* 746–748. (p. 267)

McHugh, P. R. (1995a). Witches, multiple personalities, and other psychiatric artifacts. *Nature Medicine, 1*(2), 110–114. (p. 666)

McHugh, P. R. (1995b). Resolved: Multiple personality disorder is an individually and socially created artifact. *Journal of the American Academy of Child and Adolescent Psychiatry, 34,* 957–959. (p. 667)

McKay, J. (2000). Building self-esteem in children. In M. McKay & P. Fanning (eds.), *Self-esteem.* New York: New Harbinger/St. Martins. (p. 564)

McKellar, J., Stewart, E., & Humphreys, K. (2003). Alcoholics Anonymous involvement and positive alcohol-related outcomes: Cause, consequence, or just a correlate? A prospective 2-year study of 2,319 alcohol-dependent men. *Journal of Consulting and Clinical Psychology, 71,* 302–308. (p. 689)

McKenna, K. Y. A., & Bargh, J. A. (1998). Coming out in the age of the Internet: Identity "demarginalization" through virtual group participation. *Journal of Personality and Social Psychology, 75,* 681–694. (p. 609)

McKenna, K. Y. A., & Bargh, J. A. (2000). Plan 9 from cyberspace: The implications of the Internet for personality and social psychology. *Personality and Social Psychology Review, 4,* 57–75. (p. 609)

McKenna, K. Y. A., Green, A. S., & Gleason, M. E. J. (2002). What's the big attraction? Relationship formation on the Internet. *Journal of Social Issues, 58,* 9–31. (p. 609)

McKone, E., Kanwisher, N., & Duchaine, B. C. (2007). Can generic expertise explain special processing for faces? *Trends in Cognitive Sciences, 11,* 8–15. (p. 239)

McLaughlin, C. S., Chen, C., Greenberger, E., & Biermeier, C. (1997). Family, peer, and individual correlates of sexual experience among Caucasian and Asian American late adolescents. *Journal of Personality and Social Psychology: Journal of Research on Adolescence, 7,* 33–53. (p. 439)

McLaughlin, M. (2010, October 2). JK Rowling: Depression, the 'terrible place that allowed me to come back stronger.' *The Scotsman* (www.scotsman.com). (p. 647)

McLean, C. P., & Anderson, E. R. (2009). Brave men and timid women? A review of the gender differences in fear and anxiety. *Clinical Psychology Review, 29,* 496–505. (p. 637)

McMurray, B. (2007). Defusing the childhood vocabulary explosion. *Science, 317,* 631. (p. 366)

McMurray, C. (2004, January 13). U.S., Canada, Britain: Who's getting in shape? *Gallup Poll Tuesday Briefing* (www.gallup.com). (p. 522)

McNally, R. J. (1999). EMDR and Mesmerism: A comparative historical analysis. *Journal of Anxiety Disorders, 13,* 225–236. (p. 697)

McNally, R. J. (2003). *Remembering trauma.* Cambridge, MA: Harvard University Press. (pp. 346, 347, 640)

McNally, R. J. (2007). Betrayal trauma theory: A critical appraisal. *Memory, 15,* 280–294. (p. 346)

McNally, R. J., & Geraerts, E. (2009). A new solution to the recovered memory debate. *Perspectives in Psychological Science, 4,* 126–134. (p. 346)

McNeil, B. J., Pauker, S. G., & Tversky, A. (1988). On the framing of medical decisions. In D. E. Bell, H. Raiffa, & A. Tversky (Eds.), *Decision making: Descriptive, normative, and prescriptive interactions.* New York: Cambridge University Press. (p. 358)

Mead, G. E., Morley, W., Campbell, P., Greig, C. A., McMurdo, M., & Lawlor, D. A. (2010). Exercise for depression. *Cochrance Database Systematic Reviews,* Issue 3. Art. No.: CD004366. (p. 522)

Meador, B. D., & Rogers, C. R. (1984). Person-centered therapy. In R. J. Corsini (Ed.), *Current psychotherapies* (3rd ed.). Itasca, IL: Peacock. (p. 680)

Medical Institute for Sexual Health. (1994, April). Condoms ineffective against human papilloma virus. *Sexual Health Update*, p. 2. (p. 441)

Medland, S. E., Perelle, I., De Monte, V., & Ehrman, L. (2004). Effects of culture, sex, and age on the distribution of handedness: An evaluation of the sensitivity of three measures of handedness. *Laterality: Asymmetries of Body, Brain, and Cognition, 9,* 287–297. (p. 80)

Mednick, S. A., Huttunen, M. O., & Machon, R. A. (1994). Prenatal influenza infections and adult schizophrenia. *Schizophrenia Bulletin, 20,* 263–267. (p. 661)

Mehl, M. R., Gosling, S. D., & Pennebaker, J. W. (2006). Personality in its natural habitat: Manifestations and implicit folk theories of personality in daily life. *Journal of Personality and Social Psychology, 90,* 862–877. (p. 554)

Mehl, M. R., & Pennebaker, J. W. (2003). The sounds of social life: A psychometric analysis of students' daily social environments and natural conversations. *Journal of Personality and Social Psychology, 84,* 857–870. (p. 29)

Mehl, M. R., Vazire, S., Holleran, S. E., & Clark, C. S. (2010). Eavesdropping on happiness: Well-being is related to having less small talk and more substantive conversations. *Psychological Science, 21,* 539–541. (p. 501)

Mehl, M. R., Vazire, S., Ramirez-Esparza, N., Slatcher, R. B., & Pennebaker, J. W. (2007). Are women really more talkative than men? *Science, 317,* 82. (p. 159)

Mehta, M. R. (2007). Cortico-hippocampal interaction during up-down states and memory consolidation. *Nature Neuroscience, 10,* 13–15. (p. 324)

Meichenbaum, D. (1977). *Cognitive-behavior modification: An integrative approach.* New York: Plenum Press. (p. 687)

Meichenbaum, D. (1985). *Stress inoculation training.* New York: Pergamon. (p. 687)

Meijer, E. H., & Verschuere, B. (2010). The polygraph and the detection of deception. *Journal of Forensic Psychology Practice, 10,* 525–538. (p. 482)

Meltzoff, A. N. (1988). Infant imitation after a 1-week delay: Long-term memory for novel acts and multiple stimuli. *Developmental Psychology, 24,* 470–476. (p. 305)

Meltzoff, A. N., Kuhl, P. K., Movellan, J., & Sejnowski, T. J. (2009). Foundations for a new science of learning. *Science, 325,* 284–288. (pp. 305, 367)

Meltzoff, A. N., & Moore, M. K. (1989). Imitation in newborn infants: Exploring the range of gestures imitated and the underlying mechanisms. *Developmental Psychology, 25,* 954–962. (pp. 305, 308)

Meltzoff, A. N., & Moore, M. K. (1997). Explaining facial imitation: A theoretical model. *Early Development and Parenting, 6,* 179–192. (pp. 305, 308)

Melzack, R. (1990, February). The tragedy of needless pain. *Scientific American,* pp. 27–33. (p. 116)

Melzack, R. (1992, April). Phantom limbs. *Scientific American,* pp. 120–126. (p. 264)

Melzack, R. (1998, February). Quoted in Phantom limbs. *Discover,* p. 20. (p. 264)

Melzack, R. (2005). Evolution of the neuromatrix theory of pain. *Pain Practice, 5,* 85–94. (p. 264)

Melzack, R., & Wall, P. D. (1965). Pain mechanisms: A new theory. *Science, 150,* 971–979. (p. 264)

Melzack, R., & Wall, P. D. (1983). *The challenge of pain.* New York: Basic Books. (p. 264)

Mendes, E. (2010, February 9). Six in 10 overweight or obese in U.S., more in '09 than in '08. www.gallup.com. (pp. 427, 429)

Mendes, E. (2010, June 2). U.S. exercise levels up, but demographic differences remain. www.gallup.com. (p. 523)

Mendle, J., Turkheimer, E., & Emery, R. E. (2007). Detrimental psychological outcomes associated with early pubertal timing in adolescent girls. *Developmental Review, 27,* 151–171. (p. 199)

Mendolia, M., & Kleck, R. E. (1993). Effects of talking about a stressful event on arousal: Does what we talk about make a difference? *Journal of Personality and Social Psychology, 64,* 283–292. (p. 520)

Merari, A. (2002). Explaining suicidal terrorism: Theories versus empirical evidence. Invited address to the American Psychological Association. (p. 589)

Meriac, J. P., Hoffman, B. J., Woehr, D. J., & Fleisher, M. S. (2008). Further evidence for the validity of assessment center dimensions: A meta-analysis of the incremental criterion-related validity of dimension ratings. *Journal of Applied Psychology, 93,* 1042–1052. (p. 562)

Merskey, H. (1992). The manufacture of personalities: The production of multiple personality disorder. *British Journal of Psychiatry, 160,* 327–340. (p. 666)

Merton, R. K., & Kitt, A. S. (1950). Contributions to the theory of reference group behavior. In R. K. Merton & P. F. Lazarsfeld (Eds.), *Continuities in social research: Studies in the scope and method of the American soldier.* Glencoe, IL: Free Press. (p. 500)

Mesch, G. (2001). Social relationships and Internet use among adolescents in Israel. *Social Science Quarterly, 82,* 329–340. (p. 453)

Mesoudi, A. (2009). How cultural evolutionary theory can inform social psychology and vice versa. *Psychological Review, 116,* 929–952. (p. 152)

Messinis, L., Kyprianidou, A., Malefaki, S., & Papathanasopoulos, P. (2006). Neuropsychological deficits in long-term frequent cannabis users. *Neurology, 66,* 737–739. (p. 124)

Mestel, R. (1997, April 26). Get real, Siggi. *New Scientist* (www.newscientist.com/ns/970426/siggi.html). (p. 106)

Meston, C. M., & Buss, D. M. (2007). Why humans have sex. *Archives of Sexual Behavior, 36,* 477–507. (p. 438)

Metcalfe, J. (1986). Premonitions of *insight* predict impending error. *Journal of Experimental Psychology: Learning, Memory, and Cognition, 12,* 623–634. (p. 353)

Metcalfe, J. (1998). Cognitive optimism: Self-deception or memory-based processing heuristics. *Personality and Social Psychology Review, 2,* 100–110. (p. 357)

Metzler, D. K., Jensvold, M. L., Fouts, D. H., & Fouts, R. S. (2010, Spring). Vocabulary growth in adult cross-fostered chimpanzees. *Friends of Washoe,* pp. 13–16. (p. 373)

Meyer, I. H. (2003). Prejudice, social stress, and mental health in lesbian, gay, and bisexual populations: Conceptual issues and research evidence. *Psychological Bulletin, 129,* 674–697. (p. 626)

Meyer-Bahlburg, H. F. L. (1995). Psychoneuroendocrinology and sexual pleasure: The aspect of sexual orientation. In P. R. Abramson & S. D. Pinkerton (Eds.), *Sexual nature/sexual culture.* Chicago: University of Chicago Press. (p. 446)

Mezulis, A. M., Abramson, L. Y., Hyde, J. S., & Hankin, B. L. (2004). Is there a universal positivity bias in attributions? A meta-analytic review of individual, developmental, and cultural differences in the self-serving attributional bias. *Psychological Bulletin, 130,* 711–747. (p. 565)

Michaels, J. W., Bloomel, J. M., Brocato, R. M., Linkous, R. A., & Rowe, J. S. (1982). Social facilitation and inhibition in a natural setting. *Replications in Social Psychology, 2,* 21–24. (p. 587)

Michener, J. A. (1978, February 3). External forces and inner voices. Speech at the Chapel of the Four Chaplains, Philadelphia, PA. (p. 585)

Middlebrooks, J. C., & Green, D. M. (1991). Sound localization by human listeners. *Annual Review of Psychology, 42,* 135–159. (p. 262)

Miers, R. (2009, Spring). Calum's road. *Scottish Life,* pp. 36–39, 75. (p. 463)

Mikkelsen, T. S., & 66 others. (2005). Initial sequence of the chimpanzee genome and comparison with the human genome. *Nature, 437,* 69–87. (p. 132)

Mikulincer, M., Florian, V., & Hirschberger, G. (2003). The existential function of close relationships: Introducing death into the science of love. *Personality and Social Psychology Review, 7,* 20–40. (p. 541)

Mikulincer, M., & Shaver, P. R. (2001). Attachment theory and intergroup bias: Evidence that priming the secure base schema attenuates negative reactions to outgroups. *Journal of Personality and Social Psychology, 81,* 97–115. (p. 597)

Milan, R. J., Jr., & Kilmann, P. R. (1987). Interpersonal factors in premarital contraception. *Journal of Sex Research, 23,* 289–321. (p. 439)

Miles, D. R., & Carey, G. (1997). Genetic and environmental architecture of human aggression. *Journal of Personality and Social Psychology, 72,* 207–217. (p. 600)

Milgram, S. (1963). Behavioral study of obedience. *Journal of Abnormal & Social Psychology, 67*(4), 371–378. (p. 582)

Milgram, S. (1974). *Obedience to authority.* New York: Harper & Row. (pp. 112, 582, 583, 586)

Miller, G. (2004). Axel, Buck share award for deciphering how the nose knows. *Science, 306,* 207. (p. 270)

Miller, G. (2005). The dark side of glia. *Science, 308,* 778–781. (p. 69)

Miller, G. (2008). Tackling alcoholism with drugs. *Science, 320,* 168–170. (p. 127)

Miller, G. (2010). Anything but child's play. *Science, 327,* 1192–1193. (p. 646)

Miller, G. (2010). fMRI lie detection fails a legal test. *Science, 328,* 1336–1337. (p. 482)

Miller, G., & Holden, C. (2010). Proposed revisions to psychiatry's canon unveiled. *Science, 327,* 770–771. (p. 630)

Miller, G., Tybur, J. M., & Jordan, B. D. (2007). Ovulatory cycle effects on tip earnings by lap dancers: Economic evidence for human estrus? *Evolution and Human Behavior, 28,* 375–381. (p. 437)

Miller, G. A. (1956). The magical number seven, plus or minus two: Some limits on our capacity for processing information. *Psychological Review, 63,* 81–97. (p. 317)

Miller, G. E., & Blackwell, E. (2006). Turning up the heat: Inflammation as a mechanism linking chronic stress, depression, and heart disease. *Current Directions in Psychological Science, 15,* 269–272. (p. 514)

Miller, G. E., & Chen, E. (2010). Harsh family climate in early life presages the emergence of a proinflammatory phenotype in adolescence. *Psychological Science, 21,* 848–856. (p. 514)

Miller, J. G., & Bersoff, D. M. (1995). Development in the context of everyday family relationships: Culture, interpersonal morality and adaptation. In M. Killen & D. Hart (Eds.), *Morality in everyday life: A developmental perspective.* New York: Cambridge University Press. (p. 201)

Miller, J., Shepherdson, P., & Trevena, J. (2011). Effects of clock monitoring on electroencephalographic activity: Is unconscious movement initiation an artifact of the clock? *Psychological Science, 22,* 103–109. (p. 87)

Miller, K. I., & Monge, P. R. (1986). Participation, satisfaction, and productivity: A meta-analytic review. *Academy of Management Journal, 29,* 727–753. (p. 557)

Miller, L. K. (1999). The Savant Syndrome: Intellectual impairment and exceptional skill. *Psychological Bulletin, 125,* 31–46. (p. 383)

Miller, N. E. (1985, February). Rx: Biofeedback. *Psychology Today,* pp. 54–59. (p. 523)

Miller, P. A., Eisenberg, N., Fabes, R. A., & Shell, R. (1996). Relations of moral reasoning and vicarious emotion to young children's prosocial behavior toward peers and adults. *Developmental Psychology, 32,* 210–219. (p. 202)

Miller, P. J. O., Aoki, K., Rendell, L. E., & Amano, M. (2008). Stereotypical resting behavior of the sperm whale. *Current Biology, 18,* R21–R23. (p. 93)

Miller, S. D., Blackburn, T., Scholes, G., White, G. L., & Mamalis, N. (1991). Optical differences in multiple personality disorder: A second look. *Journal of Nervous and Mental Disease, 179,* 132–135. (p. 667)

Miller, S. L., & Maner, J. K. (2010). Scent of a woman: Men's testosterone responses to olfactory ovulation cues. *Psychological Science, 21,* 276–283. (p. 437)

Miller, S. L., & Maner, J. K. (2011). Ovulation as a male mating prime: Subtle signs of women's fertility influence men's mating cognition and behavior. *Journal of Personality and Social Psychology, 100,* 295–308. (p. 437)

Miller, T. W., Nigg, J. T., & Miller, R. L. (2009). Attention deficit hyperactivity disorder in African American children: what can be concluded from the past ten years. *Clinical Psychology Review, 29,* 77–86. (p. 627)

Milner, A. D., & Goodale, M. A. (2008). Two visual systems re-viewed. *Neuropsychologia, 46,* 774–785. (p. 86)

Milyavskaya, M., Gingras, I., Mageau, G. A., Koestner, R., Gagnon, H., Fang, J., & Bolché, J. (2009). Balance across contexts: Importance of balanced need satisfaction across various life domains. *Personality and Social Psychology Bulletin, 35,* 1031–1045. (p. 450)

Mineka, S. (1985). The frightful complexity of the origins of fears. In F. R. Brush & J. B. Overmier (Eds.), *Affect, conditioning and cognition: Essays on the determinants of behavior.* Hillsdale, NJ: Erlbaum. (p. 642)

Mineka, S. (2002). Animal models of clinical psychology. In N. Smelser & P. Baltes (Eds.), *International encyclopedia of the social and behavioral sciences.* Oxford, England: Elsevier Science. (p. 642)

Mineka, S., & Oehlberg, K. (2008). The relevance of recent developments in classical conditioning to understanding the etiology and maintenance of anxiety disorders. *Acta Psychologica, 127,* 567–580. (p. 641)

Mineka, S., & Zinbarg, R. (1996). Conditioning and ethological models of anxiety disorders: Stress-in-dynamic-context anxiety models. In D. Hope (Ed.), *Perspectives on anxiety, panic, and fear* (Nebraska Symposium on Motivation). Lincoln: University of Nebraska Press. (pp. 640, 643, 701)

Mingroni, M. A. (2004). The secular rise in IQ: Giving heterosis a closer look. *Intelligence, 32,* 65–83. (p. 397)

Mingroni, M. A. (2007). Resolving the IQ paradox: Heterosis as a cause of the Flynn effect and other trends. *Psychological Review, 114,* 806–829. (p. 397)

Minsky, M. (1986). *The society of mind.* New York: Simon & Schuster. (p. 85)

Mirescu, C., & Gould, E. (2006). Stress and adult neurogenesis. *Hippocampus, 16,* 233–238. (p. 508)

Mischel, W. (1968). *Personality and assessment.* New York: Wiley. (p. 554)

Mischel, W. (1981). Current issues and challenges in personality. In L. T. Benjamin, Jr. (Ed.), *The G. Stanley Hall Lecture Series* (Vol. 1). Washington, DC: American Psychological Association. (p. 562)

Mischel, W. (2009). From *Personality and Assessment* (1968) to personality science. *Journal of Research in Personality, 43,* 282–290. (p. 554)

Mischel, W., Shoda, Y., & Peake, P. K. (1988). The nature of adolescent competencies predicted by preschool delay of gratification. *Journal of Personality and Social Psychology, 54,* 687–696. (p. 202)

Mischel, W., Shoda, Y., & Rodriguez, M. L. (1989). Delay of gratification in children. *Science, 244,* 933–938. (pp. 202, 289)

Miserandino, M. (1991). Memory and the seven dwarfs. *Teaching of Psychology, 18,* 169–171. (p. 313)

Mishkin, M. (1982). A memory system in the monkey. *Philosophical Transactions of the Royal Society of London: Biological Sciences, 298,* 83–95. (p. 325)

Mishkin, M., Suzuki, W. A., Gadian, D. G., & Vargha-Khadem, F. (1997). Hierarchical organization of cognitive memory. *Philosophical Transactions of the Royal Society of London: Biological Sciences, 352,* 1461–1467. (p. 325)

Mishra, A., & Mishra, H. (2010). Border bias: The belief that state borders can protect against disasters. *Psychological Science, 21,* 1582–1586. (p. 377)

Mita, T. H., Dermer, M., & Knight, J. (1977). Reversed facial images and the mere-exposure hypothesis. *Journal of Personality and Social Psychology, 35,* 597–601. (p. 608)

Mitani, J. C., Watts, D. P., & Amsler, S. J. (2010). Lethal intergroup aggression leads to territorial expansion in wild chimpanzees. *Current Biology, 20,* R507–R509. (p. 363)

Mitchell, D. B. (2006). Nonconscious priming after 17 years: Invulnerable implicit memory? *Psychological Science, 17,* 925–929. (p. 312)

Mitchell, J. P. (2009). Social psychology as a natural kind. *Cell, 13,* 246–251. (p. 564)

Mitchell, K. J., & Porteous, D. J. (2011). Rethinking the genetic architecture of schizophrenia. *Psychological Medicine, 41,* 19–32. (p. 662)

Mitte, K. (2005). Meta-analysis of cognitive-behavioral treatments for generalized anxiety disorder: A comparison with pharmacotherapy. *Psychological Bulletin, 131,* 785–795. (p. 688)

Mitte, K. (2008). Memory bias for threatening information in anxiety and anxiety disorders: A meta-analytic review. *Psychological Bulletin, 134,* 886–911. (p. 637)

Miyagawa, T. & 19 others. (2008). Variant between *CPT1B* and *CHKB* associated with susceptibility to narcolepsy. *Nature Genetics, 40,* 1324–1328. (p. 104)

Mobbs, D., Yu, R., Meyer, M., Passamonti, L., Seymour, B., Calder, A. J., Schweizer, S., Frith, C. D., & Dalgeish, T. (2009). A key role for similarity in vicarious reward. *Science, 324,* 900. (p. 304)

Moffitt, T. E. (2005). The new look of behavioral genetics in developmental psychopathology: Gene-environment interplay in antisocial behaviors. *Psychological Bulletin, 131,* 533–554. (p. 670)

Moffitt, T. E., Caspi, A., Harrington, H., & Milne, B. J. (2002). Males on the life-course-persistent and adolescence-limited antisocial pathways: Follow-up at age 26 years. *Development and Psychopathology, 14,* 179–207. (p. 171)

Moffitt, T. E., Caspi, A., Harrington, H., Milne, B. J., Melchior, M., Goldberg, D., & Poulton, R. (2007a). Generalized anxiety disorder and depression: Childhood risk factors in a birth cohort followed to age 32. *Psychological Medicine, 37,* 441–452. (p. 637)

Moffitt, T. E., Caspi, A., & Rutter, M. (2006). Measured gene-environment interactions in psychopathology: Concepts, research strategies, and implications for research, intervention, and public understanding of genetics. *Perspectives on Psychological Science, 1,* 5–27. (p. 652)

Moffitt, T. E., Harrington, H., Caspi, A., Kim-Cohen, J., Goldberg, D., Gregory, A. M., & Poulton, R. (2007b). Depression and generalized anxiety disorder: Cumulative and sequential comorbidity in a birth cohort followed prospectively to age 32 years. *Archives of General Psychiatry, 64,* 651–660. (p. 637)

Moffitt, T. E., & 12 others. (2011). A gradient of childhood self-control predicts health, wealth, and public safety. *Proceedings of the National Academy of Sciences, 108,* 2693–2698. (p. 171)

Moghaddam, F. M. (2005). The staircase to terrorism: A psychological exploration. *American Psychologist, 60,* 161–169. (p. 589)

Mohr, H., Pritchard, J., & Lush, T. (2010, May 29). BP has been good at downplaying disaster. *Associated Press.* (p. 357)

Moises, H. W., Zoega, T., & Gottesman, I. I. (2002, July 3). The glial growth factors deficiency and synaptic destabilization hypothesis of schizophrenia. *BMC Psychiatry, 2*(8) (www.biomedcentral.com/1471-244X/2/8). (p. 661)

Möller, I., & Krahé, B. A. (2008). Exposure to violence video games and aggression in German adolescents: A longitudinal analysis. *Aggressive Behavior, 34,* 1–14. (p. 605)

Mondloch, C. J., Lewis, T. L., Budreau, D. R., Maurer, D., Dannemiller, J. L., Stephens, B. R., & Kleiner-Gathercoal, K. A. (1999). Face perception during early infancy. *Psychological Science, 10,* 419–422. (p. 175)

Money, J. (1987). Sin, sickness, or status? Homosexual gender identity and psychoneuroendocrinology. *American Psychologist, 42*, 384–399. (pp. 445, 446)

Money, J. (1988). *Gay, straight, and in-between.* New York: Oxford University Press. (p. 603)

Money, J., Berlin, F. S., Falck, A., & Stein, M. (1983). *Antiandrogenic and counseling treatment of sex offenders.* Baltimore: Department of Psychiatry and Behavioral Sciences, The Johns Hopkins University School of Medicine. (p. 437)

Monroe, S. M., & Reid, M. W. (2009). Life stress and major depression. *Currents Directions in Psychological Science, 18*, 68–72. (p. 648)

Monti, M. M., Vanhaudenhuyse, A., Coleman, M. R., Boly, M., Pickard, J. D., Tshibanda, L., Owen, A. M., & Laureys, S. (2010). Willful modulation of brain activity in disorders of consciousness. *New England Journal of Medicine, 362*, 579–589. (p. 85)

Mooallem, J. (2009, February 19). Rescue flight. *New York Times Magazine* (www.nytimes.com). (p. 189)

Mook, D. G. (1983). In defense of external invalidity. *American Psychologist, 38*, 379–387. (p. 21)

Moorcroft, W. H. (2003). *Understanding sleep and dreaming.* New York: Kluwer/Plenum. (pp. 93, 107)

Moore, D. W. (2004, December 17). Sweet dreams go with a good night's sleep. *Gallup News Service* (www.gallup.com). (p. 96)

Moore, D. W. (2005, June 16). Three in four Americans believe in paranormal. *Gallup New Service* (www.gallup.com). (p. 253)

Moore, D. W. (2006, February 6). Britons outdrink Canadians, Americans. *Gallup News Service* (poll.gallup.com). (p. 127)

Moore, D. W. (2006, March 10). Close to 6 in 10 Americans want to lose weight. *Gallup News Service* (poll.gallup.com). (p. 432)

Moos, R. H., & Moos, B. S. (2005). Sixteen-year changes and stable remission among treated and untreated individuals with alcohol use disorders. *Drug and Alcohol Dependence, 80*, 337–347. (p. 689)

Moos, R. H., & Moos, B. S. (2006). Participation in treatment and Alcoholics Anonymous: A 16-year follow-up of initially untreated individuals. *Journal of Clinical Psychology, 62*, 735–750. (p. 689)

Mor, N., & Winquist, J. (2002). Self-focused attention and negative affect: A meta-analysis. *Psychological Bulletin, 128*, 638–662. (p. 653)

Morales, L. (2011, May 27). U.S. adults estimate that 25% of Americans are gay or lesbian. www.gallup.com. (p. 442)

More, H. L., Hutchinson, J. R., Collins, D. F., Weber, D. J., Aung, S. K. H., & Donelan, J. M. (2010). Scaling of sensorimotor control in terrestrial mammals. *Proceedings of the Royal Society B, 277*, 3563–3568. (p. 48)

Moreira, M. T., Smith, L. A., & Foxcroft, D. (2009). Social norms interventions to reduce alcohol misuse in university or college students. *Cochrane Database of Systematic Reviews.* 2009, Issue 3., Art. No.: CD006748. (p. 128)

Moreland, R. L., & Beach, S. R. (1992). Exposure effects in the classroom: The development of affinity among students. *Journal of Experimental Social Psychology, 28*, 255–276. (p. 608)

Moreland, R. L., & Zajonc, R. B. (1982). Exposure effects in person perception: Familiarity, similarity, and attraction. *Journal of Experimental Social Psychology, 18*, 395–415. (p. 608)

Morell, V. (1995). Zeroing in on how hormones affect the immune system. *Science, 269*, 773–775. (p. 510)

Morell, V. (2008, March). Minds of their own: Animals are smarter than you think. *National Geographic*, pp. 37–61. (p. 363)

Morelli, G. A., Rogoff, B., Oppenheim, D., & Goldsmith, D. (1992). Cultural variation in infants' sleeping arrangements: Questions of independence. *Developmental Psychology, 26*, 604–613. (p. 156)

Moreno, C., Laje, G., Blanco, C., Jiang, H., Schmidt, A. B., & Olfson, M. (2007). National trends in the outpatient diagnosis and treatment of bipolar disorder in youth. *Archives of General Psychiatry, 64*, 1032–1039. (p. 646)

Morewedge, C. K., & Norton, M. I. (2009). When dreaming is believing. The (motivated) interpretation of dreams. *Journal of Personality and Social Psychology, 96*, 249–264. (p. 254)

Morey, R. A., Inan, S., Mitchell, T. V., Perkins, D. O., Lieberman, J. A., & Belger, A. (2005). Imaging frontostriatal function in ultra-high-risk, early, and chronic schizophrenia during executive processing. *Archives of General Psychiatry, 62*, 254–262. (p. 660)

Morgan, A. B., & Lilienfeld, S. O. (2000). A meta-analytic review of the relation between antisocial behavior and neuropsychological measures of executive function. *Clinical Psychology Review, 20*, 113–136. (p. 669)

Mori, K., & Mori, H. (2009). Another test of the passive facial feedback hypothesis: When you face smiles, you feel happy. *Perceptual and Motor Skills, 109*, 1–3. (p. 490)

Morin, R., & Brossard, M. A. (1997, March 4). Communication breakdown on drugs. *Washington Post*, pp. A1, A6. (p. 205)

Morris, G., Baker-Ward, L., & Bauer, P. J. (2010). What remains of that day: The survival of children's autobiographical memories across time. *Applied Cognitive Psychology, 24*, 527–544. (p. 178)

Morrison, A. R. (2003). The brain on night shift. *Cerebrum, 5*(3), 23–36. (p. 95)

Morrison, C. (2007). *What does contagious yawning tell us about the mind?* Unpublished manuscript, University of Leeds. (p. 579)

Mortensen, E. L., Michaelsen, K. F., Sanders, S. A., & Reinisch, J. M. (2002). The association between duration of breastfeeding and adult intelligence. *Journal of the American Medical Association, 287*, 2365–2371. (p. 34)

Mortensen, P. B. (1999). Effects of family history and place and season of birth on the risk of schizophrenia. *New England Journal of Medicine, 340*, 603–608. (p. 661)

Moruzzi, G., & Magoun, H. W. (1949). Brain stem reticular formation and activation of the EEG. *Electroencephalography and Clinical Neurophysiology, 1*, 455–473. (p. 64)

Moscovici, S. (1985). Social influence and conformity. In G. Lindzey & E. Aronson (Eds.), *The handbook of social psychology* (3rd ed). Hillsdale, N.J.: Erlbaum. (p. 591)

Moses, E. B., & Barlow, D. H. (2006). A new unified treatment approach for emotional disorders based on emotion science. *Current Directions in Psychological Science, 15*, 146–150. (p. 687)

Mosher, W. D., Chandra, A., & Jones, J. (2005, September 15). Sexual behavior and selected health measures: Men and women 15–44 years of age, United States, 2002. *Advance Data from Vital and Health Statistics*, No. 362, National Center for Health Statistics, Centers for Disease Control and Prevention, U.S. Department of Health and Human Services. (p. 443)

Mosher, W. D., & Jones, J. (2010). Use of contraception in the United States: 1982–2008. National Center for Health Statistics, Centers for Disease Control. *Vital Health Statistics* 23(29). (p. 441)

Moss, A. C., & Albery, I. P. (2009). A dual-process model of the alcohol-behavior link for social drinking. *Psychological Bulletin, 135*, 516–530. (p. 118)

Moss, A. J., Allen, K. F., Giovino, G. A., & Mills, S. L. (1992, December 2). Recent trends in adolescent smoking, smoking-update correlates, and expectations about the future. *Advance Data No. 221* (from Vital and Health Statistics of the Centers for Disease Control and Prevention). (p. 119)

Moss, H. A., & Susman, E. J. (1980). Longitudinal study of personality development. In O. G. Brim, Jr., & J. Kagan (Eds.), *Constancy and change in human development.* Cambridge, MA: Harvard University Press. (p. 171)

Motivala, S. J., & Irwin, M. R. (2007). Sleep and immunity: Cytokine pathways linking sleep and health outcomes. *Current Directions in Psychological Science, 16*, 21–25. (p. 102)

Moyer, K. E. (1983). The physiology of motivation: Aggression as a model. In C. J. Scheier & A. M. Rogers (Eds.), *G. Stanley Hall Lecture Series* (Vol. 3). Washington, DC: American Psychological Association. (p. 600)

Mroczek, D. K., & Kolarz, D. M. (1998). The effect of age on positive and negative affect: A developmental perspective on happiness. *Journal of Personality and Social Psychology, 75*, 1333–1349. (p. 215)

Muhlnickel, W. (1998). Reorganization of auditory cortex in tinnitus. *Proceedings of the National Academy of Sciences, 95*, 10340–10343. (p. 73)

Mukamel, R., Ekstrom, A. D., Kaplan, J., Iacoboni, M., & Fried, I. (2010). Single-neuron responses in humans during execution and observation of actions. *Current Biology, 20*, 750–756. (p. 305)

Mulcahy, N. J., & Call, J. (2006). Apes save tools for future use. *Science, 312*, 1038–1040. (p. 362)

Muller, J. E., Mittleman, M. A., Maclure, M., Sherwood, J. B., & Tofler, G. H. (1996). Triggering myocardial infarction by sexual activity. *Journal of the American Medical Association, 275*, 1405–1409. (p. 435)

Muller, J. E., & Verier, R. L. (1996). Triggering of sudden death—Lessons from an earthquake. *New England Journal of Medicine, 334*, 461. (p. 506)

Mullin, C. R., & Linz, D. (1995). Desensitization and resensitization to violence against women: Effects of exposure to sexually violent films on judgments of domestic violence victims. *Journal of Personality and Social Psychology, 69*, 449–459. (p. 308)

Mulrow, C. D. (1999, March). Treatment of depression—newer pharmacotherapies, summary. *Evidence Report/Technology Assessment, 7.* Agency for Health Care Policy and Research, Rockville, MD. (http://www.ahrq.gov/clinic/deprsumm.htm). (p. 705)

Munafò, M. R., Durrant, C., Lewis, G., & Flint, J. (2009). Gene X environment interactions at the serotonin transporter locus. *Biological Psychiatry, 65*, 211–219. (p. 652)

Munsey, C. (2010, June). Medicine or menace? Psychologists' research can inform the growing debate over legalizing marijuana. *Monitor on Psychology*, pp. 50–55. (p. 124)

Murphy, G. E., & Wetzel, R. D. (1990). The lifetime risk of suicide in alcoholism. *Archives of General Psychiatry, 47*, 383–392. (p. 650)

Murphy, K. (2008, October 28). 21-year study of children set to begin. *New York Times* (www.nytimes.com). (p. 184)

Murphy, K. R., & Cleveland, J. N. (1995). *Understanding performance appraisal: Social, organizational, and goal-based perspectives*. Thousand Oaks, CA: Sage. (p. 462)

Murphy, S. T., Monahan, J. L., & Zajonc, R. B. (1995). Additivity of nonconscious affect: Combined effects of priming and exposure. *Journal of Personality and Social Psychology, 69*, 589–602. (p. 476)

Murray, B. (1998, May). Psychology is key to airline safety at Boeing. *The APA Monitor*, p. 36. (p. 470)

Murray, C. (2006). Changes over time in the Black-White difference on mental tests: Evidence from the children of the 1979 cohort of the National Longitudinal Survey of Youth. *Intelligence, 34*, 527–540. (p. 411)

Murray, C. (2007). The magnitude and components of change in the Black-White IQ difference from 1920 to 1991: A birth cohort analysis of the Woodcock-Johnson standardizations. *Intelligence, 35*, 305–318. (p. 411)

Murray, C. A., & Herrnstein, R. J. (1994, October 31). Race, genes and I.Q.—An apologia. *New Republic*, pp. 27–37. (p. 411)

Murray, C. J., & Lopez, A. D. (Eds.). (1996). *The global burden of disease: A comprehensive assessment of mortality and disability from diseases, injuries, and risk factors in 1990 and projected to 2020*. Cambridge, MA: Harvard University Press. (p. 625)

Murray, H. (1938). *Explorations in personality*. New York: Oxford University Press. (p. 463)

Murray, H. A., & Wheeler, D. R. (1937). A note on the possible clairvoyance of dreams. *Journal of Psychology, 3*, 309–313. (pp. 28, 254)

Murray, J. P. (2008). Media violence: The effects are both real and strong. *American Behavioral Scientist, 51*, 1212–1230. (p. 308)

Murray, R., Jones, P., O'Callaghan, E., Takei, N., & Sham, P. (1992). Genes, viruses, and neurodevelopmental schizophrenia. *Journal of Psychiatric Research, 26*, 225–235. (p. 661)

Murray, R. M., Morrison, P. D., Henquet, C., & Di Forti, M. (2007). Cannabis, the mind and society: The hash realities. *Nature Reviews: Neuroscience, 8*, 885–895. (p. 124)

Murray, S. L., Bellavia, G. M., Rose, P., & Griffin, D. W. (2003). Once hurt, twice hurtful: How perceived regard regulates daily marital interactions. *Journal of Personality and Social Psychology, 84*, 126–147. (p. 232)

Musallam, S., Corneil, B. D., Greger, B., Scherberger, H., & Andersen, R. A. (2004). Cognitive control signals for neural prosthetics. *Science, 305*, 258–262. (p. 71)

Musick, M. A., Herzog, A. R., & House, J. S. (1999). Volunteering and mortality among older adults: Findings from a national sample. *Journals of Gerontology, 54B*, 173–180. (p. 527)

Mustanski, B. S., & Bailey, J. M. (2003). A therapist's guide to the genetics of human sexual orientation, *Sexual and Relationship Therapy, 18*, 1468–1479. (p. 445)

Mustanski, B. S., Bailey, J. M., & Kaspar, S. (2002). Dermatoglyphics, handedness, sex, and sexual orientation. *Archives of Sexual Behavior, 31*, 113–122. (p. 447)

Mydans, S. (2002, May 17). In Pakistan, rape victims are the 'criminals.' *New York Times* (www.nytimes.com). (p. 599)

Myers, D. G. (1993). *The pursuit of happiness*. New York: Harper. (p. 500)

Myers, D. G. (2000). *The American paradox: Spiritual hunger in an age of plenty*. New Haven, CT: Yale University Press. (p. 500)

Myers, D. G. (2001, December). Do we fear the right things? *American Psychological Society Observer*, p. 3. (p. 358)

Myers, D. G. (2002). *Intuition: Its powers and perils*. New Haven, CT: Yale University Press. (p. 18)

Myers, D. G. (2008). *Social psychology*, 9th edition. New York: McGraw-Hill. (p. 565)

Myers, D. G. (2010). *Social psychology*, 10th edition. New York: McGraw-Hill. (p. 566)

Myers, D. G., & Bishop, G. D. (1970). Discussion effects on racial attitudes. *Science, 169*, 78–779. (p. 589)

Myers, D. G., & Diener, E. (1995). Who is happy? *Psychological Science, 6*, 10–19. (p. 500)

Myers, D. G., & Diener, E. (1996, May). The pursuit of happiness. *Scientific American*. (p. 500)

Myers, D. G., & Scanzoni, L. D. (2005). *What God has joined together?* San Francisco: HarperSanFrancisco. (pp. 216, 443)

Myers, I. B. (1987). *Introduction to type: A description of the theory and applications of the Myers-Briggs Type Indicator*. Palo Alto, CA: Consulting Psychologists Press. (p. 547)

Myers, T. A., & Crowther, J. H. (2009). Social comparison as a predictor of body dissatisfaction: A meta-analytic review. *Journal of Abnormal Psychology, 118*, 683–698. (p. 672)

Myerson, J., Rank, M. R., Raines, F. Q., & Schnitzler, M. A. (1998). Race and general cognitive ability: The myth of diminishing returns to education. *Psychological Science, 9*, 139–142. (p. 413)

Nagourney, A. (2002, September 25). For remarks on Iraq, Gore gets praise and scorn. *New York Times* (www.nytimes.com). (p. 574)

Nairn, R. G. (2007). Media portrayals of mental illness, or is it madness? A review. *Australian Psychologist, 42*, 138–146. (p. 632)

Napolitan, D. A., & Goethals, G. R. (1979). The attribution of friendliness. *Journal of Experimental Social Psychology, 15*, 105–113. (p. 572)

Narvaez, D. (2010). Moral complexity: The fatal attraction of truthiness and the importance of mature moral functioning. *Perspectives on Psychological Science, 5*, 163–181. (p. 202)

NAS (National Autistic Society). (2011, accessed May 11). *Statistics: How many people have autistic spectrum disorders*. www.autism.org.uk. (p. 184)

Nash, M. R. (2001, July). The truth and the hype of hypnosis. *Scientific American*, pp. 47–55. (p. 111)

National Academy of Sciences. (2001). *Exploring the biological contributions to human health: Does sex matter?* Washington, DC: Institute of Medicine, National Academy Press. (p. 161)

National Center for Complementary and Alternative Medicine. (2006). *What is complementary and alternative medicine*. www.nccam.nih.gov/health/whatiscam. (p. 526)

National Center for Health Statistics. (1990). *Health, United States, 1989*. Washington, DC: U.S. Department of Health and Human Services. (p. 211)

National Center for Health Statistics. (2004, December 15). Marital status and health: United States, 1999–2002 (by Charlotte A. Schoenborn). *Advance Data from Vital and Human Statistics, number 351*. Centers for Disease Control and Prevention. (p. 519)

National Council on Aging. (1999). *The consequences of untreated hearing loss in older persons*. Washington, DC: Author. (www.ncoa.org). (p. 371)

National Institute of Mental Health (2008). *The numbers count: Mental disorders in America*. (nimh.nih.gov). (pp. 631, 634)

National Research Council. (1990). *Human factors research needs for an aging population*. Washington, DC: National Academy Press. (p. 211)

National Safety Council. (2010). Transportation mode comparison in *Injury facts 2010 edition*. www.nsc.org. (p. 358)

National Safety Council. (2010, January 12). *NSC estimates 1.6 million crashes caused by cell phone use and texting*. www.nsc.org. (p. 88)

National Sleep Foundation (NSF). (2008). *2008 sleep in America poll*. National Sleep Foundation (sleepfoundation.org). (p. 97)

National Sleep Foundation (NSF). (2010, March 8). *2010 sleep in America poll*. www.sleepfoundation.org. (p. 97)

National Sleep Foundation. (2009) *2009 sleep in America poll: Summary of findings*. Washington, DC: National Sleep Foundation (www.sleepfoundation.org). (p. 104)

National Sleep Foundation. (2010, March 8). 2010 sleep in America poll. www.sleepfoundation.org. (p. 505)

Naumann, L. P., Vazire, S., Rentfrow, P. J., & Gosling, S. D. (2009). Personality judgments based on physical appearance. *Personality and Social Psychology Bulletin, 35*, 1661–1671. (p. 555)

Navarrete, C. D., Fessler, D. M. T., Fleischman, D. S., & Geyer, J. (2009). Race bias tracks conception risk across the menstrual cycle. *Psychological Science, 20*, 661–665. (p. 436)

Nave, C. S., Sherman, R. A., Funder, D.C., Hampson, S. E., & Goldberg, L. R. (2010). On the contextual independence of personality: Teachers' assessments predict directly observed behavior after four decades. *Social Psychological and Personality Science, 3*, 1–9. (p. 171)

Naylor, T. H. (1990). Redefining corporate motivation, Swedish style. *Christian Century, 107*, 566–570. (p. 468)

Nazimek, J. (2009). Active body, healthy mind. *The Psychologist, 22*, 206–208. (p. 211)

NCASA. (2007). *Wasting the best and the brightest: Substance abuse at America's colleges and universities*. New York: National Center on Addiction and Drug Abuse, Columbia University. (p. 128)

NCTV News. (1987, July-August). More research links harmful effects to non-violent porn, p. 12. (p. 603)

Nedeltcheva, A. V., Kilkus, J. M., Imperial, J., Schoeller, D. A., & Penev, P. D. (2010). Insufficient sleep undermines dietary efforts to reduce adiposity. *Annals of Internal Medicine, 153*, 435–441. (p. 431)

NEEF. (2011; undated, accessed 17 June 2011). *Fact sheet: children's health and nature*. National Environmental Education Foundation (www.neefusa.org). (p. 711)

Neese, R. M. (1991, November/December). What good is feeling bad? The evolutionary benefits of psychic pain. *The Sciences*, pp. 30–37. (pp. 263, 299)

Neidorf, S., & Morin, R. (2007, May 23). Four-in-ten Americans have close friends or relatives who are gay. *Pew Research Center Publications* (pewresearch.org). (p. 620)

Neimeyer, R. A., & Currier, J. M. (2009). Grief therapy: Evidence of efficacy and emerging directions. *Current Directions in Psychological Science, 18*, 352–356. (p. 220)

Neisser, U. (1979). The control of information pickup in selective looking. In A. D. Pick (Ed.), *Perception and its development: A tribute to Eleanor J. Gibson*. Hillsdale, NJ: Erlbaum. (p. 89)

Neisser, U., Boodoo, G., Bouchard, T. J., Jr., Boykin, A. W., Brody, N., Ceci, S. J., Halpern, D. F., Loehlin, J. C., Perloff, R., Sternberg, R. J., & Urbina, S. (1996). Intelligence: Knowns and unknowns. *American Psychologist, 51*, 77–101. (pp. 405, 413)

Neisser, U., Winograd, E., & Weldon, M. S. (1991). Remembering the earthquake: "What I experienced" vs. "How I heard the news." Paper presented to the Psychonomic Society convention. (p. 326)

Neitz, J., Carroll, J., & Neitz, M. (2001). Color vision: Almost reason enough for having eyes. *Optics & Photonics News 12*, 26–33. (p. 241)

Neitz, J., Geist, T., & Jacobs, G. H. (1989). Color vision in the dog. *Visual Neuroscience, 3*, 119–125. (p. 241)

Nelson, C. A., III, Furtado, E. Z., Fox, N. A., & Zeanah, C. H., Jr. (2009). The deprived human brain. *American Scientist, 97*, 222–229. (pp. 191, 407)

Nelson, M. D., Saykin, A. J., Flashman, L. A., & Riordan, H. J. (1998). Hippocampal volume reduction in schizophrenia as assessed by magnetic resonance imaging. *Archives of General Psychiatry, 55*, 433–440. (p. 660)

Nemeth, C. J., & Ormiston, M. (2007). Creative idea generation: Harmony versus stimulation. *European Journal of Social Psychology, 37*, 524–535. (p. 591)

Nes, R. B. (2010). Happiness in behaviour genetics: Findings and implications. *Journal of Happiness Studies, 11*, 369–381. (p. 501)

Nes, R. B., Czajkowski, N., & Tambs, K. (2010). Family matters: Happiness in nuclear families and twins. *Behavior Genetics, 40*, 577–590. (p. 501)

Nesca, M., & Koulack, D. (1994). Recognition memory, sleep and circadian rhythms. *Canadian Journal of Experimental Psychology, 48*, 359–379. (p. 338)

Nestoriuc, Y., Rief, W., & Martin, A. (2008). Meta-analysis of biofeedback for tension-type headache: Efficacy, specificity, and treatment moderators. *Journal of Consulting and Clinical Psychology, 76*, 379–396. (p. 523)

Neubauer, D. N. (1999). Sleep problems in the elderly. *American Family Physician, 59*, 2551–2558. (p. 96)

Neumann, R., & Strack, F. (2000). "Mood contagion": The automatic transfer of mood between persons. *Journal of Personality and Social Psychology, 79*, 211–223. (pp. 490, 579)

Newberg, A., & D'Aquili, E. (2001). *Why God won't go away: Brain science and the biology of belief*. New York: Simon & Schuster. (p. 524)

Newcomb, M. D., & Harlow, L. L. (1986). Life events and substance use among adolescents: Mediating effects of perceived loss of control and meaninglessness in life. *Journal of Personality and Social Psychology, 51*, 564–577. (p. 127)

Newell, B. R., Wong, K. Y., Cheung, J. C. H., & Rakow, T. (2008, August 23). Think, blink, or sleep on it? The impact of modes of thought on complex decision making. *Quarterly Journal of Experimental Psychology*: DOI: 10.1080/17470210802215202. (p. 360)

Newman, A. J., Bavelier, D., Corina, D., Jezzard, P., & Neville, H. J. (2002). A critical period for right hemisphere recruitment in American Sign Language processing. *Nature Neuroscience, 5*, 76–80. (p. 370)

Newman, L. S., & Baumeister, R. F. (1996). Toward an explanation of the UFO abduction phenomenon: Hypnotic elaboration, extraterrestrial sadomasochism, and spurious memories. *Psychological Inquiry, 7*, 99–126. (p. 110)

Newman, L. S., & Ruble, D. N. (1988). Stability and change in self-understanding: The early elementary school years. *Early Child Development and Care, 40*, 77–99. (p. 194)

Newman, M. L., Pennebaker, J. W., Berry, D. S., & Richards, J. M. (2003). Lying words: Predicting deception from linguistic style. *Personality and Social Psychology Bulletin, 29*, 665–675. (p. 482)

Newman, R., Ratner, N. B., Jusczyk, A. M., Jusczyk, P. W., & Dow, K. A. (2006). Infants' early ability to segment the conversational speech signal predicts later language development: A retrospective analysis. *Developmental Psychology, 42*, 643–655. (p. 367)

Newport, E. L. (1990). Maturational constraints on language learning. *Cognitive Science, 14*, 11–28. (p. 370)

Newport, F. (2001, February). Americans see women as emotional and affectionate, men as more aggressive. *The Gallup Poll Monthly*, pp. 34–38. (p. 486)

Newport, F. (2002, July 29). Bush job approval update. *Gallup News Service* (www.gallup.com/poll/releases/pr020729.asp). (p. 621)

Newport, F. (2007, June 11). Majority of Republicans doubt theory of evolution. *Gallup Poll* (www.galluppoll.com). (p. 165)

Newport, F. (2010, March 11). Americans' global warming concerns continue to drop. *Gallup* (www.gallup.com). (p. 574)

Newport, F., Argrawal, S., & Witters, D. (2010, December 23). Very religious Americans lead healthier lives. *Gallup* (www.gallup.com). (p. 527)

Newport, F., Jones, J. M., Saad, L., & Carroll, J. (2007, April 27). Gallup poll review: 10 key points about public opinion on Iraq. *The Gallup Poll* (www.gallluppoll.com). (p. 158)

Newport, F., Moore, D. W., Jones, J. M., & Saad, L. (2003, March 21). Special release: American opinion on the war. *Gallup Poll Tuesday Briefing* (www.gallup.com). (p. 577)

Newport, F., & Pelham, B. (2009, December 14). Don't worry, be 80: Worry and stress decline with age. *Gallup* (www.gallup.com). (p. 506)

Newton, E. L. (1991). The rocky road from actions to intentions. *Dissertation Abstracts International, 51*(8–B), 4105. (p. 470)

Nezlek, J. B. (2001). Daily psychological adjustment and the planfulness of day-to-day behavior. *Journal of Social and Clinical Psychology, 20*, 452–475. (p. 558)

Ng, S. H. (1990). Androcentric coding of *man* and *his* in memory by language users. *Journal of Experimental Social Psychology, 26*, 455–464. (p. 377)

Ng, T. W. H., & Feldman, D. C. (2009). How broadly does education contribute to job performance. *Personnel Psychology, 62*, 89–134. (p. 461)

Ng, T. W. H., Sorensen, K. L., & Yim, F. H. K. (2009). Does the job satisfaction—job performance relationship vary across cultures? *Journal of Cross-Cultural Psychology, 40*, 761–796. (p. 465)

Ng, W., Diener, E., Aurora, R., & Harter, J. (2009). Affluence, feelings of stress, and well-being. *Social Indicators Research, 94*, 257–271. (p. 505)

Ng, W. W. H., Sorensen, K. L., & Eby, L. T. (2006). Locus of control at work: A meta-analysis. *Journal of Organizational Behavior, 27*, 1057–1087. (p. 557)

Nguyen, H-H. D., & Ryan, A. M. (2008). Does stereotype threat affect test performance of minorities and women? A meta-analysis of experimental evidence. *Journal of Applied Psychology, 93*, 1314–1334. (p. 414)

NHTSA. (2000). *Traffic safety facts 1999: Older population*. Washington, DC: National Highway Traffic Safety Administration (National Transportation Library: www.ntl.bts.gov). (p. 211)

NICHD Early Child Care Research Network. (2002). Structure/process/outcome: Direct and indirect effects of caregiving quality on young children's development. *Psychological Science, 13*, 199–206. (p. 193)

NICHD Early Child Care Research Network. (2003). Does amount of time spent in child care predict socioemotional adjustment during the transition to kindergarten? *Child Development, 74*, 976–1005. (p. 193)

NICHD. (2006). Child-care effect sizes for the NICHD study of early child care and youth development. *American Psychologist, 61*, 99–116. (p. 193)

Nickell, J. (Ed.). (1994). *Psychic sleuths: ESP and sensational cases*. Buffalo, N.Y.: Prometheus Books. (p. 253)

Nickell, J. (1996, May/June). A study of fantasy proneness in the thirteen cases of alleged encounters in John Mack's abduction. *Skeptical Inquirer*, pp. 18–20, 54. (p. 110)

Nickell, J. (2005, July/August). The case of the psychic detectives. *Skeptical Inquirer* (skeptically.org/skepticism/id10.html). (p. 253)

Nickerson, R. S. (1998). Applied experimental psychology. *Applied Psychology: An International Review, 47*, 155–173. (p. 469)

Nickerson, R. S. (1999). How we know—and sometimes misjudge—what others know: Imputing one's own knowledge to others. *Psychological Bulletin, 125*, 737–759. (p. 470)

Nickerson, R. S. (2002). The production and perception of randomness. *Psychological Review, 109*, 330–357. (p. 17)

Nickerson, R. S. (2005). Bertrand's chord, Buffon's needles, and the concept of randomness. *Thinking & Reasoning, 11*, 67–96. (p. 17)

Nickerson, R. S., & Adams, M. J. (1979). Long-term memory for a common object. *Cognitive Psychology, 11*, 287–307. (p. 336)

Nicol, S. E., & Gottesman, I. I. (1983). Clues to the genetics and neurobiology of schizophrenia. *American Scientist, 71*, 398–404. (p. 663)

Nicolaus, L. K., Cassel, J. F., Carlson, R. B., & Gustavson, C. R. (1983). Taste-aversion conditioning of crows to control predation on eggs. *Science, 220*, 212–214. (p. 299)

Nicolelis, M. A. L., & Chapin, J. K. (2002, October). Controlling robots with the mind. *Scientific American*, pp. 46–53. (p. 71)

NIDA. (2002). Methamphetamine abuse and addiction. *Research Report Series*. National Institute on Drug Abuse, NIH Publication Number 02–4210. (p. 122)

NIDA. (2005, May). Methamphetamine. *NIDA Info Facts*. National Institute on Drug Abuse. (p. 122)

NIDCD. (2011). Quick statistics. National Institute on Deafness and Other Communication Disorders (www.nidcd.nih.gov). (p. 260)

Nie, N. H. (2001). Sociability, interpersonal relations and the Internet: Reconciling conflicting findings. *American Behavioral Scientist, 45*, 420–435. (p. 453)

Nielsen, K. M., Faergeman, O., Larsen, M. L., & Foldspang, A. (2006). Danish singles have a twofold risk of acute coronary syndrome: Data from a cohort of 138,290 persons. *Journal of Epidemiology and Community Health, 60*, 721–728. (p. 519)

Nielsen, M., & Tomaseli, K. (2010). Overimitation in Kalahari Bushman children and the origins of human cultural cognition. *Psychological Science, 21*, 729–736. (p. 305)

Niemiec, C. P., Ryan, R. M., & Deci, E. L. (2009). The path taken: Consequences of attaining intrinsic and extrinsic aspirations in post-college life. *Journal of Research in Personality, 43*, 291–306. (p. 499)

Nier, J. A. (2004). Why does the "above average effect" exist? Demonstrating idiosyncratic trait definition. *Teaching of Psychology, 31*, 53–54. (p. 566)

Nightingale, F. (1860/1969). *Notes on nursing*. Mineola, NY: Dover. (p. 520)

NIH. (2001, July 20). *Workshop summary: Scientific evidence on condom effectiveness for sexually transmitted disease (STD) prevention*. Bethesda: National Institute of Allergy and Infectious Diseases, National Institutes of Health. (p. 441)

NIH. (2006, December 4). NIDA researchers complete unprecedented scan of human genome that may help unlock the genetic contribution to tobacco addiction. *NIH News*, National Institutes of Health (www.nih.gov). (p. 126)

NIH. (2010). *Teacher's guide: Information about sleep*. National Institutes of Health (www.science.education.nih.gov). (p. 99)

Nikolas, M. A., & Burt, A. (2010). Genetic and environmental influences on ADHD symptom dimensions of inattention and hyperactivity: A meta-analysis. *Journal of Abnormal Psychology, 119*, 1–17. (p. 627)

Nir, Y., & Tononi, G. (2010). Dreaming and the brain: From phenomenology to neurophysiology. *Trends in Cognitive Sciences, 14*, 88–100. (p. 108)

Nisbett, R. E. (1987). Lay personality theory: Its nature, origin, and utility. In N. E. Grunberg, R. E. Nisbett, & others, *A distinctive approach to psychological research: The influence of Stanley Schachter*. Hillsdale, NJ: Erlbaum. (p. 460)

Nisbett, R. E. (2003). *The geography of thought: How Asians and Westerners think differently…and why*. New York: Free Press. (p. 572)

Nisbett, R. E. (2009). *Intelligence and how to get it: Why schools and culture count*. New York: Norton. (pp. 411, 412)

Nisbett, R. E., & Cohen, D. (1996). *Culture of honor: The psychology of violence in the South*. Boulder, CO: Westview Press. (p. 602)

Nixon, G. M., Thompson, J. M. D., Han, D. Y., Becroft, D. M., Clark, P. M., Robinson, E., Waldie, K E., Wild, C. J., Black, P. N., & Mitchell, E. A. (2008). Short sleep duration in middle childhood: Risk factors and consequences. *Sleep, 31*, 71–78. (p. 102)

Nock, M. K. (2010). Self-injury. *Annual Review of Clinical Psychology, 6*, 339–363. (p. 651)

Nock, M. K., Borges, G., Bromet, E. J., Alonso, J., Angermeyer, M., Beautrais, A., Bruffaerts, R., Chiu, W. T., de Girolamo, G., Gluzman, S., de Graaf, R., Gureje, O., Haro, J. M., Huang, Y., Karam, E., Kessler, R. C., Lepine, J. P., Levinson, D., Medina-Mora, M. E., Ono, Y., Posada-Villa, J., Williams, D. (2008). Cross-national prevalence and risk factors for suicidal ideation, plans, and attempts. *British Journal of Psychiatry, 192*, 98–105. (p. 651)

Nock, M. K., & Kessler, R. C. (2006). Prevalence of and risk factors for suicide attempts versus suicide gestures: Analysis of the National Comorbidity Survey. *Journal of Abnormal Psychology, 115*, 616–623. (p. 651)

Noel, J. G., Forsyth, D. R., & Kelley, K. N. (1987). Improving the performance of failing students by overcoming their self-serving attributional biases. *Basic and Applied Social Psychology, 8*, 151–162. (p. 559)

Noice, H., & Noice, T. (2006). What studies of actors and acting can tell us about memory and cognitive functioning. *Current Directions in Psychological Science, 15*, 14–18. (p. 321)

Nolen-Hoeksema, S. (2001). Gender differences in depression. *Current Directions in Psychological Science, 10*, 173–176. (p. 653)

Nolen-Hoeksema, S. (2003). *Women who think too much: How to break free of overthinking and reclaim your life*. New York: Holt. (p. 653)

Nolen-Hoeksema, S., & Larson, J. (1999). *Coping with loss*. Mahwah, NJ: Erlbaum. (p. 220)

Norberg, M. M., Krystal, J. H., & Tolin, D. F. (2008). A meta-analysis of d-cycloserine and the facilitation of fear extinction and exposure therapy. *Biological Psychiatry, 63*, 1118–1126. (p. 644)

NORC. (2010). National Opinion Research Center (University of Chicago) General Social Survey data, 1972 through 2008, accessed via sda.berkeley.edu. (p. 451)

Nordgren, L. F., van der Pligt, J., & van Harreveld, F. (2006). Visceral drives in retrospect: Explanations about the inaccessible past. *Psychological Science, 17*, 635–640. (p. 421)

Nordgren, L. F., van der Pligt, J., & van Harreveld, F. (2007). Evaluating Eve: Visceral states influence the evaluation of impulsive behavior. *Journal of Personality and Social Psychology, 93*, 75–84. (p. 421)

Nordgren, L. F., van Harreveld, F., & van der Pligt, J. (2009). The restraint bias: How the illusion of self-restraint promoted impulsive behavior. *Psychological Science, 20*, 1523–1528. (p. 560)

Norem, J. K. (2001). *The positive power of negative thinking: Using defensive pessimism to harness anxiety and perform at your peak*. New York: Basic Books. (p. 559)

Norenzayan, A., & Hansen, I. G. (2006). Belief in supernatural agents in the face of death. *Personality and Social Psychology Bulletin, 32*, 174–187. (p. 541)

Norman, D. A. (2001). The perils of home theater (www.jnd.org/dn.mss/ProblemsOfHomeTheater.html). (p. 469)

Norman, E. (2010). "The unconscious" in current psychology. *European Psychologist, 15*, 193–201. (p. 540)

Noroozian, M., Lofti, J., Gassemzadeh, H., Emami, H., & Mehrabi, Y. (2003). Academic achievement and learning abilities in left-handers: Guilt or gift? *Cortex, 38*, 779–785. (p. 80)

Norton, K. L., Olds, T. S., Olive, S., & Dank, S. (1996). Ken and Barbie at life size. *Sex Roles, 34*, 287–294. (p. 672)

Norton, M. I., & Ariely, D. (2011). Building a better America—One wealth quintile at a time. *Perspectives on Psychological Science, 6*, 9–12. (p. 38)

Norton, P. J., & Price, E. C. (2007). A meta-analytic review of adult cognitive-behavioral treatment outcome across the anxiety disorders. *Journal of Nervous and Mental Disease, 195*, 521–531. (p. 688)

Nowak, R. (1994). Nicotine scrutinized as FDA seeks to regulate cigarettes. *Science, 263*, 1555–1556. (p. 121)

NPR. (2009, July 11). Afraid to fly? Try living on a plane. www.npr.org. (p. 284)

Nurmikko, A. V., Donoghue, J. P., Hochberg, L. R., Patterson, W. R., Song, Y-K., Bull, C. W., Borton, D. A., Laiwalla, F., Park, S., Ming, Y., & Aceros, J. (2010). *Listening to brain microcircuits for interfacing with external world—Progress in wireless implantable microelectronic neuroengineering devices*. Proceedings of the *IEEE, 98*, 375–388. (p. 72)

Nurnberger, J. I., Jr., & Bierut, L. J. (2007, April). Seeking the connections: Alcoholism and our genes. *Scientific American*, pp. 46–53. (p. 126)

Nuttin, J. M., Jr. (1987). Affective consequences of mere ownership: The name letter effect in twelve European languages. *European Journal of Social Psychology, 17*, 381–402. (p. 608)

O'Connor, P., & Brown, G. W. (1984). Supportive relationships: Fact or fancy? *Journal of Social and Personal Relationships, 1*, 159–175. (p. 699)

O'Donnell, L., Stueve, A., O'Donnell, C., Duran, R., San Doval, A., Wilson, R. F., Haber, D., Perry, E., & Pleck, J. H. (2002). Long-term reduction in sexual initiation and sexual activity among urban middle schoolers in the reach for health service learning program. *Journal of Adolescent Health, 31*, 93–100. (p. 441)

O'Neil, J. (2002, September 3). Vital signs: Behavior: Parent smoking and teenage sex. *New York Times*. (p. 34)

O'Neill, M. J. (1993). The relationship between privacy, control, and stress responses in office workers. Paper presented to the Human Factors and Ergonomics Society convention. (p. 518)

O'Sullivan, M., Frank, M. G., Hurley, C. M., & Tiwana, J. (2009). Police lie detection accuracy: The effect of lie scenario. *Law and Human Behavior, 33*, 530–538. (p. 485)

Oakley, D. A., & Halligan, P. W. (2009). Hypnotic suggestion and cognitive neuroscience. *Trends in Cognitive Science, 13*, 264–270. (p. 113)

Oaten, M., & Cheng, K. (2006a). Longitudinal gains in self-regulation from regular physical exercise. *British Journal of Health Psychology, 11*, 717–733. (p. 558)

Oaten, M., & Cheng, K. (2006b). Improved self-control: The benefits of a regular program of academic study. *Basic and Applied Social Psychology, 28*, 1–16. (p. 558)

Oberlander, J., & Gill, A. J. (2006). Language with character: A stratified corpus comparison of individual differences in e-mail communication. *Discourse Processes, 42*, 239–270. (p. 555)

Oberman, L. M., & Ramachandran, V. S. (2007). The simulating social mind: The role of the mirror neuron system and simulation in the social and communicative deficits of autism spectrum disorders. *Psychological Bulletin, 133*, 310–327. (p. 185)

Ochsner, K. N., Ray, R. R., Hughes, B., McRae, K., Cooper, J. C., Weber, J., Gabrieli, J. D. E., & Gross, J. J. (2009). Bottom-up and top-down processes in emotion generation: Common and distinct neural mechanisms. *Psychological Science, 20*, 1322–1331. (pp. 476, 478)

Oddone-Paolucci, E., Genuis, M., & Violato, C. (2000). A meta-analysis of the published research on the effects of pornography. In C. Violato, E. Oddone-Paolucci, & M. Genuis (Eds.), *The changing family and child development.* Aldershot, England: Ashgate. (p. 603)

Odgers, C. L., Caspi, A., Nagin, D. S., Piquero, A. R., Slutske, W. S., Milne, B. J., Dickson, N., Poulton, R., & Moffitt, T. E. (2008). Is it important to prevent early exposure to drugs and alcohol among adolescents? *Psychological Science, 19,* 1037–1044. (p. 127)

OECD. (2010, September 23). *Obesity and the economics of prevention: Fit not fat.* Paris: Organization for Economic Co-operation and Development. (p. 431)

Oettingen, G., & Mayer, D. (2002). The motivating function of thinking about the future: Expectations versus fantasies. *Journal of Personality and Social Psychology, 83,* 1198–1212. (p. 559)

Oettingen, G., & Seligman, M. E. P. (1990). Pessimism and behavioural signs of depression in East versus West Berlin. *European Journal of Social Psychology, 20,* 207–220. (p. 559)

Offer, D., Kaiz, M., Howard, K. I., & Bennett, E. S. (2000). The altering of reported experiences. *Journal of the American Academy of Child and Adolescent Psychiatry, 39,* 735–742. (p. 344)

Offer, D., Ostrov, E., Howard, K. I., & Atkinson, R. (1988). *The teenage world: Adolescents' self-image in ten countries.* New York: Plenum. (p. 205)

Ohgami, H., Terao, T., Shiotsuki, I., Ishii, N., & Iwata, N. (2009). Lithium levels in drinking water and risk of suicide. *British Journal of Psychiatry, 194,* 464–465. (p. 707)

Öhman, A. (2009). Of snakes and fears: An evolutionary perspective on the psychology of fear. *Scandinavian Journal of Psychology, 50,* 543–552. (p. 643)

Oishi, S., Diener, E. F., Lucas, R. E., & Suh, E. M. (1999). Cross-cultural variations in predictors of life satisfaction: Perspectives from needs and values. *Personality and Social Psychology Bulletin, 25,* 980–990. (p. 421)

Oishi, S., & Schimmack, U. (2010). Culture and well-being: A new inquiry into the psychological wealth of nations. *Perspectives in Psychological Science, 5,* 463–471. (p. 502)

Oishi, S., & Schimmack, U. (2010). Residential mobility, well-being, and mortality. *Journal of Personality and Social Psychology, 98,* 980–994. (p. 451)

Okimoto, T. G., & Brescoll, V. L. (2010). The price of power: Power seeking and backlash against female politicians. *Personality and Social Psychology Bulletin, 36,* 923–936. (p. 158)

Olatunji, B. O., & Wolitzky-Taylor, K. B. (2009). Anxiety sensitivity and the anxiety disorders: A meta-analytic review and synthesis. *Psychological Bulletin, 135,* 974–999. (p. 638)

Olds, J. (1958). Self-stimulation of the brain. *Science, 127,* 315–324. (p. 66)

Olds, J. (1975). Mapping the mind onto the brain. In F. G. Worden, J. P. Swazey, & G. Adelman (Eds.), *The neurosciences: Paths of discovery.* Cambridge, MA: MIT Press. (p. 66)

Olds, J., & Milner, P. (1954). Positive reinforcement produced by electrical stimulation of the septal area and other regions of rat brain. *Journal of Comparative and Physiological Psychology, 47,* 419–427. (p. 66)

Olff, M., Langeland, W., Draijer, N., & Gersons, B. P. R. (2007). Gender differences in posttraumatic stress disorder. *Psychological Bulletin, 135,* 183–204. (p. 640)

Olfson, M., Gameroff, M. J., Marcus, S. C., & Jensen, P. S. (2003). National trends in the treatment of attention deficit hyperactivity disorder. *American Journal of Psychiatry, 160,* 1071–1077. (p. 627)

Olfson, M., & Marcus, S. C. (2009). National patterns in antidepressant medication treatment. *Archives of General Psychiatry, 66,* 848–856. (p. 706)

Olfson, M., Marcus, S. C., Wan, G. J., & Geissler, E. C. (2004). National trends in the outpatient treatment of anxiety disorders. *Journal of Clinical Psychiatry, 65,* 1166–1173. (p. 705)

Olfson, M., Shaffer, D., Marcus, S. C., & Greenberg, T. (2003). Relationship between antidepressant medication treatment and suicide in adolescents. *Archives of General Psychiatry, 60,* 978–982. (p. 706)

Olin, S. S., & Mednick, S. A. (1996). Risk factors of psychosis: Identifying vulnerable populations premorbidly. *Schizophrenia Bulletin, 22,* 223–240. (p. 663)

Oliner, S. P., & Oliner, P. M. (1988). *The altruistic personality: Rescuers of Jews in Nazi Europe.* New York: Free Press. (p. 306)

Olivola, C. Y., & Todorov, A. (2010). Elected in 100 milliseconds: Appearance-based trait inferences and voting. *Journal of Nonverbal Behavior, 54,* 83–110. (p. 484)

Olson, M. A., & Fazio, R. H. (2001). Implicit attitude formation through classical conditioning. *Psychological Science, 12,* 413–417. (p. 302)

Olson, S. (2005). Brain scans raise privacy concerns. *Science, 307,* 1548–1550. (p. 548)

Olsson, A., Nearing, K. I., & Phelps, E. A. (2007). Learning fears by observing others: The neural systems of social fear transmission. *Social Cognitive and Affective Neuroscience, 2,* 3–11. (p. 642)

Olweus, D., Mattsson, A., Schalling, D., & Low, H. (1988). Circulating testosterone levels and aggression in adolescent males: A causal analysis. *Psychosomatic Medicine, 50,* 261–272. (p. 601)

Oman, D., Kurata, J. H., Strawbridge, W. J., & Cohen, R. D. (2002). Religious attendance and cause of death over 31 years. *International Journal of Psychiatry in Medicine, 32,* 69–89. (p. 527)

Ong, A. D., Fuller-Rowell, T., & Burrow, A. L. (2009). Racial discrimination and the stress process. *Journal of Personality and Social Psychology, 96,* 1259–1271. (p. 507)

Oppenheimer, D. M., & Trail, T. E. (2010). Why leaning to the left makes you lean to the left: Effects of spatial orientation on political attitudes. *Social Cognition, 28,* 651–661. (p. 268)

Oren, D. A., & Terman, M. (1998). Tweaking the human circadian clock with light. *Science, 279,* 333–334. (p. 98)

Orne, M. T., & Evans, F. J. (1965). Social control in the psychological experiment: Antisocial behavior and hypnosis. *Journal of Personality and Social Psychology, 1,* 189–200. (p. 111)

Orth, U., Robins, R. W., & Meier, L. L. (2009). Disentangling the effects of low self-esteem and stressful events on depression: Findings from three longitudinal studies. *Personality Processes and Individual Differences, 97,* 307–321. (pp. 564, 652)

Orth, U., Robins, R. W., & Roberts, B. W. (2008). Low self-esteem prospectively predicts depression in adolescence and young adulthood. *Journal of Personality and Social Psychology, 95,* 695–708. (p. 564)

Orth, U, Robins, R. W., Trzesniewski, K. H., Maes, J., & Schmitt, M. (2009). Low self-esteem is a risk factor for depressive symptoms from young adulthood to old age. *Journal of Abnormal Psychology, 118,* 472–478. (p. 648)

Osborne, C., Manning, W. D., & Smock, P. J. (2007). Married and cohabiting parents' relationship stability: A focus on race and ethnicity. *Journal of Marriage and Family, 69,* 1345–1366. (p. 216)

Osborne, J. W. (1997). Race and academic disidentification. *Journal of Educational Psychology, 89,* 728–735. (p. 414)

Osborne, L. (1999, October 27). A linguistic big bang. *New York Times Magazine* (www.nytimes.com). (p. 369)

Osgood, C. E. (1962). *An alternative to war or surrender.* Urbana: University of Illinois Press. (p. 622)

Osgood, C. E. (1980). GRIT: A strategy for survival in mankind's nuclear age? Paper presented at the Pugwash Conference on New Directions in Disarmament. (p. 622)

Oskarsson, A. T., Van Voven, L., McClelland, G. H., & Hastie, R. (2009). What's next? Judging sequences of binary events. *Psychological Bulletin, 135,* 262–285. (p. 17)

OSS Assessment Staff. (1948). *The assessment of men.* New York: Rinehart. (p. 562)

Ost, L. G., & Hugdahl, K. (1981). Acquisition of phobias and anxiety response patterns in clinical patients. *Behaviour Research and Therapy, 16,* 439–447. (p. 642)

Ostfeld, A. M., Kasl, S. V., D'Atri, D. A., & Fitzgerald, E. F. (1987). *Stress, crowding, and blood pressure in prison.* Hillsdale, NJ: Erlbaum. (p. 518)

Osvath, M. (2009). Spontaneous planning for future stone throwing by a male chimpanzee. *Current Biology, 19,* R190–R191. (p. 363)

Oswald, A. J., & Powdthavee, N. (2006). *Does happiness adapt? A longitudinal study of disability with implications for economists and judges* (Discussion Paper No. 2208). Bonn: Institute for the Study of Labor. (p. 497)

Oswald, A. J., & Powdthavee, N. (2007). Obesity, unhappiness, and the challenge of affluence: Theory and evidence. *Economic Journal.* (p. 429)

Oswald, A. J., & Wu, S. (2010). Objective confirmation of subjective measures of human well-being: Evidence from the U.S.A. *Science, 327,* 576–579. (p. 497)

Ott, B. (2007, June 14). Investors, take note: Engagement boosts earnings. *Gallup Management Journal* (gmj.gallup.com). (p. 466)

Ott, C. H., Lueger, R. J., Kelber, S. T., & Prigerson, H. G. (2007). Spousal bereavement in older adults: Common, resilient, and chronic grief with defining characteristics. *Journal of Nervous and Mental Disease, 195,* 332–341. (p. 220)

Ott, J. C. (2010). Good governance and happiness in nations: Technical quality precedes democracy and quality beats size. *Journal of Happiness Studies, 11,* 353–368. (p. 559)

Ouellette, J. A., & Wood, W. (1998). Habit and intention in everyday life: The multiple processes by which past behavior predicts future behavior. *Psychological Bulletin, 124,* 54–74. (pp. 460, 562)

Overmier, J. B., & Murison, R. (1997). Animal models reveal the "psych" in the psychosomatics of peptic ulcers. *Current Directions in Psychological Science, 6,* 180–184. (p. 517)

Owen, A. M., Coleman, M. R., Boly, M., Davis, M. H., Laureys, S., & Pickard, J. D. (2006). Detecting awareness in the vegetative state. *Science, 313,* 1402. (p. 85)

Owen, R. (1814). First essay in *New view of society or the formation of character.* Quoted in *The story of New Lamark.* New Lamark Mills, Lamark, Scotland: New Lamark Conservation Trust, 1993. (p. 464)

Owens, J. A., Belon, K., & Moss, P. (2010). Impact of delaying school start time on adolescent sleep, mood, and behavior. *Archives of Pediatric Adolescent Medicine, 164,* 608–614. (p. 101)

Oxfam. (2005, March 26). *Three months on: New figures show tsunami may have killed up to four times as many women as men.* Oxfam Press Release (www.oxfam.org.uk). (p. 162)

Ozer, E. J., Best, S. R., Lipsey, T. L., & Weiss, D. S. (2003). Predictors of posttraumatic stress disorder and symptoms in adults: A meta-analysis. *Psychological Bulletin, 129,* 52–73. (p. 640)

Ozer, E. J., & Weiss, D. S. (2004). Who develops posttraumatic stress disorder. *Current Directions in Psychological Science, 13,* 169–172. (p. 640)

Özgen, E. (2004). Language, learning, and color perception. *Current Directions in Psychological Science, 13,* 95–98. (p. 377)

Pacifici, R., Zuccaro, P., Farre, M., Pichini, S., Di Carlo, S., Roset, P. N., Ortuno, J., Pujadus, M., Bacosi, A., Menoyo, E., Segura, J., & de la Torre, R. (2001). Effects of repeated doses of MDMA ("Ecstasy") on cell-mediated immune response in humans. *Life Sciences, 69,* 2931–2941. (p. 123)

Padgett, V. R. (1989). Predicting organizational violence: An application of 11 powerful principles of obedience. Paper presented to the American Psychological Association convention. (p. 584)

Pagani, L. S., Fitzpatrick, C., Barnett, T. A., & Dubow, E. (2010). Prospective associations between early childhood television exposure and academic, psychosocial, and physical well-being by middle childhood. *Archivers of Pediatric and Adolescent Medicine, 164,* 425–431. (p. 433)

Page, S. (1977). Effects of the mental illness label in attempts to obtain accommodation. *Canadian Journal of Behavioral Science, 9,* 84–90. (p. 632)

Page, S. E. (2007). *The difference: How the power of diversity creates better groups, firms, schools, and societies.* Princeton, NJ: Princeton University Press. (p. 591)

Palladino, J. J., & Carducci, B. J. (1983). "Things that go bump in the night": Students' knowledge of sleep and dreams. Paper presented at the meeting of the Southeastern Psychological Association. (p. 92)

Pallier, C., Colomé, A., & Sebastián-Gallés, N. (2001). The influence of native-language phonology on lexical access: Exemplar-based versus abstract lexical entries. *Psychological Science, 12,* 445–448. (p. 367)

Palmer, S., Schreiber, C., & Box, C. (1991). Remembering the earthquake: "Flashbulb" memory for experienced vs. reported events. Paper presented to the Psychonomic Society convention. (p. 326)

Pandey, J., Sinha, Y., Prakash, A., & Tripathi, R. C. (1982). Right-left political ideologies and attribution of the causes of poverty. *European Journal of Social Psychology, 12,* 327–331. (p. 573)

Panksepp, J. (2007). Neurologizing the psychology of affects: How appraisal-based constructivism and basic emotion theory can coexist. *Perspectives on Psychological Science, 2,* 281–295. (p. 480)

Pantev, C., Oostenveld, R., Engelien, A., Ross, B., Roberts, L. R., & Hoke, M. (1998). Increased auditory cortical representation in musicians. *Nature,* 392, 811–814. (p. 75)

Panzarella, C., Alloy, L. B., & Whitehouse, W. G. (2006). Expanded hopelessness theory of depression: On the mechanisms by which social support protects against depression. *Cognitive Theory and Research, 30,* 307–333. (p. 653)

Park, C. L. (2007). Religiousness/spirituality and health: A meaning systems perspective. *Journal of Behavioral Medicine, 30,* 319–328. (p. 527)

Park, G., Lubinski, D., & Benbow, C. P. (2007). Contrasting intellectual patterns predict creativity in the arts and sciences. *Psychological Science, 18,* 948–952. (p. 403)

Park, G., Lubinski, D., & Benbow, C. P. (2008). Ability differences among people who have commensurate degrees matter for scientific creativity. *Psychological Science, 19,* 957–961. (p. 387)

Park, R. L. (1999, July 12). Liars never break a sweat. *New York Times* (www.nytimes.com). (p. 482)

Parker, C. P., Baltes, B. B., Young, S. A., Huff, J. W., Altmann, R. A., LaCost, H. A., & Roberts, J. E. (2003). Relationships between psychological climate perceptions and work outcomes: A meta-analytic review. *Journal of Organizational Behavior, 24,* 389–416. (p. 465)

Parker, E. S., Cahill, L., & McGaugh, J. L. (2006). A case of unusual autobiographical remembering. *Neurocase, 12,* 35–49. (p. 334)

Parsons, T. D., & Rizzo, A. A. (2008). Affective outcomes of virtual reality exposure therapy for anxiety and specific phobias: A meta-analysis. *Journal of Behavior Therapy and Experimental Psychiatry, 39,* 250–261. (p. 682)

Pasco, J. A., Williams, L. A., Jacks, F. N., Ng, F., Henry, M. J., Nicholson, G. C., Kotowicz, M. A., & Berk, M. (2008). Tobacco smoking as a risk factor for major depressive disorder: Population-based study. *British Journal of Psychiatry, 193,* 322–326. (p. 652)

Pascoe, E. A., & Richman, L. S. (2009). Perceived discrimination and health: A meta-analytic review. *Psychological Bulletin, 135,* 531–554. (p. 507)

Passel, J. S., Wang, W., & Taylor, P. (2010, June 4). Marrying out: One-in-seven new U.S. marriages is interracial or interethnic. *Pew Research Center* (www.pewresearch.org). (p. 593)

Passell, P. (1993, March 9). Like a new drug, social programs are put to the test. *New York Times,* pp. C1, C10. (p. 37)

Pastalkova, E., Serrano, P., Pinkhasova, D., Wallace, E., Fenton, A. A., & Sacktor, T. C. (2006). Storage of spatial information by the maintenance mechanism of LTP. *Science, 313,* 1141–1144. (p. 327)

Patall, E. A., Cooper, H., & Robinson, J. C. (2008). The effects of choice on intrinsic motivation and related outcomes: A meta-analysis of research findings. *Psychological Bulletin, 134,* 270–300. (p. 303)

Pate, J. E., Pumariega, A. J., Hester, C., & Garner, D. M. (1992). Cross-cultural patterns in eating disorders: A review. *Journal of the American Academy of Child and Adolescent Psychiatry, 31,* 802–809. (p. 671)

Patel, S. R., Malhotra, A., White, D. P., Gottlieb, D. J., & Hu, F. B. (2006). Association between reduced sleep and weight gain in women. *American Journal of Epidemiology, 164,* 947–954. (p. 102)

Patten, S. B., Wang, J. L., Williams, J. V. A., Currie, S., Beck, C. A., Maxwell, C. J., & el-Guebaly, N. (2006). Descriptive epidemiology of major depression in Canada. *Canadian Journal of Psychiatry, 51,* 84–90. (p. 645)

Patterson, F. (1978, October). Conversations with a gorilla. *National Geographic,* pp. 438–465. (p. 374)

Patterson, G. R., Chamberlain, P., & Reid, J. B. (1982). A comparative evaluation of parent training procedures. *Behavior Therapy, 13,* 638–650. (pp. 293, 602)

Patterson, G. R., Reid, J. B., & Dishion, T. J. (1992). *Antisocial boys.* Eugene, OR: Castalia. (p. 602)

Patterson, M., Warr, P., & West, M. (2004). Organizational climate and company productivity: The role of employee affect and employee level. *Journal of Occupational and Organizational Psychology, 77,* 193–216. (p. 465)

Patterson, P. H. (2007). Maternal effects on schizophrenia risk. *Science, 318,* 576–577. (p. 661)

Patterson, R. (1951). *The riddle of Emily Dickinson.* Boston: Houghton Mifflin. (p. 655)

Pauker, K., Weisbuch, M., Ambady, N., Sommers, S. R., Adams, Jr., R. B., & Ivcevic, Z. (2009). Not so Black and White: Memory for ambiguous group members. *Journal of Personality and Social Psychology, 96,* 795–810. (p. 412)

Paulesu, E., Demonet, J-F., Fazio, F., McCrory, E., Chanoine, V., Brunswick, N., Cappa, S. F., Cossu, G., Habib, M., Frith, C. D., & Frith, U. (2001). Dyslexia: Cultural diversity and biological unity. *Science, 291,* 2165–2167. (p. 22)

Paus, T., Zijdenbos, A., Worsley, K., Collins, D. L., Blumenthal, J., Giedd, J. N., Rapoport, J. L., & Evans, A. C. (1999). Structural maturation of neural pathways in children and adolescents: In vivo study. *Science, 283,* 1908–1911. (p. 177)

Pavlov, I. (1927). *Conditioned reflexes: An investigation of the physiological activity of the cerebral cortex.* Oxford: Oxford University Press. (pp. 278, 282)

Payne, B. K. (2006). Weapon bias: Split-second decisions and unintended stereotyping. *Current Directions in Psychological Science, 15,* 287–291. (p. 595)

Payne, B. K., & Corrigan, E. (2007). Emotional constraints on intentional forgetting. *Journal of Experimental Social Psychology, 43,* 780–786. (p. 340)

Payne, B. K., Krosnick, J. A., Pasek, J., Lelkes, Y., Akhtar, O., & Tompson, T. (2010). Implicit and explicit prejudice in the 2008 American presidential election. *Journal of Experimental Social Psychology, 46,* 367–374. (p. 595)

Payne, J. W., Samper, A., Bettman, J. R., & Luce, M. F. (2008). Boundary conditions on unconscious thought in complex decision making. *Psychological Science, 19,* 1118–1123. (p. 360)

PCS (Prospective Studies Collaboration). (2009). Body-mass index and cause-specific mortality in 900 000 adults: Collaborative analyses of 57 prospective studies. *Lancet,* 373, 1083–1096. (p. 428)

Peckham, A. D., McHugh, R. K., & Otto, M. W. (2010). A meta-analysis of the magnitude of biased attention in depression. *Depression and Anxiety, 27,* 1135–1142. (p. 647)

Pedersen, A., Zachariae, R., & Bovbjerg, D. H. (2010). Influence of psychological stress on upper respiratory infection—A meta-analysis of prospective studies. *Psychosomatic Medicine, 72,* 823–832. (p. 510)

Pedersen, N. L., Plomin, R., McClearn, G. E., & Friberg, L. (1988). Neuroticism, extraversion, and related traits in adult twins reared apart and reared together. *Journal of Personality and Social Psychology, 55,* 950–957. (p. 136)

Peigneux, P., Laureys, S., Fuchs, S., Collette, F., Perrin, F., Reggers, J., Phillips, C., Degueldre, C., Del Fiore, G., Aerts, J., Luxen, A., & Maquet, P. (2004). Are spatial memories strengthened in the human hippocampus during slow wave sleep? *Neuron, 44,* 535–545. (pp. 99, 324)

Pekkanen, J. (1982, June). Why do we sleep? *Science, 82,* p. 86. (p. 99)

Pelham, B., & Crabtree, S. (2008, October 8). Worldwide, highly religious more likely to help others. Gallup Poll (www.gallup.com). (p. 617)

Pelham, B. W. (1993). On the highly positive thoughts of the highly depressed. In R. F. Baumeister (Ed.), *Self-esteem: The puzzle of low self-regard.* New York: Plenum. (p. 565)

Pelham, B. W. (2009, October 22). About one in six Americans report history of depression. *Gallup* (www.gallup.com). (p. 647)

Pelham, B. W. (2010, February 2). Rest eludes nearly 30% of Americans. *Gallup* (www.gallup.com). (p. 100)

Pendick, D. (1994, January/February). The mind of violence. *Brain Work: The Neuroscience Newsletter,* pp. 1–3, 5. (p. 600)

Penhune, V. B., Cismaru, R., Dorsaint-Pierre, R., Petitto, L-A., & Zatorre, R. J. (2003). The morphometry of auditory cortex in the congenitally deaf measured using MRI. *NeuroImage, 20,* 1215–1225. (p. 371)

Pennebaker, J. W. (1985). Traumatic experience and psychosomatic disease: Exploring the roles of behavioral inhibition, obsession, and confiding. *Canadian Psychology, 26,* 82–95. (p. 520)

Pennebaker, J., W. (1990). *Opening up: The healing power of confiding in others.* New York: William Morrow. (pp. 521, 540)

Pennebaker, J. W. (2002, January 28). Personal communication. (p. 621)

Pennebaker, J. W., Barger, S. D., & Tiebout, J. (1989). Disclosure of traumas and health among Holocaust survivors. *Psychosomatic Medicine, 51,* 577–589. (p. 520)

Pennebaker, J. W., & O'Heeron, R. C. (1984). Confiding in others and illness rate among spouses of suicide and accidental death victims. *Journal of Abnormal Psychology,* 93, 473–476. (p. 520)

Pennebaker, J. W., & Stone, L. D. (2003). Words of wisdom: Language use over the life span. *Journal of Personality and Social Psychology, 85,* 291–301. (p. 218)

Penny, H., & Haddock, G. (2007). Anti-fat prejudice among children: The "mere proximity" effect in 5–10 year olds. *Journal of Experimental Social Psychology, 43,* 678–683. (p. 429)

Peplau, L. A., & Fingerhut, A. W. (2007). The close relationships of lesbians and gay men. *Annual Review of Psychology, 58,* 405–424. (pp. 144, 216, 442)

Peplau, L. A., & Garnets, L. D. (2000). A new paradigm for understanding women's sexuality and sexual orientation. *Journal of Social Issues, 56,* 329–350. (p. 443)

Peppard, P. E., Szklo-Coxe, M., Hia, K. M., & Young, T. (2006). Longitudinal association of sleep-related breathing disorder and depression. *Archives of Internal Medicine, 166,* 1709–1715. (p. 104)

Pepperberg, I. M. (2006). Grey parrot numerical competence: A review. *Animal Cognition, 9,* 377–391. (p. 362)

Pepperberg, I. M. (2009). *Alex & me: How a scientist and a parrot discovered a hidden world of animal intelligence—and formed a deep bond in the process.* New York: Harper. (p. 362)

Perani, D., & Abutalebi, J. (2005). The neural basis of first and second language processing. *Current Opinion in Neurobiology, 15,* 202–206. (p. 373)

Pereira, A. C., Huddleston, D. E., Brickman, A. M., Sosunov, A. A., Hen, R., McKhann, G. M., Sloan, R., Gage, F. H., Brown, T. R., & Small, S. A. (2007). An *in vivo* correlate of exercise-induced neurogenesis in the adult dentate gyrus. *Proceedings of the National Academic of Sciences, 104,* 5638–5643. (pp. 76, 211, 212)

Pereira, G. M., & Osburn, H. G. (2007). Effects of participation in decision making on performance and employee attitudes: A quality circles meta-analysis. *Journal of Business Psychology, 22,* 145–153. (p. 467)

Pergadia, M. L. & 30 others. (2011). A 3p26-3p25 genetic linkage finding for DSM-IV major depression in heavy smoking families. *American Journal of Psychiatry. 168,* 848–852. (p. 650)

Perilloux, H. K., Webster, G. D., & Gaulin, S. J. (2010). Signals of genetic quality and maternal investment capacity: The dynamic effects of fluctuating asymmetry and waist-to-hip ratio on men's ratings of women's attractiveness *Social Psychology and Personality Science, 1,* 34–42. (pp. 145, 611)

Perlmutter, M. (1983). Learning and memory through adulthood. In M. W. Riley, B. B. Hess, & K. Bond (Eds.), *Aging in society: Selected reviews of recent research.* Hillsdale, NJ: Erlbaum. (p. 214)

Perra, O., Williams, J. H. G., Whiten, A., Fraser, L., Benzie, H., & Perrett, D. I. (2008). Imitation and 'theory of mind' competencies in discrimination of autism from other neurodevelopmental disorders. *Research in Autism Disorders, 2,* 456–468. (p. 185)

Perrett, D. (2002, October 1). Perception laboratory, Department of Psychology, University of St. Andrews, Scotland (www.perception.st-and.ac.uk). (p. 611)

Perrett, D. (2010). *In your face: The new science of human attraction.* New York: Palgrave Macmillan. (p. 611)

Perrett, D. I., Harries, M., Misflin, A. J., & Chitty, A. J. (1988). Three stages in the classification of body movements by visual neurons. In H. B. Barlow, C. Blakemore, & M. Weston Smith (Eds.), *Images and understanding.* Cambridge: Cambridge University Press. (p. 239)

Perrett, D. I., Hietanen, J. K., Oram, M. W., & Benson, P. J. (1992). Organization and functions of cells responsive to faces in the temporal cortex. *Philosophical Transactions of the Royal Society of London: Series B, 335,* 23–30. (p. 239)

Perrett, D. I., Lee, K. J., Penton-Voak, I., Rowland, D., Yoshikawa, S., Burt, D. M., Henzi, S. P., Castles, D. L., & Akamatsu, S. (1998, August). Effects of sexual dimorphism on facial attractiveness. *Nature, 394,* 884–887. (p. 596)

Perrett, D. I., May, K. A., & Yoshikawa, S. (1994). Facial shape and judgments of female attractiveness. *Nature, 368,* 239–242. (p. 239)

Perron, H., Mekaoui, L., Bernard, C., Veas, F., Stefas, I., & Leboyer, M. (2008). Endogenous retrovirus type W GAG and envelope protein antigenemia in serum of schizophrenic patients. *Biological Psychiatry, 64,* 1019–1023. (p. 661)

Person, C., Tracy, M., & Galea, S. (2006). Risk factors for depression after a disaster. *Journal of Nervous and Mental Disease, 194,* 659–666. (p. 701)

Pert, C. B. (1986). Quoted in J. Hooper & D. Teresi, *The three-pound universe.* New York: Macmillan. (p. 66)

Pert, C. B., & Snyder, S. H. (1973). Opiate receptor: Demonstration in nervous tissue. *Science, 179,* 1011–1014. (p. 51)

Perugini, E. M., Kirsch, I., Allen, S. T., Coldwell, E., Meredith, J., Montgomery, G. H., & Sheehan, J. (1998). Surreptitious observation of responses to hypnotically suggested hallucinations: A test of the compliance hypothesis. *International Journal of Clinical and Experimental Hypnosis, 46,* 191–203. (p. 113)

Peschel, E. R., & Peschel, R. E. (1987). Medical insights into the castrati in opera. *American Scientist, 75,* 578–583. (p. 437)

Pescosolido, B. A., Martin, J. K., Long, J. S., Medina, T. R., Phelan, J. C., & Link, B. G. (2010). "A disease like any other"? A decade of change in public reactions to schizophrenia, depression, and alcohol dependence. *American Journal of Psychiatry, 167,* 1321–1330. (p. 663)

Peters, M., Reimers, S., & Manning, J. T. (2006). Hand preference for writing and associations with selected demographic and behavioral variables in 255,100 subjects: The BBC Internet study. *Brain and Cognition, 62,* 177–189. (p. 80)

Peters, M., Rhodes, G., & Simmons, L. W. (2007). Contributions of the face and body to overall attractiveness. *Animal Behaviour, 73,* 937–942. (p. 611)

Peters, T. J., & Waterman, R. H., Jr. (1982). *In search of excellence; Lessons from America's best-run companies.* New York: Harper & Row. (p. 295)

Petersen, J. L., & Hyde, J. S. (2009) A meta-analytic review of research on gender differences in sexuality, 1993–2007. *Psychological Bulletin, 136,* 21–38. (p. 144)

Petersen, J. L., & Hyde, J. S. (2011). Gender differences in sexual attitudes and behaviors: A review of meta-analytic results and large datasets. *Journal of Sex Research, 48,* 149–165. (p. 437)

Peterson, C., & Barrett, L. C. (1987). Explanatory style and academic performance among university freshmen. *Journal of Personality and Social Psychology, 53,* 603–607. (p. 559)

Peterson, C., Peterson, J., & Skevington, S. (1986). Heated argument and adolescent development. *Journal of Social and Personal Relationships,* 3, 229–240. (p. 200)

Peterson, C. C., & Siegal, M. (1999). Representing inner worlds: Theory of mind in autistic, deaf, and normal hearing children. *Psychological Science, 10,* 126–129. (p. 183)

Peterson, L. R., & Peterson, M. J. (1959). Short-term retention of individual verbal items. *Journal of Experimental Psychology, 58,* 193–198. (pp. 317, 318)

Petitto, L. A., & Marentette, P. F. (1991). Babbling in the manual mode: Evidence for the ontogeny of language. *Science, 251,* 1493–1496. (p. 367)

Pettegrew, J. W., Keshavan, M. S., & Minshew, N. J. (1993). 31P nuclear magnetic resonance spectroscopy: Neurodevelopment and schizophrenia. *Schizophrenia Bulletin, 19,* 35–53. (p. 660)

Petticrew, M., Bell, R., & Hunter, D. (2002). Influence of psychological coping on survival and recurrence in people with cancer: Systematic review. *British Medical Journal, 325,* 1066. (p. 512)

Petticrew, M., Fraser, J. M., & Regan, M. F. (1999). Adverse life events and risk of breast cancer: A meta-analysis. *British Journal of Health Psychology, 4,* 1–17. (p. 512)

Pettigrew, T. F. (1998). Reactions toward the new minorities of western Europe. *Annual Review of Sociology, 24,* 77–103. (p. 594)

Pettigrew, T. F. (2006). A two-level approach to anti-immigrant prejudice and discrimination. In R. Mahalingam (Ed.), *Cultural psychology of immigrants.* Mahwah, NJ: Erlbaum. (p. 594)

Pettigrew, T. F., Christ, O., Wagner, U., & Stellmacher, J. (2007). Direct and indirect intergroup contact effects on prejudice: A normative interpretation. *International Journal of Intercultural Relations, 31,* 411–425. (p. 620)

Pettigrew, T. F., & Tropp, L. R. (2011). *When groups meet: The dynamics of intergroup contact.* New York: Psychology Press. (p. 620)

Pew. (2007, January 24). *Global warming: A divide on causes and solutions.* Pew Research Center for the People and the Press. (p. 356)

Pew. (2009, November 4). Social isolation and new technology: How the Internet and mobile phones impact Americans' social networks. Pew Research Center (www.pewresearch.org). (p. 453)

Pew. (2009, November 16). Teens and distracted driving. Internet & American Life Project, Pew Research Center (www.pewinternet.org). (p. 88)

Pew. (2010). Home broadband 2010. Pew Internet & American Life Project, Pew Research Center (www.pewinternet.org). (p. 400)

Pew. (2010, July 1). Gender equality universally embraced, but inequalities acknowledged. Pew Research Center Publications (pewresearch.org). (p. 162)

Pew Research Center. (2006, November 14). Attitudes toward homosexuality in African countries (pewresearch.org). (p. 442)

Pew Research Center. (2007, July 18). Modern marriage: "I like hugs. I like kisses. But what I really love is help with the dishes." Pew Research Center (www.pewresearch.org). (p. 614)

Pew Research Center. (2010, February 1). Almost all millennials accept interracial dating and marriage. Pew Research Center. (www.pewresearch.org). (p. 593)

Pfammatter, M., Junghan, U. M., Brenner, H. D. (2006). Efficacy of psychological therapy in schizophrenia: Conclusions from meta-analyses. *Schizophrenia Bulletin,* 32, S64–S80. (p. 696)

Phelps, J. A., Davis J. O., & Schartz, K. M. (1997). Nature, nurture, and twin research strategies. *Current Directions in Psychological Science, 6,* 117–120. (pp. 134, 662)

Philip Morris. (2003). Philip Morris USA youth smoking prevention. Teenage attitudes and behavior study, 2002. In "Raising kids who don't smoke," vol. 1(2). (p. 120)

Philip Morris Companies, Inc. (1999, October 13). Referenced in Myron Levin, Philip Morris' new campaign echoes medical experts, *Los Angeles Times.* (p. 119)

Phillips, A. C., Batty, G. D., Gale, C. R., Deary, I. J., Osborn, D., MacIntyre, K., & Carroll, D. (2009). Generalized anxiety disorder, major depressive disorder, and their comorbidity as predictors of all-cause and cardiovascular mortality: The Vietnam Experience Study. *Psychosomatic Medicine, 71,* 395–403. (p. 519)

Phillips, A. L. (2011). A walk in the woods. *American Scientist, 69,* 301–302. (p. 711)

Phillips, D. P. (1985). Natural experiments on the effects of mass media violence on fatal aggression: Strengths and weaknesses of a new approach. In L. Berkowitz (Ed.), *Advances in experimental social psychology* (Vol. 19). Orlando, FL: Academic Press. (p. 580)

Phillips, D. P., Carstensen, L. L., & Paight, D. J. (1989). Effects of mass media news stories on suicide, with new evidence on the role of story content. In D. R. Pfeffer (Ed.), *Suicide among youth: Perspectives on risk and prevention.* Washington, DC: American Psychiatric Press. (p. 580)

Phillips, J. L. (1969). *Origins of intellect: Piaget's theory.* San Francisco: Freeman. (p. 182)

Phonak. (2007). Hear the world. (www.hear-the-world.com). (p. 371)

Piaget, J. (1930). *The child's conception of physical causality.* London: Routledge & Kegan Paul. (p. 179)

Piaget, J. (1932). *The moral judgment of the child.* New York: Harcourt, Brace & World. (p. 200)

Picchioni, M. M., & Murray, R. M. (2007). Schizophrenia. *British Medical Journal, 335,* 91–95. (p. 658)

Pido-Lopez, J., Imami, N., & Aspinall, R. (2001). Both age and gender affect thymic output: More recent thymic migrants in females than males as they age. *Clinical and Experimental Immunology, 125,* 409–413. (p. 510)

Pieters, G. L. M., de Bruijn, E. R. A., Maas, Y., Hultijn, W., Vandereycken, W., Peuskens, J., & Sabbe, B. G. (2007). Action monitoring and perfectionism in anorexia nervosa. *Brain and Cognition, 63,* 42–50. (p. 671)

Pike, K. M., & Rodin, J. (1991). Mothers, daughters, and disordered eating. *Journal of Abnormal Psychology, 100,* 198–204. (p. 671)

Piliavin, J. A. (2003). Doing well by doing good: Benefits for the benefactor. In C. L. M. Keyes & J. Haidt (Eds.), *Flourishing: Positive psychology and the life well-lived.* Washington, DC: American Psychological Association. (p. 202)

Pillemer, D. B. (1995). What is remembered about early childhood events? Invited paper presentation to the American Psychological Society convention. (p. 178)

Pillemer, D. B. (1998). *Momentous events, vivid memories.* Cambridge, MA: Harvard University Press. (p. 213)

Pillemer, D. B., Ivcevic, Z., Gooze, R. A., & Collins, K. A. (2007). Self-esteem memories: Feeling good about achievement success, feeling bad about relationship distress. *Personality and Social Psychology Bulletin,* 33, 1292–1305. (p. 451)

Pilley, J. W., & Reid, A., K. (2011). Border collie comprehends object names as verbal referents. *Behavioural Processes, 86,* 184–195. (p. 374)

Pillsworth, E. G., & Haselton, M. G. (2006). Male sexual attractiveness predicts differential ovulatory shifts in female extra-pair attraction and male mate retention. *Evolution and Human Behavior, 27,* 247–258. (p. 437)

Pillsworth, M. G., Haselton, M. G., & Buss, D. M. (2004). Ovulatory shifts in female desire. *Journal of Sex Research, 41,* 55–65. (p. 436)

Pingitore, R., Dugoni, B. L., Tindale, R. S., & Spring, B. (1994). Bias against overweight job applicants in a simulated employment interview. *Journal of Applied Psychology, 79,* 909–917. (p. 429)

Pinker, S. (1990, September-October). Quoted by J. de Cuevas, "No, she holded them loosely." *Harvard Magazine,* pp. 60–67. (p. 365)

Pinker, S. (1995). The language instinct. *The General Psychologist, 31,* 63–65. (p. 374)

Pinker, S. (1998). Words and rules. *Lingua, 106,* 219–242. (p. 365)

Pinker, S. (2002, September 9). A biological understanding of human nature: A talk with Steven Pinker. *The Edge Third Culture Mail List* (www.edge.org). (pp. 137, 142)

Pinker, S. (2005, April 22). The science of gender and science: A conversation with Elizabeth Spelke. Harvard University (www.edge.org). (p. 410)

Pinker, S. (2006, January 1). Groups of people may differ genetically in their average talents and temperaments. *The Edge* (www.edge.org). (p. 413)

Pinker, S. (2007). *The stuff of thought.* New York: Viking. (p. 377)

Pinker, S. (2008). *The sexual paradox: Men, women, and the real gender gap.* New York: Scribner. (p. 159)

Pinkham, A. E., Griffin, M., Baron, R., Sasson, N. J., & Gur, R. C. (2010). The face in the crowd effect: Anger superiority when using real faces and multiple identities. *Emotion, 10,* 141–146. (p. 484)

Pinstrup-Andersen, P., & Cheng, F. (2007). Still hungry. *Scientific American, 297,* 96–103. (p. 431)

Pipe, M-E. (1996). Children's eyewitness memory. *New Zealand Journal of Psychology, 25,* 36–43. (p. 345)

Pipe, M-E., Lamb, M. E., Orbach, Y., & Esplin, P. W. (2004). Recent research on children's testimony about experienced and witnessed events. *Developmental Review, 24,* 440–468. (p. 345)

Pipher, M. (2002). *The middle of everywhere: The world's refugees come to our town.* New York: Harcourt Brace. (pp. 451, 506)

Pitcher, D., Walsh, V., Yovel, G., & Duchaine, B. (2007). TMS evidence for the involvement of the right occipital face area in early face processing. *Current Biology, 17,* 1568–1573. (p. 239)

Pitman, R. K., & Delahanty, D. L. (2005). Conceptually driven pharmacologic approaches to acute trauma. *CNS Spectrums, 10*(2), 99–106. (p. 328)

Pitman, R. K., Sanders, K. M., Zusman, R. M., Healy, A. R., Cheema, F., Lasko, N. B., Cahill, L., & Orr, S. P. (2002). Pilot study of secondary prevention of posttraumatic stress disorder with propranolol. *Biological Psychiatry, 51,* 189–192. (p. 328)

Pittenger, D. J. (1993). The utility of the Myers-Briggs Type Indicator. *Review of Educational Research, 63,* 467–488. (p. 547)

Place, S. S., Todd, P. M., Penke, L., & Asendorph, J. B. (2009). The ability to judge the romantic interest of others. *Psychological Science, 20,* 22–26. (pp. 484, 609)

Plassmann, H., O'Doherty, J., Shiv, B., & Rangel, A. (2008). Marketing actions can modulate neural representations of experienced pleasantness. *Proceedings of the National Academy of Sciences, 105,* 1050–1054. (p. 267)

Platek, S. M., & Singh, D. (2010). Optimal waist-to-hip ratios in women activate neural reward centers in men. PLoS ONE 5(2): e9042. doi:10.1371/journal.pone.0009042. (p. 611)

Pleck, J. H., Sonenstein, F. L., & Ku, L. C. (1993). Masculinity ideology: Its impact on adolescent males' heterosexual relationships. *Journal of Social Issues, 49,* 11–29. (p. 144)

Pliner, P. (1982). The effects of mere exposure on liking for edible substances. *Appetite: Journal for Intake Research,* 3, 283–290. (p. 425)

Pliner, P., Pelchat, M., & Grabski, M. (1993). Reduction of neophobia in humans by exposure to novel foods. *Appetite, 20,* 111–123. (p. 425)

Plöderl, M., & Fartacek, R. (2005). Suicidality and associated risk factors among lesbian, gay, and bisexual compared to heterosexual Austrian adults. *Suicide and Life-Threatening Behavior, 35*, 661–670. (p. 443)

Plomin, R. (1999). Genetics and general cognitive ability. *Nature, 402* (Suppl), C25–C29. (pp. 382, 406)

Plomin, R. (2001). Genetics and behaviour. *The Psychologist, 14*, 134–139. (p. 405)

Plomin, R. (2003). General cognitive ability. In R. Plomin, J. C. DeFries, I. W. Craig, & P. McGuffin (Eds.), *Behavioral genetics in a postgenomic world.* Washington, DC: APA Books. (p. 405)

Plomin, R. (2011). Why are children in the same family so different? Nonshared environment three decades later. *International Journal of Epidemiology, 40*, 582–592. (pp. 136, 150)

Plomin, R., & Bergeman, C. S. (1991). The nature of nurture: Genetic influence on "environmental" measures. *Behavioral and Brain Sciences, 14*, 373–427. (p. 140)

Plomin, R., & Crabbe, J. (2000). DNA. *Psychological Bulletin, 126*, 806–828. (p. 138)

Plomin, R., & Daniels, D. (1987). Why are children in the same family so different from one another? *Behavioral and Brain Sciences, 10*, 1–60. (p. 150)

Plomin, R., & DeFries, J. C. (1998, May). The genetics of cognitive abilities and disabilities. *Scientific American*, pp. 62–69. (p. 407)

Plomin, R., DeFries, J. C., McClearn, G. E., & Rutter, M. (1997). *Behavioral genetics.* New York: Freeman. (pp. 134, 142, 430, 446, 662)

Plomin, R., Haworth, C. M. A., & Davis, O. S. P. (2009). Common disorders are quantitative traits. *Nature Reviews: Genetics, 10*, 872–878. (p. 430)

Plomin, R., & Kovas, Y. (2005). Generalist genes and learning disabilities. *Psychological Bulletin, 131*, 592–617. (p. 405)

Plomin, R., McClearn, G. E., Pedersen, N. L., Nesselroade, J. R., & Bergeman, C. S. (1988). Genetic influence on childhood family environment perceived retrospectively from the last half of the life span. *Developmental Psychology, 24*, 37–45. (p. 140)

Plomin, R., & McGuffin, P. (2003). Psychopathology in the postgenomic era. *Annual Review of Psychology, 54*, 205–228. (p. 650)

Plomin, R., Reiss, D., Hetherington, E. M., & Howe, G. W. (January, 1994). Nature and nurture: Genetic contributions to measures of the family environment. *Developmental Psychology, 30*(1), 32–43. (p. 140)

Plotkin, H. (1994). *Darwin machines and the nature of knowledge.* Cambridge, MA: Harvard University Press. (p. 649)

Plotnik, J. M., de Waal, F. B. M., & Reiss, D. (2006). Self-recognition in an Asian elephant. *Proceedings of the National Academy of Sciences, 103*, 17053–17057. (p. 194)

Plous, S., & Herzog, H. A. (2000). Poll shows researchers favor lab animal protection. *Science, 290*, 711. (p. 23)

Poelmans, G., Pauls, D. L., Buitelaar, J. K., & Franke, B. (2011). Integrated genome-wide association study findings: Identification of a neurodevelopmental network for attention deficit hyperactivity disorder. *American Journal of Psychiatry, 168*, 365–377. (p. 627)

Pogue-Geile, M. F., & Yokley, J. L. (2010). Current research on the genetic contributors to schizophrenia. *Current Directions in Psychological Science, 19*, 214–219. (p. 662)

Polanczyk, G., De Lima, M. S., Horta, B. L., Biederman, J., & Rohde, L. A. (2007). The worldwide prevalence of ADHD: A systematic review and metaregression analysis. *American Journal of Psychiatry, 164*, 942–948. (p. 627)

Poldrack, R. A., Halchenko, Y. O., & Hanson, S. J. (2009). Decoding the large-scale structure of brain function by classifying mental states across individuals. *Psychological Science, 20*, 1364–1372. (p. 62)

Polivy, J., & Herman, C. P. (1985). Dieting and binging: A causal analysis. *American Psychologist, 40*, 193–201. (p. 433)

Polivy, J., & Herman, C. P. (1987). Diagnosis and treatment of normal eating. *Journal of Personality and Social Psychology, 55*, 635–644. (p. 433)

Polivy, J., & Herman, C. P. (2002). Causes of eating disorders. *Annual Review of Psychology, 53*, 187–213. (p. 671)

Polivy, J., Herman, C. P., & Coelho, J. S. (2008). Caloric restriction in the presence of attractive food cues: External cues, eating, and weight. *Physiology and Behavior, 94*, 729–733. (p. 426)

Pollak, S., Cicchetti, D., & Klorman, R. (1998). Stress, memory, and emotion: Developmental considerations from the study of child maltreatment. *Developmental Psychopathology, 10*, 811–828. (p. 282)

Pollak, S. D. (2008). Mechanisms linking early experience and the emergence of emotions. *Current Directions in Psychological Science, 17*, 370–375. (p. 192)

Pollak, S. D., & Kistler, D. J. (2002). Early experience is associated with the development of categorical representations for facial expressions of emotion. *Proceedings of the National Academy of Sciences, 99*, 9072–9076. (p. 485)

Pollak, S. D., & Tolley-Schell, S. A. (2003). Selective attention to facial emotion in physically abused children. *Journal of Abnormal Psychology, 112*, 323–328. (p. 485)

Pollan, M. (2009, August 2). Out of the kitchen, onto the couch. *New York Times* (www.nytimes.com). (p. 426)

Pollard, R. (1992). 100 years in psychology and deafness: A centennial retrospective. Invited address to the American Psychological Association convention, Washington, DC. (p. 374)

Pollick, A. S., & de Waal, F. B. M. (2007). Ape gestures and language evolution. *Proceedings of the National Academic of Sciences, 104*, 8184–8189. (p. 374)

Poole, D. A., & Lindsay, D. S. (1995). Interviewing preschoolers: Effects of non-suggestive techniques, parental coaching and leading questions on reports of non-experienced events. *Journal of Experimental Child Psychology, 60*, 129–154. (p. 343)

Poole, D. A., & Lindsay, D. S. (2001). Children's eyewitness reports after exposure to misinformation from parents. *Journal of Experimental Psychology: Applied, 7*, 27–50. (p. 343)

Poole, D. A., & Lindsay, D. S. (2002). Reducing child witnesses' false reports of misinformation from parents. *Journal of Experimental Child Psychology, 81*, 117–140. (p. 343)

Poon, L. W. (1987). Myths and truisms: Beyond extant analyses of speed of behavior and age. Address to the Eastern Psychological Association convention. (p. 211)

Popenoe, D. (1993). The evolution of marriage and the problem of stepfamilies: A biosocial perspective. Paper presented at the National Symposium on Stepfamilies, Pennsylvania State University. (p. 155)

Popkin, B. M. (2007, September). The world is fat. *Scientific American*, pp. 88–95. (p. 431)

Poremba, A., & Gabriel, M. (2001). Amygdalar efferents initiate auditory thalamic discriminative training-induced neuronal activity. *Journal of Neuroscience, 21*, 270–278. (p. 65)

Poropat, A. E. (2009). A meta-analysis of the five-factor model of personality and academic performance. *Psychological Bulletin, 135*, 322–338. (p. 552)

Porter, D., & Neuringer, A. (1984). Music discriminations by pigeons. *Journal of Experimental Psychology: Animal Behavior Processes, 10*, 138–148. (p. 287)

Porter, S., Birt, A. R., Yuille, J. C., & Lehman, D. R. (2000, November). Negotiating false memories: Interviewer and rememberer characteristics relate to memory distortion. *Psychological Science, 11*, 507–510. (p. 342)

Porter, S., & Peace, K. A. (2007). The scars of memory: A prospective, longitudinal investigation of the consistency of traumatic and positive emotional memories in adulthood. *Psychological Science, 18*, 435–441. (p. 347)

Porter, S., & ten Brinke, L. (2008). Reading between the lies: Identifying concealed and falsified emotions in universal facial expressions. *Psychological Science, 19*, 508–514. (p. 485)

Posner, M. I., & Carr, T. H. (1992). Lexical access and the brain: Anatomical constraints on cognitive models of word recognition. *American Journal of Psychology, 105*, 1–26. (p. 373)

Posthuma, D., & de Geus, E. J. C. (2006). Progress in the molecular-genetic study of intelligence. *Current Directions in Psychological Science, 15*, 151–155. (p. 405)

Poulton, R., & Milne, B. J. (2002). Low fear in childhood is associated with sporting prowess in adolescence and young adulthood. *Behaviour Research and Therapy, 40*, 1191–1197. (p. 668)

Powell, J. (1989). *Happiness is an inside job.* Valencia, CA: Tabor. (p. 566)

Powell, K. E., Thompson, P. D., Caspersen, C. J., & Kendrick, J. S. (1987). Physical activity and the incidence of coronary heart disease. *Annual Review of Public Health, 8*, 253–287. (p. 521)

Powell, R. A., & Boer, D. P. (1994). Did Freud mislead patients to confabulate memories of abuse? *Psychological Reports, 74*, 1283–1298. (p. 539)

PRB. (2010). *2010 world population data sheet.* Population Reference Bureau (www.pub.org). (p. 209)

Premack, D. (2007). Human and animal cognition: Continuity and discontinuity. *PNAS, 104*, 13861–13867. (p. 366)

Premack, D. G., & Woodruff, G. (1978). Does the chimpanzee have a theory of mind? *Behavioral and Brain Sciences, 1*, 515–526. (p. 183)

Prentice, D. A., & Miller, D. T. (1993). Pluralistic ignorance and alcohol use on campus: Some consequences of misperceiving the social norm. *Journal of Personality and Social Psychology, 64*, 243–256. (p. 128)

Presley, C. A., Meilman, P. W., & Lyerla, R. (1997). *Alcohol and drugs on American college campuses: Issues of violence and harassment.* Carbondale: Core Institute, Southern Illinois University. (p. 117)

Prince Charles (2000). BBC Reith Lecture. (p. 15)

Principe, G. F., Kanaya, T., Ceci, S. J., & Singh, M. (2006). Believing is seeing: How rumors can engender false memories in preschoolers. *Psychological Science, 17*, 243–248. (p. 345)

Prioleau, L., Murdock, M., & Brody, N. (1983). An analysis of psychotherapy versus placebo studies. *The Behavioral and Brain Sciences, 6,* 275–310. (p. 699)

Prior, H., Schwarz, A., & Güntürkün, O. (2008). Mirror-induced behavior in the magpie (*Pica pica*): Evidence of self-recognition. *PloS Biology, 6,* 1642–1650. (p. 194)

Proffitt, D. R. (2006a). Embodied perception and the economy of action. *Perspectives on Psychological Science, 1,* 110–122. (p. 232)

Proffitt, D.R. (2006b). Distance perception. *Current Directions in Psychological Research, 15,* 131–135. (p. 232)

Project Match Research Group. (1997). Matching alcoholism treatments to client heterogeneity: Project MATCH posttreatment drinking outcomes. *Journal of Studies on Alcohol, 58,* 7–29. (p. 689)

Pronin, E. (2007). Perception and misperception of bias in human judgment. *Trends in Cognitive Sciences, 11,* 37–43. (p. 566)

Pronin, E., Berger, J., & Molouki, S. (2007). Alone in a crowd of sheep: Asymmetric perceptions of conformity and their roots in an introspection illusion. *Journal of Personality and Social Psychology, 92,* 585–595. (p. 581)

Pronin, E., & Ross, L. (2006). Temporal differences in trait self-ascription: When the self is seen as an other. *Journal of Personality and Social Psychology, 90,* 197–209. (p. 573)

Propper, R. E., Stickgold, R., Keeley, R., & Christman, S. D. (2007). Is television traumatic? Dreams, stress, and media exposure in the aftermath of September 11, 2001. *Psychological Science, 18,* 334–340. (p. 106)

Provine, R. R., Krosnowski, K. A., & Brocato, N. W. (2009). Tearing: Breakthrough in human emotional signaling. *Evolutionary Psychology, 7,* 52–56. (p. 488)

Pryor, J. H., Hurtado, S., DeAngelo, L., Blake, L. P., & Tran, S. (2011). *The American Freshman: National Norms Fall 2010.* Higher Education Research Institute, UCLA. (pp. 158, 159, 409, 453, 504)

Pryor, J. H., Hurtado, S., Saenz, V. B., Korn, J. S., Santos, J. L., & Korn, W. S. (2006). *The American freshman: National norms for fall 2006.* Los Angeles: UCLA Higher Education Research Institute. (p. 653)

Pryor, J. H., Hurtado, S., Saenz, V. B., Lindholm, J. A., Korn, W. S., & Mahoney, K. M. (2005). *The American freshman: National norms for fall 2005.* Los Angeles: Higher Education Research Institute, UCLA. (p. 144)

Pryor, J. H., Hurtado, S., Sharkness, J., & Korn, W. S. (2007). *The American freshman: National norms for Fall 2007.* Los Angeles: UCLA Higher Education Research Institute. (p. 158)

Przbylski, A. K., Rigby, C. S., & Ryan, R. M. (2010). A motivational model of video game engagement. *Review of General Psychology, 14,* 154–166. (p. 606)

Psychologist. (2003, April). Who's the greatest? *The Psychologist, 16,* p. 17. (p. 187)

PTC. (2007, January 10). *Dying to entertain: Violence on prime time broadcast TV, 1998 to 2006.* Parents Television Council (www.parentstv.org). (p. 307)

Puetz, T. W., O'Connor, P. J., & Dishman, R. K. (2006). Effects of chronic exercise on feelings of energy and fatigue: A quantitative synthesis. *Psychological Bulletin, 132,* 866–876. (p. 522)

Puhl, R. M., & Heuer, C. A. (2009). The stigma of obesity: A review and update. *Obesity, 17,* 941–964. (p. 429)

Puhl, R. M., & Latner, J. D. (2007). Stigma, obesity, and the health of the nation's children. *Psychological Bulletin, 133,* 557–580. (p. 429)

Pulkkinen, L. (2004). A longitudinal study on social development as an impetus for school reform toward an integrated school day. *European Psychologist, 9,* 125–141. (p. 193)

Pulkkinen, L. (2006). The Jyväskylä longitudinal study of personality and social development (JYLS). In L. Pulkkinen, J. Kaprio, & R. J. Rose (Eds.), *Socioemotional development and health from adolescence to adulthood* (Cambridge studies on child and adolescent health). New York: Cambridge University Press. (p. 193)

Putnam, F. W. (1991). Recent research on multiple personality disorder. *Psychiatric Clinics of North America, 14,* 489–502. (p. 666)

Putnam, F. W. (1995). Rebuttal of Paul McHugh. *Journal of the American Academy of Child and Adolescent Psychiatry, 34,* 963. (p. 667)

Putnam, R. (2000). *Bowling alone.* New York: Simon and Schuster. (p. 153)

Pyszczynski, T. A., Hamilton, J. C., Greenberg, J., & Becker, S. E. (1991). Self-awareness and psychological dysfunction. In C. R. Snyder & D. O. Forsyth (Eds.), *Handbook of social and clinical psychology: The health perspective.* New York: Pergamon. (p. 653)

Pyszczynski, T. A., Rothschild, Z., & Abdollahi, A. (2008). Terrorism, violence, and hope for peace: A terror management perspective. *Current Directions in Psychological Science 17,* 318–322. (p. 598)

Pyszczynski, T. A., Solomon, S., & Greenberg, J. (2002). *In the wake of 9/11: The psychology of terror.* Washington, DC: American Psychological Association. (p. 598)

Quinn, P. J., Williams, G. M., Najman, J. M., Andersen, M. J., & Bor, W. (2001). The effect of breastfeeding on child development at 5 years: A cohort study. *Journal of Pediatrics & Child Health, 3,* 465–469. (p. 34)

Quinn, P. C. (2002). Category representation in young infants. *Current Directions in Psychological Science, 11,* 66–70. (p. 175)

Quinn, P. C., Bhatt, R. S., Brush, D., Grimes, A., & Sharpnack, H. (2002). Development of form similarity as a Gestalt grouping principle in infancy. *Psychological Science, 13,* 320–328. (p. 243)

Quasha, S. (1980). *Albert Einstein: An intimate portrait.* New York: Forest. (p. 400)

Quoidbach, J., Dunn, E. W., Petrides, K. V., & Mikolajczak, M. (2010). Money giveth, money taketh away: The dual effect of wealth on happiness. *Psychological Science, 21,* 759–763. (p. 498)

Qirko, H. N. (2004). "Fictive kin" and suicide terrorism. *Science, 304,* 49–50. (p. 589)

Rabbitt, P. (2006). Tales of the unexpected: 25 years of cognitive gerontology. *The Psychologist, 19,* 674–676. (p. 214)

Rabinowicz, T., Dean, D. E., Petetot, J. M., & de Courten-Myers, G. M. (1999). Gender differences in the human cerebral cortex: More neurons in males; more processes in females. *Journal of Child Neurology, 14,* 98–107. (p. 177)

Rabinowicz, T., deCourten-Myers, G. M., Petetot, J. M., Xi, G., & de los Reyes, E. (1996). Human cortex development: Estimates of neuronal numbers indicate major loss late during gestation. *Journal of Neuropathology and Experimental Neurology, 55,* 320–328. (p. 177)

Rabins, P. & 18 others. (2009). Scientific and ethical issues related to deep brain stimulation for disorders of mood, behavior, and thought. *Archives of General Psychiatry, 66,* 931–937. (p. 710)

Racsmány, M., Conway, M. A., & Demeter, G. (2010). Consolidation of episodic memories during sleep: Long-term effects of retrieval practice. *Psychological Science, 21,* 80–85. (p. 98)

Radford, B. (2010, February 18). Tiger Woods and sex addiction: Real disease or easy excuse? LiveScience.com (accessed via news.yahoo.com). (pp. 116, 253)

Rahman, Q., & Koerting, J. (2008). Sexual orientation-related differences in allocentric spatial memory tasks. *Hippocampus, 18,* 55–63. (pp. 446, 447, 448)

Rahman, Q., & Wilson, G. D. (2003). Born gay? The psychobiology of human sexual orientation. *Personality and Individual Differences, 34,* 1337–1382. (pp. 445, 448)

Rahman, Q., Wilson, G. D., & Abrahams, S. (2003). Biosocial factors, sexual orientation and neurocognitive functioning. *Psychoneuroendocrinology, 29,* 867–881. (pp. 447, 448)

Raine, A. (1999). Murderous minds: Can we see the mark of Cain? *Cerebrum: The Dana Forum on Brain Science 1*(1), 15–29. (pp. 600, 668, 669)

Raine, A. (2005). The interaction of biological and social measures in the explanation of antisocial and violent behavior. In D. M. Stoff & E. J. Susman (Eds.) *Developmental psychobiology of aggression.* New York: Cambridge University Press. (pp. 600, 668)

Raine, A., Brennan, P., Mednick, B., & Mednick, S. A. (1996). High rates of violence, crime, academic problems, and behavioral problems in males with both early neuromotor deficits and unstable family environments. *Archives of General Psychiatry, 53,* 544–549. (p. 669)

Raine, A., Lencz, T., Bihrle, S., LaCasse, L., & Colletti, P. (2000). Reduced prefrontal gray matter volume and reduced autonomic activity in antisocial personality disorder. *Archives of General Psychiatry, 57,* 119–127. (p. 669)

Rainie, L., Purcell, K., Goulet, L. S., & Hampton, K. H. (2011, June 16). Social networking sites and our lives. *Pew Research Center* (pewresearch.org). (p. 453)

Rainville, P., Duncan, G. H., Price, D. D., Carrier, B., & Bushnell, M. C. (1997). Pain affect encoded in human anterior cingulate but not somatosensory cortex. *Science, 277,* 968–971. (p. 113)

Raison, C. L., Klein, H. M., & Steckler, M. (1999). The mood and madness reconsidered. *Journal of Affective Disorders, 53,* 99–106. (p. 669)

Rajendran, G., & Mitchell, P. (2007). Cognitive theories of autism. *Developmental Review, 27,* 224–260. (p. 184)

Ralston, A. (2004). Enough rope. Interview for ABC TV, Australia, by Andrew Denton. (www.abc.net.au/enoughrope/stories/s1227885.htm). (p. 417)

Ramachandran, V. S., & Blakeslee, S. (1998). *Phantoms in the brain: Probing the mysteries of the human mind.* New York: Morrow. (pp. 56, 76, 264)

Ramírez-Esparza, N., Gosling, S. D., Benet-Martínez, V., Potter, J. P., & Pennebaker, J. W. (2006). Do bilinguals have two personalities? A special case of cultural frame switching. *Journal of Research in Personality, 40,* 99–120. (p. 376)

Rand, C. S. W., & Macgregor, A. M. C. (1990). Morbidly obese patients' perceptions of social discrimination before and after surgery for obesity. *Southern Medical Journal, 83,* 1390–1395. (p. 429)

Rand, C. S. W., & Macgregor, A. M. C. (1991). Successful weight loss following obesity surgery and perceived liability or morbid obesity. *Internal Journal of Obesity, 15,* 577–579. (p. 429)

Randi, J. (1999, February 4). 2000 club mailing list e-mail letter. (p. 255)

Randler, C. (2008). Morningness–eveningness and satisfaction with life. *Social Indicators Research, 86,* 297–302. (p. 93)

Randler, C. (2009). Proactive people are morning people. *Journal of Applied Social Psychology, 39,* 2787–2797. (p. 93)

Randler, C., & Bausback, V. (2010). Morningness-eveningness in women around the transition through menopause and its relationship with climacteric complaints. *Biological Rhythm Research, 41,* in press. (p. 93)

Randler, C., & Frech, D. (2009). Young people's time-of-day preferences affect their school performance. *Journal of Youth Studies, 12,* 653–667. (p. 93)

Rapoport, J. L. (1989, March). The biology of obsessions and compulsions. *Scientific American,* pp. 83–89. (pp. 639, 643)

Räsänen, S., Pakaslahti, A., Syvalahti, E., Jones, P. B., & Isohanni, M. (2000). Sex differences in schizophrenia: A review. *Nordic Journal of Psychiatry, 54,* 37–45. (p. 659)

Rasch, B., & Born, J. (2008). Reactivation and consolidation of memory during sleep. *Current Directions in Psychological Science, 17,* 188–192. (p. 98)

Rasmussen, H. N., Scheier, M. F., & Greenhouse, J. B. (2010). Optimism and physical health: A meta-analytic review. *Annals of Behavioral Medicine, 37,* 239–256. (p. 518)

Rath, T., & Harter, J. K. (2010, August 19). Your friends and your social wellbeing: Close friendships are vital to health, happiness, and even workplace productivity. *Gallup Management Journal* (ww.gmj.gallup.com). (p. 468)

Ray, J. (2005, April 12). U.S. teens walk away from anger: Boys and girls manage anger differently. *The Gallup Organization* (www.gallup.com). (p. 493)

Ray, O., & Ksir, C. (1990). *Drugs, society, and human behavior* (5th ed.). St. Louis: Times Mirror/Mosby. (p. 122)

Raynor, H. A., & Epstein, L. H. (2001). Dietary variety, energy regulation, and obesity. *Psychological Bulletin, 127,* 325–341. (p. 424)

Raz, A., Fan, J., & Posner, M. I. (2005). Hypnotic suggestion reduces conflict in the human brain. *PNAS, 102,* 9978–9983. (p. 113)

Read, J., & Bentall, R. (2010). The effectiveness of electroconvulsive therapy: A literature review. *Epidemiologica e Psichiatria Sociale, 19,* 333–347. (p. 708)

Reason, J. (1987). The Chernobyl errors. *Bulletin of the British Psychological Society, 40,* 201–206. (p. 590)

Reason, J., & Mycielska, K. (1982). *Absent-minded? The psychology of mental lapses and everyday errors.* Englewood Cliffs, NJ: Prentice-Hall. (p. 230)

Reece, M., Herbenick, D., Schick, V., Sanders, S.A., Dodge, B., & Fortenberry, J. D. (2010). Sexual behaviors, relationships, and perceived health among adult men in the United States: Results from a national probability sample. *Journal of Sexual Medicine, 7* (suppl 5), 291–304. (p. 209)

Reed, P. (2000). Serial position effects in recognition memory for odors. *Journal of Experimental Psychology: Learning, Memory, and Cognition, 26,* 411–422. (p. 332)

Reed, T. E., & Jensen, A. R. (1992). Conduction velocity in a brain nerve pathway of normal adults correlates with intelligence level. *Intelligence, 16,* 259–272. (p. 391)

Rees, M. (1999). *Just six numbers: The deep forces that shape the universe.* New York: Basic Books. (p. 166)

Regan, P. C., & Atkins, L. (2007). Sex differences and similarities in frequency and intensity of sexual desire. *Social Behavior and Personality, 34,* 95–102. (p. 144)

Reichardt, C. S. (2010). Testing astrological predictions about sex, marriage, and selfishness. *Skeptic Magazine, 15*(4), 40–45. (p. 550)

Reichenberg, A., Gross, R., Weiser, M., Bresnahan, M., Silverman, J., Harlap, S., Rabinoqitz, J., Shulman, C., Malaspina, D., Lubin, G., Knobler, H Y., Davidson, M., & Susser, E. (2007). Advancing paternal age and autism. *Archives of General Psychiatry, 63,* 1026–1032. (p. 185)

Reichenberg, A., & Harvey, P. D. (2007). Neuropsychological impairments in schizophrenia: Integration of performance-based and brain imaging findings. *Psychological Bulletin, 133,* 833–858. (p. 657)

Reichert, R. A., Robb, M. B., Fender, J. G., & Wartella, E. (2010). Word learning from baby videos. *Archives of Pediatrics & Adolescent Medicine, 164,* 432–437. (p. 408)

Reichle, E. D., Reineberg, A. E., & Schooler, J. W. (2010). Eye movements during mindless reading. *Psychological Science, 21,* 1300–1310. (p. 87)

Reifman, A., & Cleveland, H. H. (2007). Shared environment: A quantitative review. Paper presented to the Society for Research in Child Development, Boston, MA. (p. 137)

Reifman, A. S., Larrick, R. P., & Fein, S. (1991). Temper and temperature on the diamond: The heat-aggression relationship in major league baseball. *Personality and Social Psychology Bulletin, 17,* 580–585. (p. 601)

Reimann, F., & 24 others. (2010). Pain perception is altered by a nucleotide polymorphism in *SCN9A. PNAS, 107,* 5148–5153. (p. 263)

Reiner, W. G., & Gearhart, J. P. (2004). Discordant sexual identity in some genetic males with cloacal exstrophy assigned to female sex at birth. *New England Journal of Medicine, 350,* 333–341. (p. 161)

Reis, D., & Marino, L. (2001). Mirror self-recognition in the bottlenose dolphin: A case of cognitive convergence. *PNAS, 98,* 5937–5942. (p. 194)

Reis, H. T., & Aron, A. (2008). Love: What is it, why does it matter, and how does it operate? *Perspectives on Psychological Science, 3,* 80–86. (p. 614)

Reis, H. T., Smith, S. M., Carmichael, C. L., Caprariello, P. A., Tsa, F-F., Rodrigues, A., & Maniaci, M. R. (2010). Are you happy for me? How sharing positive events with others provides personal and interpersonal benefits. *Journal of Personality and Social Psychology, 99,* 311–329. (p. 450)

Reisenzein, R. (1983). The Schachter theory of emotion: Two decades later. *Psychological Bulletin, 94,* 239–264. (p. 476)

Reiser, M. (1982). *Police psychology.* Los Angeles: LEHI. (p. 253)

Reitzle, M. (2006). The connections between adulthood transitions and the self-perception of being adult in the changing contexts of East and West Germany. *European Psychologist, 11,* 25–38. (p. 206)

Remick, A. K., Polivy, J., & Pliner, P. (2009). Internal and external moderators of the effect of variety on food intake. *Psychological Bulletin, 135,* 434–451. (p. 426)

Remington, A., Swettenham, J., Campbell, R., & Coleman, M. (2009). Selective attention and perceptual load in autism spectrum disorder. *Psychological Science, 20,* 1388–1393. (p. 184)

Remley, A. (1988, October). From obedience to independence. *Psychology Today,* pp. 56–59. (p. 155)

Renner, M. J., & Renner, C. H. (1993). Expert and novice intuitive judgments about animal behavior. *Bulletin of the Psychonomic Society, 31,* 551–552. (p. 149)

Renner, M. J., & Rosenzweig, M. R. (1987). *Enriched and impoverished environments: Effects on brain and behavior.* New York: Springer-Verlag. (p. 148)

Renninger, K. A., & Granott, N. (2005). The process of scaffolding in learning and development. *New Ideas in Psychology, 23*(3), 111–114. (p. 186)

Rentfrow, P. J., & Gosling, S. D. (2003). The Do Re Mi's of everyday life: The structure and personality correlates of music preferences. *Journal of Personality and Social Psychology, 84,* 1236–1256. (p. 554)

Rentfrow, P. J., & Gosling, S. D. (2006). Message in a ballad: The role of music preferences in interpersonal perception. *Psychological Science, 17,* 236–242. (p. 554)

Repetti, R. L., Taylor, S. E., & Seeman, T. E. (2002). Risky families: Family social environments and the mental and physical health of offspring. *Psychological Bulletin, 128,* 330–366. (p. 505)

Repetti, R. L., Wang, S-W., & Saxbe, D. (2009). Bringing it all back home: How outside stressors shape families' everyday lives. *Current Directions in Psychological Science, 18,* 106–111. (p. 507)

Rescorla, R. A., & Wagner, A. R. (1972). A theory of Pavlovian conditioning: Variations in the effectiveness of reinforcement and nonreinforcement. In A. H. Black & W. F. Perokasy (Eds.), *Classical conditioning II: Current theory.* New York: Appleton-Century-Crofts. (p. 301)

Resnick, M. D., Bearman, P. S., Blum, R. W., Bauman, K. E., Harris, K. M., Jones, J., Tabor, J., Beuhring, T., Sieving, R., Shew, M., Bearinger, L. H., & Udry, J. R. (1997). Protecting adolescents from harm: Findings from the National Longitudinal Study on Adolescent Health. *Journal of the American Medical Association, 278,* 823–832. (pp. 33, 90, 205)

Resnick, S. M. (1992). Positron emission tomography in psychiatric illness. *Current Directions in Psychological Science, 1,* 92–98. (p. 660)

Responsive Community. (1996, Fall). Age vs. weight. Page 83 (reported from a *Wall Street Journal* survey). (p. 432)

Rethorst, C. D., Wipfli, B. M., & Landers, D. M. (2009). The antidepressive effects of exercise: A meta-analysis of randomized trials. *Sports Medicine, 39,* 491–511. (p. 522)

Reuters. (2000, July 5). Many teens regret decision to have sex (National Campaign to Prevent Teen Pregnancy survey). www.washingtonpost.com. (p. 439)

Reyna, V. F., & Farley, F. (2006). Risk and rationality in adolescent decision making: Implications for theory, practice, and public policy. *Psychological Science in the Public Interest, 7*(1), 1–44. (p. 199)

Reynolds, C. R., Niland, J., Wright, J. E., & Rosenn, M. (2010). Failure to apply the Flynn correction in death penalty litigation: Standard practice of today maybe, but certainly malpractice of tomorrow. *Journal of Psychoeducational Assessment, 28,* 477–481. (p. 402)

Reynolds, G. (2009, November 18). Phys ed: Why exercise makes you less anxious. *New York Times blog* (well.blogs.nytimes.com). (p. 523)

Rhoades, G. K., Stanley, S. M., & Markman, H. J. (2009). The pre-engagement cohabitation effect: A replication and extension of previous findings. *Journal of Family Psychology, 23,* 107–111. (p. 216)

Rhodes, G., Sumich, A., & Byatt, G. (1999). Are average facial configurations attractive only because of their symmetry? *Psychological Science, 10,* 52–58. (p. 611)

Rholes, W. S., & Simpson, J. A. (Eds.). (2004). *Adult attachment: Theory, research, and clinical implications.* New York: Guilford. (p. 191)

Rholes, W. S., Simpson, J. A., & Friedman, M. (2006). Avoidant attachment and the experience of parenting. *Personality and Social Psychology Bulletin, 32,* 275–285. (p. 191)

Ribeiro, R., Gervasoni, D., Soares, E. S., Zhou, Y., Lin, S-C., Pantoja, J., Lavine, M., & Nicolelis, M. A. L. (2004). Long-lasting novelty-induced neuronal reverberation during slow-wave sleep in multiple forebrain areas. *PloS Biology, 2*(1), e37 (www.plosbiology.org). (p. 99)

Ricciardelli, L. A., & McCabe, M. P. (2004). A biopsychosocial model of disordered eating and the pursuit of muscularity in adolescent boys. *Psychological Bulletin, 130,* 179–205. (p. 671)

Rice, M. E., & Grusec, J. E. (1975). Saying and doing: Effects on observer performance. *Journal of Personality and Social Psychology, 32,* 584–593. (p. 306)

Richardson, J. (1993). The curious case of coins: Remembering the appearance of familiar objects. *The Psychologist: Bulletin of the British Psychological Society, 6,* 360–366. (p. 336)

Richardson, J. T. E., & Zucco, G. M. (1989). Cognition and olfaction: A review. *Psychological Bulletin, 105,* 352–360. (p. 270)

Richeson, J. A., & Shelton, J. N. (2007). Negotiating interracial interactions. *Current Directions in Psychological Science, 16,* 316–320. (p. 620)

Rieff, P. (1979). *Freud: The mind of a moralist* (3rd ed.). Chicago: University of Chicago Press. (p. 540)

Rieger, G., Linsenmeier, J. A., Gygax, L., & Bailey, J. M. (2008). Sexual orientation and childhood gender nonconformity: Evidence from home videos. *Developmental Psychology, 44,* 46–58. (p. 447)

Riis, J., Loewenstein, G., Baron, J., Jepson, C., Fagerlin, A., & Ubel, P. A. (2005). Ignorance of hedonic adaptation to hemodialysis: A study using ecological momentary assessment. *Journal of Experimental Psychology: General, 134,* 3–9. (p. 497)

Riley, L. D., & Bowen, C. (2005). The sandwich generation: Challenges and coping strategies of multigenerational families. *The Family Journal, 13,* 52–58. (p. 215)

Rindermann, H., & Ceci, S. J. (2009). Educational policy and country outcomes in international cognitive competence studies. *Perspectives on Psychological Science, 4,* 551–577. (p. 412)

Ripple, C. H., & Zigler, E. F. (2003). Research, policy, and the federal role in prevention initiatives for children. *American Psychologist, 58,* 482–490. (p. 408)

Risch, N., Herrell, R., Lehner, T., Liang, K. Y., Eaves, L., Hoh, J., Griem, A., Ott, J., & Merikangas, K. R. (2009). Interaction between the serotonin transporter gene (5-HTTLPR), stressful life events, and risk of depression: a meta-analysis. *JAMA. 301,* 2462–2471. (p. 652)

Riskind, J. H., Beck, A. T., Berchick, R. J., Brown, G., & Steer, R. A. (1987). Reliability of DSM-III diagnoses for major depression and generalized anxiety disorder using the structured clinical interview for DSM-III. *Archives of General Psychiatry, 44,* 817–820. (p. 630)

Rizzolatti, G., Fadiga, L., Fogassi, L., & Gallese, V. (2002). From mirror neurons to imitation: Facts and speculations. In A. N. Meltzoff & W. Prinz (Eds.), *The imitative mind: Development, evolution, and brain bases.* Cambridge: Cambridge University Press, 2002. (p. 304)

Rizzolatti, G., Fogassi, L., & Gallese, V. (2006, November). Mirrors in the mind. *Scientific American,* pp. 54–61. (p. 304)

Roan, S. (2010, August 15). Medical treatment carries possible side effect of limiting homosexuality. *Los Angeles Times* (www.latimes.com). (p. 448)

Roberson, D., Davidoff, J., Davies, I. R. L., & Shapiro, L. R. (2004). The development of color categories in two languages: A longitudinal study. *Journal of Experimental Psychology: General, 133,* 554–571. (p. 376)

Roberson, D., Davies, I. R. L., Corbett, G. G., & Vandervyver, M. (2005). Free-sorting of colors across cultures: Are there universal grounds for grouping? *Journal of Cognition and Culture, 5,* 349–386. (p. 376)

Roberts, B. W., Caspi, A., & Moffitt, T. E. (2001). The kids are alright: Growth and stability in personality development from adolescence to adulthood. *Journal of Personality and Social Psychology, 81,* 670–683. (p. 171)

Roberts, B. W., Caspi, A., & Moffitt, T. E. (2003). Work experiences and personality development in young adulthood. *Journal of Personality and Social Psychology, 84,* 582–593. (p. 172)

Roberts, B. W., & DelVecchio, W. F. (2000). The rank-order consistency of personality traits from childhood to old age: A quantitative review of longitudinal studies. *Psychological Bulletin, 126,* 3–25. (p. 553)

Roberts, B. W., Kuncel, N. R., Shiner, R., Caspi, A., & Goldberg, L. R. (2007). The power of personality: The comparative validity of personality traits, socioeconomic status, and cognitive ability for predicting important life outcomes. *Perspectives on Psychological Science, 2,* 313–345. (p. 554)

Roberts, B. W., & Mroczek, D. (2008). Personality trait change in adulthood. *Current Directions in Psychological Science, 17,* 31–35. (p. 172)

Roberts, B. W., Walton, K. E., & Viechtbauer, W. (2006). Patterns of mean-level change in personality traits across the life course: A meta-analysis of longitudinal studies. *Psychological Bulletin, 132,* 1–25. (p. 172)

Roberts, L. (1988). Beyond Noah's ark: What do we need to know? *Science, 242,* 1247. (p. 518)

Roberts, T-A. (1991). Determinants of gender differences in responsiveness to others' evaluations. *Dissertation Abstracts International, 51*(8–B). (p. 158)

Robertson, K. F., Smeets, S., Lubinski, D., & Benbow, C. P. (2010). Beyond the threshold hypothesis: Even among the gifted and top math/science graduate students, cognitive abilitieis, vocational interests, and lifestyle preferences matter for career choice, performance, and persistence. *Current Directions in Psychological Science, 19,* 346–351. (p. 387)

Robins, L., & Regier, D. (Eds.). (1991). *Psychiatric disorders in America.* New York: Free Press. (p. 635)

Robins, L. N., Davis, D. H., & Goodwin, D. W. (1974). Drug use by U.S. Army enlisted men in Vietnam: A follow-up on their return home. *American Journal of Epidemiology, 99,* 235–249. (p. 128)

Robins, R. W., & Trzesniewski, K. H. (2005). Self-esteem development across the lifespan. *Current Directions in Psychological Science, 14*(3), 158–162. (p. 218)

Robins, R. W., Trzesniewski, K. H., Tracy, J. L., Gosling, S. D., & Potter, J. (2002). Global self-esteem across the lifespan. *Psychology and Aging, 17,* 423–434. (p. 204)

Robinson, F. P. (1970). *Effective study.* New York: Harper & Row. (p. 12)

Robinson, J. P., & Martin, S. (2008). What Do Happy People Do? *Social Indicators Research, 89,* 565–571. (pp. 97, 457)

Robinson, J. P., & Martin, S. (2009). Changes in American daily life: 1965–2005. *Social Indicators Research, 93,* 47–56. (p. 307)

Robinson, T. E., & Berridge, K. C. (2003). Addiction. *Annual Review of Psychology, 54,* 25–53. (p. 116)

Robinson, T. N. (1999). Reducing children's television viewing to prevent obesity. *Journal of the American Medical Association, 282,* 1561–1567. (p. 433)

Robinson, T. N., Borzekowski, D. L. G., Matheson, D. M., & Kraemer, H. C. (2007). Effects of fast food branding on young children's taste preferences. *Archives of Pediatric and Adolescent Medicine, 161,* 792–797. (p. 230)

Robinson, V. M. (1983). Humor and health. In P. E. McGhee & J. H. Goldstein (Eds.), *Handbook of humor research: Vol. II. Applied studies.* New York: Springer-Verlag. (p. 519)

Rochat, F. (1993). How did they resist authority? Protecting refugees in Le Chambon during World War II. Paper presented at the American Psychological Association convention. (p. 584)

Rock, I., & Palmer, S. (1990, December). The legacy of Gestalt psychology. *Scientific American,* pp. 84–90. (p. 243)

Rodenburg, R., Benjamin, A., de Roos, C., Meijer, A. M., & Stams, G. J. (2009). Efficacy of EMDR in children: A meta-analysis. *Clinical Psychology Review, 29,* 599–606. (p. 697)

Rodin, J. (1986). Aging and health: Effects of the sense of control. *Science, 233,* 1271–1276. (pp. 518, 559)

Roediger, H. L., III (2001, September). Quoted by R. Herbert, Doing a number on memory. *APS Observer,* pp. 1, 7–11. (p. 338)

Roedinger, H. L., III, & Finn, B. (2010, March/April). The pluses of getting it wrong. *Scientific American Mind,* pp. 39–41. (p. 12)

Roediger, H. L., III, & Geraci, L. (2007). Aging and the misinformation effect: A neuropsychological analysis. *Journal of Experimental Psychology, 33,* 321–334. (p. 345)

Roediger, H. L., III, & Karpicke, J. D. (2006). Test-enhanced learning: Taking memory tests improves long-term retention. *Psychological Science, 17,* 249–255. (pp. 12, 320)

Roediger, H. L., III, & McDaniel, M. A. (2007). Illusory recollection in older adults: Testing Mark Twain's conjecture. In M. Garry H. Hayne (Ed.), *Do justice and let the sky fall: Elizabeth F. Loftus and her contributions to science, law, and academic freedom.* Mahwah, NJ: Erlbaum. (p. 345)

Roediger, H. L., III, & McDermott, K. B. (1995). Creating false memories: Remembering words not presented in lists. *Journal of Experimental Psychology: Learning, Memory, and Cognition, 21*, 803–814. (p. 344)

Roediger, H. L., III, Wheeler, M. A., & Rajaram, S. (1993). Remembering, knowing, and reconstructing the past. In D. L. Medin (Ed.), *The psychology of learning and motivation: Advances in research and theory* (Vol. 30). Orlando, FL: Academic Press. (p. 341)

Roehling, M. V. (1999). Weight-based discrimination in employment: Psychological and legal aspects. *Personnel Psychology, 52*, 969–1016. (p. 429)

Roehling, M. V., Roehling, P. V., & Pichler, S. (2007). The relationship between body weight and perceived weight-related employment discrimination: The role of sex and race. *Journal of Vocational Behavior, 71*, 300–318. (p. 429)

Roehling, P. V., Roehling, M. V., Johnston, A., Brennan, A., & Drew, A. (2010). Weighty decisions: The effect of weight bias on the selection and election of U.S. political candidates. Unpublished manuscript, Hope College. (p. 429)

Roehling, P. V., Roehling, M. V., & Moen, P. (2001). The relationship between work-life policies and practices and employee loyalty: A life course perspective. *Journal of Family and Economic Issues, 22*, 141–170. (p. 468)

Roehling, P. V., Roehling, M. V., Vandlen, J. D., Blazek, J., & Guy, W. C. (2009). Weight discrimination and the glass ceiling effect among top US CEOs. *Equal Opportunities International, 28*, 179–196. (p. 429)

Roelofs, T. (2010, September 22). Somali refugee takes oath of U.S. citizenship year after his brother. *Grand Rapids Press* (www.mlive.com). (p. 465)

Roenneberg, T., Kuehnle, T., Pramstaller, P. P., Ricken, J., Havel, M., Guth, A., Merrow, M. (2004). A marker for the end of adolescence. *Current Biology, 14*, R1038–R1039. (p. 93)

Roese, N. J., & Summerville, A. (2005). What we regret most . . . and why. *Personality and Social Psychology Bulletin, 31*, 1273–1285. (p. 218)

Roesser, R. (1998). What you should know about hearing conservation. *Better Hearing Institute* (www.betterhearing.org). (p. 259)

Roest, A. M., Martens, E. J., Denollet, J., & De Jonge, P. (2010). Prognostic association of anxiety post myocardial infarction with mortality and new cardiac events: A meta-analysis. *Psychosomatic Medicine, 72*, 563–569. (p. 514)

Rofé, Y. (2008). Does repression exist? Memory, pathogenic, unconscious and clinical evidence. *Review of General Psychology, 12*, 63–85. (p. 540)

Rogers, C. R. (1958). Reinhold Niebuhr's *The self and the dramas of history*: A criticism. *Pastoral Psychology, 9*, 15–17. (p. 565)

Rogers, C. R. (1961). *On becoming a person: A therapist's view of psychotherapy*. Boston: Houghton Mifflin. (p. 679)

Rogers, C. R. (1980). *A way of being*. Boston: Houghton Mifflin. (pp. 543, 544, 679)

Rohan, K. J., Roecklein, K. A., Lindsey, K. T., Johnson, L. G., Lippy, R. D., Lacy, T. J., & Barton, F. B. (2007). A randomized controlled trial of cognitive-behavioral therapy, light therapy, and their combination for seasonal affective disorder. *Journal of Consulting and Clinical Psychology, 75*, 489–500. (p. 698)

Rohner, R. P. (1986). *The warmth dimension: Foundations of parental acceptance-rejection theory*. Newbury Park, CA: Sage. (p. 156)

Rohner, R. P., & Veneziano, R. A. (2001). The importance of father love: History and contemporary evidence. *Review of General Psychology, 5*, 382–405. (pp. 190, 195)

Rohrer, D., & Pashler, H. (2007). Increasing retention without increasing study time. *Current Directions in Psychological Science, 16*, 183–186. (p. 320)

Rohwedder, S., Willis, R. J. (2010). Mental retirement. *Journal of Economic Perspectives, 24*, 119–138. (p. 213)

Roiser, J. P., Cook, L. J., Cooper, J. D., Rubinsztein, D. C., & Sahakian, B. J. (2005). Association of a functional polymorphism in the serotonin transporter gene with abnormal emotional processing in Ecstasy users. *American Journal of Psychiatry, 162*, 609–612. (p. 123)

Rokach, A., Orzeck, T., Moya, M., & Exposito, F. (2002). Causes of loneliness in North America and Spain. *European Psychologist, 7*, 70–79. (p. 22)

Ronay, R., & von Hippel, W. (2010). The presence of an attractive woman elevates testosterone and physical risk taking in young men. *Social Psychology and Personality Science, 1*, 57–64. (p. 437)

Roney, J. R., Hanson, K. N., Durante, K. M., & Maestripieri, D. (2006). Reading men's faces: Women's mate attractiveness judgments track men's testosterone and interest in infants. *Proceedings of the Royal Society B, 273*, 2169–2175. (p. 145)

Root, T. L., Thornton, L. M., Lindroos, A. K., Stunkard, A. J., Lichtenstein, P., Pedersen, N. L., Rasmussen, F., & Bulik, C. M. (2010). Shared and unique genetic and environmental influences on binge eating and night eating: A Swedish twin study. *Eating Behaviors, 11*, 92–98. (p. 671)

Rosa-Alcázar, A. I., Sáncez-Meca, J., Gómez-Conesa, A., & Marín-Martínez, F. (2008). Psychological treatment of obsessive-compulsive disorder: A meta-analysis. *Clinical Psychology Review, 28*, 1310–1325. (p. 682)

Rosch, E. (1978). Principles of categorization. In E. Rosch & B. L. Lloyd (Eds.), *Cognition and categorization*. Hillsdale, NJ: Erlbaum. (p. 352)

Rose, A. J., & Rudolph, K. D. (2006). A review of sex differences in peer relationship processes: Potential trade-offs for the emotional and behavioral development of girls and boys. *Psychological Bulletin, 132*, 98–131. (p. 158)

Rose, J. S., Chassin, L., Presson, C. C., & Sherman, S. J. (1999). Peer influences on adolescent cigarette smoking: A prospective sibling analysis. *Merrill-Palmer Quarterly, 45*, 62–84. (pp. 119, 150)

Rose, R. J. (2004). Developmental research as impetus for school reform. *European Psychologist, 9*, 142–144. (p. 193)

Rose, R. J., Kaprio, J., Winter, T., Dick, D. M., Viken, R. J., Pulkkinen, L., & Koskenvuo, M. (2002). Femininity and fertility in sisters with twin brothers: Prenatal androgenization? Cross-sex socialization? *Psychological Science, 13*, 263–266. (p. 444)

Rose, R. J., Viken, R. J., Dick, D. M., Bates, J. E., Pulkkinen, L., & Kaprio, J. (2003). It *does* take a village: Nonfamiliar environments and children's behavior. *Psychological Science, 14*, 273–277. (p. 150)

Rose, S. (1999). Precis of lifelines: Biology, freedom, determinism. *Behavioral and Brain Sciences, 22*, 871–921. (p. 146)

Roselli, C. E., Larkin, K., Schrunk, J. M., & Stormshak, F. (2004). Sexual partner preference, hypothalamic morphology and aromatase in rams. *Physiology and Behavior, 83*, 233–245. (p. 445)

Roselli, C. E., Resko, J. A., & Stormshak, F. (2002). Hormonal influences on sexual partner preference in rams. *Archives of Sexual Behavior, 31*, 43–49. (p. 445)

Rosenbaum, J. E. (2009). Patient teenagers? A comparison of the sexual behavior of virginity pledgers and matched nonpledgers. *Pediatrics, 123*, e110–e120. (p. 441)

Rosenbaum, M. (1986). The repulsion hypothesis: On the nondevelopment of relationships. *Journal of Personality and Social Psychology, 51*, 1156–1166. (p. 612)

Rosenberg, N. A., Pritchard, J. K., Weber, J. L., Cann, H. M., Kidd, K. K., Zhivotosky, L. A., & Feldman, M. W. (2002). Genetic structure of human populations. *Science, 298*, 2381–2385. (pp. 142, 412)

Rosenberg, T. (2010, November 1). The opt-out solution. *New York Times* (www.nytimes.com). (p. 360)

Rosenhan, D. L. (1973). On being sane in insane places. *Science, 179*, 250–258. (p. 632)

Rosenthal, E. (2009, November 2). When texting kills, Britain offers path of prison. *New York Times* (www.nytimes.com). (p. 89)

Rosenthal, E. (2010, May 24). Climate fears turn to doubts among Britons. *New York Times* (www.nytimes.com). (p. 360)

Rosenthal, R., Hall, J. A., Archer, D., DiMatteo, M. R., & Rogers, P. L. (1979). The PONS test: Measuring sensitivity to nonverbal cues. In S. Weitz (Ed.), *Nonverbal communication* (2nd ed.). New York: Oxford University Press. (p. 485)

Rosenzweig, M. R. (1984). Experience, memory, and the brain. *American Psychologist, 39*, 365–376. (pp. 148, 407)

Roseth, C. J., Johnson, D. W., & Johnson, R. T. (2008). Promoting early adolescents' achievement and peer relationships: The effects of cooperative, competitive, and individualistic goal structures. *Psychological Bulletin, 134*, 223–246. (p. 621)

Rosin, H. (2010, July, August). The end of men. *The Atlantic* (www.theatlantic.com). (p. 162)

Ross, J. (2006, December). Sleep on a problem . . . it works like a dream. *The Psychologist, 19*, 738–740. (p. 99)

Ross, L. (1977). The intuitive psychologist and his shortcomings: Distortions in the attribution process. In L. Berkowitz (Ed.) *Advances in experimental social psychology* (Vol. 10). New York: Academic Press. (p. 572)

Ross, M., McFarland, C., & Fletcher, G. J. O. (1981). The effect of attitude on the recall of personal histories. *Journal of Personality and Social Psychology, 40*, 627–634. (p. 339)

Ross, M., Xun, W. Q. E., & Wilson, A. E. (2002). Language and the bicultural self. *Personality and Social Psychology Bulletin, 28*, 1040–1050. (p. 376)

Rossi, A. S., & Rossi, P. H. (1993). *Of human bonding: Parent-child relations across the life course*. Hawthorne, NY: Aldine de Gruyter. (p. 159)

Rossi, P. J. (1968). Adaptation and negative aftereffect to lateral optical displacement in newly hatched chicks. *Science, 160*, 430–432. (p. 251)

Rostosky, S. S., Riggle, E. D. G., Horne, S. G., Denton, F. N., & Huellemeier, J. D. (2010). Lesbian, gay, and bisexual individuals' psychological reactions to amendments denying access to civil marriage. *American Journal of Orthopsychiatry, 80*, 302–310. (p. 507)

Roth, T., Roehrs, T., Zwyghuizen-Doorenbos, A., Stpeanski, E., & Witting, R. (1988). Sleep and memory. In I. Hindmarch & H. Ott (Eds.), *Benzodiazepine receptor ligans, memory and information processing.* New York: Springer-Verlag. (p. 106)

Rothbart, M., Fulero, S., Jensen, C., Howard, J., & Birrell, P. (1978). From individual to group impressions: Availability heuristics in stereotype formation. *Journal of Experimental Social Psychology, 14,* 237–255. (p. 599)

Rothbart, M. K. (2007). Temperament, development, and personality. *Current Directions in Psychological Science, 16,* 207–212. (p. 137)

Rothbart, M. K., Ahadi, S. A., & Evans, D. E. (2000). Temperament and personality: Origins and outcomes. *Journal of Personality and Social Psychology, 78,* 122–135. (p. 138)

Rothbaum, F., & Tsang, B. Y-P. (1998). Lovesongs in the United States and China: On the nature of romantic love. *Journal of Cross-Cultural Psychology, 29,* 306–319. (p. 155)

Rothblum, E. D. (2007). *Same-sex couples in legalized relationships: I do, or do I?* Unpublished manuscript, Women's Studies Department, San Diego State University. (p. 145)

Rothman, A. J., & Salovey, P. (1997). Shaping perceptions to motivate healthy behavior: The role of message framing. *Psychological Bulletin, 121,* 3–19. (p. 358)

Rotton, J., & Kelly, I. W. (1985). Much ado about the full moon: A metaanalysis of lunar-lunacy research. *Psychological Bulletin, 97,* 286–306. (p. 669)

Rovee-Collier, C. (1989). The joy of kicking: Memories, motives, and mobiles. In P. R. Solomon, G. R. Goethals, C. M. Kelley, & B. R. Stephens (Eds.), *Memory: Interdisciplinary approaches.* New York: Springer-Verlag. (p. 178)

Rovee-Collier, C. (1993). The capacity for long-term memory in infancy. *Current Directions in Psychological Science, 2,* 130–135. (p. 332)

Rovee-Collier, C. (1997). Dissociations in infant memory: Rethinking the development of implicit and explicit memory. *Psychological Review, 104,* 467–498. (p. 178)

Rovee-Collier, C. (1999). The development of infant memory. *Current Directions in Psychological Science, 8,* 80–85. (p. 178)

Rowe, D. C. (1990). As the twig is bent? The myth of child-rearing influences on personality development. *Journal of Counseling and Development, 68,* 606–611. (p. 136)

Rowe, D. C. (2005). Under the skin: On the impartial treatment of genetic and environmental hypotheses of racial differences. *American Psychologist, 60,* 60–70. (p. 412)

Rowe, D. C., Almeida, D. M., & Jacobson, K. C. (1999). School context and genetic influences on aggression in adolescence. *Psychological Science, 10,* 277–280. (p. 600)

Rowe, D. C., Jacobson, K. C., & Van den Oord, E. J. C. G. (1999). Genetic and environmental influences on vocabulary IQ: Parental education level as moderator. *Child Development, 70*(5), 1151–1162. (p. 406)

Rowe, D. C., Vazsonyi, A. T., & Flannery, D. J. (1994). No more than skin deep: Ethnic and racial similarity in developmental process. *Psychological Review, 101*(3), 396. (p. 156)

Rowe, D. C., Vazsonyi, A. T., & Flannery, D. J. (1995). Ethnic and racial similarity in developmental process: A study of academic achievement. *Psychological Science, 6,* 33–38. (p. 156)

Rozin, P., Dow, S., Mosovitch, M., & Rajaram, S. (1998). What causes humans to begin and end a meal? A role for memory for what has been eaten, as evidenced by a study of multiple meal eating in amnesic patients. *Psychological Science, 9,* 392–396. (p. 425)

Rozin, P., Millman, L., & Nemeroff, C. (1986). Operation of the laws of sympathetic magic in disgust and other domains. *Journal of Personality and Social Psychology, 50,* 703–712. (p. 282)

Rubenstein, J. S., Meyer, D. E., & Evans, J. E. (2001). Executive control of cognitive processes in task switching. *Journal of Experimental Psychology: Human Perception and Performance, 27,* 763–797. (p. 88)

Rubin, D. C., Berntsen, D., & Bohni, M. K. (2008). A memory-based model of posttraumatic stress disorder: Evaluating basic assumptions underlying the PTSD diagnosis. *Psychological Review, 115,* 985–1011. (p. 640)

Rubin, D. C., Rahhal, T. A., & Poon, L. W. (1998). Things learned in early adulthood are remembered best. *Memory and Cognition, 26,* 3–19. (p. 213)

Rubin, J. Z., Pruitt, D. G., & Kim, S. H. (1994). *Social conflict: Escalation, stalemate, and settlement.* New York: McGraw-Hill. (p. 621)

Rubin, L. B. (1985). *Just friends: The role of friendship in our lives.* New York: Harper & Row. (p. 159)

Rubin, Z. (1970). Measurement of romantic love. *Journal of Personality and Social Psychology, 16,* 265–273. (p. 484)

Rubio, G., & López-Ibor, J. J. (2007). Generalized anxiety disorder: A 40-year follow-up study. *Acta Psychiatrica Scandinavica, 115,* 372–379. (p. 637)

Ruchlis, H. (1990). *Clear thinking: A practical introduction.* Buffalo, NY: Prometheus Books. (p. 353)

Rudman, L. A., & Goodwin, S. A. (2004). Gender differences in automatic ingroup bias: Why do women like women more than men like men? *Journal of Personality and Social Psychology, 87,* 494–509. (p. 596)

Rueckert, L., Doan, T., & Branch, B. (2010). Emotion and relationship effects on gender differences in empathy. Presented at the annual meeting of the Association for Psychological Science, Boston, MA, May, 2010. (p. 486)

Ruffin, C. L. (1993). Stress and health—little hassles vs. major life events. *Australian Psychologist, 28,* 201–208. (p. 507)

Rule, B. G., & Ferguson, T. J. (1986). The effects of media violence on attitudes, emotions, and cognitions. *Journal of Social Issues, 42*(3), 29–50. (p. 308)

Rule, N. O., & Ambady, N. (2008). Brief exposures: Male sexual orientation is accurately perceived at 50 ms. *Journal of Experimental Social Psychology, 44,* 1100–1105. (p. 447)

Rule, N. O., Rosen, K. S., Slepian, M. L., & Ambady, N. (2011). Mating interest improves women's accuracy in judging male sexual orientation. *Psychological Science, 22,* 881–886. (pp. 436, 447)

Rumbaugh, D. M. (1977). *Language learning by a chimpanzee: The Lana project.* New York: Academic Press. (p. 374)

Rusanen, M., Kivipelto, M., Quesenberry, C. P., Jr., Zhou, J., & Whitmer, R. A. (2011). Heavy smoking in midlife and long-term risk of Alzheimer disease and vascular dementia. *Archives of Internal Medicine, 171,* 333–339. (p. 212)

Rushton, J. P. (1975). Generosity in children: Immediate and long-term effects of modeling, preaching, and moral judgment. *Journal of Personality and Social Psychology, 31,* 459–466. (p. 306)

Rushton, J. P., & Jensen, A. R. (2005). Thirty years of research on race differences in cognitive ability. *Psychology, Public Policy, and Law, 11,* 235–294. (p. 411)

Rushton, J. P., & Jensen, A. R. (2006). The totality of available evidence shows the race IQ gap still remains. *Psychological Science, 17,* 921–922. (p. 411)

Russell, B. (1930/1985). *The conquest of happiness.* London: Unwin Paperbacks. (p. 500)

Russell, J. A. (2009). Emotion, Core Affect, and Psychological Construction. *Cognition and Emotion, 23,* 1259–1283. (p. 492)

Russell, J. A., & Carroll, J. M. (1999b). The phoenix of bipolarity: Reply to Watson and Tellegan (1999). *Psychological Bulletin, 125,* 611–614. (p. 492)

Russell, J. A., & Carroll, J. M. (1999a, January). On the bipolarity of positive and negative affect. *Psychological Bulletin, 125,* 3–30. (p. 492)

Russell, J. A., Lewicka, M., & Niit, T. (1989). A cross-cultural study of a circumplex model of affect. *Journal of Personality and Social Psychology, 57,* 848–856. (p. 492)

Rusting, C. L., & Nolen-Hoeksema, S. (1998). Regulating responses to anger: Effects of rumination and distraction on angry mood. *Journal of Personality and Social Psychology, 74,* 790–803. (p. 494)

Rutchick, A. M. (2010). Deus ex machine: The influence of polling place on voting behavior. *Political Psychology, 31,* 209–225. (p. 276)

Rutchick, A. M., Slepian, M. L., & Ferris, B. D. (2010). The pen is mightier than the word: Object priming of evaluative standards. *European Journal of Social Psychology, 40,* 704–708. (p. 276)

Ryan, C., Huebner, D., Diaz, R. M., & Sanchez, J. (2009). Family rejection as a predictor of negative health outcomes in White and Latino lesbian, gay, and bisexual young adults. *Pediatrics, 123,* 346–352. (p. 443)

Ryan, R. (1999, February 2). Quoted by Alfie Kohn, In pursuit of affluence, at a high price. *New York Times* (www.nytimes.com). (p. 499)

Ryan, R. M., & Deci, E. L. (2004). Avoiding death or engaging life as accounts of meaning and culture: Comment on Pyszczynski et al. (2004). *Psychological Bulletin, 130,* 473–477. (p. 568)

Rydell, R. J., Rydell, M. T., & Boucher, K. L. (2010). The effect of negative performance stereotypes on learning. *Journal of Personality and Social Psychology, 99,* 883–896. (p. 414)

Ryugo, D. K., Baker, C. A., Montey K. L., Chang, L.Y., Coco, A., Fallon, J. B., Shepherd, R. K. (2010). Synaptic plasticity after chemical deafening and electrical stimulation of the auditory nerve in cats. *Journal of Comparative Neurology, 518,* 1046–1063. (p. 260)

Saad, L. (2002, November 21). Most smokers wish they could quit. *Gallup News Service* (www.gallup.com). (p. 121)

Saad, L. (2006, August 10). Anti-Muslim sentiments fairly commonplace. *Gallup News Service* (poll.gallup.com). (p. 594)

Sabbagh, M. A., Xu, F., Carlson, S. M., Moses, L. J., & Lee, K. (2006). The development of executive functioning and theory of mind: A comparison of Chinese and U.S. preschoolers. *Psychological Science, 17,* 74–81. (p. 183)

Sabini, J. (1986). Stanley Milgram (1933–1984). *American Psychologist, 41,* 1378–1379. (p. 582)

Sachdev, P., & Sachdev, J. (1997). Sixty years of psychosurgery: Its present status and its future. *Australian and New Zealand Journal of Psychiatry, 31*, 457–464. (p. 711)

Sackett, P. R., Borneman, M. J., & Connelly, B. S. (2008). High-stakes testing in higher education and employment: Appraising the evidence for validity and fairness. *American Psychologist, 63*, 215–227. (p. 414)

Sackett, P. R., Hardison, C. M., & Cullen, M. J. (2004). On interpreting stereotype threat as accounting for African American-White differences on cognitive tests. *American Psychologist, 59*, 7–13. (p. 414)

Sackett, P. R., & Lievens, F. (2008). Personnel selection. *Annual Review of Psychology, 59*, 419–450. (p. 460)

Sacks, O. (1985). *The man who mistook his wife for a hat.* New York: Summit Books. (pp. 271, 335)

Sadato, N., Pascual-Leone, A., Grafman, J., Ibanez, V., Deiber, M-P., Dold, G., & Hallett, M. (1996). Activation of the primary visual cortex by Braille reading in blind subjects. *Nature, 380*, 526–528. (p. 75)

Saffran, J. A. (2009). What can statistical learning tell us about infant learning? In A. Woodward & A. Needham (eds.), *Learning and the infant mind.* New York: Oxford University Press. (p. 369)

Saffran, J. R., Aslin, R. N., & Newport, E. L. (1996). Statistical learning by 8-month-old infants. *Science, 274*, 1926–1928. (p. 369)

Sagan, C. (1979). *Broca's brain.* New York: Random House. (p. 60)

Sagan, C. (1987, February 1). The fine art of baloney detection. *Parade.* (p. 254)

Sahin, N. T., Pinker, S., Cash, S. S., Schomer, D., & Halgren, E. (2009). Sequential processing of lexical, grammatical, and phonological information within Broca's area. *Science, 326*, 445–449. (p. 372)

Salmela-Aro, K., Tolvanen, A., & Nurmi, J. (2009). Achievement strategies during university studies predict early career burnout and engagement. *Journal of Vocational Behavior, 75*, 162–172. (p. 461)

Salmon, P. (2001). Effects of physical exercise on anxiety, depression, and sensitivity to stress: A unifying theory. *Clinical Psychology Review, 21*, 33–61. (p. 523)

Salovey, P. (1990, January/February). Interview. *American Scientist*, pp. 25–29. (p. 495)

Salthouse, T. A. (2004). What and when of cognitive aging. *Current Directions in Psychological Science, 13*, 140–144. (p. 399)

Salthouse, T. A. (2009). When does age-related cognitive decline begin? *Neurobiology of Aging, 30*, 507–514. (p. 399)

Salthouse, T. A. (2010b). Selective review of cognitive aging. *Journal of the International Neuropsychological Society, 16*, 754–760. (p. 400)

Sampson, E. E. (2000). Reinterpreting individualism and collectivism: Their religious roots and monologic versus dialogic person–other relationship. *American Psychologist, 55*, 1425–1432. (p. 153)

Samuels, J., & Nestadt, G. (1997). Epidemiology and genetics of obsessive-compulsive disorder. *International Review of Psychiatry, 9*, 61–71. (p. 639)

Samuels, S., & McCabe, G. (1989). Quoted by P. Diaconis & F. Mosteller, Methods for studying coincidences. *Journal of the American Statistical Association, 84*, 853–861. (p. 18)

Sánchez-Villegas, A., Delgado-Rodríguez, M., Alonson, A., Schlatter, J., Lahortiga, F., Majem, L. S., & Martínez-González, M. A. (2009). Association of the Mediterranean dietary pattern with the incidence of depression. *Archives of General Psychiatry, 66*, 1090–1098. (p. 652)

Sanders, G., & Wright, M. (1997). Sexual orientation differences in cerebral asymmetry and in the performance of sexually dimorphic cognitive and motor tasks. *Archives of Sexual Behavior, 26*, 463–479. (p. 447)

Sanders, G., Sjodin, M., & de Chastelaine, M. (2002). On the elusive nature of sex differences in cognition hormonal influences contributing to within-sex variation. *Archives of Sexual Behavior, 31*, 145–152. (p. 447)

Sandfort, T. G. M., de Graaf, R., Bijl, R., & Schnabel, P. (2001). Same-sex sexual behavior and psychiatric disorders. *Archives of General Psychiatry, 58*, 85–91. (p. 442)

Sandkühler, S., & Bhattacharya, J. (2008). Deconstructing insight: EEG correlates of insightful problem solving. *PloS ONE, 3*, e1459 (www.plosone.org). (p. 353)

Sandler, W., Meir, I., Padden, C., & Aronoff, M. (2005). The emergence of grammar: Systematic structure in a new language. *Proceedings of the National Academy of Sciences, 102*, 2261–2265. (p. 369)

Santomauro, J., & French, C. C. (2009). Terror in the night. *The Psychologist, 22*, 672–675. (p. 95)

Santos, A., Meyer-Lindenberg, A., & Deruelle, C. (2010). Absence of racial, but not gender, stereotyping in Williams syndrome children. *Current Biology, 20*, R307–R308. (p. 598)

Sanz, C., Blicher, A., Dalke, K., Gratton-Fabri, L., McClure-Richards, T., & Fouts, R. (1998, Winter-Spring). Enrichment object use: Five chimpanzees' use of temporary and semi-permanent enrichment objects. *Friends of Washoe, 19*(1,2), 9–14. (p. 373)

Sanz, C., Morgan, D., & Gulick, S. (2004). New insights into chimpanzees, tools, and termites from the Congo Basin. *American Naturalist, 164*, 567–581. (p. 362)

Sapadin, L. A. (1988). Friendship and gender: Perspectives of professional men and women. *Journal of Social and Personal Relationships, 5*, 387–403. (p. 159)

Sapolsky, B. S., & Tabarlet, J. O. (1991). Sex in primetime television: 1979 versus 1989. *Journal of Broadcasting and Electronic Media, 35*, 505–516. (pp. 440, 603)

Sapolsky, R. (2003, September). Taming stress. *Scientific American*, pp. 87–95. (pp. 507, 648)

Sapolsky, R. (2005). The influence of social hierarchy on primate health. *Science, 308*, 648–652. (p. 518)

Sapolsky, R. (2010, November 14). This is your brain on metaphors. *New York Times* (www.nytimes.com). (p. 480)

Sato, K. (1987). Distribution of the cost of maintaining common resources. *Journal of Experimental Social Psychology, 23*, 19–31. (p. 619)

Saulny, S. (2006, June 21). A legacy of the storm: Depression and suicide. *New York Times* (www.nytimes.com). (p. 505)

Savage-Rumbaugh, E. S., Murphy, J., Sevcik, R. A., Brakke, K. E., Williams, S. L., & Rumbaugh, D. M., with commentary by Bates, E. (1993). Language comprehension in ape and child. *Monographs of the Society for Research in Child Development, 58* (233), 1–254. (p. 375)

Savage-Rumbaugh, E. S., Rumbaugh, D., & Fields, W. M. (2009). Empirical Kanzi: The ape language controversy revisited. *Skeptic, 15*, 25–33. (p. 375)

Savic, I., Berglund, H., & Lindstrom, P. (2005). Brain response to putative pheromones in homosexual men. *Proceedings of the National Academy of Sciences, 102*, 7356–7361. (p. 445)

Savic, I., & Lindström, P. (2008). PET and MRI show differences in cerebral asymmetry and functional connectivity between homo- and heterosexual subjects. *Proceedings of the National Academy of Sciences, 105*, 9403–9408. (p. 445)

Savitsky, K., Epley, N., & Gilovich, T. D. (2001). Do others judge us as harshly as we think? Overestimating the impact of our failures, shortcomings, and mishaps. *Journal of Personality and Social Psychology, 81*, 44–56. (p. 564)

Savitsky, K., & Gilovich, T. D. (2003). The illusion of transparency and the alleviation of speech anxiety. Journal *of Experimental Social Psychology, 39*, 618–625. (p. 564)

Savoy, C., & Beitel, P. (1996). Mental imagery for basketball. *International Journal of Sport Psychology, 27*, 454–462. (p. 378)

Sawyer, M. G., Arney, F. M., Baghurst, P. A., Clark, J. J., Graetz, B. W., Kosky, R. J., Nurcombe, B., Patton, G. C., Prior, M. R., Raphael, B., Rey, J., Whaites, L. C., & Zubrick, S. R. (2000). *The mental health of young people in Australia.* Canberra: Mental Health and Special Programs Branch, Commonwealth Department of Health and Aged Care. (p. 649)

Sayal, K., Heron, J., Golding, J., Alati, R., Smith, G. D., Gray, R., & Emond, A. (2009). Binge pattern of alcohol consumption during pregnancy and childhood mental health outcomes: Longitudinal population-based study. *Pediatrics, 123*, e289. (p. 174)

Sayette, M. A., Loewenstein, G., Griffin, K. M., & Black, J. J. (2008). Exploring the cold-to-hot empathy gap in smokers. *Psychological Science, 19*, 926–932. (p. 120)

Sayette, M. A., Reichle, E. D., & Schooler, J. W. (2009). Lost in the sauce: The effects of alcohol on mind wandering. *Psychological Science, 20*, 747–752. (p. 118)

Sayette, M. A., Schooler, J. W., & Reichle, E. D. (2010). Out for a smoke: The impact of cigarette craving on zoning out during reading. *Psychological Science, 21*, 26–30. (p. 120)

Sayre, R. F. (1979). The parents' last lessons. In D. D. Van Tassel (Ed.), *Aging, death, and the completion of being.* Philadelphia: University of Pennsylvania Press. (p. 212)

Sbarra, D. A. (2009). Marriage protects men from clinically meaningful elevations in C-reactive protein: Results from the National Social Life, Health, and Aging Project (NSHAP). *Psychosomatic Medicine, 71*, 828–835. (p. 519)

Scarborough, E., & Furumoto, L. (1987). *Untold lives: The first generation of American women psychologists.* New York: Columbia University Press. (p. 4)

Scarr, S. (1984, May). What's a parent to do? A conversation with E. Hall. *Psychology Today*, pp. 58–63. (p. 408)

Scarr, S. (1986). *Mother care/other care.* New York: Basic Books. (p. 192)

Scarr, S. (1989). Protecting general intelligence: Constructs and consequences for interventions. In R. J. Linn (Ed.), *Intelligence: Measurement, theory, and public policy.* Champaign: University of Illinois Press. (p. 384)

Scarr, S. (1990). Back cover comments on J. Dunn & R. Plomin (1990), *Separate lives: Why siblings are so different.* New York: Basic Books. (p. 140)

Smedley, A., & Smedley, B. D. (2005). Race as biology is fiction, racism as a social problem is real: Anthropological and historical perspectives on the social construction of race. *American Psychologist, 60,* 16–26. (p. 412)

Smelser, N. J., & Mitchell, F. (Eds.). (2002). *Terrorism: Perspectives from the behavioral and social sciences.* Washington, DC: National Research Council, National Academies Press. (p. 599)

Smilek, D., Carriere, J. S. A., & Cheyne, J. A. (2010). Out of mind, out of sight: Eye blinking as indicator and embodiment of mind wandering. *Psychological Science, 21,* 786–789. (p. 88)

Smith, A. (1983). Personal correspondence. (p. 659)

Smith, B. C. (2011, January 16). The senses and the multi-sensory. *World Question Center* (www.edge.org). (p. 268)

Smith, C. (2006, January 7). Nearly 100, LSD's father ponders his "problem child." *New York Times* (www.nytimes.com). (p. 123)

Smith, D. M., Loewenstein, G., Jankovic, A., & Ubel, P. A. (2009). Happily hopeless: Adaptation to a permanent, but not to a temporary, disability. *Health Psychology, 28,* 787–791. (p. 497)

Smith, E., & Delargy, M. (2005). Locked-in syndrome. *British Medical Journal, 330,* 406–409. (p. 497)

Smith, M. B. (1978). Psychology and values. *Journal of Social Issues, 34,* 181–199. (p. 545)

Smith, M. L., & Glass, G. V. (1977). Meta-analysis of psychotherapy outcome studies. *American Psychologist, 32,* 752–760. (p. 695)

Smith, M. L., Glass, G. V., & Miller, R. L. (1980). *The benefits of psychotherapy.* Baltimore: Johns Hopkins Press. (pp. 694, 695)

Smith, P. B., & Tayeb, M. (1989). Organizational structure and processes. In M. Bond (Ed.), *The cross-cultural challenge to social psychology.* Newbury Park, CA: Sage. (p. 468)

Smith, S. J., Axelton, A. M., & Saucier, D. A. (2009). The effects of contact on sexual prejudice: A meta-analysis. *Sex Roles, 61,* 178–191. (p. 620)

Smith, S. M., McIntosh, W. D., & Bazzini, D. G. (1999). Are the beautiful good in Hollywood? An investigation of the beauty-and-goodness stereotype on film. *Basic and Applied Social Psychology, 21,* 69–80. (p. 610)

Smith, T. B., Bartz, J., & Richards, P. S. (2007). Outcomes of religious and spiritual adaptations to psychotherapy: A meta-analytic review. *Psychotherapy Research, 17,* 643–655. (p. 700)

Smith, T. W. (1998, December). *American sexual behavior: Trends, sociodemographic differences, and risk behavior* (National Opinion Research Center GSS Topical Report No. 25). (pp. 439, 443)

Smolak, L., & Murnen, S. K. (2002). A meta-analytic examination of the relationship between child sexual abuse and eating disorders. *International Journal of Eating Disorders, 31,* 136–150. (p. 671)

Smoreda, Z., & Licoppe, C. (2000). Gender-specific use of the domestic telephone. *Social Psychology Quarterly, 63,* 238–252. (p. 159)

Snedeker, J., Geren, J., & Shafto, C. L. (2007). Starting over: International adoption as a natural experiment in language development. *Psychological Science, 18,* 79–86. (p. 368)

Snodgrass, S. E., Higgins, J. G., & Todisco, L. (1986). The effects of walking behavior on mood. Paper presented at the American Psychological Association convention. (p. 490)

Snowdon, D. A., Kemper, S. J., Mortimer, J. A., Greiner, L. H., Wekstein, D. R., & Markesbery, W. R. (1996). Linguistic ability in early life and cognitive function and Alzheimer's disease in late life: Finds from the Nun Study. *Journal of the American Medical Association, 275,* 528–532. (p. 402)

Snyder, F., & Scott, J. (1972). The psychophysiology of sleep. In N. S. Greenfield & R. A. Sterbach (Eds.), *Handbook of psychophysiology.* New York: Holt, Rinehart & Winston. (p. 108)

Snyder, S. H. (1984). Neurosciences: An integrative discipline. *Science, 225,* 1255–1257. (pp. 50, 633)

Snyder, S. H. (1986). *Drugs and the brain.* New York: Scientific American Library. (p. 707)

Social Watch. (2006, March 8). No country in the world treats its women as well as its men (www.socialwatch.org). (p. 162)

Society for Personality Assessment. (2005). The status of the Rorschach in clinical and forensic practice: An official statement by the Board of Trustees of the Society for Personality Assessment. *Journal of Personality Assessment, 85,* 219–237. (p. 538)

Sokol, D. K., Moore, C. A., Rose, R. J., Williams, C. J., Reed, T., & Christian, J. C. (1995). Intrapair differences in personality and cognitive ability among young monozygotic twins distinguished by chorion type. *Behavior Genetics, 25,* 457–466. (p. 134)

Solnick, S. J., & Hemenway, D. (1998). Is more always better?: A survey on positional concerns. *Journal of Economic Behavior & Organization, 37,* 373–383. (p. 500)

Solnick, S. J., & Hemenway, D. (2009). Do spending comparisons affect spending and satisfaction? *Journal of Socio-Economics, 38,* 568–573. (p. 500)

Solomon, D. A., Keitner, G. I., Miller, I. W., Shea, M. T., & Keller, M. B. (1995). Course of illness and maintenance treatments for patients with bipolar disorder. *Journal of Clinical Psychiatry, 56,* 5–13. (p. 707)

Solomon, J. (1996, May 20). Breaking the silence. *Newsweek,* pp. 20–22. (p. 632)

Solomon, M. (1987, December). Standard issue. *Psychology Today,* pp. 30–31. (p. 610)

Song, S. (2006, March 27). Mind over medicine. *Time,* p. 47. (p. 112)

Sontag, S. (1978). *Illness as metaphor.* New York: Farrar, Straus, & Giroux. (p. 512)

Soon, C. S., Brass, M., Heinze, H., & Haynes, J. (2008). Unconscious determinants of free decisions in the human brain. *Nature Neuroscience, 11,* 543–545. (p. 87)

Sørensen, H. J., Mortensen, E. L., Reinisch, J. M., & Mednick, S. A. (2005). Breastfeeding and risk of schizophrenia in the Copenhagen Perinatal Cohort. *Acta Psychiatrica Scandinavica, 112,* 26–29. (p. 658)

Sørensen, H. J., Mortensen, E. L., Reinisch, J. M., & Mednick, S. A. (2006). Height, weight, and body mass index in early adulthood and risk of schizophrenia. *Acta Psychiatrica Scandinavica, 114,* 49–54. (p. 658)

Sorkhabi, N. (2005). Applicability of Baumrind's parent typology to collective cultures: Analysis of cultural explanations of parent socialization effects. *International Journal of Behavioral Development, 29,* 552–563. (p. 195)

Soussignan, R. (2001). Duchenne smile, emotional experience, and autonomic reactivity: A test of the facial feedback hypothesis. *Emotion, 2,* 52–74. (p. 490)

South, S. C., Krueger, R. F., Johnson, W., & Iacono, W. G. (2008). Adolescent personality moderates genetic and environmental influences on relationships with parents. *Journal of Personality and Social Psychology, 94,* 899–912. (p. 195)

Sowell, T. (1991, May/June). Cultural diversity: A world view. *American Enterprise,* pp. 44–55. (p. 622)

Spanos, N. P. (1982). A social psychological approach to hypnotic behavior. In G. Weary & H. L. Mirels (Eds.), *Integrations of clinical and social psychology.* New York: Oxford. (p. 112)

Spanos, N. P. (1986). Hypnosis, nonvolitional responding, and multiple personality: A social psychological perspective. *Progress in Experimental Personality Research, 14,* 1–62. (p. 666)

Spanos, N. P. (1991). Hypnosis, hypnotizability, and hypnotherapy. In C. R. Snyder & D. R. Forsyth (Eds.), *Handbook of social and clinical psychology: The health perspective.* New York: Pergamon Press. (p. 111)

Spanos, N. P. (1994). Multiple identity enactments and multiple personality disorder: A sociocognitive perspective. *Psychological Bulletin, 116,* 143–165. (p. 666)

Spanos, N. P. (1996). *Multiple identities and false memories: A sociocognitive perspective.* Washington, DC: American Psychological Association Books. (pp. 111, 666)

Spanos, N. P., & Coe, W. C. (1992). A social-psychological approach to hypnosis. In E. Fromm & M. R. Nash (Eds.), *Contemporary hypnosis research.* New York: Guilford. (p. 112)

Sparrow, B., Liu, J., & Wegner, D. M. (2011). Google effects on memory: Cognitive consequences of having information at our fingertips. *Science, 333,* 776–778. (p. 316)

Speer, N. K., Reynolds, J. R., Swallow, K. M., & Zacks, J. M. (2009). Reading stories activates neural representations of visual and motor experiences. *Psychological Science, 20,* 989–999. (pp. 306, 373)

Spelke, E. S., & Kinzler, K. D. (2007). Core knowledge. *Developmental Science, 10,* 89–96. (p. 182)

Spence, I., & Feng, J. (2010). Video games and spatial cognition. *Review of General Psychology, 14,* 92–104. (p. 251)

Spencer, J., Quinn, P. C., Johnson, M. H., & Karmiloff-Smith, A. (1997). Heads you win, tails you lose: Evidence for young infants categorizing mammals by head and facial attributes. *Early Development & Parenting, 6,* 113–126. (p. 175)

Spencer, K. M., Nestor, P. G., Perlmutter, R., Niznikiewicz, M. A., Klump, M. C., Frumin, M., Shenton, M. E., & McCarley, R. W. (2004). Neural synchrony indexes disordered perception and cognition in schizophrenia. *Proceedings of the National Academy of Sciences, 101,* 17288–17293. (p. 660)

Spencer, S. J., Steele, C. M., & Quinn, D. M. (1997). Stereotype threat and women's math performance. Unpublished manuscript, Hope College. (p. 414)

Sperling, G. (1960). The information available in brief visual presentations. *Psychological Monographs, 74* (Whole No. 498). (p. 317)

Sperry, R. W. (1964). Problems outstanding in the evolution of brain function. James Arthur Lecture, American Museum of Natural History, New York. Cited by R. Ornstein (1977), *The psychology of consciousness* (2nd ed.). New York: Harcourt Brace Jovanovich. (p. 78)

Sperry, R. W. (1985). Changed concepts of brain and consciousness: Some value implications. *Zygon, 20,* 41–57. (p. 240)

Sperry, R. W. (1992, Summer). Turnabout on consciousness: A mentalist view. *Journal of Mind & Behavior, 13*(3), 259–280. (p. 81)

Spiegel, D. (2007). The mind prepared: Hypnosis in surgery. *Journal of the National Cancer Institute, 99*, 1280–1281. (p. 112)

Spiegel, D. (2008, January 31). *Coming apart: Trauma and the fragmentation of the self.* Dana Foundation (www.dana.org). (p. 667)

Spiegel, K., Leproult, R., L'Hermite-Balériaux, M., Copinschi, G., Penev, P. D., & Van Cauter, E. (2004). Leptin levels are dependent on sleep duration: Relationships with sympathovagal balance, carbohydrate regulation, cortisol, and thyrotropin. *Journal of Clinical Endocrinology and Metabolism, 89*, 5762–5771. (p. 102)

Spielberger, C., & London, P. (1982). Rage boomerangs. *American Health, 1*, 52–56. (p. 513)

Spradley, J. P., & Phillips, M. (1972). Culture and stress: A quantitative analysis. *American Anthropologist, 74*, 518–529. (p. 152)

Sprecher, S. (1989). The importance to males and females of physical attractiveness, earning potential, and expressiveness in initial attraction. *Sex Roles, 21*, 591–607. (p. 610)

Spring, B., Pingitore, R., Bourgeois, M., Kessler, K. H., & Bruckner, E. (1992). The effects and non-effects of skipping breakfast: Results of three studies. Paper presented at the American Psychological Association convention. (p. 433)

Squire, L. R. (1992). Memory and the hippocampus: A synthesis from findings with rats, monkeys, and humans. *Psychological Review, 99*, 195–231. (p. 324)

Srivastava, A., Locke, E. A., & Bartol, K. M. (2001). Money and subject well-being: It's not the money, it's the motives. *Journal of Personality and Social Psychology, 80*, 959–971. (p. 499)

Srivastava, S., John, O. P., Gosling, S. D., & Potter, J. (2003). Development of personality in early and middle adulthood: Set like plaster or persistent change? *Journal of Personality & Social Psychology, 84*, 1041–1053. (p. 552)

Srivastava, S., McGonigal, K. M., Richards, J. M., Butler, E. A., & Gross, J. J. (2006). Optimism in close relationships: How seeing things in a positive light makes them so. *Journal of Personality and Social Psychology, 91*, 143–153. (p. 559)

St. Clair, D., Xu, M., Wang, P., Yu, Y., Fang, Y., Zhang, F., Zheng, X., Gu, N., Feng, G., Sham, P., & He, L. (2005). Rates of adult schizophrenia following prenatal exposure to the Chinese famine of 1959–1961. *Journal of the American Medical Association, 294*, 557–562. (p. 660)

St. Jacques, P. L., Dolcos, F., & Cabeza, R. (2009). Effects of aging on functional connectivity of the amygdala for subsequent memory of negative pictures: A network analysis of fMRI data. *Psychological Science, 20*, 74–84. (p. 218)

Stack, S. (1992). Marriage, family, religion, and suicide. In R. Maris, A. Berman, J. Maltsberger, & R. Yufit (Eds.), *Assessment and prediction of suicide.* New York: Guilford Press. (p. 650)

Stafford, R. S., MacDonald, E. A., & Finkelstein, S. N. (2001). National patterns of medication treatment for depression, 1987 to 2001. *Primary Care Companion Journal of Clinical Psychiatry, 3*, 232–235. (p. 706)

Stager, C. L., & Werker, J. F. (1997). Infants listen for more phonetic detail in speech perception than in word-learning tasks. *Nature, 388*, 381–382. (p. 367)

Stanford University Center for Narcolepsy. (2002). Narcolepsy is a serious medical disorder and a key to understanding other sleep disorders (www.med.stanford.edu/school/Psychiatry/narcolepsy). (p. 103)

Stanley, D., Phelps, E., & Banaji, M. (2008). The neural basis of implicit attitudes. *Current Directions in Psychological Science, 17*, 164–170. (p. 595)

Stanley, J. C. (1997). Varieties of intellectual talent. *Journal of Creative Behavior, 31*, 93–119. (p. 403)

Stanovich, K. (1996). *How to think straight about psychology.* New York: HarperCollins. (p. 532)

Stark, R. (2002). Physiology and faith: Addressing the "universal" gender difference in religious commitment. *Journal for the Scientific Study of Religion, 41*, 495–507. (p. 160)

Stark, R. (2003a). *For the glory of God: How monotheism led to reformations, science, witch-hunts, and the end of slavery.* Princeton, NJ: Princeton University Press. (p. 20)

Stark, R. (2003b, October-November). False conflict: Christianity is not only compatible with science—it created it. *American Enterprise*, pp. 27–33. (p. 20)

Starr, J. M., Deary, I. J., Lemmon, H., & Whalley, L. J. (2000). Mental ability age 11 years and health status age 77 years. *Age and Ageing, 29*, 523–528. (p. 401)

Statistics Canada. (1999). *Statistical report on the health of Canadians.* Prepared by the Federal, Provincial and Territorial Advisory Committee on Population Health for the Meeting of Ministers of Health, Charlottetown, PEI, September 16–17, 1999. (p. 205)

Statistics Canada. (2010). Languages. Canada year book. 11-402-X. (p. 377)

Statistics Canada. (2010). *Victims and persons accused of homicide, by age and sex.* Table 253-0003. (p. 158)

Staub, E. (1989). *The roots of evil: The psychological and cultural sources of genocide.* New York: Cambridge University Press. (p. 576)

Steel, P., Schmidt, J., & Schultz, J. (2008). Refining the relationship between personality and subject well-being. *Psychological Bulletin, 134*, 138–161. (p. 500)

Steele, C. M. (1990, May). A conversation with Claude Steele. *APS Observer*, pp. 11–17. (p. 411)

Steele, C. M. (1995, August 31). Black students live down to expectations. *New York Times.* (p. 414)

Steele, C. M. (2010). *Whistling Vivaldi: And other clues to how stereotypes affect us.* New York: Norton. (p. 414)

Steele, C. M., & Josephs, R. A. (1990). Alcohol myopia: Its prized and dangerous effects. *American Psychologist, 45*, 921–933. (p. 118)

Steele, C. M., Spencer, S. J., & Aronson, J. (2002). Contending with group image: The psychology of stereotype and social identity threat. *Advances in Experimental Social Psychology, 34*, 379–440. (p. 414)

Steenhuysen, J. (2002, May 8). Bionic retina gives six patients partial sight. *Reuters News Service.* (See also www.optobionics.com/artificialretina.htm.). (p. 236)

Stein, D., Phillips, K., Bolton, D., Fulford, K., Sadler, J., & Kendler, K. (2010). What is a mental/psychiatric disorder? From DSM-IV to DSM-V. *Psychological Medicine, 40*, 1759–1765. (p. 626)

Stein, S. (2009, August 20). New poll: 77 percent support "choice" of public option. *Huffington Post* (huffingtonpost.com). (p. 30)

Steinberg, L. (1987, September). Bound to bicker. *Psychology Today*, pp. 36–39. (p. 205)

Steinberg, L. (2007). Risk taking in adolescence: New perspectives from brain and behavioral science. *Current Directions in Psychological Science, 16*, 55–59. (p. 199)

Steinberg, L. (2010, March). Analyzing adolescence. Interview with Sara Martin. *Monitor on Psychology*, pp. 26–29. (p. 199)

Steinberg, L., Cauffman, E., Woolard, J., Graham, S., & Banich, M. (2009). Are adolescents less mature than adults? Minors' access to abortion, the juvenile death penalty, and the alleged APA "flip-flop." *American Psychologist, 64*, 583–594. (p. 199)

Steinberg, L., & Morris, A. S. (2001). Adolescent development. *Annual Review of Psychology, 52*, 83–110. (pp. 195, 204, 205)

Steinberg, L., & Scott, E. S. (2003). Less guilty by reason of adolescence: Developmental immaturity, diminished responsibility, and the juvenile death penalty. *American Psychologist, 58*, 1009–1018. (p. 199)

Steinberg, N. (1993, February). Astonishing love stories (from an earlier United Press International report). *Games*, p. 47. (p. 608)

Steinhauer, J. (1999, November 29). Number of twins rises: So does parental stress. *New York Times* (www.nytimes.com). (p. 134)

Steinhauer, J., & Holson, L. M. (2008, September 20). As text messages fly, danger lurks. *New York Times* (www.nytimes.com). (p. 205)

Steinmetz, J. E. (1999). The localization of a simple type of learning and memory: The cerebellum and classical eyeblink conditioning. *Contemporary Psychology, 7*, 72–77. (p. 325)

Stengel, E. (1981). Suicide. In *The new Encyclopaedia Britannica, macropaedia* (Vol. 17, pp. 777–782). Chicago: Encyclopaedia Britannica. (p. 650)

Stepanikova, I., Nie, N. H., & He, X. (2010). Time on the Internet at home, loneliness, and life satisfaction: Evidence from panel time-diary data. *Computers in Human Behavior, 26*, 329–338. (p. 453)

Steptoe, A., Chida, Y., Hamer, M., & Wardle, J. (2010). Author reply: Meta-analysis of stress-related factors in cancer. *Nature Reviews: Clinical Oncology, 7*, doi:10.1038/ncponc1134-c2. (p. 512)

Stern, M., & Karraker, K. H. (1989). Sex stereotyping of infants: A review of gender labeling studies. *Sex Roles, 20*, 501–522. (p. 230)

Sternberg, E. M. (2006). A compassionate universe? *Science, 311*, 611–612. (p. 388)

Sternberg, E. M. (2009). *Healing spaces: The science of place and well-being.* Cambridge, MA: Harvard University Press. (p. 509)

Sternberg, R. J. (1985). *Beyond IQ: A triarchic theory of human intelligence.* New York: Cambridge University Press. (p. 385)

Sternberg, R. J. (1988). Applying cognitive theory to the testing and teaching of intelligence. *Applied Cognitive Psychology, 2*, 231–255. (p. 387)

Sternberg, R. J. (1999). The theory of successful intelligence. *Review of General Psychology, 3*, 292–316. (p. 385)

Sternberg, R. J. (2003). Our research program validating the triarchic theory of successful intelligence: Reply to Gottfredson. *Intelligence, 31*, 399–413. (pp. 385, 387)

Sternberg, R. J. (2006). The Rainbow Project: Enhance the SAT through assessments of analytical, practical, and creative skills. *Intelligence, 34*, 321–350. (p. 386)

Sternberg, R. J. (2007, July 6). Finding students who are wise, practical, and creative. *The Chronicle Review* (www.chronicle.com). (p. 386)

Sternberg, R. J. (2010). Assessment of gifted students for identification purposes: new techniques for a new millennium. *Learning and Individual Differences, 20,* 327–336. (p. 386)

Sternberg, R. J., & Grajek, S. (1984). The nature of love. *Journal of Personality and Social Psychology, 47,* 312–329. (p. 614)

Sternberg, R. J., & Grigorenko, E. L. (2000). Theme-park psychology: A case study regarding human intelligence and its implications for education. *Educational Psychology Review, 12,* 247–268. (p. 403)

Sternberg, R. J., & Kaufman, J. C. (1998). Human abilities. *Annual Review of Psychology, 49,* 479–502. (p. 381)

Sternberg, R. J., & Lubart, T. I. (1991). An investment theory of creativity and its development. *Human Development,* 1–31. (p. 387)

Sternberg, R. J., & Lubart, T. I. (1992). Buy low and sell high: An investment approach to creativity. *Psychological Science, 1,* 1–5. (p. 387)

Sternberg, R. J., & Wagner, R. K. (1993). The g-ocentric view of intelligence and job performance is wrong. *Current Directions in Psychological Science, 2,* 1–5. (p. 386)

Sternberg, R. J., Wagner, R. K., Williams, W. M., & Horvath, J. A. (1995). Testing common sense. *American Psychologist, 50,* 912–927. (p. 386)

Stetter, F., & Kupper, S. (2002). Autogenic training: A meta-analysis of clinical outcome studies. *Applied Psychophysiology and Biofeedback, 27,* 45–98. (p. 523)

Stevenson, H. W. (1992, December). Learning from Asian schools. *Scientific American,* pp. 70–76. (p. 412)

Stevenson, H. W., & Lee, S-Y. (1990). Contexts of achievement: A study of American, Chinese, and Japanese children. *Monographs of the Society for Research in Child Development, 55* (Serial No. 221, Nos. 1–2). (p. 403)

Stevenson, R. J., & Tomiczek, C. (2007). Olfactory-induced synesthesias: A review and model. *Psychological Bulletin, 133,* 294–309. (p. 269)

Stewart, R. E., & Chambless, D. L. (2009). Cognitive-behavioral therapy for adult anxiety disorders in clinical practice: A meta-analysis of effectiveness studies. *Journal of Consulting and Clinical Psychology, 77,* 595–606. (p. 695)

Stice, E. (2002). Risk and maintenance factors for eating pathology: A meta-analytic review. *Psychological Bulletin, 128,* 825–848. (p. 671)

Stice, E., Ng, J., & Shaw, H. (2010). Risk factors and prodromal eating pathology. *Journal of Child Psychology and Psychiatry, 51,* 518–525. (p. 671)

Stice, E., Shaw, H., Bohon, C., Marti, C. N., & Rohde, P. (2009). A meta-analytic review of depression prevention programs for children and adolescents: Factors that predict magnitude of intervention effects. *Journal of Consulting and Clinical Psychology, 77,* 486–503. (p. 702)

Stice, E., Shaw, H., & Marti, C. N. (2007). A meta-analytic review of eating disorder prevention programs: Encouraging findings. *Annual Review of Clinical Psychology, 3,* 233–257. (p. 672)

Stice, E., Spangler, D., & Agras, W. S. (2001). Exposure to media-portrayed thin-ideal images adversely affects vulnerable girls: A longitudinal experiment. *Journal of Social and Clinical Psychology, 20,* 270–288. (p. 672)

Stice, E., Spoor, S., Bohon, C., & Small, D. M. (2008). Relation between obesity and blunted striatal response to food is moderated by TaqIA A1 allele. *Science, 322,* 449–452. (p. 430)

Stickgold, R. (2000, March 7). Quoted by S. Blakeslee, For better learning, researchers endorse "sleep on it" adage. *New York Times,* p. F2. (p. 107)

Stickgold, R., & Ellenbogen, J. M. (2008, August/September). Quiet! Sleeping brain at work. *Scientific American Mind,* pp. 23–29. (p. 98)

Stickgold, R., Hobson, J. A., Fosse, R., & Fosse, M. (2001). Sleep, learning, and dreams: Off-line memory processing. *Science, 294,* 1052–1057. (p. 107)

Stickgold, R., Malia, A., Maquire, D., Roddenberry, D., & O'Connor, M. (2000, October 13). Replaying the game: Hypnagogic images in normals and amnesics. *Science, 290,* 350–353. (pp. 106, 107)

Stiglitz, J. (2009, September 13). Towards a better measure of well-being. *Financial Times* (www.ft.com). (p. 502)

Stillman, T. F., Baumeister, R. F., Vohs, K. D., Lambert, N. M., Fincham, F. D., & Brewer, L. E. (2010). Personal philosophy and personnel achievement: Belief in free will predicts better job performance. *Social Psychological and Personality Science, 1,* 43–50. (p. 557)

Stinson, D. A., Logel, C., Zanna, M. P., Holmes, J. G., Camerson, J. J., Wood, J. V., & Spencer, S. J. (2008). The cost of lower self-esteem: Testing a self- and social-bonds model of health. *Journal of Personality and Social Psychology, 94,* 412–428. (p. 521)

Stipek, D. (1992). The child at school. In M. H. Bornstein & M. E. Lamb (Eds.), *Developmental psychology: An advanced textbook.* Hillsdale, NJ: Erlbaum. (p. 194)

Stirrat, M., & Perrett, D. I. (2010). Valid facial cues to cooperation and trust: Male facial width and trustworthiness. *Psychological Science 21,* 349–354. (p. 600)

Stith, S. M., Rosen, K. H., Middleton, K. A., Busch, A. L., Lunderberg, K., & Carlton, R. P. (2000). The intergenerational transmission of spouse abuse: A meta-analysis. *Journal of Marriage and the Family, 62,* 640–654. (p. 306)

Stix, G. (2010, June). Alzheimer's: Forestalling the darkness. *Scientific American,* pp. 51–57. (p. 212)

Stix, G. (2011, March). The neuroscience of true grit. *Scientific American, 304,* 28–33. (p. 641)

Stockton, M. C., & Murnen, S. K. (1992). Gender and sexual arousal in response to sexual stimuli: A meta-analytic review. Paper presented at the American Psychological Society convention. (p. 438)

Stokoe, W. C. (1960). Sign language structure: An outline of the visual communication systems of the American Deaf. *Studies in Linguistics: Occasional papers (No. 8).* Buffalo: Dept. of Anthropology and Linguistics, University of Buffalo. (p. 370)

Stone, A. A., & Neale, J. M. (1984). Effects of severe daily events on mood. *Journal of Personality and Social Psychology, 46,* 137–144. (p. 496)

Stone, A. A., Schwartz, J. E., Broderick, J. E., & Deaton, A. (2010). A snapshot of the age distribution of psychological well-being in the United States. *PNAS, 107,* 9985–9990. (p. 218)

Stone, A. A., Schwartz, J. E., Broderick, J. E., & Shiffman, S. S. (2005). Variability of momentary pain predicts recall of weekly pain: A consequences of the peak (or salience) memory heuristic. *Personality and Social Psychology Bulletin, 31,* 1340–1346. (p. 265)

Stone, G. (2006, February 17). Homeless man discovered to be lawyer with amnesia. *ABC News* (abcnews.go.com). (p. 665)

Stone, R. (2005). In the wake: Looking for keys to posttraumatic stress. *Science, 310,* 1605. (p. 640)

Stoolmiller, M. (1999). Implications of the restricted range of family environments for estimates of heritability and nonshared environment in behavior-genetic adoption studies. *Psychological Bulletin, 125,* 392–409. (p. 137)

Storbeck, J., Robinson, M. D., & McCourt, M. E. (2006). Semantic processing precedes affect retrieval: The neurological case for cognitive primary in visual processing. *Review of General Psychology, 10,* 41–55. (p. 477)

Storm, L., Tressoldi, P. E., & Di Risio, L. (2010a). A meta-analysis with nothing to hide: Reply to Hyman (2010). *Psychological Bulletin, 136,* 491–494. (p. 254)

Storm, L., Tressoldi, P. E., & Di Risio, L. (2010b). Meta-analysis of free-response studies, 1992–2008: Assessing the noise reduction model in parapsychology *Psychological Bulletin, 136,* 471–485. (p. 254)

Storms, M. D. (1973). Videotape and the attribution process: Reversing actors' and observers' points of view. *Journal of Personality and Social Psychology, 27,* 165–175. (p. 573)

Storms, M. D. (1981). A theory of erotic orientation development. *Psychological Review, 88,* 340–353. (p. 445)

Storms, M. D. (1983). *Development of sexual orientation.* Washington, DC: Office of Social and Ethical Responsibility, American Psychological Association. (p. 444)

Storms, M. D., & Thomas, G. C. (1977). Reactions to physical closeness. *Journal of Personality and Social Psychology, 35,* 412–418. (p. 587)

Stowell, J. R., Oldham, T., & Bennett, D. (2010). Using student response systems ("clickers") to combat conformity and shyness. *Teaching of Psychology, 37,* 135–140. (p. 581)

Strack, F., Martin, L., & Stepper, S. (1988). Inhibiting and facilitating conditions of the human smile: A nonobtrusive test of the facial feedback hypothesis. *Journal of Personality and Social Psychology, 54,* 768–777. (p. 489)

Strack, S., & Coyne, J. C. (1983). Social confirmation of dysphoria: Shared and private reactions to depression. *Journal of Personality and Social Behavior, 44,* 798–806. (p. 654)

Strahan, E. J., Spencer, S. J., & Zanna, M. P. (2002). Subliminal priming and persuasion: Striking while the iron is hot. *Journal of Experimental Social Psychology, 38,* 556–568. (p. 227)

Stranahan, A. M., Khalil, D., & Gould, E. (2006). Social isolation delays the positive effects of running on adult neurogenesis. *Nature Neuroscience, 9,* 526–533. (p. 76)

Strand, S., Deary, I. J., & Smith, P. (2006). Sex differences in cognitive abilities test scores: A UK national picture. *British Journal of Educational Psychology, 76,* 463–480. (p. 409)

Strange, D., Hayne, H., & Garry, M. (2008). A photo, a suggestion, a false memory. *Applied Cognitive Psychology, 22,* 587–603. (p. 342)

Strasburger, V. C., Jordan, A. B., & Donnerstein, E. (2010). Health effects of media on children and adolescents. *Pediatrics, 125,* 756–767. (p. 307)

Stratton, G. M. (1896). Some preliminary experiments on vision without inversion of the retinal image. *Psychological Review, 3,* 611–617. (p. 251)

Straub, R. O., Seidenberg, M. S., Bever, T. G., & Terrace, H. S. (1979). Serial learning in the pigeon. *Journal of the Experimental Analysis of Behavior, 32,* 137–148. (p. 374)

Straus, M. A. (2008). Dominance and symmetry in partner violence by male and female university students in 32 nations. *Children and Youth Services Review, 30,* 252–275. (p. 158)

Straus, M. A., & Gelles, R. J. (1980). *Behind closed doors: Violence in the American family.* New York: Anchor/Doubleday. (p. 292)

Straus, M. A., Sugarman, D. B., & Giles-Sims, J. (1997). Spanking by parents and subsequent antisocial behavior of children. *Archives of Pediatric Adolescent Medicine, 151,* 761–767. (p. 292)

Strawbridge, W. J. (1999). Mortality and religious involvement: A review and critique of the results, the methods, and the measures. Paper presented at a Harvard University conference on religion and health, sponsored by the National Institute for Health Research and the John Templeton Foundation. (p. 527)

Strawbridge, W. J., Cohen, R. D., & Shema, S. J. (1997). Frequent attendance at religious services and mortality over 28 years. *American Journal of Public Health, 87,* 957–961. (p. 527)

Strawbridge, W. J., Shema, S. J., Cohen, R. D., & Kaplan, G. A. (2001). Religious attendance increases survival by improving and maintaining good health behaviors, mental health, and social relationships. *Annals of Behavioral Medicine, 23,* 68–74. (p. 527)

Strayer, D. L., & Drews, F A. (2007). Cell-phone-induced driver distraction. *Current Directions in Psychological Science, 16,* 128–131. (p. 89)

Strick, M., Dijksterhuis, A., & van Baaren, R. B. (2010). Unconscious-thought effects take place off-line, not on-line. *Psychological Science, 21,* 484–488. (p. 360)

Strickland, B. (1992, February 20). Gender differences in health and illness. Sigma Xi national lecture delivered at Hope College. (p. 209)

Stroebe, M., Stroebe, W., & Schut, H. (2001). Gender differences in adjustment to bereavement: An empirical and theoretical review. *Review of General Psychology, 5,* 62–83. (p. 220)

Stroebe, M., Stroebe, W., Schut, H., Zech, E., & van den Bout, J. (2002). Does disclosure of emotions facilitate recovery from bereavement? Evidence from two prospective studies. *Journal of Consulting and Clinical Psychology, 70,* 169–178. (p. 220)

Stroebe, W., Schut, H., & Stroebe, M. S. (2005). Grief work, disclosure and counseling: Do they help the bereaved? *Clinical Psychology Review, 25,* 395–414. (p. 220)

Stross, R. (2011, July 9). The therapist will see you now, via the web. *New York Times* (www.nytimes.com). (p. 688)

Strully, K. W. (2009). Job loss and health in the U.S. labor market. *Demography, 46,* 221–246. (p. 506)

Strupp, H. H. (1986). Psychotherapy: Research, practice, and public policy (How to avoid dead ends). *American Psychologist, 41,* 120–130. (p. 698)

Su, R., Rounds, J., & Armstrong, P. I. (2009). Men and things, women and people: A meta-analysis of sex differences in interests. *Psychological Bulletin, 135,* 859–884. (p. 159)

Subiaul, F., Cantlon, J. F., Holloway, R. L., & Terrace, H. S. (2004). Cognitive imitation in rhesus macaques. *Science, 305,* 407–410. (p. 305)

Subrahmanyam, K., & Greenfield, P. (2008). Online communication and adolescent relationships. *The Future of Children, 18,* 119–146. (p. 205)

Suddath, R. L., Christison, G. W., Torrey, E. F., Casanova, M. F., & Weinberger, D. R. (1990). Anatomical abnormalities in the brains of monozygotic twins discordant for schizophrenia. *New England Journal of Medicine, 322,* 789–794. (p. 662)

Sue, S. (2006). Research to address racial and ethnic disparities in mental health: Some lessons learned. In S. I. Donaldson, D. E. Berger, & K. Pezdek (Eds.), *Applied psychology: New frontiers and rewarding careers.* Mahwah, NJ: Erlbaum. (p. 700)

Suedfeld, P. (1998). Homo invictus: The indomitable species. *Canadian Psychology, 38,* 164–173. (p. 641)

Suedfeld, P. (2000). Reverberations of the Holocaust fifty years later: Psychology's contributions to understanding persecution and genocide. *Canadian Psychology, 41,* 1–9. (p. 641)

Suedfeld, P., & Mocellin, J. S. P. (1987). The "sensed presence" in unusual environments. *Environment and Behavior, 19,* 33–52. (p. 124)

Sugita, Y. (2004). Experience in early infancy is indispensable for color perception. *Current Biology. 14,* 1267–1271. (p. 248)

Suinn, R. M. (1997). Mental practice in sports psychology: Where have we been, Where do we go? *Clinical Psychology: Science and Practice, 4,* 189–207. (p. 378)

Sullivan, D., & von Wachter, T. (2009). Job displacement and mortality: An analysis using administrative data. *Quarterly Journal of Economics, 124,* 1265–1306. (p. 505)

Sullivan, K. T., Pasch, L. A., Johnson, M. D., & Bradbury, T. N. (2010). Social support, problem solving, and the longitudinal course of newlywed marriage. *Journal of Personality and Social Psychology, 98,* 631–644. (p. 614)

Sullivan, P. F., Neale, M. C., & Kendler, K. S. (2000). Genetic epidemiology of major depression: Review and meta-analysis. *American Journal of Psychiatry, 157,* 1552–1562. (p. 649)

Sullivan/Anderson, A. (2009, March 30). How to bring an end to the war over sex ed. *Time,* pp. 40–43. (p. 439)

Suls, J. M., & Tesch, F. (1978). Students' preferences for information about their test performance: A social comparison study. *Journal of Experimental Social Psychology, 8,* 189–197. (p. 500)

Summers, M. (1996, December 9). Mister clean. *People Weekly,* pp. 139–142. (p. 624)

Sun, Q. I., Townsend, M. K., Okereke, O., Franco, O. H., Hu, F. B., & Grodstein, F. (2009). Adiposity and weight change in mid-life in relation to healthy survival after age 70 in women: Prospective cohort study. *British Medical Journal, 339,* b3796. (p. 428)

Sundet, J. M., Borren, I., & Tambs, K. (2008). The Flynn effect is partly caused by changing fertility patterns. *Intelligence, 36,* 183–191. (p. 396)

Sundstrom, E., De Meuse, K. P., & Futrell, D. (1990). Work teams: Applications and effectiveness. *American Psychologist, 45,* 120–133. (p. 468)

Sunstein, C. R. (2007). On the divergent American reactions to terrorism and climate change. *Columbia Law Review, 107,* 503–557. (p. 356)

Suomi, S. J. (1986). Anxiety-like disorders in young nonhuman primates. In R. Gettleman (Ed.), *Anxiety disorders of childhood.* New York: Guilford Press. (p. 643)

Suppes, P. (1982). Quoted by R. H. Ennis, Children's ability to handle Piaget's propositional logic: A conceptual critique. In S. Modgil & C. Modgil (Eds.), *Jean Piaget: Consensus and controversy.* New York: Praeger. (p. 186)

Surgeon General. (1986). *The surgeon general's workshop on pornography and public health,* June 22–24. Report prepared by E. P. Mulvey & J. L. Haugaard and released by Office of the Surgeon General on August 4, 1986. (p. 604)

Surgeon General. (1999). *Mental health: A report of the surgeon general.* Rockville, MD: U.S. Department of Health and Human Services. (p. 632)

Susser, E. S. (1999). Life course cohort studies of schizophrenia. *Psychiatric Annals, 29,* 161–165. (p. 663)

Susser, E. S., Herman, D. B., & Aaron, B. (2002, August). Combating the terror of terrorism. *Scientific American,* pp. 70–77. (p. 640)

Susser, E. S., Neugenbauer, R., Hoek, H. W., Brown, A. S., Lin, S., Labovitz, D., & Gorman, J. M. (1996). Schizophrenia after prenatal famine. *Archives of General Psychiatry, 53(1),* 25–31. (p. 660)

Sutcliffe, J. S. (2008). Insights into the pathogenesis of autism. *Science, 321,* 208–209. (p. 185)

Sutherland, A. (2006, June 25). What Shamu taught me about a happy marriage, *New York Times.* (p. 295)

Swaab, D. F. (2008). Sexual orientation and its basis in brain structure and function. *PNAS, 105,* 10274–10274. (p. 445)

Swami, V., & 60 others. (2010). The attractive female body weight and female body dissatisfaction in 26 countries across 10 world regions: Results of the international body project I. *Personality and Social Psychology Bulletin, 36,* 309–325. (p. 671)

Swami, V., Henderson, G., Custance, D., & Tovée, M. J. (2011). A cross-cultural investigation of men's judgments of female body weight in Britain and Indonesia. *Journal of Cross-Cultural Psychology, 42,* 140–145. (p. 427)

Swann, W. B., Jr., Chang-Schneider, C., & McClarty, K. L. (2007). Do people's self-views matter: Self-concept and self-esteem in everyday life. *American Psychologist, 62,* 84–94. (p. 564)

Sweat, J. A., & Durm, M. W. (1993). Psychics: Do police departments really use them? *Skeptical Inquirer, 17,* 148–158. (p. 253)

Swerdlow, N. R., & Koob, G. F. (1987). Dopamine, schizophrenia, mania, and depression: Toward a unified hypothesis of cortico-stiato-pallido-thalamic function (with commentary). *Behavioral and Brain Sciences, 10,* 197–246. (p. 660)

Swim, J. K. (1994). Perceived versus meta-analytic effect sizes: An assessment of the accuracy of gender stereotypes. *Journal of Personality and Social Psychology, 66,* 21–36. (p. 596)

Swim, J. K., Johnston, K., & Pearson, N. B. (2009). Daily experiences with heterosexism: Relations between heterosexist hassles and psychological well-being. *Journal of Social and Clinical Psychology, 28,* 597–629. (p. 507)

Symbaluk, D. G., Heth, C. D., Cameron, J., & Pierce, W. D. (1997). Social modeling, monetary incentives, and pain endurance: The role of self-efficacy and pain perception. *Personality and Social Psychology Bulletin, 23,* 258–269. (p. 265)

Symond, M. B., Harris, A. W. F., Gordon, E., & Williams, L. M. (2005). "Gamma synchrony" in first-episode schizophrenia: A disorder of temporal connectivity? *American Journal of Psychiatry, 162*, 459–465. (p. 660)

Symons, C. S., & Johnson, B. T. (1997). The self-reference effect in memory: A meta-analysis. *Psychological Bulletin, 121*(3), 371–394. (p. 321)

Taha, F. A. (1972). A comparative study of how sighted and blind perceive the manifest content of dreams. *National Review of Social Sciences,* 9(3), 28. (p. 105)

Taheri, S. (2004). The genetics of sleep disorders. *Minerva Medica, 95*, 203–212. (p. 104)

Taheri, S. (2004a, 20 December). Does the lack of sleep make you fat? *University of Bristol Research News* (www.bristol.ac.uk). (p. 431)

Taheri, S., Lin, L., Austin, D., Young, T., & Mignot, E. (2004b). Short sleep duration is associated with reduced leptin, elevated ghrelin, and increased body mass index. *PloS Medicine, 1*(3), e62. (p. 431)

Taheri, S., Zeitzer, J. M., & Mignot, E. (2002). The role of hypocretins (orexins) in sleep regulation and narcolepsy. *Annual Review of Neuroscience, 25*, 283–313. (p. 104)

Tajfel, H. (Ed.). (1982). *Social identity and intergroup relations.* New York: Cambridge University Press. (p. 597)

Talal, N. (1995). Quoted by V. Morell, Zeroing in on how hormones affect the immune system. *Science, 269*, 773–775. (p. 510)

Talarico, J. M., & Rubin, D. C. (2003). Confidence, not consistency, characterizes flashbulb memories. *Psychological Science, 14*, 455–461. (p. 326)

Talarico, J. M., & Rubin, D. C. (2007). Flashbulb memories are special after all; in phenomenology, not accuracy. *Applied Cognitive Psychology, 21*, 557–578. (p. 326)

Talwar, S. K., Xu, S., Hawley, E. S., Weiss, S. A., Moxon, K. A., & Chapin, J. K. (2002). Rat navigation guided by remote control. *Nature, 417*, 37–38. (p. 66)

Tamres, L. K., Janicki, D., & Helgeson, V. S. (2002). Sex differences in coping behavior: A meta-analytic review and an examination of relative coping. *Personality and Social Psychology Review, 6*, 2–30. (p. 159)

Tang, C. Y., Eaves, E. L., Ng, J. C., Carpenter, D. M., Mai, X., Schroeder, D. H., Condon, C. A., Coliom, R., & Haier, R. J. (2010). Brain networks for working memory and factors of intelligence assessed in males and females with fMRI and DTI. *Intelligence, 38*, 293–303. (p. 390)

Tang, S-H., & Hall, V. C. (1995). The overjustification effect: A meta-analysis. *Applied Cognitive Psychology, 9*, 365–404. (p. 303)

Tangney, C. C., Kwasny, M. J., Li, H., Wilson, R. S., Evans, D. A., & Morris, M. C. (2011). Adherence to a Mediterranean-type dietary pattern and cognitive decline in a community population. *American Journal of Clinical Nutrition, 93*, 601–607. (p. 652)

Tangney, J. P., Baumeister, R. F., & Boone, A. L. (2004). High self-control predicts good adjustment, less pathology, better grades, and interpersonal success. *Journal of Personality, 72*, 271–324. (p. 558)

Tannen, D. (1990). *You just don't understand: Women and men in conversation.* New York: Morrow. (p. 159)

Tannen, D. (2001). *You just don't understand: Women and men in conversation.* New York: Harper. (p. 22)

Tannenbaum, P. (2002, February). Quoted in R. Kubey & M. Csikszentmihalyi, Television addiction is no mere metaphor. *Scientific American*, pp. 74–80. (p. 229)

Tanner, J. M. (1978). *Fetus into man: Physical growth from conception to maturity.* Cambridge, MA: Harvard University Press. (p. 198)

Tardif, T., Fletcher, P., Liang, W., Zhang, Z., Kaciroti, N., & Marchman, V. A. (2008). Baby's first 10 words. *Developmental Psychology, 44*, 929–938. (p. 368)

Tarmann, A. (2002, May/June). Out of the closet and onto the Census long form. *Population Today, 30*, pp. 1, 6. (p. 442)

Tasbihsazan, R., Nettelbeck, T., & Kirby, N. (2003). Predictive validity of the Fagan test of infant intelligence. *British Journal of Developmental Psychology, 21*, 585–597. (p. 400)

Taub, E. (2004). Harnessing brain plasticity through behavioral techniques to produce new treatments in neurorehabilitation. *American Psychologist, 59*, 692–698. (p. 75)

Taubes, G. (2001). The soft science of dietary fat. *Science, 291*, 2536–2545. (p. 433)

Taubes, G. (2002, July 7). What if it's all been a big fat lie? *New York Times* (www.nytimes.com). (p. 433)

Tausch, N., Hewstone, M., Kenworthy, J. B., Psaltis, C., Schmid, K., Popan, J. R., Cairns, E., & Hughes, J. (2010). Secondary transfer effects of intergroup contact: Alternative accounts and underlying processes. *Journal of Personality and Social Psychology, 99*, 282–302. (p. 620)

Tavris, C. (1982, November). Anger defused. *Psychology Today*, pp. 25–35. (p. 494)

Tavris, C., & Aronson, E. (2007). *Mistakes were made (but not by* me). Orlando, FL: Harcourt. (pp. 339, 576)

Tay, L., & Diener, E. (2011). Needs and subjective well-being around the world. *Journal of Personality and Social Psychology, 101*, 354–365. (p. 421)

Taylor, C. A., Manganello, J. A., Lee, S. J., & Rice, J. C. (2010). Mothers' spanking of 3-year-old children and subsequent risk of children's aggressive behavior. *Pediatrics, 125*, 1057–1065. (p. 293)

Taylor, K., & Rohrer, D. (2010). The effects of interleaved practice. *Applied Cognitive Psychology, 24*, 837–848. (p. 13)

Taylor, P. J., Gooding, P., Wood, A. M., & Tarrier, N. (2011). The role of defeat and entrapment in depression, anxiety, and suicide. *Psychological Bulletin, 137*, 391–420. (p. 650)

Taylor, P. J., Russ-Eft, D. F., & Chan, D. W. L. (2005). A meta-analytic review of behavior modeling training. *Journal of Applied Psychology, 90*, 692–709. (p. 306)

Taylor, S., Kuch, K., Koch, W. J., Crockett, D. J., & Passey, G. (1998). The structure of posttraumatic stress symptoms. *Journal of Abnormal Psychology, 107*, 154–160. (p. 640)

Taylor, S. E. (1989). *Positive illusions.* New York: Basic Books. (pp. 357, 566)

Taylor, S. E. (2002). *The tending instinct: How nurturing is essential to who we are and how we live.* New York: Times Books. (p. 159)

Taylor, S. E. (2006). Tend and befriend: Biobehavioral bases of affiliation under stress. *Current Directions in Psychological Science, 15*, 273–277. (p. 508)

Taylor, S. E., Cousino, L. K., Lewis, B. P., Gruenewald, T. L., Gurung, R. A. R., & Updegraff, J. A. (2000). Biobehavioral responses to stress in females: Tend-and-befriend, not fight-or-flight. *Psychological Review, 107*, 411–430. (p. 508)

Taylor, S. E., Pham, L. B., Rivkin, I. D., & Armor, D. A. (1998). Harnessing the imagination: Mental simulation, self-regulation, and coping. *American Psychologist, 53*, 429–439. (p. 378)

Taylor, S. P., & Chermack, S. T. (1993). Alcohol, drugs and human physical aggression. *Journal of Studies on Alcohol*, Supplement No. 11, 78–88. (p. 601)

Teasdale, T. W., & Owen, D. R. (2005). A long-term rise and recent decline in intelligence test performance: The Flynn effect in reverse. *Personality and Individual Differences, 39*, 837–843. (p. 396)

Teasdale, T. W., & Owen, D. R. (2008). Secular declines in cognitive test scores: A reversal of the Flynn effect. *Intelligence, 36*, 121–126. (p. 396)

Tedeschi, R. G., & Calhoun, L. G. (2004). Posttraumatic growth: Conceptual foundations and empirical evidence. *Psychological Inquiry, 15*, 1–18. (p. 641)

Teghtsoonian, R. (1971). On the exponents in Stevens' law and the constant in Ekinan's law. *Psychological Review, 78*, 71–80. (p. 227)

Teicher, M. H. (2002, March). The neurobiology of child abuse. *Scientific American*, pp. 68–75. (p. 192)

Teller. (2009, April 20). Quoted by J. Lehrer, Magic and the brain: Teller reveals the neuroscience of illusion. *Wired Magazine* (www.wired.com). (p. 89)

Tenopyr, M. L. (1997). Improving the workplace: Industrial/organizational psychology as a career. In R. J. Sternberg (Ed.), *Career paths in psychology: Where your degree can take you.* Washington, DC: American Psychological Association. (p. 459)

Terao, T., Ohgami, H., Shlotsuki, I., Ishil, N., & Iwata, N. (2010). Author's reply. *British Journal of Psychiatry, 196*, 160. (p. 707)

Terman, J. S., Terman, M., Lo, E-S., & Cooper, T. B. (2001). Circadian time of morning light administration and therapeutic response in winter depression. *Archives of General Psychiatry, 58*, 69–73. (p. 698)

Terman, L. M. (1916). *The measurement of intelligence.* Boston: Houghton Mifflin. (p. 394)

Terman, M., Terman, J. S., & Ross, D. C. (1998). A controlled trial of timed bright light and negative air ionization for treatment of winter depression. *Archives of General Psychiatry, 55*, 875–882. (p. 698)

Terracciano, A., Costa, P. T., Jr., & McCrae, R. R. (2006). Personality plasticity after age 30. *Personality and Social Psychology Bulletin, 32*, 999–1009. (p. 156)

Terrace, H. S. (1979, November). How Nim Chimpsky changed my mind. *Psychology Today*, pp. 65–76. (p. 374)

Terre, L., & Stoddart, R. (2000). Cutting edge specialties for graduate study in psychology. *Eye on Psi Chi*, 23–26. (p. A-1)

Tesser, A., Forehand, R., Brody, G., & Long, N. (1989). Conflict: The role of calm and angry parent-child discussion in adolescent development. *Journal of Social and Clinical Psychology, 8*, 317–330. (p. 204)

Tetlock, P. E. (1988). Monitoring the integrative complexity of American and Soviet policy rhetoric: What can be learned? *Journal of Social Issues, 44*, 101–131. (p. 621)

Tetlock, P. E. (1998). Close-call counterfactuals and belief-system defenses: I was not almost wrong but I was almost right. *Journal of Personality and Social Psychology, 75*, 639–652. (p. 17)

Tetlock, P. E. (2005). *Expert political judgement: How good is it? How can we know?* Princeton, NJ: Princeton University Press. (p. 17)

Thaler, R. H., & Sunstein, C. R. (2008). *Nudge: Improving decisions about health, wealth, and happiness.* New Haven, CT: Yale University Press. (p. 359)

Thannickal, T. C., Moore, R. Y., Nienhuis, R., Ramanathan, L., Gulyani, S., Aldrich, M., Cornford, M., & Siegel, J. M. (2000). Reduced number of hypocretin neurons in human narcolepsy. *Neuron, 27,* 469–474. (p. 104)

Thatcher, R. W., Walker, R. A., & Giudice, S. (1987). Human cerebral hemispheres develop at different rates and ages. *Science, 236,* 1110–1113. (pp. 171, 177)

Thayer, R. E. (1987). Energy, tiredness, and tension effects of a sugar snack versus moderate exercise. *Journal of Personality and Social Psychology, 52,* 119–125. (p. 522)

Thayer, R. E. (1993). Mood and behavior (smoking and sugar snacking) following moderate exercise: A partial test of self-regulation theory. *Personality and Individual Differences, 14,* 97–104. (p. 522)

Théoret, H., Halligan, H., Kobayashi, M., Fregni, F., Tager-Flusberg, H., & Pascual-Leone, A. (2005). Impaired motor facilitation during action observation in individuals with autism spectrum disorder. *Current Biology, 15,* R84–R85. (p. 185)

Thernstrom, M. (2006, May 14). My pain, my brain. *New York Times* (www.nytimes.com). (p. 266)

Thiel, A., Hadedank, B., Herholz, K., Kessler, J., Winhuisen, L., Haupt, W. F., & Heiss, W-D. (2006). From the left to the right: How the brain compensates progressive loss of language function. *Brain and Language, 98,* 57–65. (p. 76)

Thiele, T. E., Marsh, D. J., Ste. Marie, L., Bernstein, I. L., & Palmiter, R. D. (1998). Ethanol consumption and resistance are inversely related to neuropeptide Y levels. *Nature, 396,* 366–369. (p. 126)

Thomas, A., & Chess, S. (1977). *Temperament and development.* New York: Brunner/Mazel. (p. 137)

Thomas, A., & Chess, S. (1986). The New York Longitudinal Study: From infancy to early adult life. In R. Plomin & J. Dunn (Eds.), *The study of temperament: Changes, continuities, and challenges.* Hillsdale, NJ: Erlbaum. (p. 171)

Thomas, L. (1974). *The lives of a cell.* New York: Viking Press. (p. 270)

Thomas, L. (1983). *The youngest science: Notes of a medicine watcher.* New York: Viking Press. (p. 52)

Thomas, L. (1992). *The fragile species.* New York: Scribner's. (pp. 166, 369, 694)

Thompson, G. (2010). The $1 million dollar challenge. *Skeptic Magazine, 15,* 8–9. (p. 255)

Thompson, J. K., Jarvie, G. J., Lahey, B. B., & Cureton, K. J. (1982). Exercise and obesity: Etiology, physiology, and intervention. *Psychological Bulletin, 91,* 55–79. (p. 433)

Thompson, P. M., Cannon, T. D., Narr, K. L., van Erp, T., Poutanen, V-P., Huttunen, M., Lönnqvist, J., Standerskjöld-Nordenstam, C-G., Kaprio, J., Khaledy, M., Dail, R., Zoumalan, C. I., & Toga, A. W. (2001). Genetic influences on brain structure. *Nature Neuroscience, 4,* 1253–1258. (p. 405)

Thompson, P. M., Giedd, J. N., Woods, R. P., MacDonald, D., Evans, A. C., & Toga, A. W. (2000). Growth patterns in the developing brain detected by using continuum mechanical tensor maps. *Nature, 404,* 190–193. (p. 177)

Thompson, R., Emmorey, K., & Gollan, T. H. (2005). "Tip of the fingers" experiences by Deaf signers. *Psychological Science, 16,* 856–860. (p. 337)

Thomson, R., & Murachver, T. (2001). Predicting gender from electronic discourse. *British Journal of Social Psychology, 40,* 193–208 (and personal correspondence from T. Murachver, May 23, 2002). (p. 159)

Thorndike, E. L. (1898). Animal intelligence: An experimental study of the associative processes in animals. *Psychological Review Monograph Supplement 2,* 4–160. (p. 286)

Thorne, J., with Rothstein, L. (1993). *You are not alone: Words of experience and hope for the journey through depression.* New York: HarperPerennial. (p. 624)

Thornhill, R., & Gangestad, S. W. (1994). Human fluctuating asymmetry and sexual behavior. *Psychological Science, 5,* 297–302. (p. 611)

Thornton, B., & Moore, S. (1993). Physical attractiveness contrast effect: Implications for self-esteem and evaluations of the social self. *Personality and Social Psychology Bulletin, 19,* 474–480. (p. 610)

Thorpe, W. H. (1974). *Animal nature and human nature.* London: Metheun. (p. 375)

Tickle, J. J., Hull, J. G., Sargent, J. D., Dalton, M. A., & Heatherton, T. F. (2006). A structural equation model of social influences and exposure to media smoking on adolescent smoking. *Basic and Applied Social Psychology, 28,* 117–129. (p. 119)

Tiedens, L. Z. (2001). Anger and advancement versus sadness and subjugation: The effect of negative emotion expressions on social status conferral. *Journal of Personality and Social Psychology, 80,* 86–94. (p. 494)

Tiggemann, M., & Miller, J. (2010). The Internet and adolescent girls' weight satisfaction and drive for thinness. *Sex Roles, 63,* 79–90. (p. 672)

Tiihonen, J., Lönnqvist, J., Wahlbeck, K., Klaukka, T., Niskanen, L., Tanskanen, A., Haukka, J. (2009). 11-year follow-up of mortality in patients with schizophrenia: a population-based cohort study (FIN11 study). *Lancet, 374,* 260–267. (p. 705)

Time. (2009, Oct. 14). The state of the American woman. pp. 32–33. (p. 159)

***Time/CNN* Survey.** (1994, December 19). Vox pop: Happy holidays, *Time.* (p. 645)

Timmerman, T. A. (2007). "It was a thought pitch": Personal, situational, and target influences on hit-by-pitch events across time. *Journal of Applied Psychology, 92,* 876–884. (p. 601)

Tinbergen, N. (1951). *The study of instinct.* Oxford: Clarendon. (p. 418)

Tirrell, M. E. (1990). Personal communication. (p. 281)

Toews, P. (2004, December 30). *Dirk Willems: A heart undivided.* Mennonite Brethren Historical Commission (www.mbhistory.org/profiles/dirk.en.html). (p. 571)

Tolin, D. F. (2010). Is cognitive-behavioral therapy more effective than other therapies? A meta-analytic review. *Clinical Psychology Review, 30,* 710–720. (p. 695)

Tolin, D. F., & Foa, E. B. (2006). Sex differences in trauma and posttraumatic stress disorder: A quantitative review of 25 years of research. *Psychological Bulletin, 132,* 959–992. (p. 640)

Tolman, E. C., & Honzik, C. H. (1930). Introduction and removal of reward, and maze performance in rats. *University of California Publications in Psychology, 4,* 257–275. (p. 303)

Tolstoy, L. (1904). *My confessions.* Boston: Dana Estes. (p. 12)

Tondo, L., Jamison, K. R., & Baldessarini, R. J. (1997). Effect of lithium maintenance on suicidal behavior in major mood disorders. In D. M. Stoff & J. J. Mann (Eds.), *The neurobiology of suicide: From the bench to the clinic.* New York: New York Academy of Sciences. (p. 707)

Toni, N., Buchs, P.-A., Nikonenko, I., Bron, C. R., & Muller, D. (1999). LTP promotes formation of multiple spine synapses between a single axon terminal and a dendrite. *Nature, 402,* 421–442. (p. 327)

Topolinski, S., & Reber, R. (2010). Gaining insight into the "aha" experience. *Current Directions in Psychological Science, 19,* 401–405. (p. 353)

Torrey, E. F. (1986). *Witchdoctors and psychiatrists.* New York: Harper & Row. (p. 699)

Torrey, E. F., & Miller, J. (2002). *The invisible plague: The rise of mental illness from 1750 to the present.* New Brunswick, NJ: Rutgers University Press. (p. 661)

Torrey, E. F., Miller, J., Rawlings, R., & Yolken, R. H. (1997). Seasonality of births in schizophrenia and bipolar disorder: A review of the literature. *Schizophrenia Research, 28,* 1–38. (p. 661)

Totterdell, P., Kellett, S., Briner, R. B., & Teuchmann, K. (1998). Evidence of mood linkage in work groups. *Journal of Personality and Social Psychology, 74,* 1504–1515. (p. 579)

Tracy, J. L., Cheng, J. T., Robins, R. W., & Trzesniewski, K. H. (2009). Authentic and hubristic pride: The affective core of self-esteem and narcissism. *Self and Identity, 8,* 196–213. (p. 566)

Tracy, J. L., & Robins, R. W. (2004). Show your pride: Evidence for a discrete emotion expression. *Psychological Science, 15,* 194–197. (p. 492)

Trautwein, U., Lüdtke, O., Köller, O., & Baumert, J. (2006). Self-esteem, academic self-concept, and achievement: How the learning environment moderates the dynamics of self-concept. *Journal of Personality and Social Psychology, 90,* 334–349. (p. 564)

Treffert, D. A., & Christensen, D. D. (2005, December). Inside the mind of a savant. *Scientific American,* pp. 108–113. (p. 383)

Treffert, D. A., & Wallace, G. L. (2002). Island of genius—The artistic brilliance and dazzling memory that sometimes accompany autism and other disorders hint at how all brains work. *Scientific American, 286,* 76–86. (p. 383)

Treisman, A. (1987). Properties, parts, and objects. In K. R. Boff, L. Kaufman, & J. P. Thomas (Eds.), *Handbook of perception and human performance.* New York: Wiley. (p. 243)

Tremblay, R. E., Pihl, R. O., Vitaro, F., & Dobkin, P. L. (1994). Predicting early onset of male antisocial behavior from preschool behavior. *Archives of General Psychiatry, 51,* 732–739. (p. 668)

Trenholm, C., Devaney, B., Fortson, K., Quay, L., Sheeler, J., & Clark, M. (2007, April). Impacts of four Title V, Section 510 abstinence education programs. Report to U.S. Department of Health and Human Services by Mathematica Policy Research, Inc., Princeton, NJ. (p. 441)

Trewin, D. (2001). *Australian social trends 2001.* Canberra: Australian Bureau of Statistics. (p. 162)

Triandis, H. C. (1981). Some dimensions of intercultural variation and their implications for interpersonal behavior. Paper presented at the American Psychological Association convention. (p. 152)

Triandis, H. C. (1994). *Culture and social behavior.* New York: McGraw-Hill. (pp. 154, 558, 602)

Triandis, H. C., Bontempo, R., Villareal, M. J., Asai, M., & Lucca, N. (1988). Individualism and collectivism: Cross-cultural perspectives on self-ingroup relationships. *Journal of Personality and Social Psychology, 54,* 323–338. (p. 155)

Trickett, E. (2009). Community psychology: Individuals and interventions in community context. *Annual Review of Psychology, 60,* 395–419. (p. 11)

Trillin, C. (2006, March 27). Alice off the page. *The New Yorker,* p. 44. (p. 544)

Trimble, J. E. (1994). Cultural variations in the use of alcohol and drugs. In W. J. Lonner & R. Malpass (Eds.), *Psychology and culture.* Boston: Allyn & Bacon. (p. 127)

Triplett, N. (1898). The dynamogenic factors in pacemaking and competition. *American Journal of Psychology, 9,* 507–533. (p. 586)

Trut, L. N. (1999). Early canid domestication: The farm-fox experiment. *American Scientist, 87,* 160–169. (p. 142)

Tsai, J. L., & Chentsova-Dutton, Y. (2003). Variation among European Americans in emotional facial expression. *Journal of Cross-Cultural Psychology, 34,* 650–657. (p. 489)

Tsai, J. L., Miao, F. F., Seppala, E., Fung, H. H., & Yeung, D. Y. (2007). Influence and adjustment goals: Sources of cultural differences in ideal affect. *Journal of Personality and Social Psychology, 92,* 1102–1117. (p. 489)

Tsang, Y. C. (1938). Hunger motivation in gastrectomized rats. *Journal of Comparative Psychology, 26,* 1–17. (p. 422)

Tsankova, N., Renthal, W., Kumar, A., & Nestler, E. J. (2007). Epigenetic regulation in psychiatric disorders. *Nature Reviews Neuroscience, 8,* 355–367. (p. 138)

Tse, D., Langston, R. F., Kakeyama, M., Bethus, I., Spooner P. A., Wood, E. R., Witter, M. P., & Morris, R. G. M. (2007). Schemas and memory consolidation. *Science, 316,* 76–82. (p. 324)

Tsuang, M. T., & Faraone, S. V. (1990). *The genetics of mood disorders.* Baltimore, MD: Johns Hopkins University Press. (p. 649)

Tuber, D. S., Miller, D. D., Caris, K. A., Halter, R., Linden, F., & Hennessy, M. B. (1999). Dogs in animal shelters: Problems, suggestions, and needed expertise. *Psychological Science, 10,* 379–386. (p. 23)

Tucker, K. A. (2002). I believe you can fly. *Gallup Management Journal* (www.gallupjournal.com/CA/st/20020520.asp). (p. 466)

Tucker-Drob, E. M., Rhemtulla, M., Harden, K. P., Turkheimer, E., & Fask, D. (2011). Emergence of a gene x socioeconomic status interaction on infant mental ability between 10 months and 2 years. *Psychological Science, 22,* 125–133. (p. 406)

Tuerk, P. W. (2005). Research in the high-stakes era: Achievement, resources, and No Child Left Behind. *Psychological Science, 16,* 419–425. (p. 407)

Tully, T. (2003). Reply: The myth of a myth. *Current Biology, 13,* R426. (p. 278)

Turkheimer, E., Haley, A., Waldron, M., D'Onofrio, B., & Gottesman, I. I. (2003). Socioeconomic status modifies heritability of IQ in young children. *Psychological Science, 14,* 623–628. (p. 406)

Turner, J. C. (1987). *Rediscovering the social group: A self-categorization theory.* New York: Basil Blackwell. (p. 596)

Turner, J. C. (2007). Self-categorization theory. In R. Baumeister & K. Vohs (Eds.), *Encyclopedia of social psychology.* Thousand Oaks, CA: Sage. (p. 596)

Turner, N., Barling, J., & Zacharatos, A. (2002). Positive psychology at work. In C. R. Snyder & S. J. Lopez (Eds.), *The handbook of positive psychology.* New York: Oxford University Press. (p. 468)

Turpin, A. (2005, April 3). The science of psi. *FT Weekend,* pp. W1, W2. (p. 253)

Tutu, D. (1999). *No future without forgiveness.* New York: Doubleday. (p. 450)

Tversky, A. (1985, June). Quoted in K. McKean, Decisions, decisions. *Discover,* pp. 22–31. (p. 355)

Tversky, A., & Kahneman, D. (1974). Judgment under uncertainty: Heuristics and biases. *Science, 185,* 1124–1131. (p. 355)

Tversky, B. (2008, June/July). Glimpses of Chinese psychology: Reflections on the APS trip to China. *Observer,* pp. 13–14 (also at psychologicalscience.org/observer). (p. 6)

Twenge, J. M. (1997). Changes in masculine and feminine traits over time: A meta-analysis. *Sex Roles 36*(5–6), 305–325. (p. 164)

Twenge, J. M. (2006). *Generation me.* New York: Free Press. (p. 567)

Twenge, J. M., Abebe, E. M., & Campbell, W. K. (2010). Fitting in or standing out: Trends in American parents' choices for children's names, 1880–2007. *Social Psychology and Personality Science, 1,* 19–25. (pp. 154, 155)

Twenge, J. M., Baumeister, R. F., DeWall, C. N., Ciarocco, N. J., & Bartels, J. M. (2007). Social exclusion decreases prosocial behavior. *Journal of Personality and Social Psychology, 92,* 56–66. (p. 452)

Twenge, J. M., Baumeister, R. F., Tice, D. M., & Stucke, T. S. (2001). If you can't join them, beat them: Effects of social exclusion on aggressive behavior. *Journal of Personality and Social Psychology, 81,* 1058–1069. (p. 452)

Twenge, J. M., & Campbell, W. K. (2001). Age and birth cohort differences in self-esteem: A cross-temporal meta-analysis. *Personality and Social Psychology Review, 5,* 321–344. (p. 204)

Twenge, J. M., Catanese, K. R., & Baumeister, R. F. (2002). Social exclusion causes self-defeating behavior. *Journal of Personality and Social Psychology, 83,* 606–615. (p. 452)

Twenge, J. M., & Foster, J. D. (2010). Birth cohort increases in narcissistic personality traits among American college students, 1982–2009. *Social Psychological and Personality Science, 1,* 99–106. (p. 567)

Twenge, J. M., Gentile, B., DeWall, C. D., Ma, D., & Lacefield, K. (2008). *A growing disturbance: Increasing psychopathology in young people 1938–2007 in a meta-analysis of the MMPI.* Unpublished manuscript, San Diego State University. (p. 649)

Twenge, J. M., & Nolen-Hoeksema, S. (2002). Age, gender, race, socioeconomic status, and birth cohort differences on the children's depression inventory: A meta-analysis. *Journal of Abnormal Psychology, 111,* 578–588. (p. 204)

Twiss, C., Tabb, S., & Crosby, F. (1989). Affirmative action and aggregate data: The importance of patterns in the perception of discrimination. In F. Blanchard & F. Crosby (Eds.), *Affirmative action: Social psychological perspectives.* New York: Springer-Verlag. (p. 33)

U. S. Senate Select Committee on Intelligence (2004, July 9). *Report of the U.S. intelligence community's prewar intelligence assessments on Iraq.* www.gpoaccess.gov/serialset/creports/iraq.html. (pp. 26, 354)

Uchida, Y., & Kitayama, S. (2009). Happiness and unhappiness in East and West: Themes and variations. *Emotion, 9,* 441–456. (p. 501)

Uchino, B. N. (2009). Understanding the links between social support and physical health. *Perspectives on Psychological Science, 4,* 236–255. (p. 519)

Uchino, B. N., Cacioppo, J. T., & Kiecolt-Glaser, J. K. (1996). The relationship between social support and physiological processes: A review with emphasis on underlying mechanisms and implications for health. *Psychological Bulletin, 119,* 488–531. (p. 519)

Uchino, B. N., Uno, D., & Holt-Lunstad, J. (1999). Social support, physiological processes, and health. *Current Directions in Psychological Science, 8,* 145–148. (p. 519)

Udry, J. R. (2000). Biological limits of gender construction. *American Sociological Review, 65,* 443–457. (p. 160)

Uga, V., Lemut, M. C., Zampi, C., Zilli, I., & Salzarulo, P. (2006). Music in dreams. *Consciousness and Cognition, 15,* 351–357. (p. 106)

Uher, R., & McGuffin, P. (2010). The moderation by the serotonin transporter gene of environmental adversity in the etiology of depression: 2009 update. *Molecular Psychiatry, 15,* 18–22. (p. 652)

UK ECT Review Group. (2003). Efficacy and safety of electroconvulsive therapy in depressive disorders: A systematic review and meta-analysis. *Lancet, 361,* 799–808. (p. 708)

Ulrich, R. E. (1991). Animal rights, animal wrongs and the question of balance. *Psychological Science, 2,* 197–201. (p. 23)

UN. (2001). *World population ageing: 1950–2050.* United Nations (www.un.org). (p. 209)

UN. (2010). The ageing of the world's population. United Nations (www.un.org). (p. 209)

UNAIDS. (2010). *UNAIDS report on the global AIDS epidemic 2010.* www.unaids.org. (p. 511)

Unsworth, N., & Engle, R. W. (2007). The nature of individual differences in working memory capacity: Active maintenance in primary memory and controlled search from secondary memory. *Psychological Review, 114,* 104–132. (p. 318)

Urbina, I. (2010, May 29). Documents show early worries about safety of rig. *New York Times* (www.nytimes.com). (p. 357)

Urry, H. L., & Gross, J. J. (2010). Emotion regulation in older age. *Current Directions in Psychological Science, 19,* 352–357. (p. 218)

Urry, H. L., Nitschke, J. B., Dolski, I., Jackson, D. C., Dalton, K. M., Mueller, C. J., Rosenkranz, M. A., Ryff, C. D., Singer, B. H., & Davidson, R. J. (2004). Making a life worth living: Neural correlates of well-being. *Psychological Science, 15,* 367–372. (p. 481)

Ursu, S., Stenger, V. A., Shear, M. K., Jones, M. R., & Carter, C. S. (2003). Overactive action monitoring in obsessive-compulsive disorder: Evidence from functional magnetic resonance imaging. *Psychological Science, 14,* 347–353. (p. 643)

USAID. (2004, January). *The ABCs of HIV prevention.* www.usaid.gov. (p. 511)

Uttal, W. R. (2001). *The new phrenology: The limits of localizing cognitive processes in the brain.* Cambridge, MA: MIT Press. (p. 75)

Vacic, V. & 29 others. (2011). Duplications of the neuropeptide receptor gene *VIPR2* confer significant risk for schizophrenia. *Nature, 471,* 499–503. (p. 662)

Vaidya, J. G., Gray, E. K., Haig, J., & Watson, D. (2002). On the temporal stability of personality: Evidence for differential stability and the role of life experiences. *Journal of Personality and Social Psychology, 83,* 1469–1484. (p. 551)

Vaillant, G. (2009). Quoted by J. W. Shenk, What makes us happy? *The Atlantic* (www.theatlantic.com). (p. 452)

Vaillant, G. E. (1977). *Adaptation to life.* New York: Little, Brown. (p. 344)

Vaillant, G. E. (2002). *Aging well: Surprising guideposts to a happier life from the landmark Harvard study of adult development.* Boston: Little, Brown. (p. 519)

Valenstein, E. S. (1986). *Great and desperate cures: The rise and decline of psychosurgery.* New York: Basic Books. (p. 710)

Valkenburg, P. M., & Peter, J. (2009). Social consequences of the Internet for adolescents: A decade of research. *Current Directions in Psychological Science, 18,* 1–5. (pp. 205, 454, 453)

Van Anders, S. M., & Dunn, E. J. (2009). Are gonadal steroids linked with orgasm perceptions and sexual assertiveness in women and men? *Journal of Sexual Medicine, 6,* 739–751. (p. 437)

Van Baaren, R. B., Holland, R. W., Kawakami, K., & van Knippenberg, A. (2004). Mimicry and pro-social behavior. *Psychological Science, 15,* 71–74. (p. 579)

Van Baaren, R. B., Holland, R. W., Steenaert, B., & van Knippenberg, A. (2003). Mimicry for money: Behavioral consequences of imitation. *Journal of Experimental Social Psychology, 39,* 393–398. (p. 579)

van Boxtel, H. W., Orobio de Castro, B., & Goossens, F. A. (2004). High self-perceived social competence in rejected children is related to frequent fighting. *European Journal of Developmental Psychology, 1,* 205–214. (p. 566)

Van Cauter, E., Holmback, U., Knutson, K., Leproult, R., Miller, A., Nedeltcheva, A., Pannain, S., Penev, P., Tasali, E., & Spiegel, K. (2007). Impact of sleep and sleep loss on neuroendocrine and metabolic function. *Hormone Research, 67*(1), Supp. 1: 2–9. (p. 102)

van den Bos, K., & Spruijt, N. (2002). Appropriateness of decisions as a moderator of the psychology of voice. *European Journal of Social Psychology, 32,* 57–72. (p. 468)

Van den Bussche, E., Van Den Noortgate, W., & Reynvoet, B. (2009). Mechanisms of masked priming: A meta-analysis. *Psychological Bulletin, 135,* 452–477. (p. 226)

Van der Schot, A. C. & 11 others. (2009). Influence of genes and environment on brain volumes in twin pairs concordant and discordant for bipolar disorder. *Archives of General psychiatry, 66,* 142–151. (p. 652)

Van Dyke, C., & Byck, R. (1982, March). Cocaine. *Scientific American,* pp. 128–141. (p. 121)

van Engen, M. L., & Willemsen, T. M. (2004). Sex and leadership styles: A meta-analysis of research published in the 1990s. *Psychological Reports, 94,* 3–18. (p. 158)

van Goozen, S. H. M., Fairchild, G., Snoek, H., & Harold, G. T. (2007). The evidence for a neurobiological model of childhood antisocial behavior. *Psychological Bulletin, 133,* 149–182. (p. 668)

van Hemert, D. A., Poortinga, Y. H., & van de Vijver, F. J. R. (2007). Emotion and culture: A meta-analysis. *Cognition and Emotion, 21,* 913–943. (p. 489)

van Honk, J., Schutter, D. J., Bos, P. A., Kruijt, A-W., Lentje, E. G. & Baron-Cohen, S. (2011). Testosterone administration impairs cognitive empathy in women depending on second-to-fourth digit ratio. *Proceedings of the National Academy of Sciences, 108,* 3448–3452. (p. 184)

Van IJzendoorn, M. H., & Juffer, F. (2005). Adoption is a successful natural intervention enhancing adopted children's IQ and school performance. *Current Directions in Psychological Science, 14,* 326–330. (p. 406)

Van IJzendoorn, M. H., & Juffer, F. (2006). The Emanual Miller Memorial Lecture 2006: Adoption as intervention. Meta-analytic evidence for massive catch-up and plasticity in physical, socio-emotional, and cognitive development. *Journal of Child Psychology and Psychiatry, 47,* 1228–1245. (pp. 137, 406)

van IJzendoorn, M. H., & Kroonenberg, P. M. (1988). Cross-cultural patterns of attachment: A meta-analysis of the strange situation. *Child Development, 59,* 147–156. (p. 189)

Van IJzendoorn, M. H., Luijk, M. P. C. M., & Juffer, F. (2008). IQ of children growing up in children's homes: A meta-analysis on IQ delays in ophanages. *Merrill-Palmer Quarterly, 54,* 341–366. (pp. 191, 407)

Van Leeuwen, M. S. (1978). A cross-cultural examination of psychological differentiation in males and females. *International Journal of Psychology, 13,* 87–122. (p. 162)

van Praag, H. (2009). Exercise and the brain: Something to chew on. *Trends in Neuroscience, 32,* 283–290. (p. 523)

Van Rooy, D. L., & Viswesvaran, C. (2004). Emotional intelligence: A meta-analytic investigation of predictive validity and nomological net. *Journal of Vocational Behavior, 65,* 71–95. (p. 389)

Van Yperen, N. W., & Buunk, B. P. (1990). A longitudinal study of equity and satisfaction in intimate relationships. *European Journal of Social Psychology, 20,* 287–309. (p. 614)

Van Zeijl, J., Mesman, J., Van IJzendoorn, M. H., Bakermans-Kranenburg, M. J., Juffer, F., Stolk, M. N., Koot, H. M., & Alink, L. R. A. (2006). Attachment-based intervention for enhancing sensitive discipline in mothers of 1- to 3-year-old children at risk for externalizing behavior problems: A randomized controlled trial. *Journal of Consulting and Clinical Psychology, 74,* 994–1005. (p. 190)

Vance, E. B., & Wagner, N. N. (1976). Written descriptions of orgasm: A study of sex differences. *Archives of Sexual Behavior, 5,* 87–98. (p. 435)

Vandell, D. L., Belsky, J., Burchinal, M., Steinberg, L., Vandergrift, N., & NICHD Early Child Care Research Network (2010). Do effects of early child care extend to age 15 years? Results from the NICHD study of early child care and youth development. *Child Development, 81,* 737–756. (p. 192)

Vandenberg, S. G., & Kuse, A. R. (1978). Mental rotations: A group test of three-dimensional spatial visualization. *Perceptual and Motor Skills, 47,* 599–604. (p. 410)

Varnum, M. E. W., Grossmann, I., Kitayama, S., & Nisbett, R. E. (2010). The origin of cultural differences in cognition: The social orientation hypothesis. *Current Directions in Psychological Science, 19,* 9–13. (p. 155)

Vasey, P. L., & VanderLaan, D. P. (2010). An adaptive cognitive dissociation between willingness to help kin and nonkin in Samoan *Fa'afafine. Psychological Science, 21,* 292–297. (p. 446)

Vaughn, K. B., & Lanzetta, J. T. (1981). The effect of modification of expressive displays on vicarious emotional arousal. *Journal of Experimental Social Psychology, 17,* 16–30. (p. 490)

Vecera, S. P., Vogel, E. K., & Woodman, G. F. (2002). Lower region: A new cue for figure-ground assignment. *Journal of Experimental Psychology: General, 13,* 194–205. (p. 246)

Veenhoven, R. (2009). World data base of happiness: Tool for dealing with the 'data-deluge.' *Psychological Topics, 18,* 221–246. (p. 500)

Vega, V., & Malamuth, N. M. (2007). Predicting sexaul aggression: The role of pornography in the context of general and specific risk factors. *Aggressive Behavior, 33,* 104–117. (p. 603)

Vekassy, L. (1977). Dreams of the blind. *Magyar Pszichologiai Szemle, 34,* 478–491. (p. 105)

Velliste, M., Perel, S., Spalding, M. C., Whitford, A. S., & Schwartz, A. B. (2008). Cortical control of a prosthetic arm for self-feeding. *Nature, 453,* 1098–1101. (pp. 71, 72)

Veltkamp, M., Custers, R., & Aarts, H. (2011). Motivating consumer behavior by subliminal conditioning in the absence of basic needs: Striking even while the iron is cold. *Journal of Consumer Psychology, 21,* 49–56. (p. 227)

Verbeek, M. E. M., Drent, P. J., & Wiepkema, P. R. (1994). Consistent individual differences in early exploratory behaviour of male great tits. *Animal Behaviour, 48,* 1113–1121. (p. 549)

Verhaeghen, P., & Salthouse, T. A. (1997). Meta-analyses of age-cognition relations in adulthood: Estimates of linear and nonlinear age effects and structural models. *Psychological Bulletin, 122,* 231–249. (p. 211)

Verosky, S. C., & Todorov, A. (2010). Generalization of affective learning about faces to perceptually similar faces. *Psychological Science, 21,* 779–785. (p. 282)

Vertes, R., & Siegel, J. (2005). Time for the sleep community to take a critical look at the purported role of sleep in memory processing. *Sleep, 28,* 1228–1229. (p. 107)

Verwijmeren, T., Karremans, J. C., Stroebe, W., & Wigboldus, D. H. J. (2011a). The workings and limits of subliminal advertising: The role of habits. *Journal of Consumer Psychology, 21,* 206–213. (p. 227)

Verwijmeren, T., Karremans, J. C., Stroebe, W., Wigboldus, D. H. J., & Ooigen, I. (2011b). Vicary's victory: Subliminal ads in movies work! Poster presented at the Society for Personality and Social Psychology meeting, San Antonio, TX. (p. 227)

Vigil, J. M. (2009). A socio-relational framework of sex differences in the expression of emotion. *Behavioral and Brain Sciences, 32,* 375–428. (p. 486)

Vigil, J. M., Geary, D. C., & Byrd-Craven, J. (2005). A life history assessment of early childhood sexual abuse in women. *Developmental Psychology, 41,* 553–561. (p. 198)

Vigliocco, G., & Hartsuiker, R. J. (2002). The interplay of meaning, sound, and syntax in sentence production. *Psychological Bulletin, 128,* 442–472. (p. 367)

Vining, E. P. G., Freeman, J. M., Pillas, D. J., Uematsu, S., Carson, B. S., Brandt, J., Boatman, D., Pulsifer, M. B., & Zukerberg, A. (1997). Why would you remove half a brain? The outcome of 58 children after hemispherectomy—The Johns Hopkins Experience: 1968 to 1996. *Pediatrics, 100,* 163–171. (p. 75)

Vinkhuyzen, A. A. E., van der Sluis, S., Posthuma, D., & Boomsma, D. I. (2009). The heritability of aptitude and exceptional talent across different domains in adolescents and young adults. *Behavior Genetics, 39,* 380–392. (p. 405)

Visalberghi, E. Addessi, E., Truppa, V., Spagnoletti, N., Ottoni, E., Izar, P., & Fragaszy, D. (2009). Selection of effective stone tools by wild bearded capuchin monkes. *Current Biolog, 19,* 213–217. (p. 363)

Visich, P. S., & Fletcher, E. (2009). Myocardial infarction. In J. K. Ehrman, P. M., Gordon, P. S. Visich, & S. J. Keleyian (Eds.). *Clinical exercise physiology, 2nd Edition.* Champaign, IL: Human Kinetics. (p. 521)

Vita, A. J., Terry, R. B., Hubert, H. B., & Fries, J. F. (1998). Aging, health risks, and cumulative disability. *New England Journal of Medicine, 338,* 1035–1041. (p. 121)

Vitello, P. (2006, June 12). A ring tone meant to fall on deaf ears. *New York Times* (www.nytimes.com). (p. 210)

Vitiello, M. V. (2009). Recent advances in understanding sleep and sleep disturbances in older adults: Growing older does not mean sleeping poorly. *Current Directions in Psychological Science, 18,* 316–320. (p. 103)

Vitória, P. D., Salgueiro, M. F., Silva, S. A., & De Vries, H. (2009). The impact of social influence on adolescent intention to smoke: Combining types and referents of influence. *British Journal of Health Psychology, 14,* 681–699. (p. 128)

Vittengl, J. R., Clark, L. A., Dunn, T. W., & Jarrett, R. B. (2007). Reducing relapse and recurrence in unipolar depression: A comparative meta-analysis of cognitive-behavioral therapy's effects. *Journal of Consulting and Clinical Psychology, 75,* 475–488. (p. 706)

Voas, D. (2008, March/April). Ten million marriages: An astrological detective story. *Skeptical Inquirer,* pp. 52–55. (p. 550)

Vocks, S., Tuschen-Caffier, B., Pietrowsky, R., Rustenbach, S. J., Kersting, A., & Herpertz, S. (2010). Meta-analysis of the effectiveness of psychological and pharmacological treatments for binge eating disorder. *International Journal of Eating Disorders, 43,* 205–217. (p. 672)

Vogel, G. (2010). Long-fought compromise reached on European animal rules. *Science, 329,* 1588–1589. (p. 23)

Vogel, S. (1999). *The skinny on fat: Our obsession with weight control.* New York: W. H. Freeman. (p. 138)

Vohs, K. D., & Baumeister, R. F. (eds.) (2011). *Handbook of self-regulation, 2nd edition.* New York: Guilford. (p. 558)

Vohs, K. D., Mead, N. L., & Goode, M. R. (2006). The psychological consequences of money. *Science, 314,* 1154–1156. (p. 330)

Volkow, N. D., & 12 others. (2009). Evaluating dopamine reward pathway in ADHD: Clinical implications. *JAMA, 302,* 1084–1091. (p. 627)

von Békésy, G. (1957, August). The ear. *Scientific American,* pp. 66–78. (p. 261)

von Hippel, W. (2007). Aging, executive functioning, and social control. *Current Directions in Psychological Science, 16,* 240–244. (p. 211)

von Senden, M. (1932). *The perception of space and shape in the congenitally blind before and after operation.* Glencoe, IL: Free Press. (p. 250)

Vroom, V. H., & Jago, A. G. (2007). The role of the situation in leadership. *American Psychologist, 62,* 17–24. (p. 467)

VTTI. (2009, September). Driver distraction in commercial vehicle operations. Virginia Tech Transportation Institute and U.S. Department of Transportation. (p. 88)

Vul, E., Harris, C., Winkielman, P., & Pashler, H. (2009a). Puzzlingly high correlations in fMRI studies of emotion, personality, and social cognition. *Perspectives on Psychological Science, 4,* 274–290. (p. 62)

Vul, E., Harris, C., Winkielman, P., & Pashler, H. (2009b). Reply to comments on "Puzzlingly high correlations in fMRI studies of emotion, personality, and social cognition." *Perspectives on Psychological Science, 4,* 319–324. (p. 62)

Vuoksimaa, E., Kaprio, J., Kremen, W. S., Hokkanen, L., Viken, R. J., Tuulio-Henriksson, A., & Rose, R. J. (2010). Having a male co-twin masculinizes mental rotation performance in females. *Psychological Science, 21,* 1069–1071. (p. 447)

Vuoksimaa, E., Koskenvuo, M., Rose, R. J., & Kaprio, J. (2009). Origins of handedness: A nationwide study of 30,161 adults. *Neuropsychologia, 47,* 1294–1301. (p. 80)

Vyazovskiy, V. V., Cirelli, C., Pfister-Genskow, M., Faraguna, U., & Tononi, G. (2008). Molecular and electrophysiological evidence for net synaptic potentiation in wake and depression in sleep. *Nature Neuroscience, 11,* 200–208. (p. 98)

Waber, R. L., Shiv, B., Carmon, & Ariely, D. (2008). Commercial features of placebo and therapeutic efficacy. *Journal of the American Medical Association, 299,* 1016–1017. (p. 35)

Wacker, J., Chavanon, M.-L., & Stemmler, G. (2006). Investigating the dopaminergic basis of extraversion in humans: A multilevel approach. *Journal of Personality and Social Psychology, 91,* 177–187. (p. 548)

Wade, K. A., Garry, M., Read, J. D., & Lindsay, D. S. (2002). A picture is worth a thousand lies: Using false photographs to create false childhood memories. *Psychonomic Bulletin & Review, 9,* 597–603. (p. 342)

Wade, N. G., Worthington, E. L., Jr., & Vogel, D. L. (2006). Effectiveness of religiously tailored interventions in Christian therapy. *Psychotherapy Research, 17,* 91–105. (p. 700)

Wagar, B. M., & Cohen, D. (2003). Culture, memory, and the self: An analysis of the personal and collective self in long-term memory. *Journal of Experimental Social Psychology, 39,* 458–475. (p. 321)

Wagenmakers, E-J., Wetzels, R., Borsboom, D., & van der Maas, H. (2011). Why psychologists must change the way they analyze their data: The case of psi. *Journal of Personality and Social Psychology, 100,* 1–12. (p. 255)

Wager, T. D. (2005). The neural bases of placebo effects in pain. *Current Directions in Psychological Science, 14,* 175–179. (p. 266)

Wagner, A. (2010). Can neuroscience identify lies? In F. E. Bloom et al., *A judge's guide to neuroscience: A concise introduction.* Santa Barbara, CA: University of California, Santa Barbara. (p. 482)

Wagner, D. D., Cin, S. D., Sargent, J. C., Kelley, W. M., & Heatherton, T. F. (2011). Spontaneous action representation in smokers when watching movie characters smoke. *Journal of Neuroscience, 31,* 894–898. (p. 306)

Wagner, U., Gais, S., Haider, H., Verleger, R., & Born, J. (2004). Sleep inspires insight. *Nature, 427,* 352–355. (p. 99)

Wagstaff, G. (1982). Attitudes to rape: The "just world" strikes again? *Bulletin of the British Psychological Society, 13,* 275–283. (p. 573)

Wahlberg, D. (2001, October 11). We're more depressed, patriotic, poll finds. *Grand Rapids Press,* p. A15. (p. 505)

Wai, J., Cacchio, M., Putallaz, M., & Makel, M. C. (2010). Sex differences in the right tail of cognitive abilities: A 30 year examination. *Intelligence, 38,* 412–423. (p. 409)

Wai, J., Lubinski, D., & Benbow, C. P. (2005). Creativity and occupational accomplishments among intellectually precocious youths: An age 13 to age 33 longitudinal study. *Journal of Educational Psychology, 97,* 484–492. (p. 403)

Wakefield, J. C. (1992). Disorder as a harmful dysfunction: A conceptual critique of DSM-III-R's definition of mental disorder. *Psychological Review, 99,* 232–247. (p. 627)

Wakefield, J. C. (2006). What makes a mental disorder mental? *Philosophy, Psychiatry, and Psychology, 13,* 123–131. (p. 627)

Wakefield, J. C., & Spitzer, R. L. (2002). Lowered estimates—but of what? *Archives of General Psychiatry, 59,* 129–130. (p. 640)

Wakefield, J. C., Schmitz, M.F., First, M. B., & Horwitz, A. V. (2007). Extending the bereavement exclusion for major depression to other losses: Evidence from the National Comorbidity Survey. *Archives of General Psychiatry, 64,* 433–440. (p. 645)

Walker, E., Shapiro, D., Esterberg, M., & Trotman, H. (2010). Neurodevelopment and schizophrenia: Broadening the focus. *Current Directions in Psychological Science, 19,* 204–208. (pp. 660, 662)

Walker, M. P., & van der Helm, E. (2009). Overnight therapy? The role of sleep in emotional brain processing. *Psychological Bulletin, 135,* 731–748. (p. 101)

Walker, W. R., Skowronski, J. J., & Thompson, C. P. (2003). Life is pleasant—and memory helps to keep it that way! *Review of General Psychology, 7,* 203–210. (p. 218)

Walkup, J. T., & 12 others. (2008). Cognitive behavioral therapy, sertraline, or a combination in childhood anxiety. *New England Journal of Medicine, 359,* 2753–2766. (p. 706)

Wall, P. D. (2000). *Pain: The science of suffering.* New York: Columbia University Press. (p. 264)

Wallace, D. S., Paulson, R. M., Lord, C. G., & Bond, C. F., Jr. (2005). Which behaviors do attitudes predict? Meta-analyzing the effects of social pressure and perceived difficulty. *Review of General Psychology, 9(3),* 214–227. (p. 574)

Wallach, M. A., & Wallach, L. (1983). *Psychology's sanction for selfishness: The error of egoism in theory and therapy.* New York: Freeman. (p. 545)

Wallach, M. A., & Wallach, L. (1985, February). How psychology sanctions the cult of the self. *Washington Monthly,* pp. 46–56. (p. 545)

Walster (Hatfield), E., Aronson, V., Abrahams, D., & Rottman, L. (1966). Importance of physical attractiveness in dating behavior. *Journal of Personality and Social Psychology, 4,* 508–516. (p. 610)

Walters, R. G., & 94 others. (2010). A novel highly-penetrant form of obesity due to deletions on chromosome 16p11.2. *Nature, 463,* 671–675. (p. 430)

Walton, G. M., & Spencer S. J. (2009). Latent ability: Grades and test scores systematically underestimate the intellectual ability of negatively stereotyped students. *Psychological Science, 20,* 1132–1139. (p. 414)

Wampold, B. E. (2001). *The great psychotherapy debate: Models, methods, and findings.* Mahwah, NJ: Erlbaum. (pp. 698, 699)

Wampold, B. E. (2007). Psychotherapy: The humanistic (and effective) treatment. *American Psychologist, 62,* 857–873. (pp. 695, 698)

Wampold, B. E., Mondin, G. W., Moody, M., & Ahn, H. (1997). The flat earth as a metaphor for the evidence for uniform efficacy of bona fide psychotherapies: Reply to Crits-Christoph (1997) and Howard et al. (1997). *Psychological Bulletin, 122,* 226–230. (p. 695)

Wang, K-S., Liu, X-F., & Aragam, N. (2010). A genome-wide meta-analysis identified novel loci associated with schizophrenia and bipolar disorder. *Schizophrenia Research, 124,* 192–199. (p. 662)

Wang, Q., Bowling, N. A., & Eschleman, K. J. (2010). A meta-analytic examination of work and general locus of control. *Journal of Applied Psychology, 95,* 761–768. (p. 558)

Wang, S-H., Baillargeon, R., & Brueckner, L. (2004). Young infants' reasoning about hidden objects: Evidence from violation-of-expectation tasks with test trials only. *Cognition, 93,* 167–198. (p. 181)

Wansink, B. (2007). *Mindless eating: Why we eat more than we think.* New York: Bantam Dell). (p. 426)

Wansink, B., van Ittersum, K., & Painter, J. E. (2006). Ice cream illusions: Bowls, spoons, and self-served portion sizes. *American Journal of Preventive Medicine, 31,* 240–243. (p. 426)

Ward, A., & Mann, T. (2000). Don't mind if I do: Disinhibited eating under cognitive load. *Journal of Personality and Social Psychology, 78,* 753–763. (p. 433)

Ward, C. (1994). Culture and altered states of consciousness. In W. J. Lonner & R. Malpass (Eds.), *Psychology and culture.* Boston: Allyn & Bacon. (p. 115)

Ward, J. (2003). State of the art synaesthesia. *The Psychologist, 16,* 196–199. (p. 269)

Ward, K. D., Klesges, R. C., & Halpern, M. T. (1997). Predictors of smoking cessation and state-of-the-art smoking interventions. *Journal of Socies Issues, 53,* 129–145. (p. 121)

Ward, L. M., & Friedman, K. (2006). Using TV as a guide: Associations between television viewing and adolescents' sexual attitudes and behavior. *Journal of Research on Adolescence, 16,* 133–156. (p. 440)

Wardle, J., Cooke, L. J., Gibson, L., Sapochnik, M., Sheiham, A., & Lawson, M. (2003). Increasing children's acceptance of vegetables: A randomized trial of parent-led exposure. *Appetite, 40,* 155–162. (p. 267)

Wargo, E. (2007, December). Understanding the have-knots. *APS Observer,* pp. 18–21. (p. 524)

Wason, P. C. (1960). On the failure to eliminate hypotheses in a conceptual task. *Quarterly Journal of Experimental Psychology, 12,* 129–140. (p. 353)

Wason, P. C. (1981). The importance of cognitive illusions. *The Behavioral and Brain Sciences, 4,* 356. (p. 354)

Wasserman, E. A. (1993). Comparative cognition: Toward a general understanding of cognition in behavior. *Psychological Science, 4,* 156–161. (p. 287)

Wasserman, E. A. (1995). The conceptual abilities of pigeons. *American Scientist, 83,* 246–255. (p. 362)

Wastell, C. A. (2002). Exposure to trauma: The long-term effects of suppressing emotional reactions. *Journal of Nervous and Mental Disorders, 190,* 839–845. (p. 521)

Waterhouse, R. (1993, July 19). Income for 62 percent is below average pay. *The Independent,* p. 4. (p. 39)

Waterman, A. S. (1988). Identity status theory and Erikson's theory: Commonalities and differences. *Developmental Review, 8,* 185–208. (p. 204)

Watkins, E. R. (2008). Constructive and unconstructive repetitive thought. *Psychological Bulletin, 134,* 163–206. (p. 645)

Watkins, J. G. (1984). The Bianchi (L. A. Hillside Strangler) case: Sociopath or multiple personality? *International Journal of Clinical and Experimental Hypnosis, 32,* 67–101. (p. 666)

Watson, D. (2000). *Mood and temperament.* New York: Guilford Press. (pp. 496, 522)

Watson, D., Wiese, D., Vaidya, J., & Tellegen, A. (1999). The two general activation systems of affect: Structured findings, evolutionary considerations, and psychobiological evidence. *Journal of Personality and Social Psychology, 76,* 820–838. (p. 492)

Watson, J. B. (1913). Psychology as the behaviorist views it. *Psychological Review, 20,* 158–177. (pp. 84, 278, 284)

Watson, J. B. (1924). The unverbalized in human behavior. *Psychological Review, 31,* 339–347. (p. 284)

Watson, J. B., & Rayner, R. (1920). Conditioned emotional reactions. *Journal of Experimental Psychology, 3,* 1–14. (p. 284)

Watson, R. I., Jr. (1973). Investigation into deindividuation using a cross-cultural survey technique. *Journal of Personality and Social Psychology, 25,* 342–345. (p. 588)

Watson, S. J., Benson, J. A., Jr., & Joy, J. E. (2000). NEWS AND VIEWS—Marijuana and medicine: Assessing the science base: A summary of the 1999 Institute of Medicine report. *Archives of General Psychiatry, 57,* 547–553. (p. 124)

Watters, E. (2010). *Crazy like us: The globalization of the American psyche.* New York: Free Press. (p. 629)

Wayment, H. A., & Peplau, L. A. (1995). Social support and well-being among lesbian and heterosexual women: A structural modeling approach. *Personality and Social Psychology Bulletin, 21,* 1189–1199. (p. 216)

Weaver, J. B., Masland, J. L., & Zillmann, D. (1984). Effect of erotica on young men's aesthetic perception of their female sexual partners. *Perceptual and Motor Skills, 58,* 929–930. (p. 438)

Webb, W. B. (1992). *Sleep: The gentle tyrant.* Bolton, MA: Anker. (p. 103)

Webb, W. B., & Campbell, S. S. (1983). Relationships in sleep characteristics of identical and fraternal twins. *Archives of General Psychiatry, 40,* 1093–1095. (p. 97)

Webley, K. (2009, June 15). Behind the drop in Chinese adoptions. *Time,* p. 55. (p. 595)

Webster, G. D., Jonason, P. K., & Schember, T. O. (2009). Hot topics and popular papers in evolutionary psychology: Analyses of title words and citation counts in *Evolution and Human Behavior,* 1979–2008. *Evolutionary Psychology, 7,* 348–362. (p. 144)

Wechsler, D. (1972). "Hold" and "Don't Hold" tests. In S. M. Chown (Ed.), *Human aging.* New York: Penguin. (p. 398)

Wegman, H. L., & Stetler, C. (2009). A meta-analytic review of the effects of childhood abuse on medical outcomes in adulthood. *Psychosomatic Medicine, 71,* 805–812. (p. 192)

Wegner, D. M. (2002). *The illusion of conscious will.* Cambridge, MA: MIT Press. (p. 82)

Weinberger, D. R. (2001, March 10). A brain too young for good judgment. *New York Times* (www.nytimes.com). (p. 199)

Weingarten, G. (2002, March 10). Below the beltway. *Washington Post,* p. WO3. (p. 457)

Weinstein, N. D. (1980). Unrealistic optimism about future life events. *Journal of Personality and Social Psychology, 39,* 806–820. (p. 560)

Weinstein, N. D. (1982). Unrealistic optimism about susceptibility to health problems. *Journal of Behavioral Medicine, 5,* 441–460. (p. 560)

Weinstein, N. D. (1996, October 4). 1996 optimistic bias bibliography. (weinstein_c@aesop.rutgers.edu). (p. 560)

Weir, W. (2010, May 17). Middletown man, age 76, has memorized epic poem "Paradise Lost." *Hartford Courant* (www.courant.com). (p. 214)

Weis, R., & Cerankosky, B. C. (2010). Effects of video-game ownership on young boys' academic and behavioral functioning: A randomized, controlled study. *Psychological Science, 21,* 463–470. (p. 606)

Weis, S., & Süß, H-M. (2007). Reviving the search for social intelligence: A multitrait-multimethod study of its structure and construct validity. *Personality and Individual Differences, 42,* 3–14. (p. 389)

Weisbuch, M., Ivcevic, Z., & Ambady, N. (2009). On being liked on the web and in the "real world": Consistency in first impressions across personal webpages and spontaneous behavior. *Journal of Experimental Social Psychology, 45,* 573–576. (p. 454)

Weiskrantz, L. (2009). *Blindsight.* Oxford: Oxford University Press. (p. 86)

Weiskrantz, L. (2010). Blindsight in hindsight. *The Psychologist, 23,* 356–358. (p. 86)

Weiss, A., Gale, C. R., Batty, G. D., & Deary, I. J. (2009). Emotionally stable, intelligent men live longer: The Vietnam experience study cohort. *Psychosomatic Medicine, 71,* 385–394. (p. 402)

Weiss, A., King, J. E., & Enns, R. M. (2002). Subjective well-being is heritable and genetically correlated with dominance in chimpanzees (Pan troglodytes). *Journal of Personality and Social Psychology, 83,* 1141–1149. (p. 501)

Weiss, A., King, J. E., & Figueredo, A. J. (2000). The heritability of personality factors in chimpanzees (Pan troglodytes). *Behavior Genetics, 30,* 213–221. (p. 501)

Weiss, A., King, J. E., & Perkins, L. (2006). Personality and subjective well-being in orangutans *(Pongo pygmaeus* and *Pongo abelii). Journal of Personality and Social Psychology, 90,* 501–511. (p. 549)

Weiss, J. M. (1977). Psychological and behavioral influences on gastrointestinal lesions in animal models. In J. D. Maser & M. E. P. Seligman (Eds.), *Psychopathology: Experimental models.* San Francisco: Freeman. (p. 517)

Welch, J. M., Lu, J., Rodriquiz, R. M., Trotta, N. C., Peca, J., Ding, J.-D., Feliciano, C., Chen, M., Adams, J. P., Luo, J., Dudek, S. M., Weinberg, R. J., Calakos, N., Wetsel, W. C., & Feng, G. (2007). Cortico-striatal synaptic defects and OCD-like behaviours in *Sapap3*-mutant mice. *Nature, 448,* 894–900. (p. 643)

Welch, W. W. (2005, February 28). Trauma of Iraq war haunting thousands returning home. *USA Today* (www.usatoday.com). (p. 639)

Weller, S., & Davis-Beaty, K. (2002). The effectiveness of male condoms in prevention of sexually transmitted diseases (protocol). *Cochrane Database of Systematic Reviews,* Issue 4, Art. No. CD004090. (p. 441)

Wellings, K., Collumbien, M., Slaymaker, E., Singh, S., Hodges, Z., Patel, D., & Bajos, N. (2006). Sexual behaviour in context: A global perspective. *Lancet, 368,* 1706–1728. (p. 439)

Wellman, H. M., & Gelman, S. A. (1992). Cognitive development: Foundational theories of core domains. *Annual Review of Psychology, 43,* 337–375. (p. 181)

Wells, B. L. (1986). Predictors of female nocturnal orgasms: A multivariate analysis. *Journal of Sex Research, 22,* 421–437. (p. 439)

Wells, D. L. (2009). The effects of animals on human health and well-being. *Journal of Social Issues, 65,* 523–543. (p. 520)

Wells, G. L. (1981). Lay analyses of causal forces on behavior. In J. Harvey (Ed.), *Cognition, social behavior and the environment.* Hillsdale, NJ: Erlbaum. (p. 276)

Wender, P. H., Kety, S. S., Rosenthal, D., Schulsinger, F., Ortmann, J., & Lunde, I. (1986). Psychiatric disorders in the biological and adoptive families of adopted individuals with affective disorders. *Archives of General Psychiatry, 43,* 923–929. (p. 649)

Westen, D. (1996). Is Freud really dead? Teaching psychodynamic theory to introductory psychology. Presentation to the Annual Institute on the Teaching of Psychology, St. Petersburg Beach, FL. (p. 538)

Westen, D. (1998). The scientific legacy of Sigmund Freud: Toward a psychodynamically informed psychological science. *Psychological Bulletin, 124,* 333–371. (p. 539)

Westen, D. (2007). *The political brain: The role of emotion in deciding the fate of the nation.* New York: PublicAffairs. (p. 478)

Westen, D., & Morrison, K. (2001). A multidimensional meta-analysis of treatments for depression, panic, and generalized anxiety disorder: An empirical examination of the status of empirically supported therapies. *Journal of Consulting and Clinical Psychology, 69,* 875–899. (p. 695)

Whalen, P. J., Kagan, J., Cook, R. G., Davis, F. C., Kim, H., Polis, S., McLaren, D. G., Somerville, L. H., McLean, A. A., Maxwell, J. S., & Johnstone, T. (2004). Human amygdala responsibility to masked fearful eye whites. *Science, 302,* 2061. (pp. 476, 477)

Whalen, P. J., Shin, L. M., McInerney, S. C., Fisher, H., Wright, C. I., & Rauch, S. L. (2001). A functional MRI study of human amygdala responses to facial expressions of fear versus anger. *Emotion, 1,* 70–83. (p. 480)

Whaley, S. E., Sigman, M., Beckwith, L., Cohen, S. E., & Espinosa, M. P. (2002). Infant-caregiver interaction in Kenya and the United States: The importance of multiple caregivers and adequate comparison samples. *Journal of Cross-Cultural Psychology, 33,* 236–247. (p. 193)

Whalley, L. J., & Deary, I. J. (2001). Longitudinal cohort study of childhood IQ and survival up to age 76. *British Medical Journal, 322,* 1–5. (p. 402)

Whalley, L. J., Starr, J. M., Athawes, R., Hunter, D., Pattie, A., & Deary, I. J. (2000). Childhood mental ability and dementia. *Neurology, 55,* 1455–1459. (p. 401)

Whang, W., Kubzansky, L, D., Kawachi, I., Rexrode, K. M., Kroenke, C. H., Glynn, R. J., Garan, H., & Albert, C. M. (2009). Depression and risk of sudden cardiac death and coronary heart disease in women. *Journal of the American College of Cardiology, 53,* 950–958. (p. 514)

Wheelwright, J. (2004, August). Study the clones first. *Discover,* pp. 44–50. (p. 135)

Whetten, K., Ostermann J., Whetten R.A., Pence B.W., O'Donnell K., Messer L.C., Thielman N.M., & The Positive Outcomes for Orphans (POFO) Research Team. (2009, December 18). A comparison of the wellbeing of orphans and abandoned children ages 6–12 in institutional and community-based care settings in 5 less wealthy nations.." *PLoS ONE* 4.12: e8169. (p. 193)

White, G. L., & Kight, T. D. (1984). Misattribution of arousal and attraction: Effects of salience of explanations for arousal. *Journal of Experimental Social Psychology, 20,* 55–64. (p. 613)

White, H. R., Brick, J., & Hansell, S. (1993). A longitudinal investigation of alcohol use and aggression in adolescence. *Journal of Studies on Alcohol,* Supplement No. 11, 62–77. (p. 601)

White, L., & Edwards, J. (1990). Emptying the nest and parental well-being: An analysis of national panel data. *American Sociological Review, 55,* 235–242. (p. 217)

White, R. A. (1998). Intuition, heart knowledge, and parapsychology. *Journal of the American Society for Psychical Research, 92,* 158–171. (p. 254)

Whitehead, B. D., & Popenoe, D. (2001). *The state of our unions 2001: The social health of marriage in America.* Rutgers University: The National Marriage Project. (p. 216)

Whiten, A., & Boesch, C. (2001, January). Cultures of chimpanzees. *Scientific American,* pp. 60–67. (p. 362)

Whiten, A., & Byrne, R. W. (1988). Tactical deception in primates. *Behavioral and Brain Sciences, 11,* 233–244, 267–273. (p. 28)

Whiten, A., Spiteri, A., Horner, V., Bonnie, K. E., Lambeth, S. P., Schapiro, S. J., & de Waal, F. B. M. (2007). Transmission of multiple traditions within and between chimpanzee groups. *Current Biology, 17,* 1038–1043. (p. 305)

Whiting, B. B., & Edwards, C. P. (1988). *Children of different worlds: The formation of social behavior.* Cambridge, MA: Harvard University Press. (p. 156)

Whitley, B. E., Jr. (1990). The relationships of heterosexuals' attributions for the causes of homosexuality to attitudes toward lesbians and gay men. *Personality and Social Psychology Bulletin, 16,* 369–377. (p. 448)

Whitley, B. E., Jr. (1999). Right-wing authoritarianism, social dominance orientation, and prejudice. *Journal of Personality and Social Psychology, 77,* 126–134. (p. 597)

Whitlock, J. R., Heynen, A. L., Shuler, M. G., & Bear, M. F. (2006). Learning induces long-term potentiation in the hippocampus. *Science, 313,* 1093–1097. (p. 327)

Whitmer, R. A., Gustafson, D. R., Barrett-Connor, E. B., Haan, M. N., Gunderson, E. P., & Yaffe, K. (2008). Central obesity and increased risk of dementia more than three decades later. *Neurology, 71,* 1057–1064. (p. 428)

WHO. (1979). *Schizophrenia: An international followup study.* Chicester, England: Wiley. (p. 659)

WHO. (2000). *Effectiveness of male latex condoms in protecting against pregnancy and sexually transmitted infections.* World Health Organization (www.who.int). (p. 441)

WHO. (2002). *The global burden of disease.* Geneva: World Health Organization (www.who.int/msa/mnh/ems/dalys/intro.htm). (p. 645)

WHO. (2003). *The male latex condom: Specification and guidelines for condom procurement.* Department of Reproductive Health and Research, Family and Community Health, World Health Organization. (p. 441)

WHO. (2004a). Prevalence, severity, and unmet need for treatment of mental disorders in the World Health Organization World Mental Health Surveys. *Journal of the American Medical Association, 291,* 2581–2590. (pp. 634, 653)

WHO. (2008). *Mental health (nearly 1 million annual suicide deaths).* Geneva: World Health Organization (www.who.int/mental_health/en). (p. 650)

WHO. (2008). *WHO report on the global tobacco epidemic, 2008.* Geneva: World Health Organization (www.who.int). (p. 119)

WHO. (2010, September). Mental health: Strengthening our response. Fact sheet N°220. Retrieved online at www.who.int/mediacentre/factsheets/fs220/en/. (p. 625)

WHO. (2011). Country reports and charts available. Geneva: World Health Organization (int/mental_health/prevention/suicide/country_reports/en/index.html). (p. 650)

WHO. (2011). *Schizophrenia.* Geneva: World Health Organization (www.who.int). (p. 657)

Whooley, M. A., & 11 others. (2008). Depressive symptoms, health behaviors, and risk of cardiovascular events in patients with coronary heart disease. *JAMA, 300,* 2379–2388. (p. 514)

Whorf, B. L. (1956). Science and linguistics. In J. B. Carroll (Ed.), *Language, thought, and reality: Selected writings of Benjamin Lee Whorf.* Cambridge, MA: MIT Press. (p. 375)

Wicherts, J. M., Dolan, C. V., Carlson, J. S., & van der Maas, H. L. J. (2010). Raven's test performance of sub-Saharan Africans: Mean level, psychometric properties, and the Flynn Effect. *Learning and Individual Differences, 20,* 135–151. (p. 412)

Wickelgren, I. (2009, September/October). I do not feel your pain. *Scientific American Mind,* pp. 51–57. (pp. 263, 270)

Wickelgren, W. A. (1977). *Learning and memory.* Englewood Cliffs, NJ: Prentice-Hall. (p. 321)

Wielkiewicz, R. M., & Stelzner, S. P. (2005). An ecological perspective on leadership theory, research, and practice. *Review of General Psychology, 9,* 326–341. (p. 467)

Wiens, A. N., & Menustik, C. E. (1983). Treatment outcome and patient characteristics in an aversion therapy program for alcoholism. *American Psychologist, 38,* 1089–1096. (p. 683)

Wierson, M., & Forehand, R. (1994). Parent behavioral training for child noncompliance: Rationale, concepts, and effectiveness. *Current Directions in Psychological Science, 3,* 146–149. (p. 295)

Wierzbicki, M. (1993). Psychological adjustment of adoptees: A meta-analysis. *Journal of Clinical Child Psychology, 22,* 447–454. (p. 137)

Wiesel, T. N. (1982). Postnatal development of the visual cortex and the influence of environment. *Nature, 299,* 583–591. (p. 251)

Wiesner, W. H., & Cronshow, S. P. (1988). A meta-analytic investigation of the impact of interview format and degree of structure on the validity of the employment interview. *Journal of Occupational Psychology, 61,* 275–290. (p. 461)

Wigdor, A. K., & Garner, W. R. (1982). *Ability testing: Uses, consequences, and controversies.* Washington, DC: National Academy Press. (p. 413)

Wike, R., & Grim, B. J. (2007, October 30). Widespread negativity: Muslims distrust Westerners more than vice versa. *Pew Research Center* (www.pewresearch.org). (p. 594)

Wilcox, A. J., Baird, D. D., Dunson, D. B., McConnaughey, D. R., Kesner, J. S., & Weinberg, C. R. (2004). On the frequency of intercourse around ovulation: Evidence for biological influences. *Human Reproduction, 19,* 1539–1543. (p. 436)

Wilder, D. A. (1981). Perceiving persons as a group: Categorization and intergroup relations. In D. L. Hamilton (Ed.), *Cognitive processes in stereotyping and intergroup behavior.* Hillsdale, NJ: Erlbaum. (p. 597)

Wildman, D. E., Uddin, M., Liu, G., Grossman, L. I., & Goodman, M. (2003). Implications of natural selection in shaping 99.4% nonsynonymous DNA identity between humans and chimpanzees: Enlarging genus Homo. *Proceedings of the National Academy of Sciences, 100,* 7181–7188. (p. 132)

Wilford, J. N. (1999, February 9). New findings help balance the cosmological books. *New York Times* (www.nytimes.com). (p. 165)

Wilkinson, P., & Goodyer, I. (2011). Non-suicidal self-injury. *European Child & Adolescent Psychiatry, 20*, 103–108. (p. 651)

Williams, C. L., & Berry, J. W. (1991). Primary prevention of acculturative stress among refugees. *American Psychologist, 46*, 632–641. (p. 506)

Williams, J. E., & Best, D. L. (1990). *Measuring sex stereotypes: A multination study.* Newbury Park, CA: Sage. (p. 158)

Williams, J. E., Paton, C. C., Siegler, I. C., Eigenbrodt, M. L., Nieto, F. J., & Tyroler, H. A. (2000). Anger proneness predicts coronary heart disease risk: Prospective analysis from the artherosclerosis risk in communities (ARIC) study. *Circulation, 101*(17), 2034–2040. (p. 513)

Williams, J. H. G., Waister, G. D., Gilchrist, A., Perrett, D. I., Murray, A. D., & Whiten, A. (2006). Neural mechanisms of imitation and 'mirror neuron' functioning in autistic spectrum disorder. *Neuropsychogia, 44*, 610–621. (p. 218)

Williams, K. D. (2007). Ostracism. *Annual Review of Psychology, 58*, 425–452. (pp. 451, 452)

Williams, K. D. (2009). Ostracism: A temporal need-threat model. *Advances in Experimental Social Psychology, 41*, 275–313. (p. 451)

Williams, K. D., & Zadro, L. (2001). Ostracism: On being ignored, excluded and rejected. In M. Leary (Ed.), *Rejection*. New York: Oxford University Press. (p. 451)

Williams, L. A., & DeSteno, D. (2009). Adaptive social emotion or seventh sin? *Psychological Science, 20*, 284–288. (p. 566)

Williams, L. E., & Bargh, J. A. (2008). Experiencing physical warmth promotes interpersonal warmth. *Science, 322*, 606–607. (p. 268)

Williams, N. M., & 13 others. (2010). Rare chromosomal deletions and duplications in attention-deficit hyperactivity disorder: A genome-wide analysis. *Lancet, 376*, 1401–1408. (p. 627)

Williams, S. L. (1987). Self-efficacy and mastery-oriented treatment for severe phobias. Paper presented to the American Psychological Association convention. (p. 682)

Willingham, D. T. (2010, Summer). Have technology and multitasking rewired how students learn? *American Educator*, pp. 23–28, 42. (pp. 318, 455)

Willingham, W. W., Lewis, C., Morgan, R., & Ramist, L. (1990). *Predicting college grades: An analysis of institutional trends over two decades.* Princeton, NJ: Educational Testing Service. (p. 397)

Willis, J., & Todorov, A. (2006). First impressions: Making up your mind after a 100-ms. exposure to a face. *Psychological Science, 17*, 592–598. (p. 484)

Willmuth, M. E. (1987). Sexuality after spinal cord injury: A critical review. *Clinical Psychology Review, 7*, 389–412. (p. 438)

Wilson, A. E., & Ross, M. (2001). From chump to champ: People's appraisals of their earlier and present selves. *Journal of Personality and Social Psychology, 80*, 572–584. (p. 568)

Wilson, D. (2011, June 22). U.S. releases graphic images to deter smokers. *New York Times* (www.nytimes.com). (p. 356)

Wilson, R. S. (1979). Analysis of longitudinal twin data: Basic model and applications to physical growth measures. *Acta Geneticae medicae et Gemellologiae, 28*, 93–105. (p. 178)

Wilson, R. S., Arnold, S. E., Schneider, J. A., Tang, Y., & Bennett, D. A. (2007). The relationship between cerebral Alzheimer's disease pathology and odour identification in old age. *Journal of Neurology, Neurosurgery, and Psychiatry, 78*, 30–35. (p. 212)

Wilson, R. S., Beck, T. L., Bienias, J. L., & Bennett, D. A. (2007). Terminal cognitive decline: Accelerated loss of cognition in the last years of life. *Psychosomatic Medicine, 69*, 131–137. (p. 214)

Wilson, R. S., & Matheny, A. P., Jr. (1986). Behavior-genetics research in infant temperament: The Louisville twin study. In R. Plomin & J. Dunn (Eds.), *The study of temperament: Changes, continuities, and challenges.* Hillsdale, NJ: Erlbaum. (p. 137)

Wilson, T. D. (2002). *Strangers to ourselves: Discovering the adaptive unconscious.* Cambridge, MA: Harvard University Press. (p. 88)

Wilson, T. D. (2006). The power of social psychological interventions. *Science, 313*, 1251–1252. (p. 414)

Wilson, W. A., & Kuhn, C. M. (2005). How addiction hijacks our reward system. *Cerebrum, 7*(2), 53–66. (p. 127)

Windholz, G. (1989, April-June). The discovery of the principles of reinforcement, extinction, generalization, and differentiation of conditional reflexes in Pavlov's laboratories. *Pavlovian Journal of Biological Science, 26*, 64–74. (p. 282)

Windholz, G. (1997). Ivan P. Pavlov: An overview of his life and psychological work. *American Psychologist, 52*, 941–946. (p. 280)

Windle, G., Hughes, D., Linck, P., Russell, I., & Woods, B. (2010). Is exercise effective in promoting mental well-being in older age? A systematic review. *Aging and Mental Health, 14*, 652–669. (p. 522)

Wingfield, A., McCoy, S. L., Peelle, J. E., Tun, P.A., & Cox, L. C. (2005). Effects of adult aging and hearing loss on comprehension of rapid speech varying in syntactic complexity. *Journal of the American Academy of Audiology, 17*, 487–497. (p. 371)

Winner, E. (2000). The origins and ends of giftedness. *American Psychologist, 55*, 159–169. (p. 403)

Winter, W. C., Hammond, W. R., Green, N. H., Zhang, Z., & Bilwise, D. L. (2009). Measuring circadian advantage in major league baseball: A 10-year retrospective study. *Internal Journal of Sports Physiology and Performance, 4*, 394–401. (p. 98)

Wirth, J. H., & Bodenhausen, G. V. (2009). The role of gender in mental-illness stigma. *Psychological Science, 20*, 169–173. (p. 632)

Wirz-Justice, A. (2009). From the basic neuroscience of circadian clock function to light therapy for depression: On the emergence of chronotherapeutics. *Journal of Affective Disorders, 116*, 159–160. (pp. 97, 698)

Witelson, S. F., Kigar, D. L., & Harvey, T. (1999). The exceptional brain of Albert Einstein. *Lancet, 353*, 2149–2153. (pp. 74, 390)

Witt, J. K., & Proffitt, D. R. (2005). See the ball, hit the ball: Apparent ball size is correlated with batting average. *Psychological Science, 16*, 937–938. (p. 232)

Witvliet, C. V. O., Ludwig, T., & Vander Laan, K. (2001). Granting forgiveness or harboring grudges: Implications for emotions, physiology, and health. *Psychological Science, 12*, 117–123. (p. 495)

Witvliet, C. V. O., & Vrana, S. R. (1995). Psychophysiological responses as indices of affective dimensions. *Psychophysiology, 32*, 436–443. (p. 480)

Wixted, J. T., & Ebbesen, E. B. (1991). On the form of forgetting. *Psychological Science, 2*, 409–415. (p. 336)

Wolak, J., Mitchell, K., & Finkelhor, D. (2007). Unwanted and wanted exposure to online pornography in a national sample of youth Internet users. *Pediatrics, 119*, 247–257. (p. 603)

Wolfson, A. R., & Carskadon, M. A. (1998). Sleep schedules and daytime functioning in adolescents. *Child Development, 69*, 875–887. (p. 107)

Wolitzky-Taylor, K. B., Horowitz, J. D., Powers, M. B., & Telch, M. J. (2008). Psychological approaches in the treatment of specific phobias: A meta-analysis. *Clinical Psychology Review, 28*, 1021–1037. (p. 682)

Woll, S. (1986). So many to choose from: Decision strategies in videodating. *Journal of Social and Personal Relationships, 3*, 43–52. (p. 610)

Wolpe, J. (1958). *Psychotherapy by reciprocal inhibition.* Stanford, CA: Stanford University Press. (p. 682)

Wolpe, J., & Plaud, J. J. (1997). Pavlov's contributions to behavior therapy: The obvious and the not so obvious. *American Psychologist, 52*, 966–972. (p. 682)

Wonderlich, S. A., Joiner, T. E., Jr., Keel, P. K., Williamson, D. A., & Crosby, R. D. (2007). Eating disorder diagnoses: Empirical approaches to classification. *American Psychologist, 62*, 167–180. (p. 670)

Wong, D. F., Wagner, H. N., Tune, L. E., Dannals, R. F., et al. (1986). Positron emission tomography reveals elevated D_2 dopamine receptors in drug-naive schizophrenics. *Science, 234*, 1588–1593. (p. 659)

Wong, M. M., & Csikszentmihalyi, M. (1991). Affiliation motivation and daily experience: Some issues on gender differences. *Journal of Personality and Social Psychology, 60*, 154–164. (p. 158)

Wood, C. J, & Aggleton, J. P. (1989). Handedness in 'fast ball' sports: Do left-handers have an innate advantage? *British Journal of Psychology, 80*, 227–240. (p. 80)

Wood, D., Harms, P., & Vazire, S. (2010). Perceiver effects as projective tests: What your perceptions of others say about you. *Journal of Personality and Social Psychology, 99*, 174–190. (p. 541)

Wood, J. M. (2003, May 19). Quoted by R. Mestel, Rorschach tested: Blot out the famous method? Some experts say it has no place in psychiatry. *Los Angeles Times* (www.latimes.com). (p. 538)

Wood, J. M., Bootzin, R. R., Kihlstrom, J. F., & Schacter, D. L. (1992). Implicit and explicit memory for verbal information presented during sleep. *Psychological Science, 3*, 236–239. (p. 339)

Wood, J. M., Lilienfeld, S. O., Nezworski, M. T., Garb, H. N., Allen, K. H., & Wildermuth, J. L. (2010). Validity of Rorschach inkblot scores for discriminating psychopaths from nonpsychopaths in forensic populations: A meta-analysis. *Psychological Assessment, 22*, 336–349. (p. 538)

Wood, J. M., Nezworski, M. T., Garb, H. N., & Lilienfeld, S. O. (2006). The controversy over the Exner Comprehensive System and the Society for Personality Assessment's white paper on the Rorschach. *Independent Practitioner, 26*. (p. 538)

Wood, J. N., Glynn, D. D., Phillips, B. C., & Hauser, M. C. (2007). The perception of rational, goal-directed action in nonhuman primates. *Science, 317*, 1402–1405. (p. 363)

Wood, J. V., Heimpel, S. A., Manwell, L. A., & Whittington, E. J. (2009). This mood is familiar and I don't deserve to feel better anyway: Mechanisms underlying self-esteem differences in motivation to repair sad moods. *Journal of Personality and Social Psychology, 96,* 363–380. (p. 564)

Wood, J. V., Saltzberg, J. A., & Goldsamt, L. A. (1990a). Does affect induce self-focused attention? *Journal of Personality and Social Psychology, 58,* 899–908. (p. 653)

Wood, J. V., Saltzberg, J. A., Neale, J. M., Stone, A. A., & Rachmiel, T. B. (1990b). Self-focused attention, coping responses, and distressed mood in everyday life. *Journal of Personality and Social Psychology, 58,* 1027–1036. (p. 653)

Wood, W. (1987). Meta-analytic review of sex differences in group performance. *Psychological Bulletin, 102,* 53–71. (p. 158)

Wood, W., & Eagly, A. H. (2002). A cross-cultural analysis of the behavior of women and men: Implications for the origins of sex differences. *Psychological Bulletin, 128,* 699–727. (pp. 158, 164)

Wood, W., & Eagly, A. H. (2007). Social structural origins of sex differences in human mating. In S. W. Gagestad & J. A. Simpson (Eds.), *The evolution of mind: Fundamental questions and controversies.* New York: Guilford Press. (p. 158)

Wood, W., Lundgren, S., Ouellette, J. A., Busceme, S., & Blackstone, T. (1994). Minority influence: A meta-analytic review of social influence processes. *Psychological Bulletin, 115,* 323–345. (p. 591)

Wood, W., & Neal, D. T. (2007, October). A new look at habits and the habit-goal interface. *Psychological Review, 114,* 843–863. (p. 276)

Woods, N. F., Dery, G. K., & Most, A. (1983). Recollections of menarche, current menstrual attitudes, and premenstrual symptoms. In S. Golub (Ed.), *Menarche: The transition from girl to woman.* Lexington, MA: Lexington Books. (p. 198)

Woodward, B. (2002). *Bush at war.* New York: Simon & Schuster. (p. 15)

Woolcock, N. (2004, September 3). Driver thought everyone else was on wrong side. *The Times,* p. 22. (p. 581)

Woolley, A. W., Chabris, C. F., Pentland, A., Hasmi, N., & Malone, T. W. (2010). Evidence for a collective intelligence factor in the performance of human groups. *Science, 330,* 686–688. (p. 467)

World Federation for Mental Health. (2005). ADHD: The hope behind the hype (www.wfmh.org). (p. 627)

World Health Organization. (2004a). Prevalence, severity, and unmet need for treatment of mental disorders in the World Health Organization World Mental Health Surveys. *Journal of the American Medical Association, 291,* 2581–2590. (p. 653)

World Health Organization. (2004b). *Prevention of mental disorders: Effective interventions and policy options. Summary report.* Geneva: World Health Organization, Department of Mental Health and Substance Abuse. (p. 635)

World Health Organization. (2004c). *Promoting mental health: Concepts, emerging evidence, practice. Summary report.* Geneva: World Health Organization, Department of Mental Health and Substance Abuse. (p. 635)

World Health Organization. (2007). Obesity and overweight (www.who.int/dietphysicalactivity/publications/facts/obesity/en/). (p. 427)

World Health Organization. (2008). The numbers count: Mental disorders in America (www.nimh.nih.gov). (p. 115)

Worobey, J., & Blajda, V. M. (1989). Temperament ratings at 2 weeks, 2 months, and 1 year: Differential stability of activity and emotionality. *Developmental Psychology, 25,* 257–263. (p. 137)

Wortham, J. (2010, May 13). Cellphones now used more for data than for calls. *New York Times* (www.nytimes.com). (p. 453)

Worthington, E. L., Jr. (1989). Religious faith across the life span: Implications for counseling and research. *The Counseling Psychologist, 17,* 555–612. (p. 200)

Worthington, E. L., Jr., Kurusu, T. A., McCullogh, M. E., & Sandage, S. J. (1996). Empirical research on religion and psychotherapeutic processes and outcomes: A 10-year review and research prospectus. *Psychological Bulletin, 119,* 448–487. (p. 700)

Wortman, C. B., & Silver, R. C. (1989). The myths of coping with loss. *Journal of Consulting and Clinical Psychology, 57,* 349–357. (p. 220)

Wren, C. S. (1999, April 8). Drug survey of children finds middle school a pivotal time. *New York Times* (www.nytimes.com). (p. 128)

Wright, I. C., Rabe-Hesketh, S., Woodruff, P. W. R., David, A. S., Murray, R. M., & Bullmore, E. T. (2000). Meta-analysis of regional brain volumes in schizophrenia. *American Journal of Psychiatry, 157,* 16–25. (p. 660)

Wright, J. (2006, March 16). Boomers in the bedroom: Sexual attitudes and behaviours in the boomer generation. Ipsos Reid survey (www.ipsos-na.com). (p. 209)

Wright, P., Takei, N., Rifkin, L., & Murray, R. M. (1995). Maternal influenza, obstetric complications, and schizophrenia. *American Journal of Psychiatry, 152,* 1714–1720. (p. 661)

Wright, P. H. (1989). Gender differences in adults' same- and cross-gender friendships. In R. G. Adams & R. Blieszner (Eds.), *Older adult friendships: Structure and process.* Newbury Park, CA: Sage. (p. 159)

Wright, W. (1998). *Born that way: Genes, behavior, personality.* New York: Knopf. (p. 135)

Wrosch, C., & Miller, G. E. (2009). Depressive symptoms can be useful: Self-regulatory and emotional benefits of dysphoric mood in adolescence. *Journal of Personality and Social Psychology, 96,* 1181–1190. (p. 645)

Wrzesniewski, A., & Dutton, J. E. (2001). Crafting a job: Revisioning employees as active crafters of their work. *Academy of Management Review, 26,* 179–201. (p. 457)

Wrzesniewski, A., McCauley, C. R., Rozin, P., & Schwartz, B. (1997). Jobs, careers, and callings: People's relations to their work. *Journal of Research in Personality, 31,* 21–33. (p. 457)

Wu, W., & Small, S. A. (2006). Imaging the earliest stages of Alzheimer's disease. *Current Alzheimer Research, 3,* 529–539. (p. 213)

Wuethrich, B. (2001, March). Features—GETTING STUPID—Surprising new neurological behavioral research reveals that teenagers who drink too much may permanently damage their brains and seriously compromise their ability to learn. *Discover, 56,* 56–64. (p. 118)

Wulsin, L. R., Vaillant, G. E., & Wells, V. E. (1999). A systematic review of the mortality of depression. *Psychosomatic Medicine, 61,* 6–17. (p. 514)

Wyatt, J. K., & Bootzin, R. R. (1994). Cognitive processing and sleep: Implications for enhancing job performance. *Human Performance, 7,* 119–139. (pp. 106, 338)

Wyatt, R. J., Henter, I., & Sherman-Elvy, E. (2001). Tantalizing clues to preventing schizophrenia. *Cerebrum: The Dana Forum on Brain Science, 3,* pp. 15–30. (p. 661)

Wynn, K. (1992). Addition and subtraction by human infants. *Nature, 358,* 749–759. (p. 181)

Wynn, K. (2000). Findings of addition and subtraction in infants are robust and consistent: Reply to Wakeley, Rivera, and Langer. *Child Development, 71,* 1535–1536. (p. 181)

Wynne, C. D. L. (2004). *Do animals think?* Princeton, NJ: Princeton University Press. (p. 374)

Wynne, C. D. L. (2008). Aping language: A skeptical analysis of the evidence for nonhuman primate language. *Skeptic, 13*(4), 10–13. (p. 374)

Wysocki, C. J., & Gilbert, A. N. (1989). *National Geographic* Survey: Effects of age are heterogeneous. *Annals of the New York Academy of Sciences, 561,* 12–28. (p. 270)

Xu, Y., & Corkin, S. (2001). H.M. revisits the Tower of Hanoi puzzle. *Neuropsychology, 15,* 69–79. (p. 335)

Yaffe, K., Lindquist, K., Barnes, D., Covinsky, K. E., Neylan, T., Kluse, M., & Marmar, C. (2010). Posttraumatic stress disorder and risk of dementia among U.S. veterans. *Archives of General Psychiatry, 67,* 608–613. (p. 640)

Yalom, I. D. (1985). *The theory and practice of group psychotherapy* (3rd ed.). New York: Basic Books. (p. 689)

Yamagata, S., & 11 others. (2006). Is the genetic structure of human personality universal? A cross-cultural twin study from North America, Europe, and Asia. *Journal of Personality and Social Psychology, 90,* 987–998. (p. 552)

Yang, N., & Linz, D. (1990). Movie ratings and the content of adult videos: The sex-violence ratio. *Journal of Communication, 40*(2), 28–42. (p. 603)

Yang, S., Markoczy, L., & Qi, M. (2006). Unrealistic optimism in consumer credit card adoption. *Journal of Economic Psychology, 28,* 170–185. (p. 560)

Yankelovich Partners. (1995, May/June). Growing old. *American Enterprise,* p. 108. (p. 208)

Yarkoni, T. (2010). Personality in 100,000 words: A large-scale analysis of personality and word use among bloggers. *Journal of Research in Personality, 44,* 363–373. (p. 555)

Yarnell, P. R., & Lynch, S. (1970, April 25). Retrograde memory immediately after concussion. Lancet, pp. 863–865. (p. 327)

Yates, A. (1989). Current perspectives on the eating disorders: I. History, psychological and biological aspects. *Journal of the American Academy of Child and Adolescent Psychiatry, 28,* 813–828. (p. 671)

Yates, A. (1990). Current perspectives on the eating disorders: II. Treatment, outcome, and research directions. *Journal of the American Academy of Child and Adolescent Psychiatry, 29,* 1–9. (p. 671)

Yates, W. R. (2000). Testosterone in psychiatry. *Archives of General Psychiatry, 57,* 155–156. (p. 437)

Ybarra, O. (1999). Misanthropic person memory when the need to self-enhance is absent. *Personality and Social Psychology Bulletin, 25,* 261–269. (p. 565)

Yeung, J. W. K., Chan, Y, & Lee, B. L. K. (2009). Youth religiosity and substance use: A meta-analysis from 1995 to 2007. *Psychological Reports, 105,* 255–266. (p. 127)

Young, S. M., & Pinsky, D. (2006). Narcissism and celebrity. *Journal of Personality, 40*, 463–471. (p. 568)

Youngentob, S. L., & Glendinning, J. I. (2009). Fetal ethanol exposure increases ethanol intake by making it smell and taste better. *PNAS, 106*, 5359. (p. 174)

Youngentob, S. L., Kent, P. F., Scheehe, P. R., Molina, J. C., Spear, N. E., & Youngentob, L. M. (2007). Experience-induced fetal plasticity: The effect of gestational ethanol exposure on the behavioral and neurophysiologic olfactory response to ethanol odor in early postnatal and adult rats. *Behavioral Neuroscience, 121*, 1293–1305. (p. 174)

Younger, J., Aron, A., Parke, S., Chatterjee, N., & Mackey, S. (2010). Viewing Pictures of a Romantic Partner Reduces Experimental Pain: Involvement of Neural Reward Systems. *PLoS ONE* 5(10): e13309. doi:10.1371/journal.pone.0013309. (p. 452)

Yücel, M., Solowij, N., Respondek, C., Whittle, S., Fornito, A., Pantelis, C., & Lubman, D. I. (2008). Regional brain abnormalities associated with long-term cannabis use. *Archives of General Psychiatry, 65*, 694–701. (p. 124)

Yufik, T., & Simms, L. J. (2010). A meta-analytic investigation of the structure of posttraumatic stress disorder symptoms. *Journal of Abnormal Psychology, 119*, 764–776. (p. 640)

Yuki, M., Maddux, W. W., & Masuda. T. (2007). Are the windows to the soul the same in the East and West? Cultural differences in using the eyes and mouth as cues to recognize emotions in Japan and the United States. *Journal of Experimental Social Psychology, 43*, 303–311. (p. 489)

Zabin, L. S., Emerson, M. R., & Rowland, D. L. (2005). Child sexual abuse and early menarche: The direction of their relationship and its implications. *Journal of Adolescent Health, 36*, 393–400. (p. 198)

Zaccaro, S. J. (2007). Trait-based perspectives of leadership. *American Psychologist, 62*, 6–16. (p. 467)

Zadra, A., Pilon, M., & Montplairsir, J. (2008). Polysomnographic diagnosis of sleepwalking: Effects of sleep deprivation. *Annals of Neurology, 63*, 513–519. (p. 105)

Zagorsky, J. L. (2007). Do you have to be smart to be rich? The impact of IQ on wealth, income and financial distress. *Intelligence, 35*, 489–501. (p. 384)

Zajonc, R. B. (1965). Social facilitation. *Science, 149*, 269–274. (p. 587)

Zajonc, R. B. (1980). Feeling and thinking: Preferences need no inferences. *American Psychologist, 35*, 151–175. (p. 476)

Zajonc, R. B. (1984a). On the primacy of affect. *American Psychologist, 39*, 117–123. (p. 476)

Zajonc, R. B. (1984b, July 22). Quoted by D. Goleman, Rethinking IQ tests and their value. *The New York Times*, p. D22. (p. 393)

Zajonc, R. B. (1998). Emotions. In D. Gilbert, S. T. Fiske, & G. Lindzey (Eds.), *Handbook of social psychology* (4th ed.). New York: McGraw-Hill. (p. 609)

Zajonc, R. B. (2001). Mere exposure: A gateway to the subliminal. *Current Directions in Psychological Science, 10*, 224–228. (p. 608)

Zajonc, R. B., & Markus, G. B. (1975). Birth order and intellectual development. *Psychological Review, 82*, 74–88. (p. 42)

Zammit, S., Rasmussen, F., Farahmand, B., Gunnell, D., Lewis, G., Tynelius, P., & Brobert, G. P. (2007). Height and body mass index in young adulthood and risk of schizophrenia: A longitudinal study of 1,347,520 Swedish men. *Acta Psychiatrica Scandinavica, 116*, 378–385. (p. 658)

Zauberman, G., & Lynch, J. G., Jr. (2005). Resource slack and propensity to discount delayed investments of time versus money. *Journal of Experimental Psychology: General, 134*, 23–37. (p. 357)

Zeelenberg, R., Wagenmakers, E-J., & Rotteveel, M. (2006). The impact of emotion on perception. *Psychological Science, 17*, 287–291. (p. 476)

Zeidner, M. (1990). Perceptions of ethnic group modal intelligence: Reflections of cultural stereotypes or intelligence test scores? *Journal of Cross-Cultural Psychology, 21*, 214–231. (p. 411)

Zeidner, M., Roberts, R. D., & Matthews, G. (2008). The science of emotional intelligence: Current consensus and controversies. *European Psychologist, 13*, 64–78. (p. 389)

Zeineh, M. M., Engel, S. A., Thompson, P. M., & Bookheimer, S. Y. (2003). Dynamics of the hippocampus during encoding and retrieval of face-name pairs. *Science, 299*, 577–580. (p. 324)

Zell, E., & Alicke, M. D. (2010). The local dominance effect in self-evaluation: Evidence and explanations. *Personality and Social Psychology Review, 14*, 368–384. (p. 500)

Zhang, S., & Kline, S. L. (2009). Can I make my own decision? A cross-cultural study of perceived social network influence in mate selection. *Journal of Cross Cultural Psychology, 40*, 3–23. (p. 153)

Zhong, C-B., Dijksterhuis, A., & Galinsky, A. D. (2008). The merits of unconscious thought in creativity. *Psychological Science, 19*, 912–918. (p. 388)

Zhong, C-B., & Leonardelli, G. J. (2008). Cold and lonely: Does social exclusion literally feel cold? *Psychological Science, 19*, 838–842. (p. 268)

Zhu, W. X., Lu, L., & Hesketh, T. (2009). China's excess males, sex selective abortion, and one child policy: Analysis of data from 2005 national intercensus survey. *British Medical Journal (BMJ)*, 338, b1211. (p. 595)

Zietsch, B. P., Morley, K. I., Shekar, S. N., Verweij, K. J. H., Keller, M. C., Macgregor, S., Wright, M. J., Bailey, J. M., & Martin, N. G. (2008). Genetic factors predisposing to homosexuality may increase mating success in heterosexuals. *Evolution and Human Behavior, 29*, 424–433. (p. 446)

Zigler, E. F., & Styfco, S. J. (2001). Extended childhood intervention prepared children for school and beyond. *Journal of the American Medical Association, 285*, 2378–2380. (p. 408)

Zilbergeld, B. (1983). *The shrinking of America: Myths of psychological change.* Boston: Little, Brown. (pp. 692, 696)

Zillmann, D. (1986). Effects of prolonged consumption of pornography. Background paper for *The surgeon general's workshop on pornography and public health*, June 22–24. Report prepared by E. P. Mulvey & J. L. Haugaard and released by Office of the Surgeon General on August 4, 1986. (p. 476)

Zillmann, D. (1989). Effects of prolonged consumption of pornography. In D. Zillmann & J. Bryant (Eds.), *Pornography: Research advances and policy considerations.* Hillsdale, NJ: Erlbaum. (pp. 438, 603)

Zillmann, D., & Bryant, J. (1984). Effects of massive exposure to pornography. In N. Malamuth & E. Donnerstein (Eds.), *Pornography and sexual aggression.* Orlando, FL: Academic Press. (p. 604)

Zimbardo, P. G. (1970). The human choice: Individuation, reason, and order versus deindividuation, impulse, and chaos. In W. J. Arnold & D. Levine (Eds.), *Nebraska Symposium on Motivation, 1969.* Lincoln, NE: University of Nebraska Press. (p. 588)

Zimbardo, P. G. (1972, April). Pathology of imprisonment. *Transaction/Society*, pp. 4–8. (p. 575)

Zimbardo, P. G. (2001, September 16). Fighting terrorism by understanding man's capacity for evil. Op-ed essay distributed by spsp-discuss@stolaf.edu. (p. 597)

Zimbardo, P. G. (2004, May 25). *Journalist interview re: Abu Ghraib prison abuses: Eleven answers to eleven questions.* Unpublished manuscript, Stanford University. (p. 576)

Zimbardo, P. G. (2007, September). Person x situation x system dynamics. *The Observer* (Association for Psychological Science), p. 43. (p. 576)

Zimmer-Gembeck, M. J., & Helfand, M. (2008). Ten years of longitudinal research on U.S. adolescent sexual behavior: Developmental correlates of sexual intercourse, and the importance of age, gender and ethnic background. *Developmental Review, 28*, 153–224. (p. 439)

Zimmermann, T. D., & Meier, B. (2006). The rise and decline of prospective memory performance across the lifespan. *Quarterly Journal of Experimental Psychology, 59*, 2040–2046. (p. 214)

Zogby, J. (2006, March). Survey of teens and adults about the use of personal electronic devices and head phones. *Zogby International.* (p. 259)

Zou, Z., Li, F., & Buck, L. B. (2005). From the cover: Odor maps in the olfactory cortex. *Proceedings of the National Academy of Sciences, 102*, 7724–7729. (p. 270)

Zubieta, J-K., Bueller, J. A., Jackson, L. R., Scott, D. J., Xu, Y., Koeppe, R. A., Nichols, T. E., & Stohler, C. S. (2005). Placebo effects mediated by endogenous opioid activity on μ-opioid receptors. *Journal of Neuroscience, 25*, 7754–7762. (p. 266)

Zubieta, J-K., Heitzeg, M. M., Smith, Y. R., Bueller, J. A., Xu, K., Xu, Y., Koeppe, R. A., Stohler, C. S., & Goldman, D. (2003). COMT val158met genotype affects μ-opioid neurotransmitter responses to a pain stressor. *Science, 299*, 1240–1243. (p. 264)

Zucco, G. M. (2003). Anomalies in cognition: Olfactory memory. *European Psychologist, 8*, 77–86. (p. 270)

Zucker, G. S., & Weiner, B. (1993). Conservatism and perceptions of poverty: An attributional analysis. *Journal of Applied Social Psychology, 23*, 925–943. (p. 573)

Zuckerman, M. (1979). *Sensation seeking: Beyond the optimal level of arousal.* Hillsdale, NJ: Erlbaum. (p. 420)

Zvolensky, M. J., & Bernstein, A. (2005). Cigarette smoking and panic psychopathology. *Current Directions in Psychological Science, 14*, 301–305. (p. 638)

Name Index

Subject Index

The Story of Psychology: A Timeline *(continued from inside front cover)*

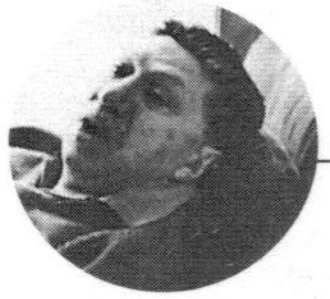

1949 In *The Organization of Behavior: A Neuropsychological Theory*, Canadian psychologist Donald O. Hebb outlines a new and influential conceptualization of how the nervous system functions.

1950 Solomon Asch publishes studies of effects of conformity on judgments of line length.

In *Childhood and Society,* Erik Erikson outlines his stages of psychosocial development.

1951 Carl Rogers publishes *Client-Centered Therapy.*

1952 The American Psychiatric Association publishes the *Diagnostic and Statistical Manual of Mental Disorders,* an influential book that will be updated periodically.

1953 Eugene Aserinski and Nathaniel Kleitman describe rapid eye movements (REM) that occur during sleep.

Janet Taylor's Manifest Anxiety Scale appears in the *Journal of Abnormal Psychology.*

1954 In *Motivation and Personality,* Abraham Maslow proposes a hierarchy of motives ranging from physiological needs to self-actualization. (Maslow later updates the hierarchy to include self-transcendence needs.)

James Olds and Peter Milner, McGill University neuropsychologists, describe rewarding effects of electrical stimulation of the hypothalamus in rats.

Gordon Allport publishes *The Nature of Prejudice.*

1956 In his *Psychological Review* article titled "The Magical Number Seven, Plus or Minus Two: Some Limits on Our Capacity for Processing Information," George Miller coins the term *chunk* for memory researchers.

1957 Robert Sears, Eleanor Maccoby, and Harry Levin publish *Patterns of Child Rearing.*

Charles Ferster and B. F. Skinner publish *Schedules of Reinforcement.*

1959 Noam Chomsky's critical review of B. F. Skinner's *Verbal Behavior* appears in the journal *Language.*

Eleanor Gibson and Richard Walk report their research on infants' depth perception in "The Visual Cliff."

Harry Harlow outlines "The Nature of Love," his work on attachment in monkeys.

Lloyd Peterson and Margaret Peterson in the *Journal of Experimental Psychology* article, "Short-Term Retention of Individual Verbal Items," highlight the importance of rehearsal in memory.

John Thibaut and Harold Kelley publish *The Social Psychology of Groups.*

1969 In his APA presidential address, "Psychology as a Means of Promoting Human Welfare," George Miller emphasizes the importance of "giving psychology away."

1971 Kenneth B. Clark becomes the first African-American president of the American Psychological Association.

Albert Bandura publishes *Social Learning Theory.*

Allan Paivio publishes *Imagery and Verbal Processes.*

B. F. Skinner publishes *Beyond Freedom and Dignity.*

1972 Elliot Aronson publishes *The Social Animal.*

Fergus Craik and Robert Lockhart's "Levels of Processing: A Framework for Memory Research" appears in the *Journal of Verbal Learning and Verbal Behavior.*

Robert Rescorla and Allan Wagner publish their associative model of Pavlovian conditioning.

Under the leadership of Derald Sue and Stanley Sue, the Asian-American Psychological Association is founded.

1973 Ethologists Karl von Frisch, Konrad Lorenz, and Nikolaas Tinbergen receive the Nobel Prize for their research on animal behavior.

1974 APA's Division 2 first publishes its journal, *Teaching of Psychology,* with Robert S. Daniel as editor.

Eleanor Maccoby (pictured) and Carol Jacklin publish *The Psychology of Sex Differences.*

1975 Biologist Edward O. Wilson's *Sociobiology* appears; it will be a controversial precursor to evolutionary psychology.

1976 Sandra Wood Scarr and Richard A. Weinberg publish "IQ Test Performance of Black Children Adopted by White Families" in *American Psychologist.*

1978 Psychologist Herbert A. Simon, Carnegie-Mellon University, wins a Nobel Prize for pioneering research on computer simulations of human thinking and problem solving.

1979 James J. Gibson publishes *The Ecological Approach to Visual Perception.*

Elizabeth Loftus publishes *Eyewitness Testimony.*

1981 Ellen Langer is the first woman to be granted tenure in Harvard University's Department of Psychology.

David Hubel and Torsten Wiesel receive a Nobel Prize for research on single-cell recordings that identified feature detector cells in the visual cortex.

Roger Sperry receives a Nobel Prize for research on split-brain patients.